CARSWELL

Watson & McGowan's ONTARIO CIVIL PRACTICE 2019 ANNUAL SURVEY, FORMS AND OTHER MATERIALS

by

GARRY D. WATSON, Q.C. and MICHAEL McGOWAN
Founding Authors

MICHAEL McGOWAN
Editor-in-Chief

DEREK McKAY
Associate Editor-in-Chief

MICHAEL FOULDS

Contributing Editor

Of the Bar of Ontario

THOMSON REUTERS®

A cataloguing record for this publication is available from Library and Archives Canada.

ISSN 1184-7433

ISBN 978-0-7798-8525-1 (bound: 2019 ed.)

ISBN 978-0-7798-8526-8 (pbk.: 2019 ed.)

Printed in the United States by Thomson Reuters.

TELL US HOW WE'RE DOING
Scan the QR code to the right with your smartphone to send your comments regarding our products and services. Free QR Code Readers are available from your mobile device app store. You can also email us at feedback.legaltaxcanada@tr.com

THOMSON REUTERS®

THOMSON REUTERS CANADA, A DIVISION OF THOMSON REUTERS CANADA LIMITED

One Corporate Plaza
2075 Kennedy Road
Toronto, Ontario
M1T 3V4

Customer Support
1-416-609-3800 (Toronto & International)
1-800-387-5164 (Toll Free Canada & U.S.)
Fax 1-416-298-5082 (Toronto)
Fax 1-877-750-9041 (Toll Free Canada Only)
Email CustomerSupport.LegalTaxCanada@TR.com

TABLE OF CONTENTS

ANNUAL SURVEY OF RECENT DEVELOPMENTS IN CIVIL PROCEDURE

Derek Mckay

and

Sean M. Grayson

Roy O'Connor LLP

with the assistance of

George Pakozdi and Tamara Markovic

TABLE OF CONTENTS

SURVEY

A. — CASE LAW DEVELOPMENTS

Overview

Arguably the most important development in the past year is new guidance regarding the availability of motions for partial summary judgment under Rule 20. The Court of Appeal has clarified that partial summary judgment is appropriate only where: (1) the issue to be decided is clearly severable from the issues that will proceed to trial; and (2) the motion will promote litigation efficiency.

Other notable developments include:

- clarification of the court's discretion to refuse a partial stay of proceedings where some but not all claims in an action are subject to a mandatory arbitration clause: see Rule 12
- additional jurisprudence to the effect that a defendant noted in default should be notified of a motion to obtain default judgment: see Rule 19
- a decision of the Court of Appeal holding that parties who fail to disclose a litigation agreement that changes the adversarial relationships between parties shall have their claims stayed: see Rule 30
- a new court-made rule that a judge designated under rule 37.15 to hear all motions is precluded from hearing a motion for summary judgment: see rule 37.15
- and new guidance regarding the enforceability of generally worded settlement releases: see rule 49.09

Courts of Justice Act — Section 137.1 — Dismissal of "SLAPP" Suits

In 2015, the Ontario legislature introduced the *Protection of Public Participation Act, 2015* S.O. 2015, c. 23, a piece of amending legislation designed to protect freedom of expression in respect of issues of public interest. As a result, s. 137.1 was added to the *Courts of Justice Act*. The new section permits a party who is sued for expressing herself on a "matter of public interest" to move to have the suit dismissed. The effect of subsections 137.1(3) and (4) is to provide that if the sued party can establish that the suit "arises from an expression made by the [defendant] that relates to a matter of public interest," the onus shifts to the suing party to justify why the suit should be permitted, failing which the suit must be dismissed. Specifically, the suing party must show both: (a) that there are "grounds to believe" that the suit has merit and that the sued party has no valid defence to the suit; and (b) the harm suffered or likely to be suffered by the suing party outweighs the public interest in protecting the expression at issue.

Section 137.1 is intended to prevent "SLAPP" suits, short for "strategic litigation against public participation," namely, the unfair use of litigation to silence public criticism or public disclosure of information. The specific intentions of the section are set out in s. 137.1(1):

(a) to encourage individuals to express themselves on matters of public interest;

(b) to promote broad participation in debates on matters of public interest;

(c) to discourage the use of litigation as a means of unduly limiting expression on matters of public interest; and

(d) to reduce the risk that participation by the public in debates on matters of public interest will be hampered by fear of legal action.

In *Bondfield Construction Co. v. The Globe and Mail*, 2018 ONSC 1880, 2018 CarswellOnt 4856 (S.C.J.), Justice E. M. Morgan suggested that the mandatory requirements of s. 137.1(4) that a suing party must satisfy to avoid dismissal may be too rigid as they mandate dismissal where the sued party has only an arguable defence, but the suit appears to have merit and the potential harm to the suing party outweighs the public's interest in protecting the expression.

The case arose from the Globe and Mail's publication of a series of articles that drew attention to certain commercial ties between a public hospital executive and the plaintiff construction company that was awarded a lucrative hospital construction contract. The plaintiff sued the Globe and Mail for defamation, in response to which the Globe and Mail brought a motion for dismissal under new s. 137.1 of the *Courts of Justice Act.* As the reported financial connection between the public office-holder and the plaintiff was a matter of public interest, the onus shifted to the plaintiff to show that its defamation action should be allowed to proceed. Morgan J. found that the plaintiff's claim had substantial merit and that public interest in articles did not outweigh the potential harm to the plaintiff. However, the Globe and Mail had an arguable "fair comment" defence to the defamation suit. Accordingly, the plaintiff could not meet the s. 137.1(4)(a)(ii) requirement of showing grounds to believe that the Globe and Mail had "no valid defence." Accordingly, Justice Morgan reluctantly dismissed the defamation action, and suggested that the scope of proceedings caught by the wording of s. 137.1 may be over extensive. As His Honour explained:

SURVEY

> While the Globe has met the specific statutory criteria for dismissal of the claim, I am not satisfied that this conclusion truly fulfills the legislative purposes of s. 371.1 of the CJA. [The plaintiff's] action strikes me as a *bona fide* attempt to recover losses it claims to have suffered as a result of the impugned series of articles. I do not think that it falls within the policy of discouraging SLAPP suits that is articulated in s. 371.1(1). In particular, it is not a claim that is designed "as a means of unduly limiting expression on matters of public interest," and so does not appear to be the type of claim at which the anti-SLAPP policy takes aim.

Rule 4.1.01 — Duty of Expert

Rule 4.1.01 codifies the longstanding common law principle that expert witnesses have a duty to be fair, objective and non-partisan. This duty is owed to the court, and it prevails over the obligations owed by the expert to the party by which she or he is retained. Recent case law has clarified the important role of the court in assuring that expert evidence is non-partisan. As the Supreme Court of Canada made clear in *White Burgess Langille Inman v. Abbott and Haliburton Co.*, 2015 SCC 23, [2015] 2 S.C.R. 182 ("*White Burgess*"), judges should act as "gatekeepers": they should exclude proposed expert evidence that is not adequately independent and impartial, rather than admit such evidence and treat its lack of independence as an issue of the weight given to it. In *White Burgess*, the court affirmed that there is a two-step process for determining the admissibility of expert evidence. First, the proponent of the evidence must establish that it meets the threshold requirements of admissibility set out in *R. v. Mohan*, [1994] 2 S.C.R. 9: (i) relevance; (ii) necessity in assisting the trier of fact; (iii) absence of an exclusionary rule; and (iv) a properly qualified expert. Second, the judge, performing her "discretionary gatekeeper" role, should balance the potential risks and benefits of admitting the evidence having regard to its independence and impartiality.

In *Bruff-Murphy v. Gunawardena*, 2017 ONCA 502; additional reasons 2017 ONCA 698; leave to appeal refused *Neloni Gunawardena v. Callum Bruff-Murphy and Hope Bruff-McArthur by their Litigation Guardian Liese Bruff-McArthur, et al.*, 2018 CarswellOnt 3656 (S.C.C.), the court ordered a new trial where the trial judge failed to exercise his gatekeeper function and permitted evidence of a defendant's expert to be presented to the jury, despite finding that the expert had "descended into the fray" as a partisan advocate.

The plaintiff in *Bruff-Murphy* had been struck in a motor vehicle accident that she claimed caused her chronic pain, anxiety and depression that left her unable to work. The impugned defence expert evidence was from a psychiatrist whose evidence was principally devoted to highlighting purported inconsistencies between what the plaintiff told the psychiatrist during a medical examination and previous statements of the plaintiff recorded in the plaintiff's medical records. The psychiatrist concluded his expert report by challenging the credibility of the plaintiff. At no time during the medical examination did the psychiatrist question the plaintiff about her previous statements. Indeed, the psychiatrist admitted that he did not review the plaintiff's medical records until after he concluded the medical examination.

The trial judge allowed the psychiatrist to give evidence but excluded him from giving testimony with respect to his challenges to the expertise and professional conduct of the plaintiff's experts and examining physicians. The trial judge concluded that he was bound to permit the psychiatrist to give evidence, stating that there is a "very high threshold" for excluding evidence on the grounds of bias. Thereafter, at trial the psychiatrist presented clearly partisan testimony to the jury aimed at discrediting the plaintiff. Despite this, the trial judge did not instruct the jury to disregard any aspects of the psychiatrist's testimony. Counsel for the plaintiff did not object to the jury charge. In the result, the jury returned a verdict assessing general damages at $23,500 and rejecting all other heads of damage, including special damages, future care costs and past and future income loss.

On appeal, the plaintiff argued that the trial judge erred by: (1) refusing to allow the plaintiff to challenge the psychiatrist's impartiality by cross-examining him about three prior decisions in which adjudicators had found that he was biased; and (2) failing to exclude the psychiatrist's evidence. The Court of Appeal disagreed with the first argument, but agreed with the second.

Regarding the plaintiff's first argument, the Court of Appeal held that prior decisions impugning an expert's impartiality are not a proper subject for cross-examination. Citing two criminal proceeding decisions dealing with the impugned credibility of police officer witnesses — *R. v. Ghorvei*, 1999 CarswellOnt 2763, 46 O.R. (3d) 63 (C.A.) and *R. v. Boyne*, 2012 SKCA 124, 2012

CarswellSask 846, 405 Sask. R. 163, 563 W.A.C. 163; leave to appeal refused (2013), 460 N.R. 397 (note) (S.C.C.) — the court reasoned that a jury, not knowing the facts of the previous cases, would be unable to assess the relevance of the previous credibility findings. Further, the court expressed concern that permitting such cross-examination would distract the jury from the real matters at issue and turn the trial into an inquiry about the reliability of the expert.

The Court of Appeal agreed, however, with the plaintiff's submission that the court erred in admitting the psychiatrist's evidence. The trial judge made no reference to the cost-benefit analysis required by *White Burgess*, and instead appeared to erroneously conclude that the court is bound to admit expert evidence that passes only the first step (the *Mohan* test) of the two-step process outlined in *White Burgess* for determining admissibility.

Conducting its own second-step gatekeeper analysis, the Court of Appeal held that there were numerous bases for concluding the risks of admitting the psychiatrist's evidence that far outweighed any benefits: the psychiatrist's "hunt for discrepancies" between what the plaintiff stated during the medical examination and what was previously recorded in her medical records, without putting the discrepancies to the plaintiff during the examination, deprived the plaintiff of the opportunity to explain the discrepancies; the psychiatrist's focus on the apparent discrepancies was not an exercise of psychiatric expertise but rather a task which could be performed by a lawyer, law student or clerk; and in offering opinions about the credibility of the plaintiff, the psychiatrist had come "dangerously close" to usurping the role of the trier of fact; and the entire tone of the report spoke to the fact that the psychiatrist was attempting to damage the plaintiff's case rather than give an objective assessment of those aspects within his area of expertise. Accordingly, the Court of Appeal concluded that the psychiatrist's evidence should not have been admitted.

Moreover, the Court of Appeal addressed the required response of a trial judge where an expert gives impermissible partisan testimony mid-trial. Holding that a judge's gatekeeping responsibility is continuous and does not end with her decision to admit expert evidence, the court stated that the trial judge "must take action" where it becomes apparent at trial that an expert is not impartial. The court held that the trial judge in *Bruff-Murphy* had two mid-trial options, both to be exercised in the absence of the jury: either (1) advise counsel that he was considering giving a mid-trial or final instruction that the psychiatrist's testimony be excluded in whole or in part from the evidence, and then hear submissions from counsel; or (2) ask for submissions from counsel on a mistrial. Further, the court clarified that a trial judge should not rely on the absence of an objection from counsel as a basis for permitting clearly biased evidence, holding that the absence of such an objection "does not impair a trial judge's ability to exercise her residual discretion to exclude evidence whose probative value is outweighed by its prejudicial effect."

Rejecting the defendant's argument that there had been "no harm, no foul," the Court of Appeal held that admission of the psychiatrist's evidence had caused a miscarriage of justice. A demonstration of the precise prejudice caused by the testimony was not required.

The Court of Appeal's decision to order a new trial and its reasoning with respect to the scope and ongoing nature of a trial judge's gate-keeper role are obviously sound. However, in the author's (Derek McKay's) respectful opinion, the issue of whether the impartiality of an expert may be challenged on the basis that he or she has previously been found biased by adjudicators warrants further consideration.

Concern about expert bias is not new. In his 2007 "Civil Justice Reform Report," the Honourable Coulter Osborne noted the common complaint "that too many experts are no more than hired guns who tailor their reports and evidence to suit the client's needs." Justice Coulter also acknowledged criticism that absent "a clear enforcement mechanism," his recommendation, now reflected in rules 4.1.01 and 53.03(2.1)(7), that experts expressly attest to their duty to be impartial, might have "no significant impact on experts unduly swayed by the parties who retain them." His principal recommendation for curbing expert bias was not implemented: granting judges the power to order that experts for opposing parties "meet and confer" on a without prejudice basis to identify areas of agreement and where possible resolve areas of disagreement. (Such a rule is however provided for in British Columbia: B.C. Rule 5-3(10(k)(iii) provides that a B.C. court may order the parties' experts to confer before serving their reports.) Leaving aside the question of whether such "meet and confers" are a workable solution, the more important point is that Justice Osborne thought that the mere express acknowledgment of duty by experts would be insufficient to curb the problem of expert bias. The question is whether the court's expanded "gate-keeping" role outlined in *White Burgess* and *Bruff-Murphy* is sufficient for the task.

The obvious incentives for biased expert evidence cannot be ignored. The expert evidence industry can be lucrative: experts frequently bill at hourly rates that rival those of lawyers, and those experts who consistently produce opinions favourable to their retaining parties' interests are likely to secure "repeat business." If a pattern of giving biased expert opinion does not exclude an expert from participating in the industry, and if such bias is not always caught, where is the incentive to abide by the expert's duty? Allowing judges to exclude the participation of experts who have a track record of bias could help to dis-incentivize partisan expert evidence.

In the author's (Derek McKay's) respectful opinion, the rationale for precluding cross-examination of an expert with respect to previous findings of bias is not entirely persuasive. Experts are accorded a special status in litigation: unlike other witnesses, they are permitted to give opinion evidence on essential issues about which the trier of fact, absent such expert opinion, could not be expected to reach a sound conclusion. Great reliance is placed on the impartiality of experts. Accordingly, analogies to other types of witnesses, such as police officers, are not on all fours. It is at least arguable that the extraordinary role afforded to experts in the resolution of essential fact issues should be matched by equally extraordinary safeguards to ensure and incentivize impartiality. Finally, the problem of misdirecting or confusing a jury need not arise. It is the trial judge that decides admissibility, and this being the case, challenges to the admissibility of an expert via cross-examination on prior instances of bias could be conducted in the absence of the jury.

Rule 12 — Class Proceedings

(a) — Partial Stay of Class Action in Favour of Arbitration Denied

In *Wellman v. TELUS Communications Company*, 2017 ONCA 433; leave to appeal allowed *TELUS Communications Inc. v. Avraham Wellman*, 2018 CarswellOnt 4703 (S.C.C.), ("*Wellman*"), the Ontario Court of Appeal rejected the notion that leading jurisprudence from the Supreme Court of Canada has lessened or removed the court's discretion to refuse to grant a partial stay of proceedings where some but not all claims in a proceeding are subject to a mandatory arbitration clause. As discussed below, in *Seidel v. TELUS Communications Inc.*, 2011 SCC 15, [2011] 1 S.C.R. 531 ("*Seidel*") a majority of the Supreme Court of Canada endorsed the principle that, absent applicable legislation to the contrary, courts ought generally to enforce mandatory arbitration clauses. In *Wellman*, the Court of Appeal held that the *Seidel* principle has no effect on the Court of Appeal's previous conclusion in *Griffin v. Dell Canada Inc.*, 2010 ONCA 29; additional reasons 2010 ONCA 164; leave to appeal refused (2010), 409 N.R. 378 (note) (S.C.C.), that a court has discretion under s. 7(5) of Ontario's *Arbitration Act, 1991* to refuse a partial stay of proceedings where in the court's estimation it would be unreasonable to require some claims to proceed to arbitration and other claims to be litigated in court.

By way of background, except in certain limited circumstances, Ontario's *Arbitration Act, 1991* governs the enforceability of a mandatory arbitration clause and generally provides for a stay of any court proceeding in respect of a matter subject to such a clause. Specifically, s. 7(1) of the *Arbitration Act* provides that where a party to an arbitration agreement commences a proceeding in respect of a matter to be submitted to arbitration, the court shall, on the motion of another party to the arbitration agreement, stay the proceeding. Section 7(2) sets out various circumstances in which the court has discretion to refuse a stay (for example, where the arbitration clause or agreement is invalid). Further, and critically, s. 7(5) provides that where only part of a court proceeding is covered by an arbitration agreement, the court may grant a partial stay, but only where it is "reasonable to separate the matters dealt with in the agreement from the other matters." Another relevant exception to the general enforceability of arbitration clauses is furnished by s. 7(2) of the *Consumer Protection Act*, which provides that an arbitration clause in a consumer agreement is invalid insofar as it prevents a consumer from commencing an action in the Superior Court of Justice.

In *Griffin v. Dell Canada Inc.*, cited above, a class action on behalf of both consumer and business purchasers of the defendant's computers, the Court of Appeal refused to stay the claims of business purchasers that were subject to enforceable mandatory arbitration clause. As the consumer claims were exempted from mandatory arbitration by s. 7(2) of the *Consumer Protection Act* and would proceed in court, the Court of Appeal declined to stay the business purchaser claims pursuant to s. 7(5) of the *Arbitration Act* which gives the court discretion to refuse a partial stay where it would be unreasonable to separate the claims. Thus, the *Griffin* court interpreted s. 7(5) as directing the court to determine which of two procedural options is more reasonable for the resolution of all claims where some but not all of the claims are subject to an enforceable arbitration clause — either: (1) allow all claims to proceed in court; or (2) bifurcate the claims, with those subject to the arbitration clause proceeding to arbitration and the remaining claims proceeding in court.

Seidel dealt with the enforceability and scope of a mandatory arbitration clause under British Columbia's consumer protection and arbitration legislation. In contrast to its Ontario counterpart, British Columbia's consumer protection legislation does not expressly stipulate that an arbitration agreement in respect of a matter covered by the act is unenforceable. It instead provides: (a) that a party other than a supplier "may bring an action in Supreme Court" for declaratory or injunctive relief in respect of a contravention of the act; and (b) that "any waiver or release by a person of the person's rights, benefits or protections under [the] Act" is void unless expressly permitted by the Act. British Columbia's arbitration legislation also differs from its Ontario counterpart in that the B.C. Act does not contain a provision analogous to s. 7(5) of the Ontario *Arbitration Act, 1991* which sets limits on when a partial stay of proceedings in favour of arbitration is appropriate. Under the British Columbia arbitration legislation, if a claim asserted in a court proceeding is subject to mandatory arbitration clause, the court must stay the proceeding unless the clause is "void, inoperative or incapable of being performed."

In *Seidel*, a proposed representative plaintiff advanced both common law and statutory consumer claims in respect of the defendant phone service provider's alleged practice of charging its customers for time it took to connect calls. The plaintiff's service contract with the defendant contained a mandatory arbitration clause. The British Columbia Court of Appeal held that none of the plaintiff's claims were exempt from mandatory arbitration and stayed all of the plaintiff's claims, including her statutory consumer protection claims. In the court's interpretation, the relevant sections of the B.C. consumer protection legislation merely provided that the Superior Court is a potential forum for advancing claims under the Act, and did not oust the exclusive jurisdiction of the arbitral regime created by the mandatory arbitration clause. The court's reasoning was rejected on appeal by a slim 5-4 majority of a highly polarized Supreme Court of Canada.

The majority of the Supreme Court held that a purposive reading of the British Columbia consumer protection legislation made clear that the legislation was intended to secure the right of the plaintiff to assert her statutory consumer protection claims in court. The majority consequently varied the order staying all of the plaintiff's claims to allow only the statutory consumer protection claims to proceed. The result was thus a partial stay order, with the bulk of the plaintiff's claims stayed in favour of mandatory arbitration. In reaching this result, the majority endorsed the following principle upon which the defendant in *Wellman* subsequently sought to rely: "Absent legislative intervention, the courts will generally give effect to the terms of a commercial contract freely entered into, even a contract of adhesion, including an arbitration clause."

In *Wellman*, the defendant phone service provider (the same defendant as in *Seidel*) argued before the Ontario Court of Appeal that the *Seidel* majority's endorsement of the principle that arbitration clauses are generally to be enforced marked an important shift in the jurisprudence in favour of arbitration. Specifically, the defendant submitted that *Seidel* had overtaken the Court of

Appeal's interpretation in *Griffin* of s. 7(5) of Ontario's *Arbitration Act, 1991*, and argued that in light of *Seidel*, the court retained little to no discretion under the section to refuse a partial stay of proceedings in cases where some but not all claims are subject to a mandatory arbitration clause. *Wellman* involves claims on behalf of both consumer and business customers of the defendant that the defendant phone service provider overcharged its customers by rounding up the duration of phone calls. The defendant's contracts (both consumer and business) during the relevant period contained mandatory arbitration clauses. The defendant conceded that the claims in respect of the consumer contracts could proceed in court, on the basis of s. 7(2) of the *Consumer Protection Act, 2002*, S.O. 2002, c. 30, Sched. A, but sought a partial stay of proceedings in respect of the business customer claims.

The defendant's stay motion in *Wellman* was denied at first instance on the basis of s. 7(5) of the *Arbitration Act, 1991*. The motions judge concluded that it would be unreasonable to bifurcate the proceeding because: consumer claims represented 70 percent of the total number of claims; issues of liability and damages for both consumer and non-consumers overlapped; no mechanism existed for arbitrating the non-consumer claims as a group; and separating the two proceedings would be inefficient and create a risk of inconsistent judgments. The defendant appealed only on the question of whether the *Griffin* analysis and framework for determining whether a partial stay of proceedings should be granted had been overtaken by *Seidel*.

The Court of Appeal concluded that *Seidel* had not overtaken *Griffin* and upheld the refusal to grant a partial stay. Justice van Rensburg (Weiler J.A. concurring) stated that the different outcomes in *Griffin* and *Seidel* are not indicative of a difference in approach to the enforceability of arbitration clauses, and in particular that the decision in *Griffin* does not contradict the general principle that contractual arbitration clauses are presumptively enforceable. Rather, the difference in outcomes is simply a consequence of differences between the respective arbitration and consumer protection legislative schemes of Ontario and British Columbia regarding the grounds upon which a court may refuse to grant a partial stay of proceedings.

Importantly, in separate reasons, Justice Blair (concurring in the result) held that *Griffin* and *Seidel* were distinguishable on a more limited basis and questioned without resolving the validity of the statutory interpretation advanced in *Griffin* and followed by his fellow panel members in *Wellman*. Firstly, Blair J.A. reasoned that *Seidel* was distinguishable because it dealt only with the right of the representative plaintiff in that case, as an individual consumer, to litigate in court a matter covered by a mandatory arbitration clause, and did not address the application of the B.C. legislative scheme to class claims on behalf of both consumers and non-consumers. Secondly, and more importantly, His Honour questioned whether *Griffin* was correctly decided. Specifically, he questioned whether s. 7(5) of the *Arbitration Act* might only have been intended to allow the court to refuse to bifurcate claims between the same contracting parties. On this alternative interpretation, s. 7(5) would have no application to cases where claims on behalf of two groups are advanced against a common defendant, but the arbitration clause at issue is enforceable against all claims of the first group (*e.g.*, non-consumers) but unenforceable against the second (*e.g.*, consumers). Finally, echoing the reasoning of the Supreme Court of Canada in *Bisaillon v. Concordia University*,

2006 SCC 19, [2006] 1 S.C.R. 666, *Union des consommateurs v. Dell Computer Corp.*, 2007 SCC 34, 284 D.L.R. (4th) 577, and *Muroff v. Rogers Wireless Inc.*, 2007 SCC 35, 284 D.L.R. (4th) 675, Blair J.A. questioned whether the *Class Proceedings Act, 1992*, "a procedural rights statute," can confer on a class of plaintiffs a right to go to court that individual claimants outside the class proceedings scheme do not enjoy.

The defendant in *Wellman* has been granted leave to appeal to the Supreme Court of Canada: (March 22, 2018), Doc. 37722, 2018 CarswellOnt 4703 (S.C.C.). The questions posed by Blair J.A. will undoubtedly figure centrally in the appeal. As discussed in previous Annual Surveys, in recent years the Supreme Court of Canada has tended to prefer complicated, formalistic statutory interpretations that favour enforcement over more purposive and pragmatic interpretations that see the court as having a residual discretion to intervene where substantive justice or procedural fairness are at risk. Markedly absent from the court's analysis has been any meaningful attention to the important "access to justice" and "litigation efficiency" goals of arbitration and class proceedings legislation. In this regard, the reasoning of Cumming J. in *Huras v. Primerica Financial Services Ltd.* (2000), 13 C.P.C. (5th) 114, [2000] O.J. No. 1474 (S.C.J.); affirmed (2001), 55 O.R. (3d) 449 (C.A.), may still provide useful guidance:

> Two of the normative purposes of an arbitration provision are to expedite the resolution of a dispute and to save costs that would be seen in a court action. The arbitration provision in the case at hand is to the opposite effect. . . . [The defendant] submits that the arbitration clause is enforceable even if utilization of the clause might prove inconvenient or more costly to the plaintiff and similarly-situated persons.
>
> I disagree. The existence of the arbitration clause in [the defendant's] contractual documents gives a superficial appearance of fairness to the unsophisticated. In reality, the arbitration clause serves to prevent any resolution of a dispute other than upon the terms dictated by [the defendant]. The existence of the arbitration clause is unfair. It would be perverse and in conflict with the normative purposes of an arbitration clause to enforce the one at hand.
>
> The *CPA* has three underlying policy objectives. First, there is a goal of facilitating access to justice for claimants of relatively small amounts of money . . . Second, the *CPA* seeks to provide for common issues to be litigated in a single proceeding involving many claimants. This achieves cost efficiencies and economies in the use of resources. Third, by facilitating access to justice, the *CPA* acts to foster deterrence of wrongful conduct. A class proceeding can be a mode of regulating business conduct in aid of public policies through the private sector seeking the remedy.
>
> The arbitration clause in the case at hand, if enforceable, would defeat the public policy inherent in the *CPA*. . . .

(b) — Absent Foreign Class Members

Class proceedings on behalf of international classes raise a unique jurisdictional problem. In ordinary, non-class action litigation, the plaintiff selects the forum in which she commences her proceeding, thereby consenting or attorning to jurisdiction, and the court's jurisdiction over the defendant may be established on any of three bases: consent of the defendant; presence of the defendant within the territorial limits of the court's jurisdiction; or a real and substantial connection between the subject-matter of the dispute and the court's territorial jurisdiction. Unlike typical litigation, class actions, which often involve global issues not confined to national territorial borders, can include the plaintiff class "absent foreign claimants" ("AFCs"): persons who are not resident in Canada and who have not consented to the jurisdiction of a Canadian court. Accordingly, if the court is to exercise jurisdiction over an AFC in a manner recognized by Canadian law, a real and substantial connection must exist between Ontario and the AFC's claim.

As discussed in the 2013 and subsequent Annual Surveys, in *Van Breda v. Village Resorts Ltd.*, 2012 SCC 17 ("*Van Breda*"), the Supreme Court of Canada held in relevant part that: (a) a real and substantial connection must be established primarily on the basis of "objective" connecting factors (*e.g.*, the commission of a tort in Ontario, or the making of contract in Ontario) that have proven or may reasonably be expected proven consistent with "order and fairness," principles that govern the court's exercise of jurisdiction and furnish a basis for "comity" (the reciprocal recognition and enforcement of judgments between courts of one territorial jurisdiction and another); but (b) "abstract concerns" about order, efficiency, fairness or comity are not themselves sufficient to establish jurisdiction (*e.g.*, the court cannot assume jurisdiction solely on the basis that an Ontario proceeding will afford all parties due process).

In *Airia Brands Inc. v. Air Canada*, 2017 ONCA 792, a price-fixing case brought on behalf of an international class that included residents of more than 100 countries, the defendants sought to exclude all AFCs from the class on the basis that the court lacked jurisdiction over their claims. Relying in part on the Supreme Court of Canada's decision in *Van Breda*, the defendants argued that use of the real and substantial connection test to assume jurisdiction over AFCs is contrary to the principles of order and fairness and constitutes an improper attempt to exercise jurisdiction beyond the court's proper territorial limits. In support of their argument, the defendants tendered evidence that with the notable exception of the United States, the majority of foreign courts do not recognize a real and substantial connection test as a basis for exercising jurisdiction and would not recognize judgments of the Ontario court in respect of claims of AFCs resident within their territorial jurisdiction. To be enforceable in such foreign courts, a judgment must be based on presence, consent or attornment (submission).

In the alternative, the defendants argued that a real and substantial connection could not be established between Ontario and the claims of AFCs. The plaintiff's claim was that the defendant airlines had conspired to fix the price of air freight into and out of Canada. The defendants argued that any torts of conspiracy would have been committed outside Canada and that the AFC's contracts with the defendants were entered into outside Canada. Further, the defendants held that the approach taken by the Manitoba Court of Appeal in *Meeking v. Cash Store Inc.*, 2013 MBCA 81, 2013 CarswellMan 458; leave to appeal allowed (2014), 472 N.R. 392 (note) (S.C.C.), to the issue of a Manitoba court's jurisdiction over out-of-province Canadian class members was inapplicable to AFCs. In that case, the Manitoba Court of Appeal held that once jurisdiction over the representative plaintiff and the defendant is established, jurisdiction over the claims of out-of-province class members arises from the existence of common issues between the claims of the out-of-province members and the representative plaintiff — in other words, on the basis of a commonality of interest. However, as the defendants in *Airia* pointed out, because

Meeking involved only a national class of Canadian class members, all provincial and territorial courts of Canada were bound by the dictates of national comity to recognize Manitoba's exercise of jurisdiction based on a proper application of the Canadian real and substantial connection test. Foreign courts would not be bound to do so.

The defendants in *Airia* were successful at first instance and the motion judge stayed the claims on behalf of AFCs. The motion judge agreed with the defendants that the real and substantial connection test does not apply to foreign class members outside the territorial limits of Canada and that, in the alternative, a real and substantial connection could not be established on the basis of either a common interest between the plaintiff and the AFCs or the procedural fairness that would be afforded to AFCs (namely, adequate representation by the representative plaintiff, notice, and the right to opt out).

The exclusion of AFCs was reversed by the Ontario Court of Appeal. Writing for the court, Pepall J.A. made short work of the motion judge's conclusion that the real and substantial connection does not apply to AFCs, noting that in *Van Breda* the Supreme Court of Canada held that the real and substantial test is a "constitutional imperative" and that where a real and substantial connection exists "the court must assume jurisdiction over all aspects of the case." Accordingly, the test is binding. Turning to the more difficult issue of whether a real and substantial connection existed in respect of the claims of the AFCs, the court acknowledged the existence of conflicting theories about the potential extra-territorial reach, if any, of Canadian class actions. Without attempting to resolve the ongoing debate, Pepall J. reviewed the extant pre-and post-*Van Breda* jurisprudence and distilled from it three factors that in combination are sufficient to have found a real and substantial connection between an Ontario court and AFCs:

> . . . [J]urisdiction may be established over AFCs where:
>
> 1) there is a real and substantial connection between the subject-matter of the action and Ontario, and jurisdiction exists over the representative plaintiff and the defendants;
>
> 2) there are common issues between the claims of the representative plaintiff and AFCs; and,
>
> 3) the procedural safeguards of adequacy of representation, adequacy of notice, and the right to opt out . . . are provided, thereby serving to enhance the real and substantial connection between AFCs and Ontario.

As Her Honour concluded, "this framework provides the necessary safeguards to establish that jurisdiction properly exists and ensures the protection of the values of order and fairness." As all three requirements were met in *Airia*, the AFCs were properly members of the proposed class.

Rule 19 — Default Judgment — Notice to Defendant

In recent years, Ontario courts have modified the default judgment regime set out under Rule 19 by affording defendants notice, contrary to the provisions of the Rule, of a plaintiff's motion to obtain default judgment against them.

The default judgment provisions of Rule 19 serve two important goals: (1) incentivizing a defendant who wishes to defend to make a timely defence; and (2) quickly clearing from the court system a claim against which the defendant does not wish to defend. Where a defendant has failed to deliver a statement of defence within the time for doing so, the plaintiff may require the registrar to note the defendant in default by filing proof that the statement of claim was served on the defendant: rule 19.01(1). Once noted in default, a defendant is deemed to admit the plaintiff's pleaded allegations of fact and is prohibited without leave from delivering a defence or taking any step in the action other than a motion to set aside the noting in default: rule 19.02(1). Further, a defendant who had been noted in default is not entitled to notice of any further step in the proceeding, including notice of any step by the plaintiff to obtain default judgment: rule 19.02(3).

In rare cases the consequences of default judgment for a defendant can be severe, as illustrated in *Beals v. Saldanha*, 2003 SCC 72, 2003 CarswellOnt 5101, 2003 CarswellOnt 5102. In that case, an action arising from what appeared to be an $8,000 mistake resulted in a Florida default judgement for $800,000 that the court enforced against an Ontario defendant.

The justifying rationale for default judgment is that the defendant has had actual notice of the claim against it and decided not to defend. Default judgment works an obvious and serious injustice if the defendant does not receive actual notice. To address the risk of such injustice, in *Elekta Ltd. v. Rodkin*, 2012 ONSC 2062, 2012 CarswellOnt 3928 (S.C.J. [Commercial List]); additional reasons 2012 ONSC 2363 (S.C.J. [Commercial List]), Justice D. M. Brown (as he then was) stated that although a defendant who has been noted in default is not entitled to a notice of a motion for default judgment, "the better practice is to serve the default judgment motion materials on the defendant in any event." As His Honour explained:

> The main reason for this practice is a simple, but important, one. Often the materials filed on a rule 19.05 motion for default judgment will raise questions about the adequacy of the service of the Statement of Claim. Some motion records do not include the affidavit of service of the originating process; that is not good practice. Even where the Registrar has noted a defendant in default, a judge will want to satisfy himself or herself that the defendant was given proper notice of the claim. By serving the default judgment motion record on the responding party and filing proof of such service, a court can satisfy itself that the person against whom default judgment is sought knew about the claim, knew about the motion for default judgment yet, nevertheless, elected not to defend or respond.

In *Canada Mortgage and Housing Corporation v. CMC Medical Centre Inc.*, 2017 ONSC 7551, 2017 CarswellOnt 20149 (S.C.J.), the court made it clear that Justice Brown's suggested practice is now an established one, but did not order that the defendant receive notice of the motion for default judgment in this case because it was clear that the defendant had actual notice of both the proceeding and the fact that the plaintiff was taking steps to note the defendant in default. Accordingly, the *Canada Mortgage* decision suggests the following attenuation of Justice Brown's suggested practice: before moving for default judgment a plaintiff should take reasonable steps to ensure that the defaulting defendant has actual notice of the proceeding.

In the author's (Derek McKay's) respectful opinion, the above-mentioned modification of Justice Brown's suggested practice is preferable to recognizing a principle that requires the plaintiff to notify the defaulting defendant of the motion for default judgment in all cases. While a judge hearing a motion for default judgment can and should exercise her discretion to require such notice where there is reason to doubt that the defaulting defendant has had actual notice of the proceeding against it, requiring such notice in all cases undermines the important incentive structure of the Rule. Despite the result in *Beals*, the risk of a defendant being stuck with a meritless adverse judgment is quite small. In the great majority of cases, the defendant can successfully move to set aside default judgment by, among other things, showing that it has a potentially tenable defence on the merits (see, for example, *Morgan v. Municipality of Toronto Police Services Board* (2003), 34 C.P.C. (5th) 46, 2003 CarswellOnt 1105 (Ont. C.A.)). Thus, in most cases successful resort to the Rule's procedures for noting in default and obtaining judgment does not bring the litigation to an end. In practice, these procedures, like the procedures for dismissal for delay, more often serve as an important tool for compelling a non-responsive party to deliver pleadings and to take such other steps as are necessary for all parties to get on with the business of resolving the dispute.

In short, where default judgment is obtained the resulting notice of default judgment to the defendant acts as a strong incentive for the defendant to engage the court process quickly and to treat the litigation seriously. Recognizing a right of a defaulting defendant to notice of the motion for default judgment in all cases would undercut that incentive.

Rule 20.01(3) — Partial Summary Judgment

Rule 20.01(3) provides for a summary judgment that dismisses "part of a claim," and thus permits "partial summary judgment." A motion for partial summary judgment may be an attractive option where the issues to be determined on the motion comprise a substantial part of the dispute or may remove from the litigation one or more parties or claims. The early resolution of a substantial issue may assist the parties in avoiding continued litigation by encouraging settlement or discontinuance. Removal of parties from the litigation — for example, third party defendants to claims for contribution and indemnity — simplifies the litigation.

In apparent response the Supreme Court of Canada's call in *Hryniak v. Mauldin*, 2014 SCC 7, for more robust use of the summary judgment procedure, motions for partial summary judgment now appear more common. However, three recent decisions of the Court of Appeal for Ontario reversing partial summary judgment — *Canadian Imperial Bank of Commerce v. Deloitte & Touche*, 2016 ONCA 922, 2016 CarswellOnt 19133, 133 O.R. (3d) 561, 404 D.L.R. (4th) 534; additional reasons 2017 ONCA 43, *Butera v. Chown, Cairns LLP*, 2017 ONCA 783, and *Toronto-Dominion Bank, N.A. v. Lloyd's Underwriters*, 2017 ONCA 1011, 2017 CarswellOnt 20445 — illustrate that the following two pre-*Hryniak* requirements for partial summary judgment continue to apply:

(1) *Claims must be clearly severable* — The issues to be resolved by partial summary judgment must be severable — that is, legally and factually distinct — from the balance of issues that will proceed to trial. Ignoring this requirement poses the risk of inconsistent judgments on the same or closely related issues (see, *e.g.*, *Corchis v. KPMG Peat Marwick Thorne*, 2002 CarswellOnt 1064, [2002] O.T.C. 475 (C.A.) at para. 3); and,

(2) *Must promote litigation efficiency* — the motion for partial summary judgment must have the potential to enhance litigation efficiency by simplifying the downstream process for resolving the entire dispute (see, *e.g.*, *Coast Foundation Society (1974) v. John Currie Architect Inc.*, 2003 BCSC 1781, 2003 CarswellBC 3001, discussed below).

In *Canadian Imperial Bank of Commerce*, cited above, a syndicate of banks advanced approximately $1 billion in financing to a public company. Soon thereafter the company announced an accounting fraud which ultimately led to bankruptcy proceedings and a restructuring. The lenders recovered less than half of the principal advanced to the company. Both the syndicate of lenders and the bankrupt company, through its receiver, sued the company's auditor variously for professional negligence, reckless misrepresentation and breach of contract. Among other things, the lenders claimed that they relied on the auditor's unqualified opinions and audits of the company in deciding to provide financing, and the company alleged that it relied on the same in deciding to pursue an aggressive course of acquisitions that ultimately resulted in its insolvency.

The auditor brought a motion for partial summary judgment on the issue of whether it owed a duty of care to the lenders. If successful, the motion promised to eliminate the lenders' claims in negligence, but would not remove any parties, as the lenders' claims for reckless misrepresentation would remain and the company's claims would be unaffected. The motion judge granted partial summary judgment, finding that no duty of care was owed. The result was reversed on appeal on the dual grounds that the issue was not necessarily severable from the balance of issues in the litigation and that partial summary judgment should not have been granted because it would not render the remaining litigation more efficient. With regard to litigation efficiency, the Court of Appeal observed that the judgment did not release any party from the proceeding and was not expected to shorten the trial, which was scheduled to take four months to complete. The court concluded that partial summary judgment "was inadvisable in the context of the litigation as a whole."

Partial summary judgment was also reversed in *Butera v. Chown*, cited above, on numerous grounds including that the claim decided on partial summary judgment was not severable from the claims that would proceed. Writing for the court, Pepall J.A. cautioned that the problems potentially associated with partial summary judgment are not limited to duplicative or inconsistent findings, but also include the following "further problems that are anathema to the stated objectives underlying *Hryniak*": (1) delay and the possibility that the moving party may use a motion for summary judgment as a tactic to cause the opposing party to expend time and money on a motion that may advance the litigation only a little or not at all; (2) the expense of the motion; and (3) such motions require the already significantly burdened judiciary to expend precious time hearing the motion and writing decisions on issues that do not dispose of the matter. Justice Pepall concluded that a "motion for partial summary judgment should be considered to be a rare procedure that is reserved for an issue or issues that may be readily bifurcated from those in the main action and that may be dealt with expeditiously and in a cost-effective manner."

The Court of Appeal reached a similar conclusion in the third case cited above, *Toronto-Dominion Bank*. The case concerned a Ponzi scheme perpe-

SURVEY

trated by a Florida lawyer who was a customer of the plaintiff bank. The Florida lawyer had defrauded 19 investors and routed the proceeds of the fraud through the plaintiff. One investor obtained judgment against the bank and the plaintiff settled the claims of the remaining 18 investors. Thereafter, the plaintiff sued its insurer for indemnity under a policy that covered employee dishonesty and errors and omissions and for breach of contract, claiming $300 million — the amount of available coverage under the policy.

In the middle of documentary productions and oral discovery, the plaintiff bank brought a motion for partial summary judgment in respect of one of many issues relating to the interpretation of the insurance policy. The proposed issue had a direct bearing on, but would not resolve, the insurer's potential liability to indemnify the plaintiff in respect of monies it paid to 3 of the 19 investors. The motions judge granted partial summary judgment, interpreting the narrow portion of the policy in favour of the plaintiff.

On appeal, the Court of Appeal for Ontario set aside the partial summary judgment on various grounds, including the failure of the judgment to promote litigation efficiency. As the court explained at para. 12:

> Such a request for an order in respect of only one of several constituent elements of a claim for which relief is sought, and then only as it might affect a portion of that claim, is not a proper request for summary judgment on "part of the claim in the statement of claim; . . . The result of the judgment is that no claim for which the Bank has sought relief has been granted, nor have any of its claims been dismissed. All of its claims for indemnification remain for determination at trial — on what will likely be a more fulsome factual record. And no party has been released from the action. Given this result, the kind of partial summary judgment granted by the motions judge was not available under Rule 20: *Canadian Imperial Bank of Commerce v. Deloitte & Touche*, 2016 ONCA 922, 133 O.R. (3d) 561 (Ont. C.A.), at para. 39. Accordingly, the motions judge failed to properly interpret the scope of relief available under Rule 20.

The requirement that partial summary judgment promote litigation efficiency deserves special comment. Partial summary judgment will often result in a bifurcated proceeding. *Canadian Imperial Bank of Commerce* and *Toronto-Dominion Bank* are illustrative. In both cases, partial summary judgment resulted in an appeal to the Court of Appeal and likely delayed the progression of these actions toward trial. Further, both cases involved complex claims for damages in the hundreds of millions of dollars. Accordingly, the cases were not ones where the costs in time and money of a plenary trial are disproportionate to the relatively simple issues and modest stakes involved in the litigation. Both actions were headed to lengthy and expensive trials regardless of the outcome of the partial summary judgment motion, and given the dollar amounts at stake, the parties on both sides in each action could reasonably be predicted to exercise every potentially advantageous procedural right afforded them under the Rules and elsewhere.

The requirement that partial summary judgment promote litigation efficiency is consistent with the more general prohibition against "litigation by installment" or "piecemeal litigation." The potential risks associated with partial summary judgment were canvassed thoroughly by Justice Groberman (as he then was) in *Coast Foundation Society (1974) v. John Currie Architect Inc.*, 2003 BCSC 1781, 2003 CarswellBC 3001, which concerned a proposed summary trial under former British Columbia Rule 18A. Groberman J.'s reasoning at paras. 16–24 as to why the court is "justifiably reluctant to decide cases in a piecemeal fashion" by means of partial summary judgment warrants quotation at length:

> [T]he primary purpose of Rule 18A [British Columbia's former summary trial procedure] is the efficient resolution of disputes. Where the court does not consider that the determination of an issue under Rule 18A will assist in the efficient resolution of the dispute, it ought not to make the determination.
>
> There are at least two aspects to be considered in gauging the efficiency of the summary trial process. First, this court must be concerned about the allocation of its own resources. Summary trial applications that will not, even if successful, reduce the length of trial, should, in general, be discouraged. The court must recognize the reality that judicial time is a scarce resource.
>
> Second, the court must consider the efficiency of a partial determination from the standpoint of the litigation itself. Piecemeal decision-making is rarely an efficient manner in which to resolve a dispute. It raises the possibility of multiple appeals on individual issues, and this will generally impede rather than hasten the orderly determination of the action.
>
> [. . .]
>
> . . . The summary procedure's chief advantages are speed and efficiency. Where the court is not convinced that the determination of an issue will be a speedy or efficient step towards resolution of the dispute, it ought not to accede to an application under Rule 18A.
>
> . . . I accept that the court should, in appropriate cases, consider the prospect of settlement as a factor in determining whether to deal with a substantive issue on a Rule 18A application. In many cases, however, it would simply be unjust to allow one party, over the objection of another, to have a single issue determined in advance of all others, in the hope that it will enhance its bargaining position. [citations omitted]

The proposed summary trial in *Coast Foundation Society* concerned a limitation defence. Although the limitation issue was discrete and there was sufficient evidence to grant judgment, Justice Groberman declined to do so on the grounds that: (a) resolving the limitation issue on the motion would not reduce the time needed to resolve the litigation as a whole; and (b) granting partial judgment would likely result in splitting the litigation into two paths through the court system. With respect to the latter ground, His Honour noted that the limitation issue was sufficiently important as to make an appeal from the partial judgment "virtually certain," and a further appeal to the Supreme Court of Canada was likely. "In the meantime," Justice Groberman warned, "the trial of the action will either be postponed, or proceed under an awkward uncertainty as to what issues will ultimately need to be decided."

Rule 28.01 — Crossclaims — Limitations Period for Crossclaim against Estate

In *Levesque v. Crampton Estate*, 2017 ONCA 455; additional reasons 2017 ONCA 676; reconsideration / rehearing refused 2018 ONCA 75, the Court of Appeal reviewed the interplay between: (a) the general two-year limitation period in the *Limitations Act, 2002*, S.O. 2002, c. 24, Sched. B, which is subject to the principle of discoverability; and (b) s. 38(3) of the *Trustee Act*, R.S.O. 1990, c. T.23, which provides that an action against an estate in respect of wrongs committed by the deceased is subject to an absolute two-year limitation period running from the date of death. The court was required to determine which limitation period applies where one joint tortfeasor has died and another brings a crossclaim for contribution and indemnity against his estate. The court held that the absolute two-year limitation period set out in the *Trustee Act* applies.

The plaintiff in this case alleged that he was sexually assaulted by the defendant priest, who died in 2010. In 2013 the plaintiff commenced an action against the priest's estate and the Roman Catholic Corporation of the Episcopal Archdiocese of Ottawa ("RCECO"). In 2014, the RCECO crossclaimed against the estate. In response, the estate brought a motion to dismiss the crossclaim on the basis that it was brought more than two years after the priest's death and therefore outside the limitation period set out in s. 38 of the *Trustee Act*. The motions judge dismissed the motion at first instance, finding that the crossclaim was governed by s. 18 of the *Limitations Act*, which provides that in the case of a claim by one joint tortfeasor against another for contribution and indemnity, the claim is "discovered" and therefore the two-year limitation period begins to run, on the day on which the wrongdoer seeking indemnity is served with the plaintiff's claim. Accordingly, the motions judge concluded that the limitation period started to run in 2013 and that the crossclaim was not time-barred.

The decision was reversed on appeal. The Court of Appeal held that s. 38 of the *Trustee Act* applied as rule 1.03(1) makes clear that a crossclaim is an "action" and s. 38 of the *Trustee Act* is included in the s. 19 *Limitations Act* schedule of statutory limitations that prevail over those listed in the *Limitations Act*. The court stated that although the application of the *Trustee Act* limitation period in this case was harsh (in that it resulted in the claim being time-barred before it was discovered), its inclusion in the schedule to the Act reflected a clear policy choice in favour of certainty and finality in estate matters after a fixed period of two years from death.

Rules 29.2 and 31.06 — Scope and Proportionality of Documentary Production

In *Inzola Group Limited v. The Corporation of the City of Brampton*, 2018 ONSC 767, 2018 CarswellOnt 2310 (S.C.J.), Daley R.S.J. refused the defendant's motion, brought just three months before trial, for production of additional documents on the issues of damages. Following a further examination for discovery of the plaintiff's corporate representative, counsel for the defendant municipality had sent a letter to the plaintiff's counsel that listed not only questions refused and taken under advisement at the examination, but also 15 additional questions that the defendant had failed to put to the plaintiff's representative during oral examination. The 15 additional questions sought extensive additional documentary disclosure from the plaintiff on matters that the defendant asserted were relevant to both quantum of damages and mitigation. The requested additional productions concerned the financial details of previous construction projects undertaken by the plaintiff with parties other than the defendant. The defendant maintained that the requested additional financial documents, although not relied upon the plaintiff's expert on damages, should have informed the expert's assessment. The plaintiff refused to answer the additional questions and refused to provide the requested additional document production. The defendant brought a motion to compel production of the refused documents under the guise of a "refusals motion."

Justice Daley concluded that the additional production was properly refused. Taking into consideration "fair and adequate disclosure, relevance, proportionality and the current state of [the] action," His Honour held that the defendant had failed to demonstrate that the additional documents dealing with the unrelated projects were relevant. Furthermore, production of the requested documentation could not be compelled under rule 31.06, which provides for the "disclosure of the findings, opinions and conclusions of an expert," because the plaintiff's expert had not relied on the requested material. Justice Daley concluded that even if relevant, the requested additional production was "entirely disproportionate" in light of: (a) the already extensive documentary productions made and the lengthy oral discoveries already conducted; (b) the extraordinary and burdensome volume of additional productions requested; and (c) the late-timing of the request.

Rule 30.02 — Production of Documents — Settlement Privilege

While settlement privilege provides a general protection against compelled disclosure, it is subject to certain exceptions, one of which arises where disclosure is necessary to prevent overcompensation of a plaintiff: *Sable Offshore Energy Inc. v. Ameron International Corp.*, [2013] 2 S.C.R. 623. In *IPEX Inc. v. AT Plastics Inc.*, 2017 ONSC 7706, 2017 CarswellOnt 20894 (S.C.J.), the defendant moved to compel disclosure of the plaintiff's settlement agreement in a related action on the grounds that disclosure was necessary to prevent double recovery. Master Graham, after carefully parsing the parties' pleadings, concluded that the defendant's motion was premature, as the necessity for disclosure, if any, turned on whether the action resulted in an award of damages to the plaintiff and, if so, the legal basis for that award. The case is interesting not only for dealing with the "double recovery" exception to settlement privilege, but also as an extraordinary illustration of how a party through artful pleading may sometimes avoid what would otherwise appear to be a foregone outcome.

The complicated background to the motion can be summarized as follows. The plaintiff IPEX, a manufacturer of plastic pipes, was sued in three product liability class actions alleging that its products were inherently defective. IPEX settled the class actions for $125 million USD. Thereafter, IPEX commenced separate actions for indemnity against the two companies that supplied it with its raw materials during the period for which it was sued in the class actions. IPEX had used the defendant ATP Plastics (Supplier A) as its supplier for the initial part of the class period, and thereafter exclusively used Supplier B, the defendant to IPEX's other action. At no point did IPEX manufacture pipes using materials from both suppliers.

IPEX and Supplier B settled their action on confidential terms, but informed Supplier A that the settlement was only in respect of the period during which Supplier B (and not Supplier A) had provided IPEX with raw materials. In response to the settlement, Supplier A did three things. First, it amended its statement of defence to plead that: (a) any damages owed to IPEX had to be apportioned between IPEX, Supplier A and itself; and (b) by reason of the settlement between IPEX and Supplier, any award of damages against it ought to be reduced by the value of that settlement to avoid double recovery. Second, Supplier A commenced a third party action against Supplier B for contribution and indemnity. Third, on the basis of its amendments to its statement of defence, Supplier A moved to compel disclosure of the settlement agreement between IPEX and Supplier B.

Responding in turn, IPEX then amended its reply to Supplier A's statement of defence to plead that, among other things: (a) its claim against Supplier A was only in respect of the materials supplied by Supplier A (and not Supplier B); (b) its primary theory against Supplier A was not based on several liability and apportionment, but rather on the theory that Supplier A was legally liable for the entire cost of the class actions settlement because Supplier A's supply of defective materials was a sufficient and foreseeable cause of the class actions and resulting class action settlement; (c) that in the event that Supplier A was found only severally liable, IPEX's claim to damages would be limited to only those damages directly attributable to the pipe manufactured using Supplier A's materials and not Supplier B's materials; and (d) in the event that the trial judge concluded that Supplier A was liable for the entirety of the $125 million USD class actions settlement (or the entirety of some lesser amount for which the court may conclude it was reasonable for IPEX to settle), if the resulting award of damages when added to the settlement monies received from Supplier B resulted in over compensation, any damages payable by Supplier A would be reduced to prevent such overcompensation.

In short, IPEX's amended pleadings provided (or at least created the strong impression) that the value of its settlement with Supplier B would only need to be disclosed to prevent double recovery in the event that a trial judge found Supplier A liable for one particular theory of liability advanced by IPEX, but not on the alternative theory it also advanced. Accordingly, Master Graham concluded that it was "therefore necessary to await the outcome of the trial to know the basis of any finding of liability against [Supplier A]."

Rule 30 — Mandatory Disclosure of Agreements that Affect Adversarial Orientation

In *Handley v. DTE Industries Limited*, 2018 ONCA 324, 2018 CarswellOnt 5118, the Ontario Court of Appeal addressed the appropriate remedy for non-disclosure of an agreement between parties that converts their adversarial relationship to a cooperative one. In this case, the non-disclosing parties submitted that the court should treat their failure to disclose their litigation agreement (described in detail below) as a species of abuse of process, a categorization which gives the court considerable discretion in fashioning a remedy. In contrast, the parties to whom disclosure was denied argued that the litigation agreement in question fundamentally changed the adversarial orientation of the litigation and the remedy for its non-disclosure was a stay of all claims advanced by the parties to the agreement.

The action involved a subrogated claim by which the plaintiff's insurer sought to recoup monies spent to rectify the plaintiff's property after a newly installed outdoor oil tank failed and flooded the property with hundreds of litres of heating oil. Just before expiry of the limitation period, the insurer through the plaintiff ("Insurer") sued the installer and vendor of the oil tank

("Installer"), the manufacturer of the tank ("Manufacturer") and the oil company that filled the tank ("Oil Company"). However, the Insurer stood little chance of recovering on any judgment that might be awarded against the first two defendants. The Installer had voluntarily dissolved, the Manufacturer was insolvent, and neither the Installer nor the Manufacturer was insured. Sometime after the Insurer's limitation expired, the Insurer changed counsel. Its new counsel thought that a claim should also have been advanced against the Installer's supplier ("Supplier"). The time for the Insurer to advance a claim against the Supplier had passed, but there was still time for the Installer or the Manufacturer to third-party the Supplier.

In a bid to recover from the Manufacturer, the Insurer entered into an agreement with the Installer whereby it was agreed that the Installer would commence a third party claim against the Supplier and the Insurer would cover the Installer's costs of prosecuting it. Shortly thereafter, the Insurer and the Installer entered into two further agreements on the same day. Under the first new agreement, which was set out in a letter, the Installer assigned all of its rights in the lawsuit to the Insurer and the Insurer agreed to indemnify the Installer against any costs or damages awarded against the Installer. Under the second new agreement, the Insurer assumed responsibility for defending the Installer and prosecuting the third party claims.

As the litigation unfolded, the Supplier became aware that the Insurer and the Installer had entered into some kind of agreement and over the next three months made unsuccessful requests for its disclosure. The Supplier then advised that it would be bringing a motion to compel disclosure, in response to which the Insurer indicated that the Supplier should direct all future correspondence to counsel for LawPro. LawPro disclosed the e-mail agreement and eventually, after abandoning claims to privilege, the original agreement and the letter agreement. Following full disclosure of the agreements, the Supplier brought an application seeking a stay of the action.

The application judge concluded that the litigation agreements should have been disclosed immediately as they had clearly changed the "adversarial orientation of the lawsuit" as discussed in *Moore v. Bertuzzi*, 2012 ONSC 3248 (S.C.J.). Accordingly, the only real issue was the appropriate remedy. In the case most directly on point, *Aecon Buildings v. Brampton (City)*, 2010 ONCA 898; leave to appeal refused (2011), 425 N.R. 400 (note) (S.C.C.), the Court of Appeal held that the failure of the plaintiff and defendant in that case to disclose a similar litigation agreement amounted to an abuse of process that required "consequences of the most serious nature for the defaulting party," namely a stay of proceedings against the third and fourth parties from which the agreement had been withheld, irrespective of whether the non-disclosure had caused prejudice. The application judge, however, was not persuaded that *Aecon* required the remedy of a stay, and instead took guidance from an earlier decision of the Court of Appeal, *Abarca v. Vargas*, 2015 ONCA 4, 2015 CarswellOnt 24, a case involving very different facts, wherein the court held that where an abuse of process has occurred the court must fashion a proportionate remedy. The application judge concluded that neither the third party Supplier nor the co-defendant Oil Company had been prejudiced by the non-disclosure because the litigation agreement had not affected their potential liability or exposure, and dismissed the application for a stay.

The decision was dismissed on appeal. The Court of Appeal clarified that parties have an obligation to immediately disclose "any agreement between or amongst parties to a lawsuit that has the effect of changing the adversarial position of the parties set out in their pleadings into a co-operative one." On the issue of remedy, the court held that its earlier decision in *Aecon* was binding as it dealt with the specific form of abuse of process at issue, the non-disclosure of litigation agreement that fundamentally changed the landscape of the litigation. Adopting its earlier reasons in *Aecon*, the court reiterated that the court must impose "consequences of the most serious nature on the defaulting party," regardless of whether the non-disclosure resulted in prejudice, because "[t]o permit the litigation to proceed without disclosure of agreements such as the one in issue renders the process a sham and amounts to a failure of justice." Further, in imposing the remedy of stay or dismissal, no issue of fairness arises where the defaulting party is a sophisticated and experienced litigant. As the court explained:

> . . . As a matter of litigation procedural policy, no unfairness is likely to arise from the application of the *Aecon* principles. At least one party to a litigation agreement usually is an insurer or other sophisticated litigation participant who should be well aware of the *Aecon* principles. Where such a sophisticated party fails to comply with its clear disclosure obligation, judicial time should not be spent on inquiring into what, if any, prejudice was caused by a breach of the party's clear obligation . . .

Rule 30.02 — Waiver of Solicitor-Client Privilege

In *Canadian Appliance Source Inc. v. Utradecanada.com Inc.*, 2017 ONSC 4959, 2017 CarswellOnt 12967 (S.C.J.); affirmed 2018 ONSC 2960 (S.C.J.), an action arising from a failed lease transaction, Master McGraw was asked to determine whether the plaintiff had waived privilege over its lawyer's file by filing an affidavit from its lawyer containing statements regarding the lawyer's legal advice and recommendations in support of a summary judgment motion. The Master noted that *Creative Career Systems Inc. v. Ontario*, 2012 ONSC 649 (S.C.J.) established a two-part test for requiring disclosure on the basis of waiver of privilege: (1) the presence of legal advice that is material to the lawsuit; and (2) the party who received the legal advice must make the receipt of it an issue in the claim or defence. Thus, a waiver of privilege occurs when the party intentionally makes its receipt of legal advice a material fact in his or her claim or defence. Further, full disclosure of that legal advice is required in accordance with the longstanding principle that a party may not disclose only selected aspects of its solicitor-client privileged communications.

Master McGraw concluded that the plaintiff had waived privilege over its lawyer's file by making an issue of its lawyer's legal advice and recommendations and ordered the plaintiff to produce all documents, correspondence, communications and notes contained in its lawyer's file regarding the parties' failed transaction.

Rule 30.10 — "Norwich Orders" — Discovery in Advance of Proceedings

In *Subway Franchise Systems of Canada, Inc. v. Trent University*, 2017 ONSC 4562 (S.C.J.), Lederer J. dismissed the plaintiff's request for a *Norwich* order on the grounds that the requested discovery could be obtained from already named defendants.

A *Norwich* order is a rarely granted remedy that permits a potential plaintiff to obtain discovery from a third party before commencing litigation. Where granted, such orders are usually made to enable a wronged party to determine the identity of the wrongdoer. They take their name from the House of Lords decision in *Norwich Pharmacal Co. v. Customs & Excise Commissioners* (1973), [1974] A.C. 133, [1973] 2 All E.R. 943, [1973] 3 W.L.R. 164 (H.L.), where the potential plaintiff Norwich, a pharmaceutical company, knew that drugs were being imported into Britain in violation of its patents, but did not know by whom. Norwich was granted an order compelling the British customs authority to disclose the identity of the importer.

In *Subway*, the plaintiff had already commenced an action for defamation against the CBC and a CBC journalist following the airing on CBC television of a program segment entitled "Chicken Challenge" in which the CBC tested samples of chicken sold by various fast food restaurants and reported the percentages of chicken and vegetable DNA they contained. The program reported that the plaintiff's "chicken" could be comprised of less than 50% actual chicken. The program also identified the organization that CBC had retained to perform the sampling and DNA testing, as well as the identity of the particular technician who performed the actual testing. Subway was unsure whether it had a cause of action against the organization, and sought a *Norwich* order compelling the organization to disclose various details regarding the mandate of its retainer by CBC and its sampling and DNA testing protocols.

Citing *Isofoton S.A. v. Toronto Dominion Bank* (2007), 85 O.R. (3d) 780 (S.C.J.), Justice Lederer identified the following considerations for determining whether a *Norwich* order should be granted:

> (a) whether the applicant has provided evidence sufficient to raise a valid, *bona fide* or reasonable claim;
>
> (b) whether the applicant has established a relationship with the third party from whom the information is sought such that it establishes that the third party is somehow involved in the acts complained of;
>
> (c) whether the third party is the only practicable source of the information available;
>
> (d) whether the third party can be indemnified for costs to which the third party may be exposed because of the disclosure; and
>
> (e) whether the interests of justice favour the obtaining of disclosure.

Lederer J. concluded that the third factor — whether the third party is the only practicable source of the information available — was dispositive of Subway's application. The information and documents sought by Subway was clearly in the possession of an existing defendant to its action, CBC, and accordingly Subway could obtain the information and documents in the usual way through discovery of CBC.

Rule 31.03 — Scope of Examination for Discovery of Corporate Representative

In *Cimtel Inc. v. TSV Holdings Ltd.*, 2018 ONSC 894, 2018 CarswellOnt 1660 (S.C.J.); additional reasons 2018 ONSC 2081 (S.C.J.), Bell J. ruled that the representative of a corporate defendant was not required on discovery to disclose knowledge he acquired in a capacity other than as an officer or employee of the defendant. Whereas the case law establishes that *at trial* a corporate representative may be compelled to disclose all relevant information, regardless of whether the information was obtained through the representative's work for the corporate party, *at discovery* the representative acts only as the "mouthpiece" of the corporation and is only obliged to divulge information known to the representative as a member of the corporation or that she or he can obtain from others employed by the corporation or from its records.

Rule 31.10 — Discovery of Non-Parties — Grounds

Pursuant to rule 31.10(1), a non-party may be examined with leave of the court where there is reason to believe that the person has information relevant to a material issue in the action. A condition for obtaining leave is that the moving party must show that she has been unable to obtain the information from the other party and the non-party: rule 31.10(2).

In *Ozdemir v. Economical Mutual Insurance Group*, 2018 ONSC 214 (S.C.J.), the defendant sought an order to compel the catastrophically injured plaintiff's caregivers to be examined and to produce certain documents. The documents related to the payment of attendant care benefits and housekeeping and maintenance expenses. The evidence before Shaw J. included conflicting information provided by the plaintiff regarding who had been providing attendant care services and how much had been paid. Further, there was no record or documentation supporting proof of payment. The defendant was the plaintiff's auto insurer and had an ongoing duty of good faith towards the plaintiff to pay the appropriate amount of accidental benefits to which he was entitled.

Applying *Famous Players Developments Corp. v. Central Capital Corp.* (1991), 6 O.R. (3d) 765 (Div. Ct.), Justice Shaw stated that before the court will compel a non-party to attend at examinations for discovery, there must be a refusal, actual or constructive, to obtain the information sought. The requirement was met in this case as the plaintiff refused to make his caregiver available and the parties' history of correspondence made it clear the defendant was unable to obtain the information it required without the assistance of the court. Accordingly, Shaw J. ordered the plaintiff's caregiver to attend at an examination for discovery to answer all relevant questions and to produce relevant documents outlined in the order.

In *Ghanim v. Ali*, 2018 ONSC 407, 2018 CarswellOnt 904 (S.C.J.), a motor vehicle accident case, the plaintiff alleged that he suffered a traumatic brain injury that left him with no memory of his life before the accident and, in particular, of his fall three days after the accident in which he hit his head. There was no dispute that the plaintiff's wife had detailed information in that regard. The plaintiff's counsel, who also represented the plaintiff's wife, indicated that the plaintiff's wife would be willing to answer questions only by way of undertakings — *i.e.*, in writing. This was not satisfactory to the defendant and the defendant moved for an order compelling examination of the plaintiff's wife as a non-party witness.

Master Champagne concluded that the case met the test under rule 31.10(2) and granted the order. The plaintiff's inability to answer questions at his examination about events before and after the accident amounted to a constructive refusal to the defendant's questions, leaving the defendant unable to obtain evidence necessary to properly defend the claim. Further the volume of information that would be the subject of questions and undertakings weighed in favour of allowing the defendant to examine the plaintiff's wife.

Rule 33.03 — Defence Medicals — Recording of Examination

In *Cruz and Cruz v. Saccucci*, 2017 ONSC 7737, 2017 CarswellOnt 20687 (S.C.J.), a motor vehicle accident case, the court ordered the plaintiff to attend a second defence medical examination and denied the plaintiff's request to have the examination recorded, after the plaintiff surreptitiously recorded the first defence medical examination. The plaintiff opposed the order and further, in the alternative, requested that he be entitled to record the examination if the order is granted.

Justice Sweeny determined that a second and fresh defence medical examination by an orthopaedic specialist was required because the plaintiff's undisclosed recording of the first had, among other things, deprived the doctor of an opportunity to ensure that his words and conduct were being accurately recorded, and would not have captured the essential non-verbal aspects of the examination. A new examination by another doctor was ordered and the plaintiff was prohibited from recording it.

Rule 37.15 — Whether Designated Motions Judge Should Hear Motion for Summary Judgment

Rule 37.15(1) provides that where a proceeding involves complicated issues or where there are two or more proceedings that involve similar issues, a judge may be designated to hear all motions in the proceeding or related proceedings. The purpose of the rule is to permit a single judge to become familiar with the complexities of the case so that all pretrial motions can be dealt with efficiently by the court. A designated rule 37.15 motions judge is precluded from presiding at the trial unless all parties consent: rule 37.15(2).

In *Trade Capital Finance Corp. v. Cook*, 2017 ONSC 3606 (S.C.J.), the court held that a judge appointed to hear motions under rule 37.15 should not hear a motion for summary judgment without the consent of the parties. The court took guidance from *Royal Bank of Canada v. Hussain*, 2016 ONCA 637, where the Court of Appeal refused to allow a summary judgment motion to be heard by the judge who presided at the pretrial conference notwithstanding that rule 50.10(1) only prohibits the pretrial judge from presiding at trial. The *Trade Capital* court noted that the relevant wording of rule 50.10(1) is essentially identical to the wording of rule 37.15(2) which precludes designated motions judge from hearing the trial.

In the author's (Derek McKay's) respectful opinion, the decision is questionable for two reasons. First, there is an important difference between the role of a designated rule 37.15 judge and a judge who presides at a pretrial conference. As the Court of Appeal observed in *Royal Bank of Canada*, the same case relied upon by the court in *Trade Capital*, a principal goal of pretrial conferences is to facilitate settlement and to that end parties must be able to trust that statements made or concessions entertained at the pretrial conference will not be shared with the trial judge. Indeed, rule 50.09 expressly provides that statements made at a pretrial conference cannot be communicated to the trial judge or judge presiding at a hearing or reference in the proceeding. The same concern does not arise in respect of rule 37.15 motions judges.

Second, the same efficiency rationale for having all motions in a complex proceeding heard by a particular judge supports having the same judge hear the summary judgment motion. The propriety of a rule 37.15 judge hearing a summary judgment motion was addressed squarely in *790668 Ontario Inc. v. D'Andrea Management Inc.*, 2013 ONSC 3188, 2013 CarswellOnt 7280 (S.C.J.), a decision that does not appear to have been brought to the court's attention in *Trade Capital*. In *D'Andrea Management*, Heeney R.S.J. denied the defendants leave to appeal from the dismissal of their motion seeking to prohibit the designated rule 37.15 motions judge from hearing a scheduled summary judgment motion. The defendants submitted that a summary judgment motion is akin to a trial and that rule 37.15(2) should be interpreted as precluding a rule 37.15 motions judge from hearing Rule 20 motions. Rejecting the defendant's submission, Heeney R.S.J. stated that having a rule 37.15 judge hear summary judgment motions promotes the efficient use of scarce judicial resources. As His Honour explained:

> The motions judge's concern for economy of judicial resources is well placed. . . . This is a complex case, and it is precisely the kind of case that rule 37.15 was designed to deal with. To assign the motion for judgment to another judge would involve an extraordinary duplication of effort, and an unwarranted consumption of judicial resources that are already stretched to the breaking point. I agree entirely with the motions judge's decision to deny the relief requested.

Justice Heeney also addressed the defendant's concern over the potential for judicial bias, stating that in the event that "the judge, in hearing one motion, clearly disclosed his or her opinion on an issue that would be central to the motion for judgment," resort could be had to existing procedures for dealing with bias and the reasonable apprehension of bias.

There is no reason to conclude that hearing all other pretrial motions in a proceeding will deprive a rule 37.15 judge of her objectivity. As Shaughnessy R.S. stated in *Bisson v. Wai-Ping*, 2005 CarswellOnt 736 (S.C.J.), "I am more than satisfied that any judge appointed under rule 37.15 (1) and faced with a Rule 20 motion for summary judgment will adequately instruct himself/herself on the requirements dictated in rule 20.04 and will not succumb to allegations that are irrelevant and immaterial."

Rule 39.02 — Leave to File Supplementary Affidavit

In *Nexim Healthcare Consultants Inc. v. Yacoob*, 2018 ONSC 91, 2018 CarswellOnt 18 (S.C.J.), following completion of the parties' cross-examinations in advance of the defendants' scheduled summary judgment motion, Master Jolley granted the plaintiff leave to file a supplementary affidavit appending a volume of documents relevant to the plaintiff's alleged damages, despite the fact that the plaintiff had no explanation for the delay. One of the principal arguments advanced in the defendants' factums on the upcoming motion was that the plaintiff had no evidence to support its claim of financial loss. The plaintiff had failed to list the documents in its affidavit of documents and had failed to produce them after requested to do so at examination for discovery. The plaintiff's representative had, however, brought them to his cross-examination as requested in the defendants' notice of examination, but was not questioned in respect of them.

Applying the test granting leave set out in *First Capital Realty Inc. v. Centrecorp Management Services Ltd.*, 2009 CarswellOnt 6914, 83 C.P.C. (6th) 310 (Div. Ct.), Master Jolley held that the plaintiff satisfied the first three, but not the fourth: (1) is the evidence relevant; (2) does the evidence respond to a matter raised on the cross-examination, not necessarily raised for the first time; (3) would granting leave to file the evidence result in non-compensable prejudice that could not be addressed by imposing costs, terms or an adjournment; and (4) did the moving party provide a reasonable or adequate explanation for why the evidence was not included at the outset.

Adopting the "flexible, contextual approach" advocated by Master Muir in *Mars Canada Inc. v. Bemco Cash & Carry Inc.*, 2015 ONSC 8078 (S.C.J.), Master Jolley concluded that the balance of considerations favoured granting the plaintiff leave to introduce the documents on the following terms: the plaintiff was to pay each of the two defendants $5,500 to cover their estimated costs of conducting new cross-examinations and revising their facta. The Master noted that her conclusion might have been different had the plaintiff's representative not previously brought the documents to his cross-examination at the request of the defendants.

Rule 39.03 — Examination of a Witness — Crown Immunity and Parliamentary Privilege

In *Canada (Procureur general) v. Thouin*, 2017 SCC 46, 2017 CarswellQue 8001, the Supreme Court of Canada held that Crown immunity precludes an employee of the Crown from being compelled to give evidence in an action in which neither the Crown nor the employee is a party. Whereas s. 27 of the *Crown Liability and Proceedings Act* ("CLPA") provides that the Crown is subject to the "rules of practice and procedure of the court" in proceedings in which the Crown is named a party, the court held that the section leaves Crown immunity undisturbed in respect of proceedings in which the Crown is merely sought as a witness.

To similar effect, in *Seelster Farms Inc. v. Ontario*, 2017 ONSC 4756, 2017 CarswellOnt 12298 (S.C.J.); additional reasons 2017 ONSC 5895 (S.C.J.), the court granted the defendants' motion to quash the plaintiff's summons to witness of two sitting members of the Ontario legislature on the grounds that the members were immune to summons by virtue of parliamentary privilege. The court held that parliamentary privilege extends absolute immunity to a sitting member of the legislature whenever the legislature is in session, and extends 40 days after the prorogation or dissolution of parliament, and 40 days before the commencement of a new session.

(*Seelster Farms Inc. v. Ontario* is also discussed below with respect to the issue of a party's standing to move to quash a summons to witness.)

Rule 39.03 — Summons to Witness — Standing to Quash

In *Seelster Farms Inc. v. Ontario*, 2017 ONSC 4756, 2017 CarswellOnt 12298 (S.C.J.); additional reasons 2017 ONSC 5895 (S.C.J.), the defendants moved to quash the plaintiff's service of summons to witness on 13 persons. The plaintiff objected, apparently without supporting authority, that the de-

SURVEY

fendants only had standing to seek to quash the summons to witness in respect of the four persons they represented and not the remaining nine. Justice Emery rejected the plaintiff's argument, holding that just as a party has the *prima facie* right under rule 39.03(1) to serve a summons to witness on a person to obtain their evidence for use on a pending motion, all other parties enjoy a corresponding right to seek to quash that summons on grounds, irrespective of the witness's representation.

Rule 40.02 — Motion to Continue Injunction — Use of Evidence Obtained from Injunction

Rule 40.02(1) provides that an interlocutory injunction or mandatory order granted on an *ex parte* motion (*i.e.*, without notice to the parties affected by the order) cannot exceed 10 days. Any subsequent motion to continue or extend the order must generally be on notice to every affected party: rule 40.02(2). A motion to continue an *ex parte* injunction is heard *de novo* (as a fresh motion), and requires the moving party to establish anew the justification for the injunction.

In *Lee v. Chang*, 2018 ONSC 930, 2018 CarswellOnt 1892 (S.C.J.), Justice Favreau confirmed the principle set out in *PricewaterhouseCoopers LLP v. Phelps*, 2010 ONSC 1061 (S.C.J.) that on a motion to continue an injunction granted on an *ex parte* basis, the moving party is precluded from relying on any evidence obtained as a result of the injunction.

The plaintiffs in *Lee v. Chang* brought an *ex parte* application, seeking a *Mareva* injunction freezing the defendants' assets and requiring the defendants' banks to produce banking records. The action related to a series of alleged loans made by the plaintiffs that the defendants had failed to repay. The plaintiffs claimed a number of causes of action, including fraud, breach of trust, fraudulent conveyance, and knowing receipt. The *Mareva* injunction was granted, and 10 days later the plaintiffs brought a motion to continue the injunction on notice to the defendants as required by rule 40.02(2). At the return of the motion, two of the four defendants argued that the injunction should be discontinued as against them on the basis that the evidence originally tendered on the *ex parte* motion was insufficient. The motions judge reserved judgment, and following the hearing of the motion, the plaintiffs sought to introduce additional evidence obtained as a result of the injunction in support of their motion. The motions judge scheduled a further hearing to determine whether the additional evidence should be admitted.

The motions judge rejected the request to admit the further evidence and terminated the injunction as against the two defendants who opposed it. The plaintiffs argued that the evidence should be accepted because it was not available at the time the original *ex parte* motion was heard, relying on the test to admit fresh evidence. The motions judge rejected this argument, ruling that in the context of a motion to continue an *ex parte* injunction, the responding party is entitled to test the record as it was before the judge who originally made the order. As Her Honour explained, "if it turns out that there was insufficient evidence to support the order, the order is essentially void *ab initio*, making it improper to rely on evidence that was obtained as a result of the order." With the benefit of argument from both sides, Justice Favreau held that the grounds for the injunction were not made out.

The decision in *Lee v. Chang* deserves further comment. In the opinion of the author (Derek McKay), an inflexible principle that a party is always precluded from relying on evidence obtained by way of an *ex parte* injunction to support a motion to continue the injunction is unnecessarily restrictive. Unquestionably, because of the absence of the affected party on the motion, a party who seeks an interim injunction on an *ex parte* basis owes a heightened duty of candour to the court, and it is incumbent on the party to make best efforts to secure all relevant evidence in advance and then present a fair and balanced picture of that evidence on the motion. If it is revealed on a subsequent motion to continue the injunction that the party has failed to meet these obligations, and that other evidence that the moving party ought to have put before the court on the original motion would have militated against granting the injunction, it is proper to sanction the moving party and to refuse to continue the injunction even in the face of compelling evidence obtained from the injunction that the injunction is justified. The court has an obligation to control its own process by seeing that it is not abused. By contrast, if with the benefit of argument from the affected party it is discovered that the moving party, through no fault of its own, lacked relevant evidence on the original motion that might have militated against granting the injunction, it is respectfully submitted that the court should be free to consider evidence obtained through the injunction. If that evidence clearly justifies continuing the injunction, the court should have the discretion to continue it where it is in the interests of justice to do so.

SURVEY

Rules 48.04 and 48.06 — Leave to Continue Discovery

Rule 48.04(1) provides that neither a party who sets an action down for trial nor a party who consents to the action being place on the trial list may initiate or continue discovery without leave of the court. In *Maxrelco Immeubles Inc. v. Jim Pattison Industries Ltd.*, 2017 ONSC 5836, 2017 CarswellOnt 15195 (S.C.J.), the plaintiff who had set the action down for trial objected to the defendant's motion to compel answers to undertakings on the basis that the defendant's agreement as to trial dates was tantamount to a consent to the action being placed on the trial list. Adopting the reasoning of Master McLeod (as he then was) in *Kechnie v. MacAllister*, 2016 ONSC 912 (S.C.J.), Justice O'Bonsawin held that the words referenced in rule 48.04(1) to consent to an action being placed on a trial list is a reference to rule 48.06(1) which provides that such a consent must be in writing and filed with the court. Accordingly, the defendant's agreement to trial dates was not a consent within the meaning of rule 48.04(1) and leave to continue discovery was not required.

(This case is also discussed above under rule 53.03(2.1).)

Rule 49 — Pierrenger Agreements — Court's Jurisdiction to Dismiss Crossclaims

A *Pierringer* settlement agreement is one where the plaintiff settles with only one or more defendants and continues the action against other defendants. Typically, the settling defendant pays an amount of money to the plaintiff and agrees to cooperate by making documents and witnesses available; in return for which the settling defendant is released from all claims, including claims for contribution or indemnity by non-settling defendants, such that non-settling defendants can only be held severally liable with the settling defendant (however, if there are multiple non-settling defendants they may be jointly liable with each other). A *Pierringer* agreement also typically includes protections for non-settling defendants, such as a requirement that a non-settling defendant be given access to the settling defendant's evidence. Further, the non-financial terms of the agreement must generally be disclosed to the court and non-settling defendants at the time of settlement, but not the settlement amount. In the event the non-settling defendant is found liable at trial, then the settlement amount is disclosed in order to determine whether the non-settling defendant is entitled to a set-off to avoid over-compensating the plaintiff. The Supreme Court of Canada approved the use of *Pierrenger* agreements in *Sable Offshore Energy Inc. v. Ameron International Corp.*, 2013 SCC 37, [2013] 2 S.C.R. 623. (For a discussion of the settling parties' disclosure obligations, see above, "Rule 30 — Mandatory Disclosure of Agreements that Affect Adversarial Orientation.")

In *Allianz v. Canada (Attorney General)*, 2017 ONSC 4484 (S.C.J.), Master MacLeod (as he then was) held that the court had jurisdiction to dismiss crossclaims by the non-settling defendant, without its consent, as against the settling defendants in order to permit a *Pierringer* agreement to be implemented.

The plaintiffs, comprised of the owners of aircraft and the owners' insurers, claimed that three defendants were liable for damage sustained to the aircraft. The plaintiffs reached a *Pierringer* settlement with two of the three defendants. A condition of the agreement required the plaintiffs to ensure that none of the settling defendants would be exposed to claims for contribution by a non-settling defendant. To give effect to the agreement, the plaintiffs brought a motion: (a) to amend their claim to remove the claims against the settling defendants and to limit the claim against the non-settling defendant to its proportionate liability for damages; and (b) for dismissal of all crossclaims in the action.

Master MacLeod held that the court had the jurisdiction to dismiss the crossclaims, without the consent of the non-settling defendant, and granted the motion on the terms intended to protect the interests of the non-settling defendant. The terms included the following:

a. the non-settling defendant would be entitled to prove at trial the proportion of liability attributable to settling defendants;

b. the plaintiffs could only recover from the non-settling defendant damages in proportion to its several liability;

c. the settling defendants were to preserve all documents listed in their affidavits of documents and any other documents subsequently produced for use in the litigation;

d. the settling defendants had to provide the plaintiffs and the non-settling defendant with the contact information for all witnesses who were deposed at the discovery, on request, and the contact information of any other former or present employees who might be required as witnesses;

e. the parties would be permitted to use the affidavits of documents, documentary production and discovery transcripts relating to the settling defendants;

f. the non-settling defendant would be permitted to bring motions, if necessary, for production and discovery orders against the settling defendants as non-parties; and

g. the action would continue under case management, with Master McLeod (now Justice McLeod) seized of the matter as the case management judge.

Rule 49.09 — Scope of Settlement Release

In *Biancaniello v. DMCT LLP*, 2017 ONCA 386, the Court of Appeal confirmed the principle that general language in a release will only bar a subsequent claim by a releasing party if the subject-matter of the subsequent claim that was specifically in the contemplation of the parties at the time the release was given, and that the court will look to the circumstances surrounding the release to determine what was in the parties' contemplation.

The facts of the case were as follows. In 2008, the corporate plaintiff settled and entered into a release with the defendant, its former accountant, after the defendant claimed for its unpaid fees relating to certain services including the structuring of a butterfly transaction (*i.e.*, the separation of business streams of a single company into separate companies). In 2011, the plaintiff learned that the butterfly transaction could be subject to a large tax liability and so sought and obtained a court order to rescind the transaction, incurring legal and accounting costs in the process. The plaintiff brought a subsequent action against the defendant seeking an order setting aside the 2008 release and claiming negligence, breach of contract, misrepresentation and breach of fiduciary duty.

The defendant brought a motion for summary judgment to dismiss the action on the basis that the plaintiff's claim was barred by the release. The motions judge dismissed the motion, finding that the release did not bar the action as it referred only to "claims existing at the present time" (*i.e.*, 2008) and that, on the evidence, the defendant failed to make the proper records and tax filings that might have revealed its negligence and so there would have been no basis for the plaintiff to have asserted at that time the claims in the later action. Leave to appeal to the Divisional Court was granted and the appeal was dismissed.

The decision was reversed by the Court of Appeal which dismissed the plaintiff's action. Adopting the decision of the UK House of Lords in *Bank of Credit and Commerce International SA v. Munawar Ali*, [2001] UKHL 8, [2001] 1 All E.R. 961, the court distilled the following principles from that case:

1. One looks first to the language of a release to find its meaning.

2. Parties may use language that releases every claim that arises, including unknown claims. However, courts will require clear language to infer that a party intended to release claims of which it was unaware.

3. General language in a release will be limited to the thing or things that were especially in the contemplation of the parties when the release was given.

4. When a release is given as part of the settlement of a claim, the parties want to wipe the slate clean between them.

5. One can look at the circumstances surrounding the giving of the release to determine what was especially in the contemplation of the parties.

Applying these principles, the court found that the release was clear and unequivocal in its intent and effect. The release referred to all claims arising from all services provided by the defendant to the plaintiff up to 2008, and released all claims that were or could have been pleaded in the earlier action.

Rule 53.01 — Admissibility of Video Surveillance as Probative Evidence

In *Rolley v. MacDonell*, 2018 ONSC 164, 2017 CarswellOnt 21233 (S.C.J.), a motor vehicle accident case, Justice Corthorn considered a mid-trial motion to determine the admissibility of surveillance videos, and provided guidance to the bar about such motions.

In the midst of the examination-in-chief of the plaintiff's first witness, the plaintiff's spouse, the defendant brought a motion for leave to admit and rely on various surveillance video recordings as substantive evidence of the plaintiff's abilities and physical condition. The defendant did not intend to rely on the surveillance videos for the purpose of impeachment. The defendant had carried out three rounds of surveillance. The video evidence contained various time gaps and time stamp deficiencies.

The plaintiff challenged the admissibility of the videos as substantive evidence on the basis that they did not satisfy the three-part test articulated by the Court of Appeal in *Iannarella v. Corbett*, 2015 ONCA 110; additional reasons 2015 ONCA 238, which requires:

1. accuracy in truly representing the facts;
2. fairness and the absence of any intention to mislead; and,
3. verification on oath by a person capable of doing so.

Corthorn J. stated that fairness and accuracy are to be addressed from two perspectives. First, the video surveillance evidence must be considered in its entirety to ensure that it satisfies the requirement of overall fairness, in the sense of providing a fair and technically accurate depiction. Second, where the proposed evidence comprises excerpts of surveillance video, the court must ensure that the excerpts are in fact representative of the events it purports to depict. Although finding that some portions of the video surveillance evidence met the *Iannarella* test, Justice Corthorn refused admission on the grounds that its prejudicial effect outweighed any probative value.

Justice Corthorn made clear that her ruling was not meant to change the legal test for the admission of surveillance evidence as substantive evidence, but rather to highlight: (a) the quality of surveillance video recordings required to satisfy the three-part test; and (b) the practicalities to be addressed by videographers and investigation companies in attempting to secure surveillance evidence of the requisite quality.

Commenting for the benefit of the bar on the amount of trial time taken by the defendant's mid-trial motion, Justice Corthorn stated that it is incumbent upon counsel to address these types of motions at pretrials or trial management conferences when timetables are being set to ensure that enough trial time is given to effectively deal with the motions. Further, Her Honour cautioned that parties seeking to rely on such type of evidence ought to give careful consideration to the quality of the video recordings before attempting to have it admitted.

Rule 53.03(2.1)3 — Disclosure of Instructions Provided to Expert

In *Maxreclo Immeubles Inc. v. Jim Pattison Industries Ltd.*, 2017 ONSC 5836, 2017 CarswellOnt 15195 (S.C.J.), the court rejected the defendant's argument that the plaintiff was required to produce all instruction letters provided by its counsel to an expert that it intended to call at trial. Rule 53.03(2.1)3 only requires that an expert include in her report a recitation of instructions with which she was provided, and does not require production of litigation-privileged communications between a party and its expert. As established by the Court of Appeal in *Moore v. Getahun*, 2015 ONCA 55; additional reasons 2015 ONCA 443; leave to appeal refused *Getahun v. Moore*, 2015 CarswellOnt 14066 (S.C.C.), absent evidence that gives rise to a reasonable suspicion that counsel improperly influenced the contents of the expert report, an opposing party cannot demand production of counsel's communications with the expert. As the defendant had not produced any such evidence, the instruction letters to the plaintiff's expert did not need to be produced.

Rule 61.06 — Security for Costs

Rule 61.06(1)(b) permits an appellate court, on motion of the respondent, to make an order for security for costs against the appellant where such an order could be made under rule 56.01, the general security for costs rule. Pursuant to rule 56.01, a court can order security for costs "as is just." On a motion for security for costs the initial onus falls on the defendant to establish that the case falls within one of the branches of rule 56.01, and once that is established, the onus shifts to the plaintiff to demonstrate that it either has sufficient assets to satisfy any costs award, that it is impecunious, or that it has a good chance of succeeding in the claim on its merits.

In *Yaiguaje v. Chevron Corporation*, 2017 ONCA 827, the Court of Appeal confirmed that an order for security for costs is discretionary and should only be made where required to do justice in a case, and set aside an order that the plaintiffs post almost $1 million as security for costs.

Yaiguaje concerns long-running, multi-jurisdictional efforts by residents of Ecuador to obtain and enforce an Ecuadorian judgment against Chevron Corporation. The plaintiffs are representative plaintiffs for approximately 30,000 indigenous Ecuadorians who have been affected by environmental pollution. The plaintiffs first commenced a proceeding in New York in 1993, which was eventually dismissed on the grounds of *forum non conveniens* and on the basis of international comity. The plaintiffs subsequently obtained a US$9.5 billion judgment in Ecuador, which they have been attempting to enforce in courts around the world. Chevron Corporation has resisted enforcement of the judgment, arguing, among other things, that it was obtained fraudulently.

The following litigation history proved relevant to the Court of Appeal's decision. In the enforcement proceedings brought in Ontario, both Chevron Corporation and its Canadian subsidiary are named as defendants. The defendants challenged the jurisdiction of the Superior Court of Justice to recognize and enforce the judgment, and their challenge eventually made its way to the

SURVEY

Supreme Court of Canada which concluded that the Superior Court does have jurisdiction: *Chevron Corp. v. Yaiguaje*, 2015 SCC 42, [2015] 3 S.C.R. 69. The defendants then moved for summary judgment, arguing that shares and assets of Chevron Canada are not exigible pursuant to the *Execution Act*, R.S.O. 1990, c. E.24, and that there is no basis to pierce the corporate veils between Chevron Corporation and the Canadian subsidiary so that the latter's shares and assets become available to satisfy the Ecuadorian judgment. On the motion, summary judgment was granted in favour of the defendants and the claims against the Canadian subsidiary were dismissed. The plaintiffs appealed the order on the summary judgment motion, which appeal is still pending at the time of writing (March 2018).

Before the appeal of the summary judgment motion could be heard, the defendants brought a motion before a single judge of the Court of Appeal seeking security for costs of the proceeding and appeal. The judge granted the motion and ordered that security of $942,951 be posted before the appeal could be heard, finding that the plaintiffs had not established impecuniosity and that they had failed to demonstrate that their claim had a good chance of success. The judge also rejected the plaintiffs' other arguments against imposing a requirement for security for costs, including the argument that the proceeding is essentially a class proceeding. The plaintiffs appealed the security for costs order.

On appeal, a panel of the Court of Appeal set aside the judge's order, finding that the judge failed to consider all the circumstances of the case and conduct a holistic analysis. The court warned against allowing a security for costs order to be used as a litigation tactic to prevent a case from being heard on its merits. While the court declined to set out a list of factors to consider in determining the justness of a security for costs order, holding that each case must be considered on its own facts, the court did set out various circumstances it considered in this case, including that the case was essentially a public interest litigation, and that it was clear from Chevron Corporation's actions over the 25 years of litigation that it would use any available means to avoid paying the Ecuadorean judgment, and that its motion for security for costs was in reality an attempt to bring the enforcement proceedings to an end.

B. — AMENDMENTS TO THE RULES

Summarized below are key amendments to the *Rules of Civil Procedure* ("Rules") made by O. Reg. 584/17, filed with registrar on December 22, 2017, all of which are now in force. The majority of the amendments deal with electronic filing of documents. An additional housekeeping amendment to rule 74.04(1) clarifies already existing evidentiary requirements for obtaining a certification of appointment of estate trustee with a will.

Rules 4.05 and 4.05.1 — Reorganization of Electronic Filing Provisions

The bulk of recent amendments are devoted to reorganizing and centralizing already existing electronic filing and issuance provisions, and introduced few procedural changes. The electronic filing provisions are now gathered together primarily under new rule 4.05.1, with some additional provisions remaining under the preceding rule 4.05.

As under the previous iteration of the Rules, rule 4.05 provides that only the software authorized by the Ministry of the Attorney General may be used to electronically issue or file materials, and deals with the software's confirmation of filing, date and timing of issuance or filing, and requirements to keep originals of electronically filed documents.

Previously existing provisions respecting what can be electronically issued and filed, and various associated requirements, are now relocated to new rule 4.05.1 so that the related provisions are now presented together in one place. Among other things, new rule 4.05.1:

- specifies for the first time the name of the Ministry's authorized software — "Civil Claims Online Portal" in English, and "Portail en ligne pour les actions civiles" in French — making the software readily locatable via an Internet search: rule 4.05.1(1).
- lists the types of documents that may be *filed* electronically at rule 4.05.1(2) (for the newly expanded list of documents, see "Rule 4.05(1) — Additional Document Types May Be Filed Electronically" below).
- lists the types of documents that may be *issued* electronically at rule 4.05.1(7): statement of claim or notice of action in Forms 14A, 14B and 14C.
- provides that in the case of an inconsistency between the information contained in an electronically filed document and information otherwise provided by the filing party through the Ministry's software, the information contained in the electronically filed document prevails, except in the case of a document that specifies the place of commencement, hearing or trial under Rule 13.1 — in which case the information provided by the filing party through the software, rather than in the electronically filed document itself, prevails (the latter exception is new): rule 4.05.1(5).
- requires a paper copy of an electronically filed statement of claim or notice of action to be filed with the registrar with the next paper filing of the plaintiff (except a document filed under subrule 19.01(1) or (2)), or at the request of the registrar (note that this requirement is revoked effective May 28, 2018 — see the summary of the May 28, 2108 amendments below): rule 4.05.1(6).

Rule 4.05(1) — Additional Document Types May Be Filed Electronically

The amendments in force May 28, 2018 expand the list of documents that may be filed electronically to include:

- a statement of claim in Form 14D (statement of claim where action commenced by notice of action): new rule 4.05.1(2)1.
- a statement of defence (Form 18A) and a notice of intent to defend (Form 18B): new rules 4.05.1.(2)2.1 and 2.2.
- any consent or court order required to be filed together with a document referred to in rule 4.05.1(2): rule 4.05.1.(2)6.
- proof of service under rule 16.09 or in Form 17A, 17B or 17C of a document that is filed electronically under rule 4.05.1(2): rule 4.05.1.(2)7.

SURVEY

Rule 4.05.1(6) — Requirement to File Paper Copy

Consistent with the amendments permitting defendants to electronically file documents, the May 28, 2018 amendments also deal comprehensively with the circumstances in which any party who has filed documents electronically is required to file a paper copy. Newly redrafted rule 4.05.1(6) provides that a party who wishes to rely upon its own electronically filed document at a hearing or conference must include a paper copy of the document with the party's materials filed for the hearing of conference. (This new filing requirement replaces the previous obligation that required a plaintiff to file a paper copy of an electronically filed statement of claim or notice of action together with the plaintiff's next paper filing in the proceeding.)

Rule 4.05(10) — Period for Retaining Originals of Signed, Certified or Commissioned Documents

To ensure that originals of certified, signed or commissioned documents remain available for the duration of a proceeding, parties must now retain the original paper format of any such document that is electronically filed until 30 days after the period for an appeal in the proceeding has expired: new rule 4.05(10)(a). Further, the filing party must make the original available for inspection and copying within five days of a request of the court or any party to the proceeding: new rule 4.05(10)(b). Under the previous iteration of the rule, parties were only required to keep the original of a signed, certified or commissioned document until the five-year anniversary of the date on which it was electronically filed.

Rule 74 — Obtaining Certificate of Appointment of Estate Trustee with a Will

As a housekeeping matter, rule 74.04(1) is reorganized to more clearly set out the existing affidavit or other evidentiary requirements on an application for a certificate of appointment of estate trustee with a will.

TABLE OF CASES

References to the Courts of Justice Act, Judicial Review Procedure Act and Statutory Powers Procedure Act are preceded by the appropriate abbreviation and "s." Class Proceedings Act cases are designated **CPA** *and are found in Volume 2, p. 1163* et seq. *Cases regarding Limitation Periods are designated* **LIM** *and are found in Volume 2, p. 1365* et seq. *All other references are to the Rules of Civil Procedure.*

T. OF C.

T. OF C.

T. OF C.

T. OF C.

TABLE OF CASES

T. OF C.

T. OF C.

T. OF C.

T. OF C.

T. OF C.

T. OF C.

T. OF C.

T. OF C.

T. OF C.

T. OF C.

T. OF C.

T. OF C.

T. OF C.

T. OF C.

T. OF C.

T. OF C.

T. OF C.

T. OF C.

T. OF C.

T. OF C.

T. OF C.

T. OF C.

T. OF C.

T. OF C.

T. OF C.

T. OF C.

T. OF C.

T. OF C.

T. OF C.

T. OF C.

T. OF C.

T. OF C.

T. OF C.

T. OF C.

T. OF C.

T. OF C.

T. OF C.

T. OF C.

T. OF C.

T. OF C.

T. OF C.

T. OF C.

T. OF C.

T. OF C.

T. OF C.

T. OF C.

T. OF C.

T. OF C.

T. OF C.

T. OF C.

T. OF C.

T. OF C.

FORMS

TABLE OF FORMS

FORMS

TABLE OF FORMS

FORMS

TABLE OF FORMS

FORMS

TABLE OF FORMS

FORMS

Made under the *Courts of Justice Act*

R.R.O. 1990, Reg. 194

as am. R.R.O. 1990, Reg. 194, r. 13.1.02(12), 24.01(2), 37.03(3), 78.14; O. Reg. 219/91; 396/91; 73/92; 175/92; 535/92; 770/92; 212/93; 465/93; 466/93; 766/93; 351/94; 484/94; 739/94; 740/94; 69/95; 70/95; 377/95; 533/95; 534/95; 60/96; 61/96; 175/96; 332/96; 333/96; 536/96; 554/96; 555/96; 118/97; 348/97; 427/97; 442/97; 171/98; 214/98; 217/98; 292/98; 452/98; 453/98 [s. 2(2) revoked O. Reg. 244/01, s. 7.]; 570/98; 627/98; 288/99; 290/99; 292/99; 484/99; 488/99 [s. 4 repealed O. Reg. 231/13, s. 12.]; 583/99; 24/00; 25/00; 504/00; 652/00; 653/00; 654/00; 113/01; 243/01; 244/01; 284/01; 427/01 [ss. 1(2), 4(2), 5(2), 6(2), (5) not in force at date of publication. Revoked O. Reg. 308/02, ss. 1(2), 2(2), 3(2), 4(3), (5).]; 447/01; 457/01; 206/02; 308/02; 336/02; 19/03; 54/03; 263/03; 419/03; 14/04; 131/04; 132/04, ss. 1–10, 11 (Fr.), 12–24; 219/04; 42/05; 168/05; 198/05; 260/05 [Corrected Ont. Gaz. 9/7/05, Vol. 138:28; 4/3/2006, Vol. 139:9.]; 77/06; 8/07; 573/07; 575/07, ss. 1–4, 5 (Fr.), 6–24, 25(1) (Fr.), (2), 26–38; 55/08; 438/08, ss. 1–12, 13(1)–(3), (4) (Fr.), 14–65, 66 (Fr.), 67; 394/09; 453/09; 186/10, ss. 1–5 (Fr.), 6; 436/10; 55/12, ss. 1, 2, 3 (Fr.), 4–7, 8 (Fr.), 9–15; 399/12; 231/13, ss. 1–9, 10 (Fr.), 11; 43/14; 170/14; CTR 9 OC 14 - 1; 259/14, ss. 1, 2, 3 (Fr.), 4–8, 9 (Fr.), 10 (Fr.), 11; 193/15, ss. 1 (Fr.), 2 (Fr.), 3, 4, 5 (Fr.), 6–18, 19(1), (2) (Fr.), 20–23; 147/16; 281/16; 487/16; 82/17, ss. 1–3, 4 (Fr.), 5–15, 16–19 (Fr.), 20; 203/17; 584/17.

FORM 2.1A — NOTICE THAT PROCEEDING (OR MOTION) MAY BE STAYED OR DISMISSED

Courts of Justice Act

(General heading)

NOTICE THAT PROCEEDING (OR MOTION) MAY BE STAYED OR DISMISSED

TO THE PLAINTIFF OR APPLICANT (OR MOVING PARTY)

The court is considering making an order staying or dismissing this proceeding *(or* motion) under Rule 2.1.01 (*or* Rule 2.1.02) because it appears on its face to be frivolous or vexatious or otherwise an abuse of the process of the court.

THIS PROCEEDING *(or* MOTION) WILL BE STAYED OR DISMISSED unless, within 15 days of receiving this notice, you file with the court a written submission, no more than

10 pages in length, responding to this notice. If you do not file a written submission that complies with this notice and Rule 2.1.01(*or* Rule 2.1.02), the court may order this proceeding (*or* motion) stayed or dismissed without further notice.

A copy of your submission may be given to any other party if the court directs it.

Date .... Signed by ....
Local registrar

(Address of court office)

TO *(Name and address of lawyer or plaintiff/applicant/moving party)*

January 23, 2014

FORM 4A — GENERAL HEADING OF DOCUMENTS — ACTIONS

Courts of Justice Act

[Repealed O. Reg. 77/06, s. 3.]

[Editor's Note: Forms 4A to 78A of the Rules of Civil Procedure have been repealed by O. Reg. 77/06, effective July 1, 2006. Pursuant to Rule of Civil Procedure 1.06, when a form is referred to by number, the reference is to the form with that number that is described in the Table of Forms at the end of these rules and which is available on the Internet through www.ontariocourtforms.on.ca. For your convenience, the government form as published on this website is reproduced below.]

ONTARIO *(Court file no.)*

SUPERIOR COURT OF JUSTICE

BETWEEN:

(name)

Plaintiff

and

(name)

Defendant

(Title of document)

(Text of document)

(For the title of the proceeding in the case of a,

(a) counterclaim against a person who is not already a party to the main action, follow Form 27B;

(b) third or subsequent party claim in an action, follow Form 29A in all documents in the main action and the third or subsequent party action;

(c) garnishment, follow Form 60H; or

(d) mortgage action in which defendants are added on a reference, follow Form 64N;

(*For the general heading in a proceeding in an appellate court, follow Form B.*)

November 1, 2005

FORM 4B — GENERAL HEADING OF DOCUMENTS — APPLICATIONS

Courts of Justice Act

[Repealed O. Reg. 77/06, s. 3.]

[Editor's Note: Forms 4A to 78A of the Rules of Civil Procedure have been repealed by O. Reg. 77/06, effective July 1, 2006. Pursuant to Rule of Civil Procedure 1.06, when a form is referred to by number, the reference is to the form with that number that is described in the Table of Forms at the end of these rules and which is available on the Internet through www.ontariocourtforms.on.ca. For your convenience, the government form as published on this website is reproduced below.]

(Court file no.)

ONTARIO

SUPERIOR COURT OF JUSTICE

BETWEEN:

(name)

Applicant

and

(name)

Respondent

APPLICATION UNDER *(statutory provision or rule under which the application is made)*

(Title of document)

(Text of document)

(In a proceeding in an appellate court, follow Form 61B.)

April 11, 2012

FORM 4C — BACKSHEET

Courts of Justice Act

[Repealed O. Reg. 77/06, s. 3.]

[Editor's Note: Forms 4A to 78A of the Rules of Civil Procedure have been repealed by O. Reg. 77/06, effective July 1, 2006. Pursuant to Rule of Civil Procedure 1.06, when a form is referred to by number, the reference is to the form with that number that is described in the Table of Forms at the end of these rules and which is available on the Internet through www.ontariocourtforms.on.ca. For your convenience, the government form as published on this website is reproduced below.]

(Short title of proceeding) *(Court file no.)*

(Name of Court)

PROCEEDING COMMENCED AT *(place)*

(Title of document)

(if affidavit, indicate name of deponent and date sworn)

(Name, address, telephone number, fax number (if any) and e-mail address (if any) of lawyer or party)

(Law society membership number of lawyer)

(Fax number, if known, and e-mail address, if known, of person on whom document is to be served)

May 1, 2016

FORM 4D — AFFIDAVIT

Courts of Justice Act

[Repealed O. Reg. 77/06, s. 3.]

[Editor's Note: Forms 4A to 78A of the Rules of Civil Procedure have been repealed by O. Reg. 77/06, effective July 1, 2006. Pursuant to Rule of Civil Procedure 1.06, when a form is referred to by number, the reference is to the form with that number that is described in the Table of Forms at the end of these rules and which is available on the Internet through www.ontariocourtforms.on.ca. For your convenience, the government form as published on this website is reproduced below.]

(*General heading*)

AFFIDAVIT OF (NAME)

I, (*full name of deponent*), of the (City, Town, *etc.*) of ...., in the (County, Regional Municipality, *etc.*) of ...., (*where the deponent is a party or the lawyer, officer, director, member or employee of a party, set out the deponent's capacity*), MAKE OATH AND SAY (*or* AFFIRM):

1. (*Set out the statements of fact in consecutively numbered paragraphs, with each paragraph being confined as far as possible to a particular statement of fact.*)

Sworn (*or* Affirmed) before me at the (City, Town, *etc.*) of .... in the (County, Regional Municipality, *etc.*) of ...., on (*date*).	
.... Commissioner for Taking Affidavits (*or as may be*)	.... (*Signature of deponent*)

July 1, 2007

FORM 4E — REQUISITION

Courts of Justice Act

[Repealed O. Reg. 77/06, s. 3.]

[Editor's Note: Forms 4A to 78A of the Rules of Civil Procedure have been repealed by O. Reg. 77/06, effective July 1, 2006. Pursuant to Rule of Civil Procedure 1.06, when a form is referred to by number, the reference is to the form with that number that is described in the Table of Forms at the end of these rules and which is available on the Internet through

www.ontariocourtforms.on.ca. For your convenience, the government form as published on this website is reproduced below.]

(*General heading*)

REQUISITION

TO THE LOCAL REGISTRAR at (*place*)

I REQUIRE (*Set out a concise statement of what is sought and include all particulars necessary for the registrar to act. Where what is sought is authorized by an order, refer to the order in the requisition and attach a copy of the entered order. Where an affidavit or other document must be filed with the requisition, refer to it in the requisition and attach it.*)

(*Date*) (*Name, address and telephone number of lawyer or person filing requisition*)

(*The following are examples of different kinds of requisition.*)

(*Simple requisition*)

I REQUIRE a certified copy of the (*identify document by nature and date*).

(*Order attached*)

I REQUIRE, in accordance with the order dated (*date*), a copy of which is attached, a commission authorizing the taking of evidence before the commissioner named in the order and a letter of request.

I REQUIRE, in accordance with the order dated (*date*), a copy of which is attached, a certificate of pending litigation in respect of the land described in the statement of claim.

(*Affidavit attached*)

I REQUIRE an order to continue this action with (*name*) as plaintiff and (*name*) as defendants. An affidavit stating that the defendant (*name*) has reached the age of majority is attached.

July 1, 2007

FORM 4F — NOTICE OF CONSTITUTIONAL QUESTION

Courts of Justice Act

[Repealed O. Reg. 77/06, s. 3.]

[Editor's Note: Forms 4A to 78A of the Rules of Civil Procedure have been repealed by O. Reg. 77/06, effective July 1, 2006. Pursuant to Rule of Civil Procedure 1.06, when a form is referred to by number, the reference is to the form with that number that is described in the Table of Forms at the end of these rules and which is available on the Internet through

www.ontariocourtforms.on.ca. For your convenience, the government form as published on this website is reproduced below.]

(GENERAL HEADING)

NOTICE OF CONSTITUTIONAL QUESTION

The *(identify party)* intends to question the constitutional validity *(or* applicability) of *(identify the particular legislative provisions or the particular rule of common law) (or* to claim a remedy under subsection 24(1) of the *Canadian Charter of Rights and Freedoms* in relation to an act or omission of the Government of Canada *(or* Ontario*))*.

The question is to be argued on *(day)*, *(date)*, at *(time)*, at *(address of court house)*.

The following are the material facts giving rise to the constitutional question: *(Set out concisely the material facts that relate to the constitutional question. Where appropriate, attach pleadings or reasons for decision.)*

The following is the legal basis for the constitutional question: *(Set out concisely the legal basis for each question, identifying the nature of the constitutional principles to be argued.)*

(Date) . . . . *(Name, address and telephone number of lawyer or party)*

TO

The Attorney General of Ontario *(as required by section 109 of the* Courts of Justice Act*)*

Constitutional Law Branch

4th floor

720 Bay Street

Toronto, Ontario M5G 2K1

fax: (416) 326-4015

The Attorney General of Canada *(as required by section 109 of the* Courts of Justice Act*)*

Suite 3400, Exchange Tower

Box 36, First Canadian Place

Toronto, Ontario M5X 1K6

fax: (416) 952-0298

(or Justice Building

234 Wellington Street

Ottawa, Ontario K1A 0H8

fax: (613) 954-1920)

(Names and addresses of lawyers

for all other parties and of all

other parties acting in person)

(This notice must be served as soon as the circumstances requiring it become known and, in any event, at least 15 days before the question is to be argued, unless the court orders otherwise.)

April 11, 2012

FORM 7A — REQUEST FOR APPOINTMENT OF LITIGATION GUARDIAN

Courts of Justice Act

[Repealed O. Reg. 77/06, s. 3.]

[Editor's Note: Forms 4A to 78A of the Rules of Civil Procedure have been repealed by O. Reg. 77/06, effective July 1, 2006. Pursuant to Rule of Civil Procedure 1.06, when a form is referred to by number, the reference is to the form with that number that is described in the Table of Forms at the end of these rules and which is available on the Internet through www.ontariocourtforms.on.ca. For your convenience, the government form as published on this website is reproduced below.]

(General heading)

REQUEST FOR APPOINTMENT OF LITIGATION GUARDIAN

THE PLAINTIFF (*or as may be*) BELIEVES THAT YOU ARE UNDER A LEGAL DISABILITY. As a party under disability, you must have a litigation guardian appointed by the court to act on your behalf in defending this proceeding.

YOU ARE REQUIRED to have some proper person make a motion to this court forthwith to be appointed as your litigation guardian.

IF YOU FAIL TO DO SO WITHIN TEN DAYS after service of this request, the plaintiff (*or as may be*) may move without further notice to have the court appoint a litigation guardian to act on your behalf.

(*Date*) (*Name, address and telephone number of lawyer or party*)

TO: (*Name and address of party under disability*)

July 1, 2007

FORM 7B — ORDER TO CONTINUE (MINOR REACHING AGE OF MAJORITY)

Courts of Justice Act

[Repealed O. Reg. 77/06, s. 3.]

[Editor's Note: Forms 4A to 78A of the Rules of Civil Procedure have been repealed by O. Reg. 77/06, effective July 1, 2006. Pursuant to Rule of Civil Procedure 1.06, when a form is referred to by number, the reference is to the form with that number that is described in the Table of Forms at the end of these rules and which is available on the Internet through www.ontariocourtforms.on.ca. For your convenience, the government form as published on this website is reproduced below.]

(*General heading*)

(*Court seal*)

ORDER TO CONTINUE

On the requisition of (*identify party*) and on reading the affidavit of (*name*), filed, which states that the minor (*name of party*) reached the age of majority on (*date*),

IT IS ORDERED that this proceeding continue by (*or* against) (*name of party*) without a litigation guardian and that the title of the proceeding be amended accordingly in all documents issued, served or filed after the date of this order.

Date .... Signed by ....

Local registrar

Address of court office ....

....

November 1, 2005

FORM 8A — NOTICE TO ALLEGED PARTNER

Courts of Justice Act

[Repealed O. Reg. 77/06, s. 3.]

[Editor's Note: Forms 4A to 78A of the Rules of Civil Procedure have been repealed by O. Reg. 77/06, effective July 1, 2006. Pursuant to Rule of Civil Procedure 1.06, when a form is referred to by number, the reference is to the form with that number that is described in the Table of Forms at the end of these rules and which is available on the Internet through

www.ontariocourtforms.on.ca. For your convenience, the government form as published on this website is reproduced below.]

(*General heading*)

NOTICE TO ALLEGED PARTNER

YOU ARE ALLEGED TO HAVE BEEN A PARTNER on (*date*) (*or* during (*period*)) in the partnership of (*firm name*) named as a party to this proceeding.

IF YOU WISH TO DENY THAT YOU WERE A PARTNER at any material time, you must defend this proceeding separately from the partnership, denying that you were a partner at the material time. If you fail to do so, you will be deemed to have been a partner on the date (*or* during the period) set out above.

AN ORDER AGAINST THE PARTNERSHIP MAY BE ENFORCED AGAINST YOU PERSONALLY if you are deemed to have been a partner, if you admit that you were a partner or if the court finds that you were a partner at the material time.

(*Date*) (*Name, address and telephone number of plaintiff's lawyer or plaintiff*)

TO (*Name and address of alleged partner*)

July 1, 2007

FORM 11A — ORDER TO CONTINUE (TRANSFER OR TRANSMISSION OF INTEREST)

Courts of Justice Act

[Repealed O. Reg. 77/06, s. 3.]

[Editor's Note: Forms 4A to 78A of the Rules of Civil Procedure have been repealed by O. Reg. 77/06, effective July 1, 2006. Pursuant to Rule of Civil Procedure 1.06, when a form is referred to by number, the reference is to the form with that number that is described in the Table of Forms at the end of these rules and which is available on the Internet through www.ontariocourtforms.on.ca. For your convenience, the government form as published on this website is reproduced below.]

(*General heading*)

(*Court seal*)

ORDER TO CONTINUE

On the requisition of (*identify party or person*) and on reading the affidavit of (*name*), filed, which indicates that on (*date*), (*recite the details of the transfer or transmission of interest or liability*),

IT IS ORDERED that this proceeding continue and that the title of the proceeding in all documents issued, served or filed after the date of this order be as follows: (*Set out new title of proceeding, deleting name of party whose interest is transferred or transmitted and showing name of new party.*)

Date .... Signed by ....

Local registrar

Address of court office ....

....

A party who wishes to set aside or vary this order must make a motion to do so forthwith after the order comes to the party's attention.

Where a transmission of interest occurs by reason of bankruptcy, leave of the bankruptcy court may be required under section 69.4 of the *Bankruptcy and Insolvency Act* (Canada) before the proceeding may continue.

November 1, 2005

FORM 14A — STATEMENT OF CLAIM (GENERAL)

Courts of Justice Act

[Repealed O. Reg. 77/06, s. 3.]

[Editor's Note: Forms 4A to 78A of the Rules of Civil Procedure have been repealed by O. Reg. 77/06, effective July 1, 2006. Pursuant to Rule of Civil Procedure 1.06, when a form is referred to by number, the reference is to the form with that number that is described in the Table of Forms at the end of these rules and which is available on the Internet through www.ontariocourtforms.on.ca. For your convenience, the government form as published on this website is reproduced below.]

(General heading)

(Court seal)

STATEMENT OF CLAIM

TO THE DEFENDANT

A LEGAL PROCEEDING HAS BEEN COMMENCED AGAINST YOU by the plaintiff. The claim made against you is set out in the following pages.

IF YOU WISH TO DEFEND THIS PROCEEDING, you or an Ontario lawyer acting for you must prepare a statement of defence in Form 18A prescribed by the *Rules of Civil Procedure*, serve it on the plaintiff's lawyer or, where the plaintiff does not have a lawyer, serve it on the plaintiff, and file it, with proof of service in this court office, WITHIN TWENTY DAYS after this statement of claim is served on you, if you are served in Ontario.

If you are served in another province or territory of Canada or in the United States of America, the period for serving and filing your statement of defence is forty days. If you are served outside Canada and the United States of America, the period is sixty days.

Instead of serving and filing a statement of defence, you may serve and file a notice of intent to defend in Form 18B prescribed by the *Rules of Civil Procedure*. This will entitle you to ten more days within which to serve and file your statement of defence.

IF YOU FAIL TO DEFEND THIS PROCEEDING, JUDGMENT MAY BE GIVEN AGAINST YOU IN YOUR ABSENCE AND WITHOUT FURTHER NOTICE TO YOU. IF YOU WISH TO DEFEND THIS PROCEEDING BUT ARE UNABLE TO PAY LEGAL FEES, LEGAL AID MAY BE AVAILABLE TO YOU BY CONTACTING A LOCAL LEGAL AID OFFICE.

(Where the claim made is for money only, include the following:)

IF YOU PAY THE PLAINTIFF'S CLAIM, and $ .... for costs, within the time for serving and filing your statement of defence you may move to have this proceeding dismissed by the court. If you believe the amount claimed for costs is excessive, you may pay the plaintiff's claim and $400 for costs and have the costs assessed by the court.

TAKE NOTICE: THIS ACTION WILL AUTOMATICALLY BE DISMISSED if it has not been set down for trial or terminated by any means within five years after the action was commenced unless otherwise ordered by the court.

Date .... Issued by ....
Local registrar

Address of court office ....
....

TO *(Name and address of each defendant)*

(In an action under the simplified procedure provided in Rule 76, add:)

THIS ACTION IS BROUGHT AGAINST YOU UNDER THE SIMPLIFIED PROCEDURE PROVIDED IN RULE 76 OF THE *RULES OF CIVIL PROCEDURE*.

CLAIM

1. The plaintiff claims: *(State here the precise relief claimed.)*

(Then set out in separate, consecutively numbered paragraphs each allegation of material fact relied on to substantiate the claim.)

(Where the statement of claim is to be served outside Ontario without a court order, set out the facts and the specific provisions of Rule 17 relied on in support of such service.)

(Date of issue) *(Name, address and telephone number of lawyer or plaintiff*

June 9, 2014

FORM 14B — STATEMENT OF CLAIM (MORTGAGE ACTION — FORECLOSURE)

Courts of Justice Act

[Repealed O. Reg. 77/06, s. 3.]

[Editor's Note: Forms 4A to 78A of the Rules of Civil Procedure have been repealed by O. Reg. 77/06, effective July 1, 2006. Pursuant to Rule of Civil Procedure 1.06, when a form is referred to by number, the reference is to the form with that number that is described in the Table of Forms at the end of these rules and which is available on the Internet through www.ontariocourtforms.on.ca. For your convenience, the government form as published on this website is reproduced below.]

(General heading)

(Court seal)

STATEMENT OF CLAIM (MORTGAGE ACTION — FORECLOSURE)

TO THE DEFENDANT

A LEGAL PROCEEDING HAS BEEN COMMENCED AGAINST YOU by the plaintiff. The claim made against you is set out in the following pages.

IF YOU WISH TO DEFEND THIS PROCEEDING, you or an Ontario lawyer acting for you must prepare a statement of defence in Form 18A prescribed by the *Rules of Civil Procedure*, serve it on the plaintiff's lawyer or, where the plaintiff does not have a lawyer, serve it on the plaintiff, and file it, with proof of service, in this court office, WITHIN 20 DAYS after this statement of claim is served on you, if you are served in Ontario.

If you are served in another province or territory of Canada or in the United States of America, the period for serving and filing your statement of defence is 40 days. If you are served outside Canada and the United States of America, the period is 60 days.

Instead of serving and filing a statement of defence, you may serve and file a notice of intent to defend in Form 18B prescribed by the *Rules of Civil Procedure*. This will entitle you to 10 more days within which to serve and file your statement of defence.

(Where payment of the mortgage debt is claimed, add:)

IF YOU PAY THE PLAINTIFF'S CLAIM, and $ .... for costs, within the time for serving and filing your statement of defence, you may move to have this proceeding dismissed by the court. If you believe the amount claimed for costs is excessive, you may pay the plaintiff's claim and $400 for costs and have the costs assessed by the court.

REQUEST TO REDEEM

Whether or not you serve and file a statement of defence, you may request the right to redeem the mortgaged property by serving a request to redeem (Form 64A) on the plaintiff and filing it in this court office within the time for serving and filing your statement of defence or at any time before being noted in default. If you do so, you will be entitled to seven days notice of the taking of the account of the amount due to the plaintiff, and to 60 days from the taking of the account within which to redeem the mortgaged property.

If you hold a lien, charge or encumbrance on the mortgaged property subsequent to the mortgage in question, you may file a request to redeem, which must contain particulars of your claim verified by an affidavit, and you will be entitled to redeem only if your claim is not disputed or, if disputed, is proved on a reference.

REQUEST FOR SALE

If you do not serve and file a statement of defence, you may request a sale of the mortgaged property by serving a request for sale (Form 64F) on the plaintiff and filing it in this court office within the time for serving and filing your statement of defence, or at any time before being noted in default. If you do so, the plaintiff will be entitled to obtain a judgment for a sale with a reference and you will be entitled to notice of the reference.

If you hold a lien, charge or encumbrance on the mortgaged property subsequent to the mortgage in question and you do not serve and file a request to redeem, you may file a request for sale which must contain particulars of your claim verified by an affidavit, and must be accompanied by a receipt showing that $250 has been paid into court as security for the costs of the plaintiff(s) and of any other party having carriage of the sale.

DEFAULT JUDGMENT

IF YOU FAIL TO SERVE AND FILE A STATEMENT OF DEFENCE, JUDGMENT MAY BE GIVEN AGAINST YOU WITHOUT FURTHER NOTICE. IF YOU WISH TO DEFEND THIS PROCEEDING BUT ARE UNABLE TO PAY LEGAL FEES, LEGAL AID MAY BE AVAILABLE TO YOU BY CONTACTING A LOCAL LEGAL AID OFFICE.

TAKE NOTICE: THIS ACTION WILL AUTOMATICALLY BE DISMISSED if it has not been set down for trial or terminated by any means within five years after the action was commenced unless otherwise ordered by the court.

Date .... Issued by ....
Local registrar

Address of
court office ....
....

TO: *(Name and address of each defendant)*

REQUEST TO REDEEM (sale action)

Whether or not you serve and file a statement of defence, you may request the right to redeem the mortgaged property by serving a request to redeem (Form 64A) on the plaintiff and filing it in this court office within the time for serving and filing your statement of defence, or at any time before being noted in default. If you do so, you will be entitled to seven days notice of the taking of the account of the amount due to the plaintiff, and to 60 days from the taking of the account within which to redeem the mortgaged property.

DEFAULT JUDGMENT

IF YOU FAIL TO SERVE AND FILE A STATEMENT OF DEFENCE, JUDGMENT MAY BE GIVEN AGAINST YOU WITHOUT FURTHER NOTICE. IF YOU WISH TO DEFEND THIS PROCEEDING BUT ARE UNABLE TO PAY LEGAL FEES, LEGAL AID MAY BE AVAILABLE TO YOU BY CONTACTING A LOCAL LEGAL AID OFFICE.

TAKE NOTICE: THIS ACTION WILL AUTOMATICALLY BE DISMISSED if it has not been set down for trial or terminated by any means within five years after the action was commenced unless otherwise ordered by the court.

Date .... Issued by ....
Local registrar

Address of
court office ....
....

TO: *(Name and address of each defendant)*

(Subsequent encumbrancers are not to be named as defendants in this statement of claim in a sale action.)

(In an action under the simplified procedure provided in Rule 76, add:)

THIS ACTION IS BROUGHT AGAINST YOU UNDER THE SIMPLIFIED PROCEDURE PROVIDED IN RULE 76 OF THE *RULES OF CIVIL PROCEDURE.*

CLAIM

1. The plaintiff claims:

(foreclosure)

(a) that the equity of redemption in the property secured by the mortgage mentioned below be foreclosed;

(or)

(sale)

(a) that the property secured by the mortgage mentioned below be sold and proceeds of sale applied towards the amount due under the mortgage, and payment to the plaintiff by the defendant *(name of defendant against whom payment of any deficiency is claimed)* personally of any deficiency if the sale proceeds are not sufficient to pay the amount found due to the plaintiff;

(possession)

(b) possession of the mortgaged property;

(payment of mortgage debt)

(c) payment by the defendant *(name of defendant against whom payment of mortgage debt is claimed)* of the sum of $ .... *(from paragraph 6 below)* now due under the mortgage together with interest at the rate of *(mortgage rate)* per cent per year until judgment;

(interest)

(d) post-judgment interest in accordance with the *Courts of Justice Act(or where the mortgage provides for interest after judgment at the mortgage rate, substitute*: post-judgment interest at the rate of *(mortgage rate)* per cent per year in accordance with the mortgage); and

(costs)

(e) the costs of this action (on a substantial indemnity basis *if the mortgage so provides, or if it provides for costs on a solicitor and client basis).*

2. The plaintiff's claim is on a mortgage dated *(date)*, made between *(name of mortgagor)* and *(name of mortgagee)*, and registered *(give particulars of registration and of any assignment of the mortgage)*, under which the defendant *(or as may be)* mortgaged the property described below for a term of .... years securing the sum of $ .... and interest on that sum at the rate of .... per cent

per year. The mortgage provides for the payment of principal and interest as follows: *(Set out terms of payment. Add a reference to provisions in the mortgage for solicitor and client costs and post-judgment interest if applicable.)*

3. The mortgage provides that on default of payment of any sum required to be paid under the mortgage, the principal becomes due and payable and the plaintiff is entitled to possession of the mortgaged property and to foreclosure of the equity of redemption in the mortgaged property (or sale of the mortgaged property *or as may be)*.

4. *(Where a claim for payment is made under section 20 of the* Mortgages Act *against a person other than the original mortgagor, add:)* The defendant *(name)* became liable under section 20 of the *Mortgages Act* to pay the amount of the mortgage debt to the plaintiff by reason of *(set out particulars of the transfer of the mortgaged property from the original mortgagor to this defendant).*

5. Default in payment of principal and interest *(or as may be)* occurred on *(date)*, and still continues.

6. There is now due under the terms of the mortgage:

(a)	for principal	$..........
(b)	for taxes paid	$..........
(c)	for premiums of insurance paid	$..........
(d)	for maintenance costs paid	$..........
(e)	for heating costs paid	$..........
(f)	for utility costs paid	$..........
	(add any other costs in similar fashion)	
(g)	for interest *(set out particulars)*	$..........
	Total now due:	$..........

The defendant *(name)* is liable to pay these sums and subsequent interest at the rate of .... per cent per year.

7. The following is a description of the mortgaged property: *(Set out a description sufficient for registration. For Land Titles land, include the parcel number.)*

(In a foreclosure action where one or more subsequent encumbrancers are named as defendants, add:)

8. The defendant (name) has been made a party to this action as a subsequent encumbrancer.

(Where the statement of claim is to be served outside Ontario without a court order, set out the facts and the specific provisions of Rule 17 relied on in support of the service.)

(Date) *(Name, address and telephone number of plaintiff's lawyer or plaintiff)*

June 9, 2014

FORM 14C — NOTICE OF ACTION

Courts of Justice Act

[Repealed O. Reg. 77/06, s. 3.]

NOTICE OF ACTION **Form 14C**

[Editor's Note: Forms 4A to 78A of the Rules of Civil Procedure have been repealed by O. Reg. 77/06, effective July 1, 2006. Pursuant to Rule of Civil Procedure 1.06, when a form is referred to by number, the reference is to the form with that number that is described in the Table of Forms at the end of these rules and which is available on the Internet through www.ontariocourtforms.on.ca. For your convenience, the government form as published on this website is reproduced below.]

(General heading)

(Court seal)

NOTICE OF ACTION

TO THE DEFENDANT

A LEGAL PROCEEDING HAS BEEN COMMENCED AGAINST YOU by the plaintiff. The claim made against you is set out in the statement of claim served with this notice of action.

IF YOU WISH TO DEFEND THIS PROCEEDING, you or an Ontario lawyer acting for you must prepare a statement of defence in Form 18A prescribed by the *Rules of Civil Procedure*, serve it on the plaintiff's lawyer or, where the plaintiff does not have a lawyer, serve it on the plaintiff, and file it, with proof of service, in this court office, WITHIN TWENTY DAYS after this notice of action is served on you, if you are served in Ontario.

If you are served in another province or territory of Canada or in the United States of America, the period for serving and filing your statement of defence is forty days. If you are served outside Canada and the United States of America, the period is sixty days.

Instead of serving and filing a statement of defence, you may serve and file a notice of intent to defend in Form 18B prescribed by the *Rules of Civil Procedure*. This will entitle you to ten more days within which to serve and file your statement of defence.

IF YOU FAIL TO DEFEND THIS PROCEEDING, JUDGMENT MAY BE GIVEN AGAINST YOU IN YOUR ABSENCE AND WITHOUT FURTHER NOTICE TO YOU. IF YOU WISH TO DEFEND THIS PROCEEDING BUT ARE UNABLE TO PAY LEGAL FEES, LEGAL AID MAY BE AVAILABLE TO YOU BY CONTACTING A LOCAL LEGAL AID OFFICE.

(Where the claim made is for money only, include the following:)

IF YOU PAY THE PLAINTIFF'S CLAIM, and $ .... for costs, within the time for serving and filing your statement of defence, you may move to have this proceeding dismissed by the court. If you believe the amount claimed for costs is excessive, you may pay the plaintiff's claim and $400 for costs and have the costs assessed by the court.

TAKE NOTICE: THIS ACTION WILL AUTOMATICALLY BE DISMISSED if it has not been set down for trial or terminated by any means within five years after the action was commenced unless otherwise ordered by the court.

Date .... Issued by ....

Local registrar

Address of court office ....

....

TO: *(Name and address of each defendant)*

(In an action under the simplified procedure provided in Rule 76, add:)

THIS ACTION IS BROUGHT AGAINST YOU UNDER THE SIMPLIFIED PROCEDURE PROVIDED IN RULE 76 OF THE *RULES OF CIVIL PROCEDURE*.

CLAIM

The plaintiff's claim is for *(set out a short statement of the nature of the plaintiff's claim).*

(Date of issue) *(Name, address and telephone number of lawyer or plaintiff)*

June 9, 2014

FORM 14D — STATEMENT OF CLAIM (ACTION COMMENCED BY NOTICE OF ACTION)

Courts of Justice Act

[Repealed O. Reg. 77/06, s. 3.]

[Editor's Note: Forms 4A to 78A of the Rules of Civil Procedure have been repealed by O. Reg. 77/06, effective July 1, 2006. Pursuant to Rule of Civil Procedure 1.06, when a form is referred to by number, the reference is to the form with that number that is described in the Table of Forms at the end of these rules and which is available on the Internet through www.ontariocourtforms.on.ca. For your convenience, the government form as published on this website is reproduced below.]

(*General heading*)

STATEMENT OF CLAIM

Notice of action issued on (*date*)

(In an action under the simplified procedure provided in Rule 76, add:)

THIS ACTION IS BROUGHT AGAINST YOU UNDER THE SIMPLIFIED PROCEDURE PROVIDED IN RULE 76 OF THE RULES OF CIVIL PROCEDURE.

1. The plaintiff claims: (*State here the precise relief claimed*).

(*Then set out in separate, consecutively numbered paragraphs each allegation of material fact relied on to substantiate the claim.*)

(*Where the statement of claim is to be served outside Ontario without a court order, set out the facts and the specific provisions of Rule 17 relied on in support of such service.*)

(*Date*) (*Name, address and telephone number of lawyer or plaintiff*)

July 1, 2007

FORM 14E — NOTICE OF APPLICATION

Courts of Justice Act

(General heading)

(Court seal)

NOTICE OF APPLICATION

TO THE RESPONDENT

A LEGAL PROCEEDING HAS BEEN COMMENCED by the applicant. The claim made by the applicant appears on the following page.

THIS APPLICATION will come on for a hearing on *(day)*, *(date)*, at *(time)*, at *(address of court house)*.

IF YOU WISH TO OPPOSE THIS APPLICATION, to receive notice of any step in the application or to be served with any documents in the application, you or an Ontario lawyer acting for you must forthwith prepare a notice of appearance in Form 38A prescribed by the *Rules of Civil Procedure*, serve it on the applicant's lawyer or, where the applicant does not have a lawyer, serve it on the applicant, and file it, with proof of service, in this court office, and you or your lawyer must appear at the hearing.

IF YOU WISH TO PRESENT AFFIDAVIT OR OTHER DOCUMENTARY EVIDENCE TO THE COURT OR TO EXAMINE OR CROSS-EXAMINE WITNESSES ON THE APPLICATION, you or your lawyer must, in addition to serving your notice of appearance, serve a copy of the evidence on the applicant's lawyer or, where the applicant does not have a lawyer, serve it on the applicant, and file it, with proof of service, in the court office where the application is to be heard as soon as possible, but at least four days before the hearing.

IF YOU FAIL TO APPEAR AT THE HEARING, JUDGMENT MAY BE GIVEN IN YOUR ABSENCE AND WITHOUT FURTHER NOTICE TO YOU. IF YOU WISH TO OPPOSE THIS APPLICATION BUT ARE UNABLE TO PAY LEGAL FEES, LEGAL AID MAY BE AVAILABLE TO YOU BY CONTACTING A LOCAL LEGAL AID OFFICE.

Date .... Issued by ....

Local registrar

Address of court office ....

....

TO *(Name and address of each respondent)*

APPLICATION

1. The applicant makes application for: *(State here the precise relief claimed.)*

2. The grounds for the application are: *(Specify the grounds to be argued, including a reference to any statutory provision or rule to be relied on.)*

3. The following documentary evidence will be used at the hearing of the application: *(List the affidavits or other documentary evidence to be relied on.)*

(Where the notice of application is to be served outside Ontario without a court order, state the facts and the specific provisions of Rule 17 relied on in support of such service.)

(Date of issue) *(Name, address and telephone number of lawyer or applicant)*

March 31, 2010

FORM 14E.1 — NOTICE OF APPLICATION UNDER SUBSECTION 140(3) OF THE COURTS OF JUSTICE ACT

Courts of Justice Act

(General heading)

(Court seal)

NOTICE OF APPLICATION UNDER SUBSECTION 140(3) OF THE COURTS OF JUSTICE ACT

TO THE ATTORNEY GENERAL OF ONTARIO AND THE RESPONDENT(S)

AN APPLICATION UNDER SUBSECTION 140(3) OF THE *COURTS OF JUSTICE ACT* HAS BEEN COMMENCED by the applicant. The claim made by the applicant appears on the following page.

THIS APPLICATION shall be heard in writing without the attendance of the parties, unless the court orders otherwise. An order under subsection 140(4) of the *Courts of Justice Act* granting leave to institute or continue a proceeding, or rescinding an order made under subsection 140(1) of that Act, shall not be made without an opportunity being provided to the Attorney General of Ontario and the respondents to serve and file a respondent's application record and factum.

Date .... Issued by ....
Local registrar

Address of court office ....

....

TO

Crown Law Office (Civil Law)

Ministry of the Attorney General

720 Bay Street, 8th Floor

Toronto, Ontario M5G 2K1

(Names and addresses of lawyers for all other parties and of allother parties acting in person)

APPLICATION UNDER SUBSECTION 140(3) OF THE COURTS OF JUSTICE ACT

1. The applicant makes application for: *(State here the precise relief claimed.)*

2. The grounds for the application are: *(Specify the grounds to be argued, including a reference to any statutory provision or rule to be relied on.)*

(Where the notice of application is to be served outside Ontario without a court order, state the facts and the specific provisions of Rule 17 relied on in support of such service.)

(Date of issue)	*(Name, address and telephone number of lawyer or applicant)*

January 23, 2014

FORM 14F — INFORMATION FOR COURT USE

Courts of Justice Act

[Repealed O. Reg. 77/06, s. 3.]

[Editor's Note: Forms 4A to 78A of the Rules of Civil Procedure have been repealed by O. Reg. 77/06, effective July 1, 2006. Pursuant to Rule of Civil Procedure 1.06, when a form is referred to by number, the reference is to the form with that number that is described in the Table of Forms at the end of these rules and which is available on the Internet through www.ontariocourtforms.on.ca. For your convenience, the government form as published on this website is reproduced below.]

Courts of Justice Act

ONTARIO

SUPERIOR COURT OF JUSTICE

(General heading)

INFORMATION FOR COURT USE

1. This proceeding is an:	❑ action	❑ application
2. Has it been commenced under the *Class Proceedings Act, 1992*?	❑ yes	❑ no
3. If the proceeding is an action, does Rule 76 (Simplified Procedure) apply?	❑ yes	❑ no

Note: *Subject to the exceptions found in subrule 76.01(1), it is MANDATORY to proceed under Rule 76 for all cases in which the money amount claimed or the value of real or personal property claimed is $100,000 or less.*

4. The claim in this proceeding (action or application) is in respect of:

(Select the one item that best describes the nature of the main claim in the proceeding.)

Bankruptcy or insolvency law	❑	Motor vehicle accident	❑
Collection of liquidated debt	❑	Municipal law	❑
Constitutional law	❑	Partnership law	❑
Construction law (other than construction lien)	❑	Personal property security	❑
Construction lien	❑	Product liability	❑
Contract law	❑	Professional malpractice (other than medical)	❑
Corporate law	❑	Real property (including leases; excluding mortgage or charge)	❑
Defamation	❑	Tort: economic injury (other than from medical or professional malpractice)	❑
Employment or labour law	❑		
Intellectual property law	❑	Tort: personal injury (other than from motor vehicle accident)	❑
Judicial review	❑	Trusts, fiduciary duty	❑
Medical malpractice	❑	Wills, estates	❑
Mortgage or charge	❑		

CERTIFICATION

I certify that the above information is correct, to the best of my knowledge.

Date: ....

Signature of lawyer
(if no lawyer, party must sign)

November 1, 2008

FORM 15A — NOTICE OF CHANGE OF LAWYERS

Courts of Justice Act

[Repealed O. Reg. 77/06, s. 3.]

[Editor's Note: Forms 4A to 78A of the Rules of Civil Procedure have been repealed by O. Reg. 77/06, effective July 1, 2006. Pursuant to Rule of Civil Procedure 1.06, when a form is referred to by number, the reference is to the form with that number that is described in the Table of Forms at the end of these rules and which is available on the Internet through www.ontariocourtforms.on.ca. For your convenience, the government form as published on this website is reproduced below.]

(*General heading*)

NOTICE OF CHANGE OF LAWYER

The plaintiff (*or as may be*), formerly represented by (*name of former lawyer*), has appointed (*name of new lawyer*) as lawyer of record.

(*Date*) (*Name, address and telephone number of new lawyer*)

TO (*Name and address of former lawyer*)

AND TO (*Names and addresses of lawyers for all other parties, or names and addresses of all other parties*)

July 1, 2007

FORM 15B — NOTICE OF APPOINTMENT OF LAWYER

Courts of Justice Act

[Repealed O. Reg. 77/06, s. 3.]

[Editor's Note: Forms 4A to 78A of the Rules of Civil Procedure have been repealed by O. Reg. 77/06, effective July 1, 2006. Pursuant to Rule of Civil Procedure 1.06, when a form is referred to by number, the reference is to the form with that number that is described in the Table of Forms at the end of these rules and which is available on the Internet through www.ontariocourtforms.on.ca. For your convenience, the government form as published on this website is reproduced below.]

(*General heading*)

NOTICE OF APPOINTMENT OF LAWYER

The plaintiff (*or as may be*) has appointed (*name*), as lawyer of record.

(*Date*) (*Name, address and telephone number of lawyer of record*)

TO (*Names and addresses of lawyers for all other parties, or names and addresses of all other parties*)

July 1, 2007

FORM 15C — NOTICE OF INTENTION TO ACT IN PERSON

Courts of Justice Act

[Repealed O. Reg. 77/06, s. 3.]

[Editor's Note: Forms 4A to 78A of the Rules of Civil Procedure have been repealed by O. Reg. 77/06, effective July 1, 2006. Pursuant to Rule of Civil Procedure 1.06, when a form is referred to by number, the reference is to the form with that number that is described in the Table of Forms at the end of these rules and which is available on the Internet through www.ontariocourtforms.on.ca. For your convenience, the government form as published on this website is reproduced below.]

(*General heading*)

NOTICE OF INTENTION TO ACT IN PERSON

The plaintiff (*or as may be*), formerly represented by (*name*) as lawyer of record, intends to act in person.

(complete if filed by the lawyer of record) The plaintiff *(or as may be)* consents to the filing of this form by the lawyer of record on his/her behalf.

Date.................................. Signed by..................................

(print name of plaintiff (or as may be))

(complete if filed by the lawyer of record) I *(name of lawyer of record)* confirm that I have explained the purpose of this form to *(name of the plaintiff or as may be)* and have confirmed his/her intention to act in person in place of me. The plaintiff *(or as may be)* signed this form at the time he/she consented to act in person.

Date.................................. Signed by..................................

(print name of lawyer of record and Law Society registration number)

(Date)

(Name, address for service and telephone number of party intending to act in person)

TO *(Name and address of former lawyer of record)*

AND TO *(Name and addresses of lawyers for all other parties, or names and addresses of all other parties)*

July 1, 2007

FORM 16A — ACKNOWLEDGMENT OF RECEIPT CARD

Courts of Justice Act

[Repealed O. Reg. 77/06, s. 3.]

[Editor's Note: Forms 4A to 78A of the Rules of Civil Procedure have been repealed by O. Reg. 77/06, effective July 1, 2006. Pursuant to Rule of Civil Procedure 1.06, when a form is referred to by number, the reference is to the form with that number that is described in the Table of Forms at the end of these rules and which is available on the Internet through www.ontariocourtforms.on.ca. For your convenience, the government form as published on this website is reproduced below.]

(*General heading*)

TO (*full name*)

You are served by mail with the documents enclosed with this card in accordance with the *Rules of Civil Procedure.*

You are requested to sign the acknowledgment below and mail this card immediately after you receive it. If you fail to do so, the documents may be served on you in another manner and you may have to pay the costs of service.

ACKNOWLEDGMENT OF RECEIPT

I ACKNOWLEDGE that I have received a copy of the following documents: (*To be completed in advance by the sender of the documents. Include sufficient particulars to identify each document.*)

....

Signature of person served

(*The reverse side of this card must bear the name and address of the sender and the required postage.*)

November 1, 2005

FORM 16B — AFFIDAVIT OF SERVICE

Courts of Justice Act

[Repealed O. Reg. 77/06, s. 3.]

[Editor's Note: Forms 4A to 78A of the Rules of Civil Procedure have been repealed by O. Reg. 77/06, effective July 1, 2006. Pursuant to Rule of Civil Procedure 1.06, when a form is referred to by number, the reference is to the form with that number that is described in the Table of Forms at the end of these rules and which is available on the Internet through www.ontariocourtforms.on.ca. For your convenience, the government form as published on this website is reproduced below.]

(If a separate document insert general heading)

AFFIDAVIT OF SERVICE

I, *(full name)*, of the *(*City, Town, *etc.)* of ...., in the *(*County, Regional Municipality, *etc.)* of ...., MAKE OATH AND SAY *(or* AFFIRM*)*:

(Personal service)

1. On *(date)*, at *(time)*, I served *(identify person served)* with the *(identify documents served)* by leaving a copy with him *(or* her*)* at *(address where service was made). (Where the rules provide for personal service on a corporation, etc. by leaving a copy of the document with another person, substitute*: by leaving a copy with *(identify person by name and title)* at *(address where service was made).)*

2. I was able to identify the person by means of *(state the means by which the person's identity was ascertained.)*

(Service by leaving a copy with an adult person in the same household as an alternative to personal service)

1. I served *(identify person served)* with the *(identify documents served)* by leaving a copy on *(date)*, at *(time)*, with a person *(insert name if known)* who appeared to be an adult member of the same household in which *(identify person served)* is residing, at *(address where service was made)*, and by sending a copy by regular lettermail *(or* registered mail*)* on *(date)* to *(identify person served)* at the same address.

2. I ascertained that the person was an adult member of the household by means of *(state how it was ascertained that the person was an adult member of the household).*

3. Before serving the documents in this way, I made an unsuccessful attempt to serve *(identify person)* personally at the same address on *(date). (If more than one attempt has been made, add:* and again on *(date).)*

(Service by mail as an alternative to personal service)

1. On *(date)*, I sent to the *(identify person served)* by regular lettermail *(or* registered mail*)* a copy of the *(identify documents served).*

2. On *(date)*, I received the attached acknowledgment of receipt card *(or* post office receipt) bearing a signature that purports to be the signature of *(identify person).*

(Service by mail on a lawyer)

1. I served *(identify party served)* with the *(identify documents served)* by sending a copy by regular lettermail *(or* registered mail*)* on *(date)* to *(name of lawyer)*, the lawyer for the *(identify party)*, at *(full mailing address)*.

(Service on a lawyer by fax)

1. I served *(identify party served)* with the *(identify documents served)* by sending a copy by fax to *(fax number)* on *(date)* to *(name of lawyer)*, the lawyer for the *(identify party)*.

(Service on a lawyer by courier)

1. I served *(identify party served)* with the *(identify documents served)* by sending a copy by *(name of courier)*, a courier, to *(name of lawyer)*, the lawyer for the *(identify party)*, at *(full address of place for delivery)*.

2. The copy was given to the courier on *(date)*.

(Service by mail on a party acting in person or a non-party)

1. I served *(identify party or person served)* with the *(identify documents served)* by sending a copy by regular lettermail *(or* registered mail*)* on *(date)* to *(full mailing address)*, the last address for service provided by *(identify party or person) (or, where no such address has been provided:* the last known address of *(identify party or person).)*

(Service on a lawyer by e-mail)

1. *(On consent of the parties or by court order)*, I served *(identify party served)* with the *(identify documents served)* by sending a copy by e-mail to *(e-mail address)* on *(date)* to *(name of lawyer)*, the lawyer for the *(identify party)*.

(Service by e-mail on a party acting in person or a non-party)

1. *(On consent of the parties or by court order)*, I served *(identify party or person served)* with the *(identify documents served)* by sending a copy by e-mail to *(e-mail address)* on *(date)*.

SWORN *(etc.)*

May 1, 2016

FORM 16C — CERTIFICATE OF SERVICE BY SHERIFF

Courts of Justice Act

[Repealed O. Reg. 77/06, s. 3.]

[Editor's Note: Forms 4A to 78A of the Rules of Civil Procedure have been repealed by O. Reg. 77/06, effective July 1, 2006. Pursuant to Rule of Civil Procedure 1.06, when a form is referred to by number, the reference is to the form with that number that is described in the Table of Forms at the end of these rules and which is available on the Internet through www.ontariocourtforms.on.ca. For your convenience, the government form as published on this website is reproduced below.]

(If a separate document insert general heading)

CERTIFICATE OF SERVICE BY SHERIFF

(*Personal service*)

I, (*full name*), Sheriff (*or* Sheriff's Officer) of the (County, District, *etc.*) of ...., certify that on (*date*), at (*time*), I served (*identify person served*) with (*identify documents served*) by leaving a copy with him (*or* her) at (*address where service was made*). (*Where the rules provide for personal service on a corporation, etc., by leaving a copy of the document with another person, substitute:* by leaving a copy with (*identify person by name and title*) at (*address where service was made*).)

I was able to identify the person by means of (*state the means by which the person's identity was ascertained.*)

(*Service by leaving a copy with an adult person in the same household as an alternative to personal service*)

I, (*full name*), Sheriff (*or* Sheriff's Officer) of the (County, District, *etc.*) of ...., certify that I served (*identify person served*) with this document by leaving a copy in a sealed envelope addressed to him (*or* her) on (*date*), at (*time*), with a person (*insert name if known*) who appeared to be an adult member of the same household in which (*identify person served*) is residing at (*address where service was made*), and by sending a copy by regular lettermail (*or* registered mail) on (*date*) to (*identify person served*) at the same address.

I ascertained that the person was an adult member of the household by means of (*state how it was ascertained that the person was an adult member of the household*).

Before serving the document in this way, I made an unsuccessful attempt to serve (*identify person*) personally at the same address on (*date*). (*If more than one attempt has been made, add:* and again on (*date*).)

Date ....

(*Signature of sheriff or sheriff's officer*)

November 1, 2005

FORM 17A — REQUEST FOR SERVICE ABROAD OF JUDICIAL OR EXTRAJUDICIAL DOCUMENTS

Courts of Justice Act

[Repealed O. Reg. 77/06, s. 3.]

[Editor's Note: Forms 4A to 78A of the Rules of Civil Procedure have been repealed by O. Reg. 77/06, effective July 1, 2006. Pursuant to Rule of Civil Procedure 1.06, when a form is referred to by number, the reference is to the form with that number that is described in the Table of Forms at the end of these rules and which is available on the Internet through www.ontariocourtforms.on.ca. For your convenience, the government form as published on this website is reproduced below.]

Convention on the service abroad of judicial and extrajudicial documents in civil or commercial matters, signed at The Hague, November 15, 1965.

Identity and address of the applicant	Address of receiving Authority

The undersigned applicant has the honour to transmit — in duplicate — the documents listed below and, in conformity with article 5 of the above-mentioned Convention, requests prompt service of one copy thereof on the addressee, i.e.

(identity and address) ....

....

(a) in accordance with the provisions of sub-paragraph (a) of the first paragraph of article 5 of the Convention*;

(b) in accordance with the following particular method (sub-paragraph (b) of the first paragraph of article 5)*: ....

....

(c) by delivery to the addressee, if the addressee accepts it voluntarily (second paragraph of article 5)*.

The authority is requested to return or to have returned to the applicant a copy of the documents — and of the annexes* — with a certificate as provided on the reverse side.

(*List of Documents*) ....

....

....

....

....

.... Done at ...., the ....

.... Signature or stamp.

* Delete if inappropriate

CERTIFICATE

The undersigned authority has the honour to certify, in conformity with article 6 of the Convention,

(1) that the document has been served*

— the (date) ....

— at (place, street, number) ....

— in one of the following methods authorized by article 5 —

(a) in accordance with the provisions of sub-paragraph (a) of the first paragraph of article 5 of the Convention*;

(b) in accordance with the following particular method*:

. . . .

. . . .;

(c) by delivery to the addressee, who accepted it voluntarily.

The documents referred to in the request have been delivered to:

— (identity and description of person) . . . .

. . . .

— relationship to the addressee (family, business or other)

. . . .

(2) that the document has not been served, by reason of the following facts*:

. . . .

. . . .

. . . .

In conformity with the second paragraph of article 12 of the Convention, the applicant is requested to pay or reimburse the expenses detailed in the attached statement*.

Annexes

Documents returned: . . . .

. . . .

. . . .

In appropriate cases, documents establishing the service: . . . .

. . . .

. . . .

. . . .

Done at ...., the ....

Signature or stamp.

* Delete if inappropriate

November 1, 2005

FORM 17B — SUMMARY OF THE DOCUMENT TO BE SERVED

Courts of Justice Act

[Repealed O. Reg. 77/06, s. 3.]

[Editor's Note: Forms 4A to 78A of the Rules of Civil Procedure have been repealed by O. Reg. 77/06, effective July 1, 2006. Pursuant to Rule of Civil Procedure 1.06, when a form is referred to by number, the reference is to the form with that number that is described in the Table of Forms at the end of these rules and which is available on the Internet through

www.ontariocourtforms.on.ca. For your convenience, the government form as published on this website is reproduced below.]

Convention on the service abroad of judicial and extrajudicial documents in civil or commercial matters, signed at The Hague, November 15, 1965.
(article 5, fourth paragraph)

Name and address of the requesting authority: . . . .

Particulars of the parties*: . . . .

. . . .

JUDICIAL DOCUMENT**

Nature and purpose of the document: . . . .

. . . .

Nature and purpose of the proceedings and, where appropriate, the amount in dispute:

. . . .

Date and place for entering appearance**: . . . .

. . . .

Court which has given judgment**: . . . .

. . . .

Date of judgment**: . . . .

. . . .

Time limits stated in the document**: . . . .

. . . .

EXTRAJUDICIAL DOCUMENT**

Nature and purpose of the document: . . . .

. . . .

Time limits stated in the document** . . . .

. . . .

* If appropriate, identity and address of the person interested in the transmission of the document.

** Delete if inappropriate

November 1, 2005

FORM 17C — NOTICE AND SUMMARY OF DOCUMENT

Courts of Justice Act

[Repealed O. Reg. 77/06, s. 3.]

[Editor's Note: Forms 4A to 78A of the Rules of Civil Procedure have been repealed by O. Reg. 77/06, effective July 1, 2006. Pursuant to Rule of Civil Procedure 1.06, when a form is referred to by number, the reference is to the form with that number that is described in the Table of Forms at the end of these rules and which is available on the Internet through www.ontariocourtforms.on.ca. For your convenience, the government form as published on this website is reproduced below.]

identity and address of the addressee

____

____

IMPORTANT

THE ENCLOSED DOCUMENT IS OF A LEGAL NATURE AND MAY AFFECT YOUR RIGHTS AND OBLIGATIONS. THE SUMMARY OF THE DOCUMENT TO BE SERVED WILL GIVE YOU SOME INFORMATION ABOUT ITS NATURE AND PURPOSE. YOU SHOULD HOWEVER READ THE DOCUMENT ITSELF CAREFULLY. IT MAY BE NECESSARY TO SEEK LEGAL ADVICE.

IF YOUR FINANCIAL RESOURCES ARE INSUFFICIENT YOU SHOULD SEEK INFORMATION ON THE POSSIBILITY OF OBTAINING LEGAL AID OR ADVICE EITHER IN THE COUNTRY WHERE YOU LIVE OR IN THE COUNTRY WHERE THE DOCUMENT WAS ISSUED.

ENQUIRIES ABOUT THE AVAILABILITY OF LEGAL AID OR ADVICE IN THE COUNTRY WHERE THE DOCUMENT WAS ISSUED MAY BE DIRECTED TO:

. . . .

(*It is recommended that the standard terms in the notice be written in English and French and where appropriate also in the official language, or in one of the official languages of the State in which the document originated. The blanks could be completed either in the language of the State to which the document is to be sent, or in English or French.*)

SUMMARY OF THE DOCUMENT TO BE SERVED: . . . .

Name and address of the requesting authority: . . . .

. . . .

*Particulars of the parties: . . . .

. . . .

**JUDICIAL DOCUMENT:

Nature and purpose of the document: . . . .

. . . .

Nature and purpose of the proceedings and where appropriate, the amount in dispute:

. . . .

**Date and place for entering appearance: ....

....

**Court which has given judgment: ....

....

**Date of judgment: ....

**Time limits stated in the document: ....

....

**EXTRAJUDICIAL DOCUMENT ....

Nature and purpose of the document: ....

....

Time limits stated in the document: ....

....

* If appropriate, identity and address of the person interested in the transmission of the document

** Delete if inappropriate

November 1, 2005

FORM 18A — STATEMENT OF DEFENCE

Courts of Justice Act

[Repealed O. Reg. 77/06, s. 3.]

[Editor's Note: Forms 4A to 78A of the Rules of Civil Procedure have been repealed by O. Reg. 77/06, effective July 1, 2006. Pursuant to Rule of Civil Procedure 1.06, when a form is referred to by number, the reference is to the form with that number that is described in the Table of Forms at the end of these rules and which is available on the Internet through www.ontariocourtforms.on.ca. For your convenience, the government form as published on this website is reproduced below.]

(*General heading*)

STATEMENT OF DEFENCE

1. The defendant admits the allegations contained in paragraphs .... of the statement of claim.

2. The defendant denies the allegations contained in paragraphs .... of the statement of claim.

3. The defendant has no knowledge in respect of the allegations contained in paragraphs .... of the statement of claim.

4. (*Set out in separate, consecutively numbered paragraphs each allegation of material fact relied on by way of defence.*)

(*Date*) (*Name, address and telephone number of defendant's lawyer or defendant*)

TO (*Name and address of plaintiff's lawyer or plaintiff*)

July 1, 2007

FORM 18B — NOTICE OF INTENT TO DEFEND

Courts of Justice Act

[Repealed O. Reg. 77/06, s. 3.]

[Editor's Note: Forms 4A to 78A of the Rules of Civil Procedure have been repealed by O. Reg. 77/06, effective July 1, 2006. Pursuant to Rule of Civil Procedure 1.06, when a form is referred to by number, the reference is to the form with that number that is described in the Table of Forms at the end of these rules and which is available on the Internet through www.ontariocourtforms.on.ca. For your convenience, the government form as published on this website is reproduced below.]

(*General heading*)

NOTICE OF INTENT TO DEFEND

The defendant (*or* defendant added by counterclaim *or* third party) intends to defend this action.

(*Date*) (*Name, address and telephone number of lawyer or party serving notice*)

TO (*Name and address of lawyer or party on whom notice is served*)

July 1, 2007

FORM 19A — DEFAULT JUDGMENT (DEBT OR LIQUIDATED DEMAND)

Courts of Justice Act

[Repealed O. Reg. 77/06, s. 3.]

[Editor's Note: Forms 4A to 78A of the Rules of Civil Procedure have been repealed by O. Reg. 77/06, effective July 1, 2006. Pursuant to Rule of Civil Procedure 1.06, when a form is referred to by number, the reference is to the form with that number that is described in the Table of Forms at the end of these rules and which is available on the Internet through www.ontariocourtforms.on.ca. For your convenience, the government form as published on this website is reproduced below.]

(*General heading*)

(*Court seal*)

JUDGMENT

On reading the statement of claim in this action and the proof of service of the statement of claim on the defendant, filed, and the defendant having been noted in default,

1. IT IS ORDERED AND ADJUDGED that the defendant pay to the plaintiff the sum of $ .... and the sum of $ .... for the costs of this action. (*Where costs are to be assessed, substitute* the costs of this action as assessed by the court.)

This judgment bears interest at the rate of .... per cent per year from its date.

Date .... Signed by ....
Local registrar

Address of court office ....
....

November 1, 2005

FORM 19B — DEFAULT JUDGMENT (RECOVERY OF POSSESSION OF LAND)

Courts of Justice Act

[Repealed O. Reg. 77/06, s. 3.]

[Editor's Note: Forms 4A to 78A of the Rules of Civil Procedure have been repealed by O. Reg. 77/06, effective July 1, 2006. Pursuant to Rule of Civil Procedure 1.06, when a form is referred to by number, the reference is to the form with that number that is described in the Table of Forms at the end of these rules and which is available on the Internet through

www.ontariocourtforms.on.ca. For your convenience, the government form as published on this website is reproduced below.]

(*General heading*)

(*Court seal*)

JUDGMENT

On reading the statement of claim in this action and the proof of service of the statement of claim on the defendant, filed, and the defendant having been noted in default,

1. IT IS ORDERED AND ADJUDGED that the defendant deliver to the plaintiff possession of the following land: (*Where the description of the land is very lengthy, substitute* the land described in the attached schedule.)

2. IT IS ORDERED AND ADJUDGED that the defendant pay to the plaintiff the sum of $ .... for the costs of this action. (*Where costs are to be assessed, substitute* the costs of this action as assessed by the court.)

The costs fixed by and payable under this judgment bear interest at the rate of .... per cent per year from its date.

Date .... Signed by ....
Local registrar

Address of court office ....
....

November 1, 2005

FORM 19C — DEFAULT JUDGMENT (RECOVERY OF POSSESSION OF PERSONAL PROPERTY)

Courts of Justice Act

[Repealed O. Reg. 77/06, s. 3.]

[Editor's Note: Forms 4A to 78A of the Rules of Civil Procedure have been repealed by O. Reg. 77/06, effective July 1, 2006. Pursuant to Rule of Civil Procedure 1.06, when a form is referred to by number, the reference is to the form with that number that is described in the Table of Forms at the end of these rules and which is available on the Internet through www.ontariocourtforms.on.ca. For your convenience, the government form as published on this website is reproduced below.]

(*General heading*)

(*Court seal*)

JUDGMENT

On reading the statement of claim in this action and the proof of service of the statement of claim on the defendant, filed, and the defendant having been noted in default,

1. IT IS ORDERED AND ADJUDGED that the defendant deliver to the plaintiff possession of the following personal property: (*or* the personal property described in the attached schedule.)

2. IT IS ORDERED AND ADJUDGED that the defendant pay to the plaintiff the sum of $ .... for the costs of this action. (*Where costs are to be assessed, substitute* the costs of this action as assessed by the court.)

The costs fixed by and payable under this judgment bear interest at the rate of .... per cent per year from its date.

Date .... Signed by ....
Local registrar

Address of court office ....
....

November 1, 2005

FORM 19D — REQUISITION FOR DEFAULT JUDGMENT

Courts of Justice Act

[Repealed O. Reg. 77/06, s. 3.]

[Editor's Note: Forms 4A to 78A of the Rules of Civil Procedure have been repealed by O. Reg. 77/06, effective July 1, 2006. Pursuant to Rule of Civil Procedure 1.06, when a form is referred to by number, the reference is to the form with that number that is described in the Table of Forms at the end of these rules and which is available on the Internet through www.ontariocourtforms.on.ca. For your convenience, the government form as published on this website is reproduced below.]

(*General heading*)

REQUISITION FOR DEFAULT JUDGMENT

TO THE LOCAL REGISTRAR at (*place*)

(*Where the defendant has not been noted in default, begin with:* I REQUIRE you to note the defendant (*name*) in default in this action on the ground that (*state nature of default*).)

I REQUIRE default judgment to be signed against the defendant (*name*).

Default judgment may properly be signed in this action because the claim is for:

❑ a debt or liquidated demand in money

❑ recovery of possession of land

❑ recovery of possession of personal property

❑ foreclosure, sale or redemption of a mortgage

(*Debt or liquidated demand*)

❑ There has been no payment on account of the claim since the statement of claim was issued. (*Complete Parts B and C.*)

OR

❑ The following payments have been made on account of the claim since the statement of claim was issued. (*Complete Parts A and C.*)

PART A — PAYMENT(S) RECEIVED BY PLAINTIFF

(*Complete this part only where part payment of the claim has been received. Where no payment has been received on account of the claim, omit this part and complete Part B.*)

1. Principal

Principal sum claimed in statement of claim (without interest) $............

Date of Payment	Amount of Payment	Payment Amount Principal	Applied to Interest	Principal Sum Owing
TOTAL	$................	$...............	$...............	A $................

2. Prejudgment interest

(*Under section 128 of the Courts of Justice Act, judgment may be obtained for prejudgment interest from the date the cause of action arose, if claimed in the statement of claim.*)

Date on which statement of claim was issued ....

Date from which prejudgment interest is claimed ....

The plaintiff is entitled to prejudgment interest on the claim, calculated as follows:

(*Calculate simple interest only unless an agreement relied on in the statement of claim specifies otherwise. Calculate interest on the principal sum owing from the date of the last payment. To calculate the interest amount, count the number of days since the last payment, multiply that number by the annual rate of interest, multiply the result by the principal sum owing and divide by 365.*)

Principal Sum Owing	Start Date	End Date (Date of Payment)	Number of Days	Rate	Interest Amount

(*The last End Date should be the date judgment is signed.*)

TOTAL B	$ ....
Principal Sum Owing (Total A above)	$ ....
Total Interest Amount (Total B above)	$ ....
SIGN JUDGMENT FOR	$ ....

REQUISITION FOR DEFAULT JUDGMENT **Form 19D**

PART B — NO PAYMENT RECEIVED BY PLAINTIFF

(*Complete this part only where no payment has been received on account of the claim.*)

1. Principal

Principal sum claimed in statement of claim (without interest) A $ ....

2. Prejudgment interest

(*Under section 128 of the Courts of Justice Act, judgment may be obtained for prejudgment interest from the date the cause of action arose, if claimed in the statement of claim.*)

Date on which statement of claim was issued ....

Date from which prejudgment interest is claimed ....

The plaintiff is entitled to prejudgment interest on the claim, calculated as follows:

(*Calculate simple interest only unless an agreement relied on in the statement of claim specifies otherwise. To calculate the interest amount, count the number of days and multiply that number by the annual rate of interest, multiply the result by the principal sum owing and divide by 365.*)

Principal Sum Owing	Start Date	End Date (Date of Payment)	Number of Days	Rate	Interest Amount
			TOTAL B		$ ....

Principal Sum Owing (Total A above)	$ ....
Total Interest Amount (Total B above)	$ ....
SIGN JUDGMENT FOR	$ ....

PART C — POSTJUDGMENT INTEREST AND COSTS

1. Postjudgment interest

The plaintiff is entitled to postjudgment interest at the rate of .... per cent per year,

❑ under the *Courts of Justice Act*, as claimed in the statement of claim.

OR

❑ in accordance with the claim made in the statement of claim.

2. Costs

The plaintiff wishes costs to be,

❑ fixed by the local registrar.

OR

❑ assessed by an assessment officer.

Date ....

(*Signature of plaintiff's lawyer or plaintiff*)

(*Name, address and telephone number of plaintiff's lawyer or plaintiff*)

July 1, 2007

FORM 22A — SPECIAL CASE

Courts of Justice Act

[Repealed O. Reg. 77/06, s. 3.]

[Editor's Note: Forms 4A to 78A of the Rules of Civil Procedure have been repealed by O. Reg. 77/06, effective July 1, 2006. Pursuant to Rule of Civil Procedure 1.06, when a form is referred to by number, the reference is to the form with that number that is described in the Table of Forms at the end of these rules and which is available on the Internet through www.ontariocourtforms.on.ca. For your convenience, the government form as published on this website is reproduced below.]

(*General heading*)

SPECIAL CASE

THE FOLLOWING CASE is stated for the opinion of the court:

1. (*Set out, in consecutively numbered paragraphs, the material facts of the case, as agreed on by the parties, that are necessary to enable the court to determine the questions stated. Refer to and include a copy of any relevant documents.*)

THE QUESTIONS for the opinion of the court are:

1. (*Set out the questions in consecutively numbered paragraphs.*)

THE RELIEF SOUGHT on the determination of the questions stated is:

1. (*Set out the relief sought, as agreed on by the parties, in respect of each possible answer to each of the questions stated, in a form that could readily be incorporated into an order.*)

(*Date*) (*Signature of all lawyers or parties in the proceeding*)
(*Names, addresses and telephone numbers of all lawyers or parties in the proceeding*)

July 1, 2007

FORM 23A — NOTICE OF DISCONTINUANCE

Courts of Justice Act

[Repealed O. Reg. 77/06, s. 3.]

[Editor's Note: Forms 4A to 78A of the Rules of Civil Procedure have been repealed by O. Reg. 77/06, effective July 1, 2006. Pursuant to Rule of Civil Procedure 1.06, when a form is referred to by number, the reference is to the form with that number that is described in the Table of Forms at the end of these rules and which is available on the Internet through www.ontariocourtforms.on.ca. For your convenience, the government form as published on this website is reproduced below.]

(*General heading*)

NOTICE OF DISCONTINUANCE

The plaintiff wholly discontinues this action. (*Where applicable, add* against the defendant (*name*).)

(*Or* The plaintiff discontinues that part of this action relating to .... *Where applicable, add* against the defendant (*name*).)

(*Date*) (*Name, address and telephone number of plaintiff's lawyer or plaintiff*)

TO (*Name and address of defendant's lawyer or defendant*)

NOTE: If there is a counterclaim, the defendant should consider rule 23.02, under which the counterclaim may be deemed to be discontinued.

NOTE: If there is a crossclaim or third party claim, the defendant should consider rule 23.03, under which the crossclaim or third party claim may be deemed to be dismissed.

July 1, 2007

FORM 23B — NOTICE OF ELECTION TO PROCEED WITH COUNTERCLAIM

Courts of Justice Act

[Repealed O. Reg. 77/06, s. 3.]

[Editor's Note: Forms 4A to 78A of the Rules of Civil Procedure have been repealed by O. Reg. 77/06, effective July 1, 2006. Pursuant to Rule of Civil Procedure 1.06, when a form is referred to by number, the reference is to the form with that number that is described in the

Table of Forms at the end of these rules and which is available on the Internet through www.ontariocourtforms.on.ca. For your convenience, the government form as published on this website is reproduced below.]

(*General heading*)

NOTICE OF ELECTION

The defendant elects to proceed with the counterclaim in this action.

(*Date*) (*Name, address and telephone number of defendant's lawyer or defendant*)

TO (*Name and address of plaintiff's lawyer or plaintiff*)

July 1, 2007

FORM 23C — NOTICE OF WITHDRAWAL OF DEFENCE

Courts of Justice Act

[Repealed O. Reg. 77/06, s. 3.]

[Editor's Note: Forms 4A to 78A of the Rules of Civil Procedure have been repealed by O. Reg. 77/06, effective July 1, 2006. Pursuant to Rule of Civil Procedure 1.06, when a form is referred to by number, the reference is to the form with that number that is described in the Table of Forms at the end of these rules and which is available on the Internet through www.ontariocourtforms.on.ca. For your convenience, the government form as published on this website is reproduced below.]

(*General heading*)

NOTICE OF WITHDRAWAL

The defendant withdraws the statement of defence in this action.

(*Or* The defendant withdraws paragraphs .... of the statement of defence in this action.)

(*Date*) (*Name, address and telephone number of defendant's lawyer or defendant*)

TO (*Name and address of plaintiff's lawyer or plaintiff*)

July 1, 2007

FORM 24.1A — NOTICE OF NAME OF MEDIATOR AND DATE OF SESSION

Courts of Justice Act

[Repealed O. Reg. 77/06, s. 3.]

[Editor's Note: Forms 4A to 78A of the Rules of Civil Procedure have been repealed by O. Reg. 77/06, effective July 1, 2006. Pursuant to Rule of Civil Procedure 1.06, when a form is referred to by number, the reference is to the form with that number that is described in the Table of Forms at the end of these rules and which is available on the Internet through www.ontariocourtforms.on.ca. For your convenience, the government form as published on this website is reproduced below.]

(GENERAL HEADING)

TO: MEDIATION CO-ORDINATOR

1. I certify that I have consulted with the parties and that the parties have chosen the following mediator for the mediation session required by Rule 24.1: *(name)*

2. The mediator is named in the list of mediators for *(name county).*

(or)

2. The mediator is not named in a list of mediators, but has been chosen by the parties under clause 24.1.08(2)(c).

3. The mediation session will take place on *(date).*

(Date) *(Name, address, telephone number and fax number of plaintiff's lawyer or of plaintiff)*

April 11, 2012

FORM 24.1B — NOTICE OF ASSIGNED MEDIATOR

Courts of Justice Act

[Repealed O. Reg. 77/06, s. 3.]

[Editor's Note: Forms 4A to 78A of the Rules of Civil Procedure have been repealed by O. Reg. 77/06, effective July 1, 2006. Pursuant to Rule of Civil Procedure 1.06, when a form is referred to by number, the reference is to the form with that number that is described in the Table of Forms at the end of these rules and which is available on the Internet through www.ontariocourtforms.on.ca. For your convenience, the government form as published on this website is reproduced below.]

(General heading)

NOTICE BY ASSIGNED MEDIATOR

TO:

AND TO:

The notice of name of mediator and date of session (Form 24.1A) required by rule 24.1.09 of the *Rules of Civil Procedure* has not been filed in this action. Accordingly, the mediation co-ordinator has assigned me to conduct the mediation session under Rule 24.1. I am a mediator named in the list of mediators for (*name county*).

The mediation session will take place on (*date*), from (*time*) to (*time*), at (*place*).

Unless the court orders otherwise, you are required to attend this mediation session. If you have a lawyer representing you in this action, he or she is also required to attend.

You are required to file a statement of issues (Form 24.1C) by (*date*) (seven days before the mediation session). A blank copy of the form is attached.

When you attend the mediation session, you should bring with you any documents that you consider of central importance in the action. You should plan to remain throughout the scheduled time. If you need another person's approval before agreeing to a settlement, you should make arrangements before the mediation session to ensure that you have ready telephone access to that person throughout the session, even outside regular business hours.

YOU MAY BE PENALIZED UNDER RULE 24.1.13 IF YOU FAIL TO FILE A STATEMENT OF ISSUES OR FAIL TO ATTEND THE MEDIATION SESSION.

(*Date*) (*Name, address, telephone number and fax number of mediator*)

cc. Mediation co-ordinator

November 1, 2005

FORM 24.1C — STATEMENT OF ISSUES

Courts of Justice Act

[Repealed O. Reg. 77/06, s. 3.]

[Editor's Note: Forms 4A to 78A of the Rules of Civil Procedure have been repealed by O. Reg. 77/06, effective July 1, 2006. Pursuant to Rule of Civil Procedure 1.06, when a form is referred to by number, the reference is to the form with that number that is described in the Table of Forms at the end of these rules and which is available on the Internet through www.ontariocourtforms.on.ca. For your convenience, the government form as published on this website is reproduced below.]

(*General heading*)

STATEMENT OF ISSUES

(*To be provided to mediator and parties at least seven days before the mediation session*)

1. Factual and legal issues in dispute

The plaintiff (or defendant) states that the following factual and legal issues are in dispute and remain to be resolved.

(*Issues should be stated briefly and numbered consecutively.*)

2. Party's position and interests (what the party hopes to achieve)

(*Brief summary.*)

3. Attached documents

Attached to this form are the following documents that the plaintiff (*or* defendant) considers of central importance in the action: (*list*)

(*date*) (*party's signature*)

(*Name, address, telephone number and fax number of lawyer of party filing statement of issues, or of party*)

NOTE: When the plaintiff provides a copy of this form to the mediator, a copy of the pleadings shall also be included.

NOTE: Rule 24.1.14 provides as follows:

> All communications at a mediation session and the mediator's notes and records shall be deemed to be without prejudice settlement discussions.

November 1, 2005

FORM 24.1D — CERTIFICATE OF NON-COMPLIANCE

Courts of Justice Act

[Repealed O. Reg. 77/06, s. 3.]

[Editor's Note: Forms 4A to 78A of the Rules of Civil Procedure have been repealed by O. Reg. 77/06, effective July 1, 2006. Pursuant to Rule of Civil Procedure 1.06, when a form is referred to by number, the reference is to the form with that number that is described in the Table of Forms at the end of these rules and which is available on the Internet through www.ontariocourtforms.on.ca. For your convenience, the government form as published on this website is reproduced below.]

(*General heading*)

CERTIFICATE OF NON-COMPLIANCE

TO: MEDIATION CO-ORDINATOR

I, (*name*), mediator, certify that this certificate of non-compliance is filed because:

( ) (*Identify party(ies)*) failed to provide a copy of a statement of issues to the mediator and the other parties (*or* to the mediator *or* to *party(ies)*).

(*Identify plaintiff*) failed to provide a copy of the pleadings to the mediator.

( ) (*Identify party(ies)*) failed to attend within the first 30 minutes of a scheduled mediation session.

(*Date*) (*Name, address, telephone number and fax number, if any, of mediator*)

November 1, 2005

FORM 25A — REPLY

Courts of Justice Act

[Repealed O. Reg. 77/06, s. 3.]

[Editor's Note: Forms 4A to 78A of the Rules of Civil Procedure have been repealed by O. Reg. 77/06, effective July 1, 2006. Pursuant to Rule of Civil Procedure 1.06, when a form is referred to by number, the reference is to the form with that number that is described in the Table of Forms at the end of these rules and which is available on the Internet through www.ontariocourtforms.on.ca. For your convenience, the government form as published on this website is reproduced below.]

(*General heading*)

REPLY

1. The plaintiff admits the allegations contained in paragraphs .... of the statement of defence.

2. The plaintiff denies the allegations contained in paragraphs .... of the statement of defence.

3. The plaintiff has no knowledge in respect of the allegations contained in paragraphs .... of the statement of defence.

4. (*Set out in separate, consecutively numbered paragraphs each allegation of material fact relied on by way of reply to the statement of defence.*)

(*Date*) (*Name, address and telephone number of plaintiff's lawyer or plaintiff*)

TO (*Name and address of defendant's*

lawyer or defendant)

July 1, 2007

FORM 27A — COUNTERCLAIM (AGAINST PARTIES TO MAIN ACTION ONLY)

Courts of Justice Act

[Repealed O. Reg. 77/06, s. 3.]

[Editor's Note: Forms 4A to 78A of the Rules of Civil Procedure have been repealed by O. Reg. 77/06, effective July 1, 2006. Pursuant to Rule of Civil Procedure 1.06, when a form is referred to by number, the reference is to the form with that number that is described in the Table of Forms at the end of these rules and which is available on the Internet through www.ontariocourtforms.on.ca. For your convenience, the government form as published on this website is reproduced below.]

(*Where the counterclaim includes as a defendant to the counterclaim a person who is not already a party to the main action, use Form 27B.*)

(*Include the counterclaim in the same document as the statement of defence, and entitle the document* STATEMENT OF DEFENCE AND COUNTERCLAIM. *The counterclaim is to follow the last paragraph of the statement of defence. Number the paragraphs in sequence commencing with the number following the number of the last paragraph of the statement of defence.*)

COUNTERCLAIM

The defendant (*name if more than one defendant*) claims: (*State here the precise relief claimed.*)

(*Then set out in separate, consecutively numbered paragraphs each allegation of material fact relied on to substantiate the counterclaim.*)

(*Where the defendant to the counterclaim is sued in a capacity other than that in which the defendant is a party to the main action, set out the capacity.*)

(*Date*) (*Name, address and telephone number of plaintiff's lawyer or plaintiff*)

TO (*Name and address of lawyer for defendant to the counterclaim or of defendant to the counterclaim*)

July 1, 2007

FORM 27B — COUNTERCLAIM (AGAINST PLAINTIFF AND PERSON NOT ALREADY PARTY TO MAIN ACTION)

Courts of Justice Act

[Repealed O. Reg. 77/06, s. 3.]

[Editor's Note: Forms 4A to 78A of the Rules of Civil Procedure have been repealed by O. Reg. 77/06, effective July 1, 2006. Pursuant to Rule of Civil Procedure 1.06, when a form is referred to by number, the reference is to the form with that number that is described in the Table of Forms at the end of these rules and which is available on the Internet through www.ontariocourtforms.on.ca. For your convenience, the government form as published on this website is reproduced below.]

(*Where all defendants to the counterclaim are already parties to the main action, use Form 27A.*)

(*General heading*)

(*Add a second title of proceeding, as follows:*)

AND BETWEEN:

(*name*)

Plaintiff by counterclaim

(*Court seal*)

and

(*name*)

Defendants to the counterclaim

STATEMENT OF DEFENCE AND COUNTERCLAIM

TO THE DEFENDANTS TO THE COUNTERCLAIM

A LEGAL PROCEEDING has been commenced against you by way of a counterclaim in an action in this court. The claim made against you is set out in the following pages.

IF YOU WISH TO DEFEND THIS COUNTERCLAIM, you or an Ontario lawyer acting for you must prepare a defence to counterclaim in Form 27C prescribed by the *Rules of Civil Procedure*, serve it on the plaintiff by counterclaim's lawyer or, where the plaintiff by counterclaim does not have a lawyer, serve it on the plaintiff by counterclaim, and file it, with proof of service, in this court, WITHIN TWENTY DAYS after this statement of defence and counterclaim is served on you.

If you are not already a party to the main action and you are served in another province or territory of Canada or in the United States of America, the period for serving and filing your defence is forty days. If you are served outside Canada and the United States of America, the period is sixty days.

If you are not already a party to the main action, instead of serving and filing a defence to counterclaim, you may serve and file a notice of intent to defend in Form 18B prescribed by the *Rules of Civil Procedure*. This will entitle you to ten more days within which to serve and file your defence to counterclaim.

IF YOU FAIL TO DEFEND THIS COUNTERCLAIM, JUDGMENT MAY BE GIVEN AGAINST YOU IN YOUR ABSENCE AND WITHOUT FURTHER NOTICE TO YOU.

IF YOU WISH TO DEFEND THIS PROCEEDING BUT ARE UNABLE TO PAY LEGAL FEES, LEGAL AID MAY BE AVAILABLE TO YOU BY CONTACTING A LOCAL LEGAL AID OFFICE.

(*Where the counterclaim is for money only, include the following:*)

IF YOU PAY THE AMOUNT OF THE COUNTERCLAIM AGAINST YOU, and $ .... for costs, within the time for serving and filing your defence to counterclaim, you may move to have the counterclaim against you dismissed by the court. If you believe the amount claimed for costs is excessive, you may pay the amount of the counterclaim and $400 for costs and have the costs assessed by the court.

Date .... Issued by ....

Local registrar

Address of court office ....

....

TO (*Name and address of defendant to the counterclaim who is not already a party to the main action*)

(*Name and address of lawyer for other defendant to the counterclaim or of other defendant to the counterclaim*)

(*The counterclaim is to follow the last paragraph of the statement of defence. Number the paragraphs in sequence commencing with the number following the number of the last paragraph of the statement of defence.*)

COUNTERCLAIM

The defendant (*name if more than one defendant*) claims: (*State here the precise relief claimed.*)

(*Then set out in separate, consecutively numbered paragraphs each allegation of material fact relied on to substantiate the counterclaim.*)

(*Where a defendant to the counterclaim who is not already a party to the main action is to be served outside Ontario without a court order, set out the facts and the specific provisions of Rule 17 relied on in support of such service.*)

(*Date of issue*)

(*Name, address and telephone number of plaintiff by counterclaim's lawyer or plaintiff by counterclaim*)

July 1, 2007

FORM 27C — DEFENCE TO COUNTERCLAIM

Courts of Justice Act

[Repealed O. Reg. 77/06, s. 3.]

[Editor's Note: Forms 4A to 78A of the Rules of Civil Procedure have been repealed by O. Reg. 77/06, effective July 1, 2006. Pursuant to Rule of Civil Procedure 1.06, when a form is referred to by number, the reference is to the form with that number that is described in the Table of Forms at the end of these rules and which is available on the Internet through www.ontariocourtforms.on.ca. For your convenience, the government form as published on this website is reproduced below.]

(*General heading, including second title of proceeding, if required*)

(*A plaintiff who delivers a reply in the main action must include the defence to counterclaim in the same document as the reply, and the document is to be entitled* REPLY AND DEFENCE TO COUNTERCLAIM. *The defence to counterclaim is to follow immediately after the last paragraph of the reply and the paragraphs are to be numbered in sequence commencing with the number following the number of the last paragraph of the reply.*)

DEFENCE TO COUNTERCLAIM

1. The defendant to the counterclaim admits the allegations contained in paragraphs .... of the counterclaim.

2. The defendant to the counterclaim denies the allegations contained in paragraphs .... of the counterclaim.

3. The defendant to the counterclaim has no knowledge in respect of the allegations contained in paragraphs .... of the counterclaim.

4. (*Set out in separate, consecutively numbered paragraphs each allegation of material fact relied on by way of defence to the counterclaim.*)

(*Date*) (*Name, address and telephone number of lawyer for defendant to the counterclaim or defendant to the counterclaim*)

TO (*Name and address of plaintiff by counterclaim's lawyer or of plaintiff by counterclaim*)

July 1, 2007

FORM 27D — REPLY TO DEFENCE TO COUNTERCLAIM

Courts of Justice Act

[Repealed O. Reg. 77/06, s. 3.]

[Editor's Note: Forms 4A to 78A of the Rules of Civil Procedure have been repealed by O. Reg. 77/06, effective July 1, 2006. Pursuant to Rule of Civil Procedure 1.06, when a form is referred to by number, the reference is to the form with that number that is described in the Table of Forms at the end of these rules and which is available on the Internet through www.ontariocourtforms.on.ca. For your convenience, the government form as published on this website is reproduced below.]

(*General heading, including second title of proceeding, if required*)

REPLY TO DEFENCE TO COUNTERCLAIM

1. The plaintiff by counterclaim admits the allegations contained in paragraphs .... of the defence to counterclaim.

2. The plaintiff by counterclaim denies the allegations contained in paragraphs .... of the defence to counterclaim.

3. The plaintiff by counterclaim has no knowledge in respect of the allegations contained in paragraphs .... of the defence to counterclaim.

4. (*Set out in separate, consecutively numbered paragraphs each allegation of material fact relied on by way of reply to the defence to counterclaim.*)

(*Date*) (*Name, address and telephone number of plaintiff by counterclaim's lawyer or plaintiff by counterclaim*)

TO (*Name and address of lawyer for the defendant to the counterclaim or defendant to the counterclaim*)

July 1, 2007

FORM 28A — CROSSCLAIM

Courts of Justice Act

[Repealed O. Reg. 77/06, s. 3.]

[Editor's Note: Forms 4A to 78A of the Rules of Civil Procedure have been repealed by O. Reg. 77/06, effective July 1, 2006. Pursuant to Rule of Civil Procedure 1.06, when a form is referred to by number, the reference is to the form with that number that is described in the Table of Forms at the end of these rules and which is available on the Internet through www.ontariocourtforms.on.ca. For your convenience, the government form as published on this website is reproduced below.]

(*Include the crossclaim in the same document as the statement of defence, and entitle the document* STATEMENT OF DEFENCE AND CROSSCLAIM. *The crossclaim is to follow the last paragraph of the statement of defence. Number the paragraphs in sequence com-*

mencing with the number following the number of the last paragraph of the statement of defence.)

CROSSCLAIM

The defendant (*name*) claims against the defendant (*name*): (*State here the precise relief claimed.*)

(*Then set out in separate, consecutively numbered paragraphs each allegation of material fact relied on to substantiate the crossclaim.*)

(*Where a defendant to the crossclaim is sued in a capacity other than that in which the defendant is a party to the main action, set out the capacity. Where the statement of defence and crossclaim is to be served outside Ontario without a court order, include the facts and the specific provisions of Rule 17 relied on in support of such service.*)

(*Date*) (*Name, address and telephone number of crossclaiming defendant's lawyer or crossclaiming defendant*)

TO (*Name and address of defendant to crossclaim's lawyer or defendant to crossclaim*)

July 1, 2007

FORM 28B — DEFENCE TO CROSSCLAIM

Courts of Justice Act

[Repealed O. Reg. 77/06, s. 3.]

[Editor's Note: Forms 4A to 78A of the Rules of Civil Procedure have been repealed by O. Reg. 77/06, effective July 1, 2006. Pursuant to Rule of Civil Procedure 1.06, when a form is referred to by number, the reference is to the form with that number that is described in the Table of Forms at the end of these rules and which is available on the Internet through www.ontariocourtforms.on.ca. For your convenience, the government form as published on this website is reproduced below.]

(*General heading*)

DEFENCE TO CROSSCLAIM

1. The defendant (*name*) admits the allegations contained in paragraphs .... of the crossclaim.

2. The defendant (*name*) denies the allegations contained in paragraphs .... of the crossclaim.

3. The defendant (*name*) has no knowledge in respect of the allegations contained in paragraphs .... of the crossclaim.

4. (*Set out in separate, consecutively numbered paragraphs each allegation of material fact relied on by way of defence to the crossclaim.*)

(*Date*)

(*Name, address and telephone number of defendant to crossclaim's lawyer or defendant to crossclaim*)

TO (*Name and address of crossclaiming defendant's lawyer or crossclaiming defendant*)

July 1, 2007

FORM 28C — REPLY TO DEFENCE TO CROSSCLAIM

Courts of Justice Act

[Repealed O. Reg. 77/06, s. 3.]

[Editor's Note: Forms 4A to 78A of the Rules of Civil Procedure have been repealed by O. Reg. 77/06, effective July 1, 2006. Pursuant to Rule of Civil Procedure 1.06, when a form is referred to by number, the reference is to the form with that number that is described in the Table of Forms at the end of these rules and which is available on the Internet through www.ontariocourtforms.on.ca. For your convenience, the government form as published on this website is reproduced below.]

(*General heading*)

REPLY TO DEFENCE TO CROSSCLAIM

1. The defendant (*name*) admits the allegations contained in paragraphs .... of the defence to crossclaim.

2. The defendant (*name*) denies the allegations contained in paragraphs .... of the defence to crossclaim.

3. The defendant (*name*) has no knowledge in respect of the allegations contained in paragraphs .... of the defence to crossclaim.

4. (*Set out in separate, consecutively numbered paragraphs each allegation of material fact relied on by way of reply to the defence to crossclaim.*)

(*Date*)

(*Name, address and telephone number of crossclaiming defendant's lawyer or crossclaiming defendant*)

TO (*Name and address of defendant to crossclaim's lawyer or defendant to crossclaim*)

July 1, 2007

FORM 29A — THIRD PARTY CLAIM

Courts of Justice Act

[Repealed O. Reg. 77/06, s. 3.]

[Editor's Note: Forms 4A to 78A of the Rules of Civil Procedure have been repealed by O. Reg. 77/06, effective July 1, 2006. Pursuant to Rule of Civil Procedure 1.06, when a form is referred to by number, the reference is to the form with that number that is described in the Table of Forms at the end of these rules and which is available on the Internet through www.ontariocourtforms.on.ca. For your convenience, the government form as published on this website is reproduced below.]

ONTARIO (*Court file no.*)

SUPERIOR COURT OF JUSTICE

BETWEEN:

(*name*)

(*Court seal*) Plaintiff

and

(*name*)

Defendant

and

(*name*)

Third Party

THIRD PARTY CLAIM

TO THE THIRD PARTY

A LEGAL PROCEEDING HAS BEEN COMMENCED AGAINST YOU by way of a third party claim in an action in this court.

The action was commenced by the plaintiff against the defendant for the relief claimed in the statement of claim served with this third party claim. The defendant has defended the action on the grounds set out in the statement of defence served with this third party claim. The defendant's claim against you is set out in the following pages.

THIRD PARTY CLAIM **Form 29A**

IF YOU WISH TO DEFEND THIS THIRD PARTY CLAIM, you or an Ontario lawyer acting for you must prepare a third party defence in Form 29B prescribed by the *Rules of Civil Procedure*, serve it on the lawyers for the other parties or, where a party does not have a lawyer, serve it on the party, and file it, with proof of service, WITHIN TWENTY DAYS after this third party claim is served on you, if you are served in Ontario.

If you are served in another province or territory of Canada or in the United States of America, the period for serving and filing your third party defence is forty days. If you are served outside Canada and the United States of America, the period is sixty days.

Instead of serving and filing a third party defence, you may serve and file a notice of intent to defend in Form 18B prescribed by the *Rules of Civil Procedure*. This will entitle you to ten more days within which to serve and file your third party defence.

YOU MAY ALSO DEFEND the action by the plaintiff against the defendant by serving and filing a statement of defence within the time for serving and filing your third party defence.

IF YOU FAIL TO DEFEND THIS THIRD PARTY CLAIM, JUDGMENT MAY BE GIVEN AGAINST YOU IN YOUR ABSENCE AND WITHOUT FURTHER NOTICE TO YOU. IF YOU WISH TO DEFEND THIS PROCEEDING BUT ARE UNABLE TO PAY LEGAL FEES, LEGAL AID MAY BE AVAILABLE TO YOU BY CONTACTING A LOCAL LEGAL AID OFFICE.

(*Where the third party claim is for money only, include the following:*)

IF YOU PAY THE AMOUNT OF THE THIRD PARTY CLAIM AGAINST YOU, and $ .... for costs, within the time for serving and filing your third party defence, you may move to have the third party claim dismissed by the court. If you believe the amount claimed for costs is excessive, you may pay the amount of the third party claim and $400 for costs and have the costs assessed by the court.

Date .... Issued by ....
Local registrar

Address of court office ....
....

TO (*Name and address of third party*)

CLAIM

1. The defendant claims against the third party: (*State here the precise relief claimed.*)

(*Then set out in separate, consecutively numbered paragraphs each allegation of material fact relied on to substantiate the third party claim.*)

(*Where the third party claim is to be served outside Ontario without a court order, set out the facts and the specific provisions of Rule 17 relied on in support of such service.*)

(*Date of issue*) (*Name, address and telephone number of defendant's lawyer or defendant*)

July 1, 2007

FORM 29B — THIRD PARTY DEFENCE

Courts of Justice Act

[Repealed O. Reg. 77/06, s. 3.]

[Editor's Note: Forms 4A to 78A of the Rules of Civil Procedure have been repealed by O. Reg. 77/06, effective July 1, 2006. Pursuant to Rule of Civil Procedure 1.06, when a form is referred to by number, the reference is to the form with that number that is described in the Table of Forms at the end of these rules and which is available on the Internet through www.ontariocourtforms.on.ca. For your convenience, the government form as published on this website is reproduced below.]

(*General heading, with title of proceeding in accordance with Form 29A*)

THIRD PARTY DEFENCE

1. The third party admits the allegations contained in paragraphs .... of the third party claim.

2. The third party denies the allegations contained in paragraphs .... of the third party claim.

3. The third party has no knowledge in respect of the allegations contained in paragraphs .... of the third party claim.

4. (*Set out in separate, consecutively numbered paragraphs each allegation of material fact relied on by way of defence to the third party claim.*)

(*Date*) (*Name, address and telephone number of third party's lawyer or third party*)

TO (*Name and address of defendant's lawyer or defendant*)

July 1, 2007

FORM 29C — REPLY TO THIRD PARTY DEFENCE

Courts of Justice Act

[Repealed O. Reg. 77/06, s. 3.]

[Editor's Note: Forms 4A to 78A of the Rules of Civil Procedure have been repealed by O. Reg. 77/06, effective July 1, 2006. Pursuant to Rule of Civil Procedure 1.06, when a form is referred to by number, the reference is to the form with that number that is described in the Table of Forms at the end of these rules and which is available on the Internet through

www.ontariocourtforms.on.ca. For your convenience, the government form as published on this website is reproduced below.]

(*General heading, with title of proceeding in accordance with Form 29A*)

REPLY TO THIRD PARTY DEFENCE

1. The defendant admits the allegations contained in paragraphs .... of the third party defence.

2. The defendant denies the allegations contained in paragraphs .... of the third party defence.

3. The defendant has no knowledge in respect of the allegations contained in paragraphs .... of the third party defence.

4. (*Set out in separate, consecutively numbered paragraphs each allegation of material fact relied on by way of reply to the third party defence.*)

(*Date*) (*Name, address and telephone number of defendant's lawyer or defendant*)

TO (*Name and address of third party's lawyer or third party*)

July 1, 2007

FORM 30A — AFFIDAVIT OF DOCUMENTS (INDIVIDUAL)

Courts of Justice Act

[Repealed O. Reg. 77/06, s. 3.]

[Editor's Note: Forms 4A to 78A of the Rules of Civil Procedure have been repealed by O. Reg. 77/06, effective July 1, 2006. Pursuant to Rule of Civil Procedure 1.06, when a form is referred to by number, the reference is to the form with that number that is described in the Table of Forms at the end of these rules and which is available on the Internet through www.ontariocourtforms.on.ca. For your convenience, the government form as published on this website is reproduced below.]

Courts of Justice Act

(*General heading*)

AFFIDAVIT OF DOCUMENTS

I, *(full name of deponent)*, of the *(*City, Town, *etc.)* of ...., in the *(*County, Regional Municipality, *etc.)* of ...., the plaintiff *(or as may be)* in this action, MAKE OATH AND SAY *(or* AFFIRM*)*:

1. I have conducted a diligent search of my records and have made appropriate enquiries of others to inform myself in order to make this affidavit. This affidavit discloses, to the full extent of my knowledge, information and belief, all documents relevant to any matter in issue in this action that are or have been in my possession, control or power.

2. I have listed in Schedule A those documents that are in my possession, control or power and that I do not object to producing for inspection.

3. I have listed in Schedule B those documents that are or were in my possession, control or power and that I object to producing because I claim they are privileged, and I have stated in Schedule B the grounds for each such claim.

4. I have listed in Schedule C those documents that were formerly in my possession, control or power but are no longer in my possession, control or power, and I have stated in Schedule C when and how I lost possession or control of or power over them and their present location.

5. I have never had in my possession, control or power any document relevant to any matter in issue in this action other than those listed in Schedules A, B and C.

6. I have listed in Schedule D the names and addresses of persons who might reasonably be expected to have knowledge of transactions or occurrences in issue. *(Strike out this paragraph if the action is not being brought under the simplified procedure.)*

SWORN *(etc.)*

....
(Signature of deponent)

LAWYER'S CERTIFICATE

I CERTIFY that I have explained to the deponent,

(a) the necessity of making full disclosure of all documents relevant to any matter in issue in the action;

(b) what kinds of documents are likely to be relevant to the allegations made in the pleadings; and

(c) if the action is brought under the simplified procedure, the necessity of providing the list required under rule 76.03.

Date ....
(Signature of lawyer)

SCHEDULE A

Documents in my possession, control or power that I do not object to producing for inspection.

(Number each document consecutively. Set out the nature and date of the document and other particulars sufficient to identify it.)

SCHEDULE B

Documents that are or were in my possession, control or power that I object to producing on the grounds of privilege.

(Number each document consecutively. Set out the nature and date of the document and other particulars sufficient to identify it. State the grounds for claiming privilege for each document.)

SCHEDULE C

Documents that were formerly in my possession, control or power but are no longer in my possession, control or power.

(Number each document consecutively. Set out the nature and date of the document and other particulars sufficient to identify it. State when and how possession or control of or power over each document was lost, and give the present location of each document.)

SCHEDULE D

(To be filled in only if the action is being brought under the simplified procedure.)

Names and addresses of persons who might reasonably be expected to have knowledge of transactions or occurrences in issue.

November 1, 2008

FORM 30B — AFFIDAVIT OF DOCUMENTS (CORPORATION OR PARTNERSHIP)

Courts of Justice Act

[Repealed O. Reg. 77/06, s. 3.]

[Editor's Note: Forms 4A to 78A of the Rules of Civil Procedure have been repealed by O. Reg. 77/06, effective July 1, 2006. Pursuant to Rule of Civil Procedure 1.06, when a form is referred to by number, the reference is to the form with that number that is described in the Table of Forms at the end of these rules and which is available on the Internet through www.ontariocourtforms.on.ca. For your convenience, the government form as published on this website is reproduced below.]

Courts of Justice Act

(General heading)

AFFIDAVIT OF DOCUMENTS

I, (*full name of deponent*), of the (City, Town, *etc.*) of ...., in the (County, Regional Municipality, *etc.*) of ...., MAKE OATH AND SAY (or AFFIRM):

1. I am the (*state the position held by the deponent in the corporation or partnership*) of the plaintiff (*or as may be*), which is a corporation (*or* partnership).

2. I have conducted a diligent search of the corporation's (*or* partnership's) records and made appropriate enquiries of others to inform myself in order to make this affidavit. This affidavit discloses, to the full extent of my knowledge, information and belief, all documents relevant to any matter in issue in this action that are or have been in the possession, control or power of the corporation (*or* partnership).

3. I have listed in Schedule A those documents that are in the possession, control or power of the corporation (*or* partnership) and that it does not object to producing for inspection.

4. I have listed in Schedule B those documents that are or were in the possession, control or power of the corporation (*or* partnership) and that it objects to producing because it claims they are privileged, and I have stated in Schedule B the grounds for each such claim.

5. I have listed in Schedule C those documents that were formerly in the possession, control or power of the corporation (*or* partnership) but are no longer in its possession, control or power and I have stated in Schedule C when and how it lost possession or control of or power over them and their present location.

6. The corporation (*or* partnership) has never had in its possession, control or power any documents relevant to any matter in issue in this action other than those listed in Schedules A, B and C.

7. I have listed in Schedule D the names and addresses of persons who might reasonably be expected to have knowledge of transactions or occurrences in issue. *(Strike out this paragraph if the action is not being brought under the simplified procedure.)*

SWORN *(etc.)*

....
(Signature of deponent)

LAWYER'S CERTIFICATE

I CERTIFY that I have explained to the deponent,

(a) the necessity of making full disclosure of all documents relevant to any matter in issue in the action;

(b) what kinds of documents are likely to be relevant to the allegations made in the pleadings; and

(c) if the action is brought under the simplified procedure, the necessity of providing the list required under rule 76.03.

Date ....
(Signature of lawyer)

SCHEDULE A

Documents in the corporation's *(or* partnership's*)* possession, control or power that it does not object to producing for inspection.

(Number each document consecutively. Set out the nature and date of the document and other particulars sufficient to identify it.)

SCHEDULE B

Documents that are or were in the corporation's *(or* partnership's*)* possession, control or power that it objects to producing on the grounds of privilege.

(Number each document consecutively. Set out the nature and date of the document and other particulars sufficient to identify it. State the grounds for claiming privilege for each document.)

SCHEDULE C

Documents that were formerly in the corporation's *(or* partnership's*)* possession, control or power but are no longer in its possession, control or power.

(Number each document consecutively. Set out the nature and date of the document and other particulars sufficient to identify it. State when and how possession or control of or power over each document was lost, and give the present location of each document.)

SCHEDULE D

(To be filled in only if the action is being brought under the simplified procedure.)

Names and addresses of persons who might reasonably be expected to have knowledge of transactions or occurrences in issue.

November 1, 2008

FORM 30C — REQUEST TO INSPECT DOCUMENTS

Courts of Justice Act

[Repealed O. Reg. 77/06, s. 3.]

[Editor's Note: Forms 4A to 78A of the Rules of Civil Procedure have been repealed by O. Reg. 77/06, effective July 1, 2006. Pursuant to Rule of Civil Procedure 1.06, when a form is referred to by number, the reference is to the form with that number that is described in the Table of Forms at the end of these rules and which is available on the Internet through www.ontariocourtforms.on.ca. For your convenience, the government form as published on this website is reproduced below.]

(General heading)

REQUEST TO INSPECT DOCUMENTS

You are requested to produce for inspection all the documents listed in Schedule A of your affidavit of documents (*or* the following documents referred to in your (*identify pleading or affidavit*):)

(*Date*) (*Name, address and telephone number of requesting lawyer or party*)

TO (*Name and address of lawyer or party requested to produce*)

July 1, 2007

FORM 34A — NOTICE OF EXAMINATION

Courts of Justice Act

[Repealed O. Reg. 77/06, s. 3.]

[Editor's Note: Forms 4A to 78A of the Rules of Civil Procedure have been repealed by O. Reg. 77/06, effective July 1, 2006. Pursuant to Rule of Civil Procedure 1.06, when a form is referred to by number, the reference is to the form with that number that is described in the Table of Forms at the end of these rules and which is available on the Internet through www.ontariocourtforms.on.ca. For your convenience, the government form as published on this website is reproduced below.]

(*To be used only for a party to the proceeding, a person to be examined for discovery or in aid of execution on behalf or in place of a party or a person to be cross-examined on an affidavit. For the examination of any other person, use a summons to witness (Form 34B).*)

(*General heading)*

NOTICE OF EXAMINATION

TO (*Name of person to be examined*)

YOU ARE REQUIRED TO ATTEND, on *(day)*, *(date)*, at *(time)*, at the office of *(name, address and telephone number of examiner)*, for *(choose one of the following)*:

[ ] Cross-examination on your affidavit dated *(date)*

[ ] Examination for discovery

[ ] Examination for discovery on behalf of or in place of *(identify party)*

[ ] Examination in aid of execution

[ ] Examination in aid of execution on behalf of or in place of *(identify party)*

(*Examination for discovery of a party or a person examined on behalf or in place of a party*)

YOU ARE REQUIRED TO BRING WITH YOU and produce at the examination the documents mentioned in subrule 30.04(4) of the *Rules of Civil Procedure*, and the following documents and things: (*Set out the nature and date of each document and give particulars sufficient to identify each document and thing.*)

(*Other examinations*)

YOU ARE REQUIRED TO BRING WITH YOU and produce at the examination the following documents and things: (*Set out the nature and date of each document and give particulars sufficient to identify each document and thing.*)

(*Date*) (*Name, address and telephone number of examining lawyer or party*)

TO (*Name and address of lawyer or of person to be examined*)

July 1, 2007

FORM 34B — SUMMONS TO WITNESS (EXAMINATION OUT OF COURT)

Courts of Justice Act

[Repealed O. Reg. 77/06, s. 3.]

[Editor's Note: Forms 4A to 78A of the Rules of Civil Procedure have been repealed by O. Reg. 77/06, effective July 1, 2006. Pursuant to Rule of Civil Procedure 1.06, when a form is referred to by number, the reference is to the form with that number that is described in the Table of Forms at the end of these rules and which is available on the Internet through www.ontariocourtforms.on.ca. For your convenience, the government form as published on this website is reproduced below.]

(*General heading*)

(*Court seal*)

SUMMONS TO WITNESS

TO (*Name and address of person to be examined*)

YOU ARE REQUIRED TO ATTEND, on *(day)*, *(date)*, at *(time)*, at the office of *(name, address and telephone number of examiner)*, for *(choose one of the following)*:

[ ] Cross-examination on your affidavit dated *(date)*

[ ] Examination for discovery with leave of the court

[ ] Examination out of court as witness before hearing

[ ] Examination in aid of execution

[ ] Taking evidence before trial

YOU ARE REQUIRED TO BRING WITH YOU and produce at the examination the following documents and things: (*Set out the nature and date of each document and give particulars sufficient to identify each document and thing.*)

ATTENDANCE MONEY for .... day(s) of attendance is served with this summons, calculated in accordance with Tariff A of the *Rules of Civil Procedure*, as follows:

Attendance allowance of $ .... daily	$ ....
Travel allowance	$ ....
Overnight accommodation and meal allowance	$ ....
	=========
TOTAL	$ ....

If further attendance is required, you will be entitled to additional attendance money.

IF YOU FAIL TO ATTEND OR REMAIN UNTIL THE END OF THIS EXAMINATION, YOU MAY BE COMPELLED TO ATTEND AT YOUR OWN EXPENSE AND YOU MAY BE FOUND IN CONTEMPT OF COURT.

Date .... Issued by ....

Local registrar

Address of court office ....

....

This summons was issued at the request of, and inquiries may be directed to:

(*Name, address and telephone number of examining lawyer or party*)

July 1, 2007

FORM 34C — COMMISSION

Courts of Justice Act

[Repealed O. Reg. 77/06, s. 3.]

[Editor's Note: Forms 4A to 78A of the Rules of Civil Procedure have been repealed by O. Reg. 77/06, effective July 1, 2006. Pursuant to Rule of Civil Procedure 1.06, when a form is referred to by number, the reference is to the form with that number that is described in the Table of Forms at the end of these rules and which is available on the Internet through www.ontariocourtforms.on.ca. For your convenience, the government form as published on this website is reproduced below.]

(*General heading*)

(*Court seal*)

COMMISSION

TO (*Name and address of commissioner*)

YOU HAVE BEEN APPOINTED A COMMISSIONER for the purpose of taking evidence in this proceeding now pending in this court by order of the court made on (*date*), a copy of which is attached.

YOU ARE GIVEN FULL AUTHORITY to do all things necessary for taking the evidence mentioned in the order authorizing this commission. (*Where the commission is issued under Rule 36, add:* You are also authorized, on consent of the parties, to take the evidence of any other witnesses who may be found in (*name of province, state or country*).)

You are to send to this court a transcript of the evidence taken, together with this commission, forthwith after the transcript is completed.

In carrying out this commission, you are to follow the terms of the attached order and the instructions contained in this commission.

THIS COMMISSION is signed and sealed by order of the court.

Date .... Issued by ....
Local registrar

Address of court office ....
....

The registrar is to attach to this commission a copy of Rules 34 and 36 and section 45 of the Evidence Act.

INSTRUCTIONS TO COMMISSIONER

1. This commission is to be conducted in accordance with Rules 34 and 36 of the Ontario Rules of Civil Procedure, a copy of which is attached, to the extent that it is possible to do so. The law of Ontario applies to the taking of the evidence.

2. Before acting on this commission, you must take the oath (*or* affirmation) set out below. You may do so before any person authorized by section 45 of the *Evidence Act* of Ontario, a copy of which is attached, to take affidavits or administer oaths or affirmations outside Ontario.

> I, ..., swear (*or* affirm) that I will, according to the best of my skill and knowledge, truly and faithfully and without partiality to any of the parties to this proceeding, take the evidence of every witness examined under this commission, and cause the evidence to be transcribed and forwarded to the court. (*In an oath, conclude:* So help me God.)
>
> Sworn (*or* Affirmed) before me at the (City, Town, *etc.*) of ...., in the (Province, State, *etc.*) of ...., on (*date*).

....
(*Signature of commissioner*)

....

(*Signature and office of person before whom oath or affirmation is taken*)

3. The examining party is required to give the person to be examined at least .... days notice of the examination and, where the order so provides, to pay attendance money to the person to be examined.

4. You must arrange to have the evidence before you recorded and transcribed. You are to administer the following oath (*or* affirmation) to the person who records and transcribes the evidence:

> You swear (*or* affirm) that you will truly and faithfully record and transcribe all questions put to all witnesses and their answers in accordance with the directions of the commissioner. (*In an oath, conclude:* So help you God.)

On consent of the parties, or where the order for this commission provides for it, the examination may be recorded by videotape or other similar means.

5. You are to administer the following oath (*or* affirmation) to each witness whose evidence is to be taken:

> You swear (*or* affirm) that the evidence to be given by you touching the matters in question between the parties to this proceeding shall be the truth, the whole truth, and nothing but the truth. (*In an oath, conclude:* So help you God.)

6. Where a witness does not understand the language or is deaf or mute, the evidence of the witness must be given through an interpreter. You are to administer the following oath (*or* affirmation) to the interpreter:

> You swear (*or* affirm) that you understand the .... language and the language in which the examination is to be conducted and that you will truly interpret the oath (*or* affirmation) to the witness, all questions put to the witness and the answers of the witness, to the best of your skill and understanding. (*In an oath, conclude:* So help you God.)

7. You are to attach to this commission the transcript of the evidence and the exhibits, and any videotape or other recording of the examination. You are to complete the certificate set out below, and mail this commission, the transcript, the exhibits and any videotape or other recording of the examination to the office of the court where the commission was issued. You are to keep a copy of the transcript and, where practicable, a copy of the exhibits until the court disposes of this proceeding. Forthwith after you mail this commission and the accompanying material to the court office, you are to notify the parties who appeared at the examination that you have done so.

CERTIFICATE OF COMMISSIONER

I, ..., certify that:

1. I administered the proper oath (*or* affirmation) to the person who recorded and transcribed the evidence, to the witness the transcript of whose evidence is attached and to any interpreter through whom the evidence was given.

2. The evidence of the witness was properly taken.

3. The evidence of the witness was accurately transcribed.

Date ....
(*Signature of commissioner*)

November 1, 2005

FORM 34D — LETTER OF REQUEST

Courts of Justice Act

[Repealed O. Reg. 77/06, s. 3.]

[Editor's Note: Forms 4A to 78A of the Rules of Civil Procedure have been repealed by O. Reg. 77/06, effective July 1, 2006. Pursuant to Rule of Civil Procedure 1.06, when a form is referred to by number, the reference is to the form with that number that is described in the Table of Forms at the end of these rules and which is available on the Internet through www.ontariocourtforms.on.ca. For your convenience, the government form as published on this website is reproduced below.]

(*General heading*)

(*Court seal*)

LETTER OF REQUEST

TO THE JUDICIAL AUTHORITIES OF (*name of province, state or country*)

A PROCEEDING IS PENDING IN THIS COURT at the (City, Town, *etc.*) of ...., in the Province of Ontario, Canada, between (*name*), plaintiff (*or as may be*), and (*name*), defendant (*or as may be*).

IT HAS BEEN SHOWN TO THIS COURT that it appears necessary for the purpose of justice that a witness residing within your jurisdiction be examined there.

THIS COURT HAS ISSUED A COMMISSION to (*name of commissioner*) of (*address of commissioner*), providing for the examination of the witness (*name of witness*), of (*address of witness*).

YOU ARE REQUESTED, in furtherance of justice, to cause (*name of witness*) (*where the commission was issued under Rule 36, add* and, on consent of the parties, any other witnesses who may be found in your jurisdiction) to appear before the commissioner by the means ordinarily used in your jurisdiction, if necessary to secure attendance, and to answer questions under oath or affirmation (*where desired, add:*) and to bring to and produce at the examination the following documents and things: (*Set out the nature and date of each document and give particulars sufficient to identify each document and thing*).

YOU ARE ALSO REQUESTED to permit the commissioner to conduct the examination of the witness in accordance with the law of evidence and Rules of Civil Procedure of Ontario and the commission issued by this court.

AND WHEN YOU REQUEST IT, the courts of Ontario are ready and willing to do the same for you in a similar case.

THIS LETTER OF REQUEST is signed and sealed by order of the court made on (*date*).

Date .... Issued by ....
Local registrar

Address of court office ....
....

November 1, 2005

FORM 34E — ORDER FOR COMMISSION AND LETTER OF REQUEST

Courts of Justice Act

[Repealed O. Reg. 77/06, s. 3.]

[Editor's Note: Forms 4A to 78A of the Rules of Civil Procedure have been repealed by O. Reg. 77/06, effective July 1, 2006. Pursuant to Rule of Civil Procedure 1.06, when a form is referred to by number, the reference is to the form with that number that is described in the Table of Forms at the end of these rules and which is available on the Internet through www.ontariocourtforms.on.ca. For your convenience, the government form as published on this website is reproduced below.]

(*Court file no.*)

(*Court*)

(*Name of judge or officer*) (*Day and date order made*)

(*Court seal*) (*Title of proceeding*)

ORDER

(*Recitals in accordance with Form 59A*)

1. THIS COURT ORDERS (*give particulars of any directions given by the court under rule 34.07*).

2. THIS COURT ORDERS that the registrar prepare and issue a commission naming (*name*), of (*address*), as commissioner to take the evidence of the witness (*name of witness*) in (*name of province, state or country*) (*where the order is made under Rule 36, add* and, on consent of the parties, any other witness who may be found there) for use at trial (*or* on examination for discovery, *etc.*).

3. THIS COURT ORDERS that the registrar prepare and issue a letter of request addressed to the judicial authorities of (*name of province, state or country*), requesting the issuing of

such process as is necessary to compel the witness (*or* witnesses) to attend and be examined before the commissioner.

(*Signature of judge, officer or registrar*)

November 1, 2005

FORM 35A — QUESTIONS ON WRITTEN EXAMINATION FOR DISCOVERY

Courts of Justice Act

[Repealed O. Reg. 77/06, s. 3.]

[Editor's Note: Forms 4A to 78A of the Rules of Civil Procedure have been repealed by O. Reg. 77/06, effective July 1, 2006. Pursuant to Rule of Civil Procedure 1.06, when a form is referred to by number, the reference is to the form with that number that is described in the Table of Forms at the end of these rules and which is available on the Internet through www.ontariocourtforms.on.ca. For your convenience, the government form as published on this website is reproduced below.]

(*General heading*)

QUESTIONS ON WRITTEN EXAMINATION FOR DISCOVERY

THE (*identify examining party*) has chosen to examine the (*identify person to be examined*) for discovery (*where the person is not a party, state whether the person is examined on behalf or in place of or in addition to a party or under a court order*) by written questions and requires that the following questions be answered by affidavit in Form 35B prescribed by the *Rules of Civil Procedure*, served within fifteen days after service of these questions.

(*Where a further list of questions is served under rule 35.04 substitute:*)

The (*identify examining party*) requires that the (*identify person to be examined*) answer the following further questions by affidavit in Form 35B prescribed by the *Rules of Civil Procedure*, served within fifteen days after service of these questions.

1. (*Number each question. Where the questions are a further list under rule 35.04, number the questions in sequence following the last question of the previous list.*)

(*Date*) (*Name, address and telephone number of examining party's lawyer or examining party*)

TO (*Name and address of lawyer for person to be examined or of person to be examined*)

July 1, 2007

FORM 35B — ANSWERS ON WRITTEN EXAMINATION FOR DISCOVERY

Courts of Justice Act

[Repealed O. Reg. 77/06, s. 3.]

[Editor's Note: Forms 4A to 78A of the Rules of Civil Procedure have been repealed by O. Reg. 77/06, effective July 1, 2006. Pursuant to Rule of Civil Procedure 1.06, when a form is referred to by number, the reference is to the form with that number that is described in the Table of Forms at the end of these rules and which is available on the Internet through www.ontariocourtforms.on.ca. For your convenience, the government form as published on this website is reproduced below.]

(General heading)

ANSWERS ON WRITTEN EXAMINATION FOR DISCOVERY

I, (*full name of deponent*), of the (City, Town, *etc.*) of ...., in the (County, Regional Municipality, *etc.*) of ...., the (*identify the capacity in which the deponent makes the affidavit*), MAKE OATH AND SAY (*or* AFFIRM) that the following answers to the questions dated (*date*) submitted by the (*identify examining party*) are true, to the best of my knowledge, information and belief:

1. (*Number each answer to correspond with the question. Where the deponent objects to answering a question, state:* I object to answering this question on the ground that it is irrelevant to the matters in issue *or* that the information sought is privileged because (*specify*) *or as may be.*)

SWORN (*etc.*)

November 1, 2005

FORM 37A — NOTICE OF MOTION

Courts of Justice Act

[Repealed O. Reg. 77/06, s. 3.]

[Editor's Note: Forms 4A to 78A of the Rules of Civil Procedure have been repealed by O. Reg. 77/06, effective July 1, 2006. Pursuant to Rule of Civil Procedure 1.06, when a form is referred to by number, the reference is to the form with that number that is described in the Table of Forms at the end of these rules and which is available on the Internet through www.ontariocourtforms.on.ca. For your convenience, the government form as published on this website is reproduced below.]

(General heading)

NOTICE OF MOTION

The (*identify moving party*) will make a motion to the court (*or* judge) on (*day*), (*date*), at (*time*), or soon after that time as the motion can be heard, at (*address of court house*).

PROPOSED METHOD OF HEARING: The motion is to be heard (*choose appropriate option*)

❑ in writing under subrule 37.12.1(1) because it is (*insert one of* on consent, unopposed *or* made without notice);

❑ in writing as an opposed motion under subrule 37.12.1(4);

❑ orally.

THE MOTION IS FOR (*state here the precise relief sought*).

THE GROUNDS FOR THE MOTION ARE (*specify the grounds to be argued, including a reference to any statutory provision or rule to be relied on*).

THE FOLLOWING DOCUMENTARY EVIDENCE will be used at the hearing of the motion: (*list the affidavits or other documentary evidence to be relied on*).

(*Date*) (*Name, address and telephone number of moving party's lawyer or moving party*)

TO (*Name and address of responding party's lawyer or responding party*)

July 1, 2007

FORM 37B — CONFIRMATION OF MOTION

Courts of Justice Act

[Repealed O. Reg. 77/06, s. 3.]

[Editor's Note: Forms 4A to 78A of the Rules of Civil Procedure have been repealed by O. Reg. 77/06, effective July 1, 2006. Pursuant to Rule of Civil Procedure 1.06, when a form is referred to by number, the reference is to the form with that number that is described in the Table of Forms at the end of these rules and which is available on the Internet through www.ontariocourtforms.on.ca. For your convenience, the government form as published on this website is reproduced below.]

(*General heading*)

I, ... *(name)*, lawyer for the moving party, confirm that the moving party has conferred or attempted to confer with the other party and confirm that the motion to be heard on .... *(date)* will proceed on the following basis:

[ ] for an adjournment on consent to .... *(date)*

[ ] for a contested adjournment to .... *(date)*, for the following reason: *(specify who is requesting the adjournment and why, and who is opposing it and why)*

[ ] for a consent order

[ ] for a hearing of all the issues

[ ] for a hearing of the following issues only *(specify)*

The presiding judge will be referred to the following materials: *(please be specific)*

I estimate that the time required for the motion, including costs submissions, will be .... minutes for the moving party*(ies)* and .... minutes for the responding party*(ies)* for a total of .... minutes.

(Date) ....

TO *(Name and address of responding party's lawyer or responding party)*

July 1, 2007

FORM 37C — REFUSALS AND UNDERTAKINGS CHART

Courts of Justice Act

[Repealed O. Reg. 77/06, s. 3.]

[Editor's Note: Forms 4A to 78A of the Rules of Civil Procedure have been repealed by O. Reg. 77/06, effective July 1, 2006. Pursuant to Rule of Civil Procedure 1.06, when a form is referred to by number, the reference is to the form with that number that is described in the Table of Forms at the end of these rules and which is available on the Internet through www.ontariocourtforms.on.ca. For your convenience, the government form as published on this website is reproduced below.]

(General heading)

REFUSALS					
Refusals to answer questions on the examination of ...., dated					
Issue & relationship to pleadings or affidavit (Group the questions by issues.)	*Question No.*	*Page No.*	*Specific question*	*Answer or precise basis for refusal*	*Disposition by the Court*
1.					
2.					
3.					

UNDERTAKINGS
Outstanding undertakings given on the examination of ...., dated ....

Issue & relationship to pleadings or affidavit (Group the undertakings by issues.)	*Question No.*	*Page No.*	*Specific undertaking*	*Date answered or precise reason for not doing so*	*Disposition by the Court*
1.					
2.					
3.					

(*Date*) (*Name, address and telephone and fax numbers of the party filing the refusals and undertakings chart*)

(*Date*) .... (*Name, address and telephone and fax numbers of the party filing the refusals and undertakings chart*) ....

November 1, 2005

FORM 38A — NOTICE OF APPEARANCE

Courts of Justice Act

[Repealed O. Reg. 77/06, s. 3.]

[Editor's Note: Forms 4A to 78A of the Rules of Civil Procedure have been repealed by O. Reg. 77/06, effective July 1, 2006. Pursuant to Rule of Civil Procedure 1.06, when a form is referred to by number, the reference is to the form with that number that is described in the Table of Forms at the end of these rules and which is available on the Internet through www.ontariocourtforms.on.ca. For your convenience, the government form as published on this website is reproduced below.]

(*General heading*)

NOTICE OF APPEARANCE

The respondent intends to respond to this application.

(*Date*) (*Name, address and telephone number of respondent's lawyer or respondent*)

TO (*Name and address of applicant's*

lawyer or applicant)

July 1, 2007

FORM 38B — CONFIRMATION OF APPLICATION

Courts of Justice Act

[Repealed O. Reg. 77/06, s. 3.]

[Editor's Note: Forms 4A to 78A of the Rules of Civil Procedure have been repealed by O. Reg. 77/06, effective July 1, 2006. Pursuant to Rule of Civil Procedure 1.06, when a form is referred to by number, the reference is to the form with that number that is described in the Table of Forms at the end of these rules and which is available on the Internet through www.ontariocourtforms.on.ca. For your convenience, the government form as published on this website is reproduced below.]

(General heading)

CONFIRMATION OF APPLICATION

I, ... *(name)*, lawyer for the applicant confirm that the application to be heard on .... *(date)* will proceed on the following basis:

[ ] for an adjournment on consent to .... *(date)*

[ ] for a contested adjournment to .... *(date)*, for the following reason: *(specify who is requesting the adjournment and why, and who is opposing it and why)*

[ ] for a consent order

[ ] for hearing of all the issues

[ ] for hearing of the following issues only *(specify)*

I estimate that the time required for the application will be: .... minutes for the applicant*(s)* and .... minutes for the respondent*(s)* for a total of .... minutes.

(Date)

TO *(Name and address of respondent's lawyer or respondent)*

July 1, 2007

FORM 42A — CERTIFICATE OF PENDING LITIGATION

Courts of Justice Act

[Repealed O. Reg. 77/06, s. 3.]

[Editor's Note: Forms 4A to 78A of the Rules of Civil Procedure have been repealed by O. Reg. 77/06, effective July 1, 2006. Pursuant to Rule of Civil Procedure 1.06, when a form is referred to by number, the reference is to the form with that number that is described in the Table of Forms at the end of these rules and which is available on the Internet through www.ontariocourtforms.on.ca. For your convenience, the government form as published on this website is reproduced below.]

(*General heading*)

(*Court seal*)

CERTIFICATE OF PENDING LITIGATION

I CERTIFY that in this proceeding an interest in the following land is in question:

(*Set out a description of the land sufficient for registration. Where the land is registered under the* Land Titles Act, *include the parcel number. Attach a schedule if necessary.*)

This certificate is issued under an order of the court made on (*date*).

Date .... Issued by ....

Local registrar

Address of court office ....

....

November 1, 2005

FORM 43A — INTERPLEADER ORDER — GENERAL

Courts of Justice Act

[Repealed O. Reg. 77/06, s. 3.]

[Editor's Note: Forms 4A to 78A of the Rules of Civil Procedure have been repealed by O. Reg. 77/06, effective July 1, 2006. Pursuant to Rule of Civil Procedure 1.06, when a form is referred to by number, the reference is to the form with that number that is described in the Table of Forms at the end of these rules and which is available on the Internet through

www.ontariocourtforms.on.ca. For your convenience, the government form as published on this website is reproduced below.]

(*Court file no.*)

(*Court*)

(*Name of judge or officer*) (*Day and date order made*)

(*Court seal*) (*Title of proceeding*)

INTERPLEADER ORDER

(*Where an interpleader application results in a judgment, amend the form accordingly.*)

(*Recitals in accordance with Form 59A or 59B*)

Payment of money into court

1. THIS COURT ORDERS that the (*identify party*) pay into court the sum of $ ...., less costs fixed at $ ...., to await the outcome of a proceeding in this court between (*identify parties*) (*or* to await the outcome of this proceeding).

2. THIS COURT DECLARES that on compliance with paragraph 1 of this order, the liability of (*identify party*) in respect of the above sum is extinguished.

3. THIS COURT ORDERS (*include any other order made by the court under rule 43.04*).

Sale of property and payment of proceeds into court

1. THIS COURT ORDERS that (*identify property*) be sold by (*method of sale*) and that the proceeds, less expenses of sale and the costs of (*identify party*) fixed at $ ...., be paid into court to await the outcome of a proceeding in this court between (*identify parties*) (*or* to await the outcome of this proceeding).

2. THIS COURT DECLARES that on compliance with paragraph 1 of this order, the liability of (*identify party*) in respect of the above sum is extinguished.

3. THIS COURT ORDERS (*include any other order made by the court under rule 43.04*).

Deposit of property with an officer of the court

1. THIS COURT ORDERS that (*identify property*) be deposited with the Sheriff of the (*county or district*) (*or as may be*) to await the outcome of a proceeding in this court between (*identify parties*) (*or* to await the outcome of this proceeding).

2. THIS COURT DECLARES that on compliance with paragraph 1 of this order, the liability of (*identify party*) in respect of the above property is extinguished.

3. THIS COURT ORDERS (*include any other order made by the court under rule 43.04*).

Trial of an issue

(*This paragraph will normally form part of an order for payment into court or deposit of property with an officer of the court.*)

4. THIS COURT ORDERS that there be a trial of the issue of (*give particulars of issue to be tried*), in which (*identify party*) shall be plaintiff and (*identify party*) shall be defendant.

5. THIS COURT ORDERS (*include any directions given by the court respecting pleadings, discovery and other matters*).

(*Signature of judge, officer or local registrar*)

November 1, 2005

FORM 44A — BOND — INTERIM RECOVERY OF PERSONAL PROPERTY

Courts of Justice Act

[Repealed O. Reg. 77/06, s. 3.]

[Editor's Note: Forms 4A to 78A of the Rules of Civil Procedure have been repealed by O. Reg. 77/06, effective July 1, 2006. Pursuant to Rule of Civil Procedure 1.06, when a form is referred to by number, the reference is to the form with that number that is described in the Table of Forms at the end of these rules and which is available on the Internet through www.ontariocourtforms.on.ca. For your convenience, the government form as published on this website is reproduced below.]

(*General heading*)

BOND

WE, (*identify party*) and (*name of surety*), jointly and severally bind ourselves and our successors to the Sheriff of the (*county or district*) in the sum of $ .... if (*identify party*) fails to return (*identify property*) to (*identify opposite party*) without delay when ordered to do so, and to pay any damages and costs that (*identify opposite party*) has sustained by reason of the interim order for recovery of possession of the property.

Date ....

.... (*seal*)

Witness .... *Signature of party*

.... (*seal*)

Witness .... *Signature of surety*

November 1, 2005

FORM 47A — JURY NOTICE

Courts of Justice Act

[Repealed O. Reg. 77/06, s. 3.]

[Editor's Note: Forms 4A to 78A of the Rules of Civil Procedure have been repealed by O. Reg. 77/06, effective July 1, 2006. Pursuant to Rule of Civil Procedure 1.06, when a form is referred to by number, the reference is to the form with that number that is described in the Table of Forms at the end of these rules and which is available on the Internet through www.ontariocourtforms.on.ca. For your convenience, the government form as published on this website is reproduced below.]

(*General heading*)

JURY NOTICE

THE (*identify party*) REQUIRES that this action be tried (*or* that the issues of fact *or* that the damages in this action be assessed) by a jury.

(*Date*) (*Name, address and telephone number of lawyer or party delivering notice*)

TO (*Name and address of lawyer or party receiving notice*)

July 1, 2007

FORM 48C — [REPEALED O. REG. 438/08, S. 67(1).]

[Repealed O. Reg. 438/08, s. 67(1).]

FORM 48C.1 — [REPEALED O. REG. 170/14, S. 24(2).]

[Repealed O. Reg. 170/14, s. 24(2).]

FORM 48C.2 — [REPEALED O. REG. 170/14, S. 24(2).]

[Repealed O. Reg. 170/14, s. 24(2).]

FORM 48D — ORDER DISMISSING ACTION FOR DELAY

Courts of Justice Act

[Repealed O. Reg. 77/06, s. 3.]

[Editor's Note: Forms 4A to 78A of the Rules of Civil Procedure *have been repealed by O. Reg. 77/06, effective July 1, 2006. Pursuant to Rule of Civil Procedure 1.06, when a form is referred to by number, the reference is to the form with that number that is described in the Table of Forms at the end of these rules and which is available on the Internet through www.ontariocourtforms.on.ca. For your convenience, the government form as published on this website is reproduced below.]*

(*General heading*)

ORDER DISMISSING ACTION

The plaintiff has not *(give particulars of plaintiff's default under rule 48.14)* and has not cured the default.

IT IS ORDERED that this action be dismissed for delay.

Date .... Signed by ....

Local registrar

(Address of court office)

NOTE: An order under rule 48.14 dismissing an action may be set aside under rule 37.14.

NOTE TO DEFENDANT(S) (AND OTHER PARTIES): When an order under rule 48.14 is made dismissing an action, rule 48.14(9) provides that any counterclaim, crossclaim or third party claim will be dismissed within 30 days thereafter in accordance with rules 24.03 and 24.04. Under rule 24.03, any counterclaim is deemed to be discontinued without costs unless the defendant delivers a notice of election to proceed with the counterclaim (Form 23B) within thirty days after the dismissal. Under rule 24.04(1) any crossclaim or third party claim made by a defendant is deemed to be dismissed, unless the court orders otherwise.

November 1, 2016

FORM 48E — [REPEALED O. REG. 170/14, S. 24(2).]

[Repealed O. Reg. 170/14, s. 24(2).]

FORM 48F — [REPEALED O. REG. 170/14, S. 24(2).]

[Repealed O. Reg. 170/14, s. 24(2).]

FORM 49A — OFFER TO SETTLE

Courts of Justice Act

[Repealed O. Reg. 77/06, s. 3.]

[Editor's Note: Forms 4A to 78A of the Rules of Civil Procedure have been repealed by O. Reg. 77/06, effective July 1, 2006. Pursuant to Rule of Civil Procedure 1.06, when a form is referred to by number, the reference is to the form with that number that is described in the Table of Forms at the end of these rules and which is available on the Internet through www.ontariocourtforms.on.ca. For your convenience, the government form as published on this website is reproduced below.]

(*General heading*)

OFFER TO SETTLE

The (*identify party*) offers to settle this proceeding (*or* the following claims in this proceeding) on the following terms: (*Set out terms in consecutively numbered paragraphs.*)

(*Date*) (*Name, address and telephone number of lawyer or party making offer*)

TO (*Name and address of lawyer or party to whom offer is made*)

FORM 49B — NOTICE OF WITHDRAWAL OF OFFER

Courts of Justice Act

[Repealed O. Reg. 77/06, s. 3.]

[Editor's Note: Forms 4A to 78A of the Rules of Civil Procedure have been repealed by O. Reg. 77/06, effective July 1, 2006. Pursuant to Rule of Civil Procedure 1.06, when a form is referred to by number, the reference is to the form with that number that is described in the Table of Forms at the end of these rules and which is available on the Internet through www.ontariocourtforms.on.ca. For your convenience, the government form as published on this website is reproduced below.]

(*General heading*)

NOTICE OF WITHDRAWAL OF OFFER

The (*identify party*) withdraws the offer to settle dated (*date*).

(*Date*) (*Name, address and telephone number of lawyer or party giving notice*)

TO (*Name and address of lawyer or party to whom notice is given*)

July 1, 2007

FORM 49C — ACCEPTANCE OF OFFER

Courts of Justice Act

[Repealed O. Reg. 77/06, s. 3.]

[Editor's Note: Forms 4A to 78A of the Rules of Civil Procedure have been repealed by O. Reg. 77/06, effective July 1, 2006. Pursuant to Rule of Civil Procedure 1.06, when a form is referred to by number, the reference is to the form with that number that is described in the Table of Forms at the end of these rules and which is available on the Internet through www.ontariocourtforms.on.ca. For your convenience, the government form as published on this website is reproduced below.]

(*General heading*)

ACCEPTANCE OF OFFER

The (*identify party*) accepts your offer to settle dated (*date*).

(*Date*) (*Name, address and telephone number of lawyer or party accepting offer*)

TO (*Name and address of lawyer or party whose offer is accepted*)

July 1, 2007

FORM 49D — OFFER TO CONTRIBUTE

Courts of Justice Act

[Repealed O. Reg. 77/06, s. 3.]

[Editor's Note: Forms 4A to 78A of the Rules of Civil Procedure have been repealed by O. Reg. 77/06, effective July 1, 2006. Pursuant to Rule of Civil Procedure 1.06, when a form is referred to by number, the reference is to the form with that number that is described in the Table of Forms at the end of these rules and which is available on the Internet through www.ontariocourtforms.on.ca. For your convenience, the government form as published on this website is reproduced below.]

(*General heading*)

OFFER TO CONTRIBUTE

The defendant (*name of defendant making offer*) offers to contribute to a settlement of the plaintiff's claim on the following terms: (*Set out terms in consecutively numbered paragraphs.*)

(*Date*) (*Name, address and telephone number of lawyer or defendant making offer*)

TO (*Name and address of lawyer or defendant to whom offer is made*)

July 1, 2007

FORM 51A — REQUEST TO ADMIT

Courts of Justice Act

[Repealed O. Reg. 77/06, s. 3.]

[Editor's Note: Forms 4A to 78A of the Rules of Civil Procedure have been repealed by O. Reg. 77/06, effective July 1, 2006. Pursuant to Rule of Civil Procedure 1.06, when a form is referred to by number, the reference is to the form with that number that is described in the Table of Forms at the end of these rules and which is available on the Internet through www.ontariocourtforms.on.ca. For your convenience, the government form as published on this website is reproduced below.]

(*General heading*)

REQUEST TO ADMIT

YOU ARE REQUESTED TO ADMIT, for the purposes of this proceeding only, the truth of the following facts: (*Set out facts in consecutively numbered paragraphs.*)

YOU ARE REQUESTED TO ADMIT, for the purposes of this proceeding only, the authenticity (see rule 51.01 of the *Rules of Civil Procedure*) of the following documents: (*Number each document and give particulars sufficient to identify each. Specify whether the document is an original or a copy and, where the document is a copy of a letter, telegram or telecommunication, state the nature of the document.*)

Attached to this request is a copy of each of the documents referred to above. (*Where it is not practicable to attach a copy or where the party already has a copy, state which documents are not attached and give the reason for not attaching them.*)

YOU MUST RESPOND TO THIS REQUEST by serving a response to request to admit in Form 51B prescribed by the *Rules of Civil Procedure* WITHIN TWENTY DAYS after this request is served on you. If you fail to do so, you will be deemed to admit, for the purposes of this proceeding only, the truth of the facts and the authenticity of the documents set out above.

(*Date*) (*Name, address and telephone number of lawyer or party serving request*)

TO (*Name and address of lawyer or party on whom request is served*)

July 1, 2007

FORM 51B — RESPONSE TO REQUEST TO ADMIT

Courts of Justice Act

[Repealed O. Reg. 77/06, s. 3.]

[Editor's Note: Forms 4A to 78A of the Rules of Civil Procedure have been repealed by O. Reg. 77/06, effective July 1, 2006. Pursuant to Rule of Civil Procedure 1.06, when a form is referred to by number, the reference is to the form with that number that is described in the Table of Forms at the end of these rules and which is available on the Internet through www.ontariocourtforms.on.ca. For your convenience, the government form as published on this website is reproduced below.]

(*General heading*)

RESPONSE TO REQUEST TO ADMIT

In response to your request to admit dated (*date*), the (*identify party responding to the request*):

1. Admits the truth of facts numbers ....

2. Admits the authenticity of documents numbers ....

3. Denies the truth of facts numbers ....

4. Denies the authenticity of documents numbers ....

5. Refuses to admit the truth of facts numbers .... for the following reasons: (*Set out reason for refusing to admit each fact.*)

6. Refuses to admit the authenticity of documents numbers .... for the following reasons: (*Set out reason for refusing to admit each document.*)

(*Date*) (*Name, address and telephone number of lawyer or party serving response*)

TO (*Name and address of lawyer or party on whom response is served*)

July 1, 2007

FORM 53 — ACKNOWLEDGMENT OF EXPERT'S DUTY

[Editor's Note: Forms 4A to 78A of the Rules of Civil Procedure have been repealed by O. Reg. 77/06, effective July 1, 2006. Pursuant to Rule of Civil Procedure 1.06, when a form is referred to by number, the reference is to the form with that number that is described in the Table of Forms at the end of these rules and which is available on the Internet through

www.ontariocourtforms.on.ca. For your convenience, the government form as published on this website is reproduced below.]

Courts of Justice Act

(General heading)

ACKNOWLEDGMENT OF EXPERT'S DUTY

1. My name is .... *(name)*. I live at .... *(city)*, in the .... *(province/state)* of .... *(name of province/state)*.

2. I have been engaged by or on behalf of .... *(name of party/parties)* to provide evidence in relation to the above-noted court proceeding.

3. I acknowledge that it is my duty to provide evidence in relation to this proceeding as follows:

(a) to provide opinion evidence that is fair, objective and non-partisan;

(b) to provide opinion evidence that is related only to matters that are within my area of expertise; and

(c) to provide such additional assistance as the court may reasonably require, to determine a matter in issue.

4. I acknowledge that the duty referred to above prevails over any obligation which I may owe to any party by whom or on whose behalf I am engaged.

Date ....

Signature

NOTE: This form must be attached to any expert report under subrules 53.03(1) or (2) and any opinion evidence provided by an expert witness on a motion or application.

July 22, 2014

FORM 53A — SUMMONS TO WITNESS (AT HEARING)

Courts of Justice Act

[Repealed O. Reg. 77/06, s. 3.]

[Editor's Note: Forms 4A to 78A of the Rules of Civil Procedure have been repealed by O. Reg. 77/06, effective July 1, 2006. Pursuant to Rule of Civil Procedure 1.06, when a form is referred to by number, the reference is to the form with that number that is described in the Table of Forms at the end of these rules and which is available on the Internet through www.ontariocourtforms.on.ca. For your convenience, the government form as published on this website is reproduced below.]

(General heading)

(*Court seal*)

SUMMONS TO WITNESS

TO (*Name and address of witness*)

YOU ARE REQUIRED TO ATTEND TO GIVE EVIDENCE IN COURT at the hearing of this proceeding on (*day*), (*date*), at (*time*), at (*address of court house*), and to remain until your attendance is no longer required.

YOU ARE REQUIRED TO BRING WITH YOU and produce at the hearing the following documents and things: (*Set out the nature and date of each document and give particulars sufficient to identify each document and thing.*)

ATTENDANCE MONEY for .... day(s) of attendance is served with this summons, calculated in accordance with Tariff A of the *Rules of Civil Procedure*, as follows:

Attendance allowance of $ .... daily	$ ....
Travel allowance	$ ....
Overnight accommodation and meal allowance	$ ....
	========
TOTAL	$ ....

If further attendance is required, you will be entitled to additional attendance money.

IF YOU FAIL TO ATTEND OR TO REMAIN IN ATTENDANCE AS REQUIRED BY THIS SUMMONS, A WARRANT MAY BE ISSUED FOR YOUR ARREST.

Date .... Issued by ....
Local registrar

Address of court office ....
....

This summons was issued at the request of, and inquiries may be directed to:

(*Name, address and telephone number of lawyer or party serving summons*)

July 1, 2007

FORM 53B — WARRANT FOR ARREST (DEFAULTING WITNESS)

Courts of Justice Act

[Repealed O. Reg. 77/06, s. 3.]

[Editor's Note: Forms 4A to 78A of the Rules of Civil Procedure have been repealed by O. Reg. 77/06, effective July 1, 2006. Pursuant to Rule of Civil Procedure 1.06, when a form is referred to by number, the reference is to the form with that number that is described in the Table of Forms at the end of these rules and which is available on the Internet through www.ontariocourtforms.on.ca. For your convenience, the government form as published on this website is reproduced below.]

(*Court file no.*)

(*Court*)

(*Name of judge*) (*Day and date*)

(*Court seal*) (*Title of Proceeding*)

WARRANT FOR ARREST

TO ALL POLICE OFFICERS in Ontario

AND TO the officers of all correctional institutions in Ontario

WHEREAS the witness (*name*), of (*address*), was served with a summons to witness to give evidence at the hearing of this proceeding, and the proper attendance money was paid or tendered,

AND WHEREAS the witness failed to obey the summons, and I am satisfied that the evidence of the witness is material to this proceeding,

YOU ARE ORDERED TO ARREST and bring the witness (*name of witness*) before the court to give evidence in this proceeding, and if the court is not then sitting or if the witness cannot be brought forthwith before the court, to deliver the witness to a provincial correctional institution or other secure facility, to be admitted and detained there until the witness can be brought before the court.

(*Signature of judge*)

November 1, 2005

FORM 53C — SUMMONS TO A WITNESS OUTSIDE ONTARIO

Courts of Justice Act

[Repealed O. Reg. 77/06, s. 3.]

[Editor's Note: Forms 4A to 78A of the Rules of Civil Procedure have been repealed by O. Reg. 77/06, effective July 1, 2006. Pursuant to Rule of Civil Procedure 1.06, when a form is referred to by number, the reference is to the form with that number that is described in the Table of Forms at the end of these rules and which is available on the Internet through

www.ontariocourtforms.on.ca. For your convenience, the government form as published on this website is reproduced below.]

(*General heading*)

(*Court seal*)

SUMMONS TO A WITNESS OUTSIDE ONTARIO

TO (*Name and address of witness*)

YOU ARE REQUIRED TO ATTEND TO GIVE EVIDENCE (in court at the hearing of this proceeding, on an examination for discovery, on a cross-examination on your affidavit dated (*date*), *etc.*) on (*day*), (*date*), at (*address of court house*), and to remain until your attendance is no longer required.

YOU ARE REQUIRED TO BRING WITH YOU and produce at the hearing the following documents and things: (*Set out the nature and date of each document and give particulars sufficient to identify each document and thing.*)

ATTENDANCE MONEY for .... day(s) of attendance is served with this summons, calculated in accordance with the *Interprovincial Summonses Act* (Ontario), as follows:

Attendance allowance of $20 daily for each day of absence from your ordinary residence (not less than $60)	$ ....
Travel allowance	$ ....
Hotel accommodation allowance for not less than three days (not less than $60)	$ ....
Meal allowance for not less than three days (not less than $48)	$ ....
	========
TOTAL	$ ....

If further attendance is required, you will be entitled to additional attendance money.

OBEDIENCE TO THIS SUMMONS may be compelled by the courts of your province under the *Interprovincial Summonses Act*.

Date .... Issued by ....

Local registrar

Address of court office ....

....

This summons was issued at the request of, and inquiries may be directed to:

(*Name, address and telephone number of lawyer or party serving summons*)

Attach or endorse the judge's certificate under section 5 of the Interprovincial Summonses Act.

July 1, 2007

FORM 53D — ORDER FOR ATTENDANCE OF WITNESS IN CUSTODY

Courts of Justice Act

[Repealed O. Reg. 77/06, s. 3.]

[Editor's Note: Forms 4A to 78A of the Rules of Civil Procedure have been repealed by O. Reg. 77/06, effective July 1, 2006. Pursuant to Rule of Civil Procedure 1.06, when a form is referred to by number, the reference is to the form with that number that is described in the Table of Forms at the end of these rules and which is available on the Internet through www.ontariocourtforms.on.ca. For your convenience, the government form as published on this website is reproduced below.]

(*Court file no.*)

(*Court*)

(*Name of judge or master*) (*Day and date order made*)

(*Court seal*) (*Title of Proceeding*)

ORDER FOR ATTENDANCE OF WITNESS IN CUSTODY

TO THE OFFICERS OF (*name of correctional institution*)

AND TO ALL POLICE OFFICERS in Ontario

WHEREAS it appears that the evidence of the witness (*name*), who is detained in custody, is material to this proceeding,

1. THIS COURT ORDERS that the witness (*name*) be brought before this court (*or as may be*) on (*day*), (*date*), at (*time*), at (*address*), to give evidence on behalf of the (*identify party*), and that the witness be returned and readmitted immediately thereafter to the correctional institution or other facility from which the witness was brought.

(*Signature of judge, officer or registrar*)

November 1, 2005

FORM 55A — NOTICE OF HEARING FOR DIRECTIONS

Courts of Justice Act

[Repealed O. Reg. 77/06, s. 3.]

[Editor's Note: Forms 4A to 78A of the Rules of Civil Procedure have been repealed by O. Reg. 77/06, effective July 1, 2006. Pursuant to Rule of Civil Procedure 1.06, when a form is referred to by number, the reference is to the form with that number that is described in the Table of Forms at the end of these rules and which is available on the Internet through www.ontariocourtforms.on.ca. For your convenience, the government form as published on this website is reproduced below.]

(*General heading*)

NOTICE OF HEARING FOR DIRECTIONS

By order of the court, a copy of which is served with this notice, a reference was directed to (*person conducting reference*) for the purpose of (*set out purpose of reference*).

The (*identify party*) has obtained an appointment with (*name of person conducting reference*) on (*day*), (*date*), at (*time*), at (*address*) for a hearing to consider directions for the conduct of the reference in this proceeding.

IF YOU FAIL TO ATTEND, in person or by an Ontario lawyer acting for you, directions may be given and the reference may proceed in your absence and without further notice to you, and you will be bound by any order made in the proceeding.

(*Date*) (*Name, address and telephone number of lawyer or party serving notice*)

TO (*Name and address of lawyer or party receiving notice*)

July 1, 2007

FORM 55B — NOTICE TO PARTY ADDED ON REFERENCE

Courts of Justice Act

[Repealed O. Reg. 77/06, s. 3.]

[Editor's Note: Forms 4A to 78A of the Rules of Civil Procedure have been repealed by O. Reg. 77/06, effective July 1, 2006. Pursuant to Rule of Civil Procedure 1.06, when a form is referred to by number, the reference is to the form with that number that is described in the Table of Forms at the end of these rules and which is available on the Internet through

www.ontariocourtforms.on.ca. For your convenience, the government form as published on this website is reproduced below.]

(*General heading*)

NOTICE TO PARTY ADDED ON REFERENCE

TO *(Name of party added on reference)*

By order of the court, a copy of which is served with this notice, a reference was directed to (*person conducting reference*) for the purpose of (*set out purpose of reference*).

YOU HAVE BEEN MADE A PARTY TO THIS PROCEEDING by order of (*name of person conducting reference*), a copy of which is also served with this notice.

THE REFERENCE WILL PROCEED on (*day*), (*date*), at (*time*), at (*address*).

YOU MAKE A MOTION to a judge of this court WITHIN TEN DAYS (*or where the person is to be served outside Ontario, such further time as the referee directs*) after this notice is served on you to set aside or vary the order directing the reference or the order adding you as a party.

IF YOU FAIL TO DO SO OR IF YOU FAIL TO ATTEND ON THE REFERENCE, in person or by an Ontario lawyer acting for you, the reference may proceed in your absence and without further notice to you, and you will be bound by any order made in this proceeding.

(*Date*) (*Name, address and telephone number of lawyer or party serving notice*)

TO (*Name and address of party added on reference*)

July 1, 2007

FORM 55C — REPORT ON REFERENCE (ADMINISTRATION OF ESTATE)

Courts of Justice Act

[Repealed O. Reg. 77/06, s. 3.]

[Editor's Note: Forms 4A to 78A of the Rules of Civil Procedure have been repealed by O. Reg. 77/06, effective July 1, 2006. Pursuant to Rule of Civil Procedure 1.06, when a form is referred to by number, the reference is to the form with that number that is described in the Table of Forms at the end of these rules and which is available on the Internet through www.ontariocourtforms.on.ca. For your convenience, the government form as published on this website is reproduced below.]

(*General heading*)

REPORT ON REFERENCE

In accordance with the order directing a reference dated (*date*), I have disposed of the matters referred to me, and I report as follows:

1. The following parties were served with the order directing a reference and a notice of hearing for directions: (*Set out names*). (*Where applicable, add:* Service on the following parties was dispensed with: (*Set out names and the reason for dispensing with service*).) The following parties were added on the reference and were served with a notice to party added on reference: (*Set out names*).

2. The following parties did not attend on the reference: (*Set out names*).

3. The personal estate not specifically bequeathed by the testator received by the executors and for which they are chargeable amounts to $ ...., and they have paid or are entitled to be allowed the sum of $ ...., leaving a balance due from (*or* to) them of $ .... (*or, where applicable:* No personal estate has been received by the executors, nor are they chargeable with any.)

4. The creditors' claims received in response to the advertisement for creditors and which I have allowed are set out in Schedule A and amount altogether to $ .... (*or, where applicable:* No creditor has sent in a claim in response to the advertisement for creditors, nor has any such claim been proved before me.)

5. The funeral expenses of the testator amounting to $ .... have been paid by the executors and are allowed to them in the account of personal estate.

6. The legacies given by the testator are set out in Schedule B, and with the interest therein mentioned, remain due to the persons named (*or as the case may be*).

7. The personal estate of the testator outstanding or undisposed of is set out in Schedule C.

8. The real estate owned by the testator and the encumbrances affecting it are set out in Schedule D.

9. The rents and profits of the testator's real estate received by the executors and for which they are chargeable amount to $ .... and they have paid or are entitled to be allowed the sum of $ ...., leaving a balance due from (*or* to) them of $ .... (*or, where applicable:* No rents and profits have been received by the executors, nor are they chargeable with any).

10. I have allowed the executors the sum of $ .... as compensation for their services in the management of the estate.

11. I have caused the real estate, other than (*identify property*), which has specifically devised, to be sold and the purchasers have paid their purchase money into court.

12. In Schedule E, I have shown how the money in court is to be dealt with.

(*Date*) (*Signature of referee*)

(*All schedules should be as brief as possible. Only the general character of the things described should be shown. Land should be described without setting out a full legal description.*)

(*In Schedule C, the personal estate not specifically bequeathed should be set out separately from the other personal property outstanding or undisposed of. Where there is no specific bequest, the report should state that fact.*)

November 1, 2005

FORM 55D — NOTICE OF CONTESTED CLAIM

Courts of Justice Act

[Repealed O. Reg. 77/06, s. 3.]

[Editor's Note: Forms 4A to 78A of the Rules of Civil Procedure have been repealed by O. Reg. 77/06, effective July 1, 2006. Pursuant to Rule of Civil Procedure 1.06, when a form is referred to by number, the reference is to the form with that number that is described in the Table of Forms at the end of these rules and which is available on the Internet through www.ontariocourtforms.on.ca. For your convenience, the government form as published on this website is reproduced below.]

(*General heading*)

NOTICE OF CONTESTED CLAIM

YOUR CLAIM IN THIS PROCEEDING IS BEING CONTESTED. You are required to prove your claim before the referee on (*day*), (*date*), (*time*), at (*address*).

IF YOU FAIL TO ATTEND AND PROVE YOUR CLAIM, YOUR CLAIM MAY BE DISALLOWED.

(*Date*) (*Name, address and telephone number of party or lawyer serving notice*)

TO (*Name and address of creditor*)

July 1, 2007

FORM 55E — NOTICE TO CREDITOR

Courts of Justice Act

[Repealed O. Reg. 77/06, s. 3.]

[Editor's Note: Forms 4A to 78A of the Rules of Civil Procedure have been repealed by O. Reg. 77/06, effective July 1, 2006. Pursuant to Rule of Civil Procedure 1.06, when a form is referred to by number, the reference is to the form with that number that is described in the Table of Forms at the end of these rules and which is available on the Internet through www.ontariocourtforms.on.ca. For your convenience, the government form as published on this website is reproduced below.]

(GENERAL HEADING)

NOTICE TO CREDITOR

YOU MAY OBTAIN PAYMENT of the amount allowed by the court in respect of your claim in this proceeding from the office of the Accountant of the Superior Court of Justice, 595 Bay Street, Suite 800, Toronto, ON M5G 2M6 *(or* the local registrar of this court at *(address))*.

(Date) . . . . . *(Name, address and telephone number of lawyer or party serving notice)*

TO *(Name and address of creditor)*

April 11, 2012

FORM 55F — CONDITIONS OF SALE

Courts of Justice Act

[Repealed O. Reg. 77/06, s. 3.]

[Editor's Note: Forms 4A to 78A of the Rules of Civil Procedure have been repealed by O. Reg. 77/06, effective July 1, 2006. Pursuant to Rule of Civil Procedure 1.06, when a form is referred to by number, the reference is to the form with that number that is described in the Table of Forms at the end of these rules and which is available on the Internet through www.ontariocourtforms.on.ca. For your convenience, the government form as published on this website is reproduced below.]

1. No person shall advance the bidding in an amount less than $10 at any bidding under $500 nor in an amount less than $20 at any bidding over $500. No person shall be allowed to retract a bid.

2. The property shall be sold to the highest bidder. Where any dispute arises as to who is the last or highest bidder, the property shall be put up again.

3. All parties to the proceeding may bid, except the party having carriage of the sale and any trustee or agent for the party or other person in a fiduciary relationship to the party.

4. The purchaser shall, at the time of sale, pay to the party having carriage of the sale or to the party's lawyer a deposit of ten per cent of the purchase price and shall pay the balance of the purchase price on completion of the sale. On payment of the balance, the purchaser shall be entitled to receive a transfer and to take possession. The purchaser shall, at the time of sale, sign an agreement for the completion of the sale.

5. The purchaser shall have the transfer prepared at the purchaser's own expense and tender it to the party having carriage of the sale for execution.

6. Where the purchaser fails to comply with any of these conditions, the deposit and all other payments made shall be forfeited and the property may be resold. Any deficiency on the

resale, together with all expenses incurred on the resale or caused by the default, shall be paid by the defaulting purchaser.

July 1, 2007

FORM 55G — INTERIM REPORT ON SALE

Courts of Justice Act

[Repealed O. Reg. 77/06, s. 3.]

[Editor's Note: Forms 4A to 78A of the Rules of Civil Procedure have been repealed by O. Reg. 77/06, effective July 1, 2006. Pursuant to Rule of Civil Procedure 1.06, when a form is referred to by number, the reference is to the form with that number that is described in the Table of Forms at the end of these rules and which is available on the Internet through www.ontariocourtforms.on.ca. For your convenience, the government form as published on this website is reproduced below.]

(*General heading*)

INTERIM REPORT ON SALE

1. In accordance with the order in this proceeding dated (*date*), in the presence of (*or* after notice to) all parties concerned, I settled the form of an advertisement and the conditions of sale for the sale of the property referred to in the judgment.

2. The advertisement was published as directed, and the property was offered for sale by public auction by me (*or* by (*name*), an auctioneer appointed by me for that purpose) on (*date*).

3. The sale was conducted in a fair, open and proper manner and (*name*) was declared the highest bidder for and became the purchaser of the property at the price of $ ...., payable as follows: (*Set out briefly the conditions of sale for payment of the purchase money.*)

(*Date*) (*Signature of referee*)

November 1, 2005

FORM 56A — ORDER FOR SECURITY FOR COSTS

Courts of Justice Act

[Repealed O. Reg. 77/06, s. 3.]

[Editor's Note: Forms 4A to 78A of the Rules of Civil Procedure have been repealed by O. Reg. 77/06, effective July 1, 2006. Pursuant to Rule of Civil Procedure 1.06, when a form is referred to by number, the reference is to the form with that number that is described in the Table of Forms at the end of these rules and which is available on the Internet through www.ontariocourtforms.on.ca. For your convenience, the government form as published on this website is reproduced below.]

(*Court file no.*)

(*Court*)

(*Name of judge or master*) (*Day and date order made*)

(*Court seal*) (*Title of Proceeding*)

ORDER FOR SECURITY FOR COSTS

(*Recitals in accordance with Form 59A*)

1. THIS COURT ORDERS that within .... days after this order is served on the plaintiff, (*or* applicant), the plaintiff (*or* applicant) shall pay into court (*or* to (*name*)) the sum of $ .... as security for the costs of this proceeding.

(*Where a plaintiff or applicant is ordered to give security for costs in some other form, give a description of the security required and vary the form of the order accordingly.*)

2. THIS COURT ORDERS that until the security required by this order has been given, the plaintiff (*or* applicant) may not take any step in this proceeding, except an appeal from this order (*or as otherwise ordered*).

(*Signature of judge, master or registrar*)

November 1, 2005

FORM 57A — BILL OF COSTS

Courts of Justice Act

[Repealed O. Reg. 77/06, s. 3.]

[Editor's Note: Forms 4A to 78A of the Rules of Civil Procedure have been repealed by O. Reg. 77/06, effective July 1, 2006. Pursuant to Rule of Civil Procedure 1.06, when a form is referred to by number, the reference is to the form with that number that is described in the Table of Forms at the end of these rules and which is available on the Internet through www.ontariocourtforms.on.ca. For your convenience, the government form as published on this website is reproduced below.]

(*General heading*)
Bill of Costs

AMOUNTS CLAIMED FOR FEES AND DISBURSEMENTS

(Following the items set out in Tariff A, itemize the claim for fees and disbursements. Indicate the names of the lawyers, students-at-law and law clerks who provided services in connection with each item.

In support of the claim for fees, attach copies of the dockets or other evidence.

In support of the claim for disbursements, attach copies of invoices or other evidence.)

STATEMENT OF EXPERIENCE

A claim for fees is being made with respect to the following lawyers:

Name of lawyer Years of experience

TO: *(name and address of lawyer or party)*

November 1, 2005

FORM 57B — COSTS OUTLINE

Courts of Justice Act

[Repealed O. Reg. 77/06, s. 3.]

[Editor's Note: Forms 4A to 78A of the Rules of Civil Procedure have been repealed by O. Reg. 77/06, effective July 1, 2006. Pursuant to Rule of Civil Procedure 1.06, when a form is referred to by number, the reference is to the form with that number that is described in the Table of Forms at the end of these rules and which is available on the Internet through www.ontariocourtforms.on.ca. For your convenience, the government form as published on this website is reproduced below.]

ONTARIO
SUPERIOR COURT OF JUSTICE
COSTS OUTLINE

The *(identify party)* provides the following outline of the submissions to be made at the hearing in support of the costs the party will seek if successful:

Fees (as detailed below)	$	
Estimated lawyer's fee for appearance	$	
Disbursements (as detailed in the attached appendix)	$	....
Total	$	

The following points are made in support of the costs sought with reference to the factors set out in subrule 57.01(1):

- the amount claimed and the amount recovered in the proceeding

- the complexity of the proceeding

ONTARIO
SUPERIOR COURT OF JUSTICE
COSTS OUTLINE

- the importance of the issues

- the conduct of any party that tended to shorten or lengthen unnecessarily the duration of the proceeding

- whether any step in the proceeding was improper, vexatious or unnecessary or taken through negligence, mistake or excessive caution

- a party's denial of or refusal to admit anything that should have been admitted

- the experience of the party's lawyer

- the hours spent, the rates sought for costs and the rate actually charged by the party's lawyer

FEE ITEMS	PERSONS	HOURS	PARTIAL INDEMNITY RATE	ACTUAL RATE*
(e.g. pleadings, affidavits, cross-examinations, preparation, hearing, etc.)	*(identify the lawyers, students, and law clerks who provided services in connection with each item together with their year of call, if applicable)*	*(specify the hours claimed for each person identified in column 2)*	*(specify the rate being sought for each person identified in column 2)*	

* Specify the rate being charged to the client for each person identified in column 2. If there is a contingency fee arrangement, state the rate that would have been charged absent such arrangement.

- any other matter relevant to the question of costs

LAWYER'S CERTIFICATE

I CERTIFY that the hours claimed have been spent, that the rates shown are correct and that each disbursement has been incurred as claimed.

Date: ....

Signature of lawyer

July 1, 2007

FORM 58A — NOTICE OF APPOINTMENT FOR ASSESSMENT OF COSTS

Courts of Justice Act

[Repealed O. Reg. 77/06, s. 3.]

[Editor's Note: Forms 4A to 78A of the Rules of Civil Procedure have been repealed by O. Reg. 77/06, effective July 1, 2006. Pursuant to Rule of Civil Procedure 1.06, when a form is referred to by number, the reference is to the form with that number that is described in the Table of Forms at the end of these rules and which is available on the Internet through www.ontariocourtforms.on.ca. For your convenience, the government form as published on this website is reproduced below.]

(*General heading*)

NOTICE OF APPOINTMENT FOR ASSESSMENT OF COSTS

TO THE PARTIES

I HAVE MADE AN APPOINTMENT to assess the costs of (*identify party*), a copy of whose bill of costs is attached to this notice, on (*day*), (*date*), at (*time*), at (*address*).

Date ....
Assessment officer

TO (*Name and address of lawyer or party on whom notice is served*)

July 1, 2007

FORM 58B — NOTICE TO DELIVER A BILL OF COSTS FOR ASSESSMENT

Courts of Justice Act

[Repealed O. Reg. 77/06, s. 3.]

[Editor's Note: Forms 4A to 78A of the Rules of Civil Procedure have been repealed by O. Reg. 77/06, effective July 1, 2006. Pursuant to Rule of Civil Procedure 1.06, when a form is referred to by number, the reference is to the form with that number that is described in the Table of Forms at the end of these rules and which is available on the Internet through www.ontariocourtforms.on.ca. For your convenience, the government form as published on this website is reproduced below.]

(*General heading*)

NOTICE TO DELIVER A BILL OF COSTS FOR ASSESSMENT

TO THE PARTIES

I HAVE MADE AN APPOINTMENT, at the request of (*identify party who obtained appointment*) to assess the costs of (*identify party entitled to costs and what costs are to be assessed*) on (*day*), (*date*), at (*time*), at (*address*).

TO (*identify party entitled to costs*)

YOU ARE REQUIRED to file your bill of costs with me and serve your bill of costs on every party interested in the assessment at least seven days before the above date.

Date ....
Assessment officer

TO (*Name and address of lawyer or party on whom notice is served*)

July 1, 2007

FORM 58C — CERTIFICATE OF ASSESSMENT OF COSTS

Courts of Justice Act

[Repealed O. Reg. 77/06, s. 3.]

[Editor's Note: Forms 4A to 78A of the Rules of Civil Procedure have been repealed by O. Reg. 77/06, effective July 1, 2006. Pursuant to Rule of Civil Procedure 1.06, when a form is referred to by number, the reference is to the form with that number that is described in the Table of Forms at the end of these rules and which is available on the Internet through www.ontariocourtforms.on.ca. For your convenience, the government form as published on this website is reproduced below.]

(*General heading*)

CERTIFICATE OF ASSESSMENT OF COSTS

I CERTIFY that I have assessed the costs of (*identify party*) in this proceeding (*or as may be*) under the authority of (*give particulars of order or specify rule or statutory provision*), and I ALLOW THE SUM OF $ ....

(Where postjudgment interest is payable, add:)

THE COSTS ALLOWED IN THIS ASSESSMENT BEAR INTEREST at the rate of ... per cent per year commencing on (*date*).

Date ....
Assessment officer

November 1, 2005

FORM 59A — ORDER

Courts of Justice Act

[Repealed O. Reg. 77/06, s. 3.]

[Editor's Note: Forms 4A to 78A of the Rules of Civil Procedure have been repealed by O. Reg. 77/06, effective July 1, 2006. Pursuant to Rule of Civil Procedure 1.06, when a form is referred to by number, the reference is to the form with that number that is described in the Table of Forms at the end of these rules and which is available on the Internet through www.ontariocourtforms.on.ca. For your convenience, the government form as published on this website is reproduced below.]

(*Court file no.*)

(*Court*)

(*Name of judge or officer*) (*Day and date order made*)

(*Court seal*) (*Title of proceeding*)

ORDER

THIS MOTION, made by (*identify moving party*) for (*state the relief sought in the notice of motion, except to the extent that it appears in the operative part of the order*), (*where applicable, add* made without notice,) was heard this day (*or* heard on (date)), at (*place*), (*recite any particulars necessary to understand the order*).

ON READING the (*give particulars of the material filed on the motion*) and on hearing the submissions of the lawyer(s) for (*identify parties*), (*where applicable, add (identify party)* appearing in person *or* no one appearing for (*identify party*), although properly served as appears from (*indicate proof of service*)),

1. THIS COURT ORDERS that ...

2. THIS COURT ORDERS that ...

(*In an order for the payment of money on which postjudgment interest is payable, add:*)

THIS ORDER BEARS INTEREST at the rate of .... per cent per year commencing on (*date*).

(*Signature of judge, officer or registrar*)

July 1, 2007

FORM 59B — JUDGMENT

Courts of Justice Act

[Repealed O. Reg. 77/06, s. 3.]

[Editor's Note: Forms 4A to 78A of the Rules of Civil Procedure have been repealed by O. Reg. 77/06, effective July 1, 2006. Pursuant to Rule of Civil Procedure 1.06, when a form is referred to by number, the reference is to the form with that number that is described in the Table of Forms at the end of these rules and which is available on the Internet through www.ontariocourtforms.on.ca. For your convenience, the government form as published on this website is reproduced below.]

(*Court file no.*)

(*Court*)

(*Name of judge or officer*) (*Day and date judgment given*)

(*Court seal*) (*Title of Proceeding*)

JUDGMENT

(*Judgment after trial or hearing of application*)

THIS ACTION (*or* APPLICATION) was heard this day (*or* heard on (*date*)) without (*or* with) a jury at (*place*) in the presence of the lawyers for all parties (*where applicable, add* (*identify party*) appearing in person, *or* no one appearing for (*identify party*) although properly served as appears from (*indicate proof of service*)),

(*Action*) ON READING THE PLEADINGS AND HEARING THE EVIDENCE and the submissions of the lawyers for the parties,

(*Application*) ON READING THE NOTICE OF APPLICATION AND THE EVIDENCE FILED BY THE PARTIES, (*where applicable, add* on hearing the oral evidence presented by the parties,) and on hearing the submissions of the lawyers for the parties.

(*Judgment on motion*)

THIS MOTION, made by (*identify moving party*), for (*state the relief sought in the notice of motion, except to the extent that it appears in the operative part of the judgment*), (*where applicable, add* made without notice,) was heard this day (*or* heard on (*date*)), at (*place*), (*recite any particulars necessary to understand the judgment*).

ON READING THE (*give particulars of the material filed on the motion*) and on hearing the submissions of the lawyer(s) for (*identify parties*), (*where applicable, add (identify party*) appearing in person *or* no one appearing for (*identify party*), although properly served as appears from (*indicate proof of service*)),

1. THIS COURT ORDERS (*or* DECLARES, *if applicable*) (*where applicable, add:* AND ADJUDGES) that . . . .

2. THIS COURT ORDERS (*or as may be*) that . . . .

(*In a judgment for the payment of money on which postjudgment interest is payable add:*)

THIS JUDGMENT BEARS INTEREST at the rate of .... per cent per year commencing on (*date*).

(*Signature of judge, officer or registrar*)

July 1, 2007

FORM 59C — ORDER ON APPEAL

Courts of Justice Act

[Repealed O. Reg. 77/06, s. 3.]

[Editor's Note: Forms 4A to 78A of the Rules of Civil Procedure have been repealed by O. Reg. 77/06, effective July 1, 2006. Pursuant to Rule of Civil Procedure 1.06, when a form is referred to by number, the reference is to the form with that number that is described in the Table of Forms at the end of these rules and which is available on the Internet through www.ontariocourtforms.on.ca. For your convenience, the government form as published on this website is reproduced below.]

(*Court file no.*)

(*Court*)

(*Name(s) of judge(s)*) (*Day and date order made*)

(*Court seal*) (*Title of Proceeding*)

ORDER

THIS APPEAL by (*identify appellant*) for (*state the relief sought in the notice of appeal, except to the extent that it is stated in the operative part of the order*) was heard this day (*or* heard on (*date*)), at (*place*), (*recite any particulars necessary to understand the order*).

ON READING the (*give particulars of the material filed on the appeal*), and on hearing the submissions of the lawyer(s) for (*identify parties*), (*where applicable, add (identify party)* appearing in person *or* no one appearing for (*identify party*) although properly served as appears from (*indicate proof of service*)),

THIS COURT ORDERS (*or* CERTIFIES, *if applicable*) that ...

THIS ORDER BEARS INTEREST at the rate of .... per cent per year commencing

on ....
(*date*)

(*Signature of judge or registrar*)

July 1, 2007

FORM 59D — NOTICE OF APPOINTMENT TO SETTLE ORDER

Courts of Justice Act

[Repealed O. Reg. 77/06, s. 3.]

[Editor's Note: Forms 4A to 78A of the Rules of Civil Procedure have been repealed by O. Reg. 77/06, effective July 1, 2006. Pursuant to Rule of Civil Procedure 1.06, when a form is referred to by number, the reference is to the form with that number that is described in the Table of Forms at the end of these rules and which is available on the Internet through www.ontariocourtforms.on.ca. For your convenience, the government form as published on this website is reproduced below.]

(General heading)

NOTICE OF APPOINTMENT TO SETTLE ORDER

The *(identify party seeking appointment)* has scheduled an appointment to settle an order with the registrar on *(day)*, *(date)*, at *(time)*, or soon after that time as the motion can be heard, at (*address of court house)*.

PROPOSED METHOD OF HEARING: The appointment is to be heard *(choose appropriate option)*

❑ in writing;

❑ in writing as an opposed appointment;

❑ by teleconference;

❑ orally.

THE APPOINTMENT IS FOR *(state here the precise relief sought).*

THE GROUNDS FOR THE APPOINTMENT ARE *(specify the grounds to be argued).*

THE FOLLOWING DOCUMENTARY EVIDENCE will be used at the appointment: *(list the affidavits or other documentary evidence to be relied on).*

(Date) *(Name, address and telephone number of lawyer of party seeking appointment or party seeking appointment)*

TO *(Name and address of lawyer of other parties represented at hearing or other parties represented at hearing)*

November 1, 2016

FORM 60A — WRIT OF SEIZURE AND SALE

Courts of Justice Act

[Repealed O. Reg. 77/06, s. 3.]

[Editor's Note: Forms 4A to 78A of the Rules of Civil Procedure have been repealed by O. Reg. 77/06, effective July 1, 2006. Pursuant to Rule of Civil Procedure 1.06, when a form is referred to by number, the reference is to the form with that number that is described in the Table of Forms at the end of these rules and which is available on the Internet through

www.ontariocourtforms.on.ca. For your convenience, the government form as published on this website is reproduced below.]

(Court file no.)

ONTARIO
SUPERIOR COURT OF JUSTICE

BETWEEN

AND

WRIT OF SEIZURE AND SALE

TO: the Sheriff of the *(name of county or district)*

Under an order of this court made on *(date)*, in favour of *(name of creditor)*, YOU ARE DIRECTED to seize and sell the real and personal property within your county or district of

Surname of individual or name of corporation/firm, etc.		
First given name (individual only)	*Second given name (individual only) (if applicable)*	*Third given name (individual only) (if applicable)*

and to realize from the seizure and sale the following sums:

(a) $ .... and interest at .... per cent per year commencing on *(date)*

(Where the writ is for two or more periodic or instalment payments, substitute:)

Amount of payment . . . . Due Date

(b) $ .... and interest at .... per cent per year on the payments in default commencing on the date of default;

(c) $ .... for costs together with interest at .... per cent per year commencing on *(date)*; and

(d) your fees and expenses in enforcing this writ.

YOU ARE DIRECTED to pay out the proceeds according to law and to report on the execution of this writ if required by the party or lawyer who filed it.

Dated at .... Issued by ....
Registrar

on ....

Address of court office
....
....
....

FORM 60A WRIT OF SEIZURE AND SALE, BACKSHEET

(Short title of proceeding) *(Court file no.)*

(Name of court)

FEES

PROCEEDING COMMENCED AT
(place)

Fee	Item	Officer

	Paid for this writ	
$50	Lawyer's fee for issuing a writ	
	First renewal	
	Second renewal	
	Third renewal	

RENEWAL

Date	Officer

WRIT OF SEIZURE AND SALE

Creditor's name ....

Creditor's address ....

....

....

....

Lawyer's name ....

....

....

Lawyer's address and telephone no.

....

....

....

July 1, 2007

FORM 60B — WRIT OF SEQUESTRATION

Courts of Justice Act

[Repealed O. Reg. 77/06, s. 3.]

[Editor's Note: Forms 4A to 78A of the Rules of Civil Procedure have been repealed by O. Reg. 77/06, effective July 1, 2006. Pursuant to Rule of Civil Procedure 1.06, when a form is referred to by number, the reference is to the form with that number that is described in the Table of Forms at the end of these rules and which is available on the Internet through www.ontariocourtforms.on.ca. For your convenience, the government form as published on this website is reproduced below.]

(*General heading*)

(*Court seal*)

TO the Sheriff of the (*name of county or district*)

Under an order of this court made on (*date*) on motion of (*name of moving party*), YOU ARE DIRECTED to take possession of and hold the following property within your county or district of (*name of person against whom order was made*): (*Set out a description of the property to be taken and held.*)

AND YOU ARE DIRECTED to collect and hold any income from the property until further order of this court.

Date .... Issued by ....
Local registrar

Address of
court office ....
....

November 1, 2005

FORM 60C — WRIT OF POSSESSION

Courts of Justice Act

[Repealed O. Reg. 77/06, s. 3.]

[Editor's Note: Forms 4A to 78A of the Rules of Civil Procedure have been repealed by O. Reg. 77/06, effective July 1, 2006. Pursuant to Rule of Civil Procedure 1.06, when a form is referred to by number, the reference is to the form with that number that is described in the Table of Forms at the end of these rules and which is available on the Internet through www.ontariocourtforms.on.ca. For your convenience, the government form as published on this website is reproduced below.]

(*General heading*)

(*Court seal*)

WRIT OF POSSESSION

To the Sheriff of the (*name of county or district*)

Under an order of this court made on (*date*) in favour of (*name of party who obtained order*), YOU ARE DIRECTED to enter and take possession of the following land and premises in your county or district: (*Set out a description of the land and premises.*)

AND YOU ARE DIRECTED to give possession of the above land and premises without delay to (*name of party who obtained order*).

Date .... Issued by ....
Local registrar

Address of
court office ....
....

Renewed by order made on (*date*).

....

Local registrar

November 1, 2005

FORM 60D — WRIT OF DELIVERY

Courts of Justice Act

[Repealed O. Reg. 77/06, s. 3.]

[Editor's Note: Forms 4A to 78A of the Rules of Civil Procedure have been repealed by O. Reg. 77/06, effective July 1, 2006. Pursuant to Rule of Civil Procedure 1.06, when a form is referred to by number, the reference is to the form with that number that is described in the Table of Forms at the end of these rules and which is available on the Internet through www.ontariocourtforms.on.ca. For your convenience, the government form as published on this website is reproduced below.]

(*General heading*)

(*Court seal*)

WRIT OF DELIVERY

TO the Sheriff of the (*name of county or district*)

Under an order of this court made on (*date*), YOU ARE DIRECTED to seize from (*name of party*) and to deliver without delay to (*name of party who obtained order*) possession of the following personal property: (*Set out a description of the property to be delivered.*)

Date .... Issued by ....

Local registrar

Address of court office ....

....

November 1, 2005

FORM 60E — REQUEST TO RENEW

Courts of Justice Act

[Repealed O. Reg. 77/06, s. 3.]

[Editor's Note: Forms 4A to 78A of the Rules of Civil Procedure have been repealed by O. Reg. 77/06, effective July 1, 2006. Pursuant to Rule of Civil Procedure 1.06, when a form is referred to by number, the reference is to the form with that number that is described in the Table of Forms at the end of these rules and which is available on the Internet through www.ontariocourtforms.on.ca. For your convenience, the government form as published on this website is reproduced below.]

(*General heading*)

REQUEST TO RENEW

TO the Sheriff of the (*name of county or district*)

YOU ARE REQUESTED TO RENEW the writ of seizure and sale issued on (*date*) in this proceeding and filed in your office for a period of six years from the date of renewal.

(*Date*) (*Signature of party or lawyer*)

(*Name, address and telephone number of party or lawyer*)

July 1, 2007

FORM 60F — DIRECTION TO ENFORCE WRIT OF SEIZURE AND SALE

Courts of Justice Act

[Repealed O. Reg. 77/06, s. 3.]

[Editor's Note: Forms 4A to 78A of the Rules of Civil Procedure have been repealed by O. Reg. 77/06, effective July 1, 2006. Pursuant to Rule of Civil Procedure 1.06, when a form is referred to by number, the reference is to the form with that number that is described in the Table of Forms at the end of these rules and which is available on the Internet through www.ontariocourtforms.on.ca. For your convenience, the government form as published on this website is reproduced below.]

(Sheriff's file no.)

(Court)

between:

(name)

Creditor(s)

and

(name)

Debtor(s)

DIRECTION TO ENFORCE WRIT

TO: the Sheriff of the *(name of county or district)*

Under an order of this court in favour of *(name of creditor)* made on *(date)*, *(name of debtor)* was ordered to pay the sum of $ .... *(where applicable, add each month or as may be)* with interest at the rate of .... per cent per year commencing on *(date)* and costs of $.......... *(as fixed or assessed)* with interest at the rate of .... per cent per year commencing on *(date)*. Since the order was made, the creditor has received the following payments:

Date of payment . . . . Amount of payment

Under rule 60.19 of the *Rules of Civil Procedure*, the creditor is entitled to costs in the amount of,

(a) $50 for the preparation of documents in connection with issuing, renewing and filing with the sheriff the writ of execution or notice of garnishment;

(b) $ .... for disbursements paid to a sheriff, registrar, official examiner, court reporter or other public officer and to which the creditor is entitled under subrule 60.19(1); *(Attach copy of all receipts.)*

(c) $ .... for an amount determined in accordance with Tariff A for conducting an examination in aid of execution; *(Attach affidavit confirming that examination was conducted, and a bill of costs.)*

(d) $ .... for any other costs to which the creditor is entitled under subrule 60.19(1). *(Attach certificate of assessment.)*

YOU ARE DIRECTED to enforce the writ of seizure and sale issued on *(date)* and filed in your office for a sum sufficient to satisfy the total of the amounts set out above, together with subsequent interest, and your fees and expenses.

Date ....

(Signature of party or lawyer)
(Name, address and telephone number of party or lawyer)

November 1, 2005

FORM 60G — REQUISITION FOR GARNISHMENT

Courts of Justice Act

[Repealed O. Reg. 77/06, s. 3.]

[Editor's Note: Forms 4A to 78A of the Rules of Civil Procedure have been repealed by O. Reg. 77/06, effective July 1, 2006. Pursuant to Rule of Civil Procedure 1.06, when a form is referred to by number, the reference is to the form with that number that is described in the Table of Forms at the end of these rules and which is available on the Internet through www.ontariocourtforms.on.ca. For your convenience, the government form as published on this website is reproduced below.]

(General heading)

REQUISITION FOR GARNISHMENT

TO: the local registrar at *(place)*

I REQUIRE a notice of garnishment to be issued in this proceeding, in accordance with the attached draft Form 60H. The total amount to be shown in the notice of garnishment is $ ...., made up as follows:

1. $ .... for principal owing under the judgment or order, including prejudgment interest.

2. $ .... for the costs of the action.

3. $50 for the preparation of documents in connection with issuing, renewing and filing with the sheriff a writ of execution or notice of garnishment.

4. $ .... for disbursements paid to a sheriff, registrar, official examiner, court reporter or other public officer and to which the creditor is entitled under subrule 60.19(1). *(Attach copies of all receipts.)*

5. $ .... for an amount determined in accordance with Tariff A for conducting an examination in aid of execution. *(Attach affidavit confirming that examination was conducted, and a bill of costs.)*

6. $ .... for any other costs to which the creditor is entitled under subrule 60.19(1). *(Attach certificate of assessment.)*

7. $ .... for postjudgment interest to today's date. *(Calculate by counting the number of days that the principal sum has been owing, multiplying that number by the annual rate of interest, then multiplying by the principal sum owing and dividing by 365.)*

Date ....

____

(Signature of creditor or creditor's lawyer)

(Name, address and telephone number of creditor or creditor's lawyer)

November 1, 2005

FORM 60G.1 — REQUISITION FOR RENEWAL OF GARNISHMENT

Courts of Justice Act

[Repealed O. Reg. 77/06, s. 3.]

[Editor's Note: Forms 4A to 78A of the Rules of Civil Procedure have been repealed by O. Reg. 77/06, effective July 1, 2006. Pursuant to Rule of Civil Procedure 1.06, when a form is referred to by number, the reference is to the form with that number that is described in the Table of Forms at the end of these rules and which is available on the Internet through

www.ontariocourtforms.on.ca. For your convenience, the government form as published on this website is reproduced below.]

ONTARIO
SUPERIOR COURT OF JUSTICE
(General heading)

REQUISITION FOR RENEWAL OF GARNISHMENT

TO: the local registrar at *(place)*

I REQUIRE a notice of renewal of garnishment to be issued in this proceeding, in accordance with the attached draft Form 60H.1. The total amount to be shown in the notice of renewal of garnishment is $ ...., made up as follows:

1. $ .... for principal owing under the judgment or order, including prejudgment interest.

2. $ .... for the costs of the action.

3. $50 for the preparation of documents in connection with issuing, renewing and filing with the sheriff a writ of execution or notice of garnishment.

4. $ .... for disbursements paid to a sheriff, registrar, official examiner, court reporter or other public officer and to which the creditor is entitled under subrule 60.19(1). *(Attach copies of all receipts.)*

5. $ .... for an amount determined in accordance with Tariff A for conducting an examination in aid of execution. *(Attach affidavit confirming that examination was conducted, and a bill of costs.)*

6. $ .... for any other costs to which the creditor is entitled under subrule 60.19(1). *(Attach certificate of assessment.)*

7. $ .... for postjudgment interest to today's date. *(Calculate by counting the number of days that the principal sum has been owing, multiplying that number by the annual rate of interest, then multiplying by the principal sum owing and dividing by 365.)*

Date ....

(Signature of creditor or creditor's lawyer)

(Name, address and telephone number of creditor or creditor's lawyer)

November 1, 2005

FORM 60H — NOTICE OF GARNISHMENT

Courts of Justice Act

[Repealed O. Reg. 77/06, s. 3.]

NOTICE OF GARNISHMENT **Form 60H**

[Editor's Note: Forms 4A to 78A of the Rules of Civil Procedure have been repealed by O. Reg. 77/06, effective July 1, 2006. Pursuant to Rule of Civil Procedure 1.06, when a form is referred to by number, the reference is to the form with that number that is described in the Table of Forms at the end of these rules and which is available on the Internet through www.ontariocourtforms.on.ca. For your convenience, the government form as published on this website is reproduced below.]

(*Court file no.*)

(*Court*)

BETWEEN

(*name*)

Creditor

(*Court seal*)

(and)

(*name*)

Debtor

(and)

(*name*)

Garnishee

NOTICE OF GARNISHMENT

To (*name and address of garnishee*)

A LEGAL PROCEEDING in this court between the creditor and the debtor has resulted in an order that the debtor pay a sum of money to the creditor. The creditor claims that you owe a debt to the debtor. A debt to the debtor includes both a debt payable to the debtor and a debt payable to the debtor and one or more co-owners. The creditor has had this notice of garnishment directed to you as garnishee in order to seize any debt that you owe or will owe to the debtor. Where the debt is payable to the debtor and to one or more co-owners, you must pay one-half of the indebtedness or the greater or lesser amount specified in an order made under subrule 60.08(16).

YOU ARE REQUIRED TO PAY to the Sheriff of the (*name of county or district*),

(a) within 10 days after this notice is served on you, all debts now payable by you to the debtor; and

(b) within 10 days after they become payable, all debts that become payable by you to the debtor within 6 years after this notice is served on you,

subject to the exemptions provided by section 7 of the *Wages Act*. The total amount of all your payments to the sheriff is not to exceed $ .... less $10 for your costs of making each payment.

EACH PAYMENT MUST BE SENT with a copy of the attached garnishee's payment notice to the sheriff at the address shown below.

IF YOU DO NOT PAY THE TOTAL AMOUNT OF $ .... LESS $10 FOR YOUR COSTS OF MAKING EACH PAYMENT WITHIN 10 DAYS after this notice is served on you, because the debt is owed to the debtor and to one or more co-owners or for any other reason, you must within that time serve on the creditor and the debtor and file with the court a garnishee's statement in Form 60I attached to this notice.

IF YOU FAIL TO OBEY THIS NOTICE, THE COURT MAY MAKE AND ENFORCE AN ORDER AGAINST YOU for payment of the amount set out above and the costs of the creditor.

IF YOU MAKE PAYMENT TO ANYONE OTHER THAN THE SHERIFF, YOU MAY BE LIABLE TO PAY AGAIN.

TO THE CREDITOR, THE DEBTOR AND THE GARNISHEE

Any party may make a motion to the court to determine any matter in relation to this notice of garnishment.

Date .... Issued by ....
Local registrar

Address of court office ....
....

Creditor's address	Debtor's address	Sheriff's address
. . . .	. . . .	. . . .
. . . .	. . . .	. . . .
telephone no.		

. . . .

(*The top portion of the garnishee's payment notice is to be completed by the creditor before the notice of garnishment is issued. Where it is anticipated that more than one payment will be made by the garnishee, the creditor should provide extra copies of the payment notice.*)

GARNISHEE PAYMENT NOTICE

Make payment by cheque or money order payable to the Sheriff of the (*the name of county or district*) and send it, along with a copy of this payment notice, to the (*address*).

Court . . . . File no. . . . .
Office at . . . .
Creditor . . . .
Debtor . . . .
Garnishee . . . .

TO BE COMPLETED BY GARNISHEE FOR EACH PAYMENT

Date of Payment . . . .
Amount enclosed $ . . . .

November 1, 2005

FORM 60H.1 — NOTICE OF RENEWAL OF GARNISHMENT

Courts of Justice Act

[Repealed O. Reg. 77/06, s. 3.]

[Editor's Note: Forms 4A to 78A of the Rules of Civil Procedure have been repealed by O. Reg. 77/06, effective July 1, 2006. Pursuant to Rule of Civil Procedure 1.06, when a form is referred to by number, the reference is to the form with that number that is described in the Table of Forms at the end of these rules and which is available on the Internet through www.ontariocourtforms.on.ca. For your convenience, the government form as published on this website is reproduced below.]

(Court file no.)

(Court)

BETWEEN *(name)*

Creditor

(Court seal) *(and)*

(name)

Debtor

(and)

(name)

Garnishee

NOTICE OF RENEWAL OF GARNISHMENT

TO *(name and address of garnishee)*

A LEGAL PROCEEDING in this court between the creditor and the debtor has resulted in an order that the debtor pay a sum of money to the creditor. The creditor claims that you owe a debt to the debtor. A debt to the debtor includes both a debt payable to the debtor and a debt payable to the debtor and one or more co-owners. The creditor has had this notice of renewal of garnishment directed to you as garnishee in order to seize any debt that you owe or will owe to the debtor. Where the debt is payable to the debtor and to one or more co-owners, you must pay one-half of the indebtedness or the greater or lesser amount specified in an order made under subrule 60.08(16).

(Where appropriate, add: This notice of renewal of garnishment enforces an order for support.)

YOU ARE REQUIRED TO PAY to the Sheriff of the *(name of county or district)*,

(a) within 10 days after this notice is served on you, all debts now payable by you to the debtor; and

(b) within 10 days after they become payable, all debts that become payable by you to the debtor within 6 years after this notice is served on you,

subject to the exemptions provided by section 7 of the *Wages Act*. The total amount of all your payments to the sheriff is not to exceed $.......... less $10 for your costs of making each payment.

EACH PAYMENT MUST BE SENT with a copy of the attached garnishee's payment notice to the sheriff at the address shown below.

IF YOU DO NOT PAY THE TOTAL AMOUNT OF $.......... LESS $10 FOR YOUR COSTS OF MAKING EACH PAYMENT WITHIN 10 DAYS after this notice is served on you, because the debt is owed to the debtor and to one or more co-owners or for any other reason, you must within that time serve on the creditor and the debtor and file with the court a garnishee's statement in Form 60I attached to this notice.

IF YOU FAIL TO OBEY THIS NOTICE, THE COURT MAY MAKE AND ENFORCE AN ORDER AGAINST YOU for payment of the amount set out above and the costs of the creditor.

IF YOU MAKE PAYMENT TO ANYONE OTHER THAN THE SHERIFF, YOU MAY BE LIABLE TO PAY AGAIN.

TO THE CREDITOR, THE DEBTOR AND THE GARNISHEE.

Any party may make a motion to the court to determine any matter in relation to this notice of renewal of garnishment.

Date .... Issued by ....
Local registrar
Address of court office ....
....

Creditor's address	Debtor's address	Sheriff's address
....	....	....
....	....	....

telephone no. ....
....

(The top portion of the garnishee's payment notice is to be completed by the creditor before the notice of renewal of garnishment is issued. Where it is anticipated that more than one payment will be made by the garnishee, the creditor should provide extra copies of the payment notice.)

GARNISHEE PAYMENT NOTICE

Make payment by cheque or money order payable to the Sheriff of the *(the name of county or district)* and send it, along with a copy of this payment notice, to the *(address)*.

Court .... File no. ....
Office at ....
Creditor ....
Debtor ....
Garnishee ....
TO BE COMPLETED BY GARNISHEE FOR EACH PAYMENT
Date of payment ....
Amount enclosed $ ....

November 1, 2005

FORM 60I — GARNISHEE'S STATEMENT

Courts of Justice Act

[Repealed O. Reg. 77/06, s. 3.]

[Editor's Note: Forms 4A to 78A of the Rules of Civil Procedure have been repealed by O. Reg. 77/06, effective July 1, 2006. Pursuant to Rule of Civil Procedure 1.06, when a form is

referred to by number, the reference is to the form with that number that is described in the Table of Forms at the end of these rules and which is available on the Internet through www.ontariocourtforms.on.ca. For your convenience, the government form as published on this website is reproduced below.]

(*The general heading on this form is to be completed by the creditor and the form is to be attached to the notice of garnishment to be served on the garnishee before the notice of garnishment is issued.*)

(*General heading as in Form 60H*)

GARNISHEE'S STATEMENT

1. I/We acknowledge that I/we owe or will owe the debtor or the debtor and one or more co-owners the sum of $ ...., payable on (*date*) because (*Give reasons why you owe the debtor or the debtor and one or more co-owners money. If you are making payment of less than the amount stated in line 2 of this paragraph because the debt is owed to the debtor and to one or more co-owners or for any other reason, give a full explanation of the reason. If you owe the debtor wages, state how often the debtor is paid. State the gross amount of the debtor's wages before any deductions and the net amount after all deductions and attach a copy of a pay slip.*)

1.1 (*If debt owed to debtor and one or more co-owners, check here* ❑ *and complete the following:*)

Co-owner(s) of the Debt (name, address) ....

2. (*If you do not owe the debtor money, explain why. Give any other information that will explain your financial relationship with the debtor.*)

3. (*If you have been served with any other notice of garnishment or a writ of execution against the debtor, give particulars.*)

Name of creditor	Location of Sheriff	Date of notice or writ	Date of service on you

4. (*If you have been served outside Ontario and you wish to object on the ground that service outside Ontario was improper, give particulars of your objection.*)

Date ....

Signature of or for garnishee ....
Name of garnishee ....
Address ....
....
Telephone number ....

November 1, 2005

FORM 60I.1 — NOTICE TO CO-OWNER OF THE DEBT

Courts of Justice Act

[Repealed O. Reg. 77/06, s. 3.]

[Editor's Note: Forms 4A to 78A of the Rules of Civil Procedure have been repealed by O. Reg. 77/06, effective July 1, 2006. Pursuant to Rule of Civil Procedure 1.06, when a form is referred to by number, the reference is to the form with that number that is described in the Table of Forms at the end of these rules and which is available on the Internet through www.ontariocourtforms.on.ca. For your convenience, the government form as published on this website is reproduced below.]

(GENERAL HEADING AS IN FORM 60H)

TO *(name and address of co-owner of the debt)*

A LEGAL PROCEEDING in this court between the creditor and the debtor has resulted in an order that the debtor pay a sum of money to the creditor. The creditor has given a notice of garnishment to *(name of garnishee)* claiming that the garnishee owes a debt to the debtor. A debt to the debtor includes both a debt payable to the debtor and a debt payable to the debtor and one or more other co-owners. The garnishee has indicated in the attached garnishee's statement that you are a co-owner. Under the notice of garnishment the garnishee has paid the greater of the debtor's ownership interest, as known to the garnishee, or one-half of the indebtedness to the sheriff.

IF YOU HAVE A CLAIM to the money being paid to the sheriff by the garnishee, you have 30 days from service of this notice to make a motion to the court for a garnishment hearing. If you fail to do so, you may not hereafter dispute the enforcement of the creditor's order for the payment or recovery of money under the *Rules of Civil Procedure* and the funds may be paid out in accordance with the *Creditors' Relief Act, 2010*.

Date ....

April 11, 2012

FORM 60J — NOTICE OF TERMINATION OF GARNISHMENT

Courts of Justice Act

[Repealed O. Reg. 77/06, s. 3.]

[Editor's Note: Forms 4A to 78A of the Rules of Civil Procedure have been repealed by O. Reg. 77/06, effective July 1, 2006. Pursuant to Rule of Civil Procedure 1.06, when a form is referred to by number, the reference is to the form with that number that is described in the Table of Forms at the end of these rules and which is available on the Internet through www.ontariocourtforms.on.ca. For your convenience, the government form as published on this website is reproduced below.]

(*General heading as in Form 60H*)

NOTICE OF TERMINATION OF GARNISHMENT

TO (*name of garnishee*)

AND TO the Sheriff of the (*name of county or district*)

THE NOTICE OF GARNISHMENT DATED (*date*) SERVED ON YOU IS TERMINATED and you are not to make any further payments under it.

(*Date*)

(*Signature of creditor or lawyer*)
(*Name, address and telephone number of creditor or lawyer*)

July 1, 2007

FORM 60K — WARRANT FOR ARREST (CONTEMPT)

Courts of Justice Act

[Repealed O. Reg. 77/06, s. 3.]

[Editor's Note: Forms 4A to 78A of the Rules of Civil Procedure have been repealed by O. Reg. 77/06, effective July 1, 2006. Pursuant to Rule of Civil Procedure 1.06, when a form is referred to by number, the reference is to the form with that number that is described in the Table of Forms at the end of these rules and which is available on the Internet through www.ontariocourtforms.on.ca. For your convenience, the government form as published on this website is reproduced below.]

(*Court file no.*)

(*Court*)

(*Name of judge*) (*Day and date*)

(*Court seal*) (*Title of proceeding*)

WARRANT FOR ARREST

TO ALL POLICE OFFICERS in Ontario

AND TO the officers of all correctional institutions in Ontario

WHEREAS it appears that (*name*), of (*address*) may be in contempt of this court,

AND WHEREAS I am of the opinion that attendance of (*name*) at the hearing of the motion for a contempt order is necessary in the interest of justice and it appears that he (*or* she) is not likely to attend voluntarily,

YOU ARE ORDERED TO ARREST and bring (*name*) before the court for the hearing of the motion for a contempt order, and if the court is not then sitting or if he (*or* she) cannot be brought forthwith before the court, you are ordered to deliver him (or her) to a provincial correctional institution or other secure facility, to be admitted and detained there until he (*or* she) can be brought before the court.

(*Signature of judge*)

November 1, 2005

FORM 60L — WARRANT OF COMMITTAL

Courts of Justice Act

[Repealed O. Reg. 77/06, s. 3.]

[Editor's Note: Forms 4A to 78A of the Rules of Civil Procedure have been repealed by O. Reg. 77/06, effective July 1, 2006. Pursuant to Rule of Civil Procedure 1.06, when a form is referred to by number, the reference is to the form with that number that is described in the Table of Forms at the end of these rules and which is available on the Internet through www.ontariocourtforms.on.ca. For your convenience, the government form as published on this website is reproduced below.]

(*Court file no.*)

(*Court*)

(*Name of judge*) (*Day and date*)

(*Court seal*) (*Title of proceeding*)

WARRANT OF COMMITTAL

TO ALL POLICE OFFICERS in Ontario

AND TO THE OFFICERS OF (*name of correctional institution*)

WHEREAS I have found that (*name*) is in contempt of this court and have ordered imprisonment as punishment for the contempt,

YOU ARE ORDERED TO ARREST (*name*) and deliver him (*or her*) to a provincial correctional institution, to be detained there for (*or* until) (*give particulars of sentence*).

(*Signature of judge*)

November 1, 2005

FORM 60M — NOTICE OF CLAIM

Courts of Justice Act

[Repealed O. Reg. 77/06, s. 3.]

[Editor's Note: Forms 4A to 78A of the Rules of Civil Procedure have been repealed by O. Reg. 77/06, effective July 1, 2006. Pursuant to Rule of Civil Procedure 1.06, when a form is referred to by number, the reference is to the form with that number that is described in the Table of Forms at the end of these rules and which is available on the Internet through www.ontariocourtforms.on.ca. For your convenience, the government form as published on this website is reproduced below.]

(*General heading*)

TO THE CREDITORS OF (*name of debtor*)

I have received notice of a claim by (*name*), of (*address*), in respect of property or the proceeds of property taken or intended to be taken in execution against the debtor. Particulars of the claim are as follows: (*Give particulars.*)

You are required to give me notice in writing, within seven days after receiving this notice, stating whether you admit or dispute the claim.

(*Date*) (*Name, address and telephone number of sheriff*)

TO (*Name and address of each creditor or lawyer*)

July 1, 2007

FORM 60N — SHERIFF'S REPORT

Courts of Justice Act

[Repealed O. Reg. 77/06, s. 3.]

[Editor's Note: Forms 4A to 78A of the Rules of Civil Procedure have been repealed by O. Reg. 77/06, effective July 1, 2006. Pursuant to Rule of Civil Procedure 1.06, when a form is referred to by number, the reference is to the form with that number that is described in the Table of Forms at the end of these rules and which is available on the Internet through www.ontariocourtforms.on.ca. For your convenience, the government form as published on this website is reproduced below.]

(*General heading*)

SHERIFF'S REPORT

In response to your request of (*date*) concerning the execution of the writ of seizure and sale (*or* possession, delivery *or* sequestration) against (*name of party*) filed with me, I report that I have taken the following action, with the following results: (*Give particulars.*)

(*Date*) (*Signature of sheriff*)

TO (*Name and address of creditor or lawyer*)

July 1, 2007

FORM 60O — REQUEST TO WITHDRAW A WRIT

Courts of Justice Act

[Repealed O. Reg. 77/06, s. 3.]

[Editor's Note: Forms 4A to 78A of the Rules of Civil Procedure have been repealed by O. Reg. 77/06, effective July 1, 2006. Pursuant to Rule of Civil Procedure 1.06, when a form is referred to by number, the reference is to the form with that number that is described in the Table of Forms at the end of these rules and which is available on the Internet through www.ontariocourtforms.on.ca. For your convenience, the government form as published on this website is reproduced below.]

ONTARIO
SUPERIOR COURT OF JUSTICE
(General heading)

REQUEST TO WITHDRAW A WRIT

TO: the Sheriff of the *(name of county or district)*

Under an order of this court in the favour of *(name of creditor)* made on *(date)*, *(name of debtor)* was ordered to pay the sum of $ .... (*where applicable, add* each month *or* as may be) with interest at the rate of .... per cent per year commencing on *(date)* and costs of $ .... *(as fixed or assessed)* with interest at the rate of .... per cent per year commencing on *(date)*.

(name of debtor) states as follows:

Order of Discharge

1. The order has been released by an order of discharge under the *Bankruptcy and Insolvency Act* (Canada). A certified copy of the order is attached.

2. The debtor has no debts under section 178 of that Act.

OR

Certificate of Full Performance

1. The order has been released by a certificate of full performance under the *Bankruptcy and Insolvency Act* (Canada). A copy of the certificate is attached.

2. The debtor has no debts under section 178 of that Act.

(name of debtor) requests that the writ of seizure and sale issued with respect to the order be withdrawn under rule 60.15 of the *Rules of Civil Procedure*.

Date ....

(Signature of debtor)
(Name, address and telephone number of debtor or debtor's lawyer)

November 1, 2005

FORM 61A — NOTICE OF APPEAL TO AN APPELLATE COURT

Courts of Justice Act

[Repealed O. Reg. 77/06, s. 3.]

[Editor's Note: Forms 4A to 78A of the Rules of Civil Procedure have been repealed by O. Reg. 77/06, effective July 1, 2006. Pursuant to Rule of Civil Procedure 1.06, when a form is referred to by number, the reference is to the form with that number that is described in the Table of Forms at the end of these rules and which is available on the Internet through www.ontariocourtforms.on.ca. For your convenience, the government form as published on this website is reproduced below.]

(*General heading in accordance with Form 61B*)

NOTICE OF APPEAL

THE (*identify party*) APPEALS to the Court of Appeal (*or* Divisional Court) from the judgment (*or* order) of (*name of judge, officer or tribunal*) dated (*date*) made at (*place*).

THE APPELLANT ASKS that the judgment be set aside and a judgment be granted as follows (*or* that the judgment be varied as follows, *or as may be*): (*Set out briefly the relief sought.*)

THE GROUNDS OF APPEAL are as follows: (*Set out briefly the grounds of appeal.*)

THE BASIS OF THE APPELLATE COURT'S JURISDICTION IS: *(State the basis for the appellate court's jurisdiction, including (i) any provision of a statute or regulation establishing jurisdiction, (ii) whether the order appealed from is final or interlocutory, (iii) whether leave to appeal is required and if so whether it has been granted, and (iv) any other facts relevant to establishing jurisdiction.)*

(*Divisional Court appeals*) The appellant requests that this appeal be heard at (*place*).

(*Date*) (*Name, address and telephone and fax numbers of appellant's lawyer or of appellant*)

TO (*Name and address of respondent's lawyer or of respondent*)

November 1, 2005

FORM 61B — GENERAL HEADING IN PROCEEDINGS IN APPELLATE COURTS

Courts of Justice Act

[Repealed O. Reg. 77/06, s. 3.]

[Editor's Note: Forms 4A to 78A of the Rules of Civil Procedure have been repealed by O. Reg. 77/06, effective July 1, 2006. Pursuant to Rule of Civil Procedure 1.06, when a form is referred to by number, the reference is to the form with that number that is described in the Table of Forms at the end of these rules and which is available on the Internet through www.ontariocourtforms.on.ca. For your convenience, the government form as published on this website is reproduced below.]

COURT OF APPEAL FOR ONTARIO (OR DIVISIONAL COURT, SUPERIOR COURT OF JUSTICE)

(*Appeal in an action*)

BETWEEN:

(*name*)

Plaintiff
(Appellant) (*or* (Respondent))

and

(*name*)

Defendant
(Respondent) (*or* (Appellant))

(*Appeal in an application*)

BETWEEN: (*name*)

Applicant
(Appellant) (*or* (Respondent in appeal))

and

(*name*)

Respondent
(Respondent in appeal) (*or* (Appellant))

APPLICATION UNDER (*statutory provision or rule under which the application is made*)

(*Where there are multiple parties in the proceeding at first instance and only some of them are parties to the appeal, include the names of all of the parties at first instance and underline the names of the parties to the appeal.*)

November 1, 2005

FORM 61C — APPELLANT'S CERTIFICATE RESPECTING EVIDENCE

Courts of Justice Act

[Repealed O. Reg. 77/06, s. 3.]

[Editor's Note: Forms 4A to 78A of the Rules of Civil Procedure have been repealed by O. Reg. 77/06, effective July 1, 2006. Pursuant to Rule of Civil Procedure 1.06, when a form is referred to by number, the reference is to the form with that number that is described in the Table of Forms at the end of these rules and which is available on the Internet through www.ontariocourtforms.on.ca. For your convenience, the government form as published on this website is reproduced below.]

(*General heading in accordance with Form 61B*)

APPELLANT'S CERTIFICATE

The appellant certifies that the following evidence is required for the appeal, in the appellant's opinion:

1. Exhibits numbers ....
2. The affidavit evidence of (*names of deponents*)
3. The oral evidence of (*names of witnesses*)

(*Date*) (*Name, address and telephone and fax numbers of appellant's lawyer or appellant*)

TO (*Name and address of respondent's lawyer or respondent*)

November 1, 2005

FORM 61D — RESPONDENT'S CERTIFICATE RESPECTING EVIDENCE

Courts of Justice Act

[Repealed O. Reg. 77/06, s. 3.]

[Editor's Note: Forms 4A to 78A of the Rules of Civil Procedure have been repealed by O. Reg. 77/06, effective July 1, 2006. Pursuant to Rule of Civil Procedure 1.06, when a form is referred to by number, the reference is to the form with that number that is described in the Table of Forms at the end of these rules and which is available on the Internet through www.ontariocourtforms.on.ca. For your convenience, the government form as published on this website is reproduced below.]

(*General heading in accordance with Form 61B*)

RESPONDENT'S CERTIFICATE

The respondent confirms the appellant's certificate (*where necessary, add* except for the following:)

ADDITIONS

1. Exhibits numbers are required for the appeal.
2. The affidavit evidence of (*names of deponents*) is required for the appeal.
3. The oral evidence of (*names of witnesses*) is required for the appeal.

DELETIONS

4. Exhibits numbers are not required for the appeal.
5. The affidavit evidence of (*names of deponents*) is not required for the appeal.
6. The oral evidence of (*names of witnesses*) is not required for the appeal.

(*Date*) (*Name, address and telephone and fax numbers of respondent's lawyer or respondent*)

TO (*Name and address of appellant's lawyer or appellant*)

November 1, 2005

FORM 61E — NOTICE OF CROSS-APPEAL

Courts of Justice Act

[Repealed O. Reg. 77/06, s. 3.]

[Editor's Note: Forms 4A to 78A of the Rules of Civil Procedure have been repealed by O. Reg. 77/06, effective July 1, 2006. Pursuant to Rule of Civil Procedure 1.06, when a form is referred to by number, the reference is to the form with that number that is described in the Table of Forms at the end of these rules and which is available on the Internet through www.ontariocourtforms.on.ca. For your convenience, the government form as published on this website is reproduced below.]

(*General heading in accordance with Form 61B*)

NOTICE OF CROSS-APPEAL

THE RESPONDENT CROSS-APPEALS in this appeal and asks that the judgment be set aside and judgment be granted as follows: (*or* that the judgment be varied as follows, *or as may be*): (*Set out briefly the relief sought.*)

THE GROUNDS FOR THIS CROSS-APPEAL are as follows: (*Set out briefly the grounds of cross-appeal.*)

(*Date*) (*Name, address and telephone and fax numbers of respondent's lawyer or respondent*)

TO (*Name and address of appellant's lawyer or appellant*)

July 1, 2007

FORM 61F — SUPPLEMENTARY NOTICE OF APPEAL OR CROSS-APPEAL

Courts of Justice Act

[Repealed O. Reg. 77/06, s. 3.]

[Editor's Note: Forms 4A to 78A of the Rules of Civil Procedure have been repealed by O. Reg. 77/06, effective July 1, 2006. Pursuant to Rule of Civil Procedure 1.06, when a form is referred to by number, the reference is to the form with that number that is described in the Table of Forms at the end of these rules and which is available on the Internet through www.ontariocourtforms.on.ca. For your convenience, the government form as published on this website is reproduced below.]

(*General heading in accordance with Form 61B*)

SUPPLEMENTARY NOTICE OF APPEAL (OR CROSS-APPEAL)

The appellant (*or* respondent) amends the notice of appeal (*or* cross-appeal) dated (*date*) in the following manner: (*Give particulars of the amendment.*)

(*Date*) (*Name, address and telephone number of lawyer or party serving notice*)

TO (*Name and address of lawyer or party on whom notice is served*)

July 1, 2007

FORM 61G — NOTICE OF LISTING FOR HEARING (APPEAL)

Courts of Justice Act

[Repealed O. Reg. 77/06, s. 3.]

[Editor's Note: Forms 4A to 78A of the Rules of Civil Procedure have been repealed by O. Reg. 77/06, effective July 1, 2006. Pursuant to Rule of Civil Procedure 1.06, when a form is referred to by number, the reference is to the form with that number that is described in the Table of Forms at the end of these rules and which is available on the Internet through www.ontariocourtforms.on.ca. For your convenience, the government form as published on this website is reproduced below.]

(*General heading in accordance with Form 61B*)

NOTICE OF LISTING FOR HEARING

THIS APPEAL HAS BEEN PERFECTED and has been listed for hearing at (*place*). You may ascertain from my office the approximate date of hearing.

Date .... Signed by ....
Registrar of the Court of Appeal
(*or* Divisional Court)
(*Address of court office*)

TO (*Name and address of every person listed in the certificate of perfection*)

November 1, 2005

FORM 61H — CERTIFICATE OF COMPLETENESS OF APPEAL BOOK AND COMPENDIUM

Courts of Justice Act

[Repealed O. Reg. 77/06, s. 3.]

[Editor's Note: Forms 4A to 78A of the Rules of Civil Procedure have been repealed by O. Reg. 77/06, effective July 1, 2006. Pursuant to Rule of Civil Procedure 1.06, when a form is referred to by number, the reference is to the form with that number that is described in the Table of Forms at the end of these rules and which is available on the Internet through www.ontariocourtforms.on.ca. For your convenience, the government form as published on this website is reproduced below.]

(*General heading in accordance with Form 61B*)

CERTIFICATE OF COMPLETENESS

I, (*name*), lawyer for the appellant (*or* appellant), certify that the appeal book and compendium in this appeal is complete and legible.

(*Date*)

(*Signature of appellant's lawyer or appellant*)

(*Name, address and telephone number of appellant's lawyer or appellant*)

July 1, 2007

FORM 61I — ORDER DISMISSING APPEAL OR CROSS-APPEAL FOR DELAY

Courts of Justice Act

[Repealed O. Reg. 77/06, s. 3.]

[Editor's Note: Forms 4A to 78A of the Rules of Civil Procedure have been repealed by O. Reg. 77/06, effective July 1, 2006. Pursuant to Rule of Civil Procedure 1.06, when a form is referred to by number, the reference is to the form with that number that is described in the Table of Forms at the end of these rules and which is available on the Internet through www.ontariocourtforms.on.ca. For your convenience, the government form as published on this website is reproduced below.]

(*General heading in accordance with Form 61B*)

ORDER DISMISSING APPEAL (OR CROSS-APPEAL)

The appellant *(or* respondent*)* has not *(give particulars of appellant's or respondent's default under rule 61.13)* and has not cured the default, although any notice that may be required by rule 61.13 has been given.

IT IS ORDERED that this appeal *(or* cross-appeal) be dismissed for delay, with costs fixed at $750, despite rule 58.13.

Date .... Signed by ....
Registrar of the Court of Appeal (or Divisional Court)

NOTE: If there is a cross-appeal, the appellant by cross-appeal should consider rule 61.15, under which the cross-appeal may be deemed to be abandoned.

November 1, 2016

FORM 61J — ORDER DISMISSING MOTION FOR LEAVE TO APPEAL FOR DELAY

Courts of Justice Act

[Repealed O. Reg. 77/06, s. 3.]

[Editor's Note: Forms 4A to 78A of the Rules of Civil Procedure have been repealed by O. Reg. 77/06, effective July 1, 2006. Pursuant to Rule of Civil Procedure 1.06, when a form is referred to by number, the reference is to the form with that number that is described in the Table of Forms at the end of these rules and which is available on the Internet through www.ontariocourtforms.on.ca. For your convenience, the government form as published on this website is reproduced below.]

Courts of Justice Act

(General heading in accordance with Form 61B)

ORDER DISMISSING MOTION FOR LEAVE

The moving party on this motion for leave to appeal from the order (*or as may be*) of *(name of court or tribunal*) dated (*date*) has not served and filed the motion record, factum and (*if necessary*) transcripts in accordance with clause 61.13(8)(a) (motion by responding party) (*or* clause 61.13(8)(b) (Registrar's notice)) of the *Rules of Civil Procedure*.

IT IS ORDERED that this motion be dismissed for delay, with costs fixed at $750, despite rule 58.13.

Date .... Signed by ....

Registrar of the Court of Appeal (or Divisional Court)

July 30, 2009

FORM 61J.1 — ORDER DISMISSING MOTION FOR DELAY

Courts of Justice Act

[Repealed O. Reg. 77/06, s. 3.]

[Editor's Note: Forms 4A to 78A of the Rules of Civil Procedure have been repealed by O. Reg. 77/06, effective July 1, 2006. Pursuant to Rule of Civil Procedure 1.06, when a form is referred to by number, the reference is to the form with that number that is described in the Table of Forms at the end of these rules and which is available on the Internet through www.ontariocourtforms.on.ca. For your convenience, the government form as published on this website is reproduced below.]

Courts of Justice Act

(General heading in accordance with Form 61B)

ORDER DISMISSING MOTION FOR DELAY

The moving party on this motion has not served and filed the motion record, factum and other material in accordance with subrule 61.16(4) of the *Rules of Civil Procedure*.

IT IS ORDERED that this motion be dismissed for delay, with costs fixed at $750, despite rule 58.13.

Date .... Signed by ....

Registrar of the Court of Appeal *(or* Divisional Court*)*

July 30, 2009

FORM 61K — NOTICE OF ABANDONMENT OF APPEAL OR CROSS-APPEAL

Courts of Justice Act

[Repealed O. Reg. 77/06, s. 3.]

[Editor's Note: Forms 4A to 78A of the Rules of Civil Procedure have been repealed by O. Reg. 77/06, effective July 1, 2006. Pursuant to Rule of Civil Procedure 1.06, when a form is referred to by number, the reference is to the form with that number that is described in the Table of Forms at the end of these rules and which is available on the Internet through www.ontariocourtforms.on.ca. For your convenience, the government form as published on this website is reproduced below.]

(*General heading in accordance with Form 61B*)

NOTICE OF ABANDONMENT

The appellant (*or* respondent) abandons this appeal (*or* cross-appeal).

(*Date*) (*Name, address and telephone number of lawyer or party serving notice*)

TO (*Name and address of lawyer or party on whom notice is served*)

NOTE: If there is a cross-appeal, the appellant by cross-appeal should consider rule 61.15, under which the cross-appeal may be deemed to be abandoned.

July 1, 2007

FORM 61L — NOTICE OF ELECTION TO PROCEED WITH CROSS-APPEAL

Courts of Justice Act

[Repealed O. Reg. 77/06, s. 3.]

[Editor's Note: Forms 4A to 78A of the Rules of Civil Procedure have been repealed by O. Reg. 77/06, effective July 1, 2006. Pursuant to Rule of Civil Procedure 1.06, when a form is referred to by number, the reference is to the form with that number that is described in the Table of Forms at the end of these rules and which is available on the Internet through www.ontariocourtforms.on.ca. For your convenience, the government form as published on this website is reproduced below.]

(*General heading in accordance with Form 61B*)

NOTICE OF ELECTION

The respondent elects to proceed with the cross-appeal.

(*Date*) (*Name, address and telephone number of respondent's lawyer or respondent*)

TO (*Name and address of appellant's lawyer or appellant*)

July 1, 2007

FORM 62A — NOTICE OF APPEAL TO A JUDGE

Courts of Justice Act

[Repealed O. Reg. 77/06, s. 3.]

[Editor's Note: Forms 4A to 78A of the Rules of Civil Procedure have been repealed by O. Reg. 77/06, effective July 1, 2006. Pursuant to Rule of Civil Procedure 1.06, when a form is referred to by number, the reference is to the form with that number that is described in the Table of Forms at the end of these rules and which is available on the Internet through www.ontariocourtforms.on.ca. For your convenience, the government form as published on this website is reproduced below.]

(*General heading*)

NOTICE OF APPEAL

THE (*identify party*) APPEALS to a judge from the order (*or* certificate) of (*name of judge or officers*) dated (*date*).

THE APPEAL WILL BE HEARD ON (*day*), (*date*), at (*time*) at (*address of court house*).

THE (*identify party*) ASKS (*state the precise relief sought*).

THE GROUNDS OF APPEAL are as follows: (*Set out briefly the grounds of appeal*).

(*Date*) (*Name, address and telephone number of lawyer or party serving notice*)

TO (*Name and address of lawyer or party on whom notice is served*)

July 1, 2007

FORM 63A — CERTIFICATE OF STAY

Courts of Justice Act

[Repealed O. Reg. 77/06, s. 3.]

[Editor's Note: Forms 4A to 78A of the Rules of Civil Procedure have been repealed by O. Reg. 77/06, effective July 1, 2006. Pursuant to Rule of Civil Procedure 1.06, when a form is referred to by number, the reference is to the form with that number that is described in the Table of Forms at the end of these rules and which is available on the Internet through www.ontariocourtforms.on.ca. For your convenience, the government form as published on this website is reproduced below.]

(*General heading*)

(*Court seal*)

CERTIFICATE OF STAY

The Registrar of the Court of Appeal (*or* Divisional Court) (*or* the local registrar of this court at (*place*)) certifies that the order (*or* judgment) of (*name of judge or officer*) dated (*date*) have been stayed by the delivery of a notice of appeal from the order (*or* judgment) (*or* by order of (*name of judge*) dated (*date*)). (*Where an order is made under Rule 63 limiting the stay, give particulars.*)

Date .... Issued by ....
Registrar

Address of court office ....
....

November 1, 2005

FORM 63B — CERTIFICATE OF STAY

Courts of Justice Act

[Repealed O. Reg. 77/06, s. 3.]

[Editor's Note: Forms 4A to 78A of the Rules of Civil Procedure have been repealed by O. Reg. 77/06, effective July 1, 2006. Pursuant to Rule of Civil Procedure 1.06, when a form is referred to by number, the reference is to the form with that number that is described in the Table of Forms at the end of these rules and which is available on the Internet through www.ontariocourtforms.on.ca. For your convenience, the government form as published on this website is reproduced below.]

(*General heading*)

(*Court Seal*)

CERTIFICATE OF STAY

The Registrar of the Divisional Court certifies that, under subsection 25(1) of the *Statutory Powers Procedure Act*, the order of the Ontario Rental Housing Tribunal dated (*date*) has been stayed by an appeal to this court.

Date .... Issued by ....
Registrar

November 1, 2005

FORM 64A — REQUEST TO REDEEM

Courts of Justice Act

[Repealed O. Reg. 77/06, s. 3.]

[Editor's Note: Forms 4A to 78A of the Rules of Civil Procedure have been repealed by O. Reg. 77/06, effective July 1, 2006. Pursuant to Rule of Civil Procedure 1.06, when a form is referred to by number, the reference is to the form with that number that is described in the Table of Forms at the end of these rules and which is available on the Internet through www.ontariocourtforms.on.ca. For your convenience, the government form as published on this website is reproduced below.]

(*General Heading*)

REQUEST TO REDEEM

The defendant (*name*) requests an opportunity to redeem the mortgaged property.

(*Date*) (*Name, address and telephone number of defendant's lawyer or defendant*)

(*Where the defendant is a subsequent encumbrancer, add:*)

AFFIDAVIT VERIFYING CLAIM

I, (*full name of deponent*), of the (City, Town, *etc.*) of ...., in the (County, Regional Municipality, *etc.*) of ...., (*where the deponent is a party or the lawyer, officer, director, member or employee of a party, set out the deponent's capacity*), MAKE OATH AND SAY (*or* AFFIRM):

1. There is now due to me under a mortgage on (*or* an execution against *or* a construction lien registered against *or as may be*) the mortgaged property,

(a) for principal	$ ....
(b) for interest (*set out particulars*)	$ ....
(c) (*set out particulars of any other amounts due*)	$ ....
Total now due	$ ....

Sworn (*etc.*)

July 1, 2007

FORM 64B — DEFAULT JUDGMENT FOR FORECLOSURE WITH A REFERENCE

Courts of Justice Act

[Repealed O. Reg. 77/06, s. 3.]

[Editor's Note: Forms 4A to 78A of the Rules of Civil Procedure have been repealed by O. Reg. 77/06, effective July 1, 2006. Pursuant to Rule of Civil Procedure 1.06, when a form is referred to by number, the reference is to the form with that number that is described in the Table of Forms at the end of these rules and which is available on the Internet through www.ontariocourtforms.on.ca. For your convenience, the government form as published on this website is reproduced below.]

(*General heading*)

(*Court seal*)

JUDGMENT

On reading the statement of claim in this action and the proof of service of the statement of claim on the defendant(s), filed, no request to redeem or request for sale having been served and filed (*or* the defendant(s) (*name(s)*) having served and filed a request to redeem) and the defendant(s) having been noted in default, and the plaintiff wishing a reference (*or* the registrar having decided to sign judgment with a reference),

1. IT IS ORDERED AND ADJUDGED that all necessary inquiries be made, accounts taken, costs fixed or assessed and steps taken for redemption or foreclosure of the equity of redemption in the mortgaged property described in the attached schedule, and that for these purposes this action be referred to the master (*or as may be*) at (*place*). The mortgage is dated and made between (*name of mortgagor*) and (*name of mortgagee*), and registered (*give particulars of registration and of any assignment of the mortgage*).

(*Where judgment is for possession, add:*)

2. IT IS ORDERED AND ADJUDGED that the defendant (*name*) deliver to the plaintiff or as the plaintiff directs possession of the mortgaged property or of such part of it as is in the possession of the defendants.

(*Where judgment is for payment of the mortgage debt and the registrar is to take the account, and the following two paragraphs:*)

3. IT IS ORDERED AND ADJUDGED that the defendant (*name*) forthwith pay to the plaintiff the sum of $ ...., being the amount due to the plaintiff (s) today for principal, interest and costs; and on payment of the amount due to the plaintiff, the plaintiff convey the mortgaged property to the defendant or as the defendants directs, in accordance with section 2 of the *Mortgages Act*, and deliver up all documents relating to the mortgaged property.

THIS JUDGMENT BEARS INTEREST at the rate of (*rate claimed in the statement of claim*) per cent per year from its date.

(*Where judgment is for payment of the mortgage debt and the plaintiff wishes the account to be taken on the reference or the registrar refers the taking of the account, substitute the following two paragraphs:*)

3. IT IS ORDERED AND ADJUDGED that the defendant (*name*) pay to the plaintiff, forthwith after confirmation of the report on the reference, the amount found due for principal, interest and costs in accordance with the report, and on payment of the amount due to the plaintiff, the plaintiff convey the mortgaged property to the defendant or as the defendant directs, in accordance with section 2 of the *Mortgages Act*, and deliver up all documents relating to the mortgaged property.

THIS JUDGMENT BEARS INTEREST at the rate set out in the report on the reference from the date of confirmation of the report.

Date .... Signed by ....

Local registrar

Address of court office ....

....

(*The description of the mortgaged property in the attached schedule must be the same as in the statement of claim.*)

November 1, 2005

FORM 64C — DEFAULT JUDGMENT FOR IMMEDIATE FORECLOSURE

Courts of Justice Act

[Repealed O. Reg. 77/06, s. 3.]

[Editor's Note: Forms 4A to 78A of the Rules of Civil Procedure have been repealed by O. Reg. 77/06, effective July 1, 2006. Pursuant to Rule of Civil Procedure 1.06, when a form is referred to by number, the reference is to the form with that number that is described in the Table of Forms at the end of these rules and which is available on the Internet through www.ontariocourtforms.on.ca. For your convenience, the government form as published on this website is reproduced below.]

(*General heading*)

(*Court seal*)

JUDGMENT

On reading the statement of claim in this action and the proof of service of the statement of claim on the defendant(s), filed, no request to redeem or request for sale having been served and filed, the defendant(s) having been noted in default, and the plaintiff not wishing a reference,

1. IT IS ORDERED AND ADJUDGED that the right, title and equity of redemption of the defendant(s) (*name(s)*) to and in the mortgaged property described in the attached schedule are foreclosed. The mortgage is dated . . . . and made between (*name of mortgagor*) and (*name of mortgagee*), and registered (*give particulars of registration and of any assignment of the mortgage*).

(*Where judgment is for possession, add:*)

2. IT IS ORDERED AND ADJUDGED that the defendant (*name*) forthwith deliver to the plaintiff or as the plaintiff directs possession of the mortgaged property or of such part of it as is in the possession of the defendant.

(*Where judgment is for payment of the mortgage debt, add the following two paragraphs:*)

3. IT IS ORDERED AND ADJUDGED that the defendant (*name*) forthwith pay to the plaintiff the sum of $ ...., being the amount due to the plaintiff today for principal, interest and costs.

THIS JUDGMENT BEARS INTEREST at the rate of (*rate claimed in the statement of claim*) per cent per year from its date.

Date .... Signed by ....

Local registrar

Address of court office ....

....

(*The description of the mortgaged property in the attached schedule must be the same as in the statement of claim.*)

November 1, 2005

FORM 64D — DEFAULT JUDGMENT FOR FORECLOSURE WITHOUT A REFERENCE

Courts of Justice Act

[Repealed O. Reg. 77/06, s. 3.]

[Editor's Note: Forms 4A to 78A of the Rules of Civil Procedure have been repealed by O. Reg. 77/06, effective July 1, 2006. Pursuant to Rule of Civil Procedure 1.06, when a form is

referred to by number, the reference is to the form with that number that is described in the Table of Forms at the end of these rules and which is available on the Internet through www.ontariocourtforms.on.ca. For your convenience, the government form as published on this website is reproduced below.]

(*General heading*)

(*Court seal*)

JUDGMENT

On reading the statement of claim in this action and the proof of service of the statement of claim on the defendant(s), filed, no request for sale having been served and filed the defendant(s) (*name(s)*) having served and filed a request to redeem and the defendant(s) having been noted in default, and the account having been taken in the presence of the lawyer(s) for the plaintiff(s) (*or* the plaintiff) and the lawyer(s) for the defendant(s) (*where applicable, add* (*identify party*) appearing in person *or* no one appearing for the defendant (*name*) although served with notice of the taking of the account as appears from the affidavit of (*name*), filed),

1. I FIND that the following sums are due to the plaintiff from the defendant (*name of owner of equity of redemption*) on (*redemption date*), the day I have fixed for payment under the mortgage in question in this action:

(a) for principal	$ ....
(b) for taxes paid	$ ....
(c) for premiums of insurance paid	$ ....
(d) for maintenance costs paid	$ ....
(e) for heating costs paid	$ ....
(f) for utility costs paid	$ ....
(*add any other costs in similar fashion*)	
(g) for interest up to (*date of judgment*)	$ ....
(h) for costs of this action	$ ....
(i) for subsequent interest on the principal at the rate of .... per cent per year up to the day fixed for payment	$ ....
making a total amount due on (*redemption date*) of	

2. IT IS ORDERED AND ADJUDGED that:

(a) on payment of the sum of $ (*total amount due from paragraph 1*) into the (*name of financial institution*) at (*address*), to the joint credit of the plaintiff and the Accountant of the Superior Court of Justice (*or* the local registrar); or

(b) on recovery by the plaintiff of the amount due under paragraph 6 of this judgment, together with post-judgment interest,

on or before (*redemption date*), the plaintiff shall convey the mortgaged property described in the attached schedule to the defendant (*name*) or as the defendant(s) direct(s), in accordance with section 2 of the *Mortgages Act*, and deliver up all documents relating to the mortgaged property. The mortgage is dated and made between (*name of mortgagor*) and (*name of mortgagee*), and registered (*give particulars of registration and of any assignment of the mortgage*).

(*Delete clause (b) where the judgment does not order payment of the mortgage debt.*)

(*Where more than one party is entitled to redeem, add:*)

3. IT IS ORDERED AND ADJUDGED that the defendant (*name of encumbrancer*) is entitled to the first right to redeem and the defendant (*name*) is entitled to the second right to

redeem (*and so on*) and the defendant (*name of owner of equity of redemption*) is entitled to the last right to redeem.

(*Foreclosure on default in payment*)

4. IT IS ORDERED AND ADJUDGED that, on default in payment as required by paragraph 2, the right, title and equity of redemption of the defendant(s) to and in the mortgaged property described in the attached schedule are foreclosed.

(*Where judgment is for possession, add:*)

5. IT IS ORDERED AND ADJUDGED that the defendant (*name*) forthwith deliver to the plaintiff or as the plaintiff directs, possession of the mortgaged property, or of such part of it as is in the possession of the defendant.

(*Where judgment is for payment of the mortgage debt, add the following two paragraphs:*)

6. IT IS ORDERED AND ADJUDGED that the defendant (*name*) forthwith pay to the plaintiff(s) the sum of $ ...., being the amount due to the plaintiff today for principal, interest and costs.

THIS JUDGMENT BEARS INTEREST at the rate of (*rate claimed in statement of claim*) per cent per year from its date.

Date .... Issued by ....

Local registrar

Address of court office ....

....

(*The description of the mortgaged property in the attached schedule must be the same as in the statement of claim.*)

July 1, 2007

FORM 64E — FINAL ORDER OF FORECLOSURE

Courts of Justice Act

[Repealed O. Reg. 77/06, s. 3.]

[Editor's Note: Forms 4A to 78A of the Rules of Civil Procedure have been repealed by O. Reg. 77/06, effective July 1, 2006. Pursuant to Rule of Civil Procedure 1.06, when a form is referred to by number, the reference is to the form with that number that is described in the Table of Forms at the end of these rules and which is available on the Internet through

www.ontariocourtforms.on.ca. For your convenience, the government form as published on this website is reproduced below.]

(*Court*)

(*Court file no.*)

(*Name of judge or officer*) (*Day and date*)

(*Court seal*) (*Title of proceeding*)

FINAL ORDER OF FORECLOSURE

THIS MOTION made by (*identify moving party*), without notice, was heard this day.

(*Order following judgment granting redemption period*)

ON READING the judgment in this action dated (*date*), (*where there is an order fixing a new day for payment, add:* the order for a new day for payment dated (*date*)), (*where a notice of change of account has been delivered, add:* the notice of change of account, with proof of service,) and the certificate of the (*title*) of the (*financial institution*) at (*place*), with affidavit of execution, and the affidavit of the plaintiff, and on hearing the submissions of the lawyer for the plaintiff, and since the defendant(s) entitled to redeem has (have) not redeemed the mortgaged property,

1. IT IS ORDERED that the right, title and equity of redemption of the defendant(s) (*names of those who failed to serve and file a request to redeem, to attend and prove a claim on the taking of account or to redeem the mortgaged property*) to and in the mortgaged property described in the attached schedule and foreclosed. The mortgage is dated .... and made between (*name of mortgagor*) and (*name of mortgagee*), and registered (*give particulars of registration and of any assignment of the mortgage*).

(*Order following report granting no redemption period*)

ON READING the judgment in this action dated (*date*), and the report in this action dated (*date*) and confirmed on (*date*), with proof of service, (*where there is an order fixing a new day for payment, add:* the order for a new day for payment dated (*date*), with proof of service,) (*where a notice of change of account has been delivered, add:* the notice of change of account, with proof of service, and the certificate of the (*title*) of the (*financial institution*) at (*place*), with affidavit of execution,) and the affidavit of the plaintiff, and on hearing the submissions of the lawyer for the plaintiff, and since the defendant(s) entitled to redeem has (have) not redeemed the mortgaged property,

1. IT IS ORDERED that the right, title and equity of redemption of the defendant(s) (*names of those who failed to serve and file a request to redeem, to attend and prove a claim on the reference or to redeem the mortgaged property*) to and in the mortgaged property described in the attached schedule are foreclosed. The mortgage is dated and made between (*name of mortgagor*) and (*name of mortgagee*), and registered (*give particulars of registration and of any assignment of the mortgage*).

(*Order following report granting no redemption period*)

ON READING the judgment in this action dated (*date*) and the report in this action dated (*date*) and confirmed on (*date*), with proof of service, and the affidavit of the plaintiff, and on hearing the submissions of the lawyer for the plaintiff, and since no defendant is entitled to redeem,

1. IT IS ORDERED that the right, title and equity of redemption of the defendant(s) (*names*) to and in the mortgaged property described in the attached schedule are foreclosed. The mortgage is dated .... and made between (*name of mortgagor*) and (*name*

of mortgagee), and registered (*give particulars of registration and of any assignment of the mortgage*).

(*Order following redemption of plaintiff by encumbrancer*)

ON READING the judgment in this action dated (*date*), (*where there is a report, add:* the report on the reference in this action dated (*date*) and confirmed on (*date*), with proof of service), the certificate of the (*title*) of the (*financial institution*) at (*place*), with affidavit of execution, and the affidavit of the defendant (*name of defendant who has redeemed*), on hearing the submissions of the lawyer for the defendant, and since the defendant has redeemed the plaintiff, and has obtained an assignment of the judgment and the mortgage and has registered the latter, and since the defendants (*names*) are in default,

1. IT IS ORDERED that the right, title and equity of redemption of the defendant(s) (*names of those who failed to serve and file a request to redeem, to attend and prove a claim on the reference or to redeem the mortgaged property*) to and in the mortgaged property described in the attached schedule and foreclosed. The mortgage is dated .... and made between (*name of mortgagor*) and (*name of mortgagee*), and registered (*give particulars of registration and of any assignment of the mortgage*).

(*Note: the preceding types of order in this form, which are for use in a foreclosure action, may be adapted for a redemption action by substituting "defendant" for "plaintiff" and "plaintiff" for "defendant", whenever those words appear.*)

(*Order following report in redemption action, where necessary to refer back to the master (or as may be) to complete redemption.*)

ON READING the judgment in this action dated (*date*), the report on the reference in this action dated (*date*) and confirmed on (*date*), with proof of service, the certificate of the (*title*) of the (*financial institution*) at (*place*), with affidavit of execution, and the affidavit of the defendant (*name*), and on hearing the submissions of the lawyer for the defendant, and since the plaintiff has failed to redeem (*where there are subsequent encumbrancers and the defendant wishes to foreclose them, add:* and it is necessary to take accounts between the defendants),

1. IT IS ORDERED that the right, title and equity of redemption of the plaintiff to and in the mortgaged property described in the attached schedule are foreclosed. The mortgage is dated .... and made between (*name of mortgagor*) and (*name of mortgagee*), and registered (*give particulars of registration and of any assignment of the mortgage*).

(*Where subsequent encumbrancers are to be foreclosed*)

2. IT IS ORDERED that all necessary inquiries be made, accounts taken, costs fixed or assessed and steps taken for redemption by or foreclosure against any subsequent encumbrancers, and that for these purposes this action be referred to the master (*or as may be*) at (*place*).

(*Where accounts are to be taken*)

3. IT IS ORDERED that all necessary inquiries be made, accounts taken, costs fixed or assessed and steps taken for the adjustment of the respective rights and liabilities of the original defendants.

(*Signature of judge, master or registrar*)

(*The description of the mortgaged property in the attached schedule must be the same as in the statement of claim.*)

July 1, 2007

FORM 64F — REQUEST FOR SALE

Courts of Justice Act

[Repealed O. Reg. 77/06, s. 3.]

[Editor's Note: Forms 4A to 78A of the Rules of Civil Procedure have been repealed by O. Reg. 77/06, effective July 1, 2006. Pursuant to Rule of Civil Procedure 1.06, when a form is referred to by number, the reference is to the form with that number that is described in the Table of Forms at the end of these rules and which is available on the Internet through www.ontariocourtforms.on.ca. For your convenience, the government form as published on this website is reproduced below.]

(*General heading*)

REQUEST FOR SALE

The defendant (*name*) requests a sale of the mortgaged property.

(Where the defendant is a subsequent encumbrancer, add:)

Attached is a certificate of the Accountant of the Superior Court of Justice (*or* the local registrar of the court at (*place*)) stating that the defendant has paid into court the sum of $250 as security for the costs of the plaintiff and of any other party having carriage of the sale.

(*Date*)	(*Name, address and telephone number of defendant's lawyer or defendant*)

(*Where the defendant is a subsequent encumbrancer, add:*)

AFFIDAVIT VERIFYING CLAIM

I, (*full name of deponent*), of the (City, Town, *etc.*) of ...., in the (County Regional Municipality, *etc.*) of ...., (*where the deponent if a party or the lawyer, officer, director, member or employee of a party, set out the deponent's capacity*), MAKE OATH AND SAY (*or* AFFIRM):

1. There is now due to me under a mortgage on (*or* an execution against *or* a construction lien registered against *or as may be*) the mortgaged property,

   (a) for principal $..........

   (b) for interest (*set out particulars*) $..........

   (c) (*set out particulars of any other amounts due*) $..........

   Total now due $..........

Sworn (*etc.*)

July 1, 2007

FORM 64G — DEFAULT JUDGMENT FOR SALE WITH A REDEMPTION PERIOD (ACTION CONVERTED FROM FORECLOSURE TO SALE)

Courts of Justice Act

[Repealed O. Reg. 77/06, s. 3.]

[Editor's Note: Forms 4A to 78A of the Rules of Civil Procedure have been repealed by O. Reg. 77/06, effective July 1, 2006. Pursuant to Rule of Civil Procedure 1.06, when a form is referred to by number, the reference is to the form with that number that is described in the Table of Forms at the end of these rules and which is available on the Internet through www.ontariocourtforms.on.ca. For your convenience, the government form as published on this website is reproduced below.]

(*General heading*)

(*Court seal*)

JUDGMENT

On reading the statement of claim in this action and the proof of service of the statement of claim on the defendant(s), filed, the defendant (*name*) having served and filed a request for sale, the defendant(s) having been noted in default and the defendant(s) (*name(s)*) having served and filed a request to redeem,

1. IT IS ORDERED AND ADJUDGED that all necessary inquiries be made, accounts taken, costs fixed or assessed and steps taken for redemption or sale of the mortgaged property described in the attached schedule, and that for these purposes this action be referred to the master (*or as may be*) at (*place*).

(*Where judgment is for possession, add:*)

2. IT IS ORDERED AND ADJUDGED that the defendant (*name*) deliver to the plaintiff or as the plaintiff directs possession of the mortgaged property or of such part of it as is in the possession of the defendant.

(*Where judgment is for payment of the mortgage debt and the registrar is to take the account, add the following two paragraphs:*)

3. IT IS ORDERED AND ADJUDGED that the defendant (*name*) forthwith pay to the plaintiff the sum of $ ...., being the amount due to the plaintiff today for principal, interest and costs; and that, on payment of the amount due to the plaintiff before the sale takes place, the plaintiff convey the mortgaged property to the defendant or as the defendant directs, in accordance with section 2 of the *Mortgages Act*, and deliver up all documents relating to the mortgage property.

THIS JUDGMENT BEARS INTEREST at the rate of (*rate claimed in statement of claim*) per cent per year from its date.

(*Where judgment is for payment of the mortgage debt and the plaintiff wishes the account to be taken on reference or the registrar refers the taking of the account, substitute the following two paragraphs:*)

3. IT IS ORDERED AND ADJUDGED that the defendant (*name*) pay to the plaintiff, forthwith after the confirmation of the report on the reference, the amount found due for principal, interest and costs in accordance with the report; and that on payment of the amount due to the plaintiff before the sale takes place, the plaintiff convey the mortgaged property to the

defendant or as the defendant directs, in accordance with section 2 of the *Mortgages Act,* and deliver up all documents relating to the mortgage property.

THIS JUDGMENT BEARS INTEREST at the rate set out in the report on the reference from the date of confirmation of the report.

Date .... Signed by ....
Local registrar

Address of court office ....
....

(*The description of the mortgaged property in the attached schedule must be the same as in the statement of claim.*)

November 1, 2005

FORM 64H — DEFAULT JUDGMENT FOR IMMEDIATE SALE (ACTION CONVERTED FROM FORECLOSURE TO SALE)

Courts of Justice Act

[Repealed O. Reg. 77/06, s. 3.]

[Editor's Note: Forms 4A to 78A of the Rules of Civil Procedure have been repealed by O. Reg. 77/06, effective July 1, 2006. Pursuant to Rule of Civil Procedure 1.06, when a form is referred to by number, the reference is to the form with that number that is described in the Table of Forms at the end of these rules and which is available on the Internet through www.ontariocourtforms.on.ca. For your convenience, the government form as published on this website is reproduced below.]

(*General heading*)

(*Court seal*)

JUDGMENT

On reading the statement of claim in this action and the proof of service of the statement of claim on the defendant(s), filed, the defendant (*name*) having served and filed a request for sale, the defendant(s) having been noted in default and no request to redeem having been served and filed (*or* a request to redeem having been served and filed by the defendant (*name of subsequent encumbrancer*)),

1. IT IS ORDERED AND ADJUDGED that all necessary inquiries be made, accounts taken, costs fixed or assessed and steps taken for the immediate sale of the mortgaged property described in the attached schedule without a redemption period, and that for these purposes this action be referred to the master (*or as may be*) at (*place*).

2. IT IS ORDERED AND ADJUDGED that the purchasers pay the purchase money into court to the credit of this action and that the purchase money be applied in payment of what

is found due to the plaintiff, together with subsequent interest and subsequent costs to be computed and fixed or assessed by the master (*or as may be*) and that the master (*or as may be*) also determine those parties or persons entitled to the balance of the money and the amounts to which they are entitled.

(*Where judgment is for possession, add:*)

3. IT IS ORDERED AND ADJUDGED that the defendant (*name*) forthwith deliver to the plaintiff or as the plaintiff directs possession of the mortgaged property, or of such part of it as is in the possession of the defendant.

(*Where judgment is for payment of the mortgage debt and the registrar is to take the account, add the following two paragraphs:*)

4. IT IS ORDERED AND ADJUDGED that the defendant (*name*) forthwith pay to the plaintiff the sum of $ ...., being the amount due to the plaintiff today for principal, interest and costs; and that on payment of the amount due to the plaintiff before the sale takes place, the plaintiff convey the mortgaged property to the defendant or as the defendant directs, in accordance with section 2 of the *Mortgages Act*, and deliver up all documents relating to the mortgaged property.

THIS JUDGMENT BEARS INTEREST at the rate of (*rate claimed in the statement of claim*) per cent per year from its date.

(*Where judgment is for payment of the mortgage debt and the plaintiff wishes the account to be taken on the reference or the registrar refers the taking of account, substitute the following two paragraphs:*)

4. IT IS ORDERED AND ADJUDGED that the defendant (*name*) pay to the plaintiff, forthwith after the confirmation of the report on the reference, the amount found due for principal, interest and costs in accordance with the report, and on payment of the amount due to the plaintiff before the sale takes place, the plaintiff convey the mortgaged property to the defendant or as the defendant directs, in accordance with section 2 of the *Mortgages Act,* and deliver up all documents relating to the mortgaged property.

THIS JUDGMENT BEARS INTEREST at the rate set out in the report on the reference from the date of confirmation of the report.

Date .... Signed by ....
Local registrar

Address of court office ....
....

(*The description of the mortgaged property in the attached schedule must be the same as in the statement of claim.*)

November 1, 2005

FORM 64I — DEFAULT JUDGMENT FOR SALE CONDITIONAL ON PROOF OF CLAIM (ACTION CONVERTED FROM FORECLOSURE TO SALE)

Courts of Justice Act

[Repealed O. Reg. 77/06, s. 3.]

[Editor's Note: Forms 4A to 78A of the Rules of Civil Procedure have been repealed by O. Reg. 77/06, effective July 1, 2006. Pursuant to Rule of Civil Procedure 1.06, when a form is referred to by number, the reference is to the form with that number that is described in the Table of Forms at the end of these rules and which is available on the Internet through www.ontariocourtforms.on.ca. For your convenience, the government form as published on this website is reproduced below.]

(*General heading*)

(*Court seal*)

JUDGMENT

On reading the statement of claim in this action and the proof of service of the statement of claim on the defendant(s), filed, no request to redeem having been served and filed (or the defendant (*name*) having served and filed a request to redeem), the defendant(s) having been noted in default, and the defendant (*name of subsequent encumbrancer*) having served and filed a request for sale and having paid into court the sum of $250 as security for costs,

1. IT IS ORDERED AND ADJUDGED that all necessary inquiries be made, accounts taken, costs fixed or assessed and steps taken for redemption or sale of the mortgaged property described in the attached schedule and that for these purposes this action be referred to the master (*or as may be*) at (*place*).

2. IT IS ORDERED AND ADJUDGED that, if the defendant (*name of subsequent encumbrancer*) fails to prove a claim on the reference for sale, the master (*or as may be*) shall proceed as on a reference for redemption or foreclosure.

(*Where judgment is for possession, add:*)

3. IT IS ORDERED AND ADJUDGED that the defendant (*name*) deliver to the plaintiff or as the plaintiff directs possession of the mortgaged property or of such part of it as is in the possession of the defendant.

(*Where judgment is for payment of the mortgage debt and the registrar is to take the account, add the following two paragraphs:*)

4. IT IS ORDERED AND ADJUDGED that the defendant (*name*) forthwith pay to the plaintiff the sum of $ ...., being the amount due to the plaintiff today for principal, interest and costs; and that on payment of the amount due to the plaintiff, the plaintiff convey the mortgaged property to the defendant or as the defendant directs, in accordance with section 2 of the *Mortgages Act,* and deliver up all documents relating to the mortgaged property.

THIS JUDGMENT BEARS INTEREST at the rate of (*rate claimed in statement of claim*) per cent per year from its date.

(*Where judgment is for payment of the mortgage debt and the plaintiff wishes the account to be taken on the reference or the registrar refers the taking of the account, substitute the following two paragraphs:*)

4. IT IS ORDERED AND ADJUDGED that the defendant (*name*) pay to the plaintiff, forthwith after the confirmation of the report on the reference, the amount found due for principal, interest and costs in accordance with the report, and on payment of the amount due to the plaintiff before the sale takes place, the plaintiff convey the mortgaged property to the defendant or as the defendant directs, in accordance with section 2 of the *Mortgages Act,* and deliver up all documents relating to the mortgaged property.

THIS JUDGMENT BEARS INTEREST at the rate set out in the report on the reference from the date of confirmation of the report.

Date .... Signed by ....
Local registrar

Address of court office ....
....

(*The description of the mortgaged property in the attached schedule must be the same as in the statement of claim.*)

November 1, 2005

FORM 64J — DEFAULT JUDGMENT FOR IMMEDIATE SALE

Courts of Justice Act

[Repealed O. Reg. 77/06, s. 3.]

[Editor's Note: Forms 4A to 78A of the Rules of Civil Procedure have been repealed by O. Reg. 77/06, effective July 1, 2006. Pursuant to Rule of Civil Procedure 1.06, when a form is referred to by number, the reference is to the form with that number that is described in the Table of Forms at the end of these rules and which is available on the Internet through www.ontariocourtforms.on.ca. For your convenience, the government form as published on this website is reproduced below.]

(*General heading*)

(*Court seal*)

JUDGMENT

On reading the statement of claim in this action and the proof of service of the statement of claim on the defendant(s), filed, no request to redeem having been served and filed and the defendant(s) having been noted in default,

1. IT IS ORDERED AND ADJUDGED that all necessary inquiries be made, accounts taken, costs fixed or assessed and steps taken for the immediate sale of the mortgaged property described in the attached schedule without a redemption period, and that for these purposes this action be referred to the master (*or as may be*) at (*place*).

2. IT IS ORDERED AND ADJUDGED that the purchasers pay the purchase money into court to the credit of this action and that the purchase money be applied in payment of what is found due to the plaintiff, together with subsequent interest and subsequent costs to be computed and fixed or assessed by the master (*or as may be*) and that the master (*or as may be*) also determine those parties or persons entitled to the balance of the money and the amounts to which they are entitled.

(*Where judgment is for possession, add:*)

3. IT IS ORDERED AND ADJUDGED that the defendant (*name*) forthwith deliver to the plaintiff or as the plaintiff directs possession of the mortgaged property, or of such part of it as is in the possession of the defendant.

(*Where judgment is for payment of the mortgage debt and the registrar is to take the account, add the following two paragraphs:*)

4. IT IS ORDERED AND ADJUDGED that the defendant (*name*) forthwith pay to the plaintiff the sum of $ ...., being the amount due to the plaintiff today for principal, interest and costs; and that on payment of the amount due to the plaintiff before the sale takes place, the plaintiff convey the mortgaged property to the defendant or as the defendant directs, in accordance with section 2 of the *Mortgages Act*, and deliver up all documents relating to the mortgaged property.

THIS JUDGMENT BEARS INTEREST at the rate of (*rate claimed in statement of claim*) per cent per year from its date.

(*Where judgment is for payment of the mortgage debt and the plaintiff wishes the account to be taken on the reference or the registrar refers the taking of the account, substitute the following two paragraphs:*)

4. IT IS ORDERED AND ADJUDGED that the defendant (*name*) pay to the plaintiff, forthwith after the confirmation of the report on the reference, the amount found due for principal, interest and costs in accordance with the report, and on payment of the amount due to the plaintiff before the sale takes place, the plaintiff convey the mortgaged property to the defendant or as the defendant directs, in accordance with section 2 of the *Mortgages Act*, and deliver up all documents relating to the mortgaged property.

THIS JUDGMENT BEARS INTEREST at the rate set out in the report on the reference from the date of confirmation of the report.

Date .... Signed by ....
Local registrar

Address of
court office ....
....

(*The description of the mortgaged property in the attached schedule must be the same as in the statement of claim.*)

November 1, 2005

FORM 64K — DEFAULT JUDGMENT FOR SALE WITH A REDEMPTION PERIOD

Courts of Justice Act

[Repealed O. Reg. 77/06, s. 3.]

[Editor's Note: Forms 4A to 78A of the Rules of Civil Procedure have been repealed by O. Reg. 77/06, effective July 1, 2006. Pursuant to Rule of Civil Procedure 1.06, when a form is referred to by number, the reference is to the form with that number that is described in the Table of Forms at the end of these rules and which is available on the Internet through

www.ontariocourtforms.on.ca. For your convenience, the government form as published on this website is reproduced below.]

(*General heading*)

(*Court seal*)

JUDGMENT

On reading the statement of claim in this action and the proof of service of the statement of claim on the defendant(s), filed, the defendant(s) having been noted in default and the defendant (*name*) having served and filed a request to redeem,

1. IT IS ORDERED AND ADJUDGED that all necessary inquiries be made, accounts taken, costs fixed or assessed and steps taken for redemption or sale of the mortgaged property described in the attached schedule, and that for these purposes this action be referred to the master (*or as may be*) at (*place*).

(*Where judgment is for possession, add:*)

2. IT IS ORDERED AND ADJUDGED that the defendant (*name*) deliver to the plaintiff or as the plaintiff directs possession of the mortgaged property or of such part of it as is in the possession of the defendant.

(*Where judgment is for payment of the mortgage debt and the registrar is to take the account, add the following two paragraphs:*)

3. IT IS ORDERED AND ADJUDGED that the defendant (*name*) forthwith pay to the plaintiff the sum of $ ...., being the amount due to the plaintiff today for principal, interest and costs; and on payment of the amount due to the plaintiff before the sale takes place, the plaintiff convey the mortgaged property to the defendant(s) or as the defendant directs, in accordance with section 2 of the *Mortgages Act*, and deliver up all documents relating to the mortgaged property.

THIS JUDGMENT BEARS INTEREST at the rate of (*rate claimed in statement of claim*) per cent per year from its date.

(*Where judgment is for payment of the mortgage debt and the plaintiff wishes the account to be taken on the reference or the registrar refers the taking of the account, substitute the following two paragraphs:*)

3. IT IS ORDERED AND ADJUDGED that the defendant (*name*) pay to the plaintiff(s), forthwith after confirmation of the report on the reference, the amount found due for principal, interest and costs in accordance with the report; and that on payment of the amount due to the plaintiff before the sale takes place, the plaintiff convey the mortgaged property to the defendant or as the defendant directs, in accordance with section 2 of the *Mortgages Act*, and deliver up all documents relating to the mortgaged property.

THIS JUDGMENT BEARS INTEREST at the rate set out in the report on the reference from the date of confirmation of the report.

Date .... Signed by ....

Local registrar

Address of court office ....

....

(The description of the mortgaged property in the attached schedule must be the same as in the statement of claim.)

November 1, 2005

FORM 64L — FINAL ORDER FOR SALE

Courts of Justice Act

[Repealed O. Reg. 77/06, s. 3.]

[Editor's Note: Forms 4A to 78A of the Rules of Civil Procedure have been repealed by O. Reg. 77/06, effective July 1, 2006. Pursuant to Rule of Civil Procedure 1.06, when a form is referred to by number, the reference is to the form with that number that is described in the Table of Forms at the end of these rules and which is available on the Internet through www.ontariocourtforms.on.ca. For your convenience, the government form as published on this website is reproduced below.]

(*Court*)

(*Court file no.*)

(*Name of judge or officer*) (*Day and date*)

(*Court seal*) (*Title of proceeding*)

FINAL ORDER FOR SALE

THIS MOTION made by the plaintiff, without notice, was heard this day.

ON READING the judgment in this action dated (*date*), and the report in this action dated (*date*) and confirmed on (*date*), with proof of service, the certificate of the (*title*) of the (*financial institution*) at (*place*), with affidavit of execution, and the affidavit of the plaintiff, and on hearing the submissions of the lawyer for the plaintiff, and since the defendant(s) entitled to redeem has (have) not redeemed the mortgaged property,

1. IT IS ORDERED that the mortgaged property described in the attached schedule be sold forthwith as directed by the judgment in this action under the direction of the master (*or as may be*) at (*place*).

(*Where appropriate, add:*)

2. IT IS ORDERED that the right, title and equity of redemption of the defendants (*names of subsequent encumbrancers who failed to attend and prove a claim on the reference*) to and in the mortgaged property described in the attached schedule are foreclosed.

(*Signature of judge, master or registrar*)

(*The description of the mortgaged property in the attached schedule must be the same as in the statement of claim.*)

July 1, 2007

FORM 64M — DEFAULT JUDGMENT FOR REDEMPTION

Courts of Justice Act

[Repealed O. Reg. 77/06, s. 3.]

[Editor's Note: Forms 4A to 78A of the Rules of Civil Procedure have been repealed by O. Reg. 77/06, effective July 1, 2006. Pursuant to Rule of Civil Procedure 1.06, when a form is referred to by number, the reference is to the form with that number that is described in the Table of Forms at the end of these rules and which is available on the Internet through www.ontariocourtforms.on.ca. For your convenience, the government form as published on this website is reproduced below.]

(*General heading*)

(*Court seal*)

JUDGMENT

On reading the statement of claim in this action and the proof of service of the statement of claim on the defendant(s), filed, and the defendant(s) having been noted in default,

1. IT IS ORDERED AND ADJUDGED that all necessary inquiries be made, accounts taken, costs fixed or assessed and steps taken for the redemption of the mortgaged property described in the attached schedule, and that for this purpose this action be referred to the master (*or as may be*) at (*place*).

2. IT IS ORDERED AND ADJUDGED that, on the plaintiff paying to the defendant (*name of mortgagee*) the amount found due on the mortgage in question, or, if nothing is found due, then forthwith after the confirmation of the report on the reference, the defendant convey the mortgaged property to the plaintiff or as the plaintiff directs, in accordance with section 2 of the *Mortgages Act*, and deliver up all documents relating to the mortgaged property.

3. IT IS ORDERED AND ADJUDGED that if the plaintiff defaults in payment of the amount found due to the defendant (*name of mortgagee*), the defendant is entitled, on motion without notice, to a final order of foreclosure against the plaintiff or to an order dismissing the action with costs.

4. IT IS ORDERED AND ADJUDGED that if nothing is found due to the defendant (*name of mortgagee*), the defendant pay the plaintiff's costs of this action and, if any balance is found due from the defendant (*name of mortgagee*) to the plaintiff, that the defendant pay the balance to the plaintiff forthwith after confirmation of the report on the reference.

THIS JUDGMENT BEARS INTEREST at the rate set out in the report on the reference from the date of confirmation of the report.

Date .... Signed by ....
Local registrar

Address of court office ....
....

(*The description of the mortgaged property in the attached schedule must be the same as in the statement of claim.*)

November 1, 2005

FORM 64N — NOTICE OF REFERENCE TO SUBSEQUENT ENCUMBRANCER ADDED ON REFERENCE

Courts of Justice Act

[Repealed O. Reg. 77/06, s. 3.]

[Editor's Note: Forms 4A to 78A of the Rules of Civil Procedure have been repealed by O. Reg. 77/06, effective July 1, 2006. Pursuant to Rule of Civil Procedure 1.06, when a form is referred to by number, the reference is to the form with that number that is described in the Table of Forms at the end of these rules and which is available on the Internet through www.ontariocourtforms.on.ca. For your convenience, the government form as published on this website is reproduced below.]

ONTARIO (*Court file no.*)

SUPERIOR COURT OF JUSTICE

BETWEEN:

(*name*)

Plaintiff

and

(*name(s)*)

Defendant(s)

and

(*name(s)*)

Defendant(s) added on the reference

NOTICE OF REFERENCE

An action has been commenced by the plaintiff for the foreclosure (*or* sale) of the mortgaged property described in the attached schedule. I have been directed by the judgment in this action dated (*date*) (*where the judgment is for sale, insert:* to conduct a sale of the property and) to inquire whether any person other than the plaintiff has a lien, charge or encumbrance on the property subsequent to the plaintiff's claim. It appears that you may have a lien, charge or encumbrance on the property. I have therefore added you as a defendant in this action.

YOU ARE REQUIRED TO APPEAR before me and prove your claim, either in person or by an Ontario lawyer acting for you, on (*day*), (*date*), at (*time*), at (*address*). At that time, I shall determine the amount of the claim of the plaintiff, and of the encumbrancers who prove their claims before me. (*Where the judgment is for sale without a redemption period, add:* At the same time, I shall settle the conditions of sale and advertisement and make any other necessary preparations for the sale of the property.)

If you wish to set aside or vary my order adding you as a defendant or the judgment in this action, you must make a motion to the court within ten days after service on you of this notice (*or where the person is to be served outside Ontario, such further time as the referee directs*). If you fail to do so, you will be bound by the judgment and the subsequent steps in this action.

IF YOU FAIL TO ATTEND AND PROVE YOUR CLAIM at the time and place set out above, you will be treated as disclaiming all interest in the property and the action will proceed in your absence and without further notice to you. The property may be dealt with as if you had no claim, and your claim may be foreclosed.

(*Date*) (*Signature of referee*)

TO (*Names and addresses of defendants added on reference who appear to be subsequent encumbrancers*)

(*The description of the mortgaged property in the attached schedule must be the same as in the statement of claim.*)

November 1, 2005

FORM 64O — NOTICE OF REFERENCE TO SUBSEQUENT ENCUMBRANCER NAMED AS ORIGINAL PARTY

Courts of Justice Act

[Repealed O. Reg. 77/06, s. 3.]

[Editor's Note: Forms 4A to 78A of the Rules of Civil Procedure have been repealed by O. Reg. 77/06, effective July 1, 2006. Pursuant to Rule of Civil Procedure 1.06, when a form is referred to by number, the reference is to the form with that number that is described in the Table of Forms at the end of these rules and which is available on the Internet through www.ontariocourtforms.on.ca. For your convenience, the government form as published on this website is reproduced below.]

ONTARIO (*Court file no.*)
SUPERIOR COURT OF JUSTICE

BETWEEN:

(*name*)

Plaintiff

and

(*name*)

Defendant(*s*)

and

(*name(s)*)

Defendant(*s*) added on the reference

NOTICE OF REFERENCE

The judgment in this action directs me (*where the judgment is for sale, insert:* to conduct a sale of the mortgaged property and) to inquire whether any person other than the plaintiff has a lien, charge or encumbrance on the mortgaged property in question in this action subsequent to the plaintiff's claim, and to take an account of the amount due to the plaintiff and any such person. It appears that you may have a lien, charge or encumbrance on the property.

YOU ARE REQUIRED TO APPEAR before me and prove your claim, either in person or by an Ontario lawyer acting for you, on (*day*), (*date*), at (*time*), at (*address*). At that time, I shall determine the amount of the claim of the plaintiff, and of the encumbrancers who prove their claims before me. (*Where the judgment is for sale without redemption period, add:* At the same time, I shall settle the conditions of sale and advertisement and make any other necessary preparations for the sale of the property.)

IF YOU FAIL TO ATTEND AND PROVE YOUR CLAIM at the time and place set out above, you will be treated as disclaiming any lien, charged or encumbrance on the property and the action will proceed in your absence and without further notice to you. The property may be dealt with as if you had no such claim and your claim may be foreclosed.

(*Date*) (*Signature of referee*)

TO (*Names and addresses of defendants named in statement of claim who appear to be subsequent encumbrancers*)

November 1, 2005

FORM 64P — NOTICE OF REFERENCE TO ORIGINAL DEFENDANTS

Courts of Justice Act

[Repealed O. Reg. 77/06, s. 3.]

[Editor's Note: Forms 4A to 78A of the Rules of Civil Procedure have been repealed by O. Reg. 77/06, effective July 1, 2006. Pursuant to Rule of Civil Procedure 1.06, when a form is referred to by number, the reference is to the form with that number that is described in the Table of Forms at the end of these rules and which is available on the Internet through www.ontariocourtforms.on.ca. For your convenience, the government form as published on this website is reproduced below.]

ONTARIO (*Court file no.*)
SUPERIOR COURT OF JUSTICE

BETWEEN:

(*name*)

Plaintiff

and

(*name(s)*)

Defendant(*s*)

and
(*name(s)*)

Defendant(*s*) added
on the reference

NOTICE OF REFERENCE

The judgment in this action directs me (*where the judgment is for sale, insert:* to conduct a sale of the mortgaged property and) to inquire whether any person other than the plaintiff has a lien, charge or encumbrance on the mortgaged property in question in this action subsequent to the plaintiff's claim, and to take an account due to the plaintiff and any such person.

It appears that the persons named in the attached schedule may have a lien, charge or encumbrance on the property (*where the judgment directs the referee to add encumbrancers, add:* and I have therefore added as defendants those persons who were not already parties to this action).

YOU ARE REQUIRED TO APPEAR before me and prove your claim, either in person or by an Ontario lawyer acting for you, on (*day*), (*date*), at (*time*), at (*address*). At that time, I shall determine whether any of the parties have a lien, charge or encumbrance on the property and ascertain the amount of those claims and of the plaintiff's claim. (*Where the judgment is for sale without a redemption period, add:* At the same time, I shall settle the conditions of sale and advertisement and make any other necessary arrangements for the sale.)

(*Where the judgment is for sale conditional on proof of a claim by a subsequent encumbrancer, add:* The defendant (*name of subsequent encumbrancer*) has requested a sale of the property. If the defendant fails to attend and prove a claim before me, there will not be a sale of the property, and the claims of those who fail to appear before me may be foreclosed.)

IF YOU FAIL TO ATTEND at the time and place set out above, the action will proceed in your absence without further notice to you and your rights in the property may be foreclosed.

If you are a subsequent encumbrancer and fail to attend and prove your claim at the time and place set out above, you will be treated as disclaiming any lien, charge or encumbrance on the property, the property may be dealt with as if you had no such claim and your claim may be foreclosed.

(*Date*) (*Signature of referee*)

TO (*Names and addresses of defendants named in statement of claim*)

SCHEDULE OF ENCUMBRANCERS

Name of encumbrancer	Nature of encumbrance	Instrument no.	Date of instrument	Date of registration

November 1, 2005

FORM 64Q — NOTICE TO ADDED DEFENDANT HAVING INTEREST IN EQUITY

Courts of Justice Act

[Repealed O. Reg. 77/06, s. 3.]

[Editor's Note: Forms 4A to 78A of the Rules of Civil Procedure have been repealed by O. Reg. 77/06, effective July 1, 2006. Pursuant to Rule of Civil Procedure 1.06, when a form is referred to by number, the reference is to the form with that number that is described in the Table of Forms at the end of these rules and which is available on the Internet through www.ontariocourtforms.on.ca. For your convenience, the government form as published on this website is reproduced below.]

ONTARIO (*Court file no.*)

SUPERIOR COURT OF JUSTICE

BETWEEN:

(*name*)

Plaintiff

and

(*name(s)*)

Defendant(s)

and

(*name(s)*)

Defendant(s) added
on the reference

NOTICE TO ADDED DEFENDANT

An action has been commenced by the plaintiff for the foreclosure (*or* sale) of the mortgaged property described in the attached schedule. I have been directed by the judgment in this action dated (*date*) (*where the judgment is for sale, insert:* to conduct a sale of the property and) to inquire whether any person other than the plaintiff has a lien, charge or encumbrance on the property subsequent to the plaintiff's claim or whether any other person has an interest in the property. It appears that you may have an interest in the property. I have therefore added you as a defendant in this action. A copy of my order and the judgment in the action are attached to this notice.

If you wish to set aside or vary my order adding you as a defendant or the judgment in this action, you must make a motion to the court within ten days after service on you of this notice (*or where the defendant is to be served outside Ontario, such further time as the referee directs*). If you fail to do so, you will be bound by the judgment and the subsequent steps in this action.

IF YOU WISH AN OPPORTUNITY TO REDEEM the property, you are required to appear before me, either in person or by an Ontario lawyer acting for you, on (*day*), (*date*), at (*time*), at (*address*).

IF YOU FAIL TO ATTEND at the time and place set out above, you may be deemed to submit to an immediate foreclosure of your interest (*or* an immediate sale of the property) and the action may proceed in your absence and without further notice to you.

(*Date*) (*Signature of referee*)

TO (*Names and addresses of defendants added on reference who appear to be interested in equity of redemption*)

(*The description of the mortgaged property in the attached schedule must be the same as in the statement of claim.*)

November 1, 2005

FORM 65A — JUDGMENT FOR ADMINISTRATION OF ESTATE

Courts of Justice Act

[Repealed O. Reg. 77/06, s. 3.]

[Editor's Note: Forms 4A to 78A of the Rules of Civil Procedure have been repealed by O. Reg. 77/06, effective July 1, 2006. Pursuant to Rule of Civil Procedure 1.06, when a form is referred to by number, the reference is to the form with that number that is described in the Table of Forms at the end of these rules and which is available on the Internet through www.ontariocourtforms.on.ca. For your convenience, the government form as published on this website is reproduced below.]

(*Court*)

(*Court file no.*)

(*Name of judge or officer*) (*Day and date judgment given*)

(*Court seal*) (*Title of proceeding*)

JUDGMENT

(*Recitals in accordance with Form 59B*)

1. THIS COURT ORDERS AND ADJUDGES that all necessary inquiries be made, accounts taken, costs assessed and steps taken by the master (*or as may be*) at (*place*) for the administration and final winding up of the estate of (*name of deceased*) and for the adjustment of the rights of all parties interested in the property.

2. THIS COURT ORDERS AND ADJUDGES that any balance found due from the applicant or the respondent(s) to the estate be paid into court to the credit of this proceeding, subject to further order of the court.

3. THIS COURT ORDERS AND ADJUDGES that the property of the estate or such parts of it as the referee directs be sold as the referee directs and that the purchasers pay the purchase money into court to the credit of this proceeding, subject to the order of the court.

4. THIS COURT ORDERS AND ADJUDGES that the referee execute transfers for any party who is a minor.

(*Signature of judge or registrar*)

November 1, 2005

FORM 66A — JUDGMENT FOR PARTITION OR SALE

Courts of Justice Act

[Repealed O. Reg. 77/06, s. 3.]

[Editor's Note: Forms 4A to 78A of the Rules of Civil Procedure have been repealed by O. Reg. 77/06, effective July 1, 2006. Pursuant to Rule of Civil Procedure 1.06, when a form is referred to by number, the reference is to the form with that number that is described in the Table of Forms at the end of these rules and which is available on the Internet through www.ontariocourtforms.on.ca. For your convenience, the government form as published on this website is reproduced below.]

(*Court*)

(*Court file no.*)

(*Name of judge or officer*) (*Day and date judgment given*)

(*Court seal*) (*Title of proceeding*)

JUDGMENT

(*Recitals in accordance with Form 59B*)

1. THIS COURT ORDERS AND ADJUDGES that all necessary inquiries be made, accounts taken, costs assessed and steps taken by the master (*or as may be*) at (*place*) for the partition or sale, or for the partition of part and sale of the remainder, of the land described in the attached schedule in accordance with the interests of the parties entitled to share in it.

2. THIS COURT ORDERS AND ADJUDGES that the land, or such part of it as the referee thinks fit, be sold under the direction of the referee, free of the claims of encumbrancers, if any, who have consented to the sale, and subject to the claims of encumbrancers who have not consented to the sale, and that the purchaser pay the purchase money into court to the credit of this proceeding, subject to the order of the court.

3. THIS COURT ORDERS AND ADJUDGES that the referee execute a transfer for any party who is a minor.

4. THIS COURT ORDERS AND ADJUDGES that, if the land is partitioned or if part of the land is partitioned and the proceeds of the sale of the remainder are insufficient to pay the costs in full, the unpaid costs be paid by the parties according to their interests in the land (*where there are parties who are minors, add:* and that the portion of the costs payable by the parties who are minors be a lien on their respective shares, and that the plaintiff (*or*

applicant) pay the costs of their litigation guardian and that those costs be added to the plaintiff's (*or* applicant's) costs.)

(*Signature of judge, officer or registrar*)

November 1, 2005

FORM 68A — NOTICE OF APPLICATION TO DIVISIONAL COURT FOR JUDICIAL REVIEW

Courts of Justice Act

[Repealed O. Reg. 77/06, s. 3.]

[Editor's Note: Forms 4A to 78A of the Rules of Civil Procedure have been repealed by O. Reg. 77/06, effective July 1, 2006. Pursuant to Rule of Civil Procedure 1.06, when a form is referred to by number, the reference is to the form with that number that is described in the Table of Forms at the end of these rules and which is available on the Internet through www.ontariocourtforms.on.ca. For your convenience, the government form as published on this website is reproduced below.]

(GENERAL HEADING)

(Court seal)

NOTICE OF APPLICATION TO DIVISIONAL COURT FOR JUDICIAL REVIEW

TO THE RESPONDENT

A LEGAL PROCEEDING HAS BEEN COMMENCED by the applicant. The claim made by the applicant appears on the following page.

THIS APPLICATION for judicial review will come on for a hearing before the Divisional Court on a date to be fixed by the registrar at the place of hearing requested by the applicant. The applicant requests that this application be heard at *(place where a Divisional Court sitting is scheduled)*.

IF YOU WISH TO OPPOSE THIS APPLICATION, to receive notice of any step in the application or to be served with any documents in the application, you or an Ontario lawyer acting for you must forthwith prepare a notice of appearance in Form 38A prescribed by the *Rules of Civil Procedure*, serve it on the applicant's lawyer or, where the applicant does not have a lawyer, serve it on the applicant, and file it, with proof of service, in the office of the Divisional Court, and you or your lawyer must appear at the hearing.

IF YOU WISH TO PRESENT AFFIDAVIT OR OTHER DOCUMENTARY EVIDENCE TO THE COURT OR TO EXAMINE OR CROSS-EXAMINE WITNESSES ON THE APPLICATION, you or your lawyer must, in additional to serving your notice of appearance, serve a copy of the evidence on the applicant's lawyer or, where the applicant does not have a lawyer, serve it on the applicant, and file it, with proof of service, in the office of the Divisional Court within thirty days after service on you of the applicant's application record, or at least four days before the hearing, whichever is earlier.

IF YOU FAIL TO APPEAR AT THE HEARING, JUDGMENT MAY BE GIVEN TO IN YOUR ABSENCE AND WITHOUT FURTHER NOTICE TO YOU. IF YOU WISH TO DEFEND THIS PROCEEDING BUT ARE UNABLE TO PAY LEGAL FEES, LEGAL AID MAY BE AVAILABLE TO YOU BY CONTACTING A LOCAL LEGAL AID OFFICE.

Date

Issued by
Registrar
Address of court office

TO *(Name and address of each respondent)*

AND TO Attorney General of Ontario *(as required by subsection 9(4) of the* Judicial Review Procedure Act*)*

Crown Law Office — Civil

720 Bay Street

8th Floor

Toronto, Ontario M7A 2S9

APPLICATION

1. The applicant makes application for: *(State here the precise relief claimed.)*

2. The grounds for the application are: *(Specify the grounds to be argued, including a reference to any statutory provision to be relied on.)*

(Where the notice of application is to be served outside Ontario without a court order, state the facts and the specific provisions of Rule 17 relied on in support of such service.)

3. The following documentary evidence will be used at the hearing of the application: *(List the affidavits or other documentary evidence to be relied on.)*

(Date) .... *(Name, address and telephone number of applicant's lawyer or applicant)*

April 11, 2012

FORM 68B — NOTICE OF LISTING FOR HEARING (JUDICIAL REVIEW)

Courts of Justice Act

[Repealed O. Reg. 77/06, s. 3.]

[Editor's Note: Forms 4A to 78A of the Rules of Civil Procedure have been repealed by O. Reg. 77/06, effective July 1, 2006. Pursuant to Rule of Civil Procedure 1.06, when a form is referred to by number, the reference is to the form with that number that is described in the Table of Forms at the end of these rules and which is available on the Internet through www.ontariocourtforms.on.ca. For your convenience, the government form as published on this website is reproduced below.]

(*General heading*)

NOTICE OF LISTING FOR HEARING

THIS APPLICATION FOR JUDICIAL REVIEW HAS BEEN PERFECTED and has been listed for hearing at (*place*). You may ascertain from my office the approximate date of hearing.

Date . . . . Signed by . . . .

Registrar of the Divisional Court
(*Address of court office*)

TO (*Name and address of every person listed in the certificate of perfection*)

November 1, 2005

FORM 68C — ORDER DISMISSING APPLICATION FOR JUDICIAL REVIEW

Courts of Justice Act

[Repealed O. Reg. 77/06, s. 3.]

[Editor's Note: Forms 4A to 78A of the Rules of Civil Procedure have been repealed by O. Reg. 77/06, effective July 1, 2006. Pursuant to Rule of Civil Procedure 1.06, when a form is referred to by number, the reference is to the form with that number that is described in the Table of Forms at the end of these rules and which is available on the Internet through www.ontariocourtforms.on.ca. For your convenience, the government form as published on this website is reproduced below.]

Courts of Justice Act

(General heading)

(Court seal)

ORDER DISMISSING APPLICATION FOR JUDICIAL REVIEW

The applicant has not *(give particulars of applicant's default under rule 68.06)* and has not cured the default, although given notice under rule 68.06 to do so.

1. IT IS ORDERED that this application be dismissed for delay, with costs fixed at $750, despite rule 58.13.

Date .... Signed by ....

Registrar of the Divisional Court

(Address of court office)

July 30, 2009

FORM 72A — NOTICE OF PAYMENT INTO COURT

Courts of Justice Act

[Repealed O. Reg. 77/06, s. 3.]

[Editor's Note: Forms 4A to 78A of the Rules of Civil Procedure have been repealed by O. Reg. 77/06, effective July 1, 2006. Pursuant to Rule of Civil Procedure 1.06, when a form is referred to by number, the reference is to the form with that number that is described in the Table of Forms at the end of these rules and which is available on the Internet through www.ontariocourtforms.on.ca. For your convenience, the government form as published on this website is reproduced below.]

(*General heading*)

NOTICE OF PAYMENT INTO COURT

The (*identify party*) paid into court on (*date*) the sum of $ .... under the offer to settle (*or acceptance of offer*) dated (*date*).

(*Date*) (*Name, address and telephone number of lawyer or party giving notice*)

TO (*Name and address of lawyer or party receiving notice*)

July 1, 2007

FORM 72B — AFFIDAVIT (MOTION FOR PAYMENT OUT OF COURT)

Courts of Justice Act

[Repealed O. Reg. 77/06, s. 3.]

[Editor's Note: Forms 4A to 78A of the Rules of Civil Procedure have been repealed by O. Reg. 77/06, effective July 1, 2006. Pursuant to Rule of Civil Procedure 1.06, when a form is referred to by number, the reference is to the form with that number that is described in the Table of Forms at the end of these rules and which is available on the Internet through www.ontariocourtforms.on.ca. For your convenience, the government form as published on this website is reproduced below.]

(*General heading*)

AFFIDAVIT

I, (*full name of deponent*) of the (City, Town, *etc.*) of ...., in the (County, Regional Municipality, *etc.*) of ...., (*where the deponent is a party or the lawyer, officer, director, member or employee of a party, set out the deponent's capacity*), MAKE OATH AND SAY (*or* AFFIRM):

1. This affidavit is filed in support of a motion for payment out of court of money belonging to (*name of person under disability*), of (*address*), who is (*state the nature of the disability*) and who was born on (*date*).

2. I am (*state the deponent's connection with the person under disability*).

3. The Accountant (*or* local registrar at (*place*)) has informed me that the sum of $ ...., including interest accrued to (*date*), is in court. There has been previously paid out the sum of $ .... on (*date*) (*or as may be*).

4. It is proposed that the sum of $ .... be paid out of court to (*name*) for the following purpose: (*Give particulars.*)

5. I believe that this expenditure is justified for the following reasons: (*Give particulars.*)

Sworn, etc.

July 1, 2007

FORM 72C — STOP ORDER

Courts of Justice Act

[Repealed O. Reg. 77/06, s. 3.]

[Editor's Note: Forms 4A to 78A of the Rules of Civil Procedure have been repealed by O. Reg. 77/06, effective July 1, 2006. Pursuant to Rule of Civil Procedure 1.06, when a form is

referred to by number, the reference is to the form with that number that is described in the Table of Forms at the end of these rules and which is available on the Internet through www.ontariocourtforms.on.ca. For your convenience, the government form as published on this website is reproduced below.]

(Court file no.)

(Court)

(Name of judge or officer) *(Day and date order made)*

(Court seal) *(Title of Proceeding)*

ORDER

(Recitals in accordance with Form 59A or 59B, followed by:) the *(identify applicant or moving party)* having undertaken through their lawyer to be bound by any order this court makes in respect of costs or damages caused by this order,

1. THIS COURT ORDERS that all money and securities held by the Accountant (*or* local registrar at (*place*)) in this proceeding now or in the future, together with any interest, to which (*identify party*) is or becomes entitled shall not be dealt with except on notice to (*identify applicant or moving party*).

(Signature of judge or officer)

July 1, 2007

FORM 73A — NOTICE OF APPLICATION FOR REGISTRATION OF UNITED KINGDOM JUDGMENT

Courts of Justice Act

[Repealed O. Reg. 77/06, s. 3.]

[Editor's Note: Forms 4A to 78A of the Rules of Civil Procedure have been repealed by O. Reg. 77/06, effective July 1, 2006. Pursuant to Rule of Civil Procedure 1.06, when a form is referred to by number, the reference is to the form with that number that is described in the Table of Forms at the end of these rules and which is available on the Internet through www.ontariocourtforms.on.ca. For your convenience, the government form as published on this website is reproduced below.]

(GENERAL HEADING)

(Court seal)

NOTICE OF APPLICATION

TO THE RESPONDENT

A LEGAL PROCEEDING HAS BEEN COMMENCED by the applicant for registration and enforcement in Ontario of a judgment granted against you by a court in the United Kingdom. The claim made by the applicant appears on the following pages.

THIS APPLICATION will come on for a hearing on (*day*), (*date*), at (*time*), at (*address of court house*).

IF YOU WISH TO OPPOSE THIS APPLICATION, to receive notice of any step in the application or to be served with any documents in the application, you or an Ontario lawyer acting for you must forthwith prepare a notice of appearance in Form 38A prescribed by the *Rules of Civil Procedure*, serve it on the applicant's lawyer or, where the applicant does not have a lawyer, serve it on the applicant, and file it, with proof of service, in this court office, and you or your lawyer must appear at the hearing.

IF YOU WISH TO PRESENT AFFIDAVIT OR OTHER DOCUMENTARY EVIDENCE TO THE COURT OR TO EXAMINE OR CROSS-EXAMINE WITNESSES ON THE APPLICATION, you or your lawyer must, in addition to serving your notice of appearance, serve a copy of the evidence on the applicant's lawyer or, where the applicant does not have a lawyer, serve it on the applicant, and file it, with proof of service, in the court office where the application is to be heard, as soon as possible, but at least four days before the hearing.

IF YOU FAIL TO APPEAR AT THE HEARING, THE UNITED KINGDOM JUDGMENT MAY BE REGISTERED AND ENFORCED AGAINST YOU WITHOUT FURTHER NOTICE.

Date ....

Issued by ....
Local registrar

Address of court office ....

....

TO *(Name and address of each respondent)*

APPLICATION

The applicant applies under the *Reciprocal Enforcement of Judgments (U.K.) Act* for registration of the following judgment of a court in the United Kingdom:

(a) Name of court ....

(b) Plaintiff *(or* applicant) ....

(c) Defendant *(or* respondent) ....

(d) Date of judgment ....

(e) Amount awarded, in the currency of the judgment, in favour of each plaintiff *(or* applicant) and against each defendant *(or* respondent)

Judgment in favour of	Judgment against	Amount of judgment	Amount awarded for costs
....	....	....	....
....	....	....	....

(f) Post judgment interest

Rate .... per year

Commencing on *(date)* ....

Payable on *(principal amount)* ....

(g) Amount unpaid, in the currency of the judgment, to each plaintiff *(or* applicant) and by each defendant *(or* respondent)

Payable to	Payable by	Amount unpaid on judgment, including interest	Amount unpaid on award of costs, including interest
....	....	....	....
....	....	....	....

2. The grounds for the application are:

(a) The judgment is one to which the Act and the Convention appearing as a schedule to the Act apply.

(b) The Act and the Convention do not preclude registration of the judgment.

( ) appeared

(c) The defendant *(or* respondent)

( ) did not appear

before the United Kingdom court that granted the judgement.

(If the defendant (or respondent) did not appear, explain in detail why registration is nevertheless permitted under the Reciprocal Enforcement of Judgments (U.K.) Act.*)*

(d) The applicant is entitled to register and enforce the judgment as,

( ) a plaintiff *(or* applicant) named in the judgment

( ) an assignee of the judgment

( ) other *(specify)* ....

3. The following documentary evidence is relied on in support of the application:

(a) the original or a certified copy of the judgment;

(b) the affidavit of ....

(c) the original or a certified copy of proof of service of the originating process of the United Kingdom court.

4. The respondent in this application resides at:

....

(Date of issue) .... *(Name, address and telephone number of lawyer or applicant)*

April 11, 2012

FORM 74.1 — NOTICE TO ESTATE REGISTRAR OF DEPOSIT OF WILL OR CODICIL

Courts of Justice Act

[Repealed O. Reg. 77/06, s. 3.]

[Editor's Note: Forms 4A to 78A of the Rules of Civil Procedure have been repealed by O. Reg. 77/06, effective July 1, 2006. Pursuant to Rule of Civil Procedure 1.06, when a form is referred to by number, the reference is to the form with that number that is described in the Table of Forms at the end of these rules and which is available on the Internet through www.ontariocourtforms.on.ca. For your convenience, the government form as published on this website is reproduced below.]

ONTARIO

SUPERIOR COURT OF JUSTICE

NOTICE

TO THE ESTATE REGISTRAR FOR ONTARIO:

A will or codicil has been deposited in this office. Particulars of the document follow.

DETAILS ABOUT THE TESTATOR

Complete in full as applicable

First given name	Second given name	Third given name	Surname

And if the testator is known by any other name(s), state below the full name(s) used including surname.

First given name	Second given name	Third given name	Surname

Birth date of testator: ______________ ______________ ______________
day *month* *year*

Date of will or codicil: ______________ ______________ ______________
day *month* *year*

Estate trustees named in will or codicil:

Name Address

Date of deposit: ______________ ______________ ______________

DEPOSIT OF WILL OR CODICIL **Form 74.1**

	day	*month*	*year*
Office of deposit:			
DATE:			
	day	*month*	*year*

Registrar
Address of court office

November 1, 2005

FORM 74.2 — NOTICE TO ESTATE REGISTRAR OF WITHDRAWAL OF WILL OR CODICIL

Courts of Justice Act

[Repealed O. Reg. 77/06, s. 3.]

[Editor's Note: Forms 4A to 78A of the Rules of Civil Procedure have been repealed by O. Reg. 77/06, effective July 1, 2006. Pursuant to Rule of Civil Procedure 1.06, when a form is referred to by number, the reference is to the form with that number that is described in the Table of Forms at the end of these rules and which is available on the Internet through www.ontariocourtforms.on.ca. For your convenience, the government form as published on this website is reproduced below.]

ONTARIO

SUPERIOR COURT OF JUSTICE

NOTICE

TO THE ESTATE REGISTRAR FOR ONTARIO:

A will or codicil has been withdrawn from this office. Particulars of the document follow.

DETAILS ABOUT THE TESTATOR

Complete in full as applicable

First given name	Second given name	Third given name	Surname

And if the testator is known by any other name(s), state below the full name(s) used including surname.

First given name	Second given name	Third given name	Surname

Birth date of testator: ____________ ____________ ____________
day *month* *year*

Date of will or codicil: ____________ ____________ ____________
day *month* *year*

Date of deposit: ____________ ____________ ____________
day *month* *year*

Date of withdrawal: ____________ ____________ ____________
day *month* *year*

WITHDRAWAL OF WILL OR CODICIL **Form 74.2**

Office of deposit: ____________________

DATE: __________ __________ __________
day *month* *year*

____
Registrar
Address of court office

November 1, 2005

FORM 74.3 — REQUEST FOR NOTICE OF COMMENCEMENT OF PROCEEDING

Courts of Justice Act

[Repealed O. Reg. 77/06, s. 3.]

[Editor's Note: Forms 4A to 78A of the Rules of Civil Procedure have been repealed by O. Reg. 77/06, effective July 1, 2006. Pursuant to Rule of Civil Procedure 1.06, when a form is referred to by number, the reference is to the form with that number that is described in the Table of Forms at the end of these rules and which is available on the Internet through www.ontariocourtforms.on.ca. For your convenience, the government form as published on this website is reproduced below.]

ONTARIO

SUPERIOR COURT OF JUSTICE

In the Estate of the deceased person described below:

DETAILS ABOUT THE DECEASED PERSON

Complete in full as applicable

First given name	Second given name	Third given name	Surname

And if the deceased was known by any other name(s), state below the full name(s) used including surname.

First given name	Second given name	Third given name	Surname

REQUEST FOR NOTICE OF COMMENCEMENT OF PROCEEDING

I have or appear to have a financial interest in the estate and desire to be informed of the commencement of any proceeding in the estate.

Notice of the commencement of any proceeding may be mailed to me at the address shown below.

DATE ______________ ______________ ______________

day *month* *year*

NAME OF INTERESTED PARTY: ADDRESS:

November 1, 2005

FORM 74.4 — APPLICATION FOR CERTIFICATE OF APPOINTMENT OF ESTATE TRUSTEE WITH A WILL (INDIVIDUAL APPLICANT)

Courts of Justice Act

[Repealed O. Reg. 77/06, s. 3.]

[Editor's Note: Forms 4A to 78A of the Rules of Civil Procedure have been repealed by O. Reg. 77/06, effective July 1, 2006. Pursuant to Rule of Civil Procedure 1.06, when a form is referred to by number, the reference is to the form with that number that is described in the Table of Forms at the end of these rules and which is available on the Internet through www.ontariocourtforms.on.ca. For your convenience, the government form as published on this website is reproduced below.]

ONTARIO

APPLICATION FOR CERTIFICATE OF APPOINTMENT OF ESTATE TRUSTEE WITH A WILL (INDIVIDUAL APPLICANT)

SUPERIOR COURT OF JUSTICE

(Form 74.4 Under the Rules)

at ____

This application is filed by (*insert name and address*)

____

DETAILS ABOUT THE DECEASED PERSON

Complete in full as applicable

First given name	Second given name	Third given name	Surname

And if the deceased was known by any other name(s), state below the full name(s) used including surname.

First given name	Second given name	Third given name	Surname

Date of birth of the deceased person, if known: (day, month, year)

____

Address of fixed place of abode (street or postal address) (city or town)	*(county or district)*

If the deceased person had no fixed place of abode in Ontario, did he or she have property in Ontario? ❑ No ❑ Yes	*Last occupation of deceased person*

Place of death (city or town; county or district)	*Date of death (day, month, year)*	*Date of last will* (marked as Exhibit "A") *(day, month, year)*

Was the deceased person 18 years of age or older at the date of the will (or 21 years of age or older if the will is dated earlier than September 1, 1971)? If not, explain why certificate is being sought. Give details in an attached schedule.	❑ No	❑ Yes

Date of codicil (marked as Exhibit "B") *(day, month, year)*	*Date of codicil* (marked as Exhibit "C") *(day, month, year)*

Marital Status ❑ Unmarried	❑ Married	❑ Widowed	❑ Divorced

Did the deceased person marry after the date of the will? If yes, explain why certificate is being sought. Give details in an attached schedule.	❑ No	❑ Yes
Was a marriage of the deceased person terminated by a judgment absolute of divorce, or declared a nullity, after the date of the will? If yes, give details in an attached schedule.	❑ No	❑ Yes
Is any person who signed the will or a codicil as witness or for the testator, or the spouse of such person, a beneficiary under the will? If yes, give details in an attached schedule.	❑ No	❑ Yes

VALUE OF ASSETS OF ESTATE

Do not include in the total amount: insurance payable to a named beneficiary or assigned for value, property held jointly and passing by survivorship, or real estate outside Ontario.

Personal Property	**Real estate, net of encumbrances**	**Total**
$	$	$

Is there any person entitled to an interest in the estate who is not an applicant?	❑ No	❑ Yes

If a person named in the will or a codicil as estate trustee is not an applicant, explain.

If a person not named in the will or a codicil as estate trustee is an applicant, explain why that person is entitled to apply.

If the spouse of the deceased is an applicant, has the spouse elected to receive the entitlement under section 5 of the *Family Law Act*? If yes, explain why the spouse is entitled to apply.	❑ No	❑ Yes

AFFIDAVIT(S) OF APPLICANT(S)
(ATTACH A SEPARATE SHEET FOR ADDITIONAL AFFIDAVITS, IF NECESSARY)

I, an applicant named in this application, make oath and say/affirm:

1. I am 18 years of age or older.

2. The exhibit(s) referred to in this application are the last will and each codicil (where applicable) of the deceased person and I do not know of any later will or codicil.

3. I will faithfully administer the deceased person's property according to law and render a complete and true account of my administration when lawfully required.

4. If I am not named as estate trustee in the will or codicil, consents of persons who together have a majority interest in the value of the assets of the estate at the date of death are attached.

5. The information contained in this application and in any attached schedules is true, to the best of my knowledge and belief.

Name (surname and forename(s))		*Occupation*	
Address (street or postal address)	*(city or town)*	*(province)*	*(postal code)*

Sworn/Affirmed before me at the ....
of ....
in the ....
of ....
this .... day of ...., 20.......... Signature of applicant

....
A Commissioner for taking Affidavits (*or as may be*)

Name (surname and forename(s))		*Occupation*	
Address (street or postal address)	*(city or town)*	*(province)*	*(postal code)*

Sworn/Affirmed before me at the ....
of ....
in the ....
of ....
this .... day of ...., 20.................................. Signature of applicant

....
A Commissioner for taking Affidavits (*or as may be*)

Notice to applicant: Information provided on this form related to the payment of estate administration tax may be forwarded to the Ministry of Finance pursuant to clause 39(1)(b) and

42(1)(c) of the *Freedom of Information and Protection of Privacy Act*. This includes the name of the deceased, name and address of estate trustee(s), value of the estate and any undertakings and tax payments made or refunded. This information will be used by the Ministry of Finance to determine the value of estates and the amount of estate administration tax payable. Questions about the collection of this information should be directed to the Senior Manager — Audit, Advisory and Compliance Branch, 33 King Street West, PO Box 625, Oshawa ON L1H 8H9, 1-866-668-8297.

February 1, 2015

FORM 74.4.1 — APPLICATION FOR CERTIFICATE OF APPOINTMENT OF ESTATE TRUSTEE WITH A WILL (INDIVIDUAL APPLICANT) LIMITED TO THE ASSETS REFERRED TO IN THE WILL

Courts of Justice Act

[Repealed O. Reg. 77/06, s. 3.]

[Editor's Note: Forms 4A to 78A of the Rules of Civil Procedure have been repealed by O. Reg. 77/06, effective July 1, 2006. Pursuant to Rule of Civil Procedure 1.06, when a form is referred to by number, the reference is to the form with that number that is described in the Table of Forms at the end of these rules and which is available on the Internet through www.ontariocourtforms.on.ca. For your convenience, the government form as published on this website is reproduced below.]

ONTARIO

SUPERIOR COURT OF JUSTICE

APPLICATION FOR CERTIFICATE OF APPOINTMENT OF ESTATE TRUSTEE WITH A WILL (INDIVIDUAL APPLICANT) LIMITED TO THE ASSETS REFERRED TO IN THE WILL

(Form 74.4.1 Under the Rules)

at

This application is filed by *(insert name and address)*

DETAILS ABOUT THE DECEASED PERSON

Complete in full as applicable

First given name	Second given name	Third given name	Surname

And if the deceased was known by any other name(s), state below the full name(s) used including surname.

First given name	Second given name	Third given name	Surname

Date of birth of the deceased person, if known: (day, month, year)

Address of fixed place of abode (street or postal address) (city or town)	*(county or district)*

If the deceased person had no fixed place of abode in Ontario, did he or she have property in Ontario? ❑ No ❑ Yes	*Last occupation of deceased person*	
Place of death (city or town; county or district)	*Date of death (day, month, year)*	*Date of last will* (marked as Exhibit "A") *(day, month, year)*

Was the deceased person 18 years of age or older at the date of the will (or 21 years of age or older if the will is dated earlier than September 1, 1971)? ❑ No ❑ Yes
If not, explain why certificate is being sought. Give details in an attached schedule.

Date of codicil (marked as Exhibit "B") *(day, month, year)*	*Date of codicil* (marked as Exhibit "C") *(day, month, year)*

Marital Status ❑ Unmarried ❑ Married ❑ Widowed ❑ Divorced

Did the deceased person marry after the date of the will? ❑ No ❑ Yes
If yes, explain why certificate is being sought. Give details in an attached schedule.

Was a marriage of the deceased person terminated by a judgment absolute of divorce, or declared a nullity, after the date of the will? ❑ No ❑ Yes
If yes, give details in an attached schedule.

Is any person who signed the will or a codicil as witness or for the testator, or the spouse of such person, a beneficiary under the will? ❑ No ❑ Yes
If yes, give details in an attached schedule.

VALUE OF ASSETS REFERRED TO IN ATTACHED WILL (MARKED AS EXHIBIT [LDQUO]A[RDQUO] TO THIS APPLICATION)

Do not include in the total amount: insurance payable to a named beneficiary or assigned for value, property held jointly and passing by survivorship, or real estate outside Ontario.

Personal Property	**Real estate, net of encumbrances**	**Total**
$	$	$

Is there any person entitled to an interest in the estate who is not an applicant? ❑ No ❑ Yes

If a person named in the will or a codicil as estate trustee is not an applicant, explain.

If a person not named in the will or a codicil as estate trustee is an applicant, explain why that person is entitled to apply.

Personal Property $	**Real estate, net of encumbrances** $	**Total** $

If the spouse of the deceased is an applicant, has the spouse elected to receive the entitlement under section 5 of the *Family Law Act*?	❑ No	❑ Yes

If yes, explain why the spouse is entitled to apply.

AFFIDAVIT(S) OF APPLICANT(S)
(ATTACH A SEPARATE SHEET FOR ADDITIONAL AFFIDAVITS, IF NECESSARY)

I, an applicant named in this application, make oath and say/affirm:

1. I am 18 years of age or older.

2. The exhibit(s) referred to in this application are the last will and each codicil (where applicable) of the deceased person relating to the assets referred to in the will and I do not know of any later will or codicil affecting those assets.

3. I will faithfully administer the deceased person's property according to law and render a complete and true account of my administration when lawfully required.

4. If I am not named as estate trustee in the will or codicil, consents of persons who together have a majority interest in the value of the assets of the estate at the date of death are attached.

5. The information contained in this application and in any attached schedules is true, to the best of my knowledge and belief.

Name (surname and forename(s))		*Occupation*	
Address *(street or postal address)*	*(city or town)*	*(province)*	*(postal code)*

Sworn/Affirmed before me at the
....
of ....
in the ....
of ....
this .... day of ...., 20..........

....
Signature of applicant

....
A Commissioner for taking Affidavits *(or as may be)*

Name (surname and forename(s))		*Occupation*	
Address (street or postal address)	*(city or town)*	*(province)*	*(postal code)*

Sworn/Affirmed before me at the
....

of ....
in the ....
of ....
this .... day of ...., 20.......... Signature of applicant

....
A Commissioner for taking Affidavits *(or as may be)*

Notice to applicant: Information provided on this form related to the payment of estate administration tax may be forwarded to the Ministry of Finance pursuant to clause 39(1)(b) and 42(1)(c) of the *Freedom of Information and Protection of Privacy Act*. This includes the name of the deceased, name and address of estate trustee(s), value of the estate and any undertakings and tax payments made or refunded. This information will be used by the Ministry of Finance to determine the value of estates and the amount of estate administration tax payable. Questions about the collection of this information should be directed to the Senior Manager — Audit, Advisory and Compliance Branch, 33 King Street West, PO Box 625, Oshawa ON L1H 8H9, 1-866-668-8297.

February 1, 2015

FORM 74.5 — APPLICATION FOR CERTIFICATE OF APPOINTMENT OF ESTATE TRUSTEE WITH A WILL (CORPORATE APPLICANT)

Courts of Justice Act

[Repealed O. Reg. 77/06, s. 3.]

[Editor's Note: Forms 4A to 78A of the Rules of Civil Procedure have been repealed by O. Reg. 77/06, effective July 1, 2006. Pursuant to Rule of Civil Procedure 1.06, when a form is referred to by number, the reference is to the form with that number that is described in the Table of Forms at the end of these rules and which is available on the Internet through www.ontariocourtforms.on.ca. For your convenience, the government form as published on this website is reproduced below.]

ONTARIO *APPLICATION FOR CERTIFICATE OF APPOINTMENT OF ESTATE TRUSTEE WITH A WILL (CORPORATE APPLICANT)*

SUPERIOR COURT OF JUSTICE

(Form 74.5 Under the Rules)

at

This application is filed by *(insert name and address)*

DETAILS ABOUT THE DECEASED PERSON

Complete in full as applicable

First given name	Second given name	Third given name	Surname

And if the deceased was known by any other name(s), state below the full name(s) used including surname.

First given name	Second given name	Third given name	Surname

Date of birth of the deceased person, if known: (day, month, year)

Address of fixed place of abode (street or postal address) (city or town)	*(county or district)*

If the deceased person had no fixed place of abode in Ontario, did he or she have property in Ontario? ❑ No ❑ Yes	*Last occupation of deceased person*

Place of death (city or town; county or district)	*Date of death (day, month, year)*	*Date of last will* (marked as Exhibit "A") *(day, month, year)*

Was the deceased person 18 years of age or older at the date of the will (or 21 years of age or older if the will is dated earlier than September 1, 1971)?	❑ No	❑ Yes

If not, explain why certificate is being sought. Give details in an attached schedule.

Date of codicil (marked as Exhibit "B") *(day, month, year)*	*Date of codicil* (marked as Exhibit "C") *(day, month, year)*

Marital Status ❑ Unmarried ❑ Married ❑ Widowed ❑ Divorced

Did the deceased person marry after the date of the will?	❑ No	❑ Yes

If yes, explain why certificate is being sought. Give details in an attached schedule.

Was a marriage of the deceased person terminated by a judgment absolute of divorce, or declared a nullity, after the date of the will?	❑ No	❑ Yes

If yes, give details in an attached schedule.

Is any person who signed the will or a codicil as witness or for the testator, or the spouse of such person, a beneficiary under the will?	❑ No	❑ Yes

If yes, give details in an attached schedule.

VALUE OF ASSETS OF ESTATE

Do not include in the total amount: insurance payable to a named beneficiary or assigned for value, property held jointly and passing by survivorship, or real estate outside Ontario.

Personal Property	**Real estate, net of encumbrances**	**Total**
$	$	$

Is there any person entitled to an interest in the estate who is not an applicant?	❏ No	❏ Yes
If a person named in the will or a codicil as estate trustee is not an applicant, explain.		
If a person not named in the will or a codicil as estate trustee is an applicant, explain why that person is entitled to apply.		
If the spouse of the deceased is an applicant, has the spouse elected to receive the entitlement under section 5 of the *Family Law Act*? If yes, explain why the spouse is entitled to apply.	❏ No	❏ Yes

AFFIDAVIT(S) OF APPLICANT(S)
(ATTACH A SEPARATE SHEET FOR ADDITIONAL AFFIDAVITS, IF NECESSARY)

I, a trust officer named in this application, make oath and say/affirm:

1. I am a trust officer of the corporate applicant.

2. I am 18 years of age or older.

3. The exhibit(s) referred to in this application are the last will and each codicil (where applicable) of the deceased person and I do not know of any later will or codicil.

4. The corporate applicant will faithfully administer the deceased person's property according to law and render a complete and true account of its administration when lawfully required.

5. If the corporate applicant is not named as estate trustee in the will or codicil, consents of persons who together have a majority interest in the value of the assets of the estate at the date of death are attached.

6. The information contained in this application and in any attached schedules is true, to the best of my knowledge and belief.

Name of corporate applicant	*Name of trust officer*		
Address of corporate applicant (street or postal address)	*(city or town)*	*(province)*	*(postal code)*

Sworn/Affirmed before me at the
....
of ....
in the ....
of ....
this .... day of ...., 20..........

....
Signature of trust officer

....
A Commissioner for taking Affidavits *(or as may be)*

I, an applicant named in this application, make oath and say/affirm:

1. I am 18 years of age or older.

2. The exhibit(s) referred to in this application are the last will and each codicil (where applicable) of the deceased person and I do not know of any later will or codicil.

3. I will faithfully administer the deceased person's property according to law and render a complete and true account of my administration when lawfully required.

4. If I am not named as estate trustee in the will or codicil, consents of persons who together have a majority interest in the value of the assets of the estate at the date of death are attached.

5. The information contained in this application and in any attached schedules is true, to the best of my knowledge and belief.

Name (surname and forename(s))		*Occupation*	
Address (street or postal address)	*(city or town)*	*(province)*	*(postal code)*

Sworn/Affirmed before me at the
....
of ....
in the ....
of ....
this .... day of ...., 20.......... Signature of applicant

....
A Commissioner for taking Affidavits *(or as may be)*

Notice to applicant: Information provided on this form related to the payment of estate administration tax may be forwarded to the Ministry of Finance pursuant to clause 39(1)(b) and 42(1)(c) of the *Freedom of Information and Protection of Privacy Act*. This includes the name of the deceased, name and address of estate trustee(s), value of the estate and any undertakings and tax payments made or refunded. This information will be used by the Ministry of Finance to determine the value of estates and the amount of estate administration tax payable. Questions about the collection of this information should be directed to the Senior Manager — Audit, Advisory and Compliance Branch, 33 King Street West, PO Box 625, Oshawa ON L1H 8H9, 1-866-668-8297.

February 1, 2015

FORM 74.5.1 — APPLICATION FOR CERTIFICATE OF APPOINTMENT OF ESTATE TRUSTEE WITH A WILL (CORPORATE APPLICANT) LIMITED TO THE ASSETS REFERRED TO IN THE WILL

Courts of Justice Act

[Repealed O. Reg. 77/06, s. 3.]

[Editor's Note: Forms 4A to 78A of the Rules of Civil Procedure have been repealed by O. Reg. 77/06, effective July 1, 2006. Pursuant to Rule of Civil Procedure 1.06, when a form is referred to by number, the reference is to the form with that number that is described in the Table of Forms at the end of these rules and which is available on the Internet through www.ontariocourtforms.on.ca. For your convenience, the government form as published on this website is reproduced below.]

ONTARIO

SUPERIOR COURT OF JUSTICE

APPLICATION FOR CERTIFICATE OF APPOINTMENT OF ESTATE TRUSTEE WITH A WILL (CORPORATE APPLICANT) LIMITED TO THE ASSETS REFERRED TO IN THE WILL

(Form 74.5.1 Under the Rules)

at

This application is filed by *(insert name and address)*

DETAILS ABOUT THE DECEASED PERSON

Complete in full as applicable

First given name	Second given name	Third given name	Surname

And if the deceased was known by any other name(s), state below the full name(s) used including surname.

First given name	Second given name	Third given name	Surname

Date of birth of the deceased person, if known: (day, month, year)

Address of fixed place of abode (street or postal address) (city or town)	*(county or district)*

If the deceased person had no fixed place of abode in Ontario, did he or she have property in Ontario? ❑ No ❑ Yes	*Last occupation of deceased person*

Place of death (city or town; county or district)	*Date of death (day, month, year)*	*Date of last will* (marked as Exhibit "A") *(day, month, year)*

Was the deceased person 18 years of age or older at the date of the will (or 21 years of age or older if the will is dated earlier than September 1, 1971)? If not, explain why certificate is being sought. Give details in an attached schedule.	❑ No	❑ Yes

Date of codicil (marked as Exhibit "B") *(day, month, year)*	*Date of codicil* (marked as Exhibit "C") *(day, month, year)*

Marital Status	❑ Unmarried	❑ Married	❑ Widowed	❑ Divorced

Did the deceased person marry after the date of the will? If yes, explain why certificate is being sought. Give details in an attached schedule.	❑ No	❑ Yes
Was a marriage of the deceased person terminated by a judgment absolute of divorce, or declared a nullity, after the date of the will? If yes, give details in an attached schedule.	❑ No	❑ Yes
Is any person who signed the will or a codicil as witness or for the testator, or the spouse of such person, a beneficiary under the will? If yes, give details in an attached schedule.	❑ No	❑ Yes

VALUE OF ASSETS REFERRED TO IN ATTACHED WILL (MARKED AS EXHIBIT [LDQUO]A[RDQUO] TO THIS APPLICATION)

Do not include in the total amount: insurance payable to a named beneficiary or assigned for value, property held jointly and passing by survivorship, or real estate outside Ontario.

Personal Property	**Real estate, net of encumbrances**	**Total**
$	$	$

Is there any person interested in the estate who is not an applicant?	❑ No	❑ Yes
If a person named in the will or a codicil as estate trustee is not an applicant, explain.		
If a person not named in the will or a codicil as estate trustee is an applicant, explain why that person is entitled to apply.		
If the spouse of the deceased is an applicant, has the spouse elected to receive the entitlement under section 5 of the *Family Law Act*? If yes, explain why the spouse is entitled to apply.	❑ No	❑ Yes

AFFIDAVIT(S) OF APPLICANT(S) (ATTACH A SEPARATE SHEET FOR ADDITIONAL AFFIDAVITS, IF NECESSARY)

I, a trust officer named in this application, make oath and say/affirm:

1. I am a trust officer of the corporate applicant.
2. I am 18 years of age or older.

3. The exhibit(s) referred to in this application are the last will and each codicil (where applicable) of the deceased person relating to the assets referred to in the will and I do not know of any later will or codicil affecting those assets.

4. The corporate applicant will faithfully administer the deceased person's property according to law and render a complete and true account of its administration when lawfully required.

5. If the corporate applicant is not named as estate trustee in the will or codicil, consents of persons who together have a majority interest in the value of the assets of the estate at the date of death are attached.

6. The information contained in this application and in any attached schedules is true, to the best of my knowledge and belief.

Name of corporate applicant		*Name of trust officer*	
Address of corporate applicant (street or postal address)	*(city or town)*	*(province)*	*(postal code)*

Sworn/Affirmed before me at the
....
of ....
in the ....
of ....
this .... day of ...., 20.......... Signature of trust officer

....
A Commissioner for taking Affidavits *(or as may be)*

I, an applicant named in this application, make oath and say/affirm:

1. I am 18 years of age or older.

2. The exhibit(s) referred to in this application are the last will and each codicil (where applicable) of the deceased person relating to the assets referred to in the will and I do not know of any later will or codicil affecting those assets.

3. I will faithfully administer the deceased person's property according to law and render a complete and true account of my administration when lawfully required.

4. If I am not named as estate trustee in the will or codicil, consents of persons who together have a majority interest in the value of the assets of the estate at the date of death are attached.

5. The information contained in this application and in any attached schedules is true, to the best of my knowledge and belief.

Name (surname and forename(s))		*Occupation*	
Address (street or postal address)	*(city or town)*	*(province)*	*(postal code)*

Sworn/Affirmed before me at the
....
of ....
in the ....

of ....
this .... day of ...., 20................................. Signature of applicant

....
A Commissioner for taking Affidavits *(or as may be)*

Notice to applicant: Information provided on this form related to the payment of estate administration tax may be forwarded to the Ministry of Finance pursuant to clause 39(1)(b) and 42(1)(c) of the *Freedom of Information and Protection of Privacy Act*. This includes the name of the deceased, name and address of estate trustee(s), value of the estate and any undertakings and tax payments made or refunded. This information will be used by the Ministry of Finance to determine the value of estates and the amount of estate administration tax payable. Questions about the collection of this information should be directed to the Senior Manager — Audit, Advisory and Compliance Branch, 33 King Street West, PO Box 625, Oshawa ON L1H 8H9, 1-866-668-8297.

February 1, 2015

FORM 74.6 — AFFIDAVIT OF SERVICE OF NOTICE

Courts of Justice Act

[Repealed O. Reg. 77/06, s. 3.]

[Editor's Note: Forms 4A to 78A of the Rules of Civil Procedure have been repealed by O. Reg. 77/06, effective July 1, 2006. Pursuant to Rule of Civil Procedure 1.06, when a form is referred to by number, the reference is to the form with that number that is described in the Table of Forms at the end of these rules and which is available on the Internet through www.ontariocourtforms.on.ca. For your convenience, the government form as published on this website is reproduced below.]

ONTARIO

SUPERIOR COURT OF JUSTICE

IN THE ESTATE OF *(insert name)* , deceased.

AFFIDAVIT OF SERVICE OF NOTICE

I, *(insert name)* , of *(insert city or town and county or district of residence)* , make oath and say/affirm:

1. I am an applicant for a certificate of appointment of estate trustee with a will in the estate.

2. I have sent or caused to be sent a notice in Form 74.7, a copy of which is marked as Exhibit "A" to this affidavit, to all adult persons and charities named in the notice (except to

an applicant who is entitled to share in the distribution of the estate), to the Public Guardian and Trustee if paragraph 6 of the notice applies, to a parent or guardian of the minor and to the Children's Lawyer if paragraph 4 applies, to the guardian or attorney if paragraph 5 applies, and to the Children's Lawyer if paragraph 7 applies, all by regular lettermail sent to the person's last known address.

3. I have attached or caused to be attached to each notice the following:

(A) In the case of a notice sent to or in respect of a person entitled only to a specified item of property or stated amount of money, an extract of the part or parts of the will or codicil relating to the gift, or a copy of the will (and codicil(s), if any).

(B) In the case of a notice sent to or in respect of any other beneficiary, a copy of the will (and codicil(s), if any).

(C) In the case of a notice sent to the Children's Lawyer or the Public Guardian and Trustee, a copy of the will (and codicil(s), if any) and a statement of the estimated value of the interest of the person represented.

4. The following persons and charities specifically named in the Will are not entitled to be served for the reasons shown:

Name of person (as it appears in will, if applicable)	Reason not served

If paragraph 4 does not apply insert "Not Applicable."

5. The following persons named in the Will or being a member of a class of beneficiaries under the Will may be entitled to be served but have not been served for the reasons shown below:

Name of person (as it appears in will, if applicable)	Reason not served

If paragraph 5 does not apply insert "Not Applicable."

6. To the best of my knowledge and belief, subject to paragraph 5 (if applicable), the persons named in the notice are all the persons who are entitled to share in the distribution of the estate.

Sworn/Affirmed before me at the . . . . . .)
)
of . . . .)
)
in the . . . .)
)
of . . . .) ______________________________
) Signature of applicant
this . . . . day of . . . ., 20 . . .)
)
)
)

____

A Commissioner for taking Affidavits *(or as may be)*

November 1, 2005

FORM 74.7 — NOTICE OF AN APPLICATION FOR A CERTIFICATE OF APPOINTMENT OF ESTATE TRUSTEE WITH A WILL

Courts of Justice Act

[Repealed O. Reg. 77/06, s. 3.]

[Editor's Note: Forms 4A to 78A of the Rules of Civil Procedure have been repealed by O. Reg. 77/06, effective July 1, 2006. Pursuant to Rule of Civil Procedure 1.06, when a form is referred to by number, the reference is to the form with that number that is described in the Table of Forms at the end of these rules and which is available on the Internet through www.ontariocourtforms.on.ca. For your convenience, the government form as published on this website is reproduced below.]

ONTARIO

SUPERIOR COURT OF JUSTICE

IN THE ESTATE OF .... *(insert name)*, deceased.

NOTICE OF AN APPLICATION FOR A CERTIFICATE OF APPOINTMENT OF ESTATE TRUSTEE WITH A WILL

1. The deceased died on (*insert date*).

2. Attached to this notice are:

(A) If the notice is sent to or in respect of a person entitled only to a specified item of property or stated amount of money, an extract of the part or parts of the will or codicil relating to the gift, or a copy of the will (and codicil(s), if any).

(B) If the notice is sent to or in respect of any other beneficiary, a copy of the will (and codicil(s), if any).

(C) If the notice is sent to the Children's Lawyer or the Public Guardian and Trustee, a copy of the will (and codicil(s), if any), and if it is not included in the notice, a statement of the estimated value of the interest of the person represented.

3. The applicant named in this notice is applying for a certificate of appointment of estate trustee with a will.

APPLICANT

Name	**Address**

4. The following persons who are less than 18 years of age are entitled, whether their interest is contingent or vested, to share in the distribution of the estate:

Name	**Date of Birth (day, month, year)**	**Name and Address of Parent or Guardian**	**Estimated Value of Interest in Estate ***

Notes:

* Note: *The Estimated Value of Interest in Estate may be omitted in the form if it is included in a separate schedule attached to the notice sent to the Children's Lawyer.*

5. The following persons who are mentally incapable within the meaning of section 6 of the *Substitute Decisions Act, 1992* in respect of an issue in the proceeding, and who have guardians or attorneys acting under powers of attorney with authority to act in the proceeding, are entitled, whether their interest is contingent or vested, to share in the distribution of the estate:

Name and Address of Person	**Name and Address of Guardian or Attorney ***

Notes:

* *Specify whether guardian or attorney*

6. The following persons who are mentally incapable within the meaning of section 6 of the *Substitute Decisions Act, 1992* in respect of an issue in the proceeding, and who do not have guardians or attorneys acting under powers of attorney with authority to act in the proceeding, are entitled, whether their interest is contingent or vested, to share in the distribution of the estate:

Name and Address of Person	**Estimated Value of Interest in Estate ***

Notes:

* Note: *The Estimated Value of Interest in Estate may be omitted in the form if it is included in a separate schedule attached to the notice sent to the Public Guardian and Trustee.*

7. Unborn or unascertained persons may be entitled to share in the distribution of the estate. *(Delete if not applicable)*

8. All other persons and charities entitled, whether their interest is contingent or vested, to share in the distribution of the estate are as follows:

Name	**Address**

9. This notice is being sent, by regular lettermail, to all adult persons and charities named above in this notice (except to an applicant who is entitled to share in the distribution of the estate), to the Public Guardian and Trustee if paragraph 6 applies, to a parent or guardian of the minor and to the Children's Lawyer if paragraph 4 applies, to the guardian or attorney if paragraph 5 applies, and to the Children's Lawyer if paragraph 7 applies.

10. The following persons named in the Will or being a member of a class of beneficiaries under the Will may be entitled to be served but have not been served for the reasons shown below:

Name of person (as it appears in will, if applicable)	**Reason not served**

If paragraph 10 does not apply insert "Not Applicable."

DATE:

February 1, 2015

FORM 74.8 — AFFIDAVIT OF EXECUTION OF WILL OR CODICIL

Courts of Justice Act

[Repealed O. Reg. 77/06, s. 3.]

[Editor's Note: Forms 4A to 78A of the Rules of Civil Procedure have been repealed by O. Reg. 77/06, effective July 1, 2006. Pursuant to Rule of Civil Procedure 1.06, when a form is referred to by number, the reference is to the form with that number that is described in the Table of Forms at the end of these rules and which is available on the Internet through www.ontariocourtforms.on.ca. For your convenience, the government form as published on this website is reproduced below.]

ONTARIO
SUPERIOR COURT OF JUSTICE

In the matter of the execution of a will or codicil of (*insert name*)

AFFIDAVIT

I, (*insert name*), of (*insert city or town and county or district, metropolitan or regional municipality of residence*), make oath and say/affirm:

1. On (*date*), I was present and saw the document marked as Exhibit "A" to this affidavit executed by (*insert name*).

2. (*Insert name*) executed the document in the presence of myself and (*insert name of other witness and city or town, county or district, metropolitan or regional municipality of residence*). We were both present at the same time, and signed the document in the testator's presence as attesting witnesses.

SWORN/AFFIRMED BEFORE	)	
me at the of	)	
in the of	)	
this day of , 20 .	)	....
	)	
	)	
	)	
	)	

....
A Commissioner for taking Affidavits
(or as may be)

NOTE: If the testator was blind or signed by making his or her mark, add the following paragraph:
3. Before its execution, the document was read over to the testator, who (was blind) (signed by making his or her mark). The testator appeared to understand the contents.

WARNING: A beneficiary or the spouse of a beneficiary should not be a witness.

November 1, 2005

FORM 74.9 — AFFIDAVIT ATTESTING TO THE HANDWRITING AND SIGNATURE OF A HOLOGRAPH WILL OR CODICIL

Courts of Justice Act

[Repealed O. Reg. 77/06, s. 3.]

[Editor's Note: Forms 4A to 78A of the Rules of Civil Procedure have been repealed by O. Reg. 77/06, effective July 1, 2006. Pursuant to Rule of Civil Procedure 1.06, when a form is referred to by number, the reference is to the form with that number that is described in the Table of Forms at the end of these rules and which is available on the Internet through www.ontariocourtforms.on.ca. For your convenience, the government form as published on this website is reproduced below.]

ONTARIO
SUPERIOR COURT OF JUSTICE

IN THE ESTATE OF (*insert name*), deceased.

AFFIDAVIT ATTESTING TO THE HANDWRITING AND SIGNATURE OF A HOLOGRAPH WILL OR CODICIL

I, (*insert name*), of (*insert city or town and county or district, metropolitan or regional municipality of residence*), make oath and say/affirm:

1. I was well acquainted with the deceased and have frequently seen the deceased's signature and handwriting.

2. I believe the whole of the document dated (*insert date*), now shown to me and marked as Exhibit "A" to this affidavit, including the signature, is in the handwriting of the deceased.

SWORN/AFFIRMED BEFORE	)	
me at the of	)	
in the of	)	
this day of , 20 .	)	....
	)	
	)	
	)	
	)	

....
A Commissioner for taking Affidavits
(or as may be)

November 1, 2005

FORM 74.10 — AFFIDAVIT OF CONDITION OF WILL OR CODICIL

Courts of Justice Act

[Repealed O. Reg. 77/06, s. 3.]

[Editor's Note: Forms 4A to 78A of the Rules of Civil Procedure have been repealed by O. Reg. 77/06, effective July 1, 2006. Pursuant to Rule of Civil Procedure 1.06, when a form is referred to by number, the reference is to the form with that number that is described in the Table of Forms at the end of these rules and which is available on the Internet through www.ontariocourtforms.on.ca. For your convenience, the government form as published on this website is reproduced below.]

ONTARIO
SUPERIOR COURT OF JUSTICE

IN THE ESTATE OF *(insert name)*, deceased.

AFFIDAVIT OF CONDITION OF WILL OR CODICIL

I, *(insert name)*, of *(insert city or town and county or district, metropolitan or regional municipality of residence)*, make oath and say/affirm:

1. On *(date)*, I was present and saw the document marked as Exhibit "A" to this affidavit executed by the deceased, in the presence of myself and *(insert name of other witness and city or town, county or district, metropolitan or regional municipality of residence)*. We were both present at the same time, and signed the document in the testator's presence as attesting witnesses.

2. The following alterations, erasures, obliterations or interlineations that have not been attested appear in the document:

3. The document is now in the same condition as when it was executed.

SWORN/AFFIRMED BEFORE	)	
me at the .... of	)	
in the .... of	)	
this .... day of ...., 20..........	)	....
	)	
	)	
	)	
	)	

....
A Commissioner for Taking Affidavits *(or as may be)*

NOTE: If paragraph 3 is not correct, add the words "except that" and give details of the exceptions.

October 24, 2017

FORM 74.11 — RENUNCIATION OF RIGHT TO A CERTIFICATE OF APPOINTMENT OF ESTATE TRUSTEE (OR SUCCEEDING ESTATE TRUSTEE) WITH A WILL

Courts of Justice Act

[Repealed O. Reg. 77/06, s. 3.]

[Editor's Note: Forms 4A to 78A of the Rules of Civil Procedure have been repealed by O. Reg. 77/06, effective July 1, 2006. Pursuant to Rule of Civil Procedure 1.06, when a form is referred to by number, the reference is to the form with that number that is described in the

Table of Forms at the end of these rules and which is available on the Internet through www.ontariocourtforms.on.ca. For your convenience, the government form as published on this website is reproduced below.]

ONTARIO
SUPERIOR COURT OF JUSTICE

IN THE ESTATE OF (*insert name*), deceased.

RENUNCIATION OF RIGHT TO A CERTIFICATE OF APPOINTMENT OF ESTATE TRUSTEE (OR SUCCEEDING ESTATE TRUSTEE) WITH A WILL

The deceased died on (*date*).

In that person's testamentary document dated (*date*), I, (*insert name*), was named an estate trustee.

I renounce my right to a certificate of appointment of estate trustee (or succeeding estate trustee) with a will.

DATE)
)
)
)
)
)
)
)

....
Signature of witness Signature of person renouncing

November 1, 2005

FORM 74.12 — CONSENT TO APPLICANT'S APPOINTMENT AS ESTATE TRUSTEE WITH A WILL

Courts of Justice Act

[Repealed O. Reg. 77/06, s. 3.]

[Editor's Note: Forms 4A to 78A of the Rules of Civil Procedure have been repealed by O. Reg. 77/06, effective July 1, 2006. Pursuant to Rule of Civil Procedure 1.06, when a form is referred to by number, the reference is to the form with that number that is described in the Table of Forms at the end of these rules and which is available on the Internet through www.ontariocourtforms.on.ca. For your convenience, the government form as published on this website is reproduced below.]

ONTARIO
SUPERIOR COURT OF JUSTICE

IN THE ESTATE OF (*insert name*), deceased.

CONSENT TO APPLICANT'S
APPOINTMENT AS ESTATE TRUSTEE WITH A WILL

The deceased died on (*date*).

No estate trustee named in a testamentary document of that person is applying for a certificate of appointment of estate trustee with a will.

I, (*insert name*), am entitled to share in the distribution of the estate.

I consent to the application by (*insert name*) for a certificate of appointment of estate trustee with a will.

I consent to an order dispensing with the filing of a bond by the applicant (*delete if inapplicable*).

DATE	))))))))	
....		....
Signature of witness		Signature of person consenting

November 1, 2005

FORM 74.12.1 — CONSENT TO APPLICANT'S APPOINTMENT AS ESTATE TRUSTEE WITH A WILL LIMITED TO THE ASSETS REFERRED TO IN THE WILL

Courts of Justice Act

[Repealed O. Reg. 77/06, s. 3.]

ONTARIO
SUPERIOR COURT OF JUSTICE

IN THE ESTATE OF *(insert name)*, deceased.

CONSENT TO APPLICANT'S
APPOINTMENT AS ESTATE TRUSTEE WITH A WILL LIMITED TO THE ASSETS REFERRED TO IN THE WILL

The deceased died on *(date)*.

No estate trustee named in a testamentary document of that person is applying for a certificate of appointment of estate trustee with a will limited to the assets referred to in the will.

I, *(insert name)*, am entitled to share in the distribution of the estate.

I consent to the application by (*insert name*) for a certificate of appointment of estate trustee with a will limited to the assets referred to in the will.

I consent to an order dispensing with the filing of a bond by the applicant (*delete if inapplicable*).

DATE	)	
	)	
	)	
	)	
	)	
....	)	....
Signature of witness	)	Signature of person consenting
	)	
	)	

February 1, 2015

FORM 74.13 — CERTIFICATE OF APPOINTMENT OF ESTATE TRUSTEE WITH A WILL

Courts of Justice Act

[Repealed O. Reg. 77/06, s. 3.]

[Editor's Note: Forms 4A to 78A of the Rules of Civil Procedure have been repealed by O. Reg. 77/06, effective July 1, 2006. Pursuant to Rule of Civil Procedure 1.06, when a form is referred to by number, the reference is to the form with that number that is described in the Table of Forms at the end of these rules and which is available on the Internet through www.ontariocourtforms.on.ca. For your convenience, the government form as published on this website is reproduced below.]

ONTARIO
SUPERIOR COURT OF JUSTICE

IN THE ESTATE OF , deceased,

late of

occupation

who died on

CERTIFICATE OF APPOINTMENT OF ESTATE TRUSTEE WITH A WILL

Applicant Address Occupation

This CERTIFICATE OF APPOINTMENT OF ESTATE TRUSTEE WITH A WILL is hereby issued under the seal of the court to the applicant named above. Attached to this certificate is a copy of the deceased's last will dated .... (and codicil(s) dated ....).

DATE ....

....
Registrar
Address of court office

February 1, 2015

FORM 74.13.1 — CERTIFICATE OF APPOINTMENT OF ESTATE TRUSTEE WITH A WILL LIMITED TO THE ASSETS REFERRED TO IN THE WILL

Courts of Justice Act

[Repealed O. Reg. 77/06, s. 3.]

[Editor's Note: Forms 4A to 78A of the Rules of Civil Procedure have been repealed by O. Reg. 77/06, effective July 1, 2006. Pursuant to Rule of Civil Procedure 1.06, when a form is referred to by number, the reference is to the form with that number that is described in the Table of Forms at the end of these rules and which is available on the Internet through www.ontariocourtforms.on.ca. For your convenience, the government form as published on this website is reproduced below.]

ONTARIO
SUPERIOR COURT OF JUSTICE

IN THE ESTATE OF , deceased,

late of

occupation

who died on

CERTIFICATE OF APPOINTMENT OF ESTATE TRUSTEE WITH A WILL LIMITED TO THE ASSETS REFERRED TO IN THE WILL

Applicant: .... Address: .... Occupation: ....

By order of a judge of the Superior Court of Justice this grant of a certificate of appointment of estate trustee with a will is limited to the assets referred to in the will dated .... (and codicils dated ....). A copy of the will (and codicils) is attached.

This will is the last will of the deceased dealing with those assets. This CERTIFICATE OF APPOINTMENT OF ESTATE TRUSTEE WITH A WILL LIMITED TO THE ASSETS REFERRED TO IN THE WILL is hereby issued under the seal of the court to the applicant named above.

DATE ....
Registrar

Address of court office

February 1, 2015

FORM 74.13.2 — ORDER FOR CERTIFICATE OF APPOINTMENT OF (SUCCEEDING) ESTATE TRUSTEE WITH A WILL LIMITED TO THE ASSETS REFERRED TO IN THE WILL

Courts of Justice Act

[Repealed O. Reg. 77/06, s. 3.]

[Editor's Note: Forms 4A to 78A of the Rules of Civil Procedure have been repealed by O. Reg. 77/06, effective July 1, 2006. Pursuant to Rule of Civil Procedure 1.06, when a form is referred to by number, the reference is to the form with that number that is described in the Table of Forms at the end of these rules and which is available on the Internet through www.ontariocourtforms.on.ca. For your convenience, the government form as published on this website is reproduced below.]

(Court file no.)

(Court)

(Name of judge or officer)

(Day and date order made)

(Court seal)

In the Estate of *(insert name)*, deceased:

ORDER

UPON the Application for a Certificate of Appointment of *(Succeeding, delete if not applicable)* Estate Trustee with a Will Limited to the Assets Referred to in the Will in the Estate of ...., deceased,

1. IT IS ORDERED that a Certificate of Appointment of *(Succeeding, delete if not applicable)* Estate Trustee with a Will Limited to the Assets Referred to in the Will be issued for the Will of the deceased dated *(insert date)*.

....

April 11, 2012

FORM 74.14 — APPLICATION FOR CERTIFICATE OF APPOINTMENT OF ESTATE TRUSTEE WITHOUT A WILL (INDIVIDUAL APPLICANT)

Courts of Justice Act

[Repealed O. Reg. 77/06, s. 3.]

[Editor's Note: Forms 4A to 78A of the Rules of Civil Procedure have been repealed by O. Reg. 77/06, effective July 1, 2006. Pursuant to Rule of Civil Procedure 1.06, when a form is referred to by number, the reference is to the form with that number that is described in the Table of Forms at the end of these rules and which is available on the Internet through www.ontariocourtforms.on.ca. For your convenience, the government form as published on this website is reproduced below.]

ONTARIO

SUPERIOR COURT OF JUSTICE

APPLICATION FOR CERTIFICATE OF APPOINTMENT OF ESTATE TRUSTEE WITHOUT A WILL (INDIVIDUAL APPLICANT)

(Form 74.14 Under the Rules)

at

This application is filed by *(insert name and address)*

DETAILS ABOUT THE DECEASED PERSON

Complete in full as applicable

First given name	Second given name	Third given name	Surname

And if the deceased was known by any other name(s), state below the full name(s) used including surname.

First given name	Second given name	Third given name	Surname

Date of birth of the deceased person, if known: (day, month, year)

Address of fixed place of abode (street or postal address) (city or town)	*(county or district)*

If the deceased person had no fixed place of abode in Ontario, did he or she have property in Ontario? ❑ No ❑ Yes	*Last occupation of deceased person*
Place of death (city or town; county or district)	*Date of death (day, month, year)*

Marital Status ❑ Unmarried ❑ Married ❑ Widowed ❑ Divorced

Was the deceased person's marriage terminated by a judgment absolute of divorce, or declared a nullity? ❑ No ❑ Yes
If yes, give details in an attached schedule.

Did the deceased person go through a form of marriage with a person where it appears uncertain whether an earlier marriage of the deceased person had been terminated by divorce or declared a nullity? ❑ No ❑ Yes
If yes, give the person's name and address, and the names and addresses of any children (including deceased children) of the marriage, in an attached schedule.

Was any earlier marriage of a person with whom the deceased person went through a form of marriage terminated by divorce or declared a nullity? ❑ No ❑ Yes
If yes, give details in an attached schedule.

Was the deceased person immediately before his or her death living with a person in a conjugal relationship outside marriage? ❑ No ❑ Yes
If yes, give the person's name and address in an attached schedule.

PERSONS ENTITLED TO SHARE IN THE ESTATE

(Attach a schedule if more space is needed. If a person entitled to share in the estate is not a spouse, child, parent, brother or sister of the deceased person, show how the relationship is traced.)

Name	**Address**	**Relationship to deceased person**	**Age (if under 18)**

VALUE OF ASSETS OF ESTATE

Do not include in the total amount: insurance payable to a named beneficiary or assigned for value, property held jointly and passing by survivorship, or real estate outside Ontario.

Personal property	**Real estate, net of encumbrances**	**Total**
$	**$**	**$**

Explain why the applicant is entitled to apply.

AFFIDAVIT(S) OF APPLICANT(S)
(ATTACH A SEPARATE SHEET FOR ADDITIONAL AFFIDAVITS, IF NECESSARY)

I, an applicant named in this application, make oath and say/affirm:

1. I am 18 years of age or older and a resident of Ontario.

2. I have made a careful search and inquiry for a will or other testamentary document of the deceased person, but none has been found. I believe that the person did not leave a will or other testamentary document.

3. I will faithfully administer the deceased person's property according to law and render a complete and true account of my administration when lawfully required.

4. Consents of persons who together have a majority interest in the value of the assets of the estate at the date of death are attached.

5. The information contained in this application and in any attached schedules is true, to the best of my knowledge and belief.

Name (surname and forename(s))		*Occupation*	
Address (street or postal address)	*(city or town)*	*(province)*	*(postal code)*

Sworn/Affirmed before me at the)
....
of ....)
in the ....)
of ....) ....
this .... day of ...., 20..........) Signature of applicant

....
A Commissioner for taking Affidavits *(or as may be)*

Name (surname and forename(s))		*Occupation*	
Address (street or postal address)	*(city or town)*	*(province)*	*(postal code)*

Sworn/Affirmed before me at the)
....

of ....)
in the ....)
of ....) ....
this .... day of ...., 20..........) Signature of applicant

....
A Commissioner for taking Affidavits (*or as may be*)

Notice to applicant: Information provided on this form related to the payment of estate administration tax may be forwarded to the Ministry of Finance pursuant to clause 39(1)(b) and 42(1)(c) of the *Freedom of Information and Protection of Privacy Act*. This includes the name of the deceased, name and address of estate trustee(s), value of the estate and any undertakings and tax payments made or refunded. This information will be used by the Ministry of Finance to determine the value of estates and the amount of estate administration tax payable. Questions about the collection of this information should be directed to the Senior Manager — Audit, Advisory and Compliance Branch, 33 King Street West, PO Box 625, Oshawa ON L1H 8H9, 1-866-668-8297.

February 1, 2015

FORM 74.15 — APPLICATION FOR CERTIFICATE OF APPOINTMENT OF ESTATE TRUSTEE WITHOUT A WILL (CORPORATE APPLICANT)

Courts of Justice Act

[Repealed O. Reg. 77/06, s. 3.]

[Editor's Note: Forms 4A to 78A of the Rules of Civil Procedure have been repealed by O. Reg. 77/06, effective July 1, 2006. Pursuant to Rule of Civil Procedure 1.06, when a form is referred to by number, the reference is to the form with that number that is described in the Table of Forms at the end of these rules and which is available on the Internet through www.ontariocourtforms.on.ca. For your convenience, the government form as published on this website is reproduced below.]

ONTARIO

SUPERIOR COURT OF JUSTICE

APPLICATION FOR CERTIFICATE OF APPOINTMENT OF ESTATE TRUSTEE WITHOUT A WILL (CORPORATE APPLICANT)

(Form 74.15 Under the Rules)

at

This application is filed by *(insert name and address)*

CORPORATE APPLICANT **Form 74.15**

DETAILS ABOUT THE DECEASED PERSON

Complete in full as applicable

First given name	Second given name	Third given name	Surname

And if the deceased was known by any other name(s), state below the full name(s) used including surname.

First given name	Second given name	Third given name	Surname

Date of birth of the deceased person, if known: (day, month, year)

Address of fixed place of abode (street or postal address) (city or town)	*(county or district)*

If the deceased person had no fixed place of abode in Ontario, did he or she have property in Ontario? ❑ No ❑ Yes	*Last occupation of deceased person*

Place of death (city or town; county or district)	*Date of death (day, month, year)*

Marital Status ❑ Unmarried ❑ Married ❑ Widowed ❑ Divorced

Was the deceased person's marriage terminated by a judgment absolute of divorce, or declared a nullity? ❑ No ❑ Yes
If yes, give details in an attached schedule.

Did the deceased person go through a form of marriage with a person where it appears uncertain whether an earlier marriage of the deceased person had been terminated by divorce or declared a nullity? ❑ No ❑ Yes
If yes, give the person's name and address, and the names and addresses of any children (including deceased children) of the marriage, in an attached schedule.

Was any earlier marriage of a person with whom the deceased person went through a form of marriage terminated by divorce or declared a nullity? ❑ No ❑ Yes
If yes, give details in an attached schedule.

Was the deceased person immediately before his or her death living with a person in a conjugal relationship outside marriage? ❑ No ❑ Yes
If yes, give the person's name in an attached schedule.

PERSONS ENTITLED TO SHARE IN THE ESTATE

(Attach a schedule if more space is needed. If a person entitled to share in the estate is not a spouse, child, parent, brother or sister of the deceased person, show how the relationship is traced.)

Name	**Address**	**Relationship to deceased person**	**Age (if under 18)**

VALUE OF ASSETS OF ESTATE

Do not include in the total amount: insurance payable to a named beneficiary or assigned for value, property held jointly and passing by survivorship, or real estate outside Ontario.

Personal property	Real estate, net of encumbrances	Total
$	$	$

Explain why the applicant is entitled to apply.

AFFIDAVIT(S) OF APPLICANT(S)
(ATTACH A SEPARATE SHEET FOR ADDITIONAL AFFIDAVITS, IF NECESSARY)

I, a trust officer named in this application, make oath and say/affirm:

1. I am a trust officer of the corporate applicant.

2. I am 18 years of age or older.

3. I have made a careful search and inquiry for a will or other testamentary document of the deceased person, but none has been found. I believe that the person did not leave a will or other testamentary document.

4. The corporate applicant will faithfully administer the deceased person's property according to law and render a complete and true account of my administration when lawfully required.

5. Consents of persons who together have a majority interest in the value of the assets of the estate at the date of death are attached.

6. The information contained in this application and in any attached schedules is true, to the best of my knowledge and belief.

Name of corporate applicant	*Name of trust officer*		
Address of corporate applicant (street or postal address)	*(city or town)*	*(province)*	*(postal code)*

Sworn/Affirmed before me at the
....
of ....
in the ....
of ....
this .... day of ...., 20.......... Signature of trust officer

....
A Commissioner for taking Affidavits *(or as may be)*

Notice to applicant: Information provided on this form related to the payment of estate administration tax may be forwarded to the Ministry of Finance pursuant to clause 39(1)(b) and 42(1)(c) of the *Freedom of Information and Protection of Privacy Act*. This includes the name of the deceased, name and address of estate trustee(s), value of the estate and any undertakings and tax payments made or refunded. This information will be used by the Ministry of Finance to determine the value of estates and the amount of estate administration tax payable. Questions about the collection of this information should be directed to the Senior Manager — Audit, Advisory and Compliance Branch, 33 King Street West, PO Box 625, Oshawa ON L1H 8H9, 1-866-668-8297.

February 1, 2015

FORM 74.16 — AFFIDAVIT OF SERVICE OF NOTICE

Courts of Justice Act

[Repealed O. Reg. 77/06, s. 3.]

[Editor's Note: Forms 4A to 78A of the Rules of Civil Procedure have been repealed by O. Reg. 77/06, effective July 1, 2006. Pursuant to Rule of Civil Procedure 1.06, when a form is referred to by number, the reference is to the form with that number that is described in the Table of Forms at the end of these rules and which is available on the Internet through www.ontariocourtforms.on.ca. For your convenience, the government form as published on this website is reproduced below.]

ONTARIO

SUPERIOR COURT OF JUSTICE

IN THE ESTATE OF (insert name) , deceased.

AFFIDAVIT OF SERVICE OF NOTICE

I, *(insert name)* , of *(insert city or town and county or district of residence)* , make oath and say/affirm:

1. I am an applicant for a certificate of appointment of estate trustee without a will in the estate.

2. I have sent or caused to be sent a notice in Form 74.17, a copy of which is marked as Exhibit "A" to this affidavit, to all adult persons named in the notice (except to an applicant who is entitled to share in the distribution of the estate), to a parent or guardian of the minor an d to the Children's Lawyer if paragraph 3 of the notice applies, to the guardian or attorney if paragraph 4 applies and to the Public Guardian and Trustee if paragraph 5 applies, all by regular lettermail sent to the person's last known address.

3. The following persons may be entitled to be served but have not been served for the reasons shown below:

Name of person (if applicable)	**Reason not served**

If paragraph 3 does not apply insert "Not Applicable."

4. To the best of my knowledge and belief, subject to paragraph 3 (if applicable), the persons named in the notice are all the persons who are entitled to share in the distribution of the estate.

Sworn/Affirmed before me at the	)	
	)	
of	)	
	)	
in the	)	
	)	
of	)	____________________
	)	Signature of applicant
this .... day of ...., 20 ...	)	
	)	
	)	

____

A Commissioner for taking Affidavits
(or as may be)

November 1, 2005

FORM 74.17 — NOTICE OF AN APPLICATION FOR A CERTIFICATE OF APPOINTMENT OF ESTATE TRUSTEE WITHOUT A WILL

Courts of Justice Act

[Repealed O. Reg. 77/06, s. 3.]

[Editor's Note: Forms 4A to 78A of the Rules of Civil Procedure have been repealed by O. Reg. 77/06, effective July 1, 2006. Pursuant to Rule of Civil Procedure 1.06, when a form is referred to by number, the reference is to the form with that number that is described in the Table of Forms at the end of these rules and which is available on the Internet through www.ontariocourtforms.on.ca. For your convenience, the government form as published on this website is reproduced below.]

ONTARIO

SUPERIOR COURT OF JUSTICE

IN THE ESTATE OF *(insert name)* , deceased.

NOTICE OF AN APPLICATION FOR A CERTIFICATE OF APPOINTMENT OF ESTATE TRUSTEE WITHOUT A WILL

1. The deceased died on *(insert date)* , without a will.

2. The applicant named in this notice is applying for a certificate of appointment of estate trustee without a will.

APPLICANT

Name	**Address**

3. The following persons who are less than 18 years of age are entitled to share in the distribution of the estate:

Name	**Date of Birth** *(day, month, year)*	**Name and Address of Parent or Guardian**	**Estimated Value of Interest in Estate**

Notes:

* Note: *The Estimated Value of Interest in Estate may be omitted in the form if it is included in a separate schedule attached to the notice sent to the Children's Lawyer.*

4. The following persons who are mentally incapable within the meaning of section 6 of the *Substitute Decisions Act, 1992* in respect of an issue in the proceeding, and who have guardians or attorneys acting under powers of attorney with authority to act in the proceeding, are entitled to share in the distribution of the estate:

Name and Address of Person	**Name and Address of Guardian or Attorney***

Notes:

* *Specify whether guardian or attorney.*

5. The following persons who are mentally incapable within the meaning of section 6 of the *Substitute Decisions Act, 1992* in respect of an issue in the proceeding, and who do not have guardians or attorneys acting under powers of attorney with authority to act in the proceeding, are enti tled to share in the distribution of the estate:

Name and Address of Person	**Estimated Value of Interest in Estate**

Notes:

* Note: *The Estimated Value of Interest in Estate may be omitted in the form if it is included in a separate schedule attached to the notice sent to the Public Guardian and Trustee.*

6. All other persons entitled to share in the distribution of the estate are as follows:

Name	**Address**

7. This notice is being sent, by regular lettermail, to all adult persons named above in this notice (except to an applicant who is entitled to share in the distribution of the estate), to a parent or guardian of the minor and to the Children's Lawyer if paragraph 3 applies, to the guardian or at torney if paragraph 4 applies, and to the Public Guardian and Trustee if paragraph 5 applies.

8. The following persons may be entitled to be served but have not been served for the reasons shown below:

Name of person	**Reason not served**

If paragraph 8 does not apply insert "Not Applicable."

DATE

November 1, 2005

FORM 74.18 — RENUNCIATION OF PRIOR RIGHT TO A CERTIFICATE OF APPOINTMENT OF ESTATE TRUSTEE WITHOUT A WILL

Courts of Justice Act

[Repealed O. Reg. 77/06, s. 3.]

[Editor's Note: Forms 4A to 78A of the Rules of Civil Procedure have been repealed by O. Reg. 77/06, effective July 1, 2006. Pursuant to Rule of Civil Procedure 1.06, when a form is referred to by number, the reference is to the form with that number that is described in the Table of Forms at the end of these rules and which is available on the Internet through www.ontariocourtforms.on.ca. For your convenience, the government form as published on this website is reproduced below.]

ONTARIO
SUPERIOR COURT OF JUSTICE

IN THE ESTATE OF (*insert name*) , deceased.

RENUNCIATION OF PRIOR RIGHT TO A CERTIFICATE OF APPOINTMENT OF ESTATE TRUSTEE WITHOUT A WILL

The deceased died on (*date*), without a will.

I, (*insert name*), am entitled to apply for a certificate of appointment of estate trustee without a will in priority to (*insert name*).

I renounce my right to a certificate of appointment of estate trustee without a will in priority to (*insert name*).

DATE)

)

)

)

)

)

) ....

....)

Signature of witness) Signature of person renouncing

November 1, 2005

FORM 74.19 — CONSENT TO APPLICANT'S APPOINTMENT AS ESTATE TRUSTEE WITHOUT A WILL

Courts of Justice Act

[Repealed O. Reg. 77/06, s. 3.]

[Editor's Note: Forms 4A to 78A of the Rules of Civil Procedure have been repealed by O. Reg. 77/06, effective July 1, 2006. Pursuant to Rule of Civil Procedure 1.06, when a form is referred to by number, the reference is to the form with that number that is described in the Table of Forms at the end of these rules and which is available on the Internet through www.ontariocourtforms.on.ca. For your convenience, the government form as published on this website is reproduced below.]

ONTARIO
SUPERIOR COURT OF JUSTICE

IN THE ESTATE OF (*insert name*), deceased.

CONSENT TO APPLICANT'S APPOINTMENT AS ESTATE TRUSTEE WITHOUT A WILL

The deceased died on (*date*), without a will.

I, (*insert name*), am entitled to share in the distribution of the estate.

I consent to the application by (*insert name*) for a certificate of appointment of estate trustee without a will.

I consent to an order dispensing with the filing of a bond by the applicant (*delete if inapplicable*).

DATE)

)

	)	
	)	
	)	
	)	
....	)	....
Signature of witness	)	Signature of person consenting

November 1, 2005

FORM 74.20 — CERTIFICATE OF APPOINTMENT OF ESTATE TRUSTEE WITHOUT A WILL

Courts of Justice Act

[Repealed O. Reg. 77/06, s. 3.]

[Editor's Note: Forms 4A to 78A of the Rules of Civil Procedure have been repealed by O. Reg. 77/06, effective July 1, 2006. Pursuant to Rule of Civil Procedure 1.06, when a form is referred to by number, the reference is to the form with that number that is described in the Table of Forms at the end of these rules and which is available on the Internet through www.ontariocourtforms.on.ca. For your convenience, the government form as published on this website is reproduced below.]

Court file no.

ONTARIO
SUPERIOR COURT OF JUSTICE

IN THE ESTATE OF , deceased,

late of

occupation

who died on

CERTIFICATE OF APPOINTMENT
OF ESTATE TRUSTEE WITHOUT A WILL

Applicant	Address	Occupation

This CERTIFICATE OF APPOINTMENT OF ESTATE TRUSTEE WITHOUT A WILL is hereby issued under the seal of the court to the applicant named above.

DATE ....

Registrar

Address of court office

November 1, 2005

FORM 74.20.1 — APPLICATION FOR CERTIFICATE OF APPOINTMENT OF A FOREIGN ESTATE TRUSTEE'S NOMINEE AS ESTATE TRUSTEE WITHOUT A WILL

Courts of Justice Act

[Repealed O. Reg. 77/06, s. 3.]

[Editor's Note: Forms 4A to 78A of the Rules of Civil Procedure have been repealed by O. Reg. 77/06, effective July 1, 2006. Pursuant to Rule of Civil Procedure 1.06, when a form is referred to by number, the reference is to the form with that number that is described in the Table of Forms at the end of these rules and which is available on the Internet through www.ontariocourtforms.on.ca. For your convenience, the government form as published on this website is reproduced below.]

ONTARIO

APPLICATION FOR CERTIFICATE OF APPOINTMENT
OF A FOREIGN ESTATE TRUSTEE'S NOMINEE AS
ESTATE TRUSTEE WITHOUT A WILL

SUPERIOR COURT OF JUSTICE

(Form 74.20.1 Under the Rules)

at

This application is filed by *(insert name)*

DETAILS ABOUT THE DECEASED PERSON

Complete in full as applicable

First given name	Second given name	Third given name	Surname

And if the deceased was known by any other name(s), state below the full name(s) used including surname.

First given name	Second given name	Third given name	Surname

Date of birth of the deceased person, if known: (day, month, year)

Address (street or postal address) (city or town) (province or state) (country)

Place of death (city or town; country)	*Date of death (day, month, year)*

Country of domicile

PARTICULARS OF FOREIGN CERTIFICATE

Country (and province or state if applicable) where issued	*Issuing court*	*Date issued (day, month, year)*
TOTAL VALUE OF ASSETS OF ESTATE		*Total* $

VALUE OF ASSETS LOCATED IN ONTARIO

Personal property	**Real estate, net of encumbrances**	**Total**
$	$	$

AFFIDAVIT(S) OF APPLICANT(S)
(ATTACH A SEPARATE SHEET FOR ADDITIONAL AFFIDAVITS, IF NECESSARY.)

I, an applicant named in this application, make oath and say/affirm:

1. I am the nominee of the foreign estate trustee appointed in the jurisdiction where the deceased was domiciled at the date of death.

2. A copy of the document appointing the foreign estate trustee, certified by the court that issued it, is marked as Exhibit "A" to this affidavit.

3. I am 18 years of age or older.

4. I will faithfully administer the deceased person's property according to law and render a complete and true account of my administration when lawfully required.

5. The information contained in this application and in any attached schedules is true, to the best of my knowledge and belief.

Name (surname and forename(s))		*Occupation*	
Address (street or postal address)	*(city or town)*	*(province)*	*(postal code)*

Sworn/Affirmed before me at the
....
of ....
in the ....
of ....
this .... day of ...., 20.......... Signature of applicant

....
A Commissioner for taking Affidavits *(or as may be)*

Name (surname and forename(s))		*Occupation*	
Address (street or postal address)	*(city or town)*	*(province)*	*(postal code)*

Sworn/Affirmed before me at the
....
of ....
in the ....
of ....
this .... day of ...., 20.......... Signature of applicant

....
A Commissioner for taking Affidavits *(or as may be)*

Notice to applicant: Information provided on this form related to the payment of estate administration tax may be forwarded to the Ministry of Finance pursuant to clause 39(1)(b) and 42(1)(c) of the *Freedom of Information and Protection of Privacy Act*. This includes the name of the deceased, name and address of estate trustee(s), value of the estate and any undertakings and tax payments made or refunded. This information will be used by the Ministry of Finance to determine the value of estates and the amount of estate administration tax payable. Questions about the collection of this information should be directed to the Senior Manager — Audit, Advisory and Compliance Branch, 33 King Street West, PO Box 625, Oshawa ON L1H 8H9, 1-866-668-8297.

February 1, 2015

FORM 74.20.2 — NOMINATION OF APPLICANT BY FOREIGN ESTATE TRUSTEE

Courts of Justice Act

[Repealed O. Reg. 77/06, s. 3.]

[Editor's Note: Forms 4A to 78A of the Rules of Civil Procedure have been repealed by O. Reg. 77/06, effective July 1, 2006. Pursuant to Rule of Civil Procedure 1.06, when a form is referred to by number, the reference is to the form with that number that is described in the Table of Forms at the end of these rules and which is available on the Internet through www.ontariocourtforms.on.ca. For your convenience, the government form as published on this website is reproduced below.]

ONTARIO
SUPERIOR COURT OF JUSTICE

IN THE ESTATE OF.......................... (insert name), deceased.

NOMINATION OF APPLICANT BY FOREIGN ESTATE TRUSTEE

1. The deceased died on (*insert date*), without a will.

2. I, ... was appointed estate trustee by the ...., in the jurisdiction where the deceased was domiciled at the date of death, on the .... day of .... 20 .

3. I nominate .... to apply in Ontario for a certificate of estate trustee without a will.

DATE:

....	....
Signature of witness	Signature of person nominating

November 1, 2005

FORM 74.20.3 — CERTIFICATE OF APPOINTMENT OF FOREIGN ESTATE TRUSTEE'S NOMINEE AS ESTATE TRUSTEE WITHOUT A WILL

Courts of Justice Act

[Repealed O. Reg. 77/06, s. 3.]

[Editor's Note: Forms 4A to 78A of the Rules of Civil Procedure have been repealed by O. Reg. 77/06, effective July 1, 2006. Pursuant to Rule of Civil Procedure 1.06, when a form is referred to by number, the reference is to the form with that number that is described in the Table of Forms at the end of these rules and which is available on the Internet through www.ontariocourtforms.on.ca. For your convenience, the government form as published on this website is reproduced below.]

Court file no.

ONTARIO
SUPERIOR COURT OF JUSTICE

IN THE ESTATE OF , deceased,

late of

occupation

who died on

CERTIFICATE OF APPOINTMENT OF FOREIGN ESTATE TRUSTEE'S NOMINEE AS ESTATE TRUSTEE WITHOUT A WILL

Applicant	Address	Occupation

This CERTIFICATE OF APPOINTMENT OF FOREIGN ESTATE TRUSTEE'S NOMINEE AS ESTATE TRUSTEE WITHOUT A WILL is hereby issued under the seal of the court to the applicant named above.

DATE ....
Registrar

Address of court office

November 1, 2005

FORM 74.21 — APPLICATION FOR CERTIFICATE OF APPOINTMENT AS SUCCEEDING ESTATE TRUSTEE WITH A WILL

Courts of Justice Act

[Repealed O. Reg. 77/06, s. 3.]

[Editor's Note: Forms 4A to 78A of the Rules of Civil Procedure have been repealed by O. Reg. 77/06, effective July 1, 2006. Pursuant to Rule of Civil Procedure 1.06, when a form is referred to by number, the reference is to the form with that number that is described in the Table of Forms at the end of these rules and which is available on the Internet through www.ontariocourtforms.on.ca. For your convenience, the government form as published on this website is reproduced below.]

ONTARIO

APPLICATION FOR CERTIFICATE OF APPOINTMENT AS SUCCEEDING ESTATE TRUSTEE WITH A WILL

SUPERIOR COURT OF JUSTICE

at

This application is filed by *(insert name and address)*

DETAILS ABOUT THE DECEASED PERSON

Complete in full as applicable

First given name	Second given name	Third given name	Surname

And if the deceased was known by any other name(s), state below the full name(s) used including surname.

First given name	Second given name	Third given name	Surname

PARTICULARS OF FIRST CERTIFICATE

Name(s) of estate trustee(s)	**Date issued** (*day, month, year*)

VALUE OF UNDISTRIBUTED ASSETS OF ESTATE

Personal property	Real estate, net of encumbrances	Total
$	$	$

Explain why the applicant is entitled to apply.

AFFIDAVIT(S) OF APPLICANT(S)

(*Attach a separate sheet for additional affidavits, if necessary.*)

I, a trust officer named in this application, make oath and say/affirm:

1. I am a trust officer of the corporate applicant.

2. I am 18 years of age or older.

3. The corporate applicant will faithfully administer the deceased person's property according to law and render a complete and true account of its administration when lawfully required.

4. If the corporate applicant is not named as estate trustee in the will or codicil, consents of persons who together have a majority interest in the value of the undistributed assets of the estate at the date of this application are attached.

5. The information contained in this application and in any attached schedules is true, to the best of my knowledge and belief.

Name of corporate applicant	Name of trust officer	
Address of corporate applicant *(street or postal address) (city or town)*	*(province)*	*(postal code)*

Sworn/Affirmed before me at the . . .
of . . . .
in the . . . .
of . . . .

Signature of trust officer

this . . . . day of . . . ., 20 . .
.

A Commissioner for taking Affidavits
(or as may be)

I, an applicant named in this application, make oath and say/affirm:

1. I am 18 years of age or older.

2. I will faithfully administer the deceased person's property according to law and render a complete and true account of my administration when lawfully required.

3. If I am not named as estate trustee in the will or codicil, consents of persons who together have a majority interest in the value of the undistributed assets of the estate at the date of this application are attached.

4. The information contained in this application and in any attached schedules is true, to the best of my knowledge and belief.

Name *(surname and forename(s))*	Occupation	
Address*(street or postal address) (city or town)*	*(province)*	*(postal code)*

Sworn/Affirmed before me at the . . . .
of . . . .
in the . . . .
of . . . .

Signature of applicant

this . . . . day of . . . ., 20 . . .

A Commissioner for taking Affidavits
(or as may be)

November 1, 2005

FORM 74.21.1 — APPLICATION FOR CERTIFICATE OF APPOINTMENT AS SUCCEEDING ESTATE TRUSTEE WITH A WILL LIMITED TO THE ASSETS REFERRED TO IN THE WILL

Courts of Justice Act

[Repealed O. Reg. 77/06, s. 3.]

[Editor's Note: Forms 4A to 78A of the Rules of Civil Procedure have been repealed by O. Reg. 77/06, effective July 1, 2006. Pursuant to Rule of Civil Procedure 1.06, when a form is referred to by number, the reference is to the form with that number that is described in the Table of Forms at the end of these rules and which is available on the Internet through www.ontariocourtforms.on.ca. For your convenience, the government form as published on this website is reproduced below.]

ONTARIO

SUPERIOR COURT OF JUSTICE

APPLICATION FOR CERTIFICATE OF APPOINTMENT AS SUCCEEDING ESTATE TRUSTEE WITH A WILL LIMITED TO THE ASSETS REFERRED TO IN THE WILL
(Form 74.21.1 Under the Rules)

at

This application is filed by *(insert name and address)*

DETAILS ABOUT THE DECEASED PERSON

Complete in full as applicable

First given name	Second given name	Third given name	Surname

And if the deceased was known by any other name(s), state below the full name(s) used including surname.

First given name	Second given name	Third given name	Surname

Date of birth of the deceased person, if known: (day, month, year)

PARTICULARS OF FIRST CERTIFICATE

Name(s) of estate trustee(s)	*Date issued (day, month, year)*

VALUE OF UNDISTRIBUTED ASSETS OF ESTATE

Personal property	**Real estate, net of encumbrances**	**Total**
$	**$**	**$**

Explain why the applicant is entitled to apply.

AFFIDAVIT(S) OF APPLICANT(S)
(ATTACH A SEPARATE SHEET FOR ADDITIONAL AFFIDAVITS, IF NECESSARY.)

I, a trust officer named in this application, make oath and say/affirm:

1. I am a trust officer of the corporate applicant.

2. I am 18 years of age or older.

3. The corporate applicant will faithfully administer the deceased person's property according to law and render a complete and true account of its administration when lawfully required.

4. If the corporate applicant is not named as estate trustee in the will or codicil, consents of persons who together have a majority interest in the value of the undistributed assets of the estate at the date of this application are attached.

5. The information contained in this application and in any attached schedules is true, to the best of my knowledge and belief.

Name of corporate applicant	*Name of trust officer*		
Address of corporate applicant (street or postal address)	*(city or town)*	*(province)*	*(postal code)*

Sworn/Affirmed before me at the
....
of ....

in the ....
of ....
this .... day of ...., 20..........

....
Signature of trust officer

....
A Commissioner for taking Affidavits *(or as may be)*

I, an applicant named in this application, make oath and say/affirm:

1. I am 18 years of age or older.

2. I will faithfully administer the deceased person's property according to law and render a complete and true account of my administration when lawfully required.

3. If I am not named as estate trustee in the will or codicil, consents of persons who together have a majority interest in the value of the undistributed assets of the estate at the date of this application are attached.

4. The information contained in this application and in any attached schedules is true, to the best of my knowledge and belief.

Name (surname and forename(s))		*Occupation*	
Address (street or postal address)	*(city or town)*	*(province)*	*(postal code)*

Sworn/Affirmed before me at the
....
of ....
in the ....
of ....
this .... day of ...., 20..........

....
Signature of applicant

....
A Commissioner for taking Affidavits *(or as may be)*

April 11, 2012

FORM 74.22 — CONSENT TO APPLICANT'S APPOINTMENT AS SUCCEEDING ESTATE TRUSTEE WITH A WILL

Courts of Justice Act

[Repealed O. Reg. 77/06, s. 3.]

[Editor's Note: Forms 4A to 78A of the Rules of Civil Procedure have been repealed by O. Reg. 77/06, effective July 1, 2006. Pursuant to Rule of Civil Procedure 1.06, when a form is referred to by number, the reference is to the form with that number that is described in the Table of Forms at the end of these rules and which is available on the Internet through www.ontariocourtforms.on.ca. For your convenience, the government form as published on this website is reproduced below.]

ONTARIO
SUPERIOR COURT OF JUSTICE

IN THE ESTATE OF (*insert name*), deceased.

CONSENT TO APPLICANT'S APPOINTMENT AS SUCCEEDING ESTATE TRUSTEE WITH A WILL

The deceased died on (*date*).

I, (*insert name*), am entitled to share in the distribution of the remaining estate.

I consent to the application by (*insert name*) for a certificate of appointment of succeeding estate trustee with a will.

I consent to an order dispensing with the filing of a bond by the applicant (*delete if inapplicable*).

DATE:	)	
	)	
	)	
	)	
	)	
. . . .	)	. . . .
Signature of witness	)	Signature of person consenting

November 1, 2005

FORM 74.22.1 — CONSENT TO APPLICANT'S APPOINTMENT AS SUCCEEDING ESTATE TRUSTEE WITH A WILL LIMITED TO THE ASSETS REFERRED TO IN THE WILL

Courts of Justice Act

[Repealed O. Reg. 77/06, s. 3.]

[Editor's Note: Forms 4A to 78A of the Rules of Civil Procedure have been repealed by O. Reg. 77/06, effective July 1, 2006. Pursuant to Rule of Civil Procedure 1.06, when a form is referred to by number, the reference is to the form with that number that is described in the Table of Forms at the end of these rules and which is available on the Internet through

www.ontariocourtforms.on.ca. For your convenience, the government form as published on this website is reproduced below.]

ONTARIO

SUPERIOR COURT OF JUSTICE

IN THE ESTATE OF *(insert name)*, deceased.

CONSENT TO APPLICANT'S APPOINTMENT AS SUCCEEDING ESTATE TRUSTEE WITH A WILL LIMITED TO THE ASSETS REFERRED TO IN THE WILL

The deceased died on *(date)*.

I, *(insert name)*, am entitled to share in the distribution of the remaining estate.

I consent to the application by (*insert name)* for a certificate of appointment of succeeding estate trustee with a will limited to the assets referred to in the will.

I consent to an order dispensing with the filing of a bond by the applicant *(delete if inapplicable)*.

DATE

....	)	....
Signature of witness	)	Signature of person consenting

April 11, 2012

FORM 74.23 — CERTIFICATE OF APPOINTMENT OF SUCCEEDING ESTATE TRUSTEE WITH A WILL

Courts of Justice Act

[Repealed O. Reg. 77/06, s. 3.]

[Editor's Note: Forms 4A to 78A of the Rules of Civil Procedure have been repealed by O. Reg. 77/06, effective July 1, 2006. Pursuant to Rule of Civil Procedure 1.06, when a form is referred to by number, the reference is to the form with that number that is described in the

Table of Forms at the end of these rules and which is available on the Internet through www.ontariocourtforms.on.ca. For your convenience, the government form as published on this website is reproduced below.]

Court file no.

ONTARIO
SUPERIOR COURT OF JUSTICE

IN THE ESTATE OF , deceased,

late of

occupation

who died on

CERTIFICATE OF APPOINTMENT OF SUCCEEDING ESTATE TRUSTEE WITH A WILL

Applicant	Address	Occupation

This CERTIFICATE OF APPOINTMENT OF SUCCEEDING ESTATE TRUSTEE WITH A WILL is hereby issued under the seal of the court to the applicant named above. Attached to this certificate is a copy of the deceased's last will dated .... (and codicil(s) dated ....).

DATE ....
Registrar
Address of court office

February 1, 2015

FORM 74.23.1 — CERTIFICATE OF APPOINTMENT OF SUCCEEDING ESTATE TRUSTEE WITH A WILL LIMITED TO THE ASSETS REFERRED TO IN THE WILL

Courts of Justice Act

[Repealed O. Reg. 77/06, s. 3.]

[Editor's Note: Forms 4A to 78A of the Rules of Civil Procedure have been repealed by O. Reg. 77/06, effective July 1, 2006. Pursuant to Rule of Civil Procedure 1.06, when a form is referred to by number, the reference is to the form with that number that is described in the Table of Forms at the end of these rules and which is available on the Internet through

www.ontariocourtforms.on.ca. For your convenience, the government form as published on this website is reproduced below.]

ONTARIO

SUPERIOR COURT OF JUSTICE

IN THE ESTATE OF , deceased,

late of

occupation

who died on

CERTIFICATE OF APPOINTMENT OF SUCCEEDING ESTATE TRUSTEE WITH A WILL LIMITED TO THE ASSETS REFERRED TO IN THE WILL

Applicant: .... Address: .... Occupation: ....

By order of a judge of the Superior Court of Justice this grant of a certificate of appointment of estate trustee with a will is limited to the assets referred to in the will dated .... (and codicils dated ....). A copy of the will (and codicils) is attached. This will is the last will of the deceased dealing with those assets.

This CERTIFICATE OF APPOINTMENT OF SUCCEEDING ESTATE TRUSTEE WITH A WILL LIMITED TO THE ASSETS REFERRED TO IN THE WILL is hereby issued under the seal of the court to the applicant named above.

DATE: ....

....

Registrar

Address of court office

February 1, 2015

FORM 74.24 — APPLICATION FOR CERTIFICATE OF APPOINTMENT AS SUCCEEDING ESTATE TRUSTEE WITHOUT A WILL

Courts of Justice Act

[Repealed O. Reg. 77/06, s. 3.]

[Editor's Note: Forms 4A to 78A of the Rules of Civil Procedure have been repealed by O. Reg. 77/06, effective July 1, 2006. Pursuant to Rule of Civil Procedure 1.06, when a form is referred to by number, the reference is to the form with that number that is described in the Table of Forms at the end of these rules and which is available on the Internet through

www.ontariocourtforms.on.ca. For your convenience, the government form as published on this website is reproduced below.]

ONTARIO

APPLICATION FOR CERTIFICATE OF APPOINTMENT AS SUCCEEDING ESTATE TRUSTEE WITHOUT A WILL

SUPERIOR COURT OF JUSTICE

at

This application is filed by *(insert name and address)*

DETAILS ABOUT THE DECEASED PERSON

Complete in full as applicable

First given name	Second given name	Third given name	Surname

And if the deceased was known by any other name(s), state below the full name(s) used including surname.

First given name	Second given name	Third given name	Surname

PARTICULARS OF FIRST CERTIFICATE

Name(s) of estate trustee(s) or administrator(s)	Date issued *(day, month, year)*

PERSONS ENTITLED TO SHARE IN THE ESTATE (AT DATE OF THIS APPLICATION)

(Attach a schedule if more space is needed. If a person entitled to share in the estate is not a spouse, child, parent, brother or sister of the deceased person, show how the relationship is traced.)

Name	**Address**	**Relationship to deceased person**	**Age (if under 18)**

VALUE OF UNDISTRIBUTED ASSETS OF ESTATE

Personal property	**Real estate, net of encumbrances**	**Total**
$	$	$

Explain why the applicant is entitled to apply.

AFFIDAVIT(S) OF APPLICANT(S)

(Attach a separate sheet for additional affidavits, if necessary.)

I, a trust officer named in this application, make oath and say/affirm:

1. I am a trust officer of the corporate applicant.

2. I am 18 years of age or older.

3. The corporate applicant will faithfully administer the deceased person's property according to law and render a complete and true account of its administration when lawfully required.

4. Consents of persons who together have a majority interest in the value of the undistributed assets of the estate at the date of this application are attached.

5. The information contained in this application and in any attached schedules is true, to the best of my knowledge and belief.

Name of corporate applicant	Name of trust officer	
Address of corporate applicant *(street or postal address) (city or town)*	*(province)*	*(postal code)*

Sworn/Affirmed before me at the . . .
of . . . .
in the . . . .
of . . . .

this . . . . day of . . . ., 20 . . .

Signature of trust officer

A Commissioner for taking Affidavits
(or as may be)

I, an applicant named in this application, make oath and say/affirm:

1. I am 18 years of age or older and a resident of Ontario.

2. I will faithfully administer the deceased person's property according to law and render a complete and true account of my administration when lawfully required.

3. Consents of persons who together have a majority interest in the value of the undistributed assets of the estate at the date of this application are attached.

4. The information contained in this application and in any attached schedules is true, to the best of my knowledge and belief.

Name (surname and forename(s))	Occupation
Address*(street or postal address) (city or town)*	*(province)* *(postal code)*

Sworn/Affirmed before me at the ......
of ....
in the ....
of ....

Signature of applicant

this .... day of ...., 20 ...

A Commissioner for taking Affidavits
(or as may be)

November 1, 2005

FORM 74.25 — CONSENT TO APPLICANT'S APPOINTMENT AS SUCCEEDING ESTATE TRUSTEE WITHOUT A WILL

Courts of Justice Act

[Repealed O. Reg. 77/06, s. 3.]

[Editor's Note: Forms 4A to 78A of the Rules of Civil Procedure have been repealed by O. Reg. 77/06, effective July 1, 2006. Pursuant to Rule of Civil Procedure 1.06, when a form is referred to by number, the reference is to the form with that number that is described in the Table of Forms at the end of these rules and which is available on the Internet through www.ontariocourtforms.on.ca. For your convenience, the government form as published on this website is reproduced below.]

ONTARIO
SUPERIOR COURT OF JUSTICE

IN THE ESTATE OF (*insert name*), deceased.

CONSENT TO APPLICANT'S APPOINTMENT AS SUCCEEDING ESTATE TRUSTEE WITHOUT A WILL

The deceased died on (*date*), without a will.

I, (*insert name*), am entitled to share in the distribution of the estate.

I consent to the application by (*insert name*) for a certificate of appointment of succeeding estate trustee without a will.

I consent to an order dispensing with the filing of a bond by the applicant (*delete if inapplicable*).

DATE:	)	
	)	
	)	
	)	
	)	
....	)	....
Signature of witness	)	Signature of person consenting

November 1, 2005

FORM 74.26 — CERTIFICATE OF APPOINTMENT OF SUCCEEDING ESTATE TRUSTEE WITHOUT A WILL

Courts of Justice Act

[Repealed O. Reg. 77/06, s. 3.]

[Editor's Note: Forms 4A to 78A of the Rules of Civil Procedure have been repealed by O. Reg. 77/06, effective July 1, 2006. Pursuant to Rule of Civil Procedure 1.06, when a form is referred to by number, the reference is to the form with that number that is described in the Table of Forms at the end of these rules and which is available on the Internet through www.ontariocourtforms.on.ca. For your convenience, the government form as published on this website is reproduced below.]

Court file no.

ONTARIO
SUPERIOR COURT OF JUSTICE

IN THE ESTATE OF , deceased,

late of

occupation

who died on

CERTIFICATE OF APPOINTMENT
OF SUCCEEDING ESTATE TRUSTEE WITHOUT A WILL

Applicant Address Occupation

This CERTIFICATE OF APPOINTMENT OF SUCCEEDING ESTATE TRUSTEE WITHOUT A WILL is hereby issued under the seal of the court to the applicant named above.

DATE

. . . .
Registrar

Address of court office

November 1, 2005

FORM 74.27 — APPLICATION FOR CONFIRMATION BY RESEALING OF APPOINTMENT OR CERTIFICATE OF ANCILLARY APPOINTMENT OF ESTATE TRUSTEE

Courts of Justice Act

[Repealed O. Reg. 77/06, s. 3.]

[Editor's Note: Forms 4A to 78A of the Rules of Civil Procedure have been repealed by O. Reg. 77/06, effective July 1, 2006. Pursuant to Rule of Civil Procedure 1.06, when a form is referred to by number, the reference is to the form with that number that is described in the Table of Forms at the end of these rules and which is available on the Internet through www.ontariocourtforms.on.ca. For your convenience, the government form as published on this website is reproduced below.]

ONTARIO

APPLICATION FOR CONFIRMATION BY RESEALING OF APPOINTMENT OR CERTIFICATE OF ANCILLARY APPOINTMENT OF ESTATE TRUSTEE

SUPERIOR COURT OF JUSTICE

(Form 74.27 Under the Rules)

at

This is an application for *(check one)*

❑ confirmation by resealing of the appointment of an estate trustee with *(or without)* a will.

❑ a certificate of ancillary appointment of an estate trustee with a will.

This application is filed by *(insert name)*

DETAILS ABOUT THE DECEASED PERSON

Complete in full as applicable

First given name	Second given name	Third given name	Surname

And if the deceased was known by any other name(s), state below the full name(s) used including surname.

First given name	Second given name	Third given name	Surname

Address (street or postal address) .... *(city or town)* .... *(province or state)* .... *(country)* ....

Place of death (city or town; country)	*Date of death (day, month, year)*

PARTICULARS OF PRIMARY CERTIFICATE OR GRANT

Country (and province or state if applicable) where issued	*Issuing court*	*Date issued (day, month, year)*

VALUE OF ASSETS LOCATED IN ONTARIO

Personal property	**Real estate, net of encumbrances**	**Total**
$	$	$

AFFIDAVIT(S) OF APPLICANT(S)
(ATTACH A SEPARATE SHEET FOR ADDITIONAL AFFIDAVITS, IF NECESSARY.)

I, an applicant named in this application, make oath and say/affirm:

1. I am an estate trustee named in the primary certificate (or primary grant of letters probate or letters of administration), a copy of which, certified by the court that issued it, is Exhibit "A" to this affidavit.

2. I am 18 years of age or older.

3. I will faithfully administer the deceased person's property according to law and render a complete and true account of my administration when lawfully required.

4. The primary certificate (or primary grant of letters probate or letters of administration) is still effective.

5. The information contained in this application and in any attached schedules is true, to the best of my knowledge and belief.

Name (surname and forename(s))		*Occupation*	
Address (street or postal address)	*(city or town)*	*(province)*	*(postal code)*

Sworn/Affirmed before me at the
....
of ....
in the ....
of ....
this .... day of ...., 20..........

....
Signature of applicant

....
A Commissioner for taking Affidavits *(or as may be)*

Notice to applicant: Information provided on this form related to the payment of estate administration tax may be forwarded to the Ministry of Finance pursuant to clause 39(1)(b) and 42(1)(c) of the *Freedom of Information and Protection of Privacy Act*. This includes the name of the deceased, name and address of estate trustee(s), value of the estate and any undertakings and tax payments made or refunded. This information will be used by the Ministry of Finance to determine the value of estates and the amount of estate administration tax payable. Questions about the collection of this information should be directed to the Senior Manager — Audit, Advisory and Compliance Branch, 33 King Street West, PO Box 625, Oshawa ON L1H 8H9, 1-866-668-8297.

February 1, 2015

FORM 74.28 — CONFIRMATION BY RESEALING OF APPOINTMENT OF ESTATE TRUSTEE

Courts of Justice Act

[Repealed O. Reg. 77/06, s. 3.]

[Editor's Note: Forms 4A to 78A of the Rules of Civil Procedure have been repealed by O. Reg. 77/06, effective July 1, 2006. Pursuant to Rule of Civil Procedure 1.06, when a form is referred to by number, the reference is to the form with that number that is described in the Table of Forms at the end of these rules and which is available on the Internet through www.ontariocourtforms.on.ca. For your convenience, the government form as published on this website is reproduced below.]

ONTARIO
SUPERIOR COURT OF JUSTICE

IN THE ESTATE OF *(insert name)*, deceased.

CONFIRMATION BY RESEALING OF APPOINTMENT OF ESTATE TRUSTEE

Sealed with the seal of the Superior Court of Justice by order of that court dated *(insert date)*, under subsection 52(1) of the *Estates Act*.

DATE

....
Registrar
Address of court office

February 1, 2015

FORM 74.29 — CERTIFICATE OF ANCILLARY APPOINTMENT OF ESTATE TRUSTEE WITH A WILL

Courts of Justice Act

[Repealed O. Reg. 77/06, s. 3.]

[Editor's Note: Forms 4A to 78A of the Rules of Civil Procedure have been repealed by O. Reg. 77/06, effective July 1, 2006. Pursuant to Rule of Civil Procedure 1.06, when a form is referred to by number, the reference is to the form with that number that is described in the Table of Forms at the end of these rules and which is available on the Internet through www.ontariocourtforms.on.ca. For your convenience, the government form as published on this website is reproduced below.]

Court file no.

ONTARIO
SUPERIOR COURT OF JUSTICE

IN THE ESTATE OF , deceased,

late of

occupation

who died on

CERTIFICATE OF ANCILLARY APPOINTMENT
OF ESTATE TRUSTEE WITH A WILL

Applicant Address Occupation

Court of foreign grant

Date of foreign grant

This CERTIFICATE OF ANCILLARY APPOINTMENT OF ESTATE TRUSTEE WITH A WILL is hereby issued under the seal of the court to the applicant named above. A certified copy of the foreign grant, to which this certificate is ancillary, is attached.

DATE ....

Registrar

Address of court office

November 1, 2005

FORM 74.30 — APPLICATION FOR CERTIFICATE OF APPOINTMENT OF ESTATE TRUSTEE DURING LITIGATION

Courts of Justice Act

[Repealed O. Reg. 77/06, s. 3.]

[Editor's Note: Forms 4A to 78A of the Rules of Civil Procedure have been repealed by O. Reg. 77/06, effective July 1, 2006. Pursuant to Rule of Civil Procedure 1.06, when a form is referred to by number, the reference is to the form with that number that is described in the Table of Forms at the end of these rules and which is available on the Internet through www.ontariocourtforms.on.ca. For your convenience, the government form as published on this website is reproduced below.]

ONTARIO

APPLICATION FOR CERTIFICATE OF APPOINTMENT OF ESTATE TRUSTEE DURING LITIGATION

SUPERIOR COURT OF JUSTICE

(Form 74.30 Under the Rules)

at ____________________

This application is filed by *(insert name)*

____

DETAILS ABOUT THE DECEASED PERSON

Complete in full as applicable

First given name	Second given name	Third given name	Surname

And if the deceased was known by any other name(s), state below the full name(s) used including surname.

First given name	Second given name	Third given name	Surname

Date of birth of the deceased person, if known: (day, month, year)

Address of fixed place of abode (street or postal address) (city or town)	*(county or district)*

If the deceased person had no fixed place of abode in Ontario, did he or she have property in Ontario? ❑ No ❑ Yes	*Last occupation of deceased person*

Place of death (city or town; county or district)	*Date of death (day, month, year)*

VALUE OF ASSETS OF ESTATE

Do not include in the total amount: insurance payable to a named beneficiary or assigned for value, property held jointly and passing by survivorship, or real estate outside Ontario.

Personal property	**Real estate, net of encumbrances**	**Total**
$	$	$

This application is made pursuant to an order for the appointment of an estate trustee during litigation, made by

(name of judge)	*(day, month, year)*
	on

AFFIDAVIT(S) OF APPLICANT(S)
(ATTACH A SEPARATE SHEET FOR ADDITIONAL AFFIDAVITS, IF NECESSARY)

I, a trust officer named in this application, make oath and say/affirm:

1. I am a trust officer of the corporate applicant.
2. I am 18 years of age or older.

3. The corporate applicant will faithfully administer the deceased person's property according to law, make no distribution without a court order, and render a complete and true account of its administration when lawfully required.

4. The information contained in this application and in any attached schedules is true, to the best of my knowledge and belief.

Name of corporate applicant		*Name of trust officer*	
Address of corporate applicant (street or postal address)	*(city or town)*	*(province)*	*(postal code)*

Sworn/Affirmed before me at the
....
of ....
in the ....
of ....
this .... day of ...., 20.......... Signature of trust officer

....
A Commissioner for taking Affidavits *(or as may be)*

I, an applicant named in this application, make oath and say/affirm:

1. I am 18 years of age or older.

2. I will faithfully administer the deceased person's property according to law, make no distribution without a court order and render a complete and true account of my administration when lawfully required.

3. The information contained in this application and in any attached schedules is true, to the best of my knowledge and belief.

Name (surname and forename(s))		*Occupation*	
Address (street or postal address)	*(city or town)*	*(province)*	*(postal code)*

Sworn/Affirmed before me at the
....
of ....
in the ....
of ....
this .... day of ...., 20.......... Signature of applicant

....
A Commissioner for taking Affidavits *(or as may be)*

April 11, 2012

FORM 74.31 — CERTIFICATE OF APPOINTMENT OF ESTATE TRUSTEE DURING LITIGATION

Courts of Justice Act

[Repealed O. Reg. 77/06, s. 3.]

[Editor's Note: Forms 4A to 78A of the Rules of Civil Procedure have been repealed by O. Reg. 77/06, effective July 1, 2006. Pursuant to Rule of Civil Procedure 1.06, when a form is referred to by number, the reference is to the form with that number that is described in the Table of Forms at the end of these rules and which is available on the Internet through www.ontariocourtforms.on.ca. For your convenience, the government form as published on this website is reproduced below.]

Court file no.

ONTARIO
SUPERIOR COURT OF JUSTICE

IN THE ESTATE OF , deceased,

late of

occupation

who died on

CERTIFICATE OF APPOINTMENT
OF ESTATE TRUSTEE DURING LITIGATION

Applicant	Address	Occupation

By order of the Superior Court of Justice, this CERTIFICATE OF APPOINTMENT OF ESTATE TRUSTEE DURING LITIGATION to determine the validity of a testamentary document of the deceased is hereby issued under the seal of the court to the applicant named above.

DATE ....
Registrar

Address of court office

November 1, 2005

FORM 74.32 — BOND — INSURANCE OR GUARANTEE COMPANY

Courts of Justice Act

[Repealed O. Reg. 77/06, s. 3.]

[Editor's Note: Forms 4A to 78A of the Rules of Civil Procedure have been repealed by O. Reg. 77/06, effective July 1, 2006. Pursuant to Rule of Civil Procedure 1.06, when a form is referred to by number, the reference is to the form with that number that is described in the Table of Forms at the end of these rules and which is available on the Internet through www.ontariocourtforms.on.ca. For your convenience, the government form as published on this website is reproduced below.]

ONTARIO
SUPERIOR COURT OF JUSTICE

BOND NO. AMOUNT: $

IN THE ESTATE OF (*insert name*), deceased.
The principal in this bond is (*insert name*)

The surety in this bond is (*insert name*), an insurer licensed under the *Insurance Act* to write surety and fidelity insurance in Ontario.

The obligee in this bond is the Accountant of the Superior Court of Justice acting for the benefit of creditors and persons entitled to share in the estate of the deceased.

The principal and the surety bind themselves, their heirs, executors, successors and assigns jointly and severally to the Accountant of the Superior Court of Justice in the amount of .... Dollars ($ ....).

The principal as an estate trustee is required to prepare a complete and true inventory of all the property of the deceased, collect the assets of the estate, pay the debts of the estate, distribute the property of the deceased according to law, and render a complete and true accounting of these activities when lawfully required.

The primary obligation under this bond belongs to the principal. The principal is liable under this bond for any amount found by the court to be owing to any creditors of the estate and persons entitled to share in the estate to whom proper payment has not been made.

The surety, provided it has been given reasonable notice of any proceeding in which judgment may be given against the principal for failure to perform the obligations of this bond shall, on order of the court, and on default of the principal to pay any final judgment made against the principal in the proceeding, pay to the obligee the amount of any deficiency in the payment by the principal, but the surety shall not be liable to pay more than the amount of the bond.

The amount of this bond shall be reduced by and to the extent of any payment made under the bond pursuant to an order of the court.

The surety is entitled to an assignment of the rights of any person who receives payment or benefit from the proceeds of this bond, to the extent of such payment or benefit received.

DATE

SIGNED, SEALED AND DELIVERED
in the presence of:

	....
	Principal
....	....
	Surety

November 1, 2005

FORM 74.33 — BOND — PERSONAL SURETIES

Courts of Justice Act

[Repealed O. Reg. 77/06, s. 3.]

[Editor's Note: Forms 4A to 78A of the Rules of Civil Procedure have been repealed by O. Reg. 77/06, effective July 1, 2006. Pursuant to Rule of Civil Procedure 1.06, when a form is referred to by number, the reference is to the form with that number that is described in the Table of Forms at the end of these rules and which is available on the Internet through www.ontariocourtforms.on.ca. For your convenience, the government form as published on this website is reproduced below.]

ONTARIO
SUPERIOR COURT OF JUSTICE

BOND NO. AMOUNT: $

IN THE ESTATE OF (*insert name*), deceased.

The principal in this bond is (*insert name*)

The sureties in this bond are (*insert names*)

The obligee in this bond is the Accountant of the Superior Court of Justice acting for the benefit of creditors and persons entitled to share in the estate of the deceased.

The principal and the sureties bind themselves, their heirs, executors, successors and assigns jointly and severally to the Accountant of the Superior Court of Justice in the amount of .... Dollars ($ ....).

The principal as an estate trustee is required to prepare a complete and true inventory of all the property of the deceased, collect the assets of the estate, pay the debts of the estate, distribute the property of the deceased according to law, and render a complete and true accounting of these activities when lawfully required.

The primary obligation under this bond belongs to the principal. The principal is liable under this bond for any amount found by the court to be owing to any creditors of the estate and persons entitled to share in the estate to whom proper payment has not been made.

The sureties, provided they have been given reasonable notice of any proceeding in which judgment may be given against the principal for failure to perform the obligations of this bond shall, on order of the court, and on default of the principal to pay any final judgment made against the principal in the proceeding, pay to the obligee the amount of any deficiency in the payment by the principal, but the sureties shall not be liable to pay more than the amount of the bond.

The amount of this bond shall be reduced by and to the extent of any payment made under the bond pursuant to an order of the court.

The sureties are entitled to an assignment of the rights of any person who receives payment or benefit from the proceeds of this bond, to the extent of such payment or benefit received.

DATE

SIGNED, SEALED AND DELIVERED
in the presence of: ....

Principal

....

Surety

AFFIDAVIT OF SURETY

I, (*insert name*), of (*insert city or town and county or district, metropolitan or regional municipality of residence*), make oath and say/affirm:

I am a proposed surety on behalf of the intended estate trustees of the property of (*insert name*), deceased, named in the attached bond.

I am eighteen years of age or over and own property worth $ .... over and above all encumbrances, and over and above what will pay my just debts and every sum for which I am now bail or for which I am liable as surety or endorser or otherwise.

SWORN/AFFIRMED BEFORE)
me at the of)
in the of)
this day of , 20 .) ....
)
)
)
)

....
A Commissioner for Taking Affidavits
(*or as may be*)

AFFIDAVIT OF SURETY

I, (*insert name*), of (*insert city or town and county or district, metropolitan or regional municipality of residence*), make oath and say/affirm:

I am a proposed surety on behalf of the intended estate trustees of the property of (*insert name*), deceased, named in the attached bond.

I am eighteen years of age or over and own property worth $ .... over and above all encumbrances, and over and above what will pay my just debts and every sum for which I am now bail or for which I am liable as surety or endorser or otherwise.

SWORN/AFFIRMED BEFORE)
the at the of)
in the of)
this day of , 20 .) ....
)
)
)
)
....)

A Commissioner for Taking Affidavits
(*or as may be*)

November 1, 2005

FORM 74.34 — REGISTRAR'S NOTICE TO ESTATE TRUSTEE NAMED IN A DEPOSITED WILL OF APPLICATION FOR CERTIFICATE OF APPOINTMENT OF ESTATE TRUSTEE WITH A WILL

Courts of Justice Act

[Repealed O. Reg. 77/06, s. 3.]

[Editor's Note: Forms 4A to 78A of the Rules of Civil Procedure have been repealed by O. Reg. 77/06, effective July 1, 2006. Pursuant to Rule of Civil Procedure 1.06, when a form is referred to by number, the reference is to the form with that number that is described in the Table of Forms at the end of these rules and which is available on the Internet through www.ontariocourtforms.on.ca. For your convenience, the government form as published on this website is reproduced below.]

ONTARIO
SUPERIOR COURT OF JUSTICE

NOTICE

Attached are a copy of an application for appointment of an estate trustee with a will in the estate of (*insert name*), deceased, and a copy of a certificate of the Estate Registrar indicating that you were named as an estate trustee in a later will or codicil of the deceased that is on deposit in the Superior Court of Justice.

DATE . . . .

Registrar

Address of court office

TO:

November 1, 2005

FORM 74.35 — REGISTRAR'S NOTICE TO ESTATE TRUSTEE NAMED IN A DEPOSITED WILL OF APPLICATION FOR CERTIFICATE OF APPOINTMENT OF ESTATE TRUSTEE WITHOUT A WILL

Courts of Justice Act

[Repealed O. Reg. 77/06, s. 3.]

[Editor's Note: Forms 4A to 78A of the Rules of Civil Procedure have been repealed by O. Reg. 77/06, effective July 1, 2006. Pursuant to Rule of Civil Procedure 1.06, when a form is referred to by number, the reference is to the form with that number that is described in the Table of Forms at the end of these rules and which is available on the Internet through www.ontariocourtforms.on.ca. For your convenience, the government form as published on this website is reproduced below.]

ONTARIO
SUPERIOR COURT OF JUSTICE

NOTICE

Attached are a copy of an application for appointment of an estate trustee without a will in the estate of (*insert name*), deceased, and a copy of a certificate of the Estate Registrar indicating that you were named as an estate trustee in a will or codicil of the deceased that is on deposit in the Superior Court of Justice.

DATE . . . .

Registrar

Address of court office

TO:

November 1, 2005

FORM 74.36 — ORDER TO ACCEPT OR REFUSE APPOINTMENT AS ESTATE TRUSTEE WITH A WILL

Courts of Justice Act

[Repealed O. Reg. 77/06, s. 3.]

[Editor's Note: Forms 4A to 78A of the Rules of Civil Procedure have been repealed by O. Reg. 77/06, effective July 1, 2006. Pursuant to Rule of Civil Procedure 1.06, when a form is referred to by number, the reference is to the form with that number that is described in the Table of Forms at the end of these rules and which is available on the Internet through www.ontariocourtforms.on.ca. For your convenience, the government form as published on this website is reproduced below.]

(*Heading in accordance with Form 59A*)

IN THE ESTATE OF (*insert name*), deceased.

ORDER TO ACCEPT OR REFUSE APPOINTMENT AS ESTATE TRUSTEE WITH A WILL

A motion for this order has been made by (*insert name of moving party*). From an affidavit made by (*insert name of maker of affidavit*) that has been filed it appears that you are named as estate trustee in a will or codicil of the deceased dated (*insert date*).

1. THIS COURT ORDERS THAT you file an application for a certificate of appointment of estate trustee with a will in the court office within .... days after this order is served on you.

2. THIS COURT ORDERS THAT if you do not do so within that time, you shall be deemed to have renounced your right to be appointed.

. . . .

Registrar

Address of court office

TO:

November 1, 2005

FORM 74.37 — ORDER TO ACCEPT OR REFUSE APPOINTMENT AS ESTATE TRUSTEE WITHOUT A WILL

Courts of Justice Act

[Repealed O. Reg. 77/06, s. 3.]

[Editor's Note: Forms 4A to 78A of the Rules of Civil Procedure have been repealed by O. Reg. 77/06, effective July 1, 2006. Pursuant to Rule of Civil Procedure 1.06, when a form is referred to by number, the reference is to the form with that number that is described in the Table of Forms at the end of these rules and which is available on the Internet through www.ontariocourtforms.on.ca. For your convenience, the government form as published on this website is reproduced below.]

(*Heading in accordance with Form 59A*)

IN THE ESTATE OF (*insert name*), deceased.

ORDER TO ACCEPT OR REFUSE APPOINTMENT AS ESTATE TRUSTEE WITHOUT A WILL

A motion for this order has been made by (*insert name of moving party*). From an affidavit made by (*insert name of maker of affidavit*) that has been filed it appears that you may have a prior right to be appointed estate trustee without a will in the deceased's estate.

1. THIS COURT ORDERS THAT you file an application for a certificate of appointment of estate trustee without a will in the court office within .... days after this order is served on you.

2. THIS COURT ORDERS THAT if you do not do so within that time, you shall be deemed to have renounced your right to be appointed.

....

Registrar

Address of court office

TO:

November 1, 2005

FORM 74.38 — ORDER TO CONSENT OR OBJECT TO A PROPOSED APPOINTMENT OF AN ESTATE TRUSTEE WITH OR WITHOUT A WILL

Courts of Justice Act

[Repealed O. Reg. 77/06, s. 3.]

[Editor's Note: Forms 4A to 78A of the Rules of Civil Procedure have been repealed by O. Reg. 77/06, effective July 1, 2006. Pursuant to Rule of Civil Procedure 1.06, when a form is referred to by number, the reference is to the form with that number that is described in the Table of Forms at the end of these rules and which is available on the Internet through www.ontariocourtforms.on.ca. For your convenience, the government form as published on this website is reproduced below.]

(*Heading in accordance with Form 59A*)

IN THE ESTATE OF (*insert name*), deceased.

ORDER TO CONSENT OR OBJECT TO A PROPOSED APPOINTMENT OF AN ESTATE TRUSTEE WITH OR WITHOUT A WILL

A motion for this order has been made by (*insert name of moving party*). From an affidavit made by (*insert name of maker of affidavit*) that has been filed it appears that (*insert name*) is applying for a certificate of appointment as estate trustee with (*or* without) a will, that you are a person with a financial interest in the estate and that your consent to the appointment is being sought.

1. THIS COURT ORDERS THAT if you oppose that person's appointment as estate trustee, you must file a notice of objection to appointment of estate trustee, in the form attached as Schedule "A", in the court office within .... days after this order is served on you.

2. THIS COURT ORDERS THAT if you do not do so within that time, you shall be deemed to have consented to that person's appointment.

. . . .
Registrar

Address of court office

TO:

Schedule "A"

ONTARIO
SUPERIOR COURT OF JUSTICE

IN THE ESTATE OF (*insert name*), deceased.

NOTICE OF OBJECTION TO APPOINTMENT OF ESTATE TRUSTEE

I, (*insert name*), object to the appointment of (*insert name*) as estate trustee because (*indicate reason*).

DATE

....
(*Name, address and telephone number of objecting person or lawyer for objecting person*)

July 1, 2007

FORM 74.39 — ORDER TO FILE A STATEMENT OF ASSETS OF THE ESTATE

Courts of Justice Act

[Repealed O. Reg. 77/06, s. 3.]

[Editor's Note: Forms 4A to 78A of the Rules of Civil Procedure have been repealed by O. Reg. 77/06, effective July 1, 2006. Pursuant to Rule of Civil Procedure 1.06, when a form is referred to by number, the reference is to the form with that number that is described in the Table of Forms at the end of these rules and which is available on the Internet through www.ontariocourtforms.on.ca. For your convenience, the government form as published on this website is reproduced below.]

(*Heading in accordance with Form 59A*)

IN THE ESTATE OF (*insert name*), deceased.

ORDER TO FILE A STATEMENT OF ASSETS OF THE ESTATE

A motion for this order has been made by (*insert name of moving party*). From an affidavit made by (*insert name of maker of affidavit*) that has been filed it appears that you are an estate trustee of the estate and that you should provide further information about the assets of the estate.

THIS COURT ORDERS THAT you file a statement of the nature of each asset of the estate and its value at the date of death in the court office within .... days after this order is served on you.

. . . .

Registrar

Address of court office

TO:

November 1, 2005

FORM 74.40 — ORDER TO BENEFICIARY WITNESS

Courts of Justice Act

[Repealed O. Reg. 77/06, s. 3.]

[Editor's Note: Forms 4A to 78A of the Rules of Civil Procedure have been repealed by O. Reg. 77/06, effective July 1, 2006. Pursuant to Rule of Civil Procedure 1.06, when a form is referred to by number, the reference is to the form with that number that is described in the Table of Forms at the end of these rules and which is available on the Internet through

www.ontariocourtforms.on.ca. For your convenience, the government form as published on this website is reproduced below.]

(*Heading in accordance with Form 59A*)

IN THE ESTATE OF (*insert name*), deceased.

ORDER TO BENEFICIARY WITNESS

A motion for this order has been made by (*insert name of moving party*). From an affidavit made by (*insert name of maker of affidavit*), it appears that (insert name of moving party) has made an application for a certificate of appointment of estate trustee with a will, that you are a beneficiary under the will or codicil dated (*insert date*) and that you or your spouse witnessed the will or codicil or signed for the testator.

1. THIS COURT ORDERS THAT if you wish the court to find that neither you nor your spouse exercised any improper or undue influence on the testator, you must make a motion, within .... days after this order is served on you, asking the court to make that finding.

2. THIS COURT ORDERS THAT if you do not make such a motion within that time, the applicant may proceed to obtain a certificate of appointment of estate trustee with a will, bearing a note stating that your benefits under the will are void under section 12 of the *Succession Law Reform Act*.

. . . .
Registrar

Address of court office

TO:

November 1, 2005

FORM 74.41 — ORDER TO FORMER SPOUSE

Courts of Justice Act

[Repealed O. Reg. 77/06, s. 3.]

[Editor's Note: Forms 4A to 78A of the Rules of Civil Procedure have been repealed by O. Reg. 77/06, effective July 1, 2006. Pursuant to Rule of Civil Procedure 1.06, when a form is referred to by number, the reference is to the form with that number that is described in the Table of Forms at the end of these rules and which is available on the Internet through www.ontariocourtforms.on.ca. For your convenience, the government form as published on this website is reproduced below.]

(*Heading in accordance with Form 59A*)

IN THE ESTATE OF (*insert name*), deceased.

ORDER TO FORMER SPOUSE

Subsection 17(2) of the *Succession Law Reform Act* provides as follows:

> "Except when a contrary intention appears by the will, where, after the testator makes a will, his or her marriage is terminated by a judgment absolute of divorce or is declared a nullity,
>
> (a) a devise or bequest of a beneficial interest in property to his or her former spouse;
>
> (b) an appointment of his or her former spouse as executor or trustee; and
>
> (c) the conferring of a general or special power of appointment on his or her former spouse,
>
> are revoked and the will shall be construed as if the former spouse had predeceased the testator."

A motion for this order has been made by (*insert name of moving party*), who has also made an application for a certificate of appointment of estate trustee with a will. From the application it appears that the will is dated (*insert date*) (*and that the codicil(s) is (are) dated* ....), that you are a former spouse of the testator and that your marriage was terminated by a judgment absolute of divorce or declared a nullity after the date of the will (*or codicil*).

1. THIS COURT ORDERS THAT if you wish to take part in the determination of the question whether the provisions in the will that affect you are revoked under subsection 17(2) of the *Succession Law Reform Act*, you must enter an appearance in the office of the registrar of the court within .... days after this order is served on you.

2. THIS COURT ORDERS THAT if you do not do so within that time, the question will be determined in your absence and you will be bound by the result.

. . . .
Registrar

Address of court office

TO:

November 1, 2005

FORM 74.42 — ORDER TO PASS ACCOUNTS

Courts of Justice Act

[Repealed O. Reg. 77/06, s. 3.]

[Editor's Note: Forms 4A to 78A of the Rules of Civil Procedure have been repealed by O. Reg. 77/06, effective July 1, 2006. Pursuant to Rule of Civil Procedure 1.06, when a form is referred to by number, the reference is to the form with that number that is described in the Table of Forms at the end of these rules and which is available on the Internet through

www.ontariocourtforms.on.ca. For your convenience, the government form as published on this website is reproduced below.]

(*Heading in accordance with Form 59A*)

IN THE ESTATE OF (*insert name*), deceased.

ORDER TO PASS ACCOUNTS

A motion for this order has been made by (*insert name of moving party*). From an affidavit made by (*insert name of maker of affidavit*) that has been filed it appears that you are an estate trustee of the estate and that you have made no accounting to the court of your dealings with the estate during the period from (*date*) to (*date*).

THIS COURT ORDERS THAT you file accounts of the estate and an application to pass accounts, in accordance with rules 74.17 and 74.18 of the Rules of Civil Procedure, in the court office within .... days after this order is served on you.

. . . .
Registrar

Address of court office

TO:

November 1, 2005

FORM 74.43 — AFFIDAVIT VERIFYING ESTATE ACCOUNTS

Courts of Justice Act

[Repealed O. Reg. 77/06, s. 3.]

[Editor's Note: Forms 4A to 78A of the Rules of Civil Procedure have been repealed by O. Reg. 77/06, effective July 1, 2006. Pursuant to Rule of Civil Procedure 1.06, when a form is referred to by number, the reference is to the form with that number that is described in the Table of Forms at the end of these rules and which is available on the Internet through www.ontariocourtforms.on.ca. For your convenience, the government form as published on this website is reproduced below.]

ONTARIO
SUPERIOR COURT OF JUSTICE

IN THE ESTATE OF (*insert name*), deceased.

AFFIDAVIT VERIFYING ESTATE ACCOUNTS

I, (*insert name*), of (*insert city or town and county or district, metropolitan or regional municipality of residence*), make oath and say/affirm:

1. I am an estate trustee for this estate.

2. The accounts marked as Exhibit "A" to this affidavit are complete and correct.

3. The information contained in the notice of application to pass accounts with respect to this estate is true.

4. All persons having a financial interest in the estate are named as respondents in the notice of application to pass accounts.

5. For any party with a disability, a representative has been identified in the notice of application.

SWORN/AFFIRMED BEFORE	)	
me at the of	)	
in the of	)	
this day of , 20 .	)	
	)	
	)	
	)	....
	)	
....	)	
A Commissioner for Taking Affidavits		
(*or as may be*)		

November 1, 2005

FORM 74.44 — NOTICE OF APPLICATION TO PASS ACCOUNTS

Courts of Justice Act

[Repealed O. Reg. 77/06, s. 3.]

[Editor's Note: Forms 4A to 78A of the Rules of Civil Procedure have been repealed by O. Reg. 77/06, effective July 1, 2006. Pursuant to Rule of Civil Procedure 1.06, when a form is referred to by number, the reference is to the form with that number that is described in the Table of Forms at the end of these rules and which is available on the Internet through www.ontariocourtforms.on.ca. For your convenience, the government form as published on this website is reproduced below.]

ONTARIO

SUPERIOR COURT OF JUSTICE

IN THE ESTATE OF *(insert name)*, deceased.

NOTICE OF APPLICATION TO PASS ACCOUNTS

This application to pass accounts will be heard on *(date)*, at *(time)*, at the court house at *(full address of court house)*, if any person with a financial interest in the estate objects to the accounts or to the compensation claimed and doesn't withdraw the objection, or if a request for increased costs is served and filed.

The deceased died on *(date)*.

A certificate of appointment of estate trustee was issued to *(insert name)* by this court on *(date)*.

The accounts are for the period from *(date)* to *(date)*.

The compensation claimed by the estate trustee, payable out of the estate, is *(insert amount)*.

The costs of the application claimed by the estate trustee under Tariff C are *(amount)*.

A person with a financial interest in the estate who retains a lawyer to review the accounts and makes no objection to them (or makes an objection and later withdraws it) but serves on the estate trustee and files with the court, with proof of service, a request for costs (Form 74.49 under the Rules of Civil Procedure) at least 10 days before the hearing date of the application, will be allowed one-half of the costs allowed to the estate trustee. However, where two or more persons are represented by the same lawyer, they are entitled to receive only one person's costs. If the Children's Lawyer or the Public Guardian and Trustee makes no objection to the accounts (or makes an objection and later withdraws it) but serves on the estate trustee and files with the court, with proof of service, a request for costs (Form 74.49.1) at least 10 days before the hearing date of the application, he or she will be allowed three-quarters of the costs allowed to the estate trustee.

Any person with a financial interest in the estate who wishes to object to the accounts shall do so by serving upon the estate trustee, or the lawyer for the estate trustee, a notice of objection to accounts (Form 74.45 under the *Rules of Civil Procedure*, a copy of which is attached to this notice of application), and by filing a copy of the notice in the court office at least 35 days before the hearing date specified in the notice of application [R.74.18(7)].

Any person who wishes to withdraw a notice of objection to accounts shall, at least 15 days before the hearing date of the application, serve on the estate trustee, and file with proof of service, a notice of withdrawal of objection (Form 74.48) [R.74.18(8.4)].

If the estate trustee or any person with a financial interest in the estate seeks costs of the application greater than the amount allowed in Tariff C, the estate trustee or other person shall serve on every other party a request for increased costs (Form 74.49.2 or 74.49.3 under the *Rules of Civil Procedure*) together with a Costs Outline in Form 57B, at least 15 days before the hearing date of the application [R.74.18(11)].

Any person with a financial interest in the estate who wishes to object or consent to a request for increased costs shall do so by returning the completed form 74.49.2 or 74.49.3, as the case may be, to the person making the request so that he or she receives it at least 10 days before the hearing date of the application. The person making the request for increased costs shall, at least 5 days before the hearing date of the application, file with the court a supplementary record described in subrule 74.18(11.3) containing (i) the documents served under subrule 74.18(11), together with an affidavit of service of those documents, (ii) an affidavit containing a summary of the responses to the request for increased costs and a list of persons who failed to respond, and (iii) the factors that contributed to the increased costs [R.74.18(11.3)].

Any person with a financial interest in the estate who does not wish to object to the accounts but wishes to receive notice of any further step in the application, including a request for costs or a request for increased costs, shall, at least 35 days before the hearing date specified in the notice of application, serve upon the estate trustee, and file with proof of service, a request for further notice in passing of accounts (Form 74.45.1), a copy of which is attached to this notice of application [R.74.18(8)].

If one or more notices of objection to accounts are filed and not withdrawn, the estate trustee shall, at least 10 days before the hearing date of the application, serve on the persons referred to in subrule 74.18(11.6), and file with proof of service, (i) a consolidation of all the remaining notices of objection to accounts and (ii) a reply to notice of objection to accounts (Form 74.49.4) [R.74.18(11.5)].

If the application to pass accounts proceeds to a hearing, the estate trustee shall, at least 5 days before the hearing date, file with the court a record containing the documents referred to in subrule 74.18(11.7). If the applicant and every other person referred to under subrule 74.18(11.6), agree to all of the terms of a draft order, the applicant shall indicate that it is a joint draft order.

If the applicant and other persons fail to agree to all of the terms of a draft order, the applicant shall indicate that it is the applicant's draft order. Any person referred to under clause 74.18(11.6)(a) may file an alternative draft order at least 3 days before the hearing date of the application or, with leave of the court, at the hearing [R.74.18(11.8)(11.9)].

At the hearing, the only issues upon which the court adjudicates are those raised in the notices of objection to accounts and requests for increased costs that have been filed, unless the court grants leave to a party to raise other issues [R.74.18(12)].

If no notice of objection to accounts is served and filed, or all objections have been withdrawn, the estate trustee may, without a hearing, obtain a judgment passing the accounts and allowing the compensation and costs claimed [R.74.18(8.5)].

On a request for increased costs, the court may, in consideration of the documents in the supplementary record, grant judgment without a hearing. If the court declines to grant a request for increased costs without a hearing, the hearing shall proceed on the date fixed [R.74.18(11.4)].

Any person may contact the estate trustee or the estate trustee's lawyer to find out whether there will be a hearing. A copy of the accounts may be obtained from the estate trustee or the estate trustee's lawyer, or may be inspected in the court office during regular business hours.

DATE ....

Registrar

(Name, address and telephone number of estate trustee or lawyer for the estate trustee)

TO: *(Name and address of each person with a financial interest in the estate)*

(For a person under disability, also indicate name and address of personal representative)

(Attach blank copy of Form 74.45 (notice of objection to accounts).)

(Attach blank copy of Form 74.45.1 (request for further notice in passing of accounts).)

January 1, 2016

FORM 74.45 — NOTICE OF OBJECTION TO ACCOUNTS

Courts of Justice Act

[Repealed O. Reg. 77/06, s. 3.]

[Editor's Note: Forms 4A to 78A of the Rules of Civil Procedure have been repealed by O. Reg. 77/06, effective July 1, 2006. Pursuant to Rule of Civil Procedure 1.06, when a form is referred to by number, the reference is to the form with that number that is described in the Table of Forms at the end of these rules and which is available on the Internet through www.ontariocourtforms.on.ca. For your convenience, the government form as published on this website is reproduced below.]

ONTARIO
SUPERIOR COURT OF JUSTICE

IN THE ESTATE OF (*insert name*), deceased.

NOTICE OF OBJECTION TO ACCOUNTS

1. I, (*insert name*), object to the amount of compensation claimed by the estate trustee on the following grounds:

(*If applicable, set out each objection in separate consecutively numbered paragraphs. Attach separate sheet if necessary.*)

2. I, (*insert name*), object to the accounts of the estate trustee on the following grounds:

(*If applicable, set out each objection in separate consecutively numbered paragraphs. Attach separate sheet if necessary.*)

DATE

(*Name, address and telephone number of objecting person or lawyer for objecting person*)

TO: (*Name and address of estate trustee or lawyer for estate trustee*)

July 1, 2007

FORM 74.45.1 — REQUEST FOR FURTHER NOTICE IN PASSING OF ACCOUNTS

Courts of Justice Act

[Repealed O. Reg. 77/06, s. 3.]

[Editor's Note: Forms 4A to 78A of the Rules of Civil Procedure have been repealed by O. Reg. 77/06, effective July 1, 2006. Pursuant to Rule of Civil Procedure 1.06, when a form is referred to by number, the reference is to the form with that number that is described in the Table of Forms at the end of these rules and which is available on the Internet through www.ontariocourtforms.on.ca. For your convenience, the government form as published on this website is reproduced below.]

ONTARIO
SUPERIOR COURT OF JUSTICE

IN THE ESTATE OF *(insert name)*, deceased.

REQUEST FOR FURTHER NOTICE IN PASSING OF ACCOUNTS

I *(insert name)* have been served with a notice of application to pass accounts. By serving this request for further notice, I acknowledge that:

I do not object to the accounts but wish to receive notice of any further step in the application, including a request for costs or a request for increased costs, and

I shall, at least 35 days before the hearing date specified in the notice of application, serve on the applicant, and file with proof of service, this request for further notice.

I further acknowledge that, unless the court orders otherwise, I am entitled to,

(a) receive notice of any further step in the application to pass accounts;

(b) receive any further document in the application;

(c) file material relating to a request for increased costs on the application at least 10 days before the hearing date of the application; and

(d) in the event of a hearing, be heard at the hearing, examine a witness and cross-examine on an affidavit, but with respect only to a request for increased costs.

DATE

(Name, address and telephone number of person requesting further notice or the lawyer for the person requesting further notice)

May 1, 2017

FORM 74.46 — NOTICE OF NO OBJECTION TO ACCOUNTS

Courts of Justice Act

[Repealed O. Reg. 77/06, s. 3.]

[Editor's Note: Forms 4A to 78A of the Rules of Civil Procedure have been repealed by O. Reg. 77/06, effective July 1, 2006. Pursuant to Rule of Civil Procedure 1.06, when a form is referred to by number, the reference is to the form with that number that is described in the Table of Forms at the end of these rules and which is available on the Internet through www.ontariocourtforms.on.ca. For your convenience, the government form as published on this website is reproduced below.]

ONTARIO
SUPERIOR COURT OF JUSTICE

IN THE ESTATE OF (*insert name*), deceased.

NOTICE OF NO OBJECTION TO ACCOUNTS

The (Public Guardian and Trustee) (Children's Lawyer) has no objection to the estate accounts and the claim for compensation by the estate trustee.

DATE

(*Name, address and telephone number of Children's Lawyer or Public Guardian and Trustee, or lawyer for Children's Lawyer or Public Guardian and Trustee*)

TO: (*Name and address of estate trustee or lawyer for estate trustee*)

July 1, 2007

FORM 74.46.1 — NOTICE OF NON-PARTICIPATION IN PASSING OF ACCOUNTS

Courts of Justice Act

[Repealed O. Reg. 77/06, s. 3.]

[Editor's Note: Forms 4A to 78A of the Rules of Civil Procedure have been repealed by O. Reg. 77/06, effective July 1, 2006. Pursuant to Rule of Civil Procedure 1.06, when a form is referred to by number, the reference is to the form with that number that is described in the

Table of Forms at the end of these rules and which is available on the Internet through www.ontariocourtforms.on.ca. For your convenience, the government form as published on this website is reproduced below.]

ONTARIO
SUPERIOR COURT OF JUSTICE

IN THE ESTATE OF (*insert name*), deceased.

NOTICE OF NON-PARTICIPATION IN PASSING OF ACCOUNTS

The (Public Guardian and Trustee) (Children's Lawyer) does not intend to participate in the passing of accounts.

DATE

(*Name, address and telephone number of Children's Lawyer or Public Guardian and Trustee, or lawyer for Children's Lawyer or Public Guardian and Trustee*)

TO: (*Name and address of estate trustee or lawyer for the estate trustee*)

July 1, 2007

FORM 74.47 — AFFIDAVIT IN SUPPORT OF UNOPPOSED JUDGMENT ON PASSING OF ACCOUNTS

Courts of Justice Act

[Repealed O. Reg. 77/06, s. 3.]

[Editor's Note: Forms 4A to 78A of the Rules of Civil Procedure have been repealed by O. Reg. 77/06, effective July 1, 2006. Pursuant to Rule of Civil Procedure 1.06, when a form is referred to by number, the reference is to the form with that number that is described in the Table of Forms at the end of these rules and which is available on the Internet through www.ontariocourtforms.on.ca. For your convenience, the government form as published on this website is reproduced below.]

ONTARIO
SUPERIOR COURT OF JUSTICE

IN THE ESTATE OF (*insert name*), deceased.

AFFIDAVIT SUPPORT OF UNOPPOSED JUDGMENT ON PASSING OF ACCOUNTS

I, (*insert name*), of (*insert city or town and county or district, metropolitan or regional municipality of residence*), make oath and say/affirm:

1. I am the applicant for an unopposed judgment on the passing of accounts in this estate with respect to estate accounts from (*date*) to (*date*).

2. A copy of the estate accounts has been provided to each person who was served with the notice of application and who requested a copy of the accounts.

3. The time for filing notices of objection to the estate accounts has expired.

4. No notice of objection has been received from any person served with the notice of application.

OR

4. Any notice of objection that was received has been withdrawn by the filing of a notice of withdrawal of objection.

SWORN/AFFIRMED BEFORE)
me at the of)
in the of)
this day of , 20 .)
)
)
) ....
)

....
A Commissioner for Taking Affidavits
(*or as may be*)

NOTE: The two versions of paragraph 4 are in the alternative. Delete the one that does not apply.

November 1, 2005

FORM 74.48 — NOTICE OF WITHDRAWAL OF OBJECTION

Courts of Justice Act

[Repealed O. Reg. 77/06, s. 3.]

[Editor's Note: Forms 4A to 78A of the Rules of Civil Procedure have been repealed by O. Reg. 77/06, effective July 1, 2006. Pursuant to Rule of Civil Procedure 1.06, when a form is referred to by number, the reference is to the form with that number that is described in the Table of Forms at the end of these rules and which is available on the Internet through www.ontariocourtforms.on.ca. For your convenience, the government form as published on this website is reproduced below.]

ONTARIO
SUPERIOR COURT OF JUSTICE

IN THE ESTATE OF (*insert name*), deceased.

NOTICE OF WITHDRAWAL OF OBJECTION

I, (*insert name*), filed a notice of objection to accounts and hereby withdraw that notice of objection.

DATE

(*Name, address and telephone number of party or party's lawyer*)

TO: (*Name and address of estate trustee or lawyer for estate trustee*)

July 1, 2007

FORM 74.49 — REQUEST FOR COSTS (PERSON OTHER THAN CHILDREN'S LAWYER OR PUBLIC GUARDIAN AND TRUSTEE)

Courts of Justice Act

[Repealed O. Reg. 77/06, s. 3.]

[Editor's Note: Forms 4A to 78A of the Rules of Civil Procedure have been repealed by O. Reg. 77/06, effective July 1, 2006. Pursuant to Rule of Civil Procedure 1.06, when a form is referred to by number, the reference is to the form with that number that is described in the Table of Forms at the end of these rules and which is available on the Internet through www.ontariocourtforms.on.ca. For your convenience, the government form as published on this website is reproduced below.]

ONTARIO
SUPERIOR COURT OF JUSTICE

IN THE ESTATE OF (*insert name*), deceased.

REQUEST FOR COSTS (PERSON OTHER THAN CHILDREN'S LAWYER OR PUBLIC GUARDIAN AND TRUSTEE)

I, (*insert name*), have retained (*insert name*) as my lawyer to review the estate accounts. I have no objection to the estate accounts and the claim for compensation by the estate trustee.

I request that I be awarded costs payable out of the estate in the amount of $ ...., representing one-half of the amount payable to the estate solicitor under Tariff C.

DATE

(Name, address and telephone number of party or party's lawyer)

TO: *(Name and address of estate trustee or lawyer for estate trustee)*

July 1, 2007

FORM 74.49.1 — REQUEST FOR COSTS (CHILDREN'S LAWYER OR PUBLIC GUARDIAN AND TRUSTEE)

Courts of Justice Act

[Repealed O. Reg. 77/06, s. 3.]

[Editor's Note: Forms 4A to 78A of the Rules of Civil Procedure have been repealed by O. Reg. 77/06, effective July 1, 2006. Pursuant to Rule of Civil Procedure 1.06, when a form is referred to by number, the reference is to the form with that number that is described in the Table of Forms at the end of these rules and which is available on the Internet through www.ontariocourtforms.on.ca. For your convenience, the government form as published on this website is reproduced below.]

ONTARIO
SUPERIOR COURT OF JUSTICE

IN THE ESTATE OF (*insert name*), deceased.

REQUEST FOR COSTS (CHILDREN'S LAWYER OR PUBLIC GUARDIAN AND TRUSTEE)

The (Public Guardian and Trustee) (Children's Lawyer) has no objection to the estate accounts and the claim for compensation by the estate trustee.

The (Public Guardian and Trustee) (Children's Lawyer) requests that he or she be awarded costs payable out of the estate in the amount of $ ...., representing three-quarters of the amount payable to the estate solicitor under Tariff C.

DATE

(Name, address and telephone number of Children's Lawyer or Public Guardian and Trustee, or lawyer for Children's Lawyer

or Public Guardian and Trustee)

TO: *(Name and address of estate trustee or lawyer for the estate trustee)*

July 1, 2007

FORM 74.49.2 — REQUEST FOR INCREASED COSTS (ESTATE TRUSTEE)

Courts of Justice Act

[Repealed O. Reg. 77/06, s. 3.]

[Editor's Note: Forms 4A to 78A of the Rules of Civil Procedure have been repealed by O. Reg. 77/06, effective July 1, 2006. Pursuant to Rule of Civil Procedure 1.06, when a form is referred to by number, the reference is to the form with that number that is described in the Table of Forms at the end of these rules and which is available on the Internet through www.ontariocourtforms.on.ca. For your convenience, the government form as published on this website is reproduced below.]

ONTARIO

SUPERIOR COURT OF JUSTICE

IN THE ESTATE OF *(insert name)*, deceased.

I request that I be awarded costs payable out of the estate in the amount of $.........., in addition to the cost of attendance at a hearing, if required, which is greater than the amount of $.......... allowed under Tariff C. I understand that this request may require a hearing on the date specified in the notice of application, in the discretion of the presiding Judge.

DATE

(Name, address and telephone number of estate trustee or lawyer for estate trustee)

TO: *(Name and address of each person with a financial interest in the estate)*

(For a person under disability, also indicate name and address of personal representative)

Response by person with a financial interest in the estate:

(A) I oppose this request for increased costs, for the following reasons:

-

-

OR

(B) I consent to this request for increased costs.

Date:

....

Signature of person listed above

Any person with a financial interest in the estate who wishes to object or consent to a request for increased costs shall do so by returning the completed form 74.49.2 to the person making the request so that such person receives it at least 12 days before the date fixed for the hearing in the Notice of Application to Pass Accounts.

The person making the request for increased costs shall, at least 10 days before the date fixed for the hearing, file with the court a supplementary record described in subrule 74.18(11.3) containing (i) the documents served under subrule 74.18(11.1), together with an affidavit of service of those documents, (ii) an affidavit containing a summary of the responses to the request for increased costs and a list of persons who failed to respond, and (iii) the factors that contributed to the increased costs.

April 11, 2012

FORM 74.49.3 — REQUEST FOR INCREASED COSTS (PERSON OTHER THAN ESTATE TRUSTEE)

Courts of Justice Act

[Repealed O. Reg. 77/06, s. 3.]

[Editor's Note: Forms 4A to 78A of the Rules of Civil Procedure have been repealed by O. Reg. 77/06, effective July 1, 2006. Pursuant to Rule of Civil Procedure 1.06, when a form is referred to by number, the reference is to the form with that number that is described in the Table of Forms at the end of these rules and which is available on the Internet through www.ontariocourtforms.on.ca. For your convenience, the government form as published on this website is reproduced below.]

ONTARIO

SUPERIOR COURT OF JUSTICE

IN THE ESTATE OF *(insert name)*, deceased.

1. I, *(insert name)*, have retained *(insert name)* as my lawyer to review the estate accounts. I have no objection to the estate accounts or to the claim for compensation by the estate trustee.

2. I request that I be awarded costs payable out of the estate in the amount of $.........., in addition to the cost of attendance at a hearing, if required, which is greater than $.........., being one-half the amount payable to the estate trustee under Tariff C. I understand that this

request may require a hearing on the date specified in the notice of application, in the discretion of the presiding Judge.

DATE

(Name, address and telephone number of person or person's lawyer)

TO: *(Name and address of every other person with a financial interest in the estate)*

(For a person under disability, also indicate name and address of personal representative)

(Name and address of estate trustee or lawyer for estate trustee)

Response by Estate Trustee or person with a financial interest in the estate:

(A) I object to this request for increased costs, for the following reasons:

-

-

OR:

(B) I consent to this request for increased costs.

Date:

....

Signature of person listed above

Any person with a financial interest in the estate who wishes to object or consent to a request for increased costs shall do so by returning the completed form 74.49.3 to the person making the request so that such person receives it at least 12 days before the date fixed for the hearing in the Notice of Application to Pass Accounts.

The person making the request for increased costs shall, at least 10 days before the date fixed for the hearing, file with the court a supplementary record described in subrule 74.18(11.3) containing (i) the documents served under subrule 74.18(11.1), together with an affidavit of service of those documents, (ii) an affidavit containing a summary of the responses to the request for increased costs and a list of persons who failed to respond, and (iii) the factors that contributed to the increased costs.

April 11, 2012

FORM 74.49.4 — REPLY TO NOTICE OF OBJECTION TO ACCOUNTS

Courts of Justice Act

[Editor's Note: Forms 4A to 78A of the Rules of Civil Procedure have been repealed by O. Reg. 77/06, effective July 1, 2006. Pursuant to Rule of Civil Procedure 1.06, when a form is referred to by number, the reference is to the form with that number that is described in the

Table of Forms at the end of these rules and which is available on the Internet through www.ontariocourtforms.on.ca. For your convenience, the government form as published on this website is reproduced below.]

ONTARIO
SUPERIOR COURT OF JUSTICE

IN THE ESTATE OF *(insert name)*, deceased.

REPLY TO NOTICE OF OBJECTION TO ACCOUNTS

1. In the attached Notice of Objection to Accounts, *(insert name)* objected to the amount of compensation claimed by the estate trustee. The reply to the objection is as follows:

(If applicable, set out a reply to each objection in separate consecutively numbered paragraphs. Attach separate sheet if necessary.)

2. In the attached Notice of Objection to Accounts, *(insert name)*, objected to the accounts of the estate trustee. The reply to the objection is as follows:

(If applicable, set out a reply to each objection in separate consecutively numbered paragraphs. Attach separate sheet if necessary.)

DATE

(Name, address and telephone number of person or lawyer replying to the objection)

February 1, 2015

FORM 74.50 — JUDGMENT ON UNOPPOSED PASSING OF ACCOUNTS

Courts of Justice Act

[Repealed O. Reg. 77/06, s. 3.]

[Editor's Note: Forms 4A to 78A of the Rules of Civil Procedure have been repealed by O. Reg. 77/06, effective July 1, 2006. Pursuant to Rule of Civil Procedure 1.06, when a form is referred to by number, the reference is to the form with that number that is described in the Table of Forms at the end of these rules and which is available on the Internet through www.ontariocourtforms.on.ca. For your convenience, the government form as published on this website is reproduced below.]

(HEADING IN ACCORDANCE WITH FORM 59B)

IN THE ESTATE OF *(insert name)*, deceased.

JUDGMENT ON PASSING OF ACCOUNTS

THIS APPLICATION was read on *(date)*, at *(place)*.

ON READING THE NOTICE OF APPLICATION TO PASS ACCOUNTS, the affidavit of service and the affidavit in support of an unopposed judgment on passing of accounts, as filed, and as there are no objections to the accounts or the claim for compensation by the estate trustee,

1. THIS COURT DECLARES that the estate accounts, as filed by the applicant for the period from *(date)* to *(date)*, are hereby passed.

2. THIS COURT DECLARES that the capital receipts and capital disbursements of the applicant for the period are as follows:

CAPITAL ACCOUNT

Credit balance forward *(if applicable)*	$	
Receipts	$..........	$.......... (total)
Debit balance forward *(if applicable)*	$	
Disbursements	$..........	$.......... (total)
Credit (or debit) balance		$..........

3. THIS COURT DECLARES that the revenue receipts and revenue disbursements of the applicant for the period are as follows:

REVENUE ACCOUNT

Credit balance forward *(if applicable)*	$	
Receipts	$..........	$.......... (total)
Debit balance forward *(if applicable)*	$	
Disbursements	$..........	$.......... (total)
Credit (or debit) balance		$..........

4. THIS COURT ORDERS that the estate trustee shall be paid as fair and reasonable compensation for services as estate trustee of the estate and for disbursements expended in administering the affairs of the estate during the period the total amount of $.......... (including H.S.T.), of which $.......... shall be paid out of the capital of the estate and $.......... shall be paid out of the revenue of the estate.

5. THIS COURT ORDERS that the costs of the passing of the accounts allowed in accordance with Tariff C, and payable out of the capital of the estate, are as follows:

To the estate trustee $.........., and H.S.T. of $.......... for a total of $..........

To *(insert names and amounts, showing each person awarded costs on a separate line)*

6. THIS COURT DECLARES that the accounts show that there remain in the estate trustee's hands the original assets as set out in Schedule "A", attached.

April 11, 2012

FORM 74.51 — JUDGMENT ON CONTESTED PASSING OF ACCOUNTS

Courts of Justice Act

[Repealed O. Reg. 77/06, s. 3.]

[Editor's Note: Forms 4A to 78A of the Rules of Civil Procedure have been repealed by O. Reg. 77/06, effective July 1, 2006. Pursuant to Rule of Civil Procedure 1.06, when a form is referred to by number, the reference is to the form with that number that is described in the Table of Forms at the end of these rules and which is available on the Internet through www.ontariocourtforms.on.ca. For your convenience, the government form as published on this website is reproduced below.]

(HEADING IN ACCORDANCE WITH FORM 59B)

IN THE ESTATE OF *(insert name)*, deceased.

JUDGMENT ON PASSING OF ACCOUNTS

THIS APPLICATION was heard on *(date)*, at *(place)* in the presence of the lawyer(s) for *(insert name) (where applicable add* and *(insert name)* appearing in person) *(where applicable add* and no one appearing for *(insert name)*, although properly served as appears from the affidavit of service filed*)*.

ON READING THE NOTICE OF APPLICATION TO PASS ACCOUNTS and on hearing the submissions made,

1. THIS COURT DECLARES that the estate accounts, as filed by the applicant for the period from *(date)* to *(date)*, are hereby passed.

2. THIS COURT DECLARES that the capital receipts and capital disbursements of the applicant for the period are as follows:

CAPITAL ACCOUNT

Credit balance forward *(if applicable)*	$	
Receipts	$..........	$.......... (total)
Debit balance forward *(if applicable)*	$	
Disbursements	$..........	$.......... (total)
Credit (or debit) balance		$..........

3. THIS COURT DECLARES that the revenue receipts and revenue disbursements of the applicant for the period are as follows:

REVENUE ACCOUNT

Credit balance forward *(if applicable)*	$	
Receipts	$..........	$.......... (total)
Debit balance forward *(if applicable)*	$	
Disbursements	$..........	$.......... (total)
Credit (or debit) balance		$..........

4. THIS COURT ORDERS that the estate trustee shall be paid as fair and reasonable compensation for services as estate trustee of the estate and for disbursements expended in ad-

ministering the affairs of the estate during the period the total amount of $.......... (including H.S.T.), of which $.......... shall be paid out of the capital of the estate and $.......... shall be paid out of the revenue of the estate.

5. THIS COURT ORDERS that the costs of the passing of the accounts allowed and payable out of the capital of the estate are as follows:

To the estate trustee $.........., and H.S.T. of $.......... for a total of $..........

To *(insert names and amounts, showing each person awarded costs on a separate line)*

6. THIS COURT DECLARES that the accounts show that there remain in the estate trustee's hands the original assets as set out in Schedule "A", attached.

April 11, 2012

FORM 75.1 — NOTICE OF OBJECTION

Courts of Justice Act

[Repealed O. Reg. 77/06, s. 3.]

[Editor's Note: Forms 4A to 78A of the Rules of Civil Procedure have been repealed by O. Reg. 77/06, effective July 1, 2006. Pursuant to Rule of Civil Procedure 1.06, when a form is referred to by number, the reference is to the form with that number that is described in the Table of Forms at the end of these rules and which is available on the Internet through www.ontariocourtforms.on.ca. For your convenience, the government form as published on this website is reproduced below.]

ONTARIO

SUPERIOR COURT OF JUSTICE

In the Estate of the deceased person described below:

DETAILS ABOUT THE DECEASED PERSON

Complete in full as applicable

First given name	Second given name	Third given name	Surname
And if the deceased was known by any other name(s), state below the full name(s) used including surname.			
First given name	Second given name	Third given name	Surname

IN THE MATTER OF an application for a certificate of appointment of estate trustee

NOTICE OF OBJECTION

I, ... *(insert name)*, object to the issuing of a certificate of appointment of estate trustee to .... *(insert name of applicant)* without notice to me because .... *(indicate reason, such as lack of testamentary capacity, undue influence or unfitness to act as estate trustee).*

The nature of my interest in the estate is: *(state relationship to the deceased and whether a named beneficiary under the will, or other basis for financial interest).* ....

DATE ....

(Name, address and telephone number of objector or lawyer for objector) ....

July 1, 2007

FORM 75.1A — REQUEST FOR ASSIGNMENT OF MEDIATOR

Courts of Justice Act

[Repealed O. Reg. 77/06, s. 3.]

[Editor's Note: Forms 4A to 78A of the Rules of Civil Procedure have been repealed by O. Reg. 77/06, effective July 1, 2006. Pursuant to Rule of Civil Procedure 1.06, when a form is referred to by number, the reference is to the form with that number that is described in the Table of Forms at the end of these rules and which is available on the Internet through www.ontariocourtforms.on.ca. For your convenience, the government form as published on this website is reproduced below.]

ONTARIO *(Court file no.)*

SUPERIOR COURT OF JUSTICE

IN THE ESTATE OF deceased,

late of ,

occupation ,

who died on ,

REQUEST FOR ASSIGNMENT OF MEDIATOR

TO: Mediation co-ordinator for (*county*)

An order giving directions was made under rule 75.1.05 on (*date of order*). A copy of the order is attached to this request.

The designated parties have not chosen a mediator under subrule 75.1.06(1). The 30-day period mentioned in subrule 75.1.07(1) has expired.

This is a request that you assign a mediator from the list for the country.

(*Date*) (*Name, address, telephone number and fax number, if any, of lawyer of party filing request, or of party*)

November 1, 2005

FORM 75.1B — NOTICE BY MEDIATOR

Courts of Justice Act

[Repealed O. Reg. 77/06, s. 3.]

[Editor's Note: Forms 4A to 78A of the Rules of Civil Procedure have been repealed by O. Reg. 77/06, effective July 1, 2006. Pursuant to Rule of Civil Procedure 1.06, when a form is referred to by number, the reference is to the form with that number that is described in the Table of Forms at the end of these rules and which is available on the Internet through www.ontariocourtforms.on.ca. For your convenience, the government form as published on this website is reproduced below.]

ONTARIO (*Court file no.*)

SUPERIOR COURT OF JUSTICE

IN THE ESTATE OF deceased,

late of ,

occupation ,

who died on ,

NOTICE BY MEDIATOR

TO:

AND TO:

I am the mediator whom the mediation co-ordinator has appointed to conduct the mediation session under Rule 75.1. (*Delete this paragraph if mediator was chosen by designated parties under clause 75.1.06(1)(a) or (c).*)

The mediation session will take place on (*date*), from (*time*) to (*time*), at (*place*).

You are required to attend this mediation session. If you have a lawyer representing you in this proceeding, he or she is also required to attend.

You are required to file a statement of issues (Form 75.1C) by (*date*) (seven days before the mediation session). A blank copy of the form is attached.

When you attend the mediation session, you should bring with you any documents that you consider of central importance in the proceeding. You should plan to remain throughout the scheduled time. If you need another person's approval before agreeing to a settlement, you should make arrangements before the mediation session to ensure that you have ready telephone access to that person throughout the session, even outside regular business hours.

YOU MAY BE PENALIZED UNDER RULE 75.1.10 IF YOU FAIL TO FILE A STATEMENT OF ISSUES OR FAIL TO ATTEND THE MEDIATION SESSION.

(*Date*) (*Name, address, telephone number and fax number, if any, of mediator*)

November 1, 2005

FORM 75.1C — STATEMENT OF ISSUES

Courts of Justice Act

[Repealed O. Reg. 77/06, s. 3.]

[Editor's Note: Forms 4A to 78A of the Rules of Civil Procedure have been repealed by O. Reg. 77/06, effective July 1, 2006. Pursuant to Rule of Civil Procedure 1.06, when a form is referred to by number, the reference is to the form with that number that is described in the Table of Forms at the end of these rules and which is available on the Internet through www.ontariocourtforms.on.ca. For your convenience, the government form as published on this website is reproduced below.]

ONTARIO (*Court file no.*)

SUPERIOR COURT OF JUSTICE

IN THE ESTATE OF deceased,

late of ,

occupation ,

who died on ,

STATEMENT OF ISSUES

(To be provided to mediator and designated parties at least seven days before the mediation session)

1. *Factual and legal issues in dispute*

The undersigned designated party states that the following factual and legal issues are in dispute and remain to be resolved.

(Issues should be stated briefly and numbered consecutively.)

2. *Party's position and interests (what the party hopes to achieve)*

(Brief summary.)

3. *Attached documents*

Attached to this form are the following documents that the designated party considers of central importance in the proceeding: *(list)*

(Date) *(party's signature)*

(Name, address, telephone number and fax number, if any, of lawyer of party filing statement of issues, or of party)

NOTE: Rule 75.1.11 provides as follows:

All communications at a mediation session and the mediator's notes and records shall be deemed to be without prejudice settlement discussions.

November 1, 2005

FORM 75.1D — CERTIFICATE OF NON-COMPLIANCE

Courts of Justice Act

[Repealed O. Reg. 77/06, s. 3.]

[Editor's Note: Forms 4A to 78A of the Rules of Civil Procedure have been repealed by O. Reg. 77/06, effective July 1, 2006. Pursuant to Rule of Civil Procedure 1.06, when a form is referred to by number, the reference is to the form with that number that is described in the Table of Forms at the end of these rules and which is available on the Internet through www.ontariocourtforms.on.ca. For your convenience, the government form as published on this website is reproduced below.]

ONTARIO *(Court file no.)*

SUPERIOR COURT OF JUSTICE

IN THE ESTATE OF deceased,

late of ,

occupation ,

who died on ,

CERTIFICATE OF NON-COMPLIANCE

TO: (*court*)

1. (*name*), mediator, certify that this certificate of non-compliance is filed because:

( ) *Identify party(ies)*) failed to provide a copy of a statement of issues to the mediator and the other parties (*or* to the mediator *or* to *party*(ies)).

( ) (*Identify party*(ies)) failed to attend within the first 30 minutes of a scheduled mediation session.

(*Date*) (*Name, address, telephone number and fax number, if any, of mediator*)

November 1, 2005

FORM 75.2 — NOTICE THAT OBJECTION HAS BEEN FILED

Courts of Justice Act

[Repealed O. Reg. 77/06, s. 3.]

[Editor's Note: Forms 4A to 78A of the Rules of Civil Procedure have been repealed by O. Reg. 77/06, effective July 1, 2006. Pursuant to Rule of Civil Procedure 1.06, when a form is referred to by number, the reference is to the form with that number that is described in the Table of Forms at the end of these rules and which is available on the Internet through www.ontariocourtforms.on.ca. For your convenience, the government form as published on this website is reproduced below.]

ONTARIO
SUPERIOR COURT OF JUSTICE

IN THE ESTATE OF (*insert name*), deceased.

IN THE MATTER OF an application for a certificate of appointment of estate trustee

NOTICE THAT OBJECTION HAS BEEN FILED

A notice of objection, a copy of which is attached, has been filed with the court.

No further action regarding issuing a certificate of appointment to you will be taken until you have complied with subrule 75.03(4) of the *Rules of Civil Procedure*.

DATE

. . . .
Registrar

Address of court office

TO: (*Name, address and telephone number of applicant or lawyer for the applicant*)

July 1, 2007

FORM 75.3 — NOTICE TO OBJECTOR

Courts of Justice Act

[Repealed O. Reg. 77/06, s. 3.]

[Editor's Note: Forms 4A to 78A of the Rules of Civil Procedure have been repealed by O. Reg. 77/06, effective July 1, 2006. Pursuant to Rule of Civil Procedure 1.06, when a form is referred to by number, the reference is to the form with that number that is described in the Table of Forms at the end of these rules and which is available on the Internet through www.ontariocourtforms.on.ca. For your convenience, the government form as published on this website is reproduced below.]

ONTARIO
SUPERIOR COURT OF JUSTICE

IN THE ESTATE OF (*insert name*), deceased.

IN THE MATTER OF an application for a certificate of appointment of estate trustee

NOTICE TO OBJECTOR

AN APPLICATION for a certificate of appointment of estate trustee in the estate has been made by (*name of applicant*).

IF YOU WISH TO OPPOSE this application, you or an Ontario lawyer acting for you must within 20 days of service on you of this notice to objector prepare a notice of appearance in Form 75.4 of the Rules of Civil Procedure, serve it on the applicant's lawyer, or where the applicant does not have a lawyer serve it on the applicant, and file it with proof of service in the court office at (*full court address where application for certificate of appointment was filed*).

IF YOU FAIL to serve and file a notice of appearance, the application for certificate of appointment of estate trustee shall proceed as if your notice of objection had not been filed.

DATE

(*Name, address and telephone number of applicant or lawyer for the applicant*)

TO: (*Name and address of the objector or lawyer for the objector*)

July 1, 2007

FORM 75.4 — NOTICE OF APPEARANCE

Courts of Justice Act

[Repealed O. Reg. 77/06, s. 3.]

[Editor's Note: Forms 4A to 78A of the Rules of Civil Procedure have been repealed by O. Reg. 77/06, effective July 1, 2006. Pursuant to Rule of Civil Procedure 1.06, when a form is referred to by number, the reference is to the form with that number that is described in the Table of Forms at the end of these rules and which is available on the Internet through www.ontariocourtforms.on.ca. For your convenience, the government form as published on this website is reproduced below.]

ONTARIO
SUPERIOR COURT OF JUSTICE

IN THE ESTATE OF (*insert name*), deceased.

IN THE MATTER OF an application for a certificate of appointment of estate trustee

NOTICE OF APPEARANCE

I desire to oppose the issuing of a certificate of appointment of estate trustee for the reasons set out in the notice of objection filed.

DATE

(*Name, address and telephone number of objector or lawyer for the objector*)

TO: (*Name, address and telephone number of applicant or lawyer for the applicant*)

July 1, 2007

FORM 75.5 — NOTICE OF APPLICATION FOR DIRECTIONS

Courts of Justice Act

[Repealed O. Reg. 77/06, s. 3.]

[Editor's Note: Forms 4A to 78A of the Rules of Civil Procedure have been repealed by O. Reg. 77/06, effective July 1, 2006. Pursuant to Rule of Civil Procedure 1.06, when a form is referred to by number, the reference is to the form with that number that is described in the Table of Forms at the end of these rules and which is available on the Internet through www.ontariocourtforms.on.ca. For your convenience, the government form as published on this website is reproduced below.]

ONTARIO
SUPERIOR COURT OF JUSTICE

IN THE ESTATE OF (*insert name*), deceased.

BETWEEN:

(*Name*)

Applicant

- and -

(*Name*)

Respondent

NOTICE OF APPLICATION FOR DIRECTIONS

TO THE RESPONDENT

A LEGAL PROCEEDING HAS BEEN COMMENCED by the applicant. The claim made by the applicant appears on the following page.

THIS APPLICATION will come on for a hearing before a judge on (*date*) at (*time*), at the Court House at (*place*).

IF YOU WISH TO OPPOSE THIS APPLICATION, you or an Ontario lawyer acting for you must forthwith prepare a notice of appearance in Form 38A prescribed by the *Rules of Civil Procedure*, serve it on the applicant's lawyer or, where the applicant does not have a lawyer, serve it on the applicant, and file it, with proof of service, in this court office, and you or your lawyer must appear at the hearing.

IF YOU WISH TO PRESENT AFFIDAVIT OR OTHER DOCUMENTARY EVIDENCE TO THE COURT OR TO EXAMINE OR CROSS-EXAMINE WITNESSES ON THE APPLICATION, you or your lawyer must, in addition to serving your notice of appearance, serve a copy of the evidence on the applicant's lawyer or, where the applicant does not have a lawyer, serve it on the applicant, and file it with proof of service, in the court office where the application is to be heard, as soon as possible, but not later than two days before the hearing.

IF YOU FAIL TO APPEAR AT THE HEARING, JUDGMENT MAY BE GIVEN IN YOUR ABSENCE AND WITHOUT FURTHER NOTICE TO YOU.

If you wish to oppose this application but are unable to pay legal fees, legal aid may be available to you by contacting a local Legal Aid office.

Date . . . . Issued by . . . .

Local registrar

Address of court office

TO: (*Name and address of respondent,*
or lawyer for respondent)

1. The applicant makes application or directions from the court with respect to: (*state nature of proceeding*)

2. The grounds for the application are rule 75.06 and (*include a reference to any statutory provision or Rule to be relied on*).

3. The following documentary evidence will be used at the hearing of the application for directions: (*list the affidavits or other documentary evidence to be relied upon*).

July 1, 2007

FORM 75.6 — NOTICE OF MOTION FOR DIRECTIONS

Courts of Justice Act

[Repealed O. Reg. 77/06, s. 3.]

[Editor's Note: Forms 4A to 78A of the Rules of Civil Procedure have been repealed by O. Reg. 77/06, effective July 1, 2006. Pursuant to Rule of Civil Procedure 1.06, when a form is referred to by number, the reference is to the form with that number that is described in the Table of Forms at the end of these rules and which is available on the Internet through www.ontariocourtforms.on.ca. For your convenience, the government form as published on this website is reproduced below.]

ONTARIO
SUPERIOR COURT OF JUSTICE

IN THE ESTATE OF (*insert name*), deceased.

BETWEEN:

(*Name*)

Moving Party

- and -

(*Name*)

Respondent

NOTICE OF MOTION FOR DIRECTIONS

The moving party will make a motion to the court on (*date*), at (*time*), or so soon after that time as the motion can be heard at (*full address of Court House*).

The motion is for directions with respect to:

(*state nature of proceeding*)

The grounds for the motion are rule 75.06 and (*specify the further grounds to be argued, including a reference to any statutory provision or Rule*).

The following documentary evidence will be used at the hearing of the motion: (*list the affidavits or other documentary evidence to be relied on*).

DATE

(*Name, address and telephone number of applicant or lawyer for the applicant*)
TO: (*Name and address of respondent or lawyer for the respondent*)

July 1, 2007

FORM 75.7 — STATEMENT OF CLAIM PURSUANT TO ORDER GIVING DIRECTIONS

Courts of Justice Act

[Repealed O. Reg. 77/06, s. 3.]

[Editor's Note: Forms 4A to 78A of the Rules of Civil Procedure have been repealed by O. Reg. 77/06, effective July 1, 2006. Pursuant to Rule of Civil Procedure 1.06, when a form is referred to by number, the reference is to the form with that number that is described in the Table of Forms at the end of these rules and which is available on the Internet through www.ontariocourtforms.on.ca. For your convenience, the government form as published on this website is reproduced below.]

ONTARIO
SUPERIOR COURT OF JUSTICE

IN THE ESTATE OF (*insert name*), deceased.

BETWEEN:

(*Name*)

Plaintiff

- and -

(*Name*)

Defendant

- and -

(*Name*)

Persons Submitting
Rights to the Court

STATEMENT OF CLAIM PURSUANT TO ORDER GIVING DIRECTIONS

TO THE DEFENDANT

A LEGAL PROCEEDING HAS BEEN COMMENCED by the Plaintiff. The claim made is set out in the following pages.

IF YOU WISH TO DEFEND THIS PROCEEDING, you or an Ontario lawyer acting for you must prepare a statement of defence in Form 18A prescribed by the *Rules of Civil Procedure*, serve it on the plaintiff's lawyer, or, where the plaintiff does not have a lawyer, serve it on the plaintiff, and file it, with proof of service, in the court office, WITHIN 20 DAYS after this statement of claim is served upon you, if you are served in Ontario.

If you are served in another province or territory of Canada or in the United States of America, the period of serving and filing your statement of defence is 40 days. If you are served outside of Canada and the United States of America, the period is 60 days.

Instead of serving and filing a statement of defence, you may serve and file a Statement of Submission or Rights to the Court in Form 75.9 prescribed by the *Rules of Civil Procedure*.

IF YOU FAIL TO DEFEND THIS PROCEEDING, JUDGMENT MAY BE GIVEN AGAINST YOU IN YOUR ABSENCE AND WITHOUT FURTHER NOTICE TO YOU. IF YOU WISH TO DEFEND THIS PROCEEDING BUT ARE UNABLE TO PAY LEGAL FEES, LEGAL AID MAY BE AVAILABLE TO YOU BY CONTACTING A LOCAL LEGAL AID OFFICE.

1. The Plaintiff claims:

November 1, 2005

FORM 75.8 — ORDER GIVING DIRECTIONS WHERE PLEADINGS DIRECTED

Courts of Justice Act

[Repealed O. Reg. 77/06, s. 3.]

[Editor's Note: Forms 4A to 78A of the Rules of Civil Procedure have been repealed by O. Reg. 77/06, effective July 1, 2006. Pursuant to Rule of Civil Procedure 1.06, when a form is referred to by number, the reference is to the form with that number that is described in the Table of Forms at the end of these rules and which is available on the Internet through

www.ontariocourtforms.on.ca. For your convenience, the government form as published on this website is reproduced below.]

(*Heading in accordance with Form 59A*)

IN THE ESTATE OF (*insert name*), deceased.

BETWEEN:

(*Name*)

Applicant
- and - (Moving Party)

(*Name*)

Respondent
- and - (Responding Party)

(*Name*)

Persons Submitting
Rights to the Court

ORDER GIVING DIRECTIONS

THIS APPLICATION (*or* MOTION) made by (*identify applicant or moving party*) for directions, was heard on (*date*), at (*place*), in the presence of the lawyer(s) for (*insert name*), and (*insert name*) appearing in person, and no one appearing for (*insert name*), although properly served as appears from the affidavit of service, filed.

ON READING the notice of application (*or* notice of motion) and on hearing the submissions made,

1. THIS COURT ORDERS that (*insert name*) shall be plaintiff and (*insert name*) shall be defendant, and that (*insert names*) are submitting their rights to the court.

2. THIS COURT ORDERS that the plaintiff(s) shall serve upon the defendant(s) and file with the court a statement of claim in Form 75.7 within .... days after this order is entered, after which pleadings shall be served and filed under rule 75.07 of the Rules of Civil Procedure.

2.1 THIS COURT ORDERS that (*insert directions relating to mandatory mediation under Rule 75.1*).

3. THIS COURT ORDERS that the applicant and respondent shall serve and file affidavits of documents and attend and submit to examinations for discovery in accordance with the *Rules of Civil Procedure.*

4. THIS COURT ORDERS that on filing the appropriate documents with the court, (*insert name*) shall be appointed as estate trustee during litigation.

5. THIS COURT ORDERS that this order giving directions shall be served by an alternative to personal service pursuant to rule 16.03 of the *Rules of Civil Procedure*, on the following persons: (*insert names*)

6. THIS COURT ORDERS that the issues be tried by a judge with (*or* without) a jury at (*place*) on a date to be fixed by the registrar.

7. THIS COURT ORDERS that the costs of this application (*or* motion) shall be (*insert amount*)

July 1, 2007

FORM 75.9 — ORDER GIVING DIRECTIONS WHERE TRIAL OF ISSUES DIRECTED

Courts of Justice Act

[Repealed O. Reg. 77/06, s. 3.]

[Editor's Note: Forms 4A to 78A of the Rules of Civil Procedure have been repealed by O. Reg. 77/06, effective July 1, 2006. Pursuant to Rule of Civil Procedure 1.06, when a form is referred to by number, the reference is to the form with that number that is described in the Table of Forms at the end of these rules and which is available on the Internet through www.ontariocourtforms.on.ca. For your convenience, the government form as published on this website is reproduced below.]

(*Heading in accordance with Form 59A*)

IN THE ESTATE OF (*insert name*), deceased.

BETWEEN:

(*Name*)

Applicant
- and - (Moving Party)

(*Name*)

Respondent
- and - (Responding Party)

(*Name*)

Persons Submitting
Rights to the Court

ORDER GIVING DIRECTIONS

THIS APPLICATION (*or* MOTION) made by (*identify applicant or moving party*) for directions, was heard on (*date*), at (*place*), in the presence of the lawyer(s) for (*insert name*), and (*insert name*) appearing in person, and no one appearing for (*insert name*), although properly served as appears from the affidavit of service, filed.

ON READING the notice of application (*or* notice of motion) and on hearing the submissions made,

1. THIS COURT ORDERS that the parties to the proceeding and the issues to be tried be as follows:

(a) (*insert name*) affirms and (*insert name*) denies that (*state nature of allegation*);

(b) (*list each issue in a separate paragraph, specifying which parties affirm and which deny*).

2. THIS COURT ORDERS that (*insert names*) are submitting their rights to the court.

2.1 THIS COURT ORDERS that (*insert directions relating to mandatory mediation under Rule 75.1*).

3. THIS COURT ORDERS that the applicant and respondent shall serve and file affidavits of documents and attend and submit to examinations for discovery in accordance with the Rules of Civil Procedure.

4. THIS COURT ORDERS that on filing the appropriate documents with the court, (*insert name*) shall be appointed as estate trustee during litigation.

5. THIS COURT ORDERS that this order giving directions shall be served by an alternative to personal service pursuant to rule 16.03 of the Rules of Civil Procedure, on the following persons (*insert names*)

6. THIS COURT ORDERS that the issues be tried by a judge with (*or* without) a jury at (*place*) on a date to be fixed by the registrar.

7. THIS COURT ORDERS that the costs of this application (*or* motion) shall be (*insert amount*)

July 1, 2007

FORM 75.10 — STATEMENT OF SUBMISSION OF RIGHTS TO THE COURT

Courts of Justice Act

[Repealed O. Reg. 77/06, s. 3.]

[Editor's Note: Forms 4A to 78A of the Rules of Civil Procedure have been repealed by O. Reg. 77/06, effective July 1, 2006. Pursuant to Rule of Civil Procedure 1.06, when a form is referred to by number, the reference is to the form with that number that is described in the Table of Forms at the end of these rules and which is available on the Internet through www.ontariocourtforms.on.ca. For your convenience, the government form as published on this website is reproduced below.]

ONTARIO
SUPERIOR COURT OF JUSTICE

IN THE ESTATE OF (*insert name*), deceased.

BETWEEN:

(*Name*)

Applicant

- and -

(*Name*)

Respondent

STATEMENT OF SUBMISSION OF RIGHTS TO THE COURT

I, (*insert name*), submit my rights to the court and understand that pursuant to rule 75.07.1 of the Rules of Civil Procedure, the following consequences apply to me:

(a) I shall not be entitled to receive any costs in the proceeding and shall not be liable to pay the costs of any party to the proceeding, except indirectly to the extent that costs are ordered by the court to be paid out of the estate;

(b) I shall not receive notice of any step taken in the proceeding except the notice of trial and a copy of the judgment disposing of the matter;

(c) If the proceeding is settled by agreement, a judgment on consent will not be given without notice to me.

DATE

(*Name, address and telephone number of the*)
person or lawyer acting for person)

TO: (*Name and address of plaintiff,*
or lawyer for plaintiff)

July 1, 2007

FORM 75.11 — NOTICE OF SETTLEMENT

Courts of Justice Act

[Repealed O. Reg. 77/06, s. 3.]

[Editor's Note: Forms 4A to 78A of the Rules of Civil Procedure have been repealed by O. Reg. 77/06, effective July 1, 2006. Pursuant to Rule of Civil Procedure 1.06, when a form is referred to by number, the reference is to the form with that number that is described in the Table of Forms at the end of these rules and which is available on the Internet through www.ontariocourtforms.on.ca. For your convenience, the government form as published on this website is reproduced below.]

ONTARIO
SUPERIOR COURT OF JUSTICE

IN THE ESTATE OF (*insert name*), deceased.

BETWEEN:

(*Name*)

Applicant

- and -

(*Name*)

Respondent

- and -

(*Name*)

Persons Submitting Rights to the Court

NOTICE OF SETTLEMENT

Pursuant to rule 75.07 of the *Rules of Civil Procedure*, attached as Schedule "A" is a copy of the settlement agreement that has been reached among the parties.

A judgment consistent with the settlement agreement will be sought. If you oppose that judgment, you or an Ontario lawyer acting for you must, within 10 days of service on you of this notice of settlement, serve a rejection of settlement in the form attached as Schedule "B" on the lawyer for the party serving this notice, or where the party serving this notice does not have a lawyer, serve it on the party serving this notice, and file it with proof of service in the court office at (*place*).

If you fail to serve and file a rejection of settlement, the court will consider the request for judgment without further notice to you.

DATE

(*Name, address and telephone number of party*) *or lawyer for the party*)

TO: (*Names and addresses of all persons who have submitted their rights to the court*)

July 1, 2007

FORM 75.12 — REJECTION OF SETTLEMENT

Courts of Justice Act

[Repealed O. Reg. 77/06, s. 3.]

[Editor's Note: Forms 4A to 78A of the Rules of Civil Procedure have been repealed by O. Reg. 77/06, effective July 1, 2006. Pursuant to Rule of Civil Procedure 1.06, when a form is referred to by number, the reference is to the form with that number that is described in the Table of Forms at the end of these rules and which is available on the Internet through www.ontariocourtforms.on.ca. For your convenience, the government form as published on this website is reproduced below.]

ONTARIO
SUPERIOR COURT OF JUSTICE

IN THE ESTATE OF (*insert name*), deceased.

BETWEEN:

(*Name*)

Applicant
(Plaintiff)

- and -

(*Name*)

Respondent
(Defendant)

- and -

(*Name*)

Persons Submitting
Rights to the Court

REJECTION OF SETTLEMENT

I, (*insert name*), reject the settlement agreement attached to the notice of settlement dated (*insert date*), for the following reasons: (*state reasons*).

DATE

(*Name, address and telephone number of person or lawyer for person*)

TO: (*Name and address of party who served the notice of settlement or the lawyer for the party*)

July 1, 2007

FORM 75.13 — NOTICE OF CONTESTATION

Courts of Justice Act

[Repealed O. Reg. 77/06, s. 3.]

[Editor's Note: Forms 4A to 78A of the Rules of Civil Procedure have been repealed by O. Reg. 77/06, effective July 1, 2006. Pursuant to Rule of Civil Procedure 1.06, when a form is referred to by number, the reference is to the form with that number that is described in the Table of Forms at the end of these rules and which is available on the Internet through www.ontariocourtforms.on.ca. For your convenience, the government form as published on this website is reproduced below.]

ONTARIO
SUPERIOR COURT OF JUSTICE

IN THE ESTATE OF (*insert name*), deceased.

BETWEEN:

(*Name*)

Estate Trustee

- and -

(*Name*)

Claimant

NOTICE OF CONTESTATION

Pursuant to section 44 or 45 of the *Estates Act*, the estate trustee of the estate contests the claim made by you against the estate, on the following grounds:

(*state grounds*)

You may apply to this court at (*insert address of court office*) for an order allowing your claim and determining its amount. If you do not apply within 30 days after receiving this notice, or within 3 months after that date if the judge on application so allows, you shall be deemed to have abandoned your claim and your claim shall be forever barred.

DATE

(*Name, address and telephone number of estate trustee or lawyer for estate trustee*)

TO: (*Name and address of person submitting claim*)

July 1, 2007

FORM 75.14 — CLAIM AGAINST ESTATE

Courts of Justice Act

[Repealed O. Reg. 77/06, s. 3.]

[Editor's Note: Forms 4A to 78A of the Rules of Civil Procedure have been repealed by O. Reg. 77/06, effective July 1, 2006. Pursuant to Rule of Civil Procedure 1.06, when a form is referred to by number, the reference is to the form with that number that is described in the Table of Forms at the end of these rules and which is available on the Internet through www.ontariocourtforms.on.ca. For your convenience, the government form as published on this website is reproduced below.]

ONTARIO
SUPERIOR COURT OF JUSTICE

IN THE ESTATE OF (*insert name*), deceased.

BETWEEN:

(*Name*)

Claimant

- and -

(*Name*)

Estate Trustee

CLAIM AGAINST ESTATE

1. The claim against the estate is for $ .... for (*state grounds for claim*).

AFFIDAVIT

I, (*name of claimant*), of (*insert city or town and country or district, metropolitan or regional municipality of residence*), MAKE OATH/AFFIRM AND SAY:

1. The grounds set out in this claim are true.

SWORN/AFFIRMED BEFORE	)	
me at the of	)	
in the of	)	
this day of , 20 .	)	
	)	
	)	
	)	....

....
A Commissioner for Taking Affidavits
(*or as may be*)

November 1, 2005

FORM 76A — NOTICE WHETHER ACTION UNDER RULE 76

Courts of Justice Act

[Repealed O. Reg. 77/06, s. 3.]

[Editor's Note: Forms 4A to 78A of the Rules of Civil Procedure have been repealed by O. Reg. 77/06, effective July 1, 2006. Pursuant to Rule of Civil Procedure 1.06, when a form is referred to by number, the reference is to the form with that number that is described in the Table of Forms at the end of these rules and which is available on the Internet through www.ontariocourtforms.on.ca. For your convenience, the government form as published on this website is reproduced below.]

Courts of Justice Act

(General heading)

NOTICE WHETHER ACTION UNDER RULE 76

The plaintiff states that this action and any related proceedings are:

(select one of the following:)

( ) continuing under Rule 76

( ) continuing as an ordinary procedure.

(Name, address and telephone and fax numbers of lawyer or plaintiff)

November 1, 2008

FORM 76B — SIMPLIFIED PROCEDURE MOTION FORM

Courts of Justice Act

[Repealed O. Reg. 77/06, s. 3.]

[Editor's Note: Forms 4A to 78A of the Rules of Civil Procedure have been repealed by O. Reg. 77/06, effective July 1, 2006. Pursuant to Rule of Civil Procedure 1.06, when a form is referred to by number, the reference is to the form with that number that is described in the Table of Forms at the end of these rules and which is available on the Internet through www.ontariocourtforms.on.ca. For your convenience, the government form as published on this website is reproduced below.]

Court File No. ....

(General heading)

SIMPLIFIED PROCEDURE MOTION FORM

JURISDICTION
( ) Judge
( ) Master
( ) Registrar

THIS FORM IS FILED BY *(Check appropriate boxes to identify the party filing this form as a moving/responding party on this motion AND to identify this party as plaintiff, defendant, etc. in the action)*

[ ] moving party

[ ] plaintiff

. . . .

[ ] responding party

[ ] defendant

. . . .

[ ] Other — specify kind of party and name

MOTION MADE

[ ] on consent of all parties

[ ] on notice to all parties and unopposed

[ ] without notice

[ ] on notice to all parties and expected to be opposed

Notice of this motion was served on (date): . . . .

by means of:

. . . .

. . . .

METHOD OF HEARING REQUESTED

[ ] by attendance

[ ] in writing only, no attendance

[ ] by fax

[ ] by telephone conference under rule 1.08

[ ] by video conference under rule 1.08

Date, time and place for conference call, telephone call or appearances

.................................(date).................................(time)..................................(place)

ORDER SOUGHT BY THIS PARTY (*Responding party is presumed to request dismissal of motion and costs*)

[ ] Extension of time — until *(give specific date)* . . . . :

[ ] serve claim

[ ] file or deliver statement of defence

[ ] Other relief — be specific

. . . .

. . . .

MATERIAL RELIED ON BY THIS PARTY

[ ] this form

[ ] pleadings

[ ] affidavits — specify

[ ] other — specify

. . . .

. . . .

GROUNDS IN SUPPORT OF/IN OPPOSITION TO MOTION (INCLUDING RULE AND STATUTORY PROVISIONS RELIED ON)

. . . .

. . . .

CERTIFICATION BY LAWYER

I certify that the above information is correct, to the best of my knowledge.

Signature of lawyer *(If no lawyer, party must sign)*

. . . .

Date

. . . .

THIS PARTY'S LAWYER *(If no lawyer, give party's name, address for service, telephone and fax number.)*

Name and firm:

Address:

Telephone:
Fax:

OTHER LAWYER *(If no lawyer, give other party's name, address for service, telephone and fax number.)*

Name and firm:

Address:

Telephone:
Fax:

THIS PARTY'S LAWYER *(If no lawyer, give party's name, address for service, telephone and fax number.)*	OTHER LAWYER *(If no lawyer, give other party's name, address for service, telephone and fax number.)*
Name and firm:	Name and firm:
Address:	Address:
Telephone:	Telephone:
Fax:	Fax:

DISPOSITION

[ ] order to go as asked

[ ] adjourned to

[ ] order refused

[ ] order to go as follows:

. . . .

. . . .

Hearing method..................................Hearing duration..................................min.

Heard in: [ ] courtroom [ ] office

[ ] Successful party MUST prepare formal order for signature

[ ] No copy of disposition to be sent to parties

[ ] Other directions — specify

. . . .

. . . .

Date . . . . Name . . . . Signature . . . .
Judge/Master/Registrar

November 1, 2005

FORM 76C — NOTICE OF READINESS FOR PRE-TRIAL CONFERENCE

Courts of Justice Act

[Repealed O. Reg. 77/06, s. 3.]

[Editor's Note: Forms 4A to 78A of the Rules of Civil Procedure have been repealed by O. Reg. 77/06, effective July 1, 2006. Pursuant to Rule of Civil Procedure 1.06, when a form is referred to by number, the reference is to the form with that number that is described in the Table of Forms at the end of these rules and which is available on the Internet through www.ontariocourtforms.on.ca. For your convenience, the government form as published on this website is reproduced below.]

(*General heading*)

NOTICE OF READINESS FOR PRE-TRIAL CONFERENCE

The *(identify party)* is ready for a pre-trial conference and is setting this action down for trial. A pre-trial conference in the action will proceed as scheduled and the trial will proceed when the action is reached on the trial list, unless the court orders otherwise.

CERTIFICATE

I CERTIFY that there was a settlement discussion under rule 76.08.

Date (*Signature*)

(Name, address and telephone and fax numbers of lawyers or party giving notice)

TO *(Name and address of lawyer or party receiving notice)*

November 1, 2005

FORM 76D — TRIAL MANAGEMENT CHECKLIST

Courts of Justice Act

[Repealed O. Reg. 77/06, s. 3.]

[Editor's Note: Forms 4A to 78A of the Rules of Civil Procedure have been repealed by O. Reg. 77/06, effective July 1, 2006. Pursuant to Rule of Civil Procedure 1.06, when a form is referred to by number, the reference is to the form with that number that is described in the Table of Forms at the end of these rules and which is available on the Internet through www.ontariocourtforms.on.ca. For your convenience, the government form as published on this website is reproduced below.]

(*General heading*)

(*Insert name of party filing this form*)

TRIAL MANAGEMENT CHECKLIST

Trial Lawyer — Plaintiff(s):

Trial Lawyer — Defendant(s):

Filed by Plaintiff

Filed by Defendant

Filed by Subsequent Party

1. Issues Outstanding

   (a) liability:

   ....

   (b) damages:

   ....

   (c) other

   ....

2. Names of Plaintiff's Witnesses

....

3. Names of Defendant's Witnesses

....

4. Admissions

....

Are the parties prepared to admit any facts for the purposes of the trial or summary trial?

yes ❑ no❑

5. Document Brief

   Will there be a document brief? yes ❑ no ❑

6. Request to Admit

   Will there be a request to admit? yes ❑ no ❑

   If so, have the parties agreed to a timetable? yes ❑ no ❑

7. Expert's Reports

   Are any expert's reports anticipated? yes ❑ no ❑

8. Amendments to Pleadings

   Are any amendments likely to be sought? yes ❑ no ❑

9. Mode of Trial

   Have the parties agreed to a summary trial? yes ❑ no ❑

   Have the parties agreed to an ordinary trial? yes ❑ no ❑

   If the parties have not agreed about the mode of trial, what mode of trial is being requested by the party filing this checklist?

   ....

10. Factum of Law

Will the parties be submitting factums of law? yes ❑ no ❑

November 1, 2005

FORM 77C — [REPEALED O. REG. 438/08, S. 67(4).]

[Repealed O. Reg. 438/08, s. 67(4).]

FORM 77D — [REPEALED O. REG. 438/08, S. 67(4).]

[Repealed O. Reg. 438/08, s. 67(4).]

FORM 78A — [REPEALED O. REG. 438/08, S. 67(4).]

[Repealed O. Reg. 438/08, s. 67(4).]

INDEX TO FORMS

S

TARIFFS

Tariff A — LAWYERS' FEES AND DISBURSEMENTS ALLOWABLE UNDER RULES 57.01 AND 58.05 [HEADING AMENDED O. REG. 42/05, S. 7(1).]

PART I — FEES

The fee for any step in a proceeding authorized by the *Rules of Civil Procedure* and the counsel fee for motions, applications, trials, references and appeals shall be determined in accordance with section 131 of the *Courts of Justice Act* and the factors set out in subrule 57.01(1).

Where students-at-law or law clerks have provided services of a nature that the Law Society of Upper Canada authorizes them to provide, fees for those services may be allowed.

PART II — DISBURSEMENTS

21.	Attendance money actually paid to a witness who is entitled to attendance money, to be calculated as follows:	
	1. Attendance allowance for each day of necessary attendance	$50
	2. Travel allowance, where the hearing or examination is held,	
	(a) in a city or town in which the witness resides, $3.00 for each day of necessary attendance;	
	(b) within 300 kilometres of where the witness resides, 24¢ a kilometre each way between his or her residence and the place of hearing or examination;	
	(c) more than 300 kilometres from where the witness resides, the minimum return air fare plus 24¢ a kilometre each way from his or her residence to the airport and from the airport to the place of hearing or examination.	
	3. Overnight accommodation and meal allowance, where the witness resides elsewhere than the place of hearing or examination and is required to remain overnight, for each overnight stay	$75
22.	Fees or expenses actually paid to a court, authorized court transcriptionist, official examiner or sheriff under the regulations under the *Administration of Justice Act*.	
23.	For service or attempted service of a document,	
	(a) in Ontario, the amount actually paid, not exceeding the fee payable to a sheriff under the regulations under the *Administration of Justice Act*;	
	(b) outside Ontario, a reasonable amount;	

(c) that was ordered to be served by publication, a reasonable amount.

23.1 Fees actually paid to a mediator in accordance with Ontario Regulation 451/98 made under the *Administration of Justice Act*.

23.2 Fees actually paid to a mediator in accordance with Ontario Regulation 291/99 made under the *Administration of Justice Act*

24. For an examination and transcript of evidence taken on the examination, the amount actually paid, not exceeding the fee payable to an official examiner under the regulations under the *Administration of Justice Act*.

25. For the preparation of a plan, model, videotape, film or photograph reasonably necessary for the conduct of the proceeding, a reasonable amount.

26. For experts' reports that were supplied to the other parties as required by the *Evidence Act* or these rules and that were reasonably necessary for the conduct of the proceeding, a reasonable amount.

27. The cost of the investigation and report of the Official Guardian.

28. For an expert who gives opinion evidence at the hearing or whose attendance was reasonably necessary at the hearing, a reasonable amount not exceeding $350 a day, subject to increase in the discretion of the assessment officer.

29. For an interpreter for services at the hearing or on an examination, a reasonable amount not exceeding $100 a day, subject to increase in the discretion of the assessment officer.

29.1 Where ordered by the presiding judge or officer, for translation into English or French of a document that has been filed, a reasonable amount.

30. Where ordered by the presiding judge or officer, such travelling and accommodation expenses incurred by a party as, in the discretion of the assessment officer, appear reasonable.

31. For copies of any documents or authorities prepared for or by a party for the use of the court and supplied to the opposite party, a reasonable amount.

32. For copies of records, appeal books and compendiums, and factums, a reasonable amount.

33. The cost of certified copies of documents such as orders, birth, marriage, and death certificates, abstracts of title, deeds, mortgages and other registered documents where reasonably necessary for the conduct of the proceeding.

34. The cost of transcripts of proceedings of courts or tribunals,

(a) where required by the court or the rules; or

(b) where reasonably necessary for the conduct of the proceeding.

35. Where ordered by the presiding judge or officer, for any other disbursement reasonably necessary for the conduct of the proceeding, a reasonable amount in the discretion of the assessment officer.

36. Harmonized sales tax (HST) actually paid or payable on the lawyer's fees and disbursements allowable under rule 58.05.

O. Reg. 219/91, s. 16; 351/94, s. 19; 533/95, s. 12; 453/98, s. 3; 290/99, s. 6; 24/00, s. 32; 652/00, s. 8; 113/01, s. 15; 243/01, s. 1; 244/01, ss. 5, 6; 284/01, s. 38; 457/01, s. 18; 19/03, s. 26; 131/04, s. 27; 42/05, s. 7; 575/07, s. 37; 55/12, s. 14; 170/14, s. 25

Tariff B — [REVOKED O. REG. 131/04, S. 28.]

[Revoked O. Reg. 131/04, s. 28.]

Tariff C — LAWYERS' COSTS ALLOWED ON PASSING OF ACCOUNTS WITHOUT A HEARING [HEADING AMENDED O. REG. 575/07, S. 38(1).]

(1) — Estate Trustee

Amount of receipts	*Amount of costs*
Less than $300,000	$2,500
$300,000 or more, but less than $500,000	3,000
$500,000 or more, but less than $1,000,000	3,500
$1,000,000 or more, but less than $3,000,000	5,000
$3,000,000 or more	7,500

(2) — Person With Financial Interest in Estate

If a person with a financial interest in an estate retains a lawyer to review the accounts, makes no objection to the accounts (or makes an objection and later withdraws it), and serves and files a request for costs, the person is entitled to one-half of the amount payable to the estate trustee.

(3) — Children's Lawyer or Public Guardian and Trustee

If the Children's Lawyer or the Public Guardian and Trustee makes no objection to the accounts (or makes an objection and later withdraws it) and serves and files a request for costs, he or she is entitled to three-quarters of the amount payable to the estate trustee.

Note: If two or more persons are represented by the same lawyer, they are entitled to receive only one person's costs.

Note: A person entitled to costs under this tariff is also entitled to the amount of harmonized sales tax (HST) on those costs.

O. Reg. 484/94, s. 14; 332/96, s. 10; 575/07, s. 38; 55/12, s. 15

PRACTICE DIRECTIONS

TABLE OF CONTENTS

MAP OF REGIONS

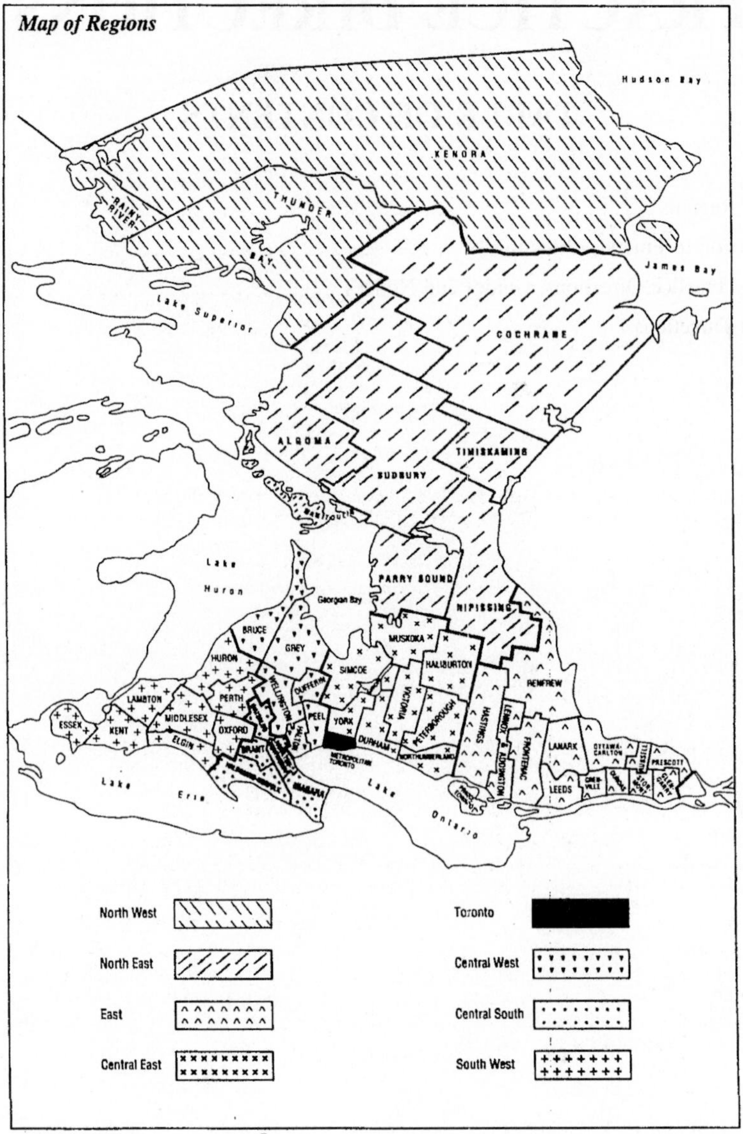

INTRODUCTION TO PRACTICE DIRECTIONS, GUIDES, AND NOTICES

Effective July 1, 2014 a series of new consolidated practice directions were introduced to supersede previous Superior Court province-wide practice directions, regional practice directions and Divisional Court practice directions. It is expected that a consolidated practice direction for the Court of Appeal will be issued soon. Two new Guides were also introduced effective July 1, 2014, one concerning electronic delivery of documents in Superior Court of Justice proceedings, and one concerning electronic service of documents in Commercial List proceedings. The Office of the Chief Justice of the Superior Court has issued an introductory note, reproduced under item 3(a) below.

The scheme of the practice directions is that the consolidated province-wide practice directions apply throughout Ontario subject to local variations contained in the regional consolidated practice directions. A map of the judicial regions is set out on the opposite page.

Effective March 1, 2017 the Court of Appeal issued a new Practice Direction Concerning Civil Appeals at the Court of Appeal for Ontario as well as (a) Guidelines for Filing Electronic Documents at the Court of Appeal for Ontario; (b) a Reference Guide for Citation Practices at the Court of Appeal for Ontario; (c) a List of Frequently Cited Civil Authorities; and (d) a Joint Request for Pre-Hearing Settlement Conference Form. Subsequently, on May 1 2017, the Court of Appeal issued Guidelines: Teleconference and Videoconference Appearances in the Court of Appeal for Ontario.

Recent Amendments. The Consolidated Practice Direction Concerning Family Cases in Central East Region was amended effective December 1, 2017. Part III H [paras. 110–115] of the Consolidated Practice Direction for the Central South Region was revoked on May 1, 2017. Part III A [paras. 75–80] of the Consolidated Practice Direction for the Central West Region was revoked on May 1, 2017 and Part I J [paragraphs 26 and 27] (family proceedings — case conferences and settlement conferences) was replaced on January 1, 2017. Effective May 1, 2017, para. 57 of the Consolidated Practice Direction for Civil Actions, Applications, Motions and Procedural Matters in the Toronto Region and the related certificate have been amended regarding mediation prior to setting an action down for trial. A Practice Advisory re Video Conferencing for Civil Practice Court, Commercial List Chambers Matters and Estates List 9:30 appointments in the Toronto Region was issued effective March 8, 2017.

Effective June 15, 2018 the Consolidated Provincial Practice Direction of the Superior Court of Justice was amended to: (a) update para. 46 regarding the times for family long motions in the Southwest Region; (b) to amend Part V, Section C regarding digital recordings of civil motions, family motions, and Small Claims Court proceedings; and (c) to add Part VI regarding books of authorities in civil proceedings.

TABLE OF PRACTICE DIRECTIONS, GUIDES AND NOTICES

PRACTICE DIRECTIONS

PD-1 — *PRACTICE DIRECTION CONCERNING CIVIL APPEALS AT THE COURT OF APPEAL FOR ONTARIO*

Effective: 1 March 2017

1. — Effective Date

This Practice Direction Concerning Civil Appeals at the Court of Appeal for Ontario revokes and replaces the Court of Appeal's previously issued Practice Direction Concerning Civil Appeals (effective 1 January 2004, updated November 2008).

This Practice Direction was filed with the Secretary of the Civil Rules Committee on 24 January 2017 and is published pursuant to rule 1.07 of the *Rules of Civil Procedure*. It is effective as of 1 March 2017.

2. — Application of the Rules of Civil Procedure

When bringing an appeal or motion in the Court of Appeal, parties must consult the *Rules of Civil Procedure*, R.R.O. 1990, Reg. 194.

Rule 61 is the primary rule governing procedures for bringing appeals and motions in writing for leave to appeal in the Court of Appeal. Rule 61.03.1 governs motions for leave to appeal. Rule 61.16 and Rule 37 are the primary rules governing procedures for bringing motions to a single judge and motions to a three-judge panel of the Court of Appeal, except for motions for leave to appeal.

Other rules that more commonly apply to appeals and motions in the Court of Appeal include:

- Rule 2 (Non-compliance with the Rules)
- Rule 2.1 (General Powers to Stay or Dismiss a Proceeding/Motion if Vexatious, etc.)
- Rule 3 (Time)
- Rule 4 (Court Documents)
- Rule 16.01(3)-(4); 16.03–16.09 (Service)
- Rule 57 (Costs of Proceedings)
- Rule 58 (Assessment of Costs)

- Rule 63 (Stay Pending Appeal)

Practice directions supplement the *Rules of Civil Procedure* and provide guidance and direction about matters not covered by the *Rules*. If there is a conflict between the *Rules of Civil Procedure* and this Practice Direction, the *Rules of Civil Procedure* take precedence.

3. — Access to Court Services in French

Motions and appeals are equally available in English and French without delay. Where you are proceeding in French or in both English and French, please note this in your correspondence.

The staff of the Court of Appeal for Ontario is pleased to serve the public in English and French. Staff will direct French inquiries to bilingual staff members.

4. — Correspondence

4.1 — Providing a Copy of all Correspondence to Opposing Parties

1. Any correspondence addressed to the Court of Appeal in relation to a court file must be copied to all parties to the proceeding or, if the parties are represented by a lawyer(s), to their lawyer(s) of record. This requirement applies, without limitation, to any correspondence addressed to the Registrar, Deputy Registrar, Senior Legal Officer, the Appeal Scheduling Unit and/or the Motions Clerk. All such correspondence must contain the Court of Appeal file number (where applicable) and title of proceeding.

2. In the event that correspondence addressed to the Court of Appeal or any of its staff is not copied to all parties or their lawyers, it will not be received, reviewed or answered.

4.2 — Correspondence to a Judge Must be Addressed to the Registrar of the Court of Appeal

1. Rule 1.09 of the *Rules of Civil Procedure* requires that all parties must consent to out-of-court communications with a judge about a court proceeding unless the court directs otherwise.

All correspondence intended to be reviewed by a judge or judges must be addressed to the Registrar and copied to all parties to the proceeding or, if the parties are represented by a lawyer(s), to their lawyer(s) of record. The Registrar will consult with the judge(s) to whom the correspondence is directed for directions as to whether the judge(s) will receive the correspondence.

2. In the event that correspondence intended to be reviewed by a judge or judges is not addressed to the Registrar or is not copied to all parties or their lawyers, it will not be received, reviewed or answered.

4.3. — Restrictions on Sending Correspondence by Email

1. The Court of Appeal E-filing address, COA.E-file@ontario.ca, must only be used to deliver electronic versions of factums, transcripts and other documents specified in this Practice Direction and in the Guidelines for Filing Electronic Documents at

the Court of Appeal for Ontario. This email address is not designed or intended to receive any inquiries or other communications about court proceedings.

2. Please consult the Guidelines for Filing Electronic Documents at the Court of Appeal for Ontario for the complete list of the type of documents that may be sent to COA.E-file@ontario.ca.

3. In order to receive a timely response to an inquiry involving proceedings in the Court of Appeal, including case searches, status inquiries, or inquiries about filing requirements, please call 416-327-5020 or toll free at 1-855-718-1756. Inquiries may also be sent via fax to (416) 327-5032. Alternatively, you may consult the Court of Appeal's website for detailed information about how best to direct your inquiry: http://www.ontariocourts.ca/coa/en/about/information.htm

5. — Service

5.1 — Service

1. The Registrar will accept copies of affidavits of service. The court will address any issues associated with proof of service as necessary.

2. The requirement in the *Rules of Civil Procedure* to serve and file electronic versions of appeal material (factums and transcripts) may be met by satisfying the Registrar that the electronic version was emailed to the opposing party(ies), together with proof of service of the paper version of the factum and transcript.

5.2 — Service on a Party Acting in Person

Rule 16 of the *Rules of Civil Procedure* describes the ways that service shall be made on a party acting in person ("self-represented party") and a party with a lawyer of record. To clarify, in the case of service on a party acting in person, service may be made by regular mail, registered mail, or by courier. If service is by courier, the deponent of the affidavit of service must indicate the date when the document was provided to the courier and the date that the courier provided the document to the self-represented party.

5.3 — Alternative Arrangements for Service of Court Documents

When a judge of the Ontario Superior Court of Justice has made an order approving a form of substituted service pursuant to rule 16.04 of the *Rules of Civil Procedure*, including an order approving and adopting the "Commercial List E-Service Guide", the parties should file a copy of such order with the Registrar of the Court of Appeal, together with the notice of appeal. When such an order has been filed, the service of documents in accordance with the order shall be considered as valid and effective service for all documents filed in the Court of Appeal, unless a judge of the Court of Appeal directs otherwise.

6. — Notice of Appeal in Civil Appeals

6.1 — Time for Commencing an Appeal

1. A party must serve a notice of appeal together with the certificate required by rule 61.05(1) of the *Rules of Civil Procedure* within 30 days after the order appealed

from was made, unless a statute or the *Rules* provide otherwise. The notice of appeal, with proof of service, must be filed in the Registrar's Office in person or by mail within 10 days after service.

The time limit for serving the notice of appeal is 30 days from the making of the order or judgment that the party is appealing from and not 30 days from the making of a subsequent, related order, such as an order dealing with costs.

2. Rules 16.05 and 16.06 specify when service of a document becomes effective. For example, if a notice of appeal is served by mail, then service of the notice of appeal only becomes effective on the fifth day after the document is mailed. In other words, the notice of appeal must be mailed at least five days before the expiry of the 30-day time period for filing the notice of appeal. Rule 3 regulates the computation of time under the *Rules of Civil Procedure*.

6.2 — Title of Proceeding

The title of a proceeding in the Court of Appeal must conform to rule 61.04(2) of the *Rules of Civil Procedure* and Form 61B. The title of proceeding should set out the parties in the same order as they appear in the title of proceeding in the court appealed from. Clearly identify the appellant and respondent as indicated in Form 61B.

The title of proceeding should include any person who has been added as a party to the proceeding by an order of the court under rule 13.01 or 13.03(2) of the *Rules of Civil Procedure*. The title of proceeding should not include any person who has been granted leave to intervene as a friend of the court under rule 13.02 or 13.03(2).

6.3 — Jurisdictional Statement — Ensuring the Court of Appeal has Jurisdiction

1. The *Rules of Civil Procedure* require that the notice of appeal includes a jurisdictional statement identifying the statutory or other basis for filing an appeal in a particular appellate court. This requirement is intended to avoid the problem of appeals being filed in the wrong court, or appeals being commenced even though there is no right to appeal from the order in question, or leave to appeal from the order is required before an appeal may be brought.

2. Parties need to be aware that there is no common law or inherent right of appeal. For there to be a right of appeal from any order or judgment, the right of appeal must be conferred by a statute. Accordingly, the jurisdictional statement in the notice of appeal must set out the basis upon which the appellant claims that the Court of Appeal has jurisdiction to entertain the appeal, including any relevant statute that provides for an appeal to the Court of Appeal.

3. The *Courts of Justice Act*, R.S.O. 1990, c. C.43, provides for the general appellate jurisdiction of the Court of Appeal and the Divisional Court in civil matters (see ss. 6, 19 and 21.9.1 of the *Courts of Justice Act*). Parties to an appeal need to consider and indicate whether the order under appeal is final or interlocutory (see s. 6(1)(b) of the *Courts of Justice Act*). In addition, if the order is only for the payment of money, then the parties need to review s. 19(1.2) of the *Courts of Justice Act* to determine if the appeal lies to the Court of Appeal or to the Divisional Court. In family law matters, the parties need to consider the application of s. 21.9.1 of the *Courts of Justice Act* to determine if the appeal lies to the Divisional Court rather than to the Court of Appeal.

4. In preparing the jurisdictional statement, parties must be aware that provisions of other statutes that govern certain types of litigation may displace the general provisions of the *Courts of Justice Act* by providing that an appeal from an order lies to the Divisional Court (for example, see s. 255 of the Ontario *Business Corporations Act*,

R.S.O. 1990, c. B.16, and s. 30 of the *Class Proceedings Act, 1992*, S.O. 1992, c. 6). Parties must also consider that orders may not be appealed if they were made under a statute that explicitly precludes a right of appeal (e.g., see the *Arbitration Act, 1991*, S.O. 1991, c. 17, ss. 7(6), 10(2), 15 and 17). In addition, some legislation requires leave to appeal before an appeal may be filed (e.g., see the *Arbitration Act, 1991*, S.O. 1991, c. 17, s. 49).

6.4 — Additional Information to Provide to the Court

On all documents filed with the court, parties shall include their telephone number, fax number, mailing address, email address (if available) and, in the case of lawyers, Law Society number.

Lawyers and self-represented parties should promptly advise the court and the other parties of any changes to their mailing or email address by emailing the Registrar's Office at COA.E-file@ontario.ca or by fax to 416-327-5032. Please include in the subject line of the email the title of proceeding and the court file number and the nature of the information being provided.

7. — Motions to the Court of Appeal in Civil Matters

7.1 — Motions to a Single Judge

7.1.1 — General

1. A single judge of the Court of Appeal hears motions Monday through Friday in chambers court located in Courtroom 7 at Osgoode Hall. From September to June, motions court starts at 10 a.m., unless the court orders otherwise. In July and August, motions court starts at 9:30 a.m., unless the court orders otherwise.

2. Lawyers do not need to wear gowns when they appear on motions before a single judge in chambers.

7.1.2 — Notice of Motion

1. The notice of motion must be formatted in accordance with Form 37A of the *Rules of Civil Procedure*.

2. The moving party may select the date for the hearing of a motion if the time limits in Rule 37 of the *Rules of Civil Procedure* for serving and filing the notice of motion and the motion record are met. Section 7.1.5 of this Practice Direction discusses the deadlines for filing a notice of motion and motion record.

3. The notice of motion must contain a statement outlining the jurisdiction of a single judge to hear the motion and to grant the relief requested.

4. The notice of motion must contain an estimated length of time for the oral argument of the motion.

5. If the hearing of a motion is expected to take more than 30 minutes, the moving party is strongly encouraged to contact the motions desk at 416-327-5020 (select your language of choice, followed by option 3) to determine the current status of the list before selecting a hearing date and serving and filing the motion material.

7.1.3 — Scheduling Motions

1. Self-represented parties, and lawyers who are bringing motions involving self-represented parties, are encouraged to schedule motions on Wednesdays or Thursdays when pro bono (free) duty counsel will be present at the court to provide advice and assistance to self-represented parties.

2. Parties who are self-represented in family law matters, and lawyers who are bringing motions against self-represented parties in family law matters, are encouraged to schedule motions on Wednesdays when pro bono (free) family law duty counsel will be available to provide advice and assistance to self-represented parties.

3. Duty counsel in motions court assists self-represented parties as *amicus curiae*, or "friend of the court".

4. More information about the duty counsel and family law duty counsel program can be obtained at the following link: http://www.ontariocourts.ca/coa/en/info/civfam/legalaid.htm

5. On Wednesdays and Thursdays, motions brought by or against self-represented parties receive priority. When all parties are represented by lawyers, they are advised to schedule motions on other days of the week if possible in order to avoid delays in having their motion heard.

6. If the moving party's estimated time for arguing a motion is 15 minutes or more, the moving party must serve and file a factum. If the moving party does not file a factum, then the moving party's time for oral argument shall be limited to 15 minutes.

7. In order to ensure the efficient use of court resources, the Registrar may direct that a motion scheduled for hearing be removed from the list and rescheduled to a different date. The parties will be consulted before the motion is removed from the list and the hearing rescheduled.

7.1.4 — Motions on Consent

1. Where all parties consent to an order, the moving party should file a notice of motion, two copies of the draft order, and a document indicating the parties' consent to the order. This document must be signed by the parties or their lawyers and contain the relevant court file number(s) and the title of proceeding. Parties are advised to include an affidavit or covering letter addressed to the Office of the Registrar setting out why the consent order is appropriate.

2. If a judge considering the proposed consent order is satisfied that it should issue, the order will be issued, usually within 2-3 business days.

3. If a judge considering the proposed order is not satisfied that it is appropriate or that it should issue, the parties will be advised and will be given an opportunity to provide oral or written argument.

7.1.5 — Requirement to Deliver a Motion Record and the Time Limits for Service and Filing

1. Rule 37.10 of the *Rules of Civil Procedure* requires the moving party to serve and file a notice of motion and a motion record together with proof of service at least seven days before the hearing date. To ensure the efficient hearing of motions by a single judge, the Registrar's office will only schedule a motion for hearing if the notice of motion and the motion record are served and filed at least seven days before the hearing date, subject to the exceptions noted in paragraphs 3 and 4 below.

2. The motion record should include the materials referred to in rule 37.10(2). In accordance with rule 37.10(2)(e), the moving party should include in the motion record a copy of the Notice of Appeal or, if the party is seeking an extension of time, the proposed Notice of Appeal. The motion record should also include any previous court order(s) made in the proceeding that is (are) relevant to the issues on the motion together with the court's reasons for the prior order(s).

3. As provided in rule 37.10(1), the moving party may seek to obtain court approval dispensing with the requirement to file a motion record. To obtain such approval, the moving party should send a letter to the attention of the Registrar setting out the reasons for the request. The letter should be copied to the responding party(ies) and be sent by email to COA.E-file@ontario.ca or by fax to 416-327-5032. The request and any response by the responding party(ies) will be placed before a judge of the Court of Appeal in advance of the hearing.

4. In situations of urgency or in unanticipated circumstances where the time limits for filing a notice of motion and/or motion record cannot be complied with, the material may be served and/or filed on shorter notice only by filing a consent or with leave of a judge.

5. When a party seeks an abridgement of the time to serve and/or file motion materials, the notice of motion should include in the relief sought a request for an abridgement of the time limits for serving and/or filing the relevant motion material. The request for an abridgement of time should be supported by a letter or affidavit explaining the reason for the request. The moving party shall deliver the letter or affidavit and accompanying motion materials to the Registrar's Office in person or by email to COA.E-file@ontario.ca or by fax to 416-327-5032. The Registrar will present the materials to a judge to determine if the material may be filed and if the motion may be heard on the date requested, and the parties will be promptly advised of the outcome.

7.1.6 — Including Materials from the Court File in the Motion Record

If the parties wish to refer at the hearing of the motion to any material from the court file that is associated with the appeal, or if they wish to refer to any material from a prior motion, the moving party must submit a letter addressed to the motions clerk asking for the specified material to be placed before the motions judge. The letter should be submitted at the same time that the motion materials must be filed pursuant to rule 37.10 of the *Rules of Civil Procedure*.

7.1.7 — Factums for Use on Motions

1. Factums greatly assist the judges in hearing and deciding motions. At the same time, it is understood that the filing of factums in some relatively simple motions may not be necessary and may cause undue expense to the parties.

2. As a result, a factum must be served and filed in motions before a single judge if the moving party's estimated time for argument is 15 minutes or more.

3. The last paragraph of a factum for a motion must indicate the amount of time estimated to argue the motion, not including reply.

4. The court requests that the parties file an electronic copy of any factum filed on a motion. For details on the procedures for filing electronic material, please consult the Guidelines for Filing Electronic Documents at the Court of Appeal for Ontario.

5. In the majority of motions, the length of the factums should be 10 pages or less. Factums shall not be more than 30 pages without a court order authorizing the filing of a longer factum.

6. If a party does not file a factum on a motion, the party will be limited to 15 minutes of oral argument at the hearing of the motion.

7.1.8 — Motions to Expedite

1. Motions to expedite the production of transcripts must be served on the opposing party and the authorized court transcriptionist.

2. Motions to expedite appeals may be brought to a judge in chambers. For more information on expedited appeals, see section 12.1 of this Practice Direction.

7.1.9 — Ex Parte Motions (Motions Without Notice to the Other Party)

When a party seeks to bring a motion without serving the notice of motion on the opposing party(ies), the moving party must indicate in the notice of motion the reasons for seeking to bring the motion without notice. A judge of the court will review the notice of motion and may grant the request to move without notice if the judge is satisfied that the nature of the motion or the circumstances render service of the notice of motion impracticable or unnecessary.

7.1.10 — Motions to Intervene in an Appeal

1. Motions to intervene in a civil proceeding in the Court of Appeal are heard by the Chief Justice or Associate Chief Justice or a judge designated for the purpose: see rule 13.03(2) of the *Rules of Civil Procedure*.

2. The parties should consult with each other to obtain mutually agreeable dates for hearing the motion and present these dates to the court through correspondence addressed to the court's Senior Legal Officer. If the parties cannot agree on suitable dates, the court will fix the date of the hearing. The moving party will be advised of the hearing date selected by the court and will be responsible for notifying the other parties.

3. After the date for the hearing of the motion to intervene is confirmed, the moving party must file a notice of motion, motion record, factum, and other material for use by the court in accordance with rule 37.10 of the *Rules of Civil Procedure* and this Practice Direction.

4. The parties may request that the motion for intervention be heard by teleconference call or videoconference. This request should be included in correspondence addressed to the Senior Legal Officer, who will put the request to the judge assigned to hear the motion.

7.2 — Motions before Three Judges

7.2.1. — Panel Motions (Except for Motions for Leave to Appeal to the Court of Appeal)

A three-judge panel of the Court of Appeal holds oral hearings on the following types of motions ("panel motions"):

- motions to quash an appeal pursuant to s. 134(3) of the *Courts of Justice Act*;
- motions under s. 7(5) of the *Courts of Justice Act* to set aside or vary the decision of a single judge of the Court of Appeal on a motion; and
- motions to introduce further evidence under s. 134(4)(b) of the *Courts of Justice Act.*

7.2.2 — Notice of Motion

1. The notice of motion must be in accordance with Form 37A of the *Rules of Civil Procedure*. The notice of motion must contain a statement outlining the jurisdiction of a panel to hear the motion and to grant the relief requested.

2. As provided in rule 61.16(3), the notice of motion should state that the moving party will make a motion to the court on a date to be fixed by the Registrar.

7.2.3 — Scheduling Panel Motions

1. Except in cases of urgency, panel motions will not be scheduled for hearing until the moving party has filed the motion record, factum and transcript, if any.

2. The oral argument for panel motions shall be limited to 15 minutes for the moving party, 10 minutes for the responding party, and 5 minutes for reply.

3. A party who seeks more time for oral argument must make a request to the civil List Judge. For details on requesting more time for oral argument, please see section 12.2 of this Practice Direction.

7.2.4 — Factums for use on Panel Motions

1. In the majority of panel motions, the length of the factums should be 10 pages or less. Factums shall not be more than 30 pages without a court order authorizing the filing of a longer factum.

2. The court requests that the parties file an electronic copy of any factum or transcript filed on a motion before a panel. For details on the procedures for filing electronic material, please consultthe Guidelines for Filing Electronic Documents at the Court of Appeal for Ontario.

7.2.5 — Motion to Quash an Appeal

1. Where the basis for a motion to quash an appeal is that the court lacks jurisdiction to hear the appeal, the motion will be scheduled at an early date.

2. A motion to quash an appeal based on an argument that the appeal is devoid of merit is heard together with the appeal because the court must consider the merits of the appeal in deciding the motion.

7.2.6 — Motion to Introduce Further Evidence

1. When a party seeks leave to file further evidence on an appeal pursuant to s. 134(4)(b) of the *Courts of Justice Act*, rule 61.16(2) of the *Rules of Civil Procedure* requires the party to bring such a motion to the panel of judges hearing the appeal.

2. The party must file three copies of the proposed further evidence in a document that is bound front and back in orange covers and identified on the cover as "Fresh Evidence Tendered by the Appellant" or "Fresh Evidence Tendered by the Respondent", as appropriate.

3. The parties should file a factum on the motion containing their arguments for or against admitting the further evidence on the appeal, including any impact the evidence may have on the resolution of the appeal.

4. Parties should consult rule 61.16(4) of the *Rules of Civil Procedure* for the timelines for serving and filing motion records and factums on a motion to introduce further evidence under s. 134(4)(b) of the *Courts of Justice Act.*

5. In situations of urgency or in unanticipated circumstances where the time limits for filing a motion record and/or factum cannot be complied with, the material may be served and/or filed on shorter notice only with the permission of a judge. For information on bringing a request to abridge the time for serving and/or filing motion materials, please refer to section 7.1.5 of this Practice Direction.

7.2.7 — Motions in Writing for Leave to Appeal

1. Pursuant to rule 61.03.1 of the *Rules of Civil Procedure*, a three-judge panel hears motions for leave to appeal to the Court of Appeal in writing without an oral hearing.

2. The court requests that the parties file an electronic copy of any factum filed on a motion in writing for leave to appeal brought under rule 61.03.1. For details on the procedures for filing electronic material, please consult the Guidelines for Filing Electronic Documents at the Court of Appeal for Ontario.

3. On a motion for leave to appeal, the court may consider whether the issue raised by the moving party involves a question of public importance. Any party that seeks to introduce additional evidence on the question of public importance must file a motion to admit this evidence and a supporting affidavit together with the motion for leave to appeal.

4. The moving party should file three copies of the proposed additional evidence bound front and back in orange covers and identified as "Additional Evidence Tendered by the Moving Party". If the respondent seeks to file its own additional evidence on the question of public importance, the respondent should file three copies of the proposed further evidence bound front and back in orange covers and identified as "Additional Evidence Tendered by the Respondent".

5. The parties may include submissions regarding the admissibility and significance of the proposed additional evidence in their factums filed on the motion for leave to appeal, provided that the factum clearly indicates that the evidence in question is being tendered as additional evidence on the leave motion.

6. Motions to strike or reject affidavits concerning the question of public importance and motions to cross-examine any witness who has sworn such an affidavit should be brought to a single judge in chambers.

7.3 — Formatting and Binding of Motion Material

1. With the exception of motions to file further or additional evidence as discussed in section 7.2.6, motion records shall have a white front cover and a light blue back sheet. Responding motion records shall have a green front cover and a light blue back sheet. The moving party's factum shall be bound in front and back white covers while the responding party's factum shall be bound in green front and back covers.

2. Parties should consult Rule 4 of the *Rules of Civil Procedure* for further information on the formatting and binding of motion material filed at the court. All text in factums must be double-spaced, except for quotations longer than four lines and footnotes. The Court of Appeal requires the use of 12-point or larger font and encourages the use of Arial or Times New Roman for all text in factums, including citations and footnotes.

3. The Registrar may refuse to accept documents or materials for filing if they do not comply with the *Rules* and/or this Practice Direction, or if they are not legible.

7.4 — Power to Stay or Dismiss a Motion

Parties should be aware that, pursuant to rule 2.1.02 of the *Rules of Civil Procedure*, the court may, on its own initiative, stay or dismiss a motion if the motion appears on its face to be frivolous or vexatious or otherwise an abuse of the process of the court.

At the Court of Appeal, the review process contemplated by rule 2.1.02 will primarily be used in relation to motions brought to a panel seeking to have a judgment of the court set aside or varied under rule 59.06 of the *Rules of Civil Procedure*. Parties who bring this type of motion should expect that the court will screen their motion in accordance with rule 2.1.02.

7.5 — Adjournment Requests

7.5.1 — Single Judge Motions

1. If all parties are prepared to consent to an adjournment of a single judge motion, then the moving party should provide a letter addressed to the motions clerk and copied to all parties advising of the adjournment request. The requesting letter may be submitted by email to COA.E-file@ontario.ca (please include "Adjournment Request" and the court file number and title of proceeding in the subject line of the email) or by fax (416-327-5032). The motions clerk will adjourn the motion to a date as agreed by the parties.

2. If the request to adjourn a single judge motion is opposed, then the party requesting the adjournment should provide a letter addressed to the motions clerk and copied to all parties advising of the reason for the adjournment request. The party opposing the request should provide a letter addressed to the motions clerk and copied to all parties advising of the reasons for opposing the adjournment request. This correspondence should be submitted by email to COA.E-file@ontario.ca (please include "Adjournment Request" and the court file number and title of proceeding in the subject line of the email) or by fax (416-327-5032). The motions clerk will present the correspondence to the motions judge for review and his or her determination will be communicated to the parties by the motions clerk before the hearing date of the motion.

7.5.2 — Panel Motions

1. If a hearing date for a panel motion is more than three weeks away, and if all parties are prepared to consent to an adjournment, then the moving party should provide a letter addressed to the Appeal Scheduling Unit and copied to all parties advising of the adjournment request. The requesting letter may be submitted by email to COA.E-file@ontario.ca (please include "Adjournment Request" and the court file number and title of proceeding in the subject line of the email) or by fax (416-327-6256). The Appeal Scheduling Unit will confirm if the matter will be adjourned and if so, will advise the parties of the new hearing date.

2. If a hearing date for a panel motion is more than three weeks away, and if the adjournment request is opposed by one or more of the parties, then the party seeking the adjournment must make the adjournment request to a judge of the court who has been designated by the Chief Justice to serve as the civil List Judge.

3. A conference call before the civil List Judge to change a hearing date must be arranged through the Appeal Scheduling Unit by contacting 416-327-5020 (select your language of choice, followed by option 4, and then press 2) or by fax (416-327-6256). The Appeal Scheduling Unit will contact the parties with the date, time and the dial-in details for the conference call.

4. If the hearing date for a panel motion is three weeks or less away, any adjournment request — whether on consent or opposed — must be made in writing to the attention of the Appeal Scheduling Unit. The requesting letter may be submitted by email to COA.E-file@ontario.ca (please include "Adjournment Request" and the court file number and title of proceeding in the subject line of the email) or by fax (416-327-6256). The request will be forwarded to the president of the panel for review and his or her determination will be communicated to the parties by the Appeal Scheduling Unit.

7.6 — Withdrawing or Abandoning a Motion

1. If the moving party withdraws or abandons a motion to be heard by a single judge or by a panel of judges, the party must serve and file a notice of abandonment in accordance with rule 37.09 (use Form 61K with necessary modifications). The moving party should also send a letter addressed to the Registrar advising that the motion has been withdrawn or abandoned. The letter should be copied to all parties and be sent by email to COA.E-file@ontario.ca (please include "Notice of Abandonment of a Motion" and the court file number and title of proceeding in the subject line of the email) or by fax to (416) 327-5032. The letter should indicate how the issue of costs has been resolved.

2. If a motion before a single judge is withdrawn or abandoned within two days of the scheduled hearing date, the moving party must advise the motions clerk that the motion will not be proceeding by calling 416-327-5020 (select your language of choice, followed by option 3).

3. If a motion before a panel of three judges is abandoned after it has been listed for hearing, the moving party must promptly advise the Appeal Scheduling Unit by contacting 416-327-5020 (select your language of choice, followed by option 4, and then press 2) or by fax (416-327-6256).

8. — Appeal Management

1. In especially complicated appeals, such as appeals involving multiple parties or grouped appeals, it may be appropriate for a judge to be assigned to manage the conduct of the appeal(s). A request for the assignment of an appeal management judge

should be made to the court by letter addressed to the Senior Legal Officer. The request should contain enough information to satisfy the court that such an appointment is appropriate. The decision to appoint an appeal management judge is made by the Chief Justice or Associate Chief Justice and is communicated to the parties.

2. The appeal management judge will conduct appeal management conferences to ensure the efficient conduct of the appeal. Appeal management conferences are held to deal with matters not otherwise governed by the *Rules of Civil Procedure*, including: the order of argument; time allocations for oral argument; the hearing date; the issues to be argued; the possibility of settling the appeal or any issues under appeal; coordination, if necessary, of the scheduling of prehearing motions; creating customized electronic appeal records; and similar matters. Such conferences are conducted in person or by teleconference or videoconference and are arranged through the Appeal Scheduling Office of the Court of Appeal.

3. In order to ensure the efficient conduct of the appeal, the appeal management judge's decisions at appeal management conferences will be communicated as required to the panel hearing the appeal, the parties, and the court's staff.

4. When the parties to a case-managed appeal seek to obtain relief from compliance with any requirements of the *Rules of Civil Procedure* or of this Practice Direction, an order of the appeal management judge dispensing with such compliance will be required. Such an order may be obtained on consent of all parties by providing two copies of the draft order, a document indicating the signed consent of the parties, and an affidavit or letter addressed to the appeal management judge with sufficient information to satisfy the appeal management judge that the order is appropriate.

9. — Pre-Hearing Settlement Conferences in Family Law Appeals

9.1 — General

The Court of Appeal for Ontario offers a voluntary pre-hearing settlement conference program. Its purpose is to attempt to resolve family law appeals at an earlier stage in order to reduce costs for litigants. The court makes available a roster of appellate judges who have particular interest in family law matters. The pre-hearing settlement conference is for those parties who would like to explore a final resolution of their legal differences before a full hearing or a narrowing of the issues requiring resolution. The court will hold a pre-hearing settlement conference only if all parties believe that a judge's assistance may assist them in resolving or narrowing the issues on appeal.

9.2 — Two-Stage Process

Pre-hearing settlement conferences are offered at two stages, as the parties require. A Stage 1 conference will take place as soon as possible after the Notice of Appeal has been filed but before the transcript has been prepared. The purpose of the conference at this stage of the proceedings is to minimize cost, if at all possible, especially the cost of the production of the transcripts. However, the parties must comply with rule 61.05(5) of the *Rules of Civil Procedure*.

A Stage 2 conference will take place after perfection of the appeal. It is designed to attempt a global resolution of the issues under appeal but, if unsuccessful, at least to offer a "good, hard look" at the issues and explore alternatives to see if the appeal, or at least some issues, can be resolved.

9.3 — Application for a Pre-hearing Settlement Conference

In order to request a conference, the parties must complete a Form entitled "Joint Request for Pre-hearing Settlement Conference" Word, PDF. They are to specify whether they are seeking a Stage 1 or Stage 2 conference although, in most cases, the timing of the application will be sufficient to advise the court. The Form must be submitted to the Appeal Scheduling Unit by email to COA.E-file@ontario.ca or by facsimile (416-327-6256). The parties should propose a range of dates and times for the conference that are suitable to all participants. The request should also contain a reasonable estimate for the length of the conference, although the court will be as flexible as required by the circumstances.

Once the "Joint Request" is received by the court, the Appeal Scheduling Unit will schedule a conference, usually within 7 to 30 days. The court will make every effort, especially in respect of Stage 1 conferences, to convene counsel and the parties as quickly as possible. Because the pre-hearing settlement conference is not intended to delay the normal progress of the appeal, a request for such a conference does not operate to suspend the obligation of the parties to comply with the requirements of Rule 61 of the *Rules of Civil Procedure*.

9.4 — Memoranda

If the parties request a Stage 1 conference, they will be required to file a copy of the reasons for judgment and a memorandum outlining the issues. It is the appellant's responsibility to deliver the reasons for judgment to the court for use at the conference. The memorandum of each party shall be no longer than 6 pages. If either party requires an exhibit from the trial or the proceeding being appealed, it may be attached to the memorandum. The court expects that the parties will attempt to isolate the real points in issue and consider ways in which they may be resolved. Since the court file will be available to the judge at the conference, the parties need not include material in the memorandums that is referred to in the notice of appeal. The parties shall serve their memorandum on the other parties.

The judgment and memorandums should be filed with the court at least 2 days before the conference.

If the parties wish a Stage 2 conference, they must file memorandums as in Stage 1. The court will also rely on the appeal book and the factums filed in preparing for the conference.

9.5 — The Conference

A Court of Appeal judge will preside over the conference. The parties and those who may have a significant influence on the outcome of the conference must be present, since they are the ultimate decision-makers. The parties are free to ask the court for whatever arrangement counsel believes to be appropriate and necessary. The process is meant to be as flexible as the parties wish. The pre-hearing settlement conference will not result in an adjournment of the appeal. The judge conducting the conference will not be assigned to the panel ultimately hearing the appeal and will not discuss any aspect of the conference with the panel.

9.6 — The Results

If the pre-hearing settlement conference results in a successful resolution of some or all of the issues, the court will expect an agreement to be drafted and signed by the parties. Counsel may also be required to provide a draft order and to speak to the settlement in court. This will depend on the circumstances of the settlement.

Except for such an agreement and draft order, the fact of the pre-hearing settlement conference, the memorandums filed and all deliberations in the process will remain strictly confidential and without prejudice to the parties' legal positions.

If the pre-hearing settlement conference is unsuccessful, the appeal will proceed as scheduled.

9.7 — Notice to Parties

To encourage parties to use the pre-hearing settlement conference facility, counsel filing or responding to a family law appeal will be required to advise their client of the availability of this service.

9.8 — Inquiries

Further information, if required, may be obtained from the Court's Appeal Scheduling Unit by telephone (416-327-5028/4615). A pre-hearing conference may be arranged by contacting the court's Appeal Scheduling Unit by telephone (416-327-5028/4615) or fax (416-327-6256).

10. — Pre-Hearing Settlement Conferences in Other Appeals

A judge of the court may conduct a pre-hearing settlement conference in any appeal in which all counsel request such a conference. Arrangements for a pre-hearing conference shall be made through the court's Appeal Scheduling Unit by telephone (416-327-5028/4615) or by fax (416-327-5256). The parties should proceed by way of analogy to the procedures set out in the program for pre-hearing settlement conferences in family law appeals.

11. — Perfecting an Appeal

11.1 — Perfection: Steps Required

1. The appellant is responsible for taking the steps prescribed by rules 61.09(2) and (3) of the *Rules of Civil Procedure* for perfecting an appeal. The appellant must file with the Registrar a certificate of perfection as described in rule 61.09(3)(c) before the appeal is perfected. After an appeal is perfected, the Registrar will assign a date for hearing the appeal.

2. Rule 61.09(4) permits an appellant to bring a motion to a single judge of the Court of Appeal for directions to vary the rules governing the material that must be served and filed to perfect an appeal. The moving party must satisfy the judge that it is in the interest of justice to grant relief from compliance with any of the *Rules*. Details about bringing motions to a single judge are found in section 7.1 of this Practice Direction and in rules 61.16 and 37 of the *Rules of Civil Procedure*.

11.2 — Child and Family Services Act *Appeals*

Rule 38(2) of the *Family Law Rules* modifies certain time periods that apply in appeals under the *Child and Family Services Act*, R.S.O. 1990, c. C.11, s. 45, including the time for perfecting the appeal. The parties should consult this rule for the deadlines that apply in these types of appeals. These deadlines are generally shorter than the time periods prescribed in the *Rules of Civil Procedure*.

11.3 — Transcripts and Exhibits

1. The phrase "transcript of evidence" as used in rule 61.09(1) of the *Rules of Civil Procedure* refers only to the oral testimony of witnesses given in the presence of a judge. Oral arguments by a lawyer or a self-represented party do not qualify as "evidence" under the *Rules*.

2. Attention is directed to rule 61.05 regarding the service of certificates (Form 61C and Form 61D) and/or an agreement respecting evidence. The appellant's certificate respecting evidence should be served and filed together with the notice of appeal. The respondent's certificate respecting evidence must be served on the appellant within 15 days of service of the appellant's certificate.

3. When a lawyer who acted at trial is not acting on the appeal, the court expects that the trial lawyer will provide timely assistance to the appellate lawyer or to the self-represented party in completing the certificates or in making an agreement respecting evidence.

4. According to rule 61.05(5), the appellant must order a transcript of all the oral evidence that the parties have not agreed to exclude.

5. In the vast majority of appeals, it is not necessary to transcribe all the testimony of the witnesses who testified in the lower court. Oral evidence should be transcribed only if the Court of Appeal needs to review the evidence in order to properly analyze the grounds of appeal and any cross-appeal.

Unnecessary transcription of the evidence of witnesses in the lower court delays the hearing of appeals and substantially increases the cost of litigation. The parties should give serious consideration to the issue of what evidence is really necessary for a proper adjudication of the appeal.

6. In appeals where the facts are not in dispute, the parties are encouraged to file an agreed statement of facts, which will take the place of a transcript. The agreed statement of facts shall be filed in the appeal book and compendium.

7. The court may impose costs sanctions where evidence is transcribed unnecessarily.

8. Unless otherwise ordered by a judge of the Court of Appeal, the transcripts of trial proceedings shall omit the following aspects of the proceedings:

(a) all proceedings on the challenge of the array or of jurors for cause;

(b) any opening address of the trial judge;

(c) the opening address of a lawyer and/or a self-represented party;

(d) all proceedings in the absence of the jury and all argument in the absence of the jury (except objections to a charge and the trial judge's related rulings together with any reasons for the rulings);

(e) all objections to the admissibility of evidence, except for a notation that an objection was made (note: the ruling of the trial judge on the objection, including any reasons for the ruling, will be transcribed.)

9. When any aspect of the proceedings mentioned in paragraph 8 is the subject of a ground of appeal, the relevant material may be transcribed without the need for a judge's order.

11.4 — Timely Preparation of Transcripts

1. Authorized court transcriptionists have been instructed that after a transcript has been ordered for a civil appeal, the completion of the transcript is not to be suspended without an order of a judge of the Court of Appeal or the receipt of a notice of abandonment of the appeal.

2. This instruction does not apply to appeals where the Area Committee has not yet decided whether to grant a Legal Aid certificate to cover the client's appeal. To ensure the timely determination of Legal Aid applications, trial lawyers are reminded of their primary responsibility to prepare an opinion letter for use on the application for Legal Aid. Every effort should be made to prepare and submit this opinion letter to Legal Aid within 30 days of the filing of the notice of appeal.

3. Lawyers are reminded that interim payments for transcripts may be obtained from Legal Aid Ontario in cases where a Legal Aid certificate has been issued.

4. The authorized court transcriptionist is requested to file with the Court of Appeal a Certificate/Proof of Ordering when the transcript has been ordered and a Certificate/Notification of Completion when the transcript has been completed. This request is in addition to any obligation imposed on the parties by the *Rules of Civil Procedure*.

5. Transcripts are generally completed within 90 days of the date of being ordered, subject to extensions for exceptional circumstances.

6. If a transcriptionist's Certificate of Completion has not been filed by the expected completion date of the transcript, the court will inquire about the status of the transcript and ascertain if the court's assistance is required to ensure its timely completion. The court may refer the issue of the outstanding transcript to a status court hearing before a judge of the Court of Appeal. The ordering party must attend the hearing, and the other parties may choose to attend in order to make submissions. The parties may attend either by way of teleconference or in person. At the hearing, the judge may order the transcriptionist to appear in order to explain the delay and to provide a plan for the timely completion of the transcript.

11.5 — Filing Transcripts

The authorized court transcriptionist must prepare an electronic version of the transcript for the court's use, and for the parties' use if they request it. The appellant is required to file an electronic version of the transcript with the court, together with a paper copy. The line and page numbering of the transcript in electronic form must correspond with that in the hard copy.

For details on the proper formatting and procedures for filing electronic documents in the Court of Appeal, please consult the Guidelines for Filing Electronic Documents at the Court of Appeal for Ontario.

11.6 — Compendiums and Exhibit Books

1. Rules 61.09 and 61.10 of the *Rules of Civil Procedure* require the appellant to file three copies of an appeal book and compendium together with the factum in order to perfect an appeal. Rule 61.12 requires a respondent to file three copies of a respondent's compendium. The appellant's appeal book and compendium shall be bound front and back in buff covers. The respondent's compendium shall be bound front and back in green covers.

2. Rules 61.09 and 61.10.1 require the appellant to file one copy of an exhibit book. The exhibit book shall be bound front and back in buff covers.

3. If an appeal is from an order made on an application or on a motion in which no exhibits were filed, then the court will not require the appellant to serve and file an exhibit book in order to perfect the appeal. The appellant shall serve the certificate of perfection on the other parties to the appeal and shall state in the certificate that an exhibit book is not required because no exhibits were filed on the application or motion.

4. The appellant's appeal book and compendium and the respondent's compendium contain documents essential to the hearing of the appeal, including the excerpts from the transcript and any exhibits that the parties will refer to in oral argument. Since the parties are only required to file one paper copy of the transcript and one paper copy of the exhibit book, it is essential to include in the compendiums all portions of the transcript that are relevant to the grounds of appeal and all relevant exhibits.

5. When the proceedings in the lower court were conducted in full or in part based on affidavit evidence, all relevant affidavits and any attached exhibits must be included in the appeal book and compendium or in the respondent's compendium.

6. In appeals from civil jury trials, if any ground of appeal relates to the charge to the jury, the trial judge's charge must be included in the appeal book and compendium.

7. In the event that the appeal book and compendium includes all the affidavits and exhibits that were filed in the lower court, then the appellant does not need to also serve and file an exhibit book in order to perfect the appeal. In such cases, the appellant's certificate of perfection should state: "All the exhibits required for this appeal are included in the appeal book and compendium." Parties should be aware, however, that the appeal book and compendium is far less useful if unnecessary exhibits or materials are included in it.

8. Filing compendiums is critical to the efficient preparation and effective argument of appeals. Thus, the requirement to file an appeal book and compendium and a respondent's compendium in all civil matters is mandatory and must be complied with, unless a judge orders relief from compliance on a motion brought under rule 61.09(4).

9. The appeal book and compendium and the respondent's compendium should be organized as described in rules 61.10(1) and 61.12(7) of the *Rules of Civil Procedure*, and should be organized in a way that enables the court to easily locate all of the documents that are referred to in the parties' factums.

10. Extracts of transcripts, affidavits or exhibits in the compendiums should include as much material as is needed to understand the context for the part of the extract that the party is relying on.

11. The Court of Appeal encourages parties to submit electronic copies of compendiums and exhibit books by CD/DVD-ROM or USB Flash Drive/USB Key, in addition to serving and filing paper copies of these materials. For details on the procedures for filing electronic material, please consult the Guidelines for Filing Electronic Documents at the Court of Appeal for Ontario.

11.7 — Factums

1. Rules 61.11 and 61.12 of the *Rules of Civil Procedure* deal with the appellant's and the respondent's factums. These rules emphasize the need for a concise summary of the relevant facts, a concise argument of the law relating to each issue, and the requirement to cross-reference the factum to the compendium. The court may impose cost sanctions on respondents who do not file their factums within the time provided in rule 61.12(2).

2. The Court of Appeal encourages the use of hyperlinks to case law referred to in electronically-filed factums. Parties may hyperlink authorities to the judgments database found on the websites of Canadian courts, www.canlii.org/en/index.html, in addition to LexisNexis Quicklaw and WestlawNext Canada.

3. The Court of Appeal requires the use of 12-point or larger font and encourages the use of Arial or Times New Roman for all text in factums, including citations and footnotes. All text in factums must be double-spaced, except for quotations longer than four lines and footnotes. The appellant's factum shall be bound in front and back white covers while the respondent's factum shall be bound in green front and back covers. The Registrar may refuse to accept materials for filing if they do not comply with the *Rules* and/or this Practice Direction, or if they are not legible.

4. In the majority of appeals, the length of the factum should be 30 pages or less. The Registrar will refuse to accept factums that use excessive footnotes or that use formatting that is inconsistent with rule 4.01(1) of the *Rules of Civil Procedure* in order to meet the 30-page limit.

5. To file a factum of longer than 30 pages, permission must be obtained by bringing a motion to a single judge of the Court of Appeal. On any such motion, the moving party must, other than in exceptional cases, include a copy of the proposed factum in the motion record.

6. If the factum refers to information that is subject to a publication ban or sealing order imposed by a court in the proceedings, or contains information the release of which would violate a legislative provision, then the party must include a prominent reference to the terms of the applicable order or legislative provision on the front cover of the factum.

7. The *Rules of Civil Procedure* require the filing of an electronic copy of all factums for use on appeals. For details on the proper formatting and procedures for preparing electronic documents for filing at the Court of Appeal, please consult the Guidelines for Filing Electronic Documents at the Court of Appeal for Ontario.

8. Parties are encouraged to consult the Reference Guide for Citation Practices at the Court of Appeal for Ontario for assistance in preparing their factums and other appeal material. This reference guide is for information purposes only.

11.8 — Books of Authorities

1. Although not required to perfect an appeal, the Court of Appeal is greatly assisted by books of authorities containing copies of the cases and relevant extracts from secondary authorities to which the parties intend to refer in arguing their appeal.

2. Parties are welcome to file joint books of authorities whenever possible.

3. If it is not feasible to provide a joint book of authorities, then do not include copies of cases that are in the other party's book of authorities. The factum should cite to the version of the case that is found in the other party's book of authorities.

4. The following practices should be followed when preparing and filing books of authorities:

(i) Include the cases being relied on in the factum and in oral argument, subject to the exception noted next.

(ii) The Court of Appeal has adopted a List of Frequently Cited Civil Authorities. Authorities on this list do not need to be included in the books of authorities. Instead, when a party's factum refers to an authority on this list, the book of authorities should only include the headnote and particular passage(s) from the authority being relied on. A complete version of the authorities on this list is available for the judges' use.

(iii) Separate the authorities in the book of authorities with a tab (either numerical or alphabetical) and include a table of contents listing where to find each authority. The authorities may be printed on both sides of the page.

(iv) Clearly mark in each authority the passage(s) that is(are) being relying on.

(v) Joint books of authorities should be bound front and back in yellow covers and marked "Joint Book of Authorities". A book of authorities filed only by the appellant should be bound front and back in white covers and marked "Appellant's Book of Authorities". A book of authorities filed only by the respondent should be bound front and back in green covers and marked "Respondent's Book of Authorities".

(vi) Because books of authorities are of great assistance to the judges in preparing for the hearing, they should be filed whenever possible at the same time as the factum. If this is not possible, then they should be filed no later than one month before the hearing date.

5. The order for selecting which print version of a case to include in the book of authorities is as follows:

(i) the decision as posted on the relevant court's website, preferably using the PDF format;

(ii) the decision as posted on CanLII (www.canlii.org), preferably using the PDF format;

(ii) the decision as it appears in an official or semi-official reporter (e.g., Supreme Court of Canada Reports, Ontario Reports, Federal Reports, and other provincial reporter series such as the B.C.L.R.'s, etc.);

(iii) the decision as it appears in an unofficial reporter (e.g., Dominion Law Reports, Business Law Reports, etc.);

(iv) the decision as posted on subscription-based databases (e.g., WestlawNext Canada, LexisNexis Quicklaw, etc.).

11.9 — Materials for Consolidated and Grouped Appeals

1. When two or more appeals are to be heard together because the appeals are from the same or related court orders, if all parties consent to filing consolidated material for the appeals, then the parties may file a letter of consent together with the consolidated material, including consolidated appeal books and compendiums, exhibit books, factums and the books of authorities for use on all the appeals.

2. If the parties to consolidated appeals are unable to agree on the use of consolidated material, a motion for directions may be brought before a single judge of the

court to authorize the preparation and filing of consolidated material as the court may approve.

3. The material filed in consolidated appeals should include the court file number of each appeal that is being heard together.

4. When two or more appeals are grouped for hearing together because they raise similar issues but the appeals are from orders made in separate proceedings, the parties must file separate material for each appeal unless a judge directs otherwise on a motion for directions.

5. Parties to consolidated or grouped appeals may seek the assistance of an appeal management judge early in the appellate process. Section 8 of this Practice Direction discusses the process for requesting the assignment of an appeal management judge.

11.10 Electronic Appeals

1. When the volume of material is large or the appeal is complex, the appeal will be much more efficiently presented to the court if the paper appeal materials are also filed in an electronic format. Thus, parties should consider the desirability of filing an electronic copy of not only the factums and transcripts but also the materials in the compendiums.

2. The electronic copies of the factums should be hyperlinked to the authorities that are cited in the factums and to the materials found in the electronic compendiums.

3. If electronic copies of any of the materials referred to in the factum are not available, then paper copies of the materials should be scanned using an optical character recognition feature to convert the scanned document into a searchable format. Generally speaking, it is not helpful to provide the court with non-searchable PDF files. To confirm that your document is searchable, use the word search feature of your software program.

12. — Appeal Scheduling Procedures

12.1 — Expedited Appeals

1. Most civil appeals will be heard within four to six months of perfection. However, it is recognized that some appeals must be heard more quickly.

2. The court automatically expedites the following types of appeals:

(a) family law appeals;

(b) appeals under the *Child and Family Services Act*, R.S.O. 1990, c. C.11, s. 45; and

(c) appeals that may delay the progress of an ongoing proceeding.

3. Such appeals will be heard at the earliest practicable date, usually within three months of perfection.

4. Appeals other than those listed in paragraph 2 may be expedited by bringing a motion to a judge of the Court of Appeal for an order expediting the appeal. The judge must be satisfied that the urgency of the matter requires an earlier hearing date.

12.2 — Estimate of Time Required for Oral Argument

1. Parties shall certify in the factum a realistic estimate of the time for oral argument of the appeal, not including reply, in fractions of an hour or hours (e.g., Â¾ of an hour, 1Â½ hours).

2. Prior to scheduling the appeal for a hearing date, a judge of the court will review the time estimate of the appellant and will assign time for the oral argument of each party, including any time for reply.

3. The parties will be notified of the time assignment for oral argument when they are notified of the hearing date of the appeal.

4. The time assignments are provided to the panel hearing the appeal. The court expects the parties to adhere to their time assignments.

5. Parties who seek more time for oral argument must make a request to a judge of the court who has been designated by the Chief Justice to serve as the civil List Judge.

6. A conference before the civil List Judge for more time for oral argument must be arranged through the Appeal Scheduling Unit by contacting 416-327-5020 (select your language of choice, followed by option 4, and then press 2) or by fax (416-327-6256).

7. Requests made for the assistance of the List Judge will be dealt with by conference call. The Appeal Scheduling Unit will contact the parties with the date, time and the dial-in details for the List Judge conference call.

12.3 — Adjournment Requests

1. If a hearing date for an appeal is more than three weeks away, and if all parties are prepared to consent to an adjournment, then the appellant should provide a letter addressed to the Appeal Scheduling Unit and copied to all parties advising of the adjournment request. The requesting letter may be submitted by email to COA.E-file@ontario.ca (please include "Adjournment Request" and the court file number and title of proceeding in the subject line of the email) or by fax (416-327-6256). The Appeal Scheduling Unit will confirm if the matter will be adjourned and if so, will advise the parties of the new hearing date.

2. If a hearing date for an appeal is more than three weeks away, and if the adjournment request is opposed by one or more of the parties, then the party seeking the adjournment must make the adjournment request to a judge of the court who has been designated by the Chief Justice to serve as the civil List Judge.

3. A conference call before the civil List Judge to change a hearing date must be arranged through the Appeal Scheduling Unit by contacting 416-327-5020 (select your language of choice, followed by option 4, and then press 2) or by fax (416-327-6256). The Appeal Scheduling Unit will contact the parties with the date, time and the dial-in details for the conference call.

4. If the hearing date for an appeal is three weeks or less away, any adjournment request — whether on consent or opposed — must be made in writing to the attention of the Appeal Scheduling Unit. The requesting letter may be submitted by email to COA.E-file@ontario.ca (please include "Adjournment Request" and the court file number and title of proceeding in the subject line of the email) or by fax (416-327-6256). The request will be forwarded to the president of the panel for review and his or her determination will be communicated to the parties by the Appeal Scheduling Unit.

12.4 — Appeals without Oral Argument

1. The court may decide appeals without oral argument on the consent of the parties. Parties who seek to have an appeal decided without oral argument shall, after delivering their factums, file a written consent with the Registrar to hear the appeal in writing.

2. In appeals without oral argument, the appellant shall be permitted to file a reply factum, which must be served and filed within ten days of the filing of the respondent's factum.

3. Where practical, the court shall render judgment within 60 days of the filing of the consent.

12.5 — The Composition of the Panel

The parties may consult the Court of Appeal's website at http://www.ontariocourts.ca/coa/en/caselist/ to see the weekly hearings lists and the composition of the panel for their appeal. The weekly hearing lists are posted on Friday at noon on the week prior to the next week's hearings.

13. — Request to Reconsider a Prior Precedential Decision of the Court of Appeal

1. When a party wishes to ask the court to decline to follow a prior precedential decision of the Court of Appeal for Ontario, the party should send a letter to the attention of the Senior Legal Officer requesting that the court convene a five-judge panel to hear the appeal. The letter should explain why there is reason to think that the court's prior precedential decision should not be followed. The letter should be copied to all parties and be submitted not later than the time for filing the requesting party's factum.

2. Any party to the proceeding in the Court of Appeal may send a letter responding to the request to convene a five-judge panel to hear the appeal.

3. The Chief or the Associate Chief Justice will review a party's request for a five-judge panel and his or her decision on the matter is final.

14. — Settling or Abandoning an Appeal or Cross-Appeal

1. If the parties agree to settle an appeal or cross-appeal, they are required to promptly submit a letter addressed to the Registrar advising that the matter has been settled. The letter should be copied to all parties and be sent by email to COA.E-file@ontario.ca (please include "Notice of Abandonment" or "Notice of Settlement" and the court file number and title of proceeding in the subject line of the email) or by fax to (416) 327-5032. The letter should indicate how the issue of costs has been resolved. The parties may attach a copy of any minutes of settlement with the letter advising of the settlement.

2. In accordance with rule 61.16(2.2) of the *Rules of Civil Procedure*, an order dismissing an appeal on consent of the parties may be obtained from a judge in chambers. When the parties settle an appeal and seek relief other than an order dismissing the appeal on consent, at least one of the parties may be directed by the court to appear in order to satisfy the court that the requested order is not inappropriate.

3. If an appeal or cross-appeal is abandoned, the relevant party is required to promptly file a notice of abandonment (Form 61K) in accordance with rule 61.14(1).

4. If an appeal and/or cross-appeal is settled or abandoned after it has been listed for hearing, the relevant party must promptly advise the Appeal Scheduling Unit of the settlement or abandonment by contacting 416-327-5020 (select your language of choice, followed by option 4, and then press 2) or by fax (416-327-6256) to ensure the efficient use of courtrooms and court resources.

15. — Courtroom Decorum

15.1 — Addressing the Court

Members of the Court of Appeal should be addressed as "Chief Justice", "Associate Chief Justice", "Justice" or "Justice (Surname)", as appropriate, and not as Madam Justice, My Lady, My Lord, Your Ladyship, Your Lordship or Your Honour.

15.2 — Courtroom Attire

Lawyers do not need to wear gowns when they appear on motions before a single judge in chambers.

Counsel who are pregnant when appearing before a panel in the Court of Appeal for Ontario are free to modify their traditional court attire in order to accommodate their pregnancy as they see fit, including dispensing with a waistcoat and tabs.

15.3 — Use of Electronic Communication Devices in the Courtroom

Unless a judge orders otherwise, electronic communication devices including cell phones and laptop computers may be used in the courtroom in a manner that is not disruptive of the proceedings. Anyone using an electronic communication device to transmit information about a court hearing has the responsibility to identify and comply with the terms of any applicable publication ban, sealing order, or other restriction on publication that has been imposed by court order or by statute.[1]

Photography and video recording of a court hearing without the authorization of a judge is prohibited by s. 136(1) of the *Courts of Justice Act*. Audio recording of a court hearing is permissible for note-taking purposes, but these audio recordings may not be transmitted. Anyone who uses an electronic communication device in a way that violates this Practice Direction may be ordered to turn off the device, leave the device outside the courtroom, leave the courtroom, abide by any other court order, and may also be subject to prosecution.

16. — Electronic Delivery of Reasons for Judgment

The court will send an HTML and PDF copy of the signed judgment by email to those lawyers and self-represented parties who have provided an email address on their materials filed with the court. Paper copies of judgments are also available at the Registrar's Office to those parties who do not have an email address, and to members of the public (who must pay the prescribed fee).

[1]For example, see *Child and Family Services Act*, R.S.O., c. C.11, s. 45; *Criminal Code of Canada*, R.S.C. 1985, c. C-46, ss. 486, 486.4-486.6, 517, 539; *Youth Criminal Justice Act*, S.C. 2002, c. 1, ss. 110, 111.

Judgments are posted on the court's website shortly after release at http://www.ontariocourts.ca/decisions_index/en/.

The court provides advance notice of release of its reserved decisions at http://www.ontariocourts.ca/decisions_index/notice.htm.

17. — Digital Audio Recordings

1. The Court of Appeal is not a "court of record". Its oral hearings are not monitored or transcribed as a matter of routine. However, the Court of Appeal records all hearings that are held in open court through the use of digital audio recording. Unless a judge orders otherwise, a copy of a digital audio recording is available upon request, provided that the proceedings are not subject to a statutory publication ban or other court order that prevents the release of the digital audio recording.

2. Requests for access to digital audio recordings should be made in the Registrar's Office and are subject to payment of the prescribed fee, unless a fee waiver certificate is produced. Such recordings are for personal use, and will not be released unless the person requesting the recording signs an undertaking agreeing to respect the limits on the permitted uses of the recording.

3. If a person wishes to have a transcript of a hearing made, he or she must first bring a motion for permission to do so before a single judge. Once the order is obtained, the person may have the recording transcribed at her or her own expense.

4. The publication, broadcasting, reproduction or other dissemination of an audio recording of a court hearing is prohibited unless expressly authorized by a court order.

18. — Costs in the Court of Appeal

1. Parties should be prepared to address all issues of costs, including the quantum of costs, at the hearing of an appeal or a motion.

2. Parties who may be entitled to costs must prepare and exchange their proposed bills of costs, to be filed at the time of argument if requested by the court. This bill should be complete to the day before the hearing and include an estimate of the costs associated with the hearing of the appeal or motion.

3. If the decision on the appeal or motion is released orally immediately after the hearing, the parties will have an opportunity to make brief submissions as to the quantum and scale of costs to be paid.

4. If the decision on the appeal or motion is reserved, the filing of the bill of costs and submissions will usually occur at the hearing.

5. The court may determine that it would be preferable to receive costs submissions after releasing its decision. In such cases, a party entitled to receive costs will deliver a bill of costs together with any submissions, in writing, in support of the requested order for costs within seven days of the release of the decision. Any party liable to pay costs may deliver a response, in writing, within 14 days of the release of the decision. The party entitled to receive costs may deliver a brief reply within 17 days of the release of the decision. These deadlines apply unless the court directs different deadlines at the hearing.

6. Unless the court orders otherwise, such material should be filed at the Registrar's Office in triplicate, together with proof of service, to the attention of the Appeal Scheduling Unit.

7. Unless the court orders otherwise, any material received in relation to costs will be forwarded to the panel for consideration 18 days after the release of the decision. The parties will be notified of the decision as to costs by way of an addendum to the decision.

19. — Post-Hearing Submissions

1. The parties are expected to fully argue all issues on an appeal in the factum and in oral submissions at the hearing of the appeal. Attempts by the parties to provide the court with additional written submissions, authorities, or other material after the hearing are improper, subject to the exceptions discussed here.

2. On occasion, after the hearing of an appeal, the court may wish to receive further submissions from the parties in respect of one or more issues. The Senior Legal Officer will advise the parties of any request by the court for further submissions and will give a timetable within which to serve and file this material.

3. The parties may become aware of a newly-decided authority that might have an impact on a reserved appeal. The authority may be sent, without submissions, to the attention of the Senior Legal Officer, who will ensure that the material is transmitted to the panel that heard the appeal.

4. If a party wishes to make submissions concerning the impact of a new authority, a request to do so should be included in a covering letter addressed to the Senior Legal Officer and copied to the other parties. The Senior Legal Officer will advise the parties whether the court is prepared to entertain such submissions and, if necessary, will give a timetable for serving and filing submissions.

5. In exceptional circumstances, a party may seek to make additional submissions to the court while an appeal is under reserve. The request, outlining the essentials of the argument and the reasons the argument was not made at the hearing of the appeal, should be made in writing to the attention of the Senior Legal Officer. Opposing parties may respond in writing to the request. The Senior Legal Officer will advise the parties whether the panel will receive further submissions. This process is not to be viewed as a substitute for properly preparing the factum and fully arguing the issues at the hearing of the appeal.

6. After a panel has released its reasons for judgment, the decision of the court is final. The normal recourse for a party who objects to the court's decision is by way of an application for leave to appeal to the Supreme Court of Canada.

7. In accordance with rule 61.16(6.1) of the *Rules of Civil Procedure*, an order or decision of a panel of the Court of Appeal may not be set aside or varied except in accordance with rules 37.14 and 59.06. Parties should be aware that rule 59.06 provides for a very narrow jurisdiction to set aside or vary an order made by a panel. This rule and the authorities that have interpreted it should be consulted before commencing a motion under rule 59.06.

8. In accordance with rule 2.1.02 of the *Rules of Civil Procedure*, the Court of Appeal will automatically screen motions under rule 59.06(2) in order to ensure that the motion is not frivolous, vexatious, or otherwise an abuse of the process of the court.

20. — Contact Information for the Court's Registrar

The office of the Registrar may be contacted at COA.Registrar@ontario.ca or by fax at 416-327-5032.

21. — Contact Information for the Court's Senior Legal Officer

The office of the Senior Legal Officer may be contacted at COA.SeniorLegalOfficer@ontario.ca or by fax at 416-327-6256.

Chief Justice George R. Strathy

January 30, 2017 Date

PD-1a — *CHANGES TO THE RULES OF CIVIL PROCEDURE AFFECTING THE COURT OF APPEAL FOR ONTARIO*

Effective July 1, 2017

The following amendments to the *Rules of Civil Procedure* come into force on July 1, 2017:

Confirmation of motion not required

A new rule (r. 61.16(1.1)) provides that a confirmation of motion (rule 37.10.1) is not required for Court of Appeal motions.

Requirement to set out reasons for granting an order on consent

In the case of a motion on consent in the Court of Appeal, a new rule (r. 37.12.1) requires filing an affidavit or other document that explains why the order should be granted on consent. This requirement is similar to s. 7.1.4 of the Practice Direction Concerning Civil Appeals at the Court of Appeal for Ontario (PDF).

Motions for leave to appeal

Rule 61.03.1 (motions for leave to appeal) has been amended as follows:

i. notices of motion for leave motions must state that the motion will be heard on a date set by the Registrar, and

ii. electronic versions of factums must be filed on leave motions.

Motion record covers

A new rule (r. 4.07(1.1)) specifies the colour of the front covers of motion records:

- green (responding party's motion record)
- orange (fresh evidence motion record)*

*Note: Court staff will accept fresh evidence motion records with an orange front cover and a back cover that is either orange or light blue: see ss. 7.3 and 7.2.6 of the Practice Direction Concerning Civil Appeals at the Court of Appeal for Ontario (PDF).

- white (all other motion records)

Rule 4.07(1) specifies that the back covers of motion records are light blue.

Appointments to settle an order

The procedures for bringing an appointment to settle an order by the Registrar of the Court of Appeal under r. 59.04 have been clarified, including the introduction of a new form, Form 59D (Notice of Appointment to Settle Order), which must be filed, with proof of service, at least seven days before the appointment date.

Materials must be both served and filed

The *Rules* have been amended to provide that the following materials must be both served and filed:

- certificates respecting evidence (rr. 61.05(1) and (3))
- certificates of perfection (r. 61.09(3))
- notice of motion to review the order of a single judge (r. 61.16(6))

Electronic version of the transcript

Rule 61.09(3) has been amended to clarify that an electronic version of the transcript of evidence must be filed, as well as one paper copy. For details on filing electronic documents, see the Guidelines for Filing Electronic Documents at the Court of Appeal for Ontario (PDF).

Dismissal by Registrar for failure to perfect by deadline imposed by a judge

Rule 61.13 empowers the Registrar to dismiss an appeal without sending out a notice of dismissal, where a party fails to meet a perfection deadline imposed by a judge.

No costs where appeal abandoned and respondent has taken no steps to respond

Rule 61.14(3) has been amended to eliminate deemed costs where an appeal is abandoned and where the appellant's only step was filing a notice of appeal/cross-appeal and the respondent has taken no action in response.

Additional amendments to French version of the Rules

The French translation of the phrase "panel" has been changed from "tribunal de juges" to "formation de juges" throughout the French version of the *Rules*.

PD-1b — *GUIDELINES FOR FILING ELECTRONIC DOCUMENTS AT THE COURT OF APPEAL FOR ONTARIO*

Effective: 1 March 2017

I. — Filing Electronic Materials

Rule 61.09 of the *Rules of Civil Procedure* requires parties to file electronic versions of their factums and transcripts on appeals.

The Court of Appeal strongly encourages parties to file electronic versions of other court documents, including appeal and motion materials filed in criminal and civil proceedings, in addition to the paper copies of these documents.

II. — Transmitting Electronic Documents by Email

1. — Types of Documents that May be Transmitted by Email

PLEASE NOTE: The COA.E-file@ontario.ca address is not designed or intended to receive any inquiries or other communications about court proceedings.

Only documents described on the following list that are less than 10 Megabytes (MBs) may be submitted to the court as an email attachment at COA.E-file@ontario.ca:

- Electronic factums
- Electronic transcripts
- Electronic versions of other documents prescribed by the *Rules of Civil Procedure* and the *Criminal Appeal Rules* including Appeal Books and Compendiums and Exhibit Books
- Electronic copies of affidavits of service
- Electronic correspondence as specified in the **Practice Direction Concerning Civil Appeals at the Court of Appeal for Ontario**:
  - Notification of change to counsel's or self-represented party's mailing or email address: see Civil Practice Direction, s. 6.4
  - Letter to the Registrar seeking court approval to dispense with the requirement to file a motion record or to abridge time to serve or file motion materials on a motion before a single judge: see Civil Practice Direction, s. 7.1.5
  - Letter to the Registrar advising that a motion to be heard by a single judge or by a panel of judges has been withdrawn or abandoned: see Civil Practice Direction, s. 7.5
  - Form entitled "Joint Request for Pre-Hearing Settlement Conference Word, PDF": see Civil Practice Direction, s. 9.3

- Letter requesting an adjournment of a single judge motion, a panel motion, or an appeal: see Civil Practice Direction, ss. 7.5 and 12.3

- Notice of abandonment or settlement of an appeal or cross-appeal: see Civil Practice Direction, s. 14

- Electronic correspondence as specified in the **Practice Direction Concerning Criminal Appeals at the Court of Appeal for Ontario**:

  - Notification of change to counsel's or self-represented party's mailing or email address: see Criminal Practice Direction, s. 6.3

  - Letter to the Registrar advising that a motion or application to be heard by a single judge or a panel of judges has been withdrawn or abandoned: see Criminal Practice Direction, s. 7.1.3

  - Letter to the Registrar seeking court approval to dispense with the requirement to file a motion record or to abridge time to serve or file motion materials on a motion before a single judge: see Criminal Practice Direction, s. 7.2.4.3

  - Letter to the Registrar, copying the designated inmate/in person Crown Counsel at Crown Law Office — Criminal or the Public Prosecution Service of Canada, requesting documents from an inmate/in person court file to be transferred to a new solicitor appeal court file: see Criminal Practice Direction, s. 9.1.4

  - Notification by an authorized court transcriptionist that a transcript has been ordered: see Criminal Practice Direction, s. 9.3.1

  - Notification by an authorized court transcriptionist that a transcript has been completed and attaching a Form 0551: see Criminal Practice Direction, s. 9.3.4

  - Notification by an authorized court transcriptionist that a transcript has not been completed within the prescribed time: see Criminal Practice Direction, s. 9.3.6

- Documents specifically requested by the Court of Appeal judiciary or staff to be transmitted via email

Please note: Electronic factums and transcripts that are 10 MBs or greater must be submitted by way of CD/DVD-ROM or USB key, as discussed below.

2. — Requirements for Sending Documents by Email

i) The sender must include in the subject line of the email the nature of the attachment and the court file number.

Examples:

Subject: Factum C12345 — Factum of the Appellant

Subject: Transcript C12345

Subject: Appeal Book and Compendium C12345

Subject: Notice of Abandonment C12345

Subject: Affidavit of Service C12345

Please be advised that if an email sent to COA.E-file@ontario.ca does not include a subject line, the email and any attachment will not be accepted by the Court of Appeal for processing.

ii) If any information in the document(s) attached to the email is subject to a publication ban, sealing order, or legislative provision banning publication, then the existence of the restriction on publication should clearly be indicated in the subject line of the email and in the body of the email.

For example:

Subject: C123456 — Appellant's Factum — Note: Publication Ban under s. 45(8) of the *Child and Family Services Act*

Please note that the materials in this factum are subject to a statutory prohibition under s. 45(8) of the *Child and Family Services Act* on publishing or publicizing information that has the effect of identifying the participants in a child protection hearing.

III. — Filing by CD/DVD-ROM or USB Key

Electronic documents may also be submitted to the Court of Appeal on a CD/DVD-ROM or USB Flash Drive/USB Key by mail, by courier, or in person.

Only one copy of a CD/DVD-ROM or USB key is required.

The CD/DVD-ROM or USB key should be labelled with the court file number. The party shall include a covering letter setting out a list of the files contained on the CD/DVD-ROM or USB key. Â The documents saved on the CD/DVD-ROM or USB key should be named by appeal or motion number and the document code identifying the type of document.Â For example:Â **C12345.FAP.docx**. The document codes are set out below.

If any information found on the CD/DVD-ROM or USB key is subject to a publication ban, sealing order, or legislative provision banning publication, then this should clearly be indicated on the covering letter and, if feasible, on a label affixed to the CD/DVD-ROM or USB key.

IV. — Formatting Electronic Material

1. Electronic materials may be submitted in the following common formats:

Text-searchable PDF (e.g., using an Optical Character Recognition format for scanned PDF documents)

Microsoft Word

HTML

2. An electronic version of a factum must be formatted so that the complete document is contained in a single electronic file. The electronic version of the factum does not need to include a scanned image of the signature from the printed version or an electronic signature.

3. If the printed version of the transcript or compendium has more than one volume, the electronic version must be saved in separate files that correspond to the printed volumes.

4. When paper documents are scanned using optical character recognition software, the resolution must be set to 300 dpi and must not be set to grayscale.

V. — Naming Electronically-Filed Material

The file names for all electronic versions of factums, transcripts and other material must start with the Court of Appeal appeal or motion number followed by one of the character codes set out below, or a longer descriptive name indicating the content of the file, and ending with the relevant extension (e.g., docx, PDF).

1. — Examples of Naming Conventions:

C55532.FAP.PDF

C55557.TRN.PDF

C55556.MPF.docx

2. — Character Codes

Appeals:

FAP	Factum of Appellant
FRE	Factum of Respondent
FXA	Factum of Cross-appellant
FXR	Factum of Respondent to the Cross-Appeal
FOI	Factum of Intervener
FOAC	Factum of Amicus Curiae
ABCO	Appeal Book and Compendium
AB	Appeal Book
RCO	Respondent Compendium
RAB	Respondent Appeal Book
EXHB	Exhibit Book

Motions:

MPF	Moving Party Factum
RPF	Responding Party Factum
MPRF	Moving Party Reply Factum (motions for leave to appeal)
MPMR	Moving Party Motion Record
RPMR	Responding Party Motion Record

Transcripts:

TRN	Transcript

VI. — Failure to Comply

The Court of Appeal will reject any electronic version of a factum, transcript or other document that does not conform to the procedures set out in these Guidelines.

PD-1c — *REFERENCE GUIDE FOR CITATION PRACTICES AT THE COURT OF APPEAL FOR ONTARIO*

Effective: 1 March 2017

This reference guide is for information purposes only.

I. — Citing Cases

1. — Citation format

Include the case name in italics (italicize the "v." between the parties' names), followed by the information indicating where the case can be found.

For example: *Smith v. Smith*, [1952] 2 S.C.R. 312

The citation should identify the jurisdiction and the court that decided the case. If this information is not obvious from the citation, then include the information in parenthesis. For example:

Correct:

Smith v. Jones, 2001 SCC 28, [2001] 3 S.C.R. 28

1234 Inc. v. 7891 Ltd. (2013), 62 O.R. (3d) 123 (S.C.)

Jones v. Jones, 1989 CanLII 3389 (AB QB)

Incorrect:

Smith v. Jones, 2001 SCC 28, [2001] 3 S.C.R. 28 (S.C.C.)

1234 Inc. v. 7891 Ltd. (2013), 117 O.R. (3d) 550

Jones v. Jones, 1989 CanLII 3389

Do not include abbreviated publisher information for electronic services such as LexisNexis Quicklaw and WestlawNext.

Correct: *Bright v. Shiny*, [2001] O.J. 3512 (Div. Ct.)

Incorrect: *Bright v. Shiny*, [2001] O.J. 3512 (Div. Ct.) (QL)

Do not cite to court summaries or headnotes, which do not form part of the court's reasons for decision.

2. — Pinpointing

Refer whenever possible to the location of the particular passage in the case that is being relied on in the factum. The citation should make it clear whether the reference is to a paragraph number ("at para. 12" or "at paras. 12–14") or to a page number ("at p. 3" or "at pp. 133-34"). If the case contains paragraph numbers, cite to the paragraph numbers rather than to the page numbers.

3. — Selecting the Source for a Citation

The order for selecting which version of a case to cite is as follows:

(i) — Neutral citation

Law v. Order, 2014 ONCA 45

(ii) — Official and semi-official reporters

Law v. Order (2014), 110 O.R. (4th) 443 (C.A.)

(iii) — Unofficial reporters

Law v. Order (2014), 395 D.L.R. (4th) 358 (Ont. C.A.)

(iv) — CanLII

Law v. Order, 2014 CanLII 45444 (ON CA)

(v) — Subscription-based electronic databases

Law v. Order, [2014] O.J. No. 4912 (C.A.)

4. — Parallel citations

Citations to more than one source for a case are not required. However, it is helpful to provide a parallel citation when the case has a neutral citation (the identifier assigned by the court to a decision), and the case has also been published in a printed reporter series.

For example: *Smith v. Jones*, 2001 SCC 28, [2001] 3 S.C.R. 28

II. — Citing Legislation

Legislation should be cited using the following format:

Personal Property Security Act, R.S.O. 1990, c. P.10, s. 5

Personal Property Security Act, O. Reg. 356/03, s. 2(2)(b)

Income Tax Act, R.S.C. 1985 (5th Supp.), c. 1, ss. 47.1 and 48.1

It is not necessary to give the full citation to the following sources:

Canadian Charter of Rights and Freedoms (Note: subsequent references should be to the *Charter*)

Constitution Act, 1982

Constitution Act, 1867

III. — Citing Secondary Sources

The following examples illustrate the proper citation styles for secondary sources:

Books:

Joel Bakan et al., *Canadian Constitutional Law*, 3d ed. (Toronto: Emond Montgomery, 2003).

Articles:

Tina Lie and Manpreet Dhaliwal, "Should Have, Could Have, Would Have: Lessons Learned from *Canadian National Railway Co. v. McKercher LLP*" (2013) 2 C.L.A.R. 54.

Loose-leaf:

Donald J.M. Brown, *Civil Appeals*, vol. 1, (loose-leaf updated July 2011), (Toronto: Carswell, 2009), at p. 2-63.

Note: The publisher information and the date of publication appear on the copyright page of the loose-leaf volume. Include in separate brackets the most recent update or release date information if that is indicated on the bottom of the page being cited. There is no need to include the date when the material was consulted.

Other:

Law Commission of Ontario, Increasing Access to Family Justice Through Comprehensive Entry Points and Inclusivity (Toronto: February 2013).

Ontario, Legislative Assembly, *Official Report of Debates (Hansard)*, 37th Parl., 2nd Sess., No. 53 (18 October 2001), at p. 2819 (Name of Speaker — if any).

IV. — Placement of Citations in the Factum

The citation should be provided in the body of the factum immediately after the paragraph containing the reference. Citations should not be provided in footnotes or endnotes.

V. — Sample Citations

1. — Legislation

Statutes

Income Tax Act, R.S.C. 1985, c. 1 (5th Supp.), s. 18(1)(m)(iv)

2. — Case law

Neutral Citation Plus Official Reporter

Housen v. Nikolaisen, 2002 SCC 33, [2002] 2 S.C.R. 235, at para. 18

Neutral Citation Plus Unofficial Reporter

MacKinnon v. National Money Mart Co., 2004 BCCA 473, 50 B.L.R. (3d) 291

No Neutral Citation Assigned

Taylor v. Law Society of Prince Edward Island (1992), 101 Nfld. & P.E.I.R. 216 (P.E.I. S.C. (A.D.))

No Neutral Citation Assigned; Only Electronic Service Available

Sousa v. Akula, 2006 CanLII 25417 (ON SC)

3. — Secondary material

Books

Ruth Sullivan, *Sullivan on the Construction of Statutes*, 5th ed. (Markham: Ont.: LexisNexis Canada, 2008).

Journal Articles

Janet Conway, "Civil Resistance and the 'Diversity of Tactics' in the Anti-Globalization Movement: Problems of Violence, Silence, and Solidarity in Activist Politics" (2003) 41 Osgoode Hall L.J. 505.

Government Documents

Ontario, Legislative Assembly, *Official Report of Debates (Hansard)*, 37th Parl., 2nd Sess., No. 53 (18 October 2001), at p. 2819 (Name of Speaker — if any).

PD-1d — *LIST OF FREQUENTLY CITED CIVIL AUTHORITIES*

Effective: 1 March 2017

Parties do not need to reproduce the full version of the authorities on the following list in their books of authorities. When a party relies on one of the following authorities in the factum, the party should only include a copy of the headnote and the passage relied on in the book of authorities.

The authorities are listed chronologically by subject matter.

Administrative Law

- *Weber v. Ontario Hydro*, [1995] 2 S.C.R. 929
- *Dunsmuir v. New Brunswick*, 2008 SCC 9, [2008] 1 S.C.R. 190

Class Proceedings

- *Hollick v. Toronto (City)*, 2001 SCC 68, [2001] 3 S.C.R. 158
- *Rumley v. British Columbia*, 2001 SCC 69, [2001] 3 S.C.R. 184
- *Western Canadian Shopping Centres Inc. v. Dutton*, 2001 SCC 46, [2001] 2 S.C.R. 534

Contracts

- *Sattva Capital Corp. v. Creston Moly Corp.*, 2014 SCC 53, [2014] 2 S.C.R. 633
- *Bhasin v. Hrynew*, 2014 SCC 71, [2014] 3 S.C.R. 494
- *MacDonald v. Chicago Title Insurance Company of Canada*, 2015 ONCA 842

Costs

- *Boucher v. Public Accountants Council for the Province of Ontario* (2004), 71 O.R. (3d) 291 (C.A.)
- *Hamilton v. Open Window Bakery Ltd.*, 2004 SCC 9, [2004] 1 S.C.R. 303

Courts — Jurisdiction

- *Morguard Investments Ltd. v. De Savoye*, [1990] 3 S.C.R. 1077
- *Club Resorts Ltd. v. Van Breda*, 2012 SCC 17, [2012] S.C.J. No. 17

Damages

- *Hill v. Church of Scientology of Toronto*, [1995] 2 S.C.R. 1130
- *Whiten v. Pilot Insurance Co.*, 2002 SCC 18, [2002] 1 S.C.R. 595
- *Fidler v. Sun Life Assurance Co. of Canada*, 2006 SCC 30, [2006] 2 S.C.R. 3
- *Honda Canada Inc. v. Keays*, 2008 SCC 39, [2008] 2 S.C.R. 362

Evidence — Standard of Proof

- *F.H. v. McDougall*, 2008 SCC 53, [2008] 3 S.C.R. 41

Family

- *Pettkus v. Becker*, [1980] 2 S.C.R. 834
- *Moge v. Moge*, [1992] 3 S.C.R. 813
- *Peter v. Beblow*, [1993] 1 S.C.R. 980
- *Gordon v. Goertz*, [1996] 2 S.C.R. 27
- *Bracklow v. Bracklow*, [1999] 1 S.C.R. 420
- *Francis v. Baker*, [1999] 3 S.C.R. 250
- *Hickey v. Hickey*, [1999] 2 S.C.R. 518
- *Van de Perre v. Edwards*, 2001 SCC 60, [2001] 2 S.C.R. 1014
- *Miglin v. Miglin*, 2003 SCC 24, [2003] 1 S.C.R. 303
- *Fisher v. Fisher*, 2008 ONCA 11, 88 O.R. (3d) 241
- *Kerr v. Baranow/Vanasse v. Seguin*, 2011 SCC 10, [2011] 1 S.C.R. 269

Injunctions

- *RJR-MacDonald Inc. v. Canada (Attorney General)*, [1994] 1 S.C.R. 311

Motions for Intervention

- *Peel (Regional Municipality) v. Great Atlantic and Pacific Co. of Canada* (1990), 74 O.R. (2d) 164 (C.A.)
- *Peixeiro v. Haberman* (1994), 20 O.R. (3d) 666 (Ont. Ct. (Gen. Div.))

- *Authorson (Litigation Guardian of) v. Canada (Attorney General)* (2001), 147 O.A.C. 355, 9 C.P.C. (5th) 218 (C.A.)
- *Zoe Childs v. Desormeaux* (2003), 67 O.R. (3d) 385 (C.A.)
- *Bedford v. Canada (Attorney General)*, 2009 NCA 669

Motions for Leave to Appeal

- *Re Sault Dock Co. Ltd. and City of Sault Ste. Marie* (1973), 2 O.R. 479 (C.A.)
- *Iness v. Canada Mortgage and Housing Corp.* (2002), 62 O.R. (3d) 255 (C.A.)

Mental Health/Jurisdiction of Administrative Boards

- *Winko v. British Columbia (Forensic Psychiatric Institute)*, [1999] 2 S.C.R. 625
- *R. v. Conway*, 2010 SCC 22, [2010] 1 S.C.R. 765

Rule 20 of the Rules of Civil Procedure (Summary Judgment)

- *Combined Air Mechanical Services Inc. v. Flesch* (2011), 2011 ONCA 764, 108 O.R. (3d) 1
- *Hryniak v. Mauldin Group*, 2014 SCC 7
- *Bruno Appliance and Furniture Inc. v. Hryniak*, 2014 SCC 8

Rule 21 of the Rules of Civil Procedure

- *Hunt v. Carey Canada Inc.*, [1990] 2 S.C.R. 959
- *R. v. Imperial Tobacco Canada Ltd.*, 2011 SCC 42, [2011] 3 S.C.R. 45

Standard of Appellate Review

- *Stein v. Kathy K (The)*, [1976] 2 S.C.R. 802
- *Equity Waste Management of Canada v. Halton Hills (Town)* (1997), 35 O.R. (3d) 321 (C.A.)
- *Housen v. Nikolaisen*, 2002 SCC 33, [2002] 2 S.C.R. 235
- *Waxman v. Waxman* (2004), 186 O.A.C. 201
- *H.L. v. Canada (Attorney General)*, 2005 SCC 25, [2005] 1 S.C.R. 401

Statutory Interpretation

- *Rizzo v. Rizzo Shoes Ltd.*, [1998] 1 S.C.R. 27
- *Bell ExpressVu Limited Partnership v. Rex*, 2002 SCC 42, [2002] 2 S.C.R. 559

Tort

- *Donoghue v. Stevenson*, [1932] A.C. 562
- *Hedley Byrne & Co. v. Heller & Partners Ltd.*, [1963] 2 All E.R. 575
- *Anns v. London Borough of Merton*, [1978] A.C. 728
- *Queen v. Cognos*, [1993] 1 S.C.R. 87
- *Athey v. Leonati*, [1996] 3 S.C.R. 458
- *Hercules Management Ltd. v. Ernst & Young*, [1997] 2 S.C.R. 165
- *Cooper v. Hobart*, 2001 SCC 79, [2001] 3 S.C.R. 537
- *Childs v. Desormeaux*, 2006 SCC 18, [2006] 1 S.C.R. 643
- *Syl Apps Secure Treatment Centre v. B.D.*, 2007 SCC 38, [2007] 3 S.C.R. 83

Tort and Contract

- *Central Trust Co. v. Rafuse*, [1986] 2 S.C.R. 147

Trusts

- *Soulos v. Korkontzilas*, [1997] 2 S.C.R. 217

PD-1e — *JOINT REQUEST FOR PRE-HEARING SETTLEMENT CONFERENCE FORM*

....
Court File No.

COURT OF APPEAL FOR ONTARIO

BETWEEN:

Plaintiff
(Appellant) (or Respondent)

and

Defendant
(Appellant) (or Respondent)

JOINT REQUEST FOR PRE-HEARING SETTLEMENT CONFERENCE FORM

We, the undersigned, jointly request a pre-hearing settlement conference for the purpose of seeking to settle the appeal in this proceeding.

We agree to respect the confidential nature of all matters discussed in the pre-hearing settlement conference by the participants in the conference.

Date:

	Name of counsel/appellant if self-represented
Name and address of appellant's law firm or of appellant if self-represented	**Name of appellant(s) being represented**

	Phone number and email address of counsel or appellant if self-represented

	Name of counsel/respondent if self-represented
Name and address of respondent's law firm or of respondent if self-represented	
	Name of respondent(s) being represented
	Phone number and email address of counsel or respondent if self-represented

PD-2 — *GUIDELINES: TELECONFERENCE AND VIDEOCONFERENCE APPEARANCES IN THE COURT OF APPEAL FOR ONTARIO*

May 1, 2017

I. — CourtCall

CourtCall is a third-party remote appearance service that may be used to make telephone and video appearances at the Court of Appeal for Ontario.

Starting May 1, 2017, CourtCall will be available to make appearances for Status Court, Purge Court and Single Judge Motions.

A CourtCall appearance is voluntary. When a CourtCall appearance is requested **without** consent of the other party, the presiding judge reserves the discretion to require a personal appearance.

To participate in a CourtCall appearance by video, the party needs a computer with sufficient bandwidth, a webcam to view the proceedings, and a fixed telephone line.

To arrange a CourtCall appearance, the interested party should take the following steps:

1. If you are not already registered with CourtCall, please register at www.courtcall.com.

2. **At least three (3) business days before the hearing**, serve and file with CourtCall (not the Court of Appeal) a Request for CourtCall Telephone or Video Appearance (see www.courtcall.com).

3. For a telephone appearance, pay a fee of $55.00 (CDN) to CourtCall.

4. For a video appearance, pay a fee of $65 (CDN) to CourtCall.

A confirmation from CourtCall will be emailed or faxed to you upon the filing and payment outlined above.

CourtCall appearances are scheduled during the Court's ordinary sitting times.

Unless notified to the contrary, all parties who have filed a **CourtCall Request to Appear by Telephone** on a timely basis and have paid the required fee to CourtCall may appear by dialing the toll-free teleconference number provided by CourtCall.

All parties who have filed a **CourtCall Request to Appear by Video** on a timely basis and have paid the required fee may appear by video by logging in using the link that will be provided and dialing the toll-free teleconference number in the Confirmation sent to you by CourtCall.

A pre-hearing check-in will occur fifteen minutes before the scheduled hearing time.

FOR MORE INFORMATION, PLEASE CONTACT COURTCALL AT 1-888-882-6878

II. — Other Teleconferencing and Videoconferencing Services at the Court of Appeal for Ontario

In addition to the services offered by CourtCall, the Court of Appeal has existing, limited facilities for facilitating a telephone or video appearance. For information about using the Court of Appeal's available facilities, please contact the general inquiry line at 416-327-5020.

Please note that you will also need to use a **fixed telephone line** to make a telephone appearance using the Court of Appeal's existing facilities. The Court's existing teleconference facilities are not compatible with mobile phone technology.

Videoconferencing Procedures

Please note that you will need to make arrangements with your local courthouse in order to make a video appearance using the Court of Appeal's existing videoconferencing facilities. In order to schedule a hearing by way of video conference, the Court of Appeal will require the following information which should be forwarded to the Appeal Scheduling Unit at the Court of Appeal for Ontario, by email to COA.E-file@ontario.ca or by fax to (416) 326-6256:

- the name and file number of the motion or appeal to be heard,
- the location of the courthouse where the appellant or moving party will
- attend to participate in the video conference

- the dial-in numbers for that facility, and
- a contact for the courthouse.

After providing this information, the Court of Appeal will contact you to advise of the scheduled date and time for the video conferencing hearing.

In order to ensure no delays are encountered when scheduling your video conferencing hearing, please ensure that the Court of Appeal Intake Office is provided with your most up-to-date contact information.

PD-3 — *AFTER HOURS CONTACT INFORMATION*

In the event of an unanticipated emergency in relation to a matter in the Court of Appeal that could not have been dealt with during regular business hours with reasonable diligence or foresight, please contact the Security Office at Osgoode Hall. The telephone number is 416-327-5115.

Huguette G. Thomson

Registrar of the Court of Appeal for Ontario

Monday, June 4th, 2007

PD-4 — *CONSOLIDATED PRACTICE DIRECTION FOR DIVISIONAL COURT PROCEEDINGS*

Effective July 1, 2014

Changes effective July 1, 2017: A new Part II was created regarding motions for leave to appeal to Divisional Court (Part III to VII have been renumbered). As of July 1, 2017, rule 62.02 requires that leave to appeal to the Divisional Court under clause 19(1) (b) of the *Courts of Justice Act*, regarding appeals of interlocutory orders of a judge, shall be obtained from a panel of that court, rather than by a single judge. Three printed copies of materials for motions for leave to appeal must now be filed in at the Divisional Court Office in Toronto.

This Practice Direction applies to Divisional Court proceedings, effective July 1, 2014. It *supersedes* all Practice Directions for Divisional Court proceedings issued prior to July 1, 2014, which are hereby revoked.

Counsel and parties are advised to refer to the relevant parts of the separate Consolidated Provincial Practice Direction and region-specific Practice Directions which may affect Divisional Court proceedings. All Superior Court of Justice Practice Directions are available on the Court's website at: www.ontariocourts.ca/scj.

Part I: — Proceedings to be heard by a Single Judge

A. — Application

1. This part applies only to motions, applications, and appeals before a single judge. It does not apply to matters to be heard by a Divisional Court panel.

2. The following proceedings in Divisional Court are directed for a hearing before one judge of the Divisional Court:

a. appeals under s. 19(1)(c) and s. 31 of the *Courts of Justice Act* and motions to quash such appeals;

b. motions incidental to appeals or applications (i.e. interim relief).

3. Paragraphs 4–11 of this Practice Direction apply **only** to the Toronto Region.

B. — Proceedings in the Toronto Region

4. In the Toronto Region only, applications for judicial review under s. 6(2) of the *Judicial Review Procedure Act*, are directed to be brought in Divisional Court for a hearing before a single judge of that court sitting as a judge of the Superior Court of Justice.

The notice of application under s. 6(2), together with all other material, will be filed with the Divisional Court at Osgoode Hall.

Confirmation of Hearing

5. In the case of appeals to a single judge and other motions incidental to appeals or applications, counsel should contact the Divisional Court office by telephone, (416) 327-6202, to arrange a hearing date. In all three-judge proceedings, a hearing date must be obtained from the Registrar by telephone, (416) 326-5400.

6. Notwithstanding that a matter is set down for a hearing, and unless otherwise ordered by a judge, the papers will not be forwarded to the presiding judge and, unless otherwise ordered, the matter will not be heard on the date scheduled unless counsel for the moving party or applicant, by 2:00 p.m. three days prior to the scheduled hearing date, files all necessary material and confirms that the motion or application is to proceed as scheduled as required under the *Rules of Civil Procedure* (see rules 37.10.1 and 38.09.1).

Counsel for the moving party or applicant may confirm the hearing date by delivering the Confirmation Forms (Form 37B or Form 38B) to the Divisional Court office at Osgoode Hall or by fax transmission to (416) 327-5549. Motions under rule 62.02 for leave to appeal the interlocutory order of a Superior Court of Justice judge are exempt from this requirement, as these motions for leave are now heard by a panel in writing only (see Part II).

7. It is expected that a factum will be filed by each party on any matter. The presiding judge may decline to hear a matter if a factum has not been filed.

8. It is the responsibility of counsel to see that the material is filed as directed.

9. Counsel are reminded that all motions for leave to appeal must include, in the motion record, a copy of the signed and entered order from which leave to appeal is sought.

Time Estimates on Argument

10. When an application under s. 6(2) of the *Judicial Review Procedure Act* or an appeal under s. 19(1)(c) and 21(2) of the *Courts of Justice Act* will require more than one hour for hearing, counsel should advise the Registrar of their best estimate when the appointment is given.

Part II: — Motions for leave to appeal to the Divisional Court

11. As of July 1, 2017, rule 62.02 requires that leave to appeal to the Divisional Court under clause 19(1)(b) of the *Courts of Justice Act*, regarding appeals of interlocutory orders of a judge, shall be obtained from a panel of that court, rather than by a single judge. These motions for leave to appeal must now be filed at the Divisional Court Office in Toronto at the following address in person or by mail/courier, together with payment of the filing fee:

Divisional Court Office

Osgoode Hall

130 Queen Street West

Toronto, ON M5H 2N5

The motion for leave will be heard in writing by a panel of three Divisional Court judges. Three printed copies of the motion record, factum and transcripts, if any, are required to be filed.

Part III: — Factums in the Divisional Court

12. Counsel and parties should refer to rules 61.11, 61.12 and 68.04(3) and (6) of the *Rules of Civil Procedure* which deal with factums on appeals and applications for judicial review. These rules require a "concise summary" of fact and law and an estimate of the time required for oral argument. If in counsel's opinion a factum of more than 30 pages is necessary, counsel should arrange an appointment with a judge of the Divisional Court through the Registrar of the Court, before filing.

Part IV: — Books of Authority

13. It is of great assistance to the Divisional Court to have books of authority filed by counsel containing copies of the authorities to which they intend to refer on the hearing of the matter. Such books of authorities:

a. Should include only the cases to which counsel actually intend to refer in the oral argument. The particular passages in the cases to which counsel wish to refer should be clearly marked.

b. Should be prepared jointly in accordance with this direction. Where counsel are unable to agree, then such case books should indicate whether they are filed by the appellant or the respondent. There should be consultation between counsel to avoid any duplication of the authorities included in their respective case books.

c. Should have a tab for each case (either numerical or by letters), should include an index of the authorities and indicate the tab where the authority is reproduced. It is not necessary to number the pages in the case-book so long as the photocopies show the page numbers of each authority.

d. Should be filed, if possible, not later than the Monday of the week preceding the hearing of the matter as they are of great assistance to the judges in preparing for the hearing.

Part V: — Filing Electronic Versions of Documents in Civil Appeals and Judicial Review Applications

A. — Application

14. This part is intended to establish a uniform approach to filing electronic documents for appeals and judicial review applications to the Divisional Court.

15. This part applies to civil appeals, including appeals from administrative tribunals, motions for leave to appeal under rule 62.02 and judicial review applications in the Divisional Court.

16. This part does not apply to motions other than motions for leave to appeal under rule 62.02. It does not apply to family appeals to the Divisional Court.

17. Parties filing electronic versions of material for Divisional Court proceedings must still file typed or printed copies of such material in accordance with Rules 61 - 62 and 68 of the *Rules of Civil Procedure*.

B. — Appeals

18. Parties are required to file electronic versions of their factums and transcripts in appeals to the Divisional Court, in accordance with Rule 61 of the *Rules of Civil Procedure*.

18.1 Parties are also encouraged to file electronic versions of all materials (e.g. appeal books and compendiums, case books, record of proceedings) in the appeal.

C. — Judicial Review Applications

19. The Court encourages parties to file electronic versions of their factums and transcripts in judicial review applications to the Divisional Court.

19.1 Parties are also encouraged to file electronic versions of all materials (e.g. application records, compendiums, case books, records of proceedings) in the judicial review application.

C.1 — Motions for Leave to Appeal

20. The Court encourages parties to file electronic versions of their factums, transcripts, motion records and books of authorities in motions for leave to appeal from an interlocutory order of a judge under rule 62.02 of the *Rules of Civil Procedure*.

D. — Providing Materials to Other Parties

21. Parties are also encouraged to give the electronic versions of documents that are filed electronically with the Court to all other parties to the proceeding.

E. — Method of Filing Electronic Documents

22. Parties may file electronic documents on CD, DVD or USB key. Three copies of the CD, DVD or USB key should be filed with the Court where the matter is being heard by a panel of three judges.

23. The CD, DVD or USB key should be accompanied by a covering letter which identifies the materials contained on the CD, DVD or USB key.

USB Key: The cover letter should include a list of the files contained on the USB key, along with the title of proceedings, Court File #, Counsel Name(s), where applicable, and Party Name. If possible, the key should be labelled with the short style of cause and the Court File #.

CD or DVD: The CD or DVD should be labelled with the title of proceedings, Court File #, Counsel Name(s), where applicable, and Party Name. Include a list of the files contained on the CD or DVD in a cover letter.

24. The electronic documents should be filed together with the hard copy of the factum filed with the Court.

F. — Format of Electronically Filed Documents

25. The electronic documents must be submitted in either Microsoft Word format (.doc or .docx) or text searchable PDF format.

26. The electronic version of factums or any other material filed in a Divisional Court appeal or judicial review application must be formatted and contained in one file and be virtually identical to the official printed version that is also filed with the Court. For example, a single file for a factum should contain the front and back pages, the index, the text and the schedules. Do not submit separate electronic files for the different sections of a factum or other document. Parties should refer to the Guide Concerning e-Delivery of Documents in the Superior Court of Justice with respect to the preparation and formatting of electronic materials to be filed with the Court.

G. — Naming of Electronically Filed Documents

27. The file names for electronic versions of factums, transcripts and other documents filed must start with the Divisional Court appeal or judicial review application file number, followed by one of the character codes set out below. Any other parties not included in this list should include their full name together with the title of the document they are filing.

Appeals

FAP	Factum of Appellant
FRE	Factum of Respondent
FXA	Factum of Cross-appellant
FXR	Factum of Cross-respondent
FOI	Factum of Intervener

FOAC	Factum of Amicus Curiae
AFAP	Amended Factum of Appellant
AFRE	Amended Factum of Respondent
FSE	Further Submissions — Appellant
FSR	Further Submissions — Respondent
ABC	Appellant's Appeal Book and Compendium
RBC	Respondent's Compendium
EXB	Exhibit Book
BOA	Book of Authorities of Appellant
BOR	Book of Authorities of Respondent

Transcripts

TRN	Transcript

Judicial Review Applications

FAPL	Factum of Applicant
FRP	Factum of Respondent
FIN	Factum of Intervener
ROP	Record of Proceeding
APAR	Application Record of Applicant
APRR	Application Record of Respondent
APINR	Application Record of Intervener
BAAP	Book of Authorities of Applicant

BARP	Book of Authorities of Respondent

Motions for Leave to Appeal

MPF	Factum of Moving Party
RPF	Factum of Responding Party
MMP	Motion Record of Moving Party
MRP	Motion Record of Responding Party

H. — Failure to Comply with this Practice Direction

28. Please note that the Divisional Court may reject any electronic version of a factum or transcript that does not conform to the procedures set out in paragraphs 14–27 of this Practice Direction.

Part VI: — Judges' Book of Authorities

29. A Judges' Book of Authorities containing authorities frequently relied on is supplied to each judge who sits in Divisional Court. There will be additions to, and deletions from, the book from time to time. An up-to-date list of the authorities in the Judges' Book will be available as of July 1, 2014, on the Court's website.

30. In preparing books of authorities, counsel need no longer include authorities contained in the Judges' Book. However, extracts from those authorities which counsel intend to refer to the court should be included in the factum or book of authorities.

Part VII: — Regional Centres for Divisional Court Filings

31. For the purpose of all filings in the Divisional Court, the following locations are designated as the regional centres. Effective June 1, 2016, the place for all Divisional Court filings for the Central East region changed from Newmarket to Oshawa (Durham Region courthouse).

Note: In accordance with Part II, all motions for leave to appeal to the Divisional Court under rule 62.02 regarding appeals of interlocutory orders of a judge must be filed at the Divisional Court in Toronto.

Region	**Regional Centre**
Central East Region	Durham Region Courthouse 150 Bond St. E. Oshawa, ON L1G 0A2

Region	**Regional Centre**
Central South Region	Hamilton (John Sopinka) Courthouse 45 Main St. E. Hamilton, ON L8N 2B7
Central West Region	Brampton (A. Grenville & William Davis) Courthouse 7755 Hurontario St. Brampton, ON L6W 4T1
East Region	Ottawa Courthouse 161 Elgin St., 2nd Fl. Ottawa On K2P 2K1
Northeast Region	Sudbury Courthouse 155 Elm St. Sudbury, ON P3C 1T9
Northwest Region	Thunder Bay Courthouse 125 Brodie St. N. Thunder Bay, ON P7C 0A3
Southwest Region	London Courthouse 80 Dundas St. London, ON N6A 6A3
Toronto Region	Osgoode Hall 130 Queen St. W. Toronto, ON M5H 2N5

Dated: April 11, 2014

Amended: July 1, 2017 (Part II); May 10, 2016 (Part VI); January 25, 2016 (Part IV)

Heather J. Smith

Chief Justice

Superior Court of Justice (Ontario)

PD-5 — *CONSOLIDATED PROVINCIAL PRACTICE DIRECTION (EFFECTIVE JULY 1, 2014)*

Notice of Amendments:

Effective June 15, 2018:

- **Part VI (Books of Authorities in Civil Proceedings) has been added;**
- **Part V C (Release of Digital Court Recordings) has been amended to clarify the process for obtaining a digital recording of a Small Claims Court proceeding and to provide that no digital recordings of civil and family motions are available to anyone unless a judge orders otherwise; and**
- **Paragraph 46 has been amended to update the information regarding long motion times in the Southwest Region.**

Effective January 1, 2017, para 57 has been amended regarding the gowning policy of the court.

Effective July 1, 2016, Section F (Publication Bans) has been added to Part V.

Effective May 1, 2016, new provisions have been added in Part I C to clarify the court's expectations regarding the confirmation of events in a family case. Amendments were also made to permit a trial scheduling conference to be scheduled in order to ensure proper completion of the Trial Scheduling Endorsement Form, which has been consolidated into one document.

Effective April 1, 2016, Part 1 B (Often Cited Family Law Cases) applies to all regions in Ontario.

February 1, 2016, Para 49 of Part III B has also been amended to indicate that all motions to transfer a civil proceeding should be brought at the court location to which the moving party seeks to have the proceeding transferred.

This Practice Direction governs proceedings in the Ontario Superior Court of Justice, province-wide *unless stated otherwise*, effective July 1, 2014.

This Practice Direction *supersedes* all previous province-wide Practice Directions issued prior to July 1, 2014, which are hereby revoked.

Counsel and parties are advised to refer to the relevant Parts of the Consolidated Practice Direction for Divisional Court Proceedings, as well as the applicable region-specific Practice Directions which are also available on the Superior Court of Justice website at: www.ontariocourts.ca/scj.

PART I: — FAMILY PROCEEDINGS IN THE SUPERIOR COURT OF JUSTICE

1. This Part applies to all Family Proceedings in the Superior Court of Justice in Ontario, *except where noted otherwise*. Counsel and parties are advised to refer to the relevant region-specific Practice Directions that supplement this Part.

A. — Dispute Resolution Officer Program

Application

2. Paragraphs 3 to 17 of this Practice Direction apply to *all* Dispute Resolution Officer (DRO) Programs in the Ontario Superior Court of Justice, including existing permanent programs, pilot projects, and any future programs.[2]

Role and Conduct of the DRO

3. DRO lawyers hearing case conferences must be appointed by the Regional Senior Judge and the Senior Family Judge, pursuant to Rule 17(9) of the *Family Law Rules*.

4. DROs shall:

a) hear *all* first case conferences for motions to change under Rule 15 of the *Family Law Rules*; and

b) complete a "Screening Report" after the conclusion of each DRO Case Conference, which will be included as part of the court file.

5. DROs may:

a) hear first case conferences on matters other than motions to change *only* when referred to the DRO by a judge and when such matters are scheduled to DROs after all first case conferences on motions to change have received priority in scheduling;

b) attempt to identify, resolve or settle outstanding issues on a consent basis;

c) assist parties in organizing their issues and disclosure documents in order to make the case "judge-ready"; and/or

d) assist parties in obtaining a signed consent order from a judge, where the parties have consented in writing at the DRO Case Conference.

6. DROs shall not:

a) write consents or draft orders on behalf of parties;

b) make orders, on consent or otherwise; or

c) award costs.

[2]As of July 1, 2014, DROs are available in the Central East Region at the Newmarket, Durham and Barrie judicial centres, the Central West Region at the Milton and Brampton judicial centres, in the Central South Region at the Hamilton judicial centre and in the Toronto Region at 393 University Avenue.

Role and Conduct of Parties Appearing before a DRO

7. Rule 17 of the *Family Law Rules* applies to case conferences including those heard by a DRO pursuant to Rule 17(9).

8. Parties attending a DRO Case Conference (DRC) must therefore comply with the document requirements under Rule 17 of the *Family Law Rules*, including advance filing of:

a) a case conference brief, which on a motion to change should at minimum include:

- a copy of the previous order that is the subject of the motion to change;
- documentation supporting the "change in circumstance";
- a description of the change being sought;

b) any relevant disclosure documents; and

c) a Form 14C Confirmation Form, filed not later than 2 pm, two business days prior to the date scheduled for the DRC.

Scheduling DRO Case Conferences (DRCs)

9. Wherever possible, motions to change will receive priority over other matters when DRCs are scheduled.

10. Wherever possible, litigants will receive the most immediate, next available date/time, accommodation may be made for reasonable conflicts.

11. Wherever possible, in advance of a DRC Hearing Date, the DRO will be advised of confirmed parties, in order to prevent any potential conflicts of interest.

DRO Screening Reports

12. At minimum, DRO Screening Reports shall include the following information, although additions may be made locally:

a) Name of DRO;

b) Whether parties were represented or unrepresented;

c) Whether the matter was scheduled before the DRO was a case conference on a motion to change or a case conference on an issue other than a motion to change;

d) Indication of whether the DRC was (1) "fully settled", (2) "partially settled", (3) resulted in no resolution, (4) resulted in disclosure only, upon conclusion;

e) Identification of any issues resolved and/or agreed upon for consideration by a judge;

f) Identification of any outstanding issues if only (1) "partially settled", (2) only disclosure arranged, or (3) no resolution;

g) Timelines for matters that must be completed (ie/disclosure by certain dates) by the parties, if issues were not resolved during the DRC; and

h) Indication of whether or not the conduct of any party has frustrated the objectives of the DRC.

13. A judge presiding at a subsequent court event for the parties may rely on the DRO's notations in the Screening Report, after hearing submissions on the issues, in determining if costs are appropriate.

Next Steps after the DRC

14. Wherever possible, on each DRC Hearing Date, at least one judge will be available to review any consent orders, minutes of settlement, or temporary orders arising out of the DRCs from the day's list. Where these settlements are reached at the end of a DRC, all efforts will be made to ensure parties and counsel will receive a judicial response on the same day as their DRC.

15. Upon completion of a DRC, parties shall be permitted to schedule as a next step:

a) a motion in front of a judge;

b) another case conference in front of a DRO if necessary;

c) a case conference in front of a judge; or

d) a settlement conference in front of a judge.

Local Schedules & Procedures Regarding DRO Programs

16. Parties attending DRCs in their respective court locations should also consult their local courthouse for any specific local procedures.

17. Local DRO Schedules in each relevant court location will be provided in the *DRO Schedule Annex*, available on the Superior Court's website at: www.ontariocourts.ca/scj/practice/practice-directions/dro/annex.

B. — Often Cited Family Law Cases

18. Paragraphs 19 to 22 of this Practice Direction apply in all Regions *except* the East, Central East and North East Regions.

19. A list of Often Cited Family Cases for Family Matters containing cases frequently relied on is now supplied to each judge who sits on the Family Team. There will be additions to, and deletions from, the list from time to time. An up-to-date list is available on the Superior Court of Justice website at: www.ontariocourts.ca/scj/practice/practice-directions/family-law-cases/list.

20. The cases in question appear on this list under various headings or topics which are not in any way intended to provide legal advice.

21. Parties in family law proceedings in the Superior Court of Justice in the Central West, Central South, Northwest, Southwest, and Toronto Regions need no longer include authorities on this list in any book of authorities relied on.

22. However, extracts from those authorities which counsel intend to refer to the court shall be included in the factum or book of authorities.

C. — Confirmation Forms

22.1 Each party to a conference or motion must file a fully completed File 14C Confirmation no later than 2 p.m. two business days before the motion or conference, except as follows:

a. Urgent motions that are being brought without notice to the other party do not need to be confirmed;

b. Long motions must be confirmed earlier than two days in advance in several locations by regional practice direction.

22.2 Form 14C Confirmations must **only** list the specific issues that are to be addressed at that event and the specific materials that the judge should review.

22.3 Where Form 14C Confirmation forms have not been properly completed and filed by the appropriate deadline by at least one party, the event will not be heard on the scheduled day without the court's permission.

D. — Form 14B Motions

23. Paragraphs 24 to 31 of this Practice Direction apply in all Regions *except* the Central East, East and Toronto Region. See the Practice Direction in your region for additional direction regarding 14B Motions.

24. The Superior Court's policy is to support timely case conferences in which parties are afforded sufficient judicial time to have a meaningful hearing. However, inadequate judicial resources present a scheduling challenge that makes consistent application of this policy across all judicial Regions difficult to achieve.

25. Consequently, in order to assist counsel and parties in making the best use of available conference time, the Superior Court will encourage greater use of Form 14B motions whenever it will make the case conference process more effective. Form 14B motions allow parties to address certain threshold issues prior to the case conference and are designed to streamline conferencing in Family Law proceedings. Such motions are limited to procedural, uncomplicated or unopposed matters that will promote the concept of fewer, but more meaningful, case conferences. In this respect, Form 14B motions procedures will be guided by paragraphs 26 to 31 below.

26. Sub-rules 14(4.2) and (10) of the *Family Law Rules* provide that motions are permissible before a case conference, if there is a situation of urgency or hardship, or if the request for relief is limited to "procedural, uncomplicated or unopposed matters". Relief is requested using Form 14B.

27. Before a case conference is held, lawyers and self-represented litigants are strongly encouraged to use Form 14B to obtain any orders that are *needed to make the case conference a more meaningful and productive process*.

28. Examples of appropriate orders include:

a. Orders of either a procedural or substantive nature that are on consent, or unopposed;

b. A request for the appointment of the Office of the Children's Lawyer;

c. Orders to add a party or obtain discovery from a third party;

d. Orders for production of documents, permission for oral questioning or other issues pertaining to discovery;

e. Enforcement of an order to provide information, produce a document or serve and file a financial statement or other document; and;

f. Any other procedural order or direction needed to promote a meaningful case conference including orders requiring that financial disclosure be provided by a party in accordance with rule 13.

29. Requests for an order shall be considered "uncomplicated" only if:

a. Oral submissions can be made in five minutes or less for each side; and

b. Affidavit material in support of the request for relief is three pages or less in length.

30. Requests that are without notice, on consent or unopposed will be determined by a judge in chambers. All other requests will be determined in motions court or by conference telephone call. The Form 14B should specify the court location, date and time for the hearing unless a conference call had been arranged under Rule 14(8).

31. A copy of Form 14B is available at the courthouse and can also be downloaded from the government website at: www.ontariocourtforms.on.ca.

E. — Settlement Conferences and Trial Scheduling Conferences

31.1 The settlement conference is an important step in family cases. The primary purpose of the settlement conference is to settle or at least narrow the issues in dispute.

31.2 Pursuant to rule 17(5)(g) of the Family Law Rules, if the case is not settled at the settlement conference, one of the additional purposes of the conference is to identify the witnesses and other evidence to be presented at trial, estimate the time needed for trial and, where appropriate, to schedule the case for trial.

31.3 If the case has not settled at the conclusion of the settlement conference, the court shall determine if the Trial Scheduling Endorsement Form can be completed at the conference or shortly thereafter and shall give directions to the parties regarding the completion of this form.

31.4 If necessary, the Court may require the parties to attend a trial scheduling conference to canvas issues regarding the scheduling of the trial and ensure proper completion of the trial scheduling endorsement form. Each party shall complete and file their portion of the Trial Scheduling Endorsement Form with the court in advance of a trial scheduling conference in accordance with the timelines in rule 17(13.1).

31.5 A trial scheduling conference's purposes include (i) ensuring that the case is ready to proceed to trial, (ii) considering each party's list of proposed witnesses and (iii) ensuring the accuracy of the estimated time for trial. Consideration should also be given to other conditions that would be appropriate under rule 1 in order to limit the duration and scope of the trial.

31.6 A trial date will not be made available until the court has reviewed and endorsed the complete Trial Scheduling Endorsement Form.

31.7 In exceptional circumstances, the court may provide litigants with a trial date before the court has endorsed the complete Trial Scheduling Endorsement form. Where this has occurred, the form must be finalized no later than 60 days in advance of the trial in order to retain the scheduled date.

F. — Trial Management Conferences

31.8 A trial management conference should be held in all family cases that have not been resolved at or before the settlement conference in order to ensure trial readiness and canvas settlement. The trial management conference should be scheduled no more than two weeks in advance of the scheduled trial date, wherever possible.

31.9 The Trial Management Conference Brief: Form 17E is no longer required. Instead of the Trial Management Conference Brief, the following documents must be filed in advance of the trial management conference by the deadlines set out in rule 17(13.1):

a. The completed Trial Scheduling Endorsement Form must be filed by either the Applicant or the party that requested the conference;

b. Each party must file an offer to settle all outstanding issues; and,

c. Each party must file an outline of their opening statement for trial.

The Endorsement Volume of the continuing record should also be put before the judge at the trial management conference.

31.10 The completed Trial Scheduling Endorsement Form shall be filed with or added to the Trial Record. No offers to settle should be included in the Trial Record.

31.11 Attendance at an assignment court or other similar scheduling event shall not be necessary where a trial management conference has been held and the trial date has been confirmed.

31.12 Where the case has been settled and the trial is no longer required, one of the parties shall immediately advise the Trial Coordinator so that the trial date can be vacated. A copy of any Minutes of Settlement or consent should be filed at the same time.

PART II: — PROCEEDINGS UNDER THE CLASS PROCEEDINGS ACT, 1992

A. — National Database of Class Proceedings

32. The Canadian Judicial Council has endorsed the recommendation of the Uniform Law Conference of Canada for the creation of a Canadian Class Proceedings Database to facilitate the exchange of information about multi-jurisdictional class proceedings. The Canadian Bar Association has announced a pilot project to establish such a Database.

33. It is anticipated that similar procedures will be implemented across the country and that lawyers and members of the public will be able to search the Database to obtain information about class action proceedings that have been commenced in any jurisdiction in Canada.

34. Within 10 days of service or filing, whichever is earlier, a copy of any:

a) originating process; or

b) Notice of Motion for certification (not including affidavits in support); or

c) amendments to the foregoing,

must be sent electronically by plaintiff's counsel to the National Class Action Database of the Canadian Bar Association at the following address:

National Class Action Database

Canadian Bar Association

E-mail: classaction@cba.org

Attention: Kerri Froc

35. A National Class Action Database Registration Form, available on the Superior Court of Justice Website, must be used when submitting documents to the National Class Action Database. Please be advised that PDF is the preferred format for documents; however, MS Word documents will also be accepted.

B. — Provincial Class Proceeding Registry

36. To promote the goals of the *Class Proceeding Act, 1992*, including judicial economy and access to the courts, each Regional Senior Judge has assigned one or more judges to coordinate all class proceedings in that Region as the "Class Proceedings Judge". To increase efficiency and provide a degree of consistency, in keeping with the case management approach ascribed to the court by the Act, the Class Proceedings Judge will preside over the majority of pre-trial class proceedings motions and certifications in that Region.

37. The purpose of the registry is to ensure that once a class is certified, other members of the same class do not attempt to certify a second proceeding.

Assigned Judges

38. The Class Proceedings Judge(s), or other judge assigned by the Regional Senior Judge, will hear motions for certification under the *Class Proceedings Act, 1992* brought in that Region.

39. The names of assigned Class Proceedings Judges may be obtained from the Regional Managers in each Region:

Region	**Telephone**	**Fax**
Northwest	(807) 343-2727	(807) 343-2758
Northeast	(705) 564-7813	(705) 564-7902
East	(613) 239-1385	(613) 239-1007
Central East	(905) 853-4822	(905) 853-4826
Toronto	(416) 327-6104	(416) 325-2872
Central West	(905) 456-4838	(905) 456-4836

Region	Telephone	Fax
Central South	(905) 645-5323	(905) 645-5374
Southwest	(519) 660-2285	(519) 660-2294

Originating Process and Court Documents

40. The title or proceeding for every class proceeding shall state that it is a "Proceeding under the *Class Proceedings Act, 1992*."

41. Every class proceeding shall have appended to the court file number the letter CP, indicating that it is a class proceeding.

42. A copy of the originating process of any proceeding commenced under the *Class Proceedings Act, 1992* must be filed with the Class Proceedings Registry at the Civil Intake Office, 393 University Avenue, Toronto, Ontario, M5G 1E6, in addition to the court office in the jurisdiction where the matter was commenced. The originating process may be sent to the Registry by registered mail, ordinary mail, facsimile (416) 327-6187, or it may be filed.

43. The solicitor of record for the party who commences the proceeding must complete a Certificate of Compliance, verifying that a copy of the originating process has been filed with the Registry. The Certificate of Compliance must be filed forthwith in the court office where the action was commenced.

Procedure on Motions and other Hearings

44. In accordance with the statutory scheme, the judge hearing the pre-trial motions will case manage the proceeding.

PART III: — CIVIL AND FAMILY MOTIONS PROCEDURE

A. — Factums for Motions

45. The following requirements apply within all judicial Regions of the Ontario Superior Court of Justice for motions in civil and family proceedings:*

a) Factums are *required* for long civil motions and encouraged for all other motions unless otherwise directed by a judge;

b) Factums or Summaries of Argument under subrule 17(8) of the *Family Law Rules* are *required* for all long family motions unless otherwise directed by a case conference judge;

*The *single exception* is family proceedings in the Toronto Region which are governed by the Consolidated Practice Direction Concerning Family Cases in the Toronto Region.

c) No factum or Summary of Argument may exceed 20 pages, unless leave is granted; and,**

d) The times for service and filing of factums or Summaries of Argument shall be in accordance with the times for service and filing of other motions materials respectively under the *Rules of Civil Procedure* or the *Family Law Rules*, *unless* a region-specific Practice Direction states otherwise.

46. The following chart sets out the times for short and long motions for civil and family proceedings in each judicial Region:

REGIONS	SHORT MOTIONS	LONG MOTIONS
Central East: Civil, Family	Under 1 hour	Over 1 hour
Central South: Civil, Family	Under 1 hour	Over 1 hour
Central West: Civil, Family	Under 1 hour	Over 1 hour
East: Civil, Family	Under 1 hour	Over 1 hour***
Northeast: Civil, Family	Under 1 hour	Over 1 hour
Northwest: Civil, Family	Under 2 hours	Over 2 hours
Southwest§: Civil, Family	Under 1/2 hour	Over 1/2 hour
Toronto: Civil	Under 2 hours	Over 2 hours

B. — Motions to Transfer a Civil Proceeding in the Central East, Central West, Central South and Toronto Regions under Rule 13.1.02 of the Rules of Civil Procedure

47. Paragraphs 48 to 51 of this Practice Direction govern motions to transfer under rule 13.1.02 in the Central East, Central West, Central South and Toronto Regions.

48. A high volume of requests to transfer civil proceedings to another county, often in another Region, are being received in the Central East, Central West, Central South and Toronto Regions. Counsel frequently seek to transfer a case, on consent. While the transfer may be appropriate in the circumstances of the case, the onus rests with the moving party to satisfy the court that a transfer is desirable in the interest of justice, having regard to the factors listed in rule 13.1.02(2)(b). It is not sufficient to bring a transfer motion orally, on consent, or to file a consent for an order to transfer a case to another county under rule 13.1.02.

49. A motion to transfer a proceeding should be brought at the court location to which the moving party seeks to have the proceeding transferred. The moving party must file a Notice of Motion with a supporting affidavit, as required under rule 13.1.02(2). The moving party's affidavit must address the factors listed in rule 13.1.02(2)(b) and, as part of the relevant matters, must identify the current stage of the proceeding (i.e., whether further motions are anticipated in the proceeding, whether a pre-trial has occurred or is scheduled, and whether mediation has been held) and why the proceeding was originally commenced in the originating county. The affidavit

**In the Toronto Region no factum may exceed 30 pages, unless leave is granted.

***The East Region has an additional "lengthy" category for long family motions more than 2 hours.

§The times stated in this chart for the Southwest Region are for general information only. It is recommended that you contact your court location to find out whether your motion will be treated as a short motion or a long motion.

should also address the estimated length of trial, whether it is a jury trial, and the number of parties and counsel.

50. Counsel are *not* required to provide affidavit evidence about the availability of judges and court facilities in the other county to satisfy factor (viii) under rule 13.1.02(2). This factor shall be addressed by the Regional Senior Judge in the Region where the motion is brought, after consulting with the local administrative judge or Regional Senior Judge for the other county.

51. The Regional Senior Judge, or his or her designate, will hear all motions to transfer. To allow the Regional Senior Judge to promptly determine all such motions, they shall be brought in writing. Responding parties are *strongly encouraged* to file and rely exclusively on written submissions to allow the motion to be heard and fully determined in writing. If an oral hearing becomes necessary, the motion shall be heard by teleconference arranged through the Office of the Regional Senior Judge in the Region where the motion is brought. In addition to filing motion material pursuant to the Rules, all parties on a motion to transfer are encouraged to submit an electronic, scanned version of their motion materials, saved as a PDF file and submitted on a USB stick appropriately tagged or marked indicating the court file number. This will facilitate the ability of the Regional Senior Judge to efficiently dispose of these motions, without the delay inherent in physical file transfers.

PART IV: — JUDICIAL MANAGEMENT OF ALL CIVIL PROCEEDINGS NOT GOVERNED BY RULE 77 OF THE RULES OF CIVIL PROCEDURE

52. Counsel and parties are reminded that all civil proceedings in Ontario, not subject to case management under Rule 77, may be judicially managed under the present provisions of the *Rules of Civil Procedure*.

53. Rule 37.15 provides that if a proceeding involves complicated issues or if two or more proceedings involve similar issues, parties and/or counsel who seek an order under the rule may make a request in writing to the Regional Senior Judge of their respective judicial Region to have a judge appointed.

54. Pursuant to Rule 48.14, the court will supervise actions that are not set down for trial on a timely basis.

55. Status Notices (Form 48C) will be issued for actions that have not been placed on the trial list or terminated by any means within two years after the filing of a statement of defence, indicating that the proceeding will be dismissed for delay within 90 days, with costs, unless:

a) the action is set down for trial; or

b) the action has been terminated by any means; or

c) a status hearing judge orders otherwise.

56. Any party who receives the Status Notice may request a Status Hearing, at which the plaintiff must show cause why the action should not be dismissed for delay and the court will review the action and may consider the range of orders set out in Rule 48.14(8).

PART V: — GENERAL PRACTICE DIRECTIONS APPLICABLE TO ALL PROCEEDINGS

A. — Gowning for Counsel

57. Counsel are required to gown for all trials, motions and appeals before the presiding judge in the Ontario Superior Court of Justice. Counsel who are pregnant are free to modify their traditional court attire in order to accommodate their pregnancy as they see fit, including dispensing with a waistcoat and tabs

58. Counsel are not required to gown for appearances before masters or judges and deputy judges of the Small Claims Court (a branch of the Superior Court of Justice).

59. Counsel are not required to gown before a Superior Court Judge of Ontario when appearing in Assignment Court, case conferences, settlement conferences, trial management conferences, trial scheduling courts, or pre-trials, *unless* a region-specific Practice Direction states otherwise.

B. — Ensuring the Integrity of Scheduled Trials, Hearing and Appeals

60. This section is intended to ensure that trials, hearings and appeals are scheduled on the basis of the chronological order in which lawyers make their commitments to appear in court. It has three important objectives:

a) to ensure that the trial lists of the Superior Court of Justice and the Ontario Court of Justice are respected;

b) to reduce court delays, the waste of court resources and the unnecessary expense and inconvenience to the public brought about by adjournments; and

c) to assist parties in civil or criminal cases in having adequate representation by a lawyer acceptable to them.

Trial Dates

61. Where a date for trial or for the hearing of a matter has been set by the Superior Court of Justice or the Ontario Court of Justice, the trial or hearing is expected to take place on that date.

Presumption of Commitment

62. By agreeing to a trial or hearing date, a lawyer is presumed to have made a commitment to appear on that date and to be bound not to make any other commitments that would make the lawyer's appearance on that date impossible.

Duty to Inform of Previous Commitments

63. When setting a date for trials, hearings or appeals in the Superior Court of Justice or the Ontario Court of Justice, every lawyer has a duty to disclose previous commitments to another court that may conflict with a proposed date for a trial, hearing or appeal.

Respect for Previous Commitments

64. In setting dates for trials, hearings or appeals, the Superior Court of Justice and the Ontario Court of Justice, as much as possible, shall avoid setting dates that would make it impossible for lawyers to keep commitments already made in other courts.

C. — Release of Digital Court Recordings

65. This section outlines the policy on the release of digital court recordings. Members of the public, counsel, litigants, accused or the media may obtain copies of digital court recordings (hereinafter referred to as "digital recordings") made from Digital Recording Devices (DRDs) of matters heard in open court, in accordance with the requirements of this section. The copies of digital court recordings will include annotations.

66. The release of digital recordings will be at the court's discretion and the use of all digital recordings will be subject to any court order and any common law or statutory restriction on publication applicable to the particular proceeding.

67. Unless this section provides otherwise, all persons must execute an undertaking with the court to access the digital recordings. The undertaking prescribes the way in which the digital recording is to be used and the terms and conditions under which the digital recording is being provided. All digital recordings are subject to the prohibition set out in s. 136 of the *Courts of Justice Act*, which prohibits the broadcast, reproduction and dissemination of audio recordings. Any person who contravenes s. 136 is guilty of an offence and subject to a penalty, in accordance with s. 136(4) of the *Courts of Justice Act*.

Exception, Small Claims Court Proceedings

68. A person requesting the release of a digital recording of a Small Claims Court proceeding must: (i) obtain a court order authorizing access, (ii) complete the "Undertaking to the Court for Access to Digital Court Recordings", and (iii) pay the prescribed fee. Paragraphs 87 to 90 of this practice direction apply to these requests. The release of a digital recording of a settlement conference is subject to rule 13.03(4) of the *Rules of the Small Claims Court*

69. For the purposes of obtaining an order for the release of a digital recording of a Small Claims Court proceeding, the provisions in paragraphs 87 to 90 apply and all references to "judge" shall be read to include "deputy judge".

Definitions

70. For the purposes of this section, "judge" means: all judges, traditional masters, and case management masters of the Superior Court of Justice.

Restrictions on Access to Digital Recordings from DRDs

71. All copies or access to digital recordings are subject to any express order the presiding judge may make. The presiding judge may expand or restrict access to the digital recordings in any particular proceeding before him or her.

72. Unless a judge of the Superior Court of Justice orders otherwise, no digital recordings are available to anyone in the following proceedings:

a. *in camera* proceedings or any portion of a proceeding that is heard *in camera*;

b. private or closed hearings (e.g. pursuant to ss. 45 or 151 of the *Child and Family Services Act*);

c. proceedings subject to a statutory, common law or court ordered restriction on the provision of transcripts or digital recordings of the proceeding (e.g., pre-trial conferences held in court with self-represented accused, pursuant to rule 28.05(4) of the *Criminal Proceedings Rules* of the Superior Court of Justice (Ontario), proceedings under the *Youth Criminal Justice Act)*; and,

d. case, settlement and trial management conferences pursuant to rule 17 of the *Family Law Rules; and,*

e. civil and family motions and applications (e.g. civil motions and applications under rule 37 and rule 38 of the *Rules of Civil Procedure*, family motions under rules 14 and 15 of the *Family Law Rules*).

Access to Digital Recordings from DRDs

Counsel of Record

73. A counsel of record in a proceeding may obtain the digital recordings of that proceeding upon completion of the "*Undertaking of Counsel/Licensed Paralegal of Record*" and payment of the prescribed fee.

74. Persons attending on behalf of counsel of record may obtain the digital recording if he or she: (i) provides a signed undertaking from counsel of record; (ii) signs the authorization included in the "*Undertaking of Counsel/Licensed Paralegal of Record*"; and (iii) pays the prescribed fee.

Litigant or Accused

75. A litigant or accused in a proceeding may obtain the digital recordings of that proceeding upon completion of the "*Undertaking to the Court for Access to Digital Court Recordings*" and payment of the prescribed fee.

The Media

76. Members of the media, identified on the "*Joint Courts' List of Designated Media for Access to Digital Court Recordings*" accessible on the Superior Court of Justice website: www.ontariocourts.ca/en/media-list.htm, may obtain the digital recordings upon completion of the "*Undertaking to the Court for Access to Digital Court Recordings*" and payment of the prescribed fee.

77. Members of the media who are not identified on the "*Joint Courts' List of Designated Media for Access to Digital Court Recordings*" may make an application for an order in accordance with this section authorizing him or her to obtain access to the digital recordings of the proceeding.

78. The applicant may obtain the digital recordings if he or she: (i) obtains a court order authorizing access, (ii) completes "*Undertaking to the Court for Access to Digital Court Recordings*", and (iii) pays the prescribed fee.

Members of the Public

79. Members of the public may make an application for an order in accordance with this section authorizing him or her to obtain access to the digital recordings of the proceeding.

80. The applicant may obtain the digital recording if he or she: (i) obtains a court order authorizing access, (ii) completes the "*Undertaking to the Court for Access to Digital Court Recordings*", and (iii) pays the prescribed fee.

Presiding Judge, Regional Senior Judge (RSJ) or Local Administrative Judge (LAJ)

81. Copies or access to digital recordings shall be provided, upon request, to the presiding judge for the proceeding in which the digital recording was prepared.

82. Copies or access to digital recordings shall be provided, upon request, to the RSJ or LAJ (or his or her designate), for administrative purposes, in the absence of the presiding judge. The presiding judge will be notified that access or copies of the digital recording were made available to the RSJ or LAJ (or his or her designate).

83. Where a judge wishes to access a digital recording from a proceeding in which another judge presided, the judge shall obtain the consent of the presiding judge to access the digital recording, subject to paragraph 83 (below).

84. Where a judge determines that he or she can deal more effectively and efficiently with a case by accessing a digital recording from a previous proceeding before another judge, in the same case or a related case, the judge can access the digital recording by obtaining permission from the presiding judge, the RSJ, the LAJ, or his or her designate, *unless it is in the interests of justice to dispense with such permission.* In that event, access to the digital recording shall be provided to the judge upon request. After access is provided, the judge who has obtained access shall notify the judge who presided at the earlier proceeding, if that judge was not notified when the issues arose.

Court Services Division Staff and Transcriptionists

85. Copies or access to digital recordings shall be provided upon request at no charge to the following:

a. Court Services Division Staff who require access in the course of their employment responsibilities; and,

b. Transcriptionists authorized by Regulation 158/03 under the *Evidence Act* who require access to transcribe court proceedings and who have signed an "Undertaking of Authorized Court Transcriptionist for Access to Audio Court Recordings".

Named Administrative Bodies or Organizations

86. Representatives of the bodies or organizations authorized pursuant to a Memorandum of Understanding with the Ministry of Attorney General to have access to digital audio recordings may obtain digital court recordings of court proceedings related directly to the matters under consideration by these bodies or organizations, upon completion of an Undertaking approved by the court and prescribed by the Memorandum of Understanding.

Hearing of the Application

87. Applications regarding access to the digital recording for any ongoing proceeding will be heard by the judge who is seized of the proceeding.

88. Applications shall be brought in accordance with the procedural rules that govern the court proceeding.

89. Applications regarding access to the digital recording for any other type of proceeding or for a proceeding that has concluded will be heard by the judge who presided at the hearing.

90. Where the judge who presided at the hearing is not available to hear the application or where no particular judge is associated with the proceeding, the RSJ, LAJ (or his or her delegate) may hear the application. Applicants should be aware that, especially for proceedings that have concluded or proceedings adjourned for a lengthy period of time, it may not always be possible to schedule an application before the appropriate judge on short notice because a judge may have many ongoing obligations in other proceedings.

91. Undertaking of Counsel/Licensed Paralegal of Record to the Court for Access to Digital Court Recordings can be obtained as *Word* or *PDF* documents on the Superior Court of Justice Website.

92. Undertaking to the Court for Access to Digital Court Recordings can be obtained as *Word* or *PDF* documents on the Superior Court of Justice Website.

D. — Electronic Devices in the Courtroom

93. This section outlines the protocol on how electronic devices may be used in courtrooms of the Ontario Superior Court of Justice by counsel, licensed paralegals, law students and law clerks assisting counsel, self-represented litigants, and media or journalists. **Note:** This section does not apply to persons who require electronic devices (or services requiring the use of electronic devices) to accommodate a disability.

Definitions

94. Electronic Devices

For the purposes of this section, "electronic devices" include all forms of computers, personal electronic and digital devices, and mobile, cellular, and smart phones.

95. Publicly Accessible Live Communications

For the purposes of this section, "publicly accessible live communications" are defined as the act of using an electronic device to transmit information from the courtroom to a publicly accessible medium (e.g. via Twitter or live blogs).

96. Judge

For the purposes of this section, "judge" means:

a. all judges, traditional masters, and case management masters of the Superior Court of Justice, and

b. judges of the Small Claims Court and deputy judges.

Prohibited Use of Electronic Devices by the Public

97. Members of the public are ***not permitted*** to use electronic devices in the courtroom unless the presiding judge orders otherwise.

Use of Electronic Devices in the Courtroom

98. ***Unless the presiding judge orders otherwise*, the use of electronic devices in silent mode and in a discreet and unobtrusive manner is *permitted*** in the courtroom by:

a. counsel;

b. paralegals who are licensed by the Law Society of Upper Canada;

c. law students and law clerks assisting counsel during the proceeding;

d. self-represented parties; and,

e. media or journalists

subject to the following restrictions:

i. The electronic device cannot interfere with courtroom decorum or otherwise interfere with the proper administration of justice.

ii. The electronic device cannot interfere with the court recording equipment or other technology in the courtroom.

iii. The electronic device cannot be used to send publicly accessible live communications where to do so would breach a restriction on publication made in the proceeding. **Note:** Anyone using an electronic device to transmit publicly accessible live communications from the courtroom has the responsibility to identify and comply with any publication bans, or other restrictions that have been imposed either by statute or by court order.

iv. The electronic device cannot be used to take photographs or videos unless the judge has granted permission to do so, in accordance with s. 136 of the *Courts of Justice Act*.

v. Only counsel, self-represented parties, the media and journalists are permitted to use electronic devices to make an audio recording of the proceeding and only for the purpose of note-taking. However, such audio recordings cannot be sent from the electronic device.

vi. Talking on electronic devices is not permitted in the courtroom.

Enforcement

99. Anyone who uses an electronic device in a manner that is inconsistent with this section, any orders of the presiding judge or that the presiding judge determines to be unacceptable may be:

a. subject to prosecution for breaches of s. 136 of the *Courts of Justice Act*, a citation and prosecution for contempt of court, or prosecution for other offences;

b. ordered to turn off the device;

c. ordered to leave the device outside the courtroom;

d. ordered to leave the courtroom; and/or

e. ordered to abide by any other order the presiding judge may make.

E. — Filing of Judicial Decisions from Electronic Databases and Citation of all Judicial Decisions

Filing of Judicial Decisions from Electronic Databases

100. Copies of judicial decisions obtained from approved electronic databases are acceptable for filing provided the report of the judicial decision contains paragraph numeration consistent with the numbering of the paragraphs in the decision as released by the court. "Approved electronic databases" are databases that are dedicated to the publication of judicial decisions (e.g. Quicklaw, CanLII, and Westlaw).

101. Counsel and parties should be aware that judicial decisions posted on electronic databases may be subject to correction or editing within a few days of the initial posting and, accordingly, parties should ensure that any decision obtained from an electronic database has not been subsequently amended.

Citation of all Judicial Decisions

101. Parties citing decisions from electronic databases should provide the citations for any paper versions of the decision in addition to the citation of the electronic database.

102. Parties should provide the date that the copy of any decision was obtained from an electronic database, as part of the citation information.

103. For decisions of the Ontario Superior Court of Justice released on or after January 1, 2010, parties should provide the neutral citation number (e.g. 2010 ONSC 1) in addition to the other required citations.

F. — Publication Bans

Application of this Part

105. This part applies to all civil, criminal and family proceedings in the Superior Court of Justice and to proceedings in the Divisional Court.

106. This part applies to all applications or motions for discretionary publication bans. It does not apply to publication bans that are mandated by statute (i.e. those that either operate automatically by virtue of statute or that a statute provides are mandatory on request)

Formal Notice of Application/Motion Required

107. Unless otherwise directed by a judge, any person seeking a discretionary order restricting publication of any Superior Court proceeding must serve and file a notice of motion or application and any supporting materials, in accordance with the applicable procedural rules.

Notification of the Media

108. Unless otherwise directed by a judge, the person seeking the publication ban (the requesting party) must provide notice to the media of the motion/application, using the procedure set out in this section.

109. The requesting party must complete and submit the "*Notice of Request for Publication Ban*" form available on the Superior Court of Justice website.

110. The length of notice required for the submission of the Notice of Request for Publication Ban is the same as the length of notice required under the applicable procedural rules for the serving and filing of the Notice of Application or Notice of Motion.

111. The information on the Notice of Request for Publication Ban will be distributed electronically to members of the media who have subscribed to receive notice of all publication ban applications/motions in the Superior Court.

112. Any member of the media who wishes to receive copies of the Notices prepared and submitted under this section should *submit a request* through the Superior Court of Justice website.

113. The requesting party may be required to produce a copy of the Notice of Request for Publication Ban to the Court at the hearing of the application/motion in order to establish that notice was provided in accordance with this section.

PART VI: — BOOKS OF AUTHORITIES IN CIVIL PROCEEDINGS

A. — Often-Cited Civil Cases

114. The List of Often-Cited Civil Cases in Civil Proceedings, which contains cases frequently relied upon, is available for each judge who presides over civil cases. There will be additions to, and deletions from, the list from time to time. The up-to-date list is available on the Superior Court of Justice website at: http://www.ontariocourts.ca/scj/practice/practice-directions/list-civil/.

115. The cases in question appear on the list under various headings or topics which are not in any way intended to provide legal advice.

116. Parties in civil proceedings need no longer include authorities on the list in any book of authorities relied on.

117. However, extracts from those authorities which counsel intend to refer to the court shall be included in the factum or book of authorities.

B. — Requirements for Books of Authorities in Civil Proceedings

118. It is of great assistance to the Court to have books of authority filed by counsel containing copies of the authorities to which they intend to refer on the hearing of the matter. Such books of authorities:

a. Should be printed double-sided.

b. Should be bound in volumes no more than three inches thick.

c. Should include only the cases to which counsel actually intend to refer in the oral argument. The particular passages in the cases to which counsel wish to refer should be clearly marked.

d. Should be prepared jointly in accordance with this direction. Where counsel are unable to agree, then such case books should indicate whether they are filed by the appellant or the respondent. There should be consultation between counsel to avoid any duplication of the authorities included in their respective case books.

e. Should have a tab for each case (either numerical or by letters), include an index of the authorities and indicate the tab where the authority is reproduced. It is not necessary to number the pages in the case book so long as the photocopies show the page numbers of each authority.

Dated: April 11, 2014

Amended: June 15, 2018; January 1, 2017; July 1, 2016; May 1, 2016; April 1, 2016; February 1, 2016; April 28, 2015

Heather J. Smith

Chief Justice

Superior Court of Justice (Ontario)

PD-6a — *THE GUIDE CONCERNING E-DELIVERY OF DOCUMENTS IN THE ONTARIO SUPERIOR COURT OF JUSTICE (EFFECTIVE JULY 1, 2014)*

This Guide applies to the e-Delivery of documents in the Ontario Superior Court of Justice, effective July 1, 2014. It *supersedes* the previous Guidelines concerning the Commercial List e-Delivery Pilot Project issued in June 2012, which is hereby revoked.

Counsel and parties are advised to refer to the relevant Parts of the Consolidated Provincial Practice Direction, the Consolidated Practice Direction for Divisional Court Proceedings as well as any other relevant Toronto region-specific Practice Directions and Guides which are available on the Superior Court of Justice website at: www.ontariocourts.ca/scj.

Introduction

Often judges sitting on the Commercial List ask counsel to provide them with an electronic copy of the materials filed for a hearing. Experience has shown that significant differences exist amongst the formats used by counsel when preparing electronic copies. As a result, the usefulness to the judge of electronic copies varies from case to case — some formats do not permit a judge to cut and paste text; some formats do not organize the scanned file by document, making quick reference to an item difficult; and, some formats are not searchable.

For electronic copies of documents to be useful to judges they must: (i) be well organized and searchable so that judges can locate quickly specific pieces of evidence or argument; (ii) enable a judge to cut and paste argument or evidence; and, (iii) enable the portability of all hearing materials.

In order to meet these needs a working group of the Commercial List Users Committee has prepared this Guide. The purpose is simple: when a judge asks counsel to submit electronic documents of filed materials, counsel now will be able to follow a uniform approach to preparing electronic copies thereby enhancing their usefulness to judges.

This Guide contemplate that in most cases counsel will deliver electronic copies of documents to the judge via a USB key, with factums in Word format and the remaining hearing materials placed in an organized PDF file. Guidelines for emailing documents to judges are also included.

Three key points should be made about the scope of this Guide:

a) Electronic copies of documents subject to a sealing order, or for which a request for a sealing order will be made, should NOT be sent to a judge. Such documents should be submitted to the court in the normal fashion for confidential documents;

b) Electronic documents sent to a judge should NOT be password protected or subject to security settings; and,

c) USB keys or, where directed, CD-ROMs, are to be delivered to a judge through the Commercial List Office.

This Guide is organized into four parts:

Part I: A *Sample Checklist* which judges may use when discussing with counsel the requirements for electronic copies of documents in any specific case;

Part II: A *Description of the Basic Steps* involved in preparing electronic copies of documents for filing with a judge;

Part III: An *Outline of the Technical Specifications* for electronic copies of documents, including Hardware and Software Requirements. The procedures set out in this Guide seek to use hardware and software which is readily accessible to all counsel at a reasonable cost. This section describes readily available software and hardware options; and,

Part IV: Detailed *Instructions on How to Create* simple and complex PDF documents.

Although the product of consultation with both the Bench and the Bar, no doubt areas of improvement will emerge as greater use is made of this Guide. The Commercial List Users Committee intends to monitor the use of the "e-Delivery" of documents and make improvements to this Guide based on the experience of the Commercial List.

PART I: — SAMPLE CHECKLIST FOR THE USE OF COMMERCIAL LIST JUDGES

Please note: a word version of the Sample Checklist is also available on the Superior Court's website at: www.ontariocourts.ca/scj.

Judge: **Court File No.:**		
Title of Proceedings: Hearing Date:		
No.	**Description**	**Yes / No**
1.	Submit electronic copy of facta in Word format?	Yes No
2.	Submit PDF copy of facta and application/motion record? (select # 3 Simple Format or # 5 Complex Format)	Yes No
3.	*Simple format*: Create bookmarks within PDF (refer to "Guidelines" document)	Yes No

Judge: **Court File No.:**		
Title of Proceedings: Hearing Date:		
No.	**Description**	**Yes / No**
4.	Make PDF OCR text searchable?	Yes No
5.	*Complex format*: Create hyperlinks & bookmarks within PDF (refer to "Guidelines" document)	Yes No
6.	Send paper copy to Judge? (use additional area below for specifics)	Yes No
7.	File with the Commercial List Office via USB key or CD Rom?	Yes No
8.	Receipt of hyperlinked PDF within 1–5 business days (based on number of pages, number of potential links and available resources)	Yes No
9.	Send electronic copy of documents to all parties	Yes No
NOTE: CONFIDENTIAL DOCUMENTS SHOULD NOT BE FILED ELECTRONICALLY		

Parties	**Names, Contact Information & File Naming Instructions**
Plaintiff/ Applicant	
Defendant/Respondent	
Third Party	
Intervener	

Additional Instructions:..................................

PART II: — THE BASIC STEPS IN PREPARING AND FILING ELECTRONIC COPIES COURT DOCUMENTS WITH A JUDGE

A. — Preparation of Electronic Word File Copy

1. Document(s) is created and finalized in word processing software. Microsoft Word (.DOC) is the standard format.

2. Create front and back covers, indices and schedules in Microsoft Word format.

3. One copy of the official court document(s), along with all attachments, is to be printed and filed as the official court copy.

4. One copy of factum is to be sent in Word format, as well as one copy in PDF format (if requested by the judge).

B. — Preparation of Electronic PDF Copy

5. Convert or scan Word document to PDF format. Conversion is preferable.

6. Convert or scan front and back covers, indices, schedules, etc., and combine with PDF.

7. Combined PDF should contain identical content and should appear the same as the official paper copy filed with the court. The PDF copy should conform to the same requirements in the *Rules of Civil Procedure* as the paper copy.

8. Scanned or converted documents are to be provided as black and white documents unless there is a relevant reason to include content in colour.

9. Image quality of scanned or converted documents is to be 200–300 dpi.

10. Update page numbering in the PDF file to reflect actual page numbers based on paper copy (see Part III: Outline of Technical Specifications).

11. Name PDF file based on pre-defined nomenclature (see Part III: Outline of Technical Specifications).

12. Perform Optical Character Recognition (OCR) within PDF to enable text searching.

13. Create bookmarks and hyperlinks within PDF to link to page references within attachments (if requested).

14. Do not apply any security settings or modification to the file properties of the PDF that may prevent the court from opening, viewing, saving, printing or searching the document.

15. Confirm the size of the Word document and / or PDF document in the properties of the file.

16. Deliver a copy of PDF document to all other parties.

C. — Transcripts

17. Electronic copies of transcripts may be filed in PDF and DOC formats as long as the copies are searchable.

D. — Sending the electronic copies to the judge

18. It is anticipated that in most circumstances judges will ask counsel to provide them with electronic copies of documents on a USB key or CD ROM. Where such a request is made by the judge, counsel should deliver the materials to the judge through the Commercial List Office. The USB key or CD ROM should be accompanied by a covering letter which identifies the materials contained on the USB key or CD ROM.

a) *USB Key*: In the cover letter include a list of the files contained on the USB key, along with the title of proceedings, Court File #, Counsel Name(s) and Party Name. If possible, label the key with the short style of cause and the Court File #.

b) *CD ROM*: Label the CD ROM with the title of proceedings, Court File #, Counsel Name(s) and Party Name. Include a list of the files contained on the CD in a cover letter.

19. In cases where the judge has requested counsel to deliver the electronic copies by email, the cover email should include the title of proceedings, Court File #, Counsel

Name(s), Party Name and type of filing. A list of the email attachments is to be included in the body of the email. See the example below.

20. PLEASE NOTE: A judge's email system cannot accept emails containing attachments of more than 6 Mb in size.

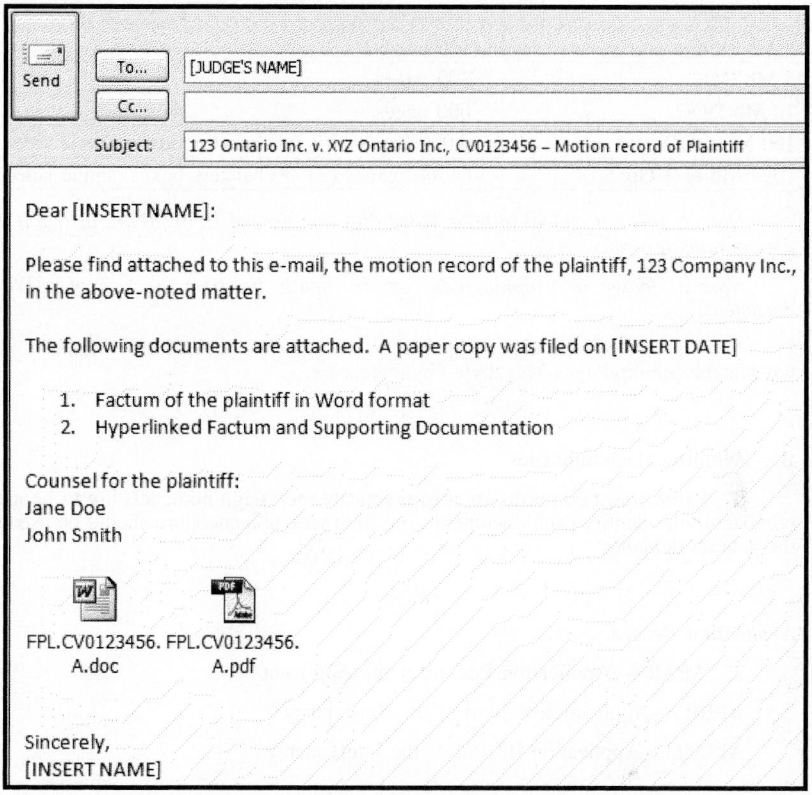
Send
To... [JUDGE'S NAME]
Cc...
Subject: 123 Ontario Inc. v. XYZ Ontario Inc., CV0123456 – Motion record of Plaintiff

Dear [INSERT NAME]:

Please find attached to this e-mail, the motion record of the plaintiff, 123 Company Inc., in the above-noted matter.

The following documents are attached. A paper copy was filed on [INSERT DATE]

1. Factum of the plaintiff in Word format
2. Hyperlinked Factum and Supporting Documentation

Counsel for the plaintiff:
Jane Doe
John Smith

FPL.CV0123456.A.doc FPL.CV0123456.A.pdf

Sincerely,
[INSERT NAME]

PART III: — OUTLINE OF TECHNICAL SPECIFICATIONS

A. — General Information on .PDF and .DOC file sizes

21. An approximation of the number of paper pages contained in a unit of PDF

Data size	Approximate Pages
1 Mb PDF	20 pages
2 Mb PDF	40 pages
5 Mb PDF	100 pages
10 Mb PDF	200 pages
100 Mb PDF	2,000 pages (3/4 — full bankers box, single sided)
1024 Mb or 1 Gig	20,480 pages (8–12 bankers boxes, single sided)
2048 Mb or 2 Gigs	40,960 pages (16–24 bankers boxes, single sided)

Note 1: Bookmarks and a table of contents somewhat affect the size of a PDF file. Hyperlinks can drastically increase the size of a PDF file. Approximate pages in Word documents versus file sizes

Data size	Approximate Pages
1 Mb .DOC	60 pages
2 Mb DOC	120 pages
5 Mb DOC	300 pages
10 Mb DOC	600 pages
100 Mb DOC	6,000 pages (2-3 full bankers boxes, single sided)
1024 Mb or 1 Gig	61,440 pages (24–30 bankers boxes, single sided)

Note 2: It is not typical to have Word files that exceed 10 or 20 Mb in size if the file contains text only.

Note 3: Image or graphic files can drastically increase the size of a Word document.

Note 4: Calculations based on web calculator found at: www.lexbe.com/hp/Pages-Megabyte-Gigabyte.aspx.

B. — Naming electronic files

22. Parties must confer as soon as practicable to assign nomenclature to be used consistently to identify each document. The following nomenclature should be used as the general default:

Application Record

23. APAR — Application Record of the Applicant

APRR — Application Record of the Respondent

APINR — Application Record of the Intervener

Motion Record

24. MPL — Motion Record of the Plaintiff

MDE — Motion Record of the Defendant

MTP — Motion Record of the Third Party

MAP — Motion Record of the Applicant

MRP — Motion Record of the Respondent

MIN — Motion Record of the Intervener

Affidavits

25. AFPL — Affidavit of or on behalf of the Plaintiff

AFDE — Affidavit of or on behalf of the Defendant

AFTP — Affidavit of or on behalf of the Third Party

AFAP — Affidavit of or on behalf of the Applicant

AFRP — Affidavit of or on behalf of the Respondent

AFIN — Affidavit of or on behalf of the Intervener

Book of Authorities

26. BAPL — Book of Authorities of the Plaintiff

BADE — Book of Authorities of the Defendant

BATP — Book of Authorities of the Third Party

BAAP — Book of Authorities of the Applicant

BARP — Book of Authorities of the Respondent

BAIN — Book of Authorities of the Intervener

Factums, including Amended and Supplementary

27. FPL — Factum of the Plaintiff

FDE — Factum of the Defendant

FTP — Factum of the Third Party

FAP — Factum of the Applicant

FRP — Factum of the Respondent

FIN — Factum of the Intervener

Note 5: suffix AM or SUP to indicate Amended or Supplemental Factum

Costs Outline

28. COPL — Cost Outline of the Plaintiff

CODE — Cost Outline of the Defendant

COTP — Cost Outline of the Third Party

COAP — Cost Outline of the Applicant

CORP — Cost Outline of the Respondent

Note 6: when there are multiple documents of the same type filed, suffix the file name with 001, 002, 003, 004, 005, etc.

C. — Page numbering in PDF files for Facta

Title page has no page number

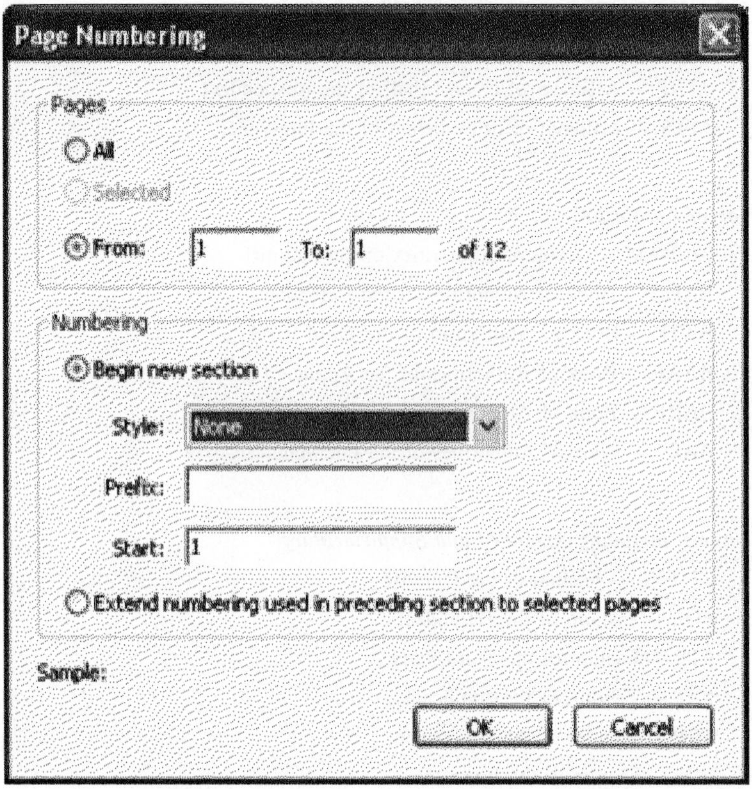

Index page numbers set using Roman numerals; e.g. i, ii, iii, iv, etc.

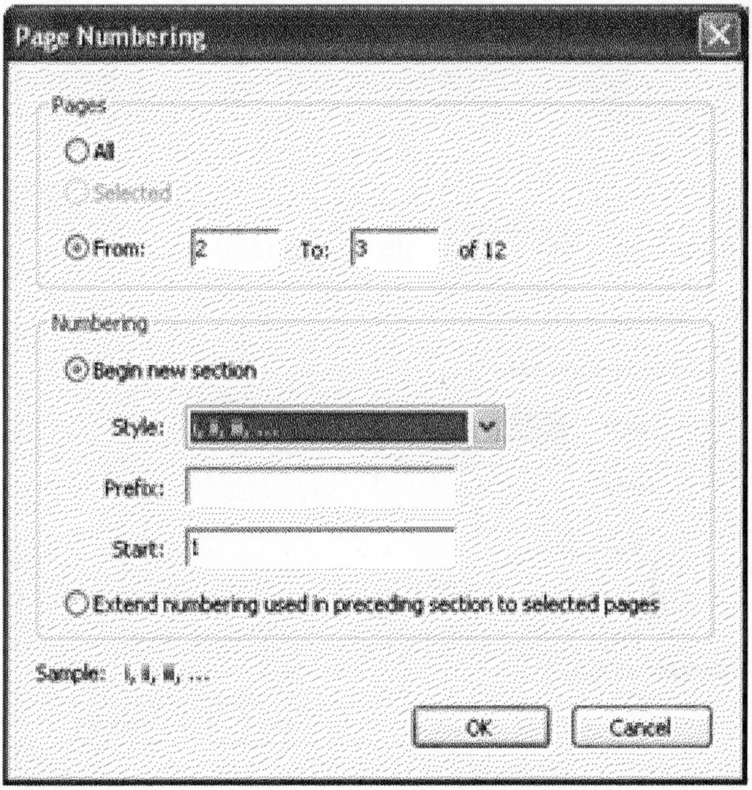

Factum pages set to use actual "hard copy" page numbers. Set pages in body of Factum to be numbered consecutively; e.g. 1, 2, 3, 4, 5, 6, etc.

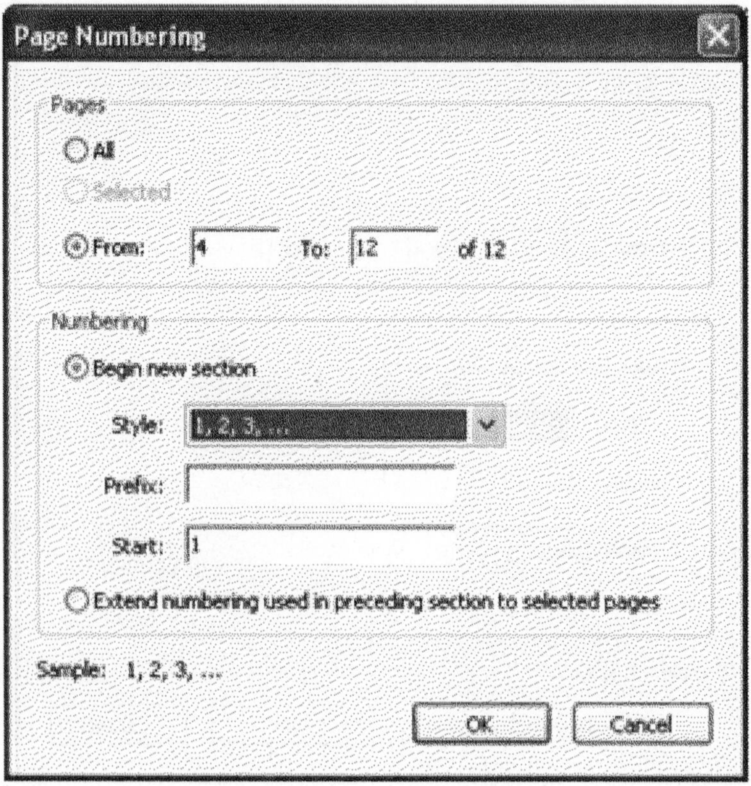

Note 7: Further instruction on how to re-number pages in Adobe Acrobat can be found by searching the "Help" menu in Adobe Acrobat Writer.

D. — Bookmarks in PDF files

29. Use Adobe Acrobat Writer or other PDF software to combine documents into one PDF file or scan the contents of the document to be filed.

30. Create bookmarks by selecting text and right clicking on text or by selecting "Add Bookmark" from the menu bar. Please note that different software and different versions of Adobe store the "Add Bookmark" function in different areas of the menu. Consult the "Help" menu for your software for more specific information.

31. The PDF document must be OCR searchable in order to highlight text. In Adobe Acrobat, highlight the heading of text in the document as it appears in the Index, right click and select "Add Bookmark" to automatically add the highlighted text to the bookmark. The bookmark function in Adobe Acrobat version X is located in the "Content" menu:

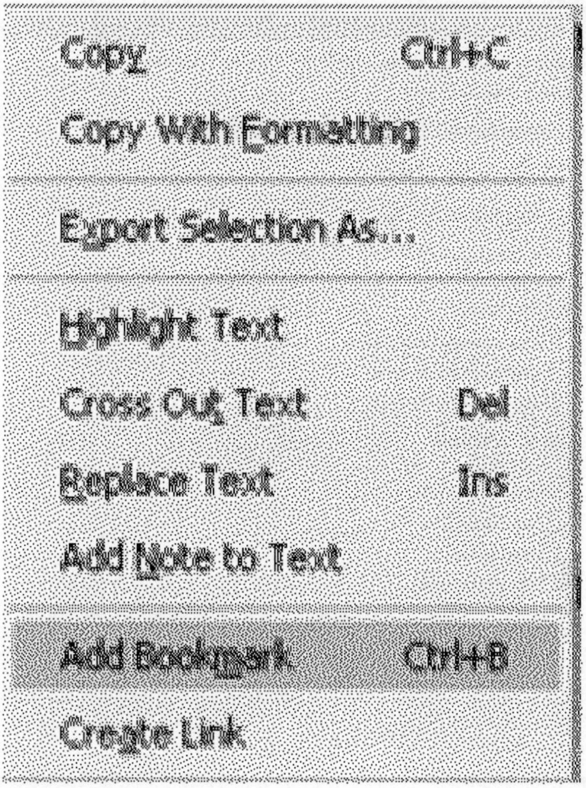

32. Each bookmark created should jump to the corresponding page of the PDF based on the Index included.

33. In the "Document Properties" of the PDF, set the "Initial View" to show the Bookmarks panel and pages. Set the "Magnification" to "Fit to Page"

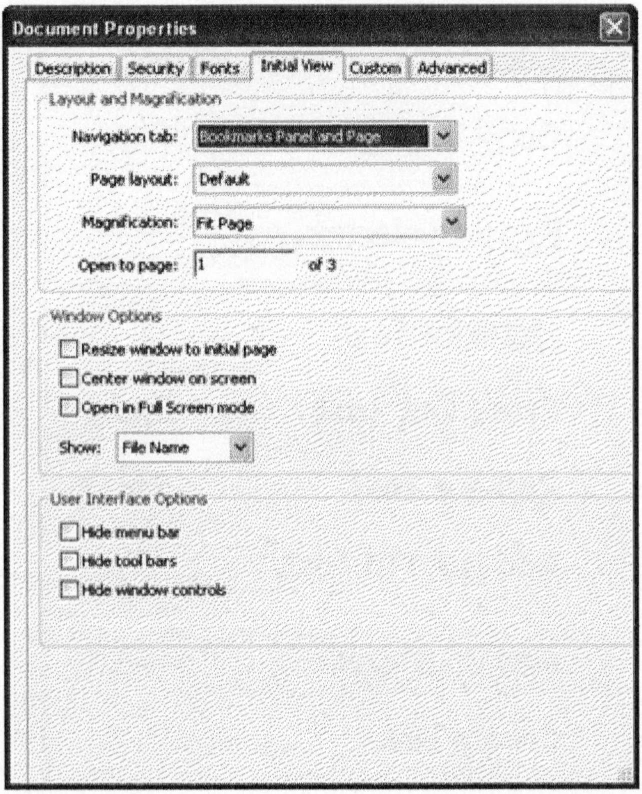

34. Where possible (and if requested) create a hyperlink to other documents contained in the PDF such as Authorities, Transcripts, Affidavits, etc.

35. Hyperlinks should only be created to documents that exist within the PDF document. Consult the "Help" menu for your software for more specific information.

E. — Hardware and Software Required

Software / Hardware	**Options**
Computer or Laptop	Minimum requirements will be included with software purchases however at this time, common minimum requirements include: 1.3 GHz or faster processor, 512 MB RAM; • 1 GB of available hard drive space; Windows XP or above; • CD / DVD writer and USB capability; • CD / DVD (for delivery) • USB Key (for delivery)
Scanner	Scanner with automatic document feeder is preferable (ADF)

Software / Hardware	**Options**
Word Processing software	Microsoft Word or Corel Word Perfect
PDF Software	Software should have capability to OCR, combine PDFs, create bookmarks, and create hyperlinks.
	Free Conversion Software: Microsoft Office 2007 and later allows for the ability to save documents in the PDF format with an Office 2007 add-in available free on the Microsoft website. *Word Perfect* (version 9 and later) saves to PDF format. *OpenOffice* is a free & open tool similar to Microsoft Office. The Word processing tool converts to PDF (MAC compatible). www.download.openoffice.org. *Primo PDF* is a free tool that you install that creates a PDF print queue that actually converts documents. www.primopdf.com/index.aspx *Other cost efficient software options: Adobe Acrobat Standard X* is one of the most commonly used PDF conversions, viewing and writing software. (Recommended). www.adobe.com/products/acrobatstandard.html. *Nuance PDF Converter Pro 7* is another commonly used PDF conversion, view and writing software www.nuance.com/products/pdf-converter-professional7/index.htm.
Scanning Software	Scanning software should be bundled with the scanner at time of installation. Consult the manual or other documentation provided with your scanner
Email application	Microsoft Outlook, Lotus Notes or other email program
Internet connection	High speed internet access preferable
Useful Resource Links	PDF help: www.pdfforlawyers.com. Consult the Help menu of your PDF software

Note: The availability of the software or hardware referred to in the above table may vary from time to time.

F. — Additional/ Optional Software

36. Meta-data cleaner to scrub Word documents and PDF documents of meta-data. A no cost option for scrubbing Word documents could be to copy the contents of a document into a new "clean" document (ensure pagination is the same). Alternately, print and scan your document to PDF.

37. Most Meta-data in PDF documents can be removed from the properties menu of the PDF or by using a compatible PDF meta-data cleaner.

38. Do not compress files using ZIP or any other file compression format. Files should not be compressed for delivery by any method.

G. — Software Options Matrix[3]

Function / Feature	**Nuance PDF Converter Pro 7**	**Adobe Acrobat X Standard**	**Adobe Acrobat Reader**	**Foxit Reader**
View, Search & Print PDF File	Yes	Yes	Yes	Yes
Preserves Hyperlink, Bookmarks & Comments	Yes	Yes	Yes	Yes
Document Review: Comments, Annotations, highlights (use arrows, sticky notes)	Yes	Yes	Yes	Yes
Modify text using "typewriter"	Yes	Yes	No	No
Export Comments or Notes in Summary	Yes	Yes	No	No
Text Search (if OCR text exists)	Yes	Yes	Yes	Yes
Digital Signature	Yes	Yes	No	No
Encryption / Security Settings	Yes	Yes	No	No
Convert from Word	Yes	Yes	No	No
Combine PDFs	Yes	Yes	No	No
OCR Capabilities	Yes	Yes	No	No
Bookmarking	Yes	Yes	No	No
Hyperlinking	Yes	Yes	No	No
Ability to support scanning	Yes	Yes	No	No
Mac Compatible Version	Yes	Yes	Yes	Yes
PRICING	*$99.99*	*$199.00*	*FREE*	*FREE*

PART IV: — HOW TO CREATE SIMPLE AND COMPLEX PDF DOCUMENTS

39. There are two ways to create PDF documents. PDF documents can be created by converting a text document into PDF format using software such as Adobe Acrobat, Adobe Distiller, Nuance, PDF Maker, or scanning documents from paper in PDF.

A. — Converting a text file to a PDF file

40. Converting text files into PDF format is the preferred method for two reasons: text conversion creates a more searchable document than scanning from paper and text conversion creates a smaller file size then scanned or imaged documents. Always convert the final version of documents to PDF format to ensure the PDF copy is the same in content and pagination as the court filed paper copy.

[3]This Matrix is not exhaustive. Further, the software programs and pricing in are not current. They reflect pricing in effect in 2012. Users are advised to check for updated programs and pricing.

a) Open the document in word processing application (Microsoft Word or Corel WordPerfect, for example)

b) From the File menu select the Print and choose the PDF printer installed.

c) Click on the settings of the printer and confirm the PDF printer is set to print to a resolution of 200 or 300 dpi.

d) Set the magnification to "Fit to Page" via File — Properties.

e) Click Print and Save the PDF file with the proper naming convention. Be sure the file has a file extension of .PDF.

B. — Creating a PDF file from a scanned document

41. For documents that must be scanned because a text version does not exist, documents should be scanned directly into PDF format using available software in conjunction with the scanner. Scanning documents into image format will require OCR to be run against the documents making the PDF searchable.

a) Refer to the manual that accompanied the scanner being used for specific details on how to scan a document.

b) Use the automatic document feeder (ADF) to scan multiple pages if one is available.

c) Ensure the resolution for scanning is set to a resolution of 200 or 300 dpi.

d) Set the magnification to "Fit to Page" via File — Properties.

e) Save scanned documents to PDF format with the proper naming convention. Ensure the file has a file extension of .PDF

C. — How to Combine PDFs

42. If there are multiple PDF documents to be combined into one file, this must be done before Bookmarks can be created. Depending on the software used, bookmarks may be automatically created at the time of combining or merging PDF files. PDF "Creator" or "Writer" is required to merge PDF files.

a) From within Adobe Acrobat Standard or Professional, click on "Create PDF" from the toolbar on the main screen.

b) The Create PDF from Multiple Documents window will appear. From the "Browse" button, browse to the location of the PDF files and add them in the order in which they should be combined.

c) Once the PDF files are in a list, they can be moved up or down depending on the location where they should be in the combined PDF document.

d) Click "OK" to begin the merge of files.

e) Select "File" — "Save As" to save the PDF with the proper naming convention. Ensure the file has a file extension of .PDF

f) Set the magnification to "Fit to Page" via File — Properties.

D. — How to Create Bookmarks

43. Bookmarks appear on the left side of a PDF document. To view bookmarks, choose Bookmarks or show Bookmarks from the View menu of your Adobe Acrobat software (the location of this menu will depend on the version of Adobe Acrobat or other software being used). Use the Table of Contents as a guideline for creating bookmarks.

a) Using Adobe Acrobat to create a bookmark, navigate to the page to be bookmarked.

b) Choose "New Bookmark" from the Document menu, click on the New Bookmark button or click "Ctrl, B" on the keyboard to create a new bookmark.

c) Click on the new untitled bookmark and enter a name for it (for example, if the bookmark is for the table of contents, enter "Table of Contents" as the name of the bookmark.

d) Repeat for each bookmark to be created.

e) Set the Initial View of the Bookmarked PDF to be "Bookmarks Panel and Page" via File — Properties — Initial View.

f) Use plain black text as the display properties for text in bookmarks. No colours, no italics.

E. — How to Rename or Delete Bookmarks

44. If bookmarks need to be renamed to match the table of contents, follow the below steps.

a) Using Adobe Acrobat, right click on the bookmark and select "Rename";

b) Type in the name as it appears in the Table of Contents;

c) To delete a bookmark, right click on it and select "Delete".

F. — How to Create Hyperlinks

45. Hyperlinks appear throughout a PDF. In a factum hyperlinks can be made to documentary evidence, oral evidence, authorities, exhibits and affidavits, etc.

a) Using Adobe Acrobat to create a hyperlink, navigate to the page where a hyperlink will be created.

b) Choose "Link Tool" from the Document menu, click on the New Bookmark button or click "Ctrl, B" on the keyboard to create a new bookmark.

c) Click on the new untitled bookmark and enter a name for it (for example, if the bookmark is for the table of contents, enter "Table of Contents" as the name of the bookmark.

d) Repeat for each bookmark to be created.

e) Set the Initial View of the Bookmarked PDF to be "Bookmarks Panel and Page" via File — Properties — Initial View.

f) Use a consistent method for creating hyperlinks. Hyperlinks should be visible on the document by either underlining, highlighting or text box using a consistent colour that does not obstruct the display of text.

G. — How to Update Page Numbering

46. Title page and back page have no page number.

47. Index page numbers set using Roman numerals; e.g., i, ii, iii, iv, etc.

48. Factum pages set to use actual "hard copy" page numbers. Set pages in body of Factum to be numbered consecutively; e.g., 1, 2, 3, 4, 5, 6, etc.

49. Update page numbering via page numbering section of the PDF software. Page numbers can be manually assigned to match the paper copy.

50. Further instruction on how to re-number pages in Adobe Acrobat or other PDF software can be found by searching the "Help" menu of the software.

H. — Questions/ Answers and FAQ

51. What is 200 or 300 dpi and why is this important?

- The quality of a scanned document largely depends on the condition of the paper document itself. If the document is older (created before 1995) or the quality of the paper is poor, the quality of the image may also be poor. If the scanning software is set to a resolution of 200 or 300 dpi, the best possible quality of image will be created, while keeping the file size to a minimum. Resolution is measured in dots per inch (dpi). A higher resolution is slower to scan (this is also dependent on the scanner and the number of pages that are scanned). The recommended resolution is 200 or 300 dpi.

52. What is OCR?

- OCR stands for Optical Character Recognition. OCR is a technology that once run against PDF files makes the files searchable and editable. OCR quality is not always 100% accurate. Accuracy of OCR text depends largely on the quality of the paper being scanned and the scanning resolution used.

53. What is PDF?

- PDF stands for Portable Document Format. It is a universal file format that preserves the fonts, images, graphics, and layout of any source document, regardless of the application and platform used to create it.

54. What is USB?

- USB stands for Universal Serial Bus. USB is a hardware format used to store and transfer files.

55. How do I know what the size is of my PDF file?

- Right click on the PDF file and check the properties tab to determine the size of the PDF file.

56. How should the PDF be named?

- Follow the guidelines provided in the naming convention list and those provided on the initial meeting checklist.

PD-6b — *NOTE FROM OFFICE OF THE CHIEF JUSTICE OF THE SUPERIOR COURT OF JUSTICE*

In 2013-2014, the Superior Court of Justice undertook to review and consolidate all of its Regional and Provincial Practice Directions. The objective of the review was an administrative re-set to identify and eliminate obsolete and redundant Practice Directions. The review also sought to consolidate, simplify and better organize the Practice Directions that were to remain in effect. The Court has now re-issued Consolidated Provincial and Regional Practice Directions for all proceedings in the Superior Court of Justice.

These Practice Directions take effect July 1, 2014 and all other previously issued Superior Court of Justice Practice Directions are revoked. Counsel are advised to check the Superior Court's website for the most recent Practice Directions: http://www.ontariocourts.on.ca/scj/practice/.

PD-6c — *PRACTICE ADVISORY — APPLICATION FOR JUDICIAL AUTHORIZATION OF PHYSICIAN ASSISTED DEATH*

In *Carter v. Canada (Attorney General)*, 2016 SCC 4, the Supreme Court of Canada directed that applications may be brought to provincial superior courts for exemptions from the *Criminal Code* prohibition against physician assisted death, in accordance with the criteria set out in *Carter v. Canada (Attorney General)*, 2015 SCC 5 [*Carter* (2015)].

This Practice Advisory is intended to provide guidance to counsel and parties who intend to bring applications to the Superior Court for an exemption to the *Criminal Code* prohibition against physician assisted death. The direction provided in this advisory is always subject to any orders made by the presiding judge on the application. In addition, this Practice Advisory refers to the types of evidence discussed in *Carter* (2015) to assist counsel and parties. However, the onus rests with the applicant to confirm and meet the evidentiary requirements set out in *Carter* (2015).

Commencement of Application

1. An application to the Superior Court of Justice for authorization for a physician assisted death shall be commenced by notice of application under Rule 14 of the Rules of Civil Procedure and be in accordance with this Practice Advisory.

Content of Notice of Application

2. The notice of application shall state that the application shall be heard by a judge on a date to be fixed by the registrar at the place of hearing, such date not being earlier than fifteen days after the application is commenced and not being later than thirty days after the application is commenced. Depending upon the circumstances, certain applications may be heard sooner on an emergency basis. The nature of the relief sought on the application must be brought to the attention of the registrar by the applicant at the time of filing so that a hearing date within these time periods, or sooner, can be fixed.

3. The notice of application shall state,

a. that the applicant is seeking authorization for a physician assisted death;

b. the date of the hearing as set by the registrar;

c. the place of the hearing; and

d. the documentary evidence to be used at the hearing of the motion.

4. In addition, the notice of application should set out if the applicant intends to seek a publication ban, an order under s. 135 of the *Courts of Justice Act* to have the application heard in the absence of the public, or an order to seal the file, as well as the grounds upon which any such orders are sought.

Application Record and Factum

5. As required under Rule 38,

a. the applicant shall serve and file an application record and factum at least seven days before the hearing;

b. the respondent(s) shall serve and file a factum and respondent(s)'s application record (if any), at least four days before the hearing.

Proof of Service

6. Proof of service of the notice of application, application record, and factum shall be filed at least seven days before the hearing date in the court office of the place of hearing.

Service of Application

7. The notice of application shall be served on,

a. the Attorney General of Canada; and

b. the Attorney General of Ontario.

8. In addition, depending upon the circumstances of the applicant, the Court may require that notice of the application be served on the applicant's spouse/partner, children, parents, grandparents, siblings, and any other person who will be affected by the order sought.

Evidence about the Applicant

9. The application record should include an affidavit from the applicant concerning,

a. the applicant's birth date;

b. the applicant's place of residence and the duration of that residency;

c. the applicant's medical condition (illness, disease, or disability);

d. whether as a result of his or her medical condition, the applicant is suffering enduring intolerable pain or distress that cannot be alleviated by any treatment acceptable to the applicant;

e. the reasons for the applicant's request for an authorization of a physician assisted death;

f. whether the applicant commenced the application after having been fully informed about his or her medical condition (illness, disease, or disability), diagnosis, prognosis, treatment options, palliative care options, the risks associated with the treatment and palliative care options, and the risks associated with a physician assisted death;

g. the manner and means and timing of the physician assisted death for which the applicant seeks an authorization;

h. whether the applicant is aware that his or her request for an authorization for a physician assisted death may be withdrawn at any time; and

i. whether the applicant is aware that if the authorization is granted, the decision to use or not use the authorization is entirely the applicant's decision to make.

Evidence of the Attending Physician

10. The application record should include an affidavit from the applicant's attending physician addressing whether,

a. the applicant has a grievous irremediable medical condition (illness, disease, or disability) that causes suffering;

b. as a result of his or her medical condition, the applicant is suffering enduring intolerable pain or distress that cannot be alleviated by any treatment acceptable to the applicant;

c. the applicant was fully informed about his or her medical condition (illness, disease, or disability), diagnosis, prognosis, treatment options, palliative care options, the risks associated with the treatment and palliative care options, and the risks associated with a physician assisted death;

d. the applicant has the mental capacity to make a clear, free, and informed decision about a physician assisted death;

e. the applicant is or will be physically incapable of ending his or her life without a physician assisted death;

f. the applicant consents without coercion, undue influence, or ambivalence to a physician assisted death;

g. the applicant is aware that his or her request for an authorization for a physician assisted death may be withdrawn at any time;

h. the applicant makes the request for authorization for a physician assisted death freely and voluntarily; and

i. the applicant is aware that if the authorization is granted, the decision to use or not use the authorization is entirely the applicant's decision to make.

Evidence of the Consulting Psychiatrist

11. The application record should include an affidavit from the applicant's consulting psychiatrist addressing whether,

a. the applicant has a grievous irremediable medical condition (illness, disease, or disability) that causes the applicant to suffer;

b. the applicant has the mental capacity to make a clear, free, and informed decision about a physician assisted death;

c. the applicant consents without coercion, undue influence, or ambivalence to a physician assisted death;

d. the applicant is aware that his or her request for an authorization for a physician assisted death may be withdrawn at any time;

e. the applicant makes the request for authorization for a physician assisted death freely and voluntarily; and

f. the applicant is aware that if the authorization is granted, the decision to use or not use the authorization is entirely the applicant's decision to make.

Evidence of Physician Proposed to Assist Death

12. The application record should include an affidavit from the physician who is proposed to be the physician authorized to assist death, who may be the applicant's attending physician or another physician, addressing,

a. the manner and means and timing of the physician assisted death;

b. whether the physician providing assistance is willing to assist the applicant in dying if that act were authorized by court order;

c. whether the physician believes that his or her providing assistance would be clearly consistent with the applicant's wishes; and

d. whether the physician understands that the decision to use or not use the authorization is entirely the applicant's decision to make.

Disposition of Application

13. On the hearing of the application, the judge may grant the relief sought, dismiss or adjourn the application for further evidence to be filed, or make such other order as is just.

January 29, 2016

Heather J. Smith

Chief Justice

Superior Court of Justice (Ontario)

PD-6d — *PROVINCIAL PRACTICE DIRECTION REGARDING APPLICATIONS UNDER S. 11(B) OF THE CANADIAN CHARTER OF RIGHTS AND FREEDOMS*

Effective September 1, 2016

This Practice Direction applies to all criminal proceedings in the Superior Court of Justice.

The provisions in this Practice Direction are subject to any orders made by the presiding judge in a specific proceeding.

In *R. v. Jordan*, 2016 SCC 27, the Supreme Court of Canada established a new framework for applications for a stay of proceedings due to unreasonable delay under s.11 (b) of the *Canadian Charter of Rights and Freedoms*. The Supreme Court also provided guidance regarding how that framework should be applied in cases that were already in the justice system prior to the release of *R. v. Jordan, i.e.* cases with a charge date before July 8, 2016.

The purpose of this Practice Direction is to ensure that s. 11(b) applications before the Superior Court of Justice are scheduled and conducted in a fair and effective manner by (i) clarifying what supporting materials are required for s. 11(b) applications; and, (ii) requiring all s. 11(b) applications be heard well in advance of the trial.

Requiring that s. 11(b) applications be heard at least 60 days in advance of the trial will allow these applications to be determined well before the trial and, in most cases, before the date on which the parties must serve and file any other pre-trial application materials. This will allow all participants to marshal their resources more effectively in a number of ways:

i. where the application is allowed and a stay is granted, the court and the parties will have sufficient time to re-allocate the time that was set aside for the trial but which is no longer needed;

ii. where the application is allowed and a stay is granted, the parties will be spared the time and expense of preparing and filing materials for other pre-trial applications, which will no longer proceed; and

iii. where the application is dismissed, cases will be ready to proceed on their scheduled trial date; this is particularly important where jury panels have been summonsed and jury selection is to begin.

All references to a rule or rules in the Practice Direction refer to the Criminal Proceedings Rules of the Superior Court of Justice (Ontario).

Part I: — Scheduling of s. 11(b) Applications

A. — Pre-trial Conference

1. Where the defence (*i.e.* an accused person or his/her counsel) intends to bring a s. 11(b) application but did not indicate this at the pre-trial conference, the defence must provide written notice of this change in position to the Crown, any other accused and the Superior Court trial coordinator, and arrange for a further pre-trial conference as soon as practicable, as required under rule 28.04(11).

2. The court may permit and/or direct that this pre-trial conference be conducted by teleconference.

3. The pre-trial conference judge will inquire about and discuss any matter that may promote a fair and expeditious hearing of the s. 11(b) application including, but not limited to, (i) the scheduling of the application; (ii) the parties' positions as to the cause of any particular periods of delay in the case, including whether the delay is attributable to the defence or to "extraordinary circumstances", as defined in *R. v. Jordan*, and (iii) the materials required to be filed in support of the application.

B. — Hearing of the s. 11(b) application

4. Unless otherwise directed by a judge, all s. 11(b) applications must be scheduled to be heard at least 60 days before the first scheduled day of trial or, where pre-

trial applications are scheduled to be heard separately in advance of the trial, at least 60 days before the first scheduled day of pre-trial applications.

5. Before filing a s. 11(b) application, the applicant must obtain a hearing date from the court. Before seeking this date from the court, the applicant will be expected to consult with the Crown and any other accused to canvass all parties' available dates and a reasonable time estimate for the hearing of the application.

6. Unless otherwise directed by a judge, the materials in support of the application must be served and filed in accordance with the timelines set out in rules 27.04 and 33:

a. the applicant's materials must be filed at least 30 days before the hearing of the application; and

b. the respondent's materials must be filed at least 10 days before the hearing of the application.

Part II: — Supporting Materials in s. 11(b) Applications

A. — Factums

7. Unless otherwise directed by a judge, factums are required for all s. 11(b) applications, as per rule 27.05(8).

8. The factums should clearly identify any periods of delay within the case that the party submits should be characterized as attributable to the defence or to "exceptional circumstances", as defined in *R. v. Jordan.*

9. In addition, in transitional cases, (*i.e.* cases with a charge date before July 8, 2016), the factum should clearly attribute each period of time in the proceeding to one of the five categories of delay identified in *R. v. Morin* ((i) inherent time requirements; (ii) delay attributable to the accused/defence; (iii) Crown delay; (iv) institutional delay and (v) other reasons for delay).

B. — Transcripts

10. Unless otherwise directed by a judge and subject to paragraph 11 below, the applicant's application record must contain the transcripts of all prior court appearances in the case. Where an appearance included the hearing of evidence and submissions, only the portion of the transcript reflecting discussions about adjournments, scheduling and selection of the next court need be provided.

11. The court encourages and expects the parties to work together to identify any periods of delay within the case that all parties agree are attributable to the defence or to "exceptional circumstances", as defined in *R. v. Jordan*, or (in transitional cases) to one of the five categories of delay identified in *R. v. Morin* ((i) inherent time requirements; (ii) delay attributable to the accused/defence; (iii) Crown delay; (iv) institutional delay and (v) other reasons for delay). Where the parties reach such an agreement, an agreed statement of fact may be filed with respect to that period, rather than transcripts.

Dated: August 29, 2016

Heather J. Smith

Chief Justice

Superior Court of Justice (Ontario)

PD-6e — *PROVINCIAL PRACTICE DIRECTION REGARDING CRIMINAL PROCEEDINGS*

Effective May 1, 2017

Part I: — Interpretation and Application of this Practice Direction

1. This Practice Direction applies to all criminal proceedings in the Superior Court of Justice.

2. The purpose of this Practice Direction is to enhance the timeliness, appropriate scheduling and trial readiness of criminal proceedings in the Superior Court of Justice.

3. Subject to section 4, this Practice Direction applies to all Indictments in the Superior Court of Justice as of May 1, 2017.

4. Part III (Factums) does not apply to Indictments that were pre-tried before May 1, 2017 unless a subsequent pre-trial is held on or after May 1, 2017.

5. The provisions of this Practice Direction are being incorporated into the Criminal Proceedings Rules of the Superior Court of Justice (Ontario). This Practice Direction will remain in effect until the revisions to the Criminal Proceedings Rules of the Superior Court of Justice (Ontario) incorporating these provisions are published in the Canada Gazette pursuant to s. 482 of the *Criminal Code*.

6. The provisions in this Practice Direction are subject to any orders made by the presiding judge in a specific proceeding.

7. All references to a rule or rules in this Practice Direction refer to the Criminal Proceedings Rules of the Superior Court of Justice (Ontario).

8. All references to the *Code* refer to the *Criminal Code*.

Part II: — Appearances on Indictments

9. On every appearance on an indictment in the Superior Court of Justice, Crown and defence counsel and any self-represented accused person must be prepared to advise the presiding judge whether any

a. previous time periods in the case in either the Superior Court of Justice or the Ontario Court of Justice; and

b. any adjournments or time periods to future scheduled events in the Superior Court of Justice

are attributable to defence delay or exceptional circumstances as described in *R. v. Jordan*, 2016 SCC 27. Counsel must also be prepared to identify the start and end dates for any such time periods.

Part III: — Factums

10. Unless otherwise ordered by a judge, factums are required for all applications:

a. change of venue applications under rule 22;

b. applications to take evidence on commission under rule 24;

c. applications regarding constitutional issues under rule 27 (including applications regarding s. 11(b) of the Charter);

d. applications to admit evidence under rule 30; and

e. applications to exclude evidence under rule 31.

11. Factums shall comply with rule 33, unless otherwise ordered by a judge.

Part IV: — Pre-trial Conferences

A. — Updated Pre-trial Forms

12. Counsel (and accused, if self-represented) shall use the updated version of the pre-trial conference report (Form 17) dated May 2017 available on the Ontario Court Forms website. As of May 15, 2017, the Court may refuse to accept filing of any previous versions of the pre-trial conference report (Form 17).

13. The pre-trial conference judge shall use the updated version of the Report to Trial Judge (Form 18-A1) dated May 2017.

B. — Directions and Orders of Pre-Trial Conference Judge

14. The pre-trial conference judge may make any order that the rules provide may be made by a judge, including an order with respect to the following:

a. directing that factums are required, or are not required, in respect of a particular application;

b. the nature, scope and content of other materials required in support of an application;

c. the manner and timelines for the service and filing of notices, application records factums or other materials in support of an application; and

d. setting time limits for oral arguments of pre-trial applications that parties should expect will be imposed subject to the discretion of the trial judge.

C. — Conducting Pre-trial Conferences by telephone or video conference

15. A judge may direct that a pre-trial conference be held by telephone conference or by video conference, either on request of one or more parties, or on his or her own initiative.

Part V: — Bail Variations pursuant to s. 515.1 of the Code

16. This part applies to consent applications under s. 515.1 of the *Code* to vary release orders issued under ss. 499, 503 or 515 of the *Code*.

17. Where the applicant has been committed for trial in the Superior Court of Justice, all applications under s. 515.1 must be brought in the Superior Court.

18. Where an application to vary a release order on consent under s. 515.1 of the *Code* without a court attendance is filed, the reviewing judge may

a. grant the order;

b. direct that a court attendance is required, including a direction that the application proceed as an application under s. 520 or s. 521 of the *Code*; or

c. give other directions regarding the application.

19. All applications under s. 515.1 seeking an order without a court attendance shall include:

a. a notice of application clearly identifying the content of the term(s) sought to be varied and supported by the following;

i. a copy of the release order that the applicant wants varied, including all previous variations of the release order;

ii. a sworn affidavit from the applicant confirming that the applicant understands that the original Undertaking or Recognizance remains in effect and that failure without lawful excuse to comply with that Undertaking or Recognizance as it has been varied is an offence contrary to the *Criminal Code*; and

iii. a sworn affidavit from each surety that includes (1) the surety's position with respect to the variation(s) being sought and (2) that the surety agrees to be bound by the order as varied and understands that if the order is varied that the surety is bound by it; or

b. a completed Form 10B with a copy of the release order that the applicant wants varied.

20. Where a judge grants a variation under s. 515.1, the Form 10B signed by the judge or, where the Form 10B is not used, the order or endorsement of the judge granting the variation, together with the original (now varied) release order, are the release orders.

Part VI: — Applications under s. 11(b) of the Canadian Charter of Rights and Freedoms

A. — Scheduling of s. 11(b) Applications

Pre-trial Conference

21. Where the defence (*e.* an accused person or his/her counsel) intends to bring a s. 11(b) application but did not indicate this at the pre-trial conference, the defence must provide written notice of this change in position to the Crown, any other accused and the Superior Court trial coordinator, and arrange for a further pre-trial conference as soon as practicable, as required under rule 28.04(11).

22. The court may permit and/or direct that this pre-trial conference be conducted by teleconference.

23. The pre-trial conference judge will inquire about and discuss any matter that may promote a fair and expeditious hearing of the s. 11(b) application including, but not limited to, (i) the scheduling of the application; (ii) the parties' positions as to the cause of any particular periods of delay in the case, including whether the delay is attributable to the defence or to "extraordinary circumstances", as defined in *R. v. Jordan*, and (iii) the materials required to be filed in support of the application.

Hearing of the s. 11(b) application

24. Unless otherwise directed by a judge, all s. 11(b) applications must be scheduled to be heard at least 60 days before the first scheduled day of trial or, where pre-trial applications are scheduled to be heard separately in advance of the trial, at least 60 days before the first scheduled day of pre-trial applications.

25. Before filing a s. 11(b) application, the applicant must obtain a hearing date from the court. Before seeking this date from the court, the applicant will be expected to consult with the Crown and any other accused to canvass all parties' available dates and a reasonable time estimate for the hearing of the application.

26. Unless otherwise directed by a judge, the materials in support of the application must be served and filed in accordance with the timelines set out in rules 27.04 and 33:

a. the applicant's materials must be filed at least 30 days before the hearing of the application; and

b. the respondent's materials must be filed at least 10 days before the hearing of the application.

B. — Supporting Materials in s. 11(b) Applications

Factums

27. Unless otherwise directed by a judge, factums are required for all s. 11(b) applications, as per rule 27.05(8).

28. The factums should clearly identify any periods of delay within the case that the party submits should be characterized as attributable to the defence or to "exceptional circumstances", as defined in *R. v. Jordan.*

29. In addition, in transitional cases, (*e.* cases with a charge date before July 8, 2016), the factum should clearly attribute each period of time in the proceeding to one of the five categories of delay identified in *R. v. Morin* ((i) inherent time requirements; (ii) delay attributable to the accused/defence; (iii) Crown delay; (iv) institutional delay and (v) other reasons for delay).

30. The information described in paragraphs 28 - 29 should be set out in a chart (or charts) attached to the factum setting out the history of the proceeding from the date of charge until the anticipated disposition of the proceeding.

Transcripts

31. Unless otherwise directed by a judge and subject to paragraph 32 below, the applicant's application record must contain the transcripts of all prior court appearances in the case. Where an appearance included the hearing of evidence and submissions, only the portion of the transcript reflecting discussions about adjournments, scheduling and selection of the next court need be provided.

32. The court encourages and expects the parties to work together to identify any periods of delay within the case that all parties agree are attributable to the defence or to "exceptional circumstances", as defined in *R. v. Jordan*, or (in transitional cases) to one of the five categories of delay identified in *R. v. Morin* ((i) inherent time requirements; (ii) delay attributable to the accused/defence; (iii) Crown delay; (iv) institutional delay and (v) other reasons for delay). Where the parties reach such an agreement, an agreed statement of fact may be filed with respect to that period, rather than transcripts.

Part VII: — Related Amendments to Other Superior Court of Justice Practice Directions

33. The following Superior Court of Justice Practice Directions (or portions thereof) are revoked:

a. the entire Provincial Practice Direction Regarding Applications under s. 11(b) of the *Canadian Charter of Rights and Freedoms*;

b. section A of part III (Bail Variations pursuant to section 515.1 of the *Criminal Code*) of the Consolidated Practice Direction for the Central West Region; and

c. section H of part III (Bail Variations pursuant to section 515.1 of the *Criminal Code*) of the Consolidated Practice Direction for the Central South Region.

Dated: April 18, 2017

Heather J. Smith

Chief Justice

Superior Court of Justice (Ontario)

PD-6f — *PRACTICE DIRECTION CONCERNING CIVIL PROCEEDINGS IN CENTRAL EAST REGION*

Effective January 1, 2017

This Practice Direction applies to all civil proceedings in the Superior Court of Justice, Central East Region, effective January 1, 2017. It *supersedes* all previous region-specific Practice Directions concerning civil proceedings for the Central East Region issued prior to January 1, 2017, which are hereby revoked.

Counsel and parties are advised to refer to the relevant Parts of the Consolidated Provincial Practice Direction as well as the Consolidated Practice Direction for Divisional Court Proceedings which are available on the Superior Court of Justice website at: www.ontariocourts.ca/scj.

Part I: — General

1. In addition to this Practice Direction, counsel and parties to civil proceedings are advised to refer to the Consolidated Provincial Practice Direction.

2. In this Practice Direction, any reference to "counsel" includes a self-represented party.

Part II: — Motions to Transfer

3. All requests for a transfer of a civil proceeding from one county to another shall be pursuant to rule 13.1.02 of the *Rules of Civil Procedure*. The motion will be granted or denied based on its merits. Counsel and parties are advised to refer to Part III of the Consolidated Provincial Practice Direction which prescribes specific requirements for motions to transfer a civil proceeding.

Part III: — Mortgage Proceedings

4. Pursuant to rule 13.1.01(3) of the *Rules of Civil Procedure*, Barrie or Oshawa are designated as the places where mortgage proceedings may be commenced for property located anywhere in the Central East Region.

Part IV: — Construction Liens

5. Construction lien pre-trials will be scheduled at intervals at the Newmarket, Barrie, and Oshawa judicial centres. To ensure continuity and efficient management, the pre-trials will be assigned to designated judges at each of the centres.

6. Construction lien pre-trials in Peterborough, Cobourg and Lindsay will be scheduled on an "as needed basis" with the Trial Co-ordinator.

7. Construction lien pre-trials from Bracebridge will be scheduled to be heard in Barrie.

8. In order to accommodate counsel, the pre-trials in construction lien matters will be scheduled on different weeks at each of the judicial centres. For a list of the scheduled dates for the pre-trials, and telephone numbers of the Trial Co-ordinator for each judicial centre, please see the "Court Locations & Schedules" section of the Court's website at: ontariocourts.ca/scj/locations/.

a) — First Pre-Trial Conference

9. It is preferred that counsel who will appear at trial and their clients attend the first pre-trial conference. Every effort will be made to discuss a resolution of the proceeding at this first appearance. In the event that a settlement cannot be achieved at this stage, then the pre-trial judge shall order:

i. the exchange of Affidavits of Documents together with a copy of each document referred to in Schedule A;

ii. the date for examinations, as well as the answering of undertakings;

iii. the date for a motion relating to refusals on examinations and any other contemplated motions;

iv. that a "Scott" Schedule and any responding Schedule be prepared and delivered prior to the next appearance date;

v. the next pre-trial date; and,

vi. that Plaintiff's counsel take out an order incorporating the above-noted terms.

b) — Second Pre-Trial Conference

10. It is mandatory that all counsel who will appear at trial and their respective clients attend the second (and, if necessary, any subsequent) pre-trial conference.

11. The pre-trial judge will discuss and assess the progress of the proceeding and will consider an appropriate award of costs for non-compliance with the First Appearance Order.

12. At the second pre-trial conference, the parties will be required to detail their respective positions with supporting documentation.

13. In the event that the proceeding is not settled at the conclusion of this second or subsequent pre-trial conference, the pre-trial conference judge shall fix a date for trial within the Civil Trial Sittings.

Part V: — Ex Parte Motions in Writing

14. All ex parte motions in writing must be filed with the court office and payment of the applicable filing fee made. They will be put before a judge in chambers for review in the normal course. Ex parte motions may not be "filed" by delivering them to the Trial Co-ordinator for a judge to review, or by sending them by email or otherwise directly to a judge of the court.

Part VI: — Civil Proceedings in Newmarket

a) — Elimination of "Placeholder" Motions

15. Where counsel or a party has booked with the Trial Co-ordinator a date for the hearing of a motion, a Notice of Motion must be filed (and the necessary filing fee paid) no later than 10 days after the motion date is booked. Unless a Notice of Motion is filed (and the necessary payment made) within this time period, any booked motion date will be vacated without notice to counsel or the moving party. The booking of "placeholder" motions will cease.

b) — Civil Motions Consent Orders

16. Where counsel and/or the parties have agreed to a consent order in a civil motion scheduled for hearing, a fully executed consent, together with a draft order, shall be emailed to the court at Newmarket.SCJ.TC@ontario.ca, along with the motion confirmation form (Form 37B) by 2 pm three days before the scheduled hearing, as required by rule 37.10.1. The materials will be put before the presiding judge in chambers for review. If satisfied that the order should issue, the presiding judge will sign the draft order. Counsel for the moving party will be notified by the court that the order is ready to be picked up and entered. Unless otherwise advised by the court, counsel and/or the parties do not have to attend at court on the scheduled hearing date, which shall be vacated.

17. Where counsel and/or the parties have resolved a motion scheduled for hearing by way of a fully executed consent and draft order, after the motion confirmation form is filed, counsel for the moving party may attend at 9:00 a.m. on the morning scheduled for hearing of the motion, and file the consent and draft order with the courtroom registrar. The consent and draft order will be put before the presiding judge in chambers for review. If the presiding judge is satisfied that the order should issue, he/she will sign the draft order. The registrar will return the signed order to counsel to be entered. Counsel is not required to remain in the courtroom after receiving the signed order.

Part VII: — Long Motions and Motions for Summary Judgment in Barrie, Bracebridge, Cobourg, Lindsay, Newmarket, Oshawa and Peterborough

18. Dates for all long motions (exceeding one hour) and all motions for summary judgment must be obtained from the Trial Co-ordinator.

19. For all motions exceeding one hour and for all summary judgment motions, counsel (and parties who are self-represented) shall file a factum no longer than 25 pages. In addition to a factum, counsel are to consult with each other and where possible file a Joint Compendium, which shall contain the key material documents to be relied on during oral argument. Where counsel cannot agree on a Joint Compendium, each will file their own separate Compendium, which shall contain the key material documents to be relied on during oral argument. The Compendium should not exceed 30 pages in length.

20. Where counsel intends to rely on case law, he or she shall file a case brief containing only those cases that will be referred to in oral argument, with the relevant passages side-barred.

21. Counsel are encouraged to file an electronic version of the factum, the Joint Compendium (or separate Compendium), and case brief on CD, DVD or USB key. The electronic documents must be submitted in either Microsoft Word format (.doc or.docx) or text searchable PDF format. The CD, DVD or USB key should be accompanied by a covering letter which identifies the materials contained on the CD, DVD or USB key, as follows:

> **USB Key**: The cover letter should include a list of the files contained on the USB key, along with the title of proceedings, Court File #, Counsel Name(s), where applicable, and Party Name. If possible, the key should be labelled with the short style of cause and the Court File #.
>
> **CD or DVD**: The CD or DVD should be labelled with the title of proceedings, Court File #, Counsel Name(s), where applicable, and Party Name. Include a list of the files contained on the CD or DVD in the cover letter.

Part VIII: — Pre-Trial Conferences

a) — Purpose

22. The purpose of this Part is to ensure that civil cases proceed to trial only after they have been properly pre-tried and endorsed as ready for trial by the presiding pre-trial conference judge. This will be achieved by the assignment of civil pre-trial conferences to judges who are experienced in civil litigation matters. Those judges will conduct all pre-trial conferences in the Region. It will also be achieved by the establishment of a Central East Trial Scheduling Court ("CETSC"), which will be held in Oshawa and presided over by the Regional Senior Judge or a judge designated by him or her. The CETSC replaces all other Trial Scheduling Courts in the Region and they will be discontinued.

b) — Obtaining a Pre-Trial Conference Date

23. All civil cases will proceed to a pre-trial conference once they are certified ready for trial by the filing of a Trial Record.

24. The existing Trial Scheduling Notice and Consent Form is replaced with a Pre-Trial Conference Confirmation Form. Counsel are required to contact the Trial Co-ordinator in the centre where the action is outstanding, to book a pre-trial conference date that is agreed to by all counsel. Counsel are to record this date on the Pre-Trial Conference Confirmation Form, and transmit it to the Trial Co-ordinator within seven days of booking the pre-trial conference date to the appropriate court location.

Barrie/Bracebridge: Barrie.SCJ.TC@ontario.ca (705-739-6099)

Newmarket: Newmarket.SCJ.TC@ontario.ca (905-853-4863)

Oshawa: Oshawa.SCJ.TC@ontario.ca (905-743-2652)

Peterborough/Cobourg/Lindsay: Peterborough.SCJ.TC@ontario.ca (705-745-3526)

25. In the event that counsel who seeks a pre-trial conference date cannot obtain the agreement of opposing counsel to one of the dates provided by the Trial Co-ordinator, counsel seeking to book the pre-trial conference shall notify the Trial Co-ordinator who will add the case to the next available CETSC.

26. All counsel are required to appear at the CETSC. Counsel opposing the fixing of the pre-trial date must establish good reason why the pre-trial conference cannot proceed on one of the dates provided by the Trial Co-ordinator. The presiding judge shall fix a date for the pre-trial conference. If the presiding judge is satisfied that no good reason was established for counsel's failure to agree to one of the dates provided by the Trial Co-ordinator, the presiding judge may make a costs award against the offending party.

c) — Pre-Trial Conference Memorandums

27. Counsel shall file their pre-trial conference memorandums with the court administration office in the centre where the action is outstanding, no later than five (5) business days before the pre-trial conference. Pre-trial memorandums will *not* be accepted for late filing. This filing requirement is intended to ensure that the pre-trial conference judge has adequate time to review the pre-trial conference memorandums in advance of the pre-trial conference.

28. If counsel fails to file the pre-trial conference memorandum in time, the pre-trial conference will be cancelled by the Trial Co-ordinator. Cancellation of the pre-trial conference, absent exceptional circumstances, may result in a costs award against the offending party.

29. If a pre-trial conference is cancelled because counsel for a party failed to file the pre-trial conference memorandum in time, counsel for any other party to the action may unilaterally fix a fresh pre-trial conference date with the Trial Co-ordinator.

30. Where a second pre-trial conference date is cancelled due again to late filing of the pre-trial conference memorandum, the Trial Co-ordinator will put the case to be spoken to at the next available CETSC. All counsel are required to attend the CETSC.

d) — The Pre-Trial Conference

31. To ensure that adequate time is allocated for a meaningful pre-trial conference, generally no more than four (4) pre-trial conferences per day will be scheduled before a single judge.

32. The pre-trial conference judge will, in accordance with rule 52.07, assist the parties in working toward a full or partial resolution of the issues in the action. In addition, the pre-trial conference judge will make such case management orders as are appropriate to ensure that the case is ready for trial. This may necessitate the holding of more than one pre-trial conference in a case.

33. The pre-trial conference judge will endorse that the case is ready for trial only when he or she is satisfied of this. The pre-trial conference judge will complete a Pre-Trial Conference Report, which will be provided to the judge presiding at the CETSC, and also to the trial judge. It will include the estimated length of the trial.

e) — Central East Trial Scheduling Court

34. Once the pre-trial conference judge has endorsed that the case is ready for trial, the case will be listed for appearance in the CETSC. The CETSC will take place in Oshawa at least once per month, usually on the last Thursday of the month. It will be presided over by the Regional Senior Judge or his or her designate.

35. Counsel of record for each party is expected to attend the CETSC. While it is preferable that counsel attend in person, attendance by telephone conference call at pre-booked times during the course of the day is permissible. Arrangements for attendance by telephone conference call can be made through the Trial Co-ordinator in the centre where the action is outstanding, or the Oshawa Trial Co-ordinator, no later than the Friday before the scheduled CETSC. In the event that counsel of record is not available to attend in person or by telephone conference call, a fully instructed lawyer acting as counsel's agent must attend the CETSC in person.

36. The purpose of the CETSC is to confirm the length of the trial and to ensure that the case is ready for trial. Civil cases will be listed to be tried at the twice-yearly regional Civil Trial Sittings. The judge presiding at the CETSC will canvass with counsel on which Civil Trial Sittings list the action will be placed. If counsel has more than one case on a particular Civil Trial Sittings list, the presiding judge must be informed of all other cases counsel has on that list and their present status. The purpose of such enquiry is to avoid the adjournments that result when counsel set multiple cases for trial at the same Civil Trial Sittings.

37. If a trial is estimated to take longer than three weeks, the judge presiding at the CETSC will decide whether the case can be tried within the twice-yearly Civil Trial Sittings, or whether the Regional Senior Judge should be asked to assign a fixed trial date.

38. A further purpose of the CETSC is to canvass whether there is any reason why a case cannot be tried at any of the courthouses in the region, so that courtroom and judicial resources can be maximized. Counsel and the parties will be required to show good reason why a case must be tried at a particular courthouse.

f) — Adjournments

39. Counsel should be prepared to proceed to trial during the Civil Trial Sittings to which the case has been assigned or on the fixed date set. Any requests to adjourn a trial must be brought at a CETSC. Counsel should expect that adjournments sought when the case is called for trial will not be granted, absent compelling reasons.

Dated: January 1, 2017

Heather J. Smith

Chief Justice

Superior Court of Justice (Ontario)

Michelle Fuerst

Regional Senior Judge

Superior Court of Justice, Central East Region

PD-7a — *CONSOLIDATED PRACTICE DIRECTION CONCERNING FAMILY CASES IN CENTRAL EAST REGION*

Effective July 1, 2014, amended May 1, 2016 and December 1, 2017

This Practice Direction applies to family law proceedings in Central East Region, other than Child Protection cases under the *Child and Family Services Act*. It supersedes all previous Practice Directions concerning family proceedings in Central East Region, which are hereby revoked. All family proceedings throughout Central East Region are conducted in the Family Court Branch of the Superior Court of Justice and are governed by the *Family Law Rules*. Counsel and parties can generally expect to attend the following court events with a judge prior to trial: one case conference; one settlement conference; one trial scheduling conference; and one trial management conference. In exceptional cases, a judge may schedule additional conferences or combine some of these conferences into one event, as permitted by the *Family Law Rules*. If a judicial decision is required prior to trial, parties may also schedule a motion as permitted by rules 14(4) to (16).

This Practice Direction explains the filing requirements and scheduling procedures for each of these events to ensure that each attendance is a meaningful appearance. **Where there is a conflict between the filing requirements of the Family Law Rules and this Practice Direction, the Practice Direction shall apply.** All filing should be done at the Family Court Filing Office for the centre in which the proceedings have been started. All references to the Trial Coordinator refer to the Family Court Trial Coordinator in the same centre. Each Family Court site also has a Family Law Information Centre (FLIC) and Mediation Service. Contact information for these services is available on the Ministry's website.

Contact information for the various court offices at each site in Central East is included at the end of this Practice Direction. Counsel and parties should also refer to the relevant parts of the Consolidated Provincial Practice Direction (Part 1 in particular). There are also additional resources that may be helpful to family law litigants at the end of this Practice Direction.

Each of the forms that are required by the *Family Law Rules* are available at the Ontario Court Forms website at: http://www.ontariocourtforms.on.ca/en/family-law-rules-forms/. In addition, the Trial Scheduling Endorsement Form for family cases is available on the Superior Court of Justice's website at: http://www.ontariocourts.ca/scj/practice/rules-forms/.

Part 1: — Confirmations

1. Each party to a conference or motion must file a fully completed Form 14C Confirmation. If the parties consult and agree on the content, they may file one joint 14C. The 14C must be filed no later than 2 p.m. two business days before the date of the motion or conference, **except for long motions which must be filed by 2 p.m. seven days before the motion.** The 14C may be faxed to the Filing Office for the court in which the event is scheduled.

2. Unless the parties do not have counsel **and** are prohibited by court order or safety issues from communicating with each other, the parties or their counsel should consult with each other in advance of the scheduled court date in order to (i) set a joint agenda of the issues they wish addressed at the conference or motion; (ii) attempt to resolve the issues in dispute; and (iii) determine how much of the scheduled time each of them will require at the court attendance to address those issues. The parties are expected to exchange proposals in advance of filing their Form 14C Confirmations. The 14C should confirm that these discussions have taken place, or set out reasons why

not, otherwise the matter may not be heard. Priority will be given to matters for which the 14C Confirmation has been fully and properly completed and reasonable efforts have been made by the parties to consult in advance, as set out above.

3. If direct communication is problematic, as only one of the two parties is represented, counsel may communicate with the other party in writing before filing their 14C. Counsel should indicate (i) the issues that must be addressed; (ii) their client's proposal to resolve the issues; and (iii) how much of the scheduled time he or she requires. The 14C should confirm that this communication has been sent and counsel should bring a copy of the communications to the conference or motion.

4. Where Form 14C Confirmations have not been filed, the conference or motion will be crossed off the court's daily schedule or event list and will not be heard by the court, unless the parties obtain a judge's order to restore it to the list. Costs may also be ordered against a party who has not filed a properly completed 14C Confirmation.

5. Form 14C Confirmations must **only** list the specific issues that are to be addressed at that event. They should also indicate which materials the judge should review. The 14C Confirmation should not direct the judge to read the entire file or any material that is not necessary for that day. A judge will generally only read the briefs and financial documents for case or settlement conferences. For motions, the 14C Confirmation should provide a clear reference to the specific volume, tab and page numbers of the Continuing Record that need to be read for the event. Normally, this will be the Notice of Motion and affidavits filed by both parties. *Failure to provide this information may result in the materials not being reviewed by the judge, the matter being placed at the bottom of the list, or the matter not being heard on that day.*

6. Form 14C Confirmations must also include a realistic time estimate for the **entire motion or conference to be completed in the time that has been booked**, including time required by the other party. See paragraphs 39 and 42 below regarding the allocation of time for motions. *Parties will be held to the time stated on their Confirmations.*

Part 2: — Adjournments

7. Once a date has been booked, the court expects counsel or parties to be ready to proceed on the scheduled day and time. In most centres, a number of cases will be scheduled at the same time, as the court cannot anticipate who will be delayed waiting to see duty counsel. Every effort will be made to give priority to cases in which the parties have exchanged properly completed material and negotiated in advance, so that they are ready to proceed at their scheduled time. However, counsel or parties should be prepared for the possibility of lengthy wait times, as the court works through the scheduled list. The court's schedule is posted online at 4:30 p.m. on the day before the scheduled attendance.

8. Due to the number of litigants requiring court dates, it is important that scheduled events are not adjourned, unless there is a reason that the parties cannot proceed. If circumstances arise that necessitate an adjournment, it should be requested as soon as possible so that the time can be made available for other matters. Unless otherwise provided in this Practice Direction, up to two administrative adjournments per case may be obtained by contacting the Trial Coordinator no later than 2:00 p.m. two business days before the scheduled event. After two administrative adjournments of any case, the parties must attend personally before the court to request an adjournment, otherwise the proceeding may be dismissed.

9. Trial scheduling conferences may not be adjourned without a judge's order, which must be obtained either by 14B motion, if there have not been two previous administrative adjournments for the case, or by appearing before the court. The ad-

journment request must set out strong reasons why the parties are not ready to go ahead, along with a proposed timetable to move the case forward.

10. Trial management conferences are peremptory on all parties and may not be adjourned without appearing before the court. Trial management conferences will only be adjourned in compelling and unforeseen circumstances, such as illness.

11. Unless a judge has ordered otherwise, once a matter has been placed on a trial list, parties and counsel must be ready to proceed on one-half days' notice at any time during that trial sittings. A trial may not be adjourned without a judge's order, which can only be obtained by attending personally, and which will only be granted in compelling and unforeseen circumstances, such as illness.

Part 3: — First Appearance

12. For cases to which Rule 39 applies (fast track matters, which do not involve claims relating to property or divorce), the first court date will be scheduled before a Rule 39 clerk. Parties must attend to ensure their case will be ready for a case conference. However, if both parties have filed all material required by the *Rules* (Application and Answer; Financial Statements; Certificate of Financial Disclosure; and Form 35.1 Affidavit in support of Custody or Access), they may jointly consent to waive the first appearance date. This may be done by filing a Joint Waiver of the first appearance with the Trial Coordinator who will then schedule a case conference date for the parties.

13. The first appearance Clerk can assist the parties by providing information and forms that need to be filed to proceed to a case conference. Duty counsel is available to provide advice to parties who qualify financially. Duty counsel and mediation services are also available to try to assist the parties to negotiate a temporary or final resolution of their issues at the first appearance date.

Part 4: — Conferences

A. — Case Conferences and Settlement Conferences

14. The parties may obtain a case conference date at their first appearance date or, if permitted by the Family Law Rules, by serving and filing a Notice of Case Conference with a date that has been obtained from the Trial Coordinator. To avoid unnecessary adjournment requests, the other side should be consulted before scheduling a date for any conference wherever possible.

15. Counsel or the parties are required to communicate before any conference in order to attempt to narrow or resolve the issues that are in dispute, unless the parties are self-represented **and** prohibited from communicating by court order.

16. Parties should serve and file a case conference brief (Form 17A) for case conferences and a settlement conference brief (Form 17C) for settlement conferences with any necessary attachments. The purposes of a case conference are set out in Rule 17(4) and the purposes of a settlement conference are set out in Rule 17(5). Parties should prepare their briefs with a view to a realistic agenda that can be completed in the time that has been scheduled for the conference.

17. Conference briefs were designed to replace adversarial pleadings and affidavits. Absent exceptional circumstances, the briefs should be prepared in a manner that will promote a climate for settlement and can realistically be read by the conference judge in the time scheduled that day. The briefs should also set out the party's proposal for any unresolved issues. **Case conference briefs should be limited to the four page**

form set out in the *Family Law Rules* with a maximum of two additional pages of narrative and proposals, other than supporting material such as lists of outstanding disclosure or professional reports. Case conference briefs that exceed the six page maximum may be returned to the parties, and the matter may be placed at the bottom of the list. Lengthy or unduly adversarial case or settlement conference briefs may not be read. The matter may also be placed at the bottom of the list and costs may be awarded.

18. At the conclusion of the case conference, the presiding judge will either schedule a settlement conference or give directions to the parties about scheduling their next step. If a motion is required, the parties should agree to deadlines to file their material, so that all material will be filed no later than 2 p.m. two business days before the motion is scheduled to be heard.

Teleconferences

19. Parties may arrange for a conference to occur by teleconference with permission obtained in advance from the judge who is scheduled to conduct the conference. The request should indicate whether the other side is consenting and, if not, the reasons. If the other party will not consent, a request for a teleconference may be made by filing a Form 14B Motion or by faxing a letter to the Trial Coordinator to be considered by the conference judge.

Motions to Change

20. A request to change a final order is made by filing a motion to change under Rule 15. The first case conference on a motion to change a final order or agreement shall be scheduled before a Dispute Resolution Officer (DRO) for those centres that have a DRO program (Barrie, Newmarket and Oshawa) in accordance with Part I of the Consolidated Provincial Practice Direction.

21. A DRO conference can be held on matters other than motions to change only as directed by the court. This may be requested by a Form 14B Motion or at another court event.

B. — Trial Scheduling Conferences

22. If the matter is not resolved at a settlement conference, the next event will be a trial scheduling conference. Where possible, the trial scheduling conference will be heard within 30 days of the settlement conference by the same judge. A trial scheduling conference will normally be scheduled by the settlement conference judge at the conclusion of the settlement conference, unless a judge has directed that the settlement conference and trial scheduling conference be combined. If the settlement conference and trial scheduling conference have been combined, the court will ensure that the Trial Scheduling Endorsement Form is completed prior to the conclusion of the combined conference.

23. The purposes of a trial scheduling conference are to ensure trial readiness and make directions regarding how the trial will proceed. The parties should serve and file a Trial Scheduling Endorsement Form in advance of the trial scheduling conference in accordance with the timelines in Rule 17(13.1), with the appropriate portions completed by each party, in lieu of the Trial Management Conference Brief (Form 17E).

24. Prior to a matter being scheduled for trial, the Trial Scheduling Endorsement Form must be fully completed and endorsed by the trial scheduling conference judge. In exceptional cases of urgency, a judge may place a matter on the trial list to secure a

trial date before the Trial Scheduling Endorsement Form is completed. In those cases, specific directions will be given about when the Trial Scheduling Endorsement Form is to be completed and when the trial management conference is to be held.

25. At the conclusion of the trial scheduling conference, a trial management conference will generally be scheduled by the presiding judge. Parties are required to advise the Trial Coordinator immediately if a matter settles so that this date can be made available to other matters.

C. — Trial Management Conferences

26. Unless otherwise ordered, a trial management conference will be held for any case that has not resolved 30 days prior to the scheduled trial date. Where possible, this event will be held within 2 weeks of the scheduled trial date. The purpose of the trial management conference is to confirm that parties are ready for trial, have filed their Trial Record and exchanged all other material required by the Trial Scheduling Endorsement Form, provide any further directions or revisions to the Trial Scheduling Endorsement Form and to explore any final possibilities for settlement to resolve the trial.

27. Additional requirements relating to the trial management conference are contained in paragraphs 47 to 50 below.

Part 5: — Motions

28. If the parties require a judge's order related to some aspect of the case, they may schedule a motion. Rule 14(4) provides that, except in urgent situations, no motion should be brought before a conference on the substantive issues in a case has been completed. Short motions are defined as motions that can be completed in less than one hour. Long motions are motions that are expected to take longer than one hour. 14B motions, which do not require a court attendance, and urgent motions, with or without notice, are also discussed below.

A. — 14B Motions

29. A Form 14B Motion may be filed for matters that are procedural, uncomplicated or unopposed, as set out in Rule 14(10). A 14B must be filed at the family court office and cannot be filed by fax.

30. The 14B Motion and supporting materials must be filed in the Continuing Record.

B. — Urgent Motions on Notice

31. A party may seek an urgent motion **on notice** without a case conference in situations of urgency or hardship regarding serious issues such as abduction, safety issues or dire financial harm. A party seeking such a motion must serve and file all of the required materials except for a Form 14C Confirmation. Prior to bringing an urgent motion, the Trial Coordinator should be contacted to see if an urgent case conference can be scheduled before the motion is heard.

32. In order to assist with having the order issued quickly, parties are encouraged to provide the court with a draft order for urgent motions.

C. — Urgent Motions without Notice

33. Motions without notice may be brought only in exceptional circumstances as set out in Rule 14(12).

34. A court will not generally make an order without allowing both parties an opportunity to participate. In addition to addressing the requirements of paragraph 31 above, a party who is seeking a motion without notice to the other party **must** address why the other party has not been served. The motion materials should set out specifically and clearly why notice is unnecessary, not reasonably possible, or any other grounds that would justify the motion being heard without notice to the other side.

35. An order obtained without notice will need to be served on the other party and the matter must be scheduled to return for another court date within 14 days, as set out in Rule 14(14).

36. If a person is requesting a restraining order as part of his or her urgent motion, he or she should also complete the pink restraining order endorsement form with the required information (such as names and birthdates of those affected, as well as addresses at which the other side is to be prohibited from attending). This form is available at the Filing Office where the urgent motion is filed.

37. If a restraining order has been granted, the court can arrange for service of the material on the other side, if requested by a party who is not represented by counsel.

D. — Short Motions

38. Motions that are expected to take one hour or less may be scheduled on the regular motion day for that centre. This date must be obtained from the Trial Coordinator. No factum should be filed for a short motion, unless ordered by the case conference or case management judge. The Notice of Motion and supporting material should be served and filed at the Family Court Office within the timelines set out in the Family Law Rules.

39. If a motion is booked for one hour, each party will be permitted a maximum of 20 minutes for argument and five minutes will be available for reply. The remaining 15 minutes is for the judge's decision and submissions regarding costs. If parties are not able to adequately deal with their matter within that time, they should schedule a long motion.

40. If a party wishes to bring a cross-motion or responding motion on the same day, it must also be scheduled through the Trial Coordinator. If no additional time is required for argument, as the issues are the same as those already raised in the motion, the responding motion may be booked for the same day. If additional time will be required for argument, and time is not available on the same short motion day, the responding motion must be scheduled on another regular motion day that has time available. Alternatively, the parties may avoid two attendances by agreeing to have both motions heard together by the same judge on a long motions day.

E. — Long Motions

41. Motions that are expected to take more than one hour, as allocated in paragraph 39, must be scheduled as long motions through the Trial Coordinator or by the presiding judge at a conference. Long motions can be scheduled either (a) with the other party's written consent or (b) with the court's permission. The moving party must serve and file all their motion material and an Offer to Settle at least 30 days prior to the scheduled motion date, otherwise the date will be vacated. The responding party must serve and file their responding material **and an Offer to Settle** at least 15 days

before the scheduled motion date. Reply material, if any, and a properly completed 14C, confirming the motion date and material to be read, must be served and filed by 2 p.m. **seven** days prior to the scheduled motion date. **If a long motion is not confirmed by 2 p.m. seven days in advance, it will be removed from the list and the date will be vacated.**

42. The time for argument of a long motion will be allocated as follows: one third of the time scheduled for the motion will be allotted to the applicant for argument; one third of the time will be allotted to the respondent; and five minutes for each hour that has been booked will be allotted for reply. The remaining time will be for allocated for the judge's decision and submissions regarding costs. The parties will be held to the time that they have scheduled.

F. — Factums and Briefs of Authorities

43. Unless otherwise directed by the conference judge, no factum should be filed for a short motion but a properly drafted factum is required on all long motions, other than Motions to Change. Each party's factum must be served and filed by no later than 2 p.m. two business days before the hearing of the motion.

44. No factum may exceed 20 pages without leave of the court.

45. The authorities that are included on the court's list of Often Cited Family Cases do not need to be provided to the court with a party's factum. Counsel and parties are advised to refer to Part I-B of the Consolidated Provincial Practice Direction. An updated list of family cases is available on the Superior Court's website at: www.ontariocourts.ca/scj.

G. — Electronic Copies of Materials

46. When a motion is complex or the volume of materials is large, the parties may file an electronic copy of their materials by providing them by USB. The USB should include a copy of their motion materials, including their factum, where required. Paper copies of the motion materials must also be filed in the Continuing Record. The factum should be filed as a separate document, which does not form part of the Continuing Record. Counsel and parties should refer to the Guide Concerning e-Delivery of Documents available on the Superior Court's website.

Part 6 — Trials and Trial Records

47. The Applicant must file a completed Trial Record, no later than 7 days before the trial management conference, containing the documents set out in Rule 23(1) and the completed Trial Scheduling Endorsement Form. The Respondent may add any documents that should have been included in the Trial Record, as set out in Rule 23(2), up to 2 p.m. **two** business days before the trial management conference. A current financial statement for each party and comparative net family property statement shall be included in the Trial Record. **The parties do not need to update their financial statements and net family property statements again prior to trial unless there is a change or an updated statement has been requested by the court.**

48. No later than 2 p.m. two business days before the trial management conference, each party must also serve and file an Offer to Settle, an outline of their Opening Trial Statement and a Draft Order.

49. If the trial record has not been filed by the trial management conference, an order may be made requiring that the trial record be prepared on an urgent basis and that costs are to be paid or alternatively the matter may be removed from the trial list.

50. Any requests to adjourn the trial should be dealt with at the trial management conference in accordance with paragraph 10 above.

Part 7 — Uncontested Trials

51. If no Answer has been filed within 30 days of the Application being served, Rule 23 allows a party to request a final order on affidavit evidence (Form 23C). Where a first appearance or case conference has been scheduled, or there is another upcoming court date, the Form 23C will not be considered by a judge in advance of the scheduled date.

52. The party filing the Form 23C should ensure that all orders requested have been claimed in the Application. As the uncontested trial is a substitute for a full trial with oral evidence, he or she should also ensure that all evidence relied upon in support of the requested order is filed as part of the 23C.

Dated: December 1, 2017

Heather J. Smith

Chief Justice

Superior Court of Justice (Ontario)

Michelle Fuerst

Regional Senior Judge

Superior Court of Justice, Central East Region

Contact information for the Family Courts in this region, including each Trial Coordinator for family cases, is attached as **Schedule A** .

Additional information about family cases in the Superior Court of Justice is available in the **Guide to Process for Family Cases** at www.ontariocourts.ca/scj/family/.

General information about family law and family cases is available from Community Legal Education Ontario at: http://yourlegalrights.on.ca/legal-topic/family-law.

Information about the mediation and information services that are available at the Family Courts in this region is available on the Ministry's website at www.attorneygeneral.jus.gov.on.ca/english/family/mediation.php.

Schedule A

Barrie / Bracebridge / Cobourg / Lindsay / Newmarket / Oshawa / Peterborough

Barrie

Family Office

Telephone: 705-739-6116

Fax: 705-739-6109

Family Trial Coordinator

Telephone: 705-739-6442

Toll Free: 1-800-410-1061

Fax: 705-739-6099

Bracebridge

Family Office

Telephone: 705-645-8793

Fax: 705-645-7901

Family Trial Coordinator

Telephone: 705-739-7121

Toll Free: 1-800-410-1061

Fax: 705-739-6099

Cobourg

Family Office

Telephone: 905-372-3751

Fax: 905-372-9952

Family Trial Coordinator

Telephone: 705-876-3823

Toll Free: 1-800-788-0977

Fax: 705-745-3526

Lindsay

Family Office

Telephone: 705-324-1400

Fax: 705-324-1401

Family Trial Coordinator

Telephone: 705-876-3823

Toll Free: 1-800-788-0977

Fax: 705-745-3526

Newmarket

Family Office

Telephone: 905-853-4809

Fax: 905-853-4864

Family Trial Coordinator

Telephone: 905-853-4823

Fax: 905-853-4880

Oshawa

Family Office

Telephone: 905-743-2800, ext 7010

Fax: 905-743-2622

Family Trial Coordinator

Telephone: 905-743-2800, ext. 7012

Fax: 905-743-2693

Peterborough

Family Office

Telephone: 705-876-3815

Fax: 705-876-3813

Family Trial Coordinator

Telephone: 705-876-3823

Toll Free: 1-800-788-0977

Fax: 705-745-3526

PD-7b — *PRACTICE ADVISORY CONCERNING LONG MOTIONS IN THE CENTRAL EAST REGION*

Effective June 19, 2017

This Practice Advisory applies to all civil, family and stand-alone pre-trial criminal long motions (e.g. 11b applications) that are scheduled for one or more hours. It *supplements* existing practice directions, including:

- Consolidated Practice Direction Concerning Family Cases in Central East Region (Regional) *Effective May 1, 2016*

- Practice Direction Concerning Civil Proceedings in the Central East Region (Regional) *Effective January 1, 2017*

Counsel and parties are advised to refer to the relevant parts of the Consolidated Provincial Practice Direction and any other applicable Central East region-specific Practice Directions or Guides, which are available on the Superior Court of Justice website at: www.ontariocourts.ca/scj.

Requirement to File Electronic Copies of Documents on USB

For civil, family and criminal long motions, parties *must* file electronic copies of their materials on a USB stick, in addition to paper copies. The pilot excludes child protection cases, criminal third party records applications, and criminal long motions heard during trial. Only stand-alone pre-trial criminal long motions (e.g. 11b applications) are included.

The USB must include a copy of the motion materials, including the factum, where required. *Paper copies of the motion materials must also be filed as required by the rules of court.*

Acceptable Formats for Electronic Documents

Two electronic versions of *each* document are required:

1. One copy must be created using Microsoft Word (.DOC), and

2. One copy must be saved in PDF format. Documents converted from Word to PDF are preferable to scanned PDF documents.

Electronic Documents Naming Convention

In order to assist court staff in storing the electronic materials and the judge in accessing them, when saving electronic documents on the USB, each document must be named using one of the prefixes below, followed by the short style of cause and court file number (e.g. *MPL Brown v. Brown*, CV-17-12345-0000):

Motion Record (containing the Notice of Motion)

MPL = Motion Record of the Plaintiff

MDE = Motion Record of the Defendant

MDM = Motion Record of the Defendant to Counterclaim

MTP = Motion Record of the Third Party

M4P = Motion Record of the Fourth Party

M5P = Motion Record of the Fifth Party

M6P = Motion Record of the Sixth Party

M7P = Motion Record of the Seventh Party

MAP = Motion Record of the Applicant

MRP = Motion Record of the Respondent

MIN = Motion Record of the Intervener

MAN = Motion Record of the Agency (Agency/Person/Special Interest)

MSL = Motion Record of the Solicitor (under the *Solicitors Act*)

MCL = Motion Record of the Client (under the *Solicitors Act*)

MNP = Motion Record of a Non-party

All relevant prior court orders and endorsements (if not already included in the Motion Record)

COE = Court Orders and Endorsements

Note: *Include only court orders and judge's endorsements that relate to the long motion.*

Affidavits

AFPL = Affidavit of or on behalf of the Plaintiff

AFDE = Affidavit of or on behalf of the Defendant

AFDM = Affidavit of or on behalf of the Defendant to Counterclaim

AFTP = Affidavit of or on behalf of the Third Party

AF4P = Affidavit of or on behalf of the Fourth Party

AF5P = Affidavit of or on behalf of the Fifth Party

AF6P = Affidavit of or on behalf of the Sixth Party

AF7P = Affidavit of or on behalf of the Seventh Party

AFAP = Affidavit of or on behalf of the Applicant

AFRP = Affidavit of or on behalf of the Respondent

AFIN = Affidavit of or on behalf of the Intervener

AFAN = Affidavit of or on behalf of the Agency (Agency/Person/Special Interest)

AFSL = Affidavit of or on behalf of the Solicitor (under the *Solicitors Act*)

AFCL = Affidavit of or on behalf of the Client (under the *Solicitors Act*)

AFNP = Affidavit of or on behalf of a Non-party

Affidavits of Service/Proof of Service

AFSPL = Affidavit of Service or Proof of Service of or on behalf of the Plaintiff

AFSDE = Affidavit of Service or Proof of Service of or on behalf of the Defendant

AFSDM = Affidavit of Service or Proof of Service of or on behalf of the Defendant to Counterclaim

AFSTP = Affidavit of Service or Proof of Service of or on behalf of the Third Party

AFS4P = Affidavit of Service or Proof of Service of or on behalf of the Fourth Party

AFS5P = Affidavit of Service or Proof of Service of or on behalf of the Fifth Party

AFS6P = Affidavit of Service or Proof of Service of or on behalf of the Sixth Party

AFS7P = Affidavit of Service or Proof of Service of or on behalf of the Seventh Party

AFSAP = Affidavit of Service or Proof of Service of or on behalf of the Applicant

AFSRP = Affidavit of Service or Proof of Service of or on behalf of the Respondent

AFSIN = Affidavit of Service or Proof of Service of or on behalf of the Intervener

AFSAN = Affidavit of Service or Proof of Service of or on behalf of the Agency (Agency/Person/Special Interest)

AFSSL = Affidavit of Service or Proof of Service of or on behalf of the Solicitor (under the *Solicitors Act*)

AFSCL = Affidavit of Service or Proof of Service of or on behalf of the Client (under the *Solicitors Act*)

AFSNP = Affidavit of Service or Proof of Service of or on behalf of a Non-party

Book of Authorities

BAPL = Book of Authorities of the Plaintiff

BADE = Book of Authorities of the Defendant

BADM = Book of Authorities of the Defendant to Counterclaim

BATP = Book of Authorities of the Third Party

BA4P = Book of Authorities of the Fourth Party

BA5P = Book of Authorities of the Fifth Party

BA6P = Book of Authorities of the Sixth Party

BA7P = Book of Authorities of the Seventh Party

BAAP = Book of Authorities of the Applicant

BARP = Book of Authorities of the Respondent

BAIN = Book of Authorities of the Intervener

BAAN = Book of Authorities of the Agency (Agency/Person/Special Interest)

BASL = Book of Authorities of the Solicitor (under the *Solicitors Act*)

BACL = Book of Authorities of the Client (under the *Solicitors Act*)

BANP = Book of Authorities of Non-party

Factums, including Amended and Supplementary

FPL = Factum of the Plaintiff

FDE = Factum of the Defendant

FDM = Factum of the Defendant to Counterclaim

FTP = Factum of the Third Party

F4P = Factum of the Fourth Party

F5P = Factum of the Fifth Party

F6P = Factum of the Sixth Party

F7P = Factum of the Seventh Party

FAP = Factum of the Applicant

FRP = Factum of the Respondent

FIN = Factum of the Intervener

FAN = Factum of the Agency (Agency/Person/Special Interest)

FSL = Factum of the Solicitor (under the *Solicitors Act*)

FCL = Factum of the Client (under the *Solicitors Act*)

FNP = Factum of a Non-party

***Note**: Add the suffix AM or SUP to indicate Amended or Supplemental Factum*

Costs Outline

COPL = Cost Outline of the Plaintiff

CODE = Cost Outline of the Defendant

CODM = Cost Outline of the Defendant to Counterclaim

COTP = Cost Outline of the Third Party

CO4P = Cost Outline of the Fourth Party

CO5P = Cost Outline of the Fifth Party

CO6P = Cost Outline of the Sixth Party

CO7P = Cost Outline of the Seventh Party

COAP = Cost Outline of the Applicant

CORP = Cost Outline of the Respondent

COIN = Cost Outline of the Intervener

COAN = Cost Outline of the Agency (Agency/Person/Special Interest)

COSL = Cost Outline of the Solicitor (under the *Solicitors Act*)

COCL = Cost Outline of the Client (under the *Solicitors Act*)

CONP = Cost Outline of a non-party

Transcripts

TRN = Transcript

Compendiums

CPL = Compendium of the Plaintiff

CDE = Compendium of the Defendant

CDM = Compendium of the Defendant to Counterclaim

CTP = Compendium of the Third Party

C4P = Compendium of the Fourth Party

C5P = Compendium of the Fifth Party

C6P = Compendium of the Sixth Party

C7P = Compendium of the Seventh Party

CAP = Compendium of the Applicant

CRP = Compendium of the Respondent

CIN = Compendium of the Intervener

CAN = Compendium of the Agency (Agency/Person/Special Interest)

CSL = Compendium of the Solicitor (under the *Solicitors Act*)

CCL = Compendium of the Client (under the *Solicitors Act*)

CNP = Compendium of a Non-party

Note: *When there is a joint compendium filed, suffix the file name with the parties (i.e. PL for plaintiff; DE for defendant, DM defendant to counterclaim, etc.)*

Note: *When there are multiple documents of the same type filed, suffix the file name with 001, 002, 003, 004, 005, etc.*

Counsel and parties may also refer to the Guide Concerning e-Delivery of Documents in the Ontario Superior Court of Justice available on the Superior Court's website.

Date: May 29, 2017

Michelle Fuerst

Regional Senior Judge

Superior Court of Justice, Central East Region

PD-7c — *CENTRAL EAST REGION LONG MOTIONS PILOT — TIPS FOR FILING MATERIALS IN CIVIL CASES*

If you have scheduled a long motion (1 hour or more) in any of the following Superior Court of Justice locations, you will need to file your materials in paper ***and on a USB stick***: Barrie, Bracebridge, Cobourg, Lindsay, Newmarket, Oshawa or Peterborough.

The pilot includes criminal, family and civil long motions, but excludes child protection cases, criminal third party records applications, and criminal long motions heard during trial (only stand-alone criminal long motions are included, such as *Charter* and other pre-trial applications).

Tip #1 — Save each document for your long motion in PDF format and in Microsoft Word format.

Tip #2 — Label each document clearly when saving it on the USB stick. This will help court staff and the judge. See the Practice Advisory for a full list of documents at: http://www.ontariocourts.ca/scj/practice/practice-directions/central-east/.

Plaintiffs — If your case is titled *Brown v. Brown*, and the court file number is CV-17-12345-0000, save your documents with the following names:

1. **Motion record** is saved as "**MPL *Brown v. Brown*, CV-17-12345-0000"**

2. Proof of service (e.g. affidavit of service) is saved as "**AFSPL** *Brown v. Brown*, CV-17-12345-0000"

3. **Affidavits** (other than proof of service) is saved as "**AFPL** *Brown v. Brown*, CV-17-12345-0000"

4. **Book of authorities** (e.g. case law) is saved as "**BAPL** *Brown v. Brown*, CV-17-12345-0000"

5. **Factum** is saved as "**FPL** *Brown v. Brown*, CV-17-12345-0000"

6. **Prior court orders and judge's endorsements** in the case related to the motion are saved as "**COE** *Brown v. Brown*, CV-17-12345-0000"

Defendants — If your case is titled *Brown v. Brown*, and the court file number is CV-17-12345-0000, name your documents as follows:

1. **Motion record** is saved as "**MDE *Brown v. Brown*, CV-17-12345-0000"**

2. Proof of service (e.g. affidavit of service) is saved as "**AFSDE** *Brown v. Brown*, CV-17-12345-0000"

3. **Affidavits** (other than affidavit of service) is saved as "**AFDE** *Brown v. Brown*, CV-17-12345-0000"

4. **Book of authorities** (e.g. case law) is saved as "**BADE** *Brown v. Brown*, CV-17-12345-0000"

5. **Factum** is saved as "**FDE** *Brown v. Brown*, CV-17-12345-0000"

6. **Prior court orders and judge's endorsements** in the case related to the motion are saved as "**COE** *Brown v. Brown*, CV-17-12345-0000"

Tip#3 — Hand your USB stick in at the court office when filing your paper documents. Staff will upload your documents and give your USB stick back to you.

PD-7d — *CENTRAL EAST REGION LONG MOTIONS PILOT — TIPS FOR FILING MATERIALS IN CRIMINAL CASES*

If you have scheduled a long motion (1 hour or more) in any of the following Superior Court of Justice locations, you will need to file your materials in paper ***and on a USB stick***: Barrie, Bracebridge, Cobourg, Lindsay, Newmarket, Oshawa or Peterborough.

The pilot includes criminal, family and civil long motions, but excludes child protection cases, criminal third party records applications, and criminal long motions heard during trial (only stand-alone criminal long motions are included, such as 11b and other pre-trial applications).

Tip #1 — Save each document for your long motion in PDF format and in Microsoft Word format.

Tip #2 — Label each document clearly when saving it on the USB stick. This will help court staff and the judge. See the Practice Advisory for a full list of documents at: http://www.ontariocourts.ca/scj/practice/practice-directions/central-east/.

Applicants — If your case is titled *R. v. Brown*, and the court file number is CR-17-87654321-0000, save your documents with the following names:

1. **Application record** is saved as "**MAP *R. v. Brown*, CR-17-87654321-0000**"

2. **Proof of service** (e.g. affidavit of service) is saved as "**AFSAP** *R. v. Brown*, CR-17-87654321-0000"

3. **Affidavits** (other than proof of service) is saved as "**AFAP** *R. v. Brown*, CR-17-87654321-0000"

4. **Book of authorities** (e.g. case law) is saved as "**BAAP** *R. v. Brown*, CR-17-87654321-0000"

5. **Factum** is saved as "**FAP** *R. v. Brown*, CR-17-87654321-0000"

6. **Prior court orders and judge's endorsements** in the case related to the motion are saved as "**COE** *R v. Brown*, CR-17-87654321-0000"

Respondents — If your case is titled *R. v. Brown*, and the court file number is CR-17-87654321-0000, name your documents as follows:

1. **Respondents record** is saved as "**MRP *R. v. Brown*, CR-17-87654321-0000**"

2. **Proof of service** (e.g. affidavit of service) is saved as "**AFSRP** *R. v. Brown*, CR-17-87654321-0000"

3. **Affidavits** (other than affidavit of service) is saved as "**AFRP** *R. v. Brown*, CR-17-87654321-0000"

4. **Book of authorities** (e.g. case law) is saved as "**BARP** *R. v. Brown*, CR-17-87654321-0000"

5. **Factum** is saved as "**FRP** *R. v. Brown*, CR-17-87654321-0000"

6. **Prior court orders and judge's endorsements** in the case related to the motion are saved as "**COE** *R. v. Brown*, CR-17-87654321-0000"

Tip#3 — Hand your USB stick in at the court office when filing your paper documents. Staff will upload your documents and give your USB stick back to you.

PD-7e — *CENTRAL EAST REGION LONG MOTIONS PILOT — TIPS FOR FILING MATERIALS IN FAMILY CASES*

If you have scheduled a long motion (1 hour or more) in any of the following Superior Court of Justice locations, you will need to file your materials in paper ***and on a USB stick***: Barrie, Bracebridge, Cobourg, Lindsay, Newmarket, Oshawa or Peterborough.

The pilot includes criminal, family and civil long motions, but excludes child protection cases, criminal third party records applications, and criminal long motions heard during trial (only stand-alone criminal long motions are included, such as *Charter* and other pre-trial applications).

Tip #1 — Save each document for your long motion in PDF format and in Microsoft Word format.

Tip #2 — Label each document clearly when saving it on the USB stick. This will help court staff and the judge. See the Practice Advisory for a full list of documents at: http://www.ontariocourts.ca/scj/practice/practice-directions/central-east/.

Applicants — If your case is titled *White v. White*, and the court file number is FC-17-12345678-0000, save your documents with the following names:

1. **Motion record** is saved as "**MAP *White v. White*, FC-17-12345678-0000"**

2. Proof of service (e.g. affidavit of service) is saved as "**AFSAP** *White v. White*, FC-17-12345678-0000"

3. **Affidavits** (other than proof of service) is saved as "**AFAP** *White v. White*, FC-17-12345678-0000"

4. **Book of authorities** (e.g. case law) is saved as "**BAAP** *White v. White*, FC-17-12345678-0000"

5. **Factum** is saved as "**FAP** *White v. White*, FC-17-12345678-0000"

6. **Prior court orders and judge's endorsements** in the case related to the motion are saved as "**COE** *White v. White*, FC-17-12345678-0000"

Respondents — If your case is titled *White v. White*, and the court file number is FC-17-12345678-0000, name your documents as follows:

1. **Motion record** is saved as "**MRP *White v. White*, FC-17-12345678-0000"**

2. Proof of service (e.g. affidavit of service) is saved as "**AFSRP** *White v. White*, FC-17-12345678-0000"

3. **Affidavits** (other than affidavit of service) is saved as "**AFRP** *White v. White*, FC-17-12345678-0000"

4. **Book of authorities** (e.g. case law) is saved as "**BARP** *White v. White*, FC-17-12345678-0000"

5. **Factum** is saved as "**FRP** *White v. White*, FC-17-12345678-0000"

6. **Prior court orders and judge's endorsements** in the case related to the motion are saved as "**COE** *White v. White*, FC-17-12345678-0000"

Tip#3 — Hand your USB stick in at the court office when filing your paper documents. Staff will upload your documents and give your USB stick back to you.

PD-8 — *CONSOLIDATED PRACTICE DIRECTION FOR THE CENTRAL SOUTH REGION*

Notice of Amendment: Part III H [paras. 110–115] was revoked on May 1, 2017.

Effective June 1, 2016

This Practice Direction applies to proceedings in the Superior Court of Justice, Central South Region, effective June 1, 2016. It replaces the previous Consolidated Practice Direction for the Central South Region that was effective on July 1, 2014.

Counsel and parties are advised to refer to the relevant Parts of the Consolidated Provincial Practice Direction as well as the Consolidated Practice Direction for Divisional Court Proceedings which are available on the Superior Court of Justice website at: www.ontariocourts.ca/scj.

Part I: — General

A. — Court Contact Information

1. Contact information for each court location in the Central South Region is available in the Central South Region's Regional Court Calendar, available on the Superior Court of Justice website.

B. — Schedule

2. The schedule for proceedings in each of the eight court sites in the Central South Region is available in the Central South Region's Regional Court Calendar.

C. — Gowning

3. Counsel are not required to gown for the following court attendances:

a. Trial scheduling court (formerly known as assignment court, "speak to" court or "purge court") in family, criminal or civil proceedings.

b. Case conferences, settlement conferences, trial scheduling conferences or trial management conferences in family proceedings.

c. Pre-trial conferences in criminal proceedings.

d. Pre-trial conferences in civil proceedings.

e. Small Claims Court proceedings.

4. Counsel must be gowned for all other proceedings.

D. — Release of Digital Court Recordings

5. Members of the public, counsel, litigants, accused or the media may obtain copies of digital court recordings of matters heard in open court, in accordance with the requirements of section C of part IV of the Court's Provincial Practice Direction.

E. — Electronic Devices in the Courtroom

6. The Superior Court of Justice's protocol relating to the use of electronic devices in the courtroom is set out in section D of part IV of the Court's Provincial Practice Direction.

Part II: — Family Proceedings

7. A reference in this part to a "rule" or the "rules" is a reference to the Family Law Rules.

A. — Mandatory Information Program (MIP)

8. Attendance at the Mandatory Information Program (MIP) is required for all matters except the matters exempted under rule 8.1(2). MIP dates are provided by court staff at the time the documents starting the legal proceeding are issued.

9. Any request to change the date of a MIP should be made directly to the courthouse's Information Referral Coordinator whose contact information is on the Ministry of the Attorney General's website under Find an Ontario Court.

B. — Conferences

Rules Applicable to all Conferences

10. All case conferences, settlement conferences, trial scheduling conferences and trial management conferences, are held before a Superior Court judge, subject to paragraph 77 (Motions to Change at locations with Dispute Resolution Officers).

11. All parties required to attend a MIP are expected to have done so and filed their certificate prior to their first case conference.

12. Briefs are required for all conferences, in accordance with rules 3 and 17.

13. Fully completed Form 14C Confirmations must be filed for all conferences, in accordance with rules 3 and 17 of the rules. The confirmation form must be filed with the court office or faxed to the trial coordinator no later than 2:00 p.m. two business days prior to the conference. If the conference has not been confirmed by at least one party, judicial permission will be required for the conference to proceed on the scheduled date. Failure to comply with the rules may also result in costs sanctions and/or postponement of the conference date.

14. Counsel and parties are expected to attend all conferences in person.

15. Counsel or a party who wishes to request to attend a conference by telephone conference call or by video under rule 17(16), must contact the trial coordinator at least 5 business days before the scheduled conference, who will seek permission from the presiding judge. Counsel or the party must make all other parties aware of the request so that they can communicate any objection to the trial coordinator. The party requesting the telephone conference call or video shall be responsible for any costs associated with it.

16. Any request for an adjournment of a conference shall initially be made through the trial coordinator. Absent an order or direction from a judge, or a consent signed by counsel or the parties and filed with the trial coordinator at least three business days before the date of the conference, counsel and the parties will be required to

attend at the scheduled time to request the adjournment. This procedure is permitted for one adjournment and thereafter the parties or their counsel must attend before the court, unless a judge directs otherwise.

Costs for Conferences

17. Rule 24 requires the presiding judge at every court event to fix costs. If a party is seeking costs for preparation for and attendance at a conference, those submissions and a costs outline should be provided to the presiding judge during the conference so that the amount of the costs can be fixed by the presiding judge who will have knowledge of the issues, the time spent, the degree of preparation required and the conduct of the parties which may entitle them or disentitle them to an order for costs. If a costs outline is not provided to the presiding judge, the judge may decline to make any costs award.

Case Conferences

18. Case conference dates may be obtained directly from the trial coordinator, subject to the practice in Family Court locations. A date will not be provided until at least one party serves and files a case conference brief. Each party must file its Form 17A: Case Conference Brief and Form 13A: Certificate of Financial Disclosure in advance of the case conference as set out in rules 13 and 17(13 and 13.1). Each party must also complete the financial disclosure required under rule 13.

19. If no answer or response to a Motion to Change is filed as required by the rules, no case conference is required and a date for an uncontested hearing may be obtained from the trial coordinator.

Settlement Conferences

20. Settlement conference dates will be set at the case conference or may be obtained directly from the trial coordinator.

21. A party attending a settlement conference must prepare a Form 17C Settlement Conference Brief with all necessary attachments and file it as required by rule 17(13.1).

22. Each party must complete their respective portion of the Trial Scheduling Endorsement Form and give it to the presiding judge at the outset of the settlement conference. Part 3 of the form will be completed by the judge after the issues have been reviewed with the parties.

23. The judge at the settlement conference may, in his or her discretion, convert the settlement conference into a trial management conference (as permitted by rule 17(7)) and have Part 3 of the Trial Scheduling Endorsement Form fully completed at that time.

24. The Trial Scheduling Endorsement Form must be fully completed before a trial date will be assigned.

25. Whenever possible, the trial date will be fixed at the conclusion of the settlement conference. A trial management conference date will be assigned at the same time, unless the presiding judge in his/her discretion feels that it will not be needed. Those will be rare and exceptional cases.

26. If there are matters that need to be completed by the parties before the case is ready for trial, the judge will fix a schedule to be followed by the parties to ensure that the case is trial ready. If the schedule is not adhered to by a party, this may be addressed by serving and filing a notice of motion to enforce the schedule, returnable at a regular motions court of the particular court location.

Trial Management Conferences

27. A trial management conference should be held in all family proceedings that have not been resolved at or before the settlement conference, no more than two weeks before the trial wherever possible, subject to paragraph 23.

28. The purposes of a trial management conference include exploring the chances of settling the case, ensuring that the parties know what witnesses will testify and what other evidence will be presented at trial and ensuring the accuracy of the estimated time needed for trial.

29. In advance of the trial management conference, the following documents must be filed by the deadlines set out in rule 17(13.1):

a. The completed Trial Scheduling Endorsement Form as endorsed by the court must be filed by either the Applicant or the party that requested the conference;

b. Each party must file an offer to settle all outstanding issues; and,

c. Each party must file an outline of their opening statement for trial.

These documents are to be filed in lieu of the requirement to file a Trial Management Conference Brief: Form 17E under rule 17(13).

30. The final Trial Scheduling Endorsement Form shall be filed with or added to the Trial Record. The parties' offers to settle must not be filed with the Trial Record.

C. — Motions

Form 14B Motions

31. Rules 14(4.2) and (10) of the rules provide that motions are permissible before a case conference if there is a situation of urgency or hardship, or if the request for relief is limited to "procedural, uncomplicated or unopposed matters". In most cases, relief should be requested using Form 14B: Motion.

32. In exceptional circumstances of urgency or hardship, permission to bring a motion before a case conference pursuant to rule (14(4.2)) can be sought when the motion is brought. A comprehensive affidavit explaining the reasons for the order sought must be filed with the motion.

33. In order to assist counsel and parties in making the best use of available conference time, the Superior Court will encourage greater use of Form 14B motions whenever it will make the case conference process more effective. Form 14B motions allow parties to address certain threshold issues prior to the case conference and are designed to streamline conferencing in family law proceedings. Such motions are limited to procedural, uncomplicated or unopposed matters that will promote the concept of fewer, but more meaningful case conferences. In this respect, Form 14B motions will be guided by the paragraphs 34 - 35.

34. Before a case conference is held, lawyers and self-represented litigants are strongly encouraged to use Form 14B to obtain any orders that are needed to make the case conference productive. Examples of appropriate orders include:

a. orders of either a procedural or substantive nature that are on consent, or unopposed;

b. a request for the appointment of the Office of the Children's Lawyer;

c. orders to add a party or obtain discovery from a third party;

d. orders for production of documents, permission for questioning or other issues pertaining to discovery;

e. enforcement of an order to provide information, produce a document or serve and file a financial statement or other document;

f. any other procedural order or direction needed to promote a meaningful case conference.

35. Motions that are without notice, on consent or unopposed will be determined by a judge in chambers, unless the court directs otherwise.

Short Motions

36. A short motion is a motion that will be argued by the parties in less than one hour including reply argument (but excluding the time required for the judge to consider the matter and render a decision).

37. Short motions shall be made returnable to a regularly scheduled motions day. These dates are listed in the Central South Region's Regional Court Calendar, available on the Superior Court of Justice website.

Factums and Other Materials

38. A factum or summary of argument is not required on a short motion, although such documents are encouraged because they provide significant assistance to the presiding judge. A factum or summary of argument shall not exceed 20 double spaced typed pages, unless leave is granted.

39. Parties are encouraged to submit draft orders with their motion materials.

40. Where a factum is being filed, the court also strongly encourages parties to deliver an electronic copy of the factum, in Word Format, at least two business days before the hearing of the motion, which can be sent to the email address for the court location where the motion will be argued:

Hamilton Family Court: Hamilton.family.superior.court@ontario.ca

Kitchener: Kitchener.superior.court@ontario.ca

Brantford: Brantford.superior.court@ontario.ca

St. Catharines: StCatharines.superior.court@ontario.ca

Simcoe: Simcoe.superior.court@ontario.ca

Welland: Welland.superior.court@ontario.ca

Cayuga: Cayuga.superior.court@ontario.ca

The covering email should identify the style of cause, the court file number and the date scheduled for the argument of the motion.

Costs

41. If counsel or a party is seeking costs for appearing on a motion, they must attend with a costs outline to be given to the presiding judge. The costs outline should specify the number of hours of work which was necessary to prepare for the motion, the nature of the work, the lawyer/clerk or other person who did the work, the number of years a lawyer has been at the bar and an itemized list of disbursements incurred with supporting invoices, if available. If the outline is not available to be given to the presiding judge, the judge may decline to make any costs award.

Adjournments of Short Motions

42. If the trial coordinator receives written confirmation that the parties have agreed to a consent adjournment not later than 2:00 p.m. two business days before the motion is returnable, the adjournment will be granted, subject to the discretion of the presiding judge and provided that the adjournment has only been requested once. The written consent must specify the date to which the matter is to be adjourned, unless the motion has been settled. If these requirements have been met, counsel and parties are not required to attend before the presiding judge at the motion date.

43. No confirmations will be accepted after 2:00 p.m. two business days before the motion is returnable.

44. If counsel and/or a self-represented party wish(es) to adjourn a matter and it is past the filing deadline for the confirmation form, they should email or fax the trial coordinator as soon as possible to advise the court of the request. If the request is opposed this should also be noted. This should be done so that the presiding judge need not read the file in preparation for the motion. However, the parties or their counsel must still attend court in these circumstances.

Long Motions

45. A long motion is a motion that is expected to require more than one hour of oral argument, including reply argument (but excluding the time required for the presiding judge to consider the matter and render his/her decision).

46. A date for a long motion must be obtained through the trial coordinator. These motions are generally set to be argued during a specified week rather than a specific date but they are scheduled on a fixed date at certain locations in the Central South Region. The trial coordinator at the specific court site should be contacted to determine the local practice.

47. The notice of motion for a long motion must be served and filed and made returnable to a regularly scheduled weekly motions list in accordance with the rules. The notice of motion must indicate whether:

a. the long motion is being scheduled to a day or week provided by the trial coordinator on consent of all parties, in which case the parties do not need to attend the regular motion date; or

b. the parties have been unable to agree on a date for the motion, in which case the parties must attend the regular motion date so that a hearing date for the long motion can be set; in these circumstances, the appearance in regular motions court must be confirmed in writing in accordance with the rules.

48. Once the date has been set for the hearing of the motion:

a. if the long motion is to be called for argument during a given week, a confirmation for the Long Motion (Form 14C) must be filed with the trial coordinator no later than 2:00 p.m. on the Thursday prior to the chosen week confirming that the motion will proceed, indicating how long the matter will be argued in total and what material is to be read by the judge hearing the long motion.

b. if the motion has been scheduled on a fixed date, a confirmation for argument of the Long Motion (Form 14C) must be filed with the trial coordinator no later than 2:00 p.m. two business days prior to the scheduled date confirming that the motion will proceed, indicating how long the matter will be argued in total and what material is to be read by the judge hearing the long motion.

Adjournments of Long Motions

49. Adjournments of long motions will not be readily granted. Any request for an adjournment of a long motion must be immediately communicated to the office of the trial coordinator. Unless otherwise directed by a judge, a request for an adjournment of a long motion must be made in court.

Long Motions Not Reached

50. If a long motion is not reached on the scheduled date or during the scheduled week, counsel and the parties are to arrange a new date with the trial coordinator. If a date cannot be agreed upon, the matter will be placed before a judge by the trial coordinator and the parties (or their counsel) will be required to attend.

51. The trial coordinator must be immediately advised in writing of settlement of any or all of the issues prior to the hearing date.

Factums and Other Materials

52. Factums are required for all long motions. The times for service and filing of factums shall be in accordance with the times for service and filing of other motion materials under the rules.

53. If case law will be relied on by a party (other than cases referred to in the Court's list of Often Cited Family Cases), a Book of Authorities should be served and filed with the factum or summary of argument with appropriate excerpts from each case highlighted or side barred.

54. A factum shall not exceed 20 double spaced typed pages, unless leave is granted. The parties are encouraged to submit draft orders with their motion materials.

55. In addition, the court strongly encourages parties to deliver an electronic copy of a factum, in Word format, at least two business days before the hearing of the motion, which can be sent to the email address for the location where the motion will be argued:

Hamilton Family Court: Hamilton.family.superior.court@ontario.ca

Kitchener: Kitchener.superior.court@ontario.ca

Brantford: Brantford.superior.court@ontario.ca

St. Catharines: StCatharines.superior.court@ontario.ca

Simcoe: Simcoe.superior.court@ontario.ca

Welland: Welland.superior.court@ontario.ca

Cayuga: Cayuga.superior.court@ontario.ca

The covering email should identify the style of cause, the court file number and the date scheduled for the argument of the motion.

56. A factum shall include the following:

a. a statement of the facts which are relevant to the motion or application;

b. the legal questions to be considered by the court;

c. the law and prior case law relating to the issues;

d. the argument of the party relating to each legal question;

e. the order which is sought from the court.

D. — Trials

Short Trials

57. A short trial is a trial that will take 15 court days or less.

Court Schedule

58. Each court location in the region holds trial sittings at different times throughout the calendar year. The trial sittings are listed in the Central South Region's Regional Court Calendar.

Trial Scheduling Court

59. Attendance at trial scheduling court will only be required by the parties where a trial date has not already been set either at the settlement conference or arranged through the trial coordinator as set out below.

60. If a trial date has not been set at the settlement conference, it should be arranged with the trial coordinator.

61. If the parties consent to a trial date or trial sittings, the consent must be filed with the trial coordinator at least three business days before that trial scheduling court date and if done, the parties do not need to attend.

62. If the parties are unable to agree on a trial date, they may speak to the matter at trial scheduling court. As a general rule, trial dates will not be arranged at the trial scheduling court unless counsel and self-represented parties have contacted the trial coordinator and tried to arrange dates in advance.

63. Subject to the practice in Family Court sites, trial scheduling courts in family proceedings are held each month at each court site in the Central South Region; these dates are listed in the Central South Region's Regional Court Calendar.

64. If there is an issue that must be addressed by the presiding judge at trial scheduling court, counsel and self-represented parties are to attend in person. In certain cases, with prior direction from a judge, counsel and/or self-represented parties may attend by telephone conference call. That conference call will take place in the courtroom on the record. A telephone conference call must be arranged through the trial coordinator at least three business days before the date of the trial scheduling court. The party requesting the telephone conference call shall be responsible for the costs associated with it.

Trial Lists

65. Cases that have been placed on the trial list will be deemed ready to proceed.

66. Counsel and parties have a duty to inform the trial coordinator of any pertinent information that may affect the trial (e.g. a case has settled or a change has occurred that will affect the status of the trial).

Trial Adjournment Requests

67. Any request for an adjournment of the trial must be communicated to the trial coordinator immediately. A motion to adjourn shall be brought on a regular weekly motion list. An adjournment can only be granted by order of a judge, even if all parties consent to the adjournment.

Long Trial Sittings

68. All trials which are expected to last longer than 15 days are deemed to be long trials.

69. There are two long trial sittings each year in the Central South Region, usually in March (commencing just after the March School Breaks) and in October. These dates are listed in the Central South Region's Regional Court Calendar.

70. Any matter placed on the long trial list is given a fixed date to commence and a judge will be made available to hear the matter in its entirety. Once a matter is placed on the long trial sittings list and a trial date is fixed, adjournments are rarely granted without significant costs ramifications.

71. Counsel and parties have a duty to inform the trial coordinator of any pertinent information that may affect the trial (e.g. a case has settled or a change has occurred that will affect the status of the trial).

72. All family cases requiring more than 15 days for trial must be referred to the Office of the Regional Senior Justice for possible assignment to a Long Trial. Where a judge determines that a matter should be referred to the long trial list, the judge will endorse the Trial Record and the Trial Scheduling Endorsement Form accordingly and forward the Form to the Office of the Regional Senior Justice.

73. The Office of the Regional Senior Justice will arrange a conference call with all parties or their counsel to assign the case to a particular long trial sittings, may order a schedule to be followed to ensure that the case is ready to proceed on the sittings to which it has been assigned and schedule a trial management conference to be held before the trial date.

74. All motions for an adjournment of a trial on the long trial list, including a consent adjournment, must be made returnable before the Regional Senior Judge or his/her designate.

E. — Family Court Sites

75. Catharines and Hamilton are Family Court sites; they are the only two Superior Court of Justice locations in the Central South Region where hearings under the *Children and Family Services Act* (child protection cases), Family Responsibility Office cases and fast track cases (under rule 39) are heard.

76. Dates for child protection, Family Responsibility Office and first appearance courts (for fast track cases) are available in the Central South Region's Regional Court Calendar or from the trial coordinator.

77. Dispute Resolution Officer programs are available in St. Catharines and Hamilton. In those locations, the first case conference on a Motion to Change a final order or agreement shall be scheduled before a Dispute Resolution Officer (DRO) in accordance with Part I of the Consolidated Provincial Practice Direction, unless the court orders otherwise.

Part III: — Criminal Proceedings

78. Any change regarding the status of a criminal matter must be brought to the immediate attention of the trial coordinator.

79. A reference in this part to a "rule" or "rules" is a reference to the Criminal Proceeding Rules for the Superior Court of Justice.

A. — Committal to Superior Court of Justice

80. Upon committal in the Ontario Court of Justice, the accused will be remanded to the next trial scheduling court (formerly assignment court) in the Superior Court of Justice that is at least three days from the date of the committal.

81. The indictment committing the accused to stand trial shall be filed in the Superior Court of Justice returnable on a fixed date at least three days before the accused's first appearance in the trial scheduling court.

B. — Trial Scheduling Court (formerly Assignment Court)

82. Criminal trial scheduling courts are held at each court site in the Central South Region one day per calendar month. These schedules can be found in the Central South Region's Regional Court Calendar, available on the Superior Court of Justice website.

Designations of Counsel

83. Counsel are encouraged to file "designations of counsel" in the Superior Court of Justice at the earliest opportunity to save clients the time and expense of attending court to address scheduling matters at trial scheduling court.

84. A designation filed in the Ontario Court of Justice does not apply in the Superior Court of Justice.

85. An original designation of counsel for the Superior Court of Justice should be filed in advance of trial scheduling court if counsel intends to appear pursuant to the Designation.

Appearance by Telephone Conference Call

86. If there is an issue that must be addressed by the presiding judge at trial scheduling court, counsel may attend in person or, subject to the discretion of the presiding judge, may attend by telephone conference call or any technological means satisfactory to the court that permits the court and all counsel to communicate simultaneously in the courtroom and will be "on the record".

87. A telephone conference call must be arranged through the office of the trial coordinator at least three business days before the date of the appearance in the trial scheduling court. Counsel attending by telephone conference call must give his/her office and cellphone numbers to the trial coordinator and must indicate the number at which he/she will be available for the conference call.

88. Telephone conference calls can be arranged between the court and counsel even when the accused is in custody and is attending by video remand, provided that the judge is satisfied that the conditions of s. 848 of the *Criminal Code* are satisfied.

Video Remands

89. In Kitchener and Hamilton, accused persons who are in custody may elect to appear at trial scheduling court by video remand, unless otherwise directed by a judge.

90. In St. Catharines, an accused who is held at the Niagara Detention Centre may attend by video remand, unless otherwise directed by a judge.

91. Where the accused has not previously appeared before the Superior Court of Justice by video on the indictment before the court, defence counsel or the accused must notify the custodian of the institution where the accused is held that he/she wishes to attend trial scheduling court by video instead of "in person". Thereafter, the accused can simply be adjourned to his or her next appearance to appear by video remand if requested by the accused, unless otherwise directed by a judge.

C. — Pre-Trial Conferences in Criminal Cases

92. A pre-trial conference date and time can be arranged by counsel with the trial coordinator and held without a judge's order and prior to the accused's first appearance in trial scheduling court.

93. Where a pre-trial conference has not been scheduled or held prior to the accused's appearance in trial scheduling court, the parties shall schedule a pre-trial conference with the trial coordinator on a date that is at least three business days before the accused's appearance in trial scheduling court; otherwise, the matter will be adjourned to the next trial scheduling court, subject to the discretion of the presiding judge.

94. A pre-trial conference in a criminal matter must be held within 60 days of the order to stand trial in the Superior Court of Justice.

95. The purpose of the pre-trial conference is to discuss the issues in the case, possible resolution of some or all of the issues, the scheduling of pre-trial motions, the

scheduling of the trial and any other matter that the pre-trial conference judge feels may promote a fair and expeditious hearing of the charges contained on the indictment.

96. Where the accused is represented by counsel, the pre-trial conference will be held before a judge of the court, in the presence of counsel and not the accused, unless the judge orders the accused to be present, in accordance with rule 28.05(8).

97. Where an accused person is self-represented, the pre-trial conference will be held in a court room closed to the public pursuant to rule 28.05(2). The conference shall be recorded, however, the recording and any transcript of the pre-trial conference will not be made available to anyone without notice to all parties and the prior written approval of the presiding judge or another judge of the court, in accordance with rules 28.05(3) and (4). Anything said in the pre-trial cannot be used for or against an accused during his/her trial.

98. Pre-trial conference reports are to be served and filed with the trial coordinator pursuant to rules 28.04(7) and (8).

99. Crown counsel and counsel of record for each accused must attend the pre-trial conference fully briefed and with specific authority to act on the matter.

100. The judge who presides at the pre-trial conference will not be the trial judge unless the parties consent.

D. — Scheduling Trial Dates for Criminal Cases

101. A trial date will not be scheduled until a pre-trial conference has taken place.

102. Trial dates must be canvassed with the trial coordinator before they can be scheduled in trial scheduling court. Counsel wishing to set a trial date must canvass trial dates with the trial coordinator at least three business days prior to trial scheduling court; otherwise the matter will be adjourned to the next trial scheduling court date to achieve compliance with this rule.

103. If the accused intends to bring a pre-trial application under s. 11(b) of the *Charter* (unreasonable delay in time to trial), that should be indicated to the trial coordinator and to the trial scheduling court so that the earliest possible trial dates can be identified and offered by the court.

E. — Adjournment of Trial or Pre-Trial Applications

104. In the event that the Crown or a defendant should need to seek an adjournment of a trial date or pre-trial application date after the date has been fixed, the trial coordinator and the opposing counsel/party shall immediately be given written notice of the request so that a date can be set for the adjournment application to be heard.

105. A formal notice of application and supporting affidavit for an adjournment must be served and filed in accordance with rules 26.03 and 26.04, unless otherwise directed by a judge.

106. The parties shall attend before the presiding judge on the date and at the time obtained from the trial coordinator. If an accused is in custody, the applicant shall take the appropriate steps to have the accused transported from the custodial institution where he/she is being held to the court house for the attendance before the presiding judge or, alternatively, to attend by video if the technology is available and appropriate and if the accused consents to an appearance by video.

F. — Abandonment of Pre-Trial Applications

107. If time has been scheduled for a pre-trial application and the applicant determines that the application will not be necessary, the applicant must immediately serve and file a Notice of Abandonment (Form 9 prescribed under the rules) and also give a copy to the trial coordinator.

G. — Non Compliance with Court Ordered Deadlines

108. In the event that a party does not comply with an order or rule of the court stipulating the date by which a party bringing a pre-trial application shall serve and file its materials and/or an order or rule stipulating the date by which a party responding to a pre-trial application must serve and file its materials, the trial coordinator is to be immediately notified.

109. If any party feels that the matter needs to be addressed in open court, the party must inform the trial coordinator, who will advise the parties when the matter is to be spoken to in open court, and the parties shall attend before the presiding judge on the date and at the time assigned. The accused shall also attend before the court at the assigned date and time. If an accused is in custody, the Crown shall take the appropriate steps to have the accused transported from the custodial institution where he/she is being held to the court house for the attendance before the presiding judge.

H. — Bail Variations pursuant to section 515.1 of the Criminal Code

This section (paragraphs 110 to 115) has been revoked and replaced by part V of the Provincial Practice Direction Regarding Criminal Proceedings.

I. — Other Bail Applications

116. Unless the application is under s. 522 or 518(2) of the *Criminal Code*, if an application for bail has never been brought by the accused at any time, it must be brought in the Ontario Court of Justice, even if the accused has been committed for trial in the Superior Court of Justice.

J. — Summary Conviction Appeals

117. Summary Conviction Appeals shall be placed on a trial scheduling court list to be spoken to, in accordance with the following timelines.

a. Defence appeals involving appellants who are out of custody shall be placed on a trial scheduling court list no more than three months from the date of the filing of Notice of Appeal. When the appeal is perfected, the court will assign a hearing date and time

b. Crown appeals and defence appeals involving appellants who are in custody on the matter from which the appeal is taken shall be placed on a trial scheduling court list which is no longer than 30 days from the date of filing the appeal.

118. In certain cases, where circumstances require it, counsel or a party may seek leave to argue an appeal without transcripts but by using alternative means, including the digital recording of the event from which the appeal is being brought.

K. — 90 Day Detention Reviews

119. Upon receipt of a Notice of Application for a 90 Day Detention Review pursuant to section 525(1) of the *Criminal Code*, the matter will be placed on the trial scheduling court list, in accordance with the procedures set out in the section.

120. If the accused is not represented by counsel,

a. The 90-Day Detention Review will be heard at the next trial scheduling court or any earlier date that is agreeable to the Crown and the accused.

b. Notice of this hearing date will be sent to the institution in which the accused is detained and the Crown Attorney's office by the trial coordinator.

c. Where necessary, the Crown Attorney's office will obtain an Order to Procure Attendance of a Prisoner to have the accused brought to the courthouse for the hearing.

121. If the accused is represented by counsel,

a. Defence counsel will be contacted by the trial coordinator and asked whether he/she requests a hearing date be set or whether there will be a waiver of the hearing.

b. If counsel waives the hearing, he/she shall immediately provide the trial coordinator with a written waiver of the hearing signed by the accused or counsel, which the trial coordinator will forward to the institution in which the accused is detained in custody and the Crown Attorney's office.

c. If counsel indicates that a hearing date is to be set,

i. The matter will be placed on the next trial scheduling court date list, so that a hearing date will be set by a judge.

ii. The accused will attend the trial scheduling court either in person or by video remand where the appropriate technology is available and the accused consents.

iii. After the hearing date is set, the trial coordinator will send a copy of the Notice of the Hearing Date to the institution in which the accused is detained.

iv. If the date is set in the absence of the accused, where necessary, the Crown Attorney's office will obtain a judge's order to have the accused brought to the courthouse for the trial scheduling court and/or for the hearing.

122. Counsel and the accused shall attend at the trial scheduling court unless a waiver signed by the accused has been received by the trial coordinator at least three days before trial scheduling court. Counsel may attend by telephone conference call in accordance with paragraphs 86–88.

Part IV: — Civil Proceedings

123. A reference in this part to a "rule" or the "rules" is a reference to the Rules of Civil Procedure.

A. — Motions and Applications

124. In the Central South Region, motions and applications in civil proceedings are classified as "long" or "short" for scheduling purposes.

Short Motions and Applications

125. A "short" motion or application is one that will be argued by the parties in less than one hour including reply argument (but excluding the time required for the judge to consider the matter and render a decision).

126. Short motions and applications are heard at the regular motions court during the weeks that the Court is scheduled to sit. The motion or application shall be made returnable to a regularly scheduled motions day. These dates are listed in the Central South Region's Regional Court Calendar on the Superior Court of Justice's website.

Long Motions and Applications

127. A "long" motion or application is one which is expected to require more than one hour for argument, including reply argument (but excluding the time required by the judge to consider the matter and render a decision).

128. A date for a long motion or application must be obtained through the trial coordinator. These motions and applications are generally set to be argued during a specified week rather than a specific date, but they are scheduled on a fixed date at certain locations in the Region. The trial coordinator at the specific court site should be contacted to determine the local practice.

129. The notice of motion or notice of application must be served and filed and made initially returnable to a regularly scheduled motions day in accordance with the rules. This date is an interim date for the matter to be spoken to, until an actual date for the hearing can be obtained from the trial coordinator and confirmed with the opposing party(ies).

a. If the parties can agree to a date/week for the long motion or application to be argued, a confirmation in writing shall be filed with the trial coordinator at least three business days before the return of the originally scheduled motion (i.e., the regularly scheduled motions day). The written confirmation must indicate:

1. that the parties have agreed to the hearing date;

2. that the parties are ready to proceed on that date;

3. the time required for the hearing of the motion or application; and

4. whether oral evidence may be required.

Once the written confirmation is received, the motion record will be endorsed to adjourn the matter to the date or week scheduled for the hearing. In that case, counsel or the parties do not have to attend at the originally scheduled motions court.

b. If the parties cannot agree to a date/week for the long motion or application to be argued, all parties must attend the originally scheduled motions court so that a date for the hearing and timetable of events (e.g., dates for responding materials to be filed, productions to be complete, cross-examinations, delivery of factums) can be ordered by the presiding judge at motions court.

130. Where a motion or application is scheduled for a specified week, the trial coordinator will contact parties or their counsel to advise when the matter will be argued during that week. When the matter is called for argument, the matter is expected to proceed.

Timetable for Long Motions and Applications

131. Parties are expected to agree and adhere to a timetable of events prior to a hearing of a long motion or application (e.g., dates for responding materials to be filed, productions to be complete, cross-examinations, delivery of factums, etc.). If an agreed upon or court ordered timetable is not complied with after a date for a long motion or application has been assigned, a party shall bring a motion returnable at an earlier regularly scheduled motions date to have the matter spoken to by all parties.

Factums & Other Material for Motions and Applications

132. A factum is required on a long motion or application. A factum is not required on a short motion or application, although factums are strongly encouraged because they provide significant assistance to the presiding judge. In either case, a factum shall not exceed 20 double spaced typed pages, unless leave is granted.

133. A factum shall include the following:

a. a statement of the facts which are relevant to the motion or application.

b. the legal questions to be considered by the court.

c. the law and prior case law relating to the issues.

d. the argument of the party relating to each legal question.

e. the order which is sought from the court.

134. When a factum is prepared, it shall be served and filed pursuant to rules 37.10(6), (7) and (8).

135. In addition, the court strongly encourages parties to deliver an electronic copy of a factum in Word format, at least two business days before the argument of the motion. The factum should be sent to by email to the court location where the motion will be argued:

Hamilton Sopinka: Hamilton.superior.court@ontario.ca

Kitchener: Kitchener.superior.court@ontario.ca

Brantford: Brantford.superior.court@ontario.ca

St. Catharines: StCatharines.superior.court@ontario.ca

Simcoe: Simcoe.superior.court@ontario.ca

Welland: Welland.superior.court@ontario.ca

Cayuga: Cayuga.superior.court@ontario.ca

The covering email should identify the style of cause, the court file number and the date scheduled for the argument of the motion.

136. Parties are also encouraged to submit draft orders with their motion materials.

137. If case law will be relied on by a party, a book of authorities should be served and filed with the factum with appropriate excerpts from each case highlighted or side barred.

138. For long motions and applications,

a. Counsel are to consult with each other and where possible file a joint compendium, which shall contain the key material documents to be relied on during oral argument. Where counsel cannot agree on a joint compendium, each will file their own separate compendium, which shall contain the key material documents to be relied on during oral argument. This may include extracts of relevant transcripts, relevant documents, photographs, etc. The compendium should not exceed 30 pages in length.

b. Counsel are strongly encouraged to deliver an electronic version of their factum, the joint compendium (or separate compendium), and book of authorities on CD, DVD or USB key to the court. These materials may not be sent by email because of the size of the materials. The electronic documents must be submitted in either Word format (.doc or.docx) or text searchable PDF The CD, DVD or USB key should be accompanied by a covering letter which identifies the materials contained on the CD, DVD or USB key, as follows:

USB Key: The cover letter should include a list of the files contained on the USB key, along with the title of proceedings, Court File #, Counsel Name(s), where applicable, and Party Name. If possible, the key should be labelled with the short style of cause and the Court File #.

CD or DVD: The CD or DVD should be labelled with the title of proceedings, Court File #, Counsel Name(s), where applicable, and Party Name. Include a list of the files contained on the CD or DVD in the cover letter.

Confirmation of Motions and Applications

139. Motion and application confirmation forms advise the trial coordinator that the matter will be proceeding as scheduled. As required under rule 37.10.1 and 38.09.1, a Confirmation Form (Form 37B or 38B) must be delivered or faxed to the trial coordinator for all motions and applications no later than 2:00 p.m. three days before the hearing date. A copy must also be faxed or emailed to the other party(ies). Parties or their counsel must ensure all confirmation forms are fully completed. Failure to do so may result in an adjournment and/or cost sanctions.

140. Subject to the discretion of the presiding judge, only the documents and material filed by parties or their counsel on the motion and specifically referred to in the confirmation form will be before the court.

Adjournments of Short Motions or Applications

141. If the trial coordinator receives an updated confirmation form advising that the parties have agreed to a consent adjournment by 2:00 p.m. the day before the short motion or application is returnable, the adjournment will be granted, subject to the discretion of the presiding judge. The updated confirmation form must specify the date to which the matter is to be adjourned, unless the motion has been settled.

142. Parties or their counsel are not required to attend before the presiding judge if the appropriate information relating to the consent adjournment is provided by 2:00 p.m. the day before the short motion or application is returnable. No confirmations will be accepted after 2:00 p.m. on the day before the motion or application is returnable.

143. If a consent or contested adjournment is sought after 2:00 pm on the day before the return of the short motion or application, counsel and/or the self-represented party should email or fax the trial coordinator that the motion will be adjourned or a contested request for adjournment will take place. It is the responsibility of parties or their counsel to address the motion in court in these circumstances.

144. Parties will be permitted three consent adjournments on a short motion or application. If a further adjournment is sought, parties or their counsel are required to attend in person, unless otherwise ordered by a judge.

Adjournment of Long Motions or Applications

145. The trial coordinator must be immediately advised of any adjournment requests for a long motion or application, and of any settlements prior to the hearing date. In particular,

a. If a fixed date has been set for the long motion to be argued and a party wishes an adjournment, that request must be spoken to before a judge. The party must bring a motion on a regularly scheduled motions day to obtain the adjournment. If the adjournment is granted, the motion will be assigned to the Long Motions List.

b. If a long motion to be argued during a given week has been adjourned, and parties consent to a further adjournment, the long motion may be adjourned by filing a consent with the trial coordinator at least three business days before the scheduled week.

c. If a long motion to be argued during a given week has been adjourned, and parties do not consent to a further adjournment, the party seeking an adjournment shall bring a motion before a judge who is presiding at a regularly scheduled motions day. If the adjournment is granted, the motion will be assigned to the Long Motions List.

Ex Parte Motions

146. All *ex parte* motions in writing must be filed with the court office with payment of the applicable filing fee. They will be placed before a judge in chambers for review in the normal course. *Ex parte* motions may not be "filed" by delivering them to the trial coordinator for a judge to review, or by sending them by email or otherwise directly to a judge of the court.

Consent Orders in Civil Motions

147. Where parties or their counsel have agreed to a consent order in a civil motion scheduled for hearing, a fully executed consent, together with a draft order, must be sent to the trial coordinator with a motion Confirmation Form (Form 37B) by 2 p.m. three days before the scheduled hearing, as required by rule 37.10.1. The materials will be put before the presiding judge in chambers for review. If satisfied that the order should issue, the presiding judge will sign the draft order. The moving party or their counsel will be notified by the court that the order is ready to be picked up and entered. Unless otherwise advised by the court, parties or their counsel do not have to attend at court on the scheduled hearing date, which shall be vacated.

148. Where parties or their counsel have resolved a motion scheduled for hearing by way of a fully executed consent and draft order *after the motion confirmation form is filed*, the trial coordinator should be advised as soon as possible. The moving party or their counsel may attend at 9:30 a.m. on the morning scheduled for the hearing of

the motion, and leave the consent and draft order with the courtroom registrar. The consent and draft order will be put before the presiding judge in chambers for review. If the presiding judge is satisfied that the order should issue, he/she will sign the draft order. The registrar will return the signed order to counsel to be entered.

B. — Construction Liens

149. All construction lien actions will proceed in a summary fashion as envisioned by the *Construction Lien Act*, R.S.O. 1990, c. 30.

C. — Trials

150. A civil action is set down for trial by filing a trial record. The filing of a trial record with proof of service shall be accompanied by a Trial Data Form.

Court Schedule

151. Each court location in the region holds trial sittings at different times throughout the calendar year. Trial scheduling courts for short civil trials (15 days or less) are held monthly in each of the court locations in the Central South Region. Dates for trial scheduling court and trial sittings can be found in the Central South Region's Regional Court Calendar.

Short Trials

152. A short civil trial is a trial that is expected to be completed in 15 days or less.

Short Trials — Trial Scheduling Court

153. Upon filing of the trial record, the registrar shall provide the listing party or their counsel with the notice of trial scheduling court. Within five days of receipt, the listing party or their counsel must serve the notice of trial scheduling court on all other parties or their counsel.

154. In advance of trial scheduling court, the listing party is expected to obtain available trial dates from the trial coordinator and canvass those dates with the other parties. Parties are then expected to agree upon a date among the available trial dates.

155. Dates for short trials will then be assigned in one of the following methods:

a. Where the parties agree to a trial date, they may file a written consent with the trial coordinator requesting that the agreed upon trial date/week be assigned to the case. If the trial coordinator receives the consent by 2:00 p.m. three business days before the scheduled trial scheduling court the parties do not need to attend trial scheduling court. The trial record will be endorsed in chambers.

b. Where the parties do not agree to a trial date, they must attend to speak to the matter at trial scheduling court so that a trial date/week will be assigned.

156. Consent procedural orders, including consent adjournments of the trial scheduling court date, will not be granted at trial scheduling court.

157. All actions may be adjourned on consent to another trial scheduling court through the trial coordinator in advance of the trial scheduling court date. Parties or their counsel must file or fax a written consent for the adjournment, signed on behalf of all parties, with the trial coordinator by 2:00 p.m. three business days before the trial scheduling court date. An action listed on the trial scheduling court list may only be adjourned two times on consent without the parties having to appear personally at trial scheduling court. After two adjournments have been granted, all parties must attend trial scheduling court in person by or telephone conference call for a further adjournment.

158. Absent a consent adjournment, or a consent to place a matter on a trial sittings of the court, parties or their counsel are expected to appear in person at trial scheduling court, although they may, in the discretion of the presiding judge, attend by telephone conference call which will be received in the courtroom and will be "on the record". A telephone conference call must be arranged through the trial coordinator by 2:00 p.m. three business days before the date of the trial scheduling court. Counsel attending by telephone conference call must give their office and cell phone numbers to the trial coordinator and must indicate the number at which they will be available for the conference call.

Long Trials

159. A long civil trial is a trial that is expected to take more than 15 days.

Procedure for Obtaining Long Trial Dates

160. Any matter placed on the long trial list is given a fixed date to commence and a judge will be available to hear the matter in its entirety. Once a matter is placed on the long trial list and a trial date is fixed, adjournments are rarely granted without significant costs ramifications.

161. All civil cases requiring more than 15 days in length for trial must be referred to the Office of the Regional Senior Justice. After a trial record is filed, cases are referred to the Office of the Regional Senior Justice for possible assignment to a long trial list in one of three ways:

a. A judge may determine that a short trial should be referred to the long trial list. The judge will endorse the trial record accordingly and refer the case to the Office of the Regional Senior Justice.

b. If all parties agree that a trial will last more than 15 days, a consent request for a long trial date can be delivered to the Office of the Regional Senior Justice.

c. If all parties do not agree that a trial will last more than 15 days, any party may write to the Office of the Regional Senior Justice seeking a teleconference to determine whether the matter should be placed on the long trial list.

162. Where a matter is referred to the Office of the Regional Senior Justice for possible assignment to a long trial list, parties or their counsel must complete the Long Trial Sittings Intake Form, available on the Superior Court of Justice website and from the registrar in each courtroom or from the trial coordinator's office. The form must be submitted to the Office of the Regional Senior Judge of the Superior Court of Justice, 45 Main Street East, Suite 721, Hamilton, ON, L8N 2B7 within 10 days of a party's request for a long trial date, or an order of judge referring the case to the Office of the Regional Senior Justice for assignment of a long trial date.

163. The Office of the Regional Senior Justice will then arrange a conference call with parties or their counsel to assign the case to a particular long trial sitting and order

a schedule to be followed to ensure that the case is ready for trial at the sittings to which it has been assigned. The matter will be determined by the Regional Senior Justice in a telephone conference call arranged with counsel or, if one of the parties is self-represented, at an "in court" attendance or by a telephone conference call which will be recorded by a court reporter.

Adjournment of Cases Set Down for Trial — Short and Long Trials

164. Once an action is placed on a short or long trial list, parties are deemed ready to proceed to trial as per rule 48.07. Cases scheduled for trial will proceed during a scheduled sitting week or designated trial week, or in the case of long trials, on the date scheduled for commencement of the long trial. Where a case is scheduled to proceed during a sitting week, parties or their counsel are expected to proceed when called.

165. All requests to adjourn a short trial or a long trial must be communicated immediately to the trial coordinator's office.

166. To obtain an adjournment of a short trial, including a consent adjournment, a motion must be served and filed to be argued before a judge at a regular weekly motions day or at the monthly trial scheduling court, supported by affidavit evidence indicating the reason for the requested adjournment. An adjournment can only be granted by the order of a judge, even if all parties agree to the adjournment.

167. To obtain an adjournment of a long trial, including a consent adjournment, a motion must be served and filed, supported by affidavit evidence indicating the reason for the requested adjournment. The motion shall be returnable before the Regional Senior Judge or his/her designate.

168. Counsel and parties are responsible to advise the trial coordinator of the status of an upcoming trial. Some examples of the information which must be communicated to the trial coordinator, as soon as it is apparent to a party, include:

a. settlement of the action or pending settlement of the action;

b. whether it is likely that a request for adjournment will be sought;

c. whether there will be any motions at the outset of the trial;

d. whether the parties may consent to dispensing with a jury;

e. the need for an interpreter to assist with the testimony of one or more witnesses; and

f. the name of a particular judge who may not be able to preside due to a potential conflict.

Restoring an Action to a Trial List

169. An action that is struck off a trial list must be restored by order of a judge, obtained at a motion, pursuant to rule 48.11. An affidavit of counsel detailing the reason for the action being removed from the trial list, along with the current status of the action, shall be filed in support of the motion. If an action is restored to the trial list, the order shall include a specific trial scheduling court date or trial sittings, or in the case of a long trial, it shall be referred to the Office of the Regional Senior Justice.

Pre Trial Conferences — for Short and Long Trials

170. Pre-trials are mandatory in all civil cases for both short and long trials. Pre-trials are scheduled for 45 minute intervals. Parties or their counsel must obtain pre-trial dates from the trial coordinator and when scheduling the pre-trial, advise if additional time is required for complex actions. Failure to provide this information in a timely manner may result in an adjournment of the pre-trial and possible cost sanctions.

171. Pre-trial conference briefs must be filed, with proof of service five business days prior to the pre-trial date, pursuant to rule 50.04. Failure to comply may result in cancellation of the pre-trial and possible cost sanctions. Self-represented parties are not excused from filing a pre-trial conference brief.

172. Pre-trial conference briefs shall contain no more than 20 double spaced typed pages. Medical reports, contracts, experts' reports and other documents are not to be attached. Relevant excerpts from such documents should be included in the typed pre-trial brief. The documents should be brought to the pre-trial conference in case the presiding judge needs to review one or more of them. The first page or two of the pre-trial brief should contain an "executive summary" of the case so that the presiding judge can quickly get a "snapshot" of the facts and issues.

173. Parties are also strongly encouraged to deliver an electronic copy of the pre-trial conference brief to the email account at the Superior Court office where the pre-trial will be held at least five days before the pre-trial. Those email addresses are found at paragraph 135 above. The covering email should indicate the title of proceedings, the court file number, for which party the pre-trial conference brief is being submitted, counsel's name or the party's name where the party is self-represented, and the date of the pre-trial conference.

174. Counsel of record, or counsel fully briefed with full authority, must attend the pre-trial with their clients, unless there is a prior order excusing counsel and/or the instructing client from attending.

175. All parties are required to participate at the pre-trial conference unless otherwise ordered by the court in advance as per rule 50.05.

176. Arrangements for a pre-trial conference by telephone for any party must be made in writing and received at least 10 days in advance so that the presiding judge can determine if such a telephone attendance is appropriate.

D. — Transfer of Cases

From Central South Region to another Region

177. If a party seeks to transfer an action commenced in the Central South Region to another region, a motion to transfer shall be filed in the court office of the county to which the transfer is sought (the receiving region), as per rules 4.05(2)4 and 13.1.02(3.1).

178. In the Central East, Central West and Toronto regions, the motion to transfer will be heard by the Regional Senior Justice, in writing. Please refer to section B of part IV of the Consolidated Provincial Practice Direction which sets out the process for motions to transfer a civil proceeding to the Central East, Central West, Central South and Toronto regions.

179. If the transfer is approved, the signed order must be issued and entered in the court location where the action was started and a requisition must then be made to transfer the file to the court location in the receiving region which has been approved in the signed transfer order.

From another Region to Central South

180. If a party seeks to transfer an action commenced in another region to the Central South Region, a motion to transfer shall be filed in the court office of the county within Central South to which the transfer is sought, as per rules 4.05(2)4 and 13.1.02(3.1).

181. The motion shall be heard by the Regional Senior Judge of the Central South Region, in writing. A copy of the materials and evidence of payment of the filing fee shall be sent to the Office of the Regional Senior Justice of the Central South Region. Please refer to section B of part IV of the Consolidated Provincial Practice Direction which sets out the process for motions to transfer a civil proceeding to the Central East, Central West, Central South and Toronto regions.

182. If the transfer is approved, the signed order must be issued and entered in the court location where the action was started and a requisition must then be made to transfer the file to the court location in the Central South Region which has been approved in the signed transfer order.

From one Superior Court location to another Superior Court location in the same Region

183. A motion to transfer a civil case from one location in the Central South Region to another location in the Central South Region should be brought in the court location in which the action was commenced.

184. If it is a consent motion, the motion shall be considered by the Local Administrative Judge at that court site. If it appears appropriate to transfer the case, before signing the order, the Local Administrative Judge will verify with the Local Administrative Judge of the court location to which the action is to be transferred that the case can be accommodated at that court site.

185. If it is not a consent motion, the motion shall be made returnable at a weekly motions court. If the presiding judge determines that the transfer order should be made, before signing the order he/she will verify with the Local Administrative Judge of the court location to which the action is to be transferred that the case can be accommodated at that court site.

E. — Mortgage Proceedings

186. Pursuant to rule 13.1.01(3), Brantford, Cayuga, Hamilton, Kitchener, St. Catharines, Simcoe, and Welland are designated as places where mortgage proceedings may be commenced for property located anywhere in the Central South Region.

F. — Class Actions: Proceedings under the **Class Proceedings Act, 1992**

187. Counsel or parties commencing a class action to be issued in the Central South Region are urged to read part II of the Consolidated Provincial Practice Direction, which applies to class proceedings throughout the province.

188. In the Central South Region, two judges have been designated as Class Action judges. The names of assigned Class Proceedings judges may be obtained from the office of the Regional Manager, Judicial Services for the Central South Region (telephone number (905) 645-5323; fax number (905) 645-5374). The Regional Manager should be notified in writing when a class action has been or is about to be commenced in the Central South Region.

Dated: June 1, 2016

Amendments: May 1, 2017 (revocation of part III H (paragraphs 110–115))

Heather J. Smith

Chief Justice

Superior Court of Justice (Ontario)

James R.H. Turnbull

Regional Senior Judge

Central South Region

PD-8a — *PRACTICE ADVISORY CONCERNING LONG MOTIONS IN THE CITY OF WELLAND*

Effective April 3, 2018

This Practice Advisory applies to all civil, family and stand-alone pre-trial criminal long motions (e.g. 11b motions) in the City of Welland that are scheduled for one or more hours. It *supplements* the *Consolidated Practice Direction for the Central South Region*, which came into effect on June 1, 2016.

Counsel and parties are advised to refer to the relevant parts of the *Consolidated Provincial Practice Direction* and any other applicable *Central South Region-specific Practice Directions or Guides*, which are available on the Superior Court of Justice website at: www.ontariocourts.ca/scj.

Requirement to File Electronic Copies of Documents on USB

For civil, family and criminal long motions, parties **must file electronic copies of their materials on a USB stick. The pilot excludes child protection cases, criminal third party records applications, and criminal long motions heard during trial. Only stand-alone pre-trial criminal long motions are included.**

The USB must include a copy of the motion materials, including the factum, where required. Paper copies of the motion materials must also be filed as required by the rules of court.

Acceptable Formats for Electronic Documents

Two electronic versions of *each* document are required:

1. One copy must be created using Microsoft Word (.DOC), and

2. One copy must be saved in PDF format. Documents converted from Word to PDF are preferable to scanned PDF documents.

Electronic Documents Naming Convention

In order to assist court staff in storing the electronic materials and the judge in accessing them, when saving electronic documents on the USB, each document must be named using one of the prefixes below, followed by the short style of cause and court file number (e.g. *MPL Brown v. Brown*, CV-17-12345-0000):

Motion Record (containing the Notice of Motion)

MPL = Motion Record of the Plaintiff

MDE = Motion Record of the Defendant

MDM = Motion Record of the Defendant to Counterclaim

MTP = Motion Record of the Third Party

M4P = Motion Record of the Fourth Party

M5P = Motion Record of the Fifth Party

M6P = Motion Record of the Sixth Party

M7P = Motion Record of the Seventh Party

MAP = Motion Record of the Applicant

MRP = Motion Record of the Respondent

MIN = Motion Record of the Intervener

MAN = Motion Record of the Agency (Agency/Person/Special Interest)

MSL = Motion Record of the Solicitor (under the *Solicitors Act*)

MCL = Motion Record of the Client (under the *Solicitors Act*)

MNP = Motion Record of a Non-party

All relevant prior court orders and endorsements (if not already included in the Motion Record)

COE = Court Orders and Endorsements

Note: *Include only court orders and judge's endorsements that relate to the long motion.*

Affidavits

AFPL = Affidavit of or on behalf of the Plaintiff

AFDE = Affidavit of or on behalf of the Defendant

AFDM = Affidavit of or on behalf of the Defendant to Counterclaim

AFTP = Affidavit of or on behalf of the Third Party

AF4P = Affidavit of or on behalf of the Fourth Party

AF5P = Affidavit of or on behalf of the Fifth Party

AF6P = Affidavit of or on behalf of the Sixth Party

AF7P = Affidavit of or on behalf of the Seventh Party

AFAP = Affidavit of or on behalf of the Applicant

AFRP = Affidavit of or on behalf of the Respondent

AFIN = Affidavit of or on behalf of the Intervener

AFAN = Affidavit of or on behalf of the Agency (Agency/Person/Special Interest)

AFSL = Affidavit of or on behalf of the Solicitor (under the *Solicitors Act*)

AFCL = Affidavit of or on behalf of the Client (under the *Solicitors Act*)

AFNP = Affidavit of or on behalf of a Non-party

Affidavits of Service/Proof of Service

AFSPL = Affidavit of Service or Proof of Service of or on behalf of the Plaintiff

AFSDE = Affidavit of Service or Proof of Service of or on behalf of the Defendant

AFSDM = Affidavit of Service or Proof of Service of or on behalf of the Defendant to Counterclaim

AFSTP = Affidavit of Service or Proof of Service of or on behalf of the Third Party

AFS4P = Affidavit of Service or Proof of Service of or on behalf of the Fourth Party

AFS5P = Affidavit of Service or Proof of Service of or on behalf of the Fifth Party

AFS6P = Affidavit of Service or Proof of Service of or on behalf of the Sixth Party

AFS7P = Affidavit of Service or Proof of Service of or on behalf of the Seventh Party

AFSAP = Affidavit of Service or Proof of Service of or on behalf of the Applicant

AFSRP = Affidavit of Service or Proof of Service of or on behalf of the Respondent

AFSIN = Affidavit of Service or Proof of Service of or on behalf of the Intervener

AFSAN = Affidavit of Service or Proof of Service of or on behalf of the Agency (Agency/Person/Special Interest)

AFSSL = Affidavit of Service or Proof of Service of or on behalf of the Solicitor (under the *Solicitors Act*)

AFSCL = Affidavit of Service or Proof of Service of or on behalf of the Client (under the *Solicitors Act*)

AFSNP = Affidavit of Service or Proof of Service of or on behalf of a Non-party

Book of Authorities

BAPL = Book of Authorities of the Plaintiff

BADE = Book of Authorities of the Defendant

BADM = Book of Authorities of the Defendant to Counterclaim

BATP = Book of Authorities of the Third Party

BA4P = Book of Authorities of the Fourth Party

BA5P = Book of Authorities of the Fifth Party

BA6P = Book of Authorities of the Sixth Party

BA7P = Book of Authorities of the Seventh Party

BAAP = Book of Authorities of the Applicant

BARP = Book of Authorities of the Respondent

BAIN = Book of Authorities of the Intervener

BAAN = Book of Authorities of the Agency (Agency/Person/Special Interest)

BASL = Book of Authorities of the Solicitor (under the *Solicitors Act*)

BACL = Book of Authorities of the Client (under the *Solicitors Act*)

BANP = Book of Authorities of Non-party

Factums, including Amended and Supplementary

FPL = Factum of the Plaintiff

FDE = Factum of the Defendant

FDM = Factum of the Defendant to Counterclaim

FTP = Factum of the Third Party

F4P = Factum of the Fourth Party

F5P = Factum of the Fifth Party

F6P = Factum of the Sixth Party

F7P = Factum of the Seventh Party

FAP = Factum of the Applicant

FRP = Factum of the Respondent

FIN = Factum of the Intervener

FAN = Factum of the Agency (Agency/Person/Special Interest)

FSL = Factum of the Solicitor (under the *Solicitors Act*)

FCL = Factum of the Client (under the *Solicitors Act*)

FNP = Factum of a Non-party

Note: *Add the suffix AM or SUP to indicate Amended or Supplemental Factum*

Costs Outline

COPL = Cost Outline of the Plaintiff

CODE = Cost Outline of the Defendant

CODM = Cost Outline of the Defendant to Counterclaim

COTP = Cost Outline of the Third Party

CO4P = Cost Outline of the Fourth Party

CO5P = Cost Outline of the Fifth Party

CO6P = Cost Outline of the Sixth Party

CO7P = Cost Outline of the Seventh Party

COAP = Cost Outline of the Applicant

CORP = Cost Outline of the Respondent

COIN = Cost Outline of the Intervener

COAN = Cost Outline of the Agency (Agency/Person/Special Interest)

COSL = Cost Outline of the Solicitor (under the *Solicitors Act*)

COCL = Cost Outline of the Client (under the *Solicitors Act*)

CONP = Cost Outline of a non-party

Transcripts

TRN = Transcript

Compendiums

CPL = Compendium of the Plaintiff

CDE = Compendium of the Defendant

CDM = Compendium of the Defendant to Counterclaim

CTP = Compendium of the Third Party

C4P = Compendium of the Fourth Party

C5P = Compendium of the Fifth Party

C6P = Compendium of the Sixth Party

C7P = Compendium of the Seventh Party

CAP = Compendium of the Applicant

CRP = Compendium of the Respondent

CIN = Compendium of the Intervener

CAN = Compendium of the Agency (Agency/Person/Special Interest)

CSL = Compendium of the Solicitor (under the *Solicitors Act*)

CCL = Compendium of the Client (under the *Solicitors Act*)

CNP = Compendium of a Non-party

Note**:** *When there is a joint compendium filed, suffix the file name with the parties (i.e. PL for plaintiff; DE for defendant, DM defendant to counterclaim, etc.)*

Note**:** *When there are multiple documents of the same type filed, suffix the file name with 001, 002, 003, 004, 005, etc.*

Counsel and parties may also refer to the *Guide Concerning e-Delivery of Documents* in the Ontario Superior Court of Justice, available on the Superior Court's website.

Date: March 26, 2018

Harrison S. Arrell

Regional Senior Judge

Superior Court of Justice, Central South Region

PD-9 — *CONSOLIDATED PRACTICE DIRECTION FOR THE CENTRAL WEST REGION (EFFECTIVE JULY 1, 2014)*

Notice of Amendment: Part III A [paras. 75–80] was revoked on May 1, 2017; Part I J [paragraphs 26 and 27] (family proceedings — case conferences and settlement conferences) was replaced on January 1, 2017.

This Practice Direction applies to proceedings in the Superior Court of Justice, Central West Region, effective July 1, 2014. It *supersedes* all previous region-specific Practice Directions for the Central West Region issued prior to July 1, 2014, which are hereby revoked.

Counsel and parties are advised to refer to the relevant Parts of the Consolidated Provincial Practice Direction as well as the Consolidated Practice Direction for Divisional Court Proceedings which are available on the Superior Court of Justice website at: www.ontariocourts.ca/scj.

PART I: — FAMILY PROCEEDINGS

1. In addition to this Part, counsel and parties in family proceedings are advised to refer to Part I of the Consolidated Provincial Practice Direction.

A. — Confirmations

2. Each party to a motion or conference must file a Form 14C Confirmation no later than 2 p.m. two business days before the date of the motion or conference. The parties may file a Form 14C Confirmation jointly.

3. The parties or their counsel should consult with each other prior to filing their Form 14C Confirmations, unless the parties are self-represented and prohibited from communicating by court order.

4. Where Form 14C Confirmations have not been filed, the conference or motion will not be scheduled on the event list and, as a result, will not be heard by the court. *Costs may be ordered against a party who has not filed the Confirmation.*

5. Form 14C Confirmations must only list the specific issues that are to be addressed at the event. They should also indicate which materials the judge should review with clear reference to the specific volume, tab and page numbers of the Continuing Record. *Failure to provide this information may result in the materials not being reviewed by the judge or the motion not being heard on that day.*

6. Form 14C Confirmations must also include an appropriate time estimate for the entire motion or conference, including time required by the other party. Parties will be held to the time stated on their Confirmations.

B. — Short Motions

7. Motions that are expected to take one hour or less may be scheduled on a regular motions day serving and filing the motion material at the court office at the location where the motion is to be heard within the timelines set out in the *Family Law Rules*.

C. — Long Motions

8. Motions that are expected to take more than one hour (including the other party's reply and cross motion, if any) must be scheduled as long motions and scheduled through the Trial Coordinator in the location where the motion is to be heard.

(i) — Long Motions in Milton

9. In Milton, a long motion must be confirmed no later than three weeks prior to the date the motion is to be heard, and all material must be filed by the moving party by that date. Counsel and parties will be advised of this requirement at the time the motion is booked.

10. If the material and the confirmation are not filed at least three weeks in advance of the date the motion is to be heard, the motion will be removed from the list and will not be heard. If possible, the time can be used to hear another motion by arrangement with the trial office.

(ii) — Long Motions in Owen Sound and Walkerton

11.In Owen Sound and Walkerton, a long motion must be confirmed no later than three weeks prior to the date the motion is to be heard. The moving party's factum must be served and filed four weeks prior to the hearing date. The respondent's factum must be served and filed three weeks prior to the hearing date. The litigant, or counsel, as the case may be, will be advised of this requirement at the time the motion is booked.

12. If the moving party's factum and the confirmation are not filed in accordance with these timelines, the motion will be removed from the list and will not be heard. If possible, the time can be used to hear another motion by arrangement with the trial office.

13.The respondent's failure to file its factum in accordance with these timelines will be addressed by the judge hearing the long motion.

14. Any request to adjourn a long motion, even if on consent, must be made by Notice of Motion, with a supporting Affidavit, returnable on the earliest available regular motions date.

D. — Form 14B Motions

15. A Form 14B Motion must be filed at the court office and cannot be filed by fax. A Form 14B Motion Form should be accompanied by four copies of a proposed Order (Form 25), a completed endorsement sheet and a self-addressed and stamped envelope for each party.

16. The 14B Motion Form shall be filed in the Continuing Record and a copy of the proposed Order shall be attached to the appropriate place in the Endorsement Volume.

17. In addition to this section, counsel and parties are advised to refer to Part I of the Consolidated Provincial Practice Direction regarding Form 14B Motions.

E. — Urgent Motions on Notice

18. A party may seek an urgent motion on notice without a case conference in situations of urgency or hardship including issues such as abduction and threats of harm where an Early Case Conference is not available. A party seeking such a motion must file all of the required materials except for a Form 14C Confirmation.

F. — Urgent Motions without Notice

19. A party that is seeking a motion without notice to the other party must also set out why notice is unnecessary or not reasonably possible. A factum or Summary of Argument is not required for an urgent motion that has been brought without notice.

G. — Factums Summaries of Arguments and Briefs of Authorities

20. A properly drafted factum or Summary of Argument is required on all long motions except where noted otherwise. If the moving party does not file a factum or Summary of Argument where required, the motion will not be scheduled.

21. For long motions, each party's factum or Summary of Argument must be filed at least seven days before the hearing of the motion.

22. No factum or Summary of Argument may exceed 20 pages without leave of the court.

23. The authorities that are included on the court's list of Often Cited Family Cases do not need to be provided to the court. Counsel and parties are advised to refer to Part I of the Consolidated Provincial Practice Direction for further direction.

H. — Compendiums

24. A Compendium containing the documents and evidence that are essential to the hearing of the motion may be provided for long or complex motions. A party wishing to file a Compendium should file it with their factum. A joint Compendium may be filed with the respondent's factum. A Compendium would normally include the Notice of Motion, Affidavits and Financial Statements, as well as excerpts from the evidence and exhibits that will be referred to in the argument of the motion.

I. — Electronic Copies of Material

25. Whenever the volume of materials is large or the motion is complex, the parties should file an electronic copy of their motion materials as well as paper copies. Counsel and parties are advised to refer to the Guide Concerning e-Delivery of documents available on the Superior Court of Justice Website.

J. — Case Conferences and Settlement Conferences

26.1 Counsel and parties are expected to attend all conferences in person.

26.2 Parties may arrange for a conference to occur by teleconference with the consent of both parties and their counsel. If the other party will not consent, a request for a teleconference may be made by filing a Form 14B Motion Form.

26.3 Counsel or the parties should communicate before any conference in order to attempt to resolve the issues that are in dispute unless the parties are self-represented and prohibited from communication by court order.

26.4 A date for a case conference may only be obtained upon one side filing a case conference brief.

26.5 Once a case or settlement conference has been scheduled no adjournments will be permitted except in **exceptional** circumstances. If exceptional circumstances arise, the party requesting the adjournment must obtain the permission, in writing, of a Superior Court Justice.

26.6 Trial management conferences may not be adjourned without a judge's order, which must be obtained either by 14B motion or by appearing before the court. The adjournment request must set out compelling reasons why the parties are not ready to go ahead, along with a proposed timetable to move the case forward.

27. Parties must serve and file a Trial Scheduling Endorsement Form with their Settlement Conference briefs, so that if the matter does not settle at the Settlement Conference a trial date can be scheduled.

K. — Dispute Resolution Officer Program — Brampton and Milton

28. If the matter is not resolved at a Settlement Conference, a Trial Scheduling Endorsement Form must be completed prior to the matter being scheduled for trial.

29. The first Case Conference on a motion to change a final order or agreement in Brampton or Milton shall be scheduled before a Dispute Resolution Officer (DRO) in accordance with Part I of the Consolidated Provincial Practice Direction. Counsel and parties are advised to refer to Part I of the Provincial Practice Direction for further direction.

30. A DRO conference may be held on matters other than motions to change only as directed by the court upon request by a 14B Motion or at another court event.

L. — Early Case Conferences — Brampton and Milton

31. Litigants who are represented by counsel, and those who are self-represented, can participate in an early case conference.

32. The case conferences will be held on Mondays. They will be listed as "Early Case Conference" (ECC) and are available only if a case conference has not already been held.

33. Fifteen ECCs will be scheduled for 10 a.m.

34. Both parties must certify they have fully discussed the issues to be litigated with the other side before their attendance at court for the ECC, or have attended court not later than 9 a.m. on the scheduled date to fully discuss the issues. If the parties have not discussed the issues fully in advance of 10 a.m., the conference will be rescheduled.

35. Litigants are required to attend the ECC.

36. Each ECC will be *limited to a total of 15 minutes* for all submissions, discussion and endorsements.

37. The litigants must file updated financial statements. Case Conference Briefs *must not to exceed five double spaced pages* setting out their positions and *must not include lengthy schedules*.

38. The parties are limited to factual assertions contained in the written material, and will not be permitted to add additional facts in submissions.

M. — Trial Records

39. If the matter is not resolved at a case conference, a completed Trial Scheduling Endorsement Form (Parts 1 and 2) must be completed by the parties and endorsed by the court prior to the matter being scheduled for trial.

40. The Applicant must file a Trial Record at least 30 days prior to the scheduled Trial date. Failure to do so will result in the matter being removed from the Trial list, unless the court orders otherwise.

N. — Cost Orders in Family Law Motions and Applications

41. Rule 57.01(6) of the *Rules of Civil Procedure* requires that, unless the parties have agreed on costs:

> every party who intends to seek costs for that step shall give to every other party involved in the same step, and bring to the hearing, a costs outline (Form 57B) not exceeding three pages in length.

42. This is to permit the presiding judge, where feasible, to summarily determine the issue of costs. The overriding principle is that "the court shall devise and adopt the simplest, least expensive, and most expeditious process for fixing costs . . ." Rule 57.01(7).

43. While Rule 24 of the *Family Law Rules*, in addressing costs, does not refer to costs outlines or bills of costs, Rule 1(7) states that if a matter is not covered by the rules, the court may give direction, and the practice shall be decided by analogy to

these rules, by reference to the *Courts of Justice Act* and, if the court considers it appropriate, by reference to the *Rules of Civil Procedure*.

44. Too frequently counsel are attending motions and applications without costs outlines, and seeking to make submissions regarding the costs to be awarded. When judges ask for the outlines or bills of costs, counsel often seek to file written submissions as to costs. This is contrary to the intention of the Rules, delays the determination of the issue, and requires judges to determine costs issues for motions and applications that were often decided months before.

45. All counsel appearing on motions and applications should attend the hearing with their costs outline in accordance with Rule 57.01 available, to provide to the presiding judge. If the outline is not available to be given to the presiding judge, the judge may decline to make any costs award.

PART II: — CIVIL PROCEEDINGS

46. In addition to this Part, counsel and parties to civil proceedings are advised to refer to Part III of the Consolidated Provincial Practice Direction.

A. — Motions to Transfer a Civil Proceeding under Rule 13.1.02 of the Rules of Civil Procedure

47. All requests for a transfer of a civil proceeding from one county to another shall be pursuant to rule 13.1.02 of the *Rules of Civil Procedure*. The motion will be granted or denied based on its merits. Counsel and parties are advised to refer to Part III the Consolidated Provincial Practice Direction which prescribes specific requirements for motions to transfer a civil proceeding.

A.1 — Designated Counties for the Commencement of Mortgage Proceedings under rule 13.1.01(3)

47.1 Pursuant to rule 13.1.01(3) of the *Rules of Civil Procedure*, which comes into effect on March 31, 2015, Brampton, Milton, Orangeville or Owen Sound have been designated as the place for commencement of mortgage proceedings for property located anywhere in the Central West Region.

B. — Applications and Motions

48. Applications and motions that require one hour or less for all parties to argue are considered short. Applications and motions that require more than one hour for all parties to argue are considered long.

C. — Short Applications or Short Motions before a Judge

49. All the materials for short motions and applications are filed in the Registrar's office. Parties must consult with each other to select a return date convenient to all parties and which will permit all parties to file all necessary materials and conduct any examinations before the return date. At the time of filing the Notice of Motion, a realistic estimate of the time required by all parties for argument must be provided.

D. — Long Motions

50. Motions that are expected to take more than one hour (including the other party's reply and cross motion, if any) must be scheduled as Long Motions and scheduled through the Trial Coordinator in the location where the motion is to be heard.

(i) — Long Motions in Milton

51. In Milton a long motion must be confirmed no later than three weeks prior to the date the motion is to be heard, and all material must be filed by the moving party by that date. The litigant, or counsel, as the case may be, will be advised of this requirement at the time the motion is booked.

52. If the material and the confirmation are not filed at least three weeks in advance of the date the motion is to be heard, the motion will be removed from the list and will not be heard. If possible, the time can be used to hear another motion by arrangement with the trial office.

(ii) — Long Motions in Owen Sound and Walkerton

53. In Owen Sound and Walkerton, a long motion must be confirmed no later than three weeks prior to the date the motion is to be heard. The moving party's factum must be served and filed four weeks prior to the hearing date. The respondent's factum must be served and filed three weeks prior to the hearing date. The litigant, or counsel, as the case may be, will be advised of this requirement at the time the motion is booked.

54. If the moving party's factum and the confirmation are not filed in accordance with these timelines, the motion will be removed from the list and will not be heard. If possible, the time can be used to hear another motion by arrangement with the trial office.

55. The respondent's failure to file its factum in accordance with these timelines will be addressed by the judge hearing the long motion.

56. Any request to adjourn a long motion, even if on consent, must be made by Notice of Motion, with a supporting Affidavit, returnable on the earliest available regular motions date.

E. — Emergency/Walk-in Motions

57. Counsel and parties who wish to have a motion added to a motions list must attend the trial office before bringing the motion into court. Counsel will be provided with a form to be completed. The trial office staff will then assign the application for leave to be added to the list to a judge who is presiding in motions court that day. The application for leave must be brought in the assigned court, unless the assigned judge directs otherwise.

58. If counsel and parties have not gone to the trial office before attending the courtroom, they will be required to go to the trial office and complete the form before the leave application is heard.

F. — Certification of an Action to Set Pre-Trial and Trial Dates

59. The practice of certifying an action ready for trial continues in Brampton. Once the trial record is filed, the Registrar will hand to the party who set the action down for trial a Certification Form to Set Pre-Trial and Trial Dates. After consultation with the opposing counsel or party, the party who received the form must complete and return the Certification Form to the trial office.

60. If a completed Certification Form is not returned within 90 days of the matter being set down for trial, the parties will be required to attend at the Assignment Court. If the parties are not ready for trial, the action will be struck from the list.

61. In order to restore an action that has been struck from the trial list, the parties must obtain an order granting leave from a judge under rule 48.11 to restore it to the trial list.

62. Once trial dates are set, the parties may adjourn the date if on consent of all parties.

63. Rule 48.04 provides that a party who sets an action down for trial or consents to placing the action on the trial list cannot initiate or continue any form of discovery or interlocutory motion without leave of the court. Leave will be granted only in rare circumstances.

G. — Material for use of the Court

Factums

64. Factums are required for all applications. Factums are required for all motions over one hour and are strongly encouraged for all other motions. No factum may exceed 20 pages, unless leave is granted. For longer or more complex motions, the court always finds it helpful for the parties to file electronic copies of their factums in Word format. Electronic copies should be attached to the hard copy of the factum with the court and should be labelled with the court file name and number, event and content of the electronic document (e.g. flash drive), as well as the return date of the matter.

Books of Authority

65. Cases contained in books of authorities should be copied on both sides of a page. Electronic copies of books of authorities are helpful in longer or more complex motions.

H. — Confirmations for Motions and Applications

66. Confirmation notices for short motions/applications must be received by fax or delivered to the court office not later than 2:00 p.m. three business days before the matter is to be heard. For example, for matters to be heard on Monday, they must be confirmed by 2:00 p.m. on the preceding Wednesday.

67. Confirmations must list only the specific issues to be addressed at the motion/application. They should also indicate the materials that the judge should review.

68. Except as otherwise provided in the Practice Direction, confirmation notices for long motions/applications must be received five business days before the matter is to proceed.

69. Only Central West confirmation notices will be accepted.

70. In Brampton and Milton, counsel should indicate on the form if they have other matters to be heard on that date, so that the court office may attempt to put their matters on one list if two or more judges are scheduled to hear the motion/application.

I. — Cost Orders in Civil Motions and Applications

71. Rule 57.01(6) of the *Rules of Civil Procedure* requires that, unless the parties have agreed on costs:

> every party who intends to seek costs for that step shall give to every other party involved in the same step, and bring to the hearing, a costs outline (Form 57B) not exceeding three pages in length.

72. This is to permit the presiding judge, where feasible, to summarily determine the issue of costs. The overriding principle is that "the court shall devise and adopt the simplest, least expensive, and most expeditious process for fixing costs . . ." Rule 57.01(7).

73. Too frequently counsel are attending motions and applications without costs outlines, and seeking to make submissions regarding the costs to be awarded. When judges ask for the outlines or bills of costs, counsel often seek to file written submissions as to costs. This is contrary to the intention of the Rules, delays the determination of the issue, and requires judges to determine costs issues for motions and applications that were often decided months before.

74. All counsel appearing on motions and applications should attend the hearing with their costs outline in accordance with Rule 57.01 available, to provide to the presiding judge. If the outline is not available to be given to the presiding judge, the judge may decline to make any costs award.

PART III: — CRIMINAL PROCEEDINGS

A. — Bail Variations pursuant to section 515.1 of the *Criminal Code*

This section (paragraphs 75 to 80) has been revoked and replaced by part V of the Provincial Practice Direction Regarding Criminal Proceedings.

Dated: April 11, 2014

Amended: May 1, 2017 (revocation of part III A (paras. 75–80)); January 1, 2017 [paragraphs 26 and 27], July 1, 2015 [modification to paragraph 39]; February 27, 2015 [addition of para 47.1]; November 7, 2014 [addition of paras 11–14 and 53–56]

Heather J. Smith

Chief Justice

Superior Court of Justice (Ontario)

Peter A. Daley

Regional Senior Judge

Superior Court of Justice, Central West Region

PD-10 — *CONSOLIDATED PRACTICE DIRECTION FOR THE EAST REGION (EFFECTIVE JULY 1, 2014)*

Notice of Amendment: Effective August 1, 2016, Part 1 (Family Proceedings) is revoked and replaced by the Practice Direction Regarding Family Cases in the Superior Court of Justice East Region.

Notice of Amendment: Part II A.1 (Designated Counties for the Commencement of Mortgage Proceedings under rule 13.1.01) has been amended to change the place of commencement of Mortgage Proceedings. These amendments were made March 11, 2016 and are in effect April 1, 2016.

Notice of Amendment: Part II A.1 (Designated Counties for the Commencement of Mortgage Proceedings under rule 13.1.01) was added on February 27, 2015 and comes into effect on March 31, 2015.

This Practice Direction applies to proceedings in the Superior Court of Justice, East Region, effective July 1, 2014. It *supersedes* all previous region-specific Practice Directions for the East Region issued prior to July 1, 2014, which are hereby revoked.

Counsel and parties are advised to refer to the relevant Parts of the Consolidated Provincial Practice Direction as well as the Consolidated Practice Direction for Divisional Court Proceedings which are available on the Superior Court of Justice website at: www.ontariocourts.ca/scj.

PART I: — FAMILY PROCEEDINGS

1. This part (paragraphs 1 to 19) has been revoked and replaced by the Practice Direction Regarding Family Cases in the Superior Court of Justice East Region.

PART II: — CIVIL PROCEEDINGS

20. In addition to this Part, counsel and parties in civil proceedings are advised to refer to Part III of the Consolidated Provincial Practice Direction.

A. — Civil Motions Court in Perth

21. In Perth, to respond to the issue of over scheduling in Friday motion courts, it is necessary to limit the number of civil motions that are set down weekly based on the time estimates provided by counsel and parties.

22. Counsel and parties must contact Court Administration to book motion time into the schedule. Counsel and parties will be held to the time estimate provided.

23. Long motions, in excess of one hour, will continue to be scheduled through the Trial Coordinator's office.

A.1 — Designated Counties for the Commencement of Mortgage Proceedings under rule 13.1.01(3)

23.1 Pursuant to rule 13.1.01(3) of the Rules of Civil Procedure, Belleville, Brockville, Cornwall, Kingston, L'Orignal, Napanee, Picton, Pembroke, Perth and Ottawa have been designated as places where mortgage proceedings may be commenced for property located anywhere in the East Region.

PART III: — CRIMINAL PROCEEDINGS

A. — Criminal Case Management Procedures for Ottawa under Rule 28 of the Criminal Proceedings Rules

24. The following criminal case management procedures, in paragraphs 25 to 29, apply in Ottawa regarding Rule 28 and the requirement for Pre-Trial Conference Reports (Rule 28.04 and Form 17), Trial Readiness Courts (Rule 28.04(18)(a)) and Trial Readiness Reports (Rule 28.04(18)(b) and Form 18-C-1).

25. Pre-Trial Conference Reports (Form 17) are not required to be filed at or before the first pre-trial in Superior Court. They may be required at a later time as directed by the pre-trial judge.

26. When the trial date is set, two other dates will be set at the same time and recorded on the indictment. The first is the filing date (usually 30 days before the trial date) for the Trial Readiness Report in Form 18-C-1. The second is a mandatory appearance in Trial Readiness Court at 12:30 p.m. on the Thursday immediately prior to the trial date.

27. Trial Readiness Court will be held each Thursday at 12:30 p.m. with a justice presiding, usually in a courtroom on the 3rd floor. Counsel are not required to gown.

28. The purpose of the Trial Readiness Report (Form 18-C-1) is to inform the court and other counsel that the case is proceeding as discussed at the most recent pre-trial.

29. If counsel or parties do not file a Trial Readiness Report by the filing date as recorded on the indictment or, if since the most recent pre-trial, there has been a change affecting the trial, all counsel and parties are required to attend the next Trial Readiness Court immediately following that filing date.

B. — Notice of Application for a 90 Day Detention Review

30. Upon receipt of a Notice of Application for a 90 Day Detention Review pursuant to section 525(1) and (2) of the *Criminal Code of Canada*, the following practice in paragraphs 31 to 34 will be followed.

31. If the accused is not represented by counsel, a hearing date will be scheduled for the next bail review court date. Notice of this hearing date will be sent to the Regional Detention Centre and the Crown Attorney's office by the Trial Coordinator. The Crown Attorney's office will prepare an Order to Produce to have the prisoner brought to the hearing.

32. If the accused is represented by counsel, defence counsel will be contacted by the Trial Coordinator and asked whether he/she requests a hearing date be set or whether there will be a waiver of the hearing.

33. If counsel waives the hearing, he/she will immediately send a letter to the Trial Coordinator confirming this waiver and a copy of this waiver will then be forwarded to the Regional Detention Centre and the Crown Attorney's office by the Trial Coordinator.

34. If counsel indicates that a hearing date is to be set, that hearing date will be set by a judge at the next bail review court date in the absence of the accused, but in the

presence of defence counsel, after which a copy of the Notice of the Hearing Date will be sent to the Regional Detention Centre, defence counsel and the Crown Attorney's office by the Trial Coordinator. The Crown Attorney's office will prepare an Order to Produce to have the prisoner brought to the hearing.

Dated: April 11, 2014

Amended: August 1, 2016; March 11, 2016; Amended: February 27, 2015 (addition of para 23.1)

Heather J. Smith

Chief Justice

Superior Court of Justice (Ontario)

James McNamara

Regional Senior Judge

Superior Court of Justice, East Region

PD-10a — *PRACTICE DIRECTION REGARDING FAMILY CASES IN THE SUPERIOR COURT OF JUSTICE EAST REGION*

Effective August 1, 2016

This Practice Direction applies to family law proceedings in the Superior Court of Justice in the East Region. It supersedes Part I: Family Proceedings of the Consolidated Practice Direction for the East Region.

Counsel and parties are advised to refer also to the relevant parts of the Consolidated Provincial Practice Direction which is available on the Superior Court of Justice website at www.ontariocourts.ca/scj.

This Practice Direction provides clarification of the process for motions (including urgent motions), case conferences, settlement conferences, trial management conferences and trials that are required under the *Family Law Rules*. This Practice Direction does not apply to cases under the *Child and Family Services Act*.

Part 1: — General Information

A. — Court Contact Information:

1. The contact information for the ten court sites in the East Region can be found on the regional court schedule section of the website of the Superior Court of Justice.

B. — Schedule:

2. The schedule for proceedings in Family Court for the ten court sites in the East Region can also be found on the regional court schedule section of the website of the Superior Court of Justice.

C. — Forms:

3. Each of the forms prescribed under the Family Law Rules is available on the Ontario Court Forms. The Trial Scheduling Endorsement Form, referred to below, is available on the Superior Court of Justice website.

Part 2: — Obtaining Dates

4. Dates for conferences and motions shall be obtained at the Family Law Counter in conjunction with the Trial Coordinator's Office. The party scheduling the date should consult in advance with the other party so that the date set is available for both parties.

5. Strict attention should be paid to the estimate of time required for the event. The parties should consult in advance so that the time estimate will include sufficient time for both parties, including for any cross motion that is expected to be heard on the same date.

6. Time allotments on the daily event lists are based on the time estimate provided when the date is obtained. Parties may be held to that time estimate, or, the motion may not be heard if the actual time required for it exceeds the initial time estimate.

Part 3: — Confirmations

7. Each party to a motion or conference must file a *Form 14C Confirmation* or the parties may file one jointly, no later than 2 p.m. two business days before the date of the motion or conference.

8. These may be filed at the Family Law Counter in the courthouse or they may be faxed to the Family Court Office. Please see the Court Contact Information link above.

9. The parties or their counsel should consult with each other prior to filing their Form 14C Confirmations, unless the parties are self-represented and prohibited from communicating by court order or by a term of judicial release.

10. Where no Form 14C Confirmation has been filed by any party, the conference or motion will be not be heard on that day. Costs may also be ordered against a party who has not filed a Confirmation.

11. Form 14C Confirmations must only list the specific issues that are to be addressed at the event. They should also indicate which materials the judge should review with clear reference to the specific volume, tab, and page numbers of the Continuing Record. *Failure to provide this information may result in the materials not being reviewed by the judge or the motion not being heard on that day.*

12. Form 14C Confirmations must also include an up-to-date time estimate for the entire motion or conference, including time required by the other party. Parties should not expect more time than originally requested nor will they be permitted more time than specified in the confirmation forms.

13. If the matter settles or the issues narrow or change parties are asked to notify the court by fax as soon as possible.

Part 4: — Motions

A. — Regular Motions

14. Regular motions are determined by the amount of time they will require to be argued. The duration for regular motions in each judicial centre is set out in Schedule 1 to this Practice Direction.

15. In all judicial centres, any regular motion requiring one hour or more for argument requires a Factum. Motion materials shall be served and filed in accordance with the timelines set out in the Family Law Rules. Motion materials must be filed at the Family Law Counter.

B. — Long Motions

16. Long Motions are all motions expected to exceed the regular motion duration in the applicable judicial centre (including the other party's reply and cross motion, if any). Long motions must be scheduled through the Trial Coordinator's Office. Long motions should be scheduled with the other party's consent as to the date.

17. A factum is required for all motions that are one hour or more. The moving party shall serve and file its Factum at least four business days before the hearing of the motion. The responding party shall serve and file its Factum at least 2 business days before the hearing of the motion.

18. No Factum may exceed 20 pages without leave of the court.

19. The authorities that are included in the Superior Court of Justice List of Often Cited Family Cases do not need to be provided to the court. However the specific paragraphs on which a party relies shall be reproduced in its Factum.

Ottawa Only

20. The moving party must provide its material for the long motion not later than ten days after the long motion date is scheduled. *Failure to do so will result in the long motion date being vacated without further notice to either party.*

Part 5: — Compendiums — Family Law Motions

21. A Compendium containing the documents and evidence essential to the hearing of a long or complex motion (e.g. summary judgment) may be served and filed with a Factum. A joint Compendium may be filed with the Respondent's Factum.

22. Normally a Compendium would include: the Notice of Motion, Affidavits or essential portions of Affidavits, Financial Statements, Net Family Property Statements, essential Exhibits and excerpts from any other evidence (e.g. transcripts) that will be referred to when arguing the motion.

A. — 14B Motions

23. A 14B Motion must be filed at the Family Law Counter and cannot be filed by fax. A Form 14B Motion Form should be accompanied by 4 copies of a proposed Order (Form 25), a self-addressed and stamped envelope for each party. For local counsel, the address may be the lawyer's court office box and no stamp is required.

24. Service requirements of a Form 14B motion are governed by the *Family Law Rules*.

25. Where a party would be unable to file documents due to their inability to obtain Canada Revenue Agency documents in a timely way, a Form 14B motion may be filed with their documents together with an affidavit stating: (a) they have filed tax returns for the particular year and have provided a copy of the return to the other party but do not yet have a notice of assessment; or (b) they have filed their tax returns for the particular year but do not have a copy or a copy of the notice of assessment — and explain why; or (c) they do not have Canadian tax returns for the particular year because they lived somewhere else and they have either provided the other return to the other party or are unable to do so for some explicable reason, and they have written to Canada Revenue Agency for the Income and Deductions printout required by *rule 13(7)(2)(B)* but have not yet received it and they attach a copy of the letter to CRA as an exhibit.

B. — Procedural Motions: Ottawa Only

26. Dates are posted at the Family Law Counter and in Family Law Information Centre when procedural motions may be brought in court. Attendance at the Family Counter by no later than 9:30 a.m. on the motion date with the served motion materials and proof of service is required.

27. A procedural motion includes a motion for a determination of urgency or hardship, seeking permission to bring a substantive motion before case conference.

28. A procedural motion should only be brought without notice to the other party in compliance with *rule 14(12)*.

29. All procedural motions, whether opposed or unopposed, are confined to 15 minutes or less in duration.

C. — Urgent Motions on Notice:

30. A party may seek an urgent motion on notice without a case conference in situations of urgency or hardship including issues such as abduction, threats of harm or dire financial harm. A party seeking such a Motion must file all of the required materials.

D. — Urgent Motions without Notice:

31. A party that is seeking a motion without notice to the other party must also set out why notice is unnecessary or not reasonably possible. A Factum or Summary of Argument is not required for an urgent motion that has been brought without notice.

Part 6: — Consent Adjournments

32. Although the court requests notice of consent adjournments as early as possible, consent adjournments of regular motions may be obtained by faxing notice to the court office not later than 4 p.m. on the last business day before the scheduled event. A notice of return of motion must be delivered to obtain a subsequent date.

33. If the motion is to be adjourned on consent on terms or on the basis of a consent order, the original signed consent and approved draft order must be filed before the matter will be taken off the list.

34. Adjournments of conferences scheduled in response to a Notice of Approaching Dismissal are only available by permission of a judge.

Part 7: — Conference Attendance by Video or Teleconference

35. Parties may arrange through the Family Law Counter in conjunction with the Trial Office for a case conference to occur by teleconference with the consent of both parties and their counsel.

36. For other conferences, or if the other party to the case conference does not consent, a request for a teleconference may be made by a *Form 14B*

37. Videoconferencing may be available in certain centres and can be used with prior judicial approval. For information contact the local Trial Coordinator.

Part 8: — Trial Scheduling

38. If a case is not resolved at a settlement conference, the Trial Scheduling Endorsement Forms must be completed and endorsed by the Court prior to the case being listed for trial.

39. The completed Forms shall be entered into the yellow Endorsement book of the Continuing Record for use at a Trial Management Conference.

40. Where the Court has directed that a Trial Scheduling Conference should be held, the parties must confirm their attendance at this conference in accordance with Rule 17(14) and file their respective portions of the Trial Scheduling Endorsement Form in advance of the conference in accordance with the timelines in rule 17(13.1).

41. Parties should refer to section 31.9 of Part 1 of the Provincial Practice Direction regarding the materials that must to be filed in advance of a Trial Management Conference.

Part 9: — Trial Records

42. The Applicant must serve and file a Trial Record at least 30 days prior to the scheduled Trial date, in compliance with *rule 23(1) and (2)*.

43. If the Applicant fails to do so, the Respondent may serve and file a Trial Record at least 20 days before the scheduled Trial date.

44. Failure of either party to file the Trial Record shall result in the case being removed from the Trial list, unless the court orders otherwise.

Dated: July 21, 2016

Heather J. Smith

Chief Justice

Superior Court of Justice (Ontario)

James E. McNamara

Regional Senior Judge

Superior Court of Justice, East Region

PD-11 — *CONSOLIDATED PRACTICE DIRECTION FOR THE NORTHEAST REGION (EFFECTIVE JULY 1, 2014)*

Notice of Amendment: Part III A (Designated Counties for the Commencement of Mortgage Proceedings under r. 13.1.01) was added on February 27, 2015 and comes into effect on March 31, 2015.

This Practice Direction applies to proceedings in the Superior Court of Justice, Northeast Region, effective July 1, 2014. It *supersedes* all previous region-specific Practice Directions for the Northeast Region issued prior to July 1, 2014, which are hereby revoked.

Counsel and parties are advised to refer to the relevant Parts of the Consolidated Provincial Practice Direction as well as the Consolidated Practice Direction for Divisional Court Proceedings which are available on the Superior Court of Justice website at: www.ontariocourts.ca/scj.

PART I: — FAMILY PROCEEDINGS

1. In addition to this Part, counsel and parties in family proceedings are advised to refer to Part I of the Consolidated Provincial Practice Direction.

A. — Form 14B Motions

2. Form 14B motions procedures are governed by Part I of the Consolidated Provincial Practice Direction. Counsel and parties are advised to refer to that Practice Direction for further direction.

PART II: — CRIMINAL PROCEEDINGS

A. — Criminal Matters arising in Chapleau and Gogama

3. The following Superior Court of Justice matters of a criminal nature arising in Chapleau or Gogama, in the District of Sudbury, may proceed at the Superior Court of Justice in Timmins, in the District of Cochrane:

a) Trials emanating from committals to stand trial in the Ontario Court of Justice in Chapleau or Gogama rendered after June 30, 2010, or preferred indictments in matters arising out of Chapleau or Gogama filed after June 30, 2010;

b) Appeals from summary convictions in the Ontario Court of Justice in Chapleau or Gogama rendered after June 30, 2010;

c) Applications for prerogative remedies relating to decisions of the Ontario Court of Justice in Chapleau or Gogama rendered after June 30, 2010;

d) Reviews of bail decisions of the Ontario Court of Justice for Chapleau or Gogama matters rendered after June 30, 2010; and,

e) Any other matters relating to charges with an alleged offence date after June 30, 2010.

PART III: — CIVIL PROCEEDINGS

A. — Designated Counties for the Commencement of Mortgage Proceedings under rule 13.1.01(3)

4. Pursuant to rule 13.1.01(3) of the *Rules of Civil Procedure*, which comes into effect on March 31, 2015, North Bay, Parry Sound, Sudbury, Haileybury, Sault St. Marie, Cochrane or Gore Bay have been designated as the place for commencement of mortgage proceedings for property located anywhere in the Northeast Region.

Dated: April 11, 2014

Amended: February 27, 2015 (addition of para 4)

Heather J. Smith

Chief Justice

Superior Court of Justice (Ontario)

Robbie D. Gordon

Regional Senior Judge

Superior Court of Justice, Northeast Region

PD-11a — *CONSOLIDATED PRACTICE DIRECTION CONCERNING FAMILY CASES IN THE NORTHEAST REGION*

Effective May 1, 2016

This Practice Direction applies to family law proceedings in the Superior Court of Justice in the Northeast Region. It supersedes Part I: Family Proceedings of the Consolidated Practice Direction for the Northeast Region.

Counsel and parties are advised to refer also to the relevant parts of the Consolidated Provincial Practice Direction which is available on the Superior Court of Justice website at www.ontariocourts.ca/scj.

Each of the forms required by the Family Law Rules is available at the Ontario Court Forms website at: http://www.ontariocourtforms.on.ca/en/family-law-rules-forms/. In addition, the Trial Scheduling Endorsement Form for family cases is available on the website of the Superior Court of Justice at: http://www.ontariocourts.ca/scj/practice/rules-forms/

Part I: — Confirmations

1. Each party to a motion or conference must file a Form 14C Confirmation, or the parties may file one jointly, no later than 2 p.m. two business days before the date of the motion or conference.

2. The parties or their counsel should consult with each other prior to filing their Form 14C Confirmations, unless the parties are self-represented and prohibited from communicating by court order.

3. Where Form 14C Confirmations have not been filed by at least one party, the conference or motion will not be scheduled on the event list and, as a result, will not be heard by the court. Costs may also be ordered against a party who has not filed the confirmation.

4. Form 14C Confirmations must only list the specific issues that are to be addressed at the event. They should also indicate which materials the judge should review with clear reference to the specific volume, tab and page numbers of the Continuing Record. Failure to provide this information may result in the materials not being reviewed by the judge or the motion or conference not being heard on that day, and costs consequences.

5. Form 14C Confirmations must also include an appropriate time estimate for the entire motion or conference, including time required by the other party. Parties will be held to the time stated on their confirmations.

6. If a Confirmation is filed for a consent adjournment, no one needs to appear to speak to the court about the adjournment unless directed to do so by the court.

Part II: — Motions

A. — Short Motions

7. Motions that are expected to take one hour or less may be scheduled on a regular motions day by serving and filing the motion material at the court office within the timelines set out in the *Family Law Rules*.

B. — Long Motions

8. In those court centres that have adopted a long motions protocol for family law matters, the protocol must be followed unless an order is obtained to the contrary. Contact the Trial Coordinator in the centre that the case is in for the latest information about long motion protocols.

9. In those court centres that have not adopted a long motions protocol,

a. Motions that are expected to take more than 1 hour (including the other party's reply and cross motion, if any) must be scheduled as long motions through the Trial Coordinator in the court office. Long motions can be scheduled either (i) with the other party's written consent or (ii) with the court's permission, by filing a Form 14B Motion Form under section 14(10) of the *Family Law Rules*; and

b. The moving party must serve and file all their motion material and an Offer to Settle at least 30 days prior to the scheduled motion date, or the date will be vacated. The responding party must serve and file their responding material and an Offer to Settle at least 15 days before the scheduled motion date. Reply material, if any, and a properly completed Form14C Confirmation, confirming the motion date and material to be read, must be served and filed by 2 p.m. seven days prior to the scheduled motion date. If a long motion is not confirmed by 2 p.m. seven days in advance, it will be removed from the list and the date will be vacated.

C. — Factums and Briefs of Authorities

10. A properly drafted factum is required on all long motions and is optional for short motions. If the moving party does not file a factum where required, the motion will not be scheduled.

11. Each party's factum must be filed by no later than 2 p.m. two business days before the hearing of the motion.

12. No factum may exceed 20 pages without leave of the court.

13. The authorities that are included on the court's list of Often Cited Family Cases do not need to be provided to the court with a party's factum. An updated list of often cited family cases is available on the Superior Court's website at: www.ontariocourts.ca/scj. However, extracts from those authorities which the court will be referred to shall be included in the factum or book of authorities, in addition to copies of any other cases that a party relies on.

D. — 14 B Motions

14. A Form 14B Motion must be filed at the family court office and cannot be filed by fax. A Form 14B Motion Form should be accompanied by one copy of a proposed Order (Form 25) and a self-addressed and stamped envelope for each party.

15. The 14B Motion Form shall be filed in the Continuing Record and a copy of the proposed Order shall be attached to the appropriate place in the Endorsement Volume.

E. — Compendiums

16. A Compendium* containing the documents and evidence that are essential to the hearing of the motion may be provided for long or complex motions. A party wishing to file a Compendium should file it with their factum. A joint Compendium may be filed with the respondent's factum.

F. — Electronic Copies of Materials

17. Whenever the volume of materials is large or the motion is complex, the parties should file an electronic copy of their motion materials as well as paper copies.

G. — Urgent Motions on Notice

17. A party may seek an urgent motion on notice without a case conference in situations of urgency or hardship including issues such as abduction, threats of harm or dire financial harm. A party seeking such a motion must file all of the required materials for a motion except for a Form 14C Confirmation.

**A compendium would normally include the Notice of Motion, Affidavits and Financial Statements, as well as excerpts from the evidence and exhibits that will be referred to in the argument of the motion.*

H. — Urgent Motions without Notice

19. A party that is seeking a motion without notice to the other party must also set out why giving notice is unnecessary, is not reasonably possible, or would have serious consequences.

I. — Case Conferences and Settlement Conferences

20. A party may by written request through the Trial Coordinator ask that a conference be conducted by teleconference or, where available, by videoconference. In any such request, the party shall indicate whether or not it is being made with consent of the opposing party and, if it is not, the reasons for the request.

21. Counsel or the parties should communicate before any conference in order to attempt to resolve the issues that are in dispute, unless the parties are self-represented and prohibited from communicating by court order.

22. The parties should each bring their Trial Scheduling Endorsement Forms to the settlement conference with their respective portions completed. If the matter is not resolved at a settlement conference, the complete Trial Scheduling Endorsement form must be endorsed by the court prior to the matter being scheduled for trial.

J. — Trial Management Conferences

23. A trial management conference will be scheduled by the court office for a date before the assigned trial date.

24. In advance of the Trial Management Conference, each party must file an Offer to Settle and Outline of Opening Statement in lieu of the Form 17E Trial Management Conference Brief. A copy of the completed Trial Scheduling Endorsement form shall be attached to these materials by the court.

K. — Trial Records

25. The Applicant must serve and file a Trial Record at least 30 days prior to the scheduled trial date. Failure to do so will result in the matter being removed from the trial list, unless the court orders otherwise. Financial Statements do not need to be updated again after the Trial Record is filed as required by Rule 13(12) unless this is required by the Trial Scheduling Endorsement Form.

Dated: May 1, 2016

Heather J. Smith

Chief Justice

Superior Court of Justice (Ontario)

Robbie D. Gordon

Regional Senior Judge

Superior Court of Justice, Northeast Region

PD-12 — *CONSOLIDATED PRACTICE DIRECTION FOR THE NORTHWEST REGION (EFFECTIVE JULY 1, 2014)*

Notice of Amendment: Part I A.1 (Designated Counties for the Commencement of Mortgage Proceedings under r. 13.1.01) was added on February 27, 2015 and comes into effect on March 31, 2015.

This Practice Direction applies to proceedings in the Superior Court of Justice, Northwest Region, effective July 1, 2014. It *supersedes* all previous region-specific Practice Directions for the Northwest Region issued prior to July 1, 2014, which are hereby revoked.

Counsel and parties are advised to refer to the relevant Parts of the Consolidated Provincial Practice Direction as well as the Consolidated Practice Direction for Divisional Court Proceedings which are available on the Superior Court of Justice website at: www.ontariocourts.ca/scj.

PART I: — ALL PROCEEDINGS

A. — Faxing or Emailing Documents and Late Filings of Documents and Confirmation Forms in all Civil, Family and Criminal Proceedings

1. There has been a marked increase in civil, family and criminal materials being faxed or e-mailed to the Superior Court of Justice, Northwest Region. This includes case conference, settlement conference, and pre-trial briefs, motion records and briefs of authorities. Often these materials are sent at the last minute. Some of the materials are voluminous.

2. In addition, there has been an increase in the number of late filings of confirmation forms and documents for specific hearings.

3. This flood of materials has, at times, overwhelmed the court's capacity to receive and process them. Faxed materials are generally less legible than original materials. They may be out of alignment. In addition, it is far from certain that all pages transmitted will be received by the court. Finally, there is a concern that pages of one document being pulled from the fax machine may be intermingled with another unrelated document.

4. Similar problems apply to the printing of e-mailed documents at the court office. Current staffing does not allow for printing and collating of e-mailed materials.

5. With respect to late filings of materials and confirmation forms as required under the applicable rules, staff are in a difficult position, not knowing whether they should accept or refuse documents.

6. In order that documents to be filed are received in a complete and legible form, all parties are asked to file original documents at the Registrar's office, complete with original affidavits of service, in compliance with the rule setting out the time for filing. Unless the filing is of an urgent nature, or the presiding judge has requested material to be delivered in this fashion, documents *should not* be sent to the court for filing by fax or e-mail. The single exception is a Pre-Trial Conference Report (From 17) which may be faxed or delivered to the trial office in accordance with timelines noted on the Form.

7. With respect to late filing of documents and confirmation forms, specific direction has been provided to staff that, if confirmations and material are not received within the prescribed time, the court file must not be forwarded to the judge. If counsel or self-represented parties appear on a specific day (and their filings are not complete)

they will need to complete a fiat to be presented to the judge and she/he will decide whether or not they will hear the matter or order the parties to select a new date.

A.1 — Designated Counties for the Commencement of Mortgage Proceedings under rule 13.1.01(3)

7.1 Pursuant to rule 13.1.01(3) of the *Rules of Civil Procedure*, which comes into effect on March 31, 2015, Fort Frances, Thunder Bay or Kenora have been designated as the place for commencement of mortgage proceedings for property located anywhere in the Northwest Region.

B. — Requests to Attend Proceedings via Teleconference or Videoconference in all Proceedings

8. Counsel and parties requesting to attend their matter via teleconference or videoconference must complete a Request Form.

9. No request shall be considered approved until approval has been duly granted by a judge of the Superior Court of Justice acting for, or in, the Northwest Region.

10. Requests are to be submitted *no less than five (5) days prior to the event.*

11. To receive a Request Form for matters in Thunder Bay contact the Trial Coordinator.

12. To receive a Request Form for matters in Kenora and Fort Frances, please contact the Assistant Trial Coordinator.

13. The contact information for the Trial Coordinator and Assistant Trial Coordinator are available on the Superior Court's website at: www.ontariocourts.ca/scj/practice/schedules/nw/directory.

PART II: — FAMILY PROCEEDINGS

14. In addition to this Part, counsel and parties in family proceedings are advised to refer to Part I of the Provincial Practice Direction.

A. — 14B Motions

15. Form 14B motions procedures are governed by Part I of the Consolidated Provincial Practice Direction. Counsel and parties are advised to refer to that Practice Direction for further direction.

PART III: — CRIMINAL PROCEEDINGS

A. — Gowning for Criminal Pre-trials

16. In addition to the gowning requirements outlined in the Consolidated Provincial Practice Direction, counsel are required to gown for criminal pre-trials in the Northwest Region.

Dated: April 11, 2014

Heather J. Smith

Chief Justice

Superior Court of Justice (Ontario)

Helen M. Pierce

Regional Senior Justice

Superior Court of Justice, Northwest Region

PD-12a — *CONSOLIDATED PRACTICE DIRECTION CONCERNING FAMILY CASES IN THE NORTHWEST REGION*

Effective June 1, 2016

This Practice Direction applies to family law proceedings in the Superior Court of Justice in the Northwest Region (Thunder Bay, Fort Frances and Kenora). It supersedes all previous Practice Directions concerning family proceedings in the Northwest Region which are hereby revoked.

Counsel and parties should also refer to the relevant parts of the Consolidated Provincial Practice Direction (Part I in particular).

All documents must be filed at the Registrar's Office in which the proceedings are commenced.

Each of the forms required by the Family Law Rules is available at the Ontario Court Forms website at: http://www.ontariocourtforms.on.ca/en/family-law-rules-forms/. In addition, the Trial Scheduling Endorsement Form for family cases is available on the website of the Superior Court of Justice at: http://www.ontariocourts.ca/scj/practice/rules-forms/

Forms to request to attend any proceeding by teleconference or videoconference are available by contacting the Trial Coordinator's office at the location in which proceedings are commenced. Contact information for the Trial Coordinator's office each centre is available in the regional schedule.

Information about additional family law services that are available in the Northwest Region is attached at Appendix A.

Part I: — Confirmations

1. Each party to a motion or conference must file, at the Registrar's Office, a Form 14C Confirmation, or the parties may file one jointly, no later than 2 p.m. two business days before the date of the motion or conference except for long motions, which must be filed by 2:00 p.m. seven days before the motion.

2. The parties or their counsel should consult with each other prior to filing their Form 14C Confirmations, unless the parties are self-represented and prohibited from communicating by court order.

3. Where Form 14C Confirmations have not been filed by at least one party, the conference or motion will not be placed on the daily event list and, as a result, will not be heard by the court.

4. Form 14C Confirmations must only list the specific issues that are to be addressed at the event. They should also include a list of which materials the judge should review with clear reference to the specific volume, tab and page numbers of the Continuing Record. Failure to provide this information may result in the materials not being reviewed by the judge or the motion or conference not being heard on that day, and costs consequences.

5. Form 14C Confirmations must also include an appropriate time estimate for the entire motion or conference, including time required by the other party. Parties will be held to the time stated on their confirmations.

6. If a Form 14C Confirmation is filed for a consent adjournment, no one needs to appear to speak to the court about the adjournment unless directed to do so by the court.

Part II: — Motions

A. — Short Motions

7. Motions that will take less than two hours (including the other party's reply and cross motion, if any) may be scheduled on a regular motions day by serving and filing the motion material at the court office within the timelines set out in the Family Law Rules.

B. — Long Motions

8. Motions that will take two hours or more (including the other party's reply and cross motion, if any) must be scheduled on a specific date, provided through the Trial Coordinator's office. Long motions are only scheduled with the court's approval, by filing a Form 14B and the parties must attend a regularly scheduled Motions Court to receive approval from that presiding motions judge to book a specific date. The moving party must serve and file all their motion material at least 30 days prior to the scheduled long motion date, or the date will be vacated. The responding party must serve and file their responding material at least 15 days before the scheduled long motion date. Reply material, if any, and a properly completed Form14C Confirmation, confirming the long motion date and material to be read, must be served and filed by 2 p.m. seven days prior to the scheduled motion date. If a long motion is not confirmed by 2 p.m. seven days in advance, it will be removed from the list and the date will be vacated.

C. — Factums and Briefs of Authorities

9. A properly drafted factum is required on all long motions but is optional for short motions. If the moving party does not file a factum where required, the motion will not proceed. The text of the factum shall be printed on good quality white paper 216 millimeters by 279 millimeters in size, on one side only, with double spaces between the lines except for quotations which may be single spaced, and margins of approximately 40 millimeters on the left hand side. The characters used shall be at least 12 point or 10 pitch size.

10. Any factum must be filed with the parties' motion materials.

11. No factum may exceed 20 pages without leave of the court.

12. The authorities that are included on the court's list of often cited family cases do not need to be provided to the court with a party's factum. An updated list of often

cited family cases referred to is available on the Superior Court's website at: www.ontariocourts.ca/scj. However, extracts from those authorities which the court will be referred to shall be included in the factum or book of authorities, in addition to copies of any other cases that a party relies on.

D. — 14B Motions

13. A Form 14B Motion must be filed at the family court office and cannot be filed by fax. A Form 14B Motion should be accompanied by one copy of a proposed Order (Form 25) and a self-addressed and stamped envelope for each party.

14. The Form 14B Motion shall be filed in the Continuing Record and a copy of the proposed Order shall be attached to the appropriate place in the Endorsement Volume.

E. — Compendium

15. A Compendium* containing the documents and evidence that are essential to the hearing of the motion may be provided for long or complex motions. A party wishing to file a Compendium should file it with their factum. A joint Compendium may be filed with the respondent's factum.

F. — Electronic Copies of Materials

16. Whenever the volume of materials is large or the motion is complex, the parties should file an electronic copy of their motion materials by e-mail to the appropriate Trial Coordinator, with the file name clearly identified for each document, as well as paper copies to be filed at the Registrar's Office.

G. — Urgent Motions With Notice

17. A party may seek an urgent motion with notice without a case conference in situations of urgency or hardship, as set out in Rule 14(4.2). A party seeking such a motion must serve and file all of the required materials except for a Form 14C Confirmation. Prior to bringing an urgent motion, the Trial Coordinator should be contacted to see if an urgent case conference can be scheduled before the motion is heard.

18. To enable the order to be issued quickly, parties are encouraged to provide the court with a draft order.

H. — Urgent Motions Without Notice

19. Motions without notice may be brought only in exceptional circumstances as set out in Rule 14(12).

20. A Court will not generally make an order without allowing both parties an opportunity to participate. In addition to addressing the requirements of paragraph 17

*A Compendium would normally include the Notice of Motion, Affidavits and Financial Statements, as well as excerpts from the evidence and exhibits that will be referred to in the argument of the motion.

above, a party who is seeking a motion without notice to the other party must address why the other party has not been served. The motions materials should set out specifically and clearly why notice is unnecessary, not reasonably possible, or any other grounds that would justify the motion being heard without notice to the other side.

21. An order obtained without notice, together with all documents used on the motion, shall be served on the other party, unless the court orders otherwise. The matter must be scheduled to come back to the court within 14 days, as set out in Rule 14(14).

22. If a person is requesting a restraining order as part of his/her urgent motion, he or she should also complete the pink restraining order endorsement form with the required information (such as names and birth dates of those affected, as well as addresses at which the other side is to be prohibited from attending.) This form is available at the Registrars' Office, where the urgent motion is filed.

23. If a restraining order has been granted, the court can arrange for service of the material on the other side, if requested by a party who is not represented by counsel.

Part III: — Case Conferences, Settlement Conferences, Trial Scheduling Conferences

I. — Conferences

24. A party may, by completing a Request for Teleconference or Videoconference form available from the Trial Coordinator, ask for court approval that a conference be conducted by teleconference or videoconference, where available. In any such request, the party shall indicate whether or not it is being made with consent of the opposing party and, if it is not, the reasons for the request.

25. Counsel or the parties should communicate before any conference in order to attempt to resolve the issues that are in dispute, unless the parties are self-represented and prohibited from communicating by court order.

26. Case conference briefs and settlement conference briefs must be filed in accordance with the Family Law Rules.

27. All conferences will be scheduled for a duration of 45 minutes, except for settlement conferences which will be scheduled for a duration of one hour.

28. The parties should bring their Trial Scheduling Endorsement Forms to the settlement conference with their respective portions completed.

29. If the case has not settled at the conclusion of the settlement conference, the court shall determine if the Trial Scheduling Endorsement Form can be completed at the conference or shortly thereafter and shall give directions to the parties regarding the completion of this form.

30. If necessary, the Court may require the parties to attend a trial scheduling conference to canvas issues regarding the scheduling of the trial and ensure proper completion of the Trial Scheduling Endorsement Form. Each party shall complete and file his or her portion of the Trial Scheduling Endorsement Form with the court in advance of a trial scheduling conference in accordance with the timelines in rule 17(13.1)

31. The purpose of a Trial Scheduling Conference includes (i) ensuring that the case is ready to proceed to trial, (ii) considering each party's list of proposed witnesses and (iii) ensuring the accuracy of the estimated time for trial. Consideration should also be given to other factors that would be appropriate under rule 1 in order to limit the duration and scope of the trial.

32. A trial date will not be made available until the court has reviewed and endorsed the completed trial scheduling endorsement form.

J. — Trial Management Conferences

33. A trial management conference shall be scheduled by the parties at the time that the trial date is assigned. The trial management conference should be scheduled to be held within two weeks of the scheduled trial date, dependent on the availability of judicial resources.

34. The Trial Management Conference Brief, Form 17E, is no longer required. Instead of the Trial Management Conference Brief, the following documents must be filed in advance of the trial management conference by the deadlines set out in rule 17(13.1)

a. The completed Trial Scheduling Endorsement Form must be filed by the applicant;

b. Each party must file an outline of his or her opening statement for trial, and

c. Each party must serve and bring to the conference, an offer to settle all outstanding issues.

35. The Trial Scheduling Endorsement Form shall be filed with or added to the Trial Record.

36. The purpose of the trial management conference is to confirm that the parties are ready for trial, have filed the Trial Record and exchanged all material required by the Trial Scheduling Endorsement Form, and to explore the final possibility of settlement of any or all trial issues.

37. Where the case has been settled and the trial is no longer required, one of the parties shall immediately advise the Trial Coordinator so that the trial date can be vacated. A copy of any Minutes of Settlement or consent should be filed with the Registrar's Office at the same time.

K. — Trial Records

38. The applicant must serve and file a Trial Record at least 30 days prior to the scheduled trial date. Failure to do so will result in the matter being removed from the trial list, unless the court orders otherwise. Financial Statements do not need to be updated again after the Trial Record is filed as required by Rule 13(12) unless this is required by the Trial Scheduling Endorsement Form.

L. — Trial Dates

39. Trials are placed on specific Running List sessions scheduled throughout the year, at each location with the Northwest Region. Please contact the appropriate Trial Coordinator for trial dates in the selected location.

40. Uncontested trial dates are also provided by contacting the Trial Coordinator at the selected location.

Dated May 24, 2016

Heather J. Smith

Chief Justice

Superior Court of Justice (Ontario)

Douglas C. Shaw

Regional Senior Judge

Superior Court of Justice, Northwest Region

Appendix A — The Family Law Information Centre

1. Mediation North is responsible for information on Family Law MIP Sessions, etc. held throughout the Northwest Region. To contact the Information Referral Coordinator please dial: 1-888-935-5455

2. Thunder Bay has a drop-in **Family Law Information (FLIC) Office** : open daily from 8:30 a.m. until 5:00 p.m. Monday–Friday and is located on the 1st floor of the Thunder Bay Court House.

— Kenora and Fort Frances do not have a local FLIC office

3. **Duty counsel** at Thunder Bay is available Tuesdays 9:00 a.m.–11:30 a.m. and 1:30 p.m.–4:00 p.m., and Thursdays 1:30 p.m.–4:00 p.m., at no cost for consultation with qualified individuals seeking legal advice.

— Kenora and Fort Frances do not have Duty Counsel available for SCJ files

PD-13 — *CONSOLIDATED PRACTICE DIRECTION FOR THE SOUTHWEST REGION (EFFECTIVE AUGUST 1, 2016)*

This Practice Direction applies to proceedings in the Superior Court of Justice, Southwest Region, effective August 1, 2016. It replaces the previous Consolidated Practice Direction for the Southwest Region that was effective on July 1, 2014.

Counsel and parties are advised to refer to the relevant Parts of the Consolidated Provincial Practice Direction as well as the Consolidated Practice Direction for Divisional Court Proceedings which are available on the Superior Court of Justice website at: www.ontariocourts.ca/scj.

Part I: — Civil Proceedings

A. — Introduction

1. This Part identifies scheduling and administrative changes to facilitate more expeditious and efficient litigation under the *Rules of Civil Procedure*.

2. Subject to paragraph 60, this Part *does not* apply to commercial motions or applications heard in London as described in Part IV of this Practice Direction. This Part does apply to contested estates matters as described in Part V below.

3. A reference in this part to a "rule" or the "rules" is a reference to the Rules of Civil Procedure.

B. — Applications and Motions

4. All applications and motions will be heard on the assigned motions court day for each respective county in the Southwest Region commencing at 10:00 a.m. unless specified otherwise in this practice direction or by court order.

5. Any motion or application that requires more than 30 minutes for all parties to argue, or requires a court reporter, will be adjourned to a special appointment date.

6. Two consent adjournments of short motions (motions scheduled for 30 minutes or less) are permitted. Any further adjournment will, if permitted, be sine die returnable on four days' notice unless otherwise ordered by the presiding judge.

7. All motions and applications (including those requiring a special appointment date) must be confirmed. Confirmation forms must be filed no later than 2:00 p.m. three days before the hearing date, as required under rules 37.10.1(1) and 38.09.1(1). Communication and cooperation in completing all parts of the prescribed form is expected by the Court. The form should accurately and fully describe all materials to which the presiding judge will be referred by any party.

8. Rules 37.10.1(2) and 38.09.1(2) provide that motions and applications that are not confirmed will not be heard by the Court. Parties will not be permitted to take unconfirmed matters into motions court to request that they be added to the list.

9. For greater certainty, the *Rules of Civil Procedure*, including all timelines, are to be strictly adhered to.

C. — Special Appointments for Motions and Applications

10. Special appointments are required for motions and applications that require more than 30 minutes for all parties to argue or require a court reporter.

11. Special appointments are scheduled for a date made available by the Trial Coordinator. To obtain a date, all parties or their counsel must complete a Certificate of Readiness of Special Appointment confirming they are, or will be on the assigned date, ready to proceed, the time required for the motion and whether a court reporter is required. The Certificate of Readiness of Special Appointment also includes a timetable for the completion of any step that remains to be completed at the time a special appointment is scheduled. The judge presiding in motions court will resolve any disputes relating to a date for such appointment and/or the timetable in motions court. Counsel and self-represented parties will be expected to strictly abide by the timetable and be ready to argue the matter on the assigned date.

12. Factums are required for all special appointments. Pursuant to the *Rules of Civil Procedure*, the moving party's factum shall be served and filed at least seven days before the scheduled hearing date of the special appointment. The responding party's factum shall be served and filed at least four days before the hearing.

13. Once the special appointment has been scheduled by the court, any adjournment requests must be spoken to before a judge. The Trial Coordinator must be advised of any adjournment requests and any settlements as far in advance of the hearing date as possible. In person attendance is required to speak to requests for an adjournment or to vacate a special appointment date. Adjournments will only be granted in exceptional cases.

14. Paragraphs 7 and 8 (confirmation forms) also apply to motions and applications that are scheduled as special appointments.

D. — Pre-Trials

15. In order to make civil pre-trials more productive and efficient, the following guidelines should be adhered to:

a. Copies of medical records and reports need not be filed with your pre-trial conference brief. Instead, relevant passages from these documents shall be copied and pasted within the pre-trial conference brief itself;

b. Each party shall bring to the conference a separate brief containing all medical and other expert reports to the conference as required by rule 50.11;

c. Pre-trial conference briefs should not exceed 20 pages in length, except in the rarest of cases. Briefs that are concise tend to be the most focussed and useful for the Court;

d. Pre-trial conference briefs must contain all of the information mandated by rule 50 including the names and anticipated length of the evidence of each witness a party is likely to call (the "witness list") and details of all steps that need to be completed before the matter is ready to be heard (including the delivery of any other expert report) and the estimated time for completion of each outstanding step. Each witness list shall be set forth in a separate, stand-alone schedule capable of being removed from the pre-trial conference brief and attached to the pre-trial conference report completed by the presiding judge pursuant to rule 50.08(1).

E. — Designated Counties for the Commencement of Mortgage Proceedings under rule 13.1.01(3)

16. Pursuant to rule 13.1.01(3), London, Windsor, St. Thomas, Chatham, Sarnia, Woodstock, Stratford and Goderich have been designated as the place for commencement of mortgage proceedings for property located anywhere in the Southwest Region.

Part II: — Family Proceedings

A. — Introduction

17. This Part identifies scheduling and administrative changes to facilitate more expeditious and efficient litigation under the *Family Law Rules*.

18. Unless otherwise stated, this Part applies to **all** family proceedings, including those in the Unified Family Court — London.

19. A reference in this part to a "rule" or the "rules" is a reference to the *Family Law Rules*.

B. — Family Motions

20. Any motion that requires less than one hour for all parties to argue is treated as a regular motion.

21. All regular motions will be heard on the assigned motions court day for each respective county in the Southwest Region commencing at 10:00 a.m. unless otherwise ordered by the court.

22. All motions requiring more than one hour to argue will require a special appointment.

23. Paragraphs 11 and 12 relating to special appointments in civil cases also apply to special appointments in family cases, including the requirements for the filing of factums. However, if the Certificate of Readiness of Special Appointment — Family Cases has been completed at the case conference, no further attendance will be required in order to obtain the date for a special appointment.

14B Motions

24. Form 14B motions are governed by Part I of the Consolidated Provincial Practice Direction. Counsel and parties are advised to refer to that Practice Direction for further direction.

C. — Confirmation Forms

25. Each party to a conference or motion must file a fully completed File 14C Confirmation no later than 2 p.m. two business days before the motion or conference, except urgent motions that are being brought without notice to the other party do not need to be confirmed.

26. Form 14C Confirmations must only list the specific issues that are to be addressed at that event and the specific materials that the judge should review. Communication and cooperation in completing all parts of the prescribed form is expected. The materials which the presiding judge will be referred to, by any party, should be fully and accurately described.

27. Where Form 14C Confirmation forms have not been properly completed and filed by the appropriate deadline, the event will not be heard on the scheduled day without the permission of the presiding judge.

D. — Conference Briefs

28. No brief or other document for use at the conference that is required to be served or filed may be served or filed after 2:00 p.m. two business days before the date scheduled for the conference (rule 17(14.1)).

29. Any attempt to file conference briefs outside of the filing dates set out in the *Family Law Rules* will be refused at the counter. However, the parties may attend in person no later than 9:00 a.m. on the day of the conference with their conference brief and file with the Trial Coordinator provided it has been served on the other party as required in the above paragraph 24 and proof of service is attached. The Trial Coordinator will stamp the brief "FILED LATE" and place it with the materials for the presiding judge to review or not, at the judge's discretion. This process allows the court staff to comply with the Rules and for conferences to proceed in a timely manner, giving the presiding judge an opportunity to read the conference brief or refuse the brief.

E. — Scheduling Family Conferences

30. Case Conferences will be limited to 7 per day to allow approximately 45 minutes for each matter scheduled.

31. Settlement Conferences will be limited to 5 per day to allow 60 minutes scheduled for each matter.

F. — Settlement Conferences and Trial Scheduling Conferences

32. The settlement conference is an important step in family cases. The primary purpose of the settlement conference is to settle or at least narrow the issues in dispute. Parties (or their counsel) are required to communicate before any conference in order to attempt to narrow or resolve the issues that are in dispute, unless the parties are self-represented and are also prohibited from communicating by court order.

33. Pursuant to rule 17(5) (g), if the case is not settled at the settlement conference, one of the additional purposes of the conference is to identify the witnesses and other evidence to be presented at trial, estimate the time needed for trial and, where appropriate, to schedule the case for trial.

34. Parties are to come to the settlement conference having completed Parts 1 and 2 of the Trial Scheduling Endorsement Form. If the case has not settled at the conclusion of the settlement conference, the presiding judge will complete Part 3 of the form, or shall give directions to the parties regarding the completion of this form.

35. If necessary, the court may require the parties to attend a trial scheduling conference to canvass issues regarding the scheduling of the trial and ensure proper completion of the Trial Scheduling Endorsement Form. Each party shall complete and file their portion of the Trial Scheduling Endorsement Form with the court in advance of a trial scheduling conference in accordance with the timelines in rule 17(13.1).

36. The purpose of a trial scheduling conference includes (i) ensuring that the case is ready to proceed to trial, (ii) considering each party's list of proposed witnesses and (iii) ensuring the accuracy of the estimated time for trial. Consideration should also be given to other conditions that would be appropriate under rule 1 in order to limit the duration and scope of the trial.

37. A trial date will not normally be made available until the court has reviewed and endorsed the complete Trial Scheduling Endorsement Form. The court may however, in its discretion, provide litigants with a provisional trial date before the court has endorsed the complete Trial Scheduling Endorsement Form, where necessary. Where this has occurred, the form must be finalized no later than 60 days in advance of the trial or as directed by the presiding judge in order to retain the scheduled trial date.

G. — Trial Management Conferences

38. A trial management conference should be held in family cases that have not been resolved at or before the settlement conference in order to ensure trial readiness and canvas settlement. The trial management conference should be scheduled no more than two weeks in advance of the scheduled trial date, wherever possible.

39. The purpose of a trial management conference is to confirm that parties are ready for trial, have filed their Trial Record exchanged all other material required by the Trial Scheduling Endorsement Form, provide any further directions or revisions to the Trial Scheduling Endorsement Form, and to explore any final possibilities for settlement to resolve the trial.

40. The Trial Management Conference Brief: Form 17E is no longer required. Instead the following documents must be filed at least 7 days before the Trial Management Conference:

a. The completed Trial Scheduling Endorsement Form must be filed by either the Applicant or the party that requested the conference;

b. Each party must file an offer to settle all outstanding issues; and,

c. Each party must file an outline of their opening statement for trial.

41. The Endorsement Volume of the continuing record should also be put before the judge at the trial management conference.

42. The judge will make any changes to Part 3 of the Trial Scheduling Endorsement Form to reflect any changes in the outstanding issues, witnesses and positions of the parties since the form was initially completed, ensure that the case is trial ready and confirm the trial sittings.

43. The completed Trial Scheduling Endorsement Form shall be filed with or added to the Trial Record. No offers to settle should be included in the Trial Record.

44. Where the case has been settled and the trial is no longer required, one of the parties shall immediately advise the Trial Coordinator so that the trial date can be vacated. A copy of any Minutes of Settlement or consent should be filed at the same time.

45. The Trial Record is to be served and filed within the timelines set out in the *Family Law Rules*.

Part III: — Additional Provisions Regarding the Unified Family Court — London

A. — *Family Law matters*

46. Paragraphs 17–23 also apply to all family law matters being heard in the Unified Family Court — London except for *Child and Family Services Act*

47. Previously scheduled settlement conferences, motions, special appointments or summary hearings may be adjourned on consent by obtaining a new date from the Trial Coordinator. A confirmation must then be sent in changing the dates. If the confirmation is sent there is no need for attendance by counsel/party. A separate confirmation must be filed to confirm attendance on the new date in accordance with the *Family Law Rules*. No more than two consent adjournments will be permitted before an in-person attendance is required.

48. Trial management conferences with a set trial sittings date may only be adjourned by attendance before the Local Administrative Judge or his/her designate at a time that may be arranged through the Trial Coordinator.

49. Trial adjournment requests may be made at the Trial Readiness Court if they have not already been addressed at the Trial Management Conference. Attendance is required. It is expected that if a matter is on the trial list it is ready for trial and, if not, it will be removed, and placed on another trial list, or adjourned to a date to be spoken to, at the presiding judge's discretion. At the Trial Readiness Court no order will be given to the trials and the parties will be expected to be ready when called.

B. — Child and Family Services Act *matters*

50. Paragraphs 51–54 apply to all *Child and Family Services Act* matters being heard in the Unified Family Court — London.

51. Trials can only be adjourned to a subsequent trial date on motion with supporting affidavit material. These motions may be brought at the Trial Readiness Court or earlier before the Local Administrative Judge or his/her designate at a time that may be arranged through the Trial Coordinator. This direction applies to requests for adjournments by Children Aid Societies and any other party.

52. Temporary Care and Custody hearings and other motions may be adjourned to a subsequent date as set out above in paragraph 47 for family matters without the

necessity of attendance by counsel or parties, provided that no more than two consent adjournments will be permitted before an in-person attendance is required.

53. Even with the consent of both parties, settlement conferences and trial management conferences may only be adjourned by filing a confirmation indicating an intention to adjourn accompanied by a personal attendance to explain the reasons for the adjournment. If the parties know ahead that a request to adjourn the settlement conference will be made, the matter may be brought forward to be spoken to. Where an adjournment has been granted, a confirmation form will have to be filed in advance of the new date as required by the *Family Law Rules*.

54. For child protection matters, the child protection Trial Scheduling Endorsement Form must be filed by all parties at the final Settlement Conference. This form is available on the Superior Court of Justice website.

C. — General

55. Trial lists are blended with *Family Law Act/Children's Law Reform Act* matters and *Child and Family Services Act* matters, bearing in mind that *Child and Family Services Act* matters have statutory timelines under both the *Child and Family Services Act* and the *Family Law Rules* that must be respected, and will be given priority.

56. Any requests for adjournments of settlement conferences, special appointments or Temporary Care and Custody hearings should be made as early as possible so that other matters may be scheduled in their stead. This will assist in reducing timeouts for these events.

Part IV: — Commercial Proceedings in London

57. The purpose of this Part is to ensure administrative steps are in place for the appropriate and timely scheduling of commercial matters.

A. — Application

58. This Part applies to commercial matters in London involving the following statutes:

a. those arising under the *Bankruptcy and Insolvency Act* (BIA) to the extent they are beyond the jurisdiction of the Deputy Registrar under section 192 of the BIA. Such matters would include, by way of example only, opposed applications for a bankruptcy order, interim receiverships;

b. matters involving the *Companies' Creditors Arrangement Act* from the initial application until completion;

c. matters involving the *Personal Property Security Act*;

d. matters involving receivers appointed under the *Courts of Justice Act* whether in conjunction with or separate from an appointment under the BIA;

e. matters involving issues arising under the *Farm Debt Mediation Act*;

f. matters involving realization or the determination of priorities of claims arising under the *Bank Act*;

g. matters under either the *Ontario Business Corporations Act* or the *Canada Business Corporations Act*;

h. matters under the *Partnerships Act* or *Limited Partnerships Act*;

i. matters under the *Bulk Sales Act*; and

j. matters incidental to a proceeding involving a statute or subject mentioned above.

B. — Procedure

59. Counsel shall identify to the Trial Coordinator that a commercial matter is time sensitive by completing the Time Sensitive — Commercial Scheduling Request A date for hearing shall be scheduled directly with the Trial Coordinator.

60. If a commercial matter is not time sensitive, motions or applications shall initially be made returnable on a regular motions date. If such a motion or application requires more than 30 minutes for all parties to argue or requires a court reporter, counsel shall complete the Certificate of Readiness of Special Appointment of Commercial Matter Form and the Region's usual procedures with respect to special appointments as set out in Part I shall apply.

61. Factums are required for all special appointments involving commercial matters. Pursuant to the *Rules of Civil Procedure*, the moving party's factum shall be served and filed at least seven days before the scheduled hearing date of the special appointment. The responding party's factum shall be served and filed at least four days before the hearing.

62. Paragraphs 7 and 8 (confirmation forms) also apply to all motions and applications for commercial proceedings in London.

63. Counsel and parties are directed to the provisions of rule 37.15 and encouraged to consider the appropriateness of a request for a direction that all motions in the commercial proceeding be heard by a single judge.

Part V: — Additional Provisions Regarding Contested Estate Matters including a Contested Passing of Accounts

64. This part (in addition to Part I) applies to all contested estates matters, including a contested passing of accounts, in the Southwest Region.

65. Unless a judge has dispensed with the requirement, a contested estate matter, including a contested passing of accounts, estimated by any party to require a hearing of more than one day will not be scheduled except in accordance with an order giving directions. An order dispensing with the requirement will only be made in exceptional circumstances. Motions for directions may also be sought for a shorter contested estate matter.

66. Orders giving directions in contested matters are designed to provide the parties with a procedural framework in which to prepare the proceeding for final adjudication. Rule 75.06 provides the court with considerable discretion and flexibility to put in place a process that will ensure the just, expeditious and least expensive determination of a proceeding on its merits. Parties are expected to take time and care in preparing proposed orders giving directions for consideration by the court.

67. Draft orders giving directions should address the following matters to the extent applicable:

a. the issue(s) to be decided;

b. the identity of the parties;

c. whether there is any party under disability who requires representation and, if so, whether notice to the Public Guardian and Trustee or the Office of the Children's Lawyer should be directed;

d. whether an estate trustee should be appointed during litigation and the amount of security, if any, such an estate trustee should file;

e. who shall be served with the order for directions, and the method of and times for service;

f. whether the parties will exchange pleadings or put before the court their respective positions and the material facts upon which they rely by some other means;

g. procedures for bringing the matter before the court in a summary way;

h. any other pre-hearing steps to be undertaken, including the scope of documentary disclosure and examinations for discovery;

i. the necessity of and means of obtaining third party records including accounting or legal records;

j. the nature of any pre-hearing motion;

k. the delivery of any expert report and the utility of a pre-hearing meeting between experts to narrow the issues in dispute;

l. the date by which the matter must be set down for hearing;

m. a pre-trial conference;

n. the witnesses each party intends to call, the issues each witness intends to address, and the anticipated length of each witness' testimony including cross-examination;

o. a timetable for each applicable step outlined above; and

p. any matter relating to the conduct of the trial or hearing, including whether affidavit(s) may or will be used as the evidence-in-chief of a witness.

68. A motion for an order giving directions should be scheduled through the Trial Coordinator at 9:30 a.m. for 15-minutes if on consent and 30-minutes if contested. If the parties cannot agree on the terms of an order giving directions, each party must file with its motion material a copy of the draft order giving directions it is seeking. Under no circumstances should any order giving directions provide that an affidavit is or affidavits are to constitute or form part of the pleadings.

69. The parties' time estimate for the hearing will be re-evaluated at the pre-trial conference. The hearing date may be vacated if the presiding judge concludes the parties have underestimated the time required.

Part VI: — Forms

70. Each of the forms prescribed under the Rules of Civil Procedure and the Family Law Rules are available on the Ontario Court Forms website

71. Additional forms referred to in this Practice Direction are as follows:

A. Certificate of Readiness of Special Appointment

B. Certificate of Readiness of Special Appointment — Family Cases

C. Time Sensitive — Commercial Scheduling Request

D. Certificate of Readiness of Special Appointment for Commercial Matter

E. Trial Scheduling Endorsement Form (TSEF — Family)

F. Trial Scheduling Endorsement Form (TSEF — Child Protection)

Dated: July 21, 2016

Heather J. Smith

Chief Justice

Superior Court of Justice (Ontario)

Thomas A. Heeney

Regional Senior Judge

Superior Court of Justice, Southwest Region

PD-14 — *CONSOLIDATED PRACTICE DIRECTION FOR CIVIL ACTIONS, APPLICATIONS, MOTIONS AND PROCEDURAL MATTERS IN THE TORONTO REGION (EFFECTIVE JULY 1, 2015)*

Effective May 1, 2017, para 57 and the related certificate have been amended regarding mediation prior to setting an action down for trial.

This Practice Direction applies to actions, applications, motions and procedural matters in the Toronto Region, effective July 1, 2015. It replaces the previous Consolidated Practice Direction for Civil Actions, Applications, Motions and Procedural Matters in the Toronto Region that was effective on July 1, 2014. Changes have been made to incorporate the numerous scheduling improvements that were introduced by the Toronto Region Pilot Practice Advisory issued by Regional Senior Justice Morawetz on October 14, 2014. These changes have proven successful in bringing about greater scheduling efficiencies. They are now been implemented on a permanent basis in Toronto through this Practice Direction.

This Practice Direction *does not apply* to motions or applications heard on the Bankruptcy List, Estates List, or under the *Class Proceedings Act, 1992*, unless specifically mentioned.

Counsel and parties are advised to refer to the relevant Parts of the Consolidated Provincial Practice Direction, the Consolidated Practice Direction for Divisional Court Proceedings as well as any other relevant Toronto region-specific Practice Directions and Guides (e.g. the Guide Concerning Best Practices for Civil Actions, Applications and Motions in the Toronto Region).

All Superior Court of Justice Practice Directions are available on the Superior Court's website at: www.ontariocourts.ca/scj

PART I: — APPLICATIONS AND MOTIONS

A. — Civil Practice Court

1. Civil Practice Court ("CPC") has been instituted in the Toronto region. It replaces the former Motions Scheduling Court. It serves the following purposes:

a) To curtail the motions culture in Toronto and to ensure that motions and applications that are ready to proceed can be heard on a timely basis.

b) To permit the CPC judge to identify cases, at any stage, which require a degree of case management. Case management, most typically, will only be invoked in complex cases or where long motions are involved.

c) To assist in the orderly hearing of long motions, long applications, and any summary judgment motion. Parties will be encouraged to submit agreed upon timetables, and where necessary, case conferences will be scheduled in advance. The CPC judge will consider the option of directing long motions to the trial list.

d) To create a judicial mechanism whereby the CPC judge can assign those cases in need of the courts intervention before other available judges.

2. The CPC is supported administratively by the Civil Practice Unit. Staff in the Civil Practice Court serve as the first contact for any long motion, long application and any summary judgment motion. They are supported by an enhanced computerized scheduling program.

B. — Rules Applicable to All Motions & Applications

3. There are four different streams for scheduling motions and applications, depending on how they are heard, their duration and the judicial officer who is to hear the motion or application:

a) Short Applications & Short Motions before Judge or Master: Applications and motions before a Judge or Master that require two hours or less for all parties to argue are considered short applications and short motions. These motions are to be booked through the Civil Scheduling Unit, per the direction below.

b) Long Applications, Long Motions, Summary Judgment Motions and Urgent Matters before a Judge: Applications and motions before a Judge that require more than two hours for all parties to argue are considered long applications and long motions. These applications and motions are booked first by contacting the Civil Practice Unit for a date in Civil Practice Court. The Civil Practice Court will confirm the date for hearing the motion, and make any necessary procedural orders that are required.

c) Motions before Masters. Different procedures exist for scheduling long motions, short motions and ex parte motions before a Master. Different procedures are also outlined below for booking long motions before a master in case-managed actions and in construction lien actions or within a reference.

d) Motions before Judges or Masters in Writing. Counsel are strongly encouraged to bring in-writing motions when appropriate, to reduce unnecessary court appearances that drain limited judicial resources and which unnecessarily add to cost.

4. Elimination of "Placeholder" Motions. Any date requisitioned for a motion before a judge or master will be vacated if the Notice of Motion is not filed with payment of the motion fee within 10 business days after the motion date is requisitioned.

5. Matters to be Heard within 100 Days of Booking. All motions will only be booked when the parties are able to confirm their availability to have the motion heard within the 100 days (14 weeks) from the date of booking. Parties who cannot proceed within that timeframe will not be provided with a motion date, except in extenuating and exceptional circumstances.

6. Costs Outline Required. On all motions before a judge or master, parties are reminded to prepare in advance, and bring to the hearing, a costs outline to the motion, as required by r. 57.01(6).

7. No Adjournments 2 Days Prior to Hearing. No adjournment for any motion before a judge or master will be granted within 2 days of the scheduled hearing date, except in extenuating and exceptional circumstances.

8. Parties' Responsibilities for All Adjourned Hearings. Where a matter has been adjourned and materials have been previously filed with the court, parties are responsible to ensure that all previously filed materials to be relied upon are pulled from the file or ordered from storage, if applicable, and brought to staff in the court office, at least one week prior to the new hearing date.

9. Materials for use of the Court. The following materials, including material in electronic format, are required by the Court:

a) Factums are required for all applications.

b) Factums are required for all motions over two hours (except undertakings and refusals motions) and are strongly encouraged for all other motions.

c) No factum may exceed 30 pages, unless leave is granted.

d) For longer or more complex motions, the court strongly encourages parties to file electronic copies of their factums in Word format. Electronic copies should be attached to the hard copy of the factum filed with the court and should be labelled with the court file name and number, event and content of the disk, as well as the return date of the matter. Counsel and parties should refer to the Guide Concerning e-Delivery of Documents available on the Superior Court's website.

e) Cases contained in books of authorities should be copied on both sides of a page. If possible, electronic copies of books of authorities are helpful in longer or more complex motions.

f) Parties are encouraged to refer to the Guide Concerning Best Practices for Civil Actions, Applications and Motions, available on the Superior Court's website, which offers further guidance to counsel and parties when bringing motions or applications, particularly on matters involving voluminous materials.

10. Motions to Transfer a Civil Proceeding. All requests for a transfer of a civil proceeding (action or application) from one county to another shall be pursuant to rule 13.1.02 of the *Rules of Civil Procedure*. The motion will be granted or denied based on its merits. Counsel and parties are advised to refer to Part III of the Consolidated Provincial Practice Direction which prescribes specific requirements for motions to transfer a civil proceeding.

11. Motions to be Heard by Masters. A master has jurisdiction to hear any motion in a civil proceeding except those specified rule 37.02(2). Masters' motions must be made to a master. Unless the relief requested in the motion is within the exclusive jurisdiction of a judge, a motion returnable by attendance or in writing must be made to "the Court" and heard by a master. Judges may refuse to hear any motion that is within the jurisdiction of a master.

12. Simplified Procedure Discovery Motions. Motions concerning issues arising from examinations for discovery in Simplified Procedure actions will be scheduled for a maximum of 30 minutes in total. All parties are expected to complete oral argument of the motion within the time scheduled, subject to leave from the presiding master in exceptional cases. Parties are encouraged to use rule 34.12 and answer questions that are objected to.

13. Confirmation of Applications and Motions. In accordance with rules 37.10.1 and 38.09.1, the Confirmation Form for motions and applications must be filed by the

applicant or moving party with the Registrar not later than 2 p.m. three days before the hearing date. Parties must confer as to the time required before sending in the Confirmation Form. Estimated time must not exceed time booked. Parties are expected to adhere to the time requested.

C. — Scheduling a Short Application or Short Motion Before a Judge or Master

14. Short applications and short motions must be booked through the Civil Practice Unit [Or Civil Scheduling Unit] (except summary judgment motions, masters' motions in construction lien actions or within a reference). These matters are to be booked by emailing the Civil Scheduling/Practice Unit at JUS.G.MAG.CSD.CivilMotionsScheduling@ontario.ca. Alternatively, parties may call or attend in person at 10th Floor, 393 University Ave., M5G 1E6, tel: 416-327-5535.

15. Parties shall consult with each other to select a return date that is convenient to all parties and which will permit all parties to file all necessary materials and conduct any examinations before the return date. At the time of booking, a realistic estimate of the time required by all parties for argument must be provided.

16. When a party books a return date for a short application or short motion by email to the Civil Scheduling/Practice Unit, it shall send by email a completed Requisition to Schedule Short Motion or Application If booking by phone, the information contained in the Requisition to Schedule Short Motion or Application form must be communicated to the booking staff. The form must be included with the motion material when filed.

17. Short motions in construction lien actions and hearings for directions within a reference are not booked through the Civil Scheduling/Practice Unit. See instructions below on booking motions before Masters.

D. — Scheduling a Long Application, Long Motion, Summary Judgment Motion or Urgent Matter before a Judge

18.An attendance at Civil Practice Court before a judge is required to schedule:

a) Long applications or long motions before a judge;

b) All summary judgment motions before a judge;

c) The urgent hearing of motions or applications before a judge; and

d) Contested requests for case management by a judge under rule 77.

e) Appeals from the Consent and Capacity Board under the *Health Care Consent Act*.

19. CPC commences at 9:30 a.m. Gowns are not required in CPC. Several CPC's may sit on a given day.

20. Appointments to appear in CPC may be booked by emailing the Civil Practice Unit at CivilPracticeCourt@ontario.ca, along with a completed Requisition to Attend Civil Practice Court.

21. Information about the current start time, location, and contact information for the CPC can be found on the Superior Court of Justice website at www.ontariocourts.ca/scj/practice/schedules/t/.

22. Before appearing at CPC, parties must seek to establish an agreed timetable for the completion of all steps required prior to the hearing of the application or motion and to bring a copy of the timetable to Civil Practice Court for approval by the judge.

23. Rule 20 of the *Rules of Civil Procedure* contemplates that some summary judgment motions will proceed by way of a hybrid hearing (written record, plus some oral evidence) or by way of a hearing on the written record followed closely by a tailored trial of issues. Scheduling the expeditious hearing of these Rule 20 motions will require greater management by the judiciary. Accordingly, all motions for summary judgment will undergo a scheduling and monitoring process commencing with an attendance at Civil Practice Court (see Summary Judgment Case Information Sheet available through court staff).

24. Parties are to advise the Civil Motions Coordinator 30 days prior to the motion hearing date about the status of the motion. In addition, in the normal course, the court will contact the parties one week before the hearing of the long motion, long application or summary judgment motion before a judge to inquire into its status, its readiness for hearing, and whether oral evidence may be required at the hearing of the motion. If the parties advise or the court determines that the motion is not ready for hearing, the parties may receive further directions from the court regarding the scheduling of the hearing of the motion.

E. — Scheduling Motions before Masters

Long Motions before a Master

25. To schedule a long motion before a master, a Requisition to Schedule Long Motion must be completed and e-mailed to Masters.Long.Motions@ontario.ca or delivered to Masters Administration on the 6th floor 393 University Ave., or by fax to 416-327-6405. Once the requisition is received, a master will be assigned to hear the motion.

26. If the action is case managed, a Requisition is not necessary and a request for a long motion may be sent directly to the Assistant Trial Coordinator for the master who is managing the action.

27. If the motion is for refusals and undertakings, both moving and responding parties are expected to have completed refusals and undertaking charts grouped by issue and completed in accordance with rules 37.10(10)(a) and (b) prior to the case conference to allow a realistic time for the hearing to be set.

Ex-Parte motions before a Master

28. After attending at the motions office, motions made without notice or consent motions may be walked into Masters' Ex-Parte Motions Court any day that a master is sitting.

29. If the motion must be heard before the next date that an ex-parte master is sitting, or if the motion must be on notice, the Civil Practice Unit will direct the moving party to appear before the Duty Master. The Duty Master will determine if the matter is urgent and if urgent, will hear the motion or attempt to have it heard by another master.

Construction Lien Motions & References before a Master

30. Long and short motions in construction lien actions require an appointment with the Construction Lien Master to be arranged through the Assistant Trial Coordinator for the Construction Lien Masters on the 6th Floor 393 University Ave., or by telephone to 416-212-9783 or 416-327-9404. All long motions require a telephone case conference with the master who will be hearing the motion in order to determine the length of time required, set a timetable for any remaining steps before the hearing of the motion and fix a return date for the motion.

31. Motions made without notice and consent motions in construction lien actions are heard daily from 9:30 to 10:00 a.m.

32. Short motions and hearings for directions within a reference are booked through the Assistant Trial Coordinator for the master assigned to conduct the reference.

Motions before a Master from the Class Proceedings, Commercial and Estates Lists

33. If the motion is under the *Class Proceedings Act, 1992*, or a proceeding on the Commercial List or Estates List, a written direction will be required from a judge on the respective list permitting the motion to be heard by a master.

34. Similarly, if the action has been assigned to a judge under rule 37.15 or rule 77.06, a direction from that judge that a master be appointed to hear motions within the master's jurisdiction will be necessary.

35. The requirement for a judge's written direction does not apply to motions under the *Bankruptcy and Insolvency Act* heard by a master exercising the authority of a registrar of the court in bankruptcy under that Act.

F. — Motions in writing

36. Counsel are encouraged to bring in-writing motions when appropriate under Rule 37.12.1 for *ex parte*, consent, and unopposed matters. Counsel must provide the consent (under Rule 37.12.1(2)) or notice that the motion is unopposed (Rule 37.12.1(3)), along with a draft order for the court. In particular, motions such as default judgments, Norwich orders, non-party production or substituted service orders may be well-suited to in-writing motions.

37. With the exception of construction lien actions and references, unless otherwise directed by a judge or master, motions in writing should be filed in the Civil Intake Office, 10th Floor, 393 University Avenue.

38. Motions in writing in a construction lien file or reference should be filed with the Assistant Trial Coordinator for the Construction Lien Masters located on the 6th Floor, 393 University Avenue.

39. A motion under Rule 7.08 must be brought in accordance with the Best Practice's Guidelines and Checklist for Rule 7.08 matters.

G. — Adjournments

40. Short applications and short motions can be adjourned once through the Civil Practice Unit (or the assistant trial coordinator for the Construction Lien Masters, if applicable); any further adjournments of these matters must be spoken to in court.

41. To adjourn a long application or long motion scheduled before a judge, counsel must appear in CPC and speak to the adjournment.

42. Long motion dates before a master may be adjourned only with leave of the assigned master at a case conference requested for that purpose before the motion date.

43. No adjournment for any motion before a judge or master will be granted within 2 days of the scheduled hearing date, except in extenuating and exceptional circumstances.

44. Where a matter has been adjourned and materials have been previously filed with the court, parties are responsible to ensure that all previously filed materials to be relied upon are pulled from the file or ordered from storage within 30 days prior to the motion, if applicable, and brought to staff in the court office, at least one week prior to the new hearing date.

PART II: — REQUESTS FOR ASSIGNMENT TO CASE MANAGEMENT — RULE 77.05

45. Under rule 77.01(2)1, parties are required to assume the greater share of responsibility for managing their own actions. However, "light touch" case management under Rule 77 is available on an "las needed/as requested" basis in accordance with the provisions of the rule.

A. — Consent Requests

46. Consent or unopposed requests for assignment to case management may be made to the Team Leader Toronto Master, or the Regional Senior Judge, or designate, in the case of a request for case management by a judge, by completing a Request for Case Management.

47. Consent by itself is insufficient and parties must explain why case management is necessary having regard to the circumstances and the criteria set out in rule 77.05(4). Case management will not be assigned to actions that fail to meet the prescribed criteria.

48. If the request is granted, the Team Leader Toronto Masters or Regional Senior Judge, or designate, will assign a master or judge to case manage the action.

B. — Opposed Requests

49. Opposed requests for assignment to case management must be brought by way of motion:

a) in the case of a request for case management by a master, on notice returnable in Masters' Motions Court before any case management master; or,

b) in the case of a request for case management by a judge, on notice returnable in Civil Practice Court.

50. If the master grants the motion he or she will become the managing master.

51. Once a master is assigned to case manage a proceeding he or she will hear all motions in that proceeding within the jurisdiction of a master and will be available for case conferences.

52. If a motion for case management by a judge is granted, the Regional Senior Judge or designate will assign a judge to case manage the proceeding.

53. Requests under rules 37.15 or 77.06 for the appointment of a judge to hear all motions or steps in a proceeding shall be made in writing to the Regional Senior Judge, or designate.

54. A judge normally will not be assigned under rules 37.15 or 77.06 unless there is a likelihood of a significant number of motions or other steps in the proceeding that are within the exclusive jurisdiction of a judge.

PART III: — MANDATORY MEDIATION

55. All actions commenced in or transferred to the Toronto Region are subject to mandatory mediation under rule 24.1 except those actions excluded in rules 24.1.04(2) and (2.1).

56. A mediation session must take place within 180 days after the first defence has been filed, unless a consent under rule 24.1.09(3) has been filed or the court orders otherwise.

57. Court staff will not accept for filing a trial record (ordinary action) or a notice of readiness for pre-trial conference (Simplified Procedure action) unless the party setting the action down for trial files a Certificate that:

a. Form 24.1A (Notice of Name of Mediator and Date of Session) has been filed with the mediation coordinator and the mediation session has taken place;

b. the report by mediator (indicating that the mediation has been concluded) has been filed with the mediation coordinator;

c. an order has been obtained from a judge or case management master exempting the action from mediation; or,

d. an order has been obtained from a judge or case management master extending the deadline for mediation until after the action is set down for trial.

These requirements will apply even where the parties have agreed to postpone a mediation session to a date more than 180 days after the first defence has been filed as permitted by rule 24.1.

58. A motion for an order exempting the action from mediation should be made to any master (unless the action is being case managed by a judge or a specific master). The motion should be returnable in motions court or by case conference if the action is case managed. Motions in writing on consent will be considered if sufficient reasons are given.

59. In keeping with the requirement for mandatory mediation and Rule 1.05, a judge may, at any stage in the proceeding, order that the parties not take any further steps in the proceeding, without leave of a judge, until a mandatory mediation has taken place.

PART IV: — CERTIFICATION OF AN ACTION TO SET PRE-TRIAL AND TRIAL DATES

60. The practice of certifying an action ready for trial continues in the Toronto Region.

61. Approximately 60 days after a trial record is filed, the Civil Trial Office will send to the party who set the action down for trial a Certification Form to Set Pre-Trial and Trial Dates, together with a list of available trial dates.

62. After consultation with the opposing counsel or party, the party who received the form must complete and return the Certification Form to the Civil Trial Office.

63. If a completed Certification Form is not returned by the date specified on the covering memo, the action will be struck from the trial list.

64.In order to restore an action that has been struck from the trial list the parties must:

a) Obtain an order granting leave from a case management master or judge under rule 48.11 to restore it to the trial list; and thereafter,

b) Attend the main file room on the 10th floor of 393 University Ave. and arrange to have the original trial record pulled and taken with the court order to the Civil Intake Counter.

The action will then be re-instated to the trial list and the trial record returned to the trial office. The trial office will treat the action as a new matter and forward new certification forms.

65. If an opposing party will not cooperate in completing the Certification Form within a reasonable time, for cases 10 days or less, a party can arrange an appearance before a judge in a "To Be Spoken To Court" which usually is held each Monday at 9:30 a.m. Contact the trial coordinator for additional information at 416-327-5320.

66. If an opposing party will not cooperate in completing the Certification Form within a reasonable time, and if a trial is anticipated to be over 10 days and, a party can arrange an appearance before the Long Trial Scheduling Court, which is normally held on Wednesdays at 9:30 a.m.

67. Once trial dates are set, there will be no adjournments of the trial except in extenuating and exceptional circumstances.

68. Rule 48.04 provides that a party who sets an action down for trial or consents to placing the action on the trial list cannot initiate or continue any form of discovery or interlocutory motion without leave of the court. Leave will be granted only in rare circumstances.

PART V: — ADMINISTRATIVE FORMS

69. Administrative forms not prescribed under the *Rules of Civil Procedure* and used by the Civil Practice Unit may be obtained from the Civil Practice Unit or can be found on the Superior Court of Justice website.

PART VI: — DESIGNATED COUNTIES FOR THE COMMENCEMENT OF MORTGAGE PROCEEDINGS UNDER RULE 13.1.01(3)

70. Pursuant to rule 13.1.01(3) of the *Rules of Civil Procedure*, which comes into effect on March 31, 2015, Toronto shall be the place for commencement of mortgage proceedings for property located anywhere in the Toronto Region.

Dated: June 26, 2015

Amended May 1, 2017

Heather J. Smith

Chief Justice

Superior Court of Justice (Ontario)

Geoffrey B. Morawetz

Regional Senior Judge

Superior Court of Justice, Toronto Region

PD-15 — *THE GUIDE CONCERNING BEST PRACTICES FOR CIVIL ACTIONS, APPLICATIONS AND MOTIONS IN THE TORONTO REGION (EFFECTIVE JULY 1, 2014)*

This Guide applies to civil actions, applications and motions in the Toronto Region, effective July 1, 2014. It *supersedes* the previous best practice document concerning civil applications and motions, which is hereby revoked.

Counsel and parties are advised to refer to the relevant Parts of the Consolidated Provincial Practice Direction, the Consolidated Practice Direction for Divisional Court Proceedings as well as other relevant Toronto region-specific Practice Directions and Guides (e.g. the Consolidated Practice Direction for Civil Actions, Applications, Motions and Procedural Matters in the Toronto Region).

All Superior Court of Justice Practice Directions and Guides are available on the Superior Court's website at: www.ontariocourts.ca/scj.

PART I: — PURPOSE

1. The Consolidated Practice Direction for Civil Actions, Applications, Motions and Procedural Matters in the Toronto Region encourages parties to refer to this Guide. This Guide describes the practices the court encourages both counsel and self-represented parties to use in preparing and conducting civil actions, applications and motions.

PART II: — CO-OPERATION AND CIVILITY BETWEEN COUNSEL AND BETWEEN COUNSEL AND SELF-REPRESENTED PARTIES

2. To be fair and just an adversarial system of litigation requires the opponents to resolve their differences in a civilized manner. Although parties conduct civil actions, applications and motions within the context of an adversarial system, the court expects counsel and self-represented parties to conduct themselves, at all times, in ways that promote cooperation, effective and timely communication, and civility, as well as applying common sense to the resolution of issues that arise during the course of a proceeding.

3. The court expects counsel to conduct applications and motions having regard to the *Principles of Professionalism for Advocates* and the *Principles of Civility for Advocates* published by The Advocates' Society, found at: www.advocates.ca/assets/files/pdf/publications/principles-of-civility.pdf.

PART III: — ASSISTANCE FOR SELF-REPRESENTED PARTIES IN PREPARING MATERIALS FOR CIVIL PROCEEDINGS

4. Self-represented parties who are involved in a civil proceeding may find it helpful to learn that Law Help Ontario, a project of Pro Bono Law Ontario, provides *pro bono* legal services to eligible individuals who cannot afford to hire a lawyer.

5. Law Help Ontario operates a walk-in centre on the main floor level of 393 University Avenue, Toronto. Information about Law Help Ontario, including the hours of operation of its walk-in centre, can be found at: www.lawhelpontario.org.

6. Counsel who are involved in civil proceedings involving a self-represented party are encouraged to consult and be guided by the *Canadian Code of Conduct for Trial Lawyers Involved in Civil Actions Involving Unrepresented Litigants* published by the American College of Trial Lawyers and found at: www.actl.com/AM/Template.cfm.

PART IV: — ELECTRONIC DOCUMENT DISCLOSURE

7. Parties are reminded of their obligation under Rule 29.1.03(4) to consult and have regard to the document titled *The Sedona Canada Principles Addressing Electronic Discovery* developed and available from the Sedona Conference. Applying the *Sedona Canada Principles Addressing Electronic Discovery* is particularly important in complex applications or motions which may involve significant documentary disclosure.

8. The *Sedona Canada Principles Addressing Electronic Discovery* may be found at: www.thesedonaconference.org/publications.

PART V: — MATERIALS FOR USE OF THE COURT IN CIVIL PROCEEDINGS

A. — Confirmation of Applications and Motions Required

9. Parties are reminded that their confirmation form must be sent to the motions office no later than 2:00 p.m. three days before the scheduled hearing date under Rule 37.10.1.

B. — Factums or Written Arguments

10. Factums are required for all applications.

11. Factums are required for all motions over two hours (except undertakings and refusals motions) and are strongly encouraged for all other motions.

12. All factums should be clear and concise.

13. For longer or more complex motions, the court finds it helpful for the parties to file electronic copies of their factums in Word format. Electronic copies of factums should be attached to the hard copy of the factum filed with the court on a disk and should be labelled with the court file name and number, event and content of the disk, as well as the return date of the matter. Counsel and parties should refer to the Guide Concerning e-Delivery of Documents available on the Superior Court's website.

C. — Books of Authorities

14. Cases contained in books of authorities should be copied on both sides of a page. Electronic copies of books of authorities are helpful in longer or more complex motions. Disks should be labelled with the court file name and number, event and content of the disk, as well as the return date of the matter.

D. — Complex Applications and Motions

15. Where a matter is on-going or the materials in the court files are voluminous, counsel are requested to facilitate the hearing of the matter by:

a) preparing a consolidated record;

b) preparing a consolidated compendium;

c) preparing a numbered list of all motion records, transcripts, casebooks and other materials; or

d) by having a representative attend at the Civil Motions List Office before a hearing to ensure that all the materials needed for the motion, application or trial are available to the court.

16. In appropriate cases, to supplement any required formal record, counsel are requested to consider preparing a compendium of the key materials to be referred to in argument (fair extracts of documents, transcripts, previous orders, authorities, etc.) to assist in focusing the case for the court. Relevant portions of the compendium should be highlighted or marked. Counsel are urged to consult among themselves in the preparation of a joint compendium, if possible.

E. — Charts and Diagrams

17. The court invites the use of diagrams, corporate organization charts, list of persons involved, point-form chronologies and other synopses of complex or technical evidence.

F. — Organization of Materials on Continuing Matters

18. Where a matter has been adjourned, parties are responsible to ensure that all the materials for the adjourned are available at least one week before the new hearing date. (This responsibility requires reviewing the court file and may require requisition documents that may have been transferred to storage.)

19. Where there are prior endorsements, orders or judgments that are relevant to a continuing matter, parties are encouraged to file an Orders Brief containing the relevant material.

20. Between 12 noon and 2:30 p.m. two days before the hearing date of a long or complex motion or application, it is recommended that a representative of the moving party attend the Civil Motions Office and organize the court file to put all relevant documents, particularly where materials are voluminous or where a matter is scheduled to reconvene.

G. — Costs

21. Parties are reminded that unless they have agreed on the costs of a motion or application, Rule 57.01(6) requires every party who intends to seek costs for a motion or application to give to the other party before the hearing of the motion or application a costs outline not exceeding three pages in length (Form 57B) and bring a copy to the hearing. It is within the discretion of the court not to entertain cost submissions unless the parties have complied with this rule.

PART VI: — COURT CONTACT INFORMATION FOR APPLICATIONS AND MOTIONS

A. — Civil Scheduling Unit

22.

10th Fl. 393 University Ave.

Tel: 416-327-5535

Fax: 416-327-9470

Short Motions or Applications (Under 2 hours before a Judge or Master)

Email: JUS.G.MAG.CSD.CivilMotionsScheduling@Ontario.ca

Motion Scheduling Court (Over 2 hours, before a Judge)

Email: MotionsSchedulingCourt@Ontario.ca

Motion Scheduling Court: Summary Judgment

Email: MotionsSchedulingCourt@Ontario.ca

Confirmations for Motions and Applications

Email: JUS.G.MAG.CSD.CivilMotionsConfirmation@Ontario.ca

Fax: 416-327-5484

B. — Masters Administration

23.

6th Fl. 393 University Ave.

Tel: 416-327-0506

Fax: 416-326-5416

Long Motions before a Master

Email: Civil.Masters.Long.Motions@Ontario.ca

Motions in Construction Lien or References

416-327-9404 or 416-212-9783

References

Telephone 416-327-0506 or attend in person to the Masters Administration on the 6th Floor, 393 University Avenue

Case Management Masters

Fax: 416-326-5416

C. — Trial Coordinators Office

24.

7th Fl. 330 University Ave.

Tel: 416-327-5320

Fax: 416-327-5697

Pre-Trial Conference (Ordinary and Simplified Procedure)

Email: Toronto.SCJ.Civil.Pre-Trials@Ontario.ca

Trial Dates

Email: MAG.CSD.Trials@Ontario.ca

PD-16 — *CONSOLIDATED PRACTICE DIRECTION CONCERNING FAMILY CASES IN THE TORONTO REGION (EFFECTIVE JULY 1, 2014, AMENDED JULY 1, 2015)*

This Practice Direction applies to family law proceedings in the Toronto Region. It *supersedes* Part III of the Consolidated Provincial Practice Direction *for family cases in Toronto*. It also *supersedes* all previous Practice Directions concerning family proceedings in the Toronto Region issued prior to July 1, 2014, which are hereby revoked.

Changes have been made to paragraphs 3, 19, 23 and 25 below which came into effect on July 1, 2015.

Counsel and parties are advised to refer to the relevant parts of the Consolidated Provincial Practice Direction, the Consolidated Practice Direction for Divisional Court Proceedings as well as any other applicable Toronto region-specific Practice Directions or Guides, which are available on the Superior Court of Justice website at: www.ontariocourts.ca/scj.

PART I: — CONFIRMATIONS

1. Each party to a motion or conference must file a Form 14C Confirmation or the parties may file one jointly, no later than 2 p.m. two business days before the date of the motion or conference.

2. The parties or their counsel should consult with each other prior to filing their Form 14C Confirmations, unless the parties are self-represented and prohibited from communicating by court order.

3. Where Form 14C Confirmations have not been filed by at least one party, the conference or motion will not be scheduled on the event list and, as a result, will not be heard by the court. *Costs may also be ordered against a party who has not filed the confirmation.*

4. Form 14C Confirmations must *only* list the specific issues that are to be addressed at the event. They should also indicate which materials the judge should review with clear reference to the specific volume, tab and page numbers of the Continuing Record. *Failure to provide this information may result in the materials not being reviewed by the judge or the motion not being heard on that day.*

5. Form 14C Confirmations must also include an appropriate time estimate for the *entire motion or conference*, including time required by the other party. Parties will be held to the time stated on their confirmations.

PART II: — MOTIONS

A. — Short Motions

6. Motions that are expected to take one hour or less may be scheduled on a Tuesday or Thursday by serving and filing the motion material (including a factum or Summary of Argument) at the family court office within the timelines set out in the *Family Law Rules.*

B. — Long Motions

7. Motions that are expected to take more than 1 hour (including the other party's reply and cross motion, if any) must be scheduled as long motions and scheduled through the Trial Coordinator in the family court office. Long motions can be scheduled either (a) with the other party's written consent or (b) with the court's permission, by filing a Form 14B Motion Form under section 14(10) of the *Family Law Rules.*

C. — Factums, Summaries of Arguments and Briefs of Authorities

8. A properly drafted factum or Summary of Argument is required on all motions except as noted below. If the moving party does not file a factum of Summary of Argument where required, the motion will not be scheduled.

9. For short motions, the times for service and filing of moving party's factum or Summary of Argument should be filed in accordance with the requirements relating to other motion materials in section 14(11) and 14(11.1) of the *Family Law Rules.*

10. For long motions, each party's factum or Summary of Argument must be filed at least seven days before the hearing of the motion.

11. No factum or Summary of Argument may exceed 20 pages without leave of the court.

12. The authorities that are included on the court's list of Often Cited Family Cases do not need to be provided to the court with a party's factum or Summary of Argument. Counsel and parties are advised to refer to Part I of the Consolidated Provincial Practice Direction. An updated list of family cases is available on the Superior Court's website at: www.ontariocourts.ca/scj.

D. — 14 B Motions

13. A Form 14B Motion must be filed at the family court office and cannot be filed by fax. A Form 14B Motion Form should be accompanied by four copies of a

proposed Order (Form 25), a completed endorsement sheet and a self-addressed and stamped envelope for each party.

14. The 14B Motion Form shall be filed in the Continuing Record and a copy of the proposed Order shall be attached to the appropriate place in the Endorsement Volume.

E. — Compendiums

15. A Compendium[4] containing the documents and evidence that are essential to the hearing of the motion may be provided for long or complex motions. A party wishing to file a Compendium should file it with their factum. A joint Compendium may be filed with the respondent's factum.

F. — Electronic Copies of Materials

16. Whenever the volume of materials is large or the motion is complex, the parties should file an electronic copy of their motion materials as well as paper copies. Counsel and parties should refer to the Guide Concerning e-Delivery of Documents available on the Superior Court's website.

G. — Urgent Motions on Notice

17. A party may seek an urgent motion *on notice* without a case conference in situations of urgency or hardship including issues such as abduction, threats of harm or dire financial harm. A party seeking such a motion must file all of the required materials except for a Form 14C Confirmation.

H. — Urgent Motions without Notice

18. A party that is seeking a motion *without notice* to the other party must also set out why notice is unnecessary or not reasonably possible. A factum or Summary of Argument is not required for an urgent motion that has been brought without notice.

I. — Case Conferences and Settlement Conferences

19. Parties may request that a conference occur by teleconference with or without the consent of both parties or their counsel by filing a Form 14B Motion Form.

20. Counsel or the parties should communicate before any conference in order to attempt to resolve the issues that are in dispute, unless the parties are self-represented and prohibited from communicating by court order.

21. The first case conference on a motion to change a final order or agreement shall be scheduled before a Dispute Resolution Officer (DRO) in accordance with Part I of the Consolidated Provincial Practice Direction.

[4]A compendium would normally include the Notice of Motion, Affidavits and Financial Statements, as well as excerpts from the evidence and exhibits that will be referred to in the argument of the motion.

22. A DRO conference can be held on matters other than motions to change only as directed by the court upon request by a 14B Motion or at another court event.

23. If the matter is not resolved at a settlement conference, a Trial Scheduling Endorsement Form (including Parts 1 and 2, endorsed by the Court) must be completed prior to the matter being scheduled for trial.

J. — Trial Management Conferences

24. A trial management conference will normally be scheduled by the family court office for the week before the assigned trial date.

25. The completed Trial Scheduling Endorsement Form must be filed by one of the parties in advance of the Trial Management Conference and each party must file an Offer to Settle and Outline of Opening Statement, in lieu of the Trial Management Conference Brief.

K. — Trial Records

26. The Applicant must file a Trial Record at least 30 days prior to the scheduled trial date. Failure to do so will result in the matter being removed from the trial list, unless the court orders otherwise.

Additional information about family cases and the mediation and information services that are available at the Toronto Superior Court of Justice, 393 University Avenue, 9th Floor, is available from Mediate 393 which is available on their website.

Dated: April 11, 2014

Heather J. Smith

Chief Justice

Superior Court of Justice (Ontario)

Geoffrey B. Morawetz

Regional Senior Judge

Superior Court of Justice, Toronto Region

PD-17 — *CONSOLIDATED PRACTICE DIRECTION CONCERNING THE ESTATES LIST IN THE TORONTO REGION (EFFECTIVE JULY 1, 2014)*

The Estates List has been established for the hearing of certain proceedings in the Toronto Region involving issues of estate, trust and capacity law.

This Practice Direction applies to matters on the Estates List in the Toronto Region, effective July 1, 2014. It *supersedes* all previous Practice Directions concerning Estates List matters in the Toronto Region issued before July 1, 2014, which are hereby revoked.

Counsel and parties are advised to refer to the relevant Parts of the Consolidated Provincial Practice Direction, the Consolidated Practice Direction for Divisional Court Proceedings as well as any other relevant Toronto region-specific Practice Directions and Guides which are available on the Superior Court of Justice website at: www.ontariocourts.ca/scj.

PART I: — THE ESTATES OFFICE

1. The Toronto Region Estates List is administered through the Estates Office, 7th floor, 330 University Avenue, Toronto, telephone number 416.326.2940 and fax number 416.326.2939. All filings relating to Estates List matters are done through the Estates Office.

PART II: — PRINCIPLES GUIDING THE ESTATES LIST

2. The following principles shall guide all proceedings conducted on the Estates List:

a) The time and expense devoted to a proceeding should be proportionate to what is at stake in the proceeding; and,

b) Co-operation, communication, civility and common sense should prevail amongst all parties and counsel.

PART III: — MATTERS HEARD ON THE ESTATES LIST

3. The Estates List hears the following matters:

a) all matters arising under Rules 74 and 75 of the *Rules of Civil Procedure*;

b) applications under Rule 14.05 regarding estates, wills and trusts, including applications for advice under section 60 of the *Trustee Act*;

c) applications relating to inter vivos trusts, whether under Rule 14.05, the *Variation of Trusts Act*, or otherwise;

d) proceedings involving the proof or validity of wills, including lost wills;

e) proceedings concerning the administration of estates;

f) summary procedures for claims against estates pursuant to the *Estates Act*, ss. 44 and 45;

g) passing of accounts of estate trustees or any other person acting in a fiduciary capacity, including guardianships and those acting under powers of attorney;

h) applications under the *Succession Law Reform Act*;

i) proceedings under the *Substitute Decisions Act, 1992*, including proceedings under that Act involving powers of attorney;

j) applications for the appointment of a guardian of property of a child under s. 47 of the *Children's Law Reform Act*, if brought in the Superior Court of Justice;

k) appeals from the Consent Capacity Board under the *Health Care Consent Act, 1996* or the *Mental Health Act*;

l) proceedings under the *Declarations of Death Act, 2002* or *Absentees Act*;

m) proceedings under the *Charities Accounting Act*, *Charitable Gifts Act* or *Religious Organizations' Lands Act*;

n) applications for the extension of time to make an election under s. 6(1) of the *Family Law Act* regarding the interest of a spouse under section 5(2) of that Act; and,

o) such other matters concerning estate, trust or capacity law as a judge may direct be heard on the Estates List. In considering whether to make such a direction, the judge may take into account the current and expected case load of matters on the Estates List.

4. Where an estate trustee(s) is either plaintiff or defendant in a civil action which does not specifically concern estate or trust law, or where an estate trustee becomes a party in such an action by virtue only of an order to continue under Rule 11.02, the action shall proceed as any other action and shall not be placed on the Estates List unless the court orders otherwise.

A. — Transfers of matters to the Estates List

5. A matter that should have been commenced on the Estates List may be transferred to it by a judge who is hearing the matter, but who is not sitting on the Estates List.

6. Matters may be transferred to the Estates List on consent, provided the matters fall within the categories outlined in sub-paragraphs 3(a)–(o), or on a motion to a judge sitting to hear matters on the Estates List.

7. The place of commencement of a proceeding is governed by Rule 13.1.01. Requests to transfer matters commenced outside the Toronto Region to the Estates List are governed by Part III of the Consolidated Provincial Practice Direction.

PART IV: — ADMINISTRATIVE MATTERS

A. — Courtrooms and Gowning

8. Matters listed on the Estates List usually are heard at 330 University Avenue, Toronto, unless notice to the contrary is given.

9. Counsel shall gown for all hearings or attendances, except pre-trial conferences and 9:30 Appointments.

B. — Estates List Documents and Forms

10. Copies of forms specified by the *Rules of Civil Procedure* can be found on the Court Services Division Forms website: www.ontariocourtforms.ca. Confirmation and other administrative forms used by the Estates List may be obtained from the Estates List Office or can be found on the Estates List webpage on the Superior Court of Justice website: www.ontariocourts.ca/scj. Counsel and parties using documents obtained from a website must remember that the *Rules of Civil Procedure* require that all documents filed in a proceeding must use characters of at least 12 point, or 10 pitch, size; as a result, some conversion of the font size of web-sourced documents may be required.

PART V: — SCHEDULING MATTERS ON THE ESTATES LIST

A. — The Daily List 9:30 Appointments and the Hearing List

11. The daily list of matters heard by a judge sitting on the Estates List consists of two parts: (i) the hearing of 9:30 Appointments of 10-minutes each, immediately followed by (ii) the hearing of contested matters or unopposed matters that require some time for a judge to review ("Hearing Matters"). 9:30 Appointments take place in chambers and deal with minor and/or unopposed matters. Counsel are not required to gown. Contested matters and application or motions are conducted in open court commencing 10:00 a.m.

12. Booking dates for a 9:30 Appointment or a Hearing Matter can be done through the Estates Office.

13. 9:30 Appointments will be for no more than 10 minutes for each matter booked and must be booked at least two days in advance. Any materials required for a 9:30 Appointment should be filed no later than 12 noon the day before the appointment.

14. If a party fails to appear at a 9:30 Appointment, the court may set a timetable and hearing date for the matter in the party's absence.

15. In order to ensure the most efficient use of court time and to enable contested matters to be heard at the earliest reasonable date, procedures for booking time on the Estates List for the hearing of a proceeding vary according to the type and length of proceeding as described below.

B. — Passing of Accounts Applications

16. When initiating an application for the passing of accounts in all circumstances — whether the passing of accounts of estate trustees or of any other person acting in a fiduciary capacity, including guardianships and those acting under powers of attorney — the applicant should book only 10 minutes on the list for Hearing Matters for the initial return date of the application.

17. If no notices of objection are received or if notices of objection are received but are withdrawn within the prescribed time in respect of the application to pass accounts, and no request for increased costs has been filed and served, the applicant may request, upon filing the material required by subrule 74.18(9), that the application proceed as an unopposed matter to be dealt with by a judge in chambers without the need for the parties to attend.

18. If no notices of objection are received or if notices of objection are received but are withdrawn within the prescribed time in respect of the application to pass accounts, and a request for increased costs has been filed and served, the judge hearing the matter on the initial return date may determine the amount of the costs at that time or, if the judge is of the view that there is not sufficient time on the initial return date to hear the matter on the initial return date, the judge can schedule a date for a further hearing on the costs issue.

19. If notices of objection are received and not withdrawn in response to the application to pass accounts, and if the parties can agree in advance of the initial return date on the terms of an order giving directions (including a timetable for each prehearing step and, where practicable, the hearing date), then parties can obtain a consent order giving directions on the scheduled initial 10 minute return date for the application.

20. If notices of objection are received and not withdrawn and if the parties cannot agree on an order for directions prior to the initial return date, the parties should file, at least two days in advance of the initial return date, copies of their respective draft orders giving directions, including timetables for each pre-hearing step and proposed hearing dates. If the dispute about directions can be resolved during the 10 minute appointment on the initial return date, the judge can issue an order giving directions, including a timetable for pre-hearing steps and a hearing date. If the argument about the terms of an order giving directions will require longer than the 10 minute appointment on the initial return date, the judge can schedule a date for the hearing of a contested motion for directions.

21. Draft orders giving directions should address the items described in paragraph 46 (below).

C. — Applications involving Wills where an Order giving Directions is required

22. Where a notice of objection has been filed to the issuance of a certificate of appointment of estate trustee and an application for directions is required, the applicant, or other person applying for directions, should book an initial 10 minute 9:30 Appointment for the initial return date of the application for directions.

23. If prior to their attendance at the 9:30 Appointment the parties can agree on the terms of a consent order giving directions, including a timetable for each pre-hearing step agreed upon, the judge at the 9:30 Appointment may issue a consent order giving directions.

24. If the parties cannot agree on an order giving directions prior to the 9:30 Appointment, the parties should file, at least two days in advance of the 9:30 Appointment, copies of their respective draft orders giving directions, including timetables for each pre-hearing step. If the dispute about directions can be resolved during the 10 minute 9:30 Appointment, the judge may issue the order giving directions, including a timetable for pre-hearing steps. If the argument about the terms of an order giving directions will require longer than the 10 minute 9:30 Appointment, the judge can schedule a date for the hearing of a contested application for directions.

D. — Guardianship Applications

25. Applications for the appointment of a guardian under the *Substitute Decisions Act* or *Children's Law Reform Act* should be commenced by booking a 10 minute 9:30 Appointment as the initial return date for the application.

26. If the application will be opposed and prior to their attendance at the 9:30 Appointment the parties can agree on the terms of a consent order giving directions, including a timetable for each step agreed upon and the hearing date, the judge at the 9:30 Appointment may issue a consent order giving directions.

27. If the application will be opposed and the parties cannot agree on an order giving directions prior to the 9:30 Appointment, the parties should file, at least two days in advance of the 9:30 Appointment, copies of their respective draft orders giving directions, including timetables for each pre-hearing step and the proposed hearing date. If the dispute about directions can be resolved during the 10 minute 9:30 Appointment, the judge may issue an order giving directions, including a timetable for pre-hearing steps and the hearing date. If the argument about the terms of an order giving directions will require longer than the 10 minute 9:30 Appointment, the judge can schedule a date for the hearing of a contested motion for directions.

28. If the application will not be opposed, at the 9:30 Appointment the court will set the date and length of time for hearing the unopposed application, unless the court is able to hear the matter as part of that day's Hearing Matters.

E. — Any other type of Application or Motion brought on the Estates List

Matters that will require less than one hour to argue on the merits

29. For other matters heard on the Estates List where the applicant or moving party realistically estimates that the argument of the matter by all parties involved will take less than one hour, an appointment may be booked on the list for Hearing Matters, through the Estates Office, for a hearing of up to one hour.

Matters that will require more than one hour to argue on the merits

30. Where an application or a motion will require more than one hour to argue on the merits and all parties to the application or motion can agree on a timetable for all pre-hearing steps and on the hearing date for argument, the applicant or moving party may obtain from the Estates Office a consent hearing date upon filing a Hearing Date Request Form that:

a) confirms that the parties have agreed on a timetable for all pre-hearing steps;

b) sets out the agreed upon timetable; and

c) sets out the agreed hearing date.

The hearing date for such a motion may be reserved by contacting the Estates Office. Confirmation of the hearing date will require the applicant or moving party to file a completed Hearing Date Request Form with the Estates Office.

31. If the parties to an application or motion that will require more than one hour to argue on the merits cannot agree on a timetable for all pre-hearing steps or on a hearing date, the applicant or moving party, on notice to all other parties, shall book a 9:30 Appointment for the court to set a timetable for pre-hearing steps and a hearing date for the application or motion to be argued on the merits. The parties should file, at least two days in advance of the 9:30 Appointment, copies of their proposed pre-hearing timetables and their proposed hearing dates.

F. — Other matters that can be dealt with at a 9:30 Appointment

32. Apart from the circumstances described above, there may be other occasions during a proceeding when the parties may wish to book a 9:30 Appointment to obtain the assistance of the court in setting timetables for further steps in the proceeding, including steps required to ready the matter for trial, or to obtain consent orders. On notice to other interested parties, such 9:30 Appointments may be booked on two days' notice.

G. — Adjournments

General Principles

33. Parties are expected to be ready to proceed with matters for which hearing dates have been agreed to or set by the court; adjournments of previously scheduled

matters shall be granted only in special circumstances and for a material reason. Parties are expected conscientiously to have sought to resolve most adjournments and waiting periods among themselves before a hearing in a way which minimizes inconvenience and difficulty for the parties.

34. Parties are expected to retain counsel promptly. A request for an adjournment because counsel has not been retained promptly or because new counsel has been retained just prior to the hearing shall be dealt with accordingly.

Where the hearing date was set at a 9:30 Appointment

35. Requests for adjournments of hearing dates which were set as a result of attendances at a 9:30 Appointment should occur infrequently since the reasonableness of the hearing date would have been canvassed at that appointment. Any such request for an adjournment, even on consent, should be made through a further 9:30 Appointment so that the court can be satisfied that the matter has reached a stage of readiness which justifies assigning a new hearing date. If the matter is not ready for hearing, it may be removed from the hearing list, leaving it to the parties to re-apply subsequently through a 9:30 Appointment for a new hearing date once the matter is ready to be heard.

Where the hearing date was not set at a 9:30 Appointment

36. Where the hearing date for a matter was not set through a 9:30 Appointment attendance, a first consent adjournment of the hearing of the matter may be arranged through the Estates Office.

37. If the parties wish to seek a second consent adjournment of the matter, they should adjourn the matter, in advance of the scheduled hearing date, to a 9:30 Appointment. If the request for a second adjournment is not made until the appearance before the judge scheduled to hear the matter, that judge may direct the matter to be adjourned to a 9:30 Appointment before it proceeds further. On the return of the matter at a 9:30 Appointment the court can determine whether the matter is ready for hearing, or whether it would be more appropriate to remove the matter from the hearing list, leaving it to the parties to reapply subsequently through a 9:30 Appointment for a new hearing date once the matter is ready to be heard.

PART VI: — CONTESTED MATTERS — GENERAL

A. — Confirmation of Applications and Motions

38. Parties must confirm the hearing of an application or motion at least three days in advance of the hearing date using the Confirmation Form (9:30 Appointment and Hearing Matter) available from the Estates Office.

B. — Urgent Applications or Motions

39. A party who considers a matter to be urgent may complete and submit to the Estates Office an Urgent Hearing Request form describing the nature of the matter, the reason for the urgency, the time required for the matter, and any scheduling discussions the party has been able to engage in with the other party or parties in the circumstances, as well as attaching a copy of the proposed Notice of Application or Notice of Motion.

40. Requests for the hearing of urgent applications or motions will be heard on an "as required" basis, by the supervising judge or designate. The Estates Office will notify the parties of the time and location for the hearing of the urgent request.

C. — Pre-Trial Conference and Trial Dates

41. Pre-trial conferences must be held in all matters proceeding to trial. Dates for pre-trial conferences and trials should be obtained from the Estates Office at the time the proceeding is set down for trial.

42. Two hours normally will be assigned for a pre-trial conference. If the parties think that a longer pre-trial conference would be appropriate in the circumstances of their case, they may book a 9:30 Appointment to secure a date for a longer pre-trial conference. If the parties are unable to agree upon a pre-trial conference date, trial date, the length of time for the trial, or any other matter concerning the conduct of the trial, a party may book a 9:30 Appointment to determine such matters.

43. At least five days prior to the date of a pre-trial conference each party must serve and file with the Estates Office an Estates List Pre-Trial Conference Form.

PART VII: — CONTESTED MATTERS — ESTATES

A. — Orders giving Directions: General

44. Orders giving directions in contested matters are designed to provide the parties with a procedural framework in which to prepare the proceeding for final adjudication. Rule 75.06 provides the court with considerable discretion and flexibility to put in place a process that will ensure the just, expeditious and least expensive determination of a proceeding on its merits. Parties are expected to take time and care in preparing proposed orders giving directions for consideration by the court.

45. If the parties cannot agree upon an order giving directions before or at a 9:30 Appointment and a contested motion for directions is required, each party must file with its motion materials a copy of the draft order giving directions it is seeking.

46. Draft orders giving directions should address, where applicable, the following matters:

a) the issues to be decided;

b) who are the parties — who is propounding the will(s) and who is challenging the will(s), and who is submitting rights to the court;

c) whether there is any party under disability who requires representation and, if so, whether notice to the Public Guardian and Trustee or the Office of the Children's Lawyer should be directed;

d) whether an estate trustee should be appointed during litigation and the amount of security, if any, such an estate trustee should file;

e) who shall be served with the order for directions, and the method of and times for service;

f) whether the parties should exchange pleadings or put before the court their respective positions and the material facts upon which they rely by some other means;

g) procedures for bringing the matter before the court in a summary way;

h) the timing of a mediation session under Rule 75.1 and its conduct, including (i) whether the parties wish the mediator to provide any report to the court on procedural issues, (ii) the desirability of multiple mediation sessions, and (iii) when a pre-trial conference should be held in the event the mediation does not result in a settlement of the proceeding;

i) any other pre-hearing steps to be undertaken, including documentary disclosure, obtaining medical, accounting or legal records, examinations for discovery, and the availability of a motion for summary judgment;

j) the timing for the delivery of any expert report and the utility of a pre-hearing meeting between experts to narrow the issues in dispute;

k) the timing of a pre-trial conference, including how long after an unsuccessful mediation session the pre-trial conference should be held; and,

l) any matter relating to the conduct of the trial or hearing, including whether affidavits be used as witnesses' evidence-in-chief.

B. — Orders giving Directions: Contested Passing of Accounts

47. Where a hearing will be held on a passing of accounts, orders giving directions proposed by the parties should address the following issues, where applicable:

a) the timing and conduct of a mediation;

b) the issues to be tried and each party's position on each issue;

c) the timing and scope of relevant disclosure;

d) the witnesses each party intends to call, the issues each witness intends to address, and the anticipated length of each witness' testimony (examination-in-chief and cross-examination); and,

e) the procedure to be followed at the hearing, including the method of adducing evidence-in-chief.

PART VIII: — MANDATORY MEDIATION — RULE 75.1

48. Rule 75.1.02(1) stipulates that mandatory mediation applies to the following proceedings:

a) contested applications to pass accounts;

b) formal proof of testamentary instruments;

c) objections to issuing a certificate of appointment;

d) return of a certificate of appointment;

e) claims against an estate;

f) proceedings under Part V of the *Succession Law Reform Act*;

g) proceedings under the *Substitute Decisions Act, 1992*;

h) proceedings under the *Absentees Act, the Charities Accounting Act, the Estates Act*, the *Trustee Act* or the *Variation of Trusts Act*;

i) applications under Rule 14.05(3) whether the matters at issue relate to an estate or trust; and,

j) proceedings under s. 5(2) of the *Family Law Act.*

49. On contested passing of accounts applications parties should be prepared to deal with the issue of directions for mandatory mediation on the initial return date specified in the notice of application.

50. In all other matters, motions for directions for the conduct of a mandatory mediation normally should form part of, or be combined with, a motion for directions under Rule 75.06. Consent mediation orders can be obtained through a 9:30 Appointment.

51. In addition to addressing the matters set out in Rule 75.1.05(4), an order giving directions for mediation should, where appropriate, deal with any further information the parties require in advance of the mediation in order to ensure a productive mediation session.

PART IX: — MATERIALS FOR USE OF THE COURT

A. — General Requirements

52. Parties are strongly encouraged to file any materials for use of the court earlier than the dates specified in the Rules, especially for more complex hearings. All materials must be filed by the moving party at least seven days before the hearing. All material must be filed by the responding party at least four days before the hearing.

53. Application/Motion Confirmation Forms must clearly specify the materials that each party wishes the court to read for use on the application/motion.

B. — Multiple-appearance Proceedings: Records for use at the Hearing

54. Many proceedings on the Estates List involve multiple attendances before the court. Over time materials can become voluminous. Parties are reminded that the Rules require that the application and motion records used at a hearing must contain *all* materials that the parties intend to use on that particular hearing.

55. The Estates List strongly discourages the practice of relying at a hearing on materials used at previously disposed of hearings in a proceeding. If a party intends to do so, the party must ensure that a representative attends at the Estates Office sufficiently in advance of the hearing to ensure that the correct materials are available for the judge. It is the responsibility of the parties, not the Estates Office or the judge, to ensure that materials from previously disposed of hearings are available for a current hearing.

56. In complex cases where a large volume of materials will be placed before the hearing judge, it is of great assistance to the court for the parties to coordinate on a common numbering scheme for the records, transcripts, factums, authorities and other materials intended for use by the court and to ensure that the materials are properly organized for use on the hearing.

C. — Multiple-appearance Proceedings: On-going Endorsements/Orders Record

57. Where a proceeding likely will involve multiple attendances before the court, it is of assistance to judges hearing matters in the proceeding to be able to review previous orders, endorsements and reasons for judgment. In such cases the person starting a case is responsible for preparing and filing with the Estates Office a red three-ring

binder, bearing the proceeding's style of cause, entitled "Endorsements/Orders Record", and containing numbered tabs.

58. The person who started the case shall keep the Endorsements/Orders Record up-to-date, under the supervision of the Estates Office personnel, by using the following procedure. Within five days of the date of the issuance of a new endorsement or reasons for judgment, or the entry of a new order in the proceeding, the person who started the case shall provide the Estates Office with (i) a copy of the new endorsement, order or reasons for judgment, (ii) a consecutively numbered tab for the new document, and (iii) an updated table of contents for filing in the *Endorsements/Orders Record* so that a continuous record of all judicial decisions in the proceeding can be kept in an ordered fashion in the court file. Where an endorsement is hand-written, the applicant should assist the Court by preparing a typed draft, in consultation with other parties, for inclusion in *the Endorsements/Order Record.*

59. An order giving directions in a proceeding may include a provision requiring the applicant to prepare and maintain such an *Endorsements/Orders Record.*

D. — Compendium of Documents

60. In appropriate cases, to supplement any required formal record, parties are requested to consider preparing a Compendium of the key materials to be referred to during oral argument (fair extracts of documents, transcripts, previous orders, authorities, etc.) to assist in focusing the case for the court. Relevant portions of the Compendium should be highlighted or marked. Parties are encouraged to consult among themselves to prepare a joint Compendium, if possible.

61. The court encourages the use of diagrams, family trees, lists of persons involved, corporate organization charts, point-form chronologies, and other synopses of complex or technical evidence.

62. The prior preparation of draft orders for consideration by the court at the end of a hearing will greatly expedite the issuance of orders.

E. — Factums and Short Statements of Issues

63. The Rules require that on applications each party must file a factum for use at the hearing.

64. Although under the Rules factums are not mandatory on the hearing of a motion, parties are reminded that factums are of great assistance to the court where the motion will be contested or where an understanding of a large amount of materials will be required in order for a court to deal with an unopposed matter. In appropriate cases filing a short, point-form or simple statement of issues, fact and/or law may provide an alternative way by which parties can assist the court in understanding the issues on the motion.

F. — Evidence at Trial

65. The court encourages the use, in appropriate circumstances, of sworn witness statements at trial in substitution for the examination-in-chief of witnesses, in whole or in part. Where sworn witness statements will be used, they must be exchanged with all other parties and counsel well in advance of the hearing and, unless a prior order is made, the witnesses should be available for cross-examination at the trial.

PART X: — MATTERS WITHOUT A HEARING

66. Judges on the Estates List deal with a variety of applications without a hearing. The most common applications involve requests to dispense with administration bonds and uncontested passing of accounts. It is important that parties filing applications without a hearing ensure that their materials contain all the information and evidence required by statute, the Rules or any published filing endorsements emanating from the Estates List, and also provide clear, detailed explanations of the reasons for the relief they are requesting.

67. Filing requirements for requests to dispense with administration bonds are set out in *Re Henderson Estate*, 2008 CanLII 69136 (ON S.C.).

68. Two copies of the draft order sought must be filed with the application materials.

69. Part XI: Costs

PART XI: — COSTS

70. Parties are reminded that the traditional practice of awarding costs in estate litigation to all parties out of the estate has been tempered by recent jurisprudence relating to the conduct of parties and their relative success in the litigation. Parties are expected to be aware of this jurisprudence and to be prepared to make submissions with respect to its application in particular cases.

PART XII: — APPLICATIONS FOR THE APPOINTMENT OF GUARDIANS UNDER THE SUBSTITUTE DECISIONS ACT OR CHILDREN'S LAW REFORM ACT

71. Part III of the *Substitute Decisions Act, 1992* specifies the procedure and filing requirements for applications to appoint guardians of adults. Part III of the *Children's Law Reform Act* sets out the procedure and filing requirements for applications to appoint guardians of minors. In addition, the general requirements of Rule 38 governing applications apply to applications to appoint guardians.

72. Parties should refer to paragraphs 25 to 28 (above) regarding the requirements for scheduling applications for the appointments of guardians.

PART XIII: — SETTLEMENTS AFFECTING PARTIES UNDER A DISABILITY

73. The partial or full settlement of a claim made by or against a person under disability requires the approval of a judge under Rule 7.08. Often the implementation of such a settlement will require the appointment of a guardian of property under Parts I and III of the *Substitute Decisions Act* or section 47 of the *Children's Law Reform Act*.

A. — Settlements of Estates List Proceedings

74. Where the settlement of a proceeding on the Estates List requires court approval, the motion for approval of the settlement and the application for the appointment of a guardian of property should be brought before a judge on the Estates List.

B. — Settlements of other Civil Proceedings

75. Where the settlement of any other civil proceeding will require the appointment of a guardian of property for a person under disability, the application for the appointment of a guardian should be brought on the Estates List. However, where the settlement occurs during the trial or pre-trial conference of a civil matter, the trial or pre-trial judge may deal with the application to appoint a guardian of property where the circumstances make it more practical to do so.

76. Where the settlement involves an adult under disability, in most circumstances the application to appoint a guardian of property should be brought on the Estates List prior to the filing of a motion for approval of the settlement so that an authorized person exists to receive any settlement funds on behalf of the party under disability prior to the approval of the settlement.

77. Since the *Children's Law Reform Act* does not authorize an amendment to a management plan for a guardian of property of a minor except by court order, where the settlement involves a minor under disability the application to appoint a guardian of property initially should be made returnable at a 9:30 Appointment on the Estates List so that the court can coordinate the hearing of the application to appoint a guardian with the motion to approve the settlement.

PART XIV: — APPLICATIONS UNDER PART V OF THE SUCCESSION LAW REFORM ACT

78. In considering an application for dependant's support under Part V of the *Succession Law Reform Act*, a court must consider numerous circumstances, including the dependant's current assets and means, the assets and means that the dependant is likely to have in the future, and the dependant's needs in light of the dependant's accustomed standard of living. Although the *Rules of Civil Procedure* do not prescribe the manner by which an applicant should place before the court evidence about these matters, applicants are encouraged to include in their application materials comprehensive lists of the dependant's assets and liabilities, as well as information about the dependant's income and expenses.

PART XV: — FAMILY LAW ACT ELECTIONS

79. An application for the extension of time to make an election under s. 6(1) of the *Family Law Act* regarding the interest of a spouse under section 5(2) of that Act should be brought on the Estates List.

Dated: April 11, 2014

Heather J. Smith

Chief Justice

Superior Court of Justice (Ontario)

Geoffrey B. Morawetz

Regional Senior Judge

Superior Court of Justice, Toronto Region

PD-18 — *CONSOLIDATED PRACTICE DIRECTION CONCERNING THE COMMERCIAL LIST (EFFECTIVE JULY 1, 2014)*

This Practice Direction applies to matters on the commercial list in the Toronto Region. It supersedes all Toronto Region Practice Directions concerning the commercial list issued before July 1, 2014, which are hereby revoked.

Counsel and parties are advised to refer to the relevant Parts of the Consolidated Provincial Practice Direction, the Consolidated Practice Direction for Divisional Court Proceedings as well as any other relevant Toronto region-specific Practice Directions and Guides which are available on the Superior Court of Justice website at: www.ontariocourts.ca/scj.

PART I: — INTRODUCTION

The Commercial List was established in 1991 for the hearing of certain actions, applications and motions in the Toronto Region involving issues of commercial law. The special procedures adopted for the hearing of matters on the Commercial List expedite the hearing and determination of these matters and have been met with considerable approval.

All counsel appearing in matters on the Commercial List are expected to know and follow the current Practice Direction.

The Commercial List remains, in the first instance, voluntary, except for bankruptcy matters. Applicants and plaintiffs may continue to set other matters that qualify for the Commercial List down for hearing either on the Commercial List or elsewhere. There is, however, a provision for any party to have a matter transferred to, or removed from, the Commercial List.

A continuous re-evaluation process by the court and the Commercial List Users' Committee determines whether (i) other matters should be added to those matters which may be listed on the Commercial List or (ii) its procedures should be further modified or continued.

This Practice Direction is to govern the conduct of matters on the Commercial List subject to further amendments as required.

PART II: — MATTERS ELIGIBLE FOR THE COMMERCIAL LIST

1. Matters which may be listed on the Commercial List are applications, motions and actions which in essence involve the following:

a) *Bankruptcy and Insolvency Act*;

b) *Bank Act*, relating to realizations and priority disputes;

c) *Bulk Sales Act*;

d) *Business Corporations Act (Ontario) and Canada Business Corporations Act*;

e) *Companies' Creditors Arrangement Act*;

f) *Limited Partnerships Act*;

g) *Pension Benefits Act*;

h) *Personal Property Security Act*;

i) receivership applications and all interlocutory motions to appoint, or give directions to, receivers and receiver/managers;

j) *Securities Act*;

k) *Winding-Up and Restructuring Act*;

l) *Credit Unions and Caisses Populaires Act*, relating to credit unions and caisses populaires under administration or that are being wound up or liquidated; and

m) such other commercial matters as a judge presiding over the Commercial List may direct to be listed on the Commercial List, including: suitably complex cases under the *Arthur Wishart Act* (Franchise Disclosure), suitable commercial matters under the *International Commercial Arbitration Act* (Ontario), *Arbitration Act, 1991* (Ontario) and *Commercial Arbitration Act* (Canada). [See *771225 Ontario Inc. v. Bramco Holdings Co. Ltd.*, [1993] O.J. No. 1772 and *Maple Valley Acres Limited v. CIBC*, [1992] O.J. No. 2610), *Piedra v. TSX Inc.*, [2009] O.J. No. 5351 (Div. Ct.)].

In considering whether to make a direction under sub-paragraph 1m), the judge may take into account the current and expected caseload of matters listed on the Commercial List.

PART III: — JUDGES, COURT OFFICIALS, COURTROOMS AND GENERAL PROCEDURES

2. The Commercial List shall be administered through the facilities of the Commercial List Office, 7th Floor, 330 University Avenue, Toronto M5G 1R7 fax: (416) 327-6228.

3. Matters listed on the Commercial List, including bankruptcy matters, shall usually be heard in courtrooms at 330 University Avenue, Toronto.

4. If counsel are aware that a judge sitting on the Commercial List should not hear a particular matter, the Commercial List Office should be advised.

5. Cooperation, communication and common sense shall continue to be the principles of operation of the Commercial List.

PART IV: — ORIGINATING PROCESS

6. Actions and applications under sub-paragraphs 1a) to l) (above) intended to be listed on the Commercial List may be issued in the Commercial List Office. Otherwise, all originating processes shall be issued from the appropriate office of the Superior Court of Justice as provided in the *Rules of Civil Procedure*.

7. For all applications, an initial return date must be obtained from the Commercial List Office or selected by counsel in conformity with the provisions of paragraphs 16 to 22 (below).

PART V: — PLACE OF HEARING

8. Only Toronto Region matters can be listed on the Commercial List (unless, for special reasons, authorization is given by the supervising judge). Aside from urgent insolvency matters, there should be a material connection to the Toronto Region over and above the location of counsel. Matters listed on the Commercial List shall only be heard in Toronto.

PART VI: — APPLICATIONS FOR TRANSFER TO/FROM THE COMMERCIAL LIST

9. Matters may be transferred to or removed from the Commercial List on a motion to a judge sitting to hear matters on the Commercial List.

10. A matter may be provisionally transferred to the Commercial List by a judge who is hearing the matter or a proceeding in the matter but who is not sitting to hear matters on the Commercial List, with the consent of all parties appearing. Such provisional transfer shall be for the purpose of bringing an application for transfer in accordance with paragraph 9 by one of the parties or as the judge may direct.

11. A matter may be transferred to the Commercial List by the Commercial List Office staff if the transfer is on consent of all parties, a Request Form and Case Timetable are fully completed and the matter is a Toronto Region matter which clearly falls within the categories of sub-paragraphs 1a) to l) (above).

PART VII: — COURT DOCUMENTS

12. The name of the court in the title of proceedings of matters listed on the Commercial List shall be: "Superior Court of Justice — Commercial List". All Notices of Application and Notices of Motion involving the Commercial List shall state that the application or motion will be made to "a judge presiding over the Commercial List at 330 University Avenue, Toronto".

13. All parts of the front and the back of a Request Form must be completed for all cases and for each proceeding (including 9:30 a.m. matters, matters added to the Commercial List and all other attendances) and the form must be signed by all counsel or an explanation for not doing so must be given. If all counsel cannot sign the same form, they may sign individual copies. Completed Request Forms may be faxed to the Commercial List Office at (416) 327-6228. Copies of the current Request Forms are available from the Commercial List Office.

14. For matters that are scheduled for a hearing time of one day or more, the Request Form shall set out an estimate of the amount of time it will take a judge to read the materials in advance.

15. A Case Timetable should be completed. If this cannot be done before the matter is first spoken to (it being recognized that the schedule may depend on the setting of a hearing date), a Case Timetable should be agreed among counsel as soon as possible thereafter and a copy sent to the Commercial List Office. In the event that counsel cannot agree on a schedule, counsel should attend before the supervising judge in chambers (see paragraph 26). It is expected that preliminary procedures shall be completed sufficiently in advance of the deadline dates to allow for consideration of the matter by counsel and for some subsequent slippage in the timetable. If a step is not completed in accordance with the Case Timetable, counsel are expected to get the matter back on schedule as soon as possible: (see *Re: Mernick* (1992), 14 C.B.R. (3d) 263). Copies of the current Case Timetable form are available from the Commercial List Office.

PART VIII: — DATES FOR APPLICATIONS, MOTIONS AND TRIALS

16. The Commercial List Office shall maintain the Commercial List. Subject to paragraphs 41 and 42 (below), the office staff, acting under the direction of the supervising judge, may assign initial hearing dates for matters other than trials.

17. The supervising judge or designate may assign initial hearing dates for matters not assigned by the office staff and for trials which, may be made in chambers at 9:30 a.m.

18. For trials and trials of issues, a motion to set a hearing date shall be made, unless the matter is otherwise scheduled by the supervising judge or designate in chambers on consent or on the appearance of all parties. The motion should be made to the supervising judge or designate, either as a chambers motion under paragraph 25 (below), or by special appointment. A trial date shall not be set unless the parties have completed a Trial Requirements Memorandum, including a brief outline of the case and its issues and witness time estimates. The Trial Requirements Memorandum form may be obtained from the Commercial List Office.

19. For a scheduling motion to a judge to be heard in chambers, counsel should try to provide a list of three mutually convenient and disparate dates from which the judge may select. Counsel are expected to check with the Commercial List Office for available dates immediately prior to the motion.

20. Except where special circumstances otherwise require, in selecting a return date for a matter, counsel are expected to allow reasonable time for all preliminary steps to take place before the return date (see paragraph 14). Counsel are encouraged and expected to consult among themselves in this regard, so that matters can be dealt with on the scheduled return date without further adjournment.

21. Counsel may specify the return date for a matter as "on a date to be established by the Commercial List Office" if there is no agreement on the return date.

22. A list of matters scheduled to be heard the following day will be posted on the bulletin board at 330 University Avenue by 4:00 p.m. Information about matters listed for the following day may also be obtained by calling (416) 327-5045 after 4:00 p.m.

PART IX: — ESTIMATES OF REQUIRED TIME

23. A realistic estimate of the time required for hearing the matter must be stated in the Request Form. If such an estimate cannot be given on the initial return of a matter, the Request Form must be appropriately amended when the matter is subsequently re-scheduled. If all parties do not sign the Request Form, the initial return of the matter shall be for only a 10 minute scheduling hearing. Counsel should allocate the estimated hearing time appropriately among themselves, failing which the court shall assume that counsel have agreed to an equal division of time. If the time estimates in the Request Form becomes obsolete, then it is to be revised by notice to the Commercial List Office, giving the reason for the change. The court expects counsel to adhere to their time estimates.

24. The court may attempt to fix not only the date, but also the time, of the hearing, in appropriate situations. This shall require the cooperation of all counsel to correctly estimate the time required for their matters, to complete them within the time previously scheduled and to minimize wasted time for all concerned.

PART X: — CHAMBERS MATTERS

25. Commercial List judges will be available in chambers at 9:30 a.m. on each day to deal with ex parte, urgent, scheduling and consent matters, each of which must take not more than 10 minutes. Counsel must book these chambers matters through the Commercial List Office and these bookings will be made to allow the Chambers Judge to hear all chambers matters by 10:00 a.m. Counsel are expected to have discussed the matter in advance and to have prepared a draft resolution for consideration by the

Chambers Judge. Counsel should file the materials for the appointment on the previous day, so that the judge is aware of the nature of the matter to be considered.

26. Ex parte matters on the Commercial List will be rare. Counsel shall be required to justify the reason for not notifying the respondents. In most cases, notice shall be required, particularly if the matter is part of an ongoing dispute and there are solicitors known to be representing the respondents, even if in respect of other matters.

27. Motions to have matters listed on the Commercial List under sub-paragraph 1m), should be accompanied by the consent of the other counsel involved or a completed Request Form so that the judge may make an order either granting or refusing the motion.

PART XI: — ADJOURNMENTS AND SETTLEMENTS

28. Counsel shall be expected to be ready to proceed with matters for which hearing times have been agreed to or set; adjournments of previously scheduled matters shall be granted only in special circumstances and for a material reason. Counsel are expected conscientiously to have sought to resolve most adjournments and waiting periods among themselves before a hearing, in a way which minimizes inconvenience and difficulty for the parties. Parties are expected to have retained counsel promptly and requests for adjournments because counsel have not been retained promptly or because new counsel have been retained just prior to the hearing shall be dealt with accordingly. Applications for adjournments on consent should be forwarded to the Commercial List Office or, if directed by the supervising judge, shall be spoken to at the next available 9:30 a.m. sittings; counsel are expected to ensure that adjournments are sought at the earliest opportunity, so that time is not blocked which could be used for other matters. It is expected that the first counsel to speak to a proposed adjournment shall be in a position to outline the position of other counsel appearing.

29. If an adjournment of a previously scheduled matter is to be sought or appears likely to be required, the Commercial List Office must be alerted as soon as possible to accommodate rescheduling of another matter or alerting counsel on standby matters.

30. If a matter is adjourned to permit the continuation of realistic settlement discussions and the matter is not settled within a reasonable time, a report should be made to the supervising judge through the Commercial List Office on the status of those discussions. This report should be made within 30 days and may be made in court, in chambers or by letter, as appropriate.

31. Where appropriate, matters may be scheduled to be heard on a "standby" basis for a particular date. In these cases, counsel should be prepared to proceed on short notice or they must keep the Commercial List Office advised of times when they become unavailable.

32. Counsel on Commercial List matters are expected to conscientiously and continuously canvass the matter of settlement and to advise promptly of all concluded settlements, or matters which are reasonably likely to settle, so that other matters may be rescheduled.

PART XII: — JUDGE TO HEAR WHOLE MATTER

33. It is anticipated that a judge who determines a substantive component of a proceeding will continue to hear all subsequent substantive components in that proceeding. Arrangements for these subsequent proceedings may be made directly with the Commercial List Office. The continuing judge should be contacted in writing about the nature of the matter to be heard and a list of times which are convenient to all

counsel, so that the judge can conveniently schedule the matter or can refer it back to the Commercial List Office for re-assignment. For matters of sufficient complexity or duration, in the event that the original judge is not sitting on the Commercial List at the time or has not then been assigned to a future Commercial List team, a request may be made for the appointment of a new continuing judge.

PART XIII: — CASE MANAGEMENT

34. It is expected that most matters of substance and of an ongoing nature on the Commercial List shall be subject to a form of case management by a Commercial List judge. Paragraph 33 already provides for significant informal case management for each case on the Commercial List. When a matter is transferred to the Commercial List, when the trial of an issue is directed or in any other matter where a party moves for case management and a Commercial List judge so directs, a specific case management judge may be appointed.

35. Where a Commercial List matter is subject to specific case management, a Scheduling Conference (if not already held at the time of transfer or otherwise) shall be held with the case management judge not later than one month after the close of pleadings or the date of the order (referred in paragraph 34) to determine a plan to process the case in a timely and reasonable fashion and to deal with any matters of a procedural nature which should be addressed at an early stage of the proceedings. The prospects for settlement should also be addressed. The results of a Scheduling Conference will be recorded in a Case Timetable.

36. Counsel will be expected to have conferred among themselves, prior to the Scheduling Conference, for the purpose of preparing a plan to process the case, including a discovery plan pursuant to rule 29.1 and a Case Timetable, for review with the case management judge.

37. Unless otherwise ordered, a Case Conference shall also be held with the case management judge not later than one month after the completion of discoveries. The plaintiff or applicant shall have the onus of arranging the Case Conference. The purpose of the Case Conference is to monitor the progress of the matter, to canvass settlement or other disposition of all or as many of the issues as possible, and to provide whatever directions as may be necessary or appropriate with respect to the disposition of the matter.

38. A Case Conference may be held at any other time during the proceeding where the parties consent or where a party moves for the scheduling of a Case Conference and the case management judge so directs.

PART XIV: — COMMERCIAL LIST MOTIONS BEFORE A MASTER

39. No Commercial List motions should be heard by a master unless referred by a Commercial List judge. The judge should indicate his/her referral by a written endorsement or direction to that effect.

40. Once there has been a referral from a Commercial List judge, counsel may book a short (two hours or less) master's motion through the scheduling unit on the 10th Floor at 393 University Avenue, but if the motion is a half day or longer or if a series of motions are anticipated where it would be beneficial for one master to be seized, no such motions shall be booked until a master is assigned by the Team Leader — Toronto Masters. The assigned Master's Registrar will then contact counsel to arrange for scheduling of the motion.

PART XV: — MOTIONS FOR SUMMARY JUDGMENT

41. If a motion for summary judgment is brought in a proceeding on the Commercial List, a motion date will not in the ordinary course be booked until:

a) The parties have exchanged all motion materials, on an agreed schedule or one fixed at a 9:30 a.m. chambers appointment, and are sufficiently advanced in the preparation of the motion to crystallize the issues and the evidence relating to them;

b) A case conference has been booked at which counsel must be prepared to address whether oral evidence should be heard on the motion in accordance with subrule 20.04(2.2), the length of time necessary for the hearing of the motion, judicial preparation time necessary and any other directions that may be required;

c) The judge hearing the case conference has directed that a motion date be booked, bearing in mind that it is expected that the case conference judge will hear the motion.

PART XVI: — APPLICATIONS

42. It is expected that applications, which can require some oral evidence, will be managed in the same manner as motions for summary judgment in paragraph 41.

PART XVII: — ALTERNATIVE DISPUTE RESOLUTION AND PRE-TRIALS

43. Resort to the techniques of "alternative dispute resolution" (ADR), where appropriate, is recognized and encouraged as an effective aid in the disposition of issues and matters on the Commercial List. Pursuant to Rule 24.01.04(2) (c), mandatory mediation does not apply to cases on the Commercial List.

44. It shall be the duty of the case management judge and the obligation of counsel to explore methods to resolve the contested issues between the parties, including the resort to ADR, at the case conferences and on whatever other occasions it may be fitting to do so.

45. At any time, particularly on consent of the parties, the case management judge may refer any issue for ADR, as appears appropriate.

46. When a matter, or any issue within a matter, has been referred to ADR, counsel shall report to the case management judge at regular intervals as to the progress of the ADR proceedings. The timing of such reports shall be agreed upon between counsel and the case management judge.

47. The court may schedule intensive pre-trials for either entire cases or for significant matters within cases. These pre-trials should be booked through the Commercial List Office, with enough time for the matters in issue and the possibility of settlement to be canvassed thoroughly. At least five days before the pre-trial, each party shall deliver to the other parties a pre-trial brief containing:

a) a concise statement of facts including the agreed facts and admissions;

b) where necessary, a concise summary of the issues;

c) any outstanding procedural issues;

d) the current settlement position of each party; and

e) an estimate of the trial time, including a list of witnesses and an estimate of the time required for hearing the evidence of each.

48. A trial management conference, which is to be arranged by counsel at least two months before trial, is to be held to deal with arrangements for managing the trial or hearing.

PART XVIII: — MATERIALS FOR USE OF COURT

49. It is expected that materials filed for the use of the court will be filed with the Commercial List Office at least within the time prescribed by the Rules. Early filing is recommended. All moving party or applicant material must be filed seven days (excluding holidays) before the hearing. All responding material must be filed four days (excluding holidays) before the hearing.

50. The Commercial List Office should be advised of what specific materials from its files are required for the hearing of any particular proceeding. This is particularly important where the matter is on-going or the materials in the court files are voluminous. It is suggested that counsel co-ordinate on a common numbering scheme for the records, transcripts, factums, authorities and other materials intended for use by the court and that a representative attend at the Commercial List Office before a hearing to ensure that the correct materials are available to the judge.

51. In appropriate cases, to supplement any required formal Record, counsel are requested to consider preparing an informal Compendium of the key materials to be referred to in argument (fair extracts of documents, transcripts, previous orders, authorities, etc.) to assist in focusing the case for the court: (see *Saskatchewan Egg Producers' Marketing Board v. Ontario*, [1993] O.J. No. 434.) Relevant portions of the Compendium should be highlighted or marked. Counsel are urged to consult among themselves in the preparation of a joint Compendium, if possible. The Compendium should contain only essential materials. The use of a loose-leaf format is particularly helpful to the court both for conducting hearings and for writing decisions.

52. All records and submissions should note on the cover page and the back page the nature of the proceeding for which the material is filed and the scheduled hearing date. When there is more than one affidavit of an individual filed in any proceeding, the affidavits should be numbered sequentially.

53. Factums should not, in the ordinary course, exceed 25 pages in length.

54. Unless it is not possible, briefs of authorities and substantial documents should be reproduced using both sides of the page.

55. Books of Authorities must be highlighted or side-barred to indicate the passages that will be referred to in argument.

56. The court invites the use of diagrams, corporate organization charts, list of persons involved, point-form chronologies and other synopses of complex or technical evidence.

57. The prior preparation of draft orders for consideration by the court at the end of a hearing will greatly expedite the issuance of orders. Where relevant model orders have been approved by the Commercial List Users' Committee, a copy of the draft order blacklined to the model order and indicating all variations sought from the model order must be filed.

58. For trials, the court encourages the use of sworn witness statements to replace examination in chief, in whole or in part, in appropriate circumstances. All such witness statements must be exchanged with all other parties and counsel well in advance

of the hearing and, unless a prior order is made, the witness should be available for cross-examination at the trial. (Also see rule 53.02).

PART XIX: — EXPERT WITNESSES

59. It is expected that counsel will comply with requirements set out in subrule 53.03(1) and (2) so as to provide notice of the intention to call an expert witness, including delivery of a signed report which contains the information mandated by subrule 53.03(2.1) within the expert report. Counsel must bring to the attention of their expert witness the duties of an expert set out in rule 4.1. Best practice should include providing the expert with the language of rule 4.1 and rule 53.03, subrules (1), (2) and (2.1).

PART XX: — REASONS FOR DECISION

60. If an endorsement, order or decision is hand-written or dictated and not transcribed by the court, counsel for the plaintiff or moving party shall assist the court in preparing a typed draft and providing to the court the typed draft for editing by the judge, along with an electronic version of the draft and a copy of the hand-written version or dictation media, highlighting any passages which were difficult to read.

PART XXI: — COSTS

61. The court will seek to award and fix costs at the end of the hearing of a matter. Counsel must submit a costs outline [subrule 57.01(6)] and be prepared to deal with costs (including liability, scale and amount) at the conclusion of the hearing of the matter or, if absolutely necessary, by written submissions immediately thereafter.

PART XXII: — USERS' COMMITTEE

62. A Commercial List Users' Committee has been established. It is comprised of members of the judiciary who sit on the Commercial List from time to time, of practitioners who are familiar with the operation of the Commercial List and who are nominated by relevant user organizations in conjunction with the Users' Committee and of a representative of Courts Administration from the Commercial List Office. The names of the members of the Users' Committee may be obtained from the Commercial List Office. The Users' Committee meets regularly to consider improvements to the organization and operation of the Commercial List and to make recommendations to the Regional Senior Justice and the Chief Justice in that regard. The Users' Committee welcomes suggestions, compliments and complaints from other practitioners who have had cases on the Commercial List. Communications may be sent to the Commercial List Office, which will direct them to the office of the Regional Senior Justice.

PART XXIII: — ENQUIRIES

63. The supervising judge of the Commercial List may be contacted about the scheduling of trials, long matters and urgent matters. In such cases, it is expected that counsel shall give details of the matter, the urgency, if any, expected length and mutually convenient dates. A Request Form and Case Timetable may be used for this purpose.

PART XXIV: — COMMERCIAL LIST FORMS

64. Current versions of the Request Forms, Case Timetable and Trial Requirements Memorandum may be obtained from the Commercial List Office.

PART XXV: — FREQUENTLY CITED CASES IN COMMERCIAL PROCEEDINGS

65. An Authorities Book for Commercial List matters containing cases frequently relied on, has been developed and approved for use in matters assigned to the Toronto Commercial List. There will be additions to, and deletions from, the list from time to time. The Authorities Book is available on the Superior Court's website at: www.ontariocourts.ca/scj/practice/practice-directions/toronto/commercial-list-authorities-book.

66. The cases in question appear on this list under various headings or topics which are not in any way intended to provide legal advice.

67. If you are relying on an authority that is contained in the Authorities Book, it need not be reproduced as part of the materials filed for the matters before the Commercial List in Toronto.

PART XXVI: — PROTOCOL CONCERNING COURT-TO-COURT COMMUNICATIONS IN CROSS BOARDER CASES

68. The Commercial List has approved the adoption of the Guidelines Applicable to Court-to-Court Communications in Cross Border Cases ("Guidelines") prepared by the American Law Institute, for matters on the Commercial List. The Guidelines are available at: www.iiiglobal.org/component/jdownloads. The Guidelines have already been applied to international insolvency cases on the Commercial List. It is expected that these Guidelines will facilitate cooperative procedures for insolvency proceedings and other types of commercial disputes involving cross-border proceedings, where court-to-court communications might facilitate in harmonizing proceedings to help ensure consistent results and increase efficiency.

69. The Guidelines will only be applied in specific cases, following adequate notice to the parties.

70. Although the Guidelines were prepared for court-to-court communications as between Canada and the United States, the Commercial List endorses their application in court-to-court communications between Canada and other countries, and as between Ontario and the other provinces and territories.

71. Counsel and/or the parties should ensure that any issues concerning the confidentiality of materials to be transmitted by the Commercial List to another jurisdiction, including the deemed undertaking rule, Rule 30.1 of the *Rules of Civil Procedure*, be addressed when consideration is given by the court to the transmittal of evidentiary or written materials from the Commercial List to another court. The Guidelines are to apply only in a manner that is consistent with the *Rules of Civil Procedure* and the practice in this jurisdiction.

72. The Commercial List confirms, as noted in the Guidelines, that the Guidelines are not meant to be static, but are meant to be adapted an modified to fit the circumstances of individual cases, and to change and evolve as experience is gained from working with them.

73. A copy of the Guidelines may also be obtained from the Commercial List Office at 393 University Avenue, 10th Floor, Toronto, Ontario M5G 1E6, Telephone 416-327-5043, Fax 416-327-6228.

Dated: April 11, 2014

Heather J. Smith

Chief Justice

Superior Court of Justice (Ontario)

Geoffrey B. Morawetz

Regional Senior Judge

Superior Court of Justice, Toronto Region

PD-19 — *GUIDE CONCERNING COMMERCIAL LIST E-SERVICE (EFFECTIVE JULY 1, 2014)*

This Guide applies to proceedings on the commercial list in the Toronto Region, effective July 1, 2014. It *supersedes* all E-Service Protocols for the Commercial List in the Toronto Region, issued before July 1, 2014, which are hereby revoked.

Counsel and parties are advised to refer to the relevant Parts of the Consolidated Provincial Practice Direction, the Consolidated Practice Direction for Divisional Court Proceedings as well as any other relevant Toronto region-specific Practice Directions and Guides which are available on the Superior Court of Justice website at: www.ontariocourts.ca/scj.

PART I: — INTRODUCTION

Proceedings on the Ontario Superior Court (Commercial List) (the "*Court*" or the "*Commercial List*") frequently involve multiple and evolving stakeholders located nationally and internationally. These proceedings involve "real time litigation" which, by its nature, requires efficient, effective and cost efficient methods of providing service and notice to stakeholders.

The usual methods of service provided for under the *Rules of Civil Procedure (Ontario)* (the "*Rules*") do not always operate efficiently in multi-party, multi-jurisdictional proceedings, nor do they take advantage of the most current technologies. Service provisions in Commercial List orders before the development of this guide evolved in an *ad hoc* manner without precision or specificity with respect to such fundamental terms as the "service list".

The purpose of this Commercial List E-Service Guide ("*E-Service Guide*") is to provide a uniform method of "substituted service", under the Rules, that engages modern and efficient processes to effect service and give notice in certain Commercial List proceedings. In order to achieve this purpose the E-Service Guide utilizes three tools:

a) Service of documents by electronic mail;

b) A "service list" with defined parameters; and

c) Mandatory websites containing defined minimum levels of information.

The E-Service Guide will be incorporated by reference in orders at the initial stages of certain Commercial List proceedings as a form of substituted service pursuant to Rule 16.04 of the Rules subject to Rule 17.05.[5] A copy of the E-Service Guide will be available on the Commercial List website at: www.ontariocourts.ca/scj/practice/practice-directions/toronto/#Commercial_List and need not be appended to the incorporating order.

The E-Service Guide permits service upon persons on the E-Service List[6] by those who have the right to serve and file material in the proceeding under the Rules, an order of the Court or otherwise. The E-Service Guide does not itself give any person the right to serve and file material. To that end, the E-Service Guide is not meant to alter or replace requirements under the Rules with respect to such matters as the delivery of Notices of Appearance. The E-Service Guide is subject to modification by the Court in appropriate cases.

Nothing in this E-Service Guide varies any requirements under the Rules or applicable practice directions with respect to the filing of Court Documents with the Court.

The E-Service Guide will be used in the following insolvency proceedings (collectively, the "*Insolvency Proceedings*") pending before the Commercial List:

a) Proceedings under the *Companies' Creditors Arrangement Act (Canada)* ("*CCAA*");

b) Receivership proceedings, including proceedings under the *Bankruptcy and Insolvency Act (Canada) ("BIA"), the Courts of Justice Act (Ontario)*, the *Securities Act (Ontario)* and other legislation which provides for the appointment of court officers;

c) Proceedings under the *Winding-Up and Restructuring Act*;

d) Division I proposal proceedings under the BIA; and

e) Any other insolvency-related proceedings, including bankruptcy proceedings under the BIA or other Commercial List proceedings, where the Court determines that it would be beneficial to use the E-Service Guide.[7]

In addition to the Insolvency Proceedings, the E-Service Guide may be used in large or complex arrangement, re-organization or similar court proceedings under the *Business Corporations Act (Canada)* and the *Business Corporations Act (Ontario)* where the Court determines that its use would be beneficial ("*Reorganization Proceedings*").[8] Insolvency Proceedings and Reorganization Proceedings are referred to collectively as "*Commercial List Proceedings*".

---

[5]Rule 17.05 deals with service of parties in a "contracting state" within the Convention on the Service Abroad of Judicial and Extrajudicial Documents in Civil or Commercial Matters signed at The Hague on November 15, 1965 — Special requirements may apply to such service which are outside the scope of this E-Service Guide.

[6]As defined in Part III below.

[7]CCAA proceedings involve, by definition, cases with more than $5 million of debt. No debt level criteria have been provided for other Insolvency Proceedings that may take advantage of the E-Service Guide — though the E-Service Guide, and in particular, the Case Website, may be inappropriate for smaller cases.

[8]Before seeking an order incorporating the E-Service Guide in Reorganization Proceedings, counsel should ensure that their firm has the capability to host the Case Website or that other suitable arrangements are made for the hosting of the site.

PART II: — SERVICE BY EMAIL

1. Electronic mail ("*Email*") will be the required mechanism to serve documents to be filed in court ("*Court Documents*") in Commercial List Proceedings. If service by Email is not practicable Court Documents may be served as provided in the Rules.

2. Court Documents are documents that must be served under the Rules with respect to motions or applications in Commercial List Proceedings such as notices of motion, notices of application, affidavits, facta, Court Officer[9] reports and orders.

3. Service by Email on the E-Service List shall be used only for the following purposes:

a) Service of Court Documents;

b) Delivery of correspondence containing information with respect to motions or applications such as the location or timing of a Commercial List Proceeding or other directions with respect to a proceeding; and

c) Circulation of material related to motions or applications such as draft orders.

4. Email sent to the E-Service List shall not be used in order to provide a party's general comments on the proceedings or to advocate positions or for any other use not specifically provided for herein.

5. The moving party in a Commercial List Proceeding shall seek Court adoption of the E-Service Guide in the order initiating the proceeding (or as soon as practicable thereafter). The following provision shall be included in such order unless varied by the Court:

Substituted Service and Case Website[10]

THIS COURT ORDERS THAT the E-Service Guide of the Commercial List (the "*Guide*") is approved and adopted by reference herein and, in this proceeding, the service of documents made in accordance with the Guide (which can be found on the Commercial List website at: www.ontariocourts.ca/scj/practice/practice-directions/toronto/#Commercial_List) shall be valid and effective service. Subject to Rule 17.05[11] this Order shall constitute an order for substituted service pursuant to Rule 16.04 of the Rules of Civil Procedure. Subject to Rule 3.01(d) of the Rules of Civil Procedure and paragraph 13 of the Guide, service of documents in accordance with the Guide will be effective on transmission. This Court further orders that a Case Website shall be established in accordance with the Guide with the following URL "<@>".

6. Except as otherwise provided herein, Email service is a sufficient mode of service of Court Documents without duplicating service by facsimile, hard copy delivery or other method of service.

[9]Court Officers include Monitors, Receivers, Information Officers, Interim Receivers, Trustees in Bankruptcy, Proposal Trustees and other similar persons.

[10]As defined in Part IV below.

[11]See Note 1.

7. Court Documents should be served by Email by way of HTML link or PDF files. If the party serving the Court Document can create an HTML link to the Court Document prior to serving the Court Document, service of such document by PDF file shall not be necessary. The HTML link must be a link directly to the document being served.[12]

8. To the extent practicable, Court Documents shall be in a format which is compliant with the Toronto Region Guide Concerning e-Delivery.

9. Where a party is serving more than one document by Email of HTML links, the Email shall specify each document being served and shall include a separate HTML link for each document being served.

10. If a Court Document is being served by way of an Email of a PDF file, the party serving the Court Document shall be cognizant of the size of the file and send the Court Document in multiple Emails if the PDF file would appear to be too large to serve in a single Email.

11. If the party serving the Court Document by Email receives notification of a transmission failure, the party serving the Court Document shall make reasonable efforts to ensure that successful Email transmission of the Court Document occurs or that the Email comes to the attention of the intended recipient or his or her firm.[13]

12. Any Court Document served by Email should clearly state in the subject line of the Email: (i) notification that a Court Document is being served; (ii) a recognizable short form name of the Commercial List Proceeding; (iii) the nature of the proceeding; and (iv) the nature of the Court Document.[14] The body of the Email should contain a description of the party serving the Court Document, a brief description of the nature of the Court Document being served, the date of the proceeding and any other specific information with respect to the proceeding such as, for example, a specific commencement time or court location if known.

13. In accordance with Rule 3.01(1)(d), a Court Document served by Email before 4:00 p.m. shall be deemed to be received that day and Court Documents served after 4:00 p.m. or at any time on a holiday shall be deemed to be received on the next day that is not a holiday.

14. Each party serving a Court Document in a Commercial List Proceeding is responsible for complying with the E-Service Guide. Nothing herein, however, is intended to change the substantive law about who is required to be served with materials in respect of any particular motion or proceeding brought within a Commercial List Proceeding.

15. Even though a Court Document has been served in accordance with this E-Service Guide, a person may show that the Court Document:

a) did not come to the person's notice;

---

[12]Where the HTML link is not to the Case Website, the party serving the Court Document shall ensure that the link remains active until the completion of the motion or proceeding relating to that Court Document.

[13]Parties who are on the E-Service List shall ensure that "out of town notifications" or other similar notifications contain the name and Email address of another member of that person's firm or business to whom the Court Document should be sent.

[14]By way of example — E-SERVICE: Nortel — Approval of Sale of Assets — Motion Record.

b) came to the person's notice later than when it was served or effectively served, or

c) was incomplete or illegible.

16. Each party serving a Court Document by Email shall prepare an affidavit of service containing the particulars of the service including the E-Service List served, the Email addresses to which Court Documents were sent and the time of the Emailing. A copy of the affidavit of service shall be filed with the Court.

PART III: — THE E-SERVICE LIST

17. The E-Service List in a Commercial List Proceeding ("*E-Service List*") is a mechanism to facilitate service of Court Documents on stakeholders who should be served with Court Documents ("*Stakeholders*"). Stakeholders include a corporation, body corporate, partnership or individual that has a legal interest in the Commercial List Proceeding. The E-Service List is not intended as a mechanism to generally disseminate information with respect to the status of a Commercial List Proceeding.

18. The E-Service List shall list the names, contact coordinates, including Email addresses, of Stakeholders or their counsel, who may be served by Email in accordance with Part III hereof. Inclusion of a party on the E-Service List allows effective service of Court Documents on such party by Email.

19. After the order is issued authorizing the use of the E-Service Guide in a Commercial List Proceeding, counsel for the party initiating the proceeding, or the appointed Court Officer, if appropriate, (the "*E-Service List Keeper*") shall prepare the initial E-Service List containing the names and e-mail addresses of Stakeholders upon whom service is to be effected by Email.

20. The E-Service List Keeper shall use its best efforts to ensure that the Email address of a Stakeholder is correct and will result in an effective transmission of Court Documents to the intended recipient when initially placed on the E-Service List. Stakeholders on the E-Service List shall notify the E-Service List Keeper of any subsequent change of their Email address.

21. The E-Service List Keeper shall send an Email to each proposed Stakeholder identifying themselves as the E-Service List Keeper and advising that: (i) the proposed Stakeholder has been placed upon the E-Service List, (ii) Court Documents will be validly served upon the proposed Stakeholder by Email; and (iii) that any Stakeholder on the E-Service List may serve Court Documents on any other Stakeholder on the E-Service List in accordance with this E-Service Guide.

22. During the course of the Commercial List Proceeding, the E-Service List Keeper shall add Stakeholders to the E-Service List from time to time as required subject to the procedure set out in paragraph 21.

23. The E-Service List must include the following parties:

a) Counsel for the applicant/moving party in the Commercial List Proceeding;

b) The Court Officer appointed in the Commercial List Proceeding and counsel for the Court Officer;

c) Counsel for any party that has delivered a Notice of Appearance under the Rules from time to time;

d) Any party or counsel to any party who should be served with Court Documents in accordance with the Rules and the practice in the Commercial List; and

e) Any Stakeholder or counsel to a Stakeholder who has filed a RES.[15]

24. Stakeholders who wish to be placed on the E-Service List in order to receive service of Court Documents in a timely and efficient manner shall Email to the E-Service List Keeper a duly completed Request for Electronic Service (*"RES"*) in the form attached as Schedule "A" hereto[16].

25. If a Stakeholder on the E-Service List no longer has an ongoing legal interest in a Commercial List Proceeding, that Stakeholder may request that the E-Service List Keeper delete that Stakeholder from the E-Service List.

26. Those persons who are interested in monitoring a Commercial List Proceeding but are not required to be served with Court Documents in accordance with the Rules or the practice in the Commercial List are not to be placed on the E-Service List. Such parties should monitor the Commercial List Proceeding by accessing the Case Website.[17]

27. A lawyer who files an RES on behalf of a client must identify such client. Lawyers receiving E-Service of Court Documents on behalf of clients must be properly accredited lawyers within the jurisdiction in which they practice. By delivery of such RES, the lawyer warrants his or her authority to receive service on behalf of his/her client.

28. In addition to the E-Service List referred to in paragraph 18 hereof, the E-Service List Keeper shall create and maintain a copyable Word document containing up to date Email addresses of the Stakeholders on the E-Service List (the "*Address List*"). The purpose of the Address List is to allow Stakeholders on the Service List to copy and paste the Email addresses of the current Stakeholders on the E-Service List into Emails serving Court Documents. This process is designed to avoid E-Service of Court Documents using out of date or inaccurate E-Service Lists. The practice of serving Court Documents by "replying to all" on a previous Email is discouraged. The E-Service List Keeper shall provide a current copy of the Address List to the WebHost[18] each time the list is updated, as Stakeholders are added or removed.

29. Any party wishing to serve a Court Document in a Commercial List Proceeding shall use the then current copy of the Address List posted on the Case Website to serve the Court Documents. If possible, the serving party shall make enquiries of the E-Service List Keeper to determine if the E-Service List Keeper is aware of parties to be added to the Address List who have not yet been added.

30. During the course of a Commercial List Proceeding, certain motions or applications require service of Court Documents on respondents with an interest in that particular motion or application only; for example, service on lien claimants with an interest only on specific property with respect to a sale approval and vesting order. In such circumstances, the party bringing the motion or application shall prepare a Supplementary E-Service List listing the names and Email addresses of the "one time" respondents that the moving party wishes to serve by Email. The cover Email shall contain the information designated in paragraph 12 and 21 hereof. The affidavit of service with respect to that motion shall include the Supplementary E-Service List.

---

[15]As defined in paragraph 24 below.

[16]Parties who do not reside in Ontario should consider whether, based upon the substantive law, the delivery of an RES constitutes attornment to the Ontario proceeding.

[17]As defined in Part IV below.

[18]As defined in Part IV herein.

31. The E-Service List Keeper shall use its best efforts to maintain the E-Service List current and accurate. In addition to any other protection that may be available to it by statute or Court order, the E-Service List Keeper shall incur no liability in carrying out the provisions of this E-Service Guide and, in particular, with respect to the creation or maintenance of the E-Service List, except for any gross negligence or wilful misconduct on its part.

PART IV: — THE CASE WEBSITE

32. The case website hereinafter described (the "*Case Website*") will be established for the purpose of:

a) Creating a comprehensive and current record of Commercial List Proceedings;

b) Allowing easy and inexpensive access to the record of proceedings to Stakeholders involved in Commercial List Proceedings and to parties with a potential interest in the proceedings;

c) Providing a mechanism to facilitate service of Court Documents by Email with HTML links to particular Court Documents; and

d) Provide a mechanism to facilitate the dissemination of notices and information to larger groups of interested parties such as employees, retirees or general unsecured creditors.

33. The Case Website shall be hosted by the Court Officer appointed in the Insolvency Proceeding or by counsel to the applicant in Reorganization Proceedings (the "*WebHost*") or as the Court may order.

34. The Case Website, or a link to the Case Website, shall be located on the WebHost's website and shall be prominently identified to ensure easy public access to the Case Website and the Court Documents posted thereon. The Case Website shall be specifically devoted to the posting, organization, storage and display of electronic versions of all Court Documents delivered in a Commercial List Proceeding.

35. The Case Website shall be organized in a manner that facilitates the ability of any interested party to easily locate Court Documents delivered in the Commercial List Proceedings and other documentation relevant to the Commercial List Proceedings such as proof of claim forms and creditor meeting documentation.

36. The WebHost shall post the following categories of documents, as served or to be served:

a) Notices of application/notices of motion;

b) All affidavits, including exhibits, and other material filed by an applicant/moving party with respect to an application/motion;

c) All responding affidavits, including exhibits, and other material delivered in response to the application or motion by all respondents;

d) All facta and written arguments delivered by any party to an application or to a motion;

e) Books of authorities;

f) All court reports filed by Court Officers;

g) All Court Orders, Reasons for Decision and Endorsements;

h) The current version of the E-Service List and Address List;

i) The name and Email address of the E-Service List Keeper; and

j) Any document that requires dissemination to interested parties, such as proof of claim forms, notices of creditor meetings, plan disclosure statements, plans of reorganization and voting letters as requested by the restructuring debtor or the Court Officer.

If the WebHost is uncertain whether a document should be posted on the Case Website as a result of its content, the WebHost may seek directions from the Court at a 9:30 appointment.

37. This list of information to be posted to the Case Website is not meant to be an exhaustive list. The WebHost may post other case-related information to the Case Website in its discretion. In the case of a Monitor under the CCAA, nothing in this E-Service Guide shall affect any requirements set out in the CCAA or the regulations thereunder with respect to the posting of documents to a website by the Monitor.

38. Documents that have been sealed by Court order or documents in respect of which sealing orders are being requested shall not be posted on the Case Website.

39. Any party intending to bring a motion or application in a Commercial List Proceeding shall, if reasonably possible, provide an electronic copy of the motion or application record to the WebHost for posting on the Case Website prior to service. If the motion or application record has been posted on the Case Website, the moving party or applicant may serve the proceeding by Email using a HTML link to the Case Website. Where time does not permit the prior posting of motion or application records on the Case Website, the applicant or moving party shall serve the Court Documents on the E-Service List by Email of a PDF or by HTML link in accordance with paragraph 7.

40. Counsel shall send an electronic copy of Court Documents to the WebHost at the time of service of the Court Documents on the E-Service List.

41. The WebHost shall use its best efforts to post documents provided to it by counsel in PDF format on the Case Website as soon as practicable.

42. The WebHost shall maintain the Case Website for a period of at least six months after the earlier of completion of the Commercial List Proceeding or the discharge of the WebHost if a Court Officer.

43. To the extent practicable the WebHost shall post links to foreign proceedings related to the Commercial List Proceedings on the Case Website.

44. The WebHost is entitled to charge for the time spent maintaining the Case Website at the usual hourly rates charged by its staff. No additional charges or fees may be claimed with respect to the establishment and maintenance of the Case Website.

45. The WebHost shall use its best efforts to maintain the Case Website current and complete. In addition to any other protection that may be available to the WebHost by statute or Court order, the WebHost shall incur no liability or obligation in carrying out the provisions of this E-Service Guide and, in particular, with respect to the creation and maintenance of the Case Website, except for any gross negligence or wilful misconduct on its part.

Schedule "A" — Request for Electronic Service ("RES")

Please refer to important notes below

In the Matter of the ❑ CCAA ❑ Receivership ❑ BIA Proposal ❑ Other ______________________ of:	XYZ Company Ltd (the "Debtor") < http://www.caseurl.com>
Legal Counsel to Stakeholder listed below: (please provide firm name, lawyer's name, address and email address) Please indicate your preference (by checking applicable box below): ❑ Serve counsel only ❑ Serve counsel & Stakeholder listed below	<LawfirmLLP > <Lawyer name > <Address line 1 > <Address line 2 > <email address >
Name of Stakeholder requesting E-Service: (please provide full legal name, address, email address and describe Stakeholder's legal relationship to the Debtor)	ABC Company Inc. <Address line 1 > <Address line 2 > <email address >
Date:	< Insert current date >

I acknowledge having read the Ontario Superior Court of Justice Commercial List E-Service Guide. I hereby request to be placed on the E-Service List. By so doing, I agree as a Stakeholder or as counsel to a Stakeholder that the Stakeholder accepts service by electronic means in this case and will be bound by that service:

Stakeholder/ Counsel to Stakeholder

PLEASE RETURN SIGNED COPY OF FORM TO <insert name of E-Service List Keeper here>: <email address> 1 *416-xxx-xxxx*

Important Notes

1. The E-Service List is intended to provide a timely and efficient method for effecting service in Commercial List Proceedings in accordance with the *E-Service Guide*, a copy of which has been posted on the Commercial List website at: www.ontariocourts.ca/scj/practice/practice-directions/toronto/#Commercial_List.

2. Persons interested solely in monitoring the proceedings should do so by reference to the Case Website noted above and should not request to be placed on the E-Service List.

3. By filing this RES form, you hereby agree that the Stakeholder accepts service by electronic means as the sole means of service and will be bound by that service.

4. Parties residing outside of Ontario should consider whether, based on substantive law, the delivery of an RES constitutes an attornment to the Ontario proceedings.

PD-20 — *NOTE REGARDING CHAMBERS APPOINTMENTS FOR TORONTO CIVIL CASES*

Parties may now request a chambers appointment on Toronto civil cases. Chambers appointments take place before a Judge for 15 minutes at a date and time to be fixed by the Judge. Parties may complete one of 3 standard chambers appointment request forms: long trials, short trials, or motions. The form is to be emailed to the appropriate court staff member (indicated on each form). These appointments are intended to be for short contested matters which do not require evidence, unopposed or on consent matters including amendments to timetables and scheduling issues. The court will contact the parties to advise if an appointment is approved and if so, schedule a date.

Civil File Number: ....

Date: ....

SUPERIOR COURT OF JUSTICE — CIVIL LIST — CHAMBERS APPOINTMENT HEARING REQUEST FORM — LONG TRIALS

A	PLEASE NOTE: The chambers appointment procedure is only for urgent, scheduling and consent matters which take no longer than 15 minutes. This restriction will be enforced. This matter is (tick one or more); ❑ urgent ❑ scheduling ❑ consent ❑ other (explain in Block D)
B	Short Title of Proceeding:
C	Date(s) Requested:
D	The following is a brief description of the matter to be considered at the chambers appointment:
E	List the materials that will be necessary for the chambers appointment. (It is the responsibility of counsel to confirm that the proper materials are available for the Court)
F	Is any Judge seized of this matter, case managing this matter, or are there any judicial conflicts? ❑ No ❑ Yes, identify case management/seized Judge .... ❑ Yes, identify conflicted Judge ....
G	Is there a self-represented party involved? ❑ Yes ❑ No

COUNSEL FOR APPLICANT/MOVING PARTY		COUNSEL FOR OTHER PARTY	
Party		**Party**	
Counsel	PRINT AND SIGN OR INITIAL	Counsel	PRINT AND SIGN OR INITIAL
Address		Address	
Phone		Phone	
Fax		Fax	
E-Mail		E-Mail	

(IF MORE THAN 2 PARTIES INVOLVED, ADD ADDITIONAL SIGNATURES AND PARTICULARS ON REVERSE OR SEPARATE PAGE)

To be submitted to: Civil List Office, 330 University Avenue, 7th Floor, Toronto, ON. E-Mail: Janice.Dickie@ontario.ca

Endorsement/Disposition ❑ See attached Yellow Endorsement Form.

Civil File Number: ....

Date: ....

SUPERIOR COURT OF JUSTICE — CIVIL LIST — CHAMBERS APPOINTMENT HEARING REQUEST FORM — MOTIONS

A	PLEASE NOTE: The chambers appointment procedure is only for urgent, scheduling and consent matters which take no longer than 15 minutes. This restriction will be enforced. This matter is (tick one or more); ❑ urgent ❑ scheduling ❑ consent ❑ other (explain in Block D)
B	Short Title of Proceeding:
C	Date(s) Requested:
D	The following is a brief description of the matter to be considered at the chambers appointment:
E	List the materials that will be necessary for the chambers appointment. (It is the responsibility of counsel to confirm that the proper materials are available for the Court)
F	Is any Judge seized of this matter, case managing this matter, or are there any judicial conflicts? ❑ No ❑ Yes, identify case management/seized Judge .... ❑ Yes, identify conflicted Judge ....
G	Is there a self-represented party involved? ❑ Yes ❑ No

COUNSEL FOR APPLICANT/MOVING PARTY		COUNSEL FOR OTHER PARTY	
Party		**Party**	
Counsel	PRINT AND SIGN OR INITIAL	Counsel	PRINT AND SIGN OR INITIAL
Address		Address	
Phone		Phone	
Fax		Fax	
E-Mail		E-Mail	

(IF MORE THAN 2 PARTIES INVOLVED, ADD ADDITIONAL SIGNATURES AND PARTICULARS ON REVERSE OR SEPARATE PAGE)

To be submitted to: Civil List Office, 330 University Avenue, 7th Floor, Toronto, ON. E-Mail: Michelle.Chen@ontario.ca

Endorsement/Disposition ❑ See attached Yellow Endorsement Form.

Civil File Number: ....

Date: ....

SUPERIOR COURT OF JUSTICE — CIVIL LIST — CHAMBERS APPOINTMENT HEARING REQUEST FORM — SHORT TRIALS

A	PLEASE NOTE: The chambers appointment procedure is only for urgent, scheduling and consent matters which take no longer than 15 minutes. This restriction will be enforced. This matter is (tick one or more); ❑ urgent ❑ scheduling ❑ consent ❑ other (explain in Block D)
B	Short Title of Proceeding:
C	Date(s) Requested:
D	The following is a brief description of the matter to be considered at the chambers appointment:
E	List the materials that will be necessary for the chambers appointment. (It is the responsibility of counsel to confirm that the proper materials are available for the Court)
F	Is any Judge seized of this matter, case managing this matter, or are there any judicial conflicts? ❑ No ❑ Yes, identify case management/seized Judge .... ❑ Yes, identify conflicted Judge ....
G	Is there a self-represented party involved? ❑ Yes ❑ No

COUNSEL FOR APPLICANT/MOVING PARTY		COUNSEL FOR OTHER PARTY	
Party		**Party**	
Counsel	PRINT AND SIGN OR INITIAL	Counsel	PRINT AND SIGN OR INITIAL
Address		Address	
Phone		Phone	
Fax		Fax	
E-Mail		E-Mail	

(IF MORE THAN 2 PARTIES INVOLVED, ADD ADDITIONAL SIGNATURES AND PARTICULARS ON REVERSE OR SEPARATE PAGE)

To be submitted to: Civil List Office, 330 University Avenue, 7th Floor, Toronto, ON. E-Mail: Theodora.Apostolopoulos@ontario.ca

Endorsement/Disposition ❑ See attached Yellow Endorsement Form.

PD-21 — *PRACTICE ADVISORY CONCERNING CIVIL LONG MOTIONS IN THE TORONTO REGION*

Effective April 3, 2018

This Practice Advisory applies to all civil long motions (over 2 hours) before judges. It does not apply to civil long motions before masters.

Counsel and parties are advised to refer to the relevant parts of the Consolidated Provincial Practice Direction and any other applicable Toronto Region-specific Practice Directions or Guides, which are available on the Superior Court of Justice website at: www.ontariocourts.ca/scj.

Requirement to File Electronic Copies of Documents on USB

For civil long motions before judges, parties **must** file electronic copies of their materials on a USB stick. The USB must include a copy of the motion materials, including the factum, where required. Paper copies of the motion materials must also be filed as required by the rules of court.

Acceptable Formats for Electronic Documents

Two electronic versions of *each* document are required:

1. One copy must be created using Microsoft Word (.DOC), and

2. One copy must be saved in PDF format. Documents converted from Word to PDF are preferable to scanned PDF documents.

Electronic Documents Naming Convention

In order to assist court staff in storing the electronic materials and the judge in accessing them, when saving electronic documents on the USB, each document must be named using one of the prefixes below, followed by the short style of cause and court file number (e.g. MPL *Brown v. Brown*, CV-17-12345-0000):

Motion Record (containing the Notice of Motion)

MPL = Motion Record of the Plaintiff

MDE = Motion Record of the Defendant

MDM = Motion Record of the Defendant to Counterclaim

MTP = Motion Record of the Third Party

M4P = Motion Record of the Fourth Party

M5P = Motion Record of the Fifth Party

M6P = Motion Record of the Sixth Party

M7P = Motion Record of the Seventh Party

MAP = Motion Record of the Applicant

MRP = Motion Record of the Respondent

MIN = Motion Record of the Intervener

MAN = Motion Record of the Agency (Agency/Person/Special Interest)

MSL = Motion Record of the Solicitor (under the *Solicitors Act*)

MCL = Motion Record of the Client (under the *Solicitors Act*)

MNP = Motion Record of a Non-party

All relevant prior court orders and endorsements (if not already included in the Motion Record)

COE = Court Orders and Endorsements

Note: *Include only court orders and judge's endorsements that relate to the long motion.*

Affidavits

AFPL = Affidavit of or on behalf of the Plaintiff

AFDE = Affidavit of or on behalf of the Defendant

AFDM = Affidavit of or on behalf of the Defendant to Counterclaim

AFTP = Affidavit of or on behalf of the Third Party

AF4P = Affidavit of or on behalf of the Fourth Party

AF5P = Affidavit of or on behalf of the Fifth Party

AF6P = Affidavit of or on behalf of the Sixth Party

AF7P = Affidavit of or on behalf of the Seventh Party

AFAP = Affidavit of or on behalf of the Applicant

AFRP = Affidavit of or on behalf of the Respondent

AFIN = Affidavit of or on behalf of the Intervener

AFAN = Affidavit of or on behalf of the Agency (Agency/Person/Special Interest)

AFSL = Affidavit of or on behalf of the Solicitor (under the *Solicitors Act*)

AFCL = Affidavit of or on behalf of the Client (under the *Solicitors Act*)

AFNP = Affidavit of or on behalf of a Non-party

Affidavits of Service/Proof of Service

AFSPL = Affidavit of Service or Proof of Service of or on behalf of the Plaintiff

AFSDE = Affidavit of Service or Proof of Service of or on behalf of the Defendant

AFSDM = Affidavit of Service or Proof of Service of or on behalf of the Defendant to Counterclaim

AFSTP = Affidavit of Service or Proof of Service of or on behalf of the Third Party

AFS4P = Affidavit of Service or Proof of Service of or on behalf of the Fourth Party

AFS5P = Affidavit of Service or Proof of Service of or on behalf of the Fifth Party

AFS6P = Affidavit of Service or Proof of Service of or on behalf of the Sixth Party

AFS7P = Affidavit of Service or Proof of Service of or on behalf of the Seventh Party

AFSAP = Affidavit of Service or Proof of Service of or on behalf of the Applicant

AFSRP = Affidavit of Service or Proof of Service of or on behalf of the Respondent

AFSIN = Affidavit of Service or Proof of Service of or on behalf of the Intervener

AFSAN = Affidavit of Service or Proof of Service of or on behalf of the Agency (Agency/Person/Special Interest)

AFSSL = Affidavit of Service or Proof of Service of or on behalf of the Solicitor (under the *Solicitors Act*)

AFSCL = Affidavit of Service or Proof of Service of or on behalf of the Client (under the *Solicitors Act*)

AFSNP = Affidavit of Service or Proof of Service of or on behalf of a Non-party

Book of Authorities

BAPL = Book of Authorities of the Plaintiff

BADE = Book of Authorities of the Defendant

BADM = Book of Authorities of the Defendant to Counterclaim

BATP = Book of Authorities of the Third Party

BA4P = Book of Authorities of the Fourth Party

BA5P = Book of Authorities of the Fifth Party

BA6P = Book of Authorities of the Sixth Party

BA7P = Book of Authorities of the Seventh Party

BAAP = Book of Authorities of the Applicant

BARP = Book of Authorities of the Respondent

BAIN = Book of Authorities of the Intervener

BAAN = Book of Authorities of the Agency (Agency/Person/Special Interest)

BASL = Book of Authorities of the Solicitor (under the *Solicitors Act*)

BACL = Book of Authorities of the Client (under the *Solicitors Act*)

BANP = Book of Authorities of Non-party

Factums, including Amended and Supplementary

FPL = Factum of the Plaintiff

FDE = Factum of the Defendant

FDM = Factum of the Defendant to Counterclaim

FTP = Factum of the Third Party

F4P = Factum of the Fourth Party

F5P = Factum of the Fifth Party

F6P = Factum of the Sixth Party

F7P = Factum of the Seventh Party

FAP = Factum of the Applicant

FRP = Factum of the Respondent

FIN = Factum of the Intervener

FAN = Factum of the Agency (Agency/Person/Special Interest)

FSL = Factum of the Solicitor (under the *Solicitors Act*)

FCL = Factum of the Client (under the *Solicitors Act*)

FNP = Factum of a Non-party

Note: *Add the suffix AM or SUP to indicate Amended or Supplemental Factum*

Costs Outline

COPL = Cost Outline of the Plaintiff

CODE = Cost Outline of the Defendant

CODM = Cost Outline of the Defendant to Counterclaim

COTP = Cost Outline of the Third Party

CO4P = Cost Outline of the Fourth Party

CO5P = Cost Outline of the Fifth Party

CO6P = Cost Outline of the Sixth Party

CO7P = Cost Outline of the Seventh Party

COAP = Cost Outline of the Applicant

CORP = Cost Outline of the Respondent

COIN = Cost Outline of the Intervener

COAN = Cost Outline of the Agency (Agency/Person/Special Interest)

COSL = Cost Outline of the Solicitor (under the *Solicitors Act*)

COCL = Cost Outline of the Client (under the *Solicitors Act*)

CONP = Cost Outline of a non-party

Transcripts

TRN = Transcript

Compendiums

CPL = Compendium of the Plaintiff

CDE = Compendium of the Defendant

CDM = Compendium of the Defendant to Counterclaim

CTP = Compendium of the Third Party

C4P = Compendium of the Fourth Party

C5P = Compendium of the Fifth Party

C6P = Compendium of the Sixth Party

C7P = Compendium of the Seventh Party

CAP = Compendium of the Applicant

CRP = Compendium of the Respondent

CIN = Compendium of the Intervener

CAN = Compendium of the Agency (Agency/Person/Special Interest)

CSL = Compendium of the Solicitor (under the *Solicitors Act*)

CCL = Compendium of the Client (under the *Solicitors Act*)

CNP = Compendium of a Non-party

Note: *When there is a joint compendium filed, suffix the file name with the parties (i.e. PL for plaintiff; DE for defendant, DM defendant to counterclaim, etc.)*

Note: *When there are multiple documents of the same type filed, suffix the file name with 001, 002, 003, 004, 005, etc.*

Counsel and parties may also refer to the *Guide Concerning e-Delivery of Documents* in the Ontario Superior Court of Justice, available on the Superior Court's website.

Dated: March 26, 2018

Geoffrey B. Morawetz

Regional Senior Judge

Superior Court of Justice, Toronto Region

PD-22 — *PRACTICE ADVISORY CONCERNING FAMILY LONG MOTIONS IN THE TORONTO REGION (EFFECTIVE SEPTEMBER 15, 2016)*

This Practice Advisory applies to all Family Law long motions (over 1 hour) in the Toronto Region. It *supplements* the Consolidated Practice Direction Concerning Family Cases in the Toronto Region which came into effect on July 1, 2014.

Counsel and parties are advised to refer to the relevant parts of the Consolidated Provincial Practice Direction and any other applicable Toronto region-specific Practice Directions or Guides, which are available on the Superior Court of Justice website at: www.ontariocourts.ca/scj.

Elimination of "Placeholder" Motions

The Trial Coordinator will continue to schedule dates for long motions when requested by the parties. The Trial Coordinator will vacate any long motion date unless the Notice of Motion along with supporting materials and affidavits are served and filed within 10 days after the motion has been scheduled.

Date: July 25, 2016

Geoffrey B. Morawetz

Regional Senior Judge

Superior Court of Justice, Toronto Region

PD-23 — *PRACTICE ADVISORY RE VIDEO CONFERENCING FOR CIVIL PRACTICE COURT, COMMERCIAL LIST CHAMBERS MATTERS AND ESTATES LIST 9:30 APPOINTMENTS IN THE TORONTO REGION*

The following Practice Advisory is in effect as of March 8, 2017.

1. In accordance with rule 1.08 of the Rules of Civil Procedure, counsel and/or parties may appear by video conference, unless otherwise directed by the court, for (i) consent matters, (ii) unopposed matters and (iii) scheduling matters in the following types of events:

a. Civil Practice Court appearances (as described in paragraphs 1 - 2 of the Consolidated Practice Direction for Civil Actions, Applications, Motions and Procedural Matters in the Toronto Region)

b. Commercial List Chambers Matters (as described in paragraphs 25–27 of the Consolidated Practice Direction Concerning the Commercial List)

c. Estates List 9:30 appointments (as described in paragraphs 11–15 of the Consolidated Practice Direction Concerning the Estates List in the Toronto Region).

2. Parties or counsel who choose to appear by video conference for one of these events must make their own arrangements to do so, in accordance with rule 1.08(6); they may do so through one of the two methods set out below.

Appearing by video conference using CourtCall (no prior Court approval required)

3. CourtCall is a third-party video conferencing service that is available for the court matters and events described in section 1.

4. A CourtCall video appearance is voluntary. Any party or counsel wishing to appear by video using CourtCall must contact CourtCall directly to make the necessary arrangements, which include the following:

i. If not already registered with CourtCall as a client, register at *courtcall.com*.

ii. **At least two (2) business days before the hearing**, book the appearance by logging into the CourtCall website (*courtcall.com*) and completing a "New Appearance" request, or by contacting CourtCall at 1-888-882-6878.

iii. Pay the fee set by CourtCall for the video appearance.

iv. CourtCall will email or fax a confirmation upon completion of the booking and payment.

v. The participant appearing by video must supply his or her own telephone and computer with a camera and internet connection with sufficient bandwidth to allow them to connect and participate.

vi. On the day of the hearing, the participant must initiate the video appearance by clicking on the link and dialing the toll-free teleconference number provided in the confirmation sent by CourtCall.

vii. A pre-hearing check-in is required fifteen minutes before the scheduled hearing time.

viii. For further information, please refer to the CourtCall website (*courtcall.com*) or contact CourtCall at 1-888-882-6878.

5. The party/counsel must also advise the Court, in writing, that he/she will be attending the court event by video using the CourtCall service. This can be done by completing the appropriate section on the scheduling/confirmation form filed with the Court.

6. All persons who have completed the necessary arrangements with CourtCall and advised the Court, in accordance with the steps outlined above, may assume that they have the Court's permission to appear for the event by video, unless otherwise directed by a judge.

Appearing by other means (prior Court approval required):

7. A party or counsel who wishes to appear for one of the court matters/events described in section 1 by video conference through means other than the CourtCall service or by telephone conference must (i) obtain the Court's prior approval to appear by the means proposed (in accordance with rule 1.08(2) or (3)) and (ii) then make the necessary arrangement in accordance with rule 1.08(6).

Dated: March 8, 2017

Heather J. Smith

Chief Justice

Superior Court of Justice (Ontario)

Geoffrey B. Morawetz

Regional Senior Judge

Superior Court of Justice, Toronto Region

Note: CourtCall can be used for video appearances at **court dates on or after March 27 2017**. Counsel/parties can begin scheduling appearances on CourtCall's website as of March 20, 2017.

COURT AND SHERIFFS' FEES

SUPERIOR COURT OF JUSTICE AND COURT OF APPEAL — FEES

Made under the *Administration of Justice Act*

O. Reg. 293/92

as am. O. Reg. 136/94 (Fr.); 272/94; 359/94; 802/94; 212/97; 248/97 (Fr.); 403/98; 329/99; 14/00; 136/04; 10/05; 272/05; 169/07; 247/12; 335/16; 344/18.

[Note: The title of this Regulation was changed from "Ontario Court (General Division) and Court of Appeal — Fees" to "Superior Court of Justice and Court of Appeal — Fees" by O. Reg. 14/00, s. 1.]

1. (1) The following fees are payable, except in respect of proceedings to which section 1.2 applies:

1. On the issue of the following:

   i. A statement of claim, notice of action or notice of application, $220.

   ii. A third or subsequent party claim, $220.

   iii. A statement of defence and counterclaim adding a party, $220.

   iv. A summons to a witness, $30.

   v. A certificate, other than a certificate of a search by the registrar required on an application for a certificate of appointment of estate trustee, $30.

   vi. A commission, $55.

   vii. A writ of execution, $70.

   viii. A notice of garnishment or notice of renewal of garnishment (including the filing of the notice with the sheriff), $140.

2. On the signing of the following:

   i. An order directing a reference, subject to subparagraph ii, $285.

ii. An order on requisition directing the assessment of a bill under the *Solicitors Act*,

A. if obtained by a client, $95,

B. if obtained by a solicitor, $175.

iii. A notice of appointment for the assessment of costs under the *Rules of Civil Procedure*, $125.

3. On the filing of the following:

i. A notice of intent to defend, $175.

ii. If no notice of intent to defend has been filed by the same party, a statement of defence, a defence to counterclaim, a defence to crossclaim or a third party defence, $175.

iii. A notice of appearance, $155.

iv. A notice of motion served on another party, a notice of motion without notice, a notice of motion for a consent order or a notice of motion for leave to appeal, other than a notice of motion in a family law appeal, $160.

v. A notice of return of motion, other than a notice of return of motion in a family law appeal, $160.

vi. In a family law appeal, a notice of motion served on another party, a notice of motion without notice, a notice of motion for a consent order or a notice of return of motion, $90.

vii. A notice of motion for leave to appeal in a family law case, $90.

viii. A requisition for signing of default judgment by registrar, $160.

ix. A trial record, $405, for the first time only.

x. A notice of appeal or cross-appeal from an interlocutory order, $220.

xi. A notice of appeal or cross-appeal to an appellate court of a final order of the Small Claims Court, $125.

xii. A notice of appeal or cross-appeal to an appellate court of a final order of any court or tribunal, other than the Small Claims Court or the Consent and Capacity Board, $220.

xiii. A request to redeem or request for sale, $125.

xiv. An affidavit under section 11 of the *Bulk Sales Act*, $95.

xv. A jury notice in a civil proceeding, $125.

4. For obtaining an appointment with a registrar for settlement of an order, $125.

5. For perfecting an appeal or judicial review application, $405.

6. For making up and forwarding of papers, documents and exhibits, $95, plus any applicable transportation costs.

7. For making copies of documents,

i. not requiring certification, $1 per page,

ii. requiring certification, $3.50 per page.

8. For the inspection of a court file by,

i. a person who has entered into an agreement with the Ministry of the Attorney General for the bulk inspection of court files, $4 per file,

ii. any other person, other than a solicitor or party in the proceeding, $10 per file.

9. For the retrieval from storage of a court file, $75.

10. For the taking of an affidavit or declaration by a commissioner for taking affidavits, $20.

11. For a copy on compact disc (CD) of a digital recording of a court hearing in respect of a case, if such a recording exists and a copy is available,

i. $22 for a single day's recording, and

ii. $10.50 for each additional day's recording, if the request is made at the same time as a request under subparagraph i.

(2) Despite subsection (1), no fee is payable under this Regulation in relation to a proceeding under Part II of the *Prevention of and Remedies for Human Trafficking Act, 2017* by or on behalf of a party to such a proceeding.

O. Reg. 359/94, s. 1; 212/97, s. 1; 248/97, s. 1; 403/98, s. 1; 329/99, s. 1; 14/00, s. 2; 136/04, s. 1; 10/05, s. 1; 272/05, s. 1; 169/07, s. 1; 247/12, s. 1; 335/16, s. 1; 344/18, s. 1

1.1 (1) If a minor or other person under disability is entitled to receive a payment or payments under a multi-provincial/territorial assistance program agreement between Ontario and a person who has been infected with the human immunodeficiency virus through the receipt by transfusion of blood or a blood product, no fee is payable for the issue of a notice of application under Rule 7.08 of the *Rules of Civil Procedure* on behalf of the minor or other person under disability, despite subparagraph 1 i of section 1.

(2) [Repealed O. Reg. 335/16, s. 2(2).]

O. Reg. 272/94; 136/04, s. 2; 335/16, s. 2

1.2 (1) The following fees are payable in respect of proceedings that are governed by Ontario Regulation 114/99 (*Family Law Rules*), except for proceedings under rule 38 (appeals), to which section 1 applies:

1.	On the filing of an application	$157.00
2.	On the filing of an answer, other than an answer referred to in item 3	125.00
3.	On the filing of an answer where the answer includes a request for a divorce by a respondent	157.00
4.	On the placing of an application on the list for hearing	280.00
5.	On the issue of a summons to a witness	19.00
6.	On the issue of a certificate with not more than five pages of copies of the Court document annexed	19.00
	For each additional page	2.00
7.	For making copies of documents,	

	i	not requiring certification, per page	1.00
	ii	requiring certification, per page	3.50
8.	For making up and forwarding papers, documents and exhibits		65.00 and the transportation costs
9.	For a copy on compact disc (CD) of a digital recording of a court hearing in respect of a case, if such a recording exists and a copy is available:		
	i	For a single day's recording	22.00
	ii	For each additional day's recording, if the request is made at the same time as a request under subitem i	10.50

(2) Despite subsection (1), no fees are payable for the filing of an application, the filing of an answer or the placing of an application on the list for hearing in respect of,

(a) proceedings under the *Children's Law Reform Act*, the *Family Law Act* (except Parts I and II), the *Family Responsibility and Support Arrears Enforcement Act, 1996*, the *Marriage Act* or the *Interjurisdictional Support Orders Act, 2002*; or

(b) proceedings to enforce an order for support, custody or access made under any of these Acts.

O. Reg. 136/04, s. 3; 169/07, s. 2; 247/12, s. 2

2. (1) The following fees are payable in estate matters:

1. For a certificate of succeeding estate trustee or a certificate of estate trustee during litigation, $125.

2. For an application of an estate trustee to pass accounts, including all services in connection with it, $390.

3. For a notice of objection to accounts, $85.

4. For an application other than an application to pass accounts, including an application for proof of lost or destroyed will, a revocation of a certificate of appointment, an application for directions or the filing of a claim and notice of contestation, $210.

5. For a notice of objection other than a notice of objection to accounts, including the filing of a notice of appearance, $85.

6. For a request for notice of commencement of proceedings, $85.

7. For the deposit of a will or codicil for safekeeping, $25.

8. For an assessment of costs, including the certificate, $60.

(2) The fees set out in section 1 are payable in estate matters in addition to the fees set out in subsection (1).

O. Reg. 293/92, s. 2; 802/94; 14/00, s. 3; 10/05, s. 2; 335/16, s. 3

3. (1) The following fees are payable in an action under the *Construction Lien Act*:

1. If the claim, crossclaim, counterclaim or third party claim does not exceed $6,000, on the issuing of a statement of claim, crossclaim, counterclaim or third party claim, $95.

2. If the claim, crossclaim, counterclaim or third party claim exceeds $6,000,

i. on the issue of a statement of claim, crossclaim, counterclaim or third party claim, $220,

ii. on the filing of a statement of defence, $155,

iii. on the issue of a certificate of action, $125,

iv. on the filing of a trial record, $405.

(2) The fees set out in section 1, except those in paragraphs 1, 2 and 3 of that section, are payable in an action under the *Construction Lien Act* in addition to the fees set out in subsection (1).

O. Reg. 359/94, s. 2; 212/97, s. 2; 14/00, s. 4; 10/05, s. 3; 335/16, s. 4

4. (1) The following fees are payable in respect of an application under the *Repair and Storage Liens Act*:

1. On the filing of an application, $220.

2. On the filing of a notice of objection, $155.

3. On the issue of an initial certificate or final certificate, $125.

4. On the issue of a writ of seizure, $70.

(2) The fees set out in section 1, except those in paragraphs 1, 2 and 3 of that section, are payable in an action under the *Repair and Storage Liens Act* in addition to the fees set out in subsection (1).

O. Reg. 359/94, s. 3; 212/97, s. 3; 14/00, s. 5; 10/05, s. 4; 335/16, s. 5

5. (1) The following fees are payable to an official examiner:

1. For the appointment, for each person examined, $9.50.

2. For the provision of facilities, $32, plus, if the examination is longer than two hours, $16 for each additional hour (or part of an hour).

3. For a reporter's attendance, $40, plus, if the examination is longer than two hours, $20 for each additional hour (or part of an hour).

4. For the transcript of an examination, regardless of the party ordering,

i. $4 per page for one copy of the first transcript ordered,

ii. $3.40 per page for one copy of each transcript ordered after the reporter has satisfied the order for a transcript described in subparagraph i, and

iii. 80 cents for each additional copy ordered before the reporter has satisfied the order for a transcript described in subparagraph i or ii.

5. For handling costs, $5.50 per invoice.

6. For cancellation of or failure to keep an appointment, with less than three working days' notice,

i. for the cancellation or failure to attend, $11.50,

ii. for the first two hours reserved for the appointment, $72, and

iii. for each additional hour (or part of an hour) reserved for the appointment, $36.

(2) The official examiner shall be paid, in addition to the fees set out in subsection (1), a travelling allowance in accordance with Regulation 11 of the Revised Regulations of Ontario, 1990 (*Kilometre Allowances*) made under the Act for attendance out of the office.

(3) If a party requires a transcript within five working days of placing the order for the transcript, the party shall pay the official examiner 75 cents per page, in addition to the fee set out in paragraph 4 of subsection (1).

(4) If a party requires a transcript within two working days of placing the order for the transcript, the party shall pay the official examiner $1.50 per page, in addition to the fee set out in paragraph 4 of subsection (1).

(5) If more than one party requires a transcript as described in subsection (3) or (4), only the first party to place the order shall be required to pay the additional fee.

Note: A solicitor who is charged more than the amounts provided in section 5 of this Regulation or who receives a transcript that does not substantially conform with Rule 4.09 of the Rules of Civil Procedure should notify the Assistant Deputy Minister, Courts Administration Division, Ministry of the Attorney General, in writing

O. Reg. 359/94, s. 4; 212/97, s. 4; 335/16, s. 6

6. (1) Beginning on January 1, 2020, and on every third January 1 thereafter, the fees payable under this Regulation shall be adjusted in accordance with the following, subject to subsection (3):

1. The fees payable immediately before the applicable January 1 date shall be increased by the percentage change between the Ontario Consumer Price Index for the calendar year that is two years before the year in which the adjustment is being made, and the Ontario Consumer Price Index for the calendar year that is five years before the year in which the adjustment is being made.

2. If the percentage change in the Ontario Consumer Price Index between the two applicable calendar years, as set out in paragraph 1, results in a negative amount, the fees shall not be increased.

3. Any fee that, once increased in accordance with paragraph 1, results in an amount that is not a whole number shall be rounded to the nearest dollar.

(2) For the purposes of subsection (1), the Ontario Consumer Price Index is the Consumer Price Index for Ontario (All-Items) as published by Statistics Canada.

(3) A fee shall not be adjusted under subsection (1) if, before the date on which the adjustment would otherwise take effect, the Minister responsible for the administration of the Act,

(a) determines that the fee as adjusted would exceed full cost recovery; and

(b) publishes notice of the determination, confirming the amount of the fee, on a Government of Ontario website.

(4) This section does not apply to the fees set out in subparagraphs 3 vi and vii of section 1 and under subsection 1.2(1).

O. Reg. 335/16, s. 7

SHERIFFS — FEES

Made under the *Administration of Justice Act*

O. Reg. 294/92

as am. O. Reg. 431/93; 137/94 (Fr.); 358/94; 213/97; 404/98; 4/99; 330/99; 217/00; 508/10; 12/11 (Fr.); 333/16.

1. (1) The following fees are payable to a sheriff:

1. For up to three attempts, whether or not successful, to serve a document, $100 for each person to be served.

2. For filing or renewing a writ of execution or order that a sheriff is liable or required to enforce and for delivering a copy of the writ or order or a renewal of it to the land registrar of a land titles division, $100.

3. For filing or renewing a writ of execution or order that a sheriff is liable or required to enforce and that is not required to be delivered to a land registrar of a land titles division, $75.

4. For filing a writ of seizure or a direction to seize under the *Repair and Storage Liens Act*, $115.

5. For each attempt, whether or not successful, to enforce a writ of delivery, a writ of sequestration, an order for interim recovery of personal property, an order for interim preservation of personal property, or a writ of seizure or direction to seize under the *Repair and Storage Liens Act*, $400.

6. For each attempt, whether or not successful, to enforce a writ of seizure and sale or an order directing a sale, $240.

7. For each attempt, whether or not successful, to enforce any other writ of execution or order, $240.

8. For a search for writs, per name searched, $11 before November 2, 2015, and the amount determined under subsection (4) on and after that date.

9. For each report showing the details of a writ, lien or order or for a copy of a writ, lien or order,

   i. before November 2, 2015, $6, up to a maximum fee of $60 for each name searched, and

   ii. on and after that date, the amount determined under subsection (4), up to a maximum fee for each name searched of the amount determined under subsection (5).

10. For preparing a schedule of distribution under the *Creditors' Relief Act*, $45 per writ or notice of garnishment listed on the schedule, up to a maximum fee of an amount equal to 20 per cent of the money received.

11. For a calculation for satisfaction of writs and garnishments, $45 per writ or notice of garnishment.

12. For any service or act ordered by a court for which no fee is provided, $55 for each hour (or part of an hour) spent performing the service or doing the act.

13. For making copies of documents, other than writs of execution, orders and certificates of lien,

i. not requiring certification, $1 per page,

ii. requiring certification, $3.50 per page.

(2) In addition to the fees set out in paragraphs 5, 6, 7 and 12 of subsection (1), the person who requests the service shall pay the sheriff his or her reasonable and necessary disbursements in carrying out the services described in those paragraphs.

(3) In subsections (4) to (8),

"actual fee" means, for a specified year, the fee that is payable on the annual effective date in the specified year;

"actual maximum fee" means, for a specified year, the maximum fee that is payable on the annual effective date in the specified year;

"annual effective date" means the first Monday in November;

"Consumer Price Index" means the Consumer Price Index for Canada, all-items, not seasonally adjusted (2002=100), as published by Statistics Canada in Table 5 of *The Consumer Price Index* (Catalogue no. 62-001-X).

(4) For the purposes of paragraphs 8 and 9 of subsection (1), the following is the amount of the fee that is payable on and after November 2, 2015:

1. The fee payable on and after November 2, 2015 and before the annual effective date in 2016 is the amount determined in accordance with the following rules:

i. Calculate the notional fee for 2015 using the formula,

$$(A \times B \times 0.5) + A$$

in which,

"A" is the actual fee payable for 2014, and

"B" is the indexation factor for 2015, as determined in accordance with subsection (6).

ii. Choose the amount that is the higher of the notional fee for 2015 and the actual fee for 2014.

iii. The amount chosen, as rounded to the nearest multiple of five cents, is the amount of the fee payable on and after November 2, 2015 and before the annual effective date in 2016.

2. The fee payable on and after the annual effective date in a specified year after 2015 and before the annual effective date in the following year is the amount determined in accordance with the following rules:

i. Calculate the notional fee for the year using the formula,

$$(C \times D \times 0.5) + C$$

in which,

"C" is the notional fee for the preceding year, and

"D" is the indexation factor for the specified year, as determined in accordance with subsection (7).

ii. Choose the amount that is the higher of the notional fee for the year and the actual fee for the preceding year.

iii. The amount chosen, as rounded to the nearest multiple of five cents, is the amount of the fee payable on and after the annual effective date in the specified year and before the annual effective date in the following year.

(5) For the purposes of paragraph 9 of subsection (1), the applicable maximum fee payable on and after November 2, 2015 is determined in accordance with the rules set out in subsection (4), with necessary modifications, to be read as if each reference to "fee", "notional fee" or "actual fee" in that subsection were a reference to "maximum fee", "notional maximum fee" or "actual maximum fee", respectively.

(6) The indexation factor for 2015 is the percentage, rounded to the nearest one-thousandth, that is calculated using the formula,

$$[(1 + E) \times (1 + F) \times (1 + G) \times (1 + H) \times (1 + J)] - 1$$

in which,

"E" is the Consumer Price Index percentage change, for June 2011, from the corresponding month of the previous year,

"F" is the Consumer Price Index percentage change, for June 2012, from the corresponding month of the previous year,

"G" is the Consumer Price Index percentage change, for June 2013, from the corresponding month of the previous year,

"H" is the Consumer Price Index percentage change, for June 2014, from the corresponding month of the previous year, and

"J" is the Consumer Price Index percentage change, for June 2015, from the corresponding month of the previous year.

(7) The indexation factor for a specified year after 2015 is the Consumer Price Index percentage change, for June of the specified year, from the corresponding month of the previous year.

(8) A reference in subsection (6) or (7) to the Consumer Price Index percentage change, for a month, from the corresponding month of the previous year is a reference to the percentage change published by Statistics Canada in Table 5 of *The Consumer Price Index* (Catalogue no. 62-001-X).

O. Reg. 213/97, s. 1; 404/98, s. 1; 4/99, s. 1; 330/99, s. 1; 217/00, s. 1; 508/10, s. 1; 333/16, s. 1

2. In addition to the fees and disbursements set out in section 1, the person who requests the service shall pay the sheriff a travel allowance as set out in Regulation 11 of the Revised Regulations of Ontario, 1990 (*Kilometre Allowances*) made under the Act for the distance he or she necessarily travels, both ways, between the court house and the place where the sheriff,

(a) [Repealed O. Reg. 431/93, s. 2.]

(b) enforces or attempts to enforce a writ or order; or

(c) performs or attempts to perform any other service directed by a court.

O. Reg. 431/93, s. 2; 333/16, s. 2

3. Ontario Regulation 392/90 is revoked.

RULES OF THE SMALL CLAIMS COURT

Made under the *Courts of Justice Act*

O. Reg. 258/98

as am. O. Reg. 295/99; 461/01 [ss. 1(2), 4(2), 7(4), 8(2), (4), 9(2), 10(3), 12(2), (4), 13(5), 14(3), 17(2), 19(3), 20(3), 22(2), 23(2) revoked O. Reg. 330/02, ss. 1(2), 3(2), 4(2), 5(2), (4), 6(2), 7(2), 8(2), (4), 9(2), 10(2), 11(2), 12(2), 13(3), 14(3), 15(2), respectively.]; 330/02, ss. 1(1), 2, 3(1), 4(1), (3), 5(1), (3), 6(1), 7(1), 8(1), (3), 9(1), 10(1), 11(1), 12(1), 13(1), (2), 14(1), (2), 15(1); 440/03; 78/06; 574/07; 56/08; 393/09, ss. 1–13, 14(1)–(3), (4) (Fr.), (5) (Fr.), (6), 15 (Fr.), 16–25; 505/09; 440/10; 56/12; 400/12; 230/13; 44/14 [s. 15 repealed O. Reg. 144/14, s. 2.]; 144/14, s. 1; 171/14; 194/15, ss. 1 (Fr.), 2 (Fr.), 3, 4; 38/16; 488/16; 202/17.

Summary of Contents

RULE 1 — GENERAL [HEADING AMENDED O. REG. 78/06, S. 1.]

CITATION

1.01 These rules may be cited as the Small Claims Court Rules.

Definitions

1.02 (1) In these rules,

"court" means the Small Claims Court;

"disability", where used in respect of a person or party, means that the person or party is,

(a) a minor,

(b) mentally incapable within the meaning of section 6 or 45 of the *Substitute Decisions Act, 1992* in respect of an issue in the proceeding, whether the person or party has a guardian or not, or

(c) an absentee within the meaning of the *Absentees Act*;

"document" includes data and information in electronic form;

"electronic" includes created, recorded, transmitted or stored in digital form in other intangible form by electronic, magnetic or optical means or by any other means that has capabilities for creation, recording, transmission or storage similar to those means, and **"electronically"** has a corresponding meaning;

"holiday" means,

(a) any Saturday or Sunday,

(b) New Year's Day,

(b.1) Family Day,

(c) Good Friday,

(d) Easter Monday,

(e) Victoria Day,

(f) Canada Day,

(g) Civic Holiday,

(h) Labour Day,

(i) Thanksgiving Day,

(j) Remembrance Day,

(k) Christmas Day,

(l) Boxing Day, and

(m) any special holiday proclaimed by the Governor General or the Lieutenant Governor, and if New Year's Day, Canada Day or Remembrance Day falls on a Saturday or Sunday, the following Monday is a holiday, and if Christmas Day falls on a Saturday or Sunday, the following Monday and Tuesday are holidays, and if Christmas Day falls on a Friday, the following Monday is a holiday;

"information technology" [Repealed O. Reg. 78/06, s. 2(1).]

"order" includes a judgment;

"paralegal" means a person licensed under the *Law Society Act* to provide legal services in Ontario;

"proof of service" means, with respect to a document, proof of service of the document in accordance with rule 8.06;

"representative" means the lawyer, paralegal or other person representing a person in a proceeding under these rules;

"self-represented", when used in reference to a person, means that the person is not represented by a representative;

"territorial division" means,

(a) a county, a district or a regional municipality, and

(b) each of the following, as they existed on December 31, 2002:

(i) The combined area of County of Brant and City of Brantford.

(ii) Municipality of Chatham-Kent.

(iii) Haldimand County.

(iv) City of Hamilton.

(v) City of Kawartha Lakes.

(vi) Norfolk County.

(vii) City of Ottawa.

(viii) County of Prince Edward.

(ix) City of Toronto.

(2) [Repealed O. Reg. 78/06, s. 2(3).]

O. Reg. 461/01, s. 1 [s. 1(2) revoked O. Reg. 330/02, s. 1(2).]; 330/02, s. 1(1); 440/03, s. 5, item 1; 78/06, s. 2; 574/07, s. 1; 393/09, s. 1; 230/13, s. 1; 44/14, s. 1

General Principle

1.03 (1) These rules shall be liberally construed to secure the just, most expeditious and least expensive determination of every proceeding on its merits in accordance with section 25 of the *Courts of Justice Act*.

Matters Not Covered in Rules

(2) If these rules do not cover a matter adequately, the court may give directions and make any order that is just, and the practice shall be decided by analogy to these rules, by reference to the *Courts of Justice Act* and the Act governing the action and, if the court considers it appropriate, by reference to the *Rules of Civil Procedure*.

O. Reg. 78/06, s. 3

ORDERS ON TERMS

1.04 When making an order under these rules, the court may impose such terms and give such directions as are just.

STANDARDS FOR DOCUMENTS

1.05 A document in a proceeding shall be printed, typewritten, written or reproduced legibly.

O. Reg. 78/06, s. 4

Electronic Filing, Issuance of Documents

1.05.1 (1) If these rules permit or require a document to be filed electronically, the software authorized by the Ministry of the Attorney General for the purpose shall be used for the filing.

(2) If these rules permit or require a document to be issued electronically, the software authorized by the Ministry of the Attorney General for the purpose shall be used for the issuance.

(3) A document issued using the authorized software is deemed to have been issued by the Small Claims Court.

Requirement for Signature

(4) If a document is filed or issued electronically, a requirement in these rules that the document contain a person's signature is satisfied if the authorized software indicates on the document that the document has been electronically filed or issued, as the case may be.

Date of Filing, Issuance

(5) The date on which a document that is filed or issued electronically is considered to have been filed or issued, as the case may be, is the date indicated for the document by the authorized software.

Filing, Issuance Outside of Business Hours

(6) A document that is filed or issued electronically outside of regular business hours is deemed to have been filed or issued, as the case may be, on the next day that is not a holiday.

Requirement to Keep Original

(7) A person who electronically files an affidavit or other signed or certified document in accordance with these rules shall,

(a) keep the original document until the third anniversary of the electronic filing, until the clerk requests that the original document be filed or until these rules require that the original document be filed, whichever is earliest; and

(b) file the original document on the clerk's request.

Limit on Application of Rule

(8) Despite subrules (1) and (2) and anything to the contrary in these rules, a rule permitting or requiring a document to be filed or issued electronically does not apply unless the Ministry of the Attorney General has authorized software to be used for the purpose for the court location at which the proceeding to which the document relates was or is to be commenced or to which it was transferred.

Inconsistencies

(9) In the event of an inconsistency between a document filed electronically by a person using the authorized software and information provided by the person using the authorized software other than the electronically filed document,

(a) the electronically filed document prevails; and

(b) the clerk may request written clarification from the person respecting the inconsistency.

O. Reg. 44/14, s. 2; 38/16, s. 1

Forms

1.06 (1) The forms prescribed by these rules shall be used where applicable and with such variations as the circumstances require.

Table of Forms

(2) In these rules, when a form is referred to by number, the reference is to the form with that number that is described in the Table of Forms at the end of these rules and is available on the Internet through *www.ontariocourtforms.on.ca*.

Additional Parties

(3) If a form does not have sufficient space to list all of the parties to the action on the first page, the remaining parties shall be listed in Form 1A, which shall be appended to the form immediately following the first page.

Additional Debtors

(4) If any of the following forms do not have sufficient space to list all of the debtors in respect of which the form applies, the remaining debtors shall be listed in Form 1A.1, which shall be appended to the form:

1. Certificate of judgment (Form 20A).

2. Writ of seizure and sale of personal property (Form 20C).

3. Writ of seizure and sale of land (Form 20D).

4. Direction to enforce writ of seizure and sale of personal property (Form 20O).

Affidavit

(5) If these rules permit or require the use of an affidavit, Form 15B may be used for the purpose unless another form is specified.

(6) [Repealed O. Reg. 78/06, s. 4.]

(7) [Repealed O. Reg. 78/06, s. 4.]

(8) [Repealed O. Reg. 78/06, s. 4.]

(9) [Repealed O. Reg. 78/06, s. 4.]

(10) [Repealed O. Reg. 78/06, s. 4.]

(11) [Repealed O. Reg. 78/06, s. 4.]

(12) [Repealed O. Reg. 78/06, s. 4.]

(13) [Repealed O. Reg. 78/06, s. 4.]

(14) [Repealed O. Reg. 78/06, s. 4.]

(15) [Repealed O. Reg. 78/06, s. 4.]

(16) [Repealed O. Reg. 78/06, s. 4.]

(17) [Revoked O. Reg. 440/03, s. 1.]

(18) [Revoked O. Reg. 440/03, s. 1.]

(19) [Revoked O. Reg. 440/03, s. 1.]

O. Reg. 461/01, s. 2; 330/02, s. 2; 440/03, s. 1; 78/06, s. 4; 393/09, s. 2

Telephone and Video Conferences — Where Available

1.07 (1) If facilities for a telephone or video conference are available at the court, all or part of any of the following may be heard or conducted by telephone or video conference as permitted by subrules (2) and (3):

1. A settlement conference.

2. A motion.

(1.1) If facilities for a video conference are available at the court, all or part of an examination of a debtor or other person under rule 20.10 may be conducted by video conference as permitted by subrules (2) and (3).

Request to be Made

(2) A settlement conference or motion may be heard or conducted by telephone or video conference or all or part of an examination under rule 20.10 may be conducted by video conference if a party files a request for the conference (Form 1B), indicating the reasons for the request, and the court grants the request.

Balance of Convenience

(3) In deciding whether to direct a telephone or video conference, the judge shall consider,

(a) the balance of convenience between the party that wants the telephone or video conference and any party that opposes it; and

(b) any other relevant matter.

Arrangements for Conference

(4) If an order directing a telephone or video conference is made, the court shall make the necessary arrangements for the conference and notify the parties of them.

Setting Aside or Varying Order

(5) A judge presiding at a proceeding or step in a proceeding may set aside or vary an order directing a telephone or video conference.

O. Reg. 78/06, s. 4; 393/09, s. 3

REPRESENTATION

1.08 For greater certainty, nothing in these rules permits or authorizes the court to permit a person to act as a representative if that person is not authorized to do so under the *Law Society Act*.

O. Reg. 230/13, s. 2

RULE 2 — NON-COMPLIANCE WITH THE RULES

EFFECT OF NON-COMPLIANCE

2.01 A failure to comply with these rules is an irregularity and does not render a proceeding or a step, document or order in a proceeding a nullity, and the court may grant all necessary amendments or other relief, on such terms as are just, to secure the just determination of the real matters in dispute.

COURT MAY DISPENSE WITH COMPLIANCE

2.02 If necessary in the interest of justice, the court may dispense with compliance with any rule at any time.

RULE 3 — TIME

COMPUTATION

3.01 If these rules or an order of the court prescribe a period of time for the taking of a step in a proceeding, the time shall be counted by excluding the first day and including the last day of the period; if the last day of the period of time falls on a holiday, the period ends on the next day that is not a holiday.

Powers of Court

3.02 (1) The court may lengthen or shorten any time prescribed by these rules or an order, on such terms as are just.

Consent

(2) A time prescribed by these rules for serving or filing a document may be lengthened or shortened by filing the consent of the parties.

O. Reg. 461/01, s. 3

RULE 4 — PARTIES UNDER DISABILITY

Plaintiff's Litigation Guardian

4.01 (1) An action by a person under disability shall be commenced or continued by a litigation guardian, subject to subrule (2).

Exception

(2) A minor may sue for any sum not exceeding $500 as if he or she were of full age.

Consent

(3) A plaintiff's litigation guardian shall, at the time of filing a claim or as soon as possible afterwards, file with the clerk a consent (Form 4A) in which the litigation guardian,

(a) states the nature of the disability;

(b) in the case of a minor, states the minor's birth date;

(c) sets out his or her relationship, if any, to the person under disability;

(d) states that he or she has no interest in the proceeding contrary to that of the person under disability;

(e) acknowledges that he or she is aware of his or her liability to pay personally any costs awarded against him or her or against the person under disability; and

(f) states whether he or she is represented by a representative and, if so, gives that person's name and confirms that the person has written authority to act in the proceeding.

O. Reg. 230/13, s. 3

Defendant's Litigation Guardian

4.02 (1) An action against a person under disability shall be defended by a litigation guardian.

(2) A defendant's litigation guardian shall file with the defence a consent (Form 4A) in which the litigation guardian,

(a) states the nature of the disability;

(b) in the case of a minor, states the minor's birth date;

(c) sets out his or her relationship, if any, to the person under disability;

(d) states that he or she has no interest in the proceeding contrary to that of the person under disability; and

(e) states whether he or she is represented by a representative and, if so, gives that person's name and confirms that the person has written authority to act in the proceeding.

(3) If it appears to the court that a defendant is a person under disability and the defendant does not have a litigation guardian the court may, after notice to the proposed litigation guardian, appoint as litigation guardian for the defendant any person who has no interest in the action contrary to that of the defendant.

O. Reg. 78/06, s. 5; 230/13, s. 4

Who May Be Litigation Guardian

4.03 (1) Any person who is not under disability may be a plaintiff's or defendant's litigation guardian, subject to subrule (2).

(2) If the plaintiff or defendant,

(a) is a minor, in a proceeding to which subrule 4.01(2) does not apply,

(i) the parent or person with lawful custody or another suitable person shall be the litigation guardian, or

(ii) if no such person is available and able to act, the Children's Lawyer shall be the litigation guardian;

(b) is mentally incapable and has a guardian with authority to act as litigation guardian in the proceeding, the guardian shall be the litigation guardian;

(c) is mentally incapable and does not have a guardian with authority to act as litigation guardian in the proceeding, but has an attorney under a power of attorney with that authority, the attorney shall be the litigation guardian;

(d) is mentally incapable and has neither a guardian with authority to act as litigation guardian in the proceeding nor an attorney under a power of attorney with that power,

(i) a suitable person who has no interest contrary to that of the incapable person may be the litigation guardian, or

(ii) if no such person is available and able to act, the Public Guardian and Trustee shall be the litigation guardian;

(e) is an absentee,

(i) the committee of his or her estate appointed under the *Absentees Act* shall be the litigation guardian,

(ii) if there is no such committee, a suitable person who has no interest contrary to that of the absentee may be the litigation guardian, or

(iii) if no such person is available and able to act, the Public Guardian and Trustee shall be the litigation guardian;

(f) is a person in respect of whom an order was made under subsection 72(1) or (2) of the *Mental Health Act* as it read before April 3, 1995, the Public Guardian and Trustee shall be the litigation guardian.

Duties of Litigation Guardian

4.04 (1) A litigation guardian shall diligently attend to the interests of the person under disability and take all steps reasonably necessary for the protection of those interests, including the commencement and conduct of a defendant's claim.

Public Guardian and Trustee, Children's Lawyer

(2) The Public Guardian and Trustee or the Children's Lawyer may act as litigation guardian without filing the consent required by subrule 4.01(3) or 4.02(2).

POWER OF COURT

4.05 The court may remove or replace a litigation guardian at any time.

SETTING ASIDE JUDGMENT, ETC.

4.06 If an action has been brought against a person under disability and the action has not been defended by a litigation guardian, the court may set aside the noting of default or any judgment against the person under disability on such terms as are just, and may set aside any step that has been taken to enforce the judgment.

SETTLEMENT REQUIRES COURT'S APPROVAL

4.07 No settlement of a claim made by or against a person under disability is binding on the person without the approval of the court.

Money to be Paid into Court

4.08 (1) Any money payable to a person under disability under an order or a settlement shall be paid into court, unless the court orders otherwise, and shall afterwards be paid out or otherwise disposed of as ordered by the court.

(2) If money is payable to a person under disability under an order or settlement, the court may order that the money shall be paid directly to the person, and payment made under the order discharges the obligation to the extent of the amount paid.

Supporting Affidavit

(3) A motion for an order under this rule shall be supported by an affidavit in Form 4B rather than an affidavit in Form 15A.

Costs

(4) In making an order under this rule, the court may order that costs payable to the moving party be paid out of the money in court directly to the moving party's representative.

O. Reg. 400/12, s. 1; 230/13, s. 5

RULE 5 — PARTNERSHIPS AND SOLE PROPRIETORSHIPS

PARTNERSHIPS

5.01 A proceeding by or against two or more persons as partners may be commenced using the firm name of the partnership.

5.02 If a proceeding is commenced against a partnership using the firm name, the partnership's defence shall be delivered in the firm name and no person who admits being a partner at any material time may defend the proceeding separately, except with leave of the court.

Notice to Alleged Partner

5.03 (1) In a proceeding against a partnership using the firm name, a plaintiff who seeks an order that would be enforceable personally against a person as a partner may serve the person with the claim, together with a notice to alleged partner (Form 5A).

(2) A person served as provided in subrule (1) is deemed to have been a partner at the material time, unless the person defends the proceeding separately denying having been a partner at the material time.

Disclosure of Partners

5.04 (1) If a proceeding is commenced by or against a partnership using the firm name, any other party may serve a notice requiring the partnership to disclose immediately in writing the names and addresses of all partners constituting the partnership at a time specified in the notice; if a partner's present address is unknown, the partnership shall disclose the last known address.

(1.1) [Repealed O. Reg. 78/06, s. 6.]

(1.1.1) [Repealed O. Reg. 78/06, s. 6.]

(2) If a partnership fails to comply with a notice under subrule (1), its claim may be dismissed or the proceeding stayed or its defence may be struck out.

O. Reg. 461/01, s. 4 [s. 4(2) revoked O. Reg. 330/02, s. 3(2).]; 330/02, s. 3(1); 440/03, s. 5, item 2; 78/06, s. 6

Enforcement of Order

5.05 (1) An order against a partnership using the firm name may be enforced against the partnership's property.

(2) An order against a partnership using the firm name may also be enforced, if the order or a subsequent order so provides, against any person who was served as provided in rule 5.03 and who,

(a) under that rule, is deemed to have been a partner at the material time;

(b) has admitted being a partner at that time; or

(c) has been adjudged to have been a partner at that time.

Against Person not Served as Alleged Partner

(3) If, after an order has been made against a partnership using the firm name, the party obtaining it claims to be entitled to enforce it against any person alleged to be a partner other than a person who was served as provided in rule 5.03, the party may make a motion for leave to do so; the judge may grant leave if the person's liability as a partner is not disputed or, if disputed, after the liability has been determined in such manner as the judge directs.

O. Reg. 78/06, s. 7

Sole Proprietorships

5.06 (1) If a person carries on business in a business name other than his or her own name, a proceeding may be commenced by or against the person using the business name.

(2) Rules 5.01 to 5.05 apply, with necessary modifications, to a proceeding by or against a sole proprietor using a business name, as though the sole proprietor were a partner and the business name were the firm name of a partnership.

RULE 6 — FORUM AND JURISDICTION

PLACE OF COMMENCEMENT AND TRIAL

6.01 (1) An action shall be commenced,

(a) in the territorial division,

(i) in which the cause of action arose, or

(ii) in which the defendant or, if there are several defendants, in which any one of them resides or carries on business; or

(b) at the court's place of sitting that is nearest to the place where the defendant or, if there are several defendants, where any one of them resides or carries on business.

(2) An action shall be tried in the place where it is commenced, but if the court is satisfied that the balance of convenience substantially favours holding the trial at another place than those described in subrule (1), the court may order that the action be tried at that other place.

(3) If, when an action is called for trial or settlement conference, the judge finds that the place where the action was commenced is not the proper place of trial, the court may order that the action be tried in any other place where it could have been commenced under this rule.

O. Reg. 78/06, s. 8(1)

6.02 A cause of action shall not be divided into two or more actions for the purpose of bringing it within the court's jurisdiction.

6.03 [Repealed O. Reg. 78/06, s. 8(2).]

RULE 7 — COMMENCEMENT OF PROCEEDINGS

Plaintiff's Claim

7.01 (1) An action shall be commenced by filing a plaintiff's claim (Form 7A) with the clerk, together with a copy of the claim for each defendant.

Contents of Claim, Attachments

(2) The following requirements apply to the claim:

1. It shall contain the following information, in concise and non-technical language:

    i. The full names of the parties to the proceeding and, if relevant, the capacity in which they sue or are sued.

    ii. The nature of the claim, with reasonable certainty and detail, including the date, place and nature of the occurences on which the claim is based.

    iii. The amount of the claim and the relief requested.

    iv. The name, address, telephone number, fax number if any, and Law Society of Upper Canada registration number if any, of the representative representing the plaintiff or, if the plaintiff is self-represented, the plaintiff's address, telephone number and fax number if any.

    v. The address where the plaintiff believes the defendant may be served.

2. If the plaintiff's claim is based in whole or in part on a document, a copy of the document shall be attached to each copy of the claim, unless it is unavailable, in which case the claim shall state the reason why the document is not attached.

(3) [Repealed O. Reg. 78/06, s. 9(2).]

O. Reg. 461/01, s. 5; 78/06, s. 9; 56/08, s. 1; 230/13, s. 6

ELECTRONIC FILING OF CLAIM

7.02 (1) A plaintiff's claim may be filed with the clerk electronically in accordance with this rule, if the following conditions are satisfied:

1. [Repealed O. Reg. 38/16, s. 2(1).]

2. Any interest payable in relation to the claim is no greater than 35 per cent per year.

3. The defendant is not a person under disability.

4. The claim is one that may, under subrule 6.01(1), be filed in a court location for which the software authorized by the Ministry of the Attorney General for the purpose may be used, as indicated by the Ministry.

(2) The plaintiff's claim shall specify at which court location referred to in paragraph 4 of subrule (1) the action is being commenced, and that court location is deemed to be the place at which the action is commenced.

(3) An email address at which the plaintiff agrees to accept service or receipt of documents from the court must be specified when filing the plaintiff's claim.

(4) If a plaintiff's claim is filed electronically, the requirement in subrule 7.01(1) to also file a copy of the claim for each defendant does not apply.

Requirement to File in Paper Format

(5) A plaintiff's claim that has been filed and issued electronically shall be filed with the clerk by the plaintiff in paper format, with proof of service, in the following circumstances and in accordance with the following rules:

1. If a defence is filed disputing all or part of the claim, the documents shall be filed at least 14 days before the date of the settlement conference, for the purposes of subrule 13.03(2).

2. If the plaintiff files a request to clerk under subrule 9.03(3) for a terms of payment hearing, the documents shall be filed together with the request.

3. If a motion is filed in the proceeding, the documents shall be filed in accordance with the following:

   i. In the case of a motion in writing for an assessment of damages filed in paper format under clause 11.03(2)(a), the documents shall be filed together with the motion.

   ii. In the case of a motion in writing for an assessment of damages filed electronically under clause 11.03(2.1)(a), the documents shall be filed within 14 days after the day the motion is filed.

   iii. In any other case, the documents shall be filed at least three days before the hearing date.

4. If the plaintiff files a request to clerk under clause 11.03(2)(b) or (2.1)(b) for an assessment hearing, the documents shall be filed at least three days before the hearing date.

5. If a garnishment hearing is requested under subrule 20.08(15), the documents shall be filed,

   i. at the time the hearing is requested, if the plaintiff is making the request, or

   ii. in any other case, at least three days before the hearing date.

6. If the plaintiff requests an examination under subrule 20.10(1), the documents shall be filed when making the request.

O. Reg. 461/01, s. 6; 44/14, s. 3; 38/16, s. 2

Issuing Claim

7.03 (1) On receiving the plaintiff's claim, the clerk shall immediately issue it by dating, signing and sealing it and assigning it a court file number.

(2) The original of the claim shall remain in the court file and the copies shall be given to the plaintiff for service on the defendant.

ELECTRONIC ISSUANCE OF CLAIM

7.04 (1) A plaintiff's claim that is filed electronically under rule 7.02 shall be issued electronically.

(2) If a plaintiff's claim is issued electronically, subrule 7.03(2) does not apply. Instead, the claim shall be retained electronically, and a copy shall be placed into the court file by the clerk only if a request is made by a person in accordance with section 137 of the *Courts of Justice Act* to see the claim.

O. Reg. 44/14, s. 3

RULE 8 — SERVICE

Service of Particular Documents — Plaintiff's or Defendant's Claim

8.01 (1) A plaintiff's claim or defendant's claim (Form 7A or 10A) shall be served personally as provided in rule 8.02 or by an alternative to personal service as provided in rule 8.03.

Time for Service of Claim

(2) A claim shall be served within six months after the date it is issued, but the court may extend the time for service, before or after the six months has elapsed.

(3) [Repealed O. Reg. 44/14, s. 4(1).]

(3.1) [Repealed O. Reg. 78/06, s. 10.]

Default Judgment

(4) A default judgment (Form 11B) shall be served by the clerk in accordance with the following:

1. The clerk shall serve the default judgment by mail or by fax on all parties named in the claim, subject to paragraph 2.

2. If a plaintiff's claim was issued electronically under rule 7.04, the clerk may instead serve the default judgment on the plaintiff by email to the email address provided by the plaintiff for the purpose.

(4.1) [Repealed O. Reg. 38/16, s. 3(1).]

(4.1.1) [Repealed O. Reg. 78/06, s. 10.]

Assessment Order

(5) An order made on a motion in writing for an assessment of damages under subrule 11.03(2) shall be served by the clerk in accordance with the following:

1. The clerk shall serve the order on the plaintiff by mail if the plaintiff provides a stamped, self-addressed envelope with the notice of motion and support affidavit, subject to paragraph 2.

2. If the plaintiff's claim was issued electronically under rule 7.04, the clerk may instead serve the order on the plaintiff by email to the email address provided by the plaintiff for the purpose.

Settlement Conference Order

(6) An order made at a settlement conference shall be served by the clerk by mail or by fax, on all parties that did not attend the settlement conference.

Summons to Witness

(7) A summons to witness (Form 18A) shall be served personally by the party who requires the presence of the witness, or by the party's representative, at least 10 days before the trial date; at the time of service, attendance money calculated in accordance with the regulations made under the *Administration of Justice Act* shall be paid or tendered to the witness.

Notice of Garnishment

(8) A notice of garnishment (Form 20E) shall be served by the creditor,

(a) together with a sworn affidavit for enforcement request (Form 20P), on the debtor, by mail, by courier, personally as provided in rule 8.02 or by an alternative to personal service as provided in rule 8.03; and

(b) together with a garnishee's statement (Form 20F), on the garnishee, by mail, by courier, personally as provided in rule 8.02 or by an alternative to personal service as provided in rule 8.03.

Notice of Garnishment Hearing

(9) A notice of garnishment hearing (Form 20Q) shall be served by the person requesting the hearing on the creditor, debtor, garnishee and co-owner of the debt, if any, and any other interested persons by mail, by courier, personally as provided in rule 8.02 or by an alternative to personal services as provided in rule 8.03.

Notice of Examination

(10) A notice of examination (Form 20H) shall be served by the creditor on the debtor or person to be examined, personally as provided in rule 8.02 or by an alternative to personal service as provided in rule 8.03.

Financial Statement

(11) If the person to be examined is the debtor and the debtor is an individual, the creditor shall serve the notice of examination on the debtor together with a blank financial information form (Form 20I).

(12) The notice of examination,

(a) shall be served, together with the financial information form if applicable, at least 30 days before the date fixed for the examination; and

(b) shall be filed, with proof of service, at least three days before the date fixed for the examination.

Notice of Contempt Hearing

(13) A notice of a contempt hearing shall be served by the creditor on the debtor or person to be examined personally as provided in rule 8.02.

Defence and Other Documents

(14) The following documents may be served by mail, by courier, by fax, personally as provided in rule 8.02 or by an alternative to personal service as provided in rule 8.03, unless the court orders otherwise:

1. A defence.

2. Any other document not referred to in subrules (1) to (13).

O. Reg. 461/01, s. 7 [s. 7(4) repealed O. Reg. 330/02, s. 4(2).]; 330/02, s. 4(1), (3); 440/03, s. 5, item 3; 78/06, s. 10; 393/09, s. 4; 230/13, s. 7; 44/14, s. 4; 38/16, s. 3

PERSONAL SERVICE

8.02 If a document is to be served personally, service shall be made,

(a) **Individual** — on an individual, other than a person under disability, by leaving a copy of the document with him or her;

(b) **Municipality** — on a municipal corporation, by leaving a copy of the document with the chair, mayor, warden or reeve of the municipality, with the clerk or deputy clerk of the municipality or with a lawyer for the municipality;

(c) **Corporation** — on any other corporation, by leaving a copy of the document with,

(i) an officer, a director or another person authorized to act on behalf of the corporation, or

(ii) a person at any place of business of the corporation who appears to be in control or management of the place of business;

(d) **Board or Commission** — on a board or commission, by leaving a copy of the document with a member or officer of the board or commission;

(e) **Person Outside Ontario Carrying on Business in Ontario** — on a person outside Ontario who carries on business in Ontario, by leaving a copy of the document with anyone carrying on business in Ontario for the person;

(f) **Crown in Right of Canada** — on Her Majesty the Queen in right of Canada, in accordance with subsection 23(2) of the *Crown Liability and Proceedings Act* (Canada);

(g) **Crown in Right of Ontario** — on Her Majesty the Queen in right of Ontario, in accordance with section 10 of the *Proceedings Against the Crown Act*;

(h) **Absentee** — on an absentee, by leaving a copy of the document with the absentee's committee, if one has been appointed or, if not, with the Public Guardian and Trustee;

(i) **Minor** — on a minor, by leaving a copy of the document with the minor and, if the minor resides with a parent or other person having his or her care or lawful custody, by leaving another copy of the document with the parent or other person;

(j) **Mentally Incapable Person** — on a mentally incapable person,

(i) if there is a guardian or an attorney acting under a validated power of attorney for personal care with authority to act in the proceeding, by leaving a copy of the document with the guardian or attorney,

(ii) if there is no guardian or attorney acting under a validated power of attorney for personal care with authority to act in the proceeding but there is an attorney under a power of attorney with authority to act in the proceeding, by leaving a copy of the document with the attorney and leaving an additional copy with the person,

(iii) if there is neither a guardian nor an attorney with authority to act in the proceeding, by leaving a copy of the document bearing the person's name and address with the Public Guardian and Trustee and leaving an additional copy with the person;

(k) **Partnership** — on a partnership, by leaving a copy of the document with,

(i) any one or more of the partners, or

(ii) a person at the principal place of business of the partnership who appears to be in control or management of the place of business; and

(l) **Sole Proprietorship** — on a sole proprietorship, by leaving a copy of the document with,

(i) the sole proprietor, or

(ii) a person at the principal place of business of the sole proprietorship who appears to be in control or management of the place of business.

O. Reg. 56/12, s. 1; 230/13, s. 8

Alternatives to Personal Service

8.03 (1) If a document is to be served by an alternative to personal service, service shall be made in accordance with subrule (2), (3) or (5); in the case of a plaintiff's claim or defendant's claim served on an individual, service may also be made in accordance with subrule (7).

At Place of Residence

(2) If an attempt is made to effect personal service at an individual's place of residence and for any reason personal service cannot be effected, the document may be served by,

(a) leaving a copy in a sealed envelope addressed to the individual at the place of residence with anyone who appears to be an adult member of the same household; and

(b) on the same day or the following day, mailing or sending by courier another copy of the document to the individual at the place of residence.

Corporation

(3) If the head office or principal place of business of a corporation or, in the case of an extra-provincial corporation, the attorney for service in Ontario cannot be found at the last address recorded with the Ministry of Government Services, service may be made on the corporation,

(a) by mailing or sending by courier a copy of the document to the corporation or to the attorney for service in Ontario, as the case may be, at that address; and

(b) by mailing or sending by courier a copy of the document to each director of the corporation as recorded with the Ministry of Government Services, at the director's address as recorded with that Ministry.

When Effective

(4) Service made under subrule (2) or (3) is effective on the fifth day after the document is mailed or verified by courier that it was delivered.

Acceptance of Service by Lawyer or Paralegal

(5) Service on a party who is represented by a lawyer or paralegal may be made by leaving a copy of the document with the lawyer or paralegal, or with an employee in the lawyer's or paralegal's office, but service under this subrule is effective only if the lawyer, paralegal or employee endorses on the document or a copy of it an acceptance of service and the date of the acceptance.

(6) By accepting service, the lawyer or paralegal is deemed to represent to the court that he or she has the client's authority to accept service.

Service of Claim

(7) Service of a plaintiff's claim or defendant's claim on an individual against whom the claim is made may be made by sending a copy of the claim by registered mail or by courier to the individual's place of residence, if the signature of the individual or any person who appears to be a member of the same household, verifying receipt of the copy, is obtained.

(8) Service under subrule (7) is effective on the date on which receipt of the copy of the claim is verified by signature, as shown in a delivery confirmation provided by or obtained from Canada Post or the commercial courier, as the case may be.

(9) [Repealed O. Reg. 393/09, s. 5(4).]

O. Reg. 78/06, s. 11; 393/09, s. 5; 440/10, s. 1; 230/13, s. 9

SUBSTITUTED SERVICE

8.04 If it is shown that it is impractical to effect prompt service of a claim personally or by an alternative to personal service, the court may allow substituted service.

SERVICE OUTSIDE ONTARIO

8.05 If the defendant is outside Ontario, the court may award as costs of the action the costs reasonably incurred in effecting service of the claim on the defendant there.

O. Reg. 78/06, s. 12

PROOF OF SERVICE

8.06 An affidavit of service (Form 8A) made by the person effecting the service constitutes proof of service of a document.

O. Reg. 461/01, s. 8 [s. 8(2) revoked O. Reg. 330/02, s. 5(2); s. 8(4) revoked 330/02, s. 5(4).]; 330/02, s. 5(1), (3); 440/03, s. 5, item 4; 78/06, s. 13

Service by Mail

8.07 (1) If a document is to be served by mail under these rules, it shall be sent, by regular lettermail or registered mail, to the last address of the person or of the person's representative that is,

(a) on file with the court, if the document is to be served by the clerk;

(b) known to the sender, if the document is to be served by any other person.

When Effective

(2) Service of a document by mail is deemed to be effective on the fifth day following the date of mailing.

Exception

(3) This rule does not apply when a claim is served by registered mail under subrule 8.03(7).

O. Reg. 78/06, s. 14; 393/09, s. 6; 230/13, s. 10

Service by Courier

8.07.1 (1) If a document is to be served by courier under these rules, it shall be sent by means of a commercial courier to the last address of the person or of the person's representative that is on file with the court or known to the sender.

When Effective

(2) Service of a document sent by courier is deemed to be effective on the fifth day following the date on which the courier verifies to the sender that the document was delivered.

Exception

(3) This rule does not apply when a claim is served by courier under subrule 8.03(7).

O. Reg. 78/06, s. 15; 393/09, s. 7; 230/13, s. 11

Service by Fax

8.08 (1) Service of a document by fax is deemed to be effective,

(a) on the day of transmission, if transmission takes place before 5 p.m. on a day that is not a holiday;

(b) on the next day that is not a holiday, in any other case.

(2) A document containing 16 or more pages, including the cover page, may be served by fax only between 5 p.m. and 8 a.m. the following day, unless the party to be served consents in advance.

O. Reg. 393/09, s. 8

NOTICE OF CHANGE OF ADDRESS

8.09 (1) A party whose address for service changes shall serve notice of the change on the court and other parties within seven days after the change takes place.

(2) Service of the notice may be proved by affidavit if the court orders that proof of service is required.

(3) [Repealed O. Reg. 78/06, s. 16.]

(4) [Repealed O. Reg. 78/06, s. 16.]

(5) [Repealed O. Reg. 78/06, s. 16.]

O. Reg. 461/01, s. 9 [s. 9(2) revoked O. Reg. 330/02, s. 6(2).]; 330/02, s. 6(1); 440/03, s. 5, item 5; 78/06, s. 16

FAILURE TO RECEIVE DOCUMENT

8.10 A person who has been served or who is deemed to have been served with a document in accordance with these rules is nevertheless entitled to show, on a motion to set aside the consequences of default, on a motion for an extension of time or in support of a request for an adjournment, that the document,

(a) did not come to the person's notice; or

(b) came to the person's notice only at some time later than when it was served or is deemed to have been served.

O. Reg. 461/01, s. 9(1)

RULE 9 — DEFENCE

DEFENCE

9.01 A defendant who wishes to dispute a plaintiff's claim shall, within 20 days of being served with the claim,

(a) serve on every other party a defence (Form 9A); and

(b) file the defence, with proof of service, with the clerk.

O. Reg. 461/01, s. 10 [s. 10(3) revoked O. Reg. 330/02, s. 7(2).]; 330/02, s. 7(1); 440/03, ss. 2, 5, item 6; 78/06, s. 17; 440/10, s. 2; 44/14, s. 5

Contents of Defence, Attachments

9.02 (1) The following requirements apply to the defence:

1. It shall contain the following information:

i. The reasons why the defendant disputes the plaintiff's claim, expressed in concise non-technical language with a reasonable amount of detail.

ii. If the defendant is self-represented, the defendant's name, address and telephone number, and fax number if any.

iii. If the defendant is represented by a representative, that person's name, address and telephone number, fax number if any, and Law Society of Upper Canada registration number if any.

2. If the defence is based in whole or in part on a document, a copy of the document shall be attached to each copy of the defence, unless it is unavailable, in which case the defence shall state the reason why the document is not attached.

(2) [Repealed O. Reg. 78/06, s. 19.]

O. Reg. 461/01, s. 11; 78/06, ss. 18, 19; 56/12, s. 2; 230/13, s. 12

Admission of Liability and Proposal of Terms of Payment

9.03 (1) A defendant who admits liability for all or part of the plaintiff's claim but wishes to arrange terms of payment may in the defence admit liability and propose terms of payment.

Where No Dispute

(2) If the plaintiff does not dispute the proposal within the 20-day period referred to in subsection (3),

(a) the defendant shall make payment in accordance with the proposal as if it were a court order;

(b) the plaintiff may serve a notice of default of payment (Form 20L) on the defendant if the defendant fails to make payment in accordance with the proposal; and

(c) the clerk shall sign judgment for the unpaid balance of the undisputed amount on the filing of an affidavit of default of payment (Form 20M) by the plaintiff swearing,

(i) that the defendant failed to make payment in accordance with the proposal,

(ii) to the amount paid by the defendant and the unpaid balance, and

(iii) that 15 days have passed since the defendant was served with a notice of default of payment.

Dispute

(3) The plaintiff may dispute the proposal within 20 days after service of the defence by filing with the clerk and serving on the defendant a request to clerk (Form 9B) for a terms of payment hearing before a referee or other person appointed by the court.

(4) The clerk shall fix a time for the hearing, allowing for a reasonable notice period after the date the request is served, and serve a notice of hearing on the parties.

Manner of Service

(4.1) The notice of hearing shall be served by mail or fax.

Financial Information Form, Defendant an Individual

(4.2) The clerk shall serve a financial information form (Form 20I) on the defendant, together with the notice of hearing, if the defendant is an individual.

(4.3) Where a defendant receives a financial information form under subrule (4.2), he or she shall complete it and serve it on the creditor before the hearing, but shall not file it with the court.

Order

(5) On the hearing, the referee or other person may make an order as to terms of payment by the defendant.

Failure to Appear, Default Judgment

(6) If the defendant does not appear at the hearing, the clerk may sign default judgment against the defendant for the part of the claim that has been admitted and shall serve a default judgment (Form 11B) on the defendant in accordance with subrule 8.01(4).

(6.1) [Repealed O. Reg. 78/06, s. 20(5).]

Failure to Make Payments

(7) Unless the referee or other person specifies otherwise in the order as to terms of payment, if the defendant fails to make payment in accordance with the order, the clerk shall sign judgment for the unpaid balance on the filing of an affidavit by the plaintiff swearing to the default and stating the amount paid and the unpaid balance.

O. Reg. 461/01, s. 12 [s. 12(2) revoked O. Reg. 330/02, s. 8(2); s. 12(4) revoked 330/02, s. 8(4).]; 330/02, s. 8(1), (3); 440/03, s. 5, item 7; 78/06, s. 20

RULE 10 — DEFENDANT'S CLAIM

Defendant's Claim

10.01 (1) A defendant may make a claim,

(a) against the plaintiff;

(b) against any other person,

(i) arising out of the transaction or occurrence relied upon by the plaintiff, or

(ii) related to the plaintiff's claim; or

(c) against the plaintiff and against another person in accordance with clause (b).

(2) The defendant's claim shall be in Form 10A and may be issued,

(a) within 20 days after the day on which the defence is filed; or

(b) after the time described in clause (a) but before trial or default judgment, with leave of the court.

Copies

(3) The defendant shall provide a copy of the defendant's claim to the court.

Contents of Defendant's Claim, Attachments

(4) The following requirements apply to the defendant's claim:

1. It shall contain the following information:

i. The full names of the parties to the defendant's claim and, if relevant, the capacity in which they sue or are sued.

ii. The nature of the claim, expressed in concise non-technical language with a reasonable amount of detail, including the date, place and nature of the occurrences on which the claim is based.

iii. The amount of the claim and the relief requested.

iv. If the defendant is self-represented, the defendant's name, address and telephone number, and fax number if any.

v. If the defendant is represented by a representative, that person's name, address and telephone number, fax number if any, and Law Society of Upper Canada registration number if any.

vi. The address where the defendant believes each person against whom the claim is made may be served.

vii. The court file number assigned to the plaintiff's claim.

2. If the defendant's claim is based in whole or in part on a document, a copy of the document shall be attached to each copy of the claim, unless it is unavailable, in which case the claim shall state the reason why the document is not attached.

(5) [Repealed O. Reg. 78/06, s. 21(4).]

Issuance

(6) On receiving the defendant's claim, the clerk shall immediately issue it by dating, signing and sealing it, shall assign it the same court file number as the plaintiff's claim and shall place the original in the court file.

(7) [Repealed O. Reg. 78/06, s. 21(4).]

(8) [Repealed O. Reg. 78/06, s. 21(4).]

O. Reg. 461/01, s. 13 [s. 13(5) revoked O. Reg. 330/02, s. 9(2).]; 330/02, s. 9(1); 440/03, s. 3; 78/06, s. 21; 56/12, s. 3; 230/13, s. 13

SERVICE

10.02 A defendant's claim shall be served by the defendant on every person against whom it is made, in accordance with subrules 8.01(1) and (2).

DEFENCE

10.03 A party who wishes to dispute the defendant's claim or a third party who wishes to dispute the plaintiff's claim shall, within 20 days after service of the defendant's claim,

(a) serve on every other party a defence (Form 9A); and

(b) file the defence, with proof of service, with the clerk.

O. Reg. 461/01, s. 14 [s. 14(3) revoked O. Reg. 330/02, s. 10(2).]; 330/02, s. 10(1); 440/03, ss. 4, 5, item 8; 78/06, s. 22; 44/14, s. 6

Defendant's Claim to be Tried with Main Action

10.04 (1) A defendant's claim shall be tried and disposed of at the trial of the action, unless the court orders otherwise.

Exception

(2) If it appears that a defendant's claim may unduly complicate or delay the trial of the action or cause undue prejudice to a party, the court may order separate trials or direct that the defendant's claim proceed as a separate action.

Rights of Third Party

(3) If the defendant alleges, in a defendant's claim, that a third party is liable to the defendant for all or part of the plaintiff's claim in the action, the third party may at the trial contest the defendant's liability to the plaintiff but only if the third party has filed a defence in accordance with subrule 10.03(1).

O. Reg. 78/06, s. 23

Application of Rules to Defendant's Claim

10.05 (1) These rules apply, with necessary modifications, to a defendant's claim as if it were a plaintiff's claim, and to a defence to a defendant's claim as if it were a defence to a plaintiff's claim.

Exception

(2) However, when a person against whom a defendant's claim is made is noted in default, judgment against that person may be obtained only in accordance with rule 11.04.

Exception, Electronic Filing, Issuance

(3) Subrule (1) does not apply to rule 7.02 (electronic filing of claim) or rule 7.04 (electronic issuance of claim).

O. Reg. 56/08, s. 2; 44/14, s. 7

RULE 11 — DEFAULT PROCEEDINGS

Noting Defendant in Default

11.01 (1) If a defendant to a plaintiff's claim or a defendant's claim fails to file a defence to all or part of the claim with the clerk within the prescribed time, the clerk may, when proof is filed that the claim was served within the territorial division, note the defendant in default.

Electronic Filing

(1.1) In the case of a plaintiff's claim that was issued electronically under rule 7.04, the plaintiff may file the proof referred to in subrule (1) electronically.

Leave Required for Person under Disability

(2) A person under disability may not be noted in default under subrule (1), except with leave of the court.

Service Outside Territorial Division

(3) If all the defendants have been served outside the court's territorial division, the clerk shall not note any defendant in default until it is proved by an affidavit for jurisdiction (Form 11A) submitted to the clerk, or by evidence presented before a judge, that the action was properly brought in that territorial division.

Electronic Filing

(4) In the case of a plaintiff's claim that was issued electronically under rule 7.04, the plaintiff may file the affidavit for jurisdiction electronically.

O. Reg. 78/06, s. 24; 44/14, s. 8

Default Judgment, Plaintiff's Claim, Debt or Liquidated Demand

11.02 (1) If a defendant has been noted in default, the clerk may sign default judgment (Form 11B) in respect of the claim or any part of the claim to which the default applies that is for a debt or liquidated demand in money, including interest if claimed.

(2) The fact that default judgment has been signed under subrule (1) does not affect the plaintiff's right to proceed on the remainder of the claim or against any other defendant for all or part of the claim.

Manner of Service of Default Judgment

(3) A default judgment (Form 11B) shall be served in accordance with subrule 8.01(4).

(4) [Repealed O. Reg. 78/06, s. 24.]

O. Reg. 78/06, s. 24; 44/14, s. 9; 38/16, s. 4

Default Judgment, Plaintiff's Claim, Unliquidated Demand

11.03 (1) If all defendants have been noted in default, the plaintiff may obtain judgment against a defendant noted in default with respect to any part of the claim to which rule 11.02 does not apply.

(2) To obtain judgment, the plaintiff may,

(a) file a notice of motion and supporting affidavit (Form 15A) requesting a motion in writing for an assessment of damages, setting out the reasons why the motion should be granted and attaching any relevant documents; or

(b) file a request to clerk (Form 9B) requesting that an assessment hearing be arranged.

Electronic Filing

(2.1) If the plaintiff wishes to obtain judgment and the plaintiff's claim was issued electronically under rule 7.04,

(a) the plaintiff may file the documents referred to in clause (2)(a) electronically, subject to subrule (2.2); or

(b) if the plaintiff wishes to request an assessment hearing, the plaintiff may file a request with the clerk electronically, and the use of Form 9B is not required for the purpose.

Requirement to File in Paper Format

(2.2) Despite clause (2.1)(a), the documents referred to in clause (2)(a) shall be filed with the clerk by the plaintiff in paper format within 14 days after the day the documents are filed electronically.

Inadequate Supporting Affidavit

(3) On a motion in writing for an assessment of damages under clause (2)(a), a judge who finds the plaintiff's affidavit inadequate or unsatisfactory may order that,

(a) a further affidavit be provided; or

(b) an assessment hearing be held.

Assessment Hearing

(4) If an assessment hearing is to be held under clause (2)(b) or (3)(b), the clerk shall fix a date for the hearing and send a notice of hearing to the plaintiff, and the assessment hearing shall proceed as a trial in accordance with rule 17.

Matters to be Proved

(5) On a motion in writing for an assessment of damages or at an assessment hearing, the plaintiff is not required to prove liability against a defendant noted in default, but is required to prove the amount of the claim.

Service of Order

(6) An order made on a motion in writing for an assessment of damages shall be served by the clerk in accordance with subrule 8.01(5).

No Assessment where Defence Filed

(7) If one or more defendants have filed a defence, a plaintiff requiring an assessment of damages against a defendant noted in default shall proceed to a settlement conference under rule 13 and, if necessary, a trial in accordance with rule 17.

O. Reg. 78/06, s. 24; 393/09, s. 9; 38/16, s. 5

DEFAULT JUDGMENT, DEFENDANT'S CLAIM

11.04 If a party against whom a defendant's claim is made has been noted in default, judgment may be obtained against the party only at trial or on motion.

O. Reg. 78/06, s. 24

CONSEQUENCES OF NOTING IN DEFAULT

11.05 (1) A defendant who has been noted in default shall not file a defence or take any other step in the proceeding, except making a motion under rule 11.06, without leave of the court or the plaintiff's consent.

(2) Any step in the proceeding may be taken without the consent of a defendant who has been noted in default.

(3) A defendant who has been noted in default is not entitled to notice of any step in the proceeding and need not be served with any other document, except the following:

1. Subrule 11.02(3) (service of default judgment).
2. Rule 12.01 (amendment of claim or defence).
3. Subrule 15.01(6) (motion after judgment).
4. Postjudgment proceedings against a debtor under rule 20.

O. Reg. 78/06, s. 24

SETTING ASIDE NOTING OF DEFAULT BY COURT ON MOTION

11.06 The court may set aside the noting in default or default judgment against a party and any step that has been taken to enforce the judgment, on such terms as are just, if the party makes a motion to set aside and the court is satisfied that,

(a) the party has a meritorious defence and a reasonable explanation for the default; and

(b) the motion is made as soon as is reasonably possible in all the circumstances.

O. Reg. 461/01, s. 15; 78/06, s. 24

RULE 11.1 — DISMISSAL BY CLERK

Dismissal

11.1.01 (1) Unless the court orders otherwise, the clerk shall make an order dismissing an action for delay if, by the second anniversary of the commencement of the action,

(a) the action has not been disposed of by order; and

(b) no step has been taken by the plaintiff under subrule 11.03(2) or (2.1) to obtain judgment, nor has a trial date been requested.

Exceptions

(2) Subrule (1) does not apply if,

(a) an offer to settle the action has been accepted and filed;

(b) the defence contains an admission of liability for the plaintiff's claim in the action and a proposal of terms of payment under subrule 9.03(1); or

(c) at the time the clerk would otherwise be required under that subrule to dismiss the action, the plaintiff is under disability.

Electronic Issuance

(2.1) An order made under subrule (1) may be issued electronically.

Service of Order

(3) The clerk shall serve a copy of an order made under subrule (1) on the parties.

(4) [Repealed O. Reg. 488/16, s. 1(3).]

(5) [Repealed O. Reg. 194/15, s. 3.]

(6) [Repealed O. Reg. 194/15, s. 3.]

(7) [Repealed O. Reg. 194/15, s. 3.]

O. Reg. 78/06, s. 24; 56/08, s. 3; 393/09, s. 10; 56/12, s. 4; 194/15, s. 3; 38/16, s. 6; 488/16, s. 1

EFFECT OF DISMISSAL ON DEFENDANT'S CLAIM

11.1.02 If an action against a defendant who has made a defendant's claim is dismissed for delay under subrule 11.1.01(1), the defendant's claim shall be deemed to be dismissed 60 days after the order under that subrule is served, unless the court orders otherwise during the 60-day period.

O. Reg. 202/17, s. 1

RULE 11.2 — REQUEST FOR CLERK'S ORDER ON CONSENT

Consent Order

11.2.01 (1) The clerk shall, on the filing of a request for clerk's order on consent (Form 11.2A), make an order granting the relief sought, including costs, if the following conditions are satisfied:

1. The relief sought is,

i. amending a claim or defence less than 30 days before the originally scheduled trial date,

ii. adding, deleting or substituting a party less than 30 days before the originally scheduled trial date,

iii. setting aside the noting in default or default judgment against a party and any specified step to enforce the judgment that has not yet been completed,

iv. restoring a matter that was dismissed under rule 11.1 to the list,

v. noting that payment has been made in full satisfaction of a judgment or terms of settlement, or

vi. dismissing an action.

2. The request is signed by all parties (including any party to be added, deleted or substituted) and states,

i. that each party has received a copy of the request, and

ii. that no party that would be affected by the order is under disability.

3. [Repealed O. Reg. 393/09, s. 11(3).]

4. [Repealed O. Reg. 393/09, s. 11(3).]

Service of order

(2) The clerk shall serve a copy of an order made under subrule (1) in accordance with subrule 8.01(14) on a party that requests it and provides a stamped, self-addressed envelope.

Same, Refusal to Make Order

(3) Where the clerk refuses to make an order, the clerk shall serve a copy of the request for clerk's order on consent (Form 11.2A), with reasons for the refusal, on all the parties.

Notice of Setting Aside of Enforcement Step

(4) Where an order is made setting aside a specified step to enforce a judgment under subparagraph 1 iii of subrule (1), a party shall file a copy of the order at each court location where the enforcement step has been requested.

O. Reg. 78/06, s. 24; 393/09, s. 11

RULE 11.3 — DISCONTINUANCE [HEADING ADDED O. REG. 393/09, S. 12.]

DISCONTINUANCE BY PLAINTIFF IN UNDEFENDED ACTION

11.3.01 (1) A plaintiff may discontinue his or her claim against a defendant who fails to file a defence to all or part of the claim with the clerk within the prescribed time by,

(a) serving a notice of discontinued claim (Form 11.3A) on all defendants who were served with the claim; and

(b) filing the notice with proof of service.

(2) A claim may not be discontinued by or against a person under disability, except with leave of the court.

Electronic Filing

(3) If the plaintiff's claim was issued electronically under rule 7.04, the plaintiff may file the notice of discontinued claim, with proof of service, electronically.

O. Reg. 393/09, s. 12; 44/14, s. 10

EFFECT OF DISCONTINUANCE ON SUBSEQUENT ACTION

11.3.02 The discontinuance of a claim is not a defence to a subsequent action on the matter, unless an order granting leave to discontinue provides otherwise.

O. Reg. 393/09, s. 12

RULE 12 — AMENDMENT, STRIKING OUT, STAY AND DISMISSAL [HEADING AMENDED O. REG. 44/14, S. 11(1).]

Right to Amend

12.01 (1) A plaintiff's or defendant's claim and a defence to a plaintiff's or defendant's claim may be amended by filing with the clerk a copy that is marked "Amended", in which any additions are underlined and any other changes are identified.

Electronic Filing

(1.1) In the case of a plaintiff's claim that was issued electronically under rule 7.04, the plaintiff may file the amended claim electronically if the claim being amended has not yet been served.

Requirement to File in Paper Format

(1.2) Subrule 7.02(5) applies, with necessary modifications, to an amended plaintiff's claim that is filed electronically under subrule (1.1).

Service

(2) The amended document shall be served by the party making the amendment on all parties, including any parties in default, in accordance with subrule 8.01(14).

Time

(3) Filing and service of the amended document shall take place at least 30 days before the originally scheduled trial date, unless,

(a) the court, on motion, allows a shorter notice period; or

(b) a clerk's order permitting the amendment is obtained under subrule 11.2.01(1).

Service on Added Party

(4) A person added as a party shall be served with the claim as amended, except that if the person is added as a party at trial, the court may dispense with service of the claim.

No Amendment Required in Response

(5) A party who is served with an amended document is not required to amend the party's defence or claim.

O. Reg. 78/06, s. 25; 393/09, s. 13; 38/16, s. 7

MOTION TO STRIKE OUT OR AMEND A DOCUMENT

12.02 (1) The court may, on motion, strike out or amend all or part of any document that,

(a) discloses no reasonable cause of action or defence;

(b) may delay or make it difficult to have a fair trial; or

(c) is inflammatory, a waste of time, a nuisance or an abuse of the court's process.

(2) In connection with an order striking out or amending a document under subrule (1), the court may do one or more of the following:

1. In the case of a claim, order that the action be stayed or dismissed.

2. In the case of a defence, strike out the defence and grant judgment.

2.1 In the case of a motion, order that the motion be stayed or dismissed.

3. Impose such terms as are just.

General Power to Stay, Dismiss Action

(3) The court may, on its own initiative, make the order referred to in paragraph 1 of subrule (2) staying or dismissing an action, if the action appears on its face to be inflammatory, a waste of time, a nuisance or an abuse of the court's process.

(4) Unless the court orders otherwise, an order under subrule (3) shall be made on the basis of written submissions in accordance with the following procedures:

1. The court shall direct the clerk to send notice by mail to the plaintiff that the court is considering making the order.

2. The plaintiff may, within 20 days after receiving the notice, file with the court a written submission, no more than four pages in length, responding to the notice.

3. If the plaintiff does not file a written submission that complies with paragraph 2, the court may make the order without any further notice to the plaintiff or to any other party.

4. If the plaintiff files a written submission that complies with paragraph 2, the court may direct the clerk to send a copy of the submission by mail to any other party.

5. A party who receives a copy of the plaintiff's submission may, within 10 days after receiving the copy, file with the court a written submission, no more than four pages in length, responding to the plaintiff's submission, and shall send a copy of the responding submission by mail to the plaintiff, and, on the request of any other party, to that party.

(5) The clerk shall send a copy of an order made under subrule (1) by mail to all the parties as soon as possible after the order is made.

(6) A document required under this rule to be sent by mail shall be mailed in the manner described in subrule 8.07(1), and is deemed to have been received on the fifth day after it is mailed.

General Power to Stay, Dismiss Motion

(7) The court may, on its own initiative, make the order referred to in paragraph 2.1 of subrule (2) staying or dismissing a motion, if the motion appears on its face to be inflammatory, a waste of time, a nuisance or an abuse of the court's process.

(8) Subrules (4) to (6) apply, with necessary modifications, to the stay or dismissal of a motion under subrule (7) and, for the purpose, a reference to the plaintiff shall be read as a reference to the moving party.

Clerk to Notify Court

(9) If the clerk becomes aware that an action could be the subject of an order under subrule (3), or that a motion could be the subject of an order under subrule (7), the clerk shall notify the court.

O. Reg. 78/06, s. 26; 44/14, s. 11(2), (3)

***Stay or Dismissal if No Leave under* Courts of Justice Act**

12.03 (1) If the court determines that a person who is subject to an order under subsection 140(1) of the *Courts of Justice Act* has instituted or continued an action without the order having been rescinded or leave granted for the action to be instituted or continued, the court shall make an order staying or dismissing the action.

Request for Order

(2) Any party to the action may file with the clerk a written request for an order under subrule (1).

Service of Order

(3) An order under subrule (1) may be made without notice, but the clerk shall send a copy of the order by mail, in the manner described in subrule 8.07(1), to every party to the action as soon as possible after the order is made.

O. Reg. 44/14, s. 11(4)

RULE 13 — SETTLEMENT CONFERENCES [HEADING AMENDED O. REG. 78/06, S. 27.]

Settlement Conference Required in Defended Action

13.01 (1) A settlement conference shall be held in every defended action.

Duty of Clerk

(2) The clerk shall fix a time, date and place for the settlement conference and serve a notice of settlement conference, together with a list of proposed witnesses (Form 13A), on the parties.

Timing

(3) The settlement conference shall be held within 90 days after the first defence is filed.

Exception

(4) Subrules (1) to (3) do not apply if the defence contains an admission of liability for all of the plaintiff's claim and a proposal of terms of payment under subrule 9.03(1).

(5) [Repealed O. Reg. 78/06, s. 27.]

(6) [Repealed O. Reg. 78/06, s. 27.]

(7) [Repealed O. Reg. 78/06, s. 27.]

O. Reg. 78/06, s. 27

Attendance

13.02 (1) A party and the party's representative, if any, shall, unless the court orders otherwise, participate in the settlement conference,

(a) by personal attendance; or

(b) by telephone or video conference in accordance with rule 1.07.

Authority to Settle

(2) A party who requires another person's approval before agreeing to a settlement shall, before the settlement conference, arrange to have ready telephone access to the other person throughout the conference, whether it takes place during or after regular business hours.

Additional Settlement Conferences

(3) The court may order the parties to attend an additional settlement conference.

(4) The clerk shall fix a time and place for any additional settlement conference and serve a notice of settlement conference, together with a list of proposed witnesses (Form 13A) on the parties.

Failure to Attend

(5) If a party who has received a notice of settlement conference fails to attend the conference, the court may,

(a) impose appropriate sanctions, by way of costs or otherwise; and

(b) order that an additional settlement conference be held, if necessary.

(6) If a defendant fails to attend a first settlement conference, receives notice of an additional settlement conference and fails to attend the additional settlement conference, the court may,

(a) strike out the defence and dismiss the defendant's claim, if any, and allow the plaintiff to prove the plaintiff's claim; or

(b) make such other order as is just.

Inadequate Preparation, Failure to File Material

(7) The court may award costs against a person who attends a settlement conference if,

(a) in the opinion of the court, the person is so inadequately prepared as to frustrate the purposes of the conference;

(b) the person fails to file the material required by subrule 13.03(2).

O. Reg. 78/06, s. 27; 230/13, s. 14

Purposes of Settlement Conference

13.03 (1) The purposes of a settlement conference are,

(a) to resolve or narrow the issues in the action;

(b) to expedite the disposition of the action;

(c) to encourage settlement of the action;

(d) to assist the parties in effective preparation for trial; and

(e) to provide full disclosure between the parties of the relevant facts and evidence.

Disclosure

(2) At least 14 days before the date of the settlement conference, each party shall serve on every other party and file with the court,

(a) a copy of any document to be relied on at the trial, including an expert report, not attached to the party's claim or defence; and

(b) a list of proposed witnesses (Form 13A) and of other persons with knowledge of the matters in dispute in the action.

(3) At the settlement conference, the parties or their representatives shall openly and frankly discuss the issues involved in the action.

Further Disclosure Restricted

(4) Except as otherwise provided or with the consent of the parties (Form 13B), the matters discussed at the settlement conference shall not be disclosed to others until after the action has been disposed of.

(5) [Repealed O. Reg. 78/06, s. 27.]

(6) [Repealed O. Reg. 78/06, s. 27.]

O. Reg. 78/06, s. 27

RECOMMENDATIONS TO PARTIES

13.04 The court may make recommendations to the parties on any matter relating to the conduct of the action, in order to fulfil the purposes of a settlement conference, including recommendations as to,

(a) the clarification and simplification of issues in the action;

(b) the elimination of claims or defences that appear to be unsupported; and

(c) the admission of facts or documents without further proof.

O. Reg. 78/06, s. 27

Orders at Settlement Conference

13.05 (1) A judge conducting a settlement conference may make any order relating to the conduct of the action that the court could make.

(2) Without limiting the generality of subrule (1), the judge may,

(a) make an order,

(i) adding or deleting parties,

(ii) consolidating actions,

(iii) with written reasons, staying or dismissing the action,

(iv) amending or striking out a claim or defence under subrule 12.02(1),

(v) [Repealed O. Reg. 44/14, s. 12(3).]

(vi) directing production of documents,

(vii) changing the place of trial under rule 6.01,

(viii) directing an additional settlement conference under subrule 13.02(3), and

(ix) ordering costs; and

(b) at an additional settlement conference, order judgment under subrule 13.02(6).

Recommendations to Judge

(3) If the settlement conference is conducted by a referee, a judge may, on the referee's recommendation, make any order that may be made under subrules (1) and (2).

Consent to Final Judgment

(4) A judge may order final judgment at a settlement conference where the matter in dispute is for an amount under the appealable limit and a party files a consent (Form 13B) signed by all parties before the settlement conference indicating that they wish to obtain final determination of the matter at the settlement conference if a mediated settlement is not reached.

Service of Order

(5) Within 10 days after the judge signs an order made at a settlement conference, the clerk shall serve the order on the parties that were not present at the settlement conference in accordance with subrule 8.01(6).

O. Reg. 78/06, s. 27; 44/14, s. 12

MEMORANDUM

13.06 (1) At the end of the settlement conference, the court shall prepare a memorandum summarizing,

(a) recommendations made under rule 13.04;

(b) the issues remaining in dispute;

(c) the matters agreed on by the parties;

(d) any evidentiary matters that are considered relevant; and

(e) information relating to the scheduling of the remaining steps in the proceeding.

(2) The memorandum shall be filed with the clerk, who shall give a copy to the trial judge.

O. Reg. 78/06, s. 27

NOTICE OF TRIAL

13.07 At or after the settlement conference, the clerk shall provide the parties with a notice stating that one of the parties must request a trial date if the action is not disposed of within 30 days after the settlement conference, and pay the fee required for setting the action down for trial.

O. Reg. 78/06, s. 27

JUDGE NOT TO PRESIDE AT TRIAL

13.08 A judge who conducts a settlement conference in an action shall not preside at the trial of the action.

O. Reg. 78/06, s. 27

WITHDRAWAL OF CLAIM

13.09 After a settlement conference has been held, a claim against a party who is not in default shall not be withdrawn or discontinued by the party who brought the claim without,

(a) the written consent of the party against whom the claim is brought; or

(b) leave of the court.

O. Reg. 78/06, s. 27

COSTS

13.10 The costs of a settlement conference, exclusive of disbursements, shall not exceed $100 unless the court orders otherwise because there are special circumstances.

O. Reg. 78/06, s. 27

RULE 14 — OFFER TO SETTLE

14.01 A party may serve on any other party an offer to settle a claim on the terms specified in the offer.

Written Documents

14.01.1 (1) An offer to settle, an acceptance of an offer to settle and a notice of withdrawal of an offer to settle shall be in writing.

Use of Forms

(2) An offer to settle may be in Form 14A, an acceptance of an offer to settle may be in Form 14B and a notice of withdrawal of an offer to settle may be in Form 14C.

Terms of Settlement

(3) The terms of an accepted offer to settle may be set out in terms of settlement (Form 14D).

O. Reg. 78/06, s. 28

Time for Making Offer

14.02 (1) An offer to settle may be made at any time.

Costs Consequences

(2) The costs consequences referred to in rule 14.07 apply only if the offer to settle is served on the party to whom it is made at least seven days before the trial commences.

O. Reg. 78/06, s. 29

Withdrawal

14.03 (1) An offer to settle may be withdrawn at any time before it is accepted, by serving a notice of withdrawal of an offer to settle on the party to whom it was made.

Deemed Withdrawal

(2) If an offer to settle specifies a date after which it is no longer available for acceptance, and has not been accepted on or before that date, the offer shall be deemed to have been withdrawn on the day after that date.

Expiry When Court Disposes of Claim

(3) An offer may not be accepted after the court disposes of the claim in respect of which the offer is made.

O. Reg. 461/01, s. 16; 78/06, s. 29

NO DISCLOSURE TO TRIAL JUDGE

14.04 If an offer to settle is not accepted, no communication about it or any related negotiations shall be made to the trial judge until all questions of liability and the relief to be granted, other than costs, have been determined.

O. Reg. 78/06, s. 29

Acceptance of an Offer to Settle

14.05 (1) An offer to settle may be accepted by serving an acceptance of an offer to settle on the party who made it, at any time before it is withdrawn or before the court disposes of the claim in respect of which it is made.

Payment Into Court As Condition

(2) An offer by a plaintiff to settle a claim in return for the payment of money by a defendant may include a term that the defendant pay the money into court; in that case, the defendant may accept the offer only by paying the money into court and notifying the plaintiff of the payment.

(3) If a defendant offers to pay money to a plaintiff in settlement of a claim, the plaintiff may accept the offer with the condition that the defendant pay the money into court; if the offer is so accepted and the defendant fails to pay the money into court, the plaintiff may proceed as provided in rule 14.06.

Costs

(4) If an accepted offer to settle does not deal with costs, the plaintiff is entitled,

(a) in the case of an offer made by the defendant, to the plaintiff's disbursements assessed to the date the plaintiff was served with the offer;

(b) in the case of an offer made by the plaintiff, to the plaintiff's disbursements assessed to the date that the notice of acceptance was served.

O. Reg. 78/06, s. 30

FAILURE TO COMPLY WITH ACCEPTED OFFER

14.06 If a party to an accepted offer to settle fails to comply with the terms of the offer, the other party may,

(a) make a motion to the court for judgment in the terms of the accepted offer; or

(b) continue the proceeding as if there had been no offer to settle.

Costs Consequences of Failure to Accept

14.07 (1) When a plaintiff makes an offer to settle that is not accepted by the defendant, the court may award the plaintiff an amount not exceeding twice the costs of the action, if the following conditions are met:

1. The plaintiff obtains a judgment as favourable as or more favourable than the terms of the offer.

2. The offer was made at least seven days before the trial.

3. The offer was not withdrawn and did not expire before the trial.

(2) When a defendant makes an offer to settle that is not accepted by the plaintiff, the court may award the defendant an amount not exceeding twice the costs awardable to a successful party, from the date the offer was served, if the following conditions are met:

1. The plaintiff obtains a judgment as favourable as or less favourable than the terms of the offer.

2. The offer was made at least seven days before the trial.

3. The offer was not withdrawn and did not expire before the trial.

(3) If an amount is awarded under subrule (1) or (2) to a self-represented party, the court may also award the party an amount not exceeding $500 as compensation for inconvenience and expense.

O. Reg. 78/06, s. 31

RULE 15 — MOTIONS

Notice of Motion and Supporting Affidavit

15.01 (1) A motion shall be made by a notice of motion and supporting affidavit (Form 15A).

(2) The moving party shall obtain a hearing date from the clerk before serving the notice of motion and supporting affidavit under subrule (3).

(3) The notice of motion and supporting affidavit,

(a) shall be served on every party who has filed a claim and any defendant who has not been noted in default, at least seven days before the hearing date; and

(b) shall be filed, with proof of service, at least three days before the hearing date.

Supporting Affidavit in Response

(4) A party who prepares an affidavit (Form 15B) in response to the moving party's notice of motion and supporting affidavit shall serve it on every party who has filed a claim or defence and file it, with proof of service, at least two days before the hearing date.

Supplementary Affidavit

(5) The moving party may serve a supplementary affidavit on every party who has filed a claim or defence and file it, with proof of service, at least two days before the hearing date.

Motion After Judgment Signed

(6) A motion that is made after judgment has been signed shall be served on all parties, including those who have been noted in default.

O. Reg. 78/06, s. 32; 393/09, s. 14(1)–(3), (6)

METHOD OF HEARING

15.02 (1) A motion may be heard,

(a) in person;

(b) by telephone or video conference in accordance with paragraph 2 of subrule 1.07(1);

(c) by a judge in writing under clause 11.03(2)(a) or (2.1)(a);

(d) by any other method that the judge determines is fair and reasonable.

(2) The attendance of the parties is not required if the motion is in writing under clause (1)(c).

O. Reg. 78/06, s. 32; 38/16, s. 8

Motion Without Notice

15.03 (1) Despite rule 15.01, a motion may be made without notice if the nature or circumstances of the motion make notice unnecessary or not reasonably possible.

Service of Order

(2) A party who obtains an order on motion without notice shall serve it on every affected party, together with a copy of the notice of motion and supporting affidavit used on the motion, within five days after the order is signed.

Motion to Set Aside or Vary Motion Made Without Notice

(3) A party who is affected by an order obtained on motion without notice may make a motion to set aside or vary the order, within 30 days after being served with the order.

O. Reg. 78/06, s. 32

NO FURTHER MOTIONS WITHOUT LEAVE

15.04 If the court is satisfied that a party has tried to delay the action, add to its costs or otherwise abuse the court's process by making numerous motions without merit, the court may, on motion, make an order prohibiting the party from making any further motions in the action without leave of the court.

O. Reg. 78/06, s. 32

ADJOURNMENT OF MOTION

15.05 A motion shall not be adjourned at a party's request before the hearing date unless the written consent of all parties is filed when the request is made, unless the court orders otherwise.

O. Reg. 78/06, s. 32

WITHDRAWAL OF MOTION

15.06 A motion shall not be withdrawn without,

(a) the written consent of all the parties; or

(b) leave of the court.

O. Reg. 78/06, s. 32

COSTS

15.07 The costs of a motion, exclusive of disbursements, shall not exceed $100 unless the court orders otherwise because there are special circumstances.

O. Reg. 78/06, s. 32

RULE 16 — NOTICE OF TRIAL

Clerk Fixes Date and Serves Notice

16.01 (1) The clerk shall fix a date for trial and serve a notice of trial on each party who has filed a claim or defence if,

(a) a settlement conference has been held; and

(b) a party has requested that the clerk fix a date for trial and has paid the required fee.

(1.1) [Repealed O. Reg. 78/06, s. 32.]

(1.2) [Repealed O. Reg. 78/06, s. 32.]

(1.3) [Repealed O. Reg. 78/06, s. 32.]

Manner of Service

(2) The notice of trial shall be served by mail or fax.

O. Reg. 461/01, s. 17 [s. 17(2) revoked O. Reg. 330/02, s. 11(2).]; 330/02, s. 11(1); 440/03, s. 5, item 9; 78/06, s. 32

RULE 17 — TRIAL

Failure to Attend

17.01 (1) If an action is called for trial and all the parties fail to attend, the trial judge may strike the action off the trial list.

(2) If an action is called for trial and a party fails to attend, the trial judge may,

(a) proceed with the trial in the party's absence;

(b) if the plaintiff attends and the defendant fails to do so, strike out the defence and dismiss the defendant's claim, if any, and allow the plaintiff to prove the plaintiff's claim, subject to subrule (3);

(c) if the defendant attends and the plaintiff fails to do so, dismiss the action and allow the defendant to prove the defendant's claim, if any; or

(d) make such other order as is just.

(2.1) In the case described in clause (2)(b) or (c), the person with the claim is not required to prove liability against the party who has failed to attend but is required to prove the amount of the claim.

(3) In the case described in clause (2)(b), if an issue as to the proper place of trial under subrule 6.01(1) is raised in the defence, the trial judge shall consider it and make a finding.

Setting Aside or Variation of Judgment

(4) The court may set aside or vary, on such terms as are just, a judgment obtained against a party who failed to attend at the trial.

Conditions to Making of Order under Subrule (4)

(5) The court may make an order under subrule (4) only if,

(a) the party who failed to attend makes a motion for the order within 30 days after becoming aware of the judgment; or

(b) the party who failed to attend makes a motion for an extension of the 30-day period mentioned in clause (a) and the court is satisfied that there are special circumstances that justify the extension.

O. Reg. 78/06, s. 33

ADJOURNMENT

17.02 (1) The court may postpone or adjourn a trial on such terms as are just, including the payment by one party to another of an amount as compensation for inconvenience and expense.

(2) If the trial of an action has been adjourned two or more times, any further adjournment may be made only on motion with notice to all the parties who were served with the notice of trial, unless the court orders otherwise.

O. Reg. 78/06, s. 34

INSPECTION

17.03 The trial judge may, in the presence of the parties or their representatives, inspect any real or personal property concerning which a question arises in the action.

Motion for New Trial

17.04 (1) A party may make a motion for a new trial within 30 days after a final order is made.

Transcript

(2) In addition to serving and filing the notice of motion and supporting affidavit (Form 15A) required under rule 15.01, the moving party shall serve and file proof that a request has been made for a transcript of,

(a) the reasons for judgment; and

(b) any other portion of the proceeding that is relevant.

Service and Filing of Transcript

(3) If available, a copy of the transcript shall, at least three days before the hearing date,

(a) be served on all parties who were served with the original notice of trial; and

(b) be filed, with proof of service.

Powers of Court on Motion

(4) On the hearing of the motion, the court may,

(a) if the party demonstrates that a condition referred to in subrule (5) is satisfied,

(i) grant a new trial, or

(ii) pronounce the judgment that ought to have been given at trial and order judgment accordingly; or

(b) dismiss the motion.

Conditions

(5) The conditions referred to in clause (4)(a) are:

1. There was a purely arithmetical error in the determination of the amount of damages awarded.

2. There is relevant evidence that was not available to the party at the time of the original trial and could not reasonably have been expected to be available at that time.

O. Reg. 78/06, s. 35; 393/09, s. 16

RULE 18 — EVIDENCE AT TRIAL

AFFIDAVIT

18.01 At the trial of an undefended action, the plaintiff's case may be proved by affidavit, unless the trial judge orders otherwise.

Written Statements, Documents and Records

18.02 (1) A document or written statement or an audio or visual record that has been served, at least 30 days before the trial date, on all parties who were served with the notice of trial, shall be received in evidence, unless the trial judge orders otherwise.

(2) Subrule (1) applies to the following written statements and documents:

1. The signed written statement of any witness, including the written report of an expert, to the extent that the statement relates to facts and opinions to which the witness would be permitted to testify in person.

2. Any other document, including but not limited to a hospital record or medical report made in the course of care and treatment, a financial record, a receipt, a bill, documentary evidence of loss of income or property damage, and a repair estimate.

Details about Witness or Author

(3) A party who serves on another party a written statement or document described in subrule (2) shall append to or include in the statement or document,

(a) the name, telephone number and address for service of the witness or author; and

(b) if the witness or author is to give expert evidence, a summary of his or her qualifications.

(4) A party who has been served with a written statement or document described in subrule (2) and who wishes to cross-examine the witness or author may summon him or her as a witness under subrule 18.03(1).

Where Witness or Author is Summoned

(5) A party who serves a summons to witness on a witness or author referred to in subrule (3) shall, at the time the summons is served, serve a copy of the summons on every other party.

(6) Service of a summons and the payment or tender of attendance money under this rule may be proved by affidavit (Form 8A).

Adjournment

(7) A party who is not served with a copy of the summons in accordance with subrule (5) may request an adjournment of the trial, with costs.

O. Reg. 78/06, s. 36

Summons to Witness

18.03 (1) A party who requires the attendance of a person in Ontario as a witness at a trial may serve the person with a summons to witness (Form 18A) requiring him or her to attend the trial at the time and place stated in the summons.

(2) The summons may also require the witness to produce at the trial the documents or other things in his or her possession, control or power relating to the matters in question in the action that are specified in the summons.

(3) A summons to witness (Form 18A) shall be served in accordance with subrule 8.01(7).

(4) Service of a summons and the payment or tender of attendance money may be proved by affidavit (Form 8A).

(5) A summons to witness continues to have effect until the attendance of the witness is no longer required.

Interpreter

(5.1) If a party serves a summons on a witness who requires an interpreter, the party shall arrange for a qualified interpreter to attend at the trial unless the interpretation is from English to French or French to English and an interpreter is provided by the Ministry of the Attorney General.

(5.2) If a party does not comply with subrule (5.1), every other party is entitled to request an adjournment of the trial, with costs.

Failure to Attend or Remain in Attendance

(6) If a witness whose evidence is material to the conduct of an action fails to attend at the trial or to remain in attendance in accordance with the requirements of a summons to witness served on him or her, the trial judge may, by warrant (Form 18B) directed to all police officers in Ontario, cause the witness to be apprehended anywhere within Ontario and promptly brought before the court.

Identification Form

(6.1) The party who served the summons on the witness may file with the clerk an identification form (Form 20K) to assist the police in apprehending the witness.

(7) On being apprehended, the witness may be detained in custody until his or her presence is no longer required or released on such terms as are just, and may be ordered to pay the costs arising out of the failure to attend or remain in attendance.

Abuse of Power to Summon Witness

(8) If satisfied that a party has abused the power to summon a witness under this rule, the court may order that the party pay directly to the witness an amount as compensation for inconvenience and expense.

O. Reg. 78/06, s. 37

RULE 19 — COSTS

Disbursements

19.01 (1) A successful party is entitled to have the party's reasonable disbursements, including any costs of effecting service or preparing a plaintiff's or defendant's claim or a defence and expenses for travel, accommodation, photocopying and experts' reports, paid by the unsuccessful party, unless the court orders otherwise.

(1.1) For greater certainty, subrule (1) includes costs associated with the electronic filing or issuance of documents under these rules.

(2) The clerk shall assess the disbursements in accordance with the regulations made under the *Administration of Justice Act* and in accordance with subrules (3) and (4); the assessment is subject to review by the court.

(3) The amount of disbursements assessed for effecting service shall not exceed $60 for each person served unless the court is of the opinion that there are special circumstances that justify assessing a greater amount.

(4) The amount of disbursements assessed for preparing a plaintiff's or defendant's claim or a defence shall not exceed $100.

O. Reg. 78/06, s. 38; 440/10, s. 3; 44/14, s. 13

LIMIT

19.02 Any power under this rule to award costs is subject to section 29 of the *Courts of Justice Act*, which limits the amount of costs that may be awarded.

O. Reg. 78/06, s. 39

19.03 [Repealed O. Reg. 440/10, s. 4.]

REPRESENTATION FEE

19.04 If a successful party is represented by a lawyer, student-at-law or paralegal, the court may award the party a reasonable representation fee at trial or at an assessment hearing.

O. Reg. 78/06, s. 39; 440/10, s. 5; 230/13, s. 15

COMPENSATION FOR INCONVENIENCE AND EXPENSE

19.05 The court may order an unsuccessful party to pay to a successful party who is self-represented an amount not exceeding $500 as compensation for inconvenience and expense.

O. Reg. 78/06, s. 39; 440/10, s. 5

PENALTY

19.06 If the court is satisfied that a party has unduly complicated or prolonged an action or has otherwise acted unreasonably, the court may order the party to pay an amount as compensation to another party.

O. Reg. 78/06, s. 39

RULE 20 — ENFORCEMENT OF ORDERS

DEFINITIONS

20.01 In rules 20.02 to 20.12,

"creditor" means a person who is entitled to enforce an order for the payment or recovery of money;

"debtor" means a person against whom an order for the payment or recovery of money may be enforced.

O. Reg. 78/06, s. 40

Power of Court

20.02 (1) The court may,

(a) stay the enforcement of an order of the court, for such time and on such terms as are just; and

(b) vary the times and proportions in which money payable under an order of the court shall be paid, if it is satisfied that the debtor's circumstances have changed.

Enforcement Limited While Periodic Payment Order in Force

(2) While an order for periodic payment is in force, no step to enforce the judgment may be taken or continued against the debtor by a creditor named in the order, except issuing a writ of seizure and sale of land and filing it with the sheriff.

Service of Notice of Default of Payment

(3) The creditor may serve the debtor with a notice of default of payment (Form 20L) in accordance with subrule 8.01(14) and file a copy of it, together with an affidavit of default of payment (Form 20M), if the debtor fails to make payments under an order for periodic payment.

Termination on Default

(4) An order for periodic payment terminates on the day that is 15 days after the creditor serves the debtor with the notice of default of payment, unless a consent (Form 13B) in which the creditor waives the default is filed within the 15-day period.

O. Reg. 78/06, s. 41

GENERAL

20.03 In addition to any other method of enforcement provided by law,

(a) an order for the payment or recovery of money may be enforced by,

(i) a writ of seizure and sale of personal property (Form 20C) under rule 20.06;

(ii) a writ of seizure and sale of land (Form 20D) under rule 20.07; and

(iii) garnishment under rule 20.08; and,

(b) a further order as to payment may be made under subrule 20.10(7).

Certificate of Judgment

20.04 (1) If there is default under an order for the payment or recovery of money, the clerk shall, at the creditor's request, supported by an affidavit for enforcement request (Form 20P) stating the amount still owing, issue a certificate of judgment (Form 20A) to the clerk at the court location specified by the creditor.

(2) The certificate of judgment shall state,

(a) the date of the order and the amount awarded;

(b) the rate of postjudgment interest payable; and

(c) the amount owing, including postjudgment interest.

O. Reg. 393/09, s. 17

Delivery of Personal Property

20.05 (1) An order for the delivery of personal property may be enforced by a writ of delivery (Form 20B) issued by the clerk to a bailiff, on the request of the person in whose favour the order was made, supported by an affidavit of that person or someone acting on that person's authority stating that the property has not been delivered.

Seizure of Other Personal Property

(2) If the property referred to in a writ of delivery cannot be found or taken by the bailiff, the person in whose favour the order was made may make a motion to the court for an order directing the bailiff to seize any other personal property of the person against whom the order was made.

(3) Unless the court orders otherwise the bailiff shall keep personal property seized under subrule (2) until the court makes a further order for its disposition.

Storage Costs

(4) The person in whose favour the order is made shall pay the bailiff's storage costs, in advance and from time to time; if the person fails to do so, the seizure shall be deemed to be abandoned.

O. Reg. 78/06, s. 42; 230/13, s. 16

Writ of Seizure and Sale of Personal Property

20.06 (1) If there is default under an order for the payment or recovery of money, the clerk shall, at the creditor's request, supported by an affidavit for enforcement request (Form 20P) stating the amount still owing, issue to a bailiff a writ of seizure and sale of personal property (Form 20C), and the bailiff shall enforce the writ for the amount owing, postjudgment interest and the bailiff's fees and expenses.

(1.1) If more than six years have passed since the order was made, a writ of seizure and sale of personal property may be issued only with leave of the court.

(1.2) If a writ of seizure and sale of personal property is not issued within one year after the date on which an order granting leave to issue it is made,

(a) the order granting leave ceases to have effect; and

(b) a writ of seizure and sale of personal property may be issued only with leave of the court on a subsequent motion.

(1.3) A writ of seizure and sale of personal property shall show the creditor's name, address and telephone number and the name, address and telephone number of the creditor's representative, if any.

Duration of Writ

(2) A writ of seizure and sale of personal property remains in force for six years after the date of its issue and for a further six years after each renewal.

Renewal of Writ

(3) A writ of seizure and sale of personal property may be renewed before its expiration by filing a request to renew a writ of seizure and sale (Form 20N) with the bailiff.

Direction to Enforce

(4) The creditor may request enforcement of a writ of seizure and sale of personal property by filing a direction to enforce writ of seizure and sale of personal property (Form 20O) with the bailiff.

Inventory of Property Seized

(5) Within a reasonable time after a request is made by someone acting on the debtor's authority, the bailiff shall deliver an inventory of personal property seized under a writ of seizure and sale of personal property.

Sale of Personal Property

(6) Personal property seized under a writ of seizure and sale of personal property shall not be sold by the bailiff unless notice of the time and place of sale has been,

(a) mailed, at least 10 days before the sale,

(i) to the creditor at the address shown on the writ, or to the creditor's representative, and

(ii) to the debtor at the debtor's last known address; and

(b) advertised in a manner that is likely to bring it to the attention of the public.

O. Reg. 78/06, s. 43; 393/09, s. 18; 230/13, s. 17

Writ of Seizure and Sale of Land

20.07 **(1)** If an order for the payment or recovery of money is unsatisfied, the clerk shall at the creditor's request, supported by an affidavit for enforcement request (Form 20P) stating the amount still owing, issue to the sheriff specified by the creditor a writ of seizure and sale of land (Form 20D).

(1.1) If more than six years have passed since the order was made, a writ of seizure and sale of land may be issued only with leave of the court.

(1.2) If a writ of seizure and sale of land is not issued within one year after the date on which an order granting leave to issue it is made,

(a) the order granting leave ceases to have effect; and

(b) a writ of seizure and sale of land may be issued only with leave of the court on a subsequent motion.

Electronic Filing, Issuance

(1.3) The following persons may electronically file a request under subrule (1) for a writ of seizure and sale of land, without the supporting affidavit for enforcement request:

1. A lawyer or a paralegal.

2. A person who has filed a requisition with the clerk to provide for the electronic filing and issuance of documents in relation to the enforcement of an order.

(1.4) If the request is filed electronically, the writ of seizure and sale of land shall be issued electronically.

(1.5) Subrule 1.05.1(6) does not apply to an electronically filed request or an electronically issued writ.

Application of **Rules of Civil Procedure** *to Issued Writ*

(2) Subject to subrules (3) and (4), the *Rules of Civil Procedure* apply for all purposes instead of these rules to an issued writ of seizure and sale of land, as if the writ were a writ of seizure and sale issued under rule 60.07 of those Rules.

Duration of Writ

(3) A writ of seizure and sale of land remains in force for six years after the date of its issue and for a further six years after each renewal.

Alternative Method of Renewal

(4) Instead of being renewed under the *Rules of Civil Procedure* in accordance with subrule (2), a writ of seizure and sale of land may be renewed before its expiration by filing a request to renew a writ of seizure and sale (Form 20N) with the sheriff.

O. Reg. 78/06, s. 44; 393/09, s. 19; 44/14, s. 14

Garnishment

20.08 (1) A creditor may enforce an order for the payment or recovery of money by garnishment of debts payable to the debtor by other persons.

Joint Debts Garnishable

(2) If a debt is payable to the debtor and to one or more co-owners, one-half of the indebtedness or a greater or lesser amount specified in an order made under subrule (15) may be garnished.

Where Leave Required

(2.1) If more than six years have passed since the order was made, or if its enforcement is subject to a condition, a notice of garnishment may be issued only with leave of the court.

(2.2) If a notice of garnishment is not issued within one year after the date on which an order granting leave to issue it is made,

(a) the order granting leave ceases to have effect; and

(b) a notice of garnishment may be issued only with leave of the court on a subsequent motion.

(2.3) A notice of renewal of garnishment may be issued under subrule (5.3) without leave of the court before the original notice of garnishment or any subsequent notice of renewal of garnishment expires.

Obtaining Notice of Garnishment

(3) A creditor who seeks to enforce an order by garnishment shall file with the clerk of a court in the territorial division in which the debtor resides or carries on business,

(a) an affidavit for enforcement request (Form 20P) naming one debtor and one garnishee and stating,

(i) the date of the order and the amount awarded,

(ii) the territorial division in which the order was made,

(iii) the rate of postjudgment interest payable,

(iv) the total amount of any payments received since the order was granted,

(v) the amount owing, including postjudgment interest,

(vi) the name and address of the named garnishee to whom a notice of garnishment is to be directed,

(vii) the creditor's belief that the named garnishee is or will become indebted to the debtor, and the grounds for the belief, and

(viii) any particulars of the debts that are known to the creditor; and

(b) a certificate of judgment (Form 20A), if the order was made in another territorial division.

(4) On the filing of the documents required by subrule (3), the clerk shall issue a notice of garnishment (Form 20E) naming as garnishee the person named in the affidavit.

(5) A notice of garnishment issued under subrule (4) shall name only one debtor and only one garnishee.

Duration and Renewal

(5.1) A notice of garnishment remains in force for six years from the date of its issue and for a further six years from each renewal.

(5.2) A notice of garnishment may be renewed before its expiration by filing with the clerk of the court in which the notice of garnishment was issued a notice of renewal of garnishment (Form 20E.1), together with an affidavit for enforcement request (Form 20P).

(5.3) On the filing of the notice and affidavit required by subrule (5.2), the clerk shall issue the notice of renewal of garnishment (Form 20E.1) naming as garnishee the person named in the affidavit.

(5.4) The provisions of these rules that apply with respect to notices of garnishment also apply with respect to notices of renewal of garnishment.

Service of Notice of Garnishment

(6) The notice of garnishment (Form 20E) shall be served by the creditor in accordance with subrule 8.01(8).

(6.1) The creditor shall serve the notice of garnishment on the debtor within five days of serving it on the garnishee.

Financial Institution

(6.2) If the garnishee is a financial institution, the notice of garnishment and all further notices required to be served under this rule shall be served at the branch at which the debt is payable.

Proof of Service

(6.3) Service of the notice of garnishment may be proved by affidavit.

Garnishee Liable From Time of Service

(7) The garnishee is liable to pay to the clerk any debt of the garnishee to the debtor, up to the amount shown in the notice of garnishment, within 10 days after service of the notice on the garnishee or 10 days after the debt becomes payable, whichever is later.

(8) For the purpose of subrule (7), a debt of the garnishee to the debtor includes,

(a) a debt payable at the time the notice of garnishment is served; and

(b) a debt payable (whether absolutely or on the fulfilment of a condition) after the notice is served and within six years after it is issued.

Payment by Garnishee

(9) A garnishee who admits owing a debt to the debtor shall pay it to the clerk in the manner prescribed by the notice of garnishment, and the amounts paid into court shall not exceed the portion of the debtor's wages that are subject to seizure or garnishment under section 7 of the *Wages Act*.

Equal Distribution Among Creditors

(10) If the clerk has issued notices of garnishment in respect of a debtor at the request of more than one creditor and receives payment under any of the notices of garnishment, he or she shall distribute the payment equally among the creditors who have filed a request for garnishment and have not been paid in full.

Disputing Garnishment

(11) A garnishee referred to in subrule (12) shall, within 10 days after service of the notice of garnishment, file with the court a statement (Form 20F) setting out the particulars.

(12) Subrule (11) applies to a garnishee who,

(a) wishes to dispute the garnishment for any reason; or

(b) pays to the clerk less than the amount set out in the notice of garnishment as owing by the garnishee to the debtor, because the debt is owed to the debtor and to one or more co-owners of the debt or for any other reason.

Service on Creditor and Debtor

(13) The garnishee shall serve a copy of the garnishee's statement on the creditor and the debtor.

Notice to Co-owner of Debt

(14) A creditor who is served with a garnishee's statement under subrule (13) shall forthwith send to any co-owners of the debt, in accordance with subrule 8.01(14), a notice to co-owner of debt (Form 20G) and a copy of the garnishee's statement.

Garnishment Hearing

(15) At the request of a creditor, debtor, garnishee, co-owner of the debt or any other interested person, the clerk shall fix a time and place for a garnishment hearing.

Service of Notice of Garnishment Hearing

(15.1) After having obtained a hearing date from the clerk, the party requesting the garnishment hearing shall serve the notice of garnishment hearing (Form 20Q) in accordance with subrule 8.01(9).

Powers of Court at Hearing

(15.2) At the garnishment hearing, the court may,

(a) if it is alleged that the garnishee's debt to the debtor has been assigned or encumbered, order the assignee or encumbrancer to appear and state the nature and particulars of the claim;

(b) determine the rights and liabilities of the garnishee, any co-owner of the debt, the debtor and any assignee or encumbrancer;

(c) vary or suspend periodic payments under a notice of garnishment; or

(d) determine any other matter in relation to a notice of garnishment.

Time to Request Hearing

(16) A person who has been served with a notice to co-owner of debt is not entitled to dispute the enforcement of the creditor's order for the payment or recovery of money or a payment made by the clerk unless the person requests a garnishment hearing within 30 days after the notice is sent.

Enforcement Against Garnishee

(17) If the garnishee does not pay to the clerk the amount set out in the notice of garnishment and does not send a garnishee's statement, the creditor is entitled to an order against the garnishee for payment of the amount set out in the notice, unless the court orders otherwise.

Payment to Person other than Clerk

(18) If, after service of a notice of garnishment, the garnishee pays a debt attached by the notice to a person other than the clerk, the garnishee remains liable to pay the debt in accordance with the notice.

Effect of Payment to Clerk

(19) Payment of a debt by a garnishee in accordance with a notice of garnishment is a valid discharge of the debt as between the garnishee and the debtor and any co-owner of the debt, to the extent of the payment.

Distribution of Payments

(20) When proof is filed that the notice of garnishment was served on the debtor, the clerk shall distribute a payment received under a notice of garnishment to a creditor in accordance with subrule (20.1), unless,

(a) a hearing has been requested under subrule (15);

(b) a notice of motion and supporting affidavit (Form 15A) has been filed under rule 8.10, 11.06 or 17.04; or

(c) a request for clerk's order on consent (Form 11.2A) has been filed seeking the relief described in subparagraph 1 iii of subrule 11.2.01(1).

(20.1) The clerk shall distribute the payment,

(a) in the case of the first payment under the notice of garnishment, 30 days after the date it is received; and

(b) in the case of every subsequent payment under the notice of garnishment, as they are received.

Notice Once Order Satisfied

(20.2) Once the amount owing under an order that is enforced by garnishment is paid, the creditor shall immediately serve a notice of termination of garnishment (Form 20R) on the garnishee and on the clerk.

Payment if Debt Jointly Owned

(21) If a payment of a debt owed to the debtor and one or more co-owners has been made to the clerk, no request for a garnishment hearing is made and the time for doing so under subrule (16) has expired, the creditor may file with the clerk, within 30 days after that expiry,

(a) proof of service of the notice to co-owner; and

(b) an affidavit stating that the creditor believes that no co-owner of the debt is a person under disability, and the grounds for the belief.

(22) The affidavit required by subrule (21) may contain statements of the deponent's information and belief, if the source of the information and the fact of the belief are specified in the affidavit.

(23) If the creditor does not file the material referred to in subrule (21) the clerk shall return the money to the garnishee.

O. Reg. 461/01, s. 18; 78/06, s. 45; 393/09, s. 20

Consolidation Order

20.09 (1) A debtor against whom there are two or more unsatisfied orders for the payment of money may make a motion to the court for a consolidation order.

(2) The debtor's notice of motion and supporting affidavit (Form 15A) shall set out, in the affidavit portion,

(a) the names and addresses of the creditors who have obtained an order for the payment of money against the debtor;

(b) the amount owed to each creditor;

(c) the amount of the debtor's income from all sources, identifying them; and

(d) the debtor's current financial obligations and any other relevant facts.

(3) For the purposes of clause 15.01(3)(a), the notice of motion and supporting affidavit shall be served on each of the creditors mentioned in it at least seven days before the hearing date.

Contents of Consolidation Order

(4) At the hearing of the motion, the court may make a consolidation order setting out,

(a) a list of unsatisfied orders for the payment of money against the debtor, indicating in each case the date, court and amount and the amount unpaid;

(b) the amounts to be paid into court by the debtor under the consolidation order; and

(c) the times of the payments.

(5) The total of the amounts to be paid into court by the debtor under a consolidation order shall not exceed the portion of the debtor's wages that are subject to seizure or garnishment under section 7 of the *Wages Act*.

Creditor May Make Submissions

(6) At the hearing of the motion, a creditor may make submissions as to the amount and times of payment.

Further Orders Obtained After Consolidation Order

(7) If an order for the payment of money is obtained against the debtor after the date of the consolidation order for a debt incurred before the date of the consolidation order, the creditor may file with the clerk a certified copy of the order; the creditor shall be added to the consolidation order and shall share in the distribution under it from that time.

(8) A consolidation order terminates immediately if an order for the payment of money is obtained against the debtor for a debt incurred after the date of the consolidation order.

Enforcement Limited While Consolidation Order in Force

(9) While the consolidation order is in force, no step to enforce the judgment may be taken or continued against the debtor by a creditor named in the order, except issuing a writ of seizure and sale of land and filing it with the sheriff.

Termination on Default

(10) A consolidation order terminates immediately if the debtor is in default under it for 21 days.

Effect of Termination

(11) If a consolidation order terminates under subrule (8) or (10), the clerk shall notify the creditors named in the consolidation order, and no further consolidation order shall be made in respect of the debtor for one year after the date of termination.

Manner of Sending Notice

(11.1) The notice that the consolidation order is terminated shall be served by mail or fax.

(11.2) [Repealed O. Reg. 78/06, s. 46(2).]

(11.3) [Repealed O. Reg. 78/06, s. 46(2).]

Equal Distribution Among Creditors

(12) All payments into a consolidation account belong to the creditors named in the consolidation order who shall share equally in the distribution of the money.

(13) The clerk shall distribute the money paid into the consolidation account at least once every six months.

O. Reg. 461/01, s. 19 [s. 19(3) revoked O. Reg. 330/02, s. 12(2).]; 330/02, s. 12(1); 440/03, s. 5, item 10; 78/06, s. 46; 393/09, s. 21

Examination of Debtor or Other Person

20.10 (1) If there is default under an order for the payment or recovery of money, the clerk of a court in the territorial division in which the debtor or other person to be examined resides or carries on business shall, at the creditor's request, issue a notice of examination (Form 20H) directed to the debtor or other person.

(2) The creditor's request shall be accompanied by,

(a) an affidavit for enforcement request (Form 20P) setting out,

(i) the date of the order and the amount awarded,

(ii) the territorial division in which the order was made,

(iii) the rate of postjudgment interest payable,

(iv) the total amount of any payments received since the order was granted, and

(v) the amount owing, including postjudgment interest; and

(b) a certificate of judgment (Form 20A), if the order was made in another territorial jurisdiction.

Service of Notice of Examination

(3) The notice of examination shall be served in accordance with subrules 8.01(10), (11) and (12).

(4) The debtor, any other persons to be examined and any witnesses whose evidence the court considers necessary may be examined in relation to,

(a) the reason for nonpayment;

(b) the debtor's income and property;

(c) the debts owed to and by the debtor;

(d) the disposal the debtor has made of any property either before or after the order was made;

(e) the debtor's present, past and future means to satisfy the order;

(f) whether the debtor intends to obey the order or has any reason for not doing so; and

(g) any other matter pertinent to the enforcement of the order.

Duties of Person to be Examined

(4.1) A person who is served with a notice of examination shall,

(a) inform himself or herself about the matters mentioned in subrule (4) and be prepared to answer questions about them; and

(b) in the case of an examination of a debtor who is an individual, complete a financial information form (Form 20I) and,

(i) serve it on the creditor requesting the examination, but not file it with the court, and

(ii) provide a copy of it to the judge presiding at the examination hearing.

(4.2) A debtor required under clause (4.1)(b) to complete a financial information form (Form 20I) shall bring such documents to the examination hearing as are necessary to support the information that he or she provides in the financial information form.

Who May Be Examined

(5) An officer or director of a corporate debtor, or, in the case of a debtor that is a partnership or sole proprietorship, the sole proprietor or any partner, may be examined on the debtor's behalf in relation to the matters set out in subrule (4).

Attendance

(5.1) A person required to attend an examination may attend,

(a) in person; or

(b) by video conference in accordance with rule 1.07.

Examinations Private, Under Oath and Recorded

(6) The examination shall be,

(a) held in the absence of the public, unless the court orders otherwise;

(b) conducted under oath; and

(c) recorded.

Order As To Payment

(7) After the examination or if the debtor's consent is filed, the court may make an order as to payment.

Enforcement Limited while Order as to Payment in Force

(8) While an order as to payment is in force, no step to enforce the judgment may be taken or continued against the debtor by a creditor named in the order, except issuing a writ of seizure and sale of land and filing it with the sheriff.

(9) [Repealed O. Reg. 78/06, s. 47(5).]

(10) [Repealed O. Reg. 78/06, s. 47(5).]

(10.1) [Repealed O. Reg. 78/06, s. 47(5).]

(11) [Repealed O. Reg. 78/06, s. 47(5).]

(12) [Repealed O. Reg. 78/06, s. 47(5).]

(13) [Repealed O. Reg. 78/06, s. 47(5).]

(14) [Repealed O. Reg. 78/06, s. 47(5).]

(15) [Repealed O. Reg. 78/06, s. 47(5).]

O. Reg. 461/01, s. 20 [s. 20(3) revoked O. Reg. 330/02, s. 13(3).]; 330/02, s. 13(1), (2); 440/03, s. 5, item 11; 78/06, s. 47; 393/09, s. 22; 440/10, s. 6

Contempt Hearing

20.11 (1) If a person on whom a notice of examination has been served under rule 20.10 attends the examination but refuses to answer questions or to produce records or documents, the court may order the person to attend before it for a contempt hearing.

Same

(2) If a person on whom a notice of examination has been served under rule 20.10 fails to attend the examination, the court may order the person to attend before it for a contempt hearing under subsection 30(1) of the *Courts of Justice Act*.

(3) If the court makes an order for a contempt hearing,

(a) the clerk shall provide the creditor with a notice of contempt hearing setting out the time, date and place of the hearing; and

(b) the creditor shall serve the notice of contempt hearing on the debtor or other person in accordance with subrule 8.01(13) and file the affidavit of service at least seven days before the hearing.

Setting Aside Order for Contempt Hearing

(4) A person who has been ordered to attend a contempt hearing under subsection 30(1) of the *Courts of Justice Act* may make a motion to set aside the order, before or after receiving the notice of contempt hearing but before the date of the hearing and, on the motion, the court may set aside the order and order that the person attend another examination under rule 20.10.

Finding of Contempt of Court

(5) At a contempt hearing held under subrule (1), the court may find the person to be in contempt of court if the person fails to show cause why the person should not be held in contempt for refusing to answer questions or produce records or documents.

Same

(6) The finding of contempt at a hearing held under subsection 30(1) of the *Courts of Justice Act* is subject to subsection 30(2) of that Act.

Other Powers of Court at Contempt Hearing

(7) At a contempt hearing, the court may order that the person,

(a) attend an examination under rule 20.10;

(b) be jailed for a period of not more than five days.

(c) attend an additional contempt hearing under subrule (1) or subsection 30(1) of the *Courts of Justice Act*, as the case may be; or

(d) comply with any other order that the judge considers necessary or just.

Warrant of Committal

(8) If a committal is ordered under clause (7)(b),

(a) the creditor may complete and file with the clerk an identification form (Form 20K) to assist the police in apprehending the person named in the warrant of committal; and

(b) the clerk shall issue a warrant of committal (Form 20J), accompanied by the identification form, if any, directed to all police officers in Ontario to apprehend the person named in the warrant anywhere in Ontario and promptly bring the person to the nearest correctional institution.

Discharge

(9) A person in custody under a warrant issued under this rule shall be discharged from custody on the order of the court or when the time prescribed in the warrant expires, whichever is earlier.

Duration and Renewal of Warrant of Committal

(10) A warrant issued under this rule remains in force for 12 months after the date of issue and may be renewed by order of the court on a motion made by the creditor for 12 months at each renewal, unless the court orders otherwise.

(11) [Repealed O. Reg. 440/10, s. 7(11).]

O. Reg. 78/06, s. 48; 440/10, s. 7

SATISFACTION OF ORDER

20.12 If payment is made in full satisfaction of an order,

(a) where all parties consent, a party may file a request for clerk's order on consent (Form 11.2A) indicating that payment has been made in full satisfaction of the order or terms of settlement; or

(b) the debtor may make a motion for an order confirming that payment has been made in full satisfaction of the order or terms of settlement.

O. Reg. 78/06, s. 48; 393/09, s. 23

RULE 21 — REFEREE

21.01 (1) A person assigned the powers and duties of a referee under subsection 73(2) of the *Courts of Justice Act* may, if directed by the regional senior justice or his or her designate,

(a) hear disputes of proposals of terms of payment under rule 9.03;

(b) conduct settlement conferences under rule 13;

(c) hear motions for consolidation orders under rule 20.09; and

(d) assess receipted disbursements for fees paid to the court, an authorized court transcriptionist or a sheriff under the regulations made under the *Administration of Justice Act*.

(2) Except under subrule 9.03(5) (order as to terms of payment), a referee shall not make a final decision in any matter referred to him or her but shall report his or her findings and recommendations to the court.

(3) [Repealed O. Reg. 78/06, s. 49.]

O. Reg. 78/06, s. 49; 393/09, s. 24; 171/14, s. 1

RULE 22 — PAYMENT INTO AND OUT OF COURT [HEADING AMENDED O. REG. 400/12, S. 2.]

22. [Repealed O. Reg. 400/12, s. 2.]

DEFINITIONS

22.01 In this Rule,

"Accountant" means the Accountant of the Superior Court of Justice;

"clerk" means the clerk in the location where the proceeding was commenced.

O. Reg. 400/12, s. 2

NON-APPLICATION OF RULE

22.02 This Rule does not apply to money paid or to be paid into court,

(a) under an order or proposal for payment made under rule 9.03;

(b) under an offer to settle a claim in return for the payment of money; or

(c) for the enforcement of an order for the payment or recovery of money under Rule 20, including enforcement by garnishment.

O. Reg. 400/12, s. 2

Payment into Court

22.03 (1) Subject to subrule (7), a party who is required to pay money into court shall do so in accordance with subrules (2) to (6).

Filing with Clerk or Accountant

(2) The party shall file the following documents with the clerk or the Accountant:

1. If the payment into court is under a statutory provision or rule, a written request for payment into court that refers to that provision or rule.

2. If the payment into court is under an order, a written request for payment into court and a copy of the order that bears the court's seal.

Direction

(3) On receiving the documents required to be filed under subrule (2), the clerk or Accountant shall give the party a direction to receive the money, addressed to a bank listed in Schedule I or II to the *Bank Act* (Canada) and specifying the account in the Accountant's name into which the money is to be paid.

Clerk to Forward Documents

(4) If the documents are filed with the clerk, the clerk shall forward the documents to the Accountant.

Payment

(5) On receiving the direction referred to in subrule (3), the party shall pay the money into the specified bank account in accordance with the direction.

Bank's Duties

(6) On receiving the money, the bank shall give a receipt to the party paying the money and immediately send a copy of the receipt to the Accountant.

Payment to Accountant by Mail

(7) A party may pay money into court by mailing to the Accountant the applicable documents referred to in subrule (2), together with the money that is payable; the written request for payment into court referred to in that subrule shall include the party's name and mailing address.

Accountant to Provide Receipt

(8) On receiving money under subrule (7), the Accountant shall send a receipt to the party paying the money.

Proof of Payment

(9) A party who pays money into court shall, immediately after receiving a receipt from the bank under subrule (6) or from the Accountant under subrule (8), as the case may be, send to every other party a copy of the receipt and file a copy of the receipt with the court.

O. Reg. 400/12, s. 2

Payment Out of Court

22.04 (1) Money may only be paid out of court under an order.

Documents to be Filed

(2) A person who seeks payment of money out of court shall file with the Accountant,

(a) a written request for payment out and supporting affidavit, in the form provided by the Ministry; and

(b) a copy of the order for payment out that bears the court's seal.

Payment Out, Children's Lawyer or Public Guardian and Trustee

(3) If the person seeking payment out is the Children's Lawyer or the Public Guardian and Trustee,

(a) the written request need not be in the form provided by the Ministry and a supporting affidavit is not required; and

(b) a single written request that deals with more than one proceeding may be filed.

Payment Out, Minor Attaining Age of Majority

(4) Despite subrule (2), money in court to which a party is entitled under an order once the party attains the age of majority may be paid out to the party on filing with the Accountant, in the forms provided by the Accountant,

(a) a written request for payment out; and

(b) an affidavit proving the identity of the party and that the party has attained the age of majority.

Accountant's Duties

(5) If the requirements of subrule (2) or (4), as the case may be, are met, the Accountant shall pay the money to the person named in the order for payment out, and the payment shall include any accrued interest, unless a court orders otherwise.

O. Reg. 400/12, s. 2

TRANSITION

22.05 This Rule applies to the payment into and out of court of money paid into court on and after the day on which Ontario Regulation 400/12 comes into force.

O. Reg. 400/12, s. 2

RULE 23

23. This Regulation comes into force on September 1, 1998.

Table of Forms

Form 1A	Additional Parties
Form 1A.1	Additional Debtors
Form 1B	Request for Telephone or Video Conference
Form 4A	Consent to Act as Litigation Guardian
Form 4B	Affidavit (Motion for Payment Out of Court)
Form 5A	Notice to Alleged Partner
Form 7A	Plaintiff's Claim
Form 8A	Affidavit of Service
Form 9A	Defence

Form 9B	Request to Clerk
Form 10A	Defendant's Claim
Form 11A	Affidavit for Jurisdiction
Form 11B	Default Judgment
Form 11.2A	Request for Clerk's Order on Consent
Form 11.3A	Notice of Discontinued Claim
Form 13A	List of Proposed Witnesses
Form 13B	Consent
Form 14A	Offer to Settle
Form 14B	Acceptance of Offer to Settle
Form 14C	Notice of Withdrawal of Offer to Settle
Form 14D	Terms of Settlement
Form 15A	Notice of Motion and Supporting Affidavit
Form 15B	Affidavit
Form 18A	Summons to Witness
Form 18B	Warrant for Arrest of Defaulting Witness
Form 20A	Certificate of Judgment
Form 20B	Writ of Delivery
Form 20C	Writ of Seizure and Sale of Personal Property
Form 20D	Writ of Seizure and Sale of Land
Form 20E	Notice of Garnishment
Form 20E.1	Notice of Renewal and Garnishment
Form 20F	Garnishee's Statement
Form 20G	Notice to Co-Owner of Debt
Form 20H	Notice of Examination
Form 20I	Financial Information Form
Form 20J	Warrant of Committal
Form 20K	Identification Form
Form 20L	Notice of Default of Payment
Form 20M	Affidavit of Default of Payment
Form 20N	Request to Renew Writ of Seizure and Sale
Form 20O	Direction to Enforce Writ of Seizure and Sale of Personal Property
Form 20P	Affidavit for Enforcement Request
Form 20Q	Notice of Garnishment Hearing
Form 20R	Notice of Termination of Garnishment

FAMILY LAW RULES

O. Reg. 114/99

FAMILY LAW RULES (SUPERIOR COURT OF JUSTICE AND ONTARIO COURT OF JUSTICE)

Made under the *Courts of Justice Act*

O. Reg. 114/99 [Corrected Gazette 8/5/99 Vol. 132:19.]

as am. O. Reg. 441/99; 544/99; 250/00; 202/01; 337/02; 56/03; 91/03; 92/03; 89/04; 76/06; 519/06; 120/07; 439/07; 561/07; 151/08, ss. 1, 2(1)–(3), (4) (Fr.), (5)–(9), 3–10; 317/09; 386/09; 6/10; 51/10; 52/10; 383/11; 186/12; 388/12; 389/12; 322/13; 142/14; 69/15; 140/15; 235/16, ss. 1–5, 6 (Fr.), 7, 8; 226/17; 298/18; 385/18.

1

---

[1]NOTICE TO THE PROFESSION FAMILY LAW RULES

The *Family Law Rules*, O. Reg. 114/99, is a new set of rules for family law cases in Superior Court of Justice, Family Court and Ontario Court of Justice locations. As a result of a delay in Family Court expansion, please note the revised implementation schedule for the new rules.

The Family Law rules will come into effect on September 15, 1999, as originally scheduled, in the following locations:

(a) all sites of the Ontario Court of Justice that are not affected by Family Court expansion and

(b) the Superior Court of Justice, Family Court site in London.

In the sites listed below, the *Family Law Rules* will come into effect on November 15, 1999. Until then, the rules of procedure that are currently in effect will continue to govern.

(a) all sites designated as expansion sites for the Superior Court of Justice, Family Court, namely:

(i) St. Catharines

(ii) York Region (Newmarket)

(iii) Durham Region (Whitby/Oshawa)

(iv) Peterborough

(v) Cobourg

RULE 1 — GENERAL

SHORT TITLE

Citation

1. (1) These rules may be cited as the *Family Law Rules*.

Cases and Courts to Which Rules Apply

(2) These rules apply to all family law cases in the Family Court of the Superior Court of Justice, in the Superior Court of Justice and in the Ontario Court of Justice,

(a) under,

(i) the *Change of Name Act*,

(ii) Parts V, VII and VIII of the *Child, Youth and Family Services Act, 2017*,

(iii) the *Children's Law Reform Act*, except sections 59 and 60,

(iii.1) the *Civil Marriage Act* (Canada),

(iv) the *Divorce Act* (Canada),

(iv.1) the *Family Homes on Reserves and Matrimonial Interests or Rights Act* (Canada),

(v) the *Family Law Act*, except Part V,

(vi) the *Family Responsibility and Support Arrears Enforcement Act, 1996*,

(vii) section 6 of the *Marriage Act*, and

(viii) the *Interjurisdictional Support Orders Act, 2002*;

(b) for the interpretation, enforcement or variation of a marriage contract, cohabitation agreement, separation agreement, paternity agreement, family arbitration agreement or family arbitration award;

(c) for a constructive or resulting trust or a monetary award as compensation for unjust enrichment between persons who have cohabited;

(vi) Lindsay

(vii) Muskoka County

(viii) Ottawa — Carleton

(ix) L'Orignal

(x) Cornwall

(xi) Brockville

(xii) Perth

and

(b) the existing Family Court sites of Hamilton — Wentworth, Simcoe County, Kingston, and Napanee

(d) for annulment of a marriage or a declaration of validity or invalidity of a marriage;

(e) for appeals of family arbitration awards under the *Arbitration Act, 1991*; and

(f) for proceedings under First Nation laws made under,

(i) the *Family Homes on Reserves and Matrimonial Interests or Rights Act* (Canada), or

(ii) the *First Nations Land Management Act* (Canada), with respect to the effect of relationship breakdown on matrimonial real property.

(2.1) [Revoked O. Reg. 89/04, s. 1(2).]

Case Management in Family Court of Superior Court of Justice

(3) Despite subrule (2), rule 39 (case management in the Family Court of the Superior Court of Justice) applies only to cases in the Family Court of the Superior Court of Justice, which has jurisdiction in the following municipalities:

Regional Municipality of Durham
County of Frontenac
County of Haliburton
City of Hamilton
County of Lanark
United Counties of Leeds and Grenville
County of Lennox and Addington
County of Middlesex
Territorial District of Muskoka
The part of The Regional Municipality of Niagara that was the County of Lincoln as it existed on December 31, 1969
County of Northumberland
City of Ottawa
County of Peterborough
United Counties of Prescott and Russell
County of Simcoe
United Counties of Stormont, Dundas and Glengarry
City of Kawartha Lakes
Regional Municipality of York

Case Management in Ontario Court of Justice

(4) Despite subrule (2), rule 40 (case management in the Ontario Court of Justice) applies only to cases in the Ontario Court of Justice.

Case Management in the Superior Court of Justice

(4.1) Despite subrule (2), rule 41 (case management in the Superior Court of Justice, other than the Family Court of the Superior Court of Justice) applies only to cases in the Superior Court of Justice that are not in the Family Court of the Superior Court of Justice.

Family Law Case Combined with Other Matter

(5) If a case in the court combines a family law case to which these rules apply with another matter to which these rules would not otherwise apply, the parties may agree or the court on motion may order that these rules apply to the combined case or part of it.

Conditions and Directions

(6) When making an order, the court may impose conditions and give directions as appropriate.

Matters not Covered in Rules

(7) If these rules do not cover a matter adequately, the court may give directions, and the practice shall be decided by analogy to these rules, by reference to the *Courts of Justice Act* and the Act governing the case and, if the court considers it appropriate, by reference to the Rules of Civil Procedure.

Certain Orders that may be made at any Time

(7.1) For greater certainty, a court may make an order under subrule (7.2), (8), (8.1) or (8.2) at any time during a case, and the power to make such an order,

(a) is in addition to any other power to make an order that these rules may specify in the circumstances; and

(b) exists unless these rules expressly provide otherwise.

Procedural Orders

(7.2) For the purposes of promoting the primary objective of these rules as required under subrules 2(4) and, particularly, (5), the court may make orders giving such directions or imposing such conditions respecting procedural matters as are just, including an order,

(a) that a party give to another party an affidavit listing documents that are relevant to the issues in a case and that are in the party's control or available to the party on request, or that a party make any other disclosure, within a specified time;

(b) limiting the number of affidavits that a party may file, or limiting the length of affidavits that a party may file (excluding any exhibits);

(c) that any motions be brought within a specified time;

(d) that a statement setting out what material facts are not in dispute be filed within a specified time (in which case the facts are deemed to be established unless a judge orders otherwise);

(e) that questioning be conducted in accordance with a plan established by the court, be subject to a time limit or be limited with respect to scope;

(f) limiting the number of witnesses;

(g) that all or part of an affidavit or any other evidence filed at any stage in a case, and any cross-examinations on it, may be used at a hearing;

(h) that a party serve and file, within a specified time, a written summary of the anticipated evidence of a witness;

(i) that a witness give all or part of his or her evidence by affidavit or another method not requiring the witness to attend in person;

(j) that oral evidence be presented, or that any oral evidence be subject to a time limit;

(k) that any expert witnesses for the parties meet to discuss the issues, and prepare a joint statement setting out the issues on which they agree and the issues that are in dispute;

(l) that a party serve and file a summary of argument;

(m) that a party provide to the court a draft order (Form 25, 25A, 25B, 25C or 25D) setting out the relief that he or she is seeking;

(n) identifying the issues to be decided at a particular hearing;

(o) that the parties appear before the court by a specified date;

(p) that a case be scheduled for trial or that a trial management conference be conducted; and

(q) that a trial be limited to a specified number of days and apportioning those days between the parties.

Effect of Order at Trial

(7.3) An order made under clause (7.2)(i) does not apply to the giving of evidence on cross-examination unless the order states so expressly.

(7.4) An order made under subrule (7.2) respecting how a trial is to proceed applies unless the trial judge orders otherwise.

Failure to Obey Order

(8) If a person fails to obey an order in a case or a related case, the court may deal with the failure by making any order that it considers necessary for a just determination of the matter, including,

(a) an order for costs;

(b) an order dismissing a claim;

(c) an order striking out any application, answer, notice of motion, motion to change, response to motion to change, financial statement, affidavit, or any other document filed by a party;

(d) an order that all or part of a document that was required to be provided but was not, may not be used in the case;

(e) if the failure to obey was by a party, an order that the party is not entitled to any further order from the court unless the court orders otherwise;

(f) an order postponing the trial or any other step in the case; and

(g) on motion, a contempt order.

Failure to Follow Rules

(8.1) If a person fails to follow these rules, the court may deal with the failure by making any order described in subrule (8), other than a contempt order under clause (8)(g).

Document that May Delay or is Inflammatory, Etc.

(8.2) The court may strike out all or part of any document that may delay or make it difficult to have a fair trial or that is inflammatory, a waste of time, a nuisance or an abuse of the court process.

(8.3) [Repealed O. Reg. 69/15, s. 1(2).]

Consequences of Striking out Certain Documents

(8.4) If an order is made striking out a party's application, answer, motion to change or response to motion to change in a case, the following consequences apply unless a court orders otherwise:

1. The party is not entitled to any further notice of steps in the case, except as provided by subrule 25(13) (service of order).

2. The party is not entitled to participate in the case in any way.

3. The court may deal with the case in the party's absence.

4. A date may be set for an uncontested trial of the case.

Reference to Forms

(9) In these rules, when a form is referred to by number, the reference is to the form with that number that is described in the Table of Forms at the end of these rules and is available on the Internet through *www.ontariocourtforms.on.ca.*

Use of Forms

(9.1) The forms authorized by these rules and set out in the Table of Forms shall be used where applicable and may be adjusted as needed to fit the situation.

Requirements for Completing Forms

(9.2) A party who is required by these rules to provide a form shall, subject to subrule (9.1),

(a) follow the instructions set out in the form;

(b) fully complete all portions of the form; and

(c) attach to the form any documents that the form requires.

Format of Written Documents

(10) Every written document in a case,

(a) shall be legibly typed or printed; and

(b) in the case of a document in paper format,

(i) shall be on white paper, or on white or nearly white paper with recycled paper content, and

(ii) may appear on one or both sides of the page.

(c) [Repealed O. Reg. 142/14, s. 1.]

Practice Directions

(11) In subrules (12), (12.1) and (12.2),

"practice direction" means a direction, notice, memorandum or guide for the purpose of governing, subject to these rules, the conduct of cases in any area.

Requirements for Practice Direction

(12) A practice direction shall be approved in advance by the Chief Justice or Chief Judge of the court, filed with the secretary of the Family Rules Committee and posted on the Ontario Courts website, and notice of the practice direction shall be published in the *Ontario Reports*.

Effective Date of Practice Direction

(12.1) A practice direction does not come into effect before it is filed and posted and notice of it is published as described in subrule (12).

Old Practice Directions

(12.2) Practice directions that were issued before these rules take effect no longer apply.

General Transition Rules, CYFSA

(13) The following rules apply in relation to cases commenced but not concluded under the *Child and Family Services Act* before its repeal:

1. If regulations made under paragraph 11 of subsection 339(1) of the *Child, Youth and Family Services Act, 2017* provide for the continued application of any portion of the repealed Act to such cases, these rules, as they read immediately before the Act's repeal, continue to apply with respect to the continued application of that portion of the repealed Act.
2. If regulations made under paragraph 11 of subsection 339(1) of the *Child, Youth and Family Services Act, 2017* provide that a reference in that Act to a matter shall be read as including a matter in the *Child and Family Services Act*, a reference in these rules to that matter in the *Child, Youth and Family Services Act, 2017* shall be read as including that matter in the *Child and Family Services Act*.

(14) [Repealed O. Reg. 76/06, s. 1(2).]

O. Reg. 441/99, s. 1; 544/99, s. 1; 202/01, s. 1; 56/03, s. 1; 89/04, s. 1; 76/06, s. 1; 439/07, s. 1; 561/07, s. 1; 388/12, s. 1; 322/13, s. 1; 142/14, s. 1; 69/15, s. 1; 226/17, s. 1; 298/18, s. 1; 385/18, s. 1

RULE 1.1 — ELECTRONIC FILING AND ISSUANCE OF DOCUMENTS [HEADING ADDED O. REG. 298/18, S. 2.]

Authorized Software

1.1 (1) If these rules permit or require a document to be filed or issued electronically, the software authorized by the Ministry of the Attorney General for the purpose shall be used for the filing or issuance.

Agreement

(2) A rule that provides that a document may be filed electronically does not apply unless the party filing the document agrees to the terms of use of the authorized software and provides an email address at which he or she agrees to accept documents from the court electronically.

Deemed Issuance

(3) A document issued electronically using the authorized software is deemed to have been issued by the court.

Date of Electronic Filing, Issuance

(4) The date on which a document that is filed or issued electronically is considered to have been filed or issued, as the case may be, is the date indicated for the document by the authorized software.

Same, Outside of Business Hours

(5) If a document is filed or issued electronically outside of regular business hours, the authorized software shall indicate that the document was filed or issued, as the case may be, on the next day on which court offices are open.

Inconsistencies

(6) In the event of an inconsistency between information provided in a document filed electronically by a person using the authorized software and information provided by the person using the authorized software that is not in the electronically filed document,

(a) the information in the electronically filed document prevails, except with respect to the municipality specified by the person for the purposes of rule 5 where the information that is not in the electronically filed document prevails; and

(b) the clerk may request from the person clarification, in the manner specified by the clerk, respecting the inconsistency, and the person shall promptly provide it.

Requirement to Keep Original

(7) A person who, in accordance with these rules, electronically files a document that was originally signed, certified or commissioned in paper format shall,

(a) retain the original document until the day on which the case is finally disposed of or, if no notice of appeal is served in the case, the time for serving the notice has expired, subject to any requirement in these rules to give the document to the clerk before that day; and

(b) promptly make the original document available for inspection and copying on the request of the court or of any party to the case.

O. Reg. 298/18, s. 2

RULE 2 — INTERPRETATION

Definitions

2. (1) In these rules,

"address" means a person's street or municipal address, mailing address, telephone number, fax number and email address;

"appellant" means a person who starts an appeal;

"applicant" means a person who starts an application;

"application" means, as the context requires, the document that starts a case or the procedure by which new cases are brought to the court for a final order or provisional order;

"arbitration agreement" means an agreement by which two or more persons agree to submit to arbitration a dispute that has arisen or may arise between them;

"authorized software" means the software referred to in rule 1.1 (electronic filing and issuance of documents);

"bond" includes a recognizance, and expressions that refer to the posting of a bond include the act of entering into a recognizance;

"case" means an application or any other method allowed in law for bringing a matter to the court for a final order or provisional order, and includes all motions, enforcements and appeals;

"change", when used to refer to an order or agreement, means to vary, suspend or discharge, or a variation, suspension or discharge (depending on whether the word is used as a verb or as a noun);

"child" means a child as defined in the Act governing the case or, if not defined in that Act, a person under the age of 18 years, and in a case under the *Divorce Act* (Canada) includes a "child of the marriage" within the meaning of that Act;

"child protection case" means a case under Part V of the *Child, Youth and Family Services Act, 2017*;

"child support guidelines" means Ontario Regulation 391/97 (*Child Support Guidelines*) made under the *Family Law Act*, or the *Federal Child Support Guidelines*, as the case may be;

"clerk" means a person who has the authority of a clerk or a registrar of the court;

"contempt motion" means a motion for a contempt order;

"contempt order" means an order finding a person in contempt of court;

"continuing record" means the record made under Rule 9 containing, in accordance with these rules, written documents in a case that are filed with the court;

"corporation" *French version only.*

"court" means the court in which a case is being heard;

"default hearing" means a hearing under section 41 of the *Family Responsibility and Support Arrears Enforcement Act, 1996* in which a payor is required to come to court to explain why payment has not been made as required by a support order;

"Director of the Family Responsibility Office" means the Director of the Family Responsibility Office under the *Family Responsibility and Support Arrears Enforcement Act, 1996*, and "Director" has the same meaning, unless the context requires otherwise;

"document" means information, sound or images recorded by any method;

"enforcement" means the use of one or more remedies mentioned in rule 26 (enforcement of orders) to enforce an order;

"family arbitration" means an arbitration that,

(a) deals with matters that could be dealt with in a marriage contract, separation agreement, cohabitation agreement or paternity agreement under Part IV of the *Family Law Act*, and

(b) is conducted exclusively in accordance with the law of Ontario or of another Canadian jurisdiction;

"family arbitration agreement" and **"family arbitration award"** have meanings that correspond to the meaning of "family arbitration";

"file" means to file with proof of service,

(a) in the court office in the municipality where the case or enforcement is started or to which the case or enforcement is transferred, or

(b) electronically in accordance with these rules;

"final order" means an order, other than a temporary order, that decides a claim in an application, including,

(a) an order made on motion that changes a final order,

(b) a judgment, and

(c) an order that decides a party's rights, in an issue between the parties or between a party and a non-party;

"government agency" means the Crown, a Crown agency, a municipal government or agency, a children's aid society or any other public body;

"income source" has the same meaning as in the *Family Responsibility and Support Arrears Enforcement Act, 1996*;

"lawyer" means a person authorized under the *Law Society Act* to practise law in Ontario;

"legal aid rate" means the rate payable by the Ontario Legal Aid Plan on an account submitted by a lawyer for copying in the lawyer's office;

"mail", when used as a noun, means ordinary or regular mail, and when used as a verb means to send by ordinary or regular mail;

"municipality" means a county, district, district municipality, regional municipality, the City of Toronto or a municipal corporation formed from the amalgamation of all the municipalities of a county, district, district municipality or regional municipality, and includes,

(a) an Indian reserve within the territorial area of a municipality, and

(b) the part of The Regional Municipality of Niagara that was the County of Lincoln as it existed on December 31, 1969;

"on motion" means on motion of a party or a person having an interest in the case;

"payment order" means a temporary or final order, but not a provisional order, requiring a person to pay money to another person, including,

(a) an order to pay an amount under Part I or II of the *Family Law Act* or the corresponding provisions of a predecessor Act,

(b) a support order,

(c) a support deduction order,

(d) an order under section 108 or subsection 213(2) of the *Child, Youth and Family Services Act, 2017*, or under the corresponding provision of a predecessor Act,

(e) a payment order made under rules 26 to 32 (enforcement measures) or under section 41 of the *Family Responsibility and Support Arrears Enforcement Act, 1996*,

(f) a fine for contempt of court,

(g) an order of forfeiture of a bond or recognizance,

(h) an order requiring a party to pay the fees and expenses of,

(i) an assessor, mediator or other expert named by the court, or

(ii) a person conducting a blood test to help determine a child's parentage, and

(i) the costs and disbursements in a case;

"payor" means a person required to pay money under an order or agreement, and includes the estate trustee of a payor who died;

"periodic payment" means an amount payable at regular intervals and includes an amount payable in instalments;

"property claim" means a claim,

(a) under Part I of the *Family Law Act*,

(b) for a constructive or resulting trust, or

(c) for a monetary award as compensation for unjust enrichment;

"provisional order" means an order that is not effective until confirmed by a court;

"recipient" means a person entitled to receive money or costs under a payment order or agreement, including,

(a) a guardian or person with custody of a child who is entitled to money for the child's benefit under an order,

(b) in the case of a support order made under the *Family Law Act*, an agency referred to in subsection 33(3) of that Act,

(c) in the case of a support order made under the *Divorce Act* (Canada), an agency referred to in subsection 20.1(1) of that Act,

(d) a children's aid society entitled to money under an order made under section 108 or subsection 213(2) of the *Child, Youth and Family Services Act, 2017*, or the corresponding provision in a predecessor Act,

(e) an assessor, mediator or other expert entitled to fees and expenses from the party named in the order, and

(f) the estate trustee of a person who was entitled to money under an order at the time of his or her death;

"Registrar General" means the Registrar General under the *Vital Statistics Act*;

"respondent" means a person against whom a claim is made in an application, answer or appeal;

"special party" means a party who is a child or who is or appears to be mentally incapable for the purposes of the *Substitute Decisions Act, 1992* in respect of an issue in the case and who, as a result, requires legal representation, but does not include a child in a custody, access, child protection, adoption or child support case;

"support deduction order" means a support deduction order as defined in section 1 of the *Family Responsibility and Support Arrears Enforcement Act, 1996*;

"support order" means an order described in subsection 34(1) of the *Family Law Act* or a support order as defined in subsection 2(1) of the *Divorce Act* (Canada) or in section 1 of the *Family Responsibility and Support Arrears Enforcement Act, 1996*;

"temporary order" means an order that says it is effective only for a limited time, and includes an interim order;

"transcript" [Repealed O. Reg. 142/14, s. 2.]

"trial" includes a hearing;

"uncontested trial" means a trial at which only the party making the claim provides evidence and submissions.

Temporary Orders

(1.1) For the purposes of the definition of "temporary order" in subrule (1), temporary orders include orders made under subsection 94(2) (custody during adjournment) of the *Child, Youth and Family Services Act, 2017* but do not include an order made under paragraph 2 of subsection 101(1) (interim society care and custody) of that Act.

Primary Objective

(2) The primary objective of these rules is to enable the court to deal with cases justly.

Dealing with Cases Justly

(3) Dealing with a case justly includes,

(a) ensuring that the procedure is fair to all parties;

(b) saving expense and time;

(c) dealing with the case in ways that are appropriate to its importance and complexity; and

(d) giving appropriate court resources to the case while taking account of the need to give resources to other cases.

Duty to Promote Primary Objective

(4) The court is required to apply these rules to promote the primary objective, and parties and their lawyers are required to help the court to promote the primary objective.

Duty to Manage Cases

(5) The court shall promote the primary objective by active management of cases, which includes,

(a) at an early stage, identifying the issues, and separating and disposing of those that do not need full investigation and trial;

(b) encouraging and facilitating use of alternatives to the court process;

(c) helping the parties to settle all or part of the case;

(d) setting timetables or otherwise controlling the progress of the case;

(e) considering whether the likely benefits of taking a step justify the cost;

(f) dealing with as many aspects of the case as possible on the same occasion; and

(g) if appropriate, dealing with the case without parties and their lawyers needing to come to court, on the basis of written documents or by holding a telephone or video conference.

O. Reg. 544/99, s. 2; 76/06, s. 2; 439/07, s. 2; 388/12, s. 2; 142/14, s. 2; 69/15, s. 2; 140/15, s. 4, item 1; 298/18, s. 3

RULE 3 — TIME

Counting Days

3. (1) In these rules or an order, the number of days between two events is counted as follows:

1. The first day is the day after the first event.
2. The last day is the day of the second event.

Counting Days — Short Periods

(2) If a rule or order provides a period of less than seven days for something to be done, Saturdays, Sundays and other days when all court offices are closed do not count as part of the period.

Day when Court Offices Closed

(3) If the last day of a period of time under these rules or an order falls on a day when court offices are closed, the period ends on the next day they are open.

Counting Days — Examples

(4) The following are examples of how time is counted under these rules:

1. Notice of a motion must be served not later than six days before the motion date (see subrule 14(11)). Saturday and Sunday are not counted, because the notice period is less than seven days (see subrule (2)). Service on the day set out in the left column below is in time for the motion to be heard on the day set out in the right column below.

Service on	Motion may be heard on
Monday	The second following Tuesday
Tuesday	The second following Wednesday
Wednesday	The second following Thursday
Thursday	The second following Friday
Friday	The second following Monday
Saturday	The second following Tuesday
Sunday	The second following Tuesday

2. A respondent who is served with an application in Canada has 30 days to serve an answer (see subrule 10(1)). A respondent who is served with an application on October 1 is in time if the answer is served on or before October 31. A respondent served on November 1 is in time if the answer is served on or before December 1.

3. If the last day for doing something under these rules or an order is New Year's Day, January 1, which is a day when court offices are closed, the time expires on January 2. If January 2 is a Saturday, Sunday or other day when court offices are closed, the time expires on January 3. If January 3 is a day when court offices are closed, the time expires on January 4.

Order to Lengthen or Shorten Time

(5) The court may make an order to lengthen or shorten any time set out in these rules or an order, except that it may lengthen a time set out in subrule 33(1) (timetable for child protection cases) only if the best interests of the child require it.

Written Consent to Change Time

(6) The parties may, by consent in writing, change any time set out in these rules, except that they may not change a time set out in,

(a) clause 14(11)(c) (confirmation of motion);

(b) clause 17(14)(c) (confirmation of conference);

(c) subrule 33(1) (timetable for child protection cases);

(d) rule 39 (case management in Family Court of Superior Court of Justice);

(e) rule 40 (case management in Ontario Court of Justice); or

(f) rule 41 (case management in the Superior Court of Justice (other than the Family Court of the Superior Court of Justice)).

Late Documents Refused by Court Office

(7) The staff at a court office shall refuse to accept a document that a person asks to file after,

(a) the time specified in these rules; or

(b) the later time specified in a consent under subrule (6), a statute that applies to the case, or a court order.

O. Reg. 544/99, s. 3; 202/01, s. 2; 76/06, s. 3; 298/18, s. 4

RULE 4 — REPRESENTATION

Definition

4. (0.1) In this rule,

"limited scope retainer" means the provision of legal services by a lawyer for part, but not all, of a party's case by agreement between the lawyer and the party.

Representation for a Party

(1) A party may,

(a) act in person;

(b) be represented by a lawyer; or

(c) be represented by a person who is not a lawyer, but only if the court gives permission in advance.

Interpretation, Acting in Person

(1.1) Where a party acts in person, anything these rules require or permit a lawyer or other representative to do shall be done by the party.

Limited Scope Retainer

(1.2) Clause (1)(b) permits a party to be represented by a lawyer acting under a limited scope retainer.

Interpretation, Limited Scope Retainer

(1.3) A party who is represented by a lawyer acting under a limited scope retainer is considered for the purposes of these rules to be acting in person, unless the lawyer is acting as the party's lawyer of record.

Private Representation of Special Party

(2) The court may authorize a person to represent a special party if the person is,

(a) appropriate for the task; and

(b) willing to act as representative.

Public Law Officer to Represent Special Party

(3) If there is no appropriate person willing to act as a special party's representative, the court may authorize the Children's Lawyer or the Public Guardian and Trustee to act as representative, but only with that official's consent.

Service of Authorization to Represent

(4) An order under subrule (2) or (3) shall be served immediately, by the person who asked for the order or by any other person named by the court,

(a) on the representative; and

(b) on every party in the case.

Representation of Party who Dies

(5) If a party dies after the start of a case, the court may make the estate trustee a party instead, on motion without notice.

Authorizing Representative for Party who Dies

(6) If the party has no estate trustee, the court may authorize an appropriate person to act as representative, with that person's consent, given in advance.

Lawyer for Child

(7) In a case that involves a child who is not a party, the court may authorize a lawyer to represent the child, and then the child has the rights of a party, unless the court orders otherwise.

Child's Rights Subject to Statute

(8) Subrule (7) is subject to section 78 (legal representation of child, protection hearing) and subsection 161(6) (legal representation of child, secure treatment hearing) of the *Child, Youth and Family Services Act, 2017*.

Choice of Lawyer

(9) A party who is acting in person may choose a lawyer by serving on every other party and filing a notice of change in representation (Form 4) containing the lawyer's consent to act.

Non-Application

(9.1) Subrule (9) does not apply if the party chooses a lawyer acting under a limited scope retainer and that lawyer is not the lawyer of record for the party.

Change in Representation

(10) Except as subrule (10.1) provides, a party represented by a lawyer may, by serving on every other party and filing a notice of change in representation (Form 4),

(a) change lawyers; or

(b) act in person.

Exception, Child Protection Case Scheduled for Trial

(10.1) In a child protection case that has been scheduled for trial or placed on a trial list, a party may act under clause (10)(b) only with the court's permission, obtained in advance by motion made with notice.

Notice of Change in Representation

(11) A notice of change in representation shall,

(a) contain the party's address for service, if the party wants to appear without a lawyer; or

(b) show the name and address of the new lawyer, if the party wants to change lawyers.

Lawyer's Removal from the Case

(12) A lawyer may make a motion for an order to be removed from the case, with notice to the client and to,

(a) the Children's Lawyer, if the client is a child;

(b) the Public Guardian and Trustee, if the client is or appears to be mentally incapable in respect of an issue in the case.

Notice of Motion to Remove Lawyer

(13) Notice of a motion to remove a lawyer shall also be served on the other parties to the case, but the evidence in support of the motion shall not be served on them, shall not be put into the continuing record and shall not be kept in the court file after the motion is heard.

Affidavit in Support of Motion to Remove Lawyer

(14) The affidavit in support of the motion shall indicate what stage the case is at, the next event in the case and any scheduled dates.

Contents and Service of Order Removing Lawyer

(15) The order removing the lawyer from the case shall,

(a) set out the client's last known address for service; and

(b) be served on all other parties, served on the client by mail, fax or email at the client's last known address and filed immediately.

O. Reg. 91/03, s. 1; 322/13, s. 2; 140/15, s. 4, item 2; 298/18, s. 5

RULE 5 — WHERE A CASE STARTS AND IS TO BE HEARD

Where Case Starts

5. (1) Subject to sections 21.8 and 21.11 of the *Courts of Justice Act* (territorial jurisdiction — Family Court), a case shall be started,

(a) in the municipality where a party resides;

(b) if the case deals with custody of or access to a child, in the municipality where the child ordinarily resides, except for cases described in,

(i) section 22 (jurisdiction of an Ontario court) of the *Children's Law Reform Act*, and

(ii) subsection 91(2) (place for child protection hearing) and subsection 203(1) (place for adoption proceeding) of the *Child, Youth and Family Services Act, 2017*; or

(c) in a municipality chosen by all parties, but only with the court's permission given in advance in that municipality.

Starting Case — Danger to Child or Party

(2) Subject to sections 21.8 and 21.11 of the *Courts of Justice Act*, if there is immediate danger that a child may be removed from Ontario or immediate danger to a child's or party's health or safety, a party may start a case in any municipality and a motion may be heard in that municipality, but the case shall be transferred to a municipality referred to in subrule (1) immediately after the motion is heard, unless the court orders otherwise.

Clerk to Refuse Documents if Case in Wrong Place

(3) The clerk shall refuse to accept an application for filing unless,

(a) the case is started in the municipality where a party resides;

(b) the case deals with custody of or access to a child and is started in the municipality where the child ordinarily resides;

(c) the case is started in a municipality chosen by all parties and the order permitting the case to be started there is filed with the application; or

(d) the lawyer or party asking to file the application says in writing that the case is one that is permitted by clause (1)(b) or subrule (2) to be started in that municipality.

Place for Steps Other than Enforcement

(4) All steps in the case, other than enforcement, shall take place in the municipality where the case is started or transferred.

Place for Enforcement — Payment Orders

(5) All steps in enforcement of a payment order, including a motion to suspend a support deduction order, shall take place,

(a) in the municipality where the recipient resides;

(b) if the recipient does not reside in Ontario, in the municipality where the order is filed with the court for enforcement;

(c) if the person enforcing the order so chooses, in the municipality where the payor resides; or

(d) in a motion under section 26 (income source dispute) of the *Family Responsibility and Support Arrears Enforcement Act, 1996*, in the municipality where the income source resides.

Place for Enforcement — Other Orders

(6) All steps in the enforcement of an order other than a payment order shall take place,

(a) if the order involves custody of or access to a child,

(i) in the municipality where the child ordinarily resides, or

(ii) if the child does not ordinarily reside in Ontario, in the municipality to which the child has the closest connection;

(b) if the order involves property, in the municipality where the person enforcing the order resides or the municipality where the property is located; or

(c) in a municipality chosen by all parties, but only with the court's permission given in advance in that municipality.

Filing Writ with Sheriff

(6.1) Despite subrules (5) and (6), a writ of seizure and sale (Form 28) may be filed with a sheriff in a different municipality.

Alternative Place for Enforcement — Order Enforced by Contempt Motion

(7) An order, other than a payment order, that is being enforced by a contempt motion may also be enforced in the municipality in which the order was made.

Place for Enforcement — Electronic Writ

(7.1) A writ of seizure and sale that is issued electronically under rule 28 (seizure and sale),

(a) shall specify the municipality in which the enforcement is taking place under subrule (5), (6) or (7), as the case may be; and

(b) is deemed to have been issued in that municipality.

Transfer to Another Municipality

(8) If it is substantially more convenient to deal with a case or any step in the case in another municipality, the court may, on motion, order that the case or step be transferred there.

Change of Place for Child Protection Case

(9) Notice of a motion under subsection 91(3) of the *Child, Youth and Family Services Act, 2017* to transfer a case to a place within the jurisdiction of another children's aid society shall be served on the parties and the other children's aid society, with the evidence in support of the motion.

O. Reg. 322/13, s. 3; 142/14, s. 3; 298/18, s. 6

RULE 6 — SERVICE OF DOCUMENTS

Methods of Service

6. (1) Service of a document under these rules may be carried out by regular service or by special service in accordance with this rule, unless an Act, rule or order provides otherwise.

Age Restriction

(1.1) No person shall serve a document under these rules unless he or she is at least 18 years of age.

Regular Service

(2) Regular service of a document on a person is carried out by,

(a) mailing a copy to the person's lawyer or, if none, to the person;

(b) sending a copy by same- or next-day courier to the person's lawyer or, if none, to the person;

(c) depositing a copy at a document exchange to which the person's lawyer or, if none, the person belongs;

(c.1) if the person consents or the court orders, using an electronic document exchange;

(d) faxing a copy to the person's lawyer or, if none, to the person; or

(e) if the person consents or the court orders, emailing a copy to the person's lawyer or, if none, to the person.

Special Service

(3) Special service of a document on a person is carried out by,

(a) leaving a copy,

(i) with the person to be served,

(ii) if the person is or appears to be mentally incapable in respect of an issue in the case, with the person and with the guardian of the person's property or, if none, with the Public Guardian and Trustee,

(iii) if the person is a child, with the child and with the child's lawyer, if any,

(iv) if the person is a corporation, with an officer, director or agent of the corporation, or with a person at any place of business of the corporation who appears to be managing the place, or

(v) if the person is a children's aid society, with an officer, director or employee of the society;

(b) leaving a copy with the person's lawyer of record in the case, or with a lawyer who accepts service in writing on a copy of the document;

(c) mailing a copy to the person, together with an acknowledgment of service in the form of a prepaid return postcard (Form 6), all in an envelope that is addressed to the person and has the sender's return address (but service under this clause is not valid unless the return postcard, signed by the person, is filed in the continuing record); or

(d) leaving a copy at the person's place of residence, in an envelope addressed to the person, with anyone who appears to be an adult person resident at the same address and, on the same day or on the next, mailing another copy to the person at that address.

Special Service — Documents that Could Lead to Imprisonment

(4) Special service of the following documents shall be carried out only by a method set out in clause (3)(a), unless the court orders otherwise:

1. A notice of contempt motion.

2. A summons to witness.

3. A notice of motion or notice of default hearing in which the person to be served faces a possibility of imprisonment.

Special Service — Restriction on Who May Serve

(4.1) Subject to subrule (4.2), special service of the following documents shall be carried out by a person other than the party required to serve the document:

1. An application (Form 8, 8A, 8B, 8B.1, 8B.2, 8C, 8D, 8D.1, 34L or 34N).

2. A motion to change (Form 15) and change information form (Form 15A) or affidavit permitted under subrule 15(22), with required attachments.

3. A document listed in subrule (4).

Exceptions

(4.2) Subrule (4.1) does not apply if,

(a) the party required to serve the document or the person being served is a person referred to in clause 8(6)(c) (officials, agencies, etc.); or

(b) the court orders otherwise.

Regular Service at Address on Latest Document

(5) Regular service may be carried out at the address for service shown on the latest document filed by the person to be served.

Notice of Address Change

(6) A party whose address for service changes shall immediately serve notice of the change on the other parties and file it.

Service By Mail, When Effective

(7) Service of a document by mail is effective on the fifth day after it was mailed.

Service By Courier, When Effective

(8) Service of a document by courier is effective on,

(a) the day after the day the courier picks it up, in the case of same-day courier service; or

(b) two days after the day the courier picks it up, in the case of next-day courier service.

Service by Document Exchange, When Effective

(9) Service of a document by deposit at a document exchange is effective only if the copy deposited and an additional copy of the document are date-stamped by the document exchange in the presence of the person depositing the copy, and then service is effective on the day after the date on the stamp.

Service by Electronic Document Exchange, When Effective

(10) Service of a document through an electronic document exchange is effective only if the electronic document exchange provides a record of service showing the date and time of service, as well as the information listed in subrule (11.4), and then service is effective on,

(a) the date shown on the record of service; or

(b) if the record of service shows that the document was served after 4 p.m., the following day.

Service by Fax or email, When Effective

(11) Service of a document by fax or email is effective on,

(a) the date shown on the first page of the fax or in the email message, as the case may be; or

(b) if the first page of the fax or the email message shows that the document was served after 4 p.m., the following day.

Special Service by leaving copy, when effective

(11.1) Special service of a document under clause (3)(a) or (b) is effective on the day the copy of the document was left in accordance with those clauses or, if the document was left after 4 p.m., the following day.

Special Service by leaving copy and mailing, when effective

(11.2) Special service of a document under clause (3)(d) is effective on the fifth day after it was mailed.

Exception, if effective date is a holiday

(11.3) Despite subrules (7) to (11.2), if the effective date of service under one of those subrules would be a day on which court offices are closed, service is instead effective on the next day on which they are open.

Information to be included in record of service

(11.4) A record of service for service of a document through an electronic document exchange shall, in addition to the date and time of service, include,

(a) the total number of pages served;

(b) the name and email address of the person who served the document;

(c) the name of the person or lawyer who was served; and

(d) the title or a description of the nature of the document.

Information to be Included with Document Served by Fax

(12) A document that is served by fax shall show, on its first page,

(a) the sender's name, telephone number and fax number;

(b) the name of the person or lawyer to be served;

(c) the date and time of the fax;

(d) the total number of pages faxed; and

(e) the name and telephone number of a person to contact in case of transmission difficulties.

Maximum Length of Document that may be Faxed

(13) Service of a document or documents relating to a single step in a case may be carried out by fax only if the total number of pages (including any cover page or back sheet) is not more than 20, unless the parties consent in advance or the court orders otherwise.

Documents that may not be Faxed

(14) A trial record, appeal record, factum or book of authorities may not be served by fax at any time unless the person to be served consents in advance.

Information to be Included with Document Served by email

(14.1) Unless the court orders otherwise, the email message to which a document served by email is attached shall include,

(a) the name of the person or lawyer to be served;

(b) the title or a description of the nature of the document;

(c) the date and time of the email; and

(d) the name and telephone number of a person to contact in case of transmission difficulties.

Substituted Service

(15) The court may, order that a document be served by substituted service, using a method chosen by the court, if the party making the motion,

(a) provides detailed evidence showing,

(i) what steps have been taken to locate the person to be served, and

(ii) if the person has been located, what steps have been taken to serve the document on that person; and

(b) shows that the method of service could reasonably be expected to bring the document to the person's attention.

Same, Notice

(15.1) An order under subrule (15) may be obtained on motion without notice, except where the person to be served is a government agency.

Service not Required

(16) The court may, on motion without notice, order that service is not required if,

(a) reasonable efforts to locate the person to be served have not been or would not be successful; and

(b) there is no method of substituted service that could reasonably be expected to bring the document to the person's attention.

Service by Advertisement

(17) If the court orders service by advertisement, Form 6A shall be used.

Approving Irregular Service

(18) When a document has been served by a method not allowed by these rules or by an order, the court may make an order approving the service if the document,

(a) came to the attention of the person to be served; or

(b) would have come to the person's attention if the person had not been evading service.

Proof of Service

(19) Service of a document may be proved by,

(a) an acceptance or admission of service, written by the person to be served or the person's lawyer;

(b) an affidavit of service (Form 6B);

(c) the return postcard mentioned in clause (3)(c);

(d) the date stamp on a copy of the document served by deposit at a document exchange; or

(e) a record of service provided by an electronic document exchange that meets the requirements of this rule.

Document That was not seen on effective date

(20) The court may, on motion, lengthen a time, set aside the consequences of failing to take a step by a specified time, order an adjournment, or make any other order that is just, if, despite service of a document having been effected on a person in accordance with this rule, the person shows that the document,

(a) did not come to his or her notice; or

(b) came to his or her notice only after the effective date of service.

O. Reg. 6/10, s. 1; 322/13, s. 4; 140/15, s. 1; 235/16, s. 1

RULE 7 — PARTIES

Who are Parties — Case

7. (1) A person who makes a claim in a case or against whom a claim is made in a case is a party to the case.

Who are Parties — Motion

(2) For purposes of a motion only, a person who is affected by a motion is also a party, but this does not apply to a child affected by a motion relating to custody, access, child protection, adoption or child support.

Persons who must be Named as Parties

(3) A person starting a case shall name,

(a) as an applicant, every person who makes a claim;

(b) as a respondent,

(i) every person against whom a claim is made, and

(ii) every other person who should be a party to enable the court to decide all the issues in the case.

Parties in Cases Involving Children

(4) In any of the following cases, every parent or other person who has care and control of the child involved, except a foster parent under the *Child, Youth and Family Services Act, 2017*, shall be named as a party, unless the court orders otherwise:

1. A case about custody of or access to a child.

2. A child protection case.

3. A secure treatment case (Part VII of the *Child, Youth and Family Services Act, 2017*).

Motion to Change Order, S. 102 of the CYFSA

(4.1) In a motion to change an order made under section 102 of the *Child, Youth and Family Services Act, 2017*, the children's aid society that was a party to the case in which the order was made is not a party to the motion to change the order, unless the court orders otherwise.

Party Added by Court Order

(5) The court may order that any person who should be a party shall be added as a party, and may give directions for service on that person.

Permanent Case Name and Court File Number

(6) The court file number given to a case and the description of the parties as applicants and respondents in the case shall remain the same on an application or motion to change an order, a status review application, an application (general) for *Child, Youth and Family Services Act, 2017* cases other than child protection and status review, an enforcement or an appeal, no matter who starts it, with the following exceptions:

1. In an enforcement of a payment order, the parties may be described instead as payors, recipients and garnishees.

2. In an appeal, the parties shall also be described as appellants and respondents.

3. When a case is transferred to another municipality, it may be given a new court file number.

4. An application under section 207 of the *Child, Youth and Family Services Act, 2017* to change or terminate an openness order shall be given a new court file number.

5. In a motion to change an order made under section 102 of the *Child, Youth and Family Services Act, 2017*,

i. the person making the motion shall be named as the applicant and every other party to the motion shall be named as the respondents, and

ii. the motion shall be given a new court file number.

6. [Repealed O. Reg. 298/18, s. 7(7).]

O. Reg. 519/06, s. 1; 383/11, s. 1; 186/12, s. 1; 298/18, s. 7

RULE 8 — STARTING A CASE

Filing an Application

8. (1) To start a case, a person shall file an application (Form 8, 8A, 8B, 8B.1, 8B.2, 8C, 8D, 8D.1, 34L or 34N).

Enforcement of Family Arbitration Award

(1.1) Despite subrule (1), a person who is entitled to the enforcement of a family arbitration award and who wants to ask the court to enforce the award under section 59.8 of the *Family Law Act* may do so by filing a request to enforce a family arbitration award (Form 32.1) under rule 32.1.

When Required to Proceed by Motion

(1.2) Despite subrules (1) and (1.1), if there is already a family law case to which these rules apply between the parties to the family arbitration agreement in the Superior Court of Justice or the Family Court of the Superior Court of Justice, the party entitled to enforcement shall make a motion in that case rather than an application under this rule or a request under rule 32.1, and subrule 14(24) applies in respect of the motion.

Change to Final Order or Agreement

(2) Subject to subrule 25(19) (changing order — fraud, mistake, lack of notice), a party who wants to ask the court to change a final order or an agreement for support filed under section 35 of the *Family Law Act* may do so only by a motion under rule 15 (if permitted to do so by that rule).

Exception

(2.1) Despite subrule (2), if a party who wants to ask the court to change a final order or agreement to which rule 15 applies also wants to make one or more related claims to which rule 15 does not apply, the party may file an application under subrule (1) to deal with the request for a change together with the related claim or claims and, in that case, subrules 15(11) to (13) apply with necessary changes to the request.

Claims in Application

(3) An application may contain,

(a) a claim against more than one person; and

(b) more than one claim against the same person.

Claim for Custody or Access

(3.1) An application containing a claim for custody of or access to a child shall be accompanied by the applicable documents referred to in Rule 35.1.

Claim Relating to Family Arbitration

(3.2) An application containing a claim under the *Arbitration Act, 1991* or the *Family Law Act* relating to a family arbitration, family arbitration agreement or family arbitration award shall be accompanied by,

(a) copies of the certificates of independent legal advice required by the *Family Law Act* for the parties;

(b) a copy of the family arbitration agreement; and

(c) if an award has been made, the original award or a certified copy.

Court Date Set when Application Filed

(4) When an application is filed, the clerk shall,

(a) set a court date, except as provided by subrule 39(7) (case management, standard track) and subrule 41(4) (case management, clerk's role); and

(b) seal the application with the court seal.

Service of Application

(5) The application shall be served immediately on every other party, and special service shall be used unless the party is listed in subrule (6).

Service on Officials, Agencies, etc.

(6) The application may be served, subject to subrule (8.1)

(a) on a foster parent, at the foster parent's residence;

(b) on a representative of a band or First Nations, Inuit or Métis community, by serving the chief or other person who appears to be in charge of its management;

(c) on any of the following persons, at their place of business:

1. A Director appointed under section 53 of the *Child, Youth and Family Services Act, 2017*.

2. A local director appointed under section 38 of the *Child, Youth and Family Services Act, 2017*.

3. An administrator in charge of a secure treatment program under Part VII of the *Child, Youth and Family Services Act, 2017*.

4. A children's aid society.

5. The Minister of Community and Social Services.

6. An agency referred to in subsection 33(3) of the *Family Law Act* or subsection 20.1(1) of the *Divorce Act* (Canada).

7. The Director of the Family Responsibility Office.

8. The Children's Lawyer.

9. The Public Guardian and Trustee.

10. The Registrar General.

Serving Protection Application on Child

(7) In a child protection case in which the child is entitled to notice, the application shall be served on the child by special service.

Serving Secure Treatment Application on Child

(8) An application for secure treatment (Part VII of the *Child, Youth and Family Services Act, 2017*) shall be served on the child by special service.

Serving Openness Applications

(8.1) An application for an openness order or an application to change or terminate an openness order (Part VIII of the *Child, Youth and Family Services Act, 2017*) shall be served by special service on,

(a) the child, if he or she is 12 years of age or older;

(b) the child's lawyer, if any; and

(c) the Children's Lawyer.

Serving Application on Child's Lawyer

(9) If an order has been made for legal representation of a child under section 78 or subsection 161(6) of the *Child, Youth and Family Services Act, 2017* or under subrule 4(7), the applicant, or another party directed by the court, shall serve all documents in the continuing record and any status review application on the child's lawyer.

Serving Protection Application Before Start of Case

(10) If a child is brought to a place of safety (section 81, 82, 84 or 85 of the *Child, Youth and Family Services Act, 2017*), an application may be served without being sealed by the clerk, if it is filed on or before the court date.

Application not Served on or Before Court Date

(11) If an application is not served on a respondent on or before the court date, at the applicant's request the clerk shall set a new court date for that respondent and the applicant shall make the necessary change to the application and serve it immediately on that respondent.

O. Reg. 337/02, s. 1; 89/04, s. 2; 519/06, s. 2; 151/08, s. 1; 6/10, s. 2; 388/12, s. 3; 142/14, s. 4; 140/15, s. 5, item 1; 298/18, s. 8

RULE 8.1 — MANDATORY INFORMATION PROGRAM IN THE SUPERIOR COURT OF JUSTICE IN TORONTO [HEADING ADDED O. REG. 89/04, S. 3.]

Application of Rule

8.1 (1) This rule applies to cases started after August 31, 2011 that deal with any of the following:

1. A claim for custody of or access to a child under the *Divorce Act* (Canada) or Part III of the *Children's Law Reform Act*.

2. A claim respecting net family property under Part I of the *Family Law Act*.

3. A claim respecting a matrimonial home under Part II of the *Family Law Act*.

4. A claim for support under the *Divorce Act* (Canada) or Part III of the *Family Law Act*.

5. A restraining order under the *Family Law Act* or the *Children's Law Reform Act*.

6. A motion to change a final order or agreement under rule 15, except motions that deal only with changing child or spousal support.

Exception

(2) Subrules (4) to (7) do not apply to,

(a) a person or agency referred to in subsection 33(3) of the *Family Law Act*;

(b) the Director of the Family Responsibility Office;

(c) parties in cases that are proceeding on consent;

(d) parties in cases in which the only claims made are for a divorce, costs or the incorporation of the terms of an agreement or prior court order;

(d.1) parties to an application in which the only claims made in the application and any answer relate to a family arbitration, family arbitration agreement or family arbitration award, unless the court orders otherwise; or

(e) parties who have already attended a mandatory information program.

Content of Program

(3) The program referred to in this rule shall provide parties to cases referred to in subrule (1) with information about separation and the legal process, and may include information on topics such as,

(a) the options available for resolving differences, including alternatives to going to court;

(b) the impact the separation of parents has on children; and

(c) resources available to deal with problems arising from separation.

Attendance Compulsory

(4) Each party to a case shall attend the program no later than 45 days after the case is started.

Appointments to Attend

(5) The applicant shall arrange his or her own appointment to attend the program, obtain an appointment for the respondent from the person who conducts the program, and serve notice of the respondent's appointment with the application.

Certificate

(6) The person who conducts the program shall provide for each party who attends a certificate of attendance, which shall be filed as soon as possible, and in any event not later than 2 p.m. on the second day before the day of the case conference, if one is scheduled.

No Other Steps

(7) A party shall not take any step in the case before his or her certificate of attendance is filed, except that a respondent may serve and file an answer and a party may make an appointment for a case conference.

Exception

(8) The court may, on motion, order that any or all of subrules (4) to (7) do not apply to the party because of urgency or hardship or for some other reason in the interest of justice.

(9) [Repealed O. Reg. 561/07, s. 2.]

O. Reg. 89/04, s. 3; 561/07, s. 2; 383/11, s. 2; 388/12, s. 4

RULE 9 — CONTINUING RECORD

Continuing Record Created

9. (1) A person starting a case shall,

(a) prepare a single continuing record of the case, to be the court's permanent record of the case; and

(b) serve it on all other parties and file it, along with the affidavits of service or other documents proving that the continuing record was served.

(2) [Repealed O. Reg. 519/06, s. 3(1).]

Support Enforcement Continuing Record

(3) If a support order is filed with the Director of the Family Responsibility Office, the person bringing the case before the court shall prepare the continuing record, and the continuing record shall be called the support enforcement continuing record.

Child Protection Continuing Record

(4) In an application for a child protection order or an application for a status review of a child protection order, the continuing record shall be called the child protection continuing record.

(5) [Repealed O. Reg. 76/06, s. 4(3).]

Formal Requirements of Continuing Record

(6) In preparing and maintaining a continuing record and support enforcement continuing record under this rule, the parties shall meet the requirements set out in the document entitled "Formal Requirements of the Continuing Record under the *Family Law Rules*", dated October 21, 2013, published by the Family Rules Committee and available on the Internet through *www.ontariocourtforms.on.ca*.

Formal Requirements of Child Protection Continuing Record

(6.1) In preparing and maintaining a child protection continuing record under this rule, the parties shall meet the requirements set out in the document entitled "Formal Requirements of the Child Protection Continuing Record under the *Family Law Rules*", dated November 1, 2005, published by the Family Rules Committee and available on the Internet through *www.ontariocourtforms.on.ca*.

Separation of Single Record

(7) Instead of the single continuing record mentioned in subrule (1), the continuing record may be separated into separate records for the applicant and the respondent, in accordance with the following:

1. In a case other than a child protection case, the court may order separate records on its own initiative or at the request of either party on motion or at a case conference, settlement conference or trial management conference.

2. [Repealed O. Reg. 519/06, s. 3(3).]

3. If the court orders separate records and there is more than one applicant and respondent, the court may order separate records for each applicant and respondent.

4. If the record consists of separate records, the separate records are called the applicant's record and the respondent's record.

Combining Separated Records

(8) If the continuing record has been separated, the court may order the records to be combined into a single record on its own initiative or at the request of either party at a case conference, settlement conference or trial management conference.

Combining Separated Records on Consent

(9) If the continuing record has been separated, the parties may, if they agree, combine the separate records into a single continuing record, in which case the parties shall arrange together for the combining of the records.

By Whom Record is Separated or Combined

(10) If the court orders that the continuing record,

(a) be separated or combined on its own initiative, the court shall give directions as to which party shall separate or combine the record, as the case requires;

(b) be separated or combined at the request of a party at a case conference, settlement conference or trial management conference, the party that makes the request shall separate or combine the record, as the case requires, unless the court orders otherwise.

Maintaining Continuing Record

(11) The parties are responsible, under the clerk's supervision, for adding to a continuing record that has not been separated all documents filed in the case and, in the case of separated records, each party is responsible, under the clerk's supervision, for adding the documents the party files to the party's own record.

Duties of Party Serving Documents

(12) A party serving documents shall,

(a) if the continuing record has not been separated,

(i) serve and file any documents that are not already in the continuing record, and

(ii) serve with the documents an updated cumulative table of contents listing the documents being filed; and

(b) if the continuing record has been separated,

(i) serve and file any documents that are not already in the party's separate record, and

(ii) serve with the documents an updated cumulative table of contents listing the documents being filed in the party's separate record.

No Service or Filing of Documents Already in Record

(13) A party shall not serve or file any document that is already in the record, despite any requirement in these rules that the document be served and filed.

(14) [Repealed O. Reg. 519/06, s. 3(4).]

Documents Referred to by Tab in Record

(15) A party who is relying on a document in the record shall refer to it by its tab in the record, except in a support enforcement continuing record.

Documents Not to be Removed from Record

(16) No document shall be removed from the continuing record except by order.

Written Reasons for Order

(17) If the court gives written reasons for making an order,

(a) they may be endorsed by hand on an endorsement sheet, or the endorsement may be a short note on the endorsement sheet saying that written reasons are being given separately;

(b) the clerk shall add a copy of the reasons to the endorsements section of the record; and

(c) the clerk shall send a copy to the parties by mail, fax or email.

(18) [Repealed O. Reg. 519/06, s. 3(5).]

Appeal

(19) If a final order is appealed, only the notice of appeal and any order of the appeal court (and no other appeal document) shall be added to the record.

Transfer of Record if Case Transferred

(20) If the court transfers a case to another municipality the clerk shall, on request, transfer the record to the clerk at the court office in the other municipality, and the record shall be used there as if the case had started in the other municipality.

Confirmation of Support Order

(21) When a provisional support order or a provisional change to a support order is sent to a court in Ontario for confirmation,

(a) if the provisional order or change was made in Ontario, the clerk shall send the continuing record to the court office where the confirmation is to take place and the respondent shall update it as this rule requires; and

(b) if the provisional order or change was not made in Ontario, the clerk shall prepare the continuing record and the respondent shall update it as this rule requires.

Cases Started Before January 1, 2007

(22) Despite this rule, if a case was started before January 1, 2007, the version of this rule that applied to the case on December 31, 2006 as its application may have been modified by the court continues, subject to subrule (23), to apply to the case unless the court orders otherwise.

Exception, Cases Started Before January 1, 2007

(23) If a motion to change a final order is made on or after January 1, 2007 in respect of a case started before that date, this rule shall apply to the motion and to all documents filed afterwards.

(24) [Repealed O. Reg. 519/06, s. 3(6).]

O. Reg. 544/99, s. 4; 89/04, s. 4; 76/06, s. 4; 519/06, s. 3; 322/13, s. 5; 140/15, s. 4, item 3

RULE 10 — ANSWERING A CASE

Serving and Filing Answer

10. (1) A person against whom an application is made shall serve an answer (Form 10, 33B, 33B.1 or 33B.2) on every other party and file it within 30 days after being served with the application.

Time for Answer — Application Served Outside Canada or U.S.A.

(2) If an application is served outside Canada or the United States of America, the time for serving and filing an answer is 60 days.

Exception — Placement for Adoption

(2.1) In an application to dispense with a parent's consent before adoption placement, (Form 8D.1), the time for serving the answer is,

(a) 20 days, if the application is served in Canada or the United States of America;

(b) 40 days, if the application is served outside Canada or the United States of America.

Answer May Include Claim

(3) A respondent may include in the answer,

(a) a claim against the applicant;

(b) a claim against any other person, who then also becomes a respondent in the case.

Answer by Added Respondent

(4) Subrules (1) to (3) apply to a respondent added under subrule (3), except that the time for serving and filing an answer is 14 days after service on the added respondent, or 30 days if the added respondent is served outside Canada or the United States of America.

Claim for Custody or Access

(4.1) An answer that includes a claim for custody of or access to a child shall be accompanied by the applicable documents referred to in Rule 35.1.

No Answer

(5) The consequences set out in paragraphs 1 to 4 of subrule 1(8.4) apply, with necessary changes, if a respondent does not serve and file an answer.

Reply

(6) A party may, within 10 days after being served with an answer, serve and file a reply (Form 10A) in response to a claim made in the answer.

O. Reg. 337/02, s. 2; 91/03, s. 2; 519/06, s. 4; 6/10, s. 3; 322/13, s. 6; 142/14, s. 5

RULE 11 — AMENDING AN APPLICATION, ANSWER OR REPLY

Amending Application without Court's Permission

11. (1) An applicant may amend the application without the court's permission as follows:

1. If no answer has been filed, by serving and filing an amended application in the manner set out in rule 8 (starting a case).

2. If an answer has been filed, by serving and filing an amended application in the manner set out in rule 8 and also filing the consent of all parties to the amendment.

Amending Answer without Court's Permission

(2) A respondent may amend the answer without the court's permission as follows:

1. If the application has been amended, by serving and filing an amended answer within 14 days after being served with the amended application.

2. If the application has not been amended, by serving and filing an amended answer and also filing the consent of all parties to the amendment.

Child Protection, Amendments Without Court's Permission

(2.1) In a child protection case, if a significant change relating to the child happens after the original document is filed,

(a) the applicant may serve and file an amended application, an amended plan of care or both; and

(b) the respondent may serve and file an amended answer and plan of care.

Amending Application or Answer with Court's Permission

(3) On motion, the court shall give permission to a party to amend an application, answer or reply, unless the amendment would disadvantage another party in a way for which costs or an adjournment could not compensate.

Claim for Custody or Access

(3.1) If an application or answer is amended to include a claim for custody of or access to a child that was not in the original application or answer, the amended application or amended answer shall be accompanied by the applicable documents referred to in Rule 35.1.

How Amendment is Shown

(4) An amendment shall be clearly shown by underlining all changes, and the rule or order permitting the amendment and the date of the amendment shall be noted in the margin of each amended page.

O. Reg. 91/03, s. 3; 6/10, s. 4

RULE 12 — WITHDRAWING, COMBINING OR SPLITTING CASES

Withdrawing Application, Answer or Reply

12. (1) A party who does not want to continue with all or part of a case may withdraw all or part of the application, answer or reply by serving a notice of withdrawal (Form 12) on every other party and filing it.

Withdrawal — Special Party's Application, Answer or Reply

(2) A special party's application, answer or reply may be withdrawn (whether in whole or in part) only with the court's permission, and the notice of motion for permission shall be served on every other party and on,

(a) the Children's Lawyer, if the special party is a child;

(b) the Public Guardian and Trustee, if the special party is not a child.

Costs Payable on Withdrawal

(3) A party who withdraws all or part of an application, answer or reply shall pay the costs of every other party in relation to the withdrawn application, answer, reply or part, up to the date of the withdrawal, unless the court orders or the parties agree otherwise.

Costs on Withdrawal by Government Agency

(4) Despite subrule (3), if the party is a government agency, costs are in the court's discretion.

Combining and Splitting Cases

(5) If it would be more convenient to hear two or more cases, claims or issues together or to split a case into two or more separate cases, claims or issues, the court may, on motion, order accordingly.

Splitting Divorce from Other Issues

(6) The court may, on motion, make an order splitting a divorce from the other issues in a case if,

(a) neither spouse will be disadvantaged by the order; and

(b) reasonable arrangements have been made for the support of any children of the marriage.

RULE 13 — FINANCIAL DISCLOSURE [HEADING AMENDED O. REG. 69/15, S. 3(1).]

Financial Statement with Application, Answer or Motion

13. (1) If an application, answer or motion contains a claim for support, a property claim, or a claim for exclusive possession of the matrimonial home and its contents,

(a) the party making the claim shall serve and file a financial statement (Form 13 or 13.1) with the document that contains the claim; and

(b) the party against whom the claim is made shall serve and file a financial statement within the time for serving and filing an answer, reply or affidavit or other document responding to the motion, whether the party is serving an answer, reply or affidavit or other document responding to the motion or not.

Form 13 for Support Claim Without Property Claim

(1.1) If the application, answer or motion contains a claim for support but does not contain a property claim or a claim for exclusive possession of the matrimonial home and its contents, the financial statement used by the parties under these rules shall be in Form 13.

Form 13.1 for Property Claim With or Without Support Claim

(1.2) If the application, answer or motion contains a property claim or a claim for exclusive possession of the matrimonial home and its contents, the financial statement used by the parties under these rules shall be in Form 13.1, whether a claim for support is also included or not.

Exception, Certain Support Claims

(1.3) If the only claim for support contained in the application, answer or motion is a claim for child support in the amount specified in the table of the applicable child support guidelines, the party making the claim is not required to file a financial statement, unless the application, answer or motion also contains a property claim or a claim for exclusive possession of the matrimonial home and its contents.

Exception, Family Arbitration Claim

(1.4) If the only claim contained in the application, answer or motion is a claim under the *Arbitration Act, 1991* or the *Family Law Act* relating to a family arbitration, family arbitration agreement or family arbitration award, the party making the claim is not required to file a financial statement, unless the court orders otherwise.

Claim for Payment Order under CFSA

(2) If an application, answer or notice of motion contains a claim for a payment order under section 108 of the *Child, Youth and Family Services Act, 2017*, clause (1)(a) does not apply to the children's aid society but clause (1)(b) applies to the party against whom the claim is made.

Financial Statements in Custody and Access Cases

(3) If an application, answer or motion contains a claim for custody of or access to a child and this rule does not otherwise require the parties to serve and file financial statements, the court may order each party to serve and file a financial statement in Form 13 within the time decided by the court.

Additional Required Financial Disclosure, Support Claim

(3.1) A party who is required under subrules (1) to (3) to serve and file a financial statement in relation to a claim for support shall, before the deadline set out in subrule (3.2), serve with the financial statement the following information, unless the court orders otherwise:

1. The income and financial information referred to in subsection 21(1) of the child support guidelines.

2. If the party became unemployed within the last three years,

i. a complete copy of the party's Record of Employment, or other evidence of termination, and

ii. a statement of any benefits or income that the party is still entitled to receive from his or her former employer despite or as a result of the termination.

3. In the case of a claim for the support of a child, proof of the amount of any special or extraordinary expenses, within the meaning of section 7 of the child support guidelines.

Timing of Requirement

(3.2) The party shall serve the information referred to in subrule (3.1),

(a) with the financial statement, if the application, answer or motion contains a claim for support but does not contain a property claim; or

(b) with the documents required to be served under subrule (3.3) or (3.4), as the case may be, if the application, answer or motion contains a property claim.

***Additional Required Financial Disclosure, Claim under Part I of the* Family Law Act**

(3.3) A party who is required under subrules (1) to (3) to serve and file a financial statement in relation to a claim under Part I of the *Family Law Act* shall, no later than 30 days after the day by which the financial statement is required to be served, serve on the other party the following information, unless the court orders otherwise:

1. The statement issued closest to the valuation date for each bank account or other account in a financial institution, pension, registered retirement or other savings plan, and any other savings or investments in which the party had an interest on that date.

2. A copy of an application or request made by the party to obtain a valuation of his or her own pension benefits, deferred pension or pension, as the case may be, if any, as of the valuation date.

3. A copy of the Municipal Property Assessment Corporation's assessment of any real property in Ontario in which the party had a right or interest on the valuation date, for the year in which that date occurred.

4. If the party owned a life insurance policy on the valuation date, the statement issued closest to that date showing the face amount and cash surrender value, if any, of the policy, and the named beneficiary.

5. If the party had an interest in a sole proprietorship or was self-employed on the valuation date, for each of the three years preceding that date,

i. the financial statements of the party's business or professional practice, other than a partnership, and

ii. a copy of every personal income tax return filed by the party, including any materials that were filed with the return.

6. If the party was a partner in a partnership on the valuation date, a copy of the partnership agreement and, for each of the three years preceding the valuation date,

i. a copy of every personal income tax return filed by the party, including any materials that were filed with the return, and

ii. the financial statements of the partnership.

7. If the party had an interest in a corporation on the valuation date, documentation showing the number and types of shares of the corporation and any other interests in the corporation that were owned by the party on that date.

8. If the corporation in which a party had an interest was privately held, for each of the three years preceding the valuation date,

i. the financial statements for the corporation and its subsidiaries, and

ii. if the interest was a majority interest, a copy of every income tax return filed by the corporation.

9. If the party was a beneficiary under a trust on the valuation date, a copy of the trust settlement agreement and the trust's financial statements for each of the three years preceding that date.

10. Documentation showing the value, on the valuation date, of any property not referred to in paragraphs 1 to 9 in which the party had an interest on that date.

11. Documentation that supports a claim, if any, for an exclusion under subsection 4(2) of the *Family Law Act*.

12. The statements or invoices issued closest to the valuation date in relation to any mortgage, line of credit, credit card balance or other debt owed by the party on that date.

13. Any available documentation showing the value, on the date of marriage, of property that the party owned or in which he or she had an interest on that date, and the amount of any debts owed by the party on that date.

Additional Required Financial Disclosure, Other Property Claims

(3.4) A party who is required under subrules (1) to (3) to serve and file a financial statement in relation to a property claim other than a claim under Part I of the *Family Law Act* shall, no later than 30 days after the day by which the financial statement is required to be served, serve on the other party any information necessary to support the claim, unless the court orders otherwise.

Financial Statement with Motion to Change Temporary Support Order

(4) Subject to subrule (1.3), the following rules respecting financial statements apply if a motion contains a request for a change in a temporary support order:

1. The party making the motion shall serve and file a financial statement (Form 13 or 13.1) with the notice of motion.

2. The party responding to the motion shall serve and file a financial statement as soon as possible after being served with the notice of motion, but in any event no later than two days before the motion date. Any affidavit in response to the motion shall be served and filed at the same time as the financial statement.

Exception — By Consent

(4.1) Parties to a consent motion to change a temporary support order do not need to serve and file financial statements if they file a consent agreeing not to serve and file them.

Financial Statement with Motion to Change Final Support Order or Support Agreement

(4.2) Subject to subrule (1.3), the following rules respecting financial statements apply if a motion is made under rule 15 requesting a change to a final support order or a support agreement:

1. The party making the motion shall serve and file a financial statement (Form 13 or 13.1) with the motion to change (Form 15).

2. The party responding to the motion shall serve and file a financial statement within the time for serving and filing the response to motion to change (Form 15B) or returning the consent motion to change (Form 15C) to the party making the motion, as set out in subrule 15(10). Any response to motion to change (Form 15B) shall be served and filed at the same time as the financial statement.

3. Parties who bring the motion by filing a consent motion to change (Form 15C) shall each file a financial statement with the form, unless they indicate in the form that they agree not to do so.

4. Parties who bring the motion by filing a consent motion to change child support (Form 15D) do not need to serve or file financial statements.

Financial Statement Required by Response

(4.3) Subrules (4) and (4.1), or subrule (4.2), as the case may be, apply with necessary changes if a party makes a motion to change an order or agreement for which the party is not required by this rule to file a financial statement, and the party responding to the motion requests a change to a support order or support agreement.

No Financial Statement from Assignee

(5) The assignee of a support order is not required to serve and file a financial statement under subrule (4) or (4.2).

Additional Required Financial Disclosure, Motion to Change Support

(5.0.1) A party who is required under subrules (4) to (4.3) to serve and file a financial statement shall serve with the financial statement the following information, unless the court orders otherwise:

1. The documents referred to in subrule (3.1).

2. A current statement of arrears from the Family Responsibility Office.

3. One of the following for each year for which the party is seeking to change or cancel arrears, as proof of the party's income:

i. The party's income tax return and,

A. the party's notice of assessment and, if any, notice of reassessment, or

B. if a notice of assessment and a notice of reassessment are unavailable for the year, a copy of the Income and Deductions printout provided by the Canada Revenue Agency for the party.

ii. If the party is not required to and has chosen not to file an income tax return because of the *Indian Act* (Canada), some other proof of income.

Requirement to Certify Financial Disclosure

(5.0.2) A party who is required to serve documents under subrule (3.1), (3.3), (3.4) or (5.0.1) shall confirm service by,

(a) serving a certificate of financial disclosure (Form 13A) together with the documents; and

(b) filing the certificate no later than,

(i) seven days before a case conference, in the case of the applicant or the party making the motion, as the case may be, and

(ii) four days before the case conference, in the case of the other party.

Financial Statement with Motion to Refrain

(5.1) A payor who makes a motion to require the Director of the Family Responsibility Office to refrain from suspending the payor's driver's licence shall, in accordance with subsection 35(7) of the *Family Responsibility and Support Arrears Enforcement Act, 1996*, serve and file with the notice of motion,

(a) a financial statement (Form 13 or 13.1) or a financial statement incorporated as Form 4 in Ontario Regulation 167/97 (*General*) made under that Act; and

(b) the proof of income specified in section 15 of the regulation referred to in clause (a).

(6) [Repealed O. Reg. 69/15, s. 3(7).]

Requirements for Filing

(7) The clerk shall not accept the financial statement of a party making or responding to a claim for support unless the following are attached to the form:

1. Proof of the party's current income.

2. One of the following, as proof of the party's income for the three previous years:

i. For each of the three previous taxation years,

A. the party's notice of assessment and, if any, notice of reassessment, or

B. if a notice of assessment and a notice of reassessment are unavailable for a taxation year, a copy of the Income and Deductions printout provided by the Canada Revenue Agency for the party for the taxation year.

ii. If the party swears or affirms a statement in the form that he or she is not required to and has chosen not to file an income tax return because of the *Indian Act* (Canada), some other proof of income for the three previous years.

Exception

(7.0.1) Subrule (7) does not apply to a financial statement filed under subrule (5.1).

Documents that are not Required to be Filed

(7.1) The following documents are not required to be filed in the continuing record unless the court orders otherwise:

1. Income tax returns, except in the case of a filing under subrule (5.1).

2. Any other document referred to in subrule (3.1), (3.3), (3.4) or (5.0.1), unless these rules provide otherwise.

No Financial Disclosure by Consent — Spousal Support in Divorce

(8) Parties to a claim for spousal support under the *Divorce Act* (Canada) do not need to serve and file financial statements or provide additional financial disclosure under this rule if they file a consent,

(a) agreeing to not serve and file financial statements or provide additional financial disclosure under this rule; or

(b) agreeing to a specified amount of support, or to no support.

(9) [Repealed O. Reg. 151/08, s. 2(8).]

Documents not to be Filed without Financial Statement

(10) The clerk shall not accept a document for filing without a financial statement if these rules require the document to be filed with a financial statement.

Insufficient Financial Information

(11) If a party believes that the financial disclosure provided by another party under this rule, whether in a financial statement or otherwise, does not provide enough information for a full understanding of the other party's financial circumstances,

(a) the party shall ask the other party to give the necessary additional information; and

(b) if the other party does not give it within seven days, the court may, on motion, order the other party to give the information or to serve and file a new financial statement.

Same

(11.1) For greater certainty, a motion form (Form 14B) may be used if making a motion for an order under subrule (3.1), (3.3), (3.4) or (5.0.1) or an order under clause (11)(b).

Updating Financial Statement

(12) Before any case conference, motion, settlement conference or trial, each party shall update the information in any financial statement that is more than 30 days old by serving and filing,

(a) a new financial statement; or

(b) an affidavit saying that the information in the last statement has not changed and is still true.

Minor Changes

(12.1) If there have been minor changes but no major changes to the information in a party's past statement, the party may serve and file, instead of a new financial statement, an affidavit with details of the changes.

Time for Updating

(12.2) The material described in subrules (12) and (12.1) shall be served and filed as follows:

1. For a case conference or settlement conference requested by a party, the requesting party shall serve and file at least seven days before the conference date and the other party shall serve and file at least four days before that date.

2. For a case conference or settlement conference that is not requested by a party, the applicant shall serve and file at least seven days before the conference date and the respondent shall serve and file at least four days before that date.

3. For a motion, the party making the motion shall serve and file at least seven days before the motion date and the other party shall serve and file at least four days before that date.

4. For a trial, the applicant shall serve and file at least seven days before the trial date and the respondent shall serve and file at least four days before that date.

Questioning on Financial Statement

(13) A party may be questioned under rule 20 on a financial statement provided under this rule, but only after a request for information has been made under clause (11)(a).

Updating Certificate of Financial Disclosure

(13.1) Before any settlement conference or trial management conference, a party who has served a corrected, updated or new version of a document referred to in subrule (3.1), (3.3), (3.4) or (5.0.1) in accordance with subrule (15), or additional documents in accordance with subrule (16), shall serve and file an updated certificate of financial disclosure (Form 13A), no later than,

(a) seven days before the conference, in the case of the party requesting the conference or, if the conference is not requested by a party, the applicant or the party making the motion, as the case may be; and

(b) four days before the conference, in the case of the other party.

Net Family Property Statement

(14) Each party to a property claim under Part I of the *Family Law Act* shall serve and file a net family property statement (Form 13B) or, if the party has already served a net family property statement, an affidavit saying that the information in that statement has not changed and is still true,

(a) not less than 30 days before a settlement conference; and

(b) not more than 30 days and not less than seven days before a trial.

Exception, Family Arbitration Claim

(14.1) Subrule (14) does not apply if the property claim arises within a claim under the *Arbitration Act, 1991* or the *Family Law Act* relating to a family arbitration, family arbitration agreement or family arbitration award.

Comparison of Net Family Properties, Joint

(14.2) Parties who have served and filed net family property statements in accordance with subrule (14) shall file a joint comparison of net family property statements (Form 13C) no later than seven days before a settlement conference, subject to subrule (14.3).

Comparison of Net Family Properties, Separate

(14.3) If the parties fail to agree on a joint comparison of net family properties, each party shall serve and file his or her own comparison of net family property statements (Form 13C) no later than,

(a) seven days before a settlement conference, in the case of the party requesting the conference or, if the settlement conference is not requested by a party, the applicant or the party making the motion, as the case may be; and

(b) four days before the settlement conference, in the case of the other party.

Duty to Correct, Update Documents

(15) As soon as a party discovers that a document that he or she has served under this rule is incorrect, incomplete or out of date, the party shall serve on the other party and, if applicable, file, a corrected, updated or new document, as the circumstances require.

Duty to Address Omissions in Financial Disclosure

(16) As soon as a party discovers that he or she failed to serve a document required to be served under subrule (3.1), (3.3), (3.4) or (5.0.1), the party shall serve the document on the other party.

Order, if Document not Provided

(17) If a party has not served or filed a document in accordance with the requirements of this rule or an Act or regulation, the court may on motion order the party to serve or file the document and, if the court makes that order, it shall also order the party to pay costs.

Other Obligations Continue to Apply

(18) The duty to provide information under this rule does not affect any other duty set out in any other Act or regulation for the party to provide information to the other party in relation to a claim to which this rule applies.

O. Reg. 544/99, s. 5; 202/01, s. 3; 92/03, s. 1; 89/04, s. 5; 76/06, s. 5; 151/08, s. 2(1)–(3), (5)–(9); 6/10, s. 5; 52/10, s. 1; 388/12, s. 5; 322/13, s. 7; 142/14, s. 6; 69/15, s. 3; 298/18, s. 9

RULE 14 — MOTIONS FOR TEMPORARY ORDERS [HEADING AMENDED O. REG. 89/04, S. 6(1).]

When to Make Motion

14. (1) A person who wants any of the following may make a motion:

1. A temporary order for a claim made in an application.

2. Directions on how to carry on the case.

3. A change in a temporary order.

Who May Make Motion

(2) A motion may be made by a party to the case or by a person with an interest in the case.

Parties to Motion

(3) A person who is affected by a motion is also a party, for purposes of the motion only, but this does not apply to a child affected by a motion relating to custody, access, child protection, adoption or child support.

No Motion Before Case Conference on Substantive Issues Completed

(4) No notice of motion or supporting evidence may be served and no motion may be heard before a conference dealing with the substantive issues in the case has been completed.

(4.1) [Repealed O. Reg. 89/04, s. 6(3).]

Urgency, Hardship Etc.

(4.2) Subrule (4) does not apply if the court is of the opinion that there is a situation of urgency or hardship or that a case conference is not required for some other reason in the interest of justice.

(5) [Repealed O. Reg. 89/04, s. 6(5).]

Other Motions

(6) Subrule (4) does not apply to a motion,

(a) to change a temporary order under subrule 25(19) (fraud, mistake, lack of notice);

(b) for a contempt order under rule 31 or an order striking out a document under subrule (22);

(c) for summary judgment under rule 16;

(d) to require the Director of the Family Responsibility Office to refrain from suspending a licence;

(e) to limit or stay a support order, the enforcement of arrears under a support order, or an alternative payment order under the *Family Responsibility and Support Arrears Enforcement Act, 1996*;

(e.1) in a child protection case;

(e.2) made without notice, made on consent, that is unopposed or that is limited to procedural, uncomplicated or unopposed matters (Form 14B);

(e.3) made in an appeal;

(f) for an oral hearing under subrule 32.1(10), 37(8) or 37.1(8); or

(g) to set aside the registration of an interjurisdictional support order made outside Canada.

Motion Involving Complicated Matters

(7) The judge who hears a motion involving complicated matters may,

(a) order that the motion or any part of it be heard as a trial; and

(b) give any directions that are necessary.

Motion by Telephone or Video Conference

(8) A party who wants a motion to be heard by telephone or video conference shall,

(a) obtain an appointment from the clerk for the hearing of the motion;

(b) make the necessary arrangements;

(c) serve a notice of the appointment and arrangements on all other parties, and file it; and

(d) participate in the motion as the notice specifies.

Documents for a Motion

(9) A motion, whether made with or without notice,

(a) requires a notice of motion (Form 14) and an affidavit (Form 14A); and

(b) may be supported by additional evidence.

Procedural, Uncomplicated or Unopposed Matters — Motion Form

(10) If a motion is limited to procedural, uncomplicated or unopposed matters, the party making the motion may use a motion form (Form 14B) instead of a notice of motion and affidavit.

(10.1) [Repealed O. Reg. 298/18, s. 10(1).]

(10.2) [Repealed O. Reg. 298/18, s. 10(1).]

Motion with Notice

(11) A party making a motion with notice shall,

(a) serve the documents mentioned in subrule (9) or (10) on all other parties, not later than six days before the motion date;

(b) file the documents as soon as possible after service, but not later than four days before the motion date;

(c) confer or attempt to confer orally or in writing with every other party about the issues that are in dispute in the motion, subject to a party being prohibited from such communication by court order;

(d) before giving the clerk confirmation of the motion in Form 14C under clause (e), give a copy of the confirmation of motion to every other party using mail, fax, email or any other method, except in a child protection case; and

(e) not later than 2 p.m. three days before the motion date, give the clerk the confirmation of motion (Form 14C) by,

(i) delivering it to the court office, or

(ii) if available in the court office, sending it by fax or by email.

Effect of Failure to Confirm

(11.1) Unless the court orders otherwise, a motion shall not be heard if confirmation of the motion is not given to the clerk in accordance with clause (11)(e).

Party to Update Confirmation

(11.2) If a party who has given a confirmation of motion determines at any time before the motion is heard that the confirmation is no longer correct, the party shall, if possible, immediately,

(a) give a copy of the corrected confirmation of motion in Form 14C to every other party using a method listed in clause (11)(d) and subsequently give the clerk the corrected confirmation of motion by a method listed in clause (11)(e); or

(b) in a child protection case, give the clerk a corrected confirmation of motion in Form 14C by a method listed in clause (11)(e).

Response to Notice of Motion

(11.3) A response by a person to a motion made using a notice of motion (Form 14) shall be served and filed not later than four days before the motion date.

Response to Motion Form

(11.4) A response by a person to a motion made using a motion form (Form 14B) shall be served and filed not later than four days after the motion form is served on the person.

Reply to Response Permitted, Notice of Motion

(11.5) A party who uses a notice of motion (Form 14) and who is served with a response to it may serve and file a reply not later than 2 p.m. three days before the motion date.

Reply to Response Not Permitted, Motion Form

(11.6) A party who uses a motion form (Form 14B) and who is served with a response to it may not serve or file a reply.

Motion Without Notice

(12) A motion may be made without notice if,

(a) the nature or circumstances of the motion make notice unnecessary or not reasonably possible;

(b) there is an immediate danger of a child's removal from Ontario, and the delay involved in serving a notice of motion would probably have serious consequences;

(c) there is an immediate danger to the health or safety of a child or of the party making the motion, and the delay involved in serving a notice of motion would probably have serious consequences; or

(d) service of a notice of motion would probably have serious consequences.

Filing for Motion Without Notice

(13) The documents for use on a motion without notice shall be filed on or before the motion date, unless the court orders otherwise.

Order Made on Motion Without Notice

(14) An order made on motion without notice (Form 14D) shall require the matter to come back to the court and, if possible, to the same judge, within 14 days or on a date chosen by the court.

Service of Order Made Without Notice

(15) An order made on motion without notice shall be served immediately on all parties affected, together with all documents used on the motion, unless the court orders otherwise.

Withdrawing a Motion

(16) A party making a motion may withdraw it in the same way as an application or answer is withdrawn under rule 12.

Evidence on a Motion

(17) Evidence on a motion may be given by any one or more of the following methods:

1. An affidavit or other admissible evidence in writing.

2. A transcript of the questions and answers on a questioning under rule 20.

3. With the court's permission, oral evidence.

Affidavit Based on Personal Knowledge

(18) An affidavit for use on a motion shall, as much as possible, contain only information within the personal knowledge of the person signing the affidavit.

Affidavit Based on Other Information

(19) The affidavit may also contain information that the person learned from someone else, but only if,

(a) the source of the information is identified by name and the affidavit states that the person signing it believes the information is true; and

(b) in addition, if the motion is a contempt motion under rule 31, the information is not likely to be disputed.

Restrictions on Evidence

(20) The following restrictions apply to evidence for use on a motion, unless the court orders otherwise:

1. The party making the motion shall serve all the evidence in support of the motion with the notice of motion.

2. The party responding to the motion shall then serve all the evidence in response.

3. The party making the motion may then serve evidence replying to any new matters raised by the evidence served by the party responding to the motion.

4. No other evidence may be used.

No Motions Without Court's Permission

(21) If a party tries to delay the case or add to its costs or in any other way to abuse the court's process by making numerous motions without merit, the court may order the party not to make any other motions in the case without the court's permission.

(22) [Repealed O. Reg. 322/13, s. 8(2).]

(23) [Repealed O. Reg. 322/13, s. 8(2).]

Motion Relating to Family Arbitration

(24) A party who wishes to make a claim under the *Arbitration Act, 1991* or the *Family Law Act* relating to a family arbitration, family arbitration agreement or family arbitration award that must or may be commenced by way of a motion may do so under this rule, even if the order being sought is a final order and, for the purpose, this rule applies with the following and any other necessary changes:

1. In addition to the documents referred to in subrule (9) or (10), the motion also requires,

   i. copies of the certificates of independent legal advice required by the *Family Law Act* for the parties,

   ii. a copy of the family arbitration agreement, and

   iii. if an award has been made, the original award or a certified copy.

2. The documents referred to in subparagraphs 1 i, ii and iii shall be served and filed in accordance with subrule (11).

3. In the case of a motion to enforce a family arbitration award under section 59.8 of the *Family Law Act*, subrules (12) to (15) do not apply.

O. Reg. 544/99, s. 6; 202/01, s. 4; 56/03, s. 2; 91/03, s. 4; 89/04, s. 6; 151/08, s. 3; 383/11, s. 3; 388/12, s. 6; 322/13, s. 8; 142/14, s. 7; 298/18, s. 10

RULE 15 — MOTIONS TO CHANGE A FINAL ORDER OR AGREEMENT [HEADING AMENDED O. REG. 89/04, S. 7(1).]

15. (0.1) [Repealed O. Reg. 151/08, s. 4.]

(0.2) [Repealed O. Reg. 151/08, s. 4.]

Definition

(1) In this rule,

"assignee" means an agency or person to whom a support order or agreement that is the subject of a motion under this rule is assigned under the *Family Law Act* or the *Divorce Act* (Canada).

Application

(2) Subject to subrule (3), this rule only applies to a motion to change,

(a) a final order; or

(b) an agreement for support filed under section 35 of the *Family Law Act.*

Same, Notice of Recalculation

(2.1) Subrule (2) applies regardless of whether a child support obligation set out in the order or agreement has been recalculated under section 39.1 of the *Family Law Act.*

Exception

(3) This rule does not apply to a motion or application to change an order made under the *Child, Youth and Family Services Act, 2017*, other than a final order made under section 102 of that Act.

Place of Motion

(4) Rule 5 (where a case starts) applies to a motion to change a final order or agreement as if the motion were a new case.

Motion to Change

(5) Subject to subrules (17) and (18), a party who wants to ask the court to change a final order or agreement shall serve and file,

(a) a motion to change (Form 15); and

(b) a change information form (Form 15A), with all required attachments.

Claim for Custody or Access

(5.1) If the motion includes a claim for custody of or access to a child, the documents referred to in subrule (5) shall be accompanied by the applicable documents referred to in Rule 35.1.

Service to Include Blank Forms

(6) The party making the motion shall serve on the other party a blank response to motion to change (Form 15B) and a blank consent motion to change (Form 15C) together with the documents referred to in subrule (5).

Special Service

(7) The documents referred to in subrules (5), (5.1) and (6) shall be served by special service (subrule 6(3)), and not by regular service.

Exception

(8) Despite subrule (7), service on the persons mentioned in subrule 8(6) (officials, agencies, etc.) may be made by regular service.

Service on Family Responsibility Office Required

(8.1) The documents referred to in subrule (5) shall be served on the Director of the Family Responsibility Office if the motion to change includes a request to change a child support obligation that,

(a) is set out in an order made under the *Divorce Act* (Canada); and

(b) was recalculated under section 39.1 of the *Family Law Act* within the 35-day period before the motion is filed.

Response or Consent to Motion

(9) The following rules apply to a party who is served with a motion to change a final order or agreement:

1. If the party does not agree to the change or if the party wants to ask the court to make an additional or a different change to the final order or agreement, the party shall

serve and file a response to motion to change (Form 15B), with all required attachments, within the time set out in clause (10)(a) or (b), as the case may be.

2. If the party agrees to the change or if the parties agree to a different change, the party shall complete the applicable portions of the consent motion to change (Form 15C) and shall, within the time set out in clause (10)(a) or (b), as the case may be,

i. return a signed copy of the consent motion to change to the party making the motion, and

ii. provide a copy of the signed consent motion to change to the assignee, if any.

Same

(10) The documents referred to in paragraphs 1 and 2 of subrule (9) shall be served and filed or returned and provided,

(a) no later than 30 days after the party responding to the motion receives the motion to change and the supporting documents, if that party resides in Canada or the United States of America; or

(b) no later than 60 days after the party responding to the motion receives the motion to change and the supporting documents, in any other case.

Service on Assignee Required

(11) In a motion to change a final order or agreement that has been assigned to an assignee, a party shall, in serving documents under subrule (5) or paragraph 1 of subrule (9), serve the documents on the assignee as if the assignee were also a party.

Assignee May Become Party

(12) On serving and filing a notice claiming a financial interest in the motion, an assignee becomes a respondent to the extent of the financial interest.

Sanctions if Assignee Not Served

(13) If an assignee is not served as required by subrule (11), the following rules apply:

1. The court may at any time, on motion by the assignee with notice to the other parties, set aside the changed order to the extent that it affects the assignee's financial interest.

2. The party who asked for the change has the burden of proving that the changed order should not be set aside.

3. If the changed order is set aside, the assignee is entitled to full recovery of its costs of the motion to set aside, unless the court orders otherwise.

No Response or Consent

(14) The consequences set out in paragraphs 1 to 4 of subrule 1(8.4) apply, with necessary changes, if a party does not serve and file a response to motion to change (Form 15B) or return a consent motion to change (Form 15C) to the party making the motion as required under subrule (9).

Same, Request for Order

(15) If a party does not serve and file a response to motion to change (Form 15B) or return a consent motion to change (Form 15C) to the party making the motion as required under subrule (9), or if the party's response is struck out by an order, the party making the motion to change may file a motion form (Form 14B) asking that the court make the order requested in the materials filed by the party, unless an assignee has filed a notice of financial interest in the motion and opposes the change.

Consent to Motion

(16) If a party returns to the party making the motion a consent motion to change (Form 15C) in accordance with subparagraph 2 i of subrule (9), the party making the motion shall complete and file the consent motion to change and, unless any assignee refuses to consent to the change being requested, the party making the motion shall file with the consent motion to change,

(a) a motion form (Form 14B) asking that the court make the order described in the consent motion to change;

(b) five copies of a draft order;

(c) a stamped envelope addressed to each party and to the assignee, if any; and

(d) if the order that is agreed on relates in whole or in part to a support obligation,

(i) a support deduction order information form prescribed under the *Family Responsibility and Support Arrears Enforcement Act, 1996*, and

(ii) a draft support deduction order.

Motion to Change on Consent

(17) Subject to subrule (18), if the parties to a final order or agreement want to ask the court to change the final order or agreement and the parties and any assignee agree to the change, the parties shall file,

(a) a change information form (Form 15A), with all required attachments;

(b) a consent motion to change (Form 15C);

(c) a motion form (Form 14B) asking that the court make the order described in the consent motion to change;

(d) five copies of a draft order;

(e) a stamped envelope addressed to each party and to the assignee, if any; and

(f) if the order that is agreed on relates in whole or in part to a support obligation,

(i) a support deduction order information form prescribed under the *Family Responsibility and Support Arrears Enforcement Act, 1996*, and

(ii) a draft support deduction order.

Motion to Change on Consent — Child Support Only

(18) If the parties to a final order or agreement want to ask the court to change the final order or agreement in relation only to a child support obligation, and the parties and any assignee agree to the change, the parties shall file,

(a) a consent motion to change child support (Form 15D), with all required attachments;

(b) five copies of a draft order;

(c) a stamped envelope addressed to each party and to the assignee, if any;

(d) a support deduction order information form prescribed under the *Family Responsibility and Support Arrears Enforcement Act, 1996*; and

(e) a draft support deduction order.

Consent After Response Filed

(19) If, at any time after a party has served and filed a response under paragraph 1 of subrule (9) and before the motion to change is heard, the parties and any assignee agree to an order that changes the final order or agreement that is the subject of the motion, the parties may proceed on consent by filing,

(a) a consent motion to change (Form 15C);

(b) a motion form (Form 14B) asking that the court make the order described in the consent motion to change;

(c) five copies of a draft order;

(d) a stamped envelope addressed to each party and to the assignee, if any; and

(e) if the order that is agreed on relates in whole or in part to a support obligation,

(i) a support deduction order information form prescribed under the *Family Responsibility and Support Arrears Enforcement Act, 1996*, and

(ii) a draft support deduction order.

Order, Agreement to be Attached

(20) A copy of any existing order or agreement that deals with custody, access or support shall be attached to every change information form (Form 15A) or consent motion to change child support (Form 15D).

Change not in Accordance with Child Support Guidelines

(21) Unless a motion to change a child support order or agreement is proceeding on the consent of the parties and any assignee, if a party asks that an order be made under this rule that is not in accordance with the tables in the applicable child support guidelines, the support recipient and the support payor shall each serve and file the evidence required by the following sections of the applicable child support guidelines, or the evidence that is otherwise necessary to satisfy the court that it should make the order asked for:

1. Section 4 (income over $150,000).

2. Section 5 (step-parent).

3. Section 7 (special expenses).

4. Section 8 (split custody).

5. Section 9 (shared custody).

6. Section 10 (undue hardship).

7. Section 21 (income and financial information) subject to subrule (21.1).

Financial Disclosure

(21.1) Subrule (21) does not require that any documents already served on the other party under subrule 13(5.0.1) be served again, but any such documents are required to be filed.

Affidavit May Be Filed

(22) A party or parties who want to ask the court to change a final order or agreement may, instead of using a change information form (Form 15A), use an affidavit containing evidence necessary to satisfy the court that it should make the order asked for and, in that case, these rules apply to the affidavit as if it were a change information form.

Same

(23) A party who responds to a motion to change a final order or agreement by serving and filing a response to motion to change (Form 15B) may use an affidavit to provide evidence supporting his or her position instead of relying on the relevant portions of the form to provide the evidence or in addition to those portions of the form and, in that case, the affidavit is deemed to be part of the form.

Requirements for Affidavit

(24) Subrules 14(18) and (19) apply with necessary changes to an affidavit provided in accordance with subrule (22) or (23).

Powers of Court — Motion on Consent or Unopposed

(25) If a motion to change a final order or agreement proceeds on the consent of the parties and any assignee or is unopposed, the clerk shall present the filed materials to a judge and the judge may,

(a) make the order asked for;

(b) require one or both parties to file further material; or

(c) require one or both parties to come to court.

Powers of Court — Directions

(26) If the court is of the opinion that a motion, whether proceeding on consent or not, cannot be properly dealt with because of the material filed, because of the matters in dispute or for any other reason, the court may give directions, including directions for a trial.

Application of Subrule 14(21)

(27) Subrule 14(21) applies with necessary changes to a motion to change a final order or agreement.

Motion Under Rule 14

(28) A motion under rule 14 may be made on a motion to change a final order or agreement.

Access to Listed Documents

(29) Subrule 19(2) (access to listed documents) applies with necessary changes to a document mentioned in a form or affidavit used under this rule.

O. Reg. 544/99, s. 7; 89/04, s. 7; 519/06, s. 5; 151/08, s. 4; 6/10, s. 6; 322/13, s. 9; 142/14, s. 8; 69/15, s. 4; 235/16, s. 2; 298/18, s. 11

RULE 16 — SUMMARY JUDGMENT

When Available

16. (1) After the respondent has served an answer or after the time for serving an answer has expired, a party may make a motion for summary judgment for a final order without a trial on all or part of any claim made or any defence presented in the case.

Available in Any Case Except Divorce

(2) A motion for summary judgment under subrule (1) may be made in any case (including a child protection case) that does not include a divorce claim.

Divorce Claim

(3) In a case that includes a divorce claim, the procedure provided in rule 36 (divorce) for an uncontested divorce may be used, or the divorce claim may be split from the rest of the case under subrule 12(6).

Evidence Required

(4) The party making the motion shall serve an affidavit or other evidence that sets out specific facts showing that there is no genuine issue requiring a trial.

Evidence of Responding Party

(4.1) In response to the affidavit or other evidence served by the party making the motion, the party responding to the motion may not rest on mere allegations or denials but shall set out, in an affidavit or other evidence, specific facts showing that there is a genuine issue for trial.

Evidence not from Personal Knowledge

(5) If a party's evidence is not from a person who has personal knowledge of the facts in dispute, the court may draw conclusions unfavourable to the party.

No Issue for Trial

(6) If there is no genuine issue requiring a trial of a claim or defence, the court shall make a final order accordingly.

Powers

(6.1) In determining whether there is a genuine issue requiring a trial, the court shall consider the evidence submitted by the parties, and the court may exercise any of the following powers for the purpose, unless it is in the interest of justice for such powers to be exercised only at a trial:

1. Weighing the evidence.

2. Evaluating the credibility of a deponent.

3. Drawing any reasonable inference from the evidence.

Oral Evidence (Mini-Trial)

(6.2) The court may, for the purposes of exercising any of the powers set out in subrule (6.1), order that oral evidence be presented by one or more parties, with or without time limits on its presentation.

Only Issue Amount of Entitlement

(7) If the only genuine issue is the amount to which a party is entitled, the court shall order a trial to decide the amount.

Only Issue Question of Law

(8) If the only genuine issue is a question of law, the court shall decide the issue and make a final order accordingly.

Order Giving Directions

(9) If the court does not make a final order, or makes an order for a trial of an issue, the court may, in addition to exercising a power listed in subrule 1(7.2),

(a) specify what facts are not in dispute, state the issues and give directions about how and when the case will go to trial (in which case the order governs how the trial proceeds, unless the trial judge orders otherwise);

(b) give directions; and

(c) impose conditions (for example, require a party to pay money into court as security, or limit a party's pretrial disclosure).

(10) [Repealed O. Reg. 69/15, s. 5(4).]

(11) [Repealed O. Reg. 69/15, s. 5(4).]

Motion for Summary Decision on Legal Issue

(12) The court may, on motion,

(a) decide a question of law before trial, if the decision may dispose of all or part of the case, substantially shorten the trial or save substantial costs;

(b) strike out an application, answer or reply because it sets out no reasonable claim or defence in law; or

(c) dismiss or suspend a case because,

(i) the court has no jurisdiction over it,

(ii) a party has no legal capacity to carry on the case,

(iii) there is another case going on between the same parties about the same matter, or

(iv) the case is a waste of time, a nuisance or an abuse of the court process.

Evidence on Motion for Summary Decision of Legal Issue

(13) On a motion under subrule (12), evidence is admissible only if the parties consent or the court gives permission.

O. Reg. 91/03, s. 5; 69/15, s. 5

RULE 17 — CONFERENCES

Conferences in Defended Cases

17. (1) Subject to subrule (1.1), in each case in which an answer is filed, a judge shall conduct at least one conference.

Exception, Case Conference Optional in Child Protection Case

(1.1) In a child protection case, a case conference may be conducted if,

(a) a party requests it; or

(b) the court considers it appropriate.

Undefended Cases

(2) If no answer is filed,

(a) the clerk shall, on request, schedule a case conference or set a date for an uncontested trial or, in an uncontested divorce case, prepare the documents for a judge; and

(b) settlement conference or trial management conference shall be conducted only if the court orders it.

Motions to Change Final Order or Agreement

(3) Subrule (1) applies, with necessary changes, to a motion to change a final order or agreement under rule 15, unless the motion is proceeding on the consent of the parties and any assignee or is unopposed.

Purposes of Case Conference

(4) The purposes of a case conference include,

(a) exploring the chances of settling the case;

(b) identifying the issues that are in dispute and those that are not in dispute;

(c) exploring ways to resolve the issues that are in dispute;

(d) ensuring disclosure of the relevant evidence;

(d.1) identifying any issues relating to any expert evidence or reports on which the parties intend to rely at trial;

(e) noting admissions that may simplify the case;

(f) setting the date for the next step in the case;

(g) setting a specific timetable for the steps to be taken in the case before it comes to trial;

(h) organizing a settlement conference, or holding one if appropriate; and

(i) giving directions with respect to any intended motion, including the preparation of a specific timetable for the exchange of material for the motion and ordering the filing of summaries of argument, if appropriate.

(4.1) A party who asks for a case conference shall serve and file a case conference notice (Form 17).

Purposes of Settlement Conference

(5) The purposes of a settlement conference include,

(a) exploring the chances of settling the case;

(b) settling or narrowing the issues in dispute;

(c) ensuring disclosure of the relevant evidence;

(c.1) settling or narrowing any issues relating to any expert evidence or reports on which the parties intend to rely at trial;

(d) noting admissions that may simplify the case;

(e) if possible, obtaining a view of how the court might decide the case;

(f) considering any other matter that may help in a quick and just conclusion of the case;

(g) if the case is not settled, identifying the witnesses and other evidence to be presented at trial, estimating the time needed for trial and scheduling the case for trial; and

(h) organizing a trial management conference, or holding one if appropriate.

Purposes of Trial Management Conference

(6) The purposes of a trial management conference include,

(a) exploring the chances of settling the case;

(b) arranging to receive evidence by a written report, an agreed statement of facts, an affidavit or another method, if appropriate;

(c) deciding how the trial will proceed;

(c.1) exploring the use of expert evidence or reports at trial, including the timing requirements for service and filing of experts' reports;

(d) ensuring that the parties know what witnesses will testify and what other evidence will be presented at trial;

(e) estimating the time needed for trial; and

(f) setting the trial date, if this has not already been done.

Combined Conference

(7) At any time on the direction of a judge, part or all of a case conference, settlement conference and trial management conference may be combined.

Orders at Conference

(8) At a case conference, settlement conference or trial management conference the judge may, if it is appropriate to do so,

(a) make an order for document disclosure (rule 19), questioning (rule 20) or filing of summaries of argument on a motion, set the times for events in the case or give directions for the next step or steps in the case;

(a.0.1) make an order respecting the use of expert witness evidence at trial or the service and filing of experts' reports;

(a.1) make an order requiring the parties to file a trial management endorsement or trial scheduling endorsement in a form determined by the court;

(b) make an order requiring one or more parties to attend,

(i) a mandatory information program,

(ii) a case conference or settlement conference conducted by a person named under subrule (9),

(iii) an intake meeting with a court-affiliated mediation service, or

(iv) a program offered through any other available community service or resource;

(b.1) if notice has been served, make a final order or any temporary order, including any of the following temporary orders to facilitate the preservation of the rights of the parties until a further agreement or order is made:

(i) an order relating to the designation of beneficiaries under a policy of life insurance, registered retirement savings plan, trust, pension, annuity or a similar financial instrument,

(ii) an order preserving assets generally or particularly,

(iii) an order prohibiting the concealment or destruction of documents or property,

(iv) an order requiring an accounting of funds under the control of one of the parties,

(v) an order preserving the health and medical insurance coverage for one of the parties and the children of the relationship, and

(vi) an order continuing the payment of periodic amounts required to preserve an asset or a benefit to one of the parties and the children;

(c) make an unopposed order or an order on consent; and

(d) on consent, refer any issue for alternative dispute resolution.

Conferences with a Non-Judge

(9) A case conference or settlement conference may be conducted by a person referred to in subrule (9.1) who has been named for the purpose by the appropriate regional senior judge, unless a party requests a conference with a judge.

Same

(9.1) For the purposes of subrule (9), the following persons may conduct a conference:

1. A person who is licensed under the *Law Society Act* to practice law in Ontario as a barrister and solicitor and whose licence is not suspended, if he or she has at least 10 years experience in the practice of family law.

2. A person who was licensed under the *Law Society Act* to practice law in Ontario as a barrister and solicitor but who has since retired, if, at the time of retirement,

i. his or her license was not suspended, and

ii. he or she had at least 10 years experience in the practice of family law.

3. A master or retired master of the Superior Court of Justice.

4. A retired judge of the Superior Court of Justice.

Settlement Conference with Judge Before Case Set for Trial

(10) A case shall not be scheduled for trial unless,

(a) a settlement conference has been conducted; or

(b) a judge has ordered that the case be scheduled for trial.

(11) [Repealed O. Reg. 151/08, s. 5(2).]

When Conferences Optional

(12) A case conference, settlement conference or trial management conference is not required, but may be held at a party's request or on a judge's direction in the following circumstances:

1. In an enforcement.

2. In a request to enforce a family arbitration award under rule 32.1.

Parties to Serve Briefs

(13) For each conference, each party shall serve and file a case conference brief (Form 17A or Form 17B), settlement conference brief (Form 17C or Form 17D) or trial management conference brief (Form 17E), as appropriate.

Case Conference Brief in Child Protection Case

(13.0.1) In a child protection case, a case conference brief shall be served and filed only if a case conference is being held under subrule (1.1).

Time for Service of Briefs

(13.1) The party requesting the conference (or, if the conference is not requested by a party, the applicant or party making the motion) shall serve and file a brief not later than six days before the date scheduled for the conference and the other party shall do so not later than four days before that date.

Parties to Confirm Attendance

(14) Each party shall,

(a) confer or attempt to confer orally or in writing with every other party about the issues that are in dispute, subject to a party being prohibited from such communication by court order;

(b) before giving the clerk confirmation of the conference in Form 17F under clause (c), give a copy of the confirmation of conference to every other party using mail, fax, email or any other method, except in a child protection case; and

(c) not later than 2 p.m. three days before the conference date, give the clerk the confirmation of conference (Form 17F) by,

(i) delivering it to the court office, or

(ii) if available in the court office, sending it by fax or by email.

Effect of Failure to Confirm

(14.1) Unless the court orders otherwise, a conference shall not be held if confirmation of the conference is not given to the clerk in accordance with clause (14)(c).

Parties to Update Confirmation

(14.1.1) If a party who has given a confirmation of conference determines at any time before the conference is held that the confirmation is no longer correct, the party shall, if possible, immediately,

(a) give a copy of the corrected confirmation of conference in Form 17F to every other party using a method listed in clause (14)(b) and subsequently give the clerk the corrected confirmation of conference by a method listed in clause (14)(c); or

(b) in a child protection case, give the clerk a corrected confirmation of conference in Form 17F by a method listed in clause (14)(c).

Requirement to Bring Documents to Settlement Conference

(14.2) The following documents shall be brought to a settlement conference:

1. Any document that supports a party's position in respect of a dispute regarding the value of property or regarding the amount of a debt, in the case of a property claim under Part I of the *Family Law Act*.

2. Any document required to be served under rule 13 (financial disclosure), if there is a dispute as to whether it was served.

Parties and Lawyers to Come to Conference

(15) The following shall come to each conference:

1. The parties, unless the court orders otherwise.

2. For each represented party, the lawyer with full knowledge of and authority in the case.

Participation by Telephone or Video Conference

(16) With permission obtained in advance from the judge who is to conduct a conference, a party or lawyer may participate in the conference by telephone or video conference.

Setting Up Telephone or Video Conference

(17) A party or lawyer who has permission to participate by telephone or video conference shall,

(a) make the necessary arrangements;

(b) serve a notice of the arrangements on all other parties and file it; and

(c) participate in the conference as the notice specifies.

Costs

(18) Costs shall not be awarded at a conference unless a party to the conference was not prepared, did not serve a required brief, did not make any required disclosure, otherwise contributed to the conference being unproductive or otherwise did not follow these rules, in which case the judge shall, despite subrule 24(10),

(a) order the party to pay the costs of the conference immediately;

(b) decide the amount of the costs; and

(c) give any directions that are needed.

Costs May be Awarded Later

(18.1) Subrule (18) does not prevent the court from awarding costs in relation to the conference at a later stage in the case, if costs are not awarded at the conference.

Conference Agreement

(19) No agreement reached at a conference is effective until it is signed by the parties, witnessed and, in a case involving a special party, approved by the court.

Agreement Filed in Continuing Record

(20) The agreement shall be filed as part of the continuing record, unless the court orders otherwise.

Continuing Record, Trial Management Conference Briefs

(21) Trial management conference briefs form part of the continuing record.

Continuing Record, Case Conference Briefs

(22) Case conference briefs do not form part of the continuing record unless the court orders otherwise and shall be returned at the end of the conference to the parties who filed them or be destroyed by court staff immediately after the conference.

Deletions from Case Conference Brief Included in Record

(22.1) If the court orders that a case conference brief form part of the continuing record, that portion of the brief that deals with settlement of the case shall be deleted.

Continuing Record, Settlement Conference Briefs

(22.2) Settlement conference briefs do not form part of the continuing record and shall be returned at the end of the conference to the parties who filed them or be destroyed by the court staff immediately after the conference.

Confidentiality of Settlement Conference

(23) No brief or evidence prepared for a settlement conference and no statement made at a settlement conference shall be disclosed to any other judge, except in,

(a) an agreement reached at a settlement conference; or

(b) an order.

Settlement Conference Judge Cannot Hear Issue

(24) A judge who conducts a settlement conference about an issue shall not hear the issue, except as subrule (25) provides.

Exception, Child Protection Case

(25) In a child protection case, if a finding that the child is in need of protection is made without a trial and a trial is needed to determine which order should be made under section 101 of the *Child, Youth and Family Services Act, 2017*, any judge who has not conducted a settlement conference on that issue may conduct the trial.

O. Reg. 544/99, s. 8; 202/01, s. 5; 91/03, s. 6; 89/04, s. 8; 151/08, s. 5; 6/10, s. 7; 383/11, s. 4; 388/12, s. 7; 322/13, s. 10; 142/14, s. 9; 69/15, s. 6; 235/16, s. 3; 298/18, s. 12

RULE 18 — OFFERS TO SETTLE

Definition

18. (1) In this rule,

"offer" means an offer to settle one or more claims in a case, motion, appeal or enforcement, and includes a counter-offer.

Application

(2) This rule applies to an offer made at any time, even before the case is started.

Making an Offer

(3) A party may serve an offer on any other party.

Offer to be Signed by Party and Lawyer

(4) An offer shall be signed personally by the party making it and also by the party's lawyer, if any.

Withdrawing an Offer

(5) A party who made an offer may withdraw it by serving a notice of withdrawal, at any time before the offer is accepted.

Time-Limited Offer

(6) An offer that is not accepted within the time set out in the offer is considered to have been withdrawn.

Offer Expires When Court Begins to Give Decision

(7) An offer may not be accepted after the court begins to give a decision that disposes of a claim dealt with in the offer.

Confidentiality of Offer

(8) The terms of an offer,

(a) shall not be mentioned in any document filed in the continuing record; and

(b) shall not be mentioned to the judge hearing the claim dealt with in the offer, until the judge has dealt with all the issues in dispute except costs.

Accepting an Offer

(9) The only valid way of accepting an offer is by serving an acceptance on the party who made the offer, at any time before,

(a) the offer is withdrawn; or

(b) the court begins to give a decision that disposes of a claim dealt with in the offer.

Offer Remains Open Despite Rejection or Counter-Offer

(10) A party may accept an offer in accordance with subrule (9) even if the party has previously rejected the offer or made a counter-offer.

Costs not Dealt with in Offer

(11) If an accepted offer does not deal with costs, either party is entitled to ask the court for costs.

Court Approval, Offer Involving Special Party

(12) A special party may make, withdraw and accept an offer, but another party's acceptance of a special party's offer and a special party's acceptance of another party's offer are not binding on the special party until the court approves.

Failure to Carry Out Terms of Accepted Offer

(13) If a party to an accepted offer does not carry out the terms of the offer, the other party may,

(a) make a motion to turn the parts of the offer within the court's jurisdiction into an order; or

(b) continue the case as if the offer had never been accepted.

Costs Consequences of Failure to Accept Offer

(14) A party who makes an offer is, unless the court orders otherwise, entitled to costs to the date the offer was served and full recovery of costs from that date, if the following conditions are met:

1. If the offer relates to a motion, it is made at least one day before the motion date.

2. If the offer relates to a trial or the hearing of a step other than a motion, it is made at least seven days before the trial or hearing date.

3. The offer does not expire and is not withdrawn before the hearing starts.

4. The offer is not accepted.

5. The party who made the offer obtains an order that is as favourable as or more favourable than the offer.

Costs Consequences — Burden of Proof

(15) The burden of proving that the order is as favourable as or more favourable than the offer to settle is on the party who claims the benefit of subrule (14).

Costs — Discretion of Court

(16) When the court exercises its discretion over costs, it may take into account any written offer to settle, the date it was made and its terms, even if subrule (14) does not apply.

RULE 19 — DOCUMENT DISCLOSURE

Affidavit Listing Documents

19. (1) Subject to subrule (1.1), every party shall, within 10 days after another party's request, give the other party an affidavit listing every document that is,

(a) relevant to any issue in the case; and

(b) in the party's control, or available to the party on request.

Exceptions

(1.1) Subrule (1) does not apply,

(a) to the Office of the Children's Lawyer or to children's aid societies; and

(b) in respect of documents required to be served under rule 13 (financial disclosure).

Access to Listed Documents

(2) The other party is entitled, on request,

(a) to examine any document listed in the affidavit, unless it is protected by a legal privilege; and

(b) to receive, at the party's own expense at the legal aid rate, a copy of any document that the party is entitled to examine under clause (a).

Access to Documents Mentioned in Court Papers

(3) Subrule (2) also applies, with necessary changes, to a document mentioned in a party's application, answer, reply, notice of motion or affidavit.

Documents Protected by Legal Privilege

(4) If a party claims that a document is protected by a legal privilege, the court may, on motion, examine it and decide the issue.

Use of Privileged Documents

(5) A party who claims that a document is protected by a legal privilege may use it at trial only,

(a) if the other party has been allowed to examine the document and been supplied with a copy, free of charge, at least 30 days before the settlement conference; or

(b) on the conditions the trial judge considers appropriate, including an adjournment if necessary.

Documents of Subsidiary or Affiliated Corporation

(6) The court may, on motion despite clause 1(7.2)(a), order a party to give another party an affidavit listing the documents that are,

(a) relevant to any issue in the case; and

(b) in the control of, or available on request to a corporation that is controlled, directly or indirectly, by the party or by another corporation that the party controls directly or indirectly.

Documents of Office of the Children's Lawyer or Children's Aid Society

(6.1) The court may, on motion despite clause 1(7.2)(a), order the Office of the Children's Lawyer or a children's aid society to give another party an affidavit listing the documents that are,

(a) relevant to any issue in the case; and

(b) in the control of, or available on request to, the Office of the Children's Lawyer or the children's aid society.

Access to Listed Documents

(7) Subrule (2) also applies, with necessary changes, to any document listed in an affidavit ordered under subrule (6) or (6.1).

Documents Omitted from Affidavit or Found Later

(8) A party who, after serving an affidavit required under subrule (1), (6) or (6.1), finds a document that should have been listed in it, or finds that the list is not correct or not complete, shall immediately serve on the other party a new affidavit listing the correct information.

Access to Additional Documents

(9) The other party is entitled, on request,

(a) to examine any document listed in an affidavit served under subrule (8), unless it is protected by a legal privilege; and

(b) to receive, free of charge, a copy of any document that the party is entitled to examine under clause (a).

Failure to Follow Rule 19 or Obey Order

(10) If a party does not follow this rule or obey an order made under this rule, the court may, in addition to any power to make an order under subrule 1(8) or (8.1),

(a) order the party to give another party an affidavit, let the other party examine a document or supply the other party with a copy free of charge;

(b) order that a document favourable to the party's case may not be used except with the court's permission; or

(c) order that the party is not entitled to obtain disclosure under these rules until the party follows the rule or obeys the order.

Document in Non-Party's Control

(11) If a document is in a non-party's control, or is available only to the non-party, and is not protected by a legal privilege, and it would be unfair to a party to go on with the case without the document, the court may, on motion with notice served on every party and served on the non-party by special service,

(a) order the non-party to let the party examine the document and to supply the party with a copy at the legal aid rate; and

(b) order that a copy be prepared and used for all purposes of the case instead of the original.

O. Reg. 383/11, s. 5; 322/13, s. 11; 69/15, s. 7

RULE 20 — QUESTIONING A WITNESS AND DISCLOSURE

Questioning — Procedure

20. (1) Questioning under this rule shall take place orally under oath or affirmation.

Cross-Examination

(2) The right to question a person includes the right to cross-examine.

Child Protection Case — Available as of Right

(3) In a child protection case, a party is entitled to obtain information from another party about any issue in the case,

(a) by questioning the other party, in which case the party shall serve the other party with a summons to witness (Form 23) by special service in accordance with subrule 6(4); or

(b) by affidavit or by another method, in which case the party shall serve the other party with a request for information (Form 20).

Other Cases — Consent or Order

(4) In a case other than a child protection case, a party is entitled to obtain information from another party about any issue in the case,

(a) with the other party's consent; or

(b) by an order under subrule (5).

Order for Questioning or Disclosure

(5) The court may, on motion, order that a person (whether a party or not) be questioned by a party or disclose information by affidavit or by another method about any issue in the case, if the following conditions are met:

1. It would be unfair to the party who wants the questioning or disclosure to carry on with the case without it.

2. The information is not easily available by any other method.

3. The questioning or disclosure will not cause unacceptable delay or undue expense.

Questioning Special Party

(6) If a person to be questioned is a special party, the court may, on motion, order that someone else be questioned in addition to or in place of the person.

Questioning About Affidavit or Net Family Property Statement

(7) The court may make an order under subrule (5) that a person be questioned or disclose details about information in an affidavit or net family property statement.

Questioning or Disclosure — Preconditions

(8) A party who wants to question a person or obtain information by affidavit or by another method may do so only if the party,

(a) has served and filed any answer, financial statement or net family property statement that these rules require; and

(b) promises in writing not to serve or file any further material for the next step in the case, except in reply to the answers or information obtained.

Notice and Summons to Non-Party

(9) The court may make an order under this rule affecting a non-party only if the non-party has been served with the notice of motion, a summons to witness (Form 23) and the witness fee required by subrule 23(4), all by special service (subrules 6(3) and (4)).

Penalty for Failure to Obey Summons

(10) Subrule 23(7) (failure to obey summons to witness) applies, with necessary changes, if a person summoned under subrule (9) fails to obey the summons.

Place of Questioning

(11) The questioning shall take place in the municipality in which the person to be questioned lives, unless that person and the party who wants to do the questioning agree to hold it in another municipality.

Other Arrangements for Questioning

(12) If the person to be questioned and the party who wants to do the questioning do not agree on one or more of the following matters, the court shall, on motion, make an order to decide the matter:

1. The date and time for the questioning.

2. The person responsible for recording the questioning.

3. The method for recording the questioning.

4. Payment of the expenses of the person to be questioned, if a non-party.

Notice to Parties

(13) The parties shall, not later than three days before the questioning, be served with notice of the name of the person to be questioned and the address, date and time of the questioning.

Questioning Person Outside Ontario

(14) If a person to be questioned lives outside Ontario and will not come to Ontario for questioning, the court may decide,

(a) the date, time and place for the questioning;

(b) how much notice the person should be given;

(c) the person before whom the questioning will be held;

(d) the amount of the witness fee to be paid to the person to be questioned;

(e) the method for recording the questioning;

(f) where necessary, that the clerk shall issue,

(i) an authorization to a commissioner (Form 20A) who is to supervise the questioning outside Ontario, and

(ii) a letter of request (Form 20B) to the appropriate court or authorities outside Ontario, asking for their assistance in getting the person to be questioned to come before the commissioner; and

(g) any other related matter.

Commissioner's Duties

(15) A commissioner authorized under subrule (14) shall,

(a) supervise the questioning according to the terms of the court's authorization, these rules and Ontario's law of evidence, unless the law of the place where the questioning is to be held requires some other manner of questioning;

(b) make and keep a copy of the record of the questioning and, if possible, of the exhibits, if any;

(c) deliver the original record, any exhibits and the authorization to the clerk who issued it; and

(d) notify the party who asked for the questioning that the record has been delivered to the clerk.

Order to Bring Documents or Things

(16) An order for questioning and a summons to witness may also require the person to bring any document or thing that is,

(a) relevant to any issue in the case; and

(b) in the person's control or available to the person on request.

Other Rules Apply

(17) Subrules 19(2), (4) and (5) (right to examine document and obtain copy, documents protected by legal privilege, use of privileged documents) apply, with necessary changes, to the documents mentioned in the order.

Scope of Questions

(18) Unless the court orders otherwise, a person to be questioned may be asked about,

(a) the names of persons who might reasonably be expected to know about the claims in the case and, with the court's permission, their addresses;

(b) the names of the witnesses whom a party intends to call at trial and, with the court's permission, their addresses;

(c) the names, addresses, findings, conclusions and opinions of expert witnesses whom a party intends to call or on whose reports the party intends to rely at trial;

(d) if it is relevant to the case, the existence and details of any insurance policy under which the insurance company may be required to pay all or part of an order for the payment of money in the case or to pay back to a party money that the party has paid under an order; and

(e) any other matter in dispute in the case.

Refusal to Answer Question

(19) If a person being questioned refuses to answer a question,

(a) the court may, on motion,

(i) decide whether the question is proper,

(ii) give directions for the person's return to the questioning, and

(iii) make a contempt order against the person; and

(b) if the person is a party or is questioned on behalf or in place of a party, the party shall not use the information that was refused as evidence in the case, unless the court gives permission under subrule (20).

Court's Permission

(20) The court shall give permission unless the use of the information would cause harm to another party or an unacceptable delay in the trial, and may impose any appropriate conditions on the permission, including an adjournment if necessary.

Duty to Correct or Update Answers

(21) A person who has been questioned or who has provided information in writing by affidavit or by another method and who finds that an answer or information given was incorrect or incomplete, or is no longer correct or complete, shall immediately provide the correct and complete information in writing to all parties.

Lawyer Answering

(22) If there is no objection, questions may be answered by the lawyer for a person being questioned, and the answer shall be taken as the person's own answer unless the person corrects or changes it before the questioning ends.

Method for Recording Questioning

(23) All the questions and answers at a questioning shall be recorded electronically or manually.

Obligation to Keep Information Confidential

(24) When a party obtains evidence under this rule, rule 13 (financial disclosure) or rule 19 (document disclosure), the party and the party's lawyer may use the evidence and any information obtained from it only for the purposes of the case in which the evidence was obtained, subject to the exceptions in subrule (25).

Use of Information Permitted

(25) Evidence and any information obtained from it may be used for other purposes,

(a) if the person who gave the evidence consents;

(b) if the evidence is filed with the court, given at a hearing or referred to at a hearing;

(c) to impeach the testimony of a witness in another case; or

(d) in a later case between the same parties or their successors, if the case in which the evidence was obtained was withdrawn or dismissed.

Court May Lift Obligation of Confidentiality

(26) The court may, on motion, give a party permission to disclose evidence or information obtained from it if the interests of justice outweigh any harm that would result to the party who provided the evidence.

O. Reg. 322/13, s. 12; 69/15, s. 8

RULE 20.1 — EXPERTS

Duty of Expert

20.1 (1) It is the duty of every expert who provides evidence in relation to a case under these rules,

(a) to provide opinion evidence that is fair, objective and non-partisan;

(b) to provide opinion evidence that is related only to matters that are within the expert's area of expertise; and

(c) to provide such additional assistance as the court may reasonably require to determine a matter in issue.

Duty Prevails

(2) In the case of an expert engaged by or on behalf of a party, the duty in subrule (1) prevails over any obligation owed by the expert to that party.

Court Appointed Experts

(3) The court may, on motion or on its own initiative, appoint one or more independent experts to inquire into and report on any question of fact or opinion relevant to an issue in a case.

Expert to be Named

(4) An order under subrule (3) appointing an expert shall name the expert and, where possible, the expert shall be a person agreed on by the parties.

Instructions

(5) An order under subrule (3) appointing an expert shall contain the instructions to be given to the expert, and the court may make any further orders that it considers necessary to enable the expert to carry out the instructions.

Fees and Expenses

(6) The court shall require the parties to pay the fees and expenses of an expert appointed under subrule (3), and shall specify the proportions or amounts of the fees and expenses that each party is required to pay.

Security

(7) If a motion by a party for the appointment of an expert under subrule (3) is opposed, the court may, as a condition of making the appointment, require the party seeking the appointment to give such security for the expert's fees and expenses as is just.

Serious Financial Hardship

(8) The court may relieve a party from responsibility for payment of any of the expert's fees and expenses, if the court is satisfied that payment would cause serious financial hardship to the party.

Report

(9) The expert shall prepare a report of the results of his or her inquiry, and shall,

(a) file the report with the clerk of the court; and

(b) provide a copy of the report to each of the parties.

Content of Report

(10) A report provided by an expert shall contain the following information:

1. The expert's name, address and area of expertise.

2. The expert's qualifications, including his or her employment and educational experiences in his or her area of expertise.

3. The instructions provided to the expert in relation to the proceeding.

4. The nature of the opinion being sought and each issue in the proceeding to which the opinion relates.

5. The expert's opinion respecting each issue and, where there is a range of opinions given, a summary of the range and the reasons for the expert's own opinion within that range.

6. The expert's reasons for his or her opinion, including,

i. a description of the factual assumptions on which the opinion is based,

ii. a description of any research conducted by the expert that led him or her to form the opinion, and

iii. a list of every document relied on by the expert in forming the opinion.

7. An acknowledgement of expert's duty (Form 20.1) signed by the expert.

Admissibility

(11) The expert's report is admissible in evidence in the case.

Cross-examination

(12) Any party may cross-examine the expert at the trial.

Non-application

(13) For greater certainty, subrules (3) to (12) do not apply in respect of,

(a) appointments of persons by the court under subsection 98(4) or (5) of the *Child, Youth and Family Services Act, 2017* or subsection 30(1) of the *Children's Law Reform Act*; or

(b) requests by the court that the Children's Lawyer act under subsection 112(1) of the *Courts of Justice Act*.

O. Reg. 383/11, s. 6; 298/18, s. 13

RULE 21 — REPORT OF CHILDREN'S LAWYER

REPORT OF CHILDREN'S LAWYER

21. When the Children's Lawyer investigates and reports on custody of or access to a child under section 112 of the *Courts of Justice Act*,

(a) the Children's Lawyer shall first serve notice on the parties and file it;

(b) the parties shall, from the time they are served with the notice, serve the Children's Lawyer with every document in the case that involves the child's custody, access, support, health or education, as if the Children's Lawyer were a party in the case;

(c) the Children's Lawyer has the same rights as a party to document disclosure (rule 19) and questioning witnesses (rule 20) about any matter involving the child's custody, access, support, health or education;

(d) within 90 days after serving the notice under clause (a), the Children's Lawyer shall serve a report on the parties and file it;

(e) within 30 days after being served with the report, a party may serve and file a statement disputing anything in it; and

(f) the trial shall not be held and the court shall not make a final order in the case until the 30 days referred to in clause (e) expire or the parties file a statement giving up their right to that time.

RULE 22 — ADMISSION OF FACTS

Meaning of Admission that Document Genuine

22. (1) An admission that a document is genuine is an admission,

(a) if the document is said to be an original, that it was written, signed or sealed as it appears to have been;

(b) if it is said to be a copy, that it is a complete and accurate copy; and

(c) if it is said to be a copy of a document that is ordinarily sent from one person to another (for example, a letter, fax or electronic message), that it was sent as it appears to have been sent and was received by the person to whom it is addressed.

Request to Admit

(2) At any time, by serving a request to admit (Form 22) on another party, a party may ask the other party to admit, for purposes of the case only, that a fact is true or that a document is genuine.

Copy of Document to be Attached

(3) A copy of any document mentioned in the request to admit shall be attached to it, unless the other party already has a copy or it is impractical to attach a copy.

Response Required within 20 Days

(4) The party on whom the request to admit is served is considered to have admitted, for purposes of the case only, that the fact is true or that the document is genuine, unless the party serves a response (Form 22A) within 20 days,

(a) denying that a particular fact mentioned in the request is true or that a particular document mentioned in the request is genuine; or

(b) refusing to admit that a particular fact mentioned in the request is true or that a particular document mentioned in the request is genuine, and giving the reasons for each refusal.

Withdrawing Admission

(5) An admission that a fact is true or that a document is genuine (whether contained in a document served in the case or resulting from subrule (4)), may be withdrawn only with the other party's consent or with the court's permission.

RULE 23 — EVIDENCE AND TRIAL

Trial Record

23. (1) At least 30 days before the start of the trial, the applicant shall serve and file a trial record containing a table of contents and the following documents:

1. The application, answer and reply, if any.

2. Any agreed statement of facts.

3. If relevant to an issue at trial, financial statements and net family property statements by all parties, completed not more than 30 days before the record is served.

3.1 If the trial involves a claim for custody of or access to a child, the applicable documents referred to in Rule 35.1.

4. Any assessment report ordered by the court or obtained by consent of the parties.

5. Any temporary order relating to a matter still in dispute.

6. Any order relating to the trial.

7. The relevant parts of any transcript on which the party intends to rely at trial.

8. Any evidence that is the subject of an order made under clause 1(7.2)(g).

Respondent May Add to Trial Record

(2) Not later than seven days before the start of the trial, a respondent may serve, file and add to the trial record any document referred to in subrule (1) that is not already in the trial record.

Summons to Witness

(3) A party who wants a witness to give evidence in court or to be questioned and to bring documents or other things shall serve on the witness a summons to witness (Form 23) by special service in accordance with subrule 6(4), together with the witness fee set out in subrule (4).

Witness Fee

(4) A person summoned as a witness shall be paid, for each day that the person is needed in court or to be questioned,

(a) $50 for coming to court or to be questioned;

(b) travel money in the amount of,

(i) $5, if the person lives in the city or town where the person gives evidence,

(ii) 30 cents per kilometre each way, if the person lives elsewhere but within 300 kilometres of the court or place of questioning,

(iii) the cheapest available air fare plus $10 a day for airport parking and 30 cents per kilometre each way from the person's home to the airport and from the airport to the court or place of questioning, if the person lives 300 or more kilometres from the court or place of questioning; and

(c) $100 per night for meals and overnight stay, if the person does not live in the city or town where the trial is held and needs to stay overnight.

Meaning of "City or Town"

(4.1) For the purposes for subrule (4), a municipality shall be considered a city or town if it was a city or town on December 31, 2002.

Continuing Effect of Summons

(5) A summons to witness remains in effect until it is no longer necessary to have the witness present.

Summons for Original Document

(6) If a document can be proved by a certified copy, a party who wants a witness to bring the original shall not serve a summons on the witness for that purpose without the court's permission.

Failure to Obey Summons

(7) The court may issue a warrant for arrest (Form 32B) to bring a witness before the court if,

(a) the witness has been served as subrule (3) requires, but has not obeyed the summons; and

(b) it is necessary to have the witness present in court or at a questioning.

Interprovincial Summons to Witness

(8) A summons to a witness outside Ontario under the *Interprovincial Summonses Act* shall be in Form 23A.

Setting Aside Summons to Witness

(9) The court may, on motion, order that a summons to witness be set aside.

Attendance of a Prisoner

(10) If it is necessary to have a prisoner come to court or to be questioned, the court may order (Form 23B) the prisoner's custodian to deliver the prisoner on payment of the fee set out in the regulations under the *Administration of Justice Act.*

Calling Opposing Party as Witness

(11) A party may call the opposing party as a witness and may cross-examine the opposing party.

Attendance of Opposing Party

(11.1) A party who wishes to call an opposing party as a witness may have the opposing party attend,

(a) by serving a summons under subrule (3) on the opposing party; or

(b) by serving on the opposing party's lawyer, at least 10 days before the start of the trial, a notice of intention to call the opposing party as a witness.

Opposing Party Disobeying Summons

(12) When an opposing party has been served with a summons under subrule (3), the court may make a final order in favour of the party calling the witness, adjourn the case or make any other appropriate order, including a contempt order, if the opposing party,

(a) does not come to or remain in court as required by the summons; or

(b) refuses to be sworn or to affirm, to answer any proper question or to bring any document or thing named in the summons.

Reading Opposing Party's Answers into Evidence

(13) An answer or information given under rule 20 (questioning) by an opposing party may be read into evidence at trial if it is otherwise proper evidence, even if the opposing party has already testified at trial.

Reading Other Person's Answers into Evidence

(14) Subrule (13) also applies, with necessary changes, to an answer or information given by a person questioned on behalf of or in place of an opposing party, unless the trial judge orders otherwise.

Using Answers — Special Circumstances

(15) Subrule (13) is subject to the following:

1. If the answer or information is being read into evidence to show that a witness's testimony at trial is not to be believed, answers or information given by the witness earlier must be put to the witness as sections 20 and 21 of the *Evidence Act* require.

2. At the request of an opposing party, the trial judge may direct the party reading the answer or information into evidence to read in, as well, any other answer or information that qualifies or explains what the party has read into evidence.

3. A special party's answer or information may be read into evidence only with the trial judge's permission.

Rebutting Answers

(16) A party who has read answers or information into evidence at trial may introduce other evidence to rebut the answers or information.

Using Answers of Witness not Available for Trial

(17) The trial judge may give a party permission to read into evidence all or part of the answers or information given under rule 20 (questioning) by a person who is unable or unwilling to testify at the trial, but before doing so the judge shall consider,

(a) the importance of the evidence;

(b) the general principle that trial evidence should be given orally in court;

(c) the extent to which the person was cross-examined; and

(d) any other relevant factor.

Taking Evidence Before Trial

(18) The court may order that a witness whose evidence is necessary at trial may give evidence before trial at a place and before a person named in the order, and then may accept the transcript as evidence.

Taking Evidence Before Trial Outside Ontario

(19) If a witness whose evidence is necessary at trial lives outside Ontario, subrules 20(14) and (15) (questioning person outside Ontario, commissioner's duties) apply, with necessary changes.

Evidence by Affidavit, Other Method

(20) A party may request that the court make an order under clause 1(7.2)(i) permitting the evidence of a witness to be heard by affidavit or another method not requiring the witness to attend in person.

(20.1) [Repealed O. Reg. 69/15, s. 9(2).]

Conditions for Use of Affidavit or Another Method not Requiring a Witness to Attend in Person

(21) Evidence at trial by affidavit or another method not requiring a witness to attend in person may be used only if,

(a) the use is in accordance with an order under clause 1(7.2)(i);

(b) the evidence is served at least 30 days before the start of the trial; and

(c) the evidence would have been admissible if given by the witness in court.

Affidavit Evidence at Uncontested Trial

(22) At an uncontested trial, evidence by affidavit in Form 14A or Form 23C and, if applicable, Form 35.1 may be used without an order under clause 1(7.2)(i), unless the court directs that oral evidence must be given.

Expert Witness Reports

(23) A party who wants to call an expert witness at trial shall serve on all other parties a report signed by the expert and containing the information listed in subrule (25),

(a) at least 90 days before the start of the trial; or

(b) in the case of a child protection case, at least 30 days before the start of the trial.

(c) [Repealed O. Reg. 6/10, s. 8(4).]

Same, Response

(24) A party who wants to call an expert witness at trial to respond to the expert witness of another party shall serve on all other parties a report signed by the expert and containing the information listed in subrule (25),

(a) at least 60 days before the start of the trial; or

(b) in the case of a child protection case, at least 14 days before the start of the trial.

Same, Contents

(25) A report provided for the purposes of subrule (1) or (2) shall contain the following information:

1. The expert's name, address and area of expertise.

2. The expert's qualifications and employment and educational experiences in his or her area of expertise.

3. The substance of the expert's proposed evidence.

Supplementary Report

(26) Any supplementary expert witness report shall be signed by the expert and served on all other parties,

(a) at least 30 days before the start of the trial; or

(b) in the case of a child protection case, at least 14 days before the start of the trial.

Failure to Serve Expert Witness Report

(27) A party who has not followed a requirement under subrule (23), (24) or (26) to serve and file an expert witness report, may not call the expert witness unless the trial judge allows otherwise.

O. Reg. 544/99, s. 9; 202/01, s. 6; 92/03, s. 2; 6/10, s. 8; 322/13, s. 13; 69/15, s. 9

RULE 24 — COSTS

Successful Party Presumed Entitled to Costs

24. (1) There is a presumption that a successful party is entitled to the costs of a motion, enforcement, case or appeal.

No Presumption in Child Protection Case or if Party is Government Agency

(2) The presumption does not apply in a child protection case or to a party that is a government agency.

Court's Discretion — Costs for or Against Government Agency

(3) The court has discretion to award costs to or against a party that is a government agency, whether it is successful or unsuccessful.

Successful Party Who has Behaved Unreasonably

(4) Despite subrule (1), a successful party who has behaved unreasonably during a case may be deprived of all or part of the party's own costs or ordered to pay all or part of the unsuccessful party's costs.

Decision on Reasonableness

(5) In deciding whether a party has behaved reasonably or unreasonably, the court shall examine,

(a) the party's behaviour in relation to the issues from the time they arose, including whether the party made an offer to settle;

(b) the reasonableness of any offer the party made; and

(c) any offer the party withdrew or failed to accept.

Divided Success

(6) If success in a step in a case is divided, the court may apportion costs as appropriate.

Absent or Unprepared Party

(7) If a party does not appear at a step in the case, or appears but is not properly prepared to deal with the issues at that step or otherwise contributes to that step being unproductive, the court shall award costs against the party unless the court orders otherwise in the interests of justice.

Bad Faith

(8) If a party has acted in bad faith, the court shall decide costs on a full recovery basis and shall order the party to pay them immediately.

Costs Caused by Fault of Lawyer or Agent

(9) If a party's lawyer or agent has run up costs without reasonable cause or has wasted costs, the court may, on motion or on its own initiative, after giving the lawyer or agent an opportunity to be heard,

(a) order that the lawyer or agent shall not charge the client fees or disbursements for work specified in the order, and order the lawyer or agent to repay money that the client has already paid toward costs;

(b) order the lawyer or agent to repay the client any costs that the client has been ordered to pay another party;

(c) order the lawyer or agent personally to pay the costs of any party; and

(d) order that a copy of an order under this subrule be given to the client.

Deciding Costs

(10) Promptly after dealing with a step in a case, the court shall, in a summary manner,

(a) determine who, if anyone, is entitled to costs in relation to that step and set the amount of any costs; or

(b) expressly reserve the decision on costs for determination at a later stage in the case.

(10.1) [Repealed O. Reg. 298/18, s. 14.]

Factors in Costs

(11) In setting the amount of costs, the court shall consider,

(a) the importance, complexity or difficulty of the issues;

(b) the reasonableness or unreasonableness of each party's behaviour in the case;

(c) the lawyer's rates;

(d) the time properly spent on the case, including conversations between the lawyer and the party or witnesses, drafting documents and correspondence, attempts to settle, preparation, hearing, argument, and preparation and signature of the order;

(e) expenses properly paid or payable; and

(f) any other relevant matter.

Same

(11) The failure of the court to act under subrule (10) in relation to a step in a case does not prevent the court from awarding costs in relation to the step at a later stage in the case.

Setting Costs Amounts

(12) In setting the amount of costs, the court shall consider,

(a) the reasonableness and proportionality of each of the following factors as it relates to the importance and complexity of the issues:

(i) each party's behaviour,

(ii) the time spent by each party,

(iii) any written offers to settle, including offers that do not meet the requirements of rule 18,

(iv) any legal fees, including the number of lawyers and their rates,

(v) any expert witness fees, including the number of experts and their rates,

(vi) any other expenses properly paid or payable; and

(b) any other relevant matter.

Supporting Materials

(12.1) Any claim for costs respecting fees or expenses shall be supported by documentation satisfactory to the court.

Order for Security for Costs

(13) A judge may, on motion, make an order for security for costs that is just, based on one or more of the following factors:

1. A party ordinarily resides outside Ontario.

2. A party has an order against the other party for costs that remains unpaid, in the same case or another case.

3. A party is a corporation and there is good reason to believe it does not have enough assets in Ontario to pay costs.

4. There is good reason to believe that the case is a waste of time or a nuisance and that the party does not have enough assets in Ontario to pay costs.

5. A statute entitles the party to security for costs.

Amount and Form of Security

(14) The judge shall determine the amount of the security, its form and the method of giving it.

Effect of Order for Security

(15) Until the security has been given, a party against whom there is an order for security for costs may not take any step in the case, except to appeal from the order, unless a judge orders otherwise.

Failure to Give Security

(16) If the party does not give the security as ordered and, as a result, a judge makes an order dismissing the party's case or striking out the party's answer or any other document filed by the party, then subrule (15) no longer applies.

Security may be Changed

(17) The amount of the security, its form and the method of giving it may be changed by order at any time.

O. Reg. 544/99, s. 10; 322/13, s. 14; 235/16, s. 4; 298/18, s. 14

RULE 25 — ORDERS

Consent Order

25. (1) If the parties agree, the court may make an order under these rules or an Act without having the parties or their lawyers come to court.

Successful Party Prepares Draft Order

(2) The party in whose favour an order is made shall prepare a draft of the order (Form 25, 25A, 25B, 25C or 25D), unless the court orders otherwise.

Other Party may Prepare Draft Order

(3) If the party in whose favour an order is made does not have a lawyer or does not prepare a draft order within 10 days after the order is made, any other party may prepare the draft order, unless the court orders otherwise.

Approval of Draft Order

(4) A party who prepares an order shall serve a draft, for approval of its form and content, on every other party who was in court or was represented when the order was made (including a child who has a lawyer).

Settling Contents of Disputed Order

(5) Unless the court orders otherwise, a party who disagrees with the form or content of a draft order shall serve, on every party who was served under subrule (4) and on the party who served the draft order,

(a) a notice disputing approval (Form 25E);

(b) a copy of the order, redrafted as proposed; and

(c) notice of a time and date at which the clerk will settle the order by telephone conference.

Time and Date

(6) The time and date shall be set by the clerk and shall be within five days after service of the notice disputing approval.

Disputed Order — Settlement by Judge

(7) If unable to settle the order at the telephone conference, the clerk shall, as soon as possible, refer the order to the judge who made it, to be settled at a further telephone conference, unless the judge orders the parties to come to court for settlement of the order.

No Approval Required if no Response from Other Party

(8) If no approval or notice disputing approval (Form 25E) is served within 10 days after the draft order is served for approval, it may be signed without approval.

No Approval Required for Certain Orders

(9) If an order dismisses a motion, case or appeal, without costs, or is prepared by the clerk under subrule (11), it may be signed without approval.

No Approval Required in Emergencies

(10) If the delay involved in getting an order approved would have serious consequences, the judge who made it may sign it without approval.

When Clerk Prepares Order

(11) The clerk shall prepare the order for signature,

(a) within 10 days after it is made, if no party has a lawyer;

(b) as soon as it is made,

(i) if it is a support deduction order or alternative payment order under the *Family Responsibility and Support Arrears Enforcement Act, 1996* or an order under the *Interjurisdictional Support Orders Act, 2002*,

(i.1) if it is a restraining order under section 35 of the *Children's Law Reform Act* or section 46 of the *Family Law Act*,

(i.2) if it is an order terminating a restraining order referred to in subclause (i.1), or

(ii) if the judge directs the clerk to do so.

Restraining Orders

(11.1) A restraining order referred to in subclause 11(b)(i.1) shall be in Form 25F or 25G.

(11.2) An order terminating a restraining order referred to in subclause 11(b)(i.1) shall be in Form 25H.

Who Signs Order

(12) An order may be signed by the judge who made it or by the clerk.

Service of Order

(13) Unless the court orders otherwise, the person who prepared an order shall serve it,

(a) on every other party, including a party to whom paragraph 1 of subrule 1(8.4) (no notice to party) applies;

(b) if a child involved in the case has a lawyer, on the lawyer; and

(c) on any other person named by the court.

Support Deduction Order Not Served

(14) A support deduction order under the *Family Responsibility and Support Arrears Enforcement Act, 1996* does not have to be served.

Service of Crown Wardship Order

(15) An order for extended society care under Part V of the *Child, Youth and Family Services Act, 2017* shall be served on the following persons, in addition to the ones mentioned in subrule (13):

1. The child, if that Act requires notice to the child.

2. Any foster parent or other person who is entitled to notice under subsection 79(3) of that Act.

3. A Director appointed under that Act.

Service of Secure Treatment Order

(16) An order for secure treatment under Part VII of the *Child, Youth and Family Services Act, 2017* shall be served on the administrator of the secure treatment program, in addition to the persons mentioned in subrule (13).

Service of Adoption Order

(17) An adoption order shall be served on the following persons, in addition to the ones mentioned in subrule (13):

1. The adopted child, if the child gave consent under subsection 180(6) of the *Child, Youth and Family Services Act, 2017*.

2. The persons mentioned in subsection 222(3) of that Act.

Effective Date

(18) An order is effective from the date on which it is made, unless it states otherwise.

Changing Order — Fraud, Mistake, Lack of Notice

(19) The court may, on motion, change an order that,

(a) was obtained by fraud;

(b) contains a mistake;

(c) needs to be changed to deal with a matter that was before the court but that it did not decide;

(d) was made without notice; or

(e) was made with notice, if an affected party was not present when the order was made because the notice was inadequate or the party was unable, for a reason satisfactory to the court, to be present.

Same

(20) Rule 14 applies with necessary changes to a motion to change a final order under subrule (19) and, for the purpose, clause 14(6)(a) shall be read as if the reference to a temporary order were a reference to a final order.

O. Reg. 56/03, s. 3; 76/06, s. 6; 151/08, s. 6; 386/09, s. 1; 322/13, s. 15; 142/14, s. 10; 140/15, s. 2; 298/18, s. 15

RULE 25.1 — PAYMENT INTO AND OUT OF COURT [HEADING ADDED O. REG. 389/12, S. 1.]

Definition

25.1 (1) In this rule,

"Accountant" means the Accountant of the Superior Court of Justice.

Non-Application of Rule

(2) This rule does not apply to,

(a) money paid or to be paid into court for the enforcement of an order for the payment or recovery of money, including enforcement by garnishment; or

(b) money for the support of a child or spouse that is paid or to be paid into court by the payor on behalf of a recipient.

Payment Into Court, Filing in Person with Clerk or Accountant

(3) Subject to subrule (9), a party who is required to pay money into court shall do so in accordance with subrules (4) to (8).

Documents to be Filed

(4) The party shall file with the clerk or Accountant a written request for payment into court and a copy of the order under which the money is payable.

Direction

(5) On receiving the documents filed under subrule (4), the clerk or Accountant shall give the party a direction to receive the money, addressed to a bank listed in Schedule I or II to the *Bank Act* (Canada) and specifying the account in the Accountant's name into which the money is to be paid.

Clerk to Forward Documents

(6) If the documents are filed with the clerk, the clerk shall forward the documents to the Accountant.

Payment

(7) On receiving from the clerk or Accountant the direction referred to in subrule (5), the party shall pay the money into the specified bank account in accordance with the direction.

Bank's Duties

(8) On receiving the money, the bank shall give a receipt to the party paying the money and immediately send a copy of the receipt to the Accountant.

Payment Into Court, Payment by Mail to Accountant

(9) A party may pay money into court by mailing to the Accountant the documents referred to in subrule (4), together with the money that is payable.

Accountant to Provide Receipt

(10) On receiving money under subrule (9), the Accountant shall give a receipt to the party paying the money.

Payment Out of Court, Authority

(11) Money may only be paid out of court under an order or on consent of all parties.

Payment Out under an Order

(12) A person who seeks payment of money out of court under an order shall file with the Accountant,

(a) a written request for payment out naming the person to whom the money is to be paid under the order;

(b) the original order for payment out or a copy certified by an official of the court, unless one or the other has already been filed with the Accountant; and

(c) an affidavit stating that the order for payment out is not under appeal and that the time for appealing the order has expired, or that any appeal of the order has been disposed of.

Children's Lawyer, Public Guardian and Trustee

(13) If the person seeking payment out under an order is the Children's Lawyer or the Public Guardian and Trustee, the documents referred to in clauses (12)(a) and (c) are not required to be filed.

Payment Out on Consent

(14) A person who seeks payment of money out of court on consent shall file with the Accountant,

(a) a written request for payment out naming the person to whom the money is to be paid, and an affidavit stating that neither the person making the request nor the person to whom the money is to be paid is a special party or a child under the age of 18 years who is not a party, with copies of the following attached as exhibits:

(i) photo identification of the requesting person,

(ii) proof of that person's date of birth,

(iii) proof of that person's current address; and

(b) the affidavit of each party or each of the other parties, as the case may be, stating that the party consents to the payment out as set out in the request and that neither the party nor the person to whom the money is to be paid is a special party or a child under the age of 18 years who is not a party, with copies of the documents referred to in subclauses (a)(i), (ii) and (iii), as they relate to the party providing the affidavit, attached as exhibits.

Accountant's Duties

(15) If the requirements of subrule (12) or (14), as the case may be, are met, the Accountant shall pay the money to the person named in the order or request for payment out, and the payment shall include any accrued interest, unless a court orders otherwise.

Order for Payment Out, Special Party or Non-Party Child

(16) The court may, on motion, order payment out of court of money for or on behalf of a special party or a child who is not a party.

Where Notice is not Required

(17) A motion under subrule (16) by the Children's Lawyer or the Public Guardian and Trustee may be made without notice, unless the court orders otherwise.

Costs

(18) In making an order under subrule (16), the court may order that costs payable to the person who made the motion be paid directly to that person's representative out of the money in court.

Application

(19) This rule applies to the payment into and out of court of money paid into court on and after the day on which Ontario Regulation 389/12 comes into force.

O. Reg. 389/12, s. 1

RULE 26 — ENFORCEMENT OF ORDERS

Where to Enforce an Order

26. (1) The place for enforcement of an order is governed by subrules 5(5), (6), (7) and (7.1) (place for starting enforcement).

How to Enforce an Order

(2) An order that has not been obeyed may, in addition to any other method of enforcement provided by law, be enforced as provided by subrules (3) and (4).

Payment Orders

(3) A payment order may be enforced by,

(a) a request for a financial statement (subrule 27(1));

(b) a request for disclosure from an income source (subrule 27(7));

(c) a financial examination (subrule 27(11));

(d) seizure and sale (rule 28);

(e) garnishment (rule 29);

(f) a default hearing (rule 30), if the order is a support order;

(g) the appointment of a receiver under section 101 of the *Courts of Justice Act*; and

(h) registration under section 42 of the *Family Responsibility and Support Arrears Enforcement Act, 1996.*

Other Orders

(4) An order other than a payment order may be enforced by,

(a) a writ of temporary seizure of property (subrule 28(10));

(b) a contempt order (rule 31); and

(c) the appointment of a receiver under section 101 of the *Courts of Justice Act.*

Statement of Money Owed

(5) A statement of money owed shall be in Form 26, with a copy of the order that is in default attached.

Special Forms for Statement of Money Owed

(6) Despite subrule (5),

(a) if the *Family Responsibility and Support Arrears Enforcement Act, 1996* applies, a statement of arrears in the form used by the Director may be used instead of Form 26;

(b) if the *Interjurisdictional Support Orders Act, 2002* applies, a document receivable under section 49 of that Act may be used instead of Form 26.

Recipient's or Director's Entitlement to Costs

(7) Unless the court orders otherwise, the recipient or the Director is entitled to the costs,

(a) of carrying out a financial examination; and

(b) of issuing, serving, filing and enforcing a writ of seizure and sale, a writ of temporary seizure and a notice of garnishment and of changing them by statutory declaration.

Enforcement of Administrative Costs

(8) For the purpose of subrule (7), the recipient or the Director may collect under a writ of seizure and sale, a notice of garnishment or a statutory declaration changing either of them,

(a) the amounts set out in the regulations under the *Administration of Justice Act* and awarded under rule 24 (costs) for filing and renewing with the sheriff a writ of seizure and sale or a writ of temporary seizure;

(b) payments made to a sheriff, clerk, official examiner, authorized court transcriptionist or other public officer in accordance with the regulations under the *Administration of Justice Act* and awarded under rule 24 (costs), on filing with the sheriff or clerk a copy of a receipt for each payment or an affidavit setting out the payments made; and

(c) the actual expense for carrying out a financial examination, or any other costs to which the recipient or the Director is entitled under subrule (7), on filing with the sheriff or clerk an affidavit (Form 26A) setting out the items of expense in detail.

Affidavit for Filing Domestic Contract

(9) An affidavit for filing a domestic contract under subsection 35(1) of the *Family Law Act* shall be in Form 26B.

Director's Status

(10) If the Director enforces an order under the *Family Responsibility and Support Arrears Enforcement Act, 1996*, anything in these rules relating to enforcement by the person in whose favour the order was made applies to the Director.

Filing and Refiling with the Director

(11) A person who files or refiles a support order in the Director's office shall immediately send notice of the filing, by mail, fax or email to the clerk at any court office where the recipient is enforcing the order.

Transferring Enforcement from Recipient to Director

(12) A recipient who files a support order in the Director's office shall, on the Director's request, assign to the Director any enforcement that the recipient has started, and then the Director may continue with the enforcement as if the Director had started it.

Transferring Enforcement from Director to Recipient

(13) If the parties withdraw a support order from the Director's office, the Director shall, on the recipient's request, given to the Director at the same time as the notice of withdrawal, assign to the recipient any enforcement that the Director has started, and then the recipient may continue with the enforcement as if the recipient had started it.

Notice of Transfer of Enforcement

(14) A person who continues an enforcement under subrule (12) or (13) shall immediately send a notice of transfer of enforcement (Form 26C), by mail, fax or email to,

(a) all parties to the enforcement;

(b) the clerk at every court office where the enforcement is being carried on; and

(c) every sheriff who is involved with the enforcement at the time of transfer.

Place of Registration of Support Order Under the* Divorce Act *(Canada)

(15) If a person wants to enforce an order for support made outside Ontario under the *Divorce Act* (Canada), the order shall be registered in a court, as defined in subsection 20(1) of that Act, as follows:

1. If the recipient resides in Ontario, in the municipality where the recipient resides.

2. If the recipient does not reside in Ontario, in the municipality where the payor resides.

3. If neither the recipient nor the payor resides in Ontario, in the municipality where any property owned by the payor is located or, if the payor doesn't have any property, in any municipality.

Place of Registration of Custody or Access Order Under the* Divorce Act *(Canada)

(16) If a person wants to enforce an order involving custody of or access to a child that is made outside Ontario under the *Divorce Act* (Canada), the order shall be registered in a court, as defined in subsection 20(1) of that Act, in accordance with clause 5(6)(a) of these rules.

Registration Requirements

(17) The person requesting the registration shall send to the court a certified copy of the order and a written request that the order be registered under paragraph 20(3)(a) of the *Divorce Act* (Canada).

O. Reg. 544/99, s. 11; 56/03, s. 4; 89/04, s. 9; 142/14, s. 11; 140/15, s. 4, item 4; 235/16, s. 5

RULE 27 — REQUIRING FINANCIAL INFORMATION

Request for Financial Statement

27. (1) If a payment order is in default, a recipient may serve a request for a financial statement (Form 27) on the payor.

Effect of Request for Financial Statement

(2) Within 15 days after being served with the request, the payor shall send a completed financial statement (Form 13) to the recipient by mail, fax or email.

Frequency of Requests for Financial Statements

(3) A recipient may request a financial statement only once in a six-month period, unless the court gives the recipient permission to do so more often.

Application of Rule 13

(4) If a party is required under this rule to give a financial statement, the following subrules apply with necessary changes:

13(6) (full disclosure)

13(7) or (7.1) (income tax documents)

13(11) (insufficient financial information)

13(12) (updating financial statement)

13(15) (correcting and updating)

13(16) (order to file statement).

Order for Financial Statement

(5) The court may, on motion, order a payor to serve and file a financial statement.

Failure to Obey Order

(6) If the payor does not serve and file a financial statement within 10 days after being served with the order, the court may, on motion with special service (subrule 6(3)), order that the payor be imprisoned continuously or intermittently for not more than 40 days.

Request for Statement of Income from Income Source

(7) If a payment order is in default, the recipient may serve a request for a statement of income (Form 27A) on an income source of the payor, requiring the income source to prepare and send to the recipient, by mail, fax or email a statement of income (Form 27B).

Frequency of Requests for Statement of Income

(8) A recipient may request a statement of income from an income source only once in a six-month period, unless the court gives the recipient permission to do so more often.

Order for Statement of Income

(9) The court may, on the recipient's motion, order an income source to serve and file a statement of income.

Income Source's Failure to Obey Order

(10) If the income source does not serve and file a statement of income within 10 days after being served with the order, the court may, on the recipient's motion, order the income source to post a bond (Form 32).

Appointment for Financial Examination

(11) If a payment order is in default, the recipient may serve on the payor, by special service (subrule 6(3)), an appointment for a financial examination (Form 27C), requiring the payor to,

(a) come to a financial examination;

(b) bring to the examination any document or thing named in the appointment that is in the payor's control or available to the payor on request, relevant to the enforcement of the order, and not protected by a legal privilege; and

(c) serve a financial statement (Form 13) on the recipient, not later than seven days before the date of the examination.

Financial Examination of Person Other than Payor

(12) If a payment order is in default and a person other than the payor may know about the matters listed in subrule (17), the recipient may require that person to come to a financial examination by serving a summons to witness (Form 23) and the witness fee (subrule 23(4)) on the person by special service (subrules 6(3) and (4)).

Place Where Financial Examination Held

(13) A financial examination shall be held,

(a) in a place where the parties and the person to be examined agree;

(b) where the person to be examined lives in Ontario, in the municipality where the person lives; or

(c) in a place chosen by the court.

Other Rules Apply

(14) Subrules 19(4), (5) and (8) (documents protected by legal privilege, use of privileged documents, documents omitted from affidavit) and 23(7) (failure to obey summons) apply to a financial examination, with necessary changes.

Notice of Time and Place of Examination

(15) A payor who is served with an appointment or a person who is served with a summons for a financial examination shall have at least 10 days' notice of the time and place of the examination.

Before Whom Examination is Held, Method of Recording

(16) A financial examination shall be held under oath or affirmation, before a person chosen by agreement of the payor and recipient or in accordance with subrule 20(12) (other arrangements for questioning), and shall be recorded by a method chosen in the same way.

Scope of Examination

(17) On a financial examination, the payor or other person may be questioned about,

(a) the reason for the payor's default;

(b) the payor's income and property;

(c) the debts owed to and by the payor;

(d) the disposal of any property by the payor either before or after the making of the order that is in default;

(e) the payor's past, present and future ability to pay under the order;

(f) whether the payor intends to obey the order, and any reason for not doing so; and

(g) any other matter relevant to the enforcement of the order.

Resistance to Examination

(18) Subrule (19) applies if a payor who is served with an appointment or a person who is served with a summons for a financial examination,

(a) does not come to the examination as required by the appointment or summons;

(b) does not serve on the recipient a financial statement as required by the appointment;

(c) comes to the examination, but does not bring a document or thing named in the appointment or summons; or

(d) comes to the examination, but refuses to take an oath or affirm or to answer a question.

Order for Another Examination

(19) The court may, on motion, make an order and give directions for another financial examination of the payor or other person and may in addition require the payor or person to post a bond (Form 32).

Imprisonment

(20) If a payor or other person, without sufficient excuse, fails to obey an order or direction made under subrule (19), the court may, on motion with special service (subrule 6(3)), order that the payor or person be imprisoned continuously or intermittently for not more than 40 days.

Imprisonment Power is Additional

(21) The court may exercise its power under subrule (20) in addition to or instead of its power of forfeiture under rule 32 (bonds, recognizances and warrants).

Frequency of Examinations

(22) A recipient may conduct only one financial examination of a payor and one financial examination of any other person in a six-month period, or more often with the court's permission.

O. Reg. 544/99, s. 12; 89/04, s. 10; 322/13, s. 16; 69/15, s. 10; 140/15, s. 4, item 5

RULE 28 — SEIZURE AND SALE

Issue of Writ of Seizure and Sale

28. (1) The clerk shall issue a writ of seizure and sale (Form 28) if a recipient files,

(a) a request for a writ of seizure and sale (Form 28A); and

(b) a statement of money owed (subrules 26(5) and (6)).

Electronic Filing of Writ

(1.1) Subject to subrule (11), a writ of seizure and sale issued under subrule (1) may be filed with a sheriff electronically.

Electronic Filing of Request, Issuance of Writ

(1.2) Subject to subrule (11), a recipient may file a request for a writ of seizure and sale electronically, in which case,

(a) clause (1)(b) does not apply to the request;

(b) the writ shall be issued electronically; and

(c) the issued writ shall automatically be filed electronically with the sheriff specified in the writ.

(1.3) [Repealed O. Reg. 298/18, s. 16.]

Error in Writ Issued Electronically

(1.4) If a person who obtained an electronically issued writ of seizure and sale discovers that the writ contains an error, the person may, no later than 5 p.m. eastern standard or daylight saving time, as the case may be, on the second day after the day on which the writ is considered under subrule (13) to have been filed with a sheriff, correct the error by using the software that was used for the issuance of the writ.

Statutory Declaration to Change Amount Owed

(2) The statutory declaration to sheriff mentioned in section 44 of the *Family Responsibility and Support Arrears Enforcement Act, 1996* shall be in Form 28B.

Statutory Declaration if Order Changed

(3) If a court changes a payment order that is being enforced by a writ of seizure and sale, a statutory declaration to sheriff (Form 28B) may be filed with the sheriff and once filed, it has the same effect as a declaration mentioned in subrule (2).

Electronic Filing

(3.1) A statutory declaration referred to in subrule (2) or (3) may be filed electronically.

Duration of Writ

(4) A writ of seizure and sale continues in effect until,

(a) the writ is withdrawn under subrule (6.5) or (7); or

(b) the court orders otherwise under subrule (8).

Writ Issued Under Former Rules

(5) A writ directing the sheriff to seize and sell a payor's property that was issued by the court under the rules that applied before these rules take effect has the same legal effect as a writ of seizure and sale issued under these rules, and does not expire except as subrule (4) provides.

Notifying Sheriff of Payment Received

(6) If a writ of seizure and sale has been filed with a sheriff,

(a) the recipient shall, on the sheriff's request, provide a statutory declaration setting out details of all payments received by or on behalf of the recipient; and

(b) the sheriff shall update the writ accordingly.

May be Filed Electronically

(6.1) Subject to subrule (11), the statutory declaration referred to in clause (6)(a) may be filed with the sheriff electronically.

Change of Address

(6.2) If the address of the recipient or his or her lawyer changes after a writ has been filed with a sheriff, the recipient shall give written notice of the new address to the sheriff, and the sheriff shall update the writ accordingly.

May be Filed Electronically

(6.3) Subject to subrule (11), notice of the new address may be filed with the sheriff electronically.

Confirmation of Electronically Filed Writ

(6.4) In order to confirm whether a writ of seizure and sale filed with a sheriff electronically has been properly issued and filed, the sheriff may require the recipient to provide to the sheriff, in the manner and within the time the sheriff specifies, a statement of money owed (subrule 26(5) or (6)).

Withdrawal by Sheriff

(6.5) The sheriff may withdraw an electronically filed writ of seizure and sale if,

(a) the sheriff determines that the writ was improperly issued or filed; or

(b) the recipient fails to comply with subrule (6.4).

Same

(6.6) A writ may be withdrawn under subrule (6.5) at any time during its enforcement.

Corrections by Sheriff

(6.7) If the sheriff makes a determination that a writ of seizure and sale filed with the sheriff electronically was properly issued or filed but contains an error or otherwise differs from the order to which the writ relates, the sheriff may correct the writ to make it consistent with the order.

Notice

(6.8) The sheriff shall give notice of a withdrawal under subrule (6.5) or a correction under subrule (6.7) to the recipient.

Withdrawing Writ

(7) The person who obtained a writ to enforce an order shall immediately withdraw it from every sheriff's office where it has been filed if,

(a) the person no longer wants to enforce the order by a writ;

(b) in the case of a payment order, the payor's obligation to make periodic payments under the order has ended and all other amounts owing under it have been paid; or

(c) in the case of any other order, the person against whom the writ was issued has obeyed the order.

Same

(7.1) A writ may be withdrawn under subrule (7) by,

(a) giving written notice to the sheriff that the writ should be withdrawn; or

(b) subject to subrule (11), filing notice of a withdrawal of writ electronically.

Order Changing, Withdrawing or Suspending Writ

(8) The court may, on motion, make an order changing the terms of a writ, withdrawing it or temporarily suspending it, even if the writ was issued by another court in Ontario.

Service of Order

(9) The person making the motion, or another person named by the court, shall serve a copy of the order on,

(a) every sheriff in whose office the writ has been filed; and

(b) if the writ was issued by the court in another place, or by another court, on the clerk of the court in the other place or the clerk of the other court.

Electronic Filing of Changes

(9.1) If the court makes an order under subrule (8) making any of the following changes to a writ that has been filed with a sheriff, the person required to serve a copy of the order under subrule (9) may, subject to subrule (11), file the changes to the writ with the sheriff electronically instead of serving a copy of the order on the sheriff under clause (9)(a):

1. The name of a party.

2. The recipient's lawyer or other representative.

3. The amount owing under the writ.

Writ of Temporary Seizure of Property

(10) The court may, on motion with special service (subrule 6(3)), give permission to issue a writ of temporary seizure (Form 28C) directing the sheriff to take possession of and hold all or part of the land and other property of a person against whom an order has been made and to hold any income from the property until the writ is withdrawn or the court orders otherwise.

Limit on Who May File Electronically

(11) The electronic filing and issuance of documents under this rule is only available for,

(a) lawyers;

(b) the Director of the Family Responsibility Office; and

(c) Ministers or bodies acting under the authority of an Act of Canada or Ontario.

(12) [Repealed O. Reg. 298/18, s. 16.]

(13) [Repealed O. Reg. 298/18, s. 16.]

Electronic Filing and Signatures, Swearing

(14) The following requirements are deemed to have been met if a document is filed or issued under this rule electronically using the authorized software:

1. A requirement that the document be signed.
2. A requirement that the document be sworn or affirmed.

O. Reg. 544/99, s. 13; 89/04, s. 11; 142/14, s. 12; 298/18, s. 16

RULE 29 — GARNISHMENT

Issue of Notice or Notices of Garnishment

29. (1) The clerk shall issue as many notices of garnishment (Form 29A or 29B) as a recipient requests if the recipient files,

(a) a request for garnishment (Form 29) or an extra-provincial garnishment process referred to in section 50 of the *Family Responsibility and Support Arrears Enforcement Act, 1996*; and

(b) a statement of money owed (subrules 26(5) and (6)).

One Recipient and One Garnishee per Notice

(2) Each notice of garnishment shall name only one recipient and one garnishee.

Service on Payor and Garnishee

(3) The notice of garnishment shall be served on the payor and on the garnishee but the payor shall, in addition, be served with the documents filed under subrule (1).

Effect of Notice of Garnishment

(4) A notice of garnishment attaches,

(a) every debt that is payable by the garnishee to the payor at the time the notice is served; and

(b) every debt that is payable by the garnishee to the payor,

(i) after the notice is served, or

(ii) on the fulfilment of a condition after the notice is served.

Duration

(5) The notice of garnishment continues in effect from the time of service on the garnishee until it is withdrawn or stopped under this rule or until the court orders otherwise under this rule.

Financial Institution

(6) If the garnishee is a financial institution, the notice of garnishment and all further notices required to be served under this rule shall be served at the branch of the institution where the debt to the payor is payable, unless subrule (6.1) applies.

Federally Regulated Financial Institution — Garnishment Re Support

(6.1) If the garnishee is a financial institution to which the *Bank Act* (Canada), the *Cooperative Credit Associations Act* (Canada) or the *Trust and Loan Companies Act* (Canada) applies and the garnishment enforces a support order, the notice of garnishment and all further notices required to be served under this rule,

(a) shall be served at the designated office of the institution established for this purpose; and

(b) shall be accompanied by a statement to garnishee financial institution re support (Form 29J).

New Accounts

(6.2) Subrules (4) and (5) do not apply to money in an account opened after a notice of garnishment is served as described in subrule (6) or (6.1).

Joint Debts Garnishable

(7) Subrules (4) and (5) also apply to debts owed to the payor and another person jointly.

Procedure When Joint Debt Garnished

(8) If a garnishee has been served with a notice of garnishment and the garnishee owes a debt to which subrules (4) and (5) apply to the payor and another person jointly,

(a) the garnishee shall pay, in accordance with subrule (11), half of the debt, or the larger or smaller amount that the court orders;

(b) the garnishee shall immediately send the other person a notice to co-owner of debt (Form 29C) by mail, fax or email, to the person's address in the garnishee's records; and

(c) the garnishee shall immediately serve the notice to co-owner of debt on the recipient or the Director, depending on who is enforcing the order, and on the sheriff or clerk if the sheriff or clerk is to receive the money under subrule (11) or (12).

Joint Debt — Money to be Held

(9) Despite subrule (12), if served with notice under clause (8)(c), the sheriff, clerk or Director shall hold the money received for 30 days, and may pay it out when the 30 days expire, unless the other person serves and files a dispute within the 30 days.

Payment of Arrears Does not End Garnishment

(10) A notice of garnishment continues to attach future periodic payments even though the total amount owed when it was served is fully paid up.

Persons to Whom Garnishee Makes Payments

(11) A garnishee who has been served with a notice of garnishment shall make the required payments to,

(a) the Director, if the notice of garnishment relates to an order being enforced by the Director;

(b) the clerk, if the notice of garnishment does not relate to an order being enforced by the Director.

Clerk or Director to Pay Out Money

(12) On receiving money under a notice of garnishment, the Director or clerk shall, even if a dispute has been filed, but subject to subrules (9) and (13), immediately pay,

(a) to the recipient, any part of the money that comes within the priority created by subsection 2(3) of the *Creditors' Relief Act, 2010*; and

(b) to the sheriff, any part of the money that exceeds that priority.

Order that Subrule (12) Does not Apply

(13) The court may, at a garnishment hearing or on a motion to change the garnishment under this rule, order that subrule (12) does not apply.

Change in Garnishment, Indexed Support

(14) If a notice of garnishment enforces a support order that indexes periodic payments for inflation, the recipient may serve on the garnishee and on the payor a statutory declaration of indexed support (Form 29D) setting out the new amount to be paid under the order, and file the declaration with the court.

Effect of Statutory Declaration of Indexed Support

(15) A statutory declaration of indexed support requires the garnishee to pay the new amount set out in the declaration from the time it is served on the garnishee.

Garnishment Dispute

(16) Within 10 days after being served with a notice of garnishment or a statutory declaration of indexed support, a payor, garnishee or co-owner of a debt may serve on the other parties and file a dispute (Form 29E, 29F or 29G).

Notice of Garnishment Hearing

(17) The clerk shall, on request, issue a notice of garnishment hearing (Form 29H),

(a) within 10 days after a dispute is served and filed; or

(b) if the recipient says that the garnishee has not paid any money or has not paid enough money.

Service of Notice

(18) The clerk shall serve and file the notice not later than 10 days before the hearing.

Garnishment Hearing

(19) At a garnishment hearing, the court may make one or more of the following temporary or final orders:

1. An order dismissing the dispute.

2. An order that changes how much is being garnished on account of a periodic payment order. The court may make an order under this paragraph even if it does not have the authority to change the payment order itself.

2.1 An order that changes how much is being garnished on account of a periodic payment order and that, at the same time, changes the payment order itself. The court may make an order under this paragraph only if,

i. the payment order is one that the court has the authority to change, and

ii. the parties to the payment order agree to the change, or one of those parties has served and filed notice of a motion to have the change made.

3. An order changing how much is being garnished on account of a non-periodic payment order.

4. An order suspending the garnishment or any term of it, while the hearing is adjourned or until the court orders otherwise.

5. An order setting aside the notice of garnishment or any statutory declaration of indexed support.

6. An order that garnished money held or received by the clerk, Director or sheriff be held in court.

7. An order that garnished money that has been paid out in error to the recipient be paid into and held in court, returned to the garnishee or sent to the payor or to the co-owner of the debt.

8. An order that garnished money held in court be returned to the garnishee or be sent to the payor, the co-owner of the debt, the sheriff, the clerk or the Director.

9. An order deciding how much remains owing under a payment order that is being enforced by garnishment against the payor or garnishee.

10. If the garnishee has not paid what was required by the notice of garnishment or statutory declaration of indexed support, an order that the garnishee pay all or part of what was required.

11. An order deciding who is entitled to the costs of the garnishment hearing and setting the amount of the costs.

Changing Garnishment at Other Times

(20) The court may also use the powers listed in subrule (19), on motion or on its own initiative, even if the notice of garnishment was issued by another court,

(a) on a motion under section 7 of the *Wages Act*;

(b) if the court replaces a temporary payment order with a final payment order;

(c) if the court indexes or changes a payment order; or

(d) if the court allows an appeal.

Changing Garnishment When Ability to Pay Changes

(21) If there has been a material change in the payor's circumstances affecting the payor's ability to pay, the court may, on motion, use the powers listed in subrule (19).

Garnishee's Payment Pays Debt

(22) Payment of a debt by a garnishee under a notice of garnishment or statutory declaration of indexed support pays off the debt between the garnishee and the payor to the extent of the payment.

Notice by Garnishee — Payor not Working or Receiving Money

(23) Within 10 days after a payor stops working for or is no longer receiving any money from a garnishee, the garnishee shall send a notice as subrule (27) requires,

(a) saying that the payor is no longer working for or is no longer receiving any money from the garnishee;

(b) giving the date on which the payor stopped working for or receiving money from the garnishee and the date of the last payment to the payor from the garnishee; and

(c) giving the name and address of any other income source of the payor, if known.

Notice by Garnishee — Payor Working or Receiving Money Again

(24) Within 10 days after the payor returns to work for or starts to receive money again from the garnishee, the garnishee shall send another notice as subrule (27) requires, saying that the payor has returned to work for or started to receive money again from the garnishee.

Notice by Payor — Working or Receiving Money Again

(25) Within 10 days after returning to work for or starting to receive money again from the garnishee, the payor shall send a notice as subrule (27) requires, saying that the payor has returned to work for or started to receive money again from the garnishee.

Notice by Payor — New Income Source

(26) Within 10 days after starting to work for or receive money from a new income source, the payor shall send a notice as subrule (27) requires, saying that the payor has started to work for or to receive money from the new income source.

Notice Sent to Clerk and Recipient or Director

(27) A notice referred to in subrule (23), (24), (25) or (26) shall be sent to the clerk, and to the recipient or the Director (depending on who is enforcing the order), by mail, fax or email.

Notice by Clerk

(28) When the clerk receives a notice under subrule (26), the clerk shall immediately notify the recipient or the Director (depending on who is enforcing the order) by mail, fax or email.

New Notice of Garnishment

(29) If no written objection is received within 10 days of the clerk notifying the recipient or the Director that a notice under subrule (26) was received, the clerk shall,

(a) issue a new notice of garnishment directed to the new garnishee, requiring the same deductions as were required to be made, under the previous notice of garnishment or statutory declaration of indexed support, on the day that the notice under subrule (26) was received; and

(b) send a copy of the new notice of garnishment to the payor and the new garnishee, by mail, fax or email.

Effect of New Notice of Garnishment

(30) Issuing a new notice of garnishment under clause (29)(a) does not cancel any previous notice of garnishment or statutory declaration of indexed support.

Notice to Stop Garnishment

(31) The recipient shall immediately send a notice to stop garnishment (Form 29I), by mail, fax or email to the garnishee and payor and file it with the clerk if,

(a) the recipient no longer wants to enforce the order by garnishment; or

(b) the requirement to make periodic payments under the order has ended and all other amounts owing under the order have been paid.

Old Orders

(32) This rule applies, with necessary changes, to,

(a) an attachment order made under section 30 of the *Family Law Reform Act* (chapter 152 of the Revised Statutes of Ontario, 1980); and

(b) a garnishment order issued by the court under the rules that were in effect before January 1, 1985.

O. Reg. 544/99, s. 14; 56/03, s. 5; 76/06, s. 7; 322/13, s. 17; 140/15, s. 4, item 6

RULE 30 — DEFAULT HEARING

Issuing Notice of Default Hearing

30. (1) The clerk shall issue a notice of default hearing (Form 30),

(a) if the support order is being enforced by the recipient, when the recipient files a request for a default hearing (Form 30A) and a statement of money owed (subrule 26(5));

(b) if it is being enforced by the Director, when the Director files a statement of money owed.

Serving Notice of Default Hearing

(2) The notice of default hearing shall be served on the payor by special service in accordance with subrule 6(4) and filed.

Payor's Dispute

(3) Within 10 days after being served with the notice, the payor shall serve on the recipient and file,

(a) a financial statement (Form 13); and

(b) a default dispute (Form 30B).

Updating Statement of Money Owed

(4) The recipient shall serve and file a new statement of money owed (subrule 26(5)) not more than seven days before the default hearing.

When Director to Update Statement

(5) Despite subrule 26(10), subrule (4) applies to the Director only if,

(a) the amount the Director is asking the court to enforce is greater than the amount shown in the notice of default hearing; or

(b) the court directs it.

Statement of Money Owed Presumed Correct

(6) The payor is presumed to admit that the recipient's statement of money owed is correct, unless the payor has filed a default dispute stating that the statement of money owed is not correct and giving detailed reasons.

Arrears Enforceable to Date of Hearing

(7) At the default hearing, the court may decide and enforce the amount owing as of the date of the hearing.

Conditional Imprisonment

(8) The court may make an order under clause 41(10)(h) or (i) of the *Family Responsibility and Support Arrears Enforcement Act, 1996*, suspending the payor's imprisonment on appropriate conditions.

Issuing Warrant of Committal

(9) If the recipient, on a motion with special service in accordance with subrule 6(4) on the payor, states by affidavit (or by oral evidence, with the court's permission) that the payor has not obeyed a condition that was imposed under subrule (8), the court may issue a warrant of committal against the payor, subject to subsection 41(15) (power to change order) of the *Family Responsibility and Support Arrears Enforcement Act, 1996*.

O. Reg. 76/06, s. 8; 322/13, s. 18

RULE 31 — CONTEMPT OF COURT

When Contempt Motion Available

31. (1) An order, other than a payment order, may be enforced by a contempt motion made in the case in which the order was made, even if another penalty is available.

Notice of Contempt Motion

(2) The notice of contempt motion (Form 31) shall be served together with a supporting affidavit, by special service in accordance with subrule 6(4), unless the court orders otherwise.

Affidavit for Contempt Motion

(3) The supporting affidavit may contain statements of information that the person signing the affidavit learned from someone else, but only if the requirements of subrule 14(19) are satisfied.

Warrant to Bring to Court

(4) To bring before the court a person against whom a contempt motion is made, the court may issue a warrant for the person's arrest if,

(a) the person's attendance is necessary in the interest of justice; and

(b) the person is not likely to attend voluntarily.

Contempt Orders

(5) If the court finds a person in contempt of the court, it may order that the person,

(a) be imprisoned for any period and on any conditions that are just;

(b) pay a fine in any amount that is appropriate;

(c) pay an amount to a party as a penalty;

(d) do anything else that the court decides is appropriate;

(e) not do what the court forbids;

(f) pay costs in an amount decided by the court; and

(g) obey any other order.

Writ of Temporary Seizure

(6) The court may also give permission to issue a writ of temporary seizure (Form 28C) against the person's property.

Limited Imprisonment or Fine

(7) In a contempt order under one of the following provisions, the period of imprisonment and the amount of a fine may not be greater than the relevant Act allows:

1. Section 38 of the *Children's Law Reform Act*.

2. Section 49 of the *Family Law Act*.

3. Section 53 of the *Family Responsibility and Support Arrears Enforcement Act, 1996*.

Conditional Imprisonment or Fine

(8) A contempt order for imprisonment or for the payment of a fine may be suspended on appropriate conditions.

Issuing Warrant of Committal

(9) If a party, on a motion with special service (subrule 6(3)) on the person in contempt, states by an affidavit in Form 32C (or by oral evidence, with the court's permission) that the person has not obeyed a condition imposed under subrule (8), the court may issue a warrant of committal against the person.

Payment of Fine

(10) A contempt order for the payment of a fine shall require the person in contempt to pay the fine,

(a) in a single payment, immediately or before a date that the court chooses; or

(b) in instalments, over a period of time that the court considers appropriate.

Corporation in Contempt

(11) If a corporation is found in contempt, the court may also make an order under subrule (5), (6) or (7) against any officer or director of the corporation.

Change in Contempt Order

(12) The court may, on motion, change an order under this rule, give directions and make any other order that is just.

O. Reg. 322/13, s. 19

RULE 32 — BONDS, RECOGNIZANCES AND WARRANTS

Warrant to Bring a Person to Court

32. (1) If a person does not come to court after being served with notice of a case, enforcement or motion that may result in an order requiring the person to post a bond,

(a) the court may issue a warrant for the person's arrest, to bring the person before the court, and adjourn the case to await the person's arrival; or

(b) the court may,

(i) hear and decide the case in the person's absence and, if appropriate, make an order requiring the person to post a bond, and

(ii) if the person has been served with the order and does not post the bond by the date set out in the order, issue a warrant for the person's arrest, on motion without notice, to bring the person before the court.

Form of Bond and Other Requirements

(2) A bond shall be in Form 32, does not need a seal, and shall,

(a) have at least one surety, unless the court orders otherwise;

(b) list the conditions that the court considers appropriate;

(c) set out an amount of money to be forfeited if the conditions are not obeyed;

(d) shall require the person posting the bond to deposit the money with the clerk immediately, unless the court orders otherwise; and

(e) name the person to whom any forfeited money is to be paid out.

Person Before Whom Recognizance to be Entered into

(3) A recognizance shall be entered into before a judge, a justice of the peace or the clerk.

Change of Conditions in a Bond

(4) The court may, on motion, change any condition in a bond if there has been a material change in a party's circumstances since the date of the order for posting the bond or the date of an order under this subrule, whichever is more recent.

***Change in Bond under* Children's Law Reform Act**

(5) In the case of a bond under the *Children's Law Reform Act*, subrule (4) also applies to a material change in circumstances that affects or is likely to affect the best interests of the child.

Removal or Replacement of Surety

(6) The court may, on motion, order that a surety be removed or be replaced by another person as surety, in which case as soon as the order is made, the surety who is removed or replaced is free from any obligation under the bond.

Motion to Enforce Bond

(7) A person requesting the court's permission to enforce a bond under subsection 143(1) (enforcement of recognizance or bond) of the *Courts of Justice Act* shall serve a notice of forfeiture motion (Form 32A), with a copy of the bond attached, on the person said to have broken the bond and on each surety.

Forfeiture if no Deposit Made

(8) If an order of forfeiture of a bond is made and no deposit was required, or a deposit was required but was not made, the order shall require the payor or surety to pay the required amount to the person to whom the bond is payable,

(a) in a single payment, immediately or before a date that the court chooses; or

(b) in instalments, over a period of time that the court considers appropriate.

Change in Payment Schedule

(9) If time is allowed for payment under subrule (8), the court may, on a later motion by the payor or a surety, allow further time for payment.

Order for Forfeiture of Deposit

(10) If an order of forfeiture of a bond is made and a deposit was required and was made, the order shall direct the clerk to pay the required amount immediately to the person to whom the bond is made payable.

Cancelling Bond

(11) The court may, on motion, make an order under subrule (4), or an order cancelling the bond and directing a refund of all or part of the deposit, if,

(a) a payor or surety made a deposit under the bond;

(b) the conditions of the bond have not been broken; and

(c) the conditions have expired or, although they have not expired or do not have an expiry date, the payor or surety has good reasons for getting the conditions of the bond changed.

Form of Warrant for Arrest

(12) A warrant for arrest issued against any of the following shall be in Form 32B:

1. A payor who does not file a financial statement ordered under subsection 40(4) of the *Family Responsibility and Support Arrears Enforcement Act, 1996* or under these rules.

2. A payor who does not come to a default hearing under section 41 of the *Family Responsibility and Support Arrears Enforcement Act, 1996.*

3. An absconding respondent under subsection 43(1) or 59(2) of the *Family Law Act.*

4. An absconding payor under subsection 49(1) of the *Family Responsibility and Support Arrears Enforcement Act, 1996.*

5. A witness who does not come to court or remain in attendance as required by a summons to witness.

6. A person who does not come to court in a case that may result in an order requiring the person to post a bond under these rules.

7. A person who does not obey an order requiring the person to post a bond under these rules.

8. A person against whom a contempt motion is made.

9. Any other person liable to arrest under an order.

10. Any other person liable to arrest for committing an offence.

Bail on Arrest

(13) Section 150 (interim release by justice of the peace) of the *Provincial Offences Act* applies, with necessary changes, to an arrest made under a warrant mentioned in paragraph 1, 2, 3 or 4 of subrule (12).

Affidavit for Warrant of Committal

(14) An affidavit in support of a motion for a warrant of committal shall be in Form 32C.

Form of Warrant of Committal

(15) A warrant of committal issued to enforce an order of imprisonment shall be in Form 32D.

RULE 32.1 — ENFORCEMENT OF FAMILY ARBITRATION AWARDS [HEADING ADDED O. REG. 388/12, S. 8.]

Requesting Enforcement

32.1 (1) A party who is entitled to the enforcement of a family arbitration award and who wants to ask the court to enforce the award under section 59.8 of the *Family Law Act* may file a request to enforce a family arbitration award (Form 32.1), together with,

(a) copies of the certificates of independent legal advice required by the *Family Law Act* for the parties to the family arbitration agreement;

(b) a copy of the family arbitration agreement; and

(c) the original award or a certified copy.

When Required to Proceed by Motion

(2) Despite subrule (1), if there is already a family law case to which these rules apply between the parties to the family arbitration agreement in the Superior Court of Justice or the Family Court of the Superior Court of Justice, the party entitled to enforcement shall make a motion in that case rather than a request under this rule, and subrule 14(24) applies in respect of the motion.

Application of Other Rules

(3) The rules that apply to an application apply to a request to enforce a family arbitration award that is proceeding under this rule, unless these rules provide otherwise.

Hearing Date

(4) When a request to enforce a family arbitration award is filed, the clerk shall set a hearing date.

Service

(5) The request shall be served immediately on every other party.

Request Not Served on or Before Hearing Date

(6) If a request to enforce a family arbitration award is not served on a respondent on or before the hearing date, the clerk shall, at the applicant's request, set a new hearing date for that respondent, and the applicant shall make the necessary change to the request and serve it immediately on that respondent.

Opposing a Request

(7) Despite subrule 10(1) (serving and filing answer), a respondent who wants to oppose a request to enforce a family arbitration award shall serve a dispute of request for enforcement (Form 32.1A) on every other party and file it,

(a) no later than 30 days after being served with the request; or

(b) if the request is served outside Canada or the United States of America, no later than 60 days after being served with the request.

Written Hearing

(8) Unless the court orders otherwise under subrule (10), the request shall be dealt with on the basis of written documents without the parties or their lawyers needing to come to court.

Request for Oral Hearing

(9) A respondent may request an oral hearing by filing a motion form (Form 14B) within seven days after being served with the request to enforce a family arbitration award.

Order for Oral Hearing

(10) The court may order an oral hearing, on motion or on its own initiative, if it is satisfied that an oral hearing is necessary to deal with the case justly.

O. Reg. 388/12, s. 8; 69/15, s. 11

RULE 33 — CHILD PROTECTION

Timetable

33. (1) Every child protection case, including a status review application, is governed by the following timetable:

Column 1 **Step in the case**	**Column 2** **Maximum time for completion, from the start of the case**
First hearing, if child has been brought to a place of safety	5 days
Service and filing of answers and plans of care	30 days
Temporary care and custody hearing	35 days
Settlement conference	80 days
Hearing	120 days

Case Management Judge

(2) Wherever possible, at the start of the case a judge shall be assigned to manage it and monitor its progress.

Court may Lengthen Times Only in Best Interests of Child

(3) The court may lengthen a time shown in the timetable only if the best interests of the child require it.

Parties may not Lengthen Times

(4) The parties may not lengthen a time shown in the timetable by consent under subrule 3(6).

Plan of Care or Supervision to be Served

(5) A party who wants the court to consider a plan of care or supervision shall serve it on the other parties and file it not later than seven days before a conference, even if that is sooner than the timetable would require.

Temporary Care and Custody Hearing — Affidavit Evidence

(6) The evidence at a temporary care and custody hearing shall be given by affidavit, unless the court orders otherwise.

Status Review

(6.1) A status review application under clause 113(2)(a)or (b) of the *Child, Youth and Family Services Act, 2017* shall be served at least 30 days before the date the order for society supervision or interim society care expires.

Forms for Child Protection Cases

(7) In a child protection case,

(a) an information for a warrant to bring a child to a place of safety shall be in Form 33;

(b) a warrant to bring a child to a place of safety shall be in Form 33A;

(c) an applicant's plan of care for a child shall be,

(i) if the applicant is a children's aid society, in Form 33B, and

(ii) if the applicant is not a children's aid society, in Form 33B.1;

(c.1) a respondent's answer and plan of care for a child shall be,

(i) if the respondent is not a children's aid society, in From 33B.1,

(ii) if the respondent is a children's aid society, in Form 10 and Form 33B;

(d) an agreed statement of facts in a child protection case shall be in Form 33C; and

(e) an agreed statement of facts in a status review application shall be in Form 33D.

Forms for Secure Treatment Cases

(8) In an application under Part VII (secure treatment) of the *Child, Youth and Family Services Act, 2017*, a consent signed by the child shall be in Form 33E and a consent signed by any other person shall be in Form 33F.

O. Reg. 91/03, s. 7; 76/06, s. 9; 298/18, s. 17

RULE 34 — ADOPTION

CYFSA Definitions Apply

34. (1) The definitions in the *Child, Youth and Family Services Act, 2017* apply to this rule and, in particular,

"Director" means a Director within the meaning of the Act.

Meaning of "Act"

(2) In this rule,

"Act" means the *Child, Youth and Family Services Act, 2017.*

"old Act" means the *Child and Family Services Act*, as it read immediately before its repeal.

Use of Initials in Documents

(2.1) An applicant or respondent may be referred to by only the first letter of his or her surname in any document in the case, except that,

(a) the applicant's full names shall appear in the adoption order; and

(b) the child's full names shall appear in the adoption order, unless the court orders that the child's first name and the first letter of his or her surname be used.

Certified Copy of Order from Outside Ontario

(3) When this rule requires a copy of an order to be filed and the order in question was made outside Ontario, it shall be a copy that is certified by an official of the court or other authority that made it.

Material to be Filed with Adoption Applications

(4) The following shall be filed with every application for an adoption:

1. A certified copy of the statement of live birth of the child, or an equivalent that satisfies the court.

2. If required, the child's consent to adoption (Form 34) or a notice of motion and supporting affidavit for an order under subsection 180(9) of the Act dispensing with the child's consent.

3. If the child is not in extended society care, an affidavit of parentage (Form 34A) or any other evidence about parentage that the court requires from the child's parent, or a person named by the court.

4. If the applicant has a spouse who has not joined in the application, a consent to the child's adoption by the spouse (Form 34B).

5. If required by the Act or by an order, a Director's or local director's statement on adoption (Form 34C) under subsection 202(1) or (7) of the Act.

6. An affidavit signed by the applicant (Form 34D) that includes details about the applicant's education, employment, health, background and ability to support and care for the child, a history of the relationship between the parent and the child and any other evidence relating to the best inter ests of the child, and states whether the child is a First Nations, Inuk or Métis person.

Report of Child's Adjustment

(5) A report under subsection 202(6) or (7) of the Act of the child's adjustment in the applicant's home shall also be filed with the application if the child is under 16 years of age, or is 16 years of age or older but has not withdrawn from parental control and has not married.

Additional Material — Child in Extended Society Care

(6) If the child is in extended society care, the following shall also be filed with the application:

1. A Director's consent to adoption (Form 34E).

1.1 If an access order was made under Part V of the Act,

0.i a copy of each access order,

i. copies of every notice given under subsection 195(2) or 197(2) of the Act or, if applicable, section 145.1.1 of the old Act,

ii. for each notice,

A. proof of service of the notice including, if applicable, a copy of an order permitting service by a method chosen by the court, or

B. a copy of an order that notice is not required, and

iii. [Repealed O. Reg. 298/18, s. 18(12).]

iv. an affidavit (Form 34G.1) signed by an employee of a children's aid society stating that,

A. no application for an openness order has been filed, or

B. if any applications for openness orders have been filed, the status of those applications, including details of any openness orders that have been made.

2. A copy of any order under Part V of the Act ending access to the child.

3. A copy of the order of extended society care.

4. Proof of service of the orders referred to in paragraphs 2 and 3, or a copy of any order dispensing with service.

5. An affidavit (Form 34G.1), signed by a person delegated by the local director of the children's aid society that has placed the child for adoption, stating,

i. that the person has made reasonable inquiries as to whether there is any outstanding access order respecting the child and that, to the best of the person's knowledge, there is no such order, and

ii. that there is no appeal in progress from an order referred to in paragraph 2 or 3, or that the appeal period has expired without an appeal being filed, or that an appeal was filed but has been withdrawn or finally dismissed.

6. If the child is a First Nations, Inuk or Métis person, proof that the written notice of intention to begin planning for the adoption of the child required under section 186 of the Act or, if applicable, section 141.2 of the old Act, was given.

Additional Material — Child Not in Extended Society Care

(7) If the child is not in extended society care and is placed for adoption by a licensee or children's aid society, the following shall also be filed with the application:

1. A copy of any custody or access order that is in force and is known to the person placing the child, or to an applicant.

2. [Revoked O. Reg. 337/02, s. 3(4).]

3. A consent to adoption (Form 34F) under section 180 of the Act from every parent, other than the applicant, of whom the person placing the child or an applicant is aware. An order under section 181 of the Act dispensing with a parent's consent may be filed instead of the consent.

4. An affidavit (Form 34G) signed by the licensee or by an authorized employee of the children's aid society (depending on who is placing the child).

5. If the child is placed by a licensee, a copy of the licensee's licence to make the placement at the time of placing the child for adoption.

6. If the child is a First Nations, Inuk or Métis person and is placed by a licensee, proof that any written notice of intention to place the child for adoption required by the regulations made under the Act or, if applicable, the old Act, was given.

7. If the child is a First Nations, Inuk or Métis person and is placed by a children's aid society, proof that the written notice of intention to begin planning for the adoption of the child required under section 186 of the Act or, if applicable, section 141.2 of the old Act, was given.

Additional Material — Relative or Step-parent

(8) If the applicant is the child's relative or the spouse of the child's parent and the child was a resident of Canada before being placed for adoption, an affidavit from each applicant (Form 34H) shall also be filed with the application.

Application By Step-Parent or Relative

(9) An application by a relative of the child or the spouse of the child's parent,

(a) shall not be commenced until the 21-day period referred to in subsection 180(8) of the Act has expired; and

(b) shall be accompanied by the applicant's affidavit confirming that he or she did not receive a withdrawal of consent during the 21-day period.

Step-Parent Adoption, Parent's Consent

(10) An application by the spouse of the child's parent shall be accompanied by the parent's consent (Form 34I).

Independent Legal Advice, Child's Consent

(11) The consent of a child to be adopted (Form 34) shall be witnessed by a representative of the Children's Lawyer, who shall complete the affidavit of execution and independent legal advice contained in the form.

Independent Legal Advice, Consent of Parent Under 18

(11.1) The consent of a person under the age of 18 years who is a parent of the child to be adopted (Form 34F) shall be witnessed by a representative of the Children's Lawyer, who shall complete an affidavit of execution and independent legal advice (Form 34J).

Independent Legal Advice, Adult Parent's Consent

(12) The consent of an adult parent of the child to be adopted shall be witnessed by an independent lawyer, who shall complete the affidavit of execution and independent legal advice.

Copy of Consent for Person Signing

(13) A person who signs a consent to an adoption shall be given a copy of the consent and of the affidavit of execution and independent legal advice.

Withdrawal of Consent by Parent

(13.1) A parent who has given consent to an adoption under subsection 180(2) of the Act may withdraw the consent under subsection 180(8) of the Act in accordance with the following:

1. If the child is placed for adoption by a children's aid society, the parent who wishes to withdraw the consent shall ensure that the children's aid society receives the written withdrawal within 21 days after the consent was given.

2. If the child is placed for adoption by a licensee, the parent who wishes to withdraw the consent shall ensure that the licensee receives the written withdrawal within 21 days after the consent was given.

3. If a relative of the child or a spouse of a parent proposes to apply to adopt the child, the parent who wishes to withdraw the consent shall ensure that the relative or spouse receives the written withdrawal within 21 days after the consent was given.

Withdrawal of Consent by Child Aged Seven or Older

(13.2) A child who has given consent to an adoption under subsection 180(6) of the Act may withdraw the consent under subsection 180(8) of the Act in accordance with the following:

1. The withdrawal shall be signed within 21 days after the consent was given, and witnessed by the person who witnesses the consent under subrule (11) or by another representative of the Children's Lawyer.

2. The person who witnesses the withdrawal shall give the original withdrawal document to the child and promptly serve a copy on the children's aid society, licensee, relative or spouse, as the case may be.

Motion to Withdraw Consent

(14) Despite subrule 5(4) (place for steps other than enforcement), a motion to withdraw a consent to an adoption under subsection 182(1) of the Act shall be made in,

(a) the municipality where the person who gave the consent lives; or

(b) in any other place that the court decides.

Clerk to Check Adoption Application

(15) Before the application is presented to a judge, the clerk shall,

(a) review the application and other documents filed to see whether they are in order; and

(b) prepare a certificate (Form 34K).

Dispensing With Consent Before Placement

(16) In an application to dispense with a parent's consent before placement for adoption,

(a) the applicant may be the licensee, a parent, the children's aid society or the person who wants to adopt;

(b) the respondent is the person who has not given consent;

(c) if an order that service is not required is sought, the request shall be made in the application and not by motion;

(d) if the application is being served, the applicant shall serve and file with it an affidavit (Form 14A) setting out the facts of the case;

(e) if the application is not being served, the applicant shall file with it an affidavit (Form 14A) setting out the facts of the case, and the clerk shall send the case to a judge for a decision on the basis of affidavit evidence.

Forms for Openness Applications

(17) In a case about an openness order under Part VIII of the Act,

(a) an application for an openness order shall be in Form 34L;

(b) a consent to an openness order under section 194 of the Act shall be in Form 34M;

(b.1) a consent to an openness order under section 196 or 197 of the Act shall be in Form 34M.1;

(c) an application to change or terminate an openness order shall be in Form 34N;

(d) an answer to an application for an openness order or an answer to an application to change or terminate an openness order shall be in Form 33B.2;

(e) the notice of intention to place a child for adoption to be served under subsection 195(2) of the Act shall be in Form 8D.2; and

(f) the notice of intention to place a First Nations, Inuk or Métis child for adoption to be served under subsection 197(2) of the Act on the child and on a representative chosen by each of the child's bands and First Nations, Inuit or Métis communities, shall be in Form 8D.3.

(g) [Repealed O. Reg. 298/18, s. 18(27).]

Service of Notice of Intention to Place a Child for Adoption

(18) In an application for an order under subsection 195(5) or clause 197(4)(b) of the Act to allow another method of service of the notice of intention to place a child for adoption (Form 8D.2 or 8D.3), or for an order under subsection 195(6) or clause 197(4)(b) of the Act that notice is not required,

(a) the applicant is the children's aid society;

(b) the respondent is the person who is entitled to receive notice under subsection 195(2) or 197(2) of the Act;

(c) the application shall be made using Form 8B.2 — Application (general) (*Child, Youth and Family Services Act, 2017* cases other than child protection and status review);

(d) the application shall be filed in the same court file as the child protection case in which the child was ordered into extended society care;

(e) the applicant shall file an affidavit (Form 14A) setting out the facts in support of the order being requested and the clerk shall send the case to a judge for a decision on the basis of the affidavit evidence.

Timelines for Openness Applications

(19) Every application for an openness order is governed by the following timetable:

Column 1 Step in the case	Column 2 Maximum time for completion, from the date the application is filed
Service and filing of answers	30 days
First hearing or settlement conference	50 days
Hearing	90 days

O. Reg. 337/02, s. 3; 519/06, s. 6; 383/11, s. 7; 388/12, s. 9; 140/15, s. 5, item 2; 298/18, s. 18

RULE 35 — CHANGE OF NAME

Time for Application

35. (1) An application under subsection 7(3) (application to court for change of name) of the *Change of Name Act* shall be made within 30 days after the applicant is notified that the Registrar General has refused to make the requested change of name.

Service on the Registrar General

(2) The applicant shall serve the application and any supporting material on the Registrar General by delivering or mailing a copy of the documents to the Deputy Registrar General.

Registrar General's Reasons for Refusal

(3) Within 15 days after being served under subrule (2), the Registrar General may file reasons for refusing to make the requested change of name.

RULE 35.1 — CUSTODY AND ACCESS [HEADING ADDED O. REG. 6/10, S. 9.]

35.1 (1) [Repealed O. Reg. 226/17, s. 2.]

Affidavit in Support of Custody or Access Claim

(2) If an application, answer or motion to change a final order contains a claim for custody of or access to a child, the party making the claim shall serve and file an affidavit in support of claim for custody or access (Form 35.1), together with any other documents required by this rule, with the document that contains the claim.

Police Records Check

(3) Every person who makes a claim for custody of a child and who is not a parent of the child shall attach to the affidavit in support of claim for custody or access,

(a) a police records check obtained not more than 60 days before the person starts the claim; or

(b) if the person requested the police records check for the purposes of the claim but has not received it by the time he or she starts the claim, proof of the request.

Same

(4) If clause (3)(b) applies, the person shall serve and file the police records check no later than 10 days after receiving it.

Request for Report from Children's Aid Society

(5) Every person required to submit a request under subsection 21.2(2) of the *Children's Law Reform Act* for a report from a children's aid society shall provide to the court a copy of the request together with the affidavit in support of claim for custody or access.

Documents Shall be Refused

(6) If these rules require a document to be accompanied by the applicable documents referred to in this rule, the clerk shall not accept the document for filing without,

(a) an affidavit in support of claim for custody or access; and

(b) the documents referred to in subrules (3) and (5), if applicable.

Corrections and Updates

(7) As soon as a person discovers that information in his or her affidavit in support of claim for custody or access is incorrect or incomplete, or that there has been a change in the information provided in the affidavit, he or she shall immediately serve and file,

(a) a new affidavit in support of claim for custody or access (Form 35.1) containing the correct or updated information; or

(b) if the correction or change is minor, an affidavit in Form 14A describing the correction or change and indicating any effect it has on the person's plan for the care and upbringing of the child.

Associated Cases

(8) If the clerk provides to a person making a claim for custody of a child information in writing under subsection 21.3(1) of the *Children's Law Reform Act* respecting any current or previous family proceedings involving the child or any person who is a party to the claim and who is not a parent of the child, the person shall serve a copy of the written information on every other party.

Same

(9) If the written information provided by the clerk contains information indicating that the person making the claim was or is involved in family proceedings in which he or she was or is not involved, the person making the claim may serve with the copy of the written information an affidavit identifying those proceedings.

O. Reg. 6/10, s. 9; 226/17, s. 2

RULE 36 — DIVORCE

Application for Divorce

36. (1) Either spouse may start a divorce case by,

(a) filing an application naming the other spouse as a respondent; or

(b) filing a joint application with no respondent.

Joint Application

(2) In a joint application, the divorce and any other order sought shall be made only with the consent of both spouses.

Allegation of Adultery

(3) In an application for divorce claiming that the other spouse committed adultery with another person, that person does not need to be named, but if named, shall be served with the application and has all the rights of a respondent in the case.

Marriage Certificate and Central Divorce Registry Certificate

(4) The court shall not grant a divorce until the following have been filed:

1. A marriage certificate or marriage registration certificate, unless the application states that it is impractical to obtain a certificate and explains why.

2. A report on earlier divorce cases started by either spouse, issued under the *Central Registry of Divorce Proceedings Regulations* (Canada).

Divorce Based on Affidavit Evidence

(5) An affidavit in Form 36 containing the following information shall be filed in accordance with subrule (5.1):

1. Confirmation that all the information in the application is correct, except as stated in the affidavit.

2. If no marriage certificate or marriage registration certificate has been filed, sufficient information to prove the marriage.

3. Proof of any previous divorce or the death of a party's previous spouse, unless the marriage took place in Canada.

4. The information about arrangements for support of any children of the marriage required by paragraph 11(1)(b) of the *Divorce Act* (Canada), and the income and financial information required by section 21 of the child support guidelines attached as exhibits.

5. Any other information necessary for the court to grant the divorce.

When Requirement Applies

(5.1) The affidavit referred to in subrule (5) shall be filed,

(a) by the applicant, if the respondent files no answer or files an answer and later withdraws it; or

(b) in the case of a joint application, by the applicants.

Draft Divorce Order

(6) The applicant shall file with the affidavit,

(a) three copies of a draft divorce order (Form 25A);

(b) a stamped envelope addressed to each party; and

(c) if the divorce order is to contain a support order,

(i) an extra copy of the draft divorce order for the clerk to file with the Director of the Family Responsibility Office, and

(ii) two copies of a draft support deduction order.

Electronic Filing of Joint Application

(6.1) Subject to subrule (6.2), a joint application under clause (1)(b) may be filed electronically, provided that the following documents are filed electronically together with the application:

1. The affidavits of the parties (Form 36).

2. A marriage certificate or marriage registration certificate, unless the application states that it is impractical to obtain a certificate and explains why.

3. A draft divorce order (Form 25A).

4. If the divorce order is to contain a support order,

i. a draft support deduction order,

ii. the support deduction order information form prescribed under the *Family Responsibility and Support Arrears Enforcement Act, 1996*, and

iii. the financial statements (Form 13) required by rule 13, if any.

5. If the divorce order is to contain an order for custody or access to a child, every affidavit in support of claim for custody or access (Form 35.1) required by rule 35.1.

6. Any supporting documents required under these rules to be filed with a document referred to in paragraphs 1 to 5.

7. Any other document the parties intend to file with the application, provided that it may be filed using the authorized software.

Where Not Available

(6.2) Subrule (6.1) does not apply if,

(a) the marriage certificate or marriage registration certificate was issued outside Canada and not in electronic format;

(b) in addition to the joint claim for a divorce, the application contains a claim for relief that is not a joint claim for support or a joint claim for custody or access to a child; or

(c) the authorized software does not permit electronic filing under subrule (6.1) for the municipality in which the application would otherwise be filed in paper format under rule 5.

Non-Application of Subrule (6)

(6.3) Subrule (6) does not apply if a joint application is filed electronically in accordance with subrule (6.1).

Continuing Record

(6.4) Rule 9 (continuing record) does not apply to a joint application that is filed electronically in accordance with subrule (6.1) unless a party is required by subrule (6.6) to give documents to the clerk in paper format, in which case, unless the court orders otherwise, rule 9 applies as if the party were the person who started the case.

Electronic Issuance of Joint Application

(6.5) A joint application that is filed electronically in accordance with subrule (6.1) may be issued electronically.

Requirement to Give Documents in Paper Format

(6.6) If, after a joint application is filed electronically in accordance with subrule (6.1), a party intends or is required to file any other document in respect of the application, the party shall, unless the court orders otherwise, give to the clerk, in paper format, the joint application and every document filed with the application.

Clerk to Present Papers to Judge

(7) When the documents mentioned in subrules (4) to (6) have been filed, the clerk shall prepare a certificate (Form 36A) and present the documents to a judge, who may,

(a) grant the divorce as set out in the draft order;

(b) have the clerk return the documents to the applicant to make any needed corrections; or

(c) grant the divorce but make changes to the draft order, or refuse to grant the divorce, after giving the applicant a chance to file an additional affidavit or come to court to explain why the order should be made without change.

Divorce Certificate

(8) When a divorce takes effect, the clerk shall, on either party's request,

(a) check the continuing record or, if there is no continuing record, the court file, to verify that,

(i) no appeal has been taken from the divorce order, or any appeal from it has been disposed of, and

(ii) no order has been made extending the time for an appeal, or any extended time has expired without an appeal; and

(b) if satisfied of those matters, issue a divorce certificate (Form 36B) and mail it to the parties, unless the court orders otherwise.

(9) [Revoked O. Reg. 89/04, s. 12.]

O. Reg. 89/04, s. 12; 298/18, s. 19

RULE 37 — INTERJURISDICTIONAL SUPPORT ORDERS ACT, 2002 [HEADING AMENDED O. REG. 56/03, S. 6.]

Application

37. (1) This rule applies to cases under the Act.

Definitions

(2) In this rule,

"Act" means the *Interjurisdictional Support Orders Act, 2002*;

"appropriate authority" has the same meaning as in the Act;

"designated authority" has the same meaning as in the Act;

"general regulation" means Ontario Regulation 55/03;

"send", when used in reference to a person, means to,

(a) mail to the person's lawyer or, if none, to the person,

(b) send by courier to the person's lawyer or, if none, to the person,

(c) deposit at a document exchange to which the person's lawyer belongs, or

(d) fax to the person's lawyer or, if none, to the person.

Notice of Hearing

(3) When the court receives a support application or a support variation application the clerk shall, under section 10 or 33 of the Act,

(a) serve on the respondent, by special service,

(i) the notice of hearing mentioned in clause 10(b) or 33(b) of the Act (Form 37),

(ii) a copy of the documents sent by the designated authority, and

(iii) blank response forms; and

(b) send to the designated authority a copy of the notice of hearing and an information sheet (Form 37A).

Information And Documents To Be Provided By Respondent

(4) The respondent shall file, within 30 days after service of the notice of hearing,

(a) an answer in Form N under the general regulation,

(i) identifying any issues the respondent intends to raise with respect to the support application, and

(ii) containing the financial information referred to in subsection 21(1) of Ontario Regulation 391/97 (*Child Support Guidelines*), if the support application includes a claim for child support;

(b) an affidavit (Form 14A) setting out the evidence on which the respondent relies; and

(c) a financial statement in Form K under the general regulation.

Respondent's Financial Statement

(5) The respondent is required to file a financial statement whether he or she intends to dispute the claim or not.

Applicant's Financial Statement

(6) The fact that the applicant has provided financial information in a form different than that required by these rules does not affect the case.

Written Hearing

(7) Unless the court orders otherwise under subrule (9), the application shall be dealt with on the basis of written documents without the parties or their lawyers needing to come to court.

Request For Oral Hearing

(8) The respondent may request an oral hearing by filing a motion form (Form 14B) within 30 days after being served with the notice of hearing.

Order For Oral Hearing

(9) The court may order an oral hearing, on the respondent's motion or on its own initiative, if it is satisfied that an oral hearing is necessary to deal with the case justly.

Direction to Request Further Information or Documents

(10) A direction to request further information or documents under clause 11(2)(a) or 34(2)(a) of the Act shall be in Form 37B, and a statement of the court's reasons for requesting further evidence shall be attached to the direction.

Direction to Be Sent to Respondent

(11) When a direction is sent to the designated authority under clause 11(2)(a) of the Act, the clerk shall also send a copy to the respondent.

Adjournment

(12) When the court adjourns the hearing under clause 11(2)(b) or 34(2)(b) of the Act, it shall specify the date on which the hearing is to continue.

Copies of Further Information or Documents

(13) When the court receives the further information or documents, the clerk shall promptly prepare a notice of continuation of hearing (Form 37C) and send it, with copies of the information or documents, to the respondent and to the designated authority.

Respondent's Affidavit

(14) If the respondent wishes to respond to the further information or documents, he or she shall file an affidavit (Form 14A) containing the response with the court, within 30 days after receiving the notice of continuation of hearing.

Preparation of Order

(15) The clerk shall prepare the order for signature as soon as it is made, in accordance with subrule 25(11).

Sending Copies of Order to Respondent and Designated Authority

(16) The court shall send,

(a) a copy of the order to the respondent, addressed to the respondent's last known address if sent by mail; and

(b) a certified copy of the order to the designated authority.

Sending Copy of Order to Appropriate Authority

(17) The designated authority shall send the certified copy of the order to the appropriate authority.

Notice of Registration, Order Made Outside Canada

(18) For the purpose of subsection 20(1) of the Act, the clerk of the Ontario court shall give notice of the registration of an order made outside Canada by providing a notice in Form 37D, as described in subrule (19), to any party to the order who is believed to ordinarily reside in Ontario.

Sending or Special Service

(19) If the party to whom notice is to be provided applied for the order in Ontario, the clerk shall send the notice to the party, but in any other case, the clerk shall serve the notice on the party by special service.

Motion to Set Aside Registration

(20) For the purpose of subsection 20(3) of the Act, a party shall give notice of a motion to set aside the registration of an order made outside Canada by,

(a) filing in the Ontario court a notice of motion (Form 14) setting out the grounds for the motion;

(b) sending the notice of motion and supporting documents to the claimant at the address shown in the order; and

(c) serving the notice of motion and supporting documents on the designated authority at least 10 days before the motion hearing date.

Designated Authority Need Not Appear On Motion

(21) The designated authority is not required to appear on the motion to set aside registration.

Notice of Decision or Order

(22) When the court makes a decision or order under section 20 of the Act, the clerk shall send copies of the order, with the court's reasons, if any,

(a) to each party, addressed to the party's last known address if sent by mail; and

(b) to the designated authority.

Party in Reciprocating Jurisdiction

(23) If a party ordinarily resides in a reciprocating jurisdiction and the order was originally sent to Ontario for registration by the appropriate authority there, the clerk may send it to that appropriate authority rather than sending it to the party as set out in clause (22)(a).

Provisional Orders

(24) When the court makes a provisional order under section 7 or 30 of the Act, the clerk shall send the following to the designated authority, to be sent to the reciprocating jurisdiction:

1. One copy of,

    i. the application (Form A under the general regulation),

ii. the applicant's financial statement (Form K under the general regulation), and

iii. a statement giving any information about the respondent's identification, whereabouts, income, assets and liabilities.

2. Three certified copies of,

i. the applicant's evidence and, if reasonably possible, the exhibits, and

ii. the provisional order.

Further Evidence

(25) When the court that made a provisional order receives a request for further evidence from the confirming court under subsection 7(4) or 30(4) of the Act, the clerk shall send to the applicant a notice for taking further evidence (Form 37E) and a copy of the documents sent by the confirming court.

O. Reg. 56/03, s. 6; 69/15, s. 12; 140/15, s. 5, item 3

RULE 37.1 — PROVISIONAL ORDERS AND CONFIRMATION OF PROVISIONAL ORDERS — DIVORCE ACT, FAMILY LAW ACT

Application

37.1 (1) This rule applies to orders made under sections 18 and 19 of the *Divorce Act* (Canada) and under section 44 of the *Family Law Act*.

Definitions

(2) In this rule,

"confirming court" means,

(a) in the case of an order under section 19 of the *Divorce Act* (Canada), the court in Ontario or another province or territory of Canada that has jurisdiction to confirm a provisional variation of the order, or

(b) for the purpose of section 44 of the *Family Law Act*,

(i) the Ontario Court of Justice sitting in the municipality where the respondent resides, or

(ii) the Family Court of the Superior Court of Justice, if the respondent resides in an area where that court has jurisdiction;

"originating court" means,

(a) in the case of an order under section 18 of the *Divorce Act* (Canada), the court in Ontario or another province or territory of Canada that has jurisdiction under section 5 of that Act to deal with an application for a provisional variation of the order, or

(b) for the purpose of section 44 of the *Family Law Act*,

(i) the Ontario Court of Justice sitting in the municipality where the provisional order is made, or

(ii) the Family Court of the Superior Court of Justice when it makes the provisional order;

"send", when used in reference to a person, means to,

(a) mail to the person's lawyer or, if none, to the person,

(b) send by courier to the person's lawyer or, if none, to the person,

(c) deposit at a document exchange to which the person's lawyer belongs, or

(d) fax to the person's lawyer or, if none, to the person.

Documents To Be Sent To Confirming Court

(3) When the court makes a provisional order under section 18 of the *Divorce Act* (Canada) or section 44 of the *Family Law Act*, the clerk shall send the following to the confirming court (if it is in Ontario) or to the Attorney General to be sent to the confirming court (if it is outside Ontario):

1. One copy of,

   i. the application (Form 8),

   ii. the applicant's financial statement (Form 13),

   iii. a statement giving any information about the respondent's identification, whereabouts, income, assets and liabilities, and

   iv. if the confirming court is in another municipality in Ontario, proof that the application was served on the respondent.

2. Three certified copies of,

   i. the applicant's evidence and, if reasonably possible, the exhibits, and

   ii. the provisional order.

No Financial Statement From Foreign Applicant

(4) When a confirming court in Ontario receives a provisional order made outside Ontario, the applicant does not have to file a financial statement.

Notice of Confirmation Hearing

(5) A clerk of a confirming court in Ontario who receives a provisional order shall,

(a) serve on the respondent, by special service (subrule 6(3)),

   (i) a notice of hearing (Form 37),

   (ii) a copy of the documents sent by the originating court, and

   (iii) blank response forms; and

(b) send a notice of hearing and an information sheet (Form 37A) to,

   (i) the applicant,

   (ii) the clerk of the originating court, and

   (iii) the Attorney General, if the provisional order was made outside Ontario.

Respondent's Financial Statement

(6) A respondent at a confirmation hearing under section 19 of the *Divorce Act* (Canada) shall serve and file a financial statement (Form 13) within 30 days after service of the notice of confirmation hearing.

Written Hearing

(7) Unless the court orders otherwise under subrule (9), the application shall be dealt with on the basis of written documents without the parties or their lawyers needing to come to court.

Request For Oral Hearing

(8) The respondent may request an oral hearing by filing a motion form (Form 14B) within 30 days after being served with the notice of hearing.

Order For Oral Hearing

(9) The court may order an oral hearing, on the applicant's motion or on its own initiative, if it is satisfied that an oral hearing is necessary to deal with the case justly.

Court Receives Request For Further Evidence

(10) When an originating court in Ontario receives a request for further evidence from the confirming court, the clerk shall send to the applicant a notice for taking further evidence (Form 37E) and a copy of the documents sent by the confirming court.

Court Sends Request For Further Evidence

(11) When a confirming court in Ontario requests further evidence from the originating court,

(a) the confirming court shall adjourn the confirmation hearing to a new date; and

(b) the clerk shall send to the originating court two certified copies of the evidence taken in the confirming court.

Continuing The Confirmation Hearing

(12) When a confirming court in Ontario receives further evidence from the originating court, the clerk shall promptly prepare a notice of continuation of hearing (Form 37C) and send it, with copies of the evidence, to the respondent and, if the provisional order was made outside Ontario, to the Attorney General.

Respondent's Affidavit

(13) If the respondent wishes to respond to the further evidence, he or she shall file an affidavit containing the response with the court, within 30 days after receiving the notice of continuation of hearing.

O. Reg. 56/03, s. 6; 69/15, s. 13

RULE 38 — APPEALS

Rules that Apply in Appeals to Divisional Court and Court of Appeal

38. (1) Rules 61, 62 and 63 of the *Rules of Civil Procedure* apply with necessary changes, including those modifications set out in subrules (2) and (3),

(a) if an appeal lies to the Divisional Court or the Court of Appeal;

(b) if leave to appeal to the Divisional Court or the Court of Appeal is required,

in a family law case as described in subrule 1(2).

Modifications in Child Protection Appeals

(2) If the appeal is brought in a case under the *Child, Youth and Family Services Act, 2017*, the following time periods apply instead of the time periods mentioned in the referenced provisions of the *Rules of Civil Procedure*:

1. The time period referred to in clause 61.09(1)(a) shall be 14 days after filing the notice of appeal if there is no transcript.

2. The time period referred to in clause 61.09(1)(b) shall be 30 days after receiving notice that the evidence has been transcribed.

3. The time period referred to in clause 61.12(2) shall be 30 days after service of the appeal book and compendium, exhibit book, transcript of evidence, if any, and appellant's factum.

4. The time period referred to in clause 61.13(2)(a) shall be 30 days after the registrar receives notice that the evidence has been transcribed.

5. The time period referred to in clause 61.13(2)(b) shall be six months after filing the notice of appeal.

6. The time period referred to in subrule 62.02(5) for serving the notice of motion for leave to appeal shall be 30 days.

Appeal of Temporary Order in* Child, Youth and Family Services Act, 2017 *Case

(3) In an appeal of a temporary order made in a case under the *Child, Youth and Family Services Act, 2017* and brought to the Divisional Court under clause 19(1)(b) of the *Courts of Justice Act*, the motion for leave to appeal shall be combined with the notice of appeal and heard together with the appeal.

Appeals to the Superior Court of Justice

(4) Subrules (5) to (45) apply to an appeal from an order of the Ontario Court of Justice to the Superior Court of Justice under,

(a) section 48 of the *Family Law Act*;

(b) section 73 of the *Children's Law Reform Act*;

(c) sections 121 and 215 of the *Child, Youth and Family Services Act, 2017*;

(d) section 40 of the *Interjurisdictional Support Orders Act, 2002*;

(e) section 40 of the *Courts of Justice Act*; and

(f) any other statute to which these rules apply, unless the statute provides for another procedure.

How to Start Appeal

(5) To start an appeal from a final order of the Ontario Court of Justice to the Superior Court of Justice under any of the provisions listed in subrule (4), a party shall,

(a) within 30 days after the date of the order or decision being appealed from, serve a notice of appeal (Form 38) on,

(i) every other party affected by the appeal or entitled to appeal,

(ii) the clerk of the court in the place where the order was made, and

(iii) if the appeal is under section 121 of the *Child, Youth and Family Services Act, 2017*, every other person entitled to notice under subsection 79(3) of that Act who appeared at the hearing; and

(b) within 10 days after serving the notice of appeal, file it.

Starting Appeal of Temporary Order

(6) Subrule (5) applies to the starting of an appeal from a temporary order of the Ontario Court of Justice to the Superior Court of Justice except that the notice of appeal shall be served within seven days after the date of the temporary order.

Same,* Child, Youth and Family Services Act, 2017 *Case

(7) To start an appeal from a temporary order of the Ontario Court of Justice to the Superior Court of Justice in a case under the *Child, Youth and Family Services Act, 2017*, subrule (5) applies and the notice of appeal shall be served within 30 days after the date of the temporary order.

Name of Case Unchanged

(8) The name of a case in an appeal shall be the same as the name of the case in the order appealed from and shall identify the parties as appellant and respondent.

Appeal by Respondent

(9) If the respondent in an appeal also wants to appeal the same order, this rule applies, with necessary changes, to the respondent's appeal, and the two appeals shall be heard together.

Grounds Stated in Notice of Appeal

(10) The notice of appeal shall state the order that the appellant wants the appeal court to make and the legal grounds for the appeal.

Other Grounds

(11) At the hearing of the appeal, no grounds other than the ones stated in the notice of appeal may be argued unless the court gives permission.

Transcript of Evidence

(12) If the appeal requires a transcript of evidence, the appellant shall, within 30 days after filing the notice of appeal, file proof that the transcript has been ordered.

Consultation With Respondent

(13) The appellant shall determine if the appeal requires a transcript of evidence in consultation with the respondent.

Agreement on Evidence to be Transcribed

(14) If the appellant and respondent agree about what evidence needs to be transcribed, the appellant shall order the agreed evidence transcribed.

No Agreement

(15) If the appellant and respondent cannot agree, the appellant shall order a transcript of all of the oral evidence from the hearing of the decision under appeal unless the court orders otherwise.

Once Transcript Completed

(16) When the authorized court transcriptionist has completed the transcript, he or she shall promptly notify the appellant, the respondent and the court office in the court where the appeal will be heard.

Contents of Appellant's Appeal Record

(17) The appellant's appeal record shall contain a copy of the following documents, in the following order:

1. A table of contents describing each document, including each exhibit, by its nature and date and, for an exhibit, by exhibit number or letter.

2. The notice of appeal.

3. The order being appealed, as signed, and any reasons given by the court appealed from, as well as a further printed copy of the reasons if they are handwritten.

4. A transcript of the oral evidence.

5. Any other material that was before the court appealed from and that is necessary for the appeal.

Contents of Appellant's Factum

(18) The appellant's factum shall be not more than 30 pages long, shall be signed by the appellant's lawyer or, if none, by the appellant and shall consist of the following parts, containing paragraphs numbered consecutively from the beginning to the end of the factum:

1. Part 1: Identification. A statement identifying the appellant and respondent and the court appealed from, and stating the result in that court.

2. Part 2: Overview. A brief overview of the case and the issues on the appeal.

3. Part 3: Facts. A brief summary of the facts relevant to the appeal, with reference to the evidence by page and line as necessary.

4. Part 4: Issues. A brief statement of each issue, followed by a brief argument referring to the law relating to that issue.

5. Part 5: Order. A precise statement of the order the appeal court is asked to make, including any order for costs.

6. Part 6: Time estimate. An estimate of how much time will be needed for the appellant's oral argument, not including reply to the respondent's argument.

7. Part 7: List of authorities. A list of all statutes, regulations, rules, cases and other authorities referred to in the factum.

8. Part 8: Legislation. A copy of all relevant provisions of statutes, regulations and rules.

Respondent's Factum and Appeal Record

(19) The respondent shall, within the timeline set out in subrule (21) or (22), serve on every other party to the appeal and file,

(a) a respondent's factum (subrule (20)); and

(b) if applicable, a respondent's appeal record containing a copy of any material that was before the court appealed from which are necessary for the appeal but are not included in the appellant's appeal record.

Contents of Respondent's Factum

(20) The respondent's factum shall be not more than 30 pages long, shall be signed by the respondent's lawyer or, if none, by the respondent and shall consist of the following parts, containing paragraphs numbered consecutively from the beginning to the end of the factum:

1. Part 1: Overview. A brief overview of the case and the issues on the appeal.

2. Part 2: Facts. A brief statement of the facts in the appellant's factum that the respondent accepts as correct and the facts that the respondent says are incorrect, and a brief summary of any additional facts relied on by the respondent, with reference to the evidence by page and line as necessary.

3. Part 3: Issues. A statement of the respondent's position on each issue raised by the appellant, followed by a brief argument referring to the law relating to that issue.

4. Part 4: Additional issues. A brief statement of each additional issue raised by the respondent, followed by a brief argument referring to the law relating to that issue.

5. Part 5: Order. A precise statement of the order the appeal court is asked to make, including any order for costs.

6. Part 6: Time estimate. An estimate of how much time will be needed for the respondent's oral argument.

7. Part 7: List of authorities. A list of all statutes, regulations, rules, cases and other authorities referred to in the factum.

8. Part 8: Legislation. A copy of all relevant provisions of statutes, regulations and rules not included in the appellant's factum.

Timelines for Serving and Filing of Records and Factums other than in CYFSA Cases

(21) Except for appeals in cases under the *Child, Youth and Family Services Act, 2017*, the following timelines for serving appeal records and factums apply:

1. If a transcript is required, the appellant's appeal record and factum shall be served on the respondent and any other person entitled to be heard in the appeal and filed within 60 days from the date of receiving notice that evidence has been transcribed.

2. If no transcript is required, the appellant's appeal record and factum shall be served on the respondent and any other person entitled to be heard in the appeal and filed within 30 days of filing of the notice of appeal.

3. The respondent's appeal record and factum shall be served on the appellant and any other person entitled to be heard on the appeal and filed within 60 days from the serving of the appellant's appeal record and factum.

Timelines for Serving and Filing of Records and Factums in CYFSA Cases

(22) For appeals of cases under the *Child, Youth and Family Services Act, 2017*, the following timelines for serving appeal records and factums apply:

1. If a transcript is required, the appellant's appeal record and factum shall be served on the respondent and any other person entitled to be heard in the appeal and filed within 30 days from the date of receiving notice that evidence has been transcribed.

2. If no transcript is required, the appellant's appeal record and factum shall be served on the respondent and any other person entitled to be heard in the appeal and filed within 14 days of filing of the notice of appeal.

3. The respondent's appeal record and factum shall be served on the appellant and any other person entitled to be heard on the appeal and filed within 30 days from the serving of the appellant's appeal record and factum.

Scheduling of Hearing

(23) When the appellant's appeal record and factum have been filed and the respondent's factum and appeal record, if any, have been filed, or the time for their filing has expired, the clerk shall schedule the appeal for hearing.

Prompt Hearing of CFSA Appeals

(24) An appeal under the *Child, Youth and Family Services Act, 2017* shall be heard within 60 days after the appellant's factum and appeal record are filed.

Motions in Appeals

(25) If a person needs to bring a motion in an appeal, rule 14 applies with necessary changes to the motion.

Security for Costs of Appeal

(26) On a motion by the respondent for security for costs, the court may make an order for security for costs that is just, if it is satisfied that,

(a) there is good reason to believe that the appeal is a waste of time, a nuisance, or an abuse of the court process and that the appellant has insufficient assets in Ontario to pay the costs of the appeal;

(b) an order for security for costs could be made against the appellant under subrule 24(13); or

(c) for other good reason, security for costs should be ordered.

Dismissal for Failure to Obey Order

(27) If an appellant does not obey an order under subrule (26), the court may on motion dismiss the appeal.

Motion for Summary Judgment in Appeal

(28) After the notice of appeal is filed, the respondent or any other person who is entitled to be heard on the appeal may make a motion for summary judgment or for summary decision on a legal issue without a hearing of the appeal, and rule 16 applies to the motion with necessary changes.

Motion to Receive Further Evidence

(29) Any person entitled to be heard in the appeal may bring a motion to admit further evidence under clause 134(4)(b) of the *Courts of Justice Act.*

Motion for Dismissal for Delay

(30) If the appellant has not,

(a) filed proof that a transcript of evidence was ordered under subrule (12);

(b) served and filed the appeal record and factum within the timelines set out in subrule (21) or (22) or such longer time as may have been ordered by the court,

the respondent may file a motion form (Form 14B) to have the appeal dismissed for delay.

Withdrawal of Appeal

(31) The appellant may withdraw an appeal by serving a notice of withdrawal (Form 12) on every other party and filing it.

Deemed Withdrawal

(32) If a person serves a notice of appeal and does not file it within 10 days as required by clause (5)(b), the appeal shall be deemed to be withdrawn unless the court orders otherwise.

Automatic Stays Pending Appeal, Support Orders

(33) The service of a notice of appeal from a temporary or final order does not stay a support order or an order that enforces a support order.

Other Payment Orders

(34) The service of a notice of appeal from a temporary or final order stays, until the disposition of the appeal, any other payment order made under the temporary or final order.

Stay by Order of Court

(35) A temporary or final order may be stayed on any conditions that the court considers appropriate,

(a) by an order of the court that made the order;

(b) by an order of the Superior Court of Justice.

Expiry of Stay Granted by Court That Made Order

(36) A stay granted under clause (35)(a) expires if no notice of appeal is served and the time for service has expired.

Powers of Superior Court of Justice

(37) A stay granted under subrule (35) may be set aside or changed by the Superior Court of Justice.

Effect of Stay Generally

(38) If an order is stayed, no steps may be taken under the order or for its enforcement, except,

(a) by order of the Superior Court of Justice; or

(b) as provided in subrules (39) and (40).

Settling of Order

(39) A stay does not prevent the settling or signing of the order.

Writ of Execution

(40) A stay does not prevent the issue of a writ of seizure and sale or the filing of the writ in a sheriff's office or land registry office, but no instruction or direction to enforce the writ shall be given to a sheriff while the stay remains in effect.

Certificate of Stay

(41) If an order is stayed, the clerk of the court that granted the stay shall, if requested by a party to the appeal, issue a certificate of stay in Form 63A under the *Rules of Civil Procedure* with necessary changes.

Stay of Support Order

(42) A party who obtains a stay of a support order shall obtain a certificate of stay under subrule (41) and file it immediately in the office of the Director of the Family Responsibility Office if the stay relates to a support order being enforced by the Director.

Certificate Filed With Sheriff's Office

(43) If a certificate of stay is filed with the sheriff's office, the sheriff shall not begin or continue enforcement of the order until satisfied that the stay is no longer in effect.

Request for Certificate

(44) A request for a certificate of stay under subrule (41) shall state whether the stay is under subrule (34) or by order under subrule (35) and, if under subrule (35), shall set out the particulars of the order.

Setting Aside Writ of Execution

(45) The court may set aside the issue or filing of a writ of seizure and sale if the party making the motion or the appellant gives security satisfactory to the court.

Appeals, Family Arbitration Awards

(46) Subrules (5), (8) to (21), (23) and (25) to (32) apply, with necessary changes, including the modifications set out in subrules (47) to (55), to the appeal of a family arbitration award under section 45 of the *Arbitration Act, 1991* and, for the purpose,

(a) a reference to the Ontario Court of Justice or to the court being appealed from shall be read as a reference to the arbitrator who made the family arbitration award; and

(b) a reference to the order or decision being appealed from shall be read as a reference to the family arbitration award.

Same, Service

(47) In addition to the persons listed under clause (5)(a), the appellant shall serve the notice of appeal on the arbitrator.

Same, Contents of Appellant's Appeal Record

(48) The material referred to in paragraph 5 of subrule (17) shall include,

(a) copies of the certificates of independent legal advice required by the *Family Law Act* for the parties;

(b) a copy of the family arbitration agreement; and

(c) the original family arbitration award or a certified copy.

Same, If Leave Required

(49) If the appeal of a family arbitration award requires the leave of the court, rule 14 applies, with necessary changes, including the modifications set out in subrules (50) to (55), to the motion for leave to appeal, other than subrules 14(4), (4.2), (6), (7), (10) to (15) and (17).

Same

(50) The notice of motion (Form 14) shall,

(a) be served on every other party affected by the appeal or entitled to appeal and on the arbitrator no later than 15 days after the making of the family arbitration award; and

(b) be filed no later than five days after service.

Same

(51) The affidavit (Form 14A) and any additional evidence mentioned in clause 14(9)(b) shall be served and filed no later than 30 days after the filing of the notice of motion for leave to appeal, together with,

(a) a copy of the notice of motion;

(b) the documents listed in subrule (48); and

(c) a factum consisting of a concise argument stating the facts and law relied on by the party making the motion.

Same

(52) The notice of motion and factum shall set out the specific questions that it is proposed the court should answer on appeal if leave to appeal is granted.

Same

(53) Any response to the motion for leave to appeal by a party shall be served and filed no later than 15 days after the materials referred to in subrule (51) were served on the party.

Same

(54) The clerk shall fix a date for the hearing of the motion, which shall not, except with the consent of the party responding to the motion, be earlier than 15 days after the filing of the materials referred to in subrule (51).

Same

(55) If leave to appeal is granted,

(a) the notice of appeal shall be served no later than seven days after the granting of leave; and

(b) the 30-day deadline set out in clause (5)(a) does not apply, but the filing deadline set out in clause (5)(b) continues to apply.

O. Reg. 89/04, s. 13; 76/06, s. 10; 388/12, s. 10; 142/14, s. 13; 69/15, s. 14; 140/15, s. 5, item 4; 298/18, s. 20

RULE 39 — CASE MANAGEMENT IN FAMILY COURT OF SUPERIOR COURT OF JUSTICE

Case Management in Certain Areas Only

39. (1) This rule applies only to cases in the Family Court of the Superior Court of Justice, which has jurisdiction in the municipalities listed in subrule 1(3).

Excluded Cases

(2) This rule does not apply to,

(a) enforcements;

(b) cases under rule 32.1, 37 or 37.1; or

(c) cases under the *Child, Youth and Family Services Act, 2017*.

(d) [Repealed O. Reg. 439/07, s. 3(1).]

Parties May not Lengthen Times

(3) A time set out in this rule may be lengthened only by order of the case management judge and not by the parties' consent under subrule 3(6).

Fast Track

(4) Applications to which this rule applies, except the ones mentioned in subrule (7), and motions to change a final order or agreement are fast track cases (subrules (5) and (6)).

Fast Track — First Court Date

(5) In a fast track case the clerk shall, on or before the first court date,

(a) confirm that all necessary documents have been served and filed;

(b) refer the parties to sources of information about the court process, alternatives to court (including mediation), the effects of separation and divorce on children and community resources that may help the parties and their children;

(c) if an answer has been filed in response to an application, or if a response to motion to change (Form 15B) or a notice of financial interest has been filed in a motion to change a final order or agreement under rule 15, confirm that the case is ready for a hearing, case conference or settlement conference and schedule it accordingly;

(d) if no answer has been filed in response to an application, send the case to a judge for a decision on the basis of affidavit evidence or, on request of the applicant, schedule a case conference; and

(e) if no response to motion to change (Form 15B), consent motion to change (Form 15C) or notice of financial interest is filed in response to a motion to change a final order or agreement under rule 15, send the case to a judge for a decision on the basis of the evidence filed in the motion.

Fast Track — Case Management Judge Assigned at Start

(6) In a fast track case, a case management judge shall be assigned by the first time the case comes before a judge.

Standard Track

(7) Applications in which the applicant makes any of the following claims are standard track cases (subrule (8)):

1. A claim for divorce.

2. A property claim.

3. A claim under the *Arbitration Act, 1991* or the *Family Law Act* relating to a family arbitration, family arbitration agreement or family arbitration award.

Features of Standard Track

(8) In a standard track case,

(a) the clerk shall not set a court date when the application is filed;

(b) a case management judge shall be assigned when a case conference or a motion is scheduled, whichever comes first; and

(c) the clerk shall schedule a case conference on any party's request.

Functions of Case Management Judge

(9) The case management judge assigned to a case,

(a) shall generally supervise its progress;

(b) shall conduct the case conference and the settlement conference;

(c) may schedule a case conference or settlement conference at any time, on the judge's own initiative; and

(d) shall hear motions in the case, when available to hear motions;

(e) [Repealed O. Reg. 76/06, s. 11(2).]

Substitute Case Management Judge

(10) If the case management judge is, for any reason, unavailable to continue as the case management judge, another case management judge may be assigned for part or all of the case.

Notice of Approaching Dismissal After 365 Days

(11) The clerk shall serve a notice of approaching dismissal (Form 39) for a case on the parties by mail, fax or email if the case has not been settled, withdrawn or scheduled or adjourned for trial before the 365th day after the date the case was started, and that time has not been lengthened by an order under subrule (3).

Exception

(11.1) Despite subrule (11), if a case conference or settlement conference is arranged before the 365th day after the date the case was started for a date on or later than the 365th day, the clerk shall not serve a notice of approaching dismissal except as set out in subrule (11.2).

Notice Sent if Conference Does Not Take Place

(11.2) If a case conference or settlement conference is arranged for a date on or later than the 365th day after the date the case was started, but the hearing does not take place on that date and is not adjourned by a judge, the clerk shall serve the notice of approaching dismissal on the parties by mail, fax or email.

Dismissal of Case

(12) A case for which a notice of approaching dismissal has been served shall be dismissed without further notice, unless one of the parties, within 60 days after the notice is served,

(a) obtains an order under subrule (3) to lengthen that time;

(b) files an agreement signed by all parties and their lawyers, if any, for a final order disposing of all issues in the case, and a notice of motion for an order carrying out the agreement;

(c) serves on all parties and files a notice of withdrawal (Form 12) that discontinues all outstanding claims in the case;

(d) schedules or adjourns the case for trial; or

(e) arranges a case conference or settlement conference for the first available date.

Same

(12.1) If a case conference or settlement conference is arranged for a date as described in clause (12)(e), but the hearing does not take place on that date and is not adjourned by a judge, the case shall be dismissed without further notice.

Dismissal After Notice

(12.2) The clerk shall dismiss a case under subrule (12) or (12.1) by preparing and signing an order dismissing the case, with no costs payable by any party.

Service of Dismissal Order by Clerk

(13) The clerk shall serve the order on each party by mail, fax or email.

Service of Dismissal Order by Lawyer on Client

(14) A lawyer who is served with a dismissal order on behalf of a client shall serve it on the client by mail, fax or email and file proof of service of the order.

Judge may Set Clerk's Order Aside

(14.1) The case management judge or another judge may, on motion, set aside an order of the clerk under subrule (12).

(15) [Repealed O. Reg. 322/13, s. 20.]

O. Reg. 202/01, s. 7; 56/03, s. 7; 89/04, s. 14; 76/06, s. 11; 439/07, s. 3; 151/08, s. 7; 388/12, s. 11; 322/13, s. 20; 140/15, s. 4, item 7; 298/18, s. 21

RULE 40 — CASE MANAGEMENT IN ONTARIO COURT OF JUSTICE

Case Management in Certain Areas Only

40. (1) This rule applies only to cases in the Ontario Court of Justice.

Excluded Cases

(2) This rule does not apply to,

(a) enforcements;

(b) cases under rule 37 or 37.1; or

(c) cases under the *Child, Youth and Family Services Act, 2017.*

(d) [Repealed O. Reg. 439/07, s. 4(1).]

Parties may not Lengthen Times

(3) A time set out in this rule may be lengthened only by order and not by the parties' consent under subrule 3(6).

First Court Date

(4) The clerk shall, on or before the first court date,

(a) confirm that all necessary documents have been served and filed;

(b) refer the parties to sources of information about the court process, alternatives to court (including mediation), the effects of separation and divorce on children and community resources that may help the parties and their children;

(c) if an answer has been filed in response to an application, or if a response to motion to change (Form 15B) or a notice of financial interest has been filed in a motion to change a final order or agreement under rule 15, confirm that the case is ready for a hearing, case conference or settlement conference and schedule it accordingly;

(d) if no answer has been filed in response to an application, send the case to a judge for a decision on the basis of affidavit evidence or, on request of the applicant, schedule a case conference; and

(e) if no response to motion to change (Form 15B), consent motion to change (Form 15C) or notice of financial interest is filed in response to a motion to change a final order or agreement under rule 15, send the case to a judge for a decision on the basis of the evidence filed in the motion.

Notice of Approaching Dismissal After 365 Days

(5) The clerk shall serve a notice of approaching dismissal (Form 39) for a case on the parties by mail, fax or email if the case has not been settled, withdrawn or scheduled or adjourned for trial before the 365th day after the date the case was started, and that time has not been lengthened by an order under subrule (3).

Exception

(5.1) Despite subrule (5), if a case conference or settlement conference is arranged before the 365th day after the date the case was started for a date on or later than the 365th day, the clerk shall not serve a notice of approaching dismissal except as set out in subrule (5.2).

Notice Sent if Conference Does Not Take Place

(5.2) If a case conference or settlement conference is arranged for a date on or later than the 365th day after the date the case was started, but the hearing does not take place on that date and is not adjourned by a judge, the clerk shall serve the notice of approaching dismissal on the parties by mail, fax or email.

Dismissal of Case

(6) A case for which a notice of approaching dismissal has been served shall be dismissed without further notice, unless one of the parties, within 60 days after the notice is served,

(a) obtains an order under subrule (3) to lengthen that time;

(b) files an agreement signed by all parties and their lawyers, if any, for a final order disposing of all issues in the case, and a notice of motion for an order carrying out the agreement;

(c) serves on all parties and files a notice of withdrawal (Form 12) that discontinues all outstanding claims in the case;

(d) schedules or adjourns the case for trial; or

(e) arranges a case conference or settlement conference for the first available date.

Same

(6.1) If a case conference or settlement conference is arranged for a date as described in clause (6)(e), but the hearing does not take place on that date and is not adjourned by a judge, the case shall be dismissed without further notice.

Dismissal After Notice

(6.2) The clerk shall dismiss a case under subrule (6) or (6.1) by preparing and signing an order dismissing the case, with no costs payable by any party.

Service of Dismissal Order by Clerk

(7) The clerk shall serve the order on each party by mail, fax or email.

Service of Dismissal Order by Lawyer on Client

(8) A lawyer who is served with a dismissal order on behalf of a client shall serve it on the client by mail, fax or email and file proof of service of the order.

Judge May Set Clerk's Order Aside

(9) A judge may, on motion, set aside an order of the clerk under subrule (6).

(10) [Repealed O. Reg. 322/13, s. 21.]

O. Reg. 202/01, s. 8; 56/03, s. 8; 89/04, s. 15; 76/06, s. 12; 439/07, s. 4; 151/08, s. 8; 322/13, s. 21; 140/15, s. 4, item 8; 298/18, s. 22

RULE 41 — CASE MANAGEMENT IN THE SUPERIOR COURT OF JUSTICE (OTHER THAN THE FAMILY COURT OF THE SUPERIOR COURT OF JUSTICE) [HEADING AMENDED O. REG. 89/04, S. 16.]

Case Management

41. (1) This rule applies only to cases in the Superior Court of Justice, other than cases in the Family Court of the Superior Court of Justice, started on or after July 1, 2004.

Excluded Cases

(2) This rule does not apply to,

(a) enforcements; or

(b) cases under rule 32.1, 37 or 37.1.

Parties May Not Lengthen Times

(3) A time set out in this rule may be lengthened only by order of the court and not by the parties' consent under subrule 3(6).

Clerk's Role

(4) The clerk shall not set a court date when the application is filed, and the case shall come before the court when a case conference or a motion is scheduled, whichever comes first, and the clerk shall schedule a case conference on any party's request.

Notice of Approaching Dismissal After 365 Days

(5) The clerk shall serve a notice of approaching dismissal (Form 39) for a case on the parties by mail, fax or email if the case has not been settled, withdrawn or scheduled or adjourned for trial before the 365th day after the date the case was started, and that time has not been lengthened by an order under subrule (3).

Exception

(5.1) Despite subrule (5), if a case conference or settlement conference is arranged before the 365th day after the date the case was started for a date on or later than the 365th day, the clerk shall not serve a notice of approaching dismissal except as set out in subrule (5.2).

Notice Sent if Conference Does Not Take Place

(5.2) If a case conference or settlement conference is arranged for a date on or later than the 365th day after the date the case was started, but the hearing does not take place on that date and is not adjourned by a judge, the clerk shall serve the notice of approaching dismissal on the parties by mail, fax or email.

Dismissal of Case

(6) A case for which a notice of approaching dismissal has been served shall be dismissed without further notice, unless one of the parties, within 60 days after the notice is served,

(a) obtains an order under subrule (3) to lengthen that time;

(b) files an agreement signed by all parties and their lawyers, if any, for a final order disposing of all issues in the case, and a notice of motion for an order carrying out the agreement;

(c) serves on all parties and files a notice of withdrawal (Form 12) that discontinues all outstanding claims in the case;

(d) schedules or adjourns the case for trial; or

(e) arranges a case conference or settlement conference for the first available date.

Same

(6.1) If a case conference or settlement conference is arranged for a date as described in clause (6)(e), but the hearing does not take place on that date and is not adjourned by a judge, the case shall be dismissed without further notice.

Dismissal After Notice

(6.2) The clerk shall dismiss a case under subrule (6) or (6.1) by preparing and signing an order dismissing the case, with no costs payable by any party.

Service of Dismissal Order

(7) The clerk shall serve the order on each party by mail, fax or email.

Service of Dismissal Order by Lawyer on Client

(8) A lawyer who is served with a dismissal order on behalf of a client shall serve it on the client by mail, fax or email and file proof of service of the order.

Judge may Set Clerk's Order Aside

(9) A judge may, on motion, set aside an order of the clerk under subrule (6).

(10) [Repealed O. Reg. 322/13, s. 22.]

O. Reg. 441/99, s. 2; 89/04, s. 16; 76/06, s. 13; 439/07, s. 5; 388/12, s. 12; 322/13, s. 22; 140/15, s. 4, item 9

RULE 42 — APPOINTMENT OF FAMILY CASE MANAGER IN THE FAMILY COURT OF THE SUPERIOR COURT OF JUSTICE IN OTTAWA

Scope

42. (1) This rule applies to cases in the Family Court of the Superior Court of Justice in the City of Ottawa if the cases relate to matters under the following Acts:

1. [Repealed O. Reg. 235/16, s. 7(1).]

2. The *Children's Law Reform Act.*

3. The *Divorce Act* (Canada).

4. The *Family Law Act.*

5. The *Family Responsibility and Support Arrears Enforcement Act, 1996.*

Same

(1.1) This rule applies in respect of a case regardless of whether it is a fast track case (rule 39) or a standard track case.

Purpose

(2) The purpose of this rule is to promote the active management, in accordance with subrule 2(5), of cases to which this rule applies by conferring specified family law jurisdiction on a Family Case Manager.

Definition

(3) In this rule,

"Family Case Manager" means a person appointed under section 86.1 of the *Courts of Justice Act* by the Lieutenant Governor in Council as a case management master who is assigned to manage cases for the purposes of this rule.

Family Case Manager, Powers and Duties

(4) In a case to which this rule applies,

(a) the Family Case Manager may only exercise the powers and carry out the duties and functions that are specified in this rule; and

(b) the exercise of those powers and the performance of those duties and functions are subject to the restrictions specified in subrule (5).

No Jurisdiction

(5) The Family Case Manager has no jurisdiction in respect of,

(a) a power, duty or function that is conferred exclusively on a judge of a superior court by law or expressly on a judge by an Act;

(b) a case involving a special party;

(c) the determination of a right or interest of a party in real property; or

(d) the making of an order or hearing of a motion for an order,

(i) to change, set aside, stay or confirm an order of a judge,

(ii) to find a person in contempt of court,

(iii) to restrain the liberty of a person, including an order for imprisonment, a warrant for arrest or a warrant of committal,

(iv) to dismiss all or part of a party's case for a failure by the party to follow these rules or obey an order in the case or a related case, if the *Family Responsibility and Support Arrears Enforcement Act, 1996* applies to the party's case,

(v) to split a divorce from other issues in a case under subrule 12(6),

(vi) [Repealed O. Reg. 235/16, s. 7(4).]

(vii) to grant summary judgment.

(6) [Repealed O. Reg. 235/16, s. 7(5).]

Motions Under Rule 14

(7) The Family Case Manager may hear motions under rule 14 relating to matters over which he or she has jurisdiction and, for the purpose, may exercise any power under that rule, other than a power under subrule 14(21).

Orders on Motion Under Rule 14

(8) If a motion under rule 14 is made in a case under an Act to which this rule applies, the Family Case Manager may make only the following orders:

0.1 Subject to subclause (5)(d)(iv), an order under subrule 1(8), other than a contempt order under clause 1(8)(g), and an order under subrule 1(8.1).

0.2 An order under subrule 1(8.2).

0.3 An order under subrule 1(8.4), if the Family Case Manager made the order striking out the document.

1. An order under rules 3, 4, 5, 6, 7, 9, 10, 11, 12, 13, 18, 19 and 20.

2. An order for costs under rule 24 relating to a step in the case that the Family Case Manager dealt with.

3. An order under rule 25 relating to an order made by the Family Case Manager.

3.1 An order under subrule 39(3) or (14.1).

4. An order to change a temporary order made by the Family Case Manager.

5. An order under section 17.2 (Blood, DNA tests) of the *Children's Law Reform Act.*

6. A temporary order for or relating to custody of or access to a child under section 21, 23, 25, 28, 29, 30, 32, 34, 39 or 40 of the *Children's Law Reform Act.*

7. A temporary order for custody of or access to a child under section 16 of the *Divorce Act* (Canada).

8. An order appointing a mediator under section 31 of the *Children's Law Reform Act* or section 3 (Mediation) of the *Family Law Act.*

9. A temporary order for or relating to support under section 33, clause 34(1)(a), (e), (f), (g) or (h), subsection 34(5) or section 37, 42 or 47 of the *Family Law Act.*

10. A temporary order for support under section 15.1 (Child support order) or 15.2 (Spousal support order) of the *Divorce Act* (Canada).

11. A temporary order under section 40 of the *Family Law Act.*

12. A temporary order dealing with property other than real property.

13. A support deduction order under section 10 (Support deduction orders to be made) of the *Family Responsibility and Support Arrears Enforcement Act, 1996.*

14. An order limiting or suspending a support deduction order.

15. An order under section 8 (Director to cease enforcement, termination of support obligation) of the *Family Responsibility and Support Arrears Enforcement Act, 1996*

that terminates a support obligation or orders repayment from a person who received support.

15.1 An order under subsection 89(3.1) or 112(2) of the *Courts of Justice Act* requesting the Children's Lawyer to act.

16. An order that is necessary and incidental to the power to make a temporary order that is within the jurisdiction of the Family Case Manager.

(9) [Repealed O. Reg. 235/16, s. 7(8).]

(10) [Repealed O. Reg. 235/16, s. 7(8).]

(11) [Repealed O. Reg. 151/08, s. 9.]

Conferences

(12) The Family Case Manager may conduct a case conference, settlement conference or trial management conference instead of a judge under rule 17.

(13) [Repealed O. Reg. 235/16, s. 7(10).]

Application of Rule 17

(14) At a case conference, settlement conference or trial management conference conducted by the Family Case Manager, rule 17 applies subject to the following changes:

1. In a case to which this rule applies, the Family Case Manager may make any order described in rule 17 and, with respect to the temporary and final orders referred to in clause 17(8)(b),

   i. the only temporary or final orders that the Family Case Manager may make are those described in subrule (8) of this rule, and

   ii. the Family Case Manager shall not make a final order unless the parties consent to the order.

2. [Repealed O. Reg. 235/16, s. 7(12).]

3. A party to the conference may not request that the conference be conducted by a judge under subrule 17(9).

4. Despite clause 17(10)(a), a case may be scheduled for trial if the Family Case Manager conducted a settlement conference.

Enforcement Powers

(15) The Family Case Manager may exercise,

(a) any power that a court may exercise under rule 27 (requiring financial information) other than a power to order a person imprisoned under subrule 27(6), (20) or (21); and

(b) the powers relating to garnishment orders set out in subrules 29(5) and (19).

Sending Case to Judge

(16) Despite anything to the contrary in this rule, the Family Case Manager may at any time order that a matter assigned to him or her be adjourned and sent to a judge.

Appeal from Temporary Order

(17) Subrules 38(5) to (45) apply with necessary changes to an appeal from a temporary order of the Family Case Manager.

Appeal from Final Order

(18) Subrules 38(1), (2) and (3) apply with necessary changes to an appeal from a final order of the Family Case Manager.

Revocation

(19) This rule is revoked on July 1, 2021.

O. Reg. 441/99, s. 2; 120/07, s. 1; 151/08, s. 9; 51/10, s. 1; 186/12, s. 2; 322/13, s. 23; 142/14, s. 14; 235/16, s. 7; 226/17, s. 3

43. This Regulation comes into force on September 15, 1999.

TABLE OF FORMS

Form Number	Form Title	Date of Form
4	Notice of change in representation	October 21, 2013
6	Acknowledgment of service	September 1, 2005
6A	Advertisement	March 19, 2015
6B	Affidavit of service	April 12, 2016
8	Application (general)	April 12, 2016
8A	Application (divorce)	April 12, 2016
8B	Application (child protection and status review)	March 1, 2018
8B.1	Application (status review for child in extended society care and child formerly in extended society care)	March 1, 2018
8B.2	Application (general) (*Child, Youth and Family Services Act, 2017* cases other than child protection and status review)	March 1, 2018
8C	Application (secure treatment)	March 1, 2018
8D	Application (adoption)	March 1, 2018
8D.1	Application (dispense with parent's consent to adoption before placement)	September 1, 2005
8D.2	Notice of intention to place child(ren) for adoption	March 1, 2018
8D.3	Notice of intention to place First Nations, Inuk or Métis child for adoption	March 1, 2018
8D.4	[Repealed O. Reg. 298/18, s. 23(2).]	
8E	[Repealed O. Reg. 519/06, s. 7(1).]	
10	Answer	March 1, 2018
10A	Reply	September 1, 2005
12	Notice of withdrawal	September 1, 2005
13	Financial statement (support claims)	January 6, 2015

TABLE OF FORMS

Form Number	Form Title	Date of Form
13.1	Financial statement (property and support claims)	January 6, 2015
13A	Certificate of financial disclosure	January 6, 2015
13B	Net family property statement	May 15, 2009
13C	Comparison of net family property statements	January 6, 2015
14	Notice of motion	March 1, 2018
14A	Affidavit (general)	September 1, 2005
14B	Motion form	September 1, 2005
14C	Confirmation of Motion	March 1, 2018
14D	Order on motion without notice	September 1, 2005
15	Motion to change	April 12, 2016
15A	Change information form	April 12, 2016
15B	Response to motion to change	April 12, 2016
15C	Consent motion to change	April 12, 2016
15D	Consent motion to change child support	April 12, 2016
17	Conference notice	September 1, 2005
17A	Case conference brief — General	November 15, 2009
17B	Case conference brief for protection application or status review	March 1, 2018
17C	Settlement conference brief — General	November 15, 2009
17D	Settlement conference brief for protection application or status review	March 1, 2018
17E	Trial management conference brief	March 1, 2018
17F	Confirmation of Conference	March 1, 2018
20	Request for information	September 1, 2005
20.1	Acknowledgement of expert's duty	August 2, 2011
20A	Authorization to commissioner	September 1, 2005
20B	Letter of request	September 1, 2005
22	Request to admit	September 1, 2005
22A	Response to request to admit	September 1, 2005
23	Summons to witness	September 1, 2005
23A	Summons to witness outside Ontario	September 1, 2005
23B	Order for prisoner's attendance	September 1, 2005
23C	Affidavit for uncontested trial	September 1, 2009
25	Order (general)	September 1, 2005
25A	Divorce order	September 1, 2005
25B	Secure treatment order	March 1, 2018
25C	Adoption order	March 1, 2018
25D	Order (uncontested trial)	September 1, 2005
25E	Notice disputing approval of order	September 1, 2005
25F	Restraining order	September 1, 2009
25G	Restraining order on motion without notice	September 1, 2009

TABLE OF FORMS

Form Number	Form Title	Date of Form
25H	Order terminating restraining order	September 1, 2009
26	Statement of money owed	April 12, 2016
26A	Affidavit of enforcement expenses	April 12, 2016
26B	Affidavit for filing domestic contract with court	April 12, 2016
26C	Notice of transfer of enforcement	April 12, 2016
27	Request for financial statement	April 12, 2016
27A	Request for statement of income	April 12, 2016
27B	Statement of income from income source	September 1, 2005
27C	Appointment for financial examination	April 12, 2016
28	Writ of seizure and sale	April 12, 2016
28A	Request for writ of seizure and sale	September 1, 2005
28B	Statutory declaration to sheriff	June 15, 2007
28C	Writ of temporary seizure	September 1, 2005
29	Request for garnishment	April 12, 2016
29A	Notice of garnishment (lump-sum debt)	April 12, 2016
29B	Notice of garnishment (periodic debt)	April 12, 2016
29C	Notice to co-owner of debt	September 1, 2005
29D	Statutory declaration of indexed support	April 12, 2016
29E	Dispute (payor)	September 1, 2005
29F	Dispute (garnishee)	September 1, 2005
29G	Dispute (co-owner of debt)	September 1, 2005
29H	Notice of garnishment hearing	September 1, 2005
29I	Notice to stop garnishment	September 1, 2005
29J	Statement to garnishee financial institution re support	April 12, 2016
30	Notice of default hearing	April 12, 2016
30A	Request for default hearing	September 1, 2005
30B	Default dispute	September 1, 2005
31	Notice of contempt motion	September 1, 2005
32	Bond (recognizance)	September 1, 2005
32A	Notice of forfeiture motion	September 1, 2005
32B	Warrant for arrest	April 12, 2016
32C	Affidavit for warrant of committal	September 1, 2005
32D	Warrant of committal	April 12, 2016
32.1	Request to enforce a family arbitration award	October 1, 2012
32.1A	Dispute of request for enforcement	October 1, 2012
33	Information for warrant to bring a child to a place of safety	March 1, 2018
33A	Warrant to bring a child to a place of safety	March 1, 2018
33B	Plan of care for child(ren) (Children's Aid Society)	March 1, 2018

TABLE OF FORMS

Form Number	Form Title	Date of Form
33B.1	Answer and plan of care (parties other than Children's Aid Society)	March 1, 2018
33B.2	Answer (*Child, Youth and Family Services Act, 2017* cases other than child protection and status review)	March 1, 2018
33C	Statement of agreed facts (child protection)	March 1, 2018
33D	Statement of agreed facts (status review)	March 1, 2018
33E	Child's consent to secure treatment	September 1, 2005
33F	Consent to secure treatment (person other than child)	December 1, 2015
34	Child's consent to adoption	April 1, 2009
34A	Affidavit of parentage	March 1, 2018
34B	Non-parent's consent to adoption by spouse	March 1, 2018
34C	Director's or local director's statement on adoption	March 1, 2018
34D	Affidavit of adoption applicant(s), sworn/affirmed	March 1, 2018
34E	Director's consent to adoption	March 1, 2018
34F	Parent's or custodian's consent to adoption	March 1, 2018
34G	Affidavit of adoption licensee or society employee	March 1, 2018
34G.1	Affidavit of society employee for adoption of a child in extended society care	March 1, 2018
34H	Affidavit of adopting relative or stepparent	March 1, 2018
34I	Parent's consent to adoption by spouse	March 1, 2018
34J	Affidavit of execution and independent legal advice (Children's Lawyer)	April 1, 2009
34K	Certificate of clerk (adoption)	March 1, 2018
34L	Application for openness order	March 1, 2018
34M	Consent to openness order under s. 194 of the *Child, Youth and Family Services Act, 2017*	March 1, 2018
34M.1	Consent to openness order under s. 196 or 197 of the *Child, Youth and Family Services Act, 2017*	March 1, 2018
34N	Application to change or terminate openness order	March 1, 2018
35.1	Affidavit in support of claim for custody or access	April 15, 2017
36	Affidavit for divorce	September 1, 2005
36A	Certificate of clerk (divorce)	March 1, 2018
36B	Certificate of divorce	September 1, 2005
37	Notice of hearing	September 1, 2005
37A	Information sheet	September 1, 2005
37B	Direction to request further information	September 1, 2005
37C	Notice of continuation of hearing	September 1, 2005

TABLE OF FORMS

Form Number	Form Title	Date of Form
37D	Notice of registration of order	September 1, 2005
37E	Notice for taking further evidence	September 1, 2005
38	Notice of appeal	September 1, 2005
39	Notice of approaching dismissal	June 15, 2007

O. Reg. 76/06, s. 14; 519/06, s. 7; 439/07, s. 6; 151/08, s. 10; 317/09, s. 1; 386/09, s. 2; 6/10, s. 10; 52/10, s. 2; 383/11, s. 8; 186/12, s. 3; 388/12, s. 13; 322/13, s. 24; 69/15, s. 15; 140/15, s. 3; 235/16, s. 8; 226/17, s. 4; 298/18, s. 23

FORMS UNDER THE FAMILY LAW RULES

Form number	Title	Rule creating form
4	Notice of change in representation	4(10)
6	Acknowledgment of service	6(3)
6A	Advertisement	6(17)
6B	Affidavit of service	6(19)
8	Application (general)	8(1)
8A	Application (divorce)	8(1)
8B	Application (child protection and status review)	8(1)
8B.1	Application (status review for Crown ward and former Crown ward)	8(1)
8B.2	Application (general) (*Child and Family Services Act* cases other than child protection and status review)	8(1)
8C	Application (secure treatment)	8(1)
8D	Application (adoption)	8(1)
8D.1	Application (dispense with parent's consent to adoption before placement)	8(1)
10	Answer	10(1)
10A	Reply	10(6)
12	Notice of withdrawal	12(1)
13	Financial statement (support claims)	13(1)
13.1	Financial statement (property and support claims)	13(1)
13B	Net family property statement	13(14)
14	Notice of motion	14(9)
14A	Affidavit (general)	14(9)
14B	Motion form	14(10)
14C	Confirmation	14(11)
14D	Order on motion without notice	14(14)
15	Change information form (motion to change child support)	15(10)
15A	Motion to Change	15(10)
15B	Response to motion to change	13(4.2)
15C	Consent motion to change	13(4.2)
15D	Consent motion to change child support	13(4.2)
17	Conference notice	17(13)
17A	Case conference brief — General	17(13)

FORMS

Form number	Title	Rule creating form
17B	Case conference brief for protection application or status review	17(13)
17C	Settlement conference brief — General	17(13)
17D	Settlement conference brief for protection application or status review	17(13)
17E	Trial management conference brief	17(13)
20	Request for information	20(3)
20A	Authorization to commissioner	20(14)
20B	Letter of request	20(14)
22	Request to admit	22(2)
22A	Response to request to admit	22(4)
23	Summons to witness	23(3)
23A	Summons to witness outside Ontario	23(8)
23B	Order for prisoner's attendance	23(10)
23C	Affidavit for uncontested trial	23(22)
25	Order (general)	25(2)
25A	Divorce order	25(2)
25B	Secure treatment order	25(2)
25C	Adoption order	25(2)
25D	Order (uncontested trial)	25(2)
25E	Notice disputing approval of order	25(5)
25F	Restraining Order	25(11.1)
25G	Restraining Order on Motion without Notice	25(11.1)
25H	Order Terminating Restraining Order	25(11.2)
26	Statement of money owed	26(5)
26A	Affidavit of enforcement expenses	26(8)
26B	Affidavit for filing domestic contract or paternity agreement with court	26(9)
26C	Notice of transfer of enforcement	26(14)
27	Request for financial statement	27(1)
27A	Request for statement of income	27(7)
27B	Statement of income from income source	27(7)
27C	Appointment for financial examination	27(11)
28	Writ of seizure and sale	28(1)
28A	Request for writ of seizure and sale	28(1)
28B	Statutory declaration to sheriff	28(2)
28C	Writ of temporary seizure	28(10)
29	Request for garnishment	29(1)
29A	Notice of garnishment (lump-sum debt)	29(1)
29B	Notice of garnishment (periodic debt)	29(1)
29C	Notice to co-owner of debt	29(8)
29D	Statutory declaration of indexed support	29(14)
29E	Dispute (payor)	29(16)
29F	Dispute (garnishee)	29(16)
29G	Dispute (co-owner of debt)	29(16)
29H	Notice of garnishment hearing	29(17)
29I	Notice to stop garnishment	29(31)

Form number	Title	Rule creating form
29J	Statement to garnishee financial institution re support	29
30	Notice of default hearing	30(1)
30A	Request for default hearing	30(1)
30B	Default dispute	30(3)
31	Notice of contempt motion	31(2)
32	Bond (recognizance)	32(2)
32.1	Request to Enforce a Family Arbitration Award	32.1(1)
32.1A	Dispute of Request for Enforcement	32.1(7)
32A	Notice of forfeiture motion	32(7)
32B	Warrant for arrest	32(12)
32C	Affidavit for warrant of committal	32(14)
32D	Warrant of committal	32(15)
33	Information for warrant to apprehend child	33(7)
33A	Warrant to apprehend child	33(7)
33B	Plan of care for child(ren) (Children's Aid Society)	33(7)
33B.1	Answer and plan of care (Parties other than Children's Aid Society)	33(7)
33B.2	Answer (*Child and Family Services Act* cases other than child protection and status review)	34(17)
33C	Statement of agreed facts (child protection)	33(7)
33D	Statement of agreed facts (status review)	33(7)
33E	Child's consent to secure treatment	33(8)
33F	Consent to secure treatment (person other than child)	33(8)
34	Child's consent to adoption	34(4)
34A	Affidavit of parentage	34(4)
34B	Non-parent's consent to adoption by spouse	34(4)
34C	Director's or local director's statement on adoption	34(4)
34D	Affidavit of adoption applicant(s)	34(4)
34E	Director's consent to adoption	34(6)
34F	Parent's or custodian's consent to adoption	34(7)
34G	Affidavit of adoption licensee or society employee	34(7)
34H	Affidavit of adopting relative or stepparent	34(8)
34I	Parent's consent to adoption by spouse	34(9)
34J	Affidavit of execution and independent legal advice (Children's Lawyer)	34(10)
34K	Certificate of clerk (adoption)	34(15)
34L	Application for openness order	34(17)
34M	Consent to openness order	34(17)
34N	Application to change or terminate openness order	34(17)
35.1	Affidavit in Support of Claim for Custody or Access	35.1(2)
36	Affidavit for divorce	36(5)
36A	Certificate of clerk (divorce)	36(7)
36B	Certificate of divorce	36(8)
37	Notice of hearing	37(3)
37A	Information sheet	37(3)
37B	Direction to request further information	37(10)
37C	Notice of continuation of hearing	37(13)

Form number	Title	Rule creating form
37D	Notice of registration of order	37(18)
37E	Notice for taking further evidence	37(25)
38	Notice of appeal	38(2)
39	Notice of approaching dismissal	39(11)

FORM 4 — NOTICE OF CHANGE IN REPRESENTATION

[Repealed O. Reg. 76/06, s. 15.]

[Editor's Note: Forms 4 to 39 of the Family Law Rules have been repealed by O. Reg. 76/06, effective May 1, 2006. Pursuant to Family Law Rule 1(9), when a form is referred to by number, the reference is to the form with that number that is described in the Table of Forms at the end of these rules and which is available at www.ontariocourtforms.on.ca. For your convenience, the government form as published on this website is reproduced below.]

Court File Number ....

.... *(Name of Court)*

at... *Court office address*

Applicant(s)

Full legal name & address for service — street & number, municipality, postal code, telephone & fax numbers and e-mail address (if any).	*Lawyer's name & address — street & number, municipality, postal code, telephone & fax numbers and e-mail address (if any).*

Respondent(s)

Full legal name & address for service — street & number, municipality, postal code, telephone & fax numbers and e-mail address (if any).	*Lawyer's name & address — street & number, municipality, postal code, telephone & fax numbers and e-mail address (if any).*

Children's Lawyer

Name & address of Children's Lawyer's agent for service (street & number, municipality, postal code, telephone & fax numbers and e-mail address (if any)) and name of person represented.

TO ALL PARTIES AND THEIR LAWYERS

FROM *(name)*.. *(Name, address, telephone & fax numbers and e-mail address)*

- ❑ I have chosen to be represented by a lawyer. See details in this box. →
- ❑ I have chosen a new lawyer. See details in this box. →
- ❑ I have decided to act in person. Documents can be served on me at the address set out in this box. →

❑ I have the court's permission to be represented by a person who is not a lawyer. See details in this box. →

❑ I have the court's permission to appear in person at a child protection trial. Documents can be served on me at the address set out in this box. →

.... (*Date of signature*)

.... (*Signature*)

Notes:

1. *You must serve this notice on the lawyers for all of the other parties. If another party does not have a lawyer, you must serve it on the party. If you have been represented by a lawyer or other person who, because of this notice, is no longer going to represent you, you must also serve this notice on that lawyer or the other person who used to represent you.*

2. *You can serve by any method set out in rule 6 of the Family Law Rules, including mail, courier, and fax.*

3. *When you have served this notice, you must file it with the clerk of the court together with proof of service (Form 6B). If you appeared without a lawyer and now you have chosen to be represented by a lawyer, you must attach that lawyer's consent to this notice.*

4. *If a child protection case has been scheduled for trial, you must receive the court's permission to remove your lawyer and represent yourself.*

October 21, 2013

FORM 6 — ACKNOWLEDGEMENT OF SERVICE

[Repealed O. Reg. 76/06, s. 15.]

[Editor's Note: Forms 4 to 39 of the Family Law Rules have been repealed by O. Reg. 76/06, effective May 1, 2006. Pursuant to Family Law Rule 1(9), when a form is referred to by number, the reference is to the form with that number that is described in the Table of Forms at the end of these rules and which is available at www.ontariocourtforms.on.ca. For your convenience, the government form as published on this website is reproduced below.]

Court File Number ....

.... (*Name of court*)

at .... *Court office address*

You are asked to fill out and sign this card and to mail it immediately. If you do not return this card, the document(s) listed below may be personally served on you and you may be ordered to pay the costs of service.

My name is: (full legal name) ....

I may be served at: (address where court documents may be mailed to you) ....

I acknowledge receiving a copy of the following document(s):

❑ *Application dated* ....
❑ *Blank form of application*

❑ *Financial statement dated* ....

❑ *Blank form of financial statement*

❑ *Answer dated* ....
❑ *Blank form of answer*

❑ *Affidavit of (name)* .... *dated* ....

❑ *Notice of motion dated* ....

❑ *Statement of money owed dated* ....

❑ *(Other. Give title and date of document.)*

❑ ....

❑ ....

❑ ....

❑ ....

.... *Signature*

.... *Date of signature*

NOTICE: The address that you give above will be used in future to serve documents by mail until you inform the other parties and the court office of a new address for service.

September 1, 2005

FORM 6A — ADVERTISEMENT

[Repealed O. Reg. 76/06, s. 15.]

[Editor's Note: Forms 4 to 39 of the Family Law Rules have been repealed by O. Reg. 76/06, effective May 1, 2006. Pursuant to Family Law Rule 1(9), when a form is referred to by number, the reference is to the form with that number that is described in the Table of Forms at the end of these rules and which is available at www.ontariocourtforms.on.ca. For your convenience, the government form as published on this website is reproduced below.]

ONTARIO

❑ *SUPERIOR COURT OF JUSTICE*

❑ *ONTARIO COURT OF JUSTICE*

NOTICE TO: (full legal name) ....

A CASE HAS BEEN STARTED AGAINST YOU IN COURT at (address: street & number, municipality, postal code)

....

The next court date is *(date)* .... at .... a.m./p.m. or as soon as possible after that time.

The court may make an order in this case that may affect your rights. You can get more information about this case from the court office at *(Write "the address above" or, if the court office is at a different address, give the street & number, municipality and postal code of the court office.)*

....

You may also get information about this case from *(name, address and telephone number of person publishing this advertisement)*

....

IF YOU DO NOT COME TO COURT, AN ORDER MAY BE MADE WITHOUT YOU AND BE ENFORCED AGAINST YOU.

March 19, 2015

FORM 6B — AFFIDAVIT OF SERVICE SWORN/AFFIRMED

[Repealed O. Reg. 76/06, s. 15.]

[Editor's Note: Forms 4 to 39 of the Family Law Rules have been repealed by O. Reg. 76/06, effective May 1, 2006. Pursuant to Family Law Rule 1(9), when a form is referred to by number, the reference is to the form with that number that is described in the Table of Forms at the end of these rules and which is available at www.ontariocourtforms.on.ca. For your convenience, the government form as published on this website is reproduced below.]

ONTARIO

Court File Number

.... *(Name of court)*

at .... *Court office address*

Applicant(s)

Full legal name & address for service — street & number, municipality, postal code, telephone & fax numbers and e-mail address (if any).	*Lawyer's name & address — street & number, municipality, postal code, telephone & fax numbers and e-mail address (if any).*

Applicant(s)

Respondent(s)

Full legal name & address for service — street & number, municipality, postal code, telephone & fax numbers and e-mail address (if any).	*Lawyer's name & address — street & number, municipality, postal code, telephone & fax numbers and e-mail address (if any)..*

My name is (full legal name) ....

I live in (municipality & province) .... *and I swear/affirm that the following is true:*

1. On *(date)* ...., at *(time)* ...., I served *(name of person to be served)* .... with the following document(s) in this case:

	Name of document	**Author (if applicable)**	**Date when document signed, issued, sworn, etc.**
	....	....	....
	....	....	....
	....	....	....
List the documents served	....	....	....
	....	....	....
	....	....	....
	....	....	....

NOTE: You can leave out any part of this form that is not applicable.

2. I served the documents mentioned in paragraph 1 by:

Check one box only and go to indicated paragraph.

❑ special service. *(Go to paragraph 3 below if you used special service.)*

❑ mail. *(Go to paragraph 4 if you used mailed service.)*

❑ same day courier. *(Go to paragraph 5 if you used courier.)*

❑ next day courier. *(Go to paragraph 5 if you used courier.)*

❑ deposit at a document exchange. *(Go to paragraph 6 if you used a document exchange.)*

❑ an electronic document exchange. *(Go to paragraph 7 if you used an electronic document exchange.)*

❑ fax. *(Go to paragraph 8 if you used fax.)*

❑ email. *(Go to paragraph 9 if you used email.)*

❑ substituted service or advertisement. *(Go to paragraph 10 if you used substituted service or advertisement.)*

3. I carried out special service of the document(s) on the person named in paragraph 1 at *(place or address)* .... by:

Check one box only. Strike out paragraphs 4 to 10 and go to paragraph 11.

❑ leaving a copy with the person.

❑ leaving a copy with *(name)* ....

❑ who is a lawyer who accepted service in writing on a copy of the document.

❑ who is the person's lawyer of record.

❑ who is the *(office or position)* .... of the corporation named in paragraph 1.

❑ mailing a copy to the person together with a prepaid return postcard in Form 6 in an envelope bearing the sender's return address. This postcard, in which receipt of the document(s) is acknowledged, was returned and is attached to this affidavit.

❑ leaving a copy in a sealed envelope addressed to the person at the person's place of residence with *(name)* ....

who provided me with identification to show that he/she was an adult person residing at the same address and by mailing another copy of the same document(s) on the same or following day to the person named in paragraph 1 at that place of residence.

❑ other *(Specify. See rule 6 for details.)*

4. I mailed the document(s) to be served by addressing the covering envelope to the person named in paragraph 1 at: *(Set out address.)* .... which is the address

Check appropriate paragraph and strike out paragraphs 3, 5, 6, 7, 8, 9 and 10.

❑ of the person's place of business.

❑ of a lawyer who accepted service on the person's behalf.

❑ of the person's lawyer of record.

❑ of the person's home.

❑ on the document most recently filed in court by the person.

❑ other *(Specify.)*

5. The document(s) to be served was/were placed in an envelope that was picked up at .... a.m./p.m. on *(date)* .... by *(name of courier service)* .... a private courier service, a copy of whose receipt is attached to this affidavit. The envelope was addressed to the person named in paragraph 1 at: *(Set out address.)* .... which is the address

Check appropriate paragraph and strike out paragraphs 3, 4, 6, 7, 8, 9 and 10.

❑ of the person's place of business.

❑ of a lawyer who accepted service on the person's behalf.

❑ of the person's lawyer of record.

❑ of the person's home.

❑ on the document most recently filed in court by the person.

❑ other *(Specify.)* ....

6. The document(s) was/were deposited at a document exchange. The exchange's date stamp on the attached copy shows the date of deposit. *(Strike out paragraphs 3, 4, 5, 7, 8, 9, 10 and 13.)*

7. The documents were served through an electronic document exchange. The record of service from the exchange is attached to this affidavit. *(Strike out paragraphs 3, 4, 5, 6, 8, 9, 10 and 13.)*

8. The document(s) to be served was/were faxed. The fax confirmation is attached to this affidavit. *(Strike out paragraphs 3, 4, 5, 6, 7, 9, 10 and 13.)*

9. The documents were served by email. Attached to this Affidavit is a copy of the email that the document was attached to. *(Strike out paragraphs 3, 4, 5, 6, 7, 8, 10 and 13.)*

10. An order of this court made on *(date)* .... allowed

❑ substituted service.

❑ service by advertisement. *(Attach advertisement.)*

The order was carried out as follows: *(Give details. Then go to paragraph 13 if you had to travel to serve substitutionally or by advertisement.)*

11. My relationship to, or affiliation with, any party in this case is as follows:

12. I am at least 18 years of age.

13. To serve the document(s), I had to travel .... kilometres. My fee for service of the document(s) is $ .... including travel.

Sworn/Affirmed before me at .... *municipality* in .... *province, state, or country* on .... *date* .... *Commissioner for taking affidavits (Type or print name below if signature is illegible.)*	.... *Signature* *(This form is to be signed in front of a lawyer, justice of the peace, notary public or commissioner for taking affidavits.)*

April 12, 2016

FORM 8 — APPLICATION (GENERAL)

[Repealed O. Reg. 76/06, s. 15.]

[Editor's Note: Forms 4 to 39 of the Family Law Rules have been repealed by O. Reg. 76/06, effective May 1, 2006. Pursuant to Family Law Rule 1(9), when a form is referred to by

number, the reference is to the form with that number that is described in the Table of Forms at the end of these rules and which is available at www.ontariocourtforms.on.ca. For your convenience, the government form as published on this website is reproduced below.]

ONTARIO

Court File Number

(SEAL)

.... *(Name of court)*

at .... *Court office address*

Applicant(s)

Full legal name & address for service — street & number, municipality, postal code, telephone & fax numbers and e-mail address (if any).	*Lawyer's name & address — street & number, municipality, postal code, telephone & fax numbers and e-mail address (if any).*

Respondent(s)

Full legal name & address for service — street & number, municipality, postal code, telephone & fax numbers and e-mail address (if any).	*Lawyer's name & address — street & number, municipality, postal code, telephone & fax numbers and e-mail address (if any).*

TO THE RESPONDENT(S):

A COURT CASE HAS BEEN STARTED AGAINST YOU IN THIS COURT. THE DETAILS ARE SET OUT ON THE ATTACHED PAGES.

❑ *THE FIRST COURT DATE IS (date)* .... *AT* .... ❑ *a.m.* ❑ *p.m.* or as soon as possible after that time, at: *(address)*

NOTE: If this is a divorce case, no date will be set unless an Answer is filed. If you have also been served with a notice of motion, there may be an earlier court date and you or your lawyer should come to court for the motion.

❑ *THIS CASE IS ON THE FAST TRACK OF THE CASE MANAGEMENT SYSTEM.* A case management judge will be assigned by the time this case first comes before a judge.

❑ *THIS CASE IS ON THE STANDARD TRACK OF THE CASE MANAGEMENT SYSTEM. No court date has been set for this case* but, if you have been served with a notice of motion, it has a court date and you or your lawyer should come to court for the motion. A case management judge will not be assigned until one of the parties asks the clerk of the court to schedule a case conference or until a motion is scheduled, whichever comes first.

IF, AFTER 365 DAYS, THE CASE HAS NOT BEEN SCHEDULED FOR TRIAL, the clerk of the court will send out a warning that the case will be dismissed within 60 days unless the parties file proof that the case has been settled or one of the parties asks for a case or a settlement conference.

IF YOU WANT TO OPPOSE ANY CLAIM IN THIS CASE, you or your lawyer must prepare an Answer (Form 10 — a blank copy should be attached), serve a copy on the applicant(s) and file a copy in the court office with an Affidavit of Service (Form 6B). *YOU HAVE ONLY*

30 DAYS AFTER THIS APPLICATION IS SERVED ON YOU (60 DAYS IF THIS APPLICATION IS SERVED ON YOU OUTSIDE CANADA OR THE UNITED STATES) TO SERVE AND FILE AN ANSWER. IF YOU DO NOT, THE CASE WILL GO AHEAD WITHOUT YOU AND THE COURT MAY MAKE AN ORDER AND ENFORCE IT AGAINST YOU.

Check the box of the paragraph that applies to your case

❑ This case includes a claim for support. It does not include a claim for property or exclusive possession of the matrimonial home and its contents. You *MUST* fill out a Financial Statement (Form 13 — a blank copy attached), serve a copy on the applicant(s) and file a copy in the court office with an Affidavit of Service even if you do not answer this case.

❑ This case includes a claim for property or exclusive possession of the matrimonial home and its contents. You *MUST* fill out a Financial Statement (Form 13.1 — a blank copy attached), serve a copy on the applicant(s) and file a copy in the court office with an Affidavit of Service even if you do not answer this case.

IF YOU WANT TO MAKE A CLAIM OF YOUR OWN, you or your lawyer must fill out the claim portion in the Answer, serve a copy on the applicant(s) and file a copy in the court office with an Affidavit of Service.

- If you want to make a claim for support but do not want to make a claim for property or exclusive possession of the matrimonial home and its contents, you *MUST* fill out a Financial Statement (Form 13), serve a copy on the applicant(s) and file a copy in the court office.

- However, if your only claim for support is for child support in the table amount specified under the Child Support Guidelines, you do not need to fill out, serve or file a Financial Statement.

- If you want to make a claim for property or exclusive possession of the matrimonial home and its contents, whether or not it includes a claim for support, you *MUST* fill out a Financial Statement (Form 13.1, not Form 13), serve a copy on the applicant(s), and file a copy in the court office.

YOU SHOULD GET LEGAL ADVICE ABOUT THIS CASE RIGHT AWAY. If you cannot afford a lawyer, you may be able to get help from your local Legal Aid Ontario office. *(See your telephone directory under LEGAL AID.)*

....	....
Date of issue	*Clerk of the court*

FAMILY HISTORY

APPLICANT: Age: .... Birthdate: *(d, m, y)* ....

Resident in *(municipality & province)* ....

since *(date)* ....

Surname at birth: .... Surname just before marriage: ....

Divorced before? ❑ No ❑ Yes *(Place and date of previous divorce)* ....

RESPONDENT: Age: .... Birthdate: *(d, m, y)* ....

Resident in *(municipality & province)* ....

since *(date)* ....

Surname at birth: .... Surname just before marriage: ....

Divorced before? ❑ No ❑ Yes *(Place and date of previous divorce)* ....

RELATIONSHIP DATES:

❑ Married on *(date)* ....

❑ Separated on *(date)* ....

❑ Started living together on *(date)* ....

❑ Never lived together

❑ Still living together

THE CHILD(REN)

List all children involved in this case, even if no claim is made for these children.

Full legal name	**Age**	**Birthdate (d, m, y)**	**Resident in (municipality & province)**	**Now Living With (name of person and relationship to child)**

PREVIOUS CASES OR AGREEMENTS

Have the parties or the children been in a court case before?

❑ No ❑ Yes

Have the parties made a written agreement dealing with any matter involved in this case?

❑ No ❑ Yes *(Give date of agreement. Indicate which of its terms are in dispute.)*

Has a Notice of Calculation and/or a Notice of Recalculation been issued by the online Child Support Service in this case?

❑ No ❑ Yes *(Give date(s) of Notice(s) of Calculation or Recalculation.)*

If yes, are you asking the court to make an order for a child support that is different from the amount set out in the Notice?

❑ No ❑ Yes *(Provide an explanation.)*

Have the parties arbitrated or agreed to arbitrate any matter involved in this case?

❑ No ❑ Yes *(Give date of agreement and family arbitration award, if any.)*

CLAIM BY APPLICANT

I ASK THE COURT FOR THE FOLLOWING:

(Claims below include claims for temporary orders.)

Claims under the *Divorce Act* **(Check boxes in this column only if you are asking for a divorce and your case is in the Superior Court of Justice or Family Court of the Superior Court of Justice.)**			**Claims under the *Family Law Act* or *Children's Law Reform Act***			**Claims relating to property** **(Check boxes in this column only if your case is in the Superior Court of Justice or Family Court of the Superior Court of Justice.)**		
00	❑	a divorce	10	❑	support for me	20	❑	equalization of net family properties
01	❑	support for me	11	❑	support for child(ren) — table amount	21	❑	exclusive possession of matrimonial home
02	❑	support for child(ren) — table amount	12	❑	support for child(ren) — other than table amount	22	❑	exclusive possession of contents of matrimonial home
03	❑	support for child(ren) — other than table amount	13	❑	custody of child(ren)	23	❑	freezing assets
04	❑	custody of child(ren)	14	❑	access to child(ren)	24	❑	sale of family property
05	❑	access to child(ren)	15	❑	restraining/non-harassment order			
	❑		16	❑	indexing spousal support			
			17	❑	declaration of parentage			
	❑		18	❑	guardianship over child's property			
Other claims			50	❑	Other *(Specify.)*			
30	❑	costs						
31	❑	annulment of marriage						
32	❑	prejudgment interest						
33	❑	claims relating to a family arbitration						

Give details of the order that you want the court to make. *(Include any amounts of support (if known) and the names of the children for whom support, custody or access is claimed.)*

IMPORTANT FACTS SUPPORTING MY CLAIM FOR DIVORCE

❑ *Separation*: The spouses have lived separate and apart since *(date)* .... and

❑ have not lived together again since that date in an unsuccessful attempt to reconcile.

❑ have lived together again during the following period(s) in an unsuccessful attempt to reconcile: *(Give dates.)*

❑ *Adultery*: The respondent has committed adultery. *(Give details. It is not necessary to name any other person involved but, if you do name the other person, then you must serve this application on the other person.)*

❑ *Cruelty*: The respondent has treated the applicant with physical or mental cruelty of such a kind as to make continued cohabitation intolerable. *(Give details.)*

IMPORTANT FACTS SUPPORTING MY OTHER CLAIM(S)

(Set out below the facts that form the legal basis for your other claim(s). Attach an additional page if you need more space.)

....

....

....

....

....

Put a line through any blank space left on this page. If additional space is needed, extra pages may be attached.

....

Date of signature *Signature of applicant*

LAWYER'S CERTIFICATE

For divorce cases only

My name is: .... and I am the applicant's lawyer in this divorce case. I certify that I have complied with the requirements of section 9 of the *Divorce Act*.

....

Date *Signature of Lawyer*

For information on accessibility of court services for people with disability-related needs, contact:
Telephone: 416-326-2220 / 1-800-518-7901 TTY: 416-326-4012 / 1-877-425-0575

April 12, 2016

FORM 8A — APPLICATION (DIVORCE)

[Editor's Note: Forms 4 to 39 of the Family Law Rules have been repealed by O. Reg. 76/06, effective May 1, 2006. Pursuant to Family Law Rule 1(9), when a form is referred to by number, the reference is to the form with that number that is described in the Table of Forms at the end of these rules and which is available at www.ontariocourtforms.on.ca. For your convenience, the government form as published on this website is reproduced below.]

ONTARIO

Court File Number

(SEAL)

.... *(Name of court)*

at .... *Court office address*

❑ *Simple (divorce only)*

❑ *Joint*

Applicant(s)

Full legal name & address for service — street & number, municipality, postal code, telephone & fax numbers and e-mail address (if any).	*Lawyer's name & address — street & number, municipality, postal code, telephone & fax numbers and e-mail address (if any).*

Applicant(s)

Respondent(s)

Full legal name & address for service — street & number, municipality, postal code, telephone & fax numbers and e-mail address (if any).	*Lawyer's name & address — street & number, municipality, postal code, telephone & fax numbers and e-mail address (if any).*

❑ *IN THIS CASE, THE APPLICANT IS CLAIMING DIVORCE ONLY.*

TO THE RESPONDENT(S): A COURT CASE FOR DIVORCE HAS BEEN STARTED AGAINST YOU IN THIS COURT. THE DETAILS ARE SET OUT ON THE ATTACHED PAGES.

THIS CASE IS ON THE STANDARD TRACK OF THE CASE MANAGEMENT SYSTEM. No court date has been set for this case but, if you have been served with a notice of motion, it has a court date and you or your lawyer should come to court for the motion. A case management judge will not be assigned until one of the parties asks the clerk of the court to schedule a case conference or until a motion is scheduled, whichever comes first.

IF, AFTER 365 DAYS, THE CASE HAS NOT BEEN SCHEDULED FOR TRIAL, the clerk of the court will send out a warning that the case will be dismissed within 60 days unless the parties file proof that the case has been settled or one of the parties asks for a case or a settlement conference.

IF YOU WANT TO OPPOSE ANY CLAIM IN THIS CASE, you or your lawyer must prepare an Answer (Form 10 — a blank copy should be attached), serve a copy on the applicant and file a copy in the court office with an Affidavit of Service (Form 6B). *YOU HAVE ONLY 30 DAYS AFTER THIS APPLICATION IS SERVED ON YOU (60 DAYS IF THIS APPLICATION IS SERVED ON YOU OUTSIDE CANADA OR THE UNITED STATES) TO SERVE AND FILE AN ANSWER. IF YOU DO NOT, THE CASE WILL GO AHEAD WITHOUT YOU AND THE COURT MAY MAKE AN ORDER AND ENFORCE IT AGAINST YOU.*

IF YOU WANT TO MAKE A CLAIM OF YOUR OWN, you or your lawyer must fill out the claim portion in the Answer, serve a copy on the applicant(s) and file a copy in the court office with an Affidavit of Service.

- If you want to make a claim for support but do not want to make a claim for property or exclusive possession of the matrimonial home and its contents, you *MUST* fill out a Financial Statement (Form 13), serve a copy on the applicant(s) and file a copy in the court office.
- However, if your only claim for support is for child support in the table amount specified under the Child Support Guidelines, you do not need to fill out, serve or file a Financial Statement.
- If you want to make a claim for property or exclusive possession of the matrimonial home and its contents, whether or not it includes a claim for support, you *MUST* fill out a Financial Statement (Form 13.1, not Form 13), serve a copy on the applicant(s), and file a copy in the court office.

YOU SHOULD GET LEGAL ADVICE ABOUT THIS CASE RIGHT AWAY. If you cannot afford a lawyer, you may be able to get help from your local Legal Aid Ontario office. *(See your telephone directory under LEGAL AID.)*

❑ *THIS CASE IS A JOINT APPLICATION FOR DIVORCE. THE DETAILS ARE SET OUT ON THE ATTACHED PAGES.* The application and affidavits in support of the application will be presented to a judge when the materials have been checked for completeness.

If you are requesting anything other than a simple divorce, such as support or property or exclusive possession of the matrimonial home and its contents, then refer to page 1 for instructions regarding the Financial Statement you should file.

....

Date of issue *Clerk of the court*

FAMILY HISTORY

APPLICANT: Age: .... Birthdate: *(d, m, y)* ....

Resident in *(municipality & province)* ....

since *(date)* ....

Surname at birth: .... Surname just before marriage: ....

Divorced before? ❑ No ❑ Yes *(Place and date of previous divorce)*

....

....

RESPONDENT/JOINT APPLICANT: Age: .... Birthdate: *(d, m, y)* ....

Resident in *(municipality & province)* ....

since *(date)* ....

Surname at birth: .... Surname just before marriage: ....

Divorced before? ❑ No ❑ Yes *(Place and date of previous divorce)*

....

....

RELATIONSHIP DATES:

❑ Married on *(date)* .... ❑ Started living together on *(date)* ....

❑ Separated on *(date)* .... ❑ Never lived together

....

THE CHILD(REN)

List all children involved in this case, even if no claim is made for these children.

Full legal name	Age	Birthdate (d,m,y)	Resident in (municipality & province)	Now Living With (name of person and relationship to child)

PREVIOUS CASES OR AGREEMENTS

Have the parties or the children been in a court case before?

❑ No ❑ Yes

Have the parties made a written agreement dealing with any matter involved in this case?

❑ No ❑ Yes *(Give date of agreement. Indicate which of its terms are in dispute. Attach an additional page if you need more space.)*

Has a Notice of Calculation and/or a Notice of Recalculation been issued by the online Child Support Service in this case?

❑ No ❑ Yes *(Give date(s) of Notice(s) of Calculation or Recalculation.)*

If yes, are you asking the court to make an order for a child support that is different from the amount set out in the Notice?

❑ No ❑ Yes *(Provide an explanation.)*

CLAIMS

USE THIS FRAME ONLY IF THIS CASE IS A JOINT APPLICATION FOR DIVORCE

WE JOINTLY ASK THE COURT FOR THE FOLLOWING:

Claims under the Divorce Act			*Claims under the* Family Law Act *or* Children's Law Reform Act			*Claims relating to property*		
00	❑	a divorce	10	❑	spousal support	20	❑	equalization of net family properties
01	❑	spousal support	11	❑	support for child(ren) — table amount	21	❑	exclusive possession of matrimonial home
02	❑	support for child(ren) — table amount	12	❑	support for child(ren) — other than table amount	22	❑	exclusive possession of contents of matrimonial home
03	❑	support for child(ren) — other than table amount	13	❑	custody of child(ren)	23	❑	freezing assets
04	❑	custody of child(ren)	14	❑	access to child(ren)	24	❑	sale of family property

05 ❑ access to child(ren)	15 ❑ restraining/non-harassment order	
	16 ❑ indexing spousal support	
	17 ❑ declaration of parentage	
	18 ❑ guardianship over child's property	
		Other claims
		30 ❑ costs
		31 ❑ annulment of marriage
		32 ❑ prejudgment interest
		50 ❑ Other *(Specify)*

USE THIS FRAME ONLY IF THE APPLICANT'S ONLY CLAIM IN THIS CASE IS FOR DIVORCE.
I ASK THE COURT FOR: *(Check if applicable.)* 00 ❑ a divorce   30 ❑ costs

IMPORTANT FACTS SUPPORTING THE CLAIM FOR DIVORCE

❑ *Separation*: The spouses have lived separate and apart since *(date)* .... and

❑ have not lived together again since that date in an unsuccessful attempt to reconcile.

❑ have lived together again during the following periods(s) in an unsuccessful attempt to reconcile: *(Give dates.)*

❑ *Adultery: (Name of spouse)* .... has committed adultery.

(Give details. It is not necessary to name any other person involved but if you do name the other person, then you must serve this application on the other person.)

❑ *Cruelty: (Name of spouse)* .... has treated *(name of spouse)* .... with physical or mental cruelty of such a kind as to make continued cohabitation intolerable. *(Give details.)*

USE THIS FRAME ONLY IF THIS CASE IS A JOINT APPLICATION FOR DIVORCE.
The details of the other order(s) that we jointly ask the court to make are as follows: *(Include any amounts of support and the names of the children for whom support, custody or access is to be ordered.)* *IMPORTANT FACTS SUPPORTING OUR CLAIM(S)* *(Set out the facts that form the legal basis for your claim(s). Attach an additional page if you need more space.)*

Put a line through any blank space left on this page.

Complete this section if your only claim is for a divorce. Your lawyer, if you are represented, must complete the Lawyer's Certificate below.

....
Date of signature *Signature of applicant*

Complete this section if you are making a joint application for divorce. Your lawyer, if you are represented, must complete the Lawyer's Certificate below.

....
Date of signature *Signature of joint applicant*

....
Date of signature *Signature of joint applicant*

LAWYER'S CERTIFICATE

My name is: .... and I am the lawyer for *(name)* .... in this divorce case. I certify that have complied with the requirements of section 9 of the *Divorce Act.*

....
Date *Signature of Lawyer*

My name is: .... and I am the lawyer for *(name)* in this divorce case. I certify that I have complied with the requirements of section 9 of the *Divorce Act.*

....
Date *Signature of Lawyer*

April 12, 2016

FORM 8B — APPLICATION (CHILD PROTECTION AND STATUS REVIEW)

[Editor's Note: Forms 4 to 39 of the Family Law Rules have been repealed by O. Reg. 76/06, effective May 1, 2006. Pursuant to Family Law Rule 1(9), when a form is referred to by number, the reference is to the form with that number that is described in the Table of Forms at the end of these rules and which is available at www.ontariocourtforms.on.ca. For your convenience, the government form as published on this website is reproduced below.]

Court File Number

SEAL

ONTARIO

.... *(Name of court)*

at .... *Court office address*

Applicant(s) (In most cases, the applicant will be a children's aid society.)

Full legal name & address for service — street & number, municipality, postal code, telephone & fax numbers and e-mail address (if any).	*Lawyer's name & address — street & number, municipality, postal code, telephone & fax numbers and e-mail address (if any).*

Respondent(s) (In most cases, a respondent will be a "parent" within the meaning of section 74 of the *Child, Youth and Family Services Act, 2017*.)

Full legal name & address for service — street & number, municipality, postal code, telephone & fax numbers and e-mail address (if any).	*Lawyer's name & address — street & number, municipality, postal code, telephone & fax numbers and e-mail address (if any).*

Children's Lawyer

Name & address of Children's Lawyer's agent for service (street & number, municipality, postal code, telephone & fax numbers and e-mail address (if any)) and name of person represented.

TO THE RESPONDENT(S):

A COURT CASE HAS BEEN STARTED AGAINST YOU IN THIS COURT. THE DETAILS ARE SET OUT ON THE ATTACHED PAGES.

THE FIRST COURT DATE IS (date) .... *AT* .... ❑ a.m. ❑ p.m. or as soon as possible after that time, at: *(address)* ....

If you have also been served with a notice of motion, there may be an earlier court date and you or your lawyer should come to court for the motion.

IF YOU WANT TO OPPOSE ANY CLAIM IN THIS CASE, you or your lawyer must prepare an Answer and Plan of Care (Form 33B.1 — a blank copy should be attached), serve a copy on the children's aid society and all other parties and file a copy in the court office with an Affidavit of Service (Form 6B).

YOU HAVE ONLY 30 DAYS AFTER THIS APPLICATION IS SERVED ON YOU (60 DAYS IF THIS APPLICATION IS SERVED ON YOU OUTSIDE CANADA OR THE UNITED STATES) TO SERVE AND FILE AN ANSWER. IF YOU DO NOT, THE CASE WILL GO AHEAD WITHOUT YOU AND THE COURT MAY MAKE AN ORDER AND ENFORCE IT AGAINST YOU.

Check this box if this paragraph applies

> ❑ The children's aid society is also making a claim for child support. You *MUST* fill out a Financial Statement (Form 13 — a blank copy attached), serve a copy on the society and file a copy in the court office with an Affidavit of Service even if you do not answer this case.

WARNING: This case is subject to case management, which means that the case runs on a timetable. That timetable says that the following steps have to be finished by the following number of days from the start of this case:

Service and filing of answers and plans of care — 30 days

Temporary care & custody hearing — 35 days

Settlement conference — 80 days

Hearing — 120 days

You should consider getting legal advice about this case right away. If you cannot afford a lawyer, you may be able to get help from your local legal aid office. *(See your telephone directory under LEGAL AID).*

....

Date of issue *Clerk of the court*

THE CHILD(REN): (List all children involved in this case.)

Child's Full Legal Name	**Birthdate**	**Age**	**Sex**	**Full Legal Name(s) of Parent(s)**		**Is the Child First Nations, Inuk, or Métis?**	**Child's Bands and First Nations, Inuit, or Métis Communities**

CLAIM BY APPLICANT

NOTE: If this case is an application for a status review, strike out paragraph 1 and go immediately to paragraph 2.

1. The applicant children's aid society asks the court to make a finding under Part V of the *Child, Youth and Family Services Act, 2017* that the child(ren) named in this application is/are in need of protection because:

> *(Check the applicable box(es). In each checked paragraph, delete those portions of the text that are not relevant.)*
>
> ❑ the child(ren) has/have suffered physical harm, inflicted by the person having charge of the child(ren) or caused by that person's
>
> > ❑ failure to care for, provide for, supervise or protect the child(ren) adequately [subclause 74(2)(a)(i)].
> >
> > ❑ pattern of neglect in caring for, providing for, supervising or protecting the child(ren) [subclause 74(2)(a)(ii)].

❑ there is a risk that the child(ren) is/are likely to suffer physical harm inflicted by the person having charge of the child(ren) or caused by that person's

❑ failure to care for, provide for, supervise or protect the child(ren) adequately [subclause 74(2)(b)(i)].

❑ pattern of neglect in caring for, providing for, supervising or protecting the child(ren) [subclause 74(2)(b)(ii)].

❑ the child(ren) has/have been sexually abused or sexually exploited, by the person having charge of the child(ren) or by another person where the person having charge knows or should know of the possibility of sexual abuse or sexual exploitation and fails to protect the child(ren) [clause 74(2)(c)].

❑ there is a risk that the child(ren) is/are likely to be sexually abused or sexually exploited, by the person having charge of the child(ren) or by another person where the person having charge knows of should know of the possibility of sexual abuse or sexual exploitation and fails to protect the child(ren) [clause 74(2)(d)].

❑ the child(ren) require(s) treatment to cure, prevent or alleviate physical harm or suffering and the child(ren)'s parent or the person having charge of the child(ren) does not provide the treatment or access to the treatment, or, where the child(ren) is/are incapable of consenting to the treatment under the *Health Care Consent Act, 1996* and the parent is a substitute decision-maker for the child(ren), the parent refuses or is unavailable or unable to consent to the treatment on the child(ren)'s behalf [clause 74(2)(e)].

❑ the child(ren) has/have suffered emotional harm, demonstrated by serious anxiety, depression, withdrawal, self-destructive or aggressive behaviour, or delayed development and there are reasonable grounds to believe that the emotional harm suffered by the child(ren) results from the actions, failure to act or pattern of neglect on the part of the child(ren)'s parent or the person having charge of the child(ren) [clause 74(2)(f)].

❑ the child(ren) has/have suffered emotional harm, demonstrated by serious anxiety, depression, withdrawal, self-destructive or aggressive behaviour, or delayed development and the child(ren)'s parent or the person having charge of the child(ren) does not provide treatment or access to treatment, or, where the child(ren) is/are incapable of consenting to treatment under the *Health Care Consent Act, 1996*, refuses or is unavailable or unable to consent to the treatment to remedy or alleviate the harm [clause 74(2)(g)].

❑ there is a risk that the child(ren) is/are likely to suffer emotional harm, demonstrated by serious anxiety, depression, withdrawal, self-destructive or aggressive behaviour, or delayed development resulting from the actions, failure to act or pattern of neglect on the part of the child(ren)'s parent or the person having charge of the child(ren) [clause 74(2)(h)].

❑ there is a risk that the child(ren) is/are likely to suffer emotional harm, demonstrated by serious anxiety, depression, withdrawal, self-destructive or aggressive behaviour, or delayed development and that the child(ren)'s parent or the person having charge of the child(ren) does not provide treatment or access to treatment, or, where the child(ren) is/are incapable of consenting to treatment under the *Health Care Consent Act, 1996*, refuses or is unavailable or unable to consent to treatment to prevent the harm [clause 74(2)(i)].

❑ the child(ren) suffer(s) from a mental, emotional or developmental condition that, if not remedied, could seriously impair the child(ren)'s development and the child(ren)'s parent or the person having charge of the child(ren) does not provide treatment or access to treatment, or, where the child(ren) is/are incapable of consenting to treatment under the *Health Care Consent Act, 1996*, refuses or is unavailable or unable to consent to the treatment to remedy or alleviate the condition [clause 74(2)(j)].

❑ the child(ren)'s parent has died or is unavailable to exercise custodial rights over the child(ren) and has not made adequate provision for the child(ren)'s care and custody, or the child(ren) is/are in a residential placement and the parent refuses or is unable or unwilling to resume the child(ren)'s care and custody [clause 74(2)(k)].

❑ the child(ren) is/are younger than twelve and has/have killed or seriously injured another person or caused serious damage to another person's property, services or treatment are necessary to prevent a recurrence and the child(ren)'s parent or the person having charge of the child(ren) does not provide services or treatment or access to services or treatment, or, where the child(ren) is/are incapable of consenting to treatment under the *Health Care Consent Act, 1996*, refuses or is unavailable or unable to consent to treatment [clause 74(2)(l)].

❑ the child(ren) is/are less than twelve years old and has/have, on more than one occasion, injured another person or caused loss or damage to another person's property, with the encouragement of the person having charge of the child(ren) or because of that person's failure or inability to supervise the child(ren) adequately [clause 74(2)(m)].

❑ the child(ren)'s parent is unable to care for the child(ren) and the child(ren) is/are brought before the court with the parent's consent and, where the child(ren) is/are twelve years of age or older, with the child(ren)'s consent, for the matter to be dealt with under Part V of the *Child, Youth and Family Services Act, 2017* [clause 74(2)(n)].

❑ the child(ren) is/are sixteen or seventeen years of age and a prescribed circumstance or condition exists [clause 74(2)(o)].

2. *(name)* .... asks for an order,

❑ that the child(ren) be placed with *(name of custodian)* .... subject to the supervision of *(full legal name of supervising society)* .... for a period of .... months, on the terms and conditions set out in the Appendix on page 7 of this Application form.

❑ that the child(ren) be placed in the interim society care of *(full legal name of society)* .... for a period of .... months

❑ that the child(ren) be placed in the interim society care of *(full legal name of society)* .... for a period of .... months and then returned to *(name of custodian)* .... subject to the supervision of *(full legal name of supervising society)* .... for a period of .... months, on the terms and conditions set out in the Appendix on page 7 of this Application form.

❑ that the child(ren) be placed in the extended society care of *(full legal name of caretaker society)* ....

❑ relating to access, the details of which are as follows:

....

❑ that *(name of person)* .... be restrained under s. 137 of the *Child, Youth and Family Services Act, 2017* from having any contact with *(name of child(ren) and/or any other caregiver)*

❑ relating to payment of support while the child(ren) is/are in care or subject to an order of supervision, the details of which are as follows:

....

❑ for court costs.

❑ other *(Specify.)* ....

❑ that the child(ren) be placed in the custody of *(name of custodian — cannot be a foster parent of the child)*

....

(This order shall be deemed to be an order under s. 28 of the Children's Law Reform Act.*)*

❑ relating to access, the details of which are as follows:

....

(This order shall be deemed to be an order under s. 28 of the Children's Law Reform Act.*)*

❑ that *(name of person)* .... be restrained under s. 102(3) of the *Child, Youth and Family Services Act, 2017* from having contact with *(name of child(ren) and/or any other caregiver)*

....

(This order shall be deemed to be an order under s. 35 of the Children's Law Reform Act.*)*

3. To the applicant's best knowledge, the child(ren)

❑ has/have never before been in the care of a society under an out-of-court agreement under s. 75 of *Child, Youth and Family Services Act, 2017.*

❑ has/have been in the care of a society under an out-of-court agreement under s. 75 of *Child, Youth and Family Services Act, 2017.* The details are as follows: *(Set out the number of times each child was in society care, when the care began and how long it lasted.)*

....

4. To the applicant's best knowledge, the parties or the child(ren) ❑ have ❑ have not been in a court case before relating to the supervision, interim or extended society care (guardianship) or custody of or access to the child(ren). *(Provide details of any existing custody order, including whether made by a superior court or under the* Divorce Act.*)*

5. The parties ❑ have ❑ have not made a written agreement dealing with any matter involved in this case. *(If you checked the first box, give date of agreement and indicate which of its terms are in dispute. Attach an additional page if you need more space.)*

6. The following is a brief statement of the facts upon which the applicant is relying in this application.

(Set out the facts in numbered paragraphs. If you need more space, you may attach a page, but you must date and sign each additional page.)

Put a line through any blank space left on this page.

....	....
Date of signature	*Signature*
....	....
If applicant is a children's aid society, give office or position of person signing.	*Print or type name.*

APPENDIX
The terms and conditions proposed for the child(ren)'s supervision are as follows: *(Set out terms and conditions in numbered paragraphs. Omit this page if no supervision is sought.)*

March 1, 2018

FORM 8B.1 — APPLICATION (STATUS REVIEW FOR CHILD IN EXTENDED SOCIETY CARE AND CHILD FORMERLY IN EXTENDED SOCIETY CARE)

[Editor's Note: Pursuant to Family Law Rule 1(9), when a form is referred to by number, the reference is to the form with that number that is described in the Table of Forms at the end of these rules and which is available at www.ontariocourtforms.on.ca. For your convenience, the government form as published on this website is reproduced below.]

Court File Number

SEAL

ONTARIO

.... *(Name of court)*

at .... *Court office address*

Applicant(s) (In most cases, the applicant will be a children's aid society.)

Full legal name & address for service — street & number, municipality, postal code, telephone & fax numbers and e-mail address (if any).	*Lawyer's name & address — street & number, municipality, postal code, telephone & fax numbers and e-mail address (if any).*

Respondent(s) (In most cases, a respondent will be a "parent" within the meaning of section 74 of the *Child, Youth and Family Services Act, 2017*.)

Full legal name & address for service — street & number, municipality, postal code, telephone & fax numbers and e-mail address (if any).	*Lawyer's name & address — street & number, municipality, postal code, telephone & fax numbers and e-mail address (if any).*

Children's Lawyer

Name & address of Children's Lawyer's agent for service (street & number, municipality, postal code, telephone & fax numbers and e-mail address (if any)) and name of person represented.

TO THE RESPONDENT(S):

A COURT CASE HAS BEEN STARTED AGAINST YOU IN THIS COURT. THE DETAILS ARE SET OUT ON THE ATTACHED PAGES.

THE FIRST COURT DATE IS (date) .... *AT* .... ❑ a.m. ❑ p.m. or as soon as possible after that time, at: *(address)* ....

If you have also been served with a notice of motion, there may be an earlier court date, and you or your lawyer should come to court for the motion.

IF YOU WANT TO OPPOSE ANY CLAIM IN THIS CASE, you or your lawyer must prepare an Answer and Plan of Care (Form 33B.1 — a blank copy should be attached), serve a copy on the children's aid society and all other parties and file a copy in the court office with an Affidavit of Service (Form 6B).

YOU HAVE ONLY 30 DAYS AFTER THIS APPLICATION IS SERVED ON YOU (60 DAYS IF THIS APPLICATION IS SERVED ON YOU OUTSIDE CANADA OR THE UNITED STATES) TO SERVE AND FILE AN ANSWER. IF YOU DO NOT, THE CASE WILL GO AHEAD WITHOUT YOU AND THE COURT MAY MAKE AN ORDER AND ENFORCE IT AGAINST YOU.

Check this box if this paragraph applies

❑ The children's aid society is also making a claim for child support. You *MUST* fill out a Financial Statement (Form 13 — a blank copy attached), serve a copy on the society and file a copy in the court office with an Affidavit of Service even if you do not answer this case.

WARNING: This case is subject to case management, which means that the case runs on a timetable. That timetable says that the following steps have to be finished by the following number of days from the start of this case:

Service and filing of answers and plans of care — 30 days

Temporary care & custody hearing — 35 days

Settlement conference — 80 days

Hearing — 120 days

You should consider getting legal advice about this case right away. If you cannot afford a lawyer, you may be able to get help from your local legal aid office. *(See your telephone directory under LEGAL AID).*

....
Date of issue *Clerk of the court*

THE CHILD

Child's Full Legal Name	**Birthdate**	**Age**	**Sex**	**Full Legal Name(s) of Parent(s)**		**Is the Child First Nations, Inuk, or Métis?**	**Child's Bands and First Nations, Inuit, or Métis Communities**

CLAIM BY (name and relationship to child, if applicable) ....

1. (name) .... asks for an order,

❑ that the child be placed in the custody of *(name of custodian)* .... under s. 116(1)(b) of the *Child, Youth and Family Services Act, 2017.*

❑ that the child be placed with *(name of custodian)* .... subject to the supervision of *(full legal name of supervising society)* .... for a period of .... months, on the terms and conditions set out in the Appendix on page 5 of this Application form.

❑ that the child be placed in the extended society care of *(full legal name of caretaker society)*

....

❑ relating to access, the details of which are as follows:

....

❑ that *(name of person)* .... be restrained under s. 137 of the *Child, Youth and Family Services Act, 2017* from having any contact with *(name of child and/or any caregiver)* .... *(Provide details of restraining order being sought.)*

❑ relating to payment of support while the child is in care or subject to an order of supervision, the details of which are as follows:

....

❑ terminating the order dated *(date of order)* .... for *(type of order)* ....

❑ for court costs.

❑ other *(Specify.)*

2. The details of the child's history in the care of a society are as follows:

(Set out number of times the child was in the care of a society, when the care began, how long it lasted and the date(s) of the order(s) for extended society care and access.)

....

3. The following is a brief statement of the facts relied upon in this application.

(Set out the facts in numbered paragraphs. If you need more space, you may attach a page, but you must date and sign each additional page.)

....

Put a line through any blank space left on this page.

....	....
Date of signature	*Signature*
....	....
If applicant is a children's aid society, give office or position of person signing.	*Print or type name.*

APPENDIX

The terms and conditions proposed for the child's supervision are as follows: *(Set out terms and conditions in numbered paragraphs. Omit this page if no supervision is sought.)*

March 1, 2018

FORM 8B.2 — APPLICATION (GENERAL) (CHILD, YOUTH AND FAMILY SERVICES ACT, 2017 CASES OTHER THAN CHILD PROTECTION AND STATUS REVIEW)

[Editor's Note: Pursuant to Family Law Rule 1(9), when a form is referred to by number, the reference is to the form with that number that is described in the Table of Forms at the end of these rules and which is available at www.ontariocourtforms.on.ca. For your convenience, the government form as published on this website is reproduced below.]

Court File Number

SEAL

ONTARIO

.... *(Name of court)*

at .... *Court office address*

Applicant(s) (In most cases, the applicant will be a children's aid society.)

Full legal name & address for service — street & number, municipality, postal code, telephone & fax numbers and e-mail address (if any).	*Lawyer's name & address — street & number, municipality, postal code, telephone & fax numbers and e-mail address (if any).*

Respondent(s) (In most cases, a respondent will be a "parent" within the meaning of section 74 of the *Child, Youth and Family Services Act, 2017*.)

Full legal name & address for service — street & number, municipality, postal code, telephone & fax numbers and e-mail address (if any).	*Lawyer's name & address — street & number, municipality, postal code, telephone & fax numbers and e-mail address (if any).*

Respondent(s) (In most cases, a respondent will be a "parent" within the meaning of section 74 of the *Child, Youth and Family Services Act, 2017*.)

Children's Lawyer

Name & address of Children's Lawyer's agent for service (street & number, municipality, postal code, telephone & fax numbers and e-mail address (if any)) and name of person represented.

TO THE RESPONDENT(S):

A COURT CASE HAS BEEN STARTED AGAINST YOU IN THIS COURT. THE DETAILS ARE SET OUT ON THE ATTACHED PAGES.

THE FIRST COURT DATE IS (date) .... *AT* .... ❑ a.m. ❑ p.m. or as soon as possible after that time, at: *(address)* ....

If you have also been served with a notice of motion, there may be an earlier court date and you or your lawyer should come to court for the motion.

IF YOU WANT TO OPPOSE ANY CLAIM IN THIS CASE, you or your lawyer must prepare an Answer (*Child, Youth and Family Services Act, 2017* Cases other than Child Protection and Status Review) (Form 33B.2 — a blank copy should be attached), serve a copy on the children's aid society and all other parties and file a copy in the court office with an Affidavit of Service (Form 6B).

YOU HAVE ONLY 30 DAYS AFTER THIS APPLICATION IS SERVED ON YOU (60 DAYS IF THIS APPLICATION IS SERVED ON YOU OUTSIDE CANADA OR THE UNITED STATES) TO SERVE AND FILE AN ANSWER. IF YOU DO NOT, THE CASE WILL GO AHEAD WITHOUT YOU AND THE COURT MAY MAKE AN ORDER AND ENFORCE IT AGAINST YOU.

Check this box if this paragraph applies

> ❑ The children's aid society is also making a claim for child support. You *MUST* fill out a Financial Statement (Form 13 — a blank copy attached), serve a copy on the society and file a copy in the court office with an Affidavit of Service even if you do not answer this case.

WARNING: This case is subject to case management, which means that the case runs on a timetable. That timetable says that the following steps have to be finished by the following number of days from the start of this case:

Service and filing of answers and plans of care — 30 days

Settlement conference — 80 days

Hearing — 120 days

You should consider getting legal advice about this case right away. If you cannot afford a lawyer, you may be able to get help from your local legal aid office. *(See your telephone directory under LEGAL AID).*

....

Date of issue *Clerk of the court*

THE CHILD(REN): (List all children involved in this case.)

Child's Full Legal Name	**Birthdate**	**Age**	**Sex**	**Full Legal Name(s) of Parent(s)**		**Is the Child First Nations, Inuk, or Métis?**	**Child's Bands and First Nations, Inuit, or Métis Communities**

CLAIM BY (name and relationship to child, if applicable) ....

1. (name) .... asks for an order: *(Specify the order being sought and the grounds upon which the application is being brought)*

❑ relating to access, the details of which are as follows:

....

❑ that *(name of person)* .... be restrained under s. 137 of the *Child, Youth and Family Services Act, 2017* from having any contact with *(name of child(ren) and/or any caregiver)* .... *(Provide details of restraining order being sought.)*

❑ relating to payment of support while the child(ren) is/are in care or subject to an order of supervision, the details of which are as follows:

....

❑ other *(Specify.)*

❑ for court costs of this application.

2. The existing orders relating to the child(ren) are as follows:

....

3. The following is a brief statement of the facts relied upon in this application.

(Set out the facts in numbered paragraphs. If you need more space, you may attach a page, but you must date and sign each additional page.)

....

Put a line through any blank space left on this page.

....

Date of signature *Signature*

....

If applicant is a children's aid society, give office or position of person signing.

Print or type name.

March 1, 2018

FORM 8C — APPLICATION FOR ❑ SECURE TREATMENT ❑ EXTENSION OF SECURE TREATMENT

[Repealed O. Reg. 76/06, s. 15.]

[Editor's Note: Forms 4 to 39 of the Family Law Rules have been repealed by O. Reg. 76/06, effective May 1, 2006. Pursuant to Family Law Rule 1(9), when a form is referred to by number, the reference is to the form with that number that is described in the Table of Forms at the end of these rules and which is available at www.ontariocourtforms.on.ca. For your convenience, the government form as published on this website is reproduced below.]

Court File Number

SEAL

ONTARIO

.... *(Name of court)*

at .... *Court office address*

Applicant(s)

Full legal name & address for service — street & number, municipality, postal code, telephone & fax numbers and e-mail address (if any).	*Lawyer's name & address — street & number, municipality, postal code, telephone & fax numbers and e-mail address (if any).*

Respondent(s)

Full legal name & address for service — street & number, municipality, postal code, telephone & fax numbers and e-mail address (if any).	*Lawyer's name & address — street & number, municipality, postal code, telephone & fax numbers and e-mail address (if any).*

Respondent(s)

Child

Full legal name of child:	*Lawyer's name & address — street & number, municipality, postal code, telephone & fax numbers and e-mail address (if any).*
Birth date (d, m, y):	
Sex:	

TO THE RESPONDENT(S) AND CHILD:

A COURT CASE HAS BEEN STARTED IN THIS COURT. THE DETAILS ARE SET OUT ON THE ATTACHED PAGES.

THE FIRST COURT DATE IS (date) .... *AT* .... ❑ a.m. ❑ p.m. or as soon as possible after that time, at *(address)* ....

Check applicable box.

1. ❑ I/We am/are the child's parent(s). *(Attach the consent of the parent(s) in Form 33F. If the child is 16 or 17 years old, the child's consent — Form 33E — must also be attached. In an application to extend treatment, the consent of the program administrator in Form 33F must also be attached. If the "child" is 18 or more years old, the "child's" consent to extend treatment in Form 33F must also be attached.)*

❑ I am an authorized officer of the applicant children's aid society that has custody of the child under an order made under Part V of the *Child, Youth and Family Services Act, 2017*. *(Attach the officer's consent in Form 33F. If the child is 16 or 17 years old, the child's consent — Form 33E — must also be attached. In an application to extend treatment, the administrator's consent in Form 33F must also be attached.)*

❑ I am a person (other than an administrator of the secure treatment program) who is caring for the child. *(To be used only where the child is less than 16 years of age. A consent of the child's parent — Form 33F — must be attached. In an application to extend treatment, the administrator's consent in Form 33F must also be attached.)*

❑ I am the child in this case and I am 16 or 17 years old. *(The child's consent — Form 33E — must be attached. In an application to extend treatment, the administrator's consent in Form 33F must also be attached.)*

❑ I am the person who has been committed to the secure treatment program in this case and I am 18 or more years old. *(To be used only in an application to extend treatment. Attach the consent of the program administrator on Form 33F.)*

❑ I am a physician qualified under the law of Ontario to practise medicine. *(To be used in an application for secure treatment only where the child is 16 years of age or more. A physician can apply to extend treatment, but only if the "child" is 18 or more years of age and only if separate consents in Form 33F, both from the administrator of the program and from the "child" are attached.)*

❑ I am the person in charge of the secure treatment program. *(To be used only in an application to extend secure treatment. Attach two consents in Form 33F — one from the administrator and the second from the child's parent or, if the child is in the care of a children's aid society, the society's consent. If the "child" is now 18 or more years old, the second consent in Form 33F must come from the "child".)*

2. I/We ask for an order under Part VII of the *Child, Youth and Family Services Act, 2017*

❑ committing the child . . . . ❑ extending the child's commitment

to the secure treatment program at: *(Name and address of secure treatment program.)*

....

3. I/We make this application because: *(NOTE: All three paragraphs — [a] and [b] and [c] — must be true in all cases.)*

❑ (a) the child has a mental disorder;

❑ (b) the secure treatment program would be effective to prevent the child from causing or attempting to cause serious bodily harm to himself/herself or to another person;

❑ (c) no less restrictive method of providing treatment appropriate for the child's mental disorder is appropriate in the circumstances;

Use this frame only in an application for commitment to a secure treatment program. In addition to paragraphs (a), (b) and (c) above, all three paragraphs below — (d) and (e) and (f) — must ALSO be true.

❑ d) the child has, as a result of the mental disorder, within 45 days immediately before,

Check only one of these three boxes

❑ the date of this application for commitment to secure treatment,

❑ the child's detention or custody under the federal *Youth Criminal Justice Act* or *Ontario's Provincial Offences Act,*

❑ the child's admission as an involuntary patient to a psychiatric facility under the *Mental Health Act,*

caused or attempted to cause serious bodily harm to himself/herself or to another person;

❑ e) the child has: {

{ ❑ within the 12 months immediately before this application for secure treatment on an occasion different from the one mentioned in clause (b) above caused or attempted to cause or by words or conduct, made a substantial threat to cause serious bodily harm to himself/herself or to another person, OR

{ ❑ caused or attempted to cause a person's death when causing or attempting to cause serious bodily harm to himself/herself or to another person; and

❑ f) treatment appropriate for the child's mental disorder is available at the program named in paragraph 2 above.

Use this frame only in an application to extend the period of commitment to a secure treatment program.

In addition to paragraphs (a), (b) and (c) above, both paragraphs below — (d) and (e) — must ALSO be true.

❑ d) the child is receiving,

❑ the treatment proposed when this court originally ordered commitment to the secure treatment program

❑ other appropriate treatment; and

❑ e) there is an appropriate plan for the child's care on release from the secure treatment program.

4. The following is a brief statement of the facts upon which this application is based. *(Set out the facts in numbered paragraphs with reference to the items in paragraph 3. If you need more space, you may attach a page, but you must date and sign each additional page.)*

Put a line through any blank space left on this page.

.... *Signature*	.... *Date of Signature*
.... *Signature*	.... *Date of Signature*

March 1, 2018

FORM 8D — APPLICATION (ADOPTION)

[Repealed O. Reg. 76/06, s. 15.]

[Editor's Note: Forms 4 to 39 of the Family Law Rules have been repealed by O. Reg. 76/06, effective May 1, 2006. Pursuant to Family Law Rule 1(9), when a form is referred to by number, the reference is to the form with that number that is described in the Table of Forms at the end of these rules and which is available at www.ontariocourtforms.on.ca. For your convenience, the government form as published on this website is reproduced below.]

Court File Number

SEAL

ONTARIO

.... *(Name of court)*

at .... *Court office address*

Applicant(s) (The first letter of the applicant's surname may be used)

Full legal name & address for service — street & number, municipality, postal code, telephone & fax numbers and e-mail address (if any).	*Lawyer's name & address — street & number, municipality, postal code, telephone & fax numbers and e-mail address (if any).*

Applicant(s) (The first letter of the applicant's surname may be used)

Respondent(s) (If there is a respondent, the first letter of the respondent's surname may be used)

Full legal name & address for service — street & number, municipality, postal code, telephone & fax numbers and e-mail address (if any).	*Lawyer's name & address — street & number, municipality, postal code, telephone & fax numbers and e-mail address (if any).*

The application is for a(n) *(check all boxes that apply)*:

❑ adoption of a child in extended society care

❑ international adoption

❑ licensed adoption

❑ relative adoption

❑ society adoption of a child who is not in extended society care

❑ stepparent adoption *(complete additional section below)*

❑ section 199(1)(b) adoption

THE APPLICANT(S) ASK FOR AN ORDER FOR THE ADOPTION OF: (Give full legal name, date of birth, sex and birth registration number of person to be adopted. If this person is in extended society care or was placed for adoption by a licensee or children's aid society, you may use an initial for the surname.)

.... *Full legal name* .... *Date of birth* .... *Sex* .... *Birth registration number*

The applicant(s) also ask for an order that the person's name after adoption be: *(full legal name of person after adoption)*

....

To be completed for a stepparent adoption:

If the adoption order is made, pursuant to s. 217(2)(b) of the *Child, Youth and Family Services Act, 2017*, the parents of the person will be:

....

YOU SHOULD CONSIDER GETTING LEGAL ADVICE ABOUT THIS RIGHT AWAY. If you cannot afford a lawyer, you may be able to get help from Legal Aid Ontario. Call *1-800-668-8258 toll-free* to get legal aid help in over 120 languages. For more information about the services available through Legal Aid Ontario, visit *www.legalaid.on.ca.*

Strike out the box below if it does not apply in this case.

NOTE TO THE RESPONDENTS: You are also being served with a notice of motion to dispense with your consent to the adoption. The details of the motion can be found on the notice of motion and the attached affidavit(s). *IF YOU WANT TO OPPOSE THIS ADOPTION*, you or your lawyer must serve and file an *Answer* (Form 10). IF YOU *DO NOT DO SO, THE COURT MAY DISPENSE WITH YOUR CONSENT WITHOUT YOU AND YOU WILL GET NO FURTHER NOTICE.*

....	....
Date of signature	*Signature of applicant*
....	....
Date of signature	*Signature of co-applicant*
....	....
Date of issue by clerk of the court	*Signature of clerk of the court*

For information on accessibility of court services for people with disability-related needs, contact:

Telephone: 416-326-2220 / 1-800-518-7901 TTY: 416-326-4012 / 1-877-425-0575

March 1, 2018

FORM 8D.1 — APPLICATION (DISPENSE WITH PARENT'S CONSENT TO ADOPTION BEFORE PLACEMENT)

[Repealed O. Reg. 76/06, s. 15.]

[Editor's Note: Forms 4 to 39 of the Family Law Rules have been repealed by O. Reg. 76/06, effective May 1, 2006. Pursuant to Family Law Rule 1(9), when a form is referred to by number, the reference is to the form with that number that is described in the Table of Forms at the end of these rules and which is available at www.ontariocourtforms.on.ca. For your convenience, the government form as published on this website is reproduced below.]

Court File Number ....

[SEAL]

.... *(Name of court)*

at .... *Court office address*

Applicant(s) (*The first letter of the applicant's surname may be used*)

Full legal name & address for service — street & number, municipality, postal code, telephone & fax numbers and e-mail address (if any).	*Lawyer's name & address — street & number, municipality, postal code, telephone & fax numbers and e-mail address (if any).*

Respondent(s) *(If there is a respondent, the first letter of respondent's surname may be used)*

Full legal name & address for service — street & number, municipality, postal code, telephone & fax numbers and e-mail address (if any).	*Lawyer's name & address — street & number, municipality, postal code, telephone & fax numbers and e-mail address (if any).*

THE APPLICANT(S) ASK FOR AN ORDER DISPENSING WITH THE CONSENT OF THE RESPONDENT(S) TO THE ADOPTION OF THE CHILD:

(Give full legal name, date of birth, sex and birth registration number (if known) of person to be adopted. If this person is to be placed for adoption by a licensee or children's aid society, you may use an initial for the surname.)

Full legal name ....

Date of birth................................

Sex......... *Birth registration number* ....

❑ The applicant(s) also ask for an order that service of the applicant on the respondent(s) is not required.

NOTE TO THE RESPONDENT(S): a court case has been started against you in this court. The details are set out in the attached affidavit.

THE FIRST COURT DATE IS (date)...................... at .... a.m./p.m. or as soon as possible after that time, at: (address)

THIS CASE IS ON THE FAST TRACK OF THE CASE MANAGEMENT SYSTEM. A case management judge will be assigned by the time this case first comes before a judge.

IF YOU WANT TO OPPOSE THIS APPLICATION, you or your lawyer must prepare an *Answer* (Form 10 — a blank copy should be attached), serve a copy on the applicant(s) and file a copy in the court office with an *Affidavit of Service* (Form 6B). YOU HAVE ONLY 20 DAYS AFTER THIS APPLICATION IS SERVED ON YOU (40 DAYS IF THIS APPLICATION IS SERVED ON YOU OUTSIDE CANADA OR THE UNITED STATES) TO SERVE AND FILE AN ANSWER. IF YOU DO NOT DO SO, THE COURT MAY DISPENSE WITH YOUR CONSENT WITHOUT YOU.

If you want to make a claim of your own, you or your lawyer must fill out the claim portion in the *Answer*, serve a copy on the applicant(s) and file a copy in the court office with an *Affidavit of Service*.

YOU SHOULD GET LEGAL ADVICE ABOUT THIS CASE RIGHT AWAY. If you cannot afford a lawyer, you may be able to get help from your local Legal Aid office. *(See your telephone directory under LEGAL AID).*

....	....
Date of signature	*Signature of applicant*
....	....
Date of signature	*Signature of co-applicant*
....	....

Date of issue by clerk of the court *Signature of clerk of the court*

September 1, 2005

FORM 8D.2 — NOTICE OF INTENTION TO PLACE CHILD(REN) FOR ADOPTION

[Editor's Note: Pursuant to Family Law Rule 1(9), when a form is referred to by number, the reference is to the form with that number that is described in the Table of Forms at the end of these rules and which is available at www.ontariocourtforms.on.ca. For your convenience, the government form as published on this website is reproduced below.]

Court File Number

ONTARIO

.... *(Name of court)*

at .... *Court office address*

TO: .... *(name of child being placed for adoption or person entitled to have access to the child)*

This notice is to advise you that the (name of children's aid society) .... *is planning to: (strike out the paragraph that does not apply. NOTE: in some cases, both paragraphs may apply.)*

❑ *place the following child(ren) for adoption: (full legal name(s) and date(s) of birth of child(ren)*

....

❑ *place you for adoption.*

This means that: *(Add more numbered lines as needed for each additional person.)*

1. Your access to .... *(name of the person to whom access is ending)* will end when .... *(name or "you" as applicable)* is placed for adoption.

2. Your access to .... *(name of the person to whom access is ending)* will end when .... *(name or "you" as applicable)* is placed for adoption.

3. Your access to .... *(name of the person to whom access is ending)* will end when .... *(name or "you" as applicable)* is placed for adoption.

Strike out the box below if it does not apply in this case

You have been granted a right of access under the Child, Youth and Family Services Act, 2017. *You have the right to apply for an openness order with respect to the following person(s): (name(s) of person(s) to whom the person receiving this notice has a right of access and may apply for an openness order.)*

You must act within 30 days if you want to ask the court for an openness order.

If you want to have a right to contact any of the persons listed above through an openness order, you or your lawyer must, *within 30 days of receiving this notice*:

1. Prepare a Form 34L: Application for Openness Order. (A blank copy should be attached; if it is not, you can obtain a copy from the court office or at *www.ontariocourtforms.on.ca.*)

2. Serve a copy of the completed Form 34L on all of the following:

    a. The children's aid society to the attention of .... at the following address:

    b. The Children's Lawyer at the Office of the Children's Lawyer, 393 University Avenue, 14th floor, Toronto, Ontario, M5G 1E6.

    c. The child's lawyer, if any.

    d. The person(s) with whom you are seeking openness, unless that person is a child under the age of 12.

3. File a copy of the completed Form 34L with a Form 6B: Affidavit of Service. You can obtain these forms from *www.ontariocourtforms.on.ca or at the court office.*

If you do not serve and file a Form 34L within 30 days of receiving this notice, you will not be able to apply to the court for any openness order.

Strike out the box below if it does not apply in this case

You are a person to whom access has been granted under the Child, Youth and Family Services Act, 2017. *You do not have a right to apply for an openness order with respect to the following person(s)*:

Every person who has been granted a right of access under the Child, Youth and Family Services Act, 2017 *may seek an openness order within 30 days after notice is received.*

Information about the order(s) that will end

Court File Number	**Court Office Address**	**Name(s) of Judge(s)**	**Date(s) of Order(s)**
Details of Access Order(s) That Will End (for example specify who has been granted a right of access and to which persons)			

You may get a lawyer to help you.

YOU SHOULD CONSIDER GETTING LEGAL ADVICE ABOUT THIS RIGHT AWAY. If you cannot afford a lawyer, you may be able to get help from Legal Aid Ontario. Call *1-800-668-8258 toll-free* to get legal aid help in over 120 languages. For more information about the services available through Legal Aid Ontario, visit *www.legalaid.on.ca.*

IF YOU ARE UNDER 18 YEARS OLD, the children's aid society must send a copy of this form to the Children's Lawyer at their place of business, which is the Office of the Children's Lawyer, 393 University Avenue, 14th floor, Toronto, Ontario, M5G 1E6. You can contact the Office of the Children's Lawyer at 416-314-8000 and ask to speak to a lawyer.

....

Signature of children's aid society employee *Date of signature*

....

(Name and position of children's aid society employee)

For information on accessibility of court services for people with disability-related needs, contact:

Telephone: 416-326-2220 / 1-800-518-7901 TTY: 416-326-4012 / 1-877-425-0575

March 1, 2018

FORM 8D.3 — NOTICE OF INTENTION TO PLACE FIRST NATIONS, INUK OR MéTIS CHILD FOR ADOPTION

[Editor's Note: Pursuant to Family Law Rule 1(9), when a form is referred to by number, the reference is to the form with that number that is described in the Table of Forms at the end of these rules and which is available at www.ontariocourtforms.on.ca. For your convenience, the government form as published on this website is reproduced below.]

Court File Number

ONTARIO

.... *(Name of court)*

at .... *Court office address*

TO: .... *(name of child being placed for adoption or representative chosen by the child's band or First Nations, Inuit or Métis community)*

This notice is to advise you that the (name of children's aid society) .... *is planning to*:

❑ *place the child, (child's full legal name and date of birth)*

.... , for adoption.

❑ *place you for adoption.*

You have a right to apply for an openness order within 30 days after receiving this notice.

If you want to have contact, you or your lawyer, *must within 30 days of receiving this notice*:

1. Prepare a Form 34L: Application for Openness Order. (A blank copy should be attached; if it is not, you can obtain a copy from the court office or at *www.ontariocourtforms.on.ca*.)

2. Serve a copy of the completed Form 34L on *all* the following:

   a. The children's aid society to the attention of .... at the following address: ....

   b. Any other person who could apply for an openness order under s. 197 of the *Child, Youth and Family Services Act, 2017 (Note: this could be the child, the child's lawyer, the Children's Lawyer, and/or the representative chosen by the child's band(s) or First Nations, Inuit or Métis communities.)*

3. File a copy of the completed Form 34L with a Form 6B: Affidavit of Service (you can obtain a copy from the court office or at *www.ontariocourtforms.on.ca*) at the court office.

If you do not serve and file a Form 34L: Application for Openness Order within 30 days of receiving this notice, you will not be able to apply to the court for an openness order.

The children's aid society also has a right to apply for an openness order within 30 days after giving this notice.

YOU SHOULD CONSIDER GETTING LEGAL ADVICE ABOUT THIS NOTICE RIGHT AWAY.

IF YOU ARE UNDER 18 YEARS OLD the children's aid society must send a copy of this form to the Children's Lawyer at their place of business, which is the Office of the Children's Lawyer, 393 University Avenue, 14th floor, Toronto, Ontario, M5G 1E6. You can contact the Office of the Children's Lawyer at 416-314-8000 and ask to speak to a lawyer.

....	....
Signature of children's aid society employee	*Date of signature*

....

(Name and position of children's aid society employee)

For information on accessibility of court services for people with disability-related needs, contact:

Telephone: 416-326-2220 / 1-800-518-7901 TTY: 416-326-4012 / 1-877-425-0575

March 1, 2018

FORM 8D.4 — [REPEALED O. REG. 298/18, S. 23(2).]

[Repealed O. Reg. 298/18, s. 23(2).]

FORM 10 — ANSWER

[Repealed O. Reg. 76/06, s. 15.]

[Editor's Note: Forms 4 to 39 of the Family Law Rules have been repealed by O. Reg. 76/06, effective May 1, 2006. Pursuant to Family Law Rule 1(9), when a form is referred to by number, the reference is to the form with that number that is described in the Table of Forms at the end of these rules and which is available at www.ontariocourtforms.on.ca. For your convenience, the government form as published on this website is reproduced below.]

Court File Number

ONTARIO

.... *(Name of court)*

at .... *Court office address*

Applicant(s)

Full legal name & address for service — street & number, municipality, postal code, telephone & fax numbers and e-mail address (if any).	*Lawyer's name & address — street & number, municipality, postal code, telephone & fax numbers and e-mail address (if any).*

Applicant(s)

Respondent(s)

Full legal name & address for service — street & number, municipality, postal code, telephone & fax numbers and e-mail address (if any).	*Lawyer's name & address — street & number, municipality, postal code, telephone & fax numbers and e-mail address (if any).*

Name & address of Children's Lawyer's agent for service (street & number, municipality, postal code, telephone & fax numbers and e-mail address (if any)) and name of person represented.

INSTRUCTIONS: FINANCIAL STATEMENT

COMPLETE A FINANCIAL STATEMENT (Form 13) IF:

- you are making or responding to a claim for spousal support; or
- you are responding to a claim for child support; or
- you are making a claim for child support in an amount different from the table amount specified under the Child Support Guidelines.

You must complete all parts of the form *UNLESS* you are *ONLY* responding to a claim for child support in the table amount specified under the Child Support Guidelines *AND* you agree with the claim. In that case, only complete Parts 1, 2 and 3.

COMPLETE A FINANCIAL STATEMENT (Form 13.1) IF:

- you are making or responding to a claim for property or exclusive possession of the matrimonial home and its contents; or
- you are making or responding to a claim for property or exclusive possession of the matrimonial home and its contents together with other claims for relief.

TO THE APPLICANT(S):

If you are making a claim against someone who is not an applicant, insert the person's name and address here.

AND TO: (full legal name) .... *an added respondent, of (address of added party)* ....

My name is *(full legal name)* ....

1. I agree with the following claim(s) made by the applicant: *(Refer to the numbers alongside the boxes on page 4 of the application form.)*

....

2. I do not agree with the following claim(s) made by the applicant: *(Again, refer to the numbers alongside the boxes on page 4 of the application form.)*

....

3. ❑ I am asking that the applicant's claim (except for the parts with which I agree) be dismissed with costs.

4. ❑ I am making a claim of my own.

(Attach a "Claim by Respondent" page and include it as page 3. Otherwise, do not attach it.)

5. ❑ The FAMILY HISTORY, as set out in the application

❑ is correct.

❑ is not correct.

(If it is not correct, attach your own FAMILY HISTORY page and underline those parts that are different from the applicant's version.)

6. The important facts that form the legal basis for my position in paragraph 2 are as follows:

(In numbered paragraphs, set out the facts for your position. Attach an additional sheet and number it if you need more space.)

1. ....

Put a line through any blank space left on this page

....	....
Date of signature	*Respondent's signature*

CLAIM BY RESPONDENT

Fill out a separate claim page for each person against whom you are making your claim(s).

7. THIS CLAIM IS MADE AGAINST

❑ THE APPLICANT

❑ AN ADDED PARTY, whose name is: *(full legal name)* ....

(If your claim is against an added party, make sure that this person's name appears on page 1 of this form.)

8. I ASK THE COURT FOR THE FOLLOWING:

(Claims below include claims for temporary orders.)

Claims under the *Divorce Act* **(Check boxes in this column only if you are asking for a divorce and your case is in the Superior Court of Justice or Family Court of the Superior Court of Justice.)**	**Claims relating to property** **(Check boxes in this column only if your case is in the Superior Court of Justice or Family Court of the Superior Court of Justice.)**	**Claims relating to child protection**
00 ❑ a divorce	20 ❑ equalization of net family properties	40 ❑ access
01 ❑ support for me	21 ❑ exclusive possession of matrimonial home	41 ❑ lesser protection order
02 ❑ support for child(ren) — table amount	21 ❑ exclusive possession of matrimonial home	42 ❑ return of child(ren) to my care
03 ❑ support for child(ren)-other than table amount	22 ❑ exclusive possession of contents of matrimonial home	43 ❑ place child(ren) into care of *(name)* ....
04 ❑ custody of child(ren)	23 ❑ freezing assets	44 ❑ interim society care and custody for .... months
05 ❑ access to child(ren)	24 ❑ sale of family property	45 ❑ society supervision of my child(ren) for .... months
Claims under the Family Law Act *or* Children's Law Reform Act	*Other claims*	
10 ❑ support for me	30 ❑ costs	
11 ❑ support for child(ren) — table amount	31 ❑ annulment of marriage	
12 ❑ support for child(ren) — other than table amount	32 ❑ prejudgment interest	
13 ❑ custody of child(ren)	33 ❑ claims relating to a family arbitration	
14 ❑ access to child(ren)		
15 ❑ restraining/non-harassment order		
16 ❑ indexing spousal support		
17 ❑ declaration of parentage		

Claims under the *Divorce Act* **(Check boxes in this column only if you are asking for a divorce and your case is in the Superior Court of Justice or Family Court of the Superior Court of Justice.)**	**Claims relating to property** **(Check boxes in this column only if your case is in the Superior Court of Justice or Family Court of the Superior Court of Justice.)**	**Claims relating to child protection**
18 ❑ guardianship over child's property		
50 ❑ Other *(Specify.)*		

Give details of the order that you want the court to make. *(Include any amounts of support (if known) and the name(s) of the child(ren) for whom support, custody or access is claimed.)*

....

IMPORTANT FACTS SUPPORTING MY CLAIM(S)

(In numbered paragraphs, set out the facts that form the legal basis for your claim(s). Attach an additional page and number it if you need more space.)

....

Put a line through any blank space left on this page.

....

Date of signature *Respondent's signature*

LAWYER'S CERTIFICATE

For divorce cases only

My name is .... and I am the respondent's lawyer in this divorce case. I certify that I have complied with the requirements of section 9 of the *Divorce Act*.

....

Date *Signature of Lawyer*

For information on accessibility of court services for people with disability-related needs, contact:

Telephone: 416-326-2220 / 1-800-518-7901 TTY: 416-326-4012 / 1-877-425-0575

March 1, 2018

FORM 10A — REPLY BY ❑ APPLICANT ❑ ADDED RESPONDENT

[Repealed O. Reg. 76/06, s. 15.]

[Editor's Note: Forms 4 to 39 of the Family Law Rules have been repealed by O. Reg. 76/06, effective May 1, 2006. Pursuant to Family Law Rule 1(9), when a form is referred to by number, the reference is to the form with that number that is described in the Table of Forms at the end of these rules and which is available at www.ontariocourtforms.on.ca. For your convenience, the government form as published on this website is reproduced below.]

Court File Number ....

.... *(Name of court)*

at.. *Court office address*

Applicant(s)

Full legal name & address for service — street & number, municipality, postal code, telephone & fax numbers and e-mail address (if any).	*Lawyer's name & address — street & number, municipality, postal code, telephone & fax numbers and e-mail address (if any).*

Respondent(s)

Full legal name & address for service — street & number, municipality, postal code, telephone & fax numbers and e-mail address (if any).	*Lawyer's name & address — street & number, municipality, postal code, telephone & fax numbers and e-mail address (if any).*

Children's Lawyer

Name & address of Children's Lawyer's agent for service (street & number, municipality, postal code, telephone & fax numbers and e-mail address (if any)) and name of person represented.

INSTRUCTIONS: FINANCIAL STATEMENT

COMPLETE A FINANCIAL STATEMENT (Form 13) IF:

- you are responding to a claim for spousal support; or
- you are responding to a claim for child support.

You must complete all parts of the form UNLESS you are ONLY responding to a claim for child support in the table amount specified under the Child Support Guidelines AND you agree with the claim. In that case, only complete Parts 1, 2 and 3.

COMPLETE A FINANCIAL STATEMENT (Form 13.1) IF:

- you are responding to a claim for property or exclusive possession of the matrimonial home and its contents; or
- you are responding to a claim for property or exclusive possession of the matrimonial home and its contents together with other claims for relief.

TO ALL PARTIES:

1. My name is *(full legal name)* ....

2. I agree with the following claim(s) made by the respondent in his/her answer: *(Refer to the numbers alongside the boxes on page 3 of the answer form.)*

3. I do not agree with the following claim(s) made by the respondent: *(Again, refer to the numbers alongside the boxes on page 3 of the answer form.)*

4. ❑ I am asking that the respondent's claim (except for the parts with which I agree) be dismissed with costs.

5. The important facts supporting my position in paragraph 3 are as follows:

(In numbered paragraphs, set out the reasons for your position. Attach an additional sheet and number it if you need more space.)

Put a line through any space left an this page.

.... *Date of signature*

.... *Signature*

September 1, 2005

FORM 12 — NOTICE OF WITHDRAWAL

[Repealed O. Reg. 76/06, s. 15.]

[Editor's Note: Forms 4 to 39 of the Family Law Rules have been repealed by O. Reg. 76/06, effective May 1, 2006. Pursuant to Family Law Rule 1(9), when a form is referred to by number, the reference is to the form with that number that is described in the Table of Forms at the end of these rules and which is available at www.ontariocourtforms.on.ca. For your convenience, the government form as published on this website is reproduced below.]

Court File Number ....

.... *(Name of court)*

at .... *Court office address*

Applicant(s)

Full legal name & address for service — street & number, municipality, postal code, telephone & fax and e-mail address (if any)	*Lawyer's name & address — street & number, municipality, postal code, telephone & fax numbers and e-mail address (if any)*

Respondent(s)

Full legal name & address for service — street & number, municipality, postal code, telephone & fax numbers and e-mail address (if any)	*Lawyer's name & address — street & number, municipality, postal code, telephone & fax numbers and e-mail address (if any)*

TO ALL PARTIES:

My name is *(full legal name)* ....

I withdraw this

❏ application dated *(date)* ....

❏ answer dated *(date)* ....

❏ notice of default hearing dated *(date)* ....

❏ notice of motion dated *(date)* ....

❏ *(Other; specify.)*

against *(names of parties against who there is to be a withdrawal)* ....

❏ completely.

❏ regarding *(state limited nature of withdrawal.)*
....
....

.... *Signature of party making withdrawal or of party's lawyer*

.... *Date of signature*

NOTE TO OTHER PARTIES: If a case, an enforcement, a motion, etc., has been wholly or partly withdrawn against you by this notice, you are entitled to your costs from the party making the withdrawal unless the court orders otherwise or unless the parties agree otherwise.

September 1, 2005

FORM 13 — FINANCIAL STATEMENT (SUPPORT CLAIMS) SWORN/AFFIRMED

[Repealed O. Reg. 76/06, s. 15.]

[Editor's Note: Forms 4 to 39 of the Family Law Rules have been repealed by O. Reg. 76/06, effective May 1, 2006. Pursuant to Family Law Rule 1(9), when a form is referred to by number, the reference is to the form with that number that is described in the Table of Forms at the end of these rules and which is available at www.ontariocourtforms.on.ca. For your convenience, the government form as published on this website is reproduced below.]

ONTARIO

Court File Number ....

.... *(Name of Court)*

at .... *Court office address*

Applicant(s)

Full legal name & address for service — street & number, municipality, postal code, telephone & fax numbers and e-mail address (if any).	Lawyer's name & address — street & number, municipality, postal code, telephone & fax numbers and e-mail address (if any).

Respondent(s)

Full legal name & address for service — street & number, municipality, postal code, telephone & fax numbers and e-mail address (if any).	Lawyer's name & address — street & number, municipality, postal code, telephone & fax numbers and e-mail address (if any).

INSTRUCTIONS

You must complete this form if you are making or responding to a claim for child or spousal support or a claim to change support, unless your only claim for support is a claim for child support in the table amount under the *Child Support Guidelines*.

You may also be required to complete and attach additional schedules based on the claims that have been made in your case or your financial circumstances:

- If you have income that is not shown in Part I of the financial statement (for example, partnership income, dividends, rental income, capital gains or RRSP income), you must also complete *Schedule A*.

- If you have made or responded to a claim for child support that involves undue hardship or a claim for spousal support, you must also complete *Schedule B*.

- If you or the other party has sought a contribution towards special or extraordinary expenses for the child(ren), you must also complete *Schedule C*.

NOTES: You must fully and truthfully complete this financial statement, including any applicable schedules. You must also provide the other party with documents relating to support and a Certificate of Financial Disclosure (Form 13A) as required by Rule 13 of the Family Law Rules.

If you are making or responding to a claim for property, an equalization payment or the matrimonial home, you must complete Form 13.1: Financial Statement (Property and Support Claims) instead of this form.

1. My name is (full legal name) ....

I live in (municipality & province) ....

and I swear/affirm that the following is true:

PART 1: — INCOME

2. I am currently

❑ employed by *(name and address of employer)*

❑ self-employed, carrying on business under the name of *(name and address of business)*

❑ unemployed since *(date when last employed)*

3. I attach proof of my year-to-date income from all sources, including my most recent *(attach all that are applicable)*:

❑ pay cheque stub ❑ social assistance stub ❑ pension stub ❑ workers' compensation stub

❑ employment insurance stub and last Record of Employment

❑ statement of income and expenses/ professional activities (for self-employed individuals)

❑ other (e.g. a letter from your employer confirming all income received to date this year)

4. Last year, my gross income from all sources was $ .... *(do not subtract any taxes that have been deducted from this income).*

5. ❑ I am attaching all of the following required documents to this financial statement as proof of my income over the past three years, if they have not already been provided:

- a copy of my personal income tax returns for each of the past three taxation years, including any materials that were filed with the returns. *(Income tax returns must be served but should NOT be filed in the continuing record, unless they are filed with a motion to refrain a driver's license suspension.)*

- a copy of my notices of assessment and any notices of reassessment for each of the past three taxation years;

- where my notices of assessment and reassessment are unavailable for any of the past three taxation years or where I have not filed a return for any of the past three taxation years, an Income and Deductions printout from the Canada Revenue Agency for each of those years, whether or not I filed an income tax return.

Note: An Income and Deductions printout is available from Canada Revenue Agency. Please call customer service at 1-800-959-8281.

OR

❑ I am an Indian within the meaning of the *Indian Act* (Canada) and I have chosen not to file income tax returns for the past three years. I am attaching the following proof of income for the last three years *(list documents you have provided)*:

(In this table you must show all of the income that you are currently receiving whether taxable or not.)

	Income Source	Amount Received/Month
1.	Employment income (before deductions)	$
2.	Commissions, tips and bonuses	$
3.	Self-employment income (Monthly amount before expenses: $..........)	$
4.	Employment Insurance benefits	$
5.	Workers' compensation benefits	$
6.	Social assistance income (including ODSP payments)	$
7.	Interest and investment income	$
8.	Pension income (including CPP and OAS)	$
9.	Spousal support received from a former spouse/partner	$
10.	Child Tax Benefits or Tax Rebates (e.g. GST)	$
11.	Other sources of income (e.g. RRSP withdrawals, capital gains) *(*attach Schedule A and divide annual amount by 12)*	$
12.	*Total monthly income from all sources*:	$
13.	*Total monthly income × 12 = Total annual income*:	$

14. Other Benefits

Provide details of any non-cash benefits that your employer provides to you or are paid for by your business such as medical insurance coverage, the use of a company car, or room and board.

Item	Details	Yearly Market Value
		$
		$
		$
		$

PART 2: — EXPENSES

Expense	**Monthly Amount**
Automatic Deductions	
CPP contributions	$
EI premiums	$
Income taxes	$
Employee pension contributions	$
Union dues	$
SUBTOTAL	$
Housing	
Rent or mortgage	$
Property taxes	$
Property insurance	$
Condominium fees	$
Repairs and maintenance	$
SUBTOTAL	$
Utilities	
Water	$
Heat	$
Electricity	$
Telephone	$
Cell phone	$
Cable	$
Internet	$
SUBTOTAL	$
Household Expenses	
Groceries	$
Household supplies	$
Meals outside the home	$
Pet care	$
Laundry and Dry Cleaning	$
SUBTOTAL	$
Childcare Costs	
Daycare expense	$
Babysitting costs	$
SUBTOTAL	$
Transportation	
Public transit, taxis	$
Gas and oil	$
Car insurance and license	$
Repairs and maintenance	$
Parking	$

Expense	Monthly Amount
Car Loan or Lease Payments	$
SUBTOTAL	$
Health	
Health insurance premiums	$
Dental expenses	$
Medicine and drugs	$
Eye care	$
SUBTOTAL	$
Personal	
Clothing	$
Hair care and beauty	$
Alcohol and tobacco	$
Education (*specify*)	$
Entertainment/recreation (including children)	$
Gifts	$
SUBTOTAL	$
Other expenses	
Life Insurance premiums	$
RRSP/RESP withdrawals	$
Vacations	$
School fees and supplies	$
Clothing for children	$
Children's activities	$
Summer camp expenses	$
Debt payments	$
Support paid for other children	$
Other expenses not shown above *(specify)*	$
SUBTOTAL	$

Total Amount of Monthly Expenses	$
Total Amount of Yearly Expenses	$

PART 3: — ASSETS

Type		Details	Value or Amount
		State Address of Each Property and Nature of Ownership	
Real Estate	1		$
	2		$
	3		$
		Year and Make	

Type		**Details**	**Value or Amount**
Cars, Boats, Vehicles	1		$
	2		$
	3		$
		Address Where Located	
Other Possessions of Value (e.g. computers, jewellery, collections)	1		$
	2		$
	3		$
		Type — Issuer — Due Date — Number of Shares	
Investments (e.g. bonds, shares, term deposits and mutual funds)	1		$
	2		$
	3		$
		Name and Address of Institution *Account Number*	
Bank Accounts	1		$
	2		$
	3		$
		Type and Issuer *Account Number*	
Savings Plans R.R.S.P.s Pension Plans R.E.S.P.s	1		$
	2		$
	3		$
		Type — Beneficiary — Face Amount	*Cash Surrender Value*
Life Insurance	1		$
	2		$
	3		$
		Name and Address of Business	
	1		$

Type		Details	Value or Amount
Interest in Business *(*attach separate year-end statement for each business)*	2		$
	3		$
		Name and Address of Debtors	
Money Owed to You *(for example, any court judgments in your favour, estate money and income tax refunds)*	1		$
	2		$
	3		$
		Description	
Other Assets	1		$
	2		$
	3		$

Total Value of All Property	$

PART 4: — DEBTS

Type of Debt	Creditor (name and address)	Full Amount Now Owing	Monthly Payments	Are Payments Being Made?
Mortgages, Lines of Credits or other Loans from a Bank, Trust or Finance Company		$	$	❑ Yes ❑ No
		$	$	❑ Yes ❑ No
		$	$	❑ Yes ❑ No
		$	$	❑ Yes ❑ No

Type of Debt	Creditor (name and address)	Full Amount Now Owing	Monthly Payments	Are Payments Being Made?
Outstanding Credit Card Balances		$	$	❑ Yes ❑ No
		$	$	❑ Yes ❑ No
Unpaid Support Amounts		$	$	❑ Yes ❑ No
		$	$	❑ Yes ❑ No
		$	$	❑ Yes ❑ No
Other Debts		$	$	❑ Yes ❑ No
		$	$	❑ Yes ❑ No
		$	$	❑ Yes ❑ No

Total Amount of Debts Outstanding	$

PART 5: — SUMMARY OF ASSETS AND LIABILITIES

Total Assets	$
Subtract Total Debts	$
Net Worth	$

NOTE: This financial statement must be updated no more than 30 days before any court event by either completing and filing:

- *a new financial statement with updated information, or*
- *an affidavit in Form 14A setting out the details of any minor changes or confirming that the information contained in this statement remains correct.*

Sworn/Affirmed before me at ....
municipality

in ....
province, state or country

on ....

date *Commissioner for taking affidavits*
(Type or print name below if signature is illegible.)

....
Signature
(This form is to be signed in front of a lawyer, justice of the peace, notary public or commissioner for taking affidavits.)

SCHEDULE A — ADDITIONAL SOURCES OF INCOME

Line	Income Source	Annual Amount
1.	Net partnership income	*$*
2.	Net rental income (Gross annual rental income of $ ....)	*$*
3.	Total amount of dividends received from taxable Canadian corporations	*$*
4.	Total capital gains ($ ....) less capital losses ($ ....)	*$*
5.	Registered retirement savings plan withdrawals	*$*
6.	Income from a Registered Retirement Income Fund or Annuity	*$*
7.	Any other income *(specify source)*	*$*

Subtotal:	*$*

SCHEDULE B — OTHER INCOME EARNERS IN THE HOME

Complete this part only if you are making or responding to a claim for undue hardship or spousal support. Check and complete all sections that apply to your circumstances.

1. ❑ I live alone.

2. ❑ I am living with *(full legal name of person you are married to or cohabiting with)*

....

3. ❑ I/we live with the following other adult(s):

....

4. ❑ I/we have *(give number)* .... child(ren) who live(s) in the home.

5. My spouse/partner ❑ works at *(place of work or business)* ....

❑ does not work outside the home.

6. My spouse/partner ❑ earns *(give amount)* $ .... per ....

❑ does not earn any income.

7. ❑ My spouse/partner or other adult residing in the home contributes about $ .... per towards the household expenses.

SCHEDULE C — SPECIAL OR EXTRAORDINARY EXPENSES FOR THE CHILD(REN)

Child's Name	Expense	Amount/yr.	Available Tax Credits or Deductions*
1.		*$*	*$*
2.		*$*	*$*
3.		*$*	*$*
4.		*$*	*$*

Child's Name	Expense	Amount/yr.	Available Tax Credits or Deductions*
5.		*$*	*$*
6.		*$*	*$*
7.		*$*	*$*
8.		*$*	*$*
9.		*$*	*$*
10.		*$*	*$*

Total Net Annual Amount	*$*
Total Net Monthly Amount	*$*

Notes:

* *Some of these expenses can be claimed in a parent's income tax return in relation to a tax credit or deduction (for example childcare costs). These credits or deductions must be shown in the above chart.*

❑ I earn $ .... per year which should be used to determine my share of the above expenses.

NOTE:

Pursuant to the *Child Support Guidelines*, a court can order that the parents of a child share the costs of the following expenses for the child:

- Necessary childcare expenses;
- Medical insurance premiums and certain health-related expenses for the child that cost more than $100 annually;
- Extraordinary expenses for the child's education;
- Post-secondary school expenses; and,
- Extraordinary expenses for extracurricular activities.

January 6, 2015

FORM 13.1 — FINANCIAL STATEMENT (PROPERTY AND SUPPORT CLAIMS) SWORN/AFFIRMED

[Repealed O. Reg. 76/06, s. 15.]

[Editor's Note: Forms 4 to 39 of the Family Law Rules have been repealed by O. Reg. 76/06, effective May 1, 2006. Pursuant to Family Law Rule 1(9), when a form is referred to by

number, the reference is to the form with that number that is described in the Table of Forms at the end of these rules and which is available at www.ontariocourtforms.on.ca. For your convenience, the government form as published on this website is reproduced below.]

ONTARIO

Court File Number ....

.... *(Name of court)*

at .... *Court office address*

Applicant(s)

Full legal name & address for service — street & number, municipality, postal code, telephone & fax numbers and e-mail address (if any).	**Lawyer's name & address — street & number, municipality, postal code, telephone & fax numbers and e-mail address (if any).**

Respondent(s)

Full legal name & address for service — street & number, municipality, postal code, telephone & fax numbers and e-mail address (if any).	**Lawyer's name & address — street & number, municipality, postal code, telephone & fax numbers and e-mail address (if any).**

INSTRUCTIONS

1. USE THIS FORM IF:

- you are making or responding to a claim for property or exclusive possession of the matrimonial home and its contents; or

- you are making or responding to a claim for property or exclusive possession of the matrimonial home and its contents together with other claims for relief.

2. USE FORM 13 INSTEAD OF THIS FORM IF:

- you are making or responding to a claim for support but NOT making or responding to a claim for property or exclusive possession of the matrimonial home and its contents.

3. If you have income that is not shown in Part I of the financial statement (for example, partnership income, dividends, rental income, capital gains or RRSP income), you must also complete *Schedule A*.

4. If you or the other party has sought a contribution towards special or extraordinary expenses for the child(ren), you must also complete *Schedule B*.

NOTE: You must fully and truthfully complete this financial statement, including any applicable schedules. You must also provide the other party with documents relating to support and property and a Certificate of Financial Disclosure (Form 13A) as required by Rule 13 of the Family Law Rules.

1. My name is (full legal name) ....

I live in (municipality & province) ....

and I swear/affirm that the following is true:

PART 1: — INCOME

2. I am currently

❑ employed by *(name and address of employer)*

❑ self-employed, carrying on business under the name of *(name and address of business)*

❑ unemployed since *(date when last employed)*

3. I attach proof of my year-to-date income from all sources, including my most recent *(attach all that are applicable)*:

❑ pay cheque stub ❑ social assistance stub ❑ pension stub ❑ workers' compensation stub

❑ employment insurance stub and last Record of Employment

❑ statement of income and expenses/ professional activities (for self-employed individuals)

❑ other (e.g. a letter from your employer confirming all income received to date this year)

4. Last year, my gross income from all sources was $ .... *(do not subtract any taxes that have been deducted from this income).*

5. ❑ I am attaching all of the following required documents to this financial statement as proof of my income over the past three years, if they have not already been provided:

- a copy of my personal income tax returns for each of the past three taxation years, including any materials that were filed with the returns. *(Income tax returns must be served but should NOT be filed in the continuing record, unless they are filed with a motion to refrain a driver's license suspension.)*

- a copy of my notices of assessment and any notices of reassessment for each of the past three taxation years;

- where my notices of assessment and reassessment are unavailable for any of the past three taxation years or where I have not filed a return for any of the past three taxation years, an Income and Deductions printout from the Canada Revenue Agency for each of those years, whether or not I filed an income tax return.

Note: An Income and Deductions printout is available from Canada Revenue Agency. Please call customer service at 1-800-959-8281.

OR

❑ I am an Indian within the meaning of the *Indian Act* (Canada) and I have chosen not to file income tax returns for the past three years. I am attaching the following proof of income for the last three years *(list documents you have provided)*:

(In this table you must show all of the income that you are currently receiving whether taxable or not.)

	Income Source	**Amount Received/Month**
1.	Employment income (before deductions)	$
2.	Commissions, tips and bonuses	$
3.	Self-employment income (Monthly amount before expenses: $..........)	$
4.	Employment Insurance benefits	$
5.	Workers' compensation benefits	$
6.	Social assistance income (including ODSP payments)	$
7.	Interest and investment income	$
8.	Pension income (including CPP and OAS)	$
9.	Spousal support received from a former spouse/partner	$
10.	Child Tax Benefits or Tax Rebates (e.g. GST)	$
11.	Other sources of income (e.g. RRSP withdrawals, capital gains) *(*attach Schedule A and divide annual amount by 12)*	$
12.	*Total monthly income from all sources*:	$
13.	*Total monthly income × 12 = Total annual income*:	$

14. Other Benefits

Provide details of any non-cash benefits that your employer provides to you or are paid for by your business such as medical insurance coverage, the use of a company car, or room and board.

Item	**Details**	**Yearly Market Value**
		$
		$
		$
		$

PART 2: — EXPENSES

Expense	**Monthly Amount**
Automatic Deductions	
CPP contributions	$
EI premiums	$
Income taxes	$
Employee pension contributions	$
Union dues	$
SUBTOTAL	$
Housing	
Rent or mortgage	$
Property taxes	$
Property insurance	$

Expense	Monthly Amount
Condominium fees	$
Repairs and maintenance	$
SUBTOTAL	$
Utilities	
Water	$
Heat	$
Electricity	$
Telephone	$
Cell phone	$
Cable	$
Internet	$
SUBTOTAL	$
Household Expenses	
Groceries	$
Household supplies	$
Meals outside the home	$
Pet care	$
Laundry and Dry Cleaning	$
SUBTOTAL	$
Childcare Costs	
Daycare expense	$
Babysitting costs	$
SUBTOTAL	$
Transportation	
Public transit, taxis	$
Gas and oil	$
Car insurance and license	$
Repairs and maintenance	$
Parking	$
Car Loan or Lease Payments	$
SUBTOTAL	$
Health	
Health insurance premiums	$
Dental expenses	$
Medicine and drugs	$
Eye care	$
SUBTOTAL	$
Personal	
Clothing	$
Hair care and beauty	$
Alcohol and tobacco	$

Expense	Monthly Amount
Education (*specify*)	$
Entertainment/recreation (including children)	$
Gifts	$
SUBTOTAL	$
Other expenses	
Life Insurance premiums	$
RRSP/RESP withdrawals	$
Vacations	$
School fees and supplies	$
Clothing for children	$
Children's activities	$
Summer camp expenses	$
Debt payments	$
Support paid for other children	$
Other expenses not shown above *(specify)*	$
SUBTOTAL	$

Total Amount of Monthly Expenses	$
Total Amount of Yearly Expenses	$

PART 3: — OTHER INCOME EARNERS IN THE HOME

Complete this part only if you are making or responding to a claim for undue hardship or spousal support. Check and complete all sections that apply to your circumstances.

1. ❑ I live alone.

2. ❑ I am living with *(full legal name of person you are married to or cohabiting with)* ....

3. ❑ I/we live with the following other adult(s): ....

4. ❑ I/we have *(give number)* .... child(ren) who live(s) in the home.

5. My spouse/partner ❑ works at *(place of work or business)* ....

❑ does not work outside the home.

6. My spouse/partner ❑ earns *(give amount)* $ .... per ....

❑ does not earn any income.

7. My spouse/partner or other adult residing in the home contributes about $ .... per towards the household expenses.

PART 4: — ASSETS IN AND OUT OF ONTARIO

If any sections of Parts 4 to 9 do not apply, do not leave blank, print "NONE" in the section.

The date of marriage is: *(give date)* ....

The valuation date is: *(give date)* ....

The date of commencement of cohabitation is (if different from date of marriage): *(give date)* ....

PART 4(A): — LAND

Include any interest in land owned on the dates in each of the columns below, including leasehold interests and mortgages. Show estimated market value of your interest, but do not deduct encumbrances or costs of disposition; these encumbrances and costs should be shown under Part 5, "Debts and Other Liabilities".

Nature & Type of Ownership (Give your percentage interest where relevant.)	Address of Property	Estimated Market Value of YOUR Interest		
		on date of marriage	on valuation date	today
		$	$	$
	15. TOTAL VALUE OF LAND		$	$

PART 4(B): — GENERAL HOUSEHOLD ITEMS AND VEHICLES

Show estimated market value, not the cost of replacement for these items owned on the dates in each of the columns below. Do not deduct encumbrances or costs of disposition; these encumbrances and costs should be shown under Part 5, "Debts and Other Liabilities".

Item	Description	Indicate if NOT in your possession	Estimated Market Value of YOUR Interest		
			on date of marriage	on valuation date	today
Household goods & furniture			$	$	$
Cars, boats, vehicles			$	$	$
Jewellery, art, electronics, tools, sports & hobby equipment			$	$	$
Other special items			$	$	$
		16. TOTAL VALUE OF GENERAL HOUSEHOLD ITEMS AND VEHICLES		$	$

PART 4(C): — BANK ACCOUNTS, SAVINGS, SECURITIES AND PENSIONS

Show the items owned on the dates in each of the columns below by category, for example, cash, accounts in financial institutions, pensions, registered retirement or other savings plans, deposit receipts, any other savings, bonds, warrants, options, notes and other securities. Give your best estimate of the market value of the securities if the items were to be sold on the open market.

Category	INSTITUTION (including location)/DESCRIPTION (including issuer and date)	Account number	Amount/Estimated Market Value		
			on date of marriage	on valuation date	today
			$	$	$
17. TOTAL VALUE OF ACCOUNTS, SAVINGS, SECURITIES AND PENSIONS				$	$

PART 4(D): — LIFE AND DISABILITY INSURANCE

List all policies in existence on the dates in each of the columns below.

Company, Type & Policy No.	Owner	Beneficiary	Face Amount	Cash Surrender Value		
				on date of marriage	on valuation date	today
				$	$	$
18. TOTAL CASH SURRENDER VALUE OF INSURANCE POLICIES					$	$

PART 4(E): — BUSINESS INTERESTS

Show any interest in an unincorporated business owned on the dates in each of the columns below. An interest in an incorporated business may be shown here or under "BANK ACCOUNTS, SAVINGS, SECURITIES, AND PENSIONS" in Part 4(c). Give your best estimate of the market value of your interest.

Name of Firm or Company	Interest	Estimated Market Value of YOUR Interest		
		on date of marriage	on valuation date	today
		$	$	$

Name of Firm or Company	Interest	Estimated Market Value of YOUR Interest		
		on date of marriage	on valuation date	today
19. TOTAL VALUE OF BUSINESS INTERESTS			$	$

PART 4(F): — MONEY OWED TO YOU

Give details of all money that other persons owe to you on the dates in each of the columns below, whether because of business or from personal dealings. Include any court judgments in your favour, any estate money and any income tax refunds owed to you.

Details	Amount Owed to You		
	on date of marriage	on valuation date	today
	$	$	$
20. TOTAL OF MONEY OWED TO YOU		$	$

PART 4(G): — OTHER PROPERTY

Show other property or assets owned on the dates in each of the columns below. Include property of any kind not listed above. Give your best estimate of market value.

Category	Details	Estimated Market Value of YOUR interest		
		on date of marriage	on valuation date	today
		$	$	$
21. TOTAL VALUE OF OTHER PROPERTY			$	$
22. VALUE OF ALL PROPERTY OWNED ON THE VALUATION DATE (Add items [15] to [21].)			$	$

PART 5: — DEBTS AND OTHER LIABILITIES

Show your debts and other liabilities on the dates in each of the columns below. List them by category such as mortgages, charges, liens, notes, credit cards, and accounts payable. Don't forget to include:

- *any money owed to the Canada Revenue Agency;*
- *contingent liabilities such as guarantees or warranties given by you (but indicate that they are contingent); and*
- *any unpaid legal or professional bills as a result of this case.*

Category	Details	Amount Owing		
		on date of marriage	on valuation date	today
		$	$	$
23. TOTAL OF DEBTS AND OTHER LIABILITIES			$	$

PART 6: — PROPERTY, DEBTS AND OTHER LIABILITIES ON DATE OF MARRIAGE

Show by category the value of your property, debts and other liabilities, calculated as of the date of your marriage. (In this part, do not include the value of a matrimonial home or debts or other liabilities directly related to its purchase or significant improvement, if you and your spouse ordinarily occupied this property as your family residence at the time of separation.)

Category and details	Value on date of marriage	
	Assets	Liabilities
Land	$	$
General household items & vehicles	$	$
Bank accounts, savings, securities & pensions	$	$
Life & disability insurance	$	$
Business interests	$	$
Money owed to you	$	$
Other property *(Specify.)*	$	$
Debts and other liabilities *(Specify.)*		

Category and details	Value on date of marriage	
	Assets	Liabilities
	$	$
TOTALS	$	$
24. NET VALUE OF PROPERTY OWNED ON DATE OF MARRIAGE *(From the total of the "Assets" column, subtract the total of the "Liabilities" column.)*	$	$
25. VALUE OF ALL DEDUCTIONS (Add items [23] and [24].)	$	$

PART 7: — EXCLUDED PROPERTY

Show by category the value of property owned on the valuation date that is excluded from the definition of "net family property" (such as gifts or inheritances received after marriage).

Category	Details	Value on valuation date
		$
	26. TOTAL VALUE OF EXCLUDED PROPERTY	$

PART 8: — DISPOSED-OF PROPERTY

Show by category the value of all property that you disposed of during the two years immediately preceding the making of this statement, or during the marriage, whichever period is shorter.

Category	Details	Value
		$
	27. TOTAL VALUE OF DISPOSED-OF PROPERTY	$

PART 9: — CALCULATION OF NET FAMILY PROPERTY

	Deductions	BALANCE
Value of all property owned on valuation date (from item [22] above)		$
Subtract value of all deductions (from item [25] above)	$	$
Subtract total value of excluded property (from item [26] above)	$	$
28. NET FAMILY PROPERTY		$

NOTE: *This financial statement must be updated no more than 30 days before any court event by either completing and filing:*

- *a new financial statement with updated information, or*
- *an affidavit in Form 14A setting out the details of any minor changes or confirming that the information contained in this statement remains correct.*

Sworn/Affirmed before me at .... *municipality* in .... *province, state or country* on .... *date* *Commissioner for taking affidavits* *(Type or print name below if signature is illegible.)*	.... *Signature* *(This form is to be signed in front of a lawyer, justice of the peace, notary public or commissioner for taking affidavits.)*

SCHEDULE A: — ADDITIONAL SOURCES OF INCOME

Line	Income Source	Annual Amount
1.	Net partnership income	$
2.	Net rental income (Gross annual rental income of $ ....)	$
3.	Total amount of dividends received from taxable Canadian corporations	$
4.	Total capital gains ($ ....) less capital losses ($ ....)	$
5.	Registered retirement savings plan withdrawals	$
6.	Income from a Registered Retirement Income Fund or Annuity	$
7.	Any other income *(specify source)*	$

Subtotal:	$

SCHEDULE B: — SPECIAL OR EXTRAORDINARY EXPENSES FOR THE CHILD(REN)

Child's Name	Expense	Amount/yr.	Available Tax Credits or Deductions*
1.		$	$
2.		$	$
3.		$	$
4.		$	$
5.		$	$
6.		$	$
7.		$	$
8.		$	$
9.		$	$
10.		$	$

Total Net Annual Amount	$
Total Net Monthly Amount	$

Notes:

* *Some of these expenses can be claimed in a parent's income tax return in relation to a tax credit or deduction (for example childcare costs). These credits or deductions must be shown in the above chart.*

❑ I earn $ .... per year which should be used to determine my share of the above expenses.

NOTE: Pursuant to the Child Support Guidelines, a court can order that the parents of a child share the costs of the following expenses for the child:

- Necessary childcare expenses;
- Medical insurance premiums and certain health-related expenses for the child that cost more than $100 annually;
- Extraordinary expenses for the child's education;
- Post-secondary school expenses; and,
- Extraordinary expenses for extracurricular activities.

January 6, 2015

FORM 13A — CERTIFICATE OF FINANCIAL DISCLOSURE

ONTARIO

Court File Number ....

.... *(Name of court)*

at .... *Court office address*

Applicant(s)

Full legal name & address for service — street & number, municipality, postal code, telephone & fax numbers and e-mail address (if any).	***Lawyer's name & address — street & number, municipality, postal code, telephone & fax numbers and e-mail address (if any).***

Respondent(s)

Full legal name & address for service — street & number, municipality, postal code, telephone & fax numbers and e-mail address (if any).	***Lawyer's name & address — street & number, municipality, postal code, telephone & fax numbers and e-mail address (if any).***

TO THE PARTIES

You must provide complete financial disclosure to the other parties in your case. A list of the documents you must provide to the other party is set out in Rule 13 of the *Family Law Rules*. You must list in this form all of the documents that you are providing to the other party in support of the information set out in your financial statement.

Once you have completed this form,

- if your case includes support with or without special expenses but does not include a claim under Part I of the *Family Law Act* (Family Property), you must:
  - attach all required documentation to the completed certificate.
  - serve this certificate (with attached documentation) on the other party with your completed Financial Statement.
- if your case includes a claim under Part I of the *Family Law Act* (Family Property) with or without a claim for support, you must:
  - attach all required documentation to the completed certificate.
  - serve this certificate (with attached documentation) on the other party within 30 days of the day that your Financial Statement was due to be served.

If you do not provide financial disclosure as required, a court may make an order against you.

You must file a copy of this certificate with the court. The documentation is not filed with the court. If you are the applicant or moving party in your case, you must file this certificate seven days before the case conference. If you are the respondent, you must serve it four days before the case conference.

If you have served any additional or updated financial disclosure before the settlement conference, you must prepare, serve and file an updated Certificate of Financial Disclosure.

Document Number	**Document Description**	**Date of Document (yyyy/mm/dd)**
Part A: Sources of Income		
Personal Income Tax Returns		
•		
•		
•		
•		
•		
Notices of Assessment and Reassessment		
•		
•		
•		
•		
•		
Employment Income		
•		
•		
•		
•		
•		
Self-Employment Income		
•		
•		
•		
•		
•		
Partnership Income and Interests in a Partnership		
•		
•		
•		
•		
•		
Income from a Privately Held Corporation		

Document Number	Document Description	Date of Document (yyyy/mm/dd)
•		
•		
•		
•		
•		
Beneficial Income from, and Interest in, a Trust		
•		
•		
•		
•		
•		
Income from Employment Insurance or Social Assistance		
•		
•		
•		
•		
•		
Pensions and Annuities		
•		
•		
•		
•		
•		
Income from Spousal Support		
•		
•		
•		
•		
•		
Tax Benefits or Rebates		
•		
•		
•		
•		
•		
Investment and Interest Income		
•		
•		
•		
•		

Document Number	Document Description	Date of Document (yyyy/mm/dd)
•		
Rental Income		
•		
•		
•		
•		
•		
Other Income		
•		
•		
•		
•		
•		
Part B: Special and Extraordinary Expenses		
•		
•		
•		
•		
•		
Part C: Claim for Equalization of Net Family Property		
Assets and Liabilities at Valuation Date		
Real Estate		
•		
•		
•		
•		
•		
Savings and Investments		
•		
•		
•		
•		
•		
Pensions		
•		
•		
•		
•		
•		
Life Insurance Policies		

Document Number	Document Description	Date of Document (yyyy/mm/dd)
•		
•		
•		
•		
•		
Interest in a Sole Proprietorship		
•		
•		
•		
•		
•		
Interest in a Partnership		
•		
•		
•		
•		
•		
Interest in a Publically Held Corporation		
•		
•		
•		
•		
•		
Interest in a Privately Held Corporation		
•		
•		
•		
•		
•		
Trust Interests		
•		
•		
•		
•		
•		
Property I own which does not belong in any of the other categories		
•		
•		
•		
•		

Document Number	Document Description	Date of Document (yyyy/mm/dd)
•		
Liabilities		
•		
•		
•		
•		
•		
Assets and Liabilities at Marriage Date		
Assets		
•		
•		
•		
•		
•		
Liabilities		
•		
•		
•		
•		
•		
Excluded Property		
•		
•		
•		
•		
•		

I am the Applicant/Respondent in this case. I certify that I have provided the opposing party with all of the documents that I have identified in this checklist.

Certified at .... *(City)* on .... *(Date)*

.... *(Signature of Party)*

January 6, 2015

FORM 13B — NET FAMILY PROPERTY STATEMENT

[Repealed O. Reg. 76/06, s. 15.]

[Editor's Note: Forms 4 to 39 of the Family Law Rules have been repealed by O. Reg. 76/06, effective May 1, 2006. Pursuant to Family Law Rule 1(9), when a form is referred to by number, the reference is to the form with that number that is described in the Table of Forms at the end of these rules and which is available at www.ontariocourtforms.on.ca. For your convenience, the government form as published on this website is reproduced below.]

ONTARIO

Court File Number

....

(Name of court)

at ....

Court office address

Applicant(s)

Full legal name & address for service — street & number, municipality, postal code, telephone & fax numbers and e-mail address (if any).	***Lawyer's name & address — street & number, municipality, postal code, telephone & fax numbers and e-mail address (if any).***

Respondent(s)

Full legal name & address for service — street & number, municipality, postal code, telephone & fax numbers and e-mail address (if any).	***Lawyer's name & address — street & number, municipality, postal code, telephone & fax numbers and e-mail address (if any).***

My name is *(full legal name)* ....

The valuation date for the following material is *(date)* ....

(Complete the tables by filling in the columns for both parties, showing your assets, debts, etc., and those of your spouse.)

TABLE 1: Value of assets owned on valuation date (List in the order of the categories in the financial statement.)		
ITEM	**APPLICANT**	**RESPONDENT**
1.	$	$

TABLE 1: Value of assets owned on valuation date (List in the order of the categories in the financial statement.)		
ITEM	**APPLICANT**	**RESPONDENT**
TOTAL 1	$	$

TABLE 2: Value of debts and liabilities on valuation date (List in the order of the categories in the financial statement.)		
ITEM	**APPLICANT**	**RESPONDENT**
1.	$	$
TOTAL 2	$	$

TABLE 3: Net value on date of marriage of property (other than a matrimonial home) after deducting debts or other liabilities on date of marriage (other than those relating directly to the purchase or significant improvement of a matrimonial home) (List in the order of the categories in the financial statement.)		
3(a) *PROPERTY ITEM*	*APPLICANT*	*RESPONDENT*
	$	$
TOTAL OF PROPERTY ITEMS	*$*	*$*
3(b) *DEBT ITEM*		

TABLE 3: Net value on date of marriage of property (other than a matrimonial home) after deducting debts or other liabilities on date of marriage (other than those relating directly to the purchase or significant improvement of a matrimonial home) (List in the order of the categories in the financial statement.)		
TOTAL OF DEBT ITEMS	$	$
NET TOTAL 3 [3(a) minus 3(b)]	$	$

TABLE 4: Value or property excluded under subsection 4(2) of the Family Law Act
(List in the order of the categories in the financial statement.)

ITEM	APPLICANT	RESPONDENT
	$	$
TOTAL 4	$	$

TOTAL 2 (from page 2)	$	$
TOTAL 3 (from page 2)	$	$
TOTAL 4 (from page 3)	$	$
TOTAL 5 ([Total 2] + [Total 3] +[Total 4])	$	$
TOTAL 1 (from page 1)	$	$
TOTAL 5 (from above)	$	$
TOTAL 6: NET FAMILY PROPERTY ([Total 1] minus [Total 5])	$	$

.... *Date of signature* .... *Signature*

May 15, 2009

FORM 13C — COMPARISON OF NET FAMILY PROPERTY STATEMENTS

This form is being prepared by

❑ the Applicant

❑ the Respondent

❑ the Applicant and Respondent jointly

ONTARIO

Court File Number ....

.... *(Name of Court)*

at .... *(Court office address)*

This document must be completed once both parties have completed and exchanged Net Family Property Statements *(Form 13B). This document can be completed jointly by the parties and filed with the court seven days before the settlement conference. If you and the other party are not able to agree on this document, then you each must prepare one, and serve it on the other party and file it with the court before the settlement conference. If you requested the settlement conference, you must serve and file the document seven days before the settlement conference, even if it is a joint statement. If no joint statement has been filed, the other party must serve and file the document four days before the settlement conference.*

Applicant(s)

Full legal name & address for service — street & number, municipality, postal code, telephone & fax numbers and e-mail address (if any).	***Lawyer's name & address — street & number, municipality, postal code, telephone & fax numbers and e-mail address (if any).***

Respondent(s)

Full legal name & address for service — street & number, municipality, postal code, telephone & fax numbers and e-mail address (if any).	***Lawyer's name & address — street & number, municipality, postal code, telephone & fax numbers and e-mail address (if any).***

Valuation Date: .... Statement Date: ....

1. — Value of Assets Owned on Valuation Date

(a) LAND

NATURE & TYPE OF OWNERSHIP (State percentage interest where relevant)	NATURE & ADDRESS OF OWNERSHIP	COMMENTS	Document Number*	Applicant's Position		Respondent's Position	
				APPLICANT	RESPONDENT	APPLICANT	RESPONDENT
Matrimonial Home				$	$	$	$
				$	$	$	$
				$	$	$	$
			(A) TOTALS: Value of Land	$	$	$	$

Notes:

* Please use the number that you used for the document in your Certificate of Financial Disclosure (Form 13A)

(b) GENERAL HOUSEHOLD ITEMS AND VEHICLES

ITEM	DESCRIPTION	COMMENTS	Document Number	Applicant's Position		Respondent's Position	
				APPLICANT	RESPONDENT	APPLICANT	RESPONDENT
Household goods & furniture				$	$	$	$
Cars, boats, vehicles				$	$	$	$
Jewellery, art, electronics, tools, sports & hobby, equipment				$	$	$	$
Other special items				$	$	$	$
				$	$	$	$
				$	$	$	$
			(B) TOTALS: Value of General Household Items and Vehicles	$	$	$	$

(c) BANK ACCOUNTS AND SAVINGS, SECURITIES AND PENSIONS

CATEGORY (Savings, Checking, GIC, RRSP, Pensions, etc.)	INSTITUTION	ACCOUNT NUMBER	COMMENTS	Document Number	Applicant's Position		Respondent's Position	
					APPLICANT	RESPONDENT	APPLICANT	RESPONDENT
					$ $ $	$ $ $	$ $ $	$ $ $
				(C) TOTALS: Value of Accounts and Savings	$	$	$	$

(d) LIFE AND DISABILITY INSURANCE

COMPANY TYPE & POLICY NO.	OWNER	BENEFICIARY	FACE AMOUNT ($)	COMMENTS	Document Number	Applicant's Position		Respondent's Position	
						APPLICANT	RESPONDENT	APPLICANT	RESPONDENT
			$ $ $			$ $ $	$ $ $	$ $ $	$ $ $
					(D) TOTALS: Cash Surrender Value of Insurance Policies	$	$	$	$

(e) BUSINESS INTERESTS

NAME OF FIRM OR COMPANY	INTERESTS	COMMENTS	Document Number	Applicant's Position		Respondent's Position	
				APPLICANT	RESPONDENT	APPLICANT	RESPONDENT
				$ $ $	$ $ $	$ $ $	$ $ $
			(E) TOTALS: Value of Business Interests	$	$	$	$

(f) MONEY OWED TO YOU

DETAILS	COMMENTS	Document Number	Applicant's Position		Respondent's Position	
			APPLICANT	RESPONDENT	APPLICANT	RESPONDENT
			$	$	$	$
			$	$	$	$
			$	$	$	$
		(F) TOTALS: Money Owed to You	$	$	$	$

(g) OTHER PROPERTY

CATEGORY	DETAILS	COMMENTS	Document Number	Applicant's Position		Respondent's Position	
				APPLICANT	RESPONDENT	APPLICANT	RESPONDENT
				$	$	$	$
				$	$	$	$
				$	$	$	$
			(G) TOTALS: Value of Other Property	$	$	$	$

VALUE OF PROPERTY OWNED ON THE VALUATION DATE, (TOTAL 1) (Add: item A to item G inclusive)	$	$	$	$

2. — Value of Debts and Other Liabilities on Valuation Date

DEBTS AND OTHER LIABILITIES

CATEGORY	DETAILS	COMMENTS	Document Number	Applicant's Position		Respondent's Position	
				APPLICANT	RESPONDENT	APPLICANT	RESPONDENT
				$ $ $	$ $ $	$ $ $	$ $ $
TOTALS: Value of Debts and Other Liabilities, (TOTAL 2)				$	$	$	$

3. — Net Value of Property (Other than a Matrimonial Home) and Debts on Date of Marriage

PROPERTY, DEBTS AND OTHER LIABILITIES ON DATE OF MARRIAGE

CATEGORY AND DETAILS	COMMENTS	Document Number	Applicant's Position		Respondent's Position	
			APPLICANT	RESPONDENT	APPLICANT	RESPONDENT
Assets			$ $	$ $	$ $	$ $
TOTAL OF PROPERTY ITEMS			$	$	$	$
Debts and other liabilities			$ $	$ $	$ $	$ $
TOTAL OF DEBTS ITEMS			$	$	$	$
NET VALUE OF PROPERTY OWNED ON DATE OF MARRIAGE (NET TOTAL 3)			$	$	$	$

4. — Value of Property Excluded Under Subs. 4(2) of "*Family Law Act*"

ITEM	COMMENTS	Document Number	Applicant's Position		Respondent's Position	
			APPLICANT	RESPONDENT	APPLICANT	RESPONDENT
			$	$	$	$
			$	$	$	$
			$	$	$	$
			$	$	$	$
			$	$	$	$
			$	$	$	$
			$	$	$	$
TOTALS: Value of Excluded Property (TOTAL 4)			*$*	*$*	*$*	*$*

TOTAL 2: Debts and Other Liabilities	$	$	$	$
TOTAL 3: Value of Property Owned on the Date of Marriage	$	$	$	$
TOTAL 4: Value of Excluded Property	$	$	$	$
TOTAL 5: (TOTAL 2 + TOTAL 3 + TOTAL 4)	*$*	*$*	*$*	*$*

TOTAL 1: Value of Property Owned on Valuation Date	$	$	$	$
TOTAL 5: *(from above)*	$	$	$	$
TOTAL 6: NET FAMILY PROPERTY (Subtract: TOTAL 1 minus TOTAL 5)	*$*	*$*	*$*	*$*

	Applicant's Position		Respondent's Position	
EQUALIZATION PAYMENTS	Applicant Pays To Respondent	Respondent Pays To Applicant	Applicant Pays To Respondent	Respondent Pays To Applicant
	$	*$*	*$*	*$*

January 6, 2015

FORM 14 — NOTICE OF MOTION

[Repealed O. Reg. 76/06, s. 15.]

[Editor's Note: Forms 4 to 39 of the Family Law Rules have been repealed by O. Reg. 76/06, effective May 1, 2006. Pursuant to Family Law Rule 1(9), when a form is referred to by number, the reference is to the form with that number that is described in the Table of Forms at the end of these rules and which is available at www.ontariocourtforms.on.ca. For your convenience, the government form as published on this website is reproduced below.]

Court File Number

ONTARIO

.... *(Name of court)*

at .... *Court office address*

Applicant(s)

Full legal name & address for service — street & number, municipality, postal code, telephone & fax numbers and e-mail address (if any).	*Lawyer's name & address — street & number, municipality, postal code, telephone & fax numbers and e-mail address (if any).*

Respondent(s)

Full legal name & address for service — street & number, municipality, postal code, telephone & fax numbers and e-mail address (if any).	*Lawyer's name & address — street & number, municipality, postal code, telephone & fax numbers and e-mail address (if any).*

The person making this motion or the person's lawyer must contact the clerk of the court by telephone or otherwise to choose a time and date when the court could hear this motion.

TO THE PARTIES:

THE COURT WILL HEAR A MOTION on (date) .... *at* ...., *or as soon as possible after that time, at (place of hearing)*

This motion will be made by *(name of person making the motion)* .... who will be asking the court for an order for the item(s) listed on page 2 of this notice.

❑ A copy of the affidavit(s) in support of this motion is/are served with this notice.

❑ A notice of a case conference is served with this notice to change an order.

If this material is missing, you should talk to the court office immediately.

The person making this motion is also relying on the following documents in the continuing record: *(List documents.)*

....

If you want to oppose this motion or to give your own views, you should talk to your own lawyer and prepare your own affidavit, serve it on all other parties and file it at the court office not later than 4 days before the date above. Only written and affidavit evidence will be allowed at a motion unless the court gives permission for oral testimony. You may bring your lawyer to the motion.

IF YOU DO NOT COME TO THE MOTION, THE COURT MAY MAKE AN ORDER WITHOUT YOU AND ENFORCE IT AGAINST YOU.

....

Date of signature

....

Signature of person making this motion or of person's lawyer

Typed or printed name of person or of person's lawyer, address for service, telephone & fax numbers and e-mail address (if any)

NOTE TO PERSON MAKING THIS MOTION: You MUST file a confirmation (Form 14C) not later than 2:00 p.m. 3 days before the date set out above.

If this is a motion to change past and future support payments under an order that has been assigned to a government agency, you must also serve this notice on that agency. If you do not, the agency can ask the court to set aside any order that you may get in this motion and can ask for costs against you.

State the order or orders requested on this motion.

March 1, 2018

FORM 14A — AFFIDAVIT (GENERAL)

[Repealed O. Reg. 76/06, s. 15.]

[Editor's Note: Forms 4 to 39 of the Family Law Rules have been repealed by O. Reg. 76/06, effective May 1, 2006. Pursuant to Family Law Rule 1(9), when a form is referred to by number, the reference is to the form with that number that is described in the Table of Forms at the end of these rules and which is available at www.ontariocourtforms.on.ca. For your convenience, the government form as published on this website is reproduced below.]

Court File Number ....

.... *(Name of court)*

at .... *Court office address*

Applicant(s)

Full legal name & address for service — street & number, municipality, postal code, telephone & fax and e-mail address (if any)	*Lawyer's name & address — street & number, municipality, postal code, telephone & fax numbers and e-mail address (if any)*

Respondent(s)

Full legal name & address for service — street & number, municipality, postal code, telephone & fax numbers and e-mail address (if any)	*Lawyer's name & address — street & number, municipality, postal code, telephone & fax numbers and e-mail address (if any)*

My name is (full legal name)

I live in (municipality & province) and I swear/affirm that the following is true:

Set out the statements of fact in consecutively numbered paragraphs. Where possible, each numbered paragraph should consist of one complete sentence and be limited to a particular statement of fact. If you learned a fact from someone else, you must give that person's name and state that you believe that fact to be true.

1.

Put a line through any blank space left on this page.

Sworn/Affirmed before me at .... *municipality* in .... *province, state or country* on .... *date* .... *Commissioner for taking affidavits (Type or print name below if signature is illegible.)*	.... *Signature* *(This form is to be signed in front of a lawyer, justice of the peace, notary public or commissioner for taking affidavits.)*

September 1, 2005

FORM 14B — MOTION FORM

[Repealed O. Reg. 76/06, s. 15.]

[Editor's Note: Forms 4 to 39 of the Family Law Rules have been repealed by O. Reg. 76/06, effective May 1, 2006. Pursuant to Family Law Rule 1(9), when a form is referred to by number, the reference is to the form with that number that is described in the Table of Forms at the end of these rules and which is available at www.ontariocourtforms.on.ca. For your convenience, the government form as published on this website is reproduced below.]

Court File Number ....

.... *(Name of court)*

at .... *Court office address*

Names of parties:

Applicant: ....

Hearing date: ....

Respondent: ....

Name of case management judge: ....

This form is filed by:

❑ applicant
❑ respondent
❑ other *(Specify.)*

....

This motion is made:

❑ with the consent of all persons affected
❑ with notice to all persons affected — opposition expected

❑ with notice to all persons affected — unopposed
❑ without notice

NOTE TO PERSON MAKING THIS MOTION: If this is a motion to change past and future support payments under an order that has been assigned to a government agency, you must also serve this Notice on that agency. If you do not, the agency can ask the court to set aside any order that you may get in this motion and can ask for court costs against you.

Order that you want the court to make: (If you need more space, add an extra sheet but do not make any changes to this form.)

Laws and rules on which you are relying: (Give name of statute and section numbers; name of regulation and section numbers; and rule numbers.)

....

....

I want the court to deal with this motion:

❑ by relying only on written material.
❑ by conference telephone call *(An appointment for such a call must be arranged in advance; see rule 14 of the Family Law Rules).)*

❑ in a hearing at which affected persons may attend personally.

At this motion, I am relying on the following material:

❑ Tabs/pages .... of the continuing record
❑ Pages .... of the transcript of the evidence of *(name of person)* ...., dated .... *(Relevant parts of transcript must be highlighted.)*

This party's lawyer (Give lawyer's name, firm, telephone & fax number and e-mail address. If no lawyer, give party's name, and address for service, telephone & fax number and e-mail address.)	Other party's lawyer (Give lawyer's name, firm, telephone & fax number and e-mail address. If no lawyer, give party's name, and address for service, telephone & fax number and e-mail address.)

.... *Signature*

.... *Date of signature*

September 1, 2005

FORM 14C — CONFIRMATION OF MOTION

[Repealed O. Reg. 76/06, s. 15.]

[Editor's Note: Forms 4 to 39 of the Family Law Rules have been repealed by O. Reg. 76/06, effective May 1, 2006. Pursuant to Family Law Rule 1(9), when a form is referred to by number, the reference is to the form with that number that is described in the Table of Forms at the end of these rules and which is available at www.ontariocourtforms.on.ca. For your convenience, the government form as published on this website is reproduced below.]

Court File Number

ONTARIO

.... *(Name of court)*

at .... *Court office address*

Applicant(s)

Full legal name & address for service — street & number, municipality, postal code, telephone & fax numbers and e-mail address (if any).	*Lawyer's name & address — street & number, municipality, postal code, telephone & fax numbers and e-mail address (if any).*

Applicant(s)

Respondent(s)

Full legal name & address for service — street & number, municipality, postal code, telephone & fax numbers and e-mail address (if any).	*Lawyer's name & address — street & number, municipality, postal code, telephone & fax numbers and e-mail address (if any).*

Name & address of Children's Lawyer's agent (street & number, municipality, postal code, telephone & fax numbers and e-mail address (if any)) and name of person represented.

1. My name is (full legal name) ....

and I am ❑ the lawyer for *(name)* ....

❑ the applicant in this case . . . . ❑ the respondent in this case

❑ other *(specify)* ....

2. Have you conferred with the opposing counsel or party regarding the issues, motion material, and time estimates, as set out in paragraphs 3 to 10 below?

❑ Yes

❑ No, because *(provide reasons)*

....

NOTE: The *Family Law Rules* require the parties or their counsel to confer, or attempt to confer, orally or in writing with each other on the issues in dispute for a motion prior to filing Confirmations. The only exception is where a party is prohibited from such communication by court order. *Failure to comply with the* Family Law Rules *may result in a cost order.*

3. The scheduled date and time for this motion is *(date)* .... at .... a.m./p.m.

4. Has a case conference been held on the substantive issues in this case?

❑ Yes, a case conference was held before Justice

❑ No, a case conference has not been held on the substantive issues in this case.

5. The case management judge for this case is Justice ....

6. This matter is

❑ going ahead on the issues listed in paragraph 7 below.

❑ going ahead for a consent order *(attach draft order)*.

❑ being adjourned on consent to *(date)* .... for a *(event)* .... because *(give reasons)*

....

❑ going ahead for a contested adjournment to *(date)* .... asked for by *(name of person asking for adjournment)* .... because *(give reasons)*

....

7. What specific orders are you seeking on this motion? *(List the specific orders below)*

a)

b)

c)

d)

e)

f)

8. ❑ I confirm that I will bring a draft order to the motion.

9. The presiding judge will be referred to the following pages/tabs:

....

10. Time estimate: .... applicant: .... minutes; respondent: .... minutes; for a total of .... minutes.

NOTE: The *Family Law Rules* require you to *deliver a copy* of this form to the opposing lawyer or party, unless this is a child protection matter. For clarification, regular or special service and an accompanying Affidavit of Service (Form 6B) under rule 6 of the *Family Law Rules* are not required. However, you must deliver this form by some method (including fax or e-mail) to the opposing lawyer or party prior to giving a copy to the court clerk.

....

Date of signature *Lawyer's or party's signature*

March 1, 2018

FORM 14D — ORDER ON MOTION WITHOUT NOTICE

[Repealed O. Reg. 76/06, s. 15.]

[Editor's Note: Forms 4 to 39 of the Family Law Rules have been repealed by O. Reg. 76/06, effective May 1, 2006. Pursuant to Family Law Rule 1(9), when a form is referred to by number, the reference is to the form with that number that is described in the Table of Forms at the end of these rules and which is available at www.ontariocourtforms.on.ca. For your convenience, the government form as published on this website is reproduced below.]

Court File Number ....

[SEAL]

.... *(Name of court)*

at .... *Court office address*

Applicant(s)

Full legal name & address for service — street & number, municipality, postal code, telephone & fax numbers and e-mail address (if any)	*Lawyer's name & address — street & number, municipality, postal code, telephone & fax numbers and e-mail address (if any)*

Respondent(s)

Full legal name & address for service — street & number, municipality, postal code, telephone & fax numbers and e-mail address (if any)	*Lawyer's name & address — street & number, municipality, postal code, telephone & fax numbers and e-mail address (if any)*

.... *Judge (print or type name)*

.... *Date of order*

The court heard a motion made by *(name of person or persons who made the motion)* .... without notice to *(name)* ....

The following persons were in court *(names of parties and lawyers in court at time of the motion)* ....

For this motion, the court read *(list the documents filed on the motion)* ....

The court also received and heard submissions on behalf of *(name or names)* ....

THIS COURT ORDERS THAT:

Put a line through any blank space left on this page.

.... *Date of signature*

.... *Signature of judge or clerk of the court*

NOTICE TO (name)

This order has been made without notice to you. If you want the court to change this order, you must act as quickly as possible after the order comes to your attention, by serving an affidavit and a notice of motion on the other parties and by filing them together with proof of service at the court office.

September 1, 2005

FORM 15 — MOTION TO CHANGE

[Repealed O. Reg. 76/06, s. 15.]

[Editor's Note: Forms 4 to 39 of the Family Law Rules have been repealed by O. Reg. 76/06, effective May 1, 2006. Pursuant to Family Law Rule 1(9), when a form is referred to by number, the reference is to the form with that number that is described in the Table of Forms at the end of these rules and which is available at www.ontariocourtforms.on.ca. For your convenience, the government form as published on this website is reproduced below.]

ONTARIO

Court File Number

(SEAL)

.... *(Name of court)*

at .... *Court office address*

❑ *the order of Justice* ...., *dated* ....

❑ *the agreement for support between the parties, dated* ...., *filed with the court on* ....

Applicant(s)

Full legal name & address for service — street & number, municipality, postal code, telephone & fax numbers and e-mail address (if any).	*Lawyer's name & address — street & number, municipality, postal code, telephone & fax numbers and e-mail address (if any).*

Respondent(s)

Full legal name & address for service — street & number, municipality, postal code, telephone & fax numbers and e-mail address (if any).	*Lawyer's name & address — street & number, municipality, postal code, telephone & fax numbers and e-mail address (if any).*

Assignee (if applicable)

Full legal name & address for service — street & number, municipality, postal code, telephone & fax numbers and e-mail address (if any).	*Lawyer's name & address — street & number, municipality, postal code, telephone & fax numbers and e-mail address (if any).*

NOTE: If you are seeking to change a support term in an agreement that has not already been filed with the court pursuant to s. 35 of the Family Law Act, *you must file the agreement and Form 26B (Affidavit for Filing Domestic Contract with Court) before bringing this motion to change.*

You may use this form if you are seeking to change an order or agreement that has been recalculated by the online Child Support Service. You must serve a copy of this form on the Family Responsibility Office if the order you recalculated was made under the Divorce Act *and the recalculation was completed within the last 35 days.*

You may not use this form to change a Notice of Calculation made by the online Child Support Service.

If the order or agreement for support has been assigned to a person or agency, the assignee must be served with this form and the Change Information Form (Form 15A). The assignee's consent to change an order or agreement for support may be necessary. It is the responsibility of the person seeking the change to the order or agreement to determine if the order or agreement has been assigned. You can do this by submitting a Confirmation of Assignment form. The Confirmation of Assignment form is available through the Ministry of the Attorney General website or at the court office.

TO: *(name(s) of party(ies))* ....

(Name of party bringing motion) .... has brought a motion to change

❑ the order of Justice ...., dated ....

❑ recalculated by the online Child Support Service on ....

❑ the agreement between you and *(name of party bringing this motion)* ...., dated .... ❑ recalculated by the online Child Support Service on ....

❑ *THE FIRST COURT DATE IS* ...., at .... ❑ a.m. ❑ p.m. or as soon as possible after that time, at *(address of court)*

❑ *NO COURT DATE HAS BEEN SET FOR THIS CASE.* A case management judge will not be assigned until one of the parties asks the clerk of the court to schedule a case conference and serves a Conference Notice (Form 17).

IF, AFTER 365 DAYS, THE CASE HAS NOT BEEN SCHEDULED FOR TRIAL, the clerk of the court will send out a warning that the case will be dismissed in 60 days unless the parties file proof that the case has been settled or one of the parties asks for a case or a settlement conference.

(To be completed by the party bringing this motion — check the box of any paragraph that applies to your case:)

❑ This case does not include any claim to change support, and a financial statement is therefore not attached.

❑ The case only includes a claim to change child support in accordance with the table amount specified under the *Child Support Guidelines* and a financial statement is therefore not attached.

❑ This case includes a claim to change support other than child support in the amount specified in the table of the applicable child support guidelines, and a financial statement is attached. You MUST fill out a Financial Statement (Form 13 or 13.1), serve a copy on the person(s) bringing the motion to change and file a copy in the court office with an Affidavit of Service (Form 6B) even if you do not respond to this case.

IF YOU CONSENT TO THE CHANGES BEING SOUGHT IN THIS MOTION, you or your lawyer must complete the Consent Motion to Change (Form 15C — a blank copy should be attached) and return a copy to the person(s) bringing the motion and any assignee, if applicable, within 30 days of being served (60 days if the motion to change is served on you outside Canada or the United States). The person(s) bringing the motion may then file the consent with the court and may obtain a court order based on the consent. If a first court date has been scheduled, you do not need to attend court on that date unless specifically directed by the court to do so.

IF YOU WANT TO OPPOSE ANY CHANGE BEING SOUGHT IN THIS MOTION OR WANT TO REQUEST A CHANGE OF YOUR OWN, you or your lawyer must complete the Response to Motion to Change (Form 15B — a blank copy should be attached), serve a copy on the person(s) bringing the motion and file a copy in the court office with an Affidavit of Service (Form 6B). *YOU HAVE ONLY 30 DAYS AFTER THIS MOTION TO CHANGE IS SERVED ON YOU (60 DAYS IF THE MOTION TO CHANGE IS SERVED ON YOU OUTSIDE CANADA OR THE UNITED STATES) TO SERVE AND FILE A RESPONSE TO A MOTION TO CHANGE. IF YOU DO NOT, THE CASE WILL GO AHEAD WITHOUT YOU AND THE COURT MAY MAKE AN ORDER AND ENFORCE IT AGAINST YOU.*

NOTE: If you want to make your own claim to change support, you MUST also fill out a Financial Statement (Form 13 or 13.1), serve a copy on the person(s) bringing the motion and file a copy in the court office with an Affidavit of Service (Form 6B) UNLESS your only claim for support is for child support in the table amount specified under the *Child Support Guidelines.*

YOU SHOULD GET LEGAL ADVICE ABOUT THIS CASE RIGHT AWAY. If you cannot afford a lawyer, you may be able to get help from your local Legal Aid Ontario Office. (See your telephone directory under LEGAL AID.)

....

Date of issue by the clerk of the court *Clerk of the court*

CLAIM BY (name(s) of person(s) bringing motion) ....

I ASK THE COURT TO CHANGE THE EXISTING COURT ORDER OR SUPPORT AGREEMENT BY MAKING AN ORDER AS FOLLOWS: *(complete only those items that affect the terms of the order or agreement that you are seeking to change.)*

❑ *1.* An order that *(name(s) of party(ies) or person(s))* ....

have custody of the following child(ren): *(name(s) and birthdate(s) of child(ren))*

....

❑ *2.* An order that *(name(s) of party(ies) or person(s))* ....

have access to the following child(ren): *(name(s) and birthdate(s) of child(ren))*

....

as follows: *(give details of access)*

....

❑ *3.* An order that *(name(s) of party(ies) and/or person(s))* .... and .... have joint custody of the following child(ren): *(name(s) and birthdate(s) of child(ren))*

....

❑ *4.* An order for the following residential/access arrangements for the child(ren): *(name(s) and birthdate(s) of child(ren)*

❑ *5.* Order(s) dealing with child support as follows:

❑ Since the order/agreement for child support was made, a Notice of Recalculation was issued by the online Child Support Service dated .... *(please attach).*

❑ The order/agreement for child support, dated ...., be terminated for the following child(ren): *(insert name(s) and birthdate(s) of child(ren))* ...., effective *(date)* ....

❑ Based on the payor's annual income of $ ...., *(name of party)* .... pay *(name of party)* .... $ .... per month for the following child(ren): *(name(s) and birthdate(s) of child(ren))* .... with payments to start on *(date)* ....

❑ This amount is the table amount listed in the *Child Support Guidelines.*

❑ This amount is more than the table amount listed in the *Child Support Guidelines.*

❑ This amount is less than the table amount listed in the *Child Support Guidelines.*

❑ Starting on *(date)* ...., *(name of party)* .... pay to *(name of party)* .... $ .... for the following special or extraordinary expenses:

Child's Name	**Type of Expense**	**Total Amount of Expense**	**Payor's Share**	**Terms of Payment (frequency of payment, date due, etc.)**
		$	$	
		$	$	
		$	$	
		$	$	
		$	$	

❑ Other: *(give details)*

6. ❑ Orders dealing with the outstanding child support owed as follows:

❑ The child support owed to *(name of recipient)* .... be fixed at $ .... as of *(date)* ....

❑ *(Name of payor)* .... pay to *(name of recipient)* .... $ .... per month, with payments to begin on *(date)* .... until the full amount owing is paid.

❑ The child support owed to *(name of agency or other person)* .... be fixed at $ .... as of *(date)* ....

❑ *(Name of payor)* .... pay to *(name of agency or other person)* .... $ .... per month, with payments to begin on *(date)* .... until the full amount owing is paid.

7. ❑ An order that the spousal support be changed as follows:

❑ The order/agreement for spousal support, dated .... be terminated effective *(date)* ....

❑ *(Name of party)* .... pay spousal support to *(name of party)* .... in the amount of $ .... per month, effective on *(date)* ....

❑ Other *(give details of the order you want the court to make)*

8. ❑ An order that the outstanding spousal support owed be paid as follows:

❑ The spousal support owed to *(name of recipient)* .... be fixed at $ .... as of *(date)* ....

❑ *(Name of payor)* pay to *(name of recipient)* .... $ .... per month, with payments to begin on *(date)* .... until the full amount owing is paid.

❑ The spousal support owed to *(name of agency or other person)* be fixed at $ .... as of *(date)* ....

❑ *(Name of payor)* .... pay to *(name of agency or other person)* .... $ .... per month, with payments to begin on *(date)* .... until the full amount owing is paid.

9. ❑ I ask that the term(s) of the order of Justice *(name of judge)* ...., dated ...., for *(give details)* .... be changed as follows: *(give details of the order you want the court to make)*

....

10. ❑ I ask the court for the following order:

....

The information and facts supporting my motion to change are set out in the Change Information Form (Form 15A) attached.

....	....
Date of signature	*Signature of person bringing the motion or person's lawyer*

April 12, 2016

FORM 15A — CHANGE INFORMATION FORM

[Repealed O. Reg. 76/06, s. 15.]

[Editor's Note: Forms 4 to 39 of the Family Law Rules have been repealed by O. Reg. 76/06, effective May 1, 2006. Pursuant to Family Law Rule 1(9), when a form is referred to by number, the reference is to the form with that number that is described in the Table of Forms at the end of these rules and which is available at www.ontariocourtforms.on.ca. For your convenience, the government form as published on this website is reproduced below.]

ONTARIO

Court File Number

.... *(Name of court)*

at .... *Court office address*

Applicant(s)

Full legal name & address for service — street & number, municipality, postal code, telephone & fax numbers and e-mail address (if any).	*Lawyer's name & address — street & number, municipality, postal code, telephone & fax numbers and e-mail address (if any).*

Respondent(s)

Full legal name & address for service — street & number, municipality, postal code, telephone & fax numbers and e-mail address (if any).	*Lawyer's name & address — street & number, municipality, postal code, telephone & fax numbers and e-mail address (if any).*

Assignee (if applicable)

Full legal name & address for service — street & number, municipality, postal code, telephone & fax numbers and e-mail address (if any).	*Lawyer's name & address — street & number, municipality, postal code, telephone & fax numbers and e-mail address (if any).*

PART 1 — GENERAL INFORMATION

(This part should be filled out to the best ability of the party asking for a change in an order or support agreement.)

My name is (full legal name) ....

I live in (municipality & province) ....

and I swear/affirm that the following is true:

1. I am the ❑ applicant ❑ Respondent

2. The applicant, *(applicant's full legal name)* .... was born on *(date of birth)* .... lives in *(municipality & province)* and, at the present time, is ❑ married ❑ living in a spousal relationship

❑ Separated ❑ other *(specify)* ....

The applicant is the ❑ support recipient ❑ support payor

3. The respondent, *(respondent's full legal name)* .... was born on *(date of birth)* .... lives in *(municipality & province)* .... and, at the present time, is ❑ Married ❑ living in a spousal relationship

❑ Separated ❑ other *(specify)* ....

The respondent is the ❑ support recipient ❑ support payor

4. This order/agreement ❑ has never been assigned

❑ has been assigned to

❑ the Ontario Ministry of Community and Social Services

❑ Ontario Works in *(name of location)* ....

❑ the municipality of *(name)* ....

❑ other *(specify)* ....

The details of the assignment are: *(Give date of assignment, indicate whether it is still in effect, add any other relevant information known to you and attach a copy of the Confirmation of Assignment Form.)*

5. The applicant and the respondent:

❑ started living together on *(date)* ....

❑ were married on *(date)* ....

❑ never lived together

❑ separated on *(date)* ....

❑ were divorced on *(date)* ....

6. The following chart gives basic information about the child(ren) in this case:

(List all child(ren) involved in this case, even those for whom no support is being claimed.)

Child's full legal name	**Age**	**Birthdate (d, m, y)**	**Lives in (municipality & province)**	**Now living with (name of person and relationship to child)**	**Support claimed for child? (YES or NO)**

7. I attach a copy of the existing ❑ court order ❑ agreement

that contains the term(s) to be changed.

8. The existing custody and access arrangements for the child(ren) are as follows:

Child's name	**Custody/Access Arrangement**

Child's name	Custody/Access Arrangement

9. The details of the existing order/agreement with respect to support are as follows:

Date of order or agreement	Present child support payment	Other terms of child support	Present support payment (if any) for spouse
	$ .... *per*		$ .... *per* ....

10. The payment status of the existing order/agreement as of today is as follows:

❑ all payments have been made

❑ arrears are owing as follows:

Child support owed to recipient	Child support owed to other(s) (such as Ministry of Community and Social Services)	Spousal support owed to recipient	Spousal support owed to other(s) (such as Ministry of Community and Social Services)
$	$	$	$ ....

CUSTODY/ACCESS

(Complete only if you are asking for a change in an order for custody or access.)

11. I ask that *(name(s) of party(ies) and/or person(s))* .... have custody of the following child(ren) *(name(s) and birthdate(s) of child(ren))* ....

12. I ask that *(name of party)* .... have access to the following child(ren) *(name(s) and birthdate(s) of child(ren))* .... as follows: *(give details of access)*

OR

13. I ask that *(name(s) of party(ies) and/or person(s))* .... and .... have joint custody of the following child(ren) *(name(s) and birthdate(s) of child(ren))* ....

14. I ask for the following residential/access arrangements for the child(ren):

(name(s) and birthdate(s) of child(ren)) ....

15. The order I am asking the court to make is in the best interests of the child(ren) for the following reasons: *(give details)*

CHILD SUPPORT

(Complete this section only if you are asking for a change in child support.)

16. I am asking to change the child support in the order/agreement because:

❑ The order/agreement was made before the applicable *Child Support Guidelines* came into effect.

❑ The following change in circumstances has taken place: *(Give details of change in circumstances.)*

❑ The parties agree to the termination of the support order/agreement, dated ...., for the following child(ren): *(name(s) and birthdate(s) of child(ren))* ...., as of *(date)* ....

Other: *(give details)*

17. I ask that the child support be changed as follows:

❑ Since the order/agreement for child support was made, a Notice of Recalculation was issued by the online Child Support Service dated .... *(please attach).*

❑ The order/agreement for child support dated .... be terminated for the following child(ren): *(insert name(s) and birthdate(s) of child(ren))* .... effective *(date)* ....

❑ Based on the payor's income of $ .... per year, *(name of party)* .... pay child support to *(name of party)* .... in the amount of $ .... per month for the following child(ren) *(name(s) and birthdate(s) of child(ren))* with payments to start on *(date)* ....

❑ This amount is the table amount listed in the *Child Support Guidelines.*

❑ This amount is more than the table amount listed in the *Child Support Guidelines.*

❑ This amount is less than the table amount listed in the *Child Support Guidelines. (If this box is checked, you must complete paragraph 18.)*

❑ Starting on *(date)* ...., *(name of party)* .... pay to *(name of party)* .... $ .... for the following special or extraordinary expenses:

Child's Name	**Type of Expense**	**Total Amount of Expense**	**Payor's Share**	**Terms of Payment (frequency of payment, date due, etc.)**
		$	$	
		$	$	
		$	$	
		$	$	
		$	$	
		$	$	

18.

❑ I am asking that child support be changed to an amount that is less than the table amount listed in the *Child Support Guidelines*. The reason(s) for my request is/are that:

❑ The parties agree to a different amount.

❑ I have attached a separate sheet to this form that explains why this is an appropriate amount of child support.

❑ The recipient is getting social assistance payments from a public agency whose consent to this arrangement is needed. I am attaching the agency's consent to this form.

❑ As can be seen from paragraphs 6 and 8 above, the parties have shared custody of the child(ren) *(the payor has a child at least 40% of the time).*

❑ I have attached a separate sheet to this form that compares the table amounts from the *Child Support Guidelines* for each of the parties, shows the increased cost of the shared custody arrangement, the financial circumstances of each party and of each child for whom support is claimed.

❑ The parties are agreeing to this arrangement and I have attached a separate sheet to this form that explains why this is an appropriate amount of child support.

❑ As can be seen from paragraphs 6 and 8 above, custody of the children is split between the parties. I have attached a separate sheet to this form that calculates the difference between the amount that each party would otherwise pay to the other under the *Child Support Guidelines.*

❑ A child is 18 or more years old and I attach to this form a separate sheet that calculates the amount of support for this child.

❑ A child contributes to his/her own support and I attach to this form a separate sheet showing the amount of the child's own income and/or assets.

❑ The payor's annual income is over $150,000 and I have attached to this form a separate sheet that calculates the amount of support that I want to be put in an order.

❑ Under the order/agreement, *(name(s) of child(ren))* .... is/are the subject of special provisions that I have detailed on a separate sheet that I have attached to this form.

❑ The payor stands in the place of a parent to *(name(s) of child(ren))* .... and I attach to this form a separate sheet that gives the details of another parent's duty to pay support for this/these child(ren), as well as the details of the calculation of the amount of support requested.

❑ The amount listed in the *Child Support Guidelines* would cause undue hardship to me or to the child(ren) for whom support is claimed. I attach to this form a separate sheet that compares the standards of living of the parties and calculates the amount of support that should be paid.

19. I ask that the outstanding child support owed be paid as follows:

❑ The child support owed to *(name of recipient)* be fixed at $ .... as of *(date)* ....

❑ *(Name of payor)* .... pay to *(name of recipient)* .... $ .... per month, with payments to begin on *(date)* .... until the full amount owing is paid.

❑ The child support owed to *(name of agency or other person)* .... be fixed at $ .... as of *(date)* ....

❑ *(Name of payor)* .... pay to *(name of agency or other person)* .... $ .... per month, with payments to begin on *(date)* .... until the full amount owing is paid.

❑ Other: *(give details)*

SPOUSAL SUPPORT

(Complete only if you are asking for a change in spousal support.)

20. I am asking to change the spousal support in the order/agreement because:

❑ The following change in circumstances has taken place: *(give details of change in circumstances.)*

❑ Spousal support should no longer be paid as of *(date)* .... for the following reasons: *(give details)*

❑ The parties consent to the termination of the spousal support order/agreement, dated ...., as of *(date)* ....

❑ Other *(give details)*:

21. I ask that the spousal support be changed as follows:

❑ The order/agreement for spousal support, dated ...., be terminated effective *(date)* ....

❑ *(Name of party)* .... pay spousal support to *(name of party)* .... in the amount of $ .... per month, effective on *(date)* ....

❑ Other *(give details of the order you want the court to make)*

22. I ask that the outstanding spousal support owed be paid as follows:

❑ The spousal support owed to *(name of recipient)* .... be fixed at $ .... as of *(date)* ....

❑ *(Name of payor)* .... pay to *(name of recipient)* .... $ .... per month, with payments to begin on *(date)* .... until the full amount owing is paid.

❑ The spousal support owed to *(name of agency or other person)* be fixed at $ .... as of *(date)* ....

❑ *(Name of payor)* .... pay to *(name of agency or other person)* .... $ .... per month, with payments to begin on *(date)* .... until the full amount owing is paid.

OTHER

(Complete if applicable.)

23. I ask that the term(s) of the order of Justice *(name of judge)* ...., dated ...., for *(give details)* .... be changed as follows: *(give details of the order you want the court to make)*

24. I ask that the court make this order for the following reasons:

Sworn/Affirmed before me at .... *municipality* in .... *province, state or country* on .... *date* .... *Commissioner for taking affidavits* *(Type or print name below if signature is illegible.)*	.... *Signature* *(This form is to be signed in front of a lawyer, justice of the peace, notary public or commissioner for taking affidavits.)*

PART 2 — INFORMATION FROM SUPPORT PAYOR

DO NOT COMPLETE THIS PART IF THE PARTIES ARE ONLY CONSENTING TO TERMINATE A SUPPORT OBLIGATION OR IF THE MOTION TO CHANGE DOES NOT INCLUDE A CLAIM TO CHANGE CHILD SUPPORT.

My name is (full legal name) ....

I live in (municipality & province) ....

and I swear/affirm that the following is true:

25. I am the support payor in this case.

26. I attach the following financial information about myself:

(a) a copy of every personal income tax return that I filed with Canada Revenue Agency for the 3 most recent taxation years;

(b) a copy of every notice of assessment or re-assessment from Canada Revenue Agency of those returns; and

(c)

❑ *(applies only if you are an employee)* proof of this year's earnings from my employer as required by clause 21(1)(c) of the *Child Support Guidelines*.

❑ *(applies only if you are self-employed, or you are a partner in a partnership or you control a corporation or are a beneficiary under a trust)* the documents listed in clauses 21(1)(d), (e), (f) or (g) of the *Child Support Guidelines*.

27. My total income

❑ will be $ .... for this year;

❑ was $ .... for last year; and

❑ was $ .... for the year before that.

28. On the basis of my annual income, the table amount from the *Child Support Guidelines* for *(number of child(ren))* .... child(ren) is $ .... per month.

29. My financial statement ❑ is attached. ❑ is not attached.

Sworn/Affirmed before me at .... *municipality* in .... *province, state or country* on .... *date* *Commissioner for taking affidavits* *(Type or print name below if signature is illegible.)*	.... *Signature* *(This form is to be signed in front of a lawyer, justice of the peace, notary public or commissioner for taking affidavits.)*

PART 3 — INFORMATION FROM SUPPORT RECIPIENT

DO NOT COMPLETE THIS PART IF THE PARTIES ARE ONLY CONSENTING TO TERMINATE A SUPPORT OBLIGATION OR IF THE MOTION TO CHANGE DOES NOT INCLUDE A CLAIM TO CHANGE CHILD SUPPORT.

My name is (full legal name) ....

I live in (municipality & province) ....

and I swear/affirm that the following is true:

30. I am the support recipient in this case.

Fill in paragraphs 31 and 32 only if:

- *the change for which you are asking is for an amount that is different from the* Child Support Guidelines;
- *the change for which you are asking relates to a child*
  - *over the age of 18 years,*
  - *for whom the payor stands in the place of a parent, or*
  - *with respect to whom the payor has access or physical custody not less than 40% of the time over the course of the year,*
- *each party has custody of one or more children*;
- *the payor's annual income as determined under the guidelines is more than $150,000*;
- *either party claims that an order according to the guidelines would result in undue hardship; or*
- *there is a claim for special or extraordinary expenses.*

31. I attach the following financial information about myself:

(a) a copy of every personal income tax return that I filed with Canada Revenue Agency for the 3 most recent taxation years;

(b) a copy of every notice of assessment or re-assessment from Canada Revenue Agency of those returns; and

(c)

❑ *(applies only if you are an employee)* proof of this year's earnings from my employer as required by clause 21(1)(c) of the *Child Support Guidelines.*

❑ *(applies only if you are self-employed, or you are a partner in a partnership or you control a corporation or are a beneficiary under a trust)* the documents listed in clauses 21(1)(d), (e), (f) or (g) of the *Child Support Guidelines.*

32. My total income

❑ will be $ .... for this year;

❑ was $ .... for last year; and

❑ was $ .... for the year before that.

33. My financial statement ❑ is attached. ❑ is not attached.

Sworn/Affirmed before me at .... *municipality*	.... *Signature* *(This form is to be signed in front of a lawyer, justice of the peace, notary public or commissioner for taking affidavits.)*
in .... *province, state or country*	
on .... *date* .... *Commissioner for taking affidavits* *(Type or print name below if signature is illegible.)*	

April 12, 2016

FORM 15B — RESPONSE TO MOTION TO CHANGE

ONTARIO

Court File Number

.... *(Name of court)*

at .... *Court office address*

Applicant(s)

Full legal name & address for service — street & number, municipality, postal code, telephone & fax numbers and e-mail address (if any).	*Lawyer's name & address — street & number, municipality, postal code, telephone & fax numbers and e-mail address (if any).*

Respondent(s)

Full legal name & address for service — street & number, municipality, postal code, telephone & fax numbers and e-mail address (if any).	*Lawyer's name & address — street & number, municipality, postal code, telephone & fax numbers and e-mail address (if any).*

Assignee (if applicable)

Full legal name & address for service — street & number, municipality, postal code, telephone & fax numbers and e-mail address (if any).	*Lawyer's name & address — street & number, municipality, postal code, telephone & fax numbers and e-mail address (if any).*

PART 1 — GENERAL INFORMATION

My name is (full legal name) ....

I live in (municipality and province) .... *and I swear/affirm that the following is true*:

1. I am the . . . . ❑ applicant ❑ Respondent

2. I am the . . . . ❑ support payor ❑ support recipient

3. This order/agreement . . . . ❑ has never been assigned

❑ has been assigned to

❑ the Ontario Ministry of Community and Social Services

❑ Ontario Works in *(name of location)* ....

❑ the municipality of *(name)* ....

❑ other *(specify)* ....

The details of the assignment are: *(give date of assignment, indicate whether it is still in effect and add any other relevant information known to you.)*

4. ❑ Since the order/agreement for child support was made, a Notice of Recalculation was issued by the online Child Support Service dated .... *(please attach).*

5. ❑ I agree with the information set out in paragraphs 1 through 10 of the Change Information Form (Form 15A), dated ....

❑ I agree with the information set out in paragraphs 1 through 10 of the Change Information Form (Form 15A), dated .... EXCEPT as follows: *(give details of the information with which you do not agree and attach any documents that support your position.)*

6. ❑ I agree with the claims made by *(name of person bringing motion to change)* .... in paragraphs .... of the Motion to Change (Form 15), dated ....

❑ I disagree with the claims made by *(name of person bringing motion to change)* .... in paragraphs .... of the Motion to Change (Form 15), dated ....

7. ❑ I am asking that the motion to change (except for the parts with which I agree) be dismissed with costs.

CLAIM BY RESPONDING PARTY
(COMPLETE ONLY IF YOU ARE ASKING THE COURT TO CHANGE THE EXISTING ORDER OR SUPPORT AGREEMENT.)

8. ❑ I am asking the court to make a change of my own, the details of which are set out below.

CUSTODY/ACCESS
(COMPLETE ONLY IF YOU ARE ASKING FOR A CHANGE IN A CUSTODY OR ACCESS ORDER.)

9. I ask that *(name of party)* .... have custody of the following child(ren): *(name(s) and birthdate(s) of child(ren))*

10. I ask that *(name of party)* .... have access to the following child(ren): *(name(s) and birthdate(s) of child(ren))*

as follows: *(give details of access)*

OR

11. I ask that *(name(s) of party(ies) and/or person(s))* .... and .... have joint custody of the following child(ren): *(name(s) and birthdate(s) of child(ren))*

12. I ask for the following residential/access arrangements for the child(ren): *(include name(s) and birthdate(s) of child(ren))*

13. The order I am asking the court to make is in the best interests of the child(ren) for the following reasons: *(give details)*

CHILD SUPPORT
(COMPLETE THIS SECTION ONLY IF YOU ARE ASKING FOR A CHANGE IN CHILD SUPPORT.)

14. I am asking to change the child support in the order/agreement because:

❑ the order/agreement was made before the applicable *Child Support Guidelines* came into effect.

❑ the following change in circumstances has taken place: *(give details of change in circumstances.)*

❑ the parties agree to the termination of the support order/agreement, dated ...., for the following child(ren): *(name(s) and birthdate(s) of child(ren))*

as of *(date)* ....

❑ Other: *(give details)*

15. I ask that the child support be changed as follows:

❑ The order/agreement for child support, dated ...., be terminated for the following child(ren): *(name(s) and birthdate(s) of child(ren))*

effective *(date)* ....

❑ Based on the payor's annual income of $ ...., *(name of party)* .... pay child support to *(name of party)* .... in the amount of $ .... per month for the following child(ren): *(name(s) and birthdate(s) of child(ren))*

with payments to start on *(date)* ....

❑ This amount is the table amount listed in the *Child Support Guidelines.*

❑ This amount is more than the table amount listed in the *Child Support Guidelines.*

❑ This amount is less than the table amount listed in the *Child Support Guidelines. (If this box is checked, you must complete paragraph 16.)*

❑ Starting on *(date)* ...., *(name of party)* .... pay to *(name of party)* .... $ .... for the following special or extraordinary expenses:

Child's Name	**Type of Expense**	**Total Amount of Expense**	**Payor's Share**	**Terms of payment (frequency of payment, date due, etc.)**
		$	$	
		$	$	
		$	$	
		$	$	
		$	$	

❑ Other: *(give details)*

16. I am asking that child support be changed to an amount that is less than the table amount listed in the *Child Support Guidelines* The reason(s) for my request is/are that:

❑ The parties agree to a different amount.

❑ I have attached a separate sheet to this form that explains why this is an appropriate amount of child support.

❑ The recipient is getting social assistance payments from a public agency whose consent to this arrangement is needed. I am attaching the agency's consent to this form.

❑ The parties have shared custody to the child(ren) *(the payor has a child at least 40% of the time).*

❑ I have attached a separate sheet to this form that compares the table amounts from the *Child Support Guidelines* for each of the parties, shows the increased cost of the shared custody arrangement, the financial circumstances of each party and of each child for whom support is claimed.

❑ The parties are agreeing to this arrangement and I have attached a separate sheet to this form that explains why this is an appropriate amount of child support.

❑ Custody of the children is split between the parties. I have attached a separate sheet to this form that calculates the difference between the amount that each party would otherwise pay to the other under the *Child Support Guidelines*.

❑ A child is 18 or more years old and I attach to this form a separate sheet that calculates the amount of support for this child.

❑ A child contributes to his/her own support and I attach to this form a separate sheet showing the amount of the child's own income and/or assets.

❑ The payor's annual income is over $150,000 and I have attached to this form a separate sheet that calculates the amount of support that I want to be put in an order.

❑ Under the order/agreement, *(name(s) of child(ren))* .... is/are the subject of special provisions that I have detailed on a separate sheet that I have attached to this form.

❑ The payor stands in the place of a parent to *(name(s) of child(ren)* .... and I attach to this form a separate sheet that gives the details of another parent's duty to pay support for this/these child(ren), as well as the details of the calculation of the amount of support requested.

❑ The amount listed in the *Child Support Guidelines* would cause undue hardship to me or to the child(ren) for whom support is claimed. I attach to this form a separate sheet that compares the standards of living of the parties and calculates the amount of support that should be paid.

17. I ask that the outstanding child support owed be paid as follows:

❑ The child support owed to *(name of recipient)* .... be fixed at $ .... as of *(date)* .... and *(name of payor)* .... pay to *(name of recipient)* .... $ .... per month, with payments to begin on *(date)* .... until the full amount owing is paid.

❑ The child support owed to *(name of agency or other person)* .... be fixed at $ .... as of *(date)* .... and *(name of payor)* .... pay to *(name of agency or other person)* .... $ .... per month, with payments to begin on *(date)* .... until the full amount owing is paid.

SPOUSAL SUPPORT
(COMPLETE ONLY IF YOU ARE ASKING FOR A CHANGE IN SPOUSAL SUPPORT.)

18. I am asking to change the spousal support in the order/agreement because:

❑ The following change in circumstances has taken place: *(give details of change in circumstances.)*

❑ Spousal support should no longer be paid as of *(date)* .... for the following reasons: *(give details)*

❑ The parties consent to the termination of the spousal support order/agreement, dated ...., as of *(date)* ....

❑ Other *(specify)*

19. I ask that the spousal support be changed as follows:

❑ The order/agreement for spousal support, dated ...., be terminated effective *(date)* ....

❑ *(Name of party)* .... pay spousal support to *(name of party)* .... in the amount of $ .... per month, effective on *(date)* ....

❑ Other: *(give details of the order you want the court to make)*

20. I ask that the outstanding spousal support owed be paid as follows:

❑ The spousal support owed to *(name of recipient)* .... be fixed at $ .... as of *(date)* ....

❑ *(Name of payor)* .... pay to *(name of recipient)* .... $ .... per month, with payments to begin on *(date)* .... until the full amount owing is paid.

❑ The spousal support owed to *(name of agency or other person)* .... be fixed at $ .... as of *(date)* ....

❑ *(Name of payor)* .... pay to *(name of agency or other person)* .... $ .... per month, with payments to begin on *(date)* .... until the full amount owing is paid.

OTHER
(COMPLETE IF APPLICABLE)

21. I ask that the term of the order of Justice *(name of judge)* ...., dated ...., for *(give details)* .... be changed as follows: *(give details of the order you want the court to make)*

22. I ask that the court make the order set out in paragraph 21 for the following reasons:

23. I ask the court to make the following additional order:

24. I ask the court to make the order set out in paragraph 23 for the following reasons:

Sworn/Affirmed before me at .... *municipality* in .... *province, state, or country* on	.... *Signature* *(This form is to be signed in front of a lawyer, justice of the peace, notary public or commissioner for taking affidavits.)*

date	*Commissioner for taking affidavits (Type or print name below if signature is illegible.)*

PART 2 — INFORMATION FROM SUPPORT PAYOR

DO NOT COMPLETE THIS PART IF THE PARTIES ARE ONLY CONSENTING TO TERMINATE A SUPPORT OBLIGATION OR IF THE MOTION TO CHANGE DOES NOT INCLUDE A CLAIM TO CHANGE CHILD SUPPORT.

My name is (full legal name) ....

I live in (municipality and province) .... *and I swear/affirm that the following is true*:

25. I am the support payor in this case.

26. I attach the following financial information about myself:

(a) a copy of every personal income tax return that I filed with Canada Revenue Agency for the 3 most recent taxation years;

(b) a copy of every notice of assessment or re-assessment from Canada Revenue Agency of those returns; and

(c) ❑ *(applies only if you are an employee)* proof of this year's earnings from my employer as required by clause 21(1)(c) of the *Child Support Guidelines.*

❑ *(applies only if you are self-employed, or you are a partner in a partnership or you control a corporation or are a beneficiary under a trust)* the documents listed in clauses 21(1)(d), (e), (f) or (g) of the *Child Support Guidelines.*

27. My total income

❑ will be $ .... for this year;

❑ was $ .... for last year; and

❑ was $ .... for the year before that.

28. On the basis of my annual income, the table amount from the *Child Support Guidelines* for *(number of children)* .... child(ren) is $ .... per month.

29. My financial statement . . . . is attached. .... is not attached.

Sworn/Affirmed before me at .... *municipality*	.... *Signature*
in .... *province, state, or country*	*(This form is to be signed in front of a lawyer, justice of the peace, notary public or commissioner for taking affidavits.)*
on	

date	*Commissioner for taking affidavits (Type or print name below if signature is illegible.)*

PART 3 — INFORMATION FROM SUPPORT RECIPIENT

DO NOT COMPLETE THIS PART IF THE PARTIES ARE ONLY CONSENTING TO TERMINATE A SUPPORT OBLIGATION OR IF THE MOTION TO CHANGE DOES NOT INCLUDE A CLAIM TO CHANGE CHILD SUPPORT.

My name is (full legal name) ....

I live in (municipality and province) .... *and I swear/affirm that the following is true*:

30. I am the support recipient in this case.

Fill in paragraphs 30 and 31 only if:

- the change for which you are asking is for an amount that is different from the *Child Support Guidelines*;
- the change for which you are asking relates to a child
  - over the age of 18 years,
  - for whom the payor stands in the place of a parent, or
  - with respect to whom the payor has access or physical custody not less than 40% of the time over the course of the year;
- each party has custody of one or more children;
- the payor's annual income as determined under the guidelines is more than $150,000;
- either party claims that an order according to the guidelines would result in undue hardship; or
- there is a claim for special or extraordinary expenses.

31. I attach the following financial information about myself:

(a) a copy of every personal income tax return that I filed with Canada Revenue Agency for the 3 most recent taxation years;

(b) a copy of every notice of assessment or re-assessment from Canada Revenue Agency of those returns; and

(c) ❑ *(applies only if you are an employee)* proof of this year's earnings from my employer as required by clause 21(1)(c) of the *Child Support Guidelines*.

❑ *(applies only if you are self-employed, or you are a partner in a partnership or you control a corporation or are a beneficiary under a trust)* the documents listed in clauses 21(1)(d), (e), (f) or (g) of the *Child Support Guidelines*.

32. My total income

❑ will be $ .... for this year;

❑ was $ .... for last year; and

❑ was $ .... for the year before that.

33. My financial statement . . . . ❑ is attached. ❑ is not attached.

Sworn/Affirmed before me at .... *municipality* in .... *province, state, or country* on .... *date* .... *Commissioner for taking affidavits (Type or print name below if signature is illegible.)*	.... *Signature* *(This form is to be signed in front of a lawyer, justice of the peace, notary public or commissioner for taking affidavits.)*

April 12, 2016

FORM 15C — CONSENT MOTION TO CHANGE

ONTARIO

Court File Number

.... *(Name of court)*

at .... *Court office address*

Applicant(s)

Full legal name & address for service — street & number, municipality, postal code, telephone & fax numbers and e-mail address (if any).	*Lawyer's name & address — street & number, municipality, postal code, telephone & fax numbers and e-mail address (if any).*

Applicant(s)

Respondent(s)

Full legal name & address for service — street & number, municipality, postal code, telephone & fax numbers and e-mail address (if any).	*Lawyer's name & address — street & number, municipality, postal code, telephone & fax numbers and e-mail address (if any).*

Assignee (if applicable)

Full legal name & address for service — street & number, municipality, postal code, telephone & fax numbers and e-mail address (if any).	*Lawyer's name & address — street & number, municipality, postal code, telephone & fax numbers and e-mail address (if any).*

YOU MAY USE THIS FORM IF YOU ARE SEEKING TO CHANGE AN ORDER OR AGREEMENT THAT HAS BEEN RECALCULATED BY THE ONLINE CHILD SUPPORT SERVICE. YOU MUST SERVE A COPY OF THIS FORM ON THE FAMILY RESPONSIBILITY OFFICE IF THE ORDER YOU RECALCULATED WAS MADE UNDER THE DIVORCE ACT *AND THE RECALCULATION WAS COMPLETED WITHIN THE LAST 35 DAYS.*

YOU MAY NOT USE THIS FORM TO CHANGE A NOTICE OF CALCULATION MADE BY THE ONLINE CHILD SUPPORT SERVICE.

EACH OF YOU SHOULD CONSIDER GETTING A LAWYER'S ADVICE BEFORE SIGNING THIS CONSENT.

IF YOU ARE SEEKING TO CHANGE A SUPPORT ORDER OR AGREEMENT THAT HAS BEEN ASSIGNED TO A PERSON OR AGENCY, YOU MUST SERVE ALL DOCUMENTS ON THE ASSIGNEE AND OBTAIN THE ASSIGNEE'S CONSENT TO ANY CHANGE THAT MAY AFFECT THE ASSIGNEE'S FINANCIAL INTEREST. FAILURE TO OBTAIN THE ASSIGNEE'S CONSENT MAY RESULT IN A COURT SETTING ASIDE AN ORDER AND ORDERING COSTS AGAINST THE PARTY WHO DID NOT PROVIDE NOTICE. IT IS THE RESPONSIBILITY OF THE PERSON SEEKING THE CHANGE TO DETERMINE IF THE ORDER HAS BEEN ASSIGNED. YOU CAN DO THIS BY SUBMITTING A CONFIRMATION OF ASSIGNMENT FORM. THE CONFIRMATION OF ASSIGNMENT FORM IS AVAILABLE THROUGH THE MINISTRY OF THE ATTORNEY GENERAL WEBSITE OR AT THE COURT OFFICE.

1. We know that each of us has the right to get advice from his or her own lawyer about this case and understand that signing this consent may result in a final court order that will be enforced.

2. ❑ We have filed/are filing Financial Statements (Form 13 or 13.1) with the court.

❑ We have agreed not to file any Financial Statements with the court.

3. ❑ We have attached the existing final order or support agreement and ask the court to make an order that changes that order or agreement as set out below.

❑ Since the order/agreement for child support was made, a Notice of Recalculation was issued by the online Child Support Service dated .... *(please attach).*

CUSTODY/ACCESS (COMPLETE ONLY IF THE PARTIES ARE ASKING FOR A CHANGE IN A CUSTODY OR ACCESS ORDER.)

4. ❑ We agree that *(name(s) of person(s) or party(ies))* .... shall have custody of the following child(ren):

Child's full legal name	**Birthdate (d, m, y)**	**Age**	**Sex**

❑ We agree that *(name(s) of person(s) or party(ies))* .... shall have access to: *(name(s) and birthdate(s) of child(ren))* .... as follows: *(give details of access order)*

....

OR

5.

❑ We agree that *(names of parties or persons)* .... and .... shall have joint custody of the following child(ren):

Child's full legal name	**Birthdate (d, m, y)**	**Age**	**Sex**

❑ We agree that the residential/access arrangements for the child(ren) *(name(s) and birthdate(s) of child(ren))* .... shall be as follows:

....

CHILD SUPPORT
(COMPLETE ONLY IF THE PARTIES ARE ASKING FOR A CHANGE IN CHILD SUPPORT.)

6. We agree to an order for child support that is:

❑ equal to or more than what is in the *Child Support Guidelines.*

❑ none (no child support).

❑ less than what is in the *Child Support Guidelines* for the following reasons:

....

7. The party receiving support ❑ is ❑ is not receiving social assistance.

8. We agree that child support shall be as follows:

❑ Based on the payor's annual income of $ ...., *(name of party)* .... shall pay to *(name of party)* .... $ .... per month for the following child(ren) *(name(s) and birthdate(s) of child(ren))* .... with payments to begin on *(date)* ....

❑ Starting on *(date)* ...., *(name of party)* .... shall pay *(name of party)* .... $ .... for the following special or extraordinary expenses:

Child's name	**Type of expense**	**Total Amount of Expense**	**Payor's Share**	**Terms of Payment (frequency of payment, date due, etc.)**
		$	$	
		$	$	
		$	$	
		$	$	
		$	$	

❑ *(Complete only if the parties are agreeing to special or extraordinary expenses.)* The recipient's total annual income is $ ....

❑ The order or agreement for child support, with respect to the child(ren) *(name(s) and birthdate(s) of child(ren))* ...., dated ...., shall be terminated as of *(date)* ....

Complete if applicable:

9. We also agree that the outstanding child support owed be paid off as follows:

❑ The child support owed to *(name of recipient)* .... shall be fixed at $ .... as of *(date)* .... and *(name of payor)* .... shall pay *(name of recipient)* .... $ .... per month, with payments to begin on *(date)* .... until the full amount owing has been paid.

❑ The child support owed to *(name of agency or other person)* .... shall be fixed at $ .... as of *(date)* .... and *(name of payor)* .... shall pay *(name of agency or other person)* .... $ .... per month, with payments to begin on *(date)* .... until the full amount owing has been paid.

SPOUSAL SUPPORT
(COMPLETE ONLY IF THE PARTIES ARE SEEKING A CHANGE IN SPOUSAL SUPPORT.)

10. We agree that the spousal support payments should be as follows:

❑ *(Name of party)* .... shall pay to *(name of party)* .... the amount of $ .... per month, with payments to begin on *(date)* ....

❑ The order or agreement for spousal support, dated ...., shall be terminated as of *(date)* ....

11. We agree that the outstanding spousal support owed be paid off as follows:

❑ The spousal support owed to *(name of recipient)* .... shall be fixed at $ .... as of *(date)* .... and *(name of payor)* .... shall pay *(name of recipient)* .... $ .... per month, with payments to begin on *(date)* .... until the full amount owing has been paid.

❑ The spousal support owed to *(name of agency or other person)* .... shall be fixed at $......... as of *(date)* .... and *(name of payor)* .... shall pay *(name of recipient)* .... $ .... per month, with payments to begin on *(date)* .... until the full amount owing has been paid.

NOTE: If money is owed to an agency or other person (an assignee), a representative of that agency or the other person must consent to the change in the order.

OTHER
(COMPLETE IF APPLICABLE.)

12. We agree that paragraph(s) *(specify which paragraphs of the order are to be changed)* .... of the order of Justice *(name of judge)* ...., dated ...., shall be changed as follows: *(give details of the order you want the court to make)*

....

The parties do not need to sign this consent at the same time. Each party must sign in the presence of his or her witness who shall sign immediately after that party.

NOTE: The witness cannot be one of the parties. If the witness does not know the party, the witness should see identification that proves that the person signing the consent is the same person who is a party to the consent.

.... *Applicant's signature*	.... *Respondent's signature*
.... *Date of applicant's signature*	.... *Date of respondent's signature*
.... *Signature of witness*	.... *Signature of witness*
.... *Type or print name of witness to applicant's signature*	.... *Type or print name of witness to respondent's signature*
.... *Address of witness*	.... *Address of witness*
.... *Telephone number of witness*	.... *Telephone number of witness*

ASSIGNEE'S CONSENT

....	....
Signature of person authorized to sign on behalf of assignee	*Date of signature*

....

Print name and title of person signing the consent

....	....
Witness's signature	*Name of witness (type or print legibly)*

April 12, 2016

FORM 15D — CONSENT MOTION TO CHANGE CHILD SUPPORT

ONTARIO

Court File Number

.... *(Name of court)*

at .... *Court office address* ....

Applicant(s)

Full legal name & address for service — street & number, municipality, postal code, telephone & fax numbers and e-mail address (if any).	*Lawyer's name & address — street & number, municipality, postal code, telephone & fax numbers and e-mail address (if any).*

Respondent(s)

Full legal name & address for service — street & number, municipality, postal code, telephone & fax numbers and e-mail address (if any).	*Lawyer's name & address — street & number, municipality, postal code, telephone & fax numbers and e-mail address (if any).*

Respondent(s)

Assignee (if applicable)

Full legal name & address for service — street & number, municipality, postal code, telephone & fax numbers and e-mail address (if any).	*Lawyer's name & address — street & number, municipality, postal code, telephone & fax numbers and e-mail address (if any).*

Instructions to the Parties:

IF YOU ARE SEEKING TO CHANGE A CHILD SUPPORT TERM IN AN AGREEMENT THAT HAS NOT ALREADY BEEN FILED WITH THE COURT PURSUANT TO SECTION 35 OF THE FAMILY LAW ACT, *YOU MUST FILE THE AGREEMENT AND FORM 26B (Affidavit for Filing Domestic Contract with Court) BEFORE BRINGING THIS MOTION TO CHANGE.*

YOU MAY USE THIS FORM IF YOU ARE SEEKING TO CHANGE AN ORDER OR AGREEMENT THAT HAS BEEN RECALCULATED BY THE ONLINE CHILD SUPPORT SERVICE. YOU MUST SERVE A COPY OF THIS FORM ON THE FAMILY RESPONSIBILITY OFFICE IF THE ORDER YOU RECALCULATED WAS MADE UNDER THE DIVORCE ACT *AND THE RECALCULATION WAS COMPLETED WITHIN THE LAST 35 DAYS.*

YOU MAY NOT USE THIS FORM TO CHANGE A NOTICE OF CALCULATION MADE BY THE ONLINE CHILD SUPPORT SERVICE.

EACH OF YOU SHOULD CONSIDER GETTING A LAWYER'S ADVICE BEFORE SIGNING THIS CONSENT.

IF YOU ARE SEEKING TO CHANGE A CHILD SUPPORT ORDER OR AGREEMENT THAT HAS BEEN ASSIGNED TO A PERSON OR AGENCY, YOU MUST OBTAIN THE ASSIGNEE'S CONSENT TO ANY CHANGE THAT MAY AFFECT THE ASSIGNEE'S FINANCIAL INTEREST. FAILURE TO OBTAIN THE ASSIGNEE'S CONSENT MAY RESULT IN A COURT SETTING ASIDE AN ORDER AND ORDERING COSTS AGAINST THE PARTY WHO DID NOT PROVIDE NOTICE. IT IS THE RESPONSIBILITY OF THE PERSON SEEKING THE CHANGE TO DETERMINE IF THE ORDER HAS BEEN ASSIGNED. YOU CAN DO THIS BY SUBMITTING A CONFIRMATION OF ASSIGNMENT FORM. THE CONFIRMATION OF ASSIGNMENT FORM IS AVAILABLE THROUGH THE MINISTRY OF THE ATTORNEY GENERAL WEBSITE OR AT THE COURT OFFICE.

TO THE COURT:

This motion to change child support is filed by the parties with the consent of the applicant and respondent and, if applicable, the assignee.

We ask the court to make the order requested in this motion by relying on this form only.

1. We know that each of us has the right to get advice from his or her own lawyer about this case and understand that signing this consent may result in a final court order that will be enforced.

2. We have attached the existing agreement or order for child support and ask the court to make an order that changes that order or agreement as set out below.

❑ Since the order/agreement for child support was made, a Notice of Recalculation was issued by the online Child Support Service dated .... *(please attach).*

Check the following box(es) that apply:

3. The total annual income of the person paying support is $ ....

The payor ❑ is ❑ is not self-employed.

4. Proof of income for the payor was provided to the recipient by: *(check at least one)*

❑ Most recent income tax return

❑ Most recent notice of income tax assessment

❑ Current pay stub

❑ Business records

❑ Other *(provide details)*

5. ❑ *(Name of party)* .... shall pay to *(name of party)* .... $ .... per month for the following child(ren) *(name(s) and birthdate(s) of child(ren))* .... with payments to begin on *(date)* ....

6. ❑ This amount is the table amount listed in the *Child Support Guidelines.*

❑ This amount is more than the table amount listed in the *Child Support Guidelines.*

❑ This amount is less than the table amount listed in the *Child Support Guidelines* for the following reasons: *(give details)*

7. Starting on *(date)* ...., *(name of party)* .... shall pay *(name of party)* .... $ .... for the following special or extraordinary expenses:

Child's Name	**Type of Expense**	**Total Amount of Expense**	**Payor's Share**	**Terms of Payment (frequency of payment, date due, etc.)**
		$	$	
		$	$	
		$	$	
		$	$	
		$	$	

(Complete paragraphs 8 and 9 only if the parties are agreeing to special or extraordinary expenses.)

8. ❑ The recipient's total annual income is $ ....

9. ❑ Proof of income for the recipient was provided to the payor by: *(check at least one)*

❑ Most recent income tax return

❑ Most recent notice of income tax assessment

❑ Current pay stub

❑ Business records

❑ Other *(provide details)*

10. ❑ The order or agreement for child support, with respect to the child(ren) *(name(s) and birthdate(s) of child(ren))* ...., dated ...., should be terminated as of *(date)* ....

Complete applicable paragraphs if there is outstanding child support owing

11. ❑ The child support owed to *(name of recipient)* .... shall be fixed at $ .... as of *(date)* ....

12. ❑ *(Name of payor)* .... shall pay *(name of recipient)* .... $ .... per month, with payments to begin on *(date)* .... until the full amount owing is paid.

13. ❑ The child support owed to *(name of agency or other person)* .... shall be fixed at $ .... as of *(date)* ....

14. ❑ *(Name of payor)* .... shall pay to *(name of agency or other person)* .... $ .... per month, with payments to begin on *(date)* .... until the full amount owing is paid.

NOTE: If money is owed to an agency or other person (an assignee), a representative of that agency or the other person must consent to the change in the order.

The parties do not need to sign this consent at the same time. Each party must sign in the presence of his or her witness who shall sign immediately after that party.

NOTE: The witness cannot be one of the parties. If the witness does not know the party, the witness should see identification that proves that the person signing the consent is the same person who is a party to the consent.

.... *Applicant's signature*	.... *Respondent's signature*
.... *Date of applicant's signature*	.... *Date of respondent's signature*
.... *Signature of witness*	.... *Signature of witness*
.... *Type or print name of witness to applicant's signature*	.... *Type or print name of witness to respondent's signature*
.... *Address of witness*	.... *Address of witness*
.... *Telephone number of witness*	.... *Telephone number of witness*

ASSIGNEE'S CONSENT

.... *Signature of person authorized to sign on behalf of assignee*	.... *Date of signature*

....

Print name and title of person signing the consent

....

Witness's signature *Name of witness (type or print legibly)*

April 12, 2016

FORM 17 — CONFERENCE NOTICE

[Repealed O. Reg. 76/06, s. 15.]

[Editor's Note: Forms 4 to 39 of the Family Law Rules have been repealed by O. Reg. 76/06, effective May 1, 2006. Pursuant to Family Law Rule 1(9), when a form is referred to by number, the reference is to the form with that number that is described in the Table of Forms at the end of these rules and which is available at www.ontariocourtforms.on.ca. For your convenience, the government form as published on this website is reproduced below.]

Court File Number

____

(Name of court)

Form 17: Conference Notice

at ______________________________

Court office address

Applicant(s)

Full legal name & address for service — street & number, municipality, postal code, telephone & fax numbers and e-mail address (if any).	*Lawyer's name & address — street & number, municipality, postal code, telephone & fax numbers and e-mail address (if any).*

Respondent(s)

Full legal name & address for service — street & number, municipality, postal code, telephone & fax numbers and e-mail address (if any).	*Lawyer's name & address — street & number, municipality, postal code, telephone & fax numbers and e-mail address (if any).*
Name & address of Children's Lawyer's agent (street & number, municipality, postal code, telephone & fax numbers and e-mail address (if any)) and name of person represented.	

TO: (name of party or parties or lawyer(s))

A ❑ *CASE CONFERENCE* ❑ *SETTLEMENT CONFERENCE* ❑ *TRIAL MANAGEMENT CONFERENCE*

WILL BE HELD at *(place of conference)* ....
at .... *a.m./p.m. on (date)* ....
The conference has been arranged at the request of

❑ the applicant ❑ the respondent
❑ the case management judge ❑ *(Other; specify.)* ....

to deal with the following issues:
You must participate at that time and date by

❑ coming to court at the address set out above.
❑ video-conference or telephone at *(location of video terminal or telephone)* ....

as agreed under arrangements already made by *(name of person)* .... for video/telephone conferencing

IF YOU DO NOT PARTICIPATE AS SET OUT ABOVE, THE CASE MAY GO ON WITHOUT YOU OR THE COURT MAY DISMISS THE CASE.

....
Date of signature *Signature of clerk of the court*

NOTE: The party requesting the conference (or, if the conference is not requested by a party, the applicant) must serve and file a case conference brief (Form 17A or 17B), settlement conference brief (Form 17C or 17D) or trial management conference brief (Form 17E) not later than seven days before the date scheduled for the conference. The other party must serve and file a brief not later than four days before the conference date. Each party must also file a confirmation (Form 14C) not later than 2 p.m. two days before the conference.

September 1, 2005

FORM 17A — CASE CONFERENCE BRIEF — GENERAL

[Repealed O. Reg. 76/06, s. 15.]

[Editor's Note: Forms 4 to 39 of the Family Law Rules have been repealed by O. Reg. 76/06, effective May 1, 2006. Pursuant to Family Law Rule 1(9), when a form is referred to by number, the reference is to the form with that number that is described in the Table of Forms at the end of these rules and which is available at www.ontariocourtforms.on.ca. For your convenience, the government form as published on this website is reproduced below.]

ONTARIO

Court File Number ....

.... *(Name of court)*

at .... *Court office address*

Name of party filing this brief	**Date of case conference**

Applicant(s)

Full legal name & address for service — street & number, municipality, postal code, telephone & fax numbers and e-mail address (if any).	*Lawyer's name & address — street & number, municipality, postal code, telephone & fax numbers and e-mail address (if any).*

Respondent(s)

Full legal name & address for service — street & number, municipality, postal code, telephone & fax numbers and e-mail address (if any).	*Lawyer's name & address — street & number, municipality, postal code, telephone & fax numbers and e-mail address (if any).*

Name & address of Children's Lawyer's agent (street & number, municipality, postal code, telephone & fax numbers and e-mail address (if any)) and name of person represented.

PART 1: — FAMILY FACTS

1. APPLICANT: . . . . Age: .... Birthdate: *(d, m, y)* ....

2. RESPONDENT: . . . . Age: .... Birthdate: *(d, m, y)* ....

3. RELATIONSHIP DATES:

- ❑ Married on *(date)* ....
- ❑ Separated on *(date)* ....
- ❑ Started living together on *(date)* ....
- ❑ Never lived together
- ❑ Other *(Explain.)* ....

4. The basic information about the child(ren) is as follows:

Child's full legal name	**Age**	**Birthdate (d, m, y)**	**Grade/Year and school**	**Now living with**

PART 2: — ISSUES

5. What are the issues in this case that *HAVE* been settled:

❑ child custody	❑ spousal support	❑ possession of home
❑ access	❑ child support	❑ equalization of net family property
❑ restraining order	❑ ownership of property	

❑ other *(Specify.)* ....

6. What are the issues in this case that have *NOT* yet been settled:

❑ child custody	❑ spousal support	❑ possession of home
❑ access	❑ child support	❑ equalization of net family property *(Attach Net Family Property Statement, Form 13B)*
❑ restraining order	❑ ownership of property	

❑ other *(Specify.)* ....

7. If child or spousal support is an issue, give the income of the parties:

Applicant: . . . . $ .... per year for the year 20..........

Respondent: . . . . $ .... per year for the year 20..........

8. Have you explored any ways to settle the issues that are still in dispute in this case?

❑ No. . . . . ❑ Yes. *(Give details.)* ....

9. Have any of the issues that have been settled been turned into a court order or a written agreement?

❑ No.
❑ Yes. ❑ an order dated ....
❑ a written agreement that is attached.

10. Have the parents attended a family law or parenting education session?

❑ No. (Should they attend one? ....)

❑ Yes. *(Give details.)* ....

PART 3: — ISSUES FOR THIS CASE CONFERENCE

11. What are the issues for this case conference? What are the important facts for this case conference?

....
....
....
....
....
....

....

12. What is your proposal to resolve these issues? ....

13. Do you want the court to make a temporary or final order at the case conference about any of these issues?

❑ No. . . . . ❑ Yes. *(Give details.)* ....

PART 4: — FINANCIAL INFORMATION

NOTE: If a claim for support has been made in this case, you must serve and file a new financial statement (Form 13 or 13.1), if it is different from the one filed in the continuing record or if the one in the continuing record is more than 30 days old. If there are minor changes but no major changes in your financial statement, you can serve and file an affidavit with details of the changes instead of a new financial statement. If you have not yet filed a financial statement in the continuing record, you must do it now. The page/tab number of the financial statement in the continuing record is ....

14. If a claim is being made for child support and a claim is made for special expenses under the child support guidelines, give details of those expenses or attach additional information.

....

....

....

....

....

....

....

....

....

....

15. If a claim is made for child support and you claim that the Child Support Guidelines table amount should not be ordered, briefly outline the reasons here or attach an additional page.

....

....

....

....

....

....

....

....

....

....

PART 5: — PROCEDURAL ISSUES

16. If custody or access issues are not yet settled:

(a) Is a custody or access assessment needed?

❑ No. . . . . ❑ Yes. *(Give names of possible assessors.)*
....

(b) Does a child or a parent under 18 years of age need legal representation from the Office of the Children's Lawyer?

❑ No. . . . . ❑ Yes. *(Give details and reasons.)*
....

17. Does any party need an order for the disclosure of documents, the questioning of witnesses, a property valuation or any other matter in this case?

❑ No. . . . . ❑ Yes. *(Give details.)* ....

18. Are any other procedural orders needed?

❑ No. . . . . ❑ Yes. *(Give details.)* ....

19. Have all the persons who should be parties in this case been added as parties?

❑ Yes. . . . . ❑ No. *(Who needs to be added?)*
....

20. Are there issues that may require expert evidence or a report?

❑ No. . . . . . . ❑ Yes. *(If yes, provide details such as: the type of expert evidence; whether the parties will be retaining a joint expert; who the expert will be; who will be paying the expert; how long it will take to obtain a report, etc.)*

....

....

....

21. Are there any other issues that should be reviewed at the case conference?

❑ No. . . . . ❑ Yes. *(Give details.)* ....

.... *Date of party's signature*	.... *Signature of party*
.... *Date of lawyer's signature*	.... *Signature of party's lawyer*

November 15, 2009

FORM 17B — CASE CONFERENCE BRIEF FOR ❏ PROTECTION APPLICATION ❏ STATUS REVIEW

[Repealed O. Reg. 76/06, s. 15.]

[Editor's Note: Forms 4 to 39 of the Family Law Rules have been repealed by O. Reg. 76/06, effective May 1, 2006. Pursuant to Family Law Rule 1(9), when a form is referred to by number, the reference is to the form with that number that is described in the Table of Forms at the end of these rules and which is available at www.ontariocourtforms.on.ca. For your convenience, the government form as published on this website is reproduced below.]

Court File Number

ONTARIO

.... *(Name of court)*

at .... *Court office address*

Name of party filing this brief	**Date of case conference**

Applicant(s)

Full legal name & address for service — street & number, municipality, postal code, telephone & fax numbers and e-mail address (if any).	*Lawyer's name & address — street & number, municipality, postal code, telephone & fax numbers and e-mail address (if any).*

Respondent(s)

Full legal name & address for service — street & number, municipality, postal code, telephone & fax numbers and e-mail address (if any).	*Lawyer's name & address — street & number, municipality, postal code, telephone & fax numbers and e-mail address (if any).*

Respondent(s)

Full legal name & address for service — street & number, municipality, postal code, telephone & fax numbers and e-mail address (if any).	*Lawyer's name & address — street & number, municipality, postal code, telephone & fax numbers and e-mail address (if any).*

Respondent(s)

Respondent(s)

Full legal name & address for service — street & number, municipality, postal code, telephone & fax numbers and e-mail address (if any).	*Lawyer's name & address — street & number, municipality, postal code, telephone & fax numbers and e-mail address (if any).*

Name & address of Children's Lawyer's agent (street & number, municipality, postal code, telephone & fax numbers and e-mail address (if any)) and name of person represented.

PART 1: — BASIC INFORMATION ABOUT THE CHILD(REN)

1. The basic information about the child(ren) is as follows:

Child's full legal name	**Age**	**Birthdate (d, m, y)**	**Full legal name of every parent of child and relationship to child (See subsection 74(1) of the *Child, Youth and Family Services Act, 2017.*)**	**Date child was brought to a place of safety**

2. Where is the child living at the time of this conference?

....

3. What is the total length of time that any child less than six years old has been in care? *(Attach more detail if necessary.)*

Name of child .... Total length of time ....

4. What is the total length of time any child six years old or more has been in care? *(Attach more details if necessary.)*

Name of child .... Total length of time ....

5. Is any child a First Nations, Inuk or Métis person?

❑ No. ❑ Yes.

5.a If the answer to question 6 is "Yes" and the child is a First Nations, Inuk or Métis person, give the name, address and telephone number of the representative chosen by each of the child's bands and First Nations, Inuit or Métis communities to which the child is a member or identifies with.

....

6. If the child was brought to a place of safety before the hearing, name the person from whose care and the place from which the child was removed.

....

7. Has everyone who is entitled to notice in this case been served?

❑ Yes. ❑ No. *(Do you want an order for substituted service on any person or an order that service is not required? Give details.)*

....

PART 2: — OUTSTANDING ISSUES

(Complete only Part 2A — Protection Application or Part 2B — Status Review, not both)

Part 2A — Protection Application

8. The parties have reached an agreement or the court has made an order on the following issues:

❑ findings of fact set out in Part 1 above

❑ temporary care and custody ❑ access

❑ finding that child is in need of protection

❑ placing the child(ren) with *(name of person)* .... for .... months under supervision.

❑ interim society care for .... months.

❑ extended society care with access

❑ extended society care without access

❑ *(Other. Specify.)*

The details of this agreement or order are:

....

9. What are the issues in this case that have *NOT* yet been resolved?

❑ findings of fact set out in Part 1 above

❑ temporary care and custody ❑ access

❑ finding that child is in need of protection

❑ placing the child(ren) with *(name of person)* .... for .... months under supervision.

❑ interim society care for .... months.

❑ extended society care with access

❑ extended society care without access

❑ *(Other. Specify.)*

Part 2B — Status Review

10. The parties have reached an agreement or the court has made an order on the following issues:

❑ temporary care and custody . . . . ❑ access

❑ placing the child(ren) with *(name of person)* .... for .... months under supervision.

❑ interim society care for .... months

❑ extended society care with access

❑ extended society care without access

❑ *(Other. Specify.)*

The details of this agreement or order are:

....

11. What are the issues in this case that have *NOT* yet been resolved?

❑ temporary care and custody . . . . ❑ access

❑ placing the child(ren) with *(name of person)* .... for .... months under supervision.

❑ interim society care for .... months.

❑ extended society care with access

❑ extended society care without access

❑ *(Other. Specify.)*

PART 3: — ISSUES FOR THIS CASE CONFERENCE

12. Have you explored any ways to settle the issues that are still in dispute in this case?

❑ No. . . . . ❑ Yes. *(Give details.)*

....

13. What are the issues for this case conference? What are the important facts for this case conference?

....

14. What is your proposal to resolve these issues?

....

15. Are any of the issues in this case urgent?

❑ . . . . No. ❑ Yes. *(Identify the issues and give details of why the issues are urgent.)*

....

PART 4: — PROCEDURAL ISSUES

16. Does any party or the Children's Lawyer want an assessment?

❑ No. . . . . . ❑ Yes. *(Give names of possible assessors and the type of assessment recommended.)*

....

17. Do the other parties agree with the proposal for an assessment?

❑ No. . . . . ❑ Yes. *(Give names of possible assessors, the type of assessment, who will be assessed, and how long it will take.)*

....

18. Have you served a plan of care on the other parties?

❑ No. . . . . ❑ Yes. *(A copy of the plan of care must be filed in the continuing record.)* The plan can be found at tab/page .... of the continuing record.

19. Does a child or a parent under 18 years of age need legal representation from the Office of the Children's Lawyer?

❑ No. . . . . ❑ Yes. *(Give details and reasons.)*

....

20. Do you want an order for the disclosure of documents, the questioning of witnesses or any other matter in this case?

❑ No. . . . . ❑ Yes. *(Give details.)*

....

21. Are there issues that may require expert evidence or a report?

❑ No. . . . . . . ❑ Yes. *(If yes, provide details such as: the type of expert evidence; whether the parties will be retaining a joint expert; who the expert will be; who will be paying the expert; how long it will take to obtain a report, etc.)*

....

22. Are there any other issues that should be reviewed at the case conference?

❑ No. . . . . ❑ Yes. *(Give details.)*

....

....	....
Date of party's signature	*Signature of party*
....	....
Date of lawyer's signature	*Signature of party's lawyer*

March 1, 2018

FORM 17C — SETTLEMENT CONFERENCE BRIEF — GENERAL

[Repealed O. Reg. 76/06, s. 15.]

[Editor's Note: Forms 4 to 39 of the Family Law Rules have been repealed by O. Reg. 76/06, effective May 1, 2006. Pursuant to Family Law Rule 1(9), when a form is referred to by number, the reference is to the form with that number that is described in the Table of Forms at the end of these rules and which is available at www.ontariocourtforms.on.ca. For your convenience, the government form as published on this website is reproduced below.]

ONTARIO

Court File Number ....

.... *(Name of court)*

at .... *Court office address*

Name of party filing this brief	**Date of settlement conference**

Applicant(s)

Full legal name & address for service — street & number, municipality, postal code, telephone & fax numbers and e-mail address (if any).	*Lawyer's name & address — street & number, municipality, postal code, telephone & fax numbers and e-mail address (if any).*

Respondent(s)

Full legal name & address for service — street & number, municipality, postal code, telephone & fax numbers and e-mail address (if any).	*Lawyer's name & address — street & number, municipality, postal code, telephone & fax numbers and e-mail address (if any).*

Name & address of Children's Lawyer's agent (street & number, municipality, postal code, telephone & fax numbers and e-mail address (if any)) and name of person represented.

PART 1: — FAMILY FACTS

1. APPLICANT: . . . . Age: .... Birthdate: *(d, m, y)* ....

2. RESPONDENT: . . . . Age: .... Birthdate: *(d, m, y)* ....

3. RELATIONSHIP DATES:

❑ Married on *(date)* ....

❑ Separated on *(date)* ....

❑ Started living together on *(date)* ....

❑ Never lived together

❑ Other *(Explain.)* ....

4. The basic information about the child(ren) is as follows:

Child's full legal name	**Age**	**Birthdate (d, m, y)**	**Grade/Year and school**	**Now living with**

PART 2: — ISSUES

If you want to refer to anything else that is not in the continuing record and that does not need to be in the continuing record, you must attach it to this brief. In particular, attach any valuations or experts' reports that are not in the record.

If you want to refer to a report or document that has already been filed in the continuing record, just give the page number(s) or tab number of that document in the continuing record.

If you are updating a document that is already in the continuing record, you must file the updated document in the continuing record and then refer to it by the page number(s) or tab numbers of that update in the continuing record.

5. What are the issues in this case that *HAVE* been settled:

❑ child custody
❑ access
❑ restraining order
❑ spousal support
❑ child support
❑ ownership of property
❑ possession of home
❑ equalization of net family property

❑ other *(Specify.)* ....

6. What are the issues in this case that have *NOT* yet been settled:

❑ child custody
❑ access
❑ restraining order
❑ spousal support
❑ child support
❑ ownership of property
❑ possession of home
❑ equalization of net family property *(Attach Net Family Property Statement, Form 13B)*

❑ other *(Specify.)* ....

7. If child or spousal support is an issue, give the income of the parties:

Applicant: . . . . $ .... per year for the year 20..........

Respondent: . . . . $ .... per year for the year 20..........

8. What are the issues for this settlement conference? What are the important facts for this settlement conference?

....

....

....

....

....

9. Do you want the court to make a temporary or final order about any of these issues at the settlement conference?

❑ No . . . . ❑ Yes. *(Give details.)* ....

10. Have any of these issues that have been settled been turned into a court order or a written agreement?

❑ No.
❑ Yes ❑ an order dated ....
❑ a written agreement that is attached.

11. Are any of the issues in this case urgent?

❑ No. . . . . ❑ Yes. *(Identify the issues and give details of why the issues are urgent.)*

....

....

....

....

....

....

PART 3: — PROCEDURAL MATTERS

12. If there is a custody or access assessment in this case, is it finished?

❑ Yes. *(If it is not already filed in the continuing record, file it now. Give the tab/page number(s) of the assessment:* ....*)*

❑ No. *(Explain why the assessment is not ready.)*

....

....

....

....

13. Are there issues that may require expert evidence or a report?

❑ No. . . . . . . ❑ Yes. *(If yes, provide details such as: the type of expert evidence; whether the parties will be retaining a joint expert; who the expert will be; who will be paying the expert; how long it will take to obtain a report, etc.)*

....

....

....

....

....

....

14. Have all of the reports you intend to rely on been provided to all of the parties and the Children's Lawyer (if involved)?

❑ No. . . . . ❑ Yes.

If not, when will they be provided? ....

15. If the Children's Lawyer is involved in this case, has the Children's Lawyer told the parties what its position is on the issues involving the children?

❑ Yes. *(What is the Children's Lawyer's position? Explain below.)*

❑ No. *(Explain below.)*

....

....

....

....

....

....

....

16. Have the parties finished the disclosing of documents and the questioning of witnesses?

❑ Yes. . . . . ❑ No. *(State what has not been done.)*

....

17. Are there any further procedural orders needed in this case?

❑ No. . . . . ❑ Yes. *(Explain.)* ....

18. I estimate that the trial time needed for my part of this trial is .... days; the other side's part of this trial is .... days.

PART 4: — OFFER TO SETTLE

19. The following is my offer to settle the outstanding issues in this case:

❑ offer to settle all issues . . . . ❑ offer to settle some of the issues

NOTE: If you have already made an offer and it is still open for acceptance, attach a copy to this brief. If you have not made an offer to settle, you must make one here. If you do not have enough information about all the issues, make a partial offer on those issues for which you do have enough information.
The other side can accept your offer. And if the other side does accept it, the accepted offer becomes a binding contract and can be turned into a court order that can be enforced against you. The other side can make a counter-offer.

In your offer for child support, give detailed calculations for any claim for special expenses or for undue hardship. If your offer deals with spousal support, it will be helpful to your case if you attach detailed calculations showing the effect of income tax on any proposed support order.

....
....
....
....
....
....
....
....
....
....
....
....
....
....
....
....
....
....
....
....
....

Put a line through any space left on this page. If additional space is needed, extra pages may be attached.

....	....
Date of party's signature	*Signature of party*
....	....
Date of lawyer's signature	*Signature of party's lawyer*

November 15, 2009

FORM 17D — SETTLEMENT CONFERENCE BRIEF FOR ❑ PROTECTION APPLICATION ❑ STATUS REVIEW

[Repealed O. Reg. 76/06, s. 15.]

[Editor's Note: Forms 4 to 39 of the Family Law Rules have been repealed by O. Reg. 76/06, effective May 1, 2006. Pursuant to Family Law Rule 1(9), when a form is referred to by number, the reference is to the form with that number that is described in the Table of Forms at the end of these rules and which is available at www.ontariocourtforms.on.ca. For your convenience, the government form as published on this website is reproduced below.]

Court File Number

ONTARIO

.... *(Name of court)*

at .... *Court office address*

Name of Party Filing this Brief	Date of settlement conference

Applicant(s)

Full legal name & address for service — street & number, municipality, postal code, telephone & fax numbers and e-mail address (if any).	*Lawyer's name & address — street & number, municipality, postal code, telephone & fax numbers and e-mail address (if any).*

Respondent(s)

Full legal name & address for service — street & number, municipality, postal code, telephone & fax numbers and e-mail address (if any).	*Lawyer's name & address — street & number, municipality, postal code, telephone & fax numbers and e-mail address (if any).*

Respondent(s)

Full legal name & address for service — street & number, municipality, postal code, telephone & fax numbers and e-mail address (if any).	*Lawyer's name & address — street & number, municipality, postal code, telephone & fax numbers and e-mail address (if any).*

Respondent(s)

Respondent(s)

Full legal name & address for service — street & number, municipality, postal code, telephone & fax numbers and e-mail address (if any).	*Lawyer's name & address — street & number, municipality, postal code, telephone & fax numbers and e-mail address (if any).*

Children's Lawyer

Name & address of Children's Lawyer's agent (street & number, municipality, postal code, telephone & fax numbers and e-mail address (if any)) and name of person represented.

PART 1: — BASIC INFORMATION ABOUT THE CHILD(REN)

1. The basic information about the child(ren) is as follows:

Child's full legal name	**Age**	**Birthdate (d, m, y)**	**Full legal name of every parent of child and relationship to child (See subsection 74(1) of the *Child, Youth and Family Services Act, 2017*.)**	**Date child was brought to a place of safety**

2. Where is the child living at the time of this conference?

....

3. What is the total length of time that any child less than six years old has been in care? *(Attach more detail if necessary).*

Name of child .... Total length of time ....

4. What is the total length of time any child six years old or more has been in care? *(Attach more details if necessary.)*

Name of child .... Total length of time ....

5. Is any child a First Nations, Inuk or Métis person?

❑ No. . . . . ❑ Yes.

5.a If the answer to question 5 if "Yes" and the child is a First Nations, Inuk or Métis person, give the name, address, and telephone number of the representative chosen by each of the child's bands and First Nations, Inuit or Métis communities to which the child is a member or identifies with.

....

6. If the child was brought to a place of safety before the hearing, name the person from whose care and the place from which the child was removed.

....

7. Has everyone who is entitled to notice in this case been served?

❑ Yes. . . . ❑ No. *(Do you want an order for substituted service on any person or an order that service is not required? Give details.)*

....

PART 2: — OUTSTANDING ISSUES

NOTE: If you want to refer to a report or document that has already been filed in the continuing record, just give the page number(s) or tab number of that document in the continuing record. If you are updating a document that is already in the continuing record, you must file the updated document in the continuing record and then refer to it by the page number(s) or tab numbers of that update in the continuing record. If you want to refer to anything else that is not in the continuing record and that does not need to be in the continuing record, you must attach it to this brief.

(Complete only Part 2A — Protection Application or Part 2B — Status Review, not both)

Part 2A — Protection Application

8. The parties have reached an agreement or the court has made an order on the following issues:

❑ findings of fact set out in Part 1 above ❑ payment order

❑ temporary care and custody ❑ access

❑ finding that child is in need of protection

❑ placing the child(ren) with *(name of person)* .... for .... months under supervision.

❑ Interim society care for .... months.

❑ extended society care with access

❑ extended society care without access

❑ *(Other. Specify.)*

The details of this agreement or order are:

....

9. What are the issues in this case that have NOT yet been resolved and what needs to happen to resolve them?

....

10. Are any of the issues in this case urgent?

❑ No. ❑ Yes. *(Identify the issues and give details of why the issues are urgent.)*

Part 2B — Status Review

11. The parties have reached an agreement or the court has made an order on the following issues:

❑ temporary care and custody ❑ payment order

❑ placing the child(ren) with *(name of person)* .... for .... months under supervision.

❑ interim society care for .... months. ❑ access

❑ extended society care with access

❑extended society care without access

❑ *(Other. Specify.)*

The details of this agreement or order are:

....

12. What are the issues in this case that have NOT yet been resolved and what needs to happen to resolve them?

....

13. Are any of the issues in this case urgent?

❑ No. ❑Yes. *(Identify the issues and give details of why the issues are urgent.)*

....

PART 3: — PROCEDURAL ISSUES

14. If there is an assessment in this case, is it finished?

❑ Yes. *(If it is not already filed in the continuing record, file it now. Give the tab/page number(s) of the assessment: ....)*

❑ No. *(Explain why the assessment is not ready.)*

15. Are there any other assessments necessary or not yet completed?

❑ No.

❑ Yes. *(Give details of the type of assessment, who will be assessed and any issues relating to the timing or completion of the assessment.)*

....

16. If the Children's Lawyer is involved in this case, has the Children's Lawyer told the parties what its position is on the issues involving the child(ren)?

❑ Yes. *(What is the Children's Lawyer's position? Explain below.)*

❑ No. *(Explain below.)*

....

17. Have you served and filed a plan of care?

❑ No.

❑ Yes. *(A copy of the plan of care must be filed in the continuing record.)* The plan can be found at tab/page .... of the continuing record.

18. Have the parties finished the disclosing of documents and the questioning of witnesses?

❑ Yes.

❑ No. *(State what has not been done.)*

....

19. Are there issues that require expert evidence or a report?

❑ No.

❑Yes. *(If yes, provide details such as: the type of expert evidence; whether the parties will be retaining a joint expert; who the expert will be; who will be paying the expert; how long it will take to obtain a report, etc.)*

....

20. Have all of the reports you intend to rely on been provided to all of the parties and the Children's Lawyer (if involved)?

❑ No. . . . . ❑ Yes.

If no, when will they be provided?

....

21. Are there any further procedural orders needed in this case?

❑ No. . . . . ❑ Yes. *(Explain.)*

....

22. Has an order been made for affidavit evidence at trial? *(Give details.)*

....

PART 4: — OFFER TO SETTLE

23. The following is my offer to settle the outstanding issues in this case:

If you have already made an offer and it is still open for acceptance, attach a copy of this brief. The other side can accept your offer. And if the other side does accept it, the accepted offer becomes a binding contract and can be turned into a court order that can be enforced against you. The other side can make a counter-offer.

Put a line through any space left on this page. If additional space is needed, extra pages may be attached.

....	....
Date of party's signature	*Signature of party*
....	....
Date of lawyer's signature	*Signature of party's lawyer*

March 1, 2018

FORM 17E — TRIAL MANAGEMENT CONFERENCE BRIEF

[Repealed O. Reg. 76/06, s. 15.]

[Editor's Note: Forms 4 to 39 of the Family Law Rules have been repealed by O. Reg. 76/06, effective May 1, 2006. Pursuant to Family Law Rule 1(9), when a form is referred to by number, the reference is to the form with that number that is described in the Table of Forms at the end of these rules and which is available at www.ontariocourtforms.on.ca. For your convenience, the government form as published on this website is reproduced below.]

Court File Number

ONTARIO

.... *(Name of court)*

at .... *Court office address*

Name of party filing this brief	**Date of trial management conference**

Applicant(s)

Full legal name & address for service — street & number, municipality, postal code, telephone & fax numbers and e-mail address (if any).	*Lawyer's name & address — street & number, municipality, postal code, telephone & fax numbers and e-mail address (if any).*

Applicant(s)

Respondent(s)

Full legal name & address for service — street & number, municipality, postal code, telephone & fax numbers and e-mail address (if any).	*Lawyer's name & address — street & number, municipality, postal code, telephone & fax numbers and e-mail address (if any).*

Name & address of Children's Lawyer's agent (street & number, municipality, postal code, telephone & fax numbers and e-mail address (if any)) and name of person represented.

PART 1: — THE ISSUES

1. What are the issues in this case that *HAVE* been settled or about which an order has been made:

Child protection cases

❑ access . . . . ❑ finding in need of protection

❑ placing the child(ren) with *(name of person)* .... for .... months under supervision.

❑ interim society care for .... months. . . . . ❑ extended society care.

❑ other *(Specify.)* ....

All other cases

❑ child custody

❑ access

❑ restraining order

❑ spousal support

❑ child support

❑ ownership of property

❑ possession of home

❑ equalization of net family property

❑ other *(Specify.)*

Attach a copy of any agreement that the judge should read to prepare for the trial management conference.

2. What are the issues in this case that have *NOT* yet been settled:

Child protection cases

❑ access . . . . ❑ finding in need of protection

❑ placing the child(ren) with *(name of person)* .... for .... months under supervision.

❑ interim society care for .... months. . . . . ❑ extended society care.

❑ other *(Specify.)* ....

All other cases

❑ child custody

❑ access

❑ restraining order

❑ spousal support

❑ child support

❑ ownership of property

❑ possession of home

❑ equalization of net family property *(Attach net family property statement, Form 13B.)*

❑ other *(Specify.)* ....

3. Where is the child living at the time of this conference?

....

4. Are any of the issues in this case urgent?

❑ No. . . . . ❑ Yes. *(Identify the issues and give details of why the issues are urgent.)*

....

PART 2: — ISSUES FOR TRIAL

5. Attach an outline of your opening statement for the trial, including:

(a) what you consider to be the undisputed facts;

(b) the theory of your case on the disputed issues;

(c) a brief summary of the evidence you plan to present at trial; and

(d) the orders you are asking the trial judge to make.

6. These are the witnesses whom I plan to have testify for me, the topics about which they will testify and my current estimate of the length of time for the testimony of each witness, including cross-examination:

Name of witness	Topic about which witness will testify	Current time estimate for witness

7. I estimate that the trial time needed for my part of this trial is .... days; the other side's part of this trial is .... days.

PART 3: — PROCEDURAL MATTERS

8. Have the parties signed a statement of agreed facts?

❑ Yes. *(Attach a copy.)* . . . . ❑ No. *(Explain why not.)*

....

9. Have the parties finished the disclosing of documents and the questioning of witnesses?

❑ Yes. . . . . ❑ No. *(Indicate what has not been done.)*

....

10. Are there any expert reports that you intend to rely on at trial?

❑ No. . . . ❑ Yes. *(Give details about the reports such as who prepared them and the issues addressed.)*

....

11. Have all of the reports you intend to rely on been provided to all of the parties and the Children's Lawyer (if involved)?

❑ No. . . . . ❑ Yes.

If no, when will they be provided?

....

12. Attach a list of the relevant orders in this case.

13. Are there any orders or directions for trial that have not been carried out?

❑ No. . . . . ❑ Yes. *(Explain.)*

....

14. Have the parties produced a joint document brief?

❑ Yes. *(Attach a copy.)* . . . . ❑ No. *(Explain why not.)*

....

15. Has an order been made for affidavit evidence at trial?

❑ Yes. . . . . ❑ No. *(Explain.)*

....

16. Are there any preliminary or procedural matters that need to be dealt with before or at the start of the trial?

❑ No. . . . . ❑ Yes. *(Explain.)*

....

17. Have you served a request to admit?

❑ Yes. . . . . ❑ No. *(Explain.)*

....

....	....
Date of party's signature	*Signature of party*
....	....
Date of lawyer's signature	*Signature of party's lawyer*

March 1, 2018

FORM 17F — CONFIRMATION OF CONFERENCE

[Repealed O. Reg. 76/06, s. 15.]

[Editor's Note: Forms 4 to 39 of the Family Law Rules have been repealed by O. Reg. 76/06, effective May 1, 2006. Pursuant to Family Law Rule 1(9), when a form is referred to by number, the reference is to the form with that number that is described in the Table of Forms at the end of these rules and which is available at www.ontariocourtforms.on.ca. For your convenience, the government form as published on this website is reproduced below.]

Court File Number

ONTARIO

.... *(Name of court)*

at .... *Court office address*

Applicant(s)

Full legal name & address for service — street & number, municipality, postal code, telephone & fax numbers and e-mail address (if any).	*Lawyer's name & address — street & number, municipality, postal code, telephone & fax numbers and e-mail address (if any).*

Applicant(s)

Respondent(s)

Full legal name & address for service — street & number, municipality, postal code, telephone & fax numbers and e-mail address (if any).	*Lawyer's name & address — street & number, municipality, postal code, telephone & fax numbers and e-mail address (if any).*

Name & address of Children's Lawyer's agent (street & number, municipality, postal code, telephone & fax numbers and e-mail address (if any)) and name of person represented.

1. My name is *(full legal name)* ....

and I am ❑ the lawyer for *(name)* ....

❑ the applicant in this case . . . . ❑ the respondent in this case

❑ other *(specify)* ....

2. Have you conferred with the opposing counsel or party regarding the issues, conference material, and time estimates, as set out in paragraphs 3 to 9 below?

❑ Yes

❑ No, because *(provide reasons)*

....

NOTE: The *Family Law Rules* require the parties or their counsel to confer, or attempt to confer, orally or in writing with each other on the issues in dispute for a conference prior to filing Confirmations. The only exception is where a party is prohibited from such communication by court order. *Failure to comply with the* Family Law Rules *may result in a cost order.*

3. The scheduled date and time for this

❑ case conference . . . . ❑ settlement conference ❑ trial management conference

is *(date)* .... at .... a.m./p.m.

4. The case management judge for this case is Justice

5. This matter is

❑ going ahead on the issues listed in paragraph 6 below.

❑ going ahead for a consent order regarding *(attach draft order)*.

❑ being adjourned on consent to *(date)* .... for a *(event)* .... because *(give reasons)* ....

❏ going ahead for a contested adjournment to *(date)* .... asked for by *(name of person asking for adjournment)* .... because *(give reasons)* ....

6. What are the most important issues to be resolved at this step in the case? *(List the issues below)*

a)

b)

c)

d)

e)

f)

7. In addition to the case conference brief, the presiding judge will be referred to the following pages/tabs:

....

8. Time estimate: .... applicant: .... minutes; respondent: .... minutes; for a total of .... minutes.

NOTE: The *Family Law Rules* require you to *deliver a copy* of this form to the opposing lawyer or party, unless this is a child protection matter. For clarification, regular or special service and an accompanying Affidavit of Service (Form 6B) under rule 6 of the *Family Law Rules* are not required. However, you must deliver this form by some method (including fax or e-mail) to the opposing lawyer or party prior to giving a copy to the court clerk.

....	....
Date of signature	*Lawyer's or party's signature*

March 1, 2018

FORM 20 — REQUEST FOR INFORMATION

[Repealed O. Reg. 76/06, s. 15.]

[Editor's Note: Forms 4 to 39 of the Family Law Rules have been repealed by O. Reg. 76/06, effective May 1, 2006. Pursuant to Family Law Rule 1(9), when a form is referred to by number, the reference is to the form with that number that is described in the Table of Forms at the end of these rules and which is available at www.ontariocourtforms.on.ca. For your convenience, the government form as published on this website is reproduced below.]

Court File Number ....

.... *(Name of court)*

at .... Court office address

Applicant(s)

Full legal name & address for service — street & number, municipality, postal code, telephone & fax and e-mail address (if any).	*Lawyer's name & address — street & number, municipality, postal code, telephone & fax numbers and e-mail address (if any).*

Respondent(s)

Full legal name & address for service — street & number, municipality, postal code, telephone & fax numbers and e-mail address (if any).	*Lawyer's name & address — street & number, municipality, postal code, telephone & fax numbers and e-mail address (if any).*

TO: (name of party) ....

This is a request for information in writing under subrule 20(2) of the *Family Law Rules*.

I request that the information be provided within .... days by

❑ an affidavit from *(name of person(s))*..................................
❑ a letter from *(name of person(s))*..................................
(Other. Specify.)
....

The information that I am requesting is as follows: (Be as specific as possible. If you want more than one piece of information, number the requested pieces of information.)

....

....

IF YOU DO NOT PROVIDE THE INFORMATION AS REQUESTED,

(1) A SUMMONS MAY BE SERVED ON YOU, REQUIRING YOU TO BE QUESTIONED ABOUT IT; or

(2) A MOTION MAY BE MADE TO THE COURT FOR AN ORDER REQUIRING YOU TO PROVIDE THE INFORMATION AND YOU MAY BE ORDERED TO PAY THE COSTS OF THE MOTION.

.... *Signature*

.... *Date of signature*

September 1, 2005

FORM 20.1 — ACKNOWLEDGEMENT OF EXPERT'S DUTY

....

ONTARIO

Court File Number ....

.... *(Name of court)*

at .... *Court office address*

Applicant(s)

Full legal name & address for service — street & number, municipality, postal code, telephone & fax numbers and e-mail address (if any).	*Lawyer's name & address — street & number, municipality, postal code, telephone & fax numbers and e-mail address (if any).*

Respondent(s)

Full legal name & address for service — street & number, municipality, postal code, telephone & fax numbers and e-mail address (if any).	*Lawyer's name & address — street & number, municipality, postal code, telephone & fax numbers and e-mail address (if any).*

Children's Lawyer

Name & address of Children's Lawyer's agent for service (street & number, municipality, postal code, telephone & fax numbers and e-mail address (if any)) and name of person represented.

1. My name is *(full legal name)* ....

2. I live in *(municipality & province)* ....

3. I have been engaged by or on behalf of *(name of party/parties)* .... to provide evidence in relation to this court proceeding.

4. I acknowledge that in relation to this proceeding, it is my duty to provide:

(a) opinion evidence that is fair, objective and non-partisan;

(b) opinion evidence that is related only to matters that are within my area of expertise; and

(c) such additional assistance as the court may reasonably require, to determine a matter in issue.

5. I acknowledge that the duty referred to above prevails over any obligation which I may owe to any party by whom or on whose behalf I am engaged.

....

Date *Signature*

NOTE: This form must be attached to any report signed by the expert and provided for the purpose of rule 20.1 of the *Family Law Rules*.

August 2, 2011

FORM 20A — AUTHORIZATION TO COMMISSIONER

[Repealed O. Reg. 76/06, s. 15.]

[Editor's Note: Forms 4 to 39 of the Family Law Rules have been repealed by O. Reg. 76/06, effective May 1, 2006. Pursuant to Family Law Rule 1(9), when a form is referred to by number, the reference is to the form with that number that is described in the Table of Forms at the end of these rules and which is available at www.ontariocourtforms.on.ca. For your convenience, the government form as published on this website is reproduced below.]

Court File Number ....

[SEAL]

.... *(Name of court)*

at .... *Court office address*

Applicant(s)

Full legal name & address for service — street and number, municipality, postal code, telephone & fax numbers and e-mail address (if any).	*Lawyer's name & address — street and number, municipality, postal code, telephone & fax numbers and e-mail address (if any).*

Respondent(s)

Full legal name & address for service — street and number, municipality, postal code, telephone & fax numbers and e-mail address (if any).	*Lawyer's name & address — street and number, municipality, postal code, telephone & fax numbers and e-mail address (if any).*

TO (full legal name and address of commissioner) ....

THE COURT HAS NAMED YOU A COMMISSIONER to take evidence in this case. A copy of the order naming you is attached.

THE COURT GIVES YOU FULL POWER to take the necessary steps to take the evidence mentioned in the attached order.

If the parties consent, you also have the power to take the evidence of any other witnesses who may be found in *(name of province, territory, state or country)* ....

In carrying out your duties under this commission, you must follow,

(a) the terms of the attached order; and

(b) the instructions set out below.

As soon as

❏ an audio recording

❏ a video recording

❏ a transcript

of the evidence is finished, you must deliver it to the clerk of the court along with this commission.

.... *Signature*

.... *Date of signature*

NOTE: Attach the court's order naming the commissioner

INSTRUCTIONS TO COMMISSIONER

1. You are to question the witness(es) according to subrules 20(14), (15) and 23(19) of the *Family Law Rules* to the extent that it is possible to do so. Subrules 20(14), (15) and 23(19) state as follows:

Questioning Person Outside Ontario

20. (14) If a person to be questioned lives outside Ontario and will not come to Ontario for questioning, the court may decide,

(a) the date, the time and place for the questioning;

(b) how much notice the person should be given;

(c) the person before whom the questioning will be held;

(d) the amount of the witness fee to be paid to the person to be questioned;

(e) the method for recording the questioning;

(f) where necessary, that the clerk shall issue,

(i) an authorization to a commissioner (Form 20A) who is to supervise the questioning outside Ontario, and

(ii) a letter of request (Form 20B) to the appropriate court or authorities outside Ontario, asking for their assistance in getting the person to be questioned to come before the commissioner; and

(g) any other related matter.

Commissioner's Duties

(15) A commissioner authorized under subrule (14) shall,

(a) supervise the questioning according to the terms of the court's authorization, these rules and Ontario's law of evidence, unless the law of the place where the questioning is to be held requires some other manner of questioning;

(b) make and keep a copy of the record of the questioning and, where possible, of the exhibits, if any;

(c) deliver the original record, any exhibits and the authorization to the clerk who issued it; and

(d) notify the party who asked for the questioning that the record has been delivered to the clerk.

Taking Evidence Before Trial Outside Ontario

23. (19) If a witness whose evidence is necessary at trial lives outside Ontario, subrules 20(14) and (15) (questioning person outside Ontario, commissioner's duties) apply with necessary changes.

2. The law of Ontario applies to the taking of evidence, unless the law of the province, territory, state or country where you supervise the questioning requires you to follow some other manner of questioning.

3. Before you begin your duties under this commission, you yourself must take the following oath or affirmation:

I, *(commissioner's name)* ....

❑ swear
❑ affirm

that I will,

(a) according to the best of my skill and knowledge, truly and faithfully and without bias to any of the parties to this case, take the evidence of every witness questioned under this commission, and

(b) cause the evidence to be

❑ recorded
❑ recorded and transcribed

and sent to the court.

(*In an oath, add the words:* "So help me God.")

Sworn/Affirmed before me at .... *municipality* in .... *province, state or country* on .... *date*	
Commissioner for taking affidavits (Type or print name below if signature is illegible.)	*Signature* *(This form is to be signed in front of a lawyer, justice of the peace, notary public or commissioner for taking affidavits.)*

You may take this oath or affirmation before any person listed in section 45 of Ontario's *Evidence Act* who is authorized to take affidavits or to administer oaths or affirmations outside Ontario. Section 45 of the *Evidence Act* states:

Oaths, etc., administered outside Ontario

45. (1) An oath, affidavit, affirmation or statutory declaration administered, sworn, affirmed or made outside Ontario before,

(a) a judge;

(b) a magistrate;

(c) an officer of a court of justice;

(d) a commissioner for taking affidavits or other competent authority of the like nature;

(e) a notary public;

(f) the head of a city, town, village, township or other municipality;

(g) an officer of any of Her Majesty's diplomatic or consular services, including an ambassador, envoy, minister, chargé d'affaires, counsellor, secretary, attaché, consul-general, consul, vice-consul, pro-consul, consular agent, acting consul-general, acting consul, acting vice-consul and acting consular agent;

(h) an officer of the Canadian diplomatic, consular or representative services, including, in addition to the diplomatic and consular officers mentioned in clause (g), a high commissioner, permanent delegate, acting high commissioner, acting permanent delegate, counsellor and secretary; or

(i) a Canadian Government trade commissioner or assistant trade commissioner,

exercising his or her functions or having jurisdiction or authority as such in the place in which it is administered, sworn, affirmed or made, is as valid and effectual to all intents and purposes as if it had been duly administered, sworn, affirmed or made in Ontario before a commissioner for taking affidavits in Ontario.

Idem

(2) An oath, affidavit, affirmation or statutory declaration administered, sworn, affirmed or made outside Ontario before a notary public for Ontario or before a commissioner for taking affidavits in Ontario is as valid and effectual to all intents and purposes as if it had been duly administered, sworn, affirmed or made in Ontario before a commissioner for taking affidavits in Ontario.

Admissibility

(3) A document that purports to be signed by a person mentioned in subsection (1) or (2) in testimony of an oath, affidavit, affirmation or statutory declaration having been administered, sworn, affirmed or made before him or her, and on which the person's office is shown below his or her signature, and

(a) in the case of a notary public, that purports to have impressed thereon or attached thereto his or her official seal;

(b) in the case of a person mentioned in clause (1)(f), that purports to have impressed thereon or attached thereto the seal of the municipality;

(c) in the case of a person mentioned in clause (1)(g), (h) or (l), that purports to have impressed thereon or attached thereto his or her seal or the seal or stamp of his or her office or of the office to which he or she is attached,

is admissible in evidence without proof of his or her signature or of his or her office or official character or of the seal or stamp and without proof that he or she was exercising his or her functions or had jurisdiction or authority in the place in which the oath, affidavit, affirmation or statutory declaration was administered, sworn, affirmed or made.

4. The party who wants the witness to be questioned must:

(a) give at least .... days notice of the date for the questioning; and,

(b) where the attached order says so, pay the witness appearance money.

5. You must arrange:

(a) to have the evidence recorded in a manner set out in the attached order; and

(b) where the order says so, to have it transcribed.

You must administer the following oath or affirmation to the person who records the evidence in shorthand and, where necessary, to the person who transcribes and written, audio or video recording of the evidence:

You

❑ swear
❑ affirm

that you will truly and accurately

❑ record
❑ transcribe
❑ record and transcribe

all questions put to all witnesses and their answers in keeping with the directions of the commissioner. (*In an oath, add the words:* "So help you God.")

6. To each witness whose evidence you take, you must administer the following oath or affirmation:

You

❑ swear

❑ affirm

that the evidence that you are about to give about the matters in dispute between the parties in this case shall be the truth, the whole truth and nothing but the truth. (*In an oath, add the words:* "So help you God.")

7. Where any witness does not understand the language in which he or she is being questioned or is deaf or mute, his or her evidence must be given through an interpreter. You must first administer the following oath or affirmation to the interpreter:

You

❑ swear
❑ affirm

that you understand the .... language and the language in which the examination is to be conducted and that you will truly interpret the

❑ oath
❑ affirmation

to all witnesses, all questions put to the witness and the answers of the witness, to the best of your skill and understanding. (*In an oath, add the words:* "So help you God.")

8. You must:

(a) fill out the certificate on the next page;

(b) make a copy of

(i) the audio or video record of the evidence,

(ii) any transcript of the evidence, and

(iii) where possible, any exhibits;

(c) keep the copies in your care until the court finishes this case;

(d) mail or deliver the originals, together with this commission and your certificate, to the clerk of the court; and

(e) immediately notify the party who asked for this questioning that the material has been sent to the clerk of the court.

COMMISSIONER'S CERTIFICATE

My name is *(full legal name)* .... and I certify that:

❑ I administered the proper to *(name)* ....

❑ oath
❑ affirmation

who was the person who
❑ recorded the evidence by shorthand.
❑ transcribed the evidence.

❑ I administered the proper to *(name of witness(es))*

❑ oath
❑ affirmation

whose evidence was taken and recorded.

❑ I administered the proper to *(name of interpreter)*

❑ oath
❑ affirmation

who was the interpreter through whom the evidence was given.

❑ The evidence of the witness(es) was properly taken and accurately

❑ recorded
❑ recorded and transcribed.

.... *Commissioner's signature*

.... *Date of signature*

September 1, 2005

FORM 20B — LETTER OF REQUEST

[Repealed O. Reg. 76/06, s. 15.]

[Editor's Note: Forms 4 to 39 of the Family Law Rules have been repealed by O. Reg. 76/06, effective May 1, 2006. Pursuant to Family Law Rule 1(9), when a form is referred to by number, the reference is to the form with that number that is described in the Table of Forms at the end of these rules and which is available at www.ontariocourtforms.on.ca. For your convenience, the government form as published on this website is reproduced below.]

Court File Number ....

[SEAL]

.... *(Name of court)*

at .... *Court office address*

Applicant(s)

Full legal name & address for service — street and number, municipality, postal code, telephone & fax numbers and e-mail address (if any).	*Lawyer's name & address — street and number, municipality, postal code, telephone & fax numbers and e-mail address (if any).*

Respondent(s)

Full legal name & address for service — street and number, municipality, postal code, telephone & fax numbers and e-mail address (if any).	*Lawyer's name & address — street and number, municipality, postal code, telephone & fax numbers and e-mail address (if any).*

TO THE JUDICIAL AUTHORITIES OF (name of province, state or country): ....

A CASE HAS BEEN STARTED IN THIS COURT INVOLVING THE PERSONS NAMED ABOVE. EVIDENCE BEFORE THIS COURT SHOWS THAT A WITNESS LIVING IN YOUR JURISDICTION SHOULD BE QUESTIONED THERE. THIS COURT HAS ISSUED A COMMISSION TO (name and address of commissioner): ....

TO QUESTION (name and address of witness): ....

YOU ARE REQUESTED to have (name of witness) ....

(a) appear before the commissioner by the method normally used in your jurisdiction;

(b) answer questions under oath or affirmation; and

(c) bring to the examination the documents or things listed on the back of this request.

YOU ARE ALSO REQUESTED TO allow the commissioner to have the witness questioned according to Ontario's law of evidence, to Ontario's rules of court and to the commission issued by this court.

AND WHEN YOU REQUEST IT, the courts in Ontario are ready and willing to do the same for you in a similar case.

THIS LETTER OF REQUEST is signed and sealed by a court order made on *(date of order)* ....

.... *Clerk of the court*

.... *Date of signature*

(Give the date of every document that the witness should bring and give enough of a description of each document or thing that the witness must bring to identify it.)

....

....

Put a line through any blank space left on this page. If you need more space, add a sheet and number the page.

September 1, 2005

FORM 22 — REQUEST TO ADMIT

[Repealed O. Reg. 76/06, s. 15.]

[Editor's Note: Forms 4 to 39 of the Family Law Rules have been repealed by O. Reg. 76/06, effective May 1, 2006. Pursuant to Family Law Rule 1(9), when a form is referred to by number, the reference is to the form with that number that is described in the Table of Forms at the end of these rules and which is available at www.ontariocourtforms.on.ca. For your convenience, the government form as published on this website is reproduced below.]

Court File Number ....

.... *(Name of court)*

at .... *Court office address*

Applicant(s)

Full legal name & address for service — street & number, municipality, postal code, telephone & fax and e-mail address (if any).	*Lawyer's name & address — street & number, municipality, postal code, telephone & fax numbers and e-mail address (if any). .*

Respondent(s)

Full legal name & address for service — street & number, municipality, postal code, telephone & fax numbers and e-mail address (if any).	*Lawyer's name & address — street & number, municipality, postal code, telephone & fax numbers and e-mail address (if any).*

TO: *(name of party)*

YOU MUST RESPOND TO THIS REQUEST WITHIN 20 DAYS AFTER BEING SERVED WITH IT.

You make your response by serving a Response to Request to Admit in Form 22A, a blank copy of which should be attached to this request. If the blank form is missing, contact your own lawyer or the court office as soon as possible.

IF YOU DO NOT RESPOND WITHIN THE TIME GIVEN, THIS CASE WILL GO TO COURT ON THE BASIS THAT YOU ARE ADMITTING, for the purposes of this case only, THAT THE FACTS SET OUT BELOW ARE TRUE AND THAT THE DOCUMENTS DESCRIBED BELOW ARE GENUINE.

You are requested to admit, only for the purposes of this case, that the following facts are true: *(If you need more space to list additional facts, attach an extra sheet.)*

1. ....

2. ....

3. ....

4. ....

5. ....

You are requested to admit, only for the purposes of this case, that the following documents are genuine. *(Being "genuine" also means:*

- *that a document that claims to be an original was written, signed or sealed as it appears to have been;*
- *that a document claiming to be a copy is a true copy of the original; and*
- *where the document claims to be a copy of a letter, fax, electronic-mail message or other document ordinarily sent from one person to another, that it was sent as it appears to have been sent and received by the person to whom it was addressed.*

Describe each document and identify it by date, type of document, author, name of person to whom it was sent, etc. Indicate whether the document is an original or a copy. If you need more space to list additional documents, attach a sheet.)

1. ....

2. ....

3. ....

4. ....

5. ....

A copy of each document named above is attached to this Request, except for: *(Give the number of any document that you are NOT attaching and state your reason for not doing so. Generally, you must attach copies of all the documents mentioned unless the other party already has a copy or it is impractical to attach a copy.)*

.... *Signature*

.... *Date of signature*

September 1, 2005

FORM 22A — RESPONSE TO REQUEST TO ADMIT

[Repealed O. Reg. 76/06, s. 15.]

[Editor's Note: Forms 4 to 39 of the Family Law Rules have been repealed by O. Reg. 76/06, effective May 1, 2006. Pursuant to Family Law Rule 1(9), when a form is referred to by number, the reference is to the form with that number that is described in the Table of Forms at the end of these rules and which is available at www.ontariocourtforms.on.ca. For your convenience, the government form as published on this website is reproduced below.]

Court File Number ....

.... (*Name of court)*

at .... *Court office address*

Applicant(s)

Full legal name & address for service — street & number, municipality, postal code, telephone & fax and e-mail address (if any).	*Lawyer's name & address — street & number, municipality, postal code, telephone & fax numbers and e-mail address (if any).*

Respondent(s)

Full legal name & address for service — street & number, municipality, postal code, telephone & fax numbers and e-mail address (if any).	*Lawyer's name & address — street & number, municipality, postal code, telephone & fax numbers and e-mail address (if any).*

TO: (name of party)

This is my response to your Request to Admit of (date) .... *that was served on me on (date)* ....

(Refer to the facts and documents according to the numbering set out in the Request to Admit.)

1. I admit that the following facts are true: *(fact numbers)* ....

2. I admit that the following documents are genuine: *(document numbers)* ....

3. I deny that the following facts are true: *(fact numbers)* ....

4. I deny that the following documents are genuine: *(document numbers)* ....

5. I refuse to admit the following facts for the following reasons: *(If you need more space, attach a sheet.)*

Fact number	My reasons

6. I refuse to admit that the following documents are genuine for the following reasons: *(If you need more space, attach a sheet.)*

Document number	My reasons

.... *Signature*

.... *Date of signature*

September 1, 2005

FORM 23 — SUMMONS TO WITNESS

[Repealed O. Reg. 76/06, s. 15.]

[Editor's Note: Forms 4 to 39 of the Family Law Rules have been repealed by O. Reg. 76/06, effective May 1, 2006. Pursuant to Family Law Rule 1(9), when a form is referred to by number, the reference is to the form with that number that is described in the Table of Forms at the end of these rules and which is available at www.ontariocourtforms.on.ca. For your convenience, the government form as published on this website is reproduced below.]

Court File Number ....

.... *(Name of court)*

at .... *Court office address*

Applicant(s)

Full legal name & address for service — street & number, municipality, postal code, telephone & fax and e-mail address (if any).	*Lawyer's name & address — street & number, municipality, postal code, telephone & fax numbers and e-mail address (if any).*

Respondent(s)

Full legal name & address for service — street & number, municipality, postal code, telephone & fax numbers and e-mail address (if any).	*Lawyer's name & address — street & number, municipality, postal code, telephone & fax numbers and e-mail address (if any).*

TO: (full legal name of witness) .... *of (address: street & number, municipality, postal code)* ....

YOU MUST:

(1) come to (address: street & number, municipality) .... *on (date)* ...., *at* .... *a.m./p.m.;*

(2) give evidence in the case or examination before (court or other person) ....

(3) bring with you the documents and things listed on the back of this summons; and

(4) remain there until this case or examination is finished or until the person conducting it says otherwise.

With this summons, you should get a fee that is calculated for .... day(s) of attendance as follows:

Appearance allowance of $ .... daily		$
Travel allowance of $ .... each way		$
Overnight hotel and meal allowance		$
	TOTAL	$

If the case or examination takes up more of your time, you will be entitled to an additional fee.

______________________ *Date of issue*	*IF YOU DO NOT COME AND REMAIN AS REQUIRED BY THIS SUMMONS, A WARRANT MAY BE ISSUED FOR YOUR ARREST.*

(Give the date of every document that the witness must bring and give enough of a description to identify each document or thing that the witness must bring.)

Draw a line through any blank space left on this page. If you need more space, you can add pages and number them.

Name, address, telephone & fax numbers and e-mail address of person or lawyer who prepared this summons.	

September 1, 2005

FORM 23A — SUMMONS TO WITNESS OUTSIDE ONTARIO

[Repealed O. Reg. 76/06, s. 15.]

[Editor's Note: Forms 4 to 39 of the Family Law Rules have been repealed by O. Reg. 76/06, effective May 1, 2006. Pursuant to Family Law Rule 1(9), when a form is referred to by number, the reference is to the form with that number that is described in the Table of Forms at the end of these rules and which is available at www.ontariocourtforms.on.ca. For your convenience, the government form as published on this website is reproduced below.]

Court File Number ....

[SEAL]

.... *(Name of court)*

at .... *Court office address*

Applicant(s)

Full legal name & address for service — street and number, municipality, postal code, telephone & fax and e-mail address (if any).	*Lawyer's name & address — street and number, municipality, postal code, telephone & fax numbers and e-mail address (if any).*

Respondent(s)

Full legal name & address for service — street and number, municipality, postal code, telephone & fax and e-mail address (if any).	*Lawyer's name & address — street and number, municipality, postal code, telephone & fax numbers and e-mail address (if any).*

TO: *(full legal name of witness)* .... of *(address: street & number, municipality, postal code)* ....

YOU MUST:

(1) come to *(address: street & number, municipality)* .... on *(date)* ...., at .... a.m./p.m.;

(2) give evidence in the case or examination before (court or other person) ....

(3) bring with you the documents and things listed on the back of this Summons; and

(4) remain there until this case or examination is finished or until the person conducting it says otherwise.

With this *Summons,* you should get a fee that is calculated for .... day(s) of attendance as follows:

Appearance allowance of $20 for each day that you are away from home ($60 minimum)		$	
Travel allowance	$		
Overnight hotel for minimum of 3 days ($60 minimum)			$
Meal allowance for minimum of 3 days ($60 minimum)			$
TOTAL		$	

If the case or examination takes up more of your time, you will be entitled to an additional fee.

IF YOU DO NOT COME AND REMAIN AS REQUIRED BY THIS SUMMONS, A WARRANT MAY BE ISSUED FOR YOUR ARREST.

.... *Date of issue*

.... *Signature of the clerk of the court*

(Give the date of every document that the witness must bring and give enough of a description to identify each document or thing that the witness must bring.)

Draw a line through any blank space left on this page. If you need more space, you can add pages and number them.

This summons was issued at the request of and inquiies may be directed to: *(Name, address, telephone number & fax numbers and e-mail address of person or lawyer who requested this summons.)*	

JUDGE'S CERTIFICATE

I, *(name)* ...., a judge of the *(name of court)* .... CERTIFY THAT I have heard and examined *(name of party or parties who have asked for this Summons or of his, her or their lawyer)* .... who seek(s) to compel the attendance of *(name of witness(es))* .... to produce documents or other articles or to testify, or both, in an Ontario case in the *(name of court in which witness is to appear)* .... involving *(names of parties in the case and court file number)* ....

I FURTHER CERTIFY THAT I am persuaded that the appearance of *(name of witness(es))* .... as a witness/witnesses in the case is necessary for the due adjudication of the case, and, in relation to the nature and importance of cause or proceeding, is reasonable and essential to the due administration of justice in Ontario.

The *Interprovincial Summonses Act* makes the following provision for the immunity of *(name of witness(es))* ....

A person who is required to attend before a court in Ontario by a summons adopted by a court outside Ontario shall be deemed, while within Ontario for the purposes for which the summons was issued, not to have submitted to the jurisdiction of the courts of Ontario other than as a witness in the proceedings in which the person is summoned and shall be absolutely immune from seizure of goods, service of process, execution of judgment, garnishment, imprisonment or molestation of any kind relating to a legal or judicial right, cause, action, proceeding or process within the jurisdiction of the Legislature of Ontario except only those proceedings grounded on events occurring during or after the required attendance of the person in Ontario.

.... *(Signature of judge)*

.... *(Date of signature)*

[SEAL OF THE COURT]

September 1, 2005

FORM 23B — ORDER FOR PRISONER'S ATTENDANCE

[Repealed O. Reg. 76/06, s. 15.]

[Editor's Note: Forms 4 to 39 of the Family Law Rules have been repealed by O. Reg. 76/06, effective May 1, 2006. Pursuant to Family Law Rule 1(9), when a form is referred to by number, the reference is to the form with that number that is described in the Table of Forms at the end of these rules and which is available at www.ontariocourtforms.on.ca. For your convenience, the government form as published on this website is reproduced below.]

Court File Number ....

[SEAL]

.... *(Name of court)*

at .... *Court office address*

Applicant(s)

Full legal name & address for service — street & number, municipality, postal code, telephone & fax numbers and e-mail address (if any).	*Lawyer's name & address — street & number, municipality, postal code, telephone & fax numbers and e-mail address (if any).*

Respondent(s)

Full legal name & address for service — street & number, municipality, postal code, telephone & fax numbers and e-mail address (if any).	*Lawyer's name & address — street & number, municipality, postal code, telephone & fax numbers and e-mail address (if any).*

.... *Judge (print or type name)*

.... *Date of order*

TO THE OFFICERS OF (name of correctional institution)

AND TO ALL PEACE OFFICERS IN ONTARIO:

THIS COURT has found that a prisoner at the institution or facility named above, *(prisoner's full legal name)* is

❑ a party in this case;

❑ a witness whose presence is necessary to decide an issue in this case.

THIS COURT ORDERS THAT:

1. You produce the prisoner before

❑ this court
❑ *(Specify other officer before whom attendance is required)*

on *(date)* ...., at .... a.m./p.m. at *(address)* .... to enable the prisoner to come to court or to an examination in this case.

2. The prisoner be returned and re-admitted immediately afterwards to the correctional institution or other facility from which he/she was brought.

.... *Date of signature*

.... *Signature of judge or clerk of the court*

September 1, 2005

FORM 23C — AFFIDAVIT FOR UNCONTESTED TRIAL, DATED

[Repealed O. Reg. 76/06, s. 15.]

[Editor's Note: Forms 4 to 39 of the Family Law Rules have been repealed by O. Reg. 76/06, effective May 1, 2006. Pursuant to Family Law Rule 1(9), when a form is referred to by number, the reference is to the form with that number that is described in the Table of Forms at the end of these rules and which is available at www.ontariocourtforms.on.ca. For your convenience, the government form as published on this website is reproduced below.]

ONTARIO

Court File Number

....

(Name of court)

at ....

Court office address

Applicant(s)

Full legal name & address for service — street & number, municipality, postal code, telephone & fax numbers and e-mail address (if any).	*Lawyer's name & address — street & number, municipality, postal code, telephone & fax numbers and e-mail address (if any).*

Respondent(s)

Full legal name & address for service — street & number, municipality, postal code, telephone & fax numbers and e-mail address (if any).	*Lawyer's name & address — street & number, municipality, postal code, telephone & fax numbers and e-mail address (if any).*

My name is (full legal name) ....

I live in (municipality & province) ....

and I swear/affirm that the following is true:

1. I am the applicant in this case.

2. There is/are *(number)* .... child(ren) from our relationship, namely:

Full Legal Name	Age	Birthdate (d, m, y)	Resident in (municipality & province)	Now living with (name of person and relationship to child)

Full Legal Name	Age	Birthdate (d, m, y)	Resident in (municipality & province)	Now living with (name of person and relationship to child)

3. I am asking for the following order:

❑ custody of the child(ren) named above

❑ access to the child(ren) named above

❑ support for *(name of recipient(s))* ....

❑ a restraining order against the respondent *(name)* .... *(date of birth)* ....

❑ other *(specify)* ....

4. The respondent and I were:

❑ married on *(date)* ....

❑ separated on *(date)* ....

❑ started living together on *(date)* ....

❑ never lived together.

CUSTODY AND ACCESS

Fill out this section if you are claiming custody of one or more of the children.

5. An order giving me custody of the child(ren) is in the best interests of the child(ren) because: *(Give reasons.)*

....

....

....

....

....

....

6. An order giving the respondent access to the children

❑ is . . . . ❑ is not

in the best interests of the child(ren) because: *(Give reasons.)*

....

....

....

....

....

....

7. If an order for access is made, it should be:

❑ reasonable access on reasonable notice;

❑ reasonable access on reasonable notice including but not limited to the terms below:

❑ on the following terms:

❑ every other weekend from .... p.m. on Friday until .... p.m. on Sunday or Monday, if Monday is a statutory holiday, starting on *(date)* ....

❑ alternate spring breaks, starting in *(year)* ....

❑ .... weeks during the summer vacation, to be decided by the parties before April 1 of each year.

❑ one half of the winter break, starting on *(date)* .... and ending on *(date)* .... to be shared as follows:

....

....

....

❑ List any other special days such as religious festivals, Christmas Day, birthdays, Mother's Day, Father's Day, etc., and indicate with which person the children will be on each day. *(Specify dates and times.)*

....

....

....

❑ other *(Specify.)* ....

CHILD SUPPORT

Fill out this section if you are claiming child support.

8. I am claiming support for *(number)* .... child(ren).

9. To the best of my knowledge, the source(s) of the respondent's income is/are *(Check one or more boxes as circumstances require.)*

❑ employment income at *(employer's name and address)* ....

❑ commissions, tips, overtime, bonuses, etc.

❑ self-employment as *(name or nature of respondent's business)* ....

❑ other *(Specify.)* ....

10. I believe that the respondent's current annual income from all income sources is $ .... for the following reasons: *(Give your reasons for believing the dollar amount set out.)*

....

....

....

....

....

....

....

....

SPOUSAL SUPPORT

Fill out this section if you are claiming support for yourself.

11. I need spousal support for the following reasons: *(Give details of your financial needs.)*

....

....

....

....

....

....

....

....

....

....

....

....

....

RESTRAINING ORDER

Fill out this section if you are claiming a restraining order against the respondent.

12. I need an order to restrain the respondent *(full legal name of person restrained)* .... *(date of birth of person restrained)* .... from

❑ a) contacting or communicating directly or indirectly with the following people *(full legal name and date(s) of birth of person[s] protected by this order)*

Name	Birthdate (d,m,y)

❑ except through *(name of person or agency)* .... to arrange access to the child(ren).

❑ except to permit access to the child(ren) *(names and birthdates)* .... on *(dates/days and times)* ....

❑ except through or in the presence of counsel.

❑ except through or in the presence of counsel or a clinical investigator from the Office of the Children's Lawyer, if the Children's Lawyer is appointed to represent the child(ren).

❑ b) coming within .... ❑ metres .... ❑ yards ❑ feet of *(locations and addresses)*

....

....

at any time or for any purpose

❑ except under the following conditions: *(provide details of conditions, including time(s), purpose(s) of exception(s) and address(es) as applicable)*

....

....

....

❑ c) *(any additional terms)* ....

I need a restraining order for the following reasons:

....

....

....

....

....

LACK OF SERVICE

Fill out this section if the respondent is not going to be served or has not been served.

NOTE: The Family Law Rules require all documents to be served on the opposing party. The court will make an order even without service, but only in very unusual circumstances such as: *1.* *An emergency situation where there is not enough time to serve documents or where serving them would put you or your child in danger or would have other serious consequences.* 2. *Where the court is satisfied that every effort has been made to find the other party and that it is impossible to serve him or her by any means.*

13. My application/motion is not being served on the respondent for the following reasons:

....

....

....
....
....
....
....

OTHER ISSUES

....
....
....
....
....
....
....
....
....
....
....
....
....
....

Put a line through any blank space left on this page.

Sworn/Affirmed before me at ....
municipality

in ....
province, state or country

on .... *Date*

.... *Commissioner for taking affidavits (Type or print name below if signature is illegible.)*

.... *Signature*

(This form is to be signed in front of a lawyer, justice of the peace, notary public or commissioner for taking affidavits.)

September 1, 2009

FORM 25 — ORDER (GENERAL) ❑ TEMPORARY ❑ FINAL

[Repealed O. Reg. 76/06, s. 15.]

[Editor's Note: Forms 4 to 39 of the Family Law Rules have been repealed by O. Reg. 76/06, effective May 1, 2006. Pursuant to Family Law Rule 1(9), when a form is referred to by number, the reference is to the form with that number that is described in the Table of Forms at the end of these rules and which is available at www.ontariocourtforms.on.ca. For your convenience, the government form as published on this website is reproduced below.]

❑ Temporary

❑ Final

Court File Number ....

[SEAL]

.... *(Name of court)*

at .... *Court office address*

Applicant(s)

Full legal name & address for service — street & number, municipality, postal code, telephone & fax numbers and e-mail address (if any)	Lawyer's name & address — street & number, municipality, postal code, telephone & fax numbers and e-mail address (if any)

Respondent(s)

Full legal name & address for service — street & number, municipality, postal code, telephone & fax numbers and e-mail address (if any)	Lawyer's name & address — street & number, municipality, postal code, telephone & fax numbers and e-mail address (if any)

.... *Judge (print or type name)*

.... *Date of order*

The court heard an application/motion made by *(name of person or persons)*

....

The following persons were in court *(names of parties and lawyers in court)*

....

The court received evidence and heard submissions on behalf of *(name or names)*

....

THIS COURT ORDERS THAT:

....

Put a line through any blank space left on this page. If additional space is needed, extra pages may be attached.

.... *Date of signature*

.... *Signature of judge or clerk of the court*

September 1, 2005

FORM 25A — DIVORCE ORDER

[Repealed O. Reg. 76/06, s. 15.]

[Editor's Note: Forms 4 to 39 of the Family Law Rules have been repealed by O. Reg. 76/06, effective May 1, 2006. Pursuant to Family Law Rule 1(9), when a form is referred to by number, the reference is to the form with that number that is described in the Table of Forms at the end of these rules and which is available at www.ontariocourtforms.on.ca. For your convenience, the government form as published on this website is reproduced below.]

Court File Number ....

[SEAL]

.... *(Name of court)*

at .... *Court office address*

Applicant(s)

Full legal name & address for service — street & number, municipality, postal code, telephone & fax numbers and e-mail address (if any)	*Lawyer's name & address — street & number, municipality, postal code, telephone & fax numbers and e-mail address (if any)*

Respondent(s)

Full legal name & address for service — street & number, municipality, postal code, telephone & fax numbers and e-mail address (if any)	*Lawyer's name & address — street & number, municipality, postal code, telephone & fax numbers and e-mail address (if any)*

.... *Judge (print or type name)*

.... *Date of order*

The court considered an application of *(name)* .... on *(date)*

The following persons were in court *(Give names of parties and lawyers in court. This paragraph may be struck out if the divorce is uncontested.)*

The court received evidence and considered submissions on behalf of *(name or names)* ....

THIS COURT ORDERS THAT:

1. *(full legal names of spouses)*

who were married at *(place)* ....

on *(date)* ....

be divorced and that the divorce take effect 31 days after the date of this order.

If the court decides that the divorce should take effect earlier, replace "31" with the smaller number.

(Add further paragraphs where the court orders other relief.) ....

Put a line through any blank space left on this page. If additional space is needed, extra pages may be attached.

.... *Date of signature*

.... *Signature of judge or clerk of the court*

NOTE: Neither spouse is free to remarry until this order takes effect, at which time you can get a Certificate of Divorce from the court office.

September 1, 2005

FORM 25B — SECURE TREATMENT ORDER

[Repealed O. Reg. 76/06, s. 15.]

[Editor's Note: Forms 4 to 39 of the Family Law Rules have been repealed by O. Reg. 76/06, effective May 1, 2006. Pursuant to Family Law Rule 1(9), when a form is referred to by number, the reference is to the form with that number that is described in the Table of Forms at the end of these rules and which is available at www.ontariocourtforms.on.ca. For your convenience, the government form as published on this website is reproduced below.]

Court File Number

SEAL

ONTARIO

.... *(Name of court)*

at .... *Court office address*

Applicant(s)

Full legal name & address for service — street & number, municipality, postal code, telephone & fax numbers and e-mail address (if any).	*Lawyer's name & address — street & number, municipality, postal code, telephone & fax numbers and e-mail address (if any).*

.... *Judge (print or type name)*

Child

Full legal name of child:
Birth date (d, m, y):
Sex:

Lawyer's name & address — street & number, municipality, postal code, telephone & fax numbers and e-mail address (if any).

.... *Date of order*

The court heard an application of *(name of person or persons)*

....

The following persons were in court (names of parties and lawyers in court)

....

The court received evidence and heard submissions on behalf of *(name or names)*

....

THIS COURT ORDERS THAT:

❑ *(child's full legal name)* .... be committed to the secure treatment program at *(name and address of program)* .... for a period of .... days, beginning on *(date)* ....

❑ the commitment of *(child's full legal name)* .... to the secure treatment program at *(name and address of program)* .... be extended for a period of .... days, beginning on *(date)* ....

❑ this application for an order . . . . ❑ of commitment

❑ extending the commitment

of *(child's full legal name)* .... to the secure treatment program at *(name and address of program)* .... be dismissed.

❑ *(Other; specify.)*

Put a line through any blank space left on this page. If additional space is needed, extra sheets may be attached.

....

Date of signature *Signature of judge or clerk of the court*

NOTE TO ADMINISTRATOR OF SECURE TREATMENT PROGRAM: Subsection 165(3) of the *Child, Youth and Family Services Act, 2017* states:

> In the calculation of a child's period of commitment, time spent in the secure treatment program before an order has been made under section 164 (commitment) or pending an application under section 167 (extension) shall be counted.

NOTE FURTHER that section 172 of the *Child, Youth and Family Services Act, 2017* authorizes a peace officer to take a child to a place where there is a secure treatment program if an order for the child's commitment to the secure treatment program has been made under section 164.

March 1, 2018

FORM 25C — ADOPTION ORDER

[Repealed O. Reg. 76/06, s. 15.]

[Editor's Note: Forms 4 to 39 of the Family Law Rules have been repealed by O. Reg. 76/06, effective May 1, 2006. Pursuant to Family Law Rule 1(9), when a form is referred to by number, the reference is to the form with that number that is described in the Table of Forms at the end of these rules and which is available at www.ontariocourtforms.on.ca. For your convenience, the government form as published on this website is reproduced below.]

Court File Number

SEAL

ONTARIO

.... *(Name of court)*

at .... *Court office address*

Applicant(s)

Full legal name & address for service — street & number, municipality, postal code, telephone & fax numbers and e-mail address (if any).	*Lawyer's name & address — street & number, municipality, postal code, telephone & fax numbers and e-mail address (if any).*

.... *Judge (print or type name)*

.... *Date of Order*

The court heard an application of *(name of person or persons)*

....

The following persons were in court *(names of parties and lawyers in court)*

....

The court received evidence and heard submissions on behalf of *(name or names)*

....

The person to be adopted is:

Name before adoption (Give full legal name of person to be adopted, unless the court orders otherwise.)	**Date of birth**	**Place of birth (municipality, province and country)**	**Sex**	**Birth registration number**

The application is for a(n) *(check all boxes that apply)*:

❑ adoption of a child in extended society care ❑ licensed adoption ❑ CAS adoption of a child who is not in extended society care ❑ section 199(1)(b) adoption

❑ international adoption ❑ relative adoption ❑ stepparent adoption *(complete additional section below)*

THIS COURT ORDERS THAT:

1. The person is adopted as the child of *(name of applicant or applicants)*

....

2. The name of the person shall now be *(person's full legal name)*

....

To be completed for a stepparent adoption:

As a result of this Order and pursuant to s. 217(2)(b) of the *Child, Youth and Family Services Act, 2017*, the parents of the person are *(full legal name of parents)*

....

....

Date of signature *Signature of judge or clerk of the court*

March 1, 2018

FORM 25D — ORDER (UNCONTESTED TRIAL) ❑ TEMPORARY ❑ FINAL

[Repealed O. Reg. 76/06, s. 15.]

[Editor's Note: Forms 4 to 39 of the Family Law Rules have been repealed by O. Reg. 76/06, effective May 1, 2006. Pursuant to Family Law Rule 1(9), when a form is referred to by number, the reference is to the form with that number that is described in the Table of Forms at the end of these rules and which is available at www.ontariocourtforms.on.ca. For your convenience, the government form as published on this website is reproduced below.]

Court File Number

____

(Name of court)

____

Form 25D: Order (Uncontested Trial)

SEAL

❑ Temporary
❑ Final

at ______________________________
Court office address

____
Judge (print or type name)

____
Date of order

Applicant(s)

Full legal name & address for service — street & number, municipality, postal code, telephone & fax numbers and e-mail address (if any).	*Lawyer's name & address — street & number, municipality, postal code, telephone & fax numbers and e-mail address (if any).*

Respondent(s)

Full legal name & address for service — street & number, municipality, postal code, telephone & fax numbers and e-mail address (if any)	*Lawyer's name & address — street & number, municipality, postal code, telephone & fax numbers and e-mail address (if any).*

Name & address of Children's Lawyer's agent (street & number, municipality, postal code, telephone & fax numbers and e-mail address (if any)) and name of person represented.

The court considered an application/motion made by *(name of person or persons)*
The following persons were in court *(names of parties and lawyers in court)*
The court received evidence and submissions on behalf of *(name or names)*

This order affects the following children:

Child's full legal name	*Date of birth (d, m, y)*	*Sex*

PARENTAGE

❑ *1.* *THIS COURT FINDS that:*

❑ each child mentioned above is a child of the marriage within the meaning of the *Divorce Act* (Canada).

❑ the applicant and respondent are parents of each child mentioned above within the meaning of the *Family Law Act* and the *Children's Law Reform Act*.

❑ other *(Specify.)*

CUSTODY

❑ *2.* *THIS COURT ORDERS that (name(s))* .... *shall have*

❑ temporary ❑ final
❑ sole ❑ joint

custody of each child mentioned above.

ACCESS

❑ *3.* *THIS COURT ORDERS that (name(s))* .... *shall have*

❑ temporary ❑ final

access to each child mentioned above. The terms of access are:

❑ reasonable access on reasonable notice;

❑ reasonable access on reasonable notice including but not limited to the terms below;

❑ as follows:

❑ every other weekend from .... p.m. on Friday until .... p.m. on Sunday or Monday, if Monday is a statutory holiday, starting on *(date)* ....

❑ alternate spring breaks, starting in *(year)* ....

❑ .... weeks during the summer vacation, to be decided by the parties before April 1 of each year.

❑ one-half of the winter break, starting on *(date)* .... and ending on *(date)* .... to be shared as follows:

❑ List any other special days such as religious festivals, Christmas Day, birthdays, Mother's Day, Father's Day, etc., and indicate with which person the children will be on each day. *(Specify dates and times.)*

❑ other *(Specify.)*

CHILD SUPPORT

❑ *4.* *THIS COURT FINDS that (name of payor)* .... has an income of $ .... *and IT ORDERS that (name of payor)* .... pay to *(name of recipient)* .... the sum of $ .... per month for the support of the child(ren) named above, starting on *(date)* ....

Fill in this frame only if there is a claim for add-ons for the child(ren).

THIS COURT FINDS that (name of recipient) .... has an income of $ .... *and IT ORDERS that (name of payor)* .... pay to *(name of recipient)* .... the sum of $ .... per month for the special or extraordinary expenses (add-ons) of the child(ren) named above, starting on *(date)* ....

The details of this amount are as follows:

Name of child	*Nature of special or extraordinary expense*	*Amount*

SPOUSAL SUPPORT

❑ *5.* *THIS COURT ORDERS that (name of payor)* .... pay to *(name of recipient)* .... ❑ temporary ❑ final spousal support in the amount of $ .... per .... starting on *(date)* ....

❑ *6.* *THIS COURT ORDERS that* the support under paragraph 5 of this order be indexed and changed annually according to the indexing factor in subsection 34(6) of the *Family Law Act.*

SUPPORT MONEY OWED

❑ *7.* *THIS COURT FINDS that* the amount of support owed is $ .... as of *(date)* ....

AND THIS COURT ORDERS that (name of payor) .... pay off this amount

❑ by *(date)* ....

❑ at the rate of $ .... per .... starting on *(date)* ....

SUPPORT — ENFORCEMENT

❑ *8.* *THIS COURT ORDERS that* unless the support order is withdrawn from the office of the Director of the Family Responsibility Office, it shall be enforced by the Director and amounts owing under the order shall be paid to the Director, who shall pay them to the person to whom they are owed.

❑ *9.* *THIS COURT ORDERS that* the clerk issue a support deduction order under section 11 of the *Family Responsibility and Support Arrears Enforcement Act* for the periodic support.

PROPERTY

❑ *10.* *THIS COURT ORDERS that*

DISCLOSURE

❑ *11.* *THIS COURT ORDERS that (name)* .... serve and file the following before the next court date:

❑ a current financial statement.

❑ other *(Specify.)*

OTHER MATTERS

❑ *12.* *THIS COURT ORDERS that*

COSTS

❑ *13.* *THIS COURT ORDERS that* costs be paid by *(name)* .... to *(name)* .... fixed at $ ....

ADJOURNMENT

❑ *14.* *THIS COURT ORDERS that* the matter(s) of .... be adjourned to *(date)* .... at *(time)* .... for: *(purpose)*

Interest

❑ *15.* *THIS COURT ORDERS that* interest be payable on amounts owing under this order at the rate of ....% per year.

Put a line through any space left on this page. If additional space is needed, extra pages may be attached.

....	....
Date of signature	*Signature of judge or clerk of the court*

September 1, 2005

FORM 25E — NOTICE DISPUTING APPROVAL OF ORDER

[Repealed O. Reg. 76/06, s. 15.]

[Editor's Note: Forms 4 to 39 of the Family Law Rules have been repealed by O. Reg. 76/06, effective May 1, 2006. Pursuant to Family Law Rule 1(9), when a form is referred to by number, the reference is to the form with that number that is described in the Table of Forms at the end of these rules and which is available at www.ontariocourtforms.on.ca. For your convenience, the government form as published on this website is reproduced below.]

Court File Number ....

.... *(Name of court)*

at .... *Court office address*

Applicant(s)

Full legal name & address for service — street & number, municipality, postal code, telephone & fax and e-mail address (if any). .	*Lawyer's name & address — street & number, municipality, postal code, telephone & fax numbers and e-mail address (if any).*

Respondent(s)

Full legal name & address for service — street & number, municipality, postal code, telephone & fax numbers and e-mail address (if any).	*Lawyer's name & address — street & number, municipality, postal code, telephone & fax numbers and e-mail address (if any).*

TO: (name of parties)

....

I disagree with the proposed wording of the order in this case for the following reasons: *(Give your reasons.)*

....

....

I am asking for a reworded order. A copy of my version of the order is attached.

THE CLERK OF THE COURT WILL SETTLE THE WORDING OF THE ORDER on *(date)* .... at .... a.m./p.m., or as soon as possible after that time at *(place for settling order)* ....

IF YOU DO NOT COME, THE CLERK OF THE COURT MAY SIGN THE ORDER WITH WORDING THAT MAY BE DIFFERENT FROM THE VERSION FIRST PROPOSED.

.... *Signature*

.... *Date of signature*

September 1, 2005

FORM 25F — RESTRAINING ORDER

SEAL

ONTARIO

Court File Number

....

(Name of court)

at ....
Court office address

❑ *Temporary* ❑ *Final*

<table>
<tr><td></td><td colspan="3">Applicant(s)</td></tr>
<tr><td>..........</td><td>Full legal name & address for service — street & number, municipality, postal code, telephone & fax numbers and e-mail address (if any).</td><td></td><td>Lawyer's name & address — street & number, municipality, postal code, telephone & fax numbers and e-mail address (if any).</td></tr>
<tr><td>Judge
(print or type name)</td><td></td><td></td><td></td></tr>
<tr><td></td><td colspan="3">Respondent(s)</td></tr>
<tr><td>..........</td><td>Full legal name & address for service — street & number, municipality, postal code, telephone & fax numbers and e-mail address (if any).</td><td></td><td>Lawyer's name & address — street & number, municipality, postal code, telephone & fax numbers and e-mail address (if any).</td></tr>
<tr><td>Date of order</td><td></td><td></td><td></td></tr>
</table>

THIS COURT ORDERS THAT:

1. ...., born ...., shall not

   (Court staff to insert here relevant clauses as ordered by judge in Endorsement.)

2. This restraining order is effective ....

3. This restraining order shall remain in effect until ....

❑ A separate order with additional terms relating to this family case was also made on this date.

In support of this order, this court heard a .... made by the .... for a restraining order under ....

The .... was made with notice to ....

The following persons were in court *(list names of parties and lawyers in court)*:

....

....

....

....

....

....

The court read the following materials filed in support of a request for this order:

....

....

....

....

....

....

The court heard submissions in support of a request for this order from:

....

....

....

....

....

....

....	....
Date of signature	*Signature of judge or clerk of the court*

Note: This order will be registered against the person being restrained on the Canadian Police Information Centre (CPIC) Database. Disobeying this order is a criminal offence punishable by fine or imprisonment. Any police or peace officer with jurisdiction over the place where the order was disobeyed may arrest the person being restrained without a warrant in accordance with section 495 of the Criminal Code of Canada.

September 1, 2009

FORM 25G — RESTRAINING ORDER ON MOTION WITHOUT NOTICE

SEAL

ONTARIO

Court File Number

....

(*Name of court*)

at ....

Court office address

	Applicant(s)	
....	*Full legal name & address for service — street & number, municipality, postal code, telephone & fax numbers and e-mail address (if any).*	*Lawyer's name & address — street & number, municipality, postal code, telephone & fax numbers and e-mail address (if any).*
Judge (print or type name)		
	Respondent(s)	
....	*Full legal name & address for service — street & number, municipality, postal code, telephone & fax numbers and e-mail address (if any).*	*Lawyer's name & address — street & number, municipality, postal code, telephone & fax numbers and e-mail address (if any).*
Date of order		

THIS COURT ORDERS THAT:

1. ...., born ...., shall not

(Court staff to insert here relevant clauses as ordered by judge in Endorsement.)

2. This restraining order is effective ....

3. This restraining order shall remain in effect until ....

4. This matter is adjourned to *(date and time)* .... to review this restraining order.

5. A copy of this order together with the notice of motion, dated ...., and affidavit of ...., sworn/affirmed on ...., shall be served immediately on *(insert full legal name of person restrained by this order)* .... by *(specify type of service)* ....

❑ A separate order with additional terms relating to this family case was also made on this date.

In support of this order, this court heard a motion made by the .... for a restraining order under ....

The motion was made without notice to ....

The following persons were in court *(list names of parties and lawyers in court)*

....

....

....

....

....

The court read the following materials filed in support of a request for this order

....

....

....

....

....

The court heard submissions in support of a request for this order from

....

....

....

....

....

....

....
Date of signature *Signature of judge or clerk of the court*

NOTICE TO (name) ....

If you want to oppose this motion or to give your own views, you must serve an Affidavit (general) (Form 14A). If you think the court should make a different order, you must serve an Affidavit (general) (Form 14A) and a Notice of Motion (Form 14). In either case, you must serve these materials on the other party and file the materials together with proof of service at the court office on or before 2 p.m. on *(insert date)* .... If you do not have a lawyer, you should ask the court office about serving the documents for you.

Note: This order will be registered against the person being restrained on the Canadian Police Information Centre (CPIC) Database. Disobeying this order is a criminal offence punishable by fine or imprisonment. Any police or peace officer with jurisdiction over the place where the order was disobeyed may arrest the person being restrained without a warrant in accordance with section 495 of the Criminal Code of Canada.

September 1, 2009

FORM 25H — ORDER TERMINATING RESTRAINING ORDER, DATED

SEAL

ONTARIO

Court File Number

....

(Name of court)

at ....
Court office address

....

	Applicant(s)	
....	*Full legal name & address for service — street & number, municipality, postal code, telephone & fax numbers and e-mail address (if any).*	*Lawyer's name & address — street & number, municipality, postal code, telephone & fax numbers and e-mail address (if any).*
Judge (print or type name)		
	Respondent(s)	
....	*Full legal name & address for service — street & number, municipality, postal code, telephone & fax numbers and e-mail address (if any).*	*Lawyer's name & address — street & number, municipality, postal code, telephone & fax numbers and e-mail address (if any).*
Date of order		

THIS COURT ORDERS THAT:

1. The restraining order made by Justice ...., on ...., shall be terminated, effective ....

In support of this order, the following persons were in court *(names of parties and lawyers in court)* ....

The court read the following materials filed in support of a request for this order ....

The court heard submissions in support of a request for this order from ....

....
Date of signature *Signature of judge or clerk of the court*

Note: This order will be sent to police services to advise them to remove the terminated restraining order from the Canadian Police Information Centre (CPIC) Database.

September 1, 2009

FORM 26 — STATEMENT OF MONEY OWED

[Repealed O. Reg. 76/06, s. 15.]

[Editor's Note: Forms 4 to 39 of the Family Law Rules have been repealed by O. Reg. 76/06, effective May 1, 2006. Pursuant to Family Law Rule 1(9), when a form is referred to by number, the reference is to the form with that number that is described in the Table of Forms at the end of these rules and which is available at www.ontariocourtforms.on.ca. For your convenience, the government form as published on this website is reproduced below.]

ONTARIO

Court File Number

.... *(Name of court)*

at .... *Court office address*

dated ....

Recipient(s)

Full legal name & address for service — street & number, municipality, postal code, telephone & fax numbers and e-mail address (if any).	*Lawyer's name & address — street & number, municipality, postal code, telephone & fax numbers and e-mail address (if any).*

Payor

Full legal name & address for service — street & number, municipality, postal code, telephone & fax numbers and e-mail address (if any).	*Lawyer's name & address — street & number, municipality, postal code, telephone & fax numbers and e-mail address (if any).*

My name is (full legal name) ....

I live in (municipality and province) .... *and I swear/affirm that the following is true*:

1. I am ❑ a person entitled to money under an order or a domestic contract that is enforceable in this court.

❑ a child's custodian or guardian entitled to money for the child's benefit under an order or a domestic contract that is enforceable in this court.

❑ an assignee of a person or of a child's custodian or guardian entitled to money under an order or a domestic contract that is enforceable in this court.

❑ an agent of the Director of the Family Responsibility Office.

❑ *(Other; specify.)* ....

2. I attach a copy of the ❏ court order ❏ domestic contract ❏ bond/recognizance and it has not been changed by a court order or agreement of the parties, except ....
(Write "NIL" if there has been no change.)

3. The total of the periodic payments that remain unpaid today is $ .... The detailed calculation of the total is attached to this statement. *(See page 2 for instructions.)*

4. The amount of interest on the unpaid periodic payments between the date of each default and today is $ .... The detailed interest calculations are attached to this statement. *(See page 2 for instructions.)*

Put a line through any blank space left on this page.

INSTRUCTIONS FOR COMPLETING FORM 26 (STATEMENT OF MONEY OWED)

Paragraph 3:

Write "NIL",

(a) if the periodic portion of your order or domestic contract is fully paid up today; or

(b) if your order or domestic contract does not require the payor to make periodic payments.

If you are claiming unpaid amounts of periodic payments under a support order, a fine or forfeiture to be paid by instalments or a domestic contract, you *MUST* attach one or more separate sheets as an appendix to this statement. There you must set out a history or a diary of the payor's payments and defaults. The diagram to the right shows one way to set out this history or diary. The final total in this diary of payments and defaults must be the same as the dollar amount in paragraph 3.

Date	**Amount Due (Add to TOTAL)**	**Amount Paid (Subtract from TOTAL)**	**TOTAL Amount Owing**
4 Sept. 1998	$250.00		$250.00
10 Sept. 1998		$250.00	$0.00
18 Sept. 1998	$250.00		$250.00
24 Sept. 1998		$150.00	$100.00
2 Oct. 1998	$250.00		$350.00
12 Oct. 1998		$125.00	$225.00
16 Oct. 1998	$250.00		$475.00
30 Oct. 1998	$250.00		$725.00
30 Oct. 1998	$250.00		$975.00

Paragraph 4:

Write "NIL",

(a) if you don't want to claim any interest on unpaid periodic payments; or

(b) if your order or domestic contract actually forbids you to claim interest. (If your order or domestic contract says nothing about interest, you can still claim it if you want.)

Even though the payor is fully paid up today on periodic payments and even though the dollar amount that you are claiming in paragraph 3 is "NIL", there may be interest owing from the times when the payor was behind in payments. You may therefore wish to make a claim for that unpaid interest here. If you are not barred from claiming interest and wish to do so, you *MUST* attach one or more work sheets as an appendix to this statement. On those work sheets,

(c) you must set out your method of computing interest. Unless the court order or domestic contract specifically allows you to compound interest, you must use simple interest.

(d) you must indicate the appropriate rate of interest. This rate can sometimes be set out in your order or domestic contract, but if it is not, then you must rely on the rate allowed by section 127 of the *Courts of Justice Act*. You can also get this information from the court office.

(e) for each overdue or partially overdue payment, calculate in dollars and cents the amount of interest allowed by subsection 129(2) of the *Courts of Justice Act*, from the date when it was due until today or until the date of full payment of that overdue amount, whichever date is earlier.

Paragraph 5:

Write "NIL",

(a) if the lump sum (whether by way of order, forfeiture, fine or support in a domestic contract) is fully paid up today; or

(b) if there is no requirement on the payor to pay any lump sum.

If there have been partial payments on the lump sum, you *MUST* attach one or more separate sheets as an appendix to this statement. There, you must set out a history or a diary of the payor's partial payments, similar to the diagram on the right. The final total in this history must be the same as the dollar amount that you are claiming in paragraph 5.

Date	Amount Due (Add to TOTAL)	Amount Paid (Subtract from TOTAL)	TOTAL Amount Owing
1 Dec. 1998	$24,000.00		$24,000.00
29 Dec. 1998		$4,700.00	$19,300/.00
12 Feb. 1999		$1,800.00	$17,500.00
6 May 1999		$1,226.00	$16,273.00

Paragraph 6:

Write "NIL",

(a) if you don't want to claim any interest on the lump-sum amount.

(b) if your order or domestic contract forbids you to claim interest.

Even though the lump sum has been paid up and even though the dollar amount that you are claiming in paragraph 5 is "NIL", the interest earned on it during a time when payment was overdue may still be owing and you may wish to claim it here. If you are not barred from claiming interest and wish to do so, you *MUST* attach one or more work sheets as an appendix to this statement. On those work sheets,

(c) you must set out your method of computing interest. You must use simple interest unless the court order or domestic contract specifically allows you to compound interest.

(d) you must indicate the appropriate rate of interest. This rate may sometimes be set out in your order or domestic contract, but if it is not, then you must rely on the rate allowed by section 127 of the *Courts of Justice Act*. You can also get this information from the court office.

(e) for each partial payment, calculate in dollars and cents the amount of interest from the date of the order or domestic contract until the date of the partial payment. Interest on any balance still outstanding today will be calculated from the date of the order, contract or agreement until today.

5. The amount of the lump-sum ❑ support ❑ equalization payment

❑ costs ❑ fine for contempt of court

❑ *(Other; specify.)* ....

that remains unpaid today is $ .... The detailed calculation is attached to this statement.

(See page 4 for instructions.)

6. The total amount of unpaid interest on the lump sum up to today is $ .... The detailed calculation is attached to this statement.

(See page 4 for instructions.)

7. The amount of court costs remaining unpaid today is $ .... The detailed calculation is attached to this statement.

(See page 4 for instructions.)

8. The amount of unpaid interest on court costs up to today is $ .... The detailed calculation is attached to this statement.

(See page 4 for instructions.)

Creditor's Relief Provisions

9. Of the money in paragraphs 5 and 6, I attribute $ .... of the total lump-sum support.

(See page 4 for instructions.)

10. Of the money in paragraphs 3 and 4, I attribute $ .... of the total periodic support.

(See page 4 for instructions.)

11. The total of the sums in paragraphs 9 and 10 is $ ....

12. I have carried out the computations in this statement and the attached sheets correctly to the best of my ability.

Final Total

13. The total amount enforceable in this court that I am claiming against the payor is as follows:

(a) unpaid amounts of periodic payments (paragraph 3)	$ ....
(b) interest on unpaid amounts of periodic payments (paragraph 4)	$ ....
(c) unpaid lump-sum debt (paragraph 5)	$ ....
(d) interest on unpaid lump-sum debt (paragraph 6)	$ ....
(e) unpaid court costs (paragraph 7)	$ ....
(f) interest on unpaid court costs (paragraph 8)	$ ....

TOTAL . . . . $ ....

Put a line through any blank space left on this page.

Sworn/Affirmed before me at .... *municipality* in .... *province, state, or country*		
on .... *date*	.... *Commissioner for taking affidavits (Type or print name below if signature is illegible.)*	.... *Signature* *(This form is to be signed in front of a lawyer, justice of the peace, notary public or commissioner for taking affidavits.)*

NOTE: To this statement, you must attach a photocopy of the order, domestic contract, bond or recognizance that you will be enforcing through the court. In the case of a bond or recognizance, you must also attach a photocopy of the order of forfeiture. If court costs were determined separately, you should include a photocopy of the order or certificate of costs.

Pages of computer print-out are acceptable provided that they generally conform to the examples or diagrams provided in the instructions above.

Paragraph 7:

Write "NIL",

(a) if the court costs are fully paid up today; or

(b) if the court did not award costs to you.

If there have been partial payments on the court costs, you *MUST* attach one or more separate sheets as an appendix to this statement. There, you must set out the history or diary of the payor's partial payments, as illustrated by the diagram alongside the note to paragraph 5. The final total in this diary must be the same as the dollar amount that you are claiming in paragraph 7.

Paragraph 8:

Write "NIL",

(a) if you don't want to claim any interest on court costs; or

(b) if your order forbids you to claim any interest on costs.

Even though the court costs may be paid up today and the dollar amount that you are claiming in paragraph 8 is "NIL", the interest earned on those costs during the time when payment on them was overdue may still be owing and you may wish to claim that interest here. If you are claiming interest on court costs, you *MUST* attach one or more work sheets as an appendix to this statement. On those work sheets,

(c) you must set out your method of computing interest. You must use simple accrual unless the court has specifically allowed you to compound your interest.

(d) you must indicate the appropriate rate of interest prevailing on the date when the order was made or the rate allowed by the court when it made the order. You can get this information from the court office.

(e) for each partial payment, you must calculate in dollars and cents the amount of interest from the date of the order until the date of the partial payment. Interest on any balance still outstanding today will run from the date of the order until today.

Paragraph 9:

Write "NIL" if your lump-sum claim has nothing to do with support or maintenance. Otherwise, figure out what portion of your lump-sum claim deals with support or maintenance. You are entitled to include the interest earned on that amount.

This figure will be needed by the clerk of the court and by others, such as the sheriff, because they are required by law to give your claim for lump-sum support priority over the claims of other people with orders against the payor under the *Creditors' Relief Act*. Section 4 of that Act states:

Priority for support orders —

4. (1) A support or maintenance order has priority over other judgment debts regardless of when an enforcement process is issued or served.

(a) if the order is for periodic payments, in the amount of the arrears owing under the order at the time of seizure or attachment; and

(b) if the order for a lump sum payment, in the amount of the lump sum.

(2) *Support orders rank equally.* — Support or maintenance orders rank equally with one another.

(3) *Enforcement process.* — Process for the enforcement or a support or maintenance order shall be identified on its face as being for support or maintenance.

(4) *Crown bound.* — Subsection (1) binds the Crown in right of Ontario.

Paragraph 10:

Write "NIL" if your claim has nothing to do with periodic support or maintenance. Otherwise, figure out what portion of your claim deals with periodic support or maintenance. You are entitled to include the interest earned on that amount. This figure together with the one in paragraph 9 will be needed by the clerk of the court and by others, such as the sheriff, to determine the priority that your support arrears should have over the claims of other people with orders against the payor. See subsection 4(1) of the *Creditors' Relief Act*.

APPENDIX .... (A, B, C, ETC.) (PAGE ....)

DATE	AMOUNT DUE (Add to TOTAL)	AMOUNT PAID (Subtract from TOTAL)	TOTAL (Amount still owing)
	$	$	$
	$	$	$
	$	$	$
	$	$	$
	$	$	$
	$	$	$
	$	$	$
	$	$	$

DATE	AMOUNT DUE (Add to TOTAL)	AMOUNT PAID (Subtract from TOTAL)	TOTAL (Amount still owing)
	$	$	$
	$	$	$
	$	$	$
	$	$	$
	$	$	$
	$	$	$
	$	$	$
	$	$	$
	$	$	$
	$	$	$
	$	$	$
	$	$	$
	$	$	$
	$	$	$
	$	$	$
	$	$	$
	$	$	$
	$	$	$
	$	$	$
	$	$	$
	$	$	$
	$	$	$
	$	$	$
	$	$	$
	$	$	$
	$	$	$
	$	$	$
	$	$	$

CALCULATION OF INTEREST

1. The calculations below relate to interest earned on *(State nature of order, judgment or contract.)* ....

2. THE CALCULATIONS BELOW USE:

❑ SIMPLE INTEREST

❑ COMPOUND INTEREST, COMPOUNDED *(State frequency of compounding)*

❑ *(Other; specify.)* ....

3. The rate of interest permitted by law is ....% per *(frequency)* ....

4. The calculation of the interest is detailed as follows:

....

April 12, 2016

FORM 26A — AFFIDAVIT OF ENFORCEMENT EXPENSES

[Repealed O. Reg. 76/06, s. 15.]

[Editor's Note: Forms 4 to 39 of the Family Law Rules have been repealed by O. Reg. 76/06, effective May 1, 2006. Pursuant to Family Law Rule 1(9), when a form is referred to by number, the reference is to the form with that number that is described in the Table of Forms at the end of these rules and which is available at www.ontariocourtforms.on.ca. For your convenience, the government form as published on this website is reproduced below.]

ONTARIO

Court File Number

.... *(Name of court)*

at .... *Court office address*

dated ....

Recipient(s)

Full legal name & address for service — street & number, municipality, postal code, telephone & fax numbers and e-mail address (if any)..	*Lawyer's name & address — street & number, municipality, postal code, telephone & fax numbers and e-mail address (if any)..*

Payor

Full legal name & address for service — street & number, municipality, postal code, telephone & fax numbers and e-mail address (if any)..	*Lawyer's name & address — street & number, municipality, postal code, telephone & fax numbers and e-mail address (if any)..*

My name is (full legal name) ....

I live in (municipality & province) .... *and I swear/affirm that the following is true*:

Attach copy of order, contract or agreement

1. I am

❑ a person entitled to money under an order or a domestic contract that is enforceable in this court.

❑ child's custodian or guardian entitled to money for the child's benefit under an order or a domestic contract that is enforceable in this court.

❑ an assignee of a person or of a child's custodian or guardian entitled to money under an order or a domestic contract that is enforceable in this court.

❑ an agent of the Director of the Family Responsibility Office.

❑ *(Other; specify.)*

2. To enforce the order or domestic contract, I took the following steps for which I am claiming costs under the rules of the court:

❑ A financial examination of the payor was carried out.

❑ A writ of seizure and sale was issued, filed and enforced.

❑ A notice of garnishment was issued, served, filed and enforced.

❑ A writ of seizure and sale was changed by way of a statutory declaration.

❑ A notice of garnishment was changed by way of a statutory declaration.

❑ *(Other; specify.)*

Put a line through any blank space left on this page.

3. The details of my claim are as follows: *(For each item of expense, give the date when it was paid and the amount. Where receipts are available, please attach them and identify them in numbered sequence.)*

ITEM OF EXPENSE	DATE	AMOUNT	Receipt No.
			1
			2
			3
			4
			5
			6
			7
			8
			9
			10
			11
			12
			13
			14
			15
			16
			17
			18
			19

ITEM OF EXPENSE	DATE	AMOUNT	Receipt No.
			20
			21
			22
			23

If you need more space, you may attach extra sheets and number them.

Sworn/Affirmed before me at .... *municipality* in .... *province, state, or country* on .... *date* .... *Commissioner for taking affidavits (Type or print name below if signature is illegible.)*	.... *Signature* *(This form is to be signed in front of a lawyer, justice of the peace, notary public or commissioner for taking affidavits.)*

April 12, 2016

FORM 26B — AFFIDAVIT FOR FILING DOMESTIC CONTRACT WITH COURT

[Repealed O. Reg. 76/06, s. 15.]

[Editor's Note: Forms 4 to 39 of the Family Law Rules have been repealed by O. Reg. 76/06, effective May 1, 2006. Pursuant to Family Law Rule 1(9), when a form is referred to by number, the reference is to the form with that number that is described in the Table of Forms at the end of these rules and which is available at www.ontariocourtforms.on.ca. For your convenience, the government form as published on this website is reproduced below.]

ONTARIO

Court File Number

.... *(Name of court)*

at .... *Court office address*

dated ....

Recipient(s)

Full legal name & address for service — street & number, municipality, postal code, telephone & fax numbers and e-mail address (if any).	*Lawyer's name & address — street & number, municipality, postal code, telephone & fax numbers and e-mail address (if any).*

Payor

Full legal name & address for service — street & number, municipality, postal code, telephone & fax numbers and e-mail address (if any).	*Lawyer's name & address — street & number, municipality, postal code, telephone & fax numbers and e-mail address (if any).*

My name is (full legal name) ....

I live in (municipality & province) ....

and I swear/affirm that the following is true:

1. I attach a copy of a ❑ marriage contract . . . . ❑ cohabitation agreement

❑ separation agreement . . . . ❑ paternity agreement

for filing with the court so that its support provisions can be enforced or changed as if they were a court order.

2. The *contract/agreement* includes the following provisions relating to child support:

a) *(Name of party)* .... to pay *(name of party)* .... child support in the monthly amount of $.......... for the following children: *(names and birthdates of children)*

....

❑ This amount includes the following special expenses:

Type	Amount
	$
	$
	$
	$

b) Child support is based on the payor's gross annual income of $........... The proportionate share of special expenses is based on the recipient's gross annual income of $..........

3. The *contract/agreement* has not been set aside or disregarded by a court nor has it been changed by agreement of the parties.

Sworn/Affirmed before me at ....
municipality

in ....
province, state, or country

....

on	....	*Signature*
date	*Commissioner for taking affidavits (Type or print name below if signature is illegible.)*	*(This form is to be signed in front of a lawyer, justice of the peace, notary public or commissioner for taking affidavits.)*

April 12, 2016

FORM 26C — NOTICE OF TRANSFER OF ENFORCEMENT

[Repealed O. Reg. 76/06, s. 15.]

[Editor's Note: Forms 4 to 39 of the Family Law Rules have been repealed by O. Reg. 76/06, effective May 1, 2006. Pursuant to Family Law Rule 1(9), when a form is referred to by number, the reference is to the form with that number that is described in the Table of Forms at the end of these rules and which is available at www.ontariocourtforms.on.ca. For your convenience, the government form as published on this website is reproduced below.]

ONTARIO

Court File Number

.... *(Name of court)*

at .... *Court office address*

Recipient(s)

Full legal name & address for service — street & number, municipality, postal code, telephone & fax numbers and e-mail address (if any).	*Lawyer's name & address — street & number, municipality, postal code, telephone & fax numbers and e-mail address (if any).*

Payor

Full legal name & address for service — street & number, municipality, postal code, telephone & fax numbers and e-mail address (if any).	*Lawyer's name & address — street & number, municipality, postal code, telephone & fax numbers and e-mail address (if any).*

TO THE PARTIES IN THIS ENFORCEMENT,

TO THE CLERK OF THE COURT at (list court locations out of which enforcement was carried out)

....

AND TO THE SHERIFF FOR (list areas where sheriff has been involved with enforcement)

....

❑ I am the recipient named above. The attached

❑ order ❑ domestic contract

has been withdrawn from the enforcement program run by the Director of the Family Responsibility Office. At my request, the Director assigned to me the enforcement measure(s) listed on page 2 of this form that were started by the Director.

❑ My name is *(full legal name)* ....

I am an authorized agent of the Director of the Family Responsibility Office. The recipient(s) *(name of recipient(s))*

....

filed the attached ❑ order ❑ domestic contract

in the Director's office to be enforced. At my request, the recipient(s) assigned to the Director the enforcement measure(s) listed on the back of this sheet that were started by the recipient(s).

....

Signature *Date of signature*

ENFORCEMENT MEASURES BEING TRANSFERRED		
Name of Enforcement Measure	**Where Started**	**When Started**

If you need more space, you may attach extra sheets and number them.

April 12, 2016

FORM 27 — REQUEST FOR FINANCIAL STATEMENT

[Repealed O. Reg. 76/06, s. 15.]

[Editor's Note: Forms 4 to 39 of the Family Law Rules have been repealed by O. Reg. 76/06, effective May 1, 2006. Pursuant to Family Law Rule 1(9), when a form is referred to by number, the reference is to the form with that number that is described in the Table of Forms at the end of these rules and which is available at www.ontariocourtforms.on.ca. For your convenience, the government form as published on this website is reproduced below.]

ONTARIO

Court File Number

.... *(Name of court)*

at .... *Court office address*

Recipient(s)

Full legal name & address for service — street & number, municipality, postal code, telephone & fax numbers and e-mail address (if any).	*Lawyer's name & address — street & number, municipality, postal code, telephone & fax numbers and e-mail address (if any).*

Payor

Full legal name & address for service — street & number, municipality, postal code, telephone & fax numbers and e-mail address (if any).	*Lawyer's name & address — street & number, municipality, postal code, telephone & fax numbers and e-mail address (if any).*

TO: (name of party) ....

I claim that you have missed payments under an order or domestic contract, a copy of which is attached to this notice.

YOU MUST PREPARE A FINANCIAL STATEMENT (Form 13) within 15 days of being served with this notice. A blank form of financial statement should accompany or be attached to this notice. If it is missing, you should contact your own lawyer or the court office immediately.

YOU MUST MAIL your completed financial statement within the next 15 days to *(person & address)*

....

....

IF YOU DO NOT MAIL THE COMPLETED FINANCIAL STATEMENT AS REQUIRED BY THIS NOTICE, THE COURT MAY ORDER YOU TO DO SO AND YOU MAY THEN BE REQUIRED TO PAY THE COSTS. IF YOU DISOBEY THE ORDER, THE COURT MAY MAKE AN ORDER FOR YOUR IMPRISONMENT.

....	....
Signature	*Date of signature*

April 12, 2016

FORM 27A — REQUEST FOR STATEMENT OF INCOME

[Repealed O. Reg. 76/06, s. 15.]

[Editor's Note: Forms 4 to 39 of the Family Law Rules have been repealed by O. Reg. 76/06, effective May 1, 2006. Pursuant to Family Law Rule 1(9), when a form is referred to by number, the reference is to the form with that number that is described in the Table of Forms at the end of these rules and which is available at www.ontariocourtforms.on.ca. For your convenience, the government form as published on this website is reproduced below.]

ONTARIO

Court File Number

.... *(Name of court)*

at .... *Court office address*

Recipient(s)

Full legal name & address for service — street & number, municipality, postal code, telephone & fax numbers and e-mail address (if any).	*Lawyer's name & address — street & number, municipality, postal code, telephone & fax numbers and e-mail address (if any).*

Payor

Full legal name & address for service — street & number, municipality, postal code, telephone & fax numbers and e-mail address (if any).	*Lawyer's name & address — street & number, municipality, postal code, telephone & fax numbers and e-mail address (if any).*

TO: *(name and address of income source)*

I claim that the payor has missed payments under an order or domestic contract.

YOU MUST PREPARE A STATEMENT OF INCOME in Form 27B concerning the payor named above. A blank form of statement of income should accompany or be attached to this notice. If it is missing, you should contact your own lawyer or the court office immediately.

YOU MUST MAIL the complete statement of income within 10 days of being served with this notice to *(person & address)*

....

....

IF YOU DO NOT MAIL THE COMPLETED STATEMENT OF INCOME AS REQUIRED BY THIS NOTICE, THE COURT MAY ORDER YOU TO DO SO AND YOU MAY THEN BE REQUIRED TO PAY THE COURT COSTS.

....

....

....

....

Signature *Date of Signature*

April 12, 2016

FORM 27B — STATEMENT OF INCOME FROM INCOME SOURCE

[Repealed O. Reg. 76/06, s. 15.]

[Editor's Note: Forms 4 to 39 of the Family Law Rules have been repealed by O. Reg. 76/06, effective May 1, 2006. Pursuant to Family Law Rule 1(9), when a form is referred to by number, the reference is to the form with that number that is described in the Table of Forms at the end of these rules and which is available at www.ontariocourtforms.on.ca. For your convenience, the government form as published on this website is reproduced below.]

Court File Number ....

.... *(Name of court)*

at .... *Court office address*

Recipient(s)

Full legal name & address for service — street & number, municipality, postal code, telephone & fax and e-mail address (if any).	*Lawyer's name & address — street & number, municipality, postal code, telephone & fax numbers and e-mail address (if any).*

Payor

Full legal name & address for service — street & number, municipality, postal code, telephone & fax numbers and e-mail address (if any).	*Lawyer's name & address — street & number, municipality, postal code, telephone & fax numbers and e-mail address (if any).*

1. My name is *(full legal name)*

   ....

2.

   ❑ I am
   - ❑ an income source of the payor.
   - ❑ an employee of an income source of the payor.
   - ❑ *(Other, specify)*
     ....
     ....

OR

❑ Neither I nor the organization for which I work is an income source of the payor for the following reasons:
- ❑ there is no money owed to the payor on any basis mentioned in paragraph 3 below.
- ❑ the payor has never worked for me or my organization.
- ❑ the payor has worked for me or my organization but stopped working on *:(date)*
  ....
- ❑ *(Other, specify.)*
  ....
  ....

(Strike out paragraph 3 if you are not an income source.)

3. I owe money to the payor on the following basis: *(check one or more boxes below)*

   ❑ wages or salary of $.......... per ....

   ❑ overtime that, over the past 6 months, has amounted to $..........

   ❑ commission, bonus, piece-work allowance or other performance-related payment that, over the past 6 months, has amounted to $..........

   ❑ benefits under an accident, disability or sickness plan that, over the past 6 months, has amounted to $..........

   ❑ a disability, retirement or other pension of $.......... per ....

   ❑ an annuity paying $.......... per ....

   ❑ vacation pay/severance pay of $ ....

❑ *(Other. specify.)*
....
....

.... *Signature*

.... *Date of signature*

September 1, 2005

FORM 27C — APPOINTMENT FOR FINANCIAL EXAMINATION

[Repealed O. Reg. 76/06, s. 15.]

[Editor's Note: Forms 4 to 39 of the Family Law Rules have been repealed by O. Reg. 76/06, effective May 1, 2006. Pursuant to Family Law Rule 1(9), when a form is referred to by number, the reference is to the form with that number that is described in the Table of Forms at the end of these rules and which is available at www.ontariocourtforms.on.ca. For your convenience, the government form as published on this website is reproduced below.]

ONTARIO

Court File Number

.... *(Name of court)*

at .... *Court office address*

Recipient(s)

Full legal name & address for service — street & number, municipality, postal code, telephone & fax numbers and e-mail address (if any).	*Lawyer's name & address — street & number, municipality, postal code, telephone & fax numbers and e-mail address (if any).*

Payor

Full legal name & address for service — street & number, municipality, postal code, telephone & fax numbers and e-mail address (if any).	*Lawyer's name & address — street & number, municipality, postal code, telephone & fax numbers and e-mail address (if any).*

TO: (full legal name of person to be examined) ....

I claim that you have missed payments under an order or domestic contract, a copy of which is attached. The purpose of this examination is to find out,

(a) your ability to pay the amount of the money owing; and

(b) your ability to continue obeying the order or domestic contract.

YOU MUST PREPARE a financial statement in Form 13 and serve it on the recipient or on the recipient's lawyer at least 7 days before the date of the examination. A blank form of financial statement should accompany or be attached to this notice. If it is missing, you should talk to your own lawyer or the court office immediately.

YOU MUST THEN COME TO A FINANCIAL EXAMINATION to be held on (date) .... *at* .... *a.m./p.m. at (place of examination)*:

You can bring your own lawyer.

YOU MUST BRING WITH YOU TO THE FINANCIAL EXAMINATION the documents or things in your possession or control that are listed on the back of this sheet.

IF YOU DO NOT COME TO THE FINANCIAL EXAMINATION, THE COURT MAY MAKE AN ORDER WITHOUT YOU AND ENFORCE IT AGAINST YOU.

....

Signature *Date of signature*

(Set out the nature and the date of every document and give enough details to identify every document and thing that the payor is to bring to the examination. Write "NIL" if no document or thing is to be brought to the examination.)

❑ A copy of the income tax return that you filed with the Canada Revenue Agency *(together with all material filed with the return)* for the years .... and a copy of any notice of assessment or reassessment that you received from the Agency for those years.

❑ Proof of your income *(including pay stubs)* for the past .... month(s).

❑ A print-out from every bank, trust company, loan corporation, credit union or caisse populaire in which you have maintained an account for the past .... month(s) showing all the transactions carried out in account during that period of time.

Put a line through any blank space left on this page.

April 12, 2016

FORM 28 — WRIT OF SEIZURE AND SALE

[Repealed O. Reg. 76/06, s. 15.]

[Editor's Note: Forms 4 to 39 of the Family Law Rules have been repealed by O. Reg. 76/06, effective May 1, 2006. Pursuant to Family Law Rule 1(9), when a form is referred to by number, the reference is to the form with that number that is described in the Table of Forms at the end of these rules and which is available at www.ontariocourtforms.on.ca. For your convenience, the government form as published on this website is reproduced below.]

ONTARIO

Court File Number

(SEAL)

.... *(Name of court)*

at .... *Court office address*

Recipient(s)

Full legal name & address for service — street & number, municipality, postal code, telephone & fax numbers and e-mail address (if any).	*Lawyer's name & address — street & number, municipality, postal code, telephone & fax numbers and e-mail address (if any).*

Payor

Full legal name & address for service — street & number, municipality, postal code, telephone & fax numbers and e-mail address (if any).	*Lawyer's name & address — street & number, municipality, postal code, telephone & fax numbers and e-mail address (if any).*

TO THE SHERIFF FOR THE (name of area) ....

An order or domestic contract that is enforceable in this court and that requires the payor to make payments to the recipient is in default.

YOU ARE THEREFORE DIRECTED TO SEIZE AND TO SELL the personal and real property within your area of *(Give full legal name of person or corporation, etc., against whom the writ shall be issued.)*

Surname of payor or name of corporation, etc.		
First given name (individual only)	*Second given name, if any (individual only)*	*Third given name, if any (individual only)*

and to realize from that sale the following sums:

Insert amount to be realized from paragraph 4(b) of the request for a writ of seizure and sale. Insert date that statement of money owed was sworn/affirmed.

(Check appropriate box)

(a) $.......... and interest on it at the rate of ....% per year, beginning on *(date)* ....; and

(b) your fees and expenses in enforcing this writ.

Priority for support payments: insert amount from paragraph 3 of request for a writ of seizure and sale.

❑ The sum to be realized includes unpaid support of $..................................

YOU ARE THEREFORE REQUIRED, under subsection 4(1) of the *Creditors' Relief Act*, to give priority to this amount over other judgments and orders.

Assignment of costs to Legal Aid Ontario: insert amount from paragraph 4(c) of request for writ of seizure and sale.

❑ *An Assignment of Judgment of Costs* in the amount of $.................................. has been made in favour of Legal Aid Ontario.

YOU ARE THEREFORE REQUIRED, under subsections 46(4) and 47(1) of the *Legal Aid Services Act, 1998*, to deduct this sum from the proceeds of the sale and to pay it to Legal Aid Ontario.

Fine, bond or recognizance

❑ This Writ enforces the sum of $.................................. as

❑ a fine for contempt of this court

❑ a forfeited bond or a forfeited recognizance

and made payable to ❑ Her Majesty the Queen

❑ other *(Specify.)* ....

YOU ARE THEREFORE REQUIRED, under subsection 143(3) of the *Courts of Justice Act*, to proceed immediately to execute this Writ without a direction to enforce.

YOU ARE FURTHER DIRECTED TO PAY OUT THESE PROCEEDS ACCORDING TO LAW AND TO REPORT ON THE EXECUTION OF THIS WRIT IF REQUIRED BY THE PARTY OR BY THE PARTY'S LAWYER WHO FILED THIS WRIT.

....

Date of signature *Signature of the clerk of the court*

Name of payor: ....

Name of recipient(s): ....

FEES		
Fee	Item	Officer
$		
$		
$		
$		
$		
$		
$		
$		
$		
$		
$		
$		
$		
$		

....

(Name of court)

at ....

Court office address

Writ of Seizure and Sale

Full legal name of filing party:

Filing party's address for service:

Name, address, telephone & fax numbers and e-mail address (if any) of filing party's lawyer:

NOTE: This writ has no automatic expiry date. It remains in effect:

(a) until it is withdrawn by or on behalf of the party who filed it; or

(b) until it is set aside or suspended by order of a court in Ontario.

April 12, 2016

FORM 28A — REQUEST FOR WRIT OF SEIZURE AND SALE

[Repealed O. Reg. 76/06, s. 15.]

[Editor's Note: Forms 4 to 39 of the Family Law Rules have been repealed by O. Reg. 76/06, effective May 1, 2006. Pursuant to Family Law Rule 1(9), when a form is referred to by number, the reference is to the form with that number that is described in the Table of Forms at the end of these rules and which is available at www.ontariocourtforms.on.ca. For your convenience, the government form as published on this website is reproduced below.]

Court File Number ....

.... *(Name of court)*

at .... *Court office address*

Recipient(s)

Full legal name & address for service — street & number, municipality, postal code, telephone & fax and e-mail address (if any).	*Lawyer's name & address — street & number, municipality, postal code, telephone & fax numbers and e-mail address (if any).*

Payor

Full legal name & address for service — street & number, municipality, postal code, telephone & fax numbers and e-mail address (if any).	*Lawyer's name & address — street & number, municipality, postal code, telephone & fax numbers and e-mail address (if any).*

TO THE CLERK OF THE COURT:

1. I am

❏ the person who signed the attached statement of money owed.
❏ the lawyer for the person who signed the attached statement of money owed.
❏ other *(Specify.)* ....

2. The attached statement of money owed contains a claim for $ .... *(Insert the sum from paragraph 13 of the statement of money owed.)*

....
....

3. This claim includes *unpaid support* of $ ...., an amount that has priority over all other judgment debts of the payor's creditors.

4. I request that a writ of seizure and sale be issued, directed to the sheriff of each of the following areas: *(list the areas)* ....

(a) to seize and sell the payor's real and personal property within that area;

(b) to realize from that seizure and sale

- ❑ the sum set out in paragraph 2 above;
- ❑ the sum of $ .... *(Set out a sum less than that in paragraph 2 above if you do not want to have all of it enforced by seizure and sale.)*; and

(c) to pay out the proceeds according to law, including payment of $ .... *(write "NIL" if no assignment was made)* to the Legal Aid Ontario in accordance with the attached *Assignment of Judgment of Costs* in favour of Legal Aid Ontario.

.... *Signature*

.... *Date of signature*

NOTE: You must file this request and a freshly prepared statement of money owed in Form 26 with the clerk of the court. If you completed paragraph 4(c) of this request with a dollar amount, a copy of the assignment of costs must be attached to this request and to each writ of seizure and sale that you file with a sheriff and a land registrar.

September 1, 2005

FORM 28B — STATUTORY DECLARATION TO SHERIFF

[Repealed O. Reg. 76/06, s. 15.]

[Editor's Note: Forms 4 to 39 of the Family Law Rules have been repealed by O. Reg. 76/06, effective May 1, 2006. Pursuant to Family Law Rule 1(9), when a form is referred to by number, the reference is to the form with that number that is described in the Table of Forms at the end of these rules and which is available at www.ontariocourtforms.on.ca. For your convenience, the government form as published on this website is reproduced below.]

Court File Number ....

.... *(Name of court)*

at .... *Court office address*

Recipient(s)

Full legal name & address for service — street & number, municipality, postal code, telephone & fax numbers and e-mail address (if any).	*Lawyer's name & address — street & number, municipality, postal code, telephone & fax numbers and e-mail address (if any).*

Payor

Full legal name & address for service — street & number, municipality, postal code, telephone & fax numbers and e-mail address (if any).	*Lawyer's name & address — street & number, municipality, postal code, telephone & fax numbers and e-mail address (if any).*

Payor

My name is (full legal name) ....

I live in (municipality & province) ....

and I declare that the following is true:

1. I am

❑ a recipient under a payment order.

❑ an assignee of a recipient under a payment order.

❑ an agent of the Director of the Family Responsibility Office.

❑ other *(Specify.)* ....

2. On *(date)* .... a writ of seizure and sale was issued in this case, a copy of which is attached.

3. Since then, the amount owed by the payor has changed and, as of today, the amount owed stands at $ .... with interest on it at the rate of .... % per year beginning on *(date when interest begins)* ....

4. Since then, the payor has:

❑ legally changed his/her name from .... to ....

❑ used the following alias(es): ....

❑ used the following spelling variation(s) of his or her name or alias(es): ....

5. The amount in paragraph 3 includes unpaid support of $ .... which, under subsection 4(1) of the *Creditors' Relief Act*, gets priority over other judgments and orders.

6. An additional *Assignment of Judgment of Costs* in the amount of *(write NIL if none)* $ .... has been made in favour of Legal Aid Ontario which, under subsections 46(4) and 47(1) of the *Legal Aid Services Act, 1998*, must be deducted from the proceeds of the sale and paid to Legal Aid Ontario.

7. The amount in paragraph 3 includes $ .... as a fine for contempt of this court, a forfeited bond or a forfeited recognizance arising out of a civil proceeding and made payable to, . . . ❑ Her Majesty the Queen ❑ other *(Specify.)* .... and, under subsection 143(3) of the *Courts of Justice Act*, the writ of seizure and sale can be executed immediately to collect that amount without a direction to enforce.

Declared before me at .... *municipality* in .... *province, state or country*	.... *Signature*

on .... *date* .... *Commissioner for taking affidavits* *(Type or print name below if signature is illegible.)*	*(This form is to be signed in front of a lawyer, justice of the peace, notary public or commissioner for taking affidavits.)*

June 15, 2007

FORM 28C — WRIT OF TEMPORARY SEIZURE

[Repealed O. Reg. 76/06, s. 15.]

[Editor's Note: Forms 4 to 39 of the Family Law Rules have been repealed by O. Reg. 76/06, effective May 1, 2006. Pursuant to Family Law Rule 1(9), when a form is referred to by number, the reference is to the form with that number that is described in the Table of Forms at the end of these rules and which is available at www.ontariocourtforms.on.ca. For your convenience, the government form as published on this website is reproduced below.]

Court File Number

[SEAL] ....

(Name of court)

at ....

Form 28C: Writ of Temporary Seizure

Court office address

Applicant(s)/Recipient(s) (Strike out inapplicable term.)

Full legal name & address for service — street & number, municipality, postal code, telephone & fax numbers & e-mail address (if any).	*Lawyer's name & address — street & number, municipality, postal code, telephone & fax numbers & e-mail address (if any).*

Respondent/Payor (Strike out inapplicable term.)

Full legal name & address for service — street & number, municipality, postal code, telephone & fax numbers & e-mail address (if any).	*Lawyer's name & address — street & number, municipality, postal code, telephone & fax numbers & e-mail address (if any).*

TO THE SHERIFF FOR THE (name of area) ....

On a motion made by *(name of moving party)* ....

the court gave its permission on *(date)* .... to issue this writ.

YOU ARE THEREFORE DIRECTED TO SEIZE AND TO HOLD the following property within your area of (Give full legal name of person or corporation, etc. against whom the writ shall be issued.)

Surname of respondent/payor or name of corporation, etc.		
First given name (individual only)	*Second given name, if any (individual only)*	*Third given name, if any (individual only)*

Give description of property to be taken and held.

YOU ARE ALSO DIRECTED TO COLLECT AND TO HOLD any income from the property until the writ is withdrawn or until further order of the court.

.... *Date of signature*

.... *Signature of the clerk of the court*

September 1, 2005

FORM 29 — REQUEST FOR GARNISHMENT

[Repealed O. Reg. 76/06, s. 15.]

[Editor's Note: Forms 4 to 39 of the Family Law Rules have been repealed by O. Reg. 76/06, effective May 1, 2006. Pursuant to Family Law Rule 1(9), when a form is referred to by number, the reference is to the form with that number that is described in the Table of Forms at the end of these rules and which is available at www.ontariocourtforms.on.ca. For your convenience, the government form as published on this website is reproduced below.]

ONTARIO

Court File Number

.... *(Name of court)*

at .... *Court office address*

Recipient(s)

Full legal name & address for service — street & number, municipality, postal code, telephone & fax numbers and e-mail address (if any).	*Lawyer's name & address — street & number, municipality, postal code, telephone & fax numbers and e-mail address (if any).*

Recipient(s)

Payor

Full legal name & address for service — street & number, municipality, postal code, telephone & fax numbers and e-mail address (if any).	*Lawyer's name & address — street & number, municipality, postal code, telephone & fax numbers and e-mail address (if any).*

TO THE CLERK OF THE COURT:

1. I am

❑ the person who signed the attached statement of money owed.

❑ the lawyer for the person who signed the attached statement of money owed.

❑ an agent for the Director of the Family Responsibility Office.

❑ *(Other; specify.)*

....

2. I want to enforce by way of garnishment the sum of $ ...., which is the money claimed in the attached statement of money owed. *(If you want to collect ongoing periodic payments as well as arrears, check the box below.)*

❑ I also want the garnishment to collect ongoing payments of $ .... per *(period)* ....

3. I request that a separate notice of garnishment be issued and sent to each person named in the Appendix to this form, who, I have reason to believe, owes or will owe money to the payor in the amounts described in that Appendix.

....

Signature of person making request or of person's lawyer *Date of signature*

NOTE: You must attach one or more sheets as an Appendix in which you name the person or persons who owe or will owe money to the payor. You must also prepare and attach a fresh statement of money owed in Form 26 (one prepared within the past 30 days) to this request and file it with the clerk of the court.

If

(a) the payor's obligation to pay the order or domestic contract that you are enforcing by this garnishment should expire or be discharged, and

(b) there is no more money owed by the payor under that order or domestic contract,

or if you simply decide that you no longer want to enforce the order or domestic contract by means of this garnishment, you must immediately fill out and serve a notice to stop garnishment in Form 29I on the payor and on each garnishee and file it, together with proof of service, with the clerk of the court at the above court office.

APPENDIX

Court File Number

Name of Garnishee: ....
Garnishee's address: ....
Amount that the garnishee owes or will owe to the payor:
❏ *periodic amounts* ❏ of $ ....
❏ *whose dollar figure I do not know*
that are or will be paid on (State frequency of payments. Write "UNKNOWN" if you do not know.) ....
❏ *lump-sum amount* ❏ *of $* ....
❏ *whose dollar figure I do not know.*
Description of debt owed by the garnishee to the payor:
❏ *wages, commissions or other employment income.* ❏ *rental payments*
❏ *money held at a bank, credit union, etc.* ❏ *pension payments*
❏ *(Other; specify.)*

Name of Garnishee: ....
Garnishee's address: ....
Amount that the garnishee owes or will owe to the payor:
❏ *periodic amounts* ❏ *of $* ....
❏ *whose dollar figure I do not know*
that are or will be paid on (State frequency of payments. Write "UNKNOWN" if you do not know.) ....
❏ *lump-sum amount* ❏ *of $* ....
❏ *whose dollar figure I do not know.*
Description of debt owed by the garnishee to the payor:
❏ *wages, commissions or other employment income.* ❏ *rental payments*
❏ *money held at a bank, credit union, etc.* ❏ *pension payments*
❏ *(Other; specify.)*

Name of Garnishee: ....
Garnishee's address: ....
Amount that the garnishee owes or will owe to the payor:
❏ *periodic amounts* ❏ *of $* ....
❏ *whose dollar figure I do not know*
that are or will be paid on (State frequency of payments. Write "UNKNOWN" if you do not know.) ....
❏ *lump-sum amount* ❏ *of $* ....
❏ *whose dollar figure I do not know.*
Description of debt owed by the garnishee to the payor:
❏ *wages, commissions or other employment income.* ❏ *rental payments*

❑ *money held at a bank, credit union, etc.* ❑ *pension payments*
❑ *(Other; specify.)*

April 12, 2016

FORM 29A — NOTICE OF GARNISHMENT (LUMP-SUM DEBT)

[Repealed O. Reg. 76/06, s. 15.]

[Editor's Note: Forms 4 to 39 of the Family Law Rules have been repealed by O. Reg. 76/06, effective May 1, 2006. Pursuant to Family Law Rule 1(9), when a form is referred to by number, the reference is to the form with that number that is described in the Table of Forms at the end of these rules and which is available at www.ontariocourtforms.on.ca. For your convenience, the government form as published on this website is reproduced below.]

ONTARIO

Court File Number

(SEAL)

.... *(Name of court)*

at .... *Court office address*

Recipient

Full legal name & address for service — street & number, municipality, postal code, telephone & fax numbers and e-mail address (if any).	*Lawyer's name & address — street & number, municipality, postal code, telephone & fax numbers and e-mail address (if any).*

Payor

Full legal name & address for service — street & number, municipality, postal code, telephone & fax numbers and e-mail address (if any).	*Lawyer's name & address — street & number, municipality, postal code, telephone & fax numbers and e-mail address (if any).*

TO: *(garnishee's full legal name and address)*

....

ALL DEDUCTIONS MADE UNDER THIS NOTICE MUST BE PAID TO

❑ the clerk of the court ❑ the Director of the Family Responsibility Office

at *(address)* ....

The payor *(name)* .... has missed payments under a court order or domestic contract that is enforceable in this court or that is enforceable by a garnishment process from outside Ontario and recognized by this court.

The recipient claims that you owe or will owe the payor a debt in the form of one or more lump-sum amounts. (A debt to the payor includes both a debt payable to the payor alone and a joint debt payable to the payor and one or more other persons.)

YOU MUST THEREFORE PAY TO the clerk of the court or the Director of the Family Responsibility Office (as indicated above)

(a) within 10 days after service of this Notice upon you, ALL MONEY THAT IS NOW PAYABLE BY YOU TO THE PAYOR; and

(b) within 10 days after any future amount becomes payable, ALL MONEY THAT BECOMES PAYABLE BY YOU TO THE PAYOR.

The total amount of your payments is not to exceed $ .... *(insert the dollar amount by adding the sums in paragraphs 5, 6, 7 and 8 of the statement of money owed or such lesser amount as the recipient chooses to have enforced by way of garnishment.)*

If your debt is jointly owed to the payor and to one or more other persons, you must pay half of the amount now payable or that becomes payable or such fraction as the court may order.

This notice is legally binding on you until it is changed or terminated.

(Check box below if appropriate.)

❑ This notice of garnishment enforces the support provisions of a court order or domestic contract. Under subsection 4(1) of the *Creditors' Relief Act, YOU MUST GIVE THIS NOTICE OF GARNISHMENT PRIORITY OVER ALL OTHER NOTICES OF GARNISHMENT,* no matter when these other competing notices of garnishment were served on you. For details of the extent of this priority, you should talk to your own lawyer.

Your payment in accordance with this notice is, to the extent of the payment, a valid discharge of your debt to the payor and, in the case of a joint debt to the payor and one or more other persons, a valid discharge of your debt to the payor and the other person(s).

If your debt is jointly owed to the payor and to one or more other persons, *YOU MUST IMMEDIATELY MAIL a notice to co-owner of the debt (Form 29C) to the following persons*:

(a) each other person to whom the joint debt is owed, at the address shown in your own records;

(b) the recipient or the Director of the Family Responsibility Office, depending on who is enforcing the order; and

(c) the clerk of the court.

A blank Form 29C should be attached to this notice. If it is missing, you should talk to your own lawyer or the court office.

If you have reason to believe that you should not be making the payments required of you by this notice, you have the right to serve a dispute in Form 29F on the parties and file it at the court office within 10 days after service of this notice upon you. You may consult with your lawyer about this. A blank Form 29F (dispute from garnishee) should be attached to this notice. If it is missing, you should talk to your own lawyer or the court office. You can serve by any method set out in rule 6 of the *Family Law Rules*, including mail, courier and fax. If you serve Form 29F and file it at the court office, the court may hold a garnishment hearing to determine the rights of the parties. In the meantime, serving and filing a dispute does not stop the operation of this notice of garnishment.

If you are the payor's employer,

(a) Section 56.1 of Ontario's *Employment Standards Act* make it unlawful to dismiss or suspend an employee or to threaten to do so on the ground that a garnishment process has been issued in respect of the employee;

(b) section 7 of the Ontario's *Wages Act* says that you cannot deduct more than:

(i) 50% of any wages (after statutory deductions) payable to your employee for the enforcement of support; and

(ii) 20% of any wages (after statutory deductions) payable to your employee for the enforcement of money not connected to support.

These percentages can be increased or decreased only by an order of the court. If a copy of such an order is attached to this notice or if it is ever served on you, you must use the percentage given in that court order; and

(c) the *Family Law Rules* state that you MUST give to the clerk of the court and to the person who asked for this garnishment, within 10 days after the end of the payor's employment with you, a written notice,

(i) indicating that the payor has ceased to be employed by you, and

(ii) setting out the date on which the employment ended and the date of the payor's last remuneration from you.

IF YOU DO NOT OBEY THIS NOTICE, THE COURT MAY ORDER YOU TO PAY THE FULL AMOUNT OWED AND THE COSTS INCURRED BY THE RECIPIENT.

IF YOU PAY ANYONE OTHER THAN AS DIRECTED ON THE FRONT OF THIS SHEET, THE COURT MAY ORDER YOU TO MAKE ANOTHER PAYMENT, BUT THIS TIME, TO THE PERSON NAMED IN THIS NOTICE.

....	....
Date of signature	*Signature of the clerk of the court*

NOTICE TO THE PAYOR: You have the right to serve and file a dispute in Form 29E at the court office within 10 days after service of this notice on you. You may want to talk to a lawyer about this. A blank Form 29E (dispute from payor) should have accompanied this notice when it was served on you. If it is missing, you should talk to your own lawyer or the court office immediately. You can serve by any method set out in rule 6 of the *Family Law Rules*, including mail, courier and fax. If you serve Form 29E and file it at the court office, the court may hold a garnishment hearing to decide the rights of the parties.

If the garnishee is your employer, the *Family Law Rules* says that you MUST, within 10 days after the end of your employment with the garnishee, give the clerk of the court and (depending on who is enforcing the garnishment) the recipient or the Director of the Family Responsibility Office, a written notice,

(a) indicating that your employment with the garnishee is ended; and

(b) setting out the date on which your employment ended and the date of your last pay from the garnishee.

Within 10 days after you start any new job or go back to your old one, you MUST give a further written notice giving the name and address of your new employer or saying that you have gone back to work with your former employer.

April 12, 2016

FORM 29B — NOTICE OF GARNISHMENT (PERIODIC DEBT)

[Repealed O. Reg. 76/06, s. 15.]

[Editor's Note: Forms 4 to 39 of the Family Law Rules have been repealed by O. Reg. 76/06, effective May 1, 2006. Pursuant to Family Law Rule 1(9), when a form is referred to by number, the reference is to the form with that number that is described in the Table of Forms at the end of these rules and which is available at www.ontariocourtforms.on.ca. For your convenience, the government form as published on this website is reproduced below.]

ONTARIO

Court File Number

(SEAL)

.... *(Name of court)*

at .... *Court office address*

Recipient

Full legal name & address for service — street & number, municipality, postal code, telephone & fax numbers and e-mail address (if any).	*Lawyer's name & address — street & number, municipality, postal code, telephone & fax numbers and e-mail address (if any).*

Payor

Full legal name & address for service — street & number, municipality, postal code, telephone & fax numbers and e-mail address (if any).	*Lawyer's name & address — street & number, municipality, postal code, telephone & fax numbers and e-mail address (if any).*

TO: (garnishee's full legal name and address)

....

ALL DEDUCTIONS MADE UNDER THIS NOTICE MUST TO BE PAID TO

❑ the clerk of the court ..... ❑ the Director of the Family Responsibility Office at *(address)* ....

The payor *(name)* .... has missed payments under a court order or domestic contract that is enforceable in this court or that is enforceable by a garnishment process from outside Ontario and recognized by this court. The recipient claims that you owe or will owe the payor a debt in the form of wages, salary, pension payments, rent, annuity or other debt that you pay out periodically or by instalments. (A debt to the payor includes both a debt payable to the payor alone and a debt payable jointly to the payor and one or more other persons.)

Check the first circle if you want the garnishment to deduct fixed dollar amounts. If you want the garnishment to deduct by way of percentage, check the second circle below.

❑ *YOU MUST IMMEDIATELY THEREFORE DEDUCT FROM ALL SUCH PAYMENTS MADE BY YOU,*

Insert the dollar amount and frequency as stated in the periodic portion of the order or domestic contract.

❑ to satisfy the payor's ongoing duty to make periodic payments under the order or domestic contract THE SUM OF $.......... on every *(state frequency)* .... or the equivalent sum according to your regular or established cycle of payment to the payor; *and*

"Accumulated debts" includes lump-sum orders, fines, forfeitures, accumulated arrears of periodic payments, court costs and interest.

❑ to reduce the payor's accumulated debts of $.......... to the recipient under the order or domestic contract, THE SUM OF $.......... on every *(state frequency)* .... or the equivalent sum according to your regular or established cycle of payment to the payor, *OR*

Check this circle only if you want the garnishment to deduct by way of percentage.

❑ *YOU MUST IMMEDIATELY THEREFORE DEDUCT FROM ALL SUCH PAYMENTS MADE BY YOU,*

Unless a court order says otherwise, you can deduct no more than 50% of the payor's wages to collect support and no more than 20% to collect money unrelated to support. There is no percentage ceiling on the deductions from non-wages.

❑ ....% of all wages that are now payable by you to the payor, and

❑ ....% of any debt (other than wages) now payable by you to the payor periodically or by instalments.

AND YOU MUST PAY THIS DEDUCTION to the clerk of the Director (as indicated above) within 10 days after service of this notice upon you. If your debt is jointly owed to the payor and to one or more other persons, you must pay half of the amount now payable or that becomes payable or such fraction as the court may order.

THIS NOTICE LEGALLY BINDS YOU TO CONTINUE PAYING THESE DEDUCTIONS within 10 days after each payment becomes payable by you to the payor, until this notice is changed or terminated.

(Check below if appropriate.)

❑ This notice of garnishment enforces the support provisions of a court order or domestic contract.

Under subsection 4(1) of the *Creditors' Relief Act, YOU MUST GIVE THIS NOTICE OF GARNISHMENT PRIORITY OVER ALL OTHER NOTICES OF GARNISHMENT*, no matter when these other competing notices of garnishment were served to you. For details of the extent of this priority, you should talk to your own lawyer.

Your payment in accordance with this notice is, to the extent of the payment, a valid discharge of your debt to the payor and, in the case of a joint debt to the payor and one or more other persons, a valid discharge of your debt to the payor and the other person(s).

If your debt is jointly owed to the payor and to one or more other persons, *YOU MUST IMMEDIATELY MAIL a notice to co-owner of the debt (Form 29C) to the following persons*:

(a) each other person to whom the joint debt is owed, at the address shown in your own records;

(b) the recipient or the Director of the Family Responsibility Office, depending on who is enforcing the order; and

(c) the clerk of the court.

A blank Form 29C should be attached to this notice. If it is missing, you should talk to your own lawyer or the court office.

If you have reason to believe that you should not be making the payments required of you by this notice, you have the right to serve and file a dispute in Form 29F at the court office within 10 days after service of this notice upon you. You may consult with your lawyer about this. A blank Form 29F (dispute from garnishee) should be attached to this notice. If it is missing, you should talk to your own lawyer or the court office. You can serve by any method set out in rule 6 of the *Family Law Rules*, including mail, courier and fax. If you serve Form 29F and file it at the court office, the court may hold a garnishment hearing to determine the rights of the parties. In the meantime, serving and filing a dispute does not stop the operation of this notice of garnishment.

If you are the payor's employer

(a) Section 56.1 of Ontario's *Employment Standards Act* makes it unlawful to dismiss or suspend an employee or to threaten to do so on the ground that a garnishment process has been issued in respect of the employee;

(b) section 7 of Ontario's *Wages Act* says that you cannot deduct more than:

(i) 50% of any wages (after statutory deductions) payable to your employee for the enforcement of support; and

(ii) 20% of any wages (after statutory deductions) payable to your employee for the enforcement of money not connected to support.

These percentages can be increased or decreased only by an order of the court. If a copy of such an order is attached to this notice or if it is ever served on you, you must use the percentage given in that court order; and

(c) the *Family Law Rules* state you MUST give to the clerk of the court and to the person who asked for this garnishment, within 10 days after the end of the payor's employment with you, a written notice,

(i) indicating that the payor has ceased to be employed by you, and

(ii) setting out the date on which the employment ended and the date of the payor's last remuneration from you.

IF YOU DO NOT OBEY THIS NOTICE, THE COURT MAY ORDER YOU TO PAY THE FULL AMOUNT OWED AND THE COSTS INCURRED BY THE RECIPIENT.

IF YOU PAY ANYONE OTHER THAN AS DIRECTED ON THE FRONT OF THIS SHEET, THE COURT MAY ORDER YOU TO MAKE ANOTHER PAYMENT, BUT THIS TIME, TO THE PERSON NAMED IN THIS NOTICE.

....	....
Date of signature	*Signature of the clerk of the court*

NOTICE TO THE PAYOR: You have the right to serve and file a dispute in Form 29E at the court office within 10 days after service of this notice on you. You may want to talk to a lawyer about this. A blank Form 29E (dispute from payor) should have accompanied this notice when it was served on you. If it is missing, you should talk to your own lawyer or the court office immediately. You can serve by any method set out in rule 6 of the *Family Law Rules*, including mail, courier and fax. If you serve From 29E and file it at the court office, the court may hold a garnishment hearing to decide the rights of the parties.

If the garnishee is your employer, the *Family Law Rules* say that you MUST, within 10 days after the end of your employment with the garnishee, give the clerk of the court and (depending on who is enforcing the garnishment) the recipient or the Director of the Family Responsibility Office, a written notice,

(a) indicating that your employment with the garnishee is ended; and

(b) setting out the date on which your employment ended and the date of your last pay from the garnishee.

Within 10 days after you start any new job or go back to your old one, you MUST give a further written notice giving the name and address of your new employer or saying that you have gone back to work with of your former employer.

April 12, 2016

FORM 29C — NOTICE TO CO-OWNER OF DEBT

[Repealed O. Reg. 76/06, s. 15.]

[Editor's Note: Forms 4 to 39 of the Family Law Rules have been repealed by O. Reg. 76/06, effective May 1, 2006. Pursuant to Family Law Rule 1(9), when a form is referred to by number, the reference is to the form with that number that is described in the Table of Forms at the end of these rules and which is available at www.ontariocourtforms.on.ca. For your convenience, the government form as published on this website is reproduced below.]

Court File Number ....

.... *(Name of court)*

at .... *Court office address*

Recipient(s)	**Payor**
Full legal name & address for service — street & number, municipality, postal code, telephone & fax and e-mail address (if any).	*Full legal name & address for service — street & number, municipality, postal code, telephone & fax and e-mail address (if any).*
Lawyer's name & address — street & number, municipality, postal code, telephone & fax numbers and e-mail address (if any).	*Lawyer's name & address — street & number, municipality, postal code, telephone & fax numbers and e-mail address (if any).*

TO: (co-owner's full legal name and address)

A court case between the recipient and the payor has resulted in a court order requiring the payor to pay money to the recipient. The recipient or a person enforcing this order on the recipient's behalf has served me or my business with a notice of garnishment, claiming to intercept a debt that I or my business is supposed to owe and to pay to the payor. Under the law, a debt to the payor includes both a debt payable to the payor alone and a debt payable jointly to the payor and one or more other persons. According to my records or the records of my business, you are such an "other person" who shares in the debt that I or my business owe to the payor.

❑ In accordance with this notice of garnishment, I have paid out one half

❑ In accordance with a court order, I have paid out $.......... of the debt that I or my business jointly owes to you and the payor. This money is being held for 30 days by:

❑ the clerk of the court

❑ the Director of the Family Responsibility Office

at *(address)* ....

IF YOU BELIEVE THAT I OR MY BUSINESS HAVE PAID OUT MONEY THAT LEGALLY BELONGS TO YOU, you have 30 days from the service of this notice to serve Form 29G (*Dispute from Co-owner of Debt*) and file it with the court. You can get a copy of this form from your own lawyer or from the court office. You must then serve a completed copy of this form to the following persons:

(a) me or my business at the address given below;

(b) the payor and the recipient; and

(c) the clerk of the court or the Director, depending on who is holding the money.

You can serve by any method set out in rule 6 of the *Family Law Rules,* including mail, courier and fax. Once you have served this form, you must then file it with the court with proof of service (Form 6B). The court may then hold a garnishment hearing to determine your rights.

IF YOU FAIL TO DO THIS WITHIN 30 DAYS, you may not later challenge the recipient's garnishment of the debt that I or my business jointly owes to you and the payor.

.... *Signature of person preparing this notice or of person's lawyer*

.... Date of signature

.... *Typed or printed name, address for service, telephone & fax numbers and e-mail address of person or of person's lawyer*

September 1, 2005

FORM 29D — STATUTORY DECLARATION OF INDEXED SUPPORT

[Repealed O. Reg. 76/06, s. 15.]

[Editor's Note: Forms 4 to 39 of the Family Law Rules have been repealed by O. Reg. 76/06, effective May 1, 2006. Pursuant to Family Law Rule 1(9), when a form is referred to by

number, the reference is to the form with that number that is described in the Table of Forms at the end of these rules and which is available at www.ontariocourtforms.on.ca. For your convenience, the government form as published on this website is reproduced below.]

ONTARIO

Court File Number

.... *(Name of court)*

at .... *Court office address*

dated ....

Recipient(s)

Full legal name & address for service — street & number, municipality, postal code, telephone & fax numbers and e-mail address (if any).	*Lawyer's name & address — street & number, municipality, postal code, telephone & fax numbers and e-mail address (if any).*

Payor

Full legal name & address for service — street & number, municipality, postal code, telephone & fax numbers and e-mail address (if any).	*Lawyer's name & address — street & number, municipality, postal code, telephone & fax numbers and e-mail address (if any).*

Garnishee

Full legal name & address for service — street & number, municipality, postal code, telephone & fax numbers and e-mail address (if any).	*Lawyer's name & address — street & number, municipality, postal code, telephone & fax numbers and e-mail address (if any).*

My name is (full legal name) ....

I live in (municipality & province) ....

and I declare that the following is true:

1. I am

❑ a recipient under a support order or the support provisions of a domestic contract.

❑ an assignee of a recipient under a support order or the support provisions of a domestic contract.

❑ an agent of the Director of the Family Responsibility Office.

❑ *(Other; specify.)*

2. On *(date)* ...., a notice of garnishment was issued to the garnishee to enforce a support order or the support provisions of a domestic contract that indexed the periodic payments for inflation.

3. On *(date)* ...., the amount of support was automatically adjusted for inflation as set out in the order, contract or agreement.

4. As a result of this adjustment, the garnishee should now be making the following deductions: *(State new level of deductions.)*

Put a line through any blank space left on this page.

....

Sworn/Affirmed before me at .... *municipality* in .... *province, state, or country*		
on .... *date*	.... *Commissioner for taking affidavits (Type or print name below if signature is illegible.)*	.... *Signature* *(This form is to be signed in front of a lawyer, justice of the peace, notary public or commissioner for taking affidavits.)*

NOTE: This declaration must be served on the garnishee and the payor together with blank forms of dispute and must then be filed with the clerk of the court. You can serve by any means allowed in rule 6 of the Family Law Rules, *including mail, courier and fax. The filing with the clerk of the court must be accompanied by proof of service (Form 6B).*

NOTICE TO GARNISHEE: From the moment that you are served with this declaration, you must treat the notice of garnishment as if it now required you to make the deductions set out in paragraph 4 of this declaration. Failure to do so is the same as disobeying the notice of garnishment.

NOTICE TO PAYOR AND GARNISHEE: You have the right to serve and file a dispute in Form 29E (dispute from payor) or Form 29F (dispute from garnishee) at the court office within 10 days after service of this declaration on you if you have legal reasons for objecting to the changes to the notice of garnishment. You may want to talk to a lawyer about this. A blank form of dispute should have accompanied this declaration when it was served on you. If it is missing, you should talk to your own lawyer or the court office immediately. If this is what you want to do, you must serve your dispute on the other parties. You can serve by any means allowed in rule 6 of the *Family Law Rules*, including mail, courier and fax. Once the dispute has been served, you must file it with the clerk of the court. The filing must be accompanied by proof of service (Form 6B). If you serve and file your dispute, the court may hold a garnishment hearing to decide the rights of the parties.

April 12, 2016

FORM 29E — DISPUTE (PAYOR)

[Repealed O. Reg. 76/06, s. 15.]

[Editor's Note: Forms 4 to 39 of the Family Law Rules have been repealed by O. Reg. 76/06, effective May 1, 2006. Pursuant to Family Law Rule 1(9), when a form is referred to by number, the reference is to the form with that number that is described in the Table of Forms at the end of these rules and which is available at www.ontariocourtforms.on.ca. For your convenience, the government form as published on this website is reproduced below.]

Court File Number ....

.... *(Name of court)*

at .... *Court office address*

Recipient(s)

Full legal name & address for service — street & number, municipality, postal code, telephone & fax and e-mail address (if any).	*Lawyer's name & address — street & number, municipality, postal code, telephone & fax numbers and e-mail address (if any).*

Payor

Full legal name & address for service — street & number, municipality, postal code, telephone & fax numbers and e-mail address (if any).	*Lawyer's name & address — street & number, municipality, postal code, telephone & fax numbers and e-mail address (if any).*

Garnishee

Full legal name & address for service — street & number, municipality, postal code, telephone & fax numbers and e-mail address (if any).	*Lawyer's name & address — street & number, municipality, postal code, telephone & fax numbers and e-mail address (if any).*

My name is (full legal name) ....

I live in (municipality & province) .... *and I swear/affirm that the following is true:*

1. I am the payor in this garnishment case.

2. I dispute

❑ the notice of garnishment issued on

❑ the statutory declaration of indexed support made on

(date) ...., for the following reason(s): *(State the reason or reasons for your dispute in numbered paragraphs.)*

Put a line through any blank space left on this page.

NOTE: Merely serving and filing this dispute will not stop the garnishment process. It can be stopped at the recipient's request if the receipient agrees with the reasons for your dispute. It can also be stopped by a court order at a garnishment hearing. If you want the court to hold a hearing, you must check the box in the frame below.

❑	NOTICE TO THE CLERK OF THE COURT AND TO ALL PARTIES: I am making a request for a garnishment hearing in which the court can rule on this dispute.

Sworn/Affirmed before me at .... *munic-ipality* in .... *province, state or country* on .... *date*

Signature

Commissioner for taking affidavits *(Type or print name below if signature is illegible.)*

(This form is to be signed in front of a lawyer, justice of the peace, notary public or commissioner for taking affidavits.)

NOTICE TO RECIPIENT: Please examine this dispute. If you disagree with it and if the payor has not asked for a garnishment hearing, you yourself may ask to have a court hearing. You may want to talk to your own lawyer about this. You have 10 days from the date of being served with this document to decide whether to have a court hearing. If you want a hearing, you or your lawyer have 10 days within which to ask the clerk of the court, either in person or in writing, to mail out to you, to the payor, to the garnishee and to the co-owner of a joint debt (if any) a notice of garnishment hearing (Form 29H). At that hearing, the judge will give you and the other parties a chance to be heard and may make an order that can affect the rights of all parties.

September 1, 2005

FORM 29F — DISPUTE (GARNISHEE)

[Repealed O. Reg. 76/06, s. 15.]

[Editor's Note: Forms 4 to 39 of the Family Law Rules have been repealed by O. Reg. 76/06, effective May 1, 2006. Pursuant to Family Law Rule 1(9), when a form is referred to by number, the reference is to the form with that number that is described in the Table of Forms at the end of these rules and which is available at www.ontariocourtforms.on.ca. For your convenience, the government form as published on this website is reproduced below.]

Court File Number ....

.... *(Name of court)*

at .... *Court office address*

Recipient(s)

Full legal name & address for service — street & number, municipality, postal code, telephone & fax and e-mail address (if any).	*Lawyer's name & address — street & number, municipality, postal code, telephone & fax numbers and e-mail address (if any).*

Payor

Full legal name & address for service — street & number, municipality, postal code, telephone & fax numbers and e-mail address (if any).	*Lawyer's name & address — street & number, municipality, postal code, telephone & fax numbers and e-mail address (if any).*

Garnishee

Full legal name & address for service — street & number, municipality, postal code, telephone & fax numbers and e-mail address (if any).	*Lawyer's name & address — street & number, municipality, postal code, telephone & fax numbers and e-mail address (if any).*

1 I am the garnishee in this garnishment case.

2. I am not legally required to pay

❑ the amounts set out in the notice of garnishment issued on
❑ the changed amounts set out in the statutory declaration of indexed support made on

(date) ...., for the following reason(s):

❑ I do not owe and do not expect to owe any money to the payor because:
- ❑ the payor has never worked for me.
- ❑ the payor stopped working for me on *(date)* ....
- ❑ I owed the payor money and paid it in full by *(date)* ....
- ❑ I do not hold any money in trust for or to the credit of the payor.
- ❑ *(Other. Specify.)*
  ....
  ....

❑ I owe or will owe money to the payor, but it cannot be seized by garnishment because *(State reasons for legal exemption.)*
❑ *(Other grounds. Specify.)*
....
....

Put a line through any blank space left on this page.

NOTE: Merely serving and filing this dispute will not stop the garnishment process. It can be stopped at the recipient's request if the receipient agrees with the reasons for your dispute. It can also be stopped by a court order at a garnishment hearing. If you want the court to hold a hearing, you must check the box in the frame below.

❑	*NOTICE TO THE CLERK OF THE COURT AND TO ALL PARTIES: I am making a request for a garnishment hearing in which the court can rule on this dispute.*

.... *Signature of garnishee*

.... *Date of signature*

NOTICE TO RECIPIENT: Please examine this dispute. If you disagree with it and if the garnishee has not asked for a garnishment hearing, you yourself may ask to have a court hearing. You may want to talk to your own lawyer about this. You have 10 days from the date of being served with this document to decide whether to have a court hearing. If you want a hearing, you or your lawyer have 10 days within which to ask the clerk of the court, either in person or in writing, to mail out to you, to the payor, to the garnishee and to the co-owner of a joint debt (if any) a notice of garnishment hearing (Form 29H). At that hearing, the judge will give you and the other parties a chance to be heard and may make an order that can affect the rights of all parties.

September 1, 2005

FORM 29G — DISPUTE (CO-OWNER OF DEBT)

[Repealed O. Reg. 76/06, s. 15.]

[Editor's Note: Forms 4 to 39 of the Family Law Rules have been repealed by O. Reg. 76/06, effective May 1, 2006. Pursuant to Family Law Rule 1(9), when a form is referred to by number, the reference is to the form with that number that is described in the Table of Forms at the end of these rules and which is available at www.ontariocourtforms.on.ca. For your convenience, the government form as published on this website is reproduced below.]

Court File Number ....

.... *(Name of court)*

at .... *Court office address*

Recipient(s)

Full legal name & address for service — street & number, municipality, postal code, telephone & fax and e-mail address (if any).	*Lawyer's name & address — street & number, municipality, postal code, telephone & fax numbers and e-mail address (if any).*

Payor

Full legal name & address for service — street & number, municipality, postal code, telephone & fax numbers and e-mail address (if any).	*Lawyer's name & address — street & number, municipality, postal code, telephone & fax numbers and e-mail address (if any).*

Garnishee

Full legal name & address for service — street & number, municipality, postal code, telephone & fax numbers and e-mail address (if any).	*Lawyer's name & address — street & number, municipality, postal code, telephone & fax numbers and e-mail address (if any).*

1. I am a person who shares in the debt that the garnishee in this garnishment case is supposed to owe to the payor.

2. I make a claim on the money that the garnishee paid out and that is being temporarily held for the recipient's benefit as follows: *(In separately numbered paragraphs, indicate the amount that you are claiming to be yours and set out the legal basis for your claim.)*

Put a line through any blank space left on this page.

NOTE: Merely serving and filing this dispute will not stop the garnishment process. It can be stopped at the recipient's request if the receipient agrees with the reasons for your dispute. It can also be stopped by a court order at a garnishment hearing. If you want the court to hold a hearing, you must check the box in the frame below.

❑	NOTICE TO THE CLERK OF THE COURT AND TO ALL PARTIES: I am making a request for a garnishment hearing in which the court can rule on this dispute.

.... *Signature of co-owner of debt*

.... *Date of signature*

NOTICE TO RECIPIENT: Please examine this dispute. If you disagree with it and if the co-owner of the debt has not asked for a garnishment hearing, you yourself may ask to have a court hearing. You may want to talk to your own lawyer about this. You have 10 days from the date of being served with this document to decide whether to have a court hearing. If you want a hearing, you or your lawyer have 10 days within which to ask the clerk of the court, either in person or in writing, to mail out to you, to the payor, to the garnishee and to the co-owner of a joint debt (if any) a notice of garnishment hearing (Form 29H). At that hearing, the judge will give you and the other parties a chance to be heard and may make an order that can affect the rights of all parties.

September 1, 2005

FORM 29H — NOTICE OF GARNISHMENT HEARING

[Repealed O. Reg. 76/06, s. 15.]

[Editor's Note: Forms 4 to 39 of the Family Law Rules have been repealed by O. Reg. 76/06, effective May 1, 2006. Pursuant to Family Law Rule 1(9), when a form is referred to by number, the reference is to the form with that number that is described in the Table of Forms at the end of these rules and which is available at www.ontariocourtforms.on.ca. For your convenience, the government form as published on this website is reproduced below.]

Court File Number ....

[SEAL]

.... *(Name of court)*

at .... *Court office address*

Recipient(s)

Full legal name & address for service — street & number, municipality, postal code, telephone & fax and e-mail address (if any).	*Lawyer's name & address — street & number, municipality, postal code, telephone & fax numbers and e-mail address (if any).*

Payor

Full legal name & address for service — street & number, municipality, postal code, telephone & fax numbers and e-mail address (if any).	*Lawyer's name & address — street & number, municipality, postal code, telephone & fax numbers and e-mail address (if any).*

Garnishee

Full legal name & address for service — street & number, municipality, postal code, telephone & fax numbers and e-mail address (if any).	*Lawyer's name & address — street & number, municipality, postal code, telephone & fax numbers and e-mail address (if any).*

TO THE PARTIES:

THE COURT WILL HOLD A HEARING on *(date)* ...., at .... a.m./p.m. or as soon as possible after that time, at *(place of hearing)* .... because *(Check the appropriate box or boxes.)*

❏ a dispute has been filed by the
  ❏ payor
  ❏ garnishee
  ❏ co-owner of a debt

❏ it is claimed that the garnishee has not paid any money

❏ it is claimed that the garnishee has paid less than the required amount money

and the clerk of the court has received a request that a garnishment hearing be held.

IF YOU DO NOT COME TO COURT, AN ORDER MAY BE MADE WITHOUT YOU AND ENFORCED AGAINST YOU.

.... *Signature of the clerk of the court*

.... *Date of signature*

NOTE: Where a dispute has been served and filed, a photocopy of it should be attached to this notice. If it is missing, you should talk to the court office immediately.

September 1, 2005

FORM 29I — NOTICE TO STOP GARNISHMENT

[Repealed O. Reg. 76/06, s. 15.]

[Editor's Note: Forms 4 to 39 of the Family Law Rules have been repealed by O. Reg. 76/06, effective May 1, 2006. Pursuant to Family Law Rule 1(9), when a form is referred to by number, the reference is to the form with that number that is described in the Table of Forms at the end of these rules and which is available at www.ontariocourtforms.on.ca. For your convenience, the government form as published on this website is reproduced below.]

Court File Number ....

.... *(Name of court)*

at .... *Court office address*

Recipient(s)

Full legal name & address for service — street & number, municipality, postal code, telephone & fax and e-mail address (if any).	*Lawyer's name & address — street & number, municipality, postal code, telephone & fax numbers and e-mail address (if any).*

Payor

Full legal name & address for service — street & number, municipality, postal code, telephone & fax numbers and e-mail address (if any).	*Lawyer's name & address — street & number, municipality, postal code, telephone & fax numbers and e-mail address (if any).*

Garnishee

Full legal name & address for service — street & number, municipality, postal code, telephone & fax numbers and e-mail address (if any).	*Lawyer's name & address — street & number, municipality, postal code, telephone & fax numbers and e-mail address (if any).*

TO: (name of garnishee) .... *AND TO*

❑ *THE CLERK OF THE COURT*:

❑ *THE SHERIFF OF (area)* ....

My name is: *(full legal name)* ....

I am

❑ the person who asked for the garnishment in this case.

❑ the lawyer for the person who asked for the garnishment in this case.

❑ the person who continued this garnishment under a transfer of enforcement.

❑ the lawyer for the person who continued this garnishment under a transfer of enforcement.

❑ an agent for the Director of the Family Responsibility Office.
❑ *(Other. Specify.)*

....

....

The notice of garnishment issued on *(date)* ...., by the clerk of the court is withdrawn today.

YOU ARE THEREFORE DIRECTED TO STOP FURTHER PAYMENTS UNDER THE GARNISHMENT.

.... *Signature of person withdrawing garnishment*

.... *Date of signature*

September 1, 2005

FORM 29J — STATEMENT TO GARNISHEE FINANCIAL INSTITUTION RE SUPPORT

[Repealed O. Reg. 76/06, s. 15.]

[Editor's Note: Forms 4 to 39 of the Family Law Rules have been repealed by O. Reg. 76/06, effective May 1, 2006. Pursuant to Family Law Rule 1(9), when a form is referred to by number, the reference is to the form with that number that is described in the Table of Forms at the end of these rules and which is available at www.ontariocourtforms.on.ca. For your convenience, the government form as published on this website is reproduced below.]

ONTARIO

Court File Number

.... *(Name of court)*

at .... *Court office address*

Recipient(s)

Full legal name & address for service — street & number, municipality, postal code, telephone & fax numbers and e-mail address (if any).	*Lawyer's name & address — street & number, municipality, postal code, telephone & fax numbers and e-mail address (if any).*

Payor

Full legal name & address for service — street & number, municipality, postal code, telephone & fax numbers and e-mail address (if any).	*Lawyer's name & address — street & number, municipality, postal code, telephone & fax numbers and e-mail address (if any).*

Payor

Garnishee

Full legal name & address for service — street & number, municipality, postal code, telephone & fax numbers and e-mail address (if any).	*Lawyer's name & address — street & number, municipality, postal code, telephone & fax numbers and e-mail address (if any).*

My name is (*full legal name*) ....

I live in (*municipality & province*) ....

The following statements are true to the best of my knowledge:

1. I am ❑ a recipient under a support order or the support provisions of a domestic contract that is enforceable by this court

❑ an assignee of a recipient under a support order or the support provisions of a domestic contract

❑ an agent of the Director of the Family Responsibility Office

2. The payor's full name is ❑ ....

❑ unknown.

3. The payor commonly uses the name(s): ....

(*Either paragraph 4 or 5 must be completed. If both known, complete both*)

4. The payor's date of birth is ....

5. The payor's social insurance number is ....

....	....
Date of signature	*Signature*

NOTE: Under rule 29(6.1) of the Family Law Rules, *this form (29J) must be attached to Forms 29A, 29B, 29D, 29E, 29G, 29H or 29I when they are served on a bank or other financial institution at a central location. Under regulations made under the federal* Bank Act, Cooperative Credit Associations Act *and* Trust and Loan Companies Act, *a notice of garnishment for support payments against a bank or other federally regulated financial institution must be served on a central location established and published by each bank or financial institution.*

April 12, 2016

FORM 30 — NOTICE OF DEFAULT HEARING

[Repealed O. Reg. 76/06, s. 15.]

[Editor's Note: Forms 4 to 39 of the Family Law Rules have been repealed by O. Reg. 76/06, effective May 1, 2006. Pursuant to Family Law Rule 1(9), when a form is referred to by number, the reference is to the form with that number that is described in the Table of Forms at the end of these rules and which is available at www.ontariocourtforms.on.ca. For your convenience, the government form as published on this website is reproduced below.]

ONTARIO

Court File Number

(SEAL)

.... *(Name of court)*

at .... *Court office address*

Recipient(s)

Full legal name & address for service — street & number, municipality, postal code, telephone & fax numbers and e-mail address (if any).	*Lawyer's name & address — street & number, municipality, postal code, telephone & fax numbers and e-mail address (if any).*

Payor

Full legal name & address for service — street & number, municipality, postal code, telephone & fax numbers and e-mail address (if any).	*Lawyer's name & address — street & number, municipality, postal code, telephone & fax numbers and e-mail address (if any).*

TO (name of payor) ....

YOU MUST COME TO COURT on (date) ...., *at* .... *a.m./p.m. or as soon after that time as the court can hear the matter, at (place of hearing)* ....

It is claimed by the recipient or on the recipient's behalf that you have missed support payments under an order or a domestic contract. Details of the claim against you can be found in the attached copy of the statement of money owed. If it is missing, you should contact the court office immediately. The court has been asked to hold a default hearing under section 41 of the *Family Responsibility and Support Arrears Enforcement Act*, in which you will be required to explain not only the missed payments mentioned in the statement of money owed, but also any payments missed right up to the day when the court holds the hearing.

YOU MUST FILL OUT the attached blank forms of the financial statement (Form 13) and the default dispute (Form 30B), serve a copy of the completed forms on the recipient's lawyer, or on the recipient if the recipient has no lawyer, or on the Director of the Family Responsibility Office, and then file the completed forms, together with proof of service (Form 6B), at the court office, all within 10 days after service of this notice on you. You can use any method of service allowed under rule 6 of the Family Law Rules, *including mail, courier or fax. If the blank forms are missing, you must talk to the court office immediately.*

IF YOU DO NOT FILL OUT AND SERVE THE FINANCIAL STATEMENT OR IF YOU DO NOT COME TO COURT AS REQUIRED BY THIS NOTICE, A WARRANT MAY BE ISSUED FOR YOUR ARREST TO BRING YOU TO COURT.

You should bring with you to the default hearing any documents (such as cancelled cheques) that you need to prove that you made payments that are claimed to be missing. You may bring your own lawyer with you.

AT THE DEFAULT HEARING, THE COURT MAY MAKE AN ORDER AGAINST YOU, INCLUDING AN ORDER FOR YOUR IMPRISONMENT FOR UP TO 180 DAYS. YOU MAY ALSO BE ORDERED TO PAY COSTS.

IF YOU PAY THE AMOUNT OF THE MISSING PAYMENTS ON OR BEFORE THE DAY OF THE HEARING, YOU MAY STILL BE REQUIRED TO COME TO COURT AND TO PAY COSTS.

....

Date of signature *Signature of clerk of the court*

April 12, 2016

FORM 30A — REQUEST FOR DEFAULT HEARING

[Repealed O. Reg. 76/06, s. 15.]

[Editor's Note: Forms 4 to 39 of the Family Law Rules have been repealed by O. Reg. 76/06, effective May 1, 2006. Pursuant to Family Law Rule 1(9), when a form is referred to by number, the reference is to the form with that number that is described in the Table of Forms at the end of these rules and which is available at www.ontariocourtforms.on.ca. For your convenience, the government form as published on this website is reproduced below.]

Court File Number ....

.... *(Name of court)*

at .... *Court office address*

Recipient(s)

Full legal name & address for service — street & number, municipality, postal code, telephone & fax and e-mail address (if any).	*Lawyer's name & address — street & number, municipality, postal code, telephone & fax numbers and e-mail address (if any).*

Payor

Full legal name & address for service — street & number, municipality, postal code, telephone & fax numbers and e-mail address (if any).	*Lawyer's name & address — street & number, municipality, postal code, telephone & fax numbers and e-mail address (if any).*

TO THE CLERK OF THE COURT:

1. I am

❑ the person who signed the attached statement of money owed.
❑ the lawyer for the person who signed the attached statement of money owed.

❑ *(Other. Specify.)*
....
....

2. The payor has missed support payments in the amount of $ ...., as detailed in the attached statement of money owed.

3. I request that a notice of default hearing be issued requiring the payor to come to court to explain the missed payments at a hearing under section 41 of the *Family Responsibility and Support Arrears Enforcement Act.*

.... *Signature*

.... *Date of signature*

NOTE: You must prepare and attach a fresh statement of money owed (one that has been prepared within the past 30 days) to this request when you file it with the clerk of the court. Then, in the week leading up to the default hearing, you must file an updated statement of money owed.

September 1, 2005

FORM 30B — DEFAULT DISPUTE

[Repealed O. Reg. 76/06, s. 15.]

[Editor's Note: Forms 4 to 39 of the Family Law Rules have been repealed by O. Reg. 76/06, effective May 1, 2006. Pursuant to Family Law Rule 1(9), when a form is referred to by number, the reference is to the form with that number that is described in the Table of Forms at the end of these rules and which is available at www.ontariocourtforms.on.ca. For your convenience, the government form as published on this website is reproduced below.]

Court File Number ....

.... *(Name of court)*

at .... *Court office address*

Recipient(s)

Full legal name & address for service — street & number, municipality, postal code, telephone & fax and e-mail address (if any).	*Lawyer's name & address — street & number, municipality, postal code, telephone & fax numbers and e-mail address (if any).*

Payor

Full legal name & address for service — street & number, municipality, postal code, telephone & fax numbers and e-mail address (if any).	*Lawyer's name & address — street & number, municipality, postal code, telephone & fax numbers and e-mail address (if any).*

My name is *(full legal name)* ....

I live in *(municipality & province)* .... and I swear/affirm that the following is true:

1. I am the person named as payor in this case.

(Check off and fill in appropriate paragraphs below. Paragraphs that do not apply to you may be struck out and initialled.)

❑ 2. I have not missed any support payments as claimed in the statement of money owed because: *(Set out your reasons for saying that there are no missed payments.)*

❑ 3. I do not owe the amount claimed in the statement of money owed. I owe instead the sum of $.......... The reason for the difference in the amounts is:

(Set out your explanation, if any and if known, for the difference. If you have paid all the money that you claim to owe here, ignore and strike out paragraphs 4 and 5 below; if not, go to paragraph 5 on the other side to give your reasons for non-payment.)

Put a line through any blank space left on this page.

❑ 4. I owe the amount claimed in the statement of money owed. *(Go to paragraph 5 below to give your reasons for not paying.)*

❑ 5. My reasons for not paying the money that I owe are: *(State your reasons.)*

Put a line through any blank space left on this page.

Sworn/Affirmed before me at .... *municipality* in .... *province, state or country* on .... *date*

Signature

Commissioner for taking affidavits (Type or print name below if signature is illegible.)

(This form is to be signed in front of a lawyer, justice of the peace, notary public or commissioner for taking affidavits.)

September 1, 2005

FORM 31 — NOTICE OF CONTEMPT MOTION

[Repealed O. Reg. 76/06, s. 15.]

[Editor's Note: Forms 4 to 39 of the Family Law Rules have been repealed by O. Reg. 76/06, effective May 1, 2006. Pursuant to Family Law Rule 1(9), when a form is referred to by number, the reference is to the form with that number that is described in the Table of Forms at the end of these rules and which is available at www.ontariocourtforms.on.ca. For your convenience, the government form as published on this website is reproduced below.]

Court File Number ....

[SEAL]

.... *(Name of court)*

at .... *Court office address*

Applicant(s)/Recipient(s) (Strike out inapplicable term.)

Full legal name & address for service — street and number, municipality, postal code, telephone & fax numbers and e-mail address (if any).	*Lawyer's name & address — street and number, municipality, postal code, telephone & fax numbers and e-mail address (if any).*

Respondent/Payor (Strike out inapplicable term.)

Full legal name & address for service — street and number, municipality, postal code, telephone & fax numbers and e-mail address (if any).	*Lawyer's name & address — street and number, municipality, postal code, telephone & fax numbers and e-mail address (if any).*

TO: (name of person against whom contempt motion is made) ....

> *The person making this motion or the person's lawyer must contact the clerk of the court by telephone or otherwise to choose a time and date when the court could hear this motion*

YOU MUST COME TO COURT AT: (place of hearing) ....

ON (date) ...., *at* .... *a.m./p.m. and to remain until the court has dealt with the case.*

A motion will be made by *(moving party's name)* .... for a finding that you are in contempt of the court because you: *(Briefly state details of contempt.)* ....

The evidence against you is set out in the affidavit(s) attached to this notice. If the document(s) is/are missing, you must talk to the court office immediately.

IF YOU ARE FOUND IN CONTEMPT OF THE COURT, THE COURT MAY MAKE AN ORDER TO IMPRISON YOU, TO PAY A FINE AND TEMPORARILY TO SEIZE YOUR PROPERTY. YOU MAY ALSO BE ORDERED TO PAY COSTS.

IF YOU DO NOT COME TO COURT, A WARRANT MAY BE ISSUED FOR YOUR ARREST TO BRING YOU TO COURT.

.... *Signature of person making this motion or of person's lawyer*

.... *Date of signature*

.... *Typed or printed name, address for service, telephone and fax numbers and e-mail address of person or of person's lawyer*

September 1, 2005

FORM 32 — BOND (RECOGNIZANCE)

[Repealed O. Reg. 76/06, s. 15.]

[Editor's Note: Forms 4 to 39 of the Family Law Rules have been repealed by O. Reg. 76/06, effective May 1, 2006. Pursuant to Family Law Rule 1(9), when a form is referred to by number, the reference is to the form with that number that is described in the Table of Forms at the end of these rules and which is available at www.ontariocourtforms.on.ca. For your convenience, the government form as published on this website is reproduced below.]

Court File Number ....

[SEAL]

.... *(Name of court)*

at .... *Court office address*

Applicant(s)/Recipient(s) (Strike out inapplicable term.)

Full legal name & address for service — street and number, municipality, postal code, telephone & fax numbers and e-mail address (if any).	*Lawyer's name & address — street and number, municipality, postal code, telephone & fax numbers and e-mail address (if any).*

Respondent/Payor (Strike out inapplicable term.)

Full legal name & address for service — street and number, municipality, postal code, telephone & fax numbers and e-mail address (if any).	*Lawyer's name & address — street and number, municipality, postal code, telephone & fax numbers and e-mail address (if any).*

TO THE COURT:

My name is *(full legal name)* ....

I live in *(municipality and province)* ....

I ACKNOWLEDGE THAT I OWE

❑ Her Majesty the Queen

❑ *(name of person who can legally collect the money from me)* ....

the amount of $ ....,

- ❑ that will be immediately deposited in full with the clerk of the court by me or by one or more of my sureties and that will be forfeited,
- ❑ that, by the court's permission, will not need to be deposited with the clerk of the court but that can be collected from me and from one or more of my sureties in the same way that an order for the payment of money may be enforced by this court,

if I do not comply with any one or more of the following conditions:

(List the conditions in numbered paragraphs. Indicate the duration of each condition with the words, "... until [expiry date]" or a similar phrase wherever the judge has imposed an expiry date.)

Put a line through any blank space left on this page or on the reverse page.

.... *Signature of person under bond (recognizance)*

NOTE: A recognizance must be signed in front of the clerk of the court or the judge. No seal is needed for a bond

(Complete the following unless the court did not require any surety. No seals are needed for a bond.)

By signing below, each surety agrees to become indebted in the same way as the person giving the bond or recognizance if that person does not comply with the terms on this form.

Full legal name and address of first surety		*Full legal name and address of second surety*
Signature of first surety		*Signature of second surety*
Full legal name and address of third surety		*Full legal name and address of fourth surety*
Signature of third surety		*Signature of fourth surety*

If this form is a recognizance, the following must be completed.

This recognizance was signed before me at *(municipality)* .... on *(date)* ....

.... *Signature of judge or clerk of the court*

NOTE TO THE BOND GIVER AND TO ANY SURETY: If there is a material change in circumstances, you may make a motion to the court to change any condition of this bond (recognizance).

September 1, 2005

FORM 32.1 — REQUEST TO ENFORCE A FAMILY ARBITRATION AWARD

[Editor's Note: Forms 4 to 39 of the Family Law Rules have been repealed by O. Reg. 76/06, effective May 1, 2006. Pursuant to Family Law Rule 1(9), when a form is referred to by number, the reference is to the form with that number that is described in the Table of Forms

at the end of these rules and which is available at www.ontariocourtforms.on.ca. For your convenience, the government form as published on this website is reproduced below.]

Court File Number

.... *(Name of court)*

at .... *Court office address*

Applicant(s)

Full legal name & address for service — street & number, municipality, postal code, telephone & fax numbers and e-mail address (if any).	*Lawyer's name & address — street & number, municipality, postal code, telephone & fax numbers and e-mail address (if any).*

Respondent(s)

Full legal name & address for service — street & number, municipality, postal code, telephone & fax numbers and e-mail address (if any).	*Lawyer's name & address — street & number, municipality, postal code, telephone & fax numbers and e-mail address (if any).*

TO THE RESPONDENT(S):

A CASE HAS BEEN STARTED IN THIS COURT TO ENFORCE THE TERMS OF A FAMILY ARBITRATION AWARD THAT RELATES TO YOU. THE DETAILS ARE SET OUT ON THE ATTACHED PAGES.

IF YOU WANT TO OPPOSE THIS REQUEST, you or your lawyer must complete Form 32.1A: Dispute of Request for Enforcement (a blank copy should be attached), serve a copy on the applicant(s) and file a copy in the court office with an Affidavit of Service (Form 6A). *YOU HAVE ONLY 30 DAYS AFTER THIS REQUEST IS SERVED ON YOU (60 DAYS IF THE APPLICATION IS SERVED ON YOU OUTSIDE CANADA OR THE UNITED STATES) TO SERVE AND FILE THE DISPUTE. IF YOU DO NOT, THE CASE WILL GO AHEAD WITHOUT YOU AND THE COURT MAY MAKE AN ORDER AND ENFORCE IT AGAINST YOU.*

YOU SHOULD GET LEGAL ADVICE ABOUT THIS CASE RIGHT AWAY. If you cannot afford a lawyer, you may be able to get help from your local Legal Aid Ontario Office. (See your telephone directory under LEGAL AID.)

....	....
Date of issue	*Clerk of the Court*

My name is (full legal name) ....

I live in (municipality & province) ....

And I swear/affirm that the following is true:

1. I attach a copy of a family arbitration agreement (attach certificates of independent legal advice for both parties) between myself and the Respondent that I signed on *(date)* .... appointing *(name)* .... to arbitrate the following issues:

❑ child custody/access ❑ child support ❑ spousal support ❑ division of property

❑ other ....

2. The family arbitration agreement has not been set aside or changed in any way.

3. The arbitration was conducted in .... *(location)* .... on the following dates: ....

4. A family arbitration award was made on *(date)* .... Attached is a copy of the award and the arbitrator's written reasons for it.

5. The family arbitration award has not been changed since it was issued.

6. ❑ Neither party to the arbitration agreement has sought to appeal or set aside the family arbitration award or brought any other proceeding relating to this arbitration.

❑ Details of any steps taken by either party to appeal or set aside the family arbitration award or to have the arbitration declared invalid are as follows:

....

....

....

....

7. I am seeking a court order as set out in paragraphs *(select particular clauses from the arbitration award)* .... of the family arbitration award.

8. I am seeking an order for child support in accordance with the provisions of the family arbitration award. Additional information regarding that claim is set out in the FAMILY HISTORY section below.

❑ This amount is the table amount listed in the *Child Support Guidelines.*

❑ This amount is more than the table amount listed in the *Child Support Guidelines.*

❑ This amount is less than the table amount listed in the *Child Support Guidelines* for the following reasons:

....

....

....

....

9. Additional information that is important to this case is as follows:

....

....

....

Sworn/Affirmed before me at .... *municipality* in .... *province, state, or country* on	.... *Signature*

date	*Commissioner for taking affidavits (Type or print name below if signature is illegible.)*	*(This form is to be signed in front of a lawyer, justice of the peace, notary public or commissioner for taking affidavits.)*

Note: If you are seeking an order that incorporates clauses relating to the custody of or access to a child, you must also serve and file a completed Form 35.1: Affidavit in Support of Claim for Custody or Access.

FAMILY HISTORY

APPLICANT: Birthdate: *(d, m, y)* ....

RESPONDENT: Birthdate: *(d, m, y)* ....

RELATIONSHIP DATES:

❑ Married on *(date)* .... ❑ Started living together on *(date)* ....

❑ Separated on *(date)* .... ❑ Never lived together ❑ Still living together

THE CHILD(REN)

List all children involved in this case, even if no claim is made for these children.

Full legal name	**Age**	**Birthdate (d, m, y)**	**Resident in (municipality & province)**	**Now Living With (name of person and relationship to child)**

IF CHILD SUPPORT IS TO BE PAID:

The ❑ Applicant ❑ Respondent is to pay child support for the following children:

....

....

....

This child support is based on the ❑ Applicant's ❑ Respondent's annual income(s) of $..........

The special or extraordinary expenses for the children, if any, are as follows:

....

....

....

....

....

....

....

....

The ❑ Applicant ❑ Respondent will pay .... percent of the above expenses, or

$ .... per

For information on accessibility of court services for people with disability-related needs, contact:
Telephone: 416-326-2220 / 1-800-518-7901 TTY: 416-326-4012 / 1-877-425-0575

October 1, 2012

FORM 32.1A — DISPUTE OF REQUEST FOR ENFORCEMENT

[Editor's Note: Forms 4 to 39 of the Family Law Rules have been repealed by O. Reg. 76/06, effective May 1, 2006. Pursuant to Family Law Rule 1(9), when a form is referred to by number, the reference is to the form with that number that is described in the Table of Forms at the end of these rules and which is available at www.ontariocourtforms.on.ca. For your convenience, the government form as published on this website is reproduced below.]

Court File Number

.... *(Name of court)*

at .... *Court office address*

Applicant(s)

Full legal name & address for service — street & number, municipality, postal code, telephone & fax numbers and e-mail address (if any).	*Lawyer's name & address — street & number, municipality, postal code, telephone & fax numbers and e-mail address (if any).*

Applicant(s)

Respondent(s)

Full legal name & address for service — street & number, municipality, postal code, telephone & fax numbers and e-mail address (if any).	*Lawyer's name & address — street & number, municipality, postal code, telephone & fax numbers and e-mail address (if any).*

My name is (full legal name) ....

I live in (municipality & province) ....

And I swear/affirm that the following is true:

1. I am the Respondent in this case.

2. I do not agree with the Applicant's request to enforce the terms of the family arbitration award dated ....

3. I dispute paragraphs (select the particular paragraphs of the request that you are disputing) .... of the Applicant's Form 32.1: Request to Enforce a Family Arbitration Award for the following reasons:

....

....

....

....

4. ❑ The Applicant's FAMILY HISTORY is correct.

❑ The Applicant's FAMILY HISTORY is incorrect and should be corrected as follows:

....

....

Sworn/Affirmed before me at ....
municipality

in ....
province, state, or country

on ....
date *Commissioner for taking affidavits (Type or print name below if signature is illegible.)*

....
Signature

(This form is to be signed in front of a lawyer, justice of the peace, notary public or commissioner for taking affidavits.)

For information on accessibility of court services for people with disability-related needs, contact:
Telephone: 416-326-2220 / 1-800-518-7901 TTY: 416-326-4012 / 1-877-425-0575

October 1, 2012

FORM 32A — NOTICE OF FORFEITURE MOTION

[Repealed O. Reg. 76/06, s. 15.]

[Editor's Note: Forms 4 to 39 of the Family Law Rules have been repealed by O. Reg. 76/06, effective May 1, 2006. Pursuant to Family Law Rule 1(9), when a form is referred to by number, the reference is to the form with that number that is described in the Table of Forms at the end of these rules and which is available at www.ontariocourtforms.on.ca. For your convenience, the government form as published on this website is reproduced below.]

Court File Number ....

.... *(Name of court)*

at .... *Court office address*

Applicant(s)/Recipient(s) (Strike out inapplicable term.)

Full legal name & address for service — street & number, municipality, postal code, telephone & fax and e-mail address (if any).	*Lawyer's name & address — street & number, municipality, postal code, telephone & fax numbers and e-mail address (if any).*

Respondent/Payor (Strike out inapplicable term.)

Full legal name & address for service — street & number, municipality, postal code, telephone & fax numbers and e-mail address (if any).	*Lawyer's name & address — street & number, municipality, postal code, telephone & fax numbers and e-mail address (if any).*

TO: *(name of person who entered into recognizance or who posted bond)* ....

AND TO: *(name of surety or sureties)* ....

The person making this motion or the person's lawyer must contact the clerk of the court by telephone or otherwise to choose a time and date when the court could hear this motion

THE COURT WILL HEAR A MOTION ON *(date)* ...., at .... a.m./p.m., or as soon as possible after that time at: *(place of hearing)* ....

The motion is being made by *(moving party's name)* .... who will be asking the court to make an order of forfeiture in respect of

❏ a recognizance entered into

❏ a bond posted

by *(name of person who entered into recognizance or who posted bond)* ....

on *(date)* .... A copy of the bond/recognizance should be attached to this notice. Details of the grounds of the motion are set out in the affidavit(s) that accompany this notice. If the document(s) is/are missing, you should talk to the court office immediately.

IF YOU DO NOT COME TO COURT FOR THIS MOTION, AN ORDER OF FORFEITURE MAY BE MADE WITHOUT YOU AND MAY BE ENFORCED AGAINST YOU.

.... *Signature of person making this motion or of person's lawyer*

.... *Date of signature*

.... *Typed or printed name, address for service, telephone and fax numbers and e-mail address of person or of person's lawyer*

September 1, 2005

FORM 32B — WARRANT FOR ARREST

[Repealed O. Reg. 76/06, s. 15.]

[Editor's Note: Forms 4 to 39 of the Family Law Rules have been repealed by O. Reg. 76/06, effective May 1, 2006. Pursuant to Family Law Rule 1(9), when a form is referred to by number, the reference is to the form with that number that is described in the Table of Forms at the end of these rules and which is available at www.ontariocourtforms.on.ca. For your convenience, the government form as published on this website is reproduced below.]

ONTARIO

Court File Number

(SEAL)

.... *(Name of court)*

at .... Court office address

TO ALL PEACE OFFICERS IN THE PROVINCE OF ONTARIO:

I COMMAND YOU TO ARREST (name of person to be arrested) ....

on the grounds that this person is:

❑ a payor who has failed to file a financial statement at the request of the Director of the Family Responsibility Office.

See subsection 40(4) of the Family Responsibility and Support Arrears Enforcement Act.

❑ a payor who has failed to file a financial statement, as required by a notice of default hearing.

See subsection 41(7) of the Family Responsibility and Support Arrears Enforcement Act.

❑ a payor who has failed to appear before the court to explain a default in a support order or domestic contract that is enforceable in this court, as required by a notice of default hearing.

See subsection 41(7) of the Family Responsibility and Support Arrears Enforcement Act.

❑ a payor who is about to leave Ontario intending to evade his or her responsibilities under a support order or domestic contract that is enforceable in this court.

See subsection 49(1) of the Family Responsibility and Support Arrears Enforcement Act.

❑ a respondent in an application for support who is about to leave Ontario, intending to evade his or her responsibilities under the *Family Law Act*.

See subsection 43(1) of the Family Law Act.

❑ a respondent in an application to incorporate a paternity agreement in an order of the court, who is about to leave Ontario, intending to evade his or her responsibilities under the agreement.

See subsection 59(2) of the Family Law Act.

❑ a witness whose presence is necessary to determine an issue in a proceeding, who has been served with a summons to witness and who has failed to attend or to remain in attendance as required by the summons to witness.

See subrules 20(9), 23(7) and 27(19) of the Family Law Rules.

❑ a person who has failed to appear at a proceeding that may result in an order requiring him or her to enter into a recognizance or to post a bond.

See rule 32(1) of the Family Law Rules.

❑ a person who has failed to enter into a recognizance or to post a bond as required by an order of this court.

See rule 32(1) of the Family Law Rules.

❑ a person against whom a motion for contempt of the court is brought, whose attendance at the motion for contempt is necessary in the interests of the justice and who appears not likely to appear voluntarily at the motion.

See subrule 31(4) of the Family Law Rules.

❑ *(Other. Specify the grounds and the statutory of regulatory authority to issue this warrant.)*

AND I FURTHER COMMAND YOU to bring this person immediately to court in the municipality in which he or she may be found to be dealt with according to law, and if the court is not then sitting, to bring this person to a justice of the peace as soon as possible to be dealt with according to law.

....	....
Signature of judge	*Date of issue*
....	....
Print or type name of judge	*Date on which this warrant expires*

(Insert all available information)

Full legal name of person to be arrested				*Birth date (d,m,y)*		*Sex*
Aliases or nicknames						
Residential address				*Telephone number*		
Employment address				*Telephone number*		
Height	*Weight*	*Hair colour*	*Hair style*	*Eye colour*	*Complexion*	
Driver's licence			*Year, make and model of automobile*			
Licence plate & province			*Social insurance number*			
Clubs, associations or union affiliation						
Most recent date & occasion when residential address was verified by personal service						
Name & address of person to be contacted for further information				*Telephone number*		

(Name of court)
Court office address
WARRANT OF ARREST

I have informed this arrested person of his/her right to a lawyer.

....
Date of arrest

....
Signature of arresting officer

....
Printed name of arresting officer

(In space below, set out address and telephone number where arresting officer may be contacted.)

April 12, 2016

FORM 32C — AFFIDAVIT FOR WARRANT OF COMMITTAL

[Repealed O. Reg. 76/06, s. 15.]

[Editor's Note: Forms 4 to 39 of the Family Law Rules have been repealed by O. Reg. 76/06, effective May 1, 2006. Pursuant to Family Law Rule 1(9), when a form is referred to by number, the reference is to the form with that number that is described in the Table of Forms at the end of these rules and which is available at www.ontariocourtforms.on.ca. For your convenience, the government form as published on this website is reproduced below.]

Court File Number ....

.... *(Name of court)*

at .... *Court office address*

Applicant(s)/Recipient(s) (Strike out inapplicable term.)

Full legal name & address for service — street & number, municipality, postal code, telephone & fax and e-mail address (if any).	*Lawyer's name & address — street & number, municipality, postal code, telephone & fax numbers and e-mail address (if any).*

Respondent/Payor (Strike out inapplicable term.)

Full legal name & address for service — street & number, municipality, postal code, telephone & fax numbers and e-mail address (if any).	*Lawyer's name & address — street & number, municipality, postal code, telephone & fax numbers and e-mail address (if any).*

My name is *(full legal name)* ....

I live in *(municipality & province)* .... and I swear/affirm that the following is true:

1. I am

❑ a recipient under a payment order.

❑ an assignee of a recipient under a payment order.

❑ an agent of the Director of the Family Responsibility Office.
❑ *(Other. Specify.)*
....
....

2. I am the person who

❑ asked the payor to file a financial statement.

❑ asked to payor to come to a financial examination.

❑ began a default hearing against the payor.

❑ made a contempt motion.

❑ *(Other; specify.)*
....
....

3. I make this motion to ask the court to issue a warrant of committal.

4. On *(date)* ...., the court made an order of imprisonment, a photocopy of which is attached to this affidavit, committing,

❑ the payor to prison for disobeying the court's order to file a financial statement,

❑ the payor to prison for disobeying the court's order or direction about a financial examination,

❑ the payor to prison for missing support payments,

❑ *(name)* .... to prison for contempt of court,

❑ *(Other; specify.)*
....
....

for a period of .... days, but the committal was suspended on certain conditions set out in the order of imprisonment.

5. The respondent/payor was

❑ in court or his/her lawyer or agent was in court when this order of conditional imprisonment was made.

❑ not in court nor was his/her lawyer or agent was in court when the order of conditional imprisonment was made, but the order was served on him/her on *(date)* ....

6. The conditions that were broken and the circumstances of the breach are as follows: *(Set out conditions of the suspended imprisonment that were broken and details of the breach.)*

❑ Payment of the sum of $.......... was due by *(date)* .... but no payment was made by that day.

❑ Payment of the sum of $.......... was due by *(date)* .... but only a partial payment of $.......... was made by that day.

❑ *(Other; specify.)*

....

....

Put a line through any blank space left on this page.

Sworn/Affirmed before me at .... *municipality* in .... *province, state or country* on .... *date*	
Commissioner for taking affidavits (Type or print name below if signature is illegible.)	*Signature* *(This form is to be signed in front of a lawyer, justice of the peace, notary public or commissioner for taking affidavits.)*

Note to Moving Party: You must attach a photocopy of the court's order of conditional imprisonment to this Affidavit

September 1, 2005

FORM 32D — WARRANT OF COMMITTAL

[Repealed O. Reg. 76/06, s. 15.]

[Editor's Note: Forms 4 to 39 of the Family Law Rules have been repealed by O. Reg. 76/06, effective May 1, 2006. Pursuant to Family Law Rule 1(9), when a form is referred to by number, the reference is to the form with that number that is described in the Table of Forms at the end of these rules and which is available at www.ontariocourtforms.on.ca. For your convenience, the government form as published on this website is reproduced below.]

ONTARIO

Court File Number

(SEAL)

.... *(Name of court)*

at .... *Court office address*

TO ALL PEACE OFFICERS IN THE PROVINCE OF ONTARIO;

AND TO THE OFFICERS OF THE: (name and address of correctional institution)

....

THIS WARRANT IS FOR THE COMMITTAL OF (full legal name of person to be imprisoned)

....

THIS COURT FOUND THAT this person:

❑ disobeyed the court's order to file a financial statement;

❑ disobeyed the court's order or direction about a financial examination;

❑ without valid reason missed support payments as required by an order or domestic contract resulting in an order being made under the *Family Responsibility and Support Arrears Enforcement Act, 1996*;

❑ was in contempt of court;

❑ other *(Specify.)*

AS PUNISHMENT, THE COURT COMMITTED THIS PERSON to prison for a term of .... days, to be served,

❑ continuously

❑ intermittently on *(pattern of intermittent sentence)* ....

and to be served ❑ consecutively with any other term of imprisonment now being served or about to be served.

❑ *(Set out alternative arrangement with respect to other terms of imprisonment.)*

Check one or both boxes as appropriate. Otherwise strike out and initial.

❑ *AND THE COURT DIRECTED THAT* this order of imprisonment be suspended on one or more conditions. The court later found that this person broke one or more of the conditions and, as a result, the court has ordered the removal of the suspension from the order of imprisonment;

❑ *AND THE COURT ORDERED THAT* this person be subject to immediate release from custody upon receipt by the officers of the correctional institution or other secure facility of the sum of *(specify amount)* $..................................

I THEREFORE COMMAND YOU TO BRING THIS PERSON SAFELY TO THE CORRECTIONAL INSTITUTION OR SECURE FACILITY NAMED ABOVE AND TO DELIVER HIM/HER TO THE OFFICERS OF THAT INSTITUTION OR FACILITY, TOGETHER WITH THIS WARRANT.

AND I COMMAND YOU, THE OFFICERS OF THE CORRECTIONAL INSTITUTION OR SECURE FACILITY, TO ADMIT THIS PERSON INTO CUSTODY IN YOUR INSTITUTION OR FACILITY AND TO DETAIN HIM/HER THERE UNTIL THIS WARRANT EXPIRES.

This warrant expires,

(a) in a case under the *Family Responsibility and Support Arrears Enforcement Act, 1996*, when this person has completed the prescribed term of imprisonment; or

(b) in other cases, when this person has completed the prescribed term of imprisonment, subject to section 28 (remission of sentence) of the Ministry of *Correctional Services Act*; or

(c) when you, the officers of the correctional institution or secure facility, receive the sum named above; or

(d) upon further order of this court,

whichever event happens first.

....

Signature of judge *Date of issue*

....

Print or type name of judge

NOTE: Completion of the prescribed term of imprisonment does not discharge arrears of support or maintenance. A description of the person to be imprisoned is set out on page 2 of this warrant.

(Insert all available information)

<table>
<tr><td colspan="4">Full legal name of person to be arrested</td><td colspan="2">Birth date (d, m, y)</td><td>Sex</td></tr>
<tr><td colspan="7">Aliases or nicknames</td></tr>
<tr><td colspan="4">Residential address</td><td colspan="3">Telephone number</td></tr>
<tr><td colspan="4">Employment address</td><td colspan="3">Telephone number</td></tr>
<tr><td>Height</td><td>Weight</td><td>Hair colour</td><td>Hair style</td><td>Eye colour</td><td colspan="2">Complexion</td></tr>
<tr><td colspan="3">Driver's licence</td><td colspan="4">Year, make and model of automobile</td></tr>
<tr><td colspan="3">Licence plate & province</td><td colspan="4">Social insurance number</td></tr>
<tr><td colspan="7">Clubs, associations or union affiliation</td></tr>
<tr><td colspan="4">Most recent date & occasion when residential address was verified by personal service</td><td colspan="3">Family Responsibility Office Case No. (if applicable)</td></tr>
<tr><td colspan="4">Name & address of person to be contacted for further information</td><td colspan="3">Telephone number</td></tr>
</table>

(Name of court)

Court office address

WARRANT OF COMMITTAL

April 12, 2016

FORM 33 — INFORMATION FOR WARRANT TO BRING A CHILD TO A PLACE OF SAFETY

[Repealed O. Reg. 76/06, s. 15.]

[Editor's Note: Forms 4 to 39 of the Family Law Rules have been repealed by O. Reg. 76/06, effective May 1, 2006. Pursuant to Family Law Rule 1(9), when a form is referred to by number, the reference is to the form with that number that is described in the Table of Forms at the end of these rules and which is available at www.ontariocourtforms.on.ca. For your convenience, the government form as published on this website is reproduced below.]

Court File Number

ONTARIO

.... *(Name of court)*

at .... *Court office address*

My name is (full legal name) ....

I live in (municipality & province) ....

and I swear/affirm that the following is true:

1. I am ❑ a child protection worker employed by *(full legal name of children's aid society)*

....

❑ *(Give occupation or title.)* .... a peace officer in the province of Ontario, employed in *(name of office out of which you work)*

....

2. I have reasonable and probable grounds to believe and do believe that *(child's full legal name)* .... is younger than 16 and is a child in need of protection for the following reasons: *(Set out grounds for belief.)*

....

3. I have reasonable and probable grounds to believe and do believe that a course of action less restrictive than the child's removal to a place of safety is not available or will not adequately protect the child, for the following reasons: *(Set out grounds for belief.)*

....

Strike out paragraph 4 if not applicable.

4. I have reasonable and probable grounds to believe that the child may be found at *(Give full municipal address or a precise description of the premises where the child may be located.)*

....

Put a line through any blank space left on this page.

Sworn/Affirmed before me at .... *municipality* in .... *province, state or country* on .... *date* *Commissioner for taking affidavits (Type or print name below if signature is illegible.)*	.... *Signature* *(This form is to be signed in front of a lawyer, justice of the peace, notary public or commissioner for taking affidavits.)*

March 1, 2018

FORM 33A — WARRANT TO BRING A CHILD TO A PLACE OF SAFETY

[Repealed O. Reg. 76/06, s. 15.]

[Editor's Note: Forms 4 to 39 of the Family Law Rules have been repealed by O. Reg. 76/06, effective May 1, 2006. Pursuant to Family Law Rule 1(9), when a form is referred to by number, the reference is to the form with that number that is described in the Table of Forms at the end of these rules and which is available at www.ontariocourtforms.on.ca. For your convenience, the government form as published on this website is reproduced below.]

Court File Number

ONTARIO

.... *(Name of court)*

at .... *Court office address*

TO ALL CHILD PROTECTION WORKERS AND PEACE OFFICERS IN THE PROVINCE OF ONTARIO:

On the basis of an information sworn before me under Part V of the *Child, Youth and Family Services Act, 2017* respecting the child named or described at the bottom of this warrant, I am satisfied that there are reasonable and probable grounds to believe:

(a) that the child is younger than 16;

(b) that the child is in need of protection; and

(c) that a course of action less restrictive than the child's removal to a place of safety is not available or will not adequately protect the child.

Check box below only if the child's whereabouts are known. Otherwise, strike out the paragraph below and initial the deletion.

❑ I am further satisfied, on the basis of that information, that the child may now be found at *(Give full municipal address or a precise description of the premises where the child may be located.)*

....

I THEREFORE AUTHORIZE YOU TO BRING THIS CHILD to a "place of safety" within the meaning of the Child, Youth and Family Services Act, 2017.

This warrant expires at .... on *(date)* ....

....	....
Signature of justice of the peace	*Date of signature*
....	....
Print or type name of justice of the peace	*Municipality where this warrant was signed*

NOTE: Any changes, alterations or corrections to this form must be initialled by the justice of the peace. It is a criminal offence for any other person to change the wording of this warrant after it has been signed by the justice of the peace.

DESCRIPTION: Insert all available information

Full legal name of child to be brought to a place of safety			*Birth date (d,m,y)*		*Sex*
Aliases or nicknames					
Residential address				*Telephone number*	
Present whereabouts of child				*Telephone number*	
Height	*Weight*	*Hair colour*	*Hair style*	*Eye colour*	*Complexion*
Other features					
Name & address of person to be contacted for further information				*Telephone number*	

....

(Name of court)

at

....

Court office address

WARRANT TO BRING A CHILD TO A PLACE OF SAFETY

March 1, 2018

FORM 33B — PLAN OF CARE FOR CHILD(REN) (CHILDREN'S AID SOCIETY)

[Editor's Note: Forms 4 to 39 of the Family Law Rules have been repealed by O. Reg. 76/06, effective May 1, 2006. Pursuant to Family Law Rule 1(9), when a form is referred to by number, the reference is to the form with that number that is described in the Table of Forms at the end of these rules and which is available at www.ontariocourtforms.on.ca. For your convenience, the government form as published on this website is reproduced below.]

Court File Number

ONTARIO

.... *(Name of court)*

at .... *Court office address*

Applicant(s) (In most cases, the applicant will be a children's aid society.)

Full legal name & address for service — street & number, municipality, postal code, telephone & fax numbers and e-mail address (if any).	*Lawyer's name & address — street & number, municipality, postal code, telephone & fax numbers and e-mail address (if any).*

Respondent(s) (In most cases, a respondent will be a "parent" within the meaning of section 74 of the *Child, Youth and Family Services Act, 2017*)

Full legal name & address for service — street & number, municipality, postal code, telephone & fax numbers and e-mail address (if any).	*Lawyer's name & address — street & number, municipality, postal code, telephone & fax numbers and e-mail address (if any).*

Respondent(s) (In most cases, a respondent will be a "parent" within the meaning of section 74 of the *Child, Youth and Family Services Act, 2017*)

Children's Lawyer

Name & address of Children's Lawyer's agent for service (street & number, municipality, postal code, telephone & fax numbers and e-mail address (if any)) and name of person represented.

Fill out only those paragraphs that apply and strike out others.

1. I am/We are *(full legal name)* .... and I am/we are *(state your position with children's aid society)* ....

2. The child(ren) in this case is/are:

Child's Full Legal Name	Birthdate	Sex

3. ❏ After the court makes a finding that the child(ren) is/are in need of protection under Part V of the *Child, Youth and Family Services Act, 2017*, I/we ask the court to make an order.

❏ The court previously found on *(date)* .... that the child(ren) was/were in need of protection under Part V of the *Child, Youth and Family Services Act, 2017*, and the court made an order on *(date)* .... I/We now ask the court to make a further order.

The details of the order that I/we now ask the court to make are as follows: *(Give details of the order you now want the court to make. If you want the order to include any supervision by the children's aid society, give details of any terms and conditions of supervision.)*

Put a line through any blank space left on this page.

4. The services that the family and child(ren) need and that will be provided are as follows: *(Give details of the service needed, who needs it and who will be providing it.)*

....

5. The children's aid society expects the respondent(s) to carry out certain conditions before it would feel that supervision or society care of the child(ren) is no longer needed. Very serious consequences could result if those conditions are broken. These conditions are: *(Set out conditions and estimate the time needed to achieve them.)*

....

Put a line through any blank space left on this page.

6. The child(ren) cannot be adequately protected while in the care of the respondent(s) because: *(State reasons.)*

....

7. The following efforts have been made in the past to protect the child(ren) while in the care of the respondent(s): *(Describe the efforts made. If no efforts were made, give explanation.)*

....

8. The following efforts are planned to keep up the child(ren)'s contact with the respondent(s): *(Describe plans. Write "Nil" if there are no plans.)*

....

9. The following arrangements have been or are being made to recognize the importance of the child's culture and to preserve his/her heritage, traditions and cultural identity:

....

Put a line through any blank space left on this page.

PART 3

10. The children's aid society has removed the child(ren) from the care of the respondent(s) and intends to make this removal

❑ temporary.

❑ permanent. *(If the children's aid society is not seeking an order of extended society care, please provide details of the efforts by the children's aid society to provide a long-term, stable placement for the child.)*

11. (To be completed if the children's aid society is seeking an order of extended society care.)

Efforts will be made to assist the child to develop a positive, secure and enduring relationship within a family through one of the following methods:

❑ adoption ..... ❑ a custody order under s. 116(1) ❑ a plan for customary care

❑ other *(Please provide available details.)*

....

12. This plan of care was served on and its details explained to the respondent(s) and others named below:

Print name of person to whom this plan was explained	**Print name of person who explained plan**	**Date of explanation**

Put a line through any blank space left on this page.

....

Date of signature *Signature*

....

Date of signature *Signature*

March 1, 2018

FORM 33B.1 — ANSWER AND PLAN OF CARE (PARTIES OTHER THAN CHILDREN'S AID SOCIETY)

[Editor's Note: Forms 4 to 39 of the Family Law Rules have been repealed by O. Reg. 76/06, effective May 1, 2006. Pursuant to Family Law Rule 1(9), when a form is referred to by number, the reference is to the form with that number that is described in the Table of Forms at the end of these rules and which is available at www.ontariocourtforms.on.ca. For your convenience, the government form as published on this website is reproduced below.]

Court File Number

ONTARIO

.... *(Name of court)*

at .... *Court office address*

Applicant(s)

Full legal name & address for service — street & number, municipality, postal code, telephone & fax numbers and e-mail address (if any).	*Lawyer's name & address — street & number, municipality, postal code, telephone & fax numbers and e-mail address (if any).*

Respondent(s)

Full legal name & address for service — street & number, municipality, postal code, telephone & fax numbers and e-mail address (if any).	*Lawyer's name & address — street & number, municipality, postal code, telephone & fax numbers and e-mail address (if any).*

Children's Lawyer

Name & address for service for Children's Lawyer's agent — street & number, municipality, postal code, telephone & fax numbers and e-mail address (if any)) and name of person represented.

TO THE APPLICANT(S):

(Note to the respondent(s): If you are making a claim against someone who is not an applicant, insert the person's name and address here.)

AND TO: (full legal name) ...., *an added respondent, of (address for service of added party)*

....

(Note to the respondent(s): You must complete, serve, file and update this form if any significant changes regarding the child(ren) occur after you sign this form.)

I am/We are *(full legal name(s))* .... and I am/we are *(state your relationship to the child(ren))*

....

PART 1

1. The child(ren) in this case is/are:

Child's Full Legal Name	**Birthdate**	**Age**	**Sex**	**Full Legal Name(s) of Parent(s)**		**Is the Child First Nations, Inuk, or Métis?**	**Child's Bands and First Nations, Inuit, or Métis Communities**

2. The following people have had the child(ren) in their care and custody during the past year:

Child's Name	**Name of Other Caregiver(s)**	**Period of Time with Caregiver(s) (d,m,y to d,m,y)**

PART 2

3. If this is a child protection application, complete this Part, then go to Part 4. *(If this is a status review, complete Part 3, then go to Part 4.)*

(Check applicable box(es).)

❑ I/We agree with the following facts in

❑ paragraph 6 of the application (Form 8B).

❑ paragraph 3 of the application (Form 8B.1).

(Refer to the numbered paragraph(s) under paragraph 6/paragraph 3 of the application.)

....

❑ I/We disagree with the following facts in

❑ paragraph 6 of the application (Form 8B).

❑ paragraph 3 of the application (Form 8B.1).

(Refer to the numbered paragraph(s) under paragraph 6/paragraph 3 of the application.)

....

NOTE: If you intend to dispute the children's aid society's position at the temporary care and custody hearing, an affidavit in Form 14A MUST also be served on the parties and filed at court.

(Attach an additional page and number it if you need more space.)

PART 3

4. If this is a status review, complete this Part, then go to Part 4. *(If this is a protection application, complete Part 2, then go to Part 4.)*

(Check applicable box(es).)

❑ I/We agree with the following facts in

❑ paragraph 6 of the application (Form 8B).

❑ paragraph 3 of the application (Form 8B.1).

(Refer to the numbered paragraph(s) under paragraph 6/paragraph 3 of the application.)

....

❑ I/We disagree with the following facts in

❑ paragraph 6 of the application (Form 8B).

❑ paragraph 3 of the application (Form 8B.1).

(Refer to the numbered paragraph(s) under paragraph 6/paragraph 3 of the application.)

....

(Attach an additional page and number it if you need more space.)

PART 4

5. What placement and terms of placement do you believe would be in the child(ren)'s best interests? *(You should include in your plan of care at least the following information. If your plan is not the same for a particular child, then complete a separate plan for that child.)*

(a) Where will you live?

(b) Who, if anyone, will live with you?

(c) Where will the child(ren) live?

(d) What school or daycare will the child(ren) attend?

(e) What days and hours will the child(ren) attend school or daycare?

(f) Are you enrolled in school or counselling?

(g) If you are enrolled in counselling, where do you attend counselling?

(h) What support services will you be using for the child(ren)?

(i) Do you have support from your family or community?

(j) If you have support from your family or community, who will help you and how will they help you?

(k) What will the child(ren)'s activities be?

(l) What will your source of income be?

(m) Do you go to work or school?

(n) If you go to work or school, what are the details, including the days and hours you work or go to school, and who will look after your child(ren) while you are there?

....

(o) State why you feel that this plan would be in the child(ren)'s best interests.

(Attach an additional page and number it if you need more space.)

6. These are the people who have information that would support my plan:

Name	Information

(Attach an additional page and number it if you need more space.)

PART 5

Claims by Respondent(s)

(Fill out a separate claim page for each person against whom you are making a claim(s).)

7. THIS CLAIM IS MADE AGAINST

❑ *THE CHILDREN'S AID SOCIETY (OR OTHER APPLICANT)*

❑ *AN ADDED PARTY*, whose name is *(full legal name)* ....

(If you claim against an added party, make sure that the person's name appears on page 1 of this form.)

8. I/WE ASK THE COURT FOR THE FOLLOWING ORDER:

(Claims below include claims for temporary orders.)

Claims relating to child protection	
❑	access
❑	lesser protection order
❑	return of child(ren) to my/our care
❑	place child(ren) into the custody of *(name)* .... *(s. 102, deemed custody order under the* Children's Law Reform Act*)*
❑	place child(ren) into the custody of *(name)* .... *(s. 116(1)(b), custody order for child formerly in extended society care)*
❑	interim society care for .... months
❑	place child(ren) into the care and custody of *(name)* .... subject to society supervision
❑	costs
❑	other *(Specify.)* ....

Give details of the order that you want the court to make. *(Include the name(s) of the child(ren) for whom custody or access is claimed.)*

....

IMPORTANT FACTS SUPPORTING MY/OUR CLAIM(S)

(In numbered paragraphs, set out the facts that form the legal basis for your claim(s). Attach an additional page and number it if you need more space.)

....

Put a line through any space left on this page.

....
Date of signature *Signature*

....
Date of signature. *Signature.*

March 1, 2018

FORM 33B.2 — ANSWER (CHILD, YOUTH AND FAMILY SERVICES ACT, 2017 CASES OTHER THAN CHILD PROTECTION AND STATUS REVIEW)

[Editor's Note: Pursuant to Family Law Rule 1(9), when a form is referred to by number, the reference is to the form with that number that is described in the Table of Forms at the end of these rules and which is available at www.ontariocourtforms.on.ca. For your convenience, the government form as published on this website is reproduced below.]

Court File Number

ONTARIO

.... *(Name of court)*

at .... *Court office address*

Applicant(s)

Full legal name & address for service — street & number, municipality, postal code, telephone & fax numbers and e-mail address (if any).	*Lawyer's name & address — street & number, municipality, postal code, telephone & fax numbers and e-mail address (if any).*

Respondent(s)

Full legal name & address for service — street & number, municipality, postal code, telephone & fax numbers and e-mail address (if any).	*Lawyer's name & address — street & number, municipality, postal code, telephone & fax numbers and e-mail address (if any).*

Children's Lawyer

Name & address for service for Children's Lawyer's agent — street & number, municipality, postal code, telephone & fax numbers and e-mail address (if any) and name of person represented.

TO THE APPLICANT(S):

(Note to the respondent(s): If you are making a claim against someone who is not an applicant, insert the person's name and address here.)

AND TO: (full legal name) ...., *an added respondent, of (address for service of added party)*

....

(Note to the respondent(s): You must complete, serve, file and update this form if any significant changes regarding the child(ren) occur after you sign this form.)

I am/We are *(full legal name(s))* .... and I am/we are *(state your relationship to the child(ren))*

....

1. The child(ren) in this case is/are:

Child's Full Legal Name	**Birthdate**	**Age**	**Sex**	**Full Legal Name(s) of Parent(s)**		**Is the Child First Nations, Inuk, or Métis?**	**Child's Bands and First Nations, Inuit, or Métis Communities**

2. ❑ I/We agree with the following facts in the application (Form 8B.2 or 34L). *(Refer to the numbered paragraph(s) in the application.)*

....

❑ I/We disagree with the following facts in the application (Form 8B.2 or 34L). *(Refer to the numbered paragraph(s) in the application.)*

(Attach an additional page and number it if you need more space.)

3. Do you agree that the court should make the order requested?

❑ Yes . . . . ❑ No

Give reasons:

....

(Attach an additional page and number it if you need more space.)

IMPORTANT FACTS SUPPORTING MY/OUR POSITION

(In numbered paragraphs, set out the facts that form the legal basis for your position. Attach an additional page and number it if you need more space.)

....

Put a line through any blank space left on this page.

....

Date of signature *Signature*

....

Date of signature *Signature*

March 1, 2018

FORM 33C — STATEMENT OF AGREED FACTS (CHILD PROTECTION)

[Repealed O. Reg. 76/06, s. 15.]

[Editor's Note: Forms 4 to 39 of the Family Law Rules have been repealed by O. Reg. 76/06, effective May 1, 2006. Pursuant to Family Law Rule 1(9), when a form is referred to by number, the reference is to the form with that number that is described in the Table of Forms at the end of these rules and which is available at www.ontariocourtforms.on.ca. For your convenience, the government form as published on this website is reproduced below.]

Court File Number

ONTARIO

.... *(Name of court)*

at .... *Court office address*

Applicant(s) [In most cases, the applicant will be a children's aid society.]

Full legal name & address for service — street & number, municipality, postal code, telephone & fax numbers and e-mail address (if any).	*Lawyer's name & address — street & number, municipality, postal code, telephone & fax numbers and e-mail address (if any).*

Respondent(s) [In most cases, a respondent will be a "parent" within the meaning of section 74 of the *Child, Youth and Family Services Act, 2017*.]

Full legal name & address for service — street & number, municipality, postal code, telephone & fax numbers and e-mail address (if any).	*Lawyer's name & address — street & number, municipality, postal code, telephone & fax numbers and e-mail address (if any).*

Respondent(s) [In most cases, a respondent will be a "parent" within the meaning of section 74 of the *Child, Youth and Family Services Act, 2017.*]

Children's Lawyer

Name & address of Children's Lawyer's agent for service (street & number, municipality, postal code, telephone & fax numbers and e-mail address (if any)) and name of person represented.

THE PEOPLE SIGNING THIS AGREEMENT ARE:

(Give full legal name. If you are a respondent, state your relationship to the child(ren). If you are an employee of the children's aid society, state your position within the society.)

Print or type full legal name	*Relationship to child OR position within children's aid society*
Signature	*Date of signature*

Print or type full legal name	*Relationship to child OR position within children's aid society*
Signature	*Date of signature*

Print or type full legal name	*Relationship to child OR position within children's aid society*
Signature	*Date of signature*

WE AGREE:

(a) that the statements made on this form are true; and

(b) that this form may be filed with the court and may be read to the court as evidence, without affecting anyone's right to test that evidence by cross-examination or to bring in other evidence.

Note that "parent" means parent as defined in section 74 of the Child, Youth and Family Services Act, 2017.

1. The information about the child(ren) in this case is as follows:

Full legal name of first child:	*Date of birth*	*Age*	*Sex*
Is the child a First Nations, Inuk, or Métis person?			

Name of each of the child's bands and First Nations, Inuit, or Métis communities and their representative(s)
If child was brought to a place of safety, address and identity of place from which the child was removed
Full legal name(s) of child's parent(s) (List everyone who is a parent of the child as defined in section 74 of the Child, Youth and Family Services Act, 2017*)*

Full legal name of second child:	*Date of birth*	*Age*	*Sex*
Is the child a First Nations, Inuk, or Métis person?			
Name of each of the child's bands and First Nations, Inuit, or Métis communities and their representative(s)			
If child was brought to a place of safety, address and identity of place from which the child was removed			
Full legal name(s) of child's parent(s) (List everyone who is a parent of the child as defined in section 74 of the Child, Youth and Family Services Act, 2017*)*			

Full legal name of third child:	*Date of birth*	*Age*	*Sex*
Is the child a First Nations, Inuk, or Métis person?			
Name of each of the child's bands and First Nations, Inuit, or Métis communities and their representative(s)			
If child was brought to a place of safety, address and identity of place from which the child was removed			
Full legal name(s) of child's parent(s) (List everyone who is a parent of the child as defined in section 74 of the Child, Youth and Family Services Act, 2017*)*			

If there are more children, attach a sheet and number it.

2. The details of the children's aid society's previous involvement with one or more of these children in this case are as follows:

> *(Write "Nil" if no involvement. Indicate any involvement with children's aid society in another part of Ontario or a child protection agency outside Ontario. Please remember that this is a statement of AGREED FACTS. That means that you must not set out something as a fact if another party disagrees with it. If you cannot agree at all about anything, write: "No agreement reached.")*

> ....

3. The child(ren) was/were brought to a place of safety because:

(If the child(ren) was/were not brought to a place of safety, write "Nil". Again, there must be full agreement by all parties. Any point on which there is disagreement must be excluded. If there is no agreement at all on anything, write: "No agreement reached.")

....

4. We agree that the court should make a finding that the child(ren) is/are in need of protection on the following reasons:

(Use only the reasons listed on page 3 of the application [form 8B]. Any reason on which there is disagreement must be excluded. If there is no agreement at all, write: "No agreement reached." In any event, the court can always make some other finding.)

....

4.1 The following important events relating to the child(ren)'s best interests have occurred since the date this application began:

....

5. We agree that the order that would best serve the best interests of the child(ren) is:

(Again, list only the terms and conditions on which there is full agreement by all parties. If there is no agreement at all, write: "No agreement reached." In any event, the court is always free to make some other order. If the order on which you all agree would remove the child(ren) from the care of the person who had the child(ren) before the case started, explain why less disruptive options would not be enough to protect the child(ren).)

....

Put a line through any space left on this page

March 1, 2018

FORM 33D — STATEMENT OF AGREED FACTS (STATUS REVIEW)

[Repealed O. Reg. 76/06, s. 15.]

[Editor's Note: Forms 4 to 39 of the Family Law Rules have been repealed by O. Reg. 76/06, effective May 1, 2006. Pursuant to Family Law Rule 1(9), when a form is referred to by number, the reference is to the form with that number that is described in the Table of Forms at the end of these rules and which is available at www.ontariocourtforms.on.ca. For your convenience, the government form as published on this website is reproduced below.]

Court File Number

ONTARIO

.... *(Name of court)*

at .... Court office address

Applicant(s) [In most child protection cases, the applicant will be a children's aid society.]

Full legal name & address for service — street & number, municipality, postal code, telephone & fax numbers and e-mail address (if any).	*Lawyer's name & address — street & number, municipality, postal code, telephone & fax numbers and e-mail address (if any).*

Respondent(s) [In most cases, a respondent will be a "parent" within the meaning of section 74 of the *Child, Youth and Family Services Act, 2017*.]

Full legal name & address for service — street & number, municipality, postal code, telephone & fax numbers and e-mail address (if any).	*Lawyer's name & address — street & number, municipality, postal code, telephone & fax numbers and e-mail address (if any).*

Children's Lawyer

Name & address of Children's Lawyer's agent for service (street & number, municipality, postal code, telephone & fax numbers and e-mail address (if any)) and name of person represented.

THE PEOPLE SIGNING THIS AGREEMENT ARE:

(Give full legal name. If you are a respondent, state your relationship to the child(ren). If you are an employee of the children's aid society, state your position within the society.)

Print or type full legal name	*Relationship to child OR position within children's aid society*
Signature	*Date of signature*

Print or type full legal name	*Relationship to child OR position within children's aid society*
Signature	*Date of signature*

Print or type full legal name	*Relationship to child OR position within children's aid society*

Signature	*Date of signature*

WE AGREE:

(a) that the statements made on this form are true; and

(b) that this form may be filed with the court and may be read to the court as evidence, without affecting anyone's right to test that evidence by cross-examination or to bring in other evidence.

Note that "parent" means parent as defined in section 74 of the Child, Youth and Family Services Act, 2017.

1. The information about the child(ren) in this case is as follows:

Full legal name of first child:	*Date of birth*	*Age*	*Sex*
Is the child a First Nations, Inuk, or Métis person?			
Name of each of the child's bands and First Nations, Inuit, or Métis communities and their representative(s)			
If child was brought to a place of safety, address and identity of place from which the child was removed			
Full legal name(s) of child's parent(s) (List everyone who is a parent of the child as defined in section 74 of the Child, Youth and Family Services Act, 2017*)*			

Full legal name of second child:	*Date of birth*	*Age*	*Sex*
Is the child a First Nations, Inuk, or Métis person?			
Name of each of the child's bands and First Nations, Inuit, or Métis communities and their representative(s)			
If child was brought to a place of safety, address and identity of place from which the child was removed			
Full legal name(s) of child's parent(s) (List everyone who is a parent of the child as defined in section 74 of the Child, Youth and Family Services Act, 2017*)*			

Full legal name of third child:	*Date of birth*	*Age*	*Sex*
Is the child a First Nations, Inuk, or Métis person?			
Name of each of the child's bands and First Nations, Inuit, or Métis communities and their representative(s)			
If child was brought to a place of safety, address and identity of place from which the child was removed			

Full legal name(s) of child's parent(s) (List everyone who is a parent of the child as defined in section 74 of the Child, Youth and Family Services Act, 2017*)*

If there are more children, attach a sheet and number it.

2. The most recent protection order dealing with the child(ren) in paragraph 1 was made on *(date)* .... and it said that: *(State substance of order.)*

3. Since the order under review was made, the following person(s) has/have become a "parent" under Part V of the *Child, Youth and Family Services Act, 2017*:

Full legal name	**Relationship to child**

4. Since that order was made, the following important events have happened:

(Describe only the events on which you can ALL agree. Please remember that this is a statement of AGREED FACTS. That means that you must not set out something as a fact if at least one of the persons signing this statement disagrees with it. If you cannot agree at all about anything, write: "No agreement reached".)

....

5. We agree that an order of the court is needed now and that it would best serve the best interests of the child(ren) because:

(If there is no agreement that an order needs to be made, write: "No agreement reached on need for an order". If you agree that an order needs to be made, give reasons for it and set out its terms and conditions. If any person disagrees with a reason, term or condition, then you must not include that reason, term or condition. If you cannot agree on any reasons, write: "No agreement reached on reasons for order". If you cannot agree on any terms or conditions of the order, write: "No agreement reached on terms and conditions of order".)

....

Put a line through any space left on this page

March 1, 2018

FORM 33E — CHILD'S CONSENT TO SECURE TREATMENT

[Repealed O. Reg. 76/06, s. 15.]

[Editor's Note: Forms 4 to 39 of the Family Law Rules have been repealed by O. Reg. 76/06, effective May 1, 2006. Pursuant to Family Law Rule 1(9), when a form is referred to by number, the reference is to the form with that number that is described in the Table of Forms at the end of these rules and which is available at www.ontariocourtforms.on.ca. For your convenience, the government form as published on this website is reproduced below.]

Court File Number ....

.... *(Name of court)*

at .... *Court office address*

Applicant(s)

Full legal name & address for service — street & number, municipality, postal code, telephone & fax numbers and e-mail address (if any).	*Lawyer's name & address — street & number, municipality, postal code, telephone & fax numbers and e-mail address (if any).*

Child

Full legal name of child: *Birthdate:* *Sex:*	*Lawyer's name & address — street and number, municipality, postal code, telephone & fax numbers and e-mail address (if any).*

1. My name is *(child's full legal name)* ....

2. I know that the applicant(s) is/are asking the court to make an order

   ❑ to send me to and maybe have me locked up for my own protection at

   ❑ to keep me for a longer time and maybe keep me locked up for my own protection at

   ❑ to get me released from

 (name and address of program) ....

3. I know that

   ❑ I have a right to be in court when this case is heard by the judge, but I agree not to come to court and to let the court make whatever order needs to be made without me.

   ❑ the court usually needs to hear witnesses before it can make an order in this case, but I agree that the court can make the order without having to hear witnesses in person and can reach its decision on evidence found in the reports and other documents that the applicant(s) can show to the judge.

4. I have talked with a lawyer

   (a) who has explained these things to me, and

   (b) who has explained what it means for me to sign this consent, and

(c) who is going to witness my signature of this form.

.... *Signature of child*

.... *Signature of lawyer*

.... *Date of signatures*

NOTE: This consent must be witnessed by an independent lawyer who is to provide an affidavit of independent legal advice on the reverse side of this sheet.

NOTE: A consent to dispense with oral evidence is not effective for more than 180 days after the court's order.

AFFIDAVIT OF EXECUTION AND INDEPENDENT LEGAL ADVICE

My name is (full legal name) .... *and I swear/affirm that the following is true:*

1. I am a member of the Bar of *(name of jurisdiction)* .... and am not acting for any other person in this secure treatment case.

2. I explained to *(child's full legal name)* .... about

❑ the nature and effect of
   ❑ secure treatment;
   ❑ an extension of secure treatment;
   ❑ release from secure treatment;

❑ the consequences of not attending the hearing; and

❑ the consequences of a hearing where a court proceeds without hearing oral evidence;

in language appropriate to his/her age to the best of my knowledge and skills.

3. After my explanation, the child told me that he/she wanted to sign this consent.

4. I was present at and witnessed the signing of this consent by the child.

Sworn/Affirmed before me at .... *municipality* in .... *province, state or country* on .... *date*

____
Signature
(This form is to be signed in front of a lawyer, justice of the peace, notary public or commissioner for taking affidavits.)

____
Commissioner for taking affidavits (Type or print name below if signature is illegible.)

September 1, 2005

FORM 33F — CONSENT TO SECURE TREATMENT (PERSON OTHER THAN CHILD)

[Repealed O. Reg. 76/06, s. 15.]

[Editor's Note: Forms 4 to 39 of the Family Law Rules have been repealed by O. Reg. 76/06, effective May 1, 2006. Pursuant to Family Law Rule 1(9), when a form is referred to by number, the reference is to the form with that number that is described in the Table of Forms at the end of these rules and which is available at www.ontariocourtforms.on.ca. For your convenience, the government form as published on this website is reproduced below.]

ONTARIO

Court File Number

.... *(Name of Court)*

at .... *Court office address*

Applicant(s)

Full legal name & address for service — street & number, municipality, postal code, telephone & fax numbers and e-mail address (if any).	*Lawyer's name & address — street & number, municipality, postal code, telephone & fax numbers and e-mail address (if any).*

Child

Full legal name of child:	*Lawyer's name & address — street & number, municipality, postal code, telephone & fax numbers and e-mail address (if any).*
Birthdate:	
Sex:	

Name and address of secure treatment program in this case

My name is *(full legal name)* .... and I am

❑ the administrator of the secure treatment program. I consent to this application for

❑ the child's commitment to the program.

❑ an extension of the child's commitment to the program.

❑ an extension of the commitment to the program of the person admitted into it who has now attained the age of eighteen years.

❑ the child's parent. I consent to

❑ this application for the commitment of my child who is in the care of a person other than the administrator of the secure treatment program.

❑ my child's commitment to the secure treatment program for a period of 180 days in this application brought by *(full legal name of applicant children's aid society)*

....

❑ this application by the administrator of the secure treatment program for an extension of my child's admission to the program.

❑ an authorized representative of the Minister of Children and Youth Services for Ontario. I consent to the admission of the child who is less than twelve years old to the secure treatment program.

❑ temporarily while this case for an order of commitment or for an order extending it is adjourned.

❑ on the court's final order of commitment or extending commitment.

❑ an officer of *(full legal name of children's aid society)* .... I am authorized, on behalf of the society, to consent to this application of the administrator of the secure treatment program for an extension of the child's commitment to that program.

❑ the person who is the subject of this case. I am 18 years of age or more. I consent to this application to extend my commitment to the secure treatment program to which I am now admitted.

....

Signature *Date of signature*

December 1, 2015

FORM 34 — CHILD'S CONSENT TO ADOPTION

[Editor's Note: Forms 4 to 39 of the Family Law Rules have been repealed by O. Reg. 76/06, effective May 1, 2006. Pursuant to Family Law Rule 1(9), when a form is referred to by number, the reference is to the form with that number that is described in the Table of Forms at the end of these rules and which is available at www.ontariocourtforms.on.ca. For your convenience, the government form as published on this website is reproduced below.]

ONTARIO

Court File Number

....

(Name of court)

at ....

Court office address

Applicant(s) (The first letter of the applicant's surname may be used)

Full legal name & address for service — street & number, municipality, postal code, telephone & fax numbers and e-mail address (if any)..	*Lawyer's name & address — street & number, municipality, postal code, telephone & fax numbers and e-mail address (if any)..*

Respondent(s) (If there is a respondent, the first letter of the respondent's surname may be used)

Full legal name & address for service — street & number, municipality, postal code, telephone & fax numbers and e-mail address (if any)..	*Lawyer's name & address — street & number, municipality, postal code, telephone & fax numbers and e-mail address (if any)..*

1. My name is *(child's full legal name)* ....

2. I was born on *(give date of birth)* ....

3. I know that the applicant(s) is/are asking the court to make an order to adopt me.

4. I agree to being adopted by the applicant(s).

5. I have been given a chance to get counselling.

6. I understand the nature and effect of this consent. I understand that I may withdraw this consent within 21 days by attending at the office of the lawyer who witnessed the consent located at *(give address)* .... or by attending at the office of another authorized representative of the Children's Lawyer and signing a written notice of withdrawal.

7. I understand that once I turn eighteen years old, I can apply for a copy of my original birth registration, if any, and a copy of my adoption order.

8. I understand that once I turn nineteen years old, my birth parent(s) can apply for information from my original birth registration, if any, any substituted birth registration and my adoption order. This information would include my full legal name after adoption.

9. I have spoken to a lawyer ❑ who has explained adoption to me,

❑ who has explained what it means for me to sign this consent,

❑ who has told me what to do if I want to change my mind about this consent,

❑ who has told me about my rights and the rights of other persons with respect to the disclosure of adoption information,

❑ who is going to witness my signing of this form.

To be completed only where the child is 12 years of age or older.

10. I agree that my name after adoption will be *(full legal name after adoption)*

....

....

Date of signatures *Signature of child*

....
Signature of Children's Lawyer

AFFIDAVIT OF EXECUTION AND INDEPENDENT LEGAL ADVICE

My name is (full legal name) ....

and I swear/affirm that the following is true:

1. I am a member of the Bar of *(name of jurisdiction)* .... and am an agent of the Office of the Children's Lawyer.

2. I am not acting for any other person in this adoption case.

3. I explained to *(child's full legal name)* .... about

❑ the nature and effect of adoption under the law of Ontario
❑ the nature and effect of this consent
❑ the circumstances under which this consent may be withdrawn
❑ his/her rights and the rights of other persons with respect to the disclosure of adoption information

in language appropriate to his/her age to the best of my knowledge and skills.

4. After my explanation, the child told me that he/she wanted to sign this consent.

5. I was present at and witnessed the signing of this consent by the child.

Sworn/Affirmed before me at .... *municipality* in .... *province, state or country* on .... *date* .... *Commissioner for taking affidavits (Type or print name below if signature is illegible.)*	.... *Signature (This form is to be signed in front of a lawyer, justice of the peace, notary public or commissioner for taking affidavits.)*

April 1, 2009

FORM 34A — AFFIDAVIT OF PARENTAGE, SWORN/AFFIRMED

[Repealed O. Reg. 76/06, s. 15.]

[Editor's Note: Forms 4 to 39 of the Family Law Rules have been repealed by O. Reg. 76/06, effective May 1, 2006. Pursuant to Family Law Rule 1(9), when a form is referred to by number, the reference is to the form with that number that is described in the Table of Forms at the end of these rules and which is available at www.ontariocourtforms.on.ca. For your convenience, the government form as published on this website is reproduced below.]

Court File Number

ONTARIO

.... *(Name of court)*

at .... *Court office address*

Applicant(s) (If the applicant is unknown at the time this affidavit is sworn/affirmed or if the applicant's name is not to be disclosed to the person swearing/affirming this affidavit, leave this box blank)

Full legal name & address for service — street & number, municipality, postal code, telephone & fax numbers and e-mail address (if any).	*Lawyer's name & address — street & number, municipality, postal code, telephone & fax numbers and e-mail address (if any).*

Respondent(s) (If there is a respondent, the first letter of the respondent's surname may be used)

Full legal name & address for service — street & number, municipality, postal code, telephone & fax numbers and e-mail address (if any).	*Lawyer's name & address — street & number, municipality, postal code, telephone & fax numbers and e-mail address (if any).*

My name is (full legal name) ....

I live in (municipality & province) ....

and I swear/affirm that the following is true:

1. The child's full legal name is: *(Give full legal name, date of birth, sex and birth registration number if known of person to be adopted. If this person was placed for adoption by a licensee or children's aid society, you may use an initial for the surname.)*

.... *Full legal name* .... *Date of birth* .... *Sex* .... *Birth registration number*

2. I am *(State your relationship to the child.)* ....

3. The child was born on *(date)* ...., in *(municipality, province, etc.)* ....

4. The child's birth was registered or registration has been requested with the vital statistics register of *(province)* .... under the following name(s):

Check applicable box(es).

5. *(Name of person familiar with legal meaning of "parent")* .... has reviewed with me those categories of persons who qualify as "parents" for the purposes of the *Child, Youth and Family Services Act, 2017* and whose consents have to be obtained or dispensed with before the child can be adopted.

Check off all boxes below that apply to your situation. Note that "birth parent" means the person who gives birth to the child.

6. The review mentioned in paragraph 5 included an examination of the following checklist:

(a) Within the 300-day period before the child's birth,

❑ the birth parent's spouse *(spouse's full legal name)* .... died.

❑ the birth parent got a divorce or annulment from *(spouse's full legal name)* ....

❑ the birth parent was living in conjugal relationship outside marriage with *(person's full legal name)* .... that lasted for a period of *(State duration of relationship.)* .... and came to an end.

❑ the birth parent was not living in a conjugal relationship of some permanence outside of marriage with anyone.

(b) At the time of the child's birth, the birth parent was

❑ not married.

❑ married to *(spouse's full legal name)* ....

❑ not living in a conjugal relationship outside marriage.

❑ living in a conjugal relationship outside marriage with *(spouse's full legal name)* .... for a period of *(state duration of relationship)* ....

(c) Where the child was conceived through assisted reproduction, at the time of the child's conception, the child's birth parent

❑ was not married.

❑ was married to *(spouse's full legal name)* ....

❑ was living in a conjugal relationship outside marriage with *(spouse's full legal name)* .... for a period of *(state duration of relationship)* ....

❑ *(not applicable)*

(d) Under *Ontario's Vital Statistics Act* or under similar legislation in another province or territory in Canada,

❑ no person, to the best of my knowledge and information,

❑ *(person's full legal name)* ....

has certified the child's birth as the child's parent.

(e) As of today's date,

❑ no other person has, to the best of my knowledge and information, been recognized by a court

❑ *(person's full legal name)* .... has been recognized by *(name of court)* ....

to be a parent to the child.

(f) In the 12 months before the child was placed for adoption,

❑ no person

❑ *(person's full legal name)* ....

has demonstrated a settled intention to treat the child as a child of his or her own family.

(g) In the 12 months before the child was placed for adoption,

❑ no person has acknowledged to me or, to the best of my knowledge and information, to any other person or agency

❑ (person's full legal name) .... acknowledged

❑ to me

❑ to *(name of other person or agency)*

parentage of the child and provided for the child's support.

(h) Prior to January 1, 2017, a statutory declaration

❑ has, to the best of my knowledge and information, never been filed by any person,

❑ was filed by *(person's full legal name)* ....

with the office of the Registrar General acknowledging parentage of the child.

(i) There is

❑ no written agreement or court order requiring any person,

❑ a written agreement made on *(date)* .... , at *(municipality, etc.)* ...., requiring *(person's full legal name)* ....,

❑ an order of *(name of court)* ...., made on *(date)* ...., at *(municipality, etc.)* ...., requiring *(person's full legal name)* ....

to provide for the child's support.

(j) There is

❑ no written agreement or court order giving any person,

❑ a written agreement made on *(date)* ...., at *(municipality, etc.)* ...., giving *(person's full legal name)* ....,

❑ an order of *(name of court)* ...., made on (date) ...., at *(municipality, etc.)* .... giving *(person's full legal name)* ....

custody of or access to the child.

7. The review in paragraphs 5 and 6 indicates that, other than the person making this affidavit,

❑ no other person

❑ *(full legal name of person(s))*

meets/meet the definition of "parent" whose consent would therefore be required before the child could be adopted.

Sworn/Affirmed before me at .... *municipality* in .... *province, state or country* on .... *date* *Commissioner for taking affidavits (Type or print name below if signature is illegible.)*	.... *Signature* *(This form is to be signed in front of a lawyer, justice of the peace, notary public or commissioner for taking affidavits.)*

March 1, 2018

FORM 34B — NON-PARENT'S CONSENT TO ADOPTION BY SPOUSE

[Repealed O. Reg. 76/06, s. 15.]

[Editor's Note: Forms 4 to 39 of the Family Law Rules have been repealed by O. Reg. 76/06, effective May 1, 2006. Pursuant to Family Law Rule 1(9), when a form is referred to by number, the reference is to the form with that number that is described in the Table of Forms at the end of these rules and which is available at www.ontariocourtforms.on.ca. For your convenience, the government form as published on this website is reproduced below.]

Court File Number

ONTARIO

.... *(Name of court)*

at .... *Court office address*

Applicant(s) (The first letter of the applicant's surname may be used)

Full legal name & address for service — street & number, municipality, postal code, telephone & fax numbers and e-mail address (if any).	*Lawyer's name & address — street & number, municipality, postal code, telephone & fax numbers and e-mail address (if any).*

Respondent(s) (If there is a respondent, the first letter of the respondent's surname may be used)

Full legal name & address for service — street & number, municipality, postal code, telephone & fax numbers and e-mail address (if any).	*Lawyer's name & address — street & number, municipality, postal code, telephone & fax numbers and e-mail address (if any).*

1. My name is *(full legal name)* .... and I live in *(municipality & province)* ....

2. The applicant is my "spouse" within the meaning of Part VIII of the *Child, Youth and Family Services Act, 2017.*

3. I am not a "parent" of the child in this case within the meaning of Part VIII of the *Child, Youth and Family Services Act, 2017.*

4. I consent to the adoption of: *(Give full legal name, date of birth, sex and birth registration number if known of person to be adopted. If this person is in extended society care or was placed for adoption by a licensee or children's aid society, you may use an initial for the surname.)*

....	....	....	....
Full legal name	*Date of birth*	*Sex*	*Birth registration number*

by my spouse *(spouse's full legal name)* ....

....	....
Date of signatures	*Signature of non-parent*
	....
	Signature of independent lawyer

NOTE: This consent must be witnessed by an independent lawyer who is to provide an affidavit of execution and independent legal advice on the next sheet of this form.

AFFIDAVIT OF EXECUTION AND INDEPENDENT LEGAL ADVICE

My name is (full legal name) ....
and I swear/affirm that the following is true:

1. I am a member of the Bar of *(name of jurisdiction)* .... and I am not acting for any other person in this adoption case.

2. I explained to *(non-parent's full legal name)* .... about

- ❏ the nature and effect of adoption under the law of Ontario;
- ❏ the nature and effect of this consent;
- ❏ the circumstances under which this consent may be withdrawn; and
- ❏ the right to counselling.

3. After my explanation, he/she told me that he/she wanted to sign this consent.

4. I was present at and witnessed the signing of this consent.

Sworn/Affirmed before me at .... *municipality* in .... *province, state or country* on .... *date* .... *Commissioner for taking affidavits (Type or print name below if signature is illegible.)*	.... *Signature* *(This form is to be signed in front of a lawyer, justice of the peace, notary public or commissioner for taking affidavits.)*

March 1, 2018

FORM 34C — DIRECTOR'S OR LOCAL DIRECTOR'S STATEMENT ON ADOPTION

[Repealed O. Reg. 76/06, s. 15.]

[Editor's Note: Forms 4 to 39 of the Family Law Rules have been repealed by O. Reg. 76/06, effective May 1, 2006. Pursuant to Family Law Rule 1(9), when a form is referred to by number, the reference is to the form with that number that is described in the Table of Forms at the end of these rules and which is available at www.ontariocourtforms.on.ca. For your convenience, the government form as published on this website is reproduced below.]

Court File Number

ONTARIO

.... *(Name of court)*

at .... *Court office address*

Applicant(s) (The first letter of the applicant's surname may be used)

Full legal name & address for service — street & number, municipality, postal code, telephone & fax numbers and e-mail address (if any).	*Lawyer's name & address — street & number, municipality, postal code, telephone & fax numbers and e-mail address (if any).*

Child ....

(Child's full legal name. If the child is in extended society care or was placed by a licensee or children's aid society, you may use an initial for the surname.)

....	....	....
Date of birth	*Sex*	*Birth registration number*

A local director of a children's aid society may complete this form only where the child was placed for adoption by the society and the child has resided in the home of the applicant(s) for at least 6 months.

1. My name is *(full legal name)* .... and I am

❑ appointed as a Director under the *Child, Youth and Family Services Act, 2017.*

❑ the local director of *(full legal name of children's aid society)*

....

2. The child in this adoption case

❑ is less than 16 years of age.

❑ is 16 years of age or more but has not withdrawn from parental control.

3. The child has resided in the home of the applicant(s) since *(date)* ....

4. Having regard to the child's best interests, I recommend:

❑ that the period of residence be dispensed with and that an order be made for the child's adoption by the applicant(s).

❑ that the court make an order of temporary custody of the child in favour of the applicant(s) for a period not exceeding one year on the terms set out on the next sheet of this form.

❑ because the child has resided in the home of the applicant(s) for at least 6 months, that an order be made for the child's adoption by the applicant(s).

❑ that an order for the child's adoption not be made for reasons set out on the next sheet of this form.

5. The report on the child's adjustment in the home of the applicant(s) is attached to this form.

6. There are

❑ no additional circumstances to which I want to draw the court's attention.

❑ additional circumstances set out on the next sheet of this form to which I want to draw the court's attention.

....

Date of signature *Signature*

NOTE TO DIRECTOR OR LOCAL DIRECTOR: If, in the Director's or local director's opinion, it would not be in the child's best interest to make the order, this form and any attachments must be filed with the court and served on the applicant(s) at least 30 days before the adoption hearing.

(Set out any additional circumstances to which the court's attention should be drawn. If more space is needed, an additional page may be attached.)

(Set out the proposed terms of the temporary custody order or the reasons for recommending against the making of an adoption order. If more space is needed, an additional page may be attached.)

March 1, 2018

FORM 34D — AFFIDAVIT OF ADOPTION APPLICANT(S), SWORN/AFFIRMED

[Editor's Note: Forms 4 to 39 of the Family Law Rules have been repealed by O. Reg. 76/06, effective May 1, 2006. Pursuant to Family Law Rule 1(9), when a form is referred to by number, the reference is to the form with that number that is described in the Table of Forms at the end of these rules and which is available at www.ontariocourtforms.on.ca. For your convenience, the government form as published on this website is reproduced below.]

Court File Number

ONTARIO

.... *(Name of court)*

at .... *Court office address*

Applicant(s) (The first letter of the applicant's surname may be used)

Full legal name & address for service — street & number, municipality, postal code, telephone & fax numbers and e-mail address (if any).	*Lawyer's name & address — street & number, municipality, postal code, telephone & fax numbers and e-mail address (if any).*

Respondent(s) (If there is a respondent, the first letter of the respondent's surname may be used)

Full legal name & address for service — street & number, municipality, postal code, telephone & fax numbers and e-mail address (if any).	*Lawyer's name & address — street & number, municipality, postal code, telephone & fax numbers and e-mail address (if any).*

Child ....

(Child's full legal name. If the child is in extended society care or was placed by a licensee or children's aid society, you may use an initial for the surname.)

....

Date of birth *Sex* *Birth registration number*

My/Our name(s) is/are (full legal name(s)) ....

I/We live in (municipality & province) ....

and I/we swear/affirm that the following is true:

1. I am/We are the applicant(s) for the adoption of the child in this case and reside in Ontario.

2. My/Our birthdate(s) is/are: *(For two persons, indicate which birthdate belongs to whom.)*

....

3. The details of my/our background are as follows: *(Give details of your health, education, employment, ability to support and care for the child and any other relevant background material. If you need more space, you may add a page.)*

....

Put a line through any blank space left on this page.

4. The child is a resident of Ontario and is *(check all boxes that apply)*:

❑ my/our grandchild.

❑ my/our grandnephew/grandniece.

❑ my/our nephew/niece.

❑ a child of my spouse.

❑ not related to me/us.

❑ a First Nations, Inuk, or Métis child.

❑ a member of the following band(s) or First Nations, Inuit, or Métis communities *(list the child's band(s) and/or First Nations, Inuit, or Métis community(ies))*:

....

5. The history of my/our relationship with the child is as follows: *(Give details of history of your relationship with the child. If you need more space, you may add a page.)*

....

Put a line through any blank space left on this page.

Check applicable box.

6. ❑ I am the sole applicant for this child's adoption and if an adoption order is made, I will be the child's only legal parent.

❑ I am the sole applicant for this child's adoption. If an adoption order is made, I will be joining with *(spouse's full legal name)* ...., who is my spouse within the meaning of Part VIII of the *Child, Youth and Family Services Act, 2017*, and together, we will be the child's only legal parents.

❑ We are applying for this child's adoption jointly as spouses within the meaning of Part VIII of the *Child, Youth and Family Services Act, 2017*. If an adoption order is made, we will be the child's only legal parents.

7. I/We understand and appreciate the special role of an adopting parent.

8. No payment or reward of any kind was made, given, received or agreed to be made, given or received by me/us or, to the best of my/our knowledge, by any other person in connection with,

(a) the adoption of this child;

(b) this child's placement for adoption;

(c) the giving of any consent to this child's adoption; or

(d) any negotiations or arrangements leading up to this child's adoption,

except for what is permitted by the *Child, Youth and Family Services Act, 2017* and the regulations made under that Act.

9. I/We understand the importance of the child's culture and will make efforts to preserve his/her traditions, heritage and cultural identity.

10. I/We understand that once the child turns eighteen years old, he/she can apply for a copy of his/her original birth registration, if any, and a copy of his/her adoption order.

11. I/We understand that once the child turns nineteen years old, his/her birth parent(s) can apply for information from his/her original birth registration, if any, any substituted birth registration, and his/her adoption order. This information would include the child's full legal name after adoption.

12. I/We understand the provisions of the *Vital Statistics Act* and the *Child, Youth and Family Services Act, 2017* related to the disclosure of adoption information.

13. I/We want to bring to the court's attention the following additional facts about the child's best interests: *(Give any additional facts. If you need more space, you may add a page.)*

....

Put a line through any blank space left on this page.

Sworn/Affirmed before me at .... *municipality* in .... *province, state or country* on .... *date* .... *Commissioner for taking affidavits (Type or print name below if signature is illegible.)*	.... *Signature* *(This form is to be signed in front of a lawyer, justice of the peace, notary public or commissioner for taking affidavits.)*

March 1, 2018

FORM 34E — DIRECTOR'S CONSENT TO ADOPTION

[Repealed O. Reg. 76/06, s. 15.]

[Editor's Note: Forms 4 to 39 of the Family Law Rules have been repealed by O. Reg. 76/06, effective May 1, 2006. Pursuant to Family Law Rule 1(9), when a form is referred to by number, the reference is to the form with that number that is described in the Table of Forms at the end of these rules and which is available at www.ontariocourtforms.on.ca. For your convenience, the government form as published on this website is reproduced below.]

Court File Number

ONTARIO

.... *(Name of court)*

at .... *Court office address*

Applicant(s) (The first letter of the applicant's surname may be used)

Full legal name & address for service — street & number, municipality, postal code, telephone & fax numbers and e-mail address (if any).	*Lawyer's name & address — street & number, municipality, postal code, telephone & fax numbers and e-mail address (if any).*

Applicant(s) (The first letter of the applicant's surname may be used)

Child ....

(Child's full legal name. If the child is in extended society care or was placed by a licensee or children's aid society, you may use an initial for the surname.)

....

Date of birth *Sex* *Birth registration number*

1. My name is *(full legal name)* .... and I am appointed as a Director under the *Child, Youth and Family Services Act, 2017.*

2. An order was made placing the child in extended society care on *(date)* .... and was placed into the care of *(full legal name of children's aid society)*

....

3. I consent to this child's adoption by the applicant(s).

....

Date of signature *Signature*

March 1, 2018

FORM 34F — PARENT'S OR CUSTODIAN'S CONSENT TO ADOPTION

[Editor's Note: Forms 4 to 39 of the Family Law Rules have been repealed by O. Reg. 76/06, effective May 1, 2006. Pursuant to Family Law Rule 1(9), when a form is referred to by number, the reference is to the form with that number that is described in the Table of Forms at the end of these rules and which is available at www.ontariocourtforms.on.ca. For your convenience, the government form as published on this website is reproduced below.]

Court File Number

ONTARIO

.... *(Name of court)*

at .... *Court office address*

1. My name is (full legal name) .... *I was born on (date of birth)* .... *and I live at (address)* ....

2. The child in this case is: *(Give child's full legal name, date of birth, sex and birth registration number, if available.)*

....	....	....	
Full legal name	Date of birth	Sex	Birth registration number

3. I am a parent of the child within the meaning of Part VIII of the Child, Youth and Family Services Act, 2017 *because I am (Check appropriate paragraph below.)*

❑ a parent of the child under section 6, 8, 9, 10, 11 or 13 of the *Children's Law Reform Act (includes a birth parent, her spouse).* I am the child's *(state your relationship to the child)*

....

❑ an individual described in subsection 7(2) of the *Children's Law Reform Act.*

❑ an individual who has been found or recognized by a court of competent jurisdiction outside of Ontario to be a parent of the child.

❑ a parent under section 217 or 218 of the *Child, Youth and Family Services Act, 2017. (includes adoptive parents)*

❑ an individual having lawful custody of the child.

❑ an individual who, during the 12 months before the child was placed for adoption, has demonstrated a settled intention to treat the child as a member of his/her family.

❑ an individual who, during the 12 months before the child was placed for adoption, has acknowledged parentage of the child and has provided for the child's support.

❑ an individual who is required to provide for the child or who has custody of or access to the child under a written agreement or a court order.

❑ an individual who has acknowledged parentage of the child under section 12 of the *Children's Law Reform Act* as it read before January 1, 2017.

4. I consent to the adoption of this child.

5. I understand the nature and effect of this consent. I understand that I may withdraw this consent in one or more of the following ways:

- If the child is placed for adoption by a children's aid society, by ensuring that the children's aid society located at *(address)* .... receives my written notice of withdrawal within 21 days after my consent was given.

- If the child is placed for adoption by a licensee, by ensuring that the licensee located at *(address)* .... receives my written notice of withdrawal within 21 days after my consent was given.

- If a relative of the child or the spouse of a parent proposes to apply to adopt the child, by ensuring that the proposed applicant receives my written notice of withdrawal within 21 days after my consent was given.

6. I understand that, after the 21 days have passed, I am not allowed to withdraw this consent unless I first get the court's permission, and then only if my child has not yet been placed for adoption and if I can show that it is in the child's best interests that this consent be withdrawn.

7. I understand the nature of an adoption order and that, if an adoption order is made, I will no longer be a legal parent to the child.

8. I understand that once the child turns eighteen years old, he/she can apply for a copy of his/her original birth registration, if any, and a copy of his/her adoption order. I understand that my full legal name may be included on such copies.

9. I understand that once the child turns nineteen years old, his/her birth parent(s) may apply for information from his/her original birth registration, if any, any substituted birth registration, and his/her adoption order. This information would include the child's full legal name after adoption.

10. I understand my right to ask and to be told whether an adoption order has been made for the child.

11. I understand my rights and the rights of other persons with respect to the disclosure of adoption information.

12. No payment or reward of any kind was made, given, received or agreed to be made, given or received by me/us or, to the best of my/our knowledge, by any other person in connection with,

(a) the adoption of this child;

(b) this child's placement for adoption;

(c) the giving of any consent to this child's adoption; or

(d) any negotiations or arrangements leading up to this child's adoption,

except for what is permitted by the *Child, Youth and Family Services Act, 2017* and the regulations made under that Act.

13. I have had a chance to get counselling about this consent.

14. I have had independent legal advice about this consent.

....

Date of signatures *Signature of parent*

....

Signature of independent lawyer

NOTE: This consent must be witnessed by an independent lawyer who is to provide an affidavit of execution and independent legal advice below. If the person giving this consent is less than 18 years old, the consent must be accompanied by Form 34J (Affidavit of Execution and Independent Legal Advice (Children's Lawyer)), instead of the Affidavit of Execution and Independent Legal Advice that accompanies this form.

AFFIDAVIT OF EXECUTION AND INDEPENDENT LEGAL ADVICE

My name is (full legal name) ....
and I swear/affirm that the following is true:

1. I am a member of the Bar of *(name of jurisdiction)* .... and I am not acting for any other person in this adoption case.

2. I explained to *(parent's full legal name)* .... about

❑ the nature and effect of adoption under the law of Ontario;
❑ the nature and effect of this consent;

- ❑ the circumstances under which this consent may be withdrawn;
- ❑ his/her rights and the rights of other persons with respect to the disclosure of adoption information;
- ❑ the right to counselling.

3. After my explanation, he/she told me that he/she wanted to sign this consent.

4. I was present at and witnessed the signing of this consent.

Sworn/Affirmed before me at .... *municipality* in .... *province, state or country* on .... *date* .... *Commissioner for taking affidavits (Type or print name below if signature is illegible.)*	.... *Signature* *(This form is to be signed in front of a lawyer, justice of the peace, notary public or commissioner for taking affidavits.)*

March 1, 2018

FORM 34G — AFFIDAVIT OF ADOPTION LICENSEE OR SOCIETY EMPLOYEE, SWORN/AFFIRMED

[Repealed O. Reg. 76/06, s. 15.]

[Editor's Note: Forms 4 to 39 of the Family Law Rules have been repealed by O. Reg. 76/06, effective May 1, 2006. Pursuant to Family Law Rule 1(9), when a form is referred to by number, the reference is to the form with that number that is described in the Table of Forms at the end of these rules and which is available at www.ontariocourtforms.on.ca. For your convenience, the government form as published on this website is reproduced below.]

Court File Number

ONTARIO

.... *(Name of court)*

at .... *Court office address*

Applicant(s) (The first letter of the applicant's surname may be used)

Full legal name & address for service — street & number, municipality, postal code, telephone & fax numbers and e-mail address (if any).	*Lawyer's name & address — street & number, municipality, postal code, telephone & fax numbers and e-mail address (if any).*

Respondent(s) (If there is a respondent, the first letter of the respondent's surname may be used)

Full legal name & address for service — street & number, municipality, postal code, telephone & fax numbers and e-mail address (if any).	*Lawyer's name & address — street & number, municipality, postal code, telephone & fax numbers and e-mail address (if any).*

My name is (full legal name) ....

I live in (municipality & province) ....

and I swear/affirm that the following is true:

1. The name of the child being placed for adoption is: *(Give full legal name, date of birth, sex and birth registration number if known of person to be adopted. If this person is in extended society care or was placed for adoption by a licensee or children's aid society, you may use an initial for the surname.)*

....	....	....	
Full legal name	Date of birth	Sex	Birth registration number

2. I am ❑ a person licensed under Part VIII of the *Child, Youth and Family Services Act, 2017* to place the child for adoption.

❑ an employee of *(full legal name of children's aid society)* .... authorized to place the child for adoption.

❑ an employee of *(full legal name of adoption agency)* .... which is licensed under Part VIII of the *Child, Youth and Family Services Act, 2017* to place the child for adoption.

3. I have made reasonable inquiries about the existence of any outstanding orders of custody of or access to the child. To the best of my knowledge,

❑ there is no outstanding order.

❑ the outstanding order(s) is/are as follows: *(For each order, give the name of the court, date of order, name of judge, court file number and full legal name(s) of the person(s) given custody or access under the order.)*

....

4. I have made reasonable inquiries about the existence of any person — other than the person(s) who already filed a consent — who is a "parent" of the child within the meaning of Part VIII of the *Child, Youth and Family Services Act, 2017.* To the best of my knowledge,

❑ There is no other "parent".

❑ the other "parent(s)" is/are: *(For each person, state his or her full legal name, address and an explanation why a consent is not yet available.)*

....

5. I have made reasonable inquiries about the existence of any other application for the adoption of this child. To the best of my knowledge,

❑ there has been no other adoption application with respect to this child.

❑ the details of the other adoption application(s) are as follows: *(For each application, state the name and location of the court before which the application was brought, the date of the application, the full legal name(s) of the applicant(s) and the result of the application.)*

....

6. I have made reasonable inquiries whether the person(s) who filed the consent(s) in this application withdrew the consent(s) or whether a court had set aside the consent(s). To the best of my knowledge,

❑ no consent was withdrawn or set aside.

❑ the details of the withdrawal or of the setting aside are as follows: *(Specify details.)*

....

7. The child in this adoption case

❑ is 7 or more years old and I have therefore offered the child a chance to get counselling about the consent. This offer of counselling

❑ was accepted and the child received counselling.

❑ was turned down by the child.

I also ensured that the child received independent legal advice from *(lawyer's name)*

....

❑ is less than 7 years old and no counselling or independent legal advice was offered.

8. I offered the child's parent(s) a chance to get counselling about the consent and the offer

❑ was accepted by *(name of parent(s) who accepted offer)* .... and counselling was provided.

❑ was turned down by *(name of parent(s) who refused offer)*

....

9. The parent(s) received independent legal advice from *(name of lawyer(s))*

....

10. To the best of my knowledge, no person has given, received or agreed to give or receive any payment or reward of any kind in connection with

(a) The adoption of the child;

(b) The child's placement for adoption;

(c) The giving of any consent to the child's adoption; or

(d) Any negotiations or arrangements leading up to the child's adoption,

except for what is permitted by the *Child, Youth and Family Services Act, 2017* and the regulations made under it.

Sworn/Affirmed before me at .... *municipality* in .... *province, state or country*	.... *Signature* *(This form is to be signed in front of a lawyer, justice of the peace, notary public or commissioner for taking affidavits.)*
on .... *date* .... *Commissioner for taking affidavits (Type or print name below if signature is illegible.)*	

March 1, 2018

FORM 34G.1 — AFFIDAVIT OF SOCIETY EMPLOYEE FOR ADOPTION OF A CHILD IN EXTENDED SOCIETY CARE, SWORN/AFFIRMED

[Editor's Note: Pursuant to Family Law Rule 1(9), when a form is referred to by number, the reference is to the form with that number that is described in the Table of Forms at the end of these rules and which is available at www.ontariocourtforms.on.ca. For your convenience, the government form as published on this website is reproduced below.]

Court File Number

ONTARIO

.... *(Name of court)*

at .... *Court office address*

Applicant(s) (The first letter of the applicant's surname may be used)

Full legal name & address for service — street & number, municipality, postal code, telephone & fax numbers and e-mail address (if any).	*Lawyer's name & address — street & number, municipality, postal code, telephone & fax numbers and e-mail address (if any).*

Applicant(s) (The first letter of the applicant's surname may be used)

Respondent(s) (If there is a respondent, the first letter of the respondent's surname may be used)

Full legal name & address for service — street & number, municipality, postal code, telephone & fax numbers and e-mail address (if any).	*Lawyer's name & address — street & number, municipality, postal code, telephone & fax numbers and e-mail address (if any).*

My name is (full legal name) ....

I live in (municipality & province) ....

and I swear/affirm that the following is true:

1. The name of the child being placed for adoption is: *(Give full legal name, date of birth, sex and birth registration number if known of person to be adopted. You may use an initial for the surname.)*

....	....	....
Full legal name	*Date of birth*	*Sex* / *Birth registration number*

2. I am an employee of *(full legal name of children's aid society)* .... authorized to place the child for adoption.

3. The child was placed in extended society care by order of Justice *(name of judge)* .... on *(date)* .... A copy of the extended society care order and proof of service of the order are attached to this affidavit.

4. I have made reasonable inquiries about the existence of any outstanding orders of access to the child. To the best of my knowledge,

❑ there is no outstanding order.

❑ A copy of the order ending access to the child made under s. 104 of the *Child, Youth and Family Services Act, 2017* made by

Justice *(name of judge)* .... on *(date of order)* .... and proof of service of the order are attached to this affidavit.

❑ A copy of the order for access to the child made under s. 104 of the *Child, Youth and Family Services Act, 2017* made by Justice *(name of judge)* .... on *(date of order)* .... is attached to this affidavit.

❑ On *(date)* ...., *(name of children's aid society)* .... gave notice to *(name(s) of person(s) entitled to notice)* .... that the child would be placed for adoption as described in the affidavit(s) of service of *(name(s) of person(s) who served notice)* .... sworn/affirmed on *(date(s) affidavit(s) of service sworn or affirmed)* ....

❑ This service was in accordance with the requirements in s. 195(4) of the *Child, Youth and Family Services Act, 2017.*

❑ This service was in accordance with the order of Justice *(name of judge)* .... pursuant to s. 195(5) of the *Child, Youth and Family Services Act, 2017.*

❑ Justice *(name of judge)* .... made an order on *(date of order)* .... dispensing with service of notice on *(name(s) of person(s) entitled to access to or contact with the child who was(were) not served)* .... pursuant to s. 195(6) of the *Child, Youth and Family Services Act, 2017.*

❑ The child is a First Nations, Inuk, or Métis person and on *(date)* ...., *(name of children's aid society)* .... gave notice to *(name(s) of person(s) entitled to notice)* .... that the child would be placed for adoption as described in the affidavit(s) of service of *(name(s) of person(s) who served notice)* .... sworn/affirmed on *(date(s) affidavit(s) of service sworn or affirmed)* ....

❑ This service was in accordance with the requirements in s. 197(4)(a) of the *Child, Youth and Family Services Act, 2017.*

❑ This service was in accordance with the order of Justice *(name of judge)* .... pursuant to s. 197(4)(b) of the *Child, Youth and Family Services Act, 2017.*

❑ Justice *(name of judge)* .... made an order on *(date of order)* .... dispensing with service of notice on *(name(s) of person(s) entitled to notice and who was/were not served)* .... pursuant to s. 197(4)(b) of the *Child, Youth and Family Services Act, 2017.*

❑ No application for an openness order was filed with respect to this child and the access order of Justice *(name of judge)* ...., dated *(date of order)* ...., was terminated upon the placement of the child for adoption on *(date child placed for adoption)* ....

❑ An openness application was filed by *(name of person(s) seeking an openness order)* .... and the following order was made:

(Give the name of the court, date of order, name of judge, court file number, full legal name(s) of the person(s) permitted to communicate or have a relationship with the child under the order and details of the order.)

....

❑ An openness application was filed by *(name of person(s) seeking an openness order)* .... and has not yet been concluded.

The status of that application is as follows: *(Provide details of the order requested, position of other parties and any court dates that have been scheduled.)*

....

5. ❑ I have made reasonable inquiries about the existence of any outstanding appeals of orders relating to the child. To the best of my knowledge,

❑ There is no appeal in progress of the order(s) for extended society care or ending access to the child.

❑ The appeal period for the order(s) for extended society care and ending access to the child have expired without an appeal being filed.

❑ An appeal of the order for extended society care was filed on *(date)* ...., and was withdrawn on *(date)* ....

❑ An appeal of the order for extended society care was filed and dismissed by *(name of judge or registrar of the Court of Appeal)* .... on *(date of order)* ....

.... An appeal of the order ending access was filed on *(date)* ...., and was withdrawn on *(date)* ....

.... An appeal of the order ending access was filed and dismissed by *(name of judge or registrar of the Court of Appeal)* .... on *(date of order)* ....

Sworn/Affirmed before me at .... *municipality* in .... *province, state or country* on .... *date* .... *Commissioner for taking affidavits (Type or print name below if signature is illegible.)*	.... *Signature* *(This form is to be signed in front of a lawyer, justice of the peace, notary public or commissioner for taking affidavits.)*

March 1, 2018

FORM 34H — AFFIDAVIT OF ADOPTING RELATIVE OR STEPPARENT, SWORN/AFFIRMED

[Repealed O. Reg. 76/06, s. 15.]

[Editor's Note: Forms 4 to 39 of the Family Law Rules have been repealed by O. Reg. 76/06, effective May 1, 2006. Pursuant to Family Law Rule 1(9), when a form is referred to by number, the reference is to the form with that number that is described in the Table of Forms at the end of these rules and which is available at www.ontariocourtforms.on.ca. For your convenience, the government form as published on this website is reproduced below.]

Court File Number

ONTARIO

.... *(Name of court)*

at .... *Court office address*

Applicant(s) (The first letter of the applicant's surname may be used)

Full legal name & address for service — street & number, municipality, postal code, telephone & fax numbers and e-mail address (if any).	*Lawyer's name & address — street & number, municipality, postal code, telephone & fax numbers and e-mail address (if any).*

Respondent(s) (If there is a respondent, the first letter of the respondent's surname may be used)

Full legal name & address for service — street & number, municipality, postal code, telephone & fax numbers and e-mail address (if any).	*Lawyer's name & address — street & number, municipality, postal code, telephone & fax numbers and e-mail address (if any).*

My name is (full legal name) ....

I live in (municipality & province) ....

and I swear/affirm that the following is true:

1. I was born on *(date of your own birth)* ....

2. The name of the child whom I want to adopt is *(Give full legal name, date of birth, sex and birth registration number if known)*

....	....	....	....
Full legal name	*Date of birth*	*Sex*	*Birth registration number*

3. I am the applicant in this adoption and am this child's

❑ stepparent. . . . . ❑ grandparent.

❑ aunt/uncle. . . . . ❑ great-aunt/great-uncle.

4. I have made reasonable inquiries about the existence of any outstanding orders of custody of or access to the child. To the best of my knowledge,

❑ there is no outstanding order.

❑ the outstanding order(s) is/are as follows: *(For each order, give the name of the court, date of order, name of judge, court file number and full legal name(s) of the person(s) given custody or access under the order.)*

....

Put a line through any space left on this page.

5. I have made reasonable inquiries about the existence of any person — other than the person(s) who already filed a consent — who is a "parent" of the child within the meaning of Part VIII of the *Child, Youth and Family Services Act, 2017*. To the best of my knowledge,

❏ there is no other "parent".

❏ the other "parent(s)" is/are: *(For each parent, state his or her full legal name, address and an explanation why a consent is not yet available.)*

....

6. I have made reasonable inquiries about the existence of any other application for the adoption of this child. To the best of my knowledge,

❏ there has been no other adoption application with respect to this child.

❏ the details of the other adoption application(s) are as follows: *(For each application, state the name and location of the court before which the application was brought, the date of the application, the full legal name(s) of the applicant(s) and the result of the application.)*

....

7. I have made reasonable inquiries whether the person(s) who filed the consent(s) in this application withdrew the consent(s) or whether a court had set aside the consent(s). To the best of my knowledge,

❏ no consent was withdrawn or set aside.

❏ the details of the withdrawal or of the setting aside are as follows: *(Specify details.)*

....

8. The child in this adoption case

❏ is 7 or more years old and I have therefore offered the child a chance to get counselling about the consent. This offer of counselling

❏ was accepted and the child received counselling.

❏ was turned down by the child.

I also ensured that the child received independent legal advice from *(lawyer's name)*

....

❏ is less than 7 years old and no counselling or independent legal advice was offered.

9. I offered the child's parent(s) a chance to get counselling about the consent and the offer

❏ was accepted by *(name of parent(s) who accepted offer)* .... and counselling was provided.

❏ was turned down by *(name of parent(s) who refused offer)*

....

Put a line through any space left on this page.

10. I also ensured that the parent(s) received independent legal advice from *(name of lawyer(s))*

....

11. To the best of my knowledge, no person has given, received or agreed to give or receive any payment or reward of any kind in connection with,

(a) the adoption of the child;

(b) the child's placement for adoption;

(c) the giving of any consent to the child's adoption; or

(d) any negotiations or arrangements leading up to the child's adoption,

except for what is permitted by the *Child, Youth and Family Services Act, 2017* and the regulations made under it.

12. I understand that once the child turns eighteen years old, he/she can apply for a copy of his/her original birth registration, if any, and a copy of his/her adoption order.

13. I understand that once the child turns nineteen years old, his/her birth parent(s) can apply for information from his/her original birth registration, if any, any substituted birth registration and his/her adoption order. This information would include the child's full legal name after adoption.

14. I understand the provisions of the *Vital Statistics Act* and the *Child, Youth and Family Services Act, 2017* related to the disclosure of adoption information.

Sworn/Affirmed before me at .... *municipality*	.... *Signature*
in .... *province, state or country*	*(This form is to be signed in front of a lawyer, justice of the peace, notary public or commissioner for taking affidavits.)*
on .... *date* .... *Commissioner for taking affidavits (Type or print name below if signature is illegible.)*	

March 1, 2018

FORM 34I — PARENT'S CONSENT TO ADOPTION BY SPOUSE

[Editor's Note: Forms 4 to 39 of the Family Law Rules have been repealed by O. Reg. 76/06, effective May 1, 2006. Pursuant to Family Law Rule 1(9), when a form is referred to by number, the reference is to the form with that number that is described in the Table of Forms at the end of these rules and which is available at www.ontariocourtforms.on.ca. For your convenience, the government form as published on this website is reproduced below.]

Court File Number

ONTARIO

.... *(Name of court)*

at .... *Court office address*

Applicant(s) (The first letter of the applicant's surname may be used)

Full legal name & address for service — street & number, municipality, postal code, telephone & fax numbers and e-mail address (if any).	*Lawyer's name & address — street & number, municipality, postal code, telephone & fax numbers and e-mail address (if any).*

Respondent(s) (If there is a respondent, the first letter of the respondent's surname may be used)

Full legal name & address for service — street & number, municipality, postal code, telephone & fax numbers and e-mail address (if any).	*Lawyer's name & address — street & number, municipality, postal code, telephone & fax numbers and e-mail address (if any).*

Child ....

(Child's full legal name. If this person is in extended society care or was placed by a licensee or children's aid society, you may use an initial for the surname.)

....

Date of birth *Sex* *Birth registration number*

1. My name is (full legal name) .... *I was born on (date of birth)* .... *and I live at (address)* ....

2. The applicant is my "spouse" within the meaning of Part VIII of the *Child, Youth and Family Services Act, 2017.*

3. I am a parent of the child within the meaning of Part VIII of the *Child, Youth and Family Services Act, 2017* because I am *(Check appropriate paragraph below.)*

❑ a parent of the child under section 6, 8, 9, 10, 11 or 13 of the *Children's Law Reform Act (includes a birth parent, her spouse).* I am the child's *(state your relationship to the child)*

....

❑ an individual described in subsection 7(2) of the *Children's Law Reform Act.*

❑ an individual who has been found or recognized by a court of competent jurisdiction outside of Ontario to be a parent of the child.

❑ a parent under section 217 or 218 of the *Child, Youth and Family Services Act, 2017. (includes adoptive parents)*

❑ an individual having lawful custody of the child.

❑ an individual who, during the 12 months before the child was placed for adoption, has demonstrated a settled intention to treat the child as a member of his/her family.

❑ an individual who, during the 12 months before the child was placed for adoption, has acknowledged parentage of the child and has provided for the child's support.

❑ an individual who is required to provide for the child or who has custody of or access to the child under a written agreement or a court order.

❑ an individual who has acknowledged parentage of the child under section 12 of the *Children's Law Reform Act* as it read before January 1, 2017.

4. I consent to the adoption of the child by my spouse.

5. I understand the nature and effect of this consent. I understand that I may withdraw my consent by ensuring that the proposed applicant and the licensee, if the child was placed for adoption by a licensee, receive(s) my written notice of withdrawal within 21 days after my consent was given.

6. I understand that, after the 21 days have passed, I am not allowed to withdraw this consent unless I first get the court's permission and if I can show that it is in the child's best interests that this consent be withdrawn.

7. I understand the nature of an adoption order. I understand that, if an adoption order were made, my spouse would be joining me in the role of a parent and, together, we would be the child's only legal parents. An adoption order would require me to share my parental rights and responsibilities with my spouse equally and permanently until a court ordered otherwise.

8. I understand my rights and the rights of other persons with respect to the disclosure of adoption information.

9. No payment or reward of any kind was made, given, received or agreed to be made, given or received by me/us or, to the best of my/our knowledge, by any other person in connection with,

(a) the adoption of this child;

(b) this child's placement for adoption;

(c) the giving of any consent to this child's adoption; or

(d) any negotiations or arrangements leading up to this child's adoption,

except for what is permitted by the *Child, Youth and Family Services Act, 2017* and the regulations made under that Act.

10. I had a chance to seek counselling with respect to this consent.

11. I have had independent legal advice with respect to this consent.

....

Date of signatures *Signature of parent*

....

NOTE: This consent must be witnessed by an independent lawyer who is to provide an affidavit of execution and independent legal advice below. If the person giving this consent is less than 18 years old, the consent must be accompanied by Form 34J (Affidavit of Execution and Independent Legal Advice (Children's Lawyer)), instead of the Affidavit of Execution and Independent Legal Advice that accompanies this form.

Signature of independent lawyer

AFFIDAVIT OF EXECUTION AND INDEPENDENT LEGAL ADVICE

My name is (full legal name) ....
and I swear/affirm that the following is true:

1. I am a member of the Bar of *(name of jurisdiction)* .... and I am not acting for any other person in this adoption case.

2. I explained to *(parent's full legal name)* .... about
- ❑ the nature and effect of adoption under the law of Ontario;
- ❑ the nature and effect of this consent;
- ❑ the circumstances under which this consent may be withdrawn;
- ❑ his/her rights and the rights of other persons with respect to the disclosure of adoption information;
- ❑ his/her rights and the rights of other persons with respect to the disclosure of adoption information;
- ❑ the right to counselling.

3. After my explanation, he/she told me that he/she wanted to sign this consent.

4. I was present at and witnessed the signing of this consent.

Sworn/Affirmed before me at .... *municipality* in .... *province, state or country* on .... *date* *Commissioner for taking affidavits (Type or print name below if signature is illegible.)*	.... *Signature* *(This form is to be signed in front of a lawyer, justice of the peace, notary public or commissioner for taking affidavits.)*

March 1, 2018

FORM 34J — AFFIDAVIT OF EXECUTION AND INDEPENDENT LEGAL ADVICE (CHILDREN'S LAWYER), SWORN/AFFIRMED

[Repealed O. Reg. 76/06, s. 15.]

[Editor's Note: Forms 4 to 39 of the Family Law Rules have been repealed by O. Reg. 76/06, effective May 1, 2006. Pursuant to Family Law Rule 1(9), when a form is referred to by number, the reference is to the form with that number that is described in the Table of Forms at the end of these rules and which is available at www.ontariocourtforms.on.ca. For your convenience, the government form as published on this website is reproduced below.]

ONTARIO

Court File Number

....

(Name of court)

at ....

Court office address

My name is (full legal name) ....

and I swear/affirm that the following is true:

1. I am an authorized representative of the Office of the Children's Lawyer in the adoption of:

Full legal name of child	*Date of birth (d, m, y) and sex*

2. I explained to *(minor parent's full legal name)* .... about

❏ the nature and effect of adoption under the law of Ontario;

❏ the nature and effect of a consent to adoption;

❏ the right to counselling;

❏ his/her rights and the rights of other persons with respect to the disclosure of adoption information;

❏ the right upon request to be advised whether an adoption order has been made,

in language appropriate to his/her age to the best of my knowledge and skills.

3. I also explained that he/she could withdraw the consent within 21 days by a written notice. I gave him/her the address where the written notice would have to be served. I also explained that, after the 21 days had passed, he/she could withdraw the consent only with the court's permission but only if the child had not yet been placed with a person for adoption and if he/she could convince the court that it would be in the child's best interests to have the consent withdrawn.

4. After my explanation, he/she told me that he/she wanted to sign the consent to adoption and I believe that this reflects his/her true wishes.

5. I was present at and witnessed the signing of the consent.

Sworn/Affirmed before me at ....

municipality *Signature*

in .... *(This form is to be signed in front of a lawyer,justice of the peace, notary public orcommissioner for taking affidavits.)*

province, state or country

on ....

date *Commissioner for taking affidavits*

(Type or print name below if signature is illegible.)

April 1, 2009

FORM 34K — CERTIFICATE OF CLERK (ADOPTION)

[Editor's Note: Forms 4 to 39 of the Family Law Rules have been repealed by O. Reg. 76/06, effective May 1, 2006. Pursuant to Family Law Rule 1(9), when a form is referred to by number, the reference is to the form with that number that is described in the Table of Forms at the end of these rules and which is available at www.ontariocourtforms.on.ca. For your convenience, the government form as published on this website is reproduced below.]

Court File Number

ONTARIO

.... *(Name of court)*

at .... *Court office address*

Applicant(s) (The first letter of the applicant's surname may be used)

Full legal name & address for service — street & number, municipality, postal code, telephone & fax numbers and e-mail address (if any).	*Lawyer's name & address — street & number, municipality, postal code, telephone & fax numbers and e-mail address (if any).*

Applicant(s) (The first letter of the applicant's surname may be used)

Respondent(s) (If there is a respondent, the first letter of the surname may be used)

Full legal name & address for service — street & number, municipality, postal code, telephone & fax numbers and e-mail address (if any).	*Lawyer's name & address — street & number, municipality, postal code, telephone & fax numbers and e-mail address (if any).*

If the appropriate box on the left cannot be checked, check the box on the right margin and describe the deficiency by the box.

The clerk of the court certifies as follows:

1. *MATERIAL COMMON TO ALL ADOPTION CASES* — *Deficiency*

(a) ❑ An application for adoption (Form 8D in *Family Law Rules*) has been filed. — 1(a) ❑

(b) ❑ A certified copy of the statement of live birth has been filed (Form 2 in regulation under *Vital Statistics Act*). — 1(b) ❑

❑ A certified copy of a change of birth registration has been filed (Form 2 in regulation under *Vital Statistics Act*).

❑ Equivalent proof of details of birth has been filed.

(c) ❑ The person to be adopted is 7 years of age or over and has filed a consent to adoption (Form 34 in *Family Law Rules*). — 1(c) ❑

❑ A court order dispensing with the consent of the person to be adopted has been filed.

(d) ❑ An affidavit of parentage has been filed (Form 34A in *Family Law Rules*). — 1(d) ❑

❑ Other evidence of who is or is not a "parent" has been filed.

(e) ❑ A report on the child's adjustment in the applicant's home: — 1(e) ❑

❑ is required by the Act (where a child had been "placed" for adoption through a licensee, a society or otherwise). That report has been filed.

❑ had been ordered by the court in the case of an adoption by a stepparent or relative. That report has been filed.

❑ has not been required in this case.

(f) ❑ The applicant has a "spouse" who is not a "parent" and who has not joined in the application. That spouse's consent (Form 34B in *Family Law Rules*) has been filed. 1(f) ❑

❑ A court order dispensing with the spouse's consent has been filed, together with,

(i) ❑ proof of service of this order.

(ii) ❑ a certified copy of an order dispensing with service.

(g) ❑ The Director's or local director's statement (with recommendations) on the adoption (Form 34C in *Family Law Rules*): 1(g) ❑

❑ is required by the Act (where a child had been "placed" for adoption through a licensee, a society or otherwise). That statement has been filed.

❑ had been ordered by the court in the case of an adoption by a stepparent or relative. That statement has been filed.

❑ has not been required in this case.

(h) ❑ The affidavit of each adoption applicant (Form 34D in *Family Law Rules*) has been filed. 1(h) ❑

(i) ❑ A draft adoption order (Form 25C in *Family Law Rules*) has been filed. 1(i) ❑

(j) ❑ This is a joint application by spouses and 1(j) ❑

(i) ❑ a certificate of the applicants' marriage had been filed.

(ii) ❑ other proof of the applicants' spousal status has been filed.

(k) ❑ Other joint application *(Specify.)* 1(k) ❑

(l) ❑ *(Other. Specify.)* 1(l) ❑

2. *ADDITIONAL MATERIAL FOR ADOPTIONS OF CHILDREN IN EXTENDED SOCIETY CARE*

(a) ❑ The Director's consent to adoption (Form 34E in *Family Law Rules*) has been filed. 2(a) ❑

(b) ❑ There is no outstanding access order to this child in extended society care, and an affidavit (Form 34G.1) has been filed confirming that fact. 2(b) ❑

❑ A certified copy of an order terminating access to this child in extended society care has been filed, together with,

(i) ❑ proof of service of this order.

(ii) ❑ a certified copy of an order dispensing with service.

(c) ❑ The outstanding access order was terminated when the child was placed for adoption and the following document(s) were filed: 2(c) ❑

❑ A copy of each access order made under Part V of the *Child, Youth and Family Services Act, 2017.*

❑ A copy of every notice of intention to place for adoption.

❑ Proof of service of notice of intention to place for adoption.

❑ A copy of the order permitting an alternative method of service.

❑ Proof of service in accordance with order for alternative service.

❑ A copy of the order dispensing with notice.

(d) ❑ The child is a First Nations, Inuk, or Métis person and the following document(s) were filed: 2(d) ❑

❑ A copy of every notice of intention to place for adoption in accordance with section 197(2) of the *Child, Youth and Family Services Act, 2017*, unless the child's First Nations, Inuk or Métis community was not listed at the time the child was placed for adoption, or the child was placed under the old Act.

❑ Proof of service of notice in accordance with s. 197(4)(a) of the *Child, Youth and Family Services Act, 2017.*

❑ A copy of the order permitting an alternative method of service pursuant to s. 197(4)(b) of the *Child, Youth and Family Services Act, 2017.*

❑ Proof of service in accordance with order for alternative service.

❑ A copy of the order dispensing with notice pursuant to s. 197(4)(b) of the *Child, Youth and Family Services Act, 2017.*

(e) ❑ A certified copy of the extended society care order has been filed together with, 2(e) ❑

(i) ❑ proof of service of this order.

(ii) ❑ a certified copy of an order dispensing with service.

(f) ❑ A copy of any openness order has been filed (if applicable). 2(f) ❑

(g) ❑ An affidavit from a society employee (Form 34G.1) has been filed, stating that no appeal of the orders mentioned in clause (b) above had been launched or that the appeal period had expired. 2(g) ❑

(h) ❑ The child is a First Nations, Inuk, or Métis person, and the following document(s) were filed: 2(h) ❑

❑ a copy of the notice provided by a society setting out the society's intention to begin planning for adoption of the child.

❑ proof of service of the notice(s).

(i) ❑ An affidavit (Form 34G.1 in *Family Law Rules*) of an authorized employee of the children's aid society has been filed. 2(i) ❑

(j) ❑ *(Other. Specify.)* 2(j) ❑

3. *ADDITIONAL MATERIAL FOR ADOPTIONS OF CHILDREN NOT IN EXTENDED SOCIETY CARE PLACED FOR ADOPTION BY LICENSEE OR SOCIETY*

(a) ❑ The child has been placed by a children's aid society. 3(a) ❑

❑ The child has been placed by a licensee, and a copy of the licensee's licence to make the placement at the time of placing the child for adoption has been filed.

(b) ❑ An affidavit (Form 34G in *Family Law Rules*) of the licensee or of an authorized employee of the children's aid society has been filed. 3(b) ❑

(c) ❑ The person filing the affidavit knows of no custody or access order involving the child. 3(c) ❑

❑ Certified copy/copies of the custody or access order(s) involving the child has/have been filed together with,

(i) ❑ proof of service of this order.

(ii) ❑ a certified copy of an order dispensing with service.

(d) ❑ A consent (Form 34F in *Family Law Rules*) to adoption from the birth parent has been filed. 3(d) ❑

❑ The consent, which was signed by the birth parent when she was under 18 years of age, is accompanied by a certificate of the Children's Lawyer (Form 34J in *Family Law Rules*).

❑ The child's birth parent has, outside Ontario, signed a form of consent that is not an Ontario consent form and that is accompanied by:

(i) ❑ a certified translation of the document into English/French.

(ii) ❑ evidence that the foreign consent complies with the laws of the place where the birth parent made it.

❑ A certified copy of an order dispensing with the birth parent's consent has been filed, together with proof of service of the order.

(e) ❑ The child is presumed to have a "parent" as defined under paragraph 2 of section 180 of the *Child, Youth and Family Services Act, 2017* and the following document(s) have been filed: 3(e) ❑

❑ A consent (Form 34F in *Family Law Rules*) to adoption from the "parent".

❑ The consent, which was signed by the "parent" when he was under 18 years of age, is accompanied by a certificate of the Children's Lawyer (Form 34J in *Family Law Rules*).

❑ The "parent" has, outside Ontario, signed a form of consent that is not an Ontario consent form and that is accompanied by:

(i) ❑ a certified translation of the document into English/French.

(ii) ❑ evidence that the foreign consent complies with the laws of the place where the "parent" made it.

❑ A certified copy of an order dispensing with the "parent's" consent, together with proof of service of the order.

❑ The court has ruled that, on a balance of probabilities, the person does not have the status of "parent" under paragraph 2 of section 180 of the *Child, Youth and Family Services Act, 2017*.

(f) ❑ A consent (Form 34F in *Family Law Rules*) to adoption from any other person who is a "parent" under Part VIII of the *Child, Youth and Family Services Act, 2017* has been filed. 3(f) ❑

❑ The consent, which was signed by the other "parent" when he/she was under 18 years of age, is accompanied by a certificate of the Children's Lawyer (Form 34J in *Family Law Rules*).

❑ This other "parent" has, outside Ontario, signed a form of consent that is not an Ontario consent form and that is accompanied by:

(i) ❑ a certified translation of the document into English/French.

(ii) ❑ evidence that the foreign consent complies with the laws of the place where the other "parent" made it.

❑ A certified copy of an order dispensing with the other "parent's" consent has been filed, together with proof of service of the order.

(g) ❑ A consent (Form 34F in *Family Law Rules*) to adoption from any other person who is a "parent" under Part VIII of the *Child, Youth and Family Services Act, 2017* has been filed. 3(g) ❑

❑ The consent, which was signed by the other "parent" when he/she was under 18 years of age, is accompanied by a certificate of the Children's Lawyer (Form 34J in *Family Law Rules*).

❑ This other "parent" has, outside Ontario, signed a form of consent that is not an Ontario consent form and that is accompanied by:

(i) ❑ a certified translation of the document into English/French.

(ii) ❑ evidence that the foreign consent complies with the laws of the place where the other "parent" made it.

❑ A certified copy of an order dispensing with the other "parent's" consent has been filed, together with proof of service of the order.

(h) ❑ The child is a First Nations, Inuk, or Métis person, and the following document(s) were filed: 3(h) ❑

❑ a copy of the notice provided by a society setting out the society's intention to begin planning for adoption of the child.

❏ a copy of the notice provided by a licensee in accordance with regulations made under the Act setting out the licensee's intention to place the child for adoption.

❏ proof of service of the notice(s).

(i) ❏ *(Other. Specify.)* 3(i) ❏

4. ADDITIONAL MATERIAL FOR ADOPTION OF CHILD RESIDENT IN CANADA BEFORE ADOPTION BY RELATIVE OR STEPPARENT OR WHERE CHILD HAS RESIDED WITH APPLICANT FOR AT LEAST TWO YEARS

(a) ❏ There are no custody or access orders involving the child. 4(a) ❏

❏ Certified copy/copies of the custody or access order(s) involving the child has/have been filed together with,

(i) ❏ proof of service of this order.

(ii) ❏ a certified copy of an order dispensing with service.

(b) ❏ A consent (Form 34F in *Family Law Rules*) to adoption from the birth parent has been filed. 4(b) ❏

❏ The consent, which was signed by the birth parent when she was under 18 years of age, is accompanied by a certificate of the Children's Lawyer (Form 34J in *Family Law Rules*).

❏ The child's birth parent has, outside Ontario, signed a form of consent that is not an Ontario consent form and that is accompanied by:

(i) ❏ a certified translation of the document into English/French.

(ii) ❏ evidence that the foreign consent complies with the laws of the place where the birth parent made it.

❏ A certified copy of an order dispensing with the birth parent's consent has been filed, together with proof of service of the order.

(c) ❏ The child is presumed to have a "parent" as defined under paragraph 2 of section 180 of the *Child, Youth and Family Services Act, 2017* and the following document(s) have been filed: 4(c) ❏

❏ A consent (Form 34F in *Family Law Rules*) to adoption from the "parent."

❑ The consent, which was signed by the "parent" when he was under 18 years of age, is accompanied by a certificate of the Children's Lawyer (Form 34J in *Family Law Rules*).

❑ The "parent" has, outside Ontario, signed a form of consent that is not an Ontario consent form and that is accompanied by:

(i) ❑ a certified translation of the document into English/French.

(ii) ❑ evidence that the foreign consent complies with the laws of the place where the "parent" made it.

❑ A certified copy of an order dispensing with the "parent's" consent has been filed, together with proof of service of the order.

❑ The court has ruled that, on a balance of probabilities, the person does not have the status of "parent" under paragraph 2 of section 180 of the *Child, Youth and Family Services Act, 2017*.

(d) ❑ A consent (Form 34F in *Family Law Rules*) to adoption from any other person who is a "parent" under Part VIII of the *Child, Youth and Family Services Act, 2017* has been filed. 4(d) ❑

❑ The consent, which was signed by the other "parent" when he/she was under 18 years of age, is accompanied by a certificate of the Children's Lawyer (Form 34J in *Family Law Rules*).

❑ This other "parent" has, outside Ontario, signed a form of consent that is not an Ontario consent and that is accompanied by:

(i) ❑ a certified translation of the document into English/French.

(ii) ❑ evidence that the foreign consent complies with the laws of the place where the other "parent" made it.

❑ A certified copy of an order dispensing with the other "parent's" consent has been filed, together with proof of service of the order.

(e) ❑ A consent (Form 34F in *Family Law Rules*) to adoption from any other person who is a "parent" under Part VIII of the *Child, Youth and Family Services Act, 2017* has been filed. 4(e) ❑

❑ The consent, which was signed by the other "parent" when he/she was under 18 years of age, is accompanied by a certificate of the Children's Lawyer (Form 34J in *Family Law Rules*).

❑ This other "parent" has, outside Ontario, signed a form of consent that is not an Ontario consent and that is accompanied by:

(i) ❑ a certified translation of the document into English/French.

(ii) ❑ evidence that the foreign consent complies with the laws of the place where the other "parent" made it.

❑ A certified copy of an order dispensing with the other "parent's" consent has been filed, together with proof of service of the order.

(f) ❑ The affidavit (Form 34H in *Family Law Rules*) of the stepparent or of each adoption applicant has been filed. 4(f) ❑

(g) ❑ This is a stepparent adoption and the spouse of the adopting stepparent has filed a consent (Form 34I in *Family Law Rules*). 4(g) ❑

(h) ❑ *(Other. Specify.)* 4(h) ❑

....

Date of Signature *Signature of clerk of the court*

March 1, 2018

FORM 34L — APPLICATION FOR OPENNESS ORDER

[Editor's Note: Pursuant to Family Law Rule 1(9), when a form is referred to by number, the reference is to the form with that number that is described in the Table of Forms at the end of these rules and which is available at www.ontariocourtforms.on.ca. For your convenience, the government form as published on this website is reproduced below.]

Court File Number

SEAL

ONTARIO

.... *(Name of court)*

at .... *Court office address*

Applicant(s)

Full legal name & address for service — street & number, municipality, postal code, telephone & fax numbers and e-mail address (if any).	*Lawyer's name & address — street & number, municipality, postal code, telephone & fax numbers and e-mail address (if any).*

Respondent(s) (Persons entitled to notice.)

Full legal name & address for service — street & number, municipality, postal code, telephone & fax numbers and e-mail address (if any).	*Lawyer's name & address — street & number, municipality, postal code, telephone & fax numbers and e-mail address (if any).*

Children's Lawyer

Name & address of Children's Lawyer's agent for service (street & number, municipality, postal code, telephone & fax numbers and e-mail address (if any)) and name of person represented.

TO THE RESPONDENT(S):

A COURT APPLICATION HAS BEEN STARTED IN THIS COURT FOR AN OPENNESS ORDER. THE DETAILS ARE SET OUT ON THE ATTACHED PAGES.

THE FIRST COURT DATE IS (date) .... *AT* .... ❑ a.m. ❑ p.m. or as soon as possible after that time, at: *(address)*

....

YOU SHOULD CONSIDER GETTING LEGAL ADVICE ABOUT THIS RIGHT AWAY. If you cannot afford a lawyer, you may be able to get help from Legal Aid Ontario. Call *1-800-668-8258 toll-free* to get legal aid help in over 120 languages. For more information about the services available through Legal Aid Ontario, visit *www.legalaid.on.ca*.

*YOU HAVE ONLY 30 DAYS AFTER THIS APPLICATION IS SERVED ON YOU (60 DAYS IF THIS APPLICATION IS SERVED ON YOU OUTSIDE CANADA OR THE UNITED STATES) TO SERVE AND FILE AN ANSWER IN FORM 33B.2: Answer (*Child, Youth and Family Services Act, 2017 *Cases other than Child Protection and Status Review). IF YOU*

DO NOT, THE CASE WILL GO AHEAD WITHOUT YOU AND THE COURT MAY MAKE AN ORDER.

....

Date of issue *Clerk of the court*

THE CHILD

Child's Full Legal Name	Birthdate	Sex	Is the Child First Nations, Inuit, or Métis?	Child's Bands or First Nations, Inuit, or Métis Communities

Extended Society Care Order:

Court File Number	Court Office Address	Name of Judge	Date of Order
Details of Order			

1. The applicant asks for an order that: *(Provide details of openness order.)*

....

2. ❑ (a) The openness order will permit the continuation of a relationship with a person that is beneficial and meaningful to the child in the following ways (*complete this section only if you are making this application under s. 194 or s. 196 of the Child, Youth and Family Services Act, 2017*):

....

❑ (b) The openness order will help the child to develop or maintain a connection with the child's First Nations, Inuit or Métis cultures, heritages and traditions and to preserve the child's cultural identity and connection to community in the following ways (*complete this section only if you are making this application under s. 197 of the Child, Youth and Family Services Act, 2017*):

....

3. The openness order is in the best interests of the child for the following reasons:

....

Put a line through any blank space left on this page.

....

Date of signature *Signature*

....

If applicant is a children's aid society, give office or position of person signing. *Print or type name.*

For information on accessibility of court services for people with disability-related needs, contact:
Telephone: 416-326-2220 / 1-800-518-7901 TTY: 416-326-4012 / 1-877-425-0575

March 1, 2018

FORM 34M — CONSENT TO OPENNESS ORDER UNDER S. 194 OF THE CHILD, YOUTH AND FAMILY SERVICES ACT, 2017

[Editor's Note: Pursuant to Family Law Rule 1(9), when a form is referred to by number, the reference is to the form with that number that is described in the Table of Forms at the end of these rules and which is available at www.ontariocourtforms.on.ca. For your convenience, the government form as published on this website is reproduced below.]

Court File Number

ONTARIO

.... *(Name of court)*

at .... *Court office address*

Applicant (In all cases, the applicant will be a children's aid society.)

Full legal name & address for service — street & number, municipality, postal code, telephone & fax numbers and e-mail address (if any).	*Lawyer's name & address — street & number, municipality, postal code, telephone & fax numbers and e-mail address (if any).*

Respondent(s) (Persons entitled to notice.)

Full legal name & address for service — street & number, municipality, postal code, telephone & fax numbers and e-mail address (if any).	*Lawyer's name & address — street & number, municipality, postal code, telephone & fax numbers and e-mail address (if any).*

Respondent(s) (Persons entitled to notice.)

Children's Lawyer

Name & address of Children's Lawyer's agent for service (street & number, municipality, postal code, telephone & fax numbers and e-mail address (if any)) and name of person represented.

THE CHILD

Child's Full Legal Name	Birthdate	Sex	Is the Child First Nations, Inuit, or Métis?	Child's Bands or First Nations, Inuit, or Métis Communities

Extended Society Care Order:

Court File Number	Court Office Address	Name of Judge	Date of Order
Details of Order			

The parties and the child, if the child is 12 years of age or older, agree to the following:

1. The openness order will permit the continuation of a relationship with a person that is beneficial and meaningful to the child for the following reasons:

....

2. The openness order is in the best interests of the child for the following reasons:

....

3. For the reasons set out above, we ask the court to make the following order: *(Provide details of openness order.)*

....

Applicant's name and position within the children's aid society:

....	....	....
Date	*Applicant's signature*	*Witness' signature*

Signature of person who will be permitted to communicate with or have a relationship with the child if order is made:

....	....	....
Date	*Respondent's signature*	*Witness' signature*

Signature of person with whom the children's aid society has placed or intends to place the child for adoption:

....	....	....
Date	*Respondent's signature*	*Witness' signature*

If applicable, children's aid society that will supervise or participate in the arrangement under the openness order:

....	....	....
Date	*Respondent's signature*	*Witness' signature*

CHILD'S CONSENT

If child is 12 years of age or older:

....	....	....
Date	*Child's signature*	*Witness' signature*

March 1, 2018

FORM 34M.1 — CONSENT TO OPENNESS ORDER UNDER S. 196 OR S. 197 OF THE CHILD, YOUTH AND FAMILY SERVICES ACT, 2017

[Editor's Note: Pursuant to Family Law Rule 1(9), when a form is referred to by number, the reference is to the form with that number that is described in the Table of Forms at the end of these rules and which is available at www.ontariocourtforms.on.ca. For your convenience, the government form as published on this website is reproduced below.]

Court File Number

ONTARIO

.... *(Name of court)*

at .... *Court office address*

Applicant

Full legal name & address for service — street & number, municipality, postal code, telephone & fax numbers and e-mail address (if any).	*Lawyer's name & address — street & number, municipality, postal code, telephone & fax numbers and e-mail address (if any).*

Applicant

Respondent(s) (Persons entitled to notice.)

Full legal name & address for service — street & number, municipality, postal code, telephone & fax numbers and e-mail address (if any).	*Lawyer's name & address — street & number, municipality, postal code, telephone & fax numbers and e-mail address (if any).*

Children's Lawyer

Name & address of Children's Lawyer's agent for service (street & number, municipality, postal code, telephone & fax numbers and e-mail address (if any)) and name of person represented.

THE CHILD

Child's Full Legal Name	Birthdate	Sex	Is the Child First Nations, Inuit, or Métis?	Child's Bands or First Nations, Inuit, or Métis Communities

Extended Society Care Order:

Court File Number	Court Office Address	Name of Judge	Date of Order
Details of Order			

The parties and the child, if the child is 12 years of age or older, agree to the following:

1. The openness order is in the best interests of the child for the following reasons:

....

2. The proposed openness order will permit the continuation of a relationship with a person that is beneficial and meaningful to the child for the following reasons (*complete this section only if you are seeking an openness order under s. 196 of the Child, Youth and Family Services Act, 2017*):

....

3. The person(s) with whom the children's aid society has placed or will place the child for adoption can comply with the terms of the proposed openness order. Details about the prospective adoptive parents' ability to comply are as follows *(complete this section only if you are seeking an openness order under s. 196 of the* Child, Youth and Family Services Act, 2017*)*:

....

4. The proposed openness order would help the child to develop or maintain a connection with the child's First Nations, Inuit or Métis cultures, heritages and traditions and preserve the child's cultural identity and connection to community for the following reasons (*complete this section only if the society is intending to place a First Nations, Inuk or Métis child for adoption and you are seeking an openness order under s. 197 of the Child, Youth and Family Services Act, 2017*):

....

5. For the reasons set out above, we ask the court to make the following order: *(Provide details of openness order.)*

....

Name of children's aid society representative and position within the children's aid society:

....

CONSENTS

....	....	....
Date	*Applicant's signature*	*Witness' signature*
....	....	....
Date	*Respondent's signature*	Witness' signature

If applicable, children's aid society that will supervise or participate in the arrangement under the openness order:

....	....	....
Date	*Respondent's signature*	*Witness' signature*

CHILD'S CONSENT

If child is 12 years of age or older:

....	....	....
Date	*Child's signature*	*Witness' signature*

March 1, 2018

FORM 34N — APPLICATION TO CHANGE OR TERMINATE OPENNESS ORDER

[Editor's Note: Pursuant to Family Law Rule 1(9), when a form is referred to by number, the reference is to the form with that number that is described in the Table of Forms at the end of these rules and which is available at www.ontariocourtforms.on.ca. For your convenience, the government form as published on this website is reproduced below.]

Court File Number

SEAL

ONTARIO

.... *(Name of court)*

at .... *Court office address*

Applicant(s)

Full legal name & address for service — street & number, municipality, postal code, telephone & fax numbers and e-mail address (if any).	*Lawyer's name & address — street & number, municipality, postal code, telephone & fax numbers and e-mail address (if any).*

Respondent(s)

Full legal name & address for service — street & number, municipality, postal code, telephone & fax numbers and e-mail address (if any).	*Lawyer's name & address — street & number, municipality, postal code, telephone & fax numbers and e-mail address (if any).*

Children's Lawyer

Name & address of Children's Lawyer's agent for service (street & number, municipality, postal code, telephone & fax numbers and e-mail address (if any)) and name of person represented.

TO THE RESPONDENT(S):

A COURT CASE HAS BEEN STARTED AGAINST YOU IN THIS COURT. THE DETAILS ARE SET OUT ON THE ATTACHED PAGES.

THE FIRST COURT DATE IS (date) .... *AT* .... ❑ a.m. ❑ p.m. or as soon as possible after that time, at: *(address)*

....

If you have also been served with a notice of motion, there may be an earlier court date, and you or your lawyer should come to court for the motion.

IF YOU WANT TO OPPOSE ANY CLAIM IN THIS CASE, you or your lawyer must prepare an Answer (*Child, Youth and Family Services Act, 2017* Cases other than Child Protection and Status Review) (Form 33B.2 — a blank copy should be attached), serve a copy on the children's aid society and all other parties and file a copy in the court office with an Affidavit of Service (Form 6B).

YOU HAVE ONLY 30 DAYS AFTER THIS APPLICATION IS SERVED ON YOU (60 DAYS IF THIS APPLICATION IS SERVED ON YOU OUTSIDE CANADA OR THE UNITED STATES) TO SERVE AND FILE AN ANSWER. IF YOU DO NOT, THE CASE WILL GO AHEAD WITHOUT YOU AND THE COURT MAY MAKE AN ORDER AND ENFORCE IT AGAINST YOU.

You should consider getting legal advice about this case right away. If you cannot afford a lawyer, you may be able to get help from your local legal aid office. *(See your telephone directory under LEGAL AID.)*

....
Date of issue *Clerk of the court*

THE CHILD

Child's Full Legal Name	Birthdate	Sex	Is the Child First Nations, Inuit, or Métis?	Child's Bands or First Nations, Inuit, or Métis Communities

Details of Openness Order to be Changed or Terminated:

Name of Judge	Date of Order	Details of Openness Order

1. The applicant asks for an order: *(if applicable)*

❑ granting permission under s. 207(2) of the *Child, Youth and Family Services Act, 2017* to *(name of person seeking contact)* .... to bring an application to change the order of Justice *(name of judge)* .... dated *(date of order)* .... for the following reasons:

....

2. The applicant asks for an order that:

❑ (a) the order, made by Justice *(name of judge)* .... on *(date of order)* .... be changed as follows:

....

OR

❑ (b) the order, made by Justice *(name of judge)* .... on *(date of order)* .... be terminated.

3. The following circumstances have changed:

....

4. The proposed order is in the best interests of the child for the following reasons:

....

5. If you are seeking to change (not terminate) an openness order:

❑ (a) In the case of an openness order made under s. 194 or s. 196 of the *Child, Youth and Family Services Act, 2017*, the proposed change to the openness order would continue a relationship that is beneficial and meaningful to the child for the following reasons:

....

❑ (b) in the case of an openness order made under s. 197 of the *Child, Youth and Family Services Act, 2017*, the proposed change to the openness order would help the child to develop or maintain a connection with the child's First Nations, Inuit or Métis cultures, heritages and traditions and preserve the child's cultural identity and connection to community for the following reasons:

....

6. If you are seeking to terminate (not change) an openness order made under s. 194 or 196 of the *Child, Youth and Family Services Act, 2017*, the proposed termination of the openness order would terminate a relationship that is no longer beneficial and meaningful to the child for the following reasons:

....

Put a line through any blank space left on this page.

....	....
Date of signature	*Signature*
....	....
If applicant is a children's aid society, give office or position of person signing.	*Print or type name.*

March 1, 2018

FORM 35.1 — AFFIDAVIT IN SUPPORT OF CLAIM FOR CUSTODY OR ACCESS, DATED

Court File Number

ONTARIO

.... *(Name of court)*

at .... Court office address

Applicant(s)

Full legal name & address for service — street & number, municipality, postal code, telephone & fax numbers and e-mail address (if any).	*Lawyer's name & address — street & number, municipality, postal code, telephone & fax numbers and e-mail address (if any).*

Respondent(s)

Full legal name & address for service — street & number, municipality, postal code, telephone & fax numbers and e-mail address (if any).	*Lawyer's name & address — street & number, municipality, postal code, telephone & fax numbers and e-mail address (if any).*

AFFIDAVIT IN SUPPORT OF CLAIM FOR CUSTODY OR ACCESS
(IF YOU NEED MORE SPACE, ATTACH EXTRA PAGES.)

My name is (full legal name) ....

My date of birth is (d, m, y) ....

I live in: (name of city, town or municipality and province, state or country if outside of Ontario)

....

I swear/affirm that the following is true:

PART A: — TO BE COMPLETED BY ALL PERSONS SEEKING CUSTODY OR ACCESS
(WRITE [LDQUO]N/A[RDQUO] IF ANY OF THE PARAGRAPHS DO NOT APPLY TO YOU OR THE CHILD(REN).)

1. During my life, I have also used or been known by the following names:

2. The child(ren) in this case is/are:

Child's full legal name	**Birthdate (d, m, y)**	**Age**	**Full legal name(s) of parent(s)**	**Name(s) of all people the child lives with now (include address if the child does not live with you)**	**My relationship to the child (specify if parent, grandparent, family friend, etc.)**

Child's full legal name	Birthdate (d, m, y)	Age	Full legal name(s) of parent(s)	Name(s) of all people the child lives with now (include address if the child does not live with you)	My relationship to the child (specify if parent, grandparent, family friend, etc.)

3. I am also the parent of or have acted as a parent (for example, as a step-parent, legal guardian etc.) to the following child(ren): (include the full legal names and birthdates of any child(ren) not already listed in paragraph 2)

Child's full legal name	Birthdate (d, m, y)	My relationship to the child (specify if parent, step-parent, grandparent, etc.)	Name(s) of the person(s) with whom the child lives now (if the child is under 18 years old)

4. I am or have been a party in the following court case(s) involving custody of or access to any child: (Including the child(ren) in this case or any other child(ren). Do not include cases involving a children's aid society in this section. Attach a copy of any custody or access court order(s) or endorsement(s) you have.)

Court location	Names of parties in the case	Name(s) of child(ren)	Court orders made (include dates of orders)

5. I have been a party or person responsible for the care of a child in the following child protection court case(s): (attach a copy of any relevant court order(s) or endorsement(s) you have)

Court location	Names of people involved in the case	Name of children's aid society	Court orders made (include dates of orders)

6. I have been found guilty of the following criminal offence(s) for which I have not received a pardon:

Charge	Approximate date of finding of guilt	Sentence received

Charge	**Approximate date of finding of guilt**	**Sentence received**

7. I am now charged with the following criminal offence(s):

Charge	**Date of next court appearance**	**Terms of release while waiting for trial (attach copy of bail or other release conditions, if any)**

8. When the court is assessing a person's ability to act as a parent, s. 24(4) of the Children's Law Reform Act *requires the court to consider whether the person has at any time committed violence or abuse against*:

- his or her spouse;
- a parent of the child to whom the claim for custody or access relates;
- a member of the person's household; or
- any child.

I am aware of the following violence or abuse the court should consider under s. 24(4) of the Children's Law Reform Act*: (describe incident(s) or episode(s) and provide information about the nature of the violence or abuse, who committed the violence and who the victim(s) was/were)*

9. To the best of my knowledge, since birth, the child(ren) in this case has/have lived with the following caregiver(s): (including a parent, legal guardian, children's aid society etc.)

Child's Name	**Name(s) of Caregiver(s) (if the child was in the care of a children's aid society, give the name of that children's aid society)**	**Period(s) of Time with Caregiver(s) (d,m,y to d,m,y)**

10. My plan for the care and upbringing of the child(ren) is as follows:

a) I plan to live at the following address: ....

b) The following people (other than the child(ren) involved in this case) will be living with me:

Full legal name and other names this person has used	Birthdate (d, m, y)	Relationship to you	Has a child of this person ever been in the care of a children's aid society? (if yes, give details)	Has this person been found guilty of a criminal offence (for which he/she has not received a pardon) or is he/she currently facing criminal charges? (if yes, give details)

c) *Decisions for the child(ren) (including education, medical care, religious upbringing, extra-curricular activities, etc.) will be made as follows*:

❑ *jointly by me and (name(s) of person(s))* ....

by me

by (name(s) of person(s)) ....

(If necessary, provide additional details below.)

d) ❑ *I am a stay-at-home parent.*

❑ *I work*: ❑ *full time.* ❑ *part time.*

❑ *I attend school*: ❑ *full time.* ❑ *part time.*

at: (name of your place of work or school) ....

I anticipate that my plans for work and/or school may change as follows: (complete if you know or expect that you will be doing something different from what you are doing now))

e) *The child(ren) will attend school, daycare or be cared for by others on a regular basis as follows*:

f) *My plan for the child(ren) to have regular contact with others, including the child(ren)'s parent(s) and family members, is as follows*:

g) Check the appropriate box:

❑ *The child(ren) does not/do not have any special medical, educational, mental health or developmental needs.*

❑ *The child or one or more of the children has/have the following special needs and will receive support and services for those needs as follows: (if a child does not have special needs, you do not have to include information about that child below)*

Name of child	Special need(s)	Description of child's needs	Support or service child will be receiving (include the names of any doctors, counsellors, treatment centres, etc. that are or will be providing support or services to the child)
	❑ medical ❑ educational ❑ mental health ❑ developmental ❑ other		
	❑ medical ❑ educational ❑ mental health ❑ developmental ❑ other		
	❑ medical ❑ educational ❑ mental health ❑ developmental ❑ other		
	❑ medical ❑ educational ❑ mental health ❑ developmental ❑ other		
	❑ medical ❑ educational ❑ mental health ❑ developmental ❑ other		

h) *I will have support from the following relatives, friends or community services in caring for the child(ren)*:

11. I acknowledge that the court needs up-to-date and accurate information about my plan in order to make a custody or access order in the best interests of the child(ren) (subrule 35.1(7)). If, at any time before a final order is made in this case,

a) there are any changes in my life or circumstances that affect the information provided in this affidavit; or

b) I discover that the information in this affidavit is incorrect or incomplete,

I will immediately serve and file either:

a) an updated affidavit in support of claim for custody or access (Form 35.1); or,

b) if the correction or change is minor, an affidavit in Form 14A describing the correction or change and indicating any effect it has on my plan for the care and upbringing of the child(ren).

.... *(Initial here to show you have read this paragraph and you understand it.)*

NOTE: If you are not a parent of the child, as determined under the Children's Law Reform Act, *for whom you are seeking an order of custody, you must complete Part B of this affidavit.*

For the purposes of this form and under the Children's Law Reform Act, *a parent may include*:

- *The person who gives birth to a child (a "birth parent").*
- *Where a child is conceived through sexual intercourse, the person who is married to or living with the person who gives birth to the child at the time that the child is born (a "spouse").*
- *The person certified as a parent of the child under the* Vital Statistics Act.
- *A person found or recognized by a court as a parent to the child.*

For more information about whether you are a parent for the purposes of this form, see the Children's Law Reform Act *or talk to a lawyer.*

If you are completing Part B, you do not have to swear/affirm the affidavit at this point. You will swear/affirm at the end of Part B.

Sworn/Affirmed before me at .... *municipality* in .... *province, state, or country* on .... *Date* .... *Commissioner for taking affidavits (Type or print name below if signature is illegible.)*	.... *Signature* *(This form is to be signed in front of a lawyer, justice of the peace, notary public or commissioner for taking affidavits.)*

PART B — TO BE COMPLETED ONLY BY A NON-PARENT SEEKING A CUSTODY ORDER

If you are a parent of the child, as determined under the *Children's Law Reform Act*, for whom you are seeking an order of custody, you are not required to complete this Part of the form.

Individuals who may *not* be a parent may include:

- A grandparent, aunt, or uncle.
- A sperm donor.
- A surrogate.
- A step-parent.

For more information about whether you are a parent for the purposes of this form, see the *Children's Law Reform Act* or talk to a lawyer.

NOTICE: If you are a non-parent claiming custody of a child, court staff will conduct a search of the databases maintained by the Ontario courts to identify previous or current family court cases in which you or the child(ren) may have been or may be involved and provide you with a list of those cases. This information will be shared with the court and you must provide a copy to any other party.

If the list contains information about someone other than you, you may swear or affirm an affidavit indicating that you are not the same person as the person named in the list.

In addition to the information in Part A, I swear/affirm that the following is true:

12. To the best of my knowledge, the child(ren) in this case has/have been involved in the following custody/access or child protection court cases: (do NOT include cases in which the child was charged under the Youth Criminal Justice Act (Canada)*)*

Child(ren)'s name(s)	**Type of Case**	**Details of Case**

13. You must file a police records check with the court. Choose the option below that applies to you:

❑ *I have attached to this affidavit a copy of my police records check, dated (date of report from local police force)* .... *Since the date that the attached police records check was completed, I have been found guilty of or charged with the following offence(s)*:

❑ *On (date)* ...., *I sent a request to (name of local police force)* .... *for a police records check.*

I agree to serve and file the police records check with the court within 10 days after the day I receive it. I understand that the court may not make an order for custody of the child(ren) until I have filed the police records check.

14. Since I turned 18 years old or became a parent, whichever was earlier, I have lived in the following places:

Approximate dates (month/year to month/year)	**City, town or municipality where you lived (if outside of Ontario, give name of province, state or country)**

15. I have provided a signed consent form to the court, which authorizes each of the children's aid societies listed below to send a report to me and to the court indicating:

- *whether the society has any records within the meaning of the* Children's Law Reform Act *regulations relating to me; and*

- *the date(s) on which any files were opened and/or closed (if applicable).*

i) Name of children's aid society: ....

ii) Name of children's aid society: ....

iii) Name of children's aid society: ....

iv) Name of children's aid society: ....

v) Name of children's aid society: ....

vi) Name of children's aid society: ....

16. I understand that if any report from a children's aid society indicates that the children's aid society has records related to me, then, unless the court orders otherwise, that report will be shared with:

a) the court;

b) any other parties in this case; and

c) the child(ren)'s lawyer, if there is one in this case.

If I wish to bring a motion asking the court not to release all or part of this report, I understand that I must file my motion with the court no later than *20 days* from the day that the last report is received by the court.

I also understand that any report indicating that a children's aid society has no records relating to me will not be shared with the court, any other party or the child(ren)'s lawyer.

.... *(Initial here to show that you have read this paragraph and you understand it.)*

Sworn/Affirmed before me at .... *Municipality* in .... *province, state, or country* on .... *Date* *Commissioner for taking affidavits (Type or print name below if signature is illegible.)*	.... *Signature* *(This form is to be signed in front of a lawyer, justice of the peace, notary public or commissioner for taking affidavits.)*

April 15, 2017

FORM 36 — AFFIDAVIT FOR DIVORCE

[Repealed O. Reg. 76/06, s. 15.]

[Editor's Note: Forms 4 to 39 of the Family Law Rules have been repealed by O. Reg. 76/06, effective May 1, 2006. Pursuant to Family Law Rule 1(9), when a form is referred to by number, the reference is to the form with that number that is described in the Table of Forms at the end of these rules and which is available at www.ontariocourtforms.on.ca. For your convenience, the government form as published on this website is reproduced below.]

Court File Number ....

.... *(Name of court)*

at .... *Court office address*

Applicant

Full legal name & address for service — street & number, municipality, postal code, telephone & fax and e-mail address (if any).	*Lawyer's name & address — street & number, municipality, postal code, telephone & fax numbers and e-mail address (if any).*

Respondent(s)

Full legal name & address for service — street & number, municipality, postal code, telephone & fax numbers and e-mail address (if any).	*Lawyer's name & address — street & number, municipality, postal code, telephone & fax numbers and e-mail address (if any).*

My name is (full legal name) ....

I live in (municipality & province) .... *and I swear/affirm that the following is true:*

1. I am the applicant in this divorce case.

2. There is no chance of a reconciliation between the respondent and me.

3. All the information in the application in this case is correct, except: *(State any corrections or changes to the information in the application. Write "NONE" if there are no corrections or changes.)*

4.

❑ The certificate or registration of my marriage to the respondent has been signed and sealed by the Registrar General of Ontario and

❑ has been filed with the application.

❑ is attached to this affidavit.

❑ The certificate of my marriage to the respondent was issued outside Ontario. It is called *(title of certificate)* .... It was issued at *(place of issue)* .... on *(date)* .... by *(name and title of person who issued certificate)* .... and the information in it about my marriage is correct.

❑ I have not been able to get a certificate or registration of my marriage. I was married to the respondent on *(date)* .... at *(place of marriage)* .... The marriage was performed by *(name and title)*

.... who had the authority to perform marriages in that place.

5. The legal basis for the divorce is:

❑ that the respondent and I have been separated for at least one year. We separated on *(date)* ....

❑ *(Other. Specify.)*

....

....

6. I do not know about and I am not involved in any arrangement to make up or to hide evidence or to deceive the court in this divorce case.

Strike out the following paragraphs if they do not apply.

7. I do not want to make a claim for a division of property in this divorce case, even though I know that it may be legally impossible to make such a claim after the divorce.

8. I want the divorce order to include the following paragraph numbers of the attached consent, settlement, separation agreement or previous court order: *(List the numbers of the paragraphs that you want included in the divorce order.)*

....

9. There are (number) .... children of the marriage. They are:

Full legal name of child	Birthdate (d,m,y)

10. The custody and access arrangements for the child(ren) are as follows: *(Give summary.)*

....

....

11. These are the arrangements that have been made for the support of the child(ren) of the marriage:

(a) The income of the party paying child support is $.......... per year.

(b) The number of children for whom support is supposed to be paid is *(number)* ....

(c) The amount of support that should be paid according to the applicable table in the child support guidelines is $.......... per month.

(d) The amount of child support actually being paid is $.......... per month.

(NOTE: — Where the dollar amounts in clauses (c) and (d) are different, you must fill out the frame on the next page. If the amounts in clauses (c) and (d) are the same, skip the frame and go directly to paragraph 12.)

Fill out the information in this frame only if the amounts in paragraphs 11(c) and 11(d) are different. If they are the same, go to paragraph 12

(a) Child support is already covered by:

(i) ❑ a court order dated *(date)* .... that was made before the child support guidelines came into effect (before 1 May 1997). I attach a copy of the order

(ii) ❑ a domestic contract order dated *(date)* .... that was made before the child support guidelines came into effect (before 1 May 1997). I attach a copy of the contract

(iii) ❑ a court order or written agreement dated *(date)* .... made after the guidelines came into effect that has some direct or indirect benefits for the child(ren). I attach a copy.

(iv) ❑ a written consent between the parties dated *(date)* .... agreeing to the payment of an amount different from that set out in the guidelines.

(b) The child support clauses of this order or agreement require payment of $ .... per .... in child support.

(c) These child support clauses

❑ are not indexed for any automatic cost-of-living increases.

❑ are indexed according to *(Give indexing formula)*

....

(d) These child support clauses

❑ have not been changed since the day the order or agreement was made.

❑ have been changed on *(Give dates and details of changes)*

....

(e) *(If you ticked off box (i) above, you can go to paragraph 12. If you ticked off boxes (ii), (iii) or (iv) above, then fill out the information after box of the corresponding number below. For example, if you ticked off box (iii) above, you would fill out the information alongside box (iii) below.)*

(ii) ❑ The amount being paid under this agreement is a fair and reasonable arrangement for the support of the child(ren) because: *(Give reasons.)*

....

....

(iii) ❑ The order or agreement directly or indirectly benefits the child(ren) because: *(Give details of benefits.)*

....

....

(iv) ❑ The amount to which the parties have consented is reasonable for the support of the child(ren) because: *(Give reasons.)*

....

....

12. I am claiming costs in this case. The details of this claim are as follows: *(Give details.)*

....

....

13. The respondent's address last known to me is: *(Give address.)*

....

....

Put a line through any blank space left on this page.

Sworn/Affirmed before me at .... *municipality* in .... *province, state or country* on .... *date*	
Commissioner for taking affidavits *(Type or print name below if signature is illegible.)*	*Signature* *(This form is to be signed in front of a lawyer, justice of the peace, notary public or commissioner for taking affidavits.)*

September 1, 2005

FORM 36A — CERTIFICATE OF CLERK (DIVORCE)

[Repealed O. Reg. 76/06, s. 15.]

[Editor's Note: Forms 4 to 39 of the Family Law Rules have been repealed by O. Reg. 76/06, effective May 1, 2006. Pursuant to Family Law Rule 1(9), when a form is referred to by number, the reference is to the form with that number that is described in the Table of Forms at the end of these rules and which is available at www.ontariocourtforms.on.ca. For your convenience, the government form as published on this website is reproduced below.]

Court File Number

ONTARIO

.... *(Name of court)*

at .... *Court office address*

Applicant's last name .... *Respondent's last name* ....

If the appropriate box on the left cannot be checked, check the box on the right margin and describe the deficiency by that box. If the divorce application was filed electronically, write "N/A" in the blank spaces relating to the Continuing Record.

The clerk of the court certifies as follows:

Check if applicable and complete the rest of the certificate as if the divorce had been claimed by the applicant.

❑ Divorce claimed only by the respondent.

Deficiency

1. *PRELIMINARY*

(a) ❑ Jurisdiction — Application filed in correct municipality 1(a) ❑

❑ No answer filed ....

❑ Answer was withdrawn — Continuing record tab/page number ....

❑ Order dated ...., under subrule 12(6), splitting divorce from rest of the case — continuing record tab/page number ....

❑ Answer struck out by order dated .... — Continuing record tab/page number ....

❑ Joint application — no respondent ....

(b) ❑ Clearance certificate from Central Divorce Registry .... 1(b) ❑

2. *PROOF OF SERVICE* 2 ❑

❑ Affidavit of service

❑ Person's lawyer accepted service

❑ Joint application — no service necessary

3. *METHOD OF SERVICE* 3 ❑

❑ Left copy with person to be served

❑ Left copy with person's lawyer

❑ Mailed copy to person and received acknowledgement signed by person

❑ Left copy at person's residence with adult resident and mailed another copy

❑ Signed acknowledgement of service filed

❑ Other *(specify.)* ....

Service took place in *(province or country)* ....

Service was carried out on *(date)* ....

4. *GROUNDS FOR DIVORCE* 4 ❑

❑ Separation since *(date)* ...., affidavit sworn more than one year after separation

❑ Adultery

❑ Cruelty

5. *ONTARIO RESIDENCE* 5 ❑

Application should indicate that at least one spouse must have been Ontario resident for at least a year.

❑ Applicant resident in Ontario since *(date)* ....

❑ Respondent resident in Ontario since *(date)* ....

6. *CLAIMS* 6 ❑

❑ Only claim for divorce

❑ Claim for child support *[details in part 9 below]*

❑ Claim for custody/access — details in application

❑ Claim for spousal support — details in application

❑ Claim for property — details in application

❑ Claim to include provisions of consent, agreement or previous court order — details in application

❑ Costs

7. *PROOF OF MARRIAGE* 7 ❑

Marriage took place ❑ in Canada ❑ outside Canada

❑ Marriage certificate or registration of marriage filed — details agree with those in application — Continuing record tab/page number ....

❑ No certificate — details of marriage set out in affidavit — Continuing record tab/page number ....

❑ Previous divorce or death certificate filed — Continuing record tab/page number ....

8. AFFIDAVITS 8 ❑

❑ Applicant's affidavit — Continuing record tab/page number ....

❑ Respondent's affidavit — Continuing record tab/page number ....

❑ Affidavit of *(name)* .... — Continuing record tab/page number ....

❑ Affidavit complies with Form 36 and is properly completed — Continuing record tab/page number ....

9. CHILDREN 9 ❑

❑ No children of the marriage ❑ There are children of the marriage

❑ Child support guidelines information supplied — Continuing record tab/page number ....

- ❑ Payor's income ❑ table amount
- ❑ recipient's income *[REQUIRED for special expenses (add-ons), split custody, shared custody, payor is stepparent, child over 18, payor's income more than $150,000, claim of undue hardship]*
- ❑ details of special expenses (add-ons)
- ❑ agreement/consent with explanation for claim less than table amount

10. DRAFT ORDER 10 ❑

The following material has been filed:

❑ Draft Order — no support claimed.

- ❑ 3 copies — filed in paper format ❑ Filed electronically

❑ Draft order and draft support deduction order — support claimed

- ❑ 4 copies of draft order + 2 copies of draft support deduction order — filed in paper format
- ❑ Filed electronically

❑ Service of order on parties

- ❑ Stamped envelope for each party — application filed in paper format
- ❑ Email address of at least one party — application filed electronically

❑ Address for service of order on respondent is same as

- ❑ on application ❑ on documents filed by respondent ❑ in applicant's affidavit

❑ Draft order in same terms as application

❑ Draft order in same terms as consent, minutes of settlement, or agreement filed — Continuing record tab/page number ....

❑ Request for early effective date for divorce; agreements and undertakings filed not to appeal — Continuing record tab/page number ....

11. NOTICE TO APPLICANT 11 ❑

❑ Applicant notified of deficiencies but requests to submit papers to judge despite them.

.... *Date of signature* .... *Signature of clerk of the court*

March 1, 2018

FORM 36B — CERTIFICATE OF DIVORCE

[Repealed O. Reg. 76/06, s. 15.]

[Editor's Note: Forms 4 to 39 of the Family Law Rules have been repealed by O. Reg. 76/06, effective May 1, 2006. Pursuant to Family Law Rule 1(9), when a form is referred to by number, the reference is to the form with that number that is described in the Table of Forms at the end of these rules and which is available at www.ontariocourtforms.on.ca. For your convenience, the government form as published on this website is reproduced below.]

Court File Number ....

[SEAL]

.... *(Name of court)*

at .... *Court office address*

Applicant

Full legal name & address for service — street and number, municipality, postal code, telephone & fax numbers and e-mail address (if any).	*Lawyer's name & address — street and number, municipality, postal code, telephone & fax numbers and e-mail address (if any).*

Respondent(s)

Full legal name & address for service — street and number, municipality, postal code, telephone & fax numbers and e-mail address (if any).	*Lawyer's name & address — street and number, municipality, postal code, telephone & fax numbers and e-mail address (if any).*

I CERTIFY THAT the marriage of *(full legal names of the spouses)* .... that was solemnized at *(place of marriage)* on *(date of marriage)* .... was dissolved by an order of this court made on *(date of divorce order)* ....

The divorce took effect on *(date when order took effect)* ....

.... *Signature of clerk of the court*

.... *Date of signature*

NOTE: This certificate can only be issued on or after the date on which the divorce takes effect.

September 1, 2005

FORM 37 — NOTICE OF HEARING

[Repealed O. Reg. 76/06, s. 15.]

[Editor's Note: Forms 4 to 39 of the Family Law Rules have been repealed by O. Reg. 76/06, effective May 1, 2006. Pursuant to Family Law Rule 1(9), when a form is referred to by number, the reference is to the form with that number that is described in the Table of Forms at the end of these rules and which is available at www.ontariocourtforms.on.ca. For your convenience, the government form as published on this website is reproduced below.]

Court File Number ....

[SEAL]

____

(Name of court)

at _______________________________

Court office address

Applicant(s)

Full legal name & address for service — street & number, municipality, postal code, telephone & fax numbers and e-mail address (if any).	*Lawyer's name & address — street & number, municipality, postal code, telephone & fax numbers and e-mail address (if any).*

Respondent(s)

Full legal name & address for service — street & number, municipality, postal code, telephone & fax numbers and e-mail address (if any).	*Lawyer's name & address — street & number, municipality, postal code, telephone & fax numbers and e-mail address (if any).*

NOTICE:

THE COURT WILL HOLD A WRITTEN HEARING on *(date)* . . . .

at .... a.m./p.m., or as soon as possible after that time at *(place of hearing)* . . . .

This court has received

❑ An application under the *Interjurisdictional Support Orders Act, 2002* for

❑ an order ❑ a change of an order

❑ A provisional ❑ an order ❑ change of an order

❑ in another part of Ontario ❑ outside Ontario

The details are set out in the attached materials.

IF YOU WANT TO OPPOSE ANY CLAIM IN THIS CASE, you or your lawyer must prepare an Answer (a blank copy of which is attached) and file a copy in the court office. YOU HAVE ONLY 30 DAYS AFTER THIS NOTICE IS SERVED ON YOU TO FILE AN ANSWER TO THIS CASE.

Whether or not you wish to oppose a claim in this case, YOU MUST FILE A FINANCIAL STATEMENT (a blank copy of which is attached) with the court office WITHIN 30 DAYS AFTER THIS NOTICE IS SERVED ON YOU.

If you want to ask for an oral hearing, you must prepare a motion (Form 14B — blank copy attached), and file a copy in the court office WITHIN 30 DAYS AFTER THIS NOTICE IS SERVED ON YOU.

The court will only consider the written materials in this case on the date noted above. UNLESS THE COURT ORDERS OTHERWISE, THERE IS NO NEED FOR YOU TO COME TO COURT OR TO HAVE A LAWYER THERE TO ARGUE YOUR CASE. If an order is made or the judge requires you to be present or provide further evidence, you will be notified.

IF YOU DO NOT FILE WRITTEN MATERIALS, THE COURT MAY MAKE AN ORDER WITHOUT YOUR WRITTEN ANSWER AND ENFORCE IT AGAINST YOU.

You should get legal advice about this case right away. If you cannot afford a lawyer, you may be able to get help from your local Legal Aid office. (See your telephone directory under LEGAL AID.)

Date of signature	*Signature of registrar or clerk of the court*

NOTE: *A copy of the application should be attached to this notice, along with a copy of the applicant's financial statement, a copy of any provisional order and a copy of the applicant's evidence. Also attached to this notice should be a blank Financial Statement that you must fill out and file. If a provisional order was made in another part of Ontario, you must serve and file your financial statement.*

If any of these documents is missing, you should talk to the court office at the address at the top of this form immediately.

September 1, 2005

FORM 37A — INFORMATION SHEET

[Repealed O. Reg. 76/06, s. 15.]

[Editor's Note: Forms 4 to 39 of the Family Law Rules have been repealed by O. Reg. 76/06, effective May 1, 2006. Pursuant to Family Law Rule 1(9), when a form is referred to by number, the reference is to the form with that number that is described in the Table of Forms at the end of these rules and which is available at www.ontariocourtforms.on.ca. For your convenience, the government form as published on this website is reproduced below.]

Court File Number ....

____

(Name of court)

at ______________________________

Court office address

Applicant(s)

Full legal name & address for service — street & number, municipality, postal code, telephone & fax numbers and e-mail address (if any).	*Lawyer's name & address — street & number, municipality, postal code, telephone & fax numbers and e-mail address (if any).*

Respondent(s)

Full legal name & address for service — street & number, municipality, postal code, telephone & fax numbers and e-mail address (if any).	*Lawyer's name & address — street & number, municipality, postal code, telephone & fax numbers and e-mail address (if any).*

TO THE APPLICANT(S):

The respondent(s) was/were served with a notice of

❑ *Interjurisdictional Support Orders Act, 2002* hearing.
❑ confirmation hearing.

A copy of this notice is attached to this sheet. It is being sent to you FOR YOUR INFORMATION ONLY.

THERE IS NO NEED FOR YOU TO COME TO THIS HEARING OR TO HAVE A LAWYER THERE TO ARGUE YOUR CASE FOR YOU.

You will be told about what happens at the hearing by the office where you submitted your application. If you have any questions, you should talk to your own lawyer or the office where you submitted your application.

______________________________ ______________________________

Date of signature *Signature of registrar or clerk of the court*

September 1, 2005

FORM 37B — DIRECTION TO REQUEST FURTHER INFORMATION

[Repealed O. Reg. 76/06, s. 15.]

[Editor's Note: Forms 4 to 39 of the Family Law Rules have been repealed by O. Reg. 76/06, effective May 1, 2006. Pursuant to Family Law Rule 1(9), when a form is referred to by number, the reference is to the form with that number that is described in the Table of Forms at the end of these rules and which is available at www.ontariocourtforms.on.ca. For your convenience, the government form as published on this website is reproduced below.]

Court File Number ....

[SEAL]

____

(Name of court)

at ______________________________

Court office address

Applicant(s)

Full legal name & address for service — street & number, municipality, postal code, telephone & fax numbers and e-mail address (if any).	*Lawyer's name & address — street & number, municipality, postal code, telephone & fax numbers and e-mail address (if any).*

Respondent(s)

Full legal name & address for service — street & number, municipality, postal code, telephone & fax numbers and e-mail address (if any).	*Lawyer's name & address — street & number, municipality, postal code, telephone & fax numbers and e-mail address (if any).*

TO THE (check appropriate box(es))

❑ APPLICANT(S):
❑ THE ONTARIO INTERJURISDICTIONAL SUPPORT ORDERS UNIT:

This court considered the application for support or the application to change a support order on *(date)* . . . .

THE COURT ADJOURNED THE HEARING OF THE CASE TO *(date)* . . . .

❑ You, the applicant, are directed to provide the information or documents required by the court.

❑ You, the Ontario Interjurisdictional Support Orders Unit, are directed to contact the applicant or appropriate authority in the reciprocating jurisdiction to request the information or documents required by the court.

This court requires the following information or documents: *(attach extra paper if necessary, or transcript noting information and documents required).*

. . . .

. . . .

The information or documents must be filed with this court at the address at the top of this form at least 30 days before the court date. At the hearing, a temporary order:

- ❑ was not made;
- ❑ was made — details will be sent; or
- ❑ was made — a certified copy of the temporary order is attached.

Date of signature	*Signature of registrar or clerk of the court*

NOTE: *A copy of the respondent's evidence and a copy of the court's reasons for seeking further evidence should be attached to this form. If either of these is missing, you should talk to the court office at the address at the top of this form immediately.*

September 1, 2005

FORM 37C — NOTICE OF CONTINUATION OF HEARING

[Repealed O. Reg. 76/06, s. 15.]

[Editor's Note: Forms 4 to 39 of the Family Law Rules have been repealed by O. Reg. 76/06, effective May 1, 2006. Pursuant to Family Law Rule 1(9), when a form is referred to by number, the reference is to the form with that number that is described in the Table of Forms at the end of these rules and which is available at www.ontariocourtforms.on.ca. For your convenience, the government form as published on this website is reproduced below.]

Court File Number ....

[SEAL]

(Name of court)

at ______________________

Court office address

Applicant(s)

Full legal name & address for service — street & number, municipality, postal code, telephone & fax numbers and e-mail address (if any).	*Lawyer's name & address — street & number, municipality, postal code, telephone & fax numbers and e-mail address (if any).*

Applicant(s)

Respondent(s)

Full legal name & address for service — street & number, municipality, postal code, telephone & fax numbers and e-mail address (if any).	*Lawyer's name & address — street & number, municipality, postal code, telephone & fax numbers and e-mail address (if any).*

TO THE RESPONDENT(S):

THE COURT WILL CONTINUE A WRITTEN HEARING on *(date)* . . . .

at .... a.m./p.m., or as soon as possible after that time at *(place of hearing)* . . . .

This case was adjourned on *(adjournment date)* . . . .

so that the case could be sent to the originating jurisdiction for further evidence.

The originating jurisdiction has now sent to this court further evidence, a copy of which is attached. This court will therefore consider this case at the time and place shown above.

IF YOU WISH TO RESPOND TO THE FURTHER EVIDENCE, YOU OR YOUR LAWYER MUST FILE AN AFFIDAVIT IN RESPONSE (Form 14A — blank copy attached) WITHIN 30 DAYS AFTER YOU RECEIVE THIS NOTICE.

If you want to ask for an oral hearing, you must prepare a motion (Form 14B — blank copy attached), and file a copy in the court office WITHIN 30 DAYS AFTER THIS NOTICE IS SERVED ON YOU.

The court will only consider the written materials in this case on the date noted above. UNLESS THE COURT ORDERS OTHERWISE, THERE IS NO NEED FOR YOU TO COME TO COURT OR TO HAVE A LAWYER THERE TO ARGUE YOUR CASE. If an order is made or the judge requires you to be present or provide further evidence, you will be notified.

Date of signature	*Signature of registrar or clerk of the court*

NOTE: *A copy of the applicant's further evidence taken in the originating jurisdiction should be attached to this notice. If it is missing, you should talk to the court office at the address at the top of this form immediately.*

September 1, 2005

FORM 37D — NOTICE OF REGISTRATION OF ORDER

[Repealed O. Reg. 76/06, s. 15.]

[Editor's Note: Forms 4 to 39 of the Family Law Rules have been repealed by O. Reg. 76/06, effective May 1, 2006. Pursuant to Family Law Rule 1(9), when a form is referred to by number, the reference is to the form with that number that is described in the Table of Forms

at the end of these rules and which is available at www.ontariocourtforms.on.ca. For your convenience, the government form as published on this website is reproduced below.]

Court File Number ....

[SEAL]

____
(Name of court)

at ______________________________
Court office address

Applicant(s)

Full legal name & address for service — street & number, municipality, postal code, telephone & fax numbers and e-mail address (if any).	*Lawyer's name & address — street & number, municipality, postal code, telephone & fax numbers and e-mail address (if any).*

Respondent(s)

Full legal name & address for service — street & number, municipality, postal code, telephone & fax numbers and e-mail address (if any).	*Lawyer's name & address — street & number, municipality, postal code, telephone & fax numbers and e-mail address (if any).*

TO THE *(check appropriate box(es))*

❑ APPLICANT(S):
❑ RESPONDENT(S):

The *(name of court)* . . . .

at *(place where court presides)* . . . .

has asked the courts in Ontario to enforce

❑ an order for the payment of support for dependants.
❑ the support provisions of a written agreement between you and the other party.

This order/agreement has been registered with this Ontario court on *(date of registration)* .... under the *Interjurisdictional Support Orders Act, 2002*.

If you have reason to believe that:

(a) you did not have notice or a reasonable opportunity to be heard;

(b) the order/agreement is contrary to public policy in Ontario; or

(c) the court that made the order did not have jurisdiction to make it,

you may make a motion (Forms 14 and 14A) to have the registration set aside, but you must do so within 30 days after receiving this notice. You must mail notice of your own motion to the Ontario Interjurisdictional Support Orders Unit at: (address)

. . . .

You may use any method of service set out in rule 6 of the *Family Law Rules*, including mail, courier or fax.

If you choose not to challenge the registration, the order/agreement will be enforced against you as if it were an order of an Ontario court. You have the right at any time to apply for a change of this order/agreement if there has been a material change in circumstances since the making of the order/agreement.

Date of signature	*Signature of registrar or clerk of the court*

September 1, 2005

FORM 37E — NOTICE FOR TAKING FURTHER EVIDENCE

[Repealed O. Reg. 76/06, s. 15.]

[Editor's Note: Forms 4 to 39 of the Family Law Rules have been repealed by O. Reg. 76/06, effective May 1, 2006. Pursuant to Family Law Rule 1(9), when a form is referred to by number, the reference is to the form with that number that is described in the Table of Forms at the end of these rules and which is available at www.ontariocourtforms.on.ca. For your convenience, the government form as published on this website is reproduced below.]

Court File Number ....

[SEAL]

(Name of court)

at

Court office address

Applicant(s)

Full legal name & address for service — street & number, municipality, postal code, telephone & fax numbers and e-mail address (if any).	*Lawyer's name & address — street & number, municipality, postal code, telephone & fax numbers and e-mail address (if any).*

Respondent(s)

Full legal name & address for service — street & number, municipality, postal code, telephone & fax numbers and e-mail address (if any).	*Lawyer's name & address — street & number, municipality, postal code, telephone & fax numbers and e-mail address (if any).*

TO THE APPLICANT(S):

The provisional

❑ order in this case

❏ change of the order made by the *(name of court)* . . . .
on (date) . . . .

has come before a judge of the *(name and address of court)* . . . .

That other court requires further evidence from you. The details are set out in the attached material.

If you want to continue your application for support or for a change in support, you or your lawyer must prepare an affidavit (Form 14A — blank copy attached) of your further evidence and file it in this court office.

The other court will continue the hearing on *(insert date, if known)* ....
Your affidavit evidence must be filed in this court 30 days before that date so it can be sent to the other court in time for the hearing.

IF YOU DO NOT FILE FURTHER AFFIDAVIT EVIDENCE, THE PROVISIONAL ORDER/CHANGE OF AN ORDER MAY NOT BE CONFIRMED BY THE OTHER COURT.

Date of signature	*Signature of registrar or clerk of the court*

NOTE: *A copy of the respondent's evidence and a copy of the other court's reasons for seeking further evidence should be attached to this notice. If either of these is missing, you should talk to the court office at the address at the top of this form immediately.*

September 1, 2005

FORM 38 — NOTICE OF APPEAL

[Repealed O. Reg. 76/06, s. 15.]

[Editor's Note: Forms 4 to 39 of the Family Law Rules have been repealed by O. Reg. 76/06, effective May 1, 2006. Pursuant to Family Law Rule 1(9), when a form is referred to by number, the reference is to the form with that number that is described in the Table of Forms at the end of these rules and which is available at www.ontariocourtforms.on.ca. For your convenience, the government form as published on this website is reproduced below.]

Court File Number

____
(Name of court)

Form 38:
Notice of Appeal

at ______________________________
Court office address

Applicant(s) *Check the appropriate box:* ❑ *Appellant* ❑ *Respondent in this appeal*

Full legal name & address for service — street & number, municipality, postal code, telephone & fax numbers and e-mail address (if any).	*Lawyer's name & address — street & number, municipality, postal code, telephone & fax numbers and e-mail address (if any).*

Respondent(s) *Check the appropriate box:* ❑ *Appellant* ❑ *Respondent in this appeal*

Full legal name & address for service — street & number, municipality, postal code, telephone & fax numbers and e-mail address (if any).	*Lawyer's name & address — street & number, municipality, postal code, telephone & fax numbers and e-mail address (if any).*
Name & address of Children's Lawyer's agent (street & number, municipality, postal code, telephone & fax numbers and e-mail address (if any)) and name of person represented.	

My name is (name of party making this appeal) ....
I APPEAL TO THE (name of court) ....
at (municipality) ....
from the following order or decision:

Date of order: ....
Name of court that made it: ....
Name of judge who made it: ....
Place where it was made: ....
It was: ❑ a final order. ❑ a temporary order.

I ask that this order be set aside and that an order be made as follows: (Set out briefly the order that you want the appeal court to make.)

The legal grounds for my appeal are: (Set out in numbered paragraphs the legal basis of your appeal.)

Draw a line through any space left on this page.

NOTE TO THE APPELLANT: You have 30 days to serve this notice on the other parties in the case and you must file it with the clerk of the appeal court with proof of service (Form 6B) within 10 days after that.

NOTE TO THE RESPONDENT: If you want to oppose this appeal, you or your lawyer must prepare a respondent's factum required by subrule 38(9) of the *Family Law Rules*, serve a copy on the appellant(s) and file a copy with the clerk of the appeal court with proof of service (Form 6B). You must serve and file a respondent's factum at least 3 days before the hearing of the appeal. If you do not, the appeal will go ahead without you and the court may make a new order and enforce it against you.

....
Date of signature

....
Signature

September 1, 2005

FORM 39 — NOTICE OF APPROACHING DISMISSAL

[Repealed O. Reg. 76/06, s. 15.]

[Editor's Note: Forms 4 to 39 of the Family Law Rules have been repealed by O. Reg. 76/06, effective May 1, 2006. Pursuant to Family Law Rule 1(9), when a form is referred to by number, the reference is to the form with that number that is described in the Table of Forms at the end of these rules and which is available at www.ontariocourtforms.on.ca. For your convenience, the government form as published on this website is reproduced below.]

Court File Number ....

.... *(Name of court)*

at .... *Court office address*

Applicant(s)

Full legal name & address for service — street & number, municipality, postal code, telephone & fax numbers and e-mail address (if any).	*Lawyer's name & address — street & number, municipality, postal code, telephone & fax numbers and e-mail address (if any).*

Respondent(s)

Full legal name & address for service — street & number, municipality, postal code, telephone & fax numbers and e-mail address (if any).	*Lawyer's name & address — street & number, municipality, postal code, telephone & fax numbers and e-mail address (if any).*

TO ALL PARTIES:

1. *THE CLERK OF THE COURT WILL DISMISS THIS CASE WITHOUT FURTHER NOTICE* unless, within 60 days after service of this notice, one of the parties:

(a) obtains an order under subrule 39(3), 40(3) or 41(3) to lengthen the time to do anything described below;

(b) files an agreement signed by all parties and their lawyers, if any, for a final order disposing of all issues in the case, and a notice of motion for an order carrying out the agreement;

(c) serves on all parties and files a notice of withdrawal (Form 12) that discontinues all outstanding claims in the case;

(d) schedules or adjourns the case for trial; or

(e) arranges a case conference or settlement conference for the first available date.

2. If a case conference or settlement conference is arranged for a date as described in clause 1(e) but the hearing does not take place on that date and is not adjourned by a judge, the case will be dismissed without further notice.

3. Any temporary orders, including temporary orders for support and interim restraining orders under section 46 of the *Family Law Act* or under section 35 of the *Children's Law Reform Act*, will expire upon the dismissal of the case.

Put a line through any blank space left on this page.

....

Date of signature *Signature of clerk of the court*

June 15, 2007

CLASS PROCEEDINGS

TABLE OF CONTENTS

INTRODUCTION

This section contains the various components of the class proceedings legislative package, *i.e.*, the two Acts — the *Class Proceedings Act, 1992*, S.O. 1992, c. 6 (which establishes the procedure for class actions) and the *Law Society Amendment Act (Class Proceedings Funding)*, 1992, S.O. 1992, c. 7 (which provides a funding mechanism for class actions) — and the regulations made under the latter Act (O. Reg. 771/92) which regulate applications to the Class Proceedings Committee for financial assistance from the Class Proceedings Fund. (The Class Proceedings Committee has issued several practice directions and guidelines that can be found at the Committee's website: http://www.lawfoundation.on.ca/practice-directions/)

The text of U.S. Federal Rules of Civil Procedure, Rule 23 is also included.

In the Annual Survey of Recent Developments in Civil Procedure in this and earlier editions will be found an analysis of the case law decided under the Act.

Some Recent Cases. The most interesting recent class action decision is *Quenneville v. Volkswagen Group Canada Inc.*, 2018 ONSC 1020, 2018 CarswellOnt 2159 (S.C.J.), where, after the opt-out deadline passed and after the court approved a settlement, 66 class members decided they wished to opt-out and sue in a separate joint action, all represented by the same counsel.

Though class counsel could have flatly opposed the motion to permit late opt-outs, and the presiding judge would have dismissed the motion, class counsel proposed that each of the moving class members be given an opportunity to provide personalized individual information explaining why they wished to opt-out. The judge agreed and 34 class members provided such information. The court ultimately found that none of the reasons given were compelling or warranted an extension of the opt-out deadline, which is an important component in the management and administration of a class action.

It is submitted that allowing each dissatisfied class member an opportunity to explain individually why they wished to opt-out is the best practice in such circumstances, and that class counsel properly fulfilled their duties owed to all class members by asking the judge not to immediately dismiss the motion, but rather to give the class members an opportunity to explain. It is quite conceivable that one of the class members might have had a valid reason to extend the opt-out deadline, *e.g.*, if a class member with an unusually large individual claim did not receive actual notice of the opt-out deadline or the settlement approval hearing.

As usual, the majority of recent certification motions were successful. By our count the court certified 12 reported cases and refused only three.

The subject-matter of the class actions varied widely. One dealt with competition law: in *Airia Brands Inc. v. Air Canada*, 2017 ONCA 792, 2017 CarswellOnt 15877, 11 C.P.C. (8th) 35, 417 D.L.R. (4th) 467, the court certified a claim for price-fixing airfreight charges, including claims on behalf of absent foreign class members. Three involved consumers' rights: in *Bennett v. Hydro One Inc.*, 2017 ONSC 7065, 2017 CarswellOnt 18775 (S.C.J.), the court refused to certify a claim that an electric utility overcharged its customers; in *Hodge v. Neinstein*, 2017 ONCA 494, 2017 CarswellOnt 9036, 136 O.R. (3d) 81, 7 C.P.C. (8th) 221, 414 D.L.R. (4th) 303; leave to appeal refused *Gary Neinstein, et al. v. Cassie Hodge*, 2017 CarswellOnt 19577, 2017 CarswellOnt 19578 (S.C.C.), the court certified a claim against a law firm for improperly charging contingent fees; and in *Wellman v. TELUS Communications Company*, 2017 ONCA 433, 2017 CarswellOnt 8100, 138 O.R. (3d) 413, 100 C.P.C. (7th) 1, 413 D.L.R. (4th) 684; leave to appeal allowed *TELUS Communications Inc. v. Avraham Wellman*, 2018 CarswellOnt 4703, 2018 CarswellOnt 4704 (S.C.C.), the court certified a claim for overbilling by telecommunications companies despite an arbitration clause in the subject contracts.

Two certification decisions dealt with employment law: in *Sondhi v. Deloitte Management Services LP*, 2018 ONSC 271, 2018 CarswellOnt 364, 45 C.C.E.L. (4th) 217 (S.C.J.); additional reasons 2018 ONSC 1504, 2018 CarswellOnt 3330 (S.C.J.), the court certified a claim for employee benefits, despite the likelihood that many class members would opt-out. The potential number of opt-outs is an insufficient reason to refuse certification, and the actual number of opt-outs is no basis for decertification unless, perhaps, it changes what is the preferable procedure; and in *Freeman Bartholomew v. Coco Paving Inc. and LaFarge Canada Inc.*, 2017 ONSC 6014, 2017 CarswellOnt 16082 (S.C.J.), the court refused to certify a claim for lost overtime.

Two more decisions involved product liability: in *Bennett v. Lenovo (Canada) Inc.*, 2017 ONSC 5853, 2017 CarswellOnt 15375 (S.C.J.); additional reasons 2017 ONSC 6839, 2017 CarswellOnt 18122 (S.C.J.), the court certified a claim for defective computers; and in *Kaira v. Mercedes Benz*, 2017 ONSC 3795, 2017 CarswellOnt 10042, 15 C.E.L.R. (4th) 145 (S.C.J.); additional reasons 2017 ONSC 4692, 2017 CarswellOnt 12008 (S.C.J.), the court certified a claim for defeat devices in automobiles' emission control systems.

Other recent decision dealt with (a) inmates' rights: in *Dadzie v. Her Majesty the Queen in Right of Ontario*, 2017 ONSC 7101, 2017 CarswellOnt 18589 (S.C.J.), on consent the court certified a claim for staffing-related lockdowns at correctional institutions; (b) pharmaceuticals: in *Batten v. Boehringer Ingelheim (Canada) Ltd.*, 2017

ONSC 6098, 2017 CarswellOnt 17148 (Div. Ct.), the court refused to certify a claim regarding the drug Pradaxa; (c) professional liability: in *Green v. The Hospital for Sick Children*, 2017 ONSC 6545, 2017 CarswellOnt 16865, 14 C.P.C. (8th) 311 (S.C.J.), the court refused to certify a claim for negligent laboratory tests; (d) securities/investors' rights: in *Barkley v. Tier 1 Capital Management Inc.*, 2018 ONSC 1956, 2018 CarswellOnt 4767 (S.C.J.), the court certified a claim by investors in a syndicated mortgage arrangement; and in *LBP Holdings Ltd. v. Hycroft Mining Corporation*, 2017 ONSC 6342, 2017 CarswellOnt 16283 (S.C.J.), the court certified a securities claim against some but not all defendants; and (e) miscellaneous topics: in *Metro Taxi Ltd. v. City of Ottawa*, 2018 ONSC 509, 2018 CarswellOnt 523, 13 C.P.C. (8th) 325 (S.C.J.), the court certified a claim by taxi operators against a municipality for permitting Uber to operate in the city, and in *Daniells v. McLellan*, 2017 ONSC 3466, 2017 CarswellOnt 14307, 6 C.P.C. (8th) 317 (S.C.J.), the court certified a breach of privacy claim for improperly accessing patients' health records.

With respect to the timing of certification motions, s. 2(3)(b) of the *Class Proceedings Act* provides that, technically, leave is required to make a certification motion more than 90 days after the statement of defence (or notice of intent to defend, or notice of appearance, as the case may be) was, or ought to have been, delivered. Delays over 90 days are common if not universal, but in *Smith v. Armstrong*, 2018 ONSC 2435, 2018 CarswellOnt 6120 (S.C.J.), the court was faced with a 17-year delay and denied leave, stating at para. 50 "It is neither desirable nor appropriate that a defendant be required to answer a lawsuit that has languished for over 16 years with very minimal progress."

Regarding appeals from certification, in *LBP Holdings Ltd. v. Hycroft Gold Corp.*, 2018 ONSC 1794, 2018 CarswellOnt 3806 (Div. Ct.), the Divisional Court held that the plaintiff requires leave to appeal if the court certifies a claim against some but not all defendants and the plaintiff wishes to contest the exclusion of some defendants.

Two recent decisions dealt with multi-jurisdictional issues: in *Romeo v. Ford Motor Co.*, 2017 ONSC 6674, 2017 CarswellOnt 17377 (S.C.J.), the court refused to permit plaintiffs in an overlapping Saskatchewan class action to intervene in the Ontario certification motion; and in *Babin v. Bayer Inc.*, 2017 ONSC 3200, 2017 CarswellOnt 7813, 6 C.P.C. (8th) 358 (S.C.J.), where four class actions were commenced in various provinces and the plaintiffs' consortium of law firms informally "parked" the Ontario action in favour of the Alberta action, but later sought to proceed in Ontario when difficulties arose in Alberta, the court formally stayed the Ontario action. Alberta was the *forum conveniens*.

Regarding pleadings, in *Castrillo v. Workplace Safety and Insurance Board*, 2017 ONCA 121, 2017 CarswellOnt 1765, 136 O.R. (3d) 654, the court refused to strike a claim by injured workers against the Workplace Safety and Insurance Board for misfeasance in public office and negligence.

Regarding evidence for certification, in *K. (J.) v. Ontario*, 2016 ONSC 8040, 2016 CarswellOnt 21094, 136 O.R. (3d) 67 (S.C.J.); appeal quashed 2017 ONCA 332, 2017 CarswellOnt 5949, 9 C.P.C. (8th) 22, pre-certification, the court ordered the plaintiff to apply to the Youth Justice Court to obtain some of the plaintiff's youth records, which were subject to the *Youth Criminal Justice Act*, S.C. 2002, c. 1.

With respect to carriage motions, in *David v. Loblaw*, 2018 ONSC 1298, 2018 CarswellOnt 3172 (S.C.J.), the court enumerated 16 factors to be considered on carriage motions, and awarded carriage of that price-fixing claim to the more proactive of the two competing consortiums. In *Quenneville v. Audi AG*, 2018 ONSC 1530, 2018 CarswellOnt 3459 (S.C.J.), the court added a 17th factor, holding that the rival law firms' preparation and performance on the carriage motion is itself a factor in determining to whom carriage should be given. And in *Kaplan v. Casino Rama Services Inc.*, 2017 ONSC 2671, 2017 CarswellOnt 6888, 9 C.P.C. (8th) 439 (S.C.J.), the court awarded carriage of the action to the law firm consortium which was more experienced, better prepared, and had a more workable theory of the case.

Interestingly, in *Quenneville* Justice Perell suggested that law firms seeking carriage of a class action should hire independent counsel. He noted with regret that it had become commonplace on carriage motions for the rival lawyers to extol their own virtues and badmouth their competitors. It is certainly true that retaining independent counsel would give the appearance of some objectivity. However it also would open the door for a silver-tongued ringer being brought in for the carriage motion and then disappear, leaving the actual conduct of the class action to her less stellar clients. It is submitted that there is considerable value in the case management judge seeing the whites-of-the-eyes of the lawyers who will actually be conducting the litigation. If, as Justice Perell rightly held, the rival lawyers' performance on a carriage motion is to be a factor in determining to whom carriage is given, then it is the rival lawyers themselves who should argue the motion.

Regarding assessment and distribution of damages, in *Daniells v. McLellan*, 2017 ONSC 6887, 2017 CarswellOnt 18716, 14 C.P.C. (8th) 303 (S.C.J.), the court permitted an aggregate assessment of damages in an action for breach of confidentiality of health records.

Numerous recent cases deal with settlement approval motions: in *Marchand v. Ford Motor Company*, 2018 ONSC 685, 2018 CarswellOnt 2895 (S.C.J.), the court approved a settlement of this action for defective automobile exhausts that provided partial reimbursement for the repair costs of the vehicles; in *Calhoun v. Barkervill Gold Mines Ltd.*, 2018 ONSC 1055, 2018 CarswellOnt 2287 (S.C.J.), the court certified a securities case on consent and approved a $250,000 settlement; in *David v. Loblaw*, 2018 ONSC 198, 2018 CarswellOnt 168, 14 C.P.C. (8th) 273 (S.C.J.), the court refused to interfere with the defendant's voluntary compensation program for its price-fixing activities, and deferred determination of the issues of enforceability of the releases and credit against any ultimate damage award; in *Mancinelli v. Royal Bank of Canada*, 2017 ONSC 5503, 2017 CarswellOnt 14511 (S.C.J.), the court approved the settlement of six price-fixing claims with a total value of $51.5 million; in *Gerard v. Detour Gold Corporation*, 2017 ONSC 3966, 2017 CarswellOnt 9956 (S.C.J.), the court approved the $6 million settlement of this securities case, approved class counsel's $1.6 million fee, and awarded $15,000 honoraria to each of the two representative plaintiffs; in *Barwin v. IKO*, 2017 ONSC 3520, 2017 CarswellOnt 9580, 4 C.P.C. (8th) 305 (S.C.J.), the court approved a $4.7 million settlement of a defective roofing shingles claim, approved class counsel's 25% fee, and awarded a $5,000 honorarium to the representative plaintiff; in *Seed v. Ontario*, 2017 ONSC 3534, 2017 CarswellOnt 8867, 10 C.P.C. (8th) 126 (S.C.J.), the court approved the $8 million settlement of an institutional abuse claim, set class counsel's fees at $2.52 million, and awarded a $15,000 honorarium to the representative plaintiff; in *Drew v. Walmart Canada Inc.*, 2017 ONSC 3308, 2017 CarswellOnt 8159, 10 C.P.C. (8th) 182 (S.C.J.), the court approved a settlement of a data breach claim providing credit monitoring for the class members and $250,000 for class counsel's fees; and in *Cannon v. Funds for Canada Foundation*, 2017 ONSC 2670, 2017 CarswellOnt 6889, 9 C.P.C. (8th) 431, 2017 D.T.C. 5060 (S.C.J.), the court approved the $17.5 million settlement of a claim regarding a charitable tax donation scheme and approved class counsel's 33% contingency fee and a $50,000 honorarium for the representative plaintiff.

Regarding fee approval outside the context of a settlement approval motion, in *McDonald v. Home Capital Group*, 2017 ONSC 5195, 2017 CarswellOnt 13563, 13 C.P.C. (8th) 213 (S.C.J.), a securities case, the court set class counsel's fees at $2.775 million representing 15% of the recovery or a multiplier of 4.6.

With respect to funding issues, in *Marriott v. General Motors of Canada Company*, 2018 ONSC 2535, 2018 CarswellOnt 6254 (S.C.J.), the court approved a funding agreement to pay certain disbursements and adverse costs awards in exchange for 7% of the proceeds of the case; and in *Houle v. St. Jude Medical Inc.*, 2017 ONSC 5129,

2017 CarswellOnt 13215, 9 C.P.C. (8th) 321 (S.C.J.), the court approved a Litigation Funding Agreement subject to certain amendments. The latter decision resulted in *Houle v. St. Jude Medical Inc.*, 2018 ONCA 88, 2018 CarswellOnt 1035, where the Court of Appeal held that an order conditionally approving a class action funding agreement is interlocutory for purposes of appeal, and could not be appealed as of right.

CLASS PROCEEDINGS ACT CASE LAW

CPA — *CASE LAW*

Authors' Note on Organization of Cases

Cases under the *Class Proceedings Act* have been organized as follows:

Disposition of Certification Motions — New Decisions

Smith v. Armstrong, 2018 ONSC 2435, 2018 CarswellOnt 6120 (S.C.J.)

The court refused leave to bring a certification motion after a 17-year delay.

Barkley v. Tier 1 Capital Management Inc., 2018 ONSC 1956, 2018 CarswellOnt 4767 (S.C.J.)

The court certified this claim by investors in a syndicated mortgage arrangement.

Metro Taxi Ltd. v. City of Ottawa, 2018 ONSC 509, 2018 CarswellOnt 523, 45 C.C.E.L. (4th) 130, 13 C.P.C. (8th) 325, 71 M.P.L.R. (5th) 311 (S.C.J.)

The court certified this claim by taxi operators against a municipality for permitting Uber to operate in the city.

Sondhi v. Deloitte Management Services LP, 2018 ONSC 271, 2018 CarswellOnt 364, 45 C.C.E.L. (4th) 217 (S.C.J.); additional reasons 2018 ONSC 1504, 2018 CarswellOnt 3330, 45 C.C.E.L. (4th) 256 (S.C.J.)

The court certified this claim for employee benefits, despite the likelihood that many class members would opt-out. The potential number of opt-outs is an insufficient reason to refuse certification, and the actual number of opt-outs is no basis for decertification unless, perhaps, it changes what is the preferable procedure.

Dadzie v. Her Majesty the Queen in Right of Ontario, 2017 ONSC 7101, 2017 CarswellOnt 18589 (S.C.J.)

On consent the court certified this claim for staffing-related lockdowns at correctional institutions.

Bennett v. Hydro One Inc., 2017 ONSC 7065, 2017 CarswellOnt 18775 (S.C.J.)

The court refused to certify a claim that an electric utility overcharged its customers.

Green v. The Hospital for Sick Children, 2017 ONSC 6545, 2017 CarswellOnt 16865, 14 C.P.C. (8th) 311 (S.C.J.)

The court refused to certify this claim for negligent laboratory tests.

LBP Holdings Ltd. v. Hycroft Mining Corporation, 2017 ONSC 6342, 2017 CarswellOnt 16283 (S.C.J.)

The court certified this securities claim against some but not all defendants.

Batten v. Boehringer Ingelheim (Canada) Ltd., 2017 ONSC 6098, 2017 CarswellOnt 17148 (Div. Ct.)

The court refused to certify this claim regarding the drug Pradaxa.

Freeman Bartholomew v. Coco Paving Inc. and LaFarge Canada Inc., 2017 ONSC 6014, 2017 CarswellOnt 16082, 43 C.C.E.L. (4th) 104 (S.C.J.)

The court refused to certify this claim for lost overtime.

Bennett v. Lenovo (Canada) Inc., 2017 ONSC 5853, 2017 CarswellOnt 15375 (S.C.J.); additional reasons 2017 ONSC 6839, 2017 CarswellOnt 18122 (S.C.J.)

The court certified this claim for defective computers.

Airia Brands Inc. v. Air Canada, 2017 ONCA 792, 2017 CarswellOnt 15877, 11 C.P.C. (8th) 35, 417 D.L.R. (4th) 467

The court certified this claim for price-fixing airfreight charges, including claims on behalf of absent foreign class members.

Daniells v. McLellan, 2017 ONSC 3466, 2017 CarswellOnt 14307, 39 C.C.L.T. (4th) 263, 6 C.P.C. (8th) 317 (S.C.J.)

The court certified this breach of privacy claim for improperly accessing patients' health records.

Kaira v. Mercedes Benz, 2017 ONSC 3795, 2017 CarswellOnt 10042, 15 C.E.L.R. (4th) 145 (S.C.J.); additional reasons 2017 ONSC 4692, 2017 CarswellOnt 12008, 15 C.E.L.R. (4th) 172 (S.C.J.)

The court certified this claim for defeat devices in automobiles' emission control systems.

Hodge v. Neinstein, 2017 ONCA 494, 2017 CarswellOnt 9036, 136 O.R. (3d) 81, 7 C.P.C. (8th) 221, 414 D.L.R. (4th) 303; leave to appeal refused

Gary Neinstein, et al. v. Cassie Hodge, 2017 CarswellOnt 19577, 2017 CarswellOnt 19578 (S.C.C.)

The court certified a claim against a law firm for improperly charging contingent fees.

Wellman v. TELUS Communications Company, 2017 ONCA 433, 2017 CarswellOnt 8100, 138 O.R. (3d) 413, 100 C.P.C. (7th) 1, 413 D.L.R. (4th) 684; leave to appeal allowed *TELUS Communications Inc. v. Avraham Wellman*, 2018 CarswellOnt 4703, 2018 CarswellOnt 4704 (S.C.C.)

The court certified a claim for overbilling by telecommunications companies despite an arbitration clause in the subject contracts.

Disposition of Certification Motions — Child Abuse

Templin v. Ontario, 2016 ONSC 7853, 2016 CarswellOnt 20472, 6 C.P.C. (8th) 410 (S.C.J.)

On consent, the court certified this institutional abuse action.

Brown v. Canada (Attorney General) (2014), 2014 ONSC 6967, 2014 CarswellOnt 16807, 123 O.R. (3d) 369, 14 C.C.L.T. (4th) 187, 60 C.P.C. (7th) 229, [2015] 1 C.N.L.R. 1, 329 O.A.C. 140 (Div. Ct.); additional reasons 2015 ONSC 717, 2015 CarswellOnt 1288, 17 C.C.L.T. (4th) 255, 71 C.P.C. (7th) 54 (Div. Ct.)

The court certified this claim arising from welfare authorities removing aboriginal children from their families and placing them with foster or adoptive parents.

Cavanaugh v. Grenville Christian College, 2014 ONSC 290, 2014 CarswellOnt 2109, [2014] O.J. No. 849 (Div. Ct.)

The court certified this claim for residential school abuse.

Brown v. Canada (Attorney General) (2013), 2013 ONSC 5637, 2013 CarswellOnt 13591, 5 C.C.L.T. (4th) 243, 45 C.P.C. (7th) 186, [2014] 1 C.N.L.R. 1 (S.C.J.); additional reasons 2013 ONSC 6887, 2013 CarswellOnt 15475, 5 C.C.L.T. (4th) 275, 45 C.P.C. (7th) 217 (S.C.J.); affirmed 2014 ONSC 6967, 2014 CarswellOnt 16807, 123 O.R. (3d) 369, 14 C.C.L.T. (4th) 187, 60 C.P.C. (7th) 229, [2015] 1 C.N.L.R. 1, 329 O.A.C. 140 (Div. Ct.); additional reasons 2015 ONSC 717, 2015 CarswellOnt 1288, 17 C.C.L.T. (4th) 255, 71 C.P.C. (7th) 54 (Div. Ct.)

The court certified a claim regarding a 1960s government program to remove aboriginal children from their families and place them with non-aboriginal foster or adoptive parents.

Seed v. Ontario, 2012 ONSC 2681, 2012 CarswellOnt 5544, 31 C.P.C. (7th) 76, [2012] O.J. No. 2006 (S.C.J.); additional reasons 2012 ONSC 4588, 2012 CarswellOnt 9789, 31 C.P.C. (7th) 116 (S.C.J.)

The court certified this claim relating to Ontario's operation of a school for the visually impaired.

Cloud v. Canada (Attorney General) (2004), [2004] O.J. No. 4924, 2004 CarswellOnt 5026, 2 C.P.C. (6th) 199, 27 C.C.L.T. (3d) 50, [2005] 1 C.N.L.R. 8, 247 D.L.R. (4th) 667, 192 O.A.C. 239, 73 O.R. (3d) 401 (C.A.); additional reasons at (2004), 2004 CarswellOnt 5926, 7 C.P.C. (6th) 137 (C.A.); leave to appeal refused (May 12, 2005), Doc. 30759, 2005 CarswellOnt 1866, 2005 CarswellOnt 1867 (S.C.C.)

The court certified a claim for abuse by former students of a residential school.

Rumley v. British Columbia, 2001 SCC 69, [2001] S.C.J. No. 39, 2001 CarswellBC 2166, 2001 CarswellBC 2167, 9 C.P.C. (5th) 1, 205 D.L.R. (4th) 39, [2001] 11 W.W.R. 207, 95 B.C.L.R. (3d) 1, 157 B.C.A.C. 1, 256 W.A.C. 1, 275 N.R. 342, 10 C.C.L.T. (3d) 1, [2001] 3 S.C.R. 184

The court certified a class action regarding abuse of students at a residential school for the deaf over a 42-year period.

Disposition of Certification Motions — Competition Law

Airia Brands Inc. v. Air Canada, 2017 ONCA 792, 2017 CarswellOnt 15877, 11 C.P.C. (8th) 35, 417 D.L.R. (4th) 467

The court certified this claim for price-fixing airfreight charges, including claims on behalf of absent foreign class members.

Shah v. LG Chem, Ltd., 2017 ONSC 2586, 2017 CarswellOnt 6145, 100 C.P.C. (7th) 165, 413 D.L.R. (4th) 546 (Div. Ct.)

The court certified this claim for price fixing lithium ion batteries, including an unlawful means conspiracy claim.

Fanshawe College of Applied Arts and Technology v. Hitachi, Ltd., 2016 ONSC 5118, 2016 CarswellOnt 12972, 88 C.P.C. (7th) 284 (S.C.J.); leave to appeal refused *Fanshawe v. Hitachi*, 2017 ONSC 2791, 2017 CarswellOnt 11443 (S.C.J.)

The court certified this claim for price fixing colour display tubes used in televisions etc.

Airia Brands Inc. v. Air Canada, 2015 ONSC 5352, 2015 CarswellOnt 12958, 78 C.P.C. (7th) 95 (S.C.J.)

The court certified this claim for price fixing airfreight charges.

Bancroft-Snell v. Visa Canada Corp., 2014 ONSC 5772, 2014 CarswellOnt 13750, 69 C.P.C. (7th) 366 (S.C.J.)

For settlement purposes, the court certified this claim for price-fixing credit card fees.

Crosslink Technology Inc. v. BASF Canada, 2014 ONSC 1682, 2014 CarswellOnt 2757, 54 C.P.C. (7th) 111, [2014] O.J. No. 1080 (S.C.J.); leave to appeal refused 2014 ONSC 4529, 2014 CarswellOnt 12138 (S.C.J.)

The court certified a claim for price-fixing polyether polyol products.

Option consommateurs v. Infineon Technologies AG, 2013 SCC 59, 2013 CarswellQue 10520, 2013 CarswellQue 10521, (sub nom. *Infineon Technologies AG v. Option Consommateurs)* [2013] 3 S.C.R. 600, 20 B.L.R. (5th) 1, 45 C.P.C. (7th) 99, 364 D.L.R. (4th) 668, 450 N.R. 355, [2013] S.C.J. No. 59

The court certified this Quebec class action against international manufacturers for inflating the price of microchips.

Bratton v. Samsung Electronics Co., 2012 ONSC 5231, 2012 CarswellOnt 11458, 40 C.P.C. (7th) 415 (S.C.J.)

For settlement purposes, the court certified a price fixing claim regarding dynamic random access memory devices.

Fanshawe College of Applied Arts and Technology v. LG Philips LCD Co., 2011 ONSC 2484, 2011 CarswellOnt 3712, 9 C.P.C. (7th) 184 (S.C.J.)

The court certified a claim for price fixing liquid crystal display panels.

Irving Paper Ltd. v. Atofina Chemicals Inc., 2010 ONSC 2705, 2010 CarswellOnt 3898, [2010] O.J. No. 2472, 103 O.R. (3d) 296, 95 C.P.C. (6th) 170 (S.C.J.)

The court certified a class action alleging a price fixing conspiracy for hydrogen peroxide.

Nutech Brands Inc. v. Air Canada (2008), 2008 CarswellOnt 1494, [2008] O.J. No. 1065, 59 C.P.C. (6th) 166 (S.C.J.)

The court certified a claim for fixing prices of airfreight in advance of a motion to approve a settlement with some but not all defendants.

Axiom Plastics Inc. v. E.I. Dupont Canada Co. (2007), 2007 CarswellOnt 5641, 87 O.R. (3d) 352, 46 C.P.C. (6th) 234, [2007] O.J. No. 3327 (S.C.J.); leave to appeal refused (2008), [2008] O.J. No. 1973, 2008 CarswellOnt 2912, 55 C.P.C. (6th) 118, 237 O.A.C. 221, 90 O.R. (3d) 782 (Div. Ct.)

The court certified a claim alleging price-fixing related to resins used by auto manufacturers.

Chadha v. Bayer Inc. (2003), 2003 CarswellOnt 49, 223 D.L.R. (4th) 158, 168 O.A.C. 143, 63 O.R. (3d) 22, 31 B.L.R. (3d) 214, 23 C.L.R. (3d) 1, 31 C.P.C. (5th) 40, [2003] O.J. No. 27 (C.A.); additional reasons at (2003), 2003 CarswellOnt 1205, 170 O.A.C. 126 (C.A.); leave to appeal refused (2003), 2003 CarswellOnt 2810, 2003 CarswellOnt 2811, 65 O.R. (3d) xvii, 191 O.A.C. 397 (note), 320 N.R. 399 (note) (S.C.C.)

The court refused to certify a claim for alleged price-fixing.

Price v. Panasonic Canada Inc. (2002), 22 C.P.C. (5th) 379, 2002 CarswellOnt 2087, [2002] O.J. No. 2362 (S.C.J.)

Certification was refused in respect of claims arising from breaches of the *Combines Investigation Act* and *Competition Act* involving an estimated 20 million purchasers of electronic equipment over a 19-year period.

Disposition of Certification Motions — Consumers' Rights

Bennett v. Hydro One Inc., 2017 ONSC 7065, 2017 CarswellOnt 18775 (S.C.J.)

The court refused to certify a claim that an electric utility overcharged its customers.

Hodge v. Neinstein, 2017 ONCA 494, 2017 CarswellOnt 9036, 136 O.R. (3d) 81, 7 C.P.C. (8th) 221, 414 D.L.R. (4th) 303; leave to appeal refused *Gary Neinstein, et al. v. Cassie Hodge*, 2017 CarswellOnt 19577, 2017 CarswellOnt 19578 (S.C.C.)

The court certified a claim against a law firm for improperly charging contingent fees.

Wellman v. TELUS Communications Company, 2017 ONCA 433, 2017 CarswellOnt 8100, 138 O.R. (3d) 413, 100 C.P.C. (7th) 1, 413 D.L.R. (4th) 684; leave to appeal allowed *TELUS Communications Inc. v. Avraham Wellman*, 2018 CarswellOnt 4703, 2018 CarswellOnt 4704 (S.C.C.)

The court certified a claim for overbilling by telecommunications companies despite an arbitration clause in the subject contracts.

Bernstein v. Peoples Trust Co., 2017 ONSC 752, 2017 CarswellOnt 1361, 97 C.P.C. (7th) 286 (S.C.J.); additional reasons 2017 ONSC 2189, 2017 CarswellOnt 5120 (S.C.J.)

The court certified this claim alleging unfair practices in issuing prepaid payment cards.

Hodge v. Neinstein, 2015 ONSC 7345, 2015 CarswellOnt 18937, 129 O.R. (3d) 111, 84 C.P.C. (7th) 93, 342 O.A.C. 306 (Div. Ct.); reversed in part 2017 ONCA 494, 2017 CarswellOnt 9036, 136 O.R. (3d) 81, 7 C.P.C. (8th) 221, 414 D.L.R. (4th) 303; leave to appeal refused *Gary Neinstein, et al. v. Cassie Hodge* (December 7, 2017), Doc. 37739, 2017 CarswellOnt 19577, 2017 CarswellOnt 19578 (S.C.C.)

The court certified a claim against a law firm for improperly charging contingent fees.

Wright v. United Parcel Service (Canada) Ltd., 2015 ONSC 2220, 2015 CarswellOnt 7474, 73 C.P.C. (7th) 244, 336 O.A.C. 21 (Div. Ct.); additional reasons 2015 ONSC 6778, 2015 CarswellOnt 16688 (Div. Ct.)

The court certified a claim that a courier company charged unwarranted fees.

Wellman v. TELUS Communications Co., 2014 ONSC 3318, 2014 CarswellOnt 16562, 63 C.P.C. (7th) 50 (S.C.J.)

The court certified a claim for overbilling by telecommunications companies.

Hodge v. Neinstein, 2014 ONSC 4503, 2014 CarswellOnt 10316, 58 C.P.C. (7th) 37, [2014] O.J. No. 3572 (S.C.J.); additional reasons 2014 ONSC 6366, 2014 CarswellOnt 15274, 59 C.P.C. (7th) 248 (S.C.J.); reversed in part 2017 ONCA 494, 2017 CarswellOnt 9036, 136 O.R. (3d) 81, 7 C.P.C. (8th) 221, 414 D.L.R. (4th) 303; leave to appeal refused *Gary Neinstein, et al. v. Cassie Hodge* (December 7, 2017), Doc. 37739, 2017 CarswellOnt 19577, 2017 CarswellOnt 19578 (S.C.C.); reversed 2015 ONSC 7345, 2015 CarswellOnt 18937, 129 O.R. (3d) 111, 84 C.P.C. (7th) 93, 342 O.A.C. 306 (Div. Ct.)

The court refused to certify a claim against a law firm for improperly charging contingent fees.

Sankar v. Bell Mobility Inc., 2013 ONSC 5916, 2013 CarswellOnt 13796, 52 C.P.C. (7th) 75 (S.C.J.); additional reasons 2013 ONSC 6886, 2013 CarswellOnt 15481, 52 C.P.C. (7th) 111 (S.C.J.); leave to appeal refused 2013 ONSC 7529, 2013 CarswellOnt 18414 (Div. Ct.)

The court certified this claim for premature expiry of prepaid phone cards.

Magill v. Expedia, Inc., 2013 ONSC 683, 2013 CarswellOnt 1073, 36 C.P.C. (7th) 74 (S.C.J.)

The court certified a claim for wrongful service charges imposed by a hotel reservation website.

MacDonald v. BMO Trust Co., 2012 ONSC 759, 2012 CarswellOnt 1035, 20 C.P.C. (7th) 284, [2012] O.J. No. 407 (S.C.J.); additional reasons 2012 ONSC 2654, 2012 CarswellOnt 5374, 35 C.P.C. (7th) 199 (S.C.J.)

The court certified a claim regarding fees charged when converting foreign currency into Canadian dollars.

Loveless v. Ontario Lottery & Gaming Corp., 2011 ONSC 4744, 2011 CarswellOnt 8820, 21 C.P.C. (7th) 340, 340 D.L.R. (4th) 120, [2011] O.J. No. 3783 (S.C.J.)

The court refused to certify a claim for failure of the defendant to protect lottery ticket buyers from fraud committed by the defendant's retailer network.

Elder Advocates of Alberta Society v. Alberta, 2011 SCC 24, 2011 CarswellAlta 763, 2011 CarswellAlta 764, EYB 2011-190431, [2011] S.C.J. No. 24, [2011] 2 S.C.R. 261, 499 A.R. 345, [2011] 6 W.W.R. 191, 81 C.C.L.T. (3d) 1, 416 N.R. 198, 331 D.L.R. (4th) 257, 514 W.A.C. 345, 2 C.P.C. (7th) 1, 41 Alta. L.R. (5th) 1, [2011] A.C.S. No. 24

The court certified claims of unjust enrichment and discrimination under s. 15(1) of the *Charter* relating to the alleged overcharging of residents of long term care facilities.

*Re*Collections Inc. v. Toronto Dominion Bank*, 2010 ONSC 6560, 2010 CarswellOnt 9950, [2010] O.J. No. 5686, 5 C.P.C. (7th) 214 (S.C.J.); additional reasons 2011 ONSC 3477, 2011 CarswellOnt 4522, 20 C.P.C. (7th) 195 (S.C.J.)

The court refused to certify a claim regarding the bank's practice of placing a "hold" on cheques deposited to customers' accounts.

Penney v. Bell Canada, 2010 ONSC 2801, 2010 CarswellOnt 3315, 93 C.P.C. (6th) 306 (S.C.J.)

The court refused to certify a claim regarding delays in telephone installations.

Wilkins v. Rogers Communications Inc. (2008), [2008] O.J. No. 4381, 66 C.P.C. (6th) 251, 2008 CarswellOnt 6450 (S.C.J.)

The court certified this claim for interruption of service to digital cable subscribers.

Dean v. Mister Transmission (International) Ltd. (2008), 2008 CarswellOnt 6445, 66 C.P.C. (6th) 287 (S.C.J.); additional reasons at (2009), 2009 CarswellOnt 1308, [2009] O.J. No. 992 (S.C.J.)

The court certified a claim the defendants had improperly charged for "estimates" contrary to the *Motor Vehicle Repair Act*, R.S.O. 1990, c. M-43 and the *Consumer Protection Act, 2002*.

*Arabi v. Toronto Dominion Bank, (*sub nom. *McLaine v. London Life Insurance Co.)* [2007] O.J. No. 5035, 233 O.A.C. 275, 53 C.P.C. (6th) 135, 2007 CarswellOnt 8294 (Div. Ct.); additional reasons at (2008), 2008 CarswellOnt 3579, 59 C.P.C. (6th) 235, 239 O.A.C. 293 (Div. Ct.)

The court refused to certify a claim against banks regarding prepayment provisions in mortgages.

Lee Valley Tools Ltd. v. Canada Post Corp., 57 C.P.C. (6th) 223, 2007 CarswellOnt 8216, [2007] O.J. No. 4942 (S.C.J.)

The court certified a claim for allegedly collecting shipping charges in violation of the *Weights and Measures Act*.

Cassano v. Toronto Dominion Bank, [2007] O.J. No. 4406, 2007 CarswellOnt 7341, 47 C.P.C. (6th) 209, 87 O.R. (3d) 401, 2007 ONCA 781, 230 O.A.C. 231, 287 D.L.R. (4th) 703 (C.A.); leave to appeal refused (2008), 2008 CarswellOnt 1729, 2008 CarswellOnt 1730, [2008] S.C.C.A. No. 15, 386 N.R. 389 (note), 252 O.A.C. 399 (note) (S.C.C.)

The court certified this action for unauthorized bank charges regarding foreign currency transactions.

Macleod v. Viacom Entertainment Canada Inc. (2003), 2003 CarswellOnt 305, 28 C.P.C. (5th) 160, [2003] O.J. No. 331 (S.C.J.)

The court refused to certify a claim regarding late fees and unreturned video fees against a chain of video rental stores.

Despault v. King West Village Lofts Ltd. (2001), [2001] O.J. No. 2933, 2001 CarswellOnt 2598, 10 C.P.C. (5th) 89 (S.C.J.)

The court certified a claim by purchasers of condominium units regarding allegedly improper charges imposed by the seller.

Disposition of Certification Motions — Disease Outbreaks

Sherman v. University Health Network, 2011 ONSC 6941, 2011 CarswellOnt 13165 (S.C.J.)

On consent, the court certified a claim regarding an outbreak of the *pseudomonas* bacteria "superbug".

Glover v. Toronto (City), 2009 CarswellOnt 1985, [2009] O.J. No. 1523, 70 C.P.C. (6th) 303 (S.C.J.); leave to appeal refused 2010 ONSC 2366, 2010 CarswellOnt 2466, 95 C.P.C. (6th) 206 (Div. Ct.)

The court certified a claim regarding an outbreak of Legionnaire's disease subject to amending the litigation plan.

Lavier v. MyTravel Canada Holidays Inc. (2009), 2009 CarswellOnt 1688, [2009] O.J. No. 1314, 72 C.P.C. (6th) 87, 248 O.A.C. 378 (Div. Ct.)

The court set aside an order refusing to certify a claim against a tour operator regarding an outbreak of gastrointestinal illness at resorts in the Dominican Republic, and permitted the plaintiffs to revise their litigation plan.

Sauer v. Canada (Minister of Agriculture) (September 3, 2008), Doc. Toronto 05-CV-287428CP, [2008] O.J. No. 3419, 2008 CarswellOnt 5081

(S.C.J.); leave to appeal refused (2009), [2009] O.J. No. 402, 2009 CarswellOnt 680, 246 O.A.C. 256 (Div. Ct.)

The court certified a claim against the Canadian government for negligence relating to the spread of "mad cow disease."

Healey v. Lakeridge Health Corp. (2006), 2006 CarswellOnt 6574, [2006] O.J. No. 4277, 38 C.P.C. (6th) 145 (S.C.J.); additional reasons at (December 8, 2006), Doc. 04-CV-267728, 2006 CarswellOnt 9528 (S.C.J.)

The court found that this action for persons exposed to tuberculosis satisfied three of the five certification requirements and adjourned to motion to permit further materials to be filed regarding the remaining requirements.

Eliopoulos v. Ontario (Minister of Health & Long Term Care) (2006), 2006 CarswellOnt 6777, [2006] O.J. No. 4400, 35 C.P.C. (6th) 7, 43 C.C.L.T. (3d) 163, 82 O.R. (3d) 321, 217 O.A.C. 69, 276 D.L.R. (4th) 411 (C.A.); leave to appeal refused (May 24, 2007), Doc. 31783, 2007 CarswellOnt 3256, 2007 CarswellOnt 3257, [2006] S.C.C.A. No. 514

The court refused to certify a claim for failure to prevent an outbreak of West Nile virus because the claim did not disclose a cause of action.

Vezina v. Loblaw Cos. (2005), 17 C.P.C. (6th) 307, 2005 CarswellOnt 1942, [2005] O.J. No. 1974 (S.C.J.); additional reasons at (August 3, 2005), Doc. 02-CV-234964 CP, 2005 CarswellOnt 4646 (S.C.J.)

The court certified a claim for negligence and breach of contract where a grocery store exposed shoppers to Hepatitis A.

Rose v. Pettle (2004), 43 C.P.C. (5th) 183, [2004] O.J. No. 739, 2004 CarswellOnt 774, 23 C.C.L.T. (3d) 21 (S.C.J.)

The court certified a claim arising from an outbreak of infection at an acupuncture clinic.

MacDonald (Litigation Guardian of) v. Dufferin-Peel Catholic District School Board (2000), 2000 CarswellOnt 5048, 20 C.P.C. (5th) 345 (S.C.J.)

The court refused to certify a claim regarding toxic mold in schoolrooms.

Anderson v. Wilson (1999), 44 O.R. (3d) 673, 122 O.A.C. 69, 175 D.L.R. (4th) 409, 36 C.P.C. (4th) 17, 1999 CarswellOnt 2073, [1999] O.J. No. 2494 (C.A.); leave to appeal refused (2000), 258 N.R. 194 (note), 138 O.A.C. 200 (note), 2000 CarswellOnt 1837, 2000 CarswellOnt 1838, [1999] S.C.C.A. No. 476

The court certified a class action arising from a Hepatitis B outbreak.

Sutherland v. Canadian Red Cross Society (1994), 17 O.R. (3d) 645, 21 C.P.C. (3d) 137, 112 D.L.R. (4th) 504 (Gen. Div.)

Certification was refused in a proposed class action to recover damages for people who had contracted HIV as a result of receiving contaminated blood and blood products. Certification was refused on the ground that (1) the claims of the class members did not raise common issues; (2) a class action was not the preferable procedure to resolve the controversy; (3) a multitude of disparate third party claims would make the proceeding unduly complicated and unmanageable; and (4) the named plaintiff was not an adequate representative plaintiff for the class.

Disposition of Certification Motions — Education

Turner v. York University, 2012 ONSC 4272, 2012 CarswellOnt 10191, 40 C.P.C. (7th) 156, 298 O.A.C. 174 (Div. Ct.)

The court refused to certify a claim by students whose classes were disrupted by a strike.

Ramdath v. George Brown College of Applied Arts & Technology, 2010 CarswellOnt 2038, 2010 ONSC 2019, [2010] O.J. No. 1411, 93 C.P.C. (6th) 106 (S.C.J.)

The court certified a misrepresentation claim by students against a college.

Matoni v. C.B.S. Interactive Multimedia Inc. (2008), 2008 CarswellOnt 228, [2008] O.J. No. 197 (S.C.J.); additional reasons at (August 29, 2008), Doc. 06-CV-310529CP, 2008 CarswellOnt 5077 (S.C.J.); additional reasons (December 3, 2008), 06-CV-310529CP, 2008 CarswellOnt 7185 (S.C.J.); additional reasons at (August 29, 2008), Doc. 06-CV-310529CP, 2008 CarswellOnt 5076 (S.C.J.); additional reasons at (December 3, 2008), Doc. 06-CV-310529CP, 2008 CarswellOnt 7185 (S.C.J.)

The court certified this consumer protection claim for students of a non-accredited dental hygienist training program, subject to adding an appropriate class representative.

Hickey-Button v. Loyalist College of Applied Arts & Technology (2006), 31 C.P.C. (6th) 390, 2006 CarswellOnt 3618, [2006] O.J. No. 2393, 267 D.L.R. (4th) 601, 211 O.A.C. 301 (C.A.)

The court certified a claim by nursing students who had been promised a certain option which was not made available to them.

Nieberg (Litigation Guardian of) v. Simcoe County District School Board (2004), 48 C.P.C. (5th) 164, [2004] O.J. No. 2524, 2004 CarswellOnt 2409 (S.C.J.)

The court refused to certify a class action for failure to meet the educational and physical needs of 17 disabled students.

Olar v. Laurentian University (2003), 37 C.P.C. (5th) 129, 2003 CarswellOnt 2591 (S.C.J.); additional reasons at (January 8, 2004), Doc. 00-GD-49743, 2004 CarswellOnt 44, [2004] O.J. No. 35 (S.C.J.); affirmed (2004), 2004 CarswellOnt 3684, [2004] O.J. No. 3716, 6 C.P.C. (6th) 276 (Div. Ct.)

The court refused to certify a claim by students against a university for misrepresentation.

Mouhteros v. DeVry Canada Inc. (1998), 41 O.R. (3d) 63, 22 C.P.C. (4th) 198, 1998 CarswellOnt 2704, [1998] O.J. No. 2786 (Gen. Div.)

The court refused to certify a misrepresentation claim against an educational institution.

Disposition of Certification Motions — Employment — General

Sondhi v. Deloitte Management Services LP, 2018 ONSC 271, 2018 CarswellOnt 364, 45 C.C.E.L. (4th) 217 (S.C.J.); additional reasons 2018 ONSC 1504, 2018 CarswellOnt 3330, 45 C.C.E.L. (4th) 256 (S.C.J.)

The court certified this claim for employee benefits, despite the likelihood that many class members would opt-out. The potential number of opt-outs is an insufficient reason to refuse certification, and the actual number of opt-outs is no basis for decertification unless, perhaps, it changes what is the preferable procedure.

Freeman Bartholomew v. Coco Paving Inc. and LaFarge Canada Inc., 2017 ONSC 6014, 2017 CarswellOnt 16082, 43 C.C.E.L. (4th) 104 (S.C.J.); additional reasons 2017 ONSC 5382, 2017 CarswellOnt 14108 (S.C.J.)

The court refused to certify this claim for lost overtime.

Berg v. Canadian Hockey League, 2017 ONSC 2608, 2017 CarswellOnt 6227 (S.C.J.); additional reasons 2017 ONSC 5382, 2017 CarswellOnt 14108 (S.C.J.)

The court certified a claim for breach of employment standards legislation on behalf of a class of amateur hockey players.

Sondhi v. Deloitte Management Services LP, 2017 ONSC 2122, 2017 CarswellOnt 5540, 1 C.P.C. (8th) 49 (S.C.J.)

The court certified a claim that a class of persons doing work for the defendant were employees, not independent contractors.

Bozsik v. Livingston International Inc., 2016 ONSC 7168, 2016 CarswellOnt 18149, 38 C.C.E.L. (4th) 43 (S.C.J.)

The court certified this claim for unpaid overtime.

Omarali v. Just Energy Group Inc., 2016 ONSC 4094, 2016 CarswellOnt 12236, 89 C.P.C. (7th) 113, 2016 C.L.L.C. 210-054, [2016] O.J. No. 3997 (S.C.J.); leave to appeal refused 2016 ONSC 7096, 2016 CarswellOnt 18098 (Div. Ct.)

The court certified this claim for *Employment Standards Act* benefits including minimum wage and overtime pay.

Bakshi v. Global Credit & Collection Inc., 2015 ONSC 6842, 2015 CarswellOnt 17310 (S.C.J.)

On consent, the court certified this claim for commissions by former employees.

Baroch v. Canada Cartage Diversified GP Inc., 2015 ONSC 40, 2015 CarswellOnt 1157, 66 C.P.C. (7th) 72, 2015 C.L.L.C. 210-028 (S.C.J.); additional reasons 2015 ONSC 1147, 2015 CarswellOnt 2431, 71 C.P.C. (7th) 151 (S.C.J.); leave to appeal refused 2015 ONSC 3227, 2015 CarswellOnt 8885, 2015 C.L.L.C. 210-052 (Div. Ct.)

The court certified a claim for unpaid overtime based on the employer's systemic policies and practices.

Brown v. Canadian Imperial Bank of Commerce, 2014 ONCA 677, 2014 CarswellOnt 13747, 57 C.P.C. (7th) 243, 2015 C.L.L.C. 210-001, 326 O.A.C. 159

The court refused to certify this claim for overtime pay.

Rosen v. BMO Nesbitt Burns Inc., 2013 ONSC 2144, 2013 CarswellOnt 11561, 9 C.C.E.L. (4th) 315, 44 C.P.C. (7th) 149, 2013 C.L.L.C. 210-053 (S.C.J.); additional reasons 2013 ONSC 6356, 2013 CarswellOnt 15428, 56 C.P.C. (7th) 182 (S.C.J.); leave to appeal refused 2013 ONSC 7762, [2013] O.J. No. 6258 (Div. Ct.)

The court certified this claim for overtime pay.

Brown v. CIBC, 2013 ONSC 1284, 2013 CarswellOnt 4766, 34 C.P.C. (7th) 270, 2013 C.L.L.C. 210-031, 307 O.A.C. 90 (Div. Ct.); affirmed 2014 ONCA 677, 2014 CarswellOnt 13747, 57 C.P.C. (7th) 243, 2015 C.L.L.C. 210-001, 326 O.A.C. 159

The court refused to certify this claim for overtime pay.

Perrenoud v. eHealth Ontario, 2012 ONSC 6704, 2012 CarswellOnt 14757, 33 C.P.C. (7th) 60 (S.C.J.)

The court certified a claim by employees regarding performance awards and merit increases.

McCracken v. Canadian National Railway Co., 2012 ONCA 445, 2012 CarswellOnt 8010, 111 O.R. (3d) 745, 100 C.C.E.L. (3d) 27, 21 C.P.C. (7th) 57, 2012 C.L.L.C. 210-041, 293 O.A.C. 274, [2012] O.J. No. 2884; additional reasons 2012 ONCA 797, 2012 CarswellOnt 14475, 5 C.C.E.L. (4th) 327

The court refused to certify this claim for overtime based on the alleged misclassification of front line supervisors as managerial employees.

Fresco v. Canadian Imperial Bank of Commerce, 2012 ONCA 444, 2012 CarswellOnt 7956, 111 O.R. (3d) 501, 100 C.C.E.L. (3d) 81, 21 C.P.C. (7th) 223, 2012 C.L.L.C. 210-040, 293 O.A.C. 248; leave to appeal refused 2013 CarswellOnt 3154, 2013 CarswellOnt 3155, 452 N.R. 394 (note), 314 O.A.C. 402 (note), [2012] S.C.C.A. No. 379

The court certified claims for overtime by customer service employees.

Fulawka v. Bank of Nova Scotia (2011), 2011 ONSC 530, 2011 CarswellOnt 5491, [2011] O.J. No. 2561, 337 D.L.R. (4th) 319, 10 C.P.C. (7th) 12, 2012 C.L.L.C. 210-009 (Div. Ct.); reversed in part 2012 ONCA 443, 2012 CarswellOnt 7951, 111 O.R. (3d) 346, 100 C.C.E.L. (3d) 119, 21 C.P.C. (7th) 1, 352 D.L.R. (4th) 1, 2012 C.L.L.C. 210-039, 293 O.A.C. 204, [2012] O.J. No. 2885; leave to appeal refused 2013 CarswellOnt 3152, 2013 CarswellOnt 3153, 452 N.R. 393 (note), 314 O.A.C. 402 (note) (S.C.C.)

The court certified a claim for overtime pay by sales staff in a bank's retail branches.

Wilson v. Re/Max Metro-City Realty Ltd (2003), 2003 CarswellOnt 46, 22 C.C.E.L. (3d) 307, 27 C.P.C. (5th) 350, [2003] O.J. No. 79, 63 O.R. (3d) 131 (S.C.J.)

The court certified a claim by a class of sales agents for overpayment of expenses deducted by their employer pursuant to a standard form contract.

Berry v. Pulley (2001), 8 C.P.C. (5th) 367, 2001 CarswellOnt 738, 197 D.L.R. (4th) 317 (S.C.J.)

The court certified a claim by a plaintiff class of airline pilots against a defendant class of airline pilots arising from the merger of their employers.

Kumar v. Sharp Business Forms Inc. (2001), 5 C.P.C. (5th) 128, 2001 CarswellOnt 1569, 9 C.C.E.L. (3d) 75 (S.C.J.)

The court certified a claim for overtime pay, holiday pay, and vacation pay. Availability of proceedings under the *Employment Standards Act* did not prevent the employees from bringing a class action.

Huras v. Com Dev Ltd. (1999), 36 C.P.C. (4th) 31, 46 C.C.E.L. (2d) 67, 1999 CarswellOnt 2079, [1999] O.J. No. 2560 (S.C J.); affirmed (2001), 2001 CarswellOnt 1683, 8 C.P.C. (5th) 277 (Div. Ct.)

The court refused to certify a claim by approximately 50 employees alleging that their contracts of employment were breached by the employer's failure to provide them with shares pursuant to an Employee Stock Plan.

Wicke v. Canadian Occidental Petroleum Ltd. (1998), 40 O.R. (3d) 731, 1998 CarswellOnt 2863 (Gen. Div.)

The court certified a class action by former employees for unpaid overtime wages, *etc.*

Halabi v. Becker Milk Co. (1998), 39 O.R. (3d) 153, 38 C.C.E.L. (2d) 89 (Gen. Div.)

The court refused to certify a class action for overtime pay, vacation pay, *etc.*

Atkinson v. Ault Foods Ltd. (December 23, 1997), Doc. 887/97 (Ont. Gen. Div.)

The court certified a claim by a class against their former employer for bonus and vacation pay.

Disposition of Certification Motions — Employment — Pensions

Chapman v. Benefit Plan Administration, 2013 ONSC 3318, 2013 CarswellOnt 9017, 43 C.P.C. (7th) 40 (S.C.J.); additional reasons 2014 ONSC 537, 2014 CarswellOnt 890, 11 C.C.P.B. (2nd) 56 (S.C.J.)

The court certified this pension plan claim.

Lacroix v. Canada Mortgage & Housing Corp., 2012 ONCA 243, 2012 CarswellOnt 4342, 15 C.P.C. (7th) 1, 75 E.T.R. (3d) 42, 110 O.R. (3d) 81, 96 C.C.P.B. 222, 349 D.L.R. (4th) 1, 2012 C.E.B. & P.G.R. 8482, (sub nom. *McCann v. Canada Mortgage & Housing Corp.)* 290 O.A.C. 99; leave to appeal refused 2012 CarswellOnt 13928, 2012 CarswellOnt 13929, (sub nom. *McCann v. Canada Mortgage and Housing Corp.)* 443 N.R. 391 (note) (S.C.C.)

In this pension class action, the court declined to certify new common issues with respect to partial termination of a pension plan.

Kidd v. Canada Life Assurance Co., 2011 ONSC 6324, 2011 CarswellOnt 11407, 93 C.C.P.B. 211, 2011 C.E.B. & P.G.R. 8458, 22 C.P.C. (7th) 156 (S.C.J.)

For settlement purposes, the court certified a claim for a pension plan surplus.

Sunnybrook Health Sciences Centre v. Lorenz, 2009 CarswellOnt 4576, 82 C.P.C. (6th) 330, 2009 C.E.B. & P.G.R. 8352, 76 C.C.P.B. 230 (S.C.J.)

The court refused to certify a class action that attempted to implement an agreement to divide the surplus of a pension plan and there was no *lis* between the parties.

McGee v. London Life Insurance Co. (2008), 63 C.P.C. (6th) 107, 2008 CarswellOnt 2534, [2008] O.J. No. 1760, 2008 C.E.B. & P.G.R. 8295, 70 C.C.P.B. 2 (S.C.J.); leave to appeal refused (2008), 2008 CarswellOnt 3850, 70 C.C.P.B. 266 (Div. Ct.); additional reasons at (2008), 2008 CarswellOnt 4822, 70 C.C.P.B. 269 (Div. Ct.); additional reasons at (2008), 2008 CarswellOnt 7983, 72 C.C.P.B. 302 (S.C.J.)

The court certified a claim regarding the partial winding up of a pension plan.

Caponi v. Canada Life Assurance Co. (2009), 2009 CarswellOnt 113, 70 C.C.L.I. (4th) 148, 2009 C.E.B. & P.G.R. 8326 (S.C.J.)

The court certified this claim regarding the partial wind-up of a pension plan.

MacDougall v. Ontario Northland Transportation Commission, 2007 CarswellOnt 881, 221 O.A.C. 150, 39 C.P.C. (6th) 63, 59 C.C.P.B. 194, 2007

C.E.B. & P.G.R. 8236 (Div. Ct.); additional reasons at (2007), 2007 CarswellOnt 3331, 39 C.P.C. (6th) 207, 60 C.C.P.B. 119 (Div. Ct.); leave to appeal refused (July 31, 2007), Doc. CA M34862, 2007 CarswellOnt 8994 (C.A.); leave to appeal refused (2008), 2008 CarswellOnt 826, 2008 CarswellOnt 827, 385 N.R. 393 (note), 252 O.A.C. 400 (note) (S.C.C.)

The court refused to certify a claim by pension plan members where there were irreconcilable conflicts between subclasses.

Boucher v. P.S.A.C. (2005), 18 C.P.C. (6th) 391, [2005] O.J. No. 2693, 2005 CarswellOnt 2742, 47 C.C.P.B. 5 (S.C.J.); additional reasons at (2005), 2005 CarswellOnt 5677, 48 C.C.P.B. 28 (S.C.J.); affirmed (2006), 25 C.P.C. (6th) 219, 2006 CarswellOnt 1658, 51 C.C.P.B. 18 (Ont. Div. Ct.)

The court dismissed the plaintiffs' motion for certification in their action against their former employer for its management of the pension plan fund.

Paramount Pictures (Canada) Inc. v. Dillon, 29 C.P.C. (6th) 13, 2006 CarswellOnt 3536, 53 C.C.P.B. 88, 24 E.T.R. (3d) 189, 2006 C.E.B. & P.G.R. 8205 (S.C.J.)

An application by the employer for a determination of the beneficial ownership of a pension surplus was certified as a class proceeding.

Sutherland v. Hudson's Bay Co. (2005), 74 O.R. (3d) 608, [2005] O.J. No. 1455, 2005 CarswellOnt 2564, 46 C.C.P.B. 225, 17 E.T.R. (3d) 287, 17 C.P.C. (6th) 199 (S.C.J.); additional reasons at (2006), 53 C.C.P.B. 154, 2006 CarswellOnt 3095, 24 E.T.R. (3d) 253 (S.C.J.)

Subject to the determination of some outstanding matters, the court was satisfied that the plaintiffs' claims involving the employer's use of surplus pension funds would be appropriate for certification.

O.P.S.E.U. v. Ontario (2005), 13 C.P.C. (6th) 178, (sub nom. *Ontario Public Service Employees Union v. Ontario)* 2005 CarswellOnt 1809, C.E.B. & P.G.R. 8156, 46 C.C.P.B. 200 (S.C.J.)

The court certified a claim regarding employees whose employment was transferred to a new employer resulting in losses in pension entitlements.

McLaughlin v. Falconbridge Ltd. (1999), 36 C.P.C. (4th) 40, C.E.B. & P.G.R. 8360 (headnote only), 21 C.C.P.B. 133, 1999 CarswellOnt 1965 (S.C J.)

The court certified a claim by members of an employee pension plan alleging breach of fiduciary duty by the actuary for the pension plan.

Disposition of Certification Motions — Employment — Retiree Issues

Vivendi Canada Inc. v. Dell'Aniello, 2014 CSC 1, 2014 SCC 1, 2014 CarswellQue 28, 2014 CarswellQue 29, [2014] 1 S.C.R. 1, 8 C.C.P.B. (2nd)

163, 51 C.P.C. (7th) 1, 369 D.L.R. (4th) 195, 2014 C.E.B. & P.G.R. 8066, 453 N.R. 150, [2014] S.C.J. No. 1

The court certified this Quebec class action regarding the unilateral amendment of retirees' health insurance plan. The court of first instance overstepped its bounds by ruling on the merits, and seeking common answers rather than merely identifying common questions.

O'Neill v. General Motors of Canada Ltd., 2011 ONSC 6291, 2011 CarswellOnt 13316, [2011] O.J. No. 4785 (S.C.J.)

On consent, the court certified a claim by retired employees for reduction of their retirement benefits.

Nadolny v. Peel (Region) (2009), 78 C.P.C. (6th) 252, 2009 CarswellOnt 5901, [2009] O.J. No. 4006 (S.C.J.)

The court refused to certify a claim regarding post retirement benefits for non-unionized employees.

Kranjcec v. Ontario (2004), 2004 CarswellOnt 31, C.E.B. & P.G.R. 8084, 39 C.C.P.B. 32, 69 O.R. (3d) 231, 44 C.P.C. (5th) 376, 40 C.C.E.L. (3d) 24 (S.C.J.)

The court certified an action regarding retirement benefits.

Ormrod v. Etobicoke (City) Hydro-Electric Commission (2001), 2001 CarswellOnt 614, 3 C.P.C. (5th) 253, 8 C.C.E.L. (3d) 48, (sub nom. *Ormrod v. Etobicoke (Hydro-Electric Commission))* 53 O.R. (3d) 285, 28 C.C.P.B. 261 (S.C.J.)

The court certified a claim by the defendant's retired employees regarding withdrawal of promised health care benefits.

Schweyer v. Laidlaw Carriers Inc. (2000), 49 C.C.E.L. (2d) 308, 23 C.C.P.B. 200, 44 C.P.C. (4th) 236, 2000 CarswellOnt 511, [2000] O.J. No. 575 (S.C.J.)

The court certified a claim regarding an early retirement package.

Disposition of Certification Motions — Employment — Wrongful Dismissal

Brigaitis v. IQT Ltd., 2014 ONSC 7, 2014 CarswellOnt 504, 22 B.L.R. (5th) 297, 50 C.P.C. (7th) 9 (S.C.J.); additional reasons 2014 ONSC 1192, 2014 CarswellOnt 2207, 50 C.P.C. (7th) 54 (S.C.J.)

The court certified this claim for wrongful dismissal.

Kafka v. Allstate Insurance Co. of Canada, 2012 ONSC 1035, 2012 CarswellOnt 4089, 98 C.C.E.L. (3d) 53, 23 C.P.C. (7th) 400, 2012 C.L.L.C. 210-034, 289 O.A.C. 292, [2012] O.J. No. 1520 (Div. Ct.)

The court refused to certify a claim for termination and severance pay under the *Employment Standards Act* as there were no common issues.

Downey v. Mitel Networks Corp. (2004), 21 C.P.C. (6th) 346, 2004 CarswellOnt 6686 (S.C.J.)

The court certified this wrongful dismissal claim as a class proceeding.

Isaacs v. Nortel Networks Corp. (2001), 2001 CarswellOnt 4404, 15 C.C.E.L. (3d) 78 (S.C.J.)

The court certified a claim for mass wrongful dismissal.

Dillon v. Novi Canadian Ltd. (1999), 36 C.P.C. (4th) 28, 45 C.C.E.L. (2d) 23, 1999 CarswellOnt 2246 (S.C.J.)

The court certified a mass wrongful dismissal claim resulting from a restructuring of the defendant's business operations.

Webb v. K-Mart Canada Ltd. (1999), 45 O.R. (3d) 389, 36 C.P.C. (4th) 99, 99 C.L.L.C. 210-038, 45 C.C.E.L. (2d) 165, 1999 CarswellOnt 1899 (S.C.J.); additional reasons at (1999), 45 O.R. (3d) 425, 46 C.C.E.L. (2d) 293, 43 C.P.C. (4th) 26, 1999 CarswellOnt 2832, [1999] O.J. No. 3285 (S.C.J.); leave to appeal refused (1999), 45 O.R. (3d) 638, 49 C.C.E.L. (2d) 59, 1999 CarswellOnt 4624, [1999] O.J. No. 3286 (Div. Ct.)

The court certified a mass wrongful dismissal claim involving persons dismissed in several provinces.

Disposition of Certification Motions — Franchise Law

1291079 Ontario Ltd. v. Sears Canada Ltd., 2014 ONSC 5190, 2014 CarswellOnt 12200 (S.C.J.)

The court certified this claim by franchisees against franchisors.

Trillium Motor World Ltd. v. General Motors of Canada Ltd., 2012 ONSC 1443, 2012 CarswellOnt 4207, 92 C.C.L.T. (3d) 204, 37 C.P.C. (7th) 30, 76 E.T.R. (3d) 294, [2012] O.J. No. 1579 (Div. Ct.)

The court certified a claim for lawyers' negligence in giving advice regarding termination of automobile dealership franchises.

1250264 Ontario Inc. v. Pet Valu Canada Inc., 2011 ONSC 287, 2011 CarswellOnt 9662, 16 C.P.C. (7th) 52, [2011] O.J. No. 1618 (S.C.J.); additional reasons 2011 ONSC 3475, 2011 CarswellOnt 4521, 16 C.P.C. (7th) 92 (S.C.J.)

The court certified a claim against a franchisor for failure to share volume rebates with its franchisees.

2038724 Ontario Ltd. v. Quizno's Canada Restaurant Corp., 2010 ONCA 466, 2010 CarswellOnt 4305, [2010] O.J. No. 2683, 100 O.R. (3d) 721, 87 C.P.C. (6th) 375, 320 D.L.R. (4th) 612, 265 O.A.C. 134 (C.A.); additional reasons 2010 ONCA 611, 2010 CarswellOnt 6924, 89 C.P.C. (6th) 199; leave to appeal refused (2010), 2011 CarswellOnt 499, 2011 CarswellOnt 500, [2010] S.C.C.A. No. 348, [2010] C.S.C.R. No. 348, [2011] 1 S.C.R. x (note), 417 N.R. 397 (note), 284 O.A.C. 396 (note) (S.C.C.)

The court certified this franchise class action.

Landsbridge Auto Corp. v. Midas Canada Inc. (2009), 2009 CarswellOnt 1655, [2009] O.J. No. 1279, 73 C.P.C. (6th) 10 (S.C.J.)

The court certified this claim for breach of a franchise agreement.

1176560 Ontario Ltd. v. Great Atlantic & Pacific Co. of Canada Ltd. (2002), 2002 CarswellOnt 4272, 28 C.P.C. (5th) 135, [2002] O.J. No. 4781, 62 O.R. (3d) 535 (S.C.J.); leave to appeal allowed (2003), 2003 CarswellOnt 998, [2003] O.J. No. 1089, 169 O.A.C. 343, 64 O.R. (3d) 42 (Div. Ct.); affirmed (2004), 2004 CarswellOnt 945, [2004] O.J. No. 865, 50 C.P.C. (5th) 25, 70 O.R. (3d) 182, 184 O.A.C. 298 (Div. Ct.); leave to appeal refused (2004), 2004 CarswellOnt 3045, 50 C.P.C. (5th) 34 (C.A.)

The court certified a claim by a class of franchisees against the franchisor.

909787 Ontario Ltd. v. Bulk Barn Foods Ltd. (2000), 2 C.P.C. (5th) 61, 2000 CarswellOnt 3539, [2000] O.J. No. 3649, 138 O.A.C. 180 (Div. Ct.); additional reasons at (2000), 2000 CarswellOnt 3981, 138 O.A.C. 180 (Div. Ct.)

The court refused to certify this claim by franchisees against a franchisor.

Mont-Bleu Ford Inc. v. Ford Motor Co. of Canada (2000), [2000] O.J. No. 1815, 48 O.R. (3d) 753, 134 O.A.C. 66, 48 C.P.C. (4th) 353, 2000 CarswellOnt 1826 (Div. Ct.)

The Divisional Court held that a claim seeking interpretation of an automobile dealership contract should be certified. The fact that the putative class members were economically advantaged and sophisticated, and could have sued independently, did not prevent certification.

Rosedale Motors Inc. v. Petro-Canada Inc. (1998), 42 O.R. (3d) 776, 86 C.P.R. (3d) 1, 31 C.P.C. (4th) 340, 1998 CarswellOnt 5009, [1998] O.J. No. 5461 (Gen. Div.); additional reasons at (March 21, 2000), Doc. 94-CQ-53786 CP, 2000 CarswellOnt 861, [2000] O.J. No. 938 (S.C.J.)

The court refused to certify an action by a class of franchisees based on various misrepresentations made largely in separate meetings with each franchisee. While in principle misrepresentation class actions may be certified, in this case there were no common issues the adjudication of which would move the litigation forward in a meaningful way.

Disposition of Certification Motions — Inmates' Rights

Dadzie v. Her Majesty the Queen in Right of Ontario, 2017 ONSC 7101, 2017 CarswellOnt 18589 (S.C.J.)

On consent the court certified this claim for staffing-related lockdowns at correctional institutions.

Brazeau v. Canada (Attorney General), 2016 ONSC 7836, 2016 CarswellOnt 19654, 6 C.P.C. (8th) 434, 370 C.R.R. (2d) 212 (S.C.J.)

On consent, the court certified a claim for placing inmates in solitary confinement.

Johnson v. Ontario, 2016 ONSC 5314, 2016 CarswellOnt 16353, 364 C.R.R. (2d) 17 (S.C.J.)

The court certified a claim by inmates of a correctional institution for overcrowding and lack of proper supervision.

Lauzon v. Canada (Attorney General), 2015 ONSC 2620, 2015 CarswellOnt 6940, 67 C.P.C. (7th) 337, 384 D.L.R. (4th) 532, 335 O.A.C. 126 (Div. Ct.)

The court refused to certify a claim by Joyceville inmates for the government's banning t-shirts designed for Prisoner Justice Day.

Good v. Toronto Police Services Board, 2014 ONSC 4583, 2014 CarswellOnt 10726, 121 O.R. (3d) 413, 54 C.P.C. (7th) 1, 375 D.L.R. (4th) 200, 317 C.R.R. (2d) 62, 321 O.A.C. 358 (Div. Ct.); additional reasons 2014 ONSC 6115, 2014 CarswellOnt 15068, 69 C.P.C. (7th) 291 (Div. Ct.); reversed 2016 ONCA 250, 2016 CarswellOnt 5047, 130 O.R. (3d) 241, 82 C.P.C. (7th) 1, 396 D.L.R. (4th) 411, 347 O.A.C. 307; leave to appeal refused (November 10, 2016), Doc. 37050, 2016 CarswellOnt 17619, 2016 CarswellOnt 17620, [2016] S.C.C.A. No. 255; affirmed 2016 ONCA 250, 2016 CarswellOnt 5047, 130 O.R. (3d) 241, 82 C.P.C. (7th) 1, 396 D.L.R. (4th) 411, 347 O.A.C. 307

The court certified a claim regarding the arrest or mass detention of protestors and members of the public during the 2010 G20 summit.

Lauzon v. Canada (Attorney General), 2014 ONSC 2811, 2014 CarswellOnt 6633, 58 C.P.C. (7th) 201, 312 C.R.R. (2d) 1, [2014] O.J. No. 2402 (S.C.J.); additional reasons 2014 ONSC 3618, 2014 CarswellOnt 8177, 68 C.P.C. (7th) 332 (S.C.J.); affirmed 2015 ONSC 2620, 2015 CarswellOnt 6940, 67 C.P.C. (7th) 337, 384 D.L.R. (4th) 532, 335 O.A.C. 126 (Div. Ct.)

The court refused to certify a claim by Joyceville inmates for the government's banning t-shirts designed for Prisoner Justice Day.

Phaneuf v. Ontario, 2010 ONCA 901, 2010 CarswellOnt 9755, [2010] O.J. No. 5631, 97 C.P.C. (6th) 281, 104 O.R. (3d) 392, 222 C.R.R. (2d) 150, (sub nom. *R. v. Phaneuf*) 275 O.A.C. 160

The court refused to certify a claim on behalf of persons detained in prison while awaiting assessment under s. 672.11 of the *Criminal Code*.

Slark (Litigation Guardian of) v. Ontario, 2010 ONSC 1726, 2010 CarswellOnt 9465, 6 C.P.C. (7th) 168, [2010] O.J. No. 5187 (S.C.J.); leave to appeal refused 2010 ONSC 6131, 2010 CarswellOnt 9235, 6 C.P.C. (7th) 221, [2010] O.J. No. 5172 (Div. Ct.)

The court certified a claim for mistreatment of patients at a facility for persons with developmental disabilities.

Joanisse v. Barker (2003), 38 C.P.C. (5th) 386, [2003] O.J. No. 3137, 2003 CarswellOnt 3054 (S.C.J.); additional reasons at [2003] O.J. No. 4081, 2003 CarswellOnt 3983, [2003] O.T.C. 733, 46 C.P.C. (5th) 348 (S.C.J.)

The court refused to certify claims for battery and breach of fiduciary duty by inmates of an institution for the criminally insane regarding alleged human experimentation.

Disposition of Certification Motions — Insurance

Jeffery v. London Life Insurance Co. (2008), 59 C.P.C. (6th) 30, 65 C.C.L.I. (4th) 10, 241 O.A.C. 101, 2008 CarswellOnt 5169, [2008] O.J. No. 3428 (Div. Ct.)

The court certified a claim by participating policyholders for denial of benefits based on the insurer's financial performance, for which the policyholders paid higher premiums.

Hague v. Liberty Mutual Insurance Co. (2004), 13 C.P.C. (6th) 1, [2004] O.J. No. 3057, 2004 CarswellOnt 6141, 21 C.C.L.I. (4th) 264 (S.C.J.); additional reasons at (2004), 2004 CarswellOnt 6142, 13 C.P.C. (6th) 31, 21 C.C.L.I. (4th) 294 (S.C.J.); additional reasons at (2005), [2005] O.J. No. 1660, 2005 CarswellOnt 1361, 13 C.P.C. (6th) 37, 21 C.C.L.I. (4th) 300 (S.C.J.); leave to appeal refused (March 29, 2005), Doc. Toronto 3-05, 2005 CarswellOnt 1830 (Div. Ct.)

The court certified a claim that the defendant used substandard automotive parts when repairing insured vehicles.

Bellaire v. Independent Order of Foresters (2004), 2004 CarswellOnt 5608, 5 C.P.C. (6th) 68, [2004] O.J. No. 2242, 19 C.C.L.I. (4th) 35 (S.C.J.); additional reasons at (2004), 2004 CarswellOnt 5609, 5 C.P.C. (6th) 84, 19 C.C.L.I. (4th) 51 (S.C.J.)

The court refused to certify a misrepresentation case regarding life insurance premiums.

McNaughton Automotive Ltd. v. Co-operators General Insurance Co., 66 O.R. (3d) 466, (sub nom. *Segnitz v. Royal & Sun Alliance Insurance Co. of*

Canada) [2003] O.J. No. 3267, 2003 CarswellOnt 3181, [2003] I.L.R. I-4249, 10 C.C.L.I. (4th) 258, 47 C.P.C. (5th) 370 (S.C.J); additional reasons at 49 C.P.C. (5th) 383, 2003 CarswellOnt 4323, [2003] O.J. No. 4168, 10 C.C.L.I. (4th) 273, [2003] I.L.R. I-4250 (S.C.J)

The court certified a claim based on breach of a statutory condition in an automobile insurance policy.

Kumar v. Mutual Life Assurance Co. of Canada, 2003 CarswellOnt 1209, [2003] O.J. No. 1160, [2003] I.L.R. I-4181, 31 C.P.C. (5th) 205, 47 C.C.L.I. (3d) 43, 170 O.A.C. 165, 226 D.L.R. (4th) 112 (C.A.); additional reasons at (April 16, 2003), Doc. CA C37858, 2003 CarswellOnt 1444 (C.A.); leave to appeal refused (2004), 2004 CarswellOnt 238, 2004 CarswellOnt 239, (sub nom. *Williams v. Mutual Life Assurance Co. of Canada)* 328 N.R. 197 (note), (sub nom. *Williams v. Mutual Life Assurance Co. of Canada)* 195 O.A.C. 195 (note) (S.C.C.)

The court refused to certify a "vanishing premium" life insurance case where litigation of the individual issues would result in no costs savings for the class members.

MacRae v. Mutual of Omaha Insurance Co. (2000), 2 C.P.C. (5th) 121, 2000 CarswellOnt 2473, (sub nom. *MaCrae v. Mutual of Omaha Insurance Co.)* [2001] I.L.R. I-3890 (S.C.J.)

The court certified a claim and approved a settlement regarding alleged misrepresentations in the marketing of life insurance policies.

Williams v. Mutual Life Assurance Co. of Canada (2000), 51 O.R. (3d) 54, [2001] I.L.R. I-3896, 24 C.C.L.I. (3d) 298, 2000 CarswellOnt 3739, [2000] O.J. No. 3821 (S.C.J.); additional reasons at (2001), 2001 CarswellOnt 370, (sub nom. *Kumar v. Mutual Life Assurance Co. of Canada)* [2001] O.J. No. 445, 27 C.C.L.I. (3d) 256, 6 C.P.C. (5th) 194 (S.C.J.)

The court refused to certify a "vanishing premium" life insurance case. Certifying negligent misrepresentation claims is very problematic.

S.R. Gent (Canada) Inc. v. Ontario (Workplace Safety & Insurance Board) (1999), 45 O.R. (3d) 106, 46 C.C.E.L. (2d) 273, 43 C.P.C. (4th) 176, 1999 CarswellOnt 2858 (S.C.J.)

The court denied certification of a claim regarding retroactive premiums imposed by the Workplace Safety and Insurance Board where an application for judicial review was the preferable procedure.

Dabbs v. Sun Life Assurance Co. of Canada (1998), 40 O.R. (3d) 429, 22 C.P.C. (4th) 381, 5 C.C.L.I. (3d) 18, [1998] I.L.R. I-3575, 1998 CarswellOnt 2758, [1998] O.J. No. 2811 (Gen. Div.); additional reasons at (1998), 47 C.P.C. (4th) 105, 22 C.C.L.I. (3d) 198, 1998 CarswellOnt 5915 (Gen. Div.); set aside/quashed (1998), 41 O.R. (3d) 97, 165 D.L.R. (4th) 482, [1999] I.L.R. I-3629, 113 O.A.C. 307, 7 C.C.L.I. (3d) 38, 27 C.P.C. (4th) 243, 1998 CarswellOnt 3539, [1998] O.J. No. 3622 (C.A.);

leave to appeal refused (1998), 235 N.R. 390 (note), 118 O.A.C. 399 (note) (S.C.C.)

The court certified a "vanishing premium" class action against a life insurer based on alleged misrepresentations by its agents as to future investment performance.

Disposition of Certification Motions — Intellectual Property

Keatley Surveying Ltd. v. Teranet Inc., 2015 ONCA 248, 2015 CarswellOnt 5147, 125 O.R. (3d) 447, 66 C.P.C. (7th) 223, 384 D.L.R. (4th) 147, 331 O.A.C. 324, [2015] O.J. No. 1828

The court certified a claim for copyright infringement of surveys filed in land registry offices which the defendant copied and sold to the public.

Waldman v. Thomson Reuters Corp., 2012 ONSC 1138, 2012 CarswellOnt 2225, 99 C.P.R. (4th) 303, 22 C.P.C. (7th) 33, [2012] O.J. No. 792 (S.C.J.); leave to appeal refused 2012 ONSC 3436, 2012 CarswellOnt 7472 (Div. Ct.)

The court certified a copyright infringement claim regarding distributing copies of documents authored by lawyers and filed in court files.

Robertson v. Thomson Corp. (1999), 171 D.L.R. (4th) 171, 85 C.P.R. (3d) 1, 43 O.R. (3d) 161, 30 C.P.C. (4th) 182, 1999 CarswellOnt 301, [1999] O.J. No. 280 (Gen. Div.); additional reasons at (1999), 43 O.R. (3d) 389, 43 C.P.C. (4th) 166, 1999 CarswellOnt 2822 (Gen. Div.)

The court certified a claim for infringement of copyright through electronic media.

Disposition of Certification Motions — Mass Torts

Da Silva v. 2162095 Ontario Ltd., 2016 ONSC 2069, 2016 CarswellOnt 7324 (S.C.J.)

The court certified a claim by customers of a self-storage facility for negligence in failing to have a functioning sprinkler system.

Carillo v. Vinen Atlantic S.A., 2014 ONSC 5269, 2014 CarswellOnt 12436, 62 C.P.C. (7th) 90 (S.C.J.)

The court certified this fire claim by residents of an apartment building.

Durling v. Sunrise Propane Energy Group Inc., 2014 ONSC 1041, 2014 CarswellOnt 2028, 81 C.E.L.R. (3d) 341, 40 R.P.R. (5th) 223 (Div. Ct.)

The court certified this claim against the landlords of a propane handling business where explosions and fires occurred.

Quinte v. Eastwood Mall Inc., 2014 ONSC 249, 2014 CarswellOnt 1826, 59 C.P.C. (7th) 301 (S.C.J.); additional reasons 2014 ONSC 1661, 2014 CarswellOnt 4202, 59 C.P.C. (7th) 321 (S.C.J.)

The court certified this claim arising from the collapse of a roof-top parking lot.

Plaunt v. Renfrew Power Generation Inc., 2011 ONSC 4087, 2011 CarswellOnt 5648, 7 R.P.R. (5th) 304, 13 C.P.C. (7th) 173, 63 C.E.L.R. (3d) 173, [2011] O.J. No. 2995 (S.C.J.); additional reasons 2011 ONSC 5777, 2011 CarswellOnt 10267, 13 C.P.C. (7th) 203, 63 C.E.L.R. (3d) 203 (S.C.J.)

The court certified a claim for flooding caused by operation of a dam.

Durling v. Sunrise Propane Energy Group Inc., 2011 ONSC 7506, 2011 CarswellOnt 14414, [2011] O.J. No. 5806 (S.C.J.)

The court refused a consent certification of this claim arising from a propane explosion because one of the consent terms barred the claims of class members who did not register within six months after certification.

Charmley v. Deltera Construction Ltd., 2010 ONSC 7153, 2010 CarswellOnt 9818, 8 C.P.C. (7th) 61, 97 C.L.R. (3d) 264 (S.C.J.)

The court certified a claim arising out of an explosion and fire.

Maggisano v. Skyservice Airlines Inc., 2010 ONSC 6203, 2010 CarswellOnt 8536, 6 C.P.C. (7th) 394 (S.C.J.)

The court certified a claim arising from a hard landing of an airplane in the Dominican Republic.

DeFazio v. Ontario (Ministry of Labour) (2007), 2007 CarswellOnt 8314, 49 C.P.C. (6th) 144, 232 O.A.C. 48 (Div. Ct.); additional reasons at (2008), 2008 CarswellOnt 533, 53 C.P.C. (6th) 192 (Div. Ct.)

The court refused to certify a claim for exposure to asbestos dust during construction at the Sheppard subway station.

Politzer v. 170498 Canada Inc. (2005), 2005 CarswellOnt 7035, 20 C.P.C. (6th) 288, 39 R.P.R. (4th) 90 (S.C.J.)

The court certified a claim by residents of an apartment building for damages arising from a burst water pipe.

Pearson v. Inco Ltd. (2005), 2005 CarswellOnt 6598, 205 O.A.C. 30, 78 O.R. (3d) 641, [2005] O.J. No. 4918, 261 D.L.R. (4th) 629, 20 C.E.L.R. (3d) 258, 43 R.P.R. (4th) 43, 18 C.P.C. (6th) 77 (C.A.); additional reasons at (2006), 2006 CarswellOnt 1527, 20 C.E.L.R. (3d) 292, 208 O.A.C. 284, 25 C.P.C. (6th) 1, 79 O.R. (3d) 427, [2006] O.J. No. 991, 267 D.L.R. (4th) 111 (C.A.); leave to appeal refused (June 29, 2006), Doc. 31249, 2006 CarswellOnt 4020, 2006 CarswellOnt 4021 (S.C.C.)

The court certified a claim for devaluation of real property values resulting from pollution caused by the defendant.

Ludwig v.1099029 Ontario Ltd. (2004), 4 C.P.C. (6th) 251, 2004 CarswellOnt 4516 (S.C.J.)

The court certified a claim for damages by neighbours of a manufacturing facility which caught fire.

Nunes v. Air Transat A.T. Inc. (February 28, 2003), Doc. 01-CV-217295CP, [2003] O.J. No. 2006, 2003 CarswellOnt 5856 (S.C.J.)

The court adjourned a motion to certify claims arising from an emergency landing to deal with certain details, but indicated certification would be granted.

Hollick v. Metropolitan Toronto (Municipality), (sub nom. *Hollick v. Toronto (City)*) 2001 SCC 68, [2001] S.C.J. No. 67, 2001 CarswellOnt 3577, 2001 CarswellOnt 3578, (sub nom. *Hollick v. Toronto (City)*) 205 D.L.R. (4th) 19, (sub nom. *Hollick v. Toronto (City)*) 56 O.R. (3d) 214 (headnote only), 24 M.P.L.R. (3d) 9, 277 N.R. 51, 13 C.P.C. (5th) 1, 42 C.E.L.R. (N.S.) 26, 153 O.A.C. 279, (sub nom. *Hollick v. Toronto (City)*) [2001] 3 S.C.R. 158

The court refused to certify this environmental action where a pre-existing no-fault small claims trust fund administered by the Ministry of the Environment was available to satisfy the class members' claims.

Bywater v. Toronto Transit Commission (1998), 27 C.P.C. (4th) 172, 1998 CarswellOnt 4645, [1998] O.J. No. 4913 (Gen. Div.); additional reasons at (1999), 30 C.P.C. (4th) 131, 1999 CarswellOnt 201, [1999] O.J. No. 67 (Gen. Div.)

The court certified a claim for damages arising from a fire in a subway system.

Disposition of Certification Motions — Pharmaceuticals

Batten v. Boehringer Ingelheim (Canada) Ltd., 2017 ONSC 6098, 2017 CarswellOnt 17148 (Div. Ct.)

The court refused to certify this claim regarding the drug Pradaxa.

Norman v. Thunder Bay Regional Health Sciences Centre, 2015 ONSC 3252, 2015 CarswellOnt 10287, 74 C.P.C. (7th) 184 (S.C.J.)

The court refused to certify a claim regarding the chemotherapy drug Taxotere.

Waheed v. Pfizer Canada Inc., 2011 ONSC 5057, 2011 CarswellOnt 8634 (S.C.J.)

For settlement purposes, the court certified claims regarding the drugs Bextra and Celebrex.

Schick v. Boehringer Ingelheim (Canada) Ltd., 2011 ONSC 1942, 2011 CarswellOnt 2096, 18 C.P.C. (7th) 128, [2011] O.J. No. 1381 (S.C.J.)

The court certified a product liability claim regarding the drug Mirapex.

Goodridge v. Pfizer Canada, 2010 CarswellOnt 896, 2010 ONSC 1095, [2010] O.J. No. 655, 101 O.R. (3d) 202, 85 C.P.C. (6th) 267, 73 C.C.L.T. (3d) 211 (S.C.J.)

The court certified some claims regarding the drug gabapentin, but refused to certify claims based on the defendant promoting "off label" uses for the drug and based on other companies manufacturing and marketing generic gabapentin.

Heward v. Eli Lilly & Co. (2007), 2007 CarswellOnt 611, [2007] O.J. No. 404, 39 C.P.C. (6th) 153, 47 C.C.L.T. (3d) 114 (S.C.J.); leave to appeal allowed (2007), 2007 CarswellOnt 4363, [2007] O.J. No. 2709, 51 C.C.L.T. (3d) 167, 45 C.P.C. (6th) 309 (S.C.J.); affirmed (2008), [2008] O.J. No. 2610, 2008 CarswellOnt 3837, 56 C.P.C. (6th) 309, 91 O.R. (3d) 691, 239 O.A.C. 273, 295 D.L.R. (4th) 175, 58 C.C.L.T. (3d) 99 (Div. Ct.)

The court certified a claim regarding side effects of the anti-psychotic drug Zyprexa.

Boulanger v. Johnson & Johnson Corp. (2007), 2007 CarswellOnt 252, [2007] O.J. No. 179, 40 C.P.C. (6th) 170 (S.C.J.); additional reasons at (May 23, 2007), Doc. 00-CV-197409CP, 2007 CarswellOnt 3238 (S.C.J.); leave to appeal refused (May 16, 2007), Doc. 56/07, [2007] O.J. No. 1991, 2007 CarswellOnt 3360 (Div. Ct.); leave to appeal refused (September 13, 2007), Doc. D56/07, 2007 CarswellOnt 6100 (Div. Ct.); further additional reasons at (July 11, 2007), Doc. 00-CV-197409CP, 2007 CarswellOnt 4454, [2007] O.J. No. 2766 (S.C.J.)

The court certified a claim regarding side effects of the drug Prepulsid.

Wilson v. Servier Canada Inc. (2000), 50 O.R. (3d) 219, 49 C.P.C. (4th) 233, 2000 CarswellOnt 3257, [2000] O.J. No. 3392 (S.C.J.); leave to appeal refused (2000), 52 O.R. (3d) 20, 2000 CarswellOnt 4399, 143 O.A.C. 279 (Div. Ct.); leave to appeal refused (2001), 2001 CarswellOnt 3077, 2001 CarswellOnt 3078, [2001] S.C.C.A. No. 88, 276 N.R. 197 (note), 154 O.A.C. 198 (note)

A national class was certified in this class action against the Ontario distributor of a weight loss pill and its French parent.

Disposition of Certification Motions — Product Liability

Bennett v. Lenovo (Canada) Inc., 2017 ONSC 5853, 2017 CarswellOnt 15375 (S.C.J.); additional reasons 2017 ONSC 6839, 2017 CarswellOnt 18122 (S.C.J.)

The court certified this claim for defective computers.

Kaira v. Mercedes Benz, 2017 ONSC 3795, 2017 CarswellOnt 10042, 15 C.E.L.R. (4th) 145 (S.C.J.); additional reasons 2017 ONSC 4692, 2017 CarswellOnt 12008, 15 C.E.L.R. (4th) 172 (S.C.J.)

The court certified this claim for defeat devices in automobiles' emission control systems.

Vester v. Boston Scientific Ltd., 2017 ONSC 1095, 2017 CarswellOnt 2324, 97 C.P.C. (7th) 236 (S.C.J.)

The court certified this claim against the manufacturer of allegedly defective transvaginal mesh medical devices.

Quenneville v. Volkswagen Group Canada Inc., 2016 ONSC 7959, 2016 CarswellOnt 20027, 6 C.E.L.R. (4th) 109, 5 C.P.C. (8th) 338 (S.C.J.)

For settlement purposes, the court certified a national class action regarding "defeat devices" installed in automobiles.

1688782 Ontario Inc. v. Maple Leaf Foods Inc., 2016 ONSC 4233, 2016 CarswellOnt 16995 (S.C.J.); additional reasons 2017 ONSC 4612, 2017 CarswellOnt 12269 (S.C.J.)

The court certified a claim by franchisees of a restaurant chain against a supplier who provided meat contaminated with listeria.

Dine v. Biomet Inc., 2015 ONSC 7050, 2015 CarswellOnt 19419 (S.C.J.); additional reasons 2016 ONSC 857, 2016 CarswellOnt 1750 (S.C.J.); leave to appeal refused 2016 ONSC 4039, 2016 CarswellOnt 9694, 132 O.R. (3d) 605 (Div. Ct.)

The court certified this claim for defective hip implants.

Paus v. Concord Adex Developments Corp., 2015 ONSC 5122, 2015 CarswellOnt 12416, 78 C.P.C. (7th) 136 (S.C.J.)

On consent the court certified this claim regarding defective balconies in condominium units.

Harper v. American Medical Systems Canada Inc., 2015 ONSC 3434, 2015 CarswellOnt 7877, 74 C.P.C. (7th) 424 (S.C.J.)

On consent, the court certified this claim regarding a transvaginal mesh and approved a notice program.

McSherry v. Zimmer GMBH, 2014 ONSC 5527, 2014 CarswellOnt 12988, 69 C.P.C. (7th) 399 (S.C.J.)

On consent the court certified this products liability claim.

Arora v. Whirlpool Canada LP, 2013 ONCA 657, 2013 CarswellOnt 15260, 118 O.R. (3d) 113, 19 B.L.R. (5th) 279, 6 C.C.L.T. (4th) 1, 44 C.P.C. (7th) 223, 370 D.L.R. (4th) 59, 311 O.A.C. 203; leave to appeal refused

2014 CarswellOnt 3031, 2014 CarswellOnt 3032, 473 N.R. 387 (note), [2013] S.C.C.A. No. 498 (S.C.C.)

The court refused to certify a claim for poorly designed washing machines.

Nolevaux v. King and John Festival Corp., 2013 ONSC 5451, 2013 ONSC 5525, 2013 ONSC 5526, 2013 CarswellOnt 13729 (S.C.J.)

The court certified this claim for falling balcony glass from a Toronto condominium tower.

Crisante v. DePuy Orthopaedics Inc., 2013 ONSC 5186, 2013 CarswellOnt 11831, 56 C.P.C. (7th) 162 (S.C.J.); additional reasons 2013 ONSC 6351, 2013 CarswellOnt 15417, 57 C.P.C. (7th) 399 (S.C.J.)

The court certified a claim regarding defective hip replacement implants.

Williams v. Canon Canada Inc., 2012 ONSC 3692, 2012 CarswellOnt 8439, 34 C.P.C. (7th) 403, 294 O.A.C. 251, [2012] O.J. No. 3120 (Div. Ct.)

The court refused to certify a claim for defective cameras where the common issue requirement was not satisfied.

Toronto Community Housing Corp. v. Thyssenrkupp Elevator (Canada) Ltd., 2011 ONSC 4914, 2011 CarswellOnt 8341, [2011] O.J. No. 3746, 19 C.P.C. (7th) 280 (S.C.J.); additional reasons 2011 ONSC 7588, 2011 CarswellOnt 14476, 19 C.P.C. (7th) 352, [2011] O.J. No. 5866 (S.C.J.); leave to appeal refused 2012 ONSC 225, 2012 CarswellOnt 504, 19 C.P.C. (7th) 364, [2012] O.J. No. 143 (Div. Ct.)

The court certified a claim for a defective elevator braking device.

Ducharme v. Solarium de Paris Inc., 2010 ONSC 5667, 2010 CarswellOnt 7852, 98 C.P.C. (6th) 386, [2010] O.J. No. 4436, 98 C.P.C. (6th) 386 (S.C.J.)

The court certified a class action involving the design, manufacture and sale of solariums.

Singer v. Schering-Plough Canada Inc., 2010 ONSC 42, 2010 CarswellOnt 79, [2010] O.J. No. 113, 87 C.P.C. (6th) 276 (S.C.J.); additional reasons 2010 ONSC 1737, 2010 CarswellOnt 1820, [2010] O.J. No. 1243, 87 C.P.C. (6th) 345 (S.C.J.)

The court refused to certify a class proceeding relating to alleged faulty labelling of sun screen products.

Robinson v. Medtronic, 80 C.P.C. (6th) 87, 2009 CarswellOnt 6337, [2009] O.J. No. 4366 (S.C.J.); affirmed 79 C.C.L.T. (3d) 26, 267 O.A.C. 126, [2010] O.J. No. 3056, 2010 ONSC 3777, 2010 CarswellOnt 5221, 97 C.P.C. (6th) 392 (Div. Ct.)

The court certified a claim regarding defective components of implantable heart defibrillators.

Lambert v. Guidant Corp. (2009), [2009] O.J. No. 1910, 2009 CarswellOnt 2535, 72 C.P.C. (6th) 120 (S.C.J.); leave to appeal refused (2009), [2009] O.J. No. 4464, 2009 CarswellOnt 6512 (Div. Ct.)

The court certified a claim for defective pacemakers.

Ronald Smith & Associates Inc. v. Intuit Canada (2009), 78 C.P.C. (6th) 49, 2009 CarswellOnt 1333 (S.C.J.)

The court certified a claim for defective computer software which allegedly caused the deletion of data.

Griffin v. Dell Canada Inc., 2009 CarswellOnt 560, [2009] O.J. No. 418, 72 C.P.C. (6th) 158 (S.C.J.); affirmed 2009 CarswellOnt 2085, [2009] O.J. No. 1592, 76 C.P.C. (6th) 173, 64 B.L.R. (4th) 186 (S.C.J.); affirmed 2010 ONCA 29, 2010 CarswellOnt 177, [2010] O.J. No. 177, 98 O.R. (3d) 481, 315 D.L.R. (4th) 723, 259 O.A.C. 108, 64 B.L.R. (4th) 199, 80 C.P.C. (6th) 154 (C.A.); additional reasons at 2010 ONCA 164, 2010 CarswellOnt 1192 (C.A.); leave to appeal refused 2010 CarswellOnt 3417, 2010 CarswellOnt 3418, 275 O.A.C. 398 (note), [2010] S.C.C.A. No. 75, 409 N.R. 378 (note) (S.C.C.); leave to appeal refused (July 31, 2009), Doc. Toronto 271/09, 2009 CarswellOnt 4742, [2009] O.J. No. 3438 (Div. Ct.)

The court certified this claim for defective computers despite arbitration provisions in the sale contracts.

Poulin v. Ford Motor Co. of Canada Ltd./Ford du Canada Ltée (2008), [2008] O.J. No. 4153, 2008 CarswellOnt 6184, 301 D.L.R. (4th) 610, 65 C.P.C. (6th) 247, 242 O.A.C. 209 (Div. Ct.) (Div. Ct.)

The court refused to certify a claim alleging defects in door latch mechanisms of certain vehicles.

Attis v. Canada (Minister of Health), 93 O.R. (3d) 35, [2008] O.J. No. 3766, 2008 ONCA 660, 2008 CarswellOnt 5661, 300 D.L.R. (4th) 415, 254 O.A.C. 91, 59 C.P.C. (6th) 195 (C.A.); leave to appeal refused 2009 CarswellOnt 2343, 2009 CarswellOnt 2344, [2008] S.C.C.A. No. 491, [2009] 1 S.C.R. v (note), 396 N.R. 397 (note)

The court refused to certify a claim against the federal government for failing to properly regulate breast implants where the statement of claim failed to disclose a cause of action.

Ragoonanan Estate v. Imperial Tobacco Canada Ltd. (2008), [2008] O.J. No. 1644, 2008 CarswellOnt 2399, (sub nom. *Ragoonanan v. Imperial Tobacco Canada Ltd.)* 236 O.A.C. 199, 54 C.P.C. (6th) 167 (Div. Ct.); additional reasons at (2009), 2009 CarswellOnt 609, 71 C.P.C. (6th) 394 (Div. Ct.)

The court refused to certify a claim regarding cigarettes starting fires where the class definition was fatally merit-based, a class action was not the preferable procedure, and the litigation plan was not satisfactory.

LeFrancois v. Guidant Corp. (2008), [2008] O.J. No. 1397, 2008 CarswellOnt 2073, 56 C.P.C. (6th) 268 (S.C.J.); additional reasons at (2008), 2008 CarswellOnt 3566, 65 C.P.C. (6th) 32, [2008] O.J. No. 2402 (S.C.J.); leave to appeal refused (2009), 2009 CarswellOnt 30, [2009] O.J. No. 36, (sub nom. *Guidant Corp. v. LeFrancois)* 245 O.A.C. 213, 67 C.P.C. (6th) 9 (Div. Ct.); additional reasons at (2008), 2008 CarswellOnt 5201, [2008] O.J. No. 3459 further (S.C.J.)

The court certified a claim regarding defective defibrillators.

Taylor v. Canada (Minister of Health) (2007), 49 C.P.C. (6th) 36, [2007] O.J. No. 3312, 2007 CarswellOnt 5541, 285 D.L.R. (4th) 296 (S.C.J.); leave to appeal refused (2007), 2007 CarswellOnt 8122, (sub nom. *Taylor v. Canada (Attorney General))* 233 O.A.C. 111, 289 D.L.R. (4th) 567 (Div. Ct.)

The court certified a claim regarding the federal government's actions concerning the importation, sale and distribution of TMJ implants.

Peter v. Medtronic Inc. (2007), 2007 CarswellOnt 7975, [2007] O.J. No. 4828, 50 C.P.C. (6th) 133 (S.C.J.); additional reasons at (2008), 2008 CarswellOnt 2475, [2008] O.J. No. 1700, 65 C.P.C. (6th) 23 (S.C.J.); leave to appeal refused (2008), 2008 CarswellOnt 2759, [2008] O.J. No. 1916, 55 C.P.C. (6th) 242 (Div. Ct.)

The court certified a claim regarding defective batteries in implanted medical devices.

Bondy v. Toshiba of Canada Ltd. (2007), [2007] O.J. No. 784, 39 C.P.C. (6th) 339, 2007 CarswellOnt 1419 (S.C.J.)

The court certified a claim regarding allegedly defective notebook computers.

Caputo v. Imperial Tobacco Ltd. (2004), 2004 CarswellOnt 423, [2004] O.J. No. 299, 236 D.L.R. (4th) 348, 42 B.L.R. (3d) 276, 22 C.C.L.T. (3d) 261, 44 C.P.C. (5th) 350 (S.C.J.); additional reasons at (2005), 2005 CarswellOnt 856, [2005] O.J. No. 842, 74 O.R. (3d) 728, 9 C.P.C. (6th) 175, 250 D.L.R. (4th) 756 (S.C.J.)

The court refused to certify this tobacco class action.

Andersen v. St. Jude Medical Inc. (2003), [2003] O.J. No. 3556, 2003 CarswellOnt 3478, 38 C.P.C. (5th) 122, 67 O.R. (3d) 136 (S.C.J.); additional reasons at (2004), [2004] O.J. No. 132, 2004 CarswellOnt 136, 48 C.P.C. (5th) 312 (S.C.J.); leave to appeal refused (January 28, 2005), Doc. Toronto 191/04, 192/04, 2005 CarswellOnt 318 (Div. Ct.)

The court certified an action based on allegedly defective mechanical heart valves.

Knowles v. Wyeth-Ayerst Canada Inc. (May 14, 2001), Doc. 33778, 2001 CarswellOnt 1623, [2001] O.J. No. 1812 (S.C.J.); additional reasons at

(July 11, 2001), Doc. 00-CP-33778, 2001 CarswellOnt 2549, [2001] O.J. No. 2881 (S.C.J.)

The court conditionally certified this product liability case for settlement purposes.

Bunn v. Ribcor Holdings Inc. (1998), [1998] O.J. No. 1790, 20 C.P.C. (4th) 145, 1998 CarswellOnt 2033 (Gen. Div.)

The court certified a claim by a class of subdivision purchasers against the developer and the municipality arising from defects in the homes.

Nantais v. Telectronics Proprietary (Canada) Ltd. (1995), 25 O.R. (3d) 331, 40 C.P.C. (3d) 245, 127 D.L.R. (4th) 552 (Gen. Div.); leave to appeal refused 25 O.R. (3d) 331 at 347, 40 C.P.C. (3d) 263, 129 D.L.R. (4th) 110 (Gen. Div.)

The court certified a class action on behalf of the recipients of allegedly defective pacemakers.

Bendall v. McGhan Medical Corp. (1993), 14 O.R. (3d) 734, 16 C.P.C. (3d) 156, 106 D.L.R. (4th) 339 (Gen. Div.)

A class action commenced on behalf of persons who had received silicone gel breast implants was certified as a class proceeding. A large number of women would not be able to access the judicial system except by way of class action, and the cost of individual litigation would be prohibitive. A class action would avoid that problem because of the system of regulated contingent fees.

Disposition of Certification Motions — Professional Negligence

Green v. The Hospital for Sick Children, 2017 ONSC 6545, 2017 CarswellOnt 16865, 14 C.P.C. (8th) 311 (S.C.J.)

The court refused to certify this claim for negligent laboratory tests.

Excalibur Special Opportunities LP v. Schwartz Levitsky Feldman LLP, 2016 ONCA 916, 2016 CarswellOnt 19121, 135 O.R. (3d) 743, 66 B.L.R. (5th) 1, 95 C.P.C. (7th) 284, 406 D.L.R. (4th) 201; leave to appeal refused (June 8, 2017), Doc. 37436, 2017 CarswellOnt 8835, 2017 CarswellOnt 8836, [2017] S.C.C.A. No. 54

The court certified a claim for a negligent audit report.

Lipson v. Cassels Brock & Blackwell LLP, 2013 ONCA 165, 2013 CarswellOnt 2953, 114 O.R. (3d) 481, 31 C.P.C. (7th) 128, [2013] 4 C.T.C. 116, 360 D.L.R. (4th) 577, 303 O.A.C. 124, [2013] O.J. No. 1195; additional reasons 2013 ONCA 391, 2013 CarswellOnt 7677

The court certified a claim for negligent tax advice.

Trillium Motor World Ltd. v. General Motors of Canada Ltd., 2012 ONSC 463, 2012 CarswellOnt 4166, 92 C.C.L.T. (3d) 193, 37 C.P.C. (7th) 19, [2012] O.J. No. 1578 (S.C.J.)

The court certified a claim regarding termination of automobile dealership franchises.

Jean-Marie v. Green (2000), 13 C.P.C. (5th) 173, 2000 CarswellOnt 3976 (S.C.J.)

The court refused to certify a class proceeding against a lawyer for negligence as the statement of claim disclosed no cause of action.

Delgrosso v. Paul (1999), 45 O.R. (3d) 605, 48 C.C.L.T. (2d) 315, 41 C.P.C. (4th) 390, 1999 CarswellOnt 4561 (Gen. Div.); leave to appeal refused (1999), 46 C.P.C. (4th) 140, 1999 CarswellOnt 4562 (Div. Ct.)

The court certified an action against a solicitor by a class of mortgage investors.

Disposition of Certification Motions — Securities/Investors Rights

Barkley v. Tier 1 Capital Management Inc., 2018 ONSC 1956, 2018 CarswellOnt 4767 (S.C.J.)

The court certified this claim by investors in a syndicated mortgage arrangement.

LBP Holdings Ltd. v. Hycroft Mining Corporation, 2017 ONSC 6342, 2017 CarswellOnt 16283 (S.C.J.)

The court certified this securities claim against some but not all defendants.

Mask v. Silvercorp Metals Inc., 2016 ONCA 641, 2016 CarswellOnt 13364, 132 O.R. (3d) 161, 408 D.L.R. (4th) 706, 352 O.A.C. 380

Having refused leave under s. 138.8 of the *Securities Act*, the court refused to certify common law misrepresentation and negligence claims.

Fantl v. Transamerica Life Canada, 2016 ONCA 633, 2016 CarswellOnt 13309, 133 O.R. (3d) 422, 59 C.C.L.I. (5th) 88, 89 C.P.C. (7th) 1, 351 O.A.C. 326; leave to appeal refused (February 23, 2017), Doc. 37258, 2017 CarswellOnt 2686, 2017 CarswellOnt 2687 (S.C.C.)

The court certified a negligent misrepresentation claim on behalf of a class of investors. Such claims are not necessarily unsuitable for certification.

Swisscanto Fondsleitung AG v. BlackBerry Ltd., 2016 ONSC 534, 2016 CarswellOnt 960, 90 C.P.C. (7th) 386 (S.C.J.)

The court certified a claim for misrepresentations in financial statements.

Canadian Imperial Bank of Commerce v. Green, 2015 CSC 60, 2015 SCC 60, 2015 CarswellOnt 18335, 2015 CarswellOnt 18336, [2015] 3 S.C.R. 801,

135 O.R. (3d) 334 (note), 44 B.L.R. (5th) 1, 77 C.P.C. (7th) 1, 391 D.L.R. (4th) 567, 478 N.R. 202, 346 O.A.C. 204, [2015] S.C.J. No. 60

The court discussed when claims under s. 138.3 of the *Ontario Securities Act* should be certified.

Coffin v. Atlantic Power Corp., 2015 ONSC 3686, 2015 CarswellOnt 11280, 127 O.R. (3d) 199, 77 C.P.C. (7th) 324 (S.C.J.)

The court refused to certify this securities claim by shareholders and debenture holders, but permitted the debenture holders to reconstitute their claim.

Labourers' Pension Fund of Central and Eastern Canada (Trustees of) v. Sino-Forest Corp., 2015 ONSC 439, 2015 CarswellOnt 621, 124 O.R. (3d) 687 (S.C.J.)

The court certified a securities class action alleging negligent misrepresentations made in the defendants' public disclosure documents.

Abdula v. Canadian Solar Inc., 2015 ONSC 53, 2015 CarswellOnt 183, 126 O.R. (3d) 459 (S.C.J.); additional reasons 2015 ONSC 1421, 2015 CarswellOnt 3055 (S.C.J.); affirmed 2015 ONSC 4322, 2015 CarswellOnt 10244, 46 B.L.R. (5th) 222 (S.C.J.)

The court certified the claims for negligent misrepresentation and for statutory misrepresentation pursuant to Part XXIII.1 of the *Securities Act*, R.S.O. 1990, c. S.5.

Fantl v. Transamerica Life Canada, 2015 ONSC 1367, 2015 CarswellOnt 3067, 125 O.R. (3d) 230, 46 C.C.L.I. (5th) 30, 71 C.P.C. (7th) 56, 331 O.A.C. 358 (Div. Ct.); additional reasons 2015 ONSC 2917, 2015 CarswellOnt 7060, 73 C.P.C. (7th) 384 (Div. Ct.); affirmed 2016 ONCA 633, 2016 CarswellOnt 13309, 133 O.R. (3d) 422, 59 C.C.L.I. (5th) 88, 89 C.P.C. (7th) 1, 351 O.A.C. 326; leave to appeal refused (February 23, 2017), Doc. 37258, 2017 CarswellOnt 2686, 2017 CarswellOnt 2687 (S.C.C.)

The court certified a negligent misrepresentation claim on behalf of a class of investors.

Musicians' Pension Fund of Canada (Trustee of) v. Kinross Gold Corp., 2014 ONCA 901, 2014 CarswellOnt 17766, 61 C.P.C. (7th) 1, (sub nom. *Bayens v. Kinross Gold Corp.)* 327 O.A.C. 156

The court refused to certify this securities claim based on common law negligent misrepresentation. Generally such claims are not suitable for certification.

Millwright Regional Council of Ontario Pension Trust Fund (Trustees of) v. Celestica Inc., 2014 ONSC 1057, 2014 CarswellOnt 1872, 49 C.P.C. (7th) 12, [2014] O.J. No. 744 (S.C.J.)

The court certified a misrepresentation claim in this securities case.

Fischer v. IG Investment Management Ltd., 2013 SCC 69, 2013 CarswellOnt 17258, 2013 CarswellOnt 17259, (sub nom. *AIC Limited v. Fischer)* [2013] 3 S.C.R. 949, 45 C.P.C. (7th) 227, 366 D.L.R. (4th) 1, 482 N.R. 80, 312 O.A.C. 128, [2013] S.C.J. No. 69

The court certified this market timing class action despite a related Ontario Securities Commission proceeding.

Tucci v. Smart Technologies Inc., 2013 ONSC 802, 2013 CarswellOnt 1122, 114 O.R. (3d) 294, 11 B.L.R. (5th) 319 (S.C.J.)

The court certified this securities class action but revised the class definition.

Musicians' Pension Fund of Canada (Trustee of) v. Kinross Gold Corp., 2013 ONSC 6864, 2013 CarswellOnt 15676, 20 B.L.R. (5th) 284, 45 C.P.C. (7th) 371, [2013] O.J. No. 5071 (S.C.J.); affirmed 2014 ONCA 901, 2014 CarswellOnt 17766, 61 C.P.C. (7th) 1, (sub nom. *Bayens v. Kinross Gold Corp.)* 327 O.A.C. 156

The court refused leave under Part XXIII.1 of the Ontario *Securities Act* to bring a misrepresentation claim, and therefore refused to certify the claim.

Ironworkers Ontario Pension Fund (Trustee of) v. Manulife Financial Corp., 2013 ONSC 4083, 2013 CarswellOnt 10277, 44 C.P.C. (7th) 80, [2013] O.J. No. 3455 (S.C.J.); additional reasons 2013 ONSC 6354, 2013 CarswellOnt 15419, [2013] O.J. No. 5088 (S.C.J.)

The court certified this securities claim, and gave leave under s. 138 of the *Securities Act*.

Ivany v. Financiere Telco Inc., 2013 ONSC 6347, 2013 CarswellOnt 5402, 41 C.P.C. (7th) 249 (S.C.J.); leave to appeal refused 2013 ONSC 6969, 2013 CarswellOnt 15506 (S.C.J.)

The court certified this claim arising from a failed investment scheme regarding tax-free withdrawal from RSPs.

AFA Livförsäkringsaktiebolag v. Agnico-Eagle Mines Ltd., 2013 ONSC 2290, 2013 CarswellOnt 4524, 51 C.P.C. (7th) 202 (S.C.J.)

On consent, the court certified this securities claim and granted leave under Part XXIII.1 of the Ontario *Securities Act.*

Drywall Acoustic Lathing and Insulation Local 675 Pension Fund (Trustees) v. SNC-Lavelin Group Inc., 2012 ONSC 5288, 2012 CarswellOnt 11520, 112 O.R. (3d) 569, 41 C.P.C. (7th) 375, [2012] O.J. No. 4389 (S.C.J.)

On an unopposed motion, the court certified this securities class action, granted leave under Part XXIII.1 of the *Securities Act*, and gave leave to discontinue certain claims.

Pardham v. Bank of Montreal, 2012 ONSC 4681, 2012 CarswellOnt 9946, 96 C.C.L.T. (3d) 260, 26 C.P.C. (7th) 186 (S.C.J.)

The court certified a claim for investment fraud.

Green v. Canadian Imperial Bank of Commerce, 2012 ONSC 3637, 2012 CarswellOnt 8382, 29 C.P.C. (7th) 225, [2012] O.J. No. 3072 (S.C.J.); reversed 2014 ONCA 90, 2014 CarswellOnt 1143, (sub nom. *Millwright Regional Council of Ontario Pension Trust Fund (Trustess of) v. Celestica Inc.)* 118 O.R. (3d) 641, 50 C.P.C. (7th) 113, 370 D.L.R. (4th) 402, 314 O.A.C. 315, [2014] O.J. No. 419; additional reasons 2014 ONCA 344, 2014 CarswellOnt 5625, 68 C.P.C. (7th) 99; affirmed 2015 CSC 60, 2015 SCC 60, 2015 CarswellOnt 18335, 2015 CarswellOnt 18336, [2015] 3 S.C.R. 801, 135 O.R. (3d) 334 (note), 44 B.L.R. (5th) 1, 77 C.P.C. (7th) 1, 391 D.L.R. (4th) 567, 478 N.R. 202, 346 O.A.C. 204, [2015] S.C.J. No. 60; additional reasons 2016 ONSC 3829, 2016 CarswellOnt 9114 (S.C.J.)

The court refused to certify this securities class action because it was time-barred. Otherwise the court would have certified it and granted leave under s. 138.3 of the *Securities Act*.

Kherani v. Bank of Montreal, 2012 ONSC 2230, 2012 CarswellOnt 4326, 26 C.P.C. (7th) 195, [2012] O.J. No. 1623 (S.C.J.); additional reasons 2012 ONSC 4679, 2012 CarswellOnt 10150, 26 C.P.C. (7th) 276 (S.C.J.); leave to appeal refused *Pardhan v. Bank of Montreal*, 2013 ONSC 355, 2013 CarswellOnt 662, 100 C.C.L.T. (3d) 181, 303 O.A.C. 45, [2013] O.J. No. 329 (Div. Ct.)

Where this investment fraud claim satisfied all criteria except for the litigation plan, the court adjourned the certification motion to permit the plaintiff to produce an acceptable plan.

Sorenson v. easyhome Ltd., 2012 ONSC 1946, 2012 CarswellOnt 3672, 40 C.P.C. (7th) 16 (S.C.J.)

On consent, the court granted leave to bring a secondary market claim under the *Securities Act* and certified the claim.

French v. Investia Financial Services Inc., 2012 ONSC 1150, 2012 CarswellOnt 2140, 29 C.P.C. (7th) 191, [2012] O.J. No. 712 (S.C.J.)

The court certified a claim regarding an alleged mutual fund leveraging scheme.

McKenna v. Gammon Gold. Inc., 2011 ONSC 3782, 2011 CarswellOnt 5931, 13 C.P.C. (7th) 232, [2011] O.J. No. 3240, 87 C.C.L.T. (3d) 123 (Div. Ct.); additional reasons at 2011 ONSC 5882, 2011 CarswellOnt 11093, 87 C.C.L.T. (3d) 141 (Div. Ct.)

The court affirmed certification of a claim under s. 130 of the *Securities Act*, but overruled the motion judge's refusal to certify a conspiracy claim unless the plaintiff established the conspiracy claim caused separate damages. It was not plain and obvious the conspiracy claim merged with the s. 130 claim.

Dobbie v. Arctic Glacier Income Fund, 2011 ONSC 25, 2011 CarswellOnt 1301, [2011] O.J. No. 932, 3 C.P.C. (7th) 261 (S.C.J.); leave to appeal allowed 2012 ONSC 773, 2012 CarswellOnt 886, 109 O.R. (3d) 607 (S.C.J.)

The court certified a claim for misrepresentations regarding securities in both the primary and secondary market.

Topacio v. Batac, 2011 ONSC 1008, 2011 CarswellOnt 977, 14 C.P.C. (7th) 63, [2011] O.J. No. 711 (S.C.J.); additional reasons 2011 ONSC 2155, 2011 CarswellOnt 2403, 14 C.P.C. (7th) 100 (S.C.J.); additional reasons 2011 ONSC 2157, 2011 CarswellOnt 2404, 14 C.P.C. (7th) 103 (S.C.J.)

The court certified a claim regarding a misappropriation scheme victimizing members of an investment club.

Silver v. Imax Corp. (December 14, 2009), Doc. CV-06-3257-00, 2009 CarswellOnt 7873, [2009] O.J. No. 5573 (S.C.J.)

The court certified this securities class action based on misrepresentation in the secondary market.

Allen v. Aspen Group Resources Corp. (December 4, 2009), Doc. 02-CV-241587CP, 2009 CarswellOnt 7620, [2009] O.J. No. 5213 (S.C.J.)

The court certified a securities class action based on misrepresentations in a take-over circular.

Zopf v. Soberan Tessis Inc. (2009), 78 C.P.C. (6th) 323, 2009 CarswellOnt 1386, [2009] O.J. No. 1104 (S.C.J.)

The court certified a claim regarding the sale of debentures to unaccredited investors and the mass redemption of the debentures.

Moyes v. Fortune Financial Corp. (2002), 2002 CarswellOnt 3810, 61 O.R. (3d) 770, [2002] O.J. No. 4297, 32 C.P.C. (5th) 150 (S.C.J.); additional reasons at (November 8, 2002), Doc. 00-CV-198979CP, 2002 CarswellOnt 3804, [2002] O.J. No. 4298 (S.C.J.); affirmed (2003), 2003 CarswellOnt 4245, [2003] O.J. No. 4731, 178 O.A.C. 236, 38 C.P.C. (5th) 67, 67 O.R. (3d) 795 (Div. Ct.); leave to appeal refused (2004), 2004 CarswellOnt 1406, 44 C.P.C. (5th) 85 (C.A.)

The court refused to certify a claim by investors in a failed technology company.

Ward-Price v. Mariners Haven Inc. (2002), 2002 CarswellOnt 3728, [2002] O.J. No. 4260, 36 C.P.C. (5th) 189 (S.C.J.)

The court certified an action by investors in a condominium project against the developer.

Kerr v. Danier Leather Inc. (2001), [2001] O.J. No. 4000, 2001 CarswellOnt 3586, 19 B.L.R. (3d) 254, 14 C.P.C. (5th) 293 (S.C.J.)

The court certified a claim based on misrepresentations in a prospectus.

Carom v. Bre-X Minerals Ltd. (2000), 51 O.R. (3d) 236, 1 C.P.C. (5th) 62, 138 O.A.C. 55, 11 B.L.R. (3d) 1, 196 D.L.R. (4th) 344, 2000 CarswellOnt 3838, [2000] O.J. No. 4014 (C.A.); leave to appeal refused (2001), 2001 CarswellOnt 3609, 2001 CarswellOnt 3610, [2000] S.C.C.A. No. 660, 283 N.R. 399 (note), 157 O.A.C. 399 (note) (S.C.C.)

The Court of Appeal reversed the lower courts and certified a claim for negligent misrepresentation. The lower courts had certified a claim for fraudulent misrepresentation and there was no good reason to certify one but not the other. The *Class Proceedings Act* should be used to deal with as many issues as possible.

Joncas v. Spruce Falls Power & Paper Co. (1999), 45 C.P.C. (4th) 241, 1999 CarswellOnt 1805, [1999] O.J. No. 2359 (Gen. Div.)

The court certified a claim for negligence, breach of fiduciary duty and oppression in the distribution of shares in a corporation.

Millgate Financial Corp. v. BF Realty Holdings Ltd. (1998), [1998] O.J. No. 4537, 28 C.P.C. (4th) 72, 1998 CarswellOnt 4294 (Gen. Div. [Commercial List])

The court refused to certify a claim by debenture holders but ordered a trial of a key issue. The defendants agreed the decision would be binding on them in favour of any class which may be certified in the future.

Nash v. CIBC Trust Corp. (1996), 7 C.P.C. (4th) 260 (Ont. Gen. Div.); affirmed (March 13, 1997), CAC25819 (Ont. C.A.)

The court certified a class action on behalf of investors concerning alleged misconduct by the trustee. Discussion of contents of certification order.

Maxwell v. MLG Ventures Ltd. (1995), 7 C.C.L.S. 155 (Ont. Gen. Div.)

The court certified a class action by former shareholders who had sold shares based on alleged misrepresentations in an offering circular.

Abdool v. Anaheim Management Ltd. (1995), 21 O.R. (3d) 453, 31 C.P.C. (3d) 197, 121 D.L.R. (4th) 496, 78 O.A.C. 377 (Div. Ct.)

The court refused to certify a class action by condominium investors where there were numerous individual issues, individual discovery of class members was likely, and the class members' claims were individually viable. The goals of the *Class Proceedings Act* are (1) access to justice, (2) judicial economy, and (3) modification of behaviour.

Rogers Broadcasting Ltd. v. Alexander (1994), 25 C.P.C. (3d) 159, 4 C.C.L.S. 227 (Ont. Gen. Div. [Commercial List])

Where a corporation applied under the *Canada Business Corporations Act* to fix the fair value of shares of shareholders who dissented to a proposed amalgamation, a dissenting shareholder made a counter-application seeking damages for oppression and certification of a class proceeding on behalf of all minority shareholders contending that the amalgamation and subsequent privatization was effected in a manner which was oppressive and unfairly prejudicial to the minority. In refusing certification it was held that (1) since the non-dissenting minority shareholders had made no complaint about oppression and unfairness it would be wrong to include them in any class; (2) since there was little evidence of oppression or unfairness except with regard to the representative plaintiff, oppression was not a common issue; and (3) even if there was a common issue the preferable procedure to resolve the claims of the dissenting shareholders was to proceed with the valuation pursuant to s. 190(15) of the *CBCA* as there was no judicial economy to be gained by a class proceeding where a mechanism was in place for valuation under the *CBCA*.

Peppiatt v. Nicol (1993), 16 O.R. (3d) 133, 20 CP.C. (3d) 272 (Gen. Div.)

A class action commenced on behalf of the equity members of a golf club was certified where the representative plaintiffs had no conflict of interest, had been widely selected, had retained experienced counsel, and had demonstrated a willingness and ability to act. Without certification, a large number of members would be denied access to the legal system.

Disposition of Certification Motions — Tenant Issues

Williams v. Toronto (City), 2012 ONCA 915, 2012 CarswellOnt 16441, 30 C.P.C. (7th) 8, 358 D.L.R. (4th) 69, 300 O.A.C. 339

The court certified a claim for the municipality's failure to provide notices of rent reductions to rooming house tenants, resulting in their paying excess rent.

Zeigler v. Sherkston Resorts Inc. (1996), 30 O.R. (3d) 375, 4 C.P.C. (4th) 225 (Gen. Div.)

Certification was refused of claims based upon the *Rent Control Act, 1992*, which provided a complete code of procedure for seeking redress.

Disposition of Certification Motions — Usury/Criminal Interest

De Wolf v. Bell ExpressVu Inc. (2008), 2008 CarswellOnt 818, [2008] O.J. No. 592, 58 C.P.C. (6th) 110 (S.C.J.)

The court certified a claim that late fees charged by the defendant offended s. 347 of the *Criminal Code*.

Markson v. MBNA Canada Bank, [2007] O.J. No. 1684, 2007 CarswellOnt 2716, 43 C.P.C. (6th) 10, 2007 ONCA 334, 282 D.L.R. (4th) 385, 32 B.L.R. (4th) 273, 224 O.A.C. 71, 85 O.R. (3d) 321 (C.A.); leave to appeal refused 2007 CarswellOnt 7420, 2007 CarswellOnt 7421, [2007] S.C.C.A. No. 346, 383 N.R. 381, [2007] 3 S.C.R. xii (note), 248 O.A.C. 396 (note) (S.C.C.)

The court certified a criminal rate of interest claim against a credit card company charging a flat transaction fee as well as compound interest.

Smith v. National Money Mart Co. (2007), 2007 CarswellOnt 29, 29 E.T.R. (3d) 199, 37 C.P.C. (6th) 171, [2007] O.J. No. 46 (S.C.J.); leave to appeal refused (2007), 2007 CarswellOnt 2177, 30 E.T.R. (3d) 163, [2007] O.J. No. 2160 (Div. Ct.)

The court certified a usury claim against a payday loan lender.

Disposition of Certification Motions — Miscellaneous

Smith v. Armstrong, 2018 ONSC 2435, 2018 CarswellOnt 6120 (S.C.J.)

The court refused leave to bring a certification motion after a 17-year delay.

Metro Taxi Ltd. v. City of Ottawa, 2018 ONSC 509, 2018 CarswellOnt 523, 45 C.C.E.L. (4th) 130, 13 C.P.C. (8th) 325, 71 M.P.L.R. (5th) 311 (S.C.J.)

The court certified this claim by taxi operators against a municipality for permitting Uber to operate in the city.

Daniells v. McLellan, 2017 ONSC 3466, 2017 CarswellOnt 14307, 39 C.C.L.T. (4th) 263, 6 C.P.C. (8th) 317 (S.C.J.)

The court certified this breach of privacy claim for improperly accessing patients' health records.

Heyde v. Theberge Developments Ltd., 2017 ONSC 1574, 2017 CarswellOnt 3790, 99 C.P.C. (7th) 131 (S.C.J.); additional reasons 2017 ONSC 3462, 2017 CarswellOnt 8335 (S.C.J.)

The court certified this claim by purchasers of condominium units for the developer's failure to provide the promised heating system and other deficiencies.

Noble v. North Halton Golf and Country Club Ltd., 2016 ONSC 2962, 2016 CarswellOnt 7556, 58 B.L.R. (5th) 122, 87 C.P.C. (7th) 315 (S.C.J.)

The court certified an oppression claim by members of a golf club.

Lalani v. Reeves, 2016 ONSC 424, 2016 CarswellOnt 958, 90 C.P.C. (7th) 404 (S.C.J.)

The court certified a claim for knowing assistance and knowing receipt of proceeds of a Ponzi scheme, despite a four-year delay in seeking certification.

Amyotrophic Lateral Sclerosis Society of Essex County v. Windsor (City), 2015 ONCA 572, 2015 CarswellOnt 12140, 76 C.P.C. (7th) 276, 387 D.L.R. (4th) 603, 38 M.P.L.R. (5th) 175, 337 O.A.C. 315, [2015] O.J. No. 4267

The court certified this claim for unconstitutional taxation but restricted the class period to reflect the applicable limitation period.

Evans v. Bank of Nova Scotia, 2014 ONSC 2135, 2014 CarswellOnt 7666, 55 C.P.C. (7th) 141, [2014] O.J. No. 2708 (S.C.J.); leave to appeal refused 2014 ONSC 7249, 2014 CarswellOnt 17769 (S.C.J.)

The court certified claims for "intrusion upon seclusion," etc. where a rogue bank employee gave confidential customer information to third parties who committed identity theft and fraud.

Dennis v. Ontario Lottery and Gaming Corp., 2013 ONCA 501, 2013 CarswellOnt 10539, 116 O.R. (3d) 321, 37 C.P.C. (7th) 268, 365 D.L.R. (4th) 145, 307 O.A.C. 377; leave to appeal refused 2014 CarswellOnt 1724, 2014 CarswellOnt 1725, 471 N.R. 394 (note), 335 O.A.C. 399 (note) (S.C.C.)

The court certified a claim for failure to deny persons subject to voluntary self-exclusion contracts from the defendant's gambling venues.

Arenson v. Toronto (City), 2012 ONSC 3944, 2012 CarswellOnt 9734, 35 C.P.C. (7th) 207, 1 M.P.L.R. (5th) 57 (S.C.J.); additional reasons 2012 ONSC 4488, 2012 CarswellOnt 9706 (S.C.J.); affirmed 2013 ONSC 5837, 2013 CarswellOnt 13045, 40 C.P.C. (7th) 215 (Div. Ct.)

The court refused to certify a claim regarding defective parking meters.

Cannon v. Funds for Canada Foundation, 2012 ONSC 399, 2012 CarswellOnt 503, 13 C.P.C. (7th) 250, [2012] 3 C.T.C. 132, [2012] O.J. No. 168 (S.C.J.); additional reasons 2012 ONSC 3009, 2012 CarswellOnt 7212, [2012] O.J. No. 2611 (S.C.J.); leave to appeal refused 2012 ONSC 6101, 2012 CarswellOnt 13625, 112 O.R. (3d) 641 (Div. Ct.)

The court certified a claim by donors regarding charitable donations disallowed by the Canada Revenue Agency.

St. John's Evangelical Lutheran Church of Toronto v. Steers, 2011 ONSC 6308, 2011 CarswellOnt 11456 (S.C.J.); additional reasons 2011 ONSC 7416, 2011 CarswellOnt 14446, 38 C.P.C. (7th) 121 (S.C.J.)

For settlement purposes, the court certified a claim regarding the ownership and operation of church property.

Rowlands v. Durham Region Health, 2011 ONSC 719, 2011 CarswellOnt 3228, 20 C.P.C. (7th) 253, [2011] O.J. No. 1864 (S.C.J.)

The court certified a claim regarding accidental loss of confidential health information.

Amytrophic Lateral Sclerosis Society of Essex (County) v. Windsor (City), 2011 ONSC 91, 2011 CarswellOnt 397, 79 M.P.L.R. (4th) 314, [2011] O.J. No. 321, 8 C.P.C. (7th) 217 (S.C.J.); leave to appeal allowed 2011 ONSC 4327, 2011 CarswellOnt 6912 (S.C.J.)

The court certified a claim for illegal taxes in the form of fees charged by municipalities for bingo licences.

KRP Enterprises Inc. v. Haldimand (County), 2010 CarswellOnt 675, 2010 ONSC 901, [2010] O.J. No. 500, 88 C.P.C. (6th) 387 (S.C.J.)

The court certified this action on behalf of various subclasses adversely affected by First Nations protesters occupying land and blockading a highway.

Robinson v. Rochester Financial Ltd., 2010 CarswellOnt 206, 2010 ONSC 463, [2010] O.J. No. 187, 89 C.P.C. (6th) 91 (S.C.J.); leave to appeal refused 2010 ONSC 1899, 2010 CarswellOnt 2153, [2010] O.J. No. 1481, 89 C.P.C. (6th) 118, 262 O.A.C. 148 (Div. Ct.)

The court certified a claim against promoters of a gift program which was determined by the Canada Revenue Agency to be a sham.

Grant v. Canada (Attorney General) (December 4, 2009), Doc. 04-CV-263007, 2009 CarswellOnt 7642, [2009] O.J. No. 5232 (S.C.J.)

The court certified a claim by members of a First Nation regarding defective housing constructed by the Crown.

Roach v. Canada (Attorney General), 2009 CarswellOnt 922, 74 C.P.C. (6th) 22 (S.C.J.); affirmed 84 C.P.C. (6th) 276, 2009 CarswellOnt 8324, [2009] O.J. No. 5286 (Div. Ct.)

The court refused to certify a claim challenging the constitutionality of the requirement that new citizens swear or affirm their allegiance to the Queen.

Serhan Estate v. Johnson & Johnson (2006), (sub nom. *Serhan (Trustee of) v. Johnson & Johnson)* 2006 CarswellOnt 3705, [2006] O.J. No. 2421, 28 C.P.C. (6th) 83, 85 O.R. (3d) 665, 269 D.L.R. (4th) 279, 213 O.A.C. 298, 24 E.T.R. (3d) 265 (Div. Ct.)

The decision certifying a class proceeding for damages based in part on waiver of tort was upheld.

L. (A.) v. Ontario (Minister of Community & Social Services) (2006), 2006 CarswellOnt 7393, 274 D.L.R. (4th) 431, 218 O.A.C. 150, [2006] O.J. No. 4673, 83 O.R. (3d) 512, 35 R.F.L. (6th) 56, 36 C.P.C. (6th) 265, 45 C.C.L.T. (3d) 207 (C.A.); leave to appeal refused (May 10, 2007), Doc. 31825, 2007 CarswellOnt 3059, 2007 CarswellOnt 3060 (S.C.C.)

The court refused to certify an action based on claims related to the provision of special needs programs under the *Child and Family Services Act* on the basis the statement of claim did not disclose a cause of action.

Mandeville v. Manufacturers Life Insurance Co. (2002), 40 C.P.C. (5th) 182, [2002] O.J. No. 5386, 2002 CarswellOnt 5381, 2 C.C.L.I. (4th) 211 (S.C.J.)

The court certified a class action regarding demutualization of the defendant insurer.

Larcade v. Ontario (Minister of Community & Social Services) (2003), 36 C.P.C. (5th) 382, 2003 CarswellOnt 2368, (sub nom. *A.L. v. Ontario*

(Minister of Community & Social Services)) [2003] O.J. No. 2405, *(*sub nom. *L. (A.) v. Ontario (Minister of Community & Social Services)* 65 O.R. (3d) 289, 41 R.F.L. (5th) 123 (S.C.J.)

The court dismissed a motion for certification of a claim alleging that the defendant ministry had breached its statutory duty and acted negligently.

Fehringer v. Sun Media Corp. (2002), 27 C.P.C. (5th) 155, 2002 CarswellOnt 3569, [2002] O.J. No. 4110 (S.C.J.); affirmed (2003), 39 C.P.C. (5th) 151, 2003 CarswellOnt 3841, [2003] O.J. No. 3918 (Div. Ct.)

The court refused to certify a claim on behalf of "Sunshine Girls" for misconduct by a newspaper photographer.

Perron v. Canada (Attorney General), 2003 CarswellOnt 1187, [2003] O.J. No. 1348, 105 C.R.R. (2d) 92, 32 C.P.C. (5th) 165, [2003] 3 C.N.L.R. 198 (S.C.J.)

The court refused to certify a claim for a declaration that a provision of the *Indian Act* is unconstitutional. It is generally undesirable to pursue a class action for a declaration of constitutional invalidity.

Cheung v. Kings Land Development Inc. (2001), *(*sub nom. *Cheung v. Kings Land Developments Inc.))* 55 O.R. (3d) 747, 2001 CarswellOnt 3227, 14 C.P.C. (5th) 374 (S.C.J.); leave to appeal refused (2002), 2002 CarswellOnt 270, 156 O.A.C. 73 (Div. Ct.)

The court certified a claim arising from a failed condominium project.

Buffett v. Ontario (Attorney General) (1998), 42 O.R. (3d) 53, 27 C.P.C. (4th) 282, 1998 CarswellOnt 3546, [1998] O.J. No. 3740 (Gen. Div.)

Certification was refused where the applicant sought to certify a class action to obtain a declaration of constitutional invalidity.

Controltech Engineering Inc. v. Ontario Hydro (1998), 72 O.T.C. 351, 1998 CarswellOnt 4918, [1998] O.J. No. 5350 (Gen. Div.); affirmed (2000), (sub nom. *Controltech Engineering Inc. v. Ontario Power Generation Inc.)* 130 O.A.C. 367, 2000 CarswellOnt 340, [2000] O.J. No. 379 (Div. Ct.)

The court refused to certify a claim for misrepresentation on behalf of a class of participants in a contract bidding process.

Kenora (Town) Police Services Board v. Savino (1997), 20 C.P.C. (4th) 13 (Ont. Div. Ct.); leave to appeal refused (1997), 20 C.P.C. (4th) 15 (Ont. C.A.)

The court refused to certify this defamation action.

Tampa Hall Ltd. v. Canadian Imperial Bank of Commerce (1998), 37 O.R. (3d) 150, 17 C.P.C. (4th) 371, 37 C.L.R. (2d) 274 (Gen. Div.)

The court refused to certify a class action by *Construction Lien Act* trust fund claimants because there were no common issues. Even the issue of whether the defendant bank had actual or constructive knowledge of the unpaid trust beneficiaries required separate proof for each class member and was not a common issue.

Multi-Jurisdictional Issues

Romeo v. Ford Motor Co., 2017 ONSC 6674, 2017 CarswellOnt 17377 (S.C.J.)

The court refused to permit plaintiffs in an overlapping Saskatchewan class action to intervene in the Ontario certification motion.

Babin v. Bayer Inc., 2017 ONSC 3200, 2017 CarswellOnt 7813, 6 C.P.C. (8th) 358 (S.C.J.)

Where four class actions were commenced in various provinces and the plaintiffs' consortium of law firms informally "parked" the Ontario action in favour of the Alberta action, but later sought to proceed in Ontario when difficulties arose in Alberta, the court formally stayed the Ontario action. Alberta was the *forum conveniens*.

Endean v. British Columbia, 2016 CSC 42, 2016 SCC 42, 2016 CarswellBC 2891, 2016 CarswellBC 2892, [2016] 2 S.C.R. 162, 88 B.C.L.R. (5th) 1, 91 C.P.C. (7th) 1, 401 D.L.R. (4th) 577, [2016] 12 W.W.R. 1, (sub nom. *Endean v. Canadian Red Cross Society)* 488 N.R. 246

Judges involved in pan-national class actions have discretion to hold hearings outside their home provinces in conjunction with other judges managing related class actions. Video links to their home provinces are permissible but not mandatory.

Airia Brands Inc. v. Air Canada, 2015 ONSC 5332, 2015 CarswellOnt 12787, 126 O.R. (3d) 756, 78 C.P.C. (7th) 49 (S.C.J.); additional reasons 2016 ONSC 1220, 2016 CarswellOnt 2791 (S.C.J.); reversed 2017 ONCA 792, 2017 CarswellOnt 15877, 11 C.P.C. (8th) 35, 417 D.L.R. (4th) 467

In this claim for price fixing airfreight charges, the court stayed the claim of absent foreign class members because Ontario was *forum non-conveniens*.

Eidoo v. Infineon Technologies AG, 2013 ONSC 853, 2013 CarswellOnt 1303 (S.C.J.)

In motions heard simultaneously by video conference by courts in Ontario, Quebec and British Columbia pursuant to the *Canadian Judicial Protocol for the Management of Multijurisdictional Class Actions*, the court approved a partial settlement of a price fixing claim and set class counsel's fee.

Turon v. Abbott Laboratories Ltd., 2011 ONSC 4343, 2011 CarswellOnt 7405, 38 C.P.C. (7th) 215, 340 D.L.R. (4th) 510 (S.C.J.); leave to appeal refused 2011 ONSC 4676, 2011 CarswellOnt 7934, 340 D.L.R. (4th) 519 (Div. Ct.)

The court refused the plaintiffs' request to temporarily stay the action pending the outcome of a certification motion in a similar B.C. case. A party who commences an action should move forward with reasonable dispatch.

Speers Estate v. Reader's Digest Assn. (Canada) ULC (2009), [2009] O.J. No. 2332, 2009 CarswellOnt 3161, 73 C.P.C. (6th) 281 (S.C.J.); additional reasons at (July 17, 2009), Doc. 08-CV-350312 CP, 2009 CarswellOnt 4198 (S.C.J.)

The court refused to restrain the defendants from prosecuting a Quebec defamation claim against the plaintiff for allegedly defamatory statements made in the statement of claim of this Ontario class action.

Lépine v. Société Canadienne des postes, 2009 CarswellQue 2490, 2009 CarswellQue 2491, EYB 2009-156806, 2009 SCC 16, (sub nom. *Canada Post Corp. v. Lépine)* 387 N.R. 91, (sub nom. *Société canadienne des postes v. Lépine)* 304 D.L.R. (4th) 539, [2009] 1 S.C.R. 549, 67 C.P.C. (6th) 201

In dealing with a national class action the court has a duty to ensure that the conduct of the proceeding, the choice of remedies, and the enforcement of the judgment take account of the interests of the class members from various provinces, and must ensure that clear information is provided to them. In this case the Quebec courts refused to recognize an Ontario class action settlement where, *inter alia*, the notices published in Quebec were confusing and did not mention a similar action pending in Quebec.

Tiboni v. Merck Frosst Canada Ltd. (2009), [2009] O.J. No. 821, 2009 CarswellOnt 1248, (sub nom. *Mignacca v. Merch Frosst Canada Ltd.)* 247 O.A.C. 322, (sub nom. *Mignacca v. Merch Frosst Canada Ltd.)* 95 O.R. (3d) 269, 71 C.P.C. (6th) 350 (Div. Ct.) (Div. Ct.)

The court refused to stay this Ontario multi-jurisdictional class action despite an overlapping multi-jurisdictional class action having been certified in Saskatchewan.

Sollen v. Pfizer Canada Inc. (2008), 2008 CarswellOnt 1258, [2008] O.J. No. 866, 290 D.L.R. (4th) 603, 55 C.P.C. (6th) 340 (S.C.J.); affirmed 2008 CarswellOnt 7152, 2008 ONCA 803, 63 C.P.C. (6th) 1, 305 D.L.R. (4th) 184 (C.A.)

Where similar actions were commenced in several provinces, and the Saskatchewan court held that there was no more convenient forum than Saskatchewan, the Ontario court dismissed the defendant's motion to enjoin the plaintiffs from continuing the Saskatchewan action, and granted the plaintiffs' motion to discontinue the Ontario action.

Wilson v. Servier Canada Inc. (2002), 2002 CarswellOnt 1416, [2002] O.J. No. 1002, 58 O.R. (3d) 753, 23 C.P.C. (5th) 193 (S.C.J.)

The court held that a product liability claim against a French pharmaceutical company had a real and substantial connection with Ontario, and permitted the action to proceed.

Parsons v. Canadian Red Cross Society (March 9, 2000), Doc. 98-CV-141369 CP, 98-CV-146405, 2000 CarswellOnt 716 (S.C.J.)

Where an Administrator of a class action settlement was to be jointly appointed by courts in British Columbia, Ontario and Quebec, and the Quebec court conducted a thorough hearing on the issue, the Ontario court reviewed the Quebec court's record, concurred in its decision, and adopted its reasons.

McCutcheon v. Cash Store Inc. (2006), 80 O.R. (3d) 644, [2006] O.J. No. 1860, 27 C.P.C. (6th) 293, 2006 CarswellOnt 2973 (S.C.J.)

The inclusion of non-residents in the definition of the class will not *per se* amount to an excess of the court's jurisdiction. In this case, there was a real and substantial connection between Ontario and the claims of residents outside Ontario. Further, considerations of order and fairness mitigated in favour of extending the class to include persons outside of Ontario.

Andersen v. St. Jude Medical Inc. (2004), 2004 CarswellOnt 136, [2004] O.J. No. 132, 48 C.P.C. (5th) 312 (S.C.J.); additional reasons at (May 21, 2004), Doc. 00-CV-195906CP, [2004] O.J. No. 3102, 2004 CarswellOnt 8144 (S.C.J.); affirmed (February 8, 2006), Doc. Toronto 367/04, 2006 CarswellOnt 710, [2006] O.J. No. 508 (Div. Ct.)

The court discussed the definition of a national class including *Family Law Act* claimants.

Wilson v. Servier Canada Inc. (2002), 59 O.R. (3d) 656, 2002 CarswellOnt 1859, 213 D.L.R. (4th) 751 (S.C.J.); appeal quashed (2002), 2002 CarswellOnt 3300, [2002] O.J. No. 3856, 23 C.P.C. (5th) 1, 220 D.L.R. (4th) 191 (C.A.)

A national class may be certified. The *Class Proceedings Act* recognizes and affirms the court's inherent jurisdiction to include non-resident claimants within an Ontario action where there is a real and substantial connection.

Carom v. Bre-X Minerals Ltd. (1999), 43 O.R. (3d) 441, 30 C.P.C. (4th) 133, 1999 CarswellOnt 326, [1999] O.J. No. 281 (Gen. Div.)

A class may include persons residing outside Ontario. Ontario had a real and substantial connection to the subject-matter of the case and the outcome would be recognized in other provinces pursuant to *Morguard Investments Ltd. v. De Savoye* (1990), 46 C.P.C. (2d) 1, 52 B.C.L.R. (2d) 160, 76 D.L.R. (4th) 256, 122 N.R. 81, 15 R.P.R. (2d) 1, [1990] 3 S.C.R. 1077, [1991] 2 W.W.R. 217.

Nantais v. Telectronics Proprietary (Canada) Ltd. (1995), 25 O.R. (3d) 331, 40 C.P.C. (3d) 245, 127 D.L.R. (4th) 552 (Gen. Div.); leave to appeal refused 25 O.R. (3d) 331 at 347, 40 C.P.C. (3d) 263, 129 D.L.R. (4th) 110 (Gen. Div.)

A nation wide class was certified. For the reasons given in *Morguard Investments Ltd. v. De Savoye*, [1990] 3 S.C.R. 1077, and to accomplish the goals of the *Class Proceedings Act*, it is eminently sensible that the question of liability be determined as far as possible once and for all for all Canadians.

Wilson v. Servier Canada Inc. (2001), [2001] O.J. No. 1615, 2001 Carswell-Ont 1507, 11 C.P.C. (5th) 374 (S.C.J.)

After certification, the court granted the plaintiff's request to appoint a sub-class representative regarding B.C. class members.

Parsons v. McDonald's Restaurants of Canada Ltd. (2004), 2004 CarswellOnt 76, [2004] O.J. No. 83, 45 C.P.C. (5th) 304 (S.C.J.); affirmed (2005), 2005 CarswellOnt 544, (sub nom. *Currie v. McDonald's Restaurants of Canada Ltd.)* 74 O.R. (3d) 321, 7 C.P.C. (6th) 60, (sub nom. *Currie v. McDonald's Restaurants of Canada Ltd.)* 250 D.L.R. (4th) 224, (sub nom. *Currie v. McDonald's Restaurants of Canada Ltd.)* 195 O.A.C. 244 (C.A.)

Where the plaintiff had previously and unsuccessfully opposed settlement of a U.S. class action, the court held the plaintiff's claim was barred by the U.S. settlement and permanently stayed the action. However a second Ontario action by a plaintiff who was not aware of the U.S. action was permitted to proceed.

Overlapping Actions

Quizno's Canada Restaurant Corp. v. Kileel Developments Ltd., 241 O.A.C. 148, 92 O.R. (3d) 347, 2008 CarswellOnt 5525, 2008 ONCA 644, [2008] O.J. No. 3674 (C.A.)

The court refused to stay a counterclaim which raised claims similar to those in an uncertified class action where it was unknown whether the claimant would opt out if certification were granted.

Northfield Capital Corp. v. Aurelian Resources Inc. (2007), 2007 CarswellOnt 1374, 29 B.L.R. (4th) 149, 84 O.R. (3d) 748 (S.C.J.)

The court refused to consolidate the plaintiffs' individual actions with the class action. The court's jurisdiction to grant a stay should be exercised sparingly and only in the clearest of cases where there would be an injustice or prejudice to the moving party. In this case, the plaintiffs would face considerable delay and increased costs if the actions are consolidated or tried together.

Knowles v. Wyeth-Ayerst Canada Inc. (2001), 2001 CarswellOnt 2550, [2001] O.J. No. 2880, 16 C.P.C. (5th) 343 (S.C.J.)

The court refused to consolidate two product liability class actions involving different parties but the same product, and refused to let one defendant intervene in the other action.

Blatt Holdings Ltd. v. Traders General Insurance Co. (2001), 9 C.P.C. (5th) 256, 2001 CarswellOnt 1822 (S.C.J.)

The court ordered that three actions involving separate parties but analogous facts and legal issues should be managed by separate case management judges.

Carriage Motions

Quenneville v. Audi AG, 2018 ONSC 1530, 2018 CarswellOnt 3459 (S.C.J.)

The rival law firms' preparation and performance on the carriage motion is itself a factor in determining to whom carriage should be given.

David v. Loblaw; *Breckon v. Loblaw*, 2018 ONSC 1298, 2018 CarswellOnt 3172 (S.C.J.)

The court enumerated 16 factors to be considered on carriage motions, and awarded carriage of this price-fixing claim to the more proactive of the two competing consortiums.

Kaplan v. Casino Rama Services Inc., 2017 ONSC 2671, 2017 CarswellOnt 6888, 9 C.P.C. (8th) 439 (S.C.J.)

The court awarded carriage of this action to the law firm consortium which was more experienced, better prepared, and had a more workable theory of the case.

Mancinelli v. Barrick Gold Corp., 2016 ONCA 571, 2016 CarswellOnt 11222, 131 O.R. (3d) 497, 30 C.C.L.T. (4th) 188, 89 C.P.C. (7th) 225, 400 D.L.R. (4th) 550, 350 O.A.C. 389

The court awarded carriage of this action to the consortium of lawyers with the better theory of the case and more advanced preparation.

Kowalyshyn v. Valeant Pharmaceuticals International, Inc., 2016 ONSC 3819, 2016 CarswellOnt 9329 (S.C.J.)

The court held the interrelationship of multi-jurisdiction litigation to be determinative in this carriage motion, with the other factors being neutral or non-determinative.

Wilson v. LG Chem Ltd., 2014 ONSC 1875, 2014 CarswellOnt 3562, 68 C.P.C. (7th) 147, [2014] O.J. No. 1388 (S.C.J.)

The court awarded carriage to the counsel which were more proactive and considered in their approach to this price-fixing litigation.

Waheed v. Glaxosmithkline Inc., 2013 ONSC 5792, 2013 CarswellOnt 13883, 117 O.R. (3d) 680, 46 C.P.C. (7th) 180 (S.C.J.)

Where a law firm was awarded carriage of a class action but failed to bring a certification motion within three years, the court refused to transfer carriage to another law firm. The test on such motions is whether (a) the delay was clearly unreasonable; (b) there is prejudice or harm to the class members; (c) the explanation for the delay is inadequate; and (d) an order setting a deadline for the certification motion is not workable or in the best interests of the class.

Locking v. Armtec Infrastructure Inc., 2013 ONSC 331, 2013 CarswellOnt 1252, 46 C.P.C. (7th) 427, 303 O.A.C. 299, [2013] O.J. No. 531 (Div. Ct.)

While it is preferable to avoid any analysis of the merits of the claim on a carriage motion, some analysis may be necessary to determine which action is in the best interests of the class.

McSherry v. Zimmer GMBH (2012), 2010 ONSC 4113, 2012 CarswellOnt 17147, 36 C.P.C. (7th) 318 (S.C.J.)

The court awarded carriage of an Ontario class action where ten related class actions were commenced in six provinces. The court refused to use the carriage motion to regulate sharing of class action litigation in the marketplace.

Smith v. Sino-Forest Corp., 2012 ONSC 24, 2012 CarswellOnt 485, 34 C.P.C. (7th) 76 (S.C.J.)

The court awarded carriage of this claim to one of three groups of plaintiff's counsel.

Simmonds v. Armtec Infrastructure Inc., 2012 ONSC 44, 2012 CarswellOnt 1112, 35 C.P.C. (7th) 269 (S.C.J.); leave to appeal allowed 2012 ONSC 5228, 2012 CarswellOnt 11654 (S.C.J.)

In deciding which of two sets of plaintiff counsel should have carriage of this securities claim, the court considered (a) the nature and scope of the causes of action advanced, (b) the theories supporting those causes of action, (c) the best interests of the class, (d) fairness to the defendant, and (e) what is consistent with the policy objectives of the *Class Proceedings Act.*

McQuade v. Toronto Police Services Board, 2011 ONSC 5086, 2011 CarswellOnt 11685, 38 C.P.C. (7th) 168 (S.C.J.)

Where two proceedings were commenced asserting claims regarding police conduct at the G20 Summit, the court granted carriage to counsel in one action, and stayed the second action.

Fantl v. Transamerica Life Canada, 2009 CarswellOnt 2383, 2009 ONCA 377, [2009] O.J. No. 1826, 72 C.P.C. (6th) 1, 249 O.A.C. 58, 95 O.R. (3d) 767 (C.A.)

A representative plaintiff is a genuine plaintiff who chooses, retains and instructs counsel. In reviewing the choice of counsel, the court should consider: (a) has the plaintiff chosen competent counsel, (b) were there any improper considerations in the choice of counsel, and (c) is there prejudice to the class as a result of the choice of counsel. In this case the court refused to interfere with the plaintiff's choice of new counsel after the original law firm representing the plaintiff dissolved.

DeFazio v. Ontario (Ministry of Labour) (December 5, 2007), Doc. Toronto 163/07, 2007 CarswellOnt 8034, [2007] O.J. No. 4871 (Div. Ct.); additional reasons at (2007), 2007 CarswellOnt 8314, 49 C.P.C. (6th) 144, 232 O.A.C. 48 (Div. Ct.); additional reasons at (2008), 2008 CarswellOnt 533, 53 C.P.C. (6th) 192 (Div. Ct.)

Section 12 applies both before and after certification. Where two class actions were commenced regarding the same matter, the court determined which of the two actions should proceed.

Whiting v. Menu Foods Operating Ltd. (2007), [2007] O.J. No. 3996, 2007 CarswellOnt 6726, 53 C.P.C. (6th) 124 (S.C.J.)

Where two class actions had been commenced about the same subject, the court determined which action would proceed based on the best interests of the class members.

Setterington v. Merck Frosst Canada Ltd. (2006), 26 C.P.C. (6th) 173, 2006 CarswellOnt 506 (S.C.J.)

Where two class proceedings had been commenced for the same claim, the court awarded carriage of the claim to the plaintiffs whose counsel could better serve the class. It was not appropriate for the court to require the successful plaintiffs to retain counsel for the unsuccessful plaintiffs as co-counsel.

Holmes v. London Life Insurance Co. (December 13, 2005), Doc. 99-CV-182772, London 46300CP, 2005 CarswellOnt 7421 (S.C.J.)

Plaintiffs involved in a motion to determine who should have carriage of the action were required to answer questions about any indemnities they had received regarding the costs of the action. Fee arrangements in class actions are subject to disclosure and approval by the court, which trumps the assertion that the arrangements are subject to solicitor-and-client privilege.

Genier v. CCI Capital Canada Ltd. (2005), 2005 CarswellOnt 1141, 14 C.P.C. (6th) 297 (S.C.J.)

In determining which of two overlapping class actions should proceed, the task of the court is to determine which proceedings will best protect the interests of the class members as a whole.

Gorecki v. Canada (Attorney General) (2004), 47 C.P.C. (5th) 151, 2004 CarswellOnt 1266, C.E.B. & P.G.R. 8091 (S.C.J.)

The court stayed one of two overlapping class actions.

Ricardo v. Air Transat A.T. Inc. (2002), 2002 CarswellOnt 1394, [2002] O.J. No. 1090, 21 C.P.C. (5th) 297 (S.C.J.); leave to appeal refused (2002), 2002 CarswellOnt 1764, [2002] O.J. No. 2122, 22 C.P.C. (5th) 285 (Div. Ct.)

Where two plaintiffs and groups of counsel seek to represent a class, the task of the court is to choose the group which best serve the interests of the class.

VitaPharm Canada Ltd. v. F. Hoffman-LaRoche Ltd. (2000), 2000 CarswellOnt 4681, [2000] O.J. No. 4594, 4 C.P.C. (5th) 169 (S.C.J.)

Where several class actions are commenced regarding the same matter and the plaintiffs are unable to reach an agreement, the court will determine which actions should be stayed and who should act as counsel. The court may appoint different or additional counsel to ensure adequacy of representation. Discussion of the factors considered in determining who should be solicitors of record.

Sequence of Hearings

Smith v. Sino-Forest Corp., 2012 ONSC 1924, 2012 CarswellOnt 3480, (sub nom. *Labourers' Pension Fund of Central and Eastern Canada v. Sino-Forest Corp.)* 110 O.R. (3d) 173 (S.C.J.)

The court ordered that a motion for leave to commence a secondary market action under s. 138.8 of the *Securities Act* be combined with the certification motion.

Patel v. Groupon Inc., 2012 ONSC 1799, 2012 CarswellOnt 3449, 40 C.P.C. (7th) 29 (S.C.J.)

The court ordered that the certification motion precede a motion for summary judgment.

Pennyfeather v. Timminco Limited, 2011 ONSC 4257, 2011 CarswellOnt 6829, 107 O.R. (3d) 201, [2011] O.J. No. 3286 (S.C.J.)

As a general rule, the defendant should deliver its defence prior to certification. The court ordered the plaintiff to provide particulars, and the defendants to then deliver their defence.

Berkovits v. Canon Canada Inc., 2010 ONSC 395, 2010 CarswellOnt 5173, 98 C.P.C. (6th) 91 (S.C.J.)

The court decided to hear the motion to strike an affidavit in support of the certification motion at the same time as the certification motion.

Martin v. AstraZeneca Pharmaceuticals PLC, 2009 CarswellOnt 5499, [2009] O.J. No. 3847, 83 C.P.C. (6th) 79 (S.C.J.); leave to appeal refused 2009 CarswellOnt 7673, [2009] O.J. No. 5265, 259 O.A.C. 155 (Div. Ct.)

The court refused to permit the defendant to move for summary judgment prior to the certification motion. There was no reason to depart from the general rule that certification motions be given priority.

McKenna v. Gammon Gold Inc., 2009 CarswellOnt 7551, [2009] O.J. No. 5151, 84 C.P.C. (6th) 148 (S.C.J.)

The court ordered that the defendants' summary judgment motion should be brought following the certification motion.

Lacroix v. Canada Mortgage & Housing Corp. (2007), 50 C.P.C. (6th) 95, 2007 CarswellOnt 2582, [2007] O.J. No. 1648 (S.C.J.); additional reasons (March 27, 2007), Doc. 99-CV-10694, 2007 CarswellOnt 2583 (S.C.J.)

Where a certified action was amended to add new claims and parties, but certification was subsequently denied regarding the new claims, such claims were severed and permitted to proceed as a separate action. In hindsight, the court should not have bifurcated the motion to amend from the motion to certify the new claims.

Attis v. Canada (Minister of Health) (2005), 28 C.P.C. (6th) 209, [2005] O.J. No. 1337, 2005 CarswellOnt 1341, 75 O.R. (3d) 302 (S.C.J.)

Generally, the certification motion ought to be the first procedural matter to be heard and determined.

Potter v. Bank of Canada (2005), 2005 CarswellOnt 778, 45 C.C.P.B. 98, 9 C.P.C. (6th) 36, C.E.B. & P.G.R. 8149 (S.C.J.)

The court directed that the defendants' motion to strike part of the statement of claim and declare that the *Class Proceedings Act* does not apply to the plaintiffs' claim be heard prior to the plaintiffs' motion for certification.

D.L.T.E. Holdings Ltd. v. Horseshoe Resort Corp. (2003), 37 C.P.C. (5th) 369, 2003 CarswellOnt 1962 (S.C.J.); leave to appeal allowed (2003), 2003 CarswellOnt 6353, 5 C.P.C. (6th) 388 (S.C.J.)

The court ordered the trial of a key issue which would shorten the proceedings.

Gariepy v. Shell Oil Co. (2003), 2003 CarswellOnt 8, 63 O.R. (3d) 91, 29 C.P.C. (5th) 305 (S.C.J.)

The defendant's motion for summary judgment was adjourned pending final disposition of all appeals respecting the issue of certification.

Andersen v. St. Jude Medical Inc. (2002), 2002 CarswellOnt 4014, [2002] O.J. No. 4478, 29 C.P.C. (5th) 234 (S.C.J.)

The court adjourned a motion attacking the admissibility of affidavit evidence filed on a certification motion to the date of hearing of the certification motion.

Ward-Price v. Mariners Haven Inc. (2002), 2002 CarswellOnt 3728, [2002] O.J. No. 4260, 36 C.P.C. (5th) 189 (S.C.J.)

Generally, the certification motion should be the first matter dealt with in a proposed class proceeding.

McNaughton Automotive Ltd. v. Co-operators General Insurance Co. (2002), 2002 CarswellOnt 4928, 32 C.P.C. (5th) 294 (S.C.J.)

Where the court was managing over 30 similar class proceedings and the parties wished to bring various certification, rule 20 and rule 21 motions, the court directed that all motions be heard together.

Hague v. Liberty Mutual Insurance Co. (2001), 2001 CarswellOnt 4338, [2001] O.J. No. 4872, 17 C.P.C. (5th) 316 (S.C.J.); additional reasons at (February 6, 2002), Doc. 01-CV-204787CP, 2002 CarswellOnt 372 (S.C.J.)

The court refused to stay one class action pending a motion for summary judgment in a similar case involving different parties.

Moyes v. Fortune Financial Corp. (2001), [2001] O.J. No. 4455, 2001 CarswellOnt 4062, 13 C.P.C. (5th) 147 (S.C.J.); additional reasons at (November 27, 2001), Doc. 00-CV-198979CP, 2001 CarswellOnt 4220 (S.C.J.)

Ordinarily certification is the first order of business, subject to exceptions for motions to strike as disclosing no cause of action, and for motions regarding evidence for the certification motion. The court deferred the hearing of a summary judgment motion until after certification.

Holmes v. London Life Insurance Co. (2000), 50 O.R. (3d) 388, 23 C.C.L.I. (3d) 148, 1 C.P.C. (5th) 95, 2000 CarswellOnt 3463 (S.C.J.)

It is a matter of discretion whether the certification motion should be heard prior to an application to adjudicate the merits of the claim. In this case, the court dealt with the merits first.

Tang Estate v. Huang & Danczkay Properties (1997), 10 C.P.C. (4th) 344 (Ont. Gen. Div.)

This class action was stayed pending disposition of an appeal in a related action.

Sutherland v. Canadian Red Cross Society (1994), 17 O.R. (3d) 645, 21 C.P.C. (3d) 137, 112 D.L.R. (4th) 504 (Gen. Div.)

The court declined to rule on an argument that the action was statute-barred where no separate motion was brought under rule 21 in that regard. A certification motion includes affidavit evidence which may be inappropriate to mix with a rule 21 motion.

Andersen v. St. Jude Medical Inc., 2010 CarswellOnt 3, 2010 ONSC 77, [2010] O.J. No. 8, 87 C.P.C. (6th) 45 (S.C.J.)

Shortly before trial the court amended the certification order to include waiver of tort as a common issue and bifurcated the trial to defer determination of punitive damage issues.

Parties and Joinder

Hudspeth v. Whatcott, 2017 ONSC 1708, 2017 CarswellOnt 3918, 98 C.P.C. (7th) 40 (S.C.J.)

The court permitted the plaintiffs to amend their claim to create an opt-in joinder action for defamation, civil conspiracy to injure, and intentional infliction of mental suffering against defendants who distributed hateful pamphlets at a gay pride parade. The plaintiffs could seek declaratory and injunctive relief similar to that available under Rule 23 of the US Federal *Rules of Civil Procedure*.

Ledyit v. Bristol-Myers Squibb Canada Inc., 2008 CarswellOnt 2613, 2008 ONCA 372, 53 C.P.C. (6th) 209 (C.A.)

Where the named plaintiff did not have a claim against one of several defendants, the court added as a plaintiff a class member residing in Quebec who did have such a claim.

Matoni v. C.B.S. Interactive Multimedia Inc. (January 22, 2008), Doc. 06-CV-310529CP, 2008 CarswellOnt 228, [2008] O.J. No. 197 (S.C.J.); additional reasons at (August 29, 2008), Doc. 06-CV-310529CP, 2008 CarswellOnt 5077 (S.C.J.); additional reasons at (December 3, 2008), Doc. 06-CV-310529CP, 2008 CarswellOnt 7185 (S.C.J.); additional reasons at (August 29, 2008), Doc. 06-CV-310529CP, 2008 CarswellOnt 5076 (Ont. S.C.J.); additional reasons at (December 3, 2008), Doc. 06-CV-310529CP, 2008 CarswellOnt 7185 (S.C.J.)

Where the named plaintiffs did not have a valid claim, but the case was otherwise suitable for certification, the court gave the plaintiffs a reasonable opportunity, free from interference by the defendants, to find a suitable representative plaintiff.

Heron v. Guidant Corp. (June 8, 2007), Doc. 05-CV-295630 CP, 2007 CarswellOnt 9010, [2007] O.J. No. 3823 (Ont. S.C.J.)

Where a class action had been commenced regarding defective defibrillators and a second class action was commenced regarding both defective defibrillators and defective pacemakers, the court permitted the second action to be limited to pacemakers, removed from the second action the plaintiff who had received a defibrillator, and added him as a plaintiff in the first action.

Lawrence v. Atlas Cold Storage Holdings Inc. (2006), 34 C.P.C. (6th) 41, 2006 CarswellOnt 5716 (S.C.J.); additional reasons at (January 30, 2007), Doc. 04-CV-263289 CP, 2007 CarswellOnt 479 (S.C.J.)

The court added a plaintiff, on terms, where the class action was at an early stage and there was no prejudice to the defendants.

Parsons v. McDonald's Restaurants of Canada Ltd. (2005), [2005] O.J. No. 506, 2005 CarswellOnt 544, (sub nom. *Currie v. McDonald's Restaurants of Canada Ltd.*) 74 O.R. (3d) 321, 7 C.P.C. (6th) 60, (sub nom. *Currie v. McDonald's Restaurants of Canada Ltd.*) 250 D.L.R.

(4th) 224, (sub nom. *Currie v. McDonald's Restaurants of Canada Ltd.)* 195 O.A.C. 244 (C.A.)

The court found that commencement of two similar class actions by plaintiffs represented by the same counsel was not an abuse of process where it was done to protect the interests of the class members. Plaintiff's counsel's job was to protect the legal interests of the proposed class. The legal rights of the plaintiffs were not affected by their lawyers' pecuniary interest in the litigation.

Shaw v. Zurich Canada (2004), 72 O.R. (3d) 452, 2004 CarswellOnt 3809, 9 M.V.R. (5th) 250 (S.C.J.)

The court refused to add a new representative plaintiff after it was determined or conceded that the current representative plaintiff has no cause of action.

Veley v. CGU Insurance Co. of Canada (2004), 2004 CarswellOnt 164, 7 C.C.L.I. (4th) 128, 43 C.P.C. (5th) 400 (S.C.J.)

Where a class action was brought based on a widespread industry practice, and the defendant corporation was the product of an amalgamation of two predecessor companies which had followed the industry practice, the court held that the plaintiff could serve as representative plaintiff notwithstanding he was a customer of only one of the predecessor companies. *Segnitz v. Royal & Sunalliance Insurance Co. of Canada* (2003), 29 C.P.C. (5th) 359, [2003] O.J. No. 78, 2003 CarswellOnt 50, 44 C.C.L.I. (3d) 248 (S.C.J.); additional reasons at (January 20, 2003), Doc. 37188/01, 2003 CarswellOnt 139, [2003] O.J. No. 102 (S.C.J.); additional reasons at (2004), 2004 CarswellOnt 1287, [2004] O.J. No. 1376, 49 C.P.C. (5th) 167, 12 C.C.L.I. (4th) 143 (S.C.J.) held to be wrongly decided.

Veley v. CGU Insurance Co. of Canada (2004), 2004 CarswellOnt 164, 7 C.C.L.I. (4th) 128, 43 C.P.C. (5th) 400 (S.C.J.)

Where the defendant's motion to dismiss the action based on the plaintiff's individual claim being statute barred was heard together with the plaintiff's motion to substitute a new plaintiff whose claim was not statute barred, the court dismissed the named plaintiff's individual claim but permitted a new plaintiff to be added.

Farquhar v. Liberty Mutual Insurance Co. (2004), 2004 CarswellOnt 166, 6 C.C.L.I. (4th) 193, [2004] O.J. No. 148, 43 C.P.C. (5th) 361 (S.C.J.)

Where the defendant's motion to dismiss the action based on the plaintiff's individual claim being statute barred was granted but before the order was issued and entered the plaintiff' brought a motion to substitute a new plaintiff whose claim was not statute barred, the court refused to permit a new plaintiff to be added, and the entire action was dismissed.

Giuliano v. Allstate Insurance Co. (2003), 66 O.R. (3d) 238, [2003] O.J. No. 3266, 2003 CarswellOnt 3159, 3 C.C.L.I. (4th) 216, 40 C.P.C. (5th) 140, 46 M.V.R. (4th) 143 (S.C.J.)

Where the named plaintiff did not have a valid claim, the court permitted another class member who had a tenable claim to be added as a representative plaintiff.

Logan v. Ontario (Minister of Health) (2003), 2003 CarswellOnt 425, [2003] O.J. No. 418, 36 C.P.C. (5th) 176 (S.C.J.); affirmed (2004), [2004] O.J. No. 2769, 2004 CarswellOnt 2662, 71 O.R. (3d) 451, 47 C.P.C. (5th) 1, (sub nom. *Logan v. Canada (Minister of Health)*) 188 O.A.C. 294 (C.A.)

The court permitted the named plaintiff to withdraw and be replaced by other class members.

Boulanger v. Johnson & Johnson Corp. (2003), 2003 CarswellOnt 1405, 170 O.A.C. 333, 64 O.R. (3d) 208, 226 D.L.R. (4th) 747, 32 C.P.C. (5th) 203 (Div. Ct.)

A representative plaintiff is entitled to advance claims for class members which the representative plaintiff does not have in her personal capacity. However, the representative plaintiff must have some claim against the defendant in her personal capacity. *Andersen v. St. Jude Medical Inc.*, [2002] O.J. No. 260, 2002 CarswellOnt 150, [2002] O.T.C. 53 (S.C.J.) overruled.

Wilson v. Servier Canada Inc. (2003), 2002 CarswellOnt 5665, [2002] O.J. No. 2138, 46 C.P.C. (5th) 359 (S.C.J.); leave to appeal refused (October 4, 2002), Doc. 584/02, 2002 CarswellOnt 5663 (Div. Ct.)

The court amended a certification order to add new defendants who were not parties at the time of the original certification hearing.

Young v. Janssen-Ortho Inc. (2002), 15 C.P.C. (6th) 327, 2002 CarswellOnt 6214 (S.C.J.); affirmed (2003), 2003 CarswellOnt 697, (sub nom. *Young Estate v. Janssen-Ortho Inc.*) 169 O.A.C. 158, 32 C.P.C. (5th) 47 (C.A.)

The court consolidated two class proceedings and substituted a new representative plaintiff.

Egglestone v. Barker (2001), [2001] O.J. No. 1617, 2001 CarswellOnt 1508, 9 C.P.C. (5th) 304 (S.C.J.)

The court granted a motion adding a co-representative plaintiff.

Western Canadian Shopping Centres Inc. v. Dutton (2001), 2001 SCC 46, (sub nom. *Western Canadian Shopping Centres Inc. v. Bennett Jones Verchere*) 201 D.L.R. (4th) 385, [2000] S.C.J. No. 63, 2001 CarswellAlta 884, 2001 CarswellAlta 885, 94 Alta. L.R. (3d) 1, 272 N.R. 135, 8 C.P.C. (5th) 1, [2002] 1 W.W.R. 1, 286 A.R. 201, 253 W.A.C. 201, [2001] 2 S.C.R. 534

In assessing whether the proposed representative is adequate, the court may look to the motivation of the representative, the competence of the representative's counsel, and the capacity of the representative to bear any costs that may be incurred by the representative in particular (as opposed to by counsel or by the class members generally). The proposed representative need not be "typical" of the class, nor the "best" possible representative but must vigorously and capably prosecute the interests of the class.

Ragoonanan Estate v. Imperial Tobacco Canada Ltd. (2000), 51 O.R. (3d) 603, 2000 CarswellOnt 4613, [2000] O.J. No. 4597, 4 C.C.L.T. (3d) 132 (S.C.J.)

Where the plaintiff had no reasonable cause of action against a defendant, the court struck out the statement of claim. The fact that putative class members may have a cause of action against that defendant was insufficient.

Anderson v. Wilson (1999), 44 O.R. (3d) 673, 122 O.A.C. 69, 175 D.L.R. (4th) 409, 36 C.P.C. (4th) 17, 1999 CarswellOnt 2073, [1999] O.J. No. 2494 (C.A.); leave to appeal refused (2000), 258 N.R. 194 (note), 138 O.A.C. 200 (note), 2000 CarswellOnt 1837, 2000 CarswellOnt 1838, [1999] S.C.C.A. No. 476

Representatives who did not share all the same complaints as some of the class members were approved. There was no conflict of interest and no reality to the suggestion they would not adequately represent all class members. If and when real problems arose it would not be difficult to create separate representation.

Bywater v. Toronto Transit Commission (1998), 27 C.P.C. (4th) 172, 1998 CarswellOnt 4645, [1998] O.J. No. 4913 (Gen. Div.); additional reasons at (1999), 30 C.P.C. (4th) 131, 1999 CarswellOnt 201, [1999] O.J. No. 67 (Gen. Div.)

A representative plaintiff need not be typical of the class or share every characteristic of every other member of the class. It is sufficient that he or she would fairly and adequately represent the interests of the class and be without interests in conflict on the common issues.

Ontario New Home Warranty Program v. General Electric Co. (1998), 36 O.R. (3d) 787, 17 C.P.C. (4th) 183, 1998 CarswellOnt 138 (Gen. Div.)

Where the plaintiff may not have had capacity to assert several of the claims contained in the statement of claim, the court added to additional plaintiffs *nunc pro tunc*.

Maxwell v. MLG Ventures Ltd. (1995), 7 C.C.L.S. 155 (Ont. Gen. Div.)

Lack of a complete knowledge of issues involved in the class proceeding did not mean that the representative plaintiff could not adequately represent the class. The representative had adequate knowledge and was clearly able to instruct counsel.

Abdool v. Anaheim Management Ltd. (1995), 21 O.R. (3d) 453, 31 C.P.C. (3d) 197, 121 D.L.R. (4th) 496, 78 O.A.C. 377 (Div. Ct.)

The class representative need not be typical of class members provided he or she has no conflict of interest and will fairly and adequately advance the class claims.

Bendall v. McGhan Medical Corp. (1993), 14 O.R. (3d) 734, 16 C.P.C. (3d) 156, 106 D.L.R. (4th) 339 (Gen. Div.)

In cases involving multiple plaintiffs and defendants it is not necessary that each plaintiff have a cause of action against each defendant so long as each defendant has a cause of action asserted against it by at least one plaintiff.

Defendant Class Issues

General Motors of Canada Ltd. v. Abrams, 2011 ONSC 5338, 2011 CarswellOnt 9366, [2011] O.J. No. 4175, 93 C.C.P.B. 97, 2011 C.L.L.C. 220-056, 2011 C.E.B. & P.G.R. 8455, 13 C.P.C. (7th) 130 (S.C.J.)

For settlement purposes, the court certified a claim against the plaintiff's retired employees regarding termination or alteration of their health care benefits.

Chippewas of Sarnia Band v. Canada (A.G.) (1996), 29 O.R. (3d) 549, 137 D.L.R. (4th) 239; additional reasons (1996), 138 D.L.R. (4th) 574 (Gen. Div.)

Where an Indian Band asserted a land claim, the court appointed representative defendants to act on behalf of up to six classes of defendants. All potential defendants need not be named prior to certification. The representative defendant need not consent or be willing to assume that role.

MacDougall v. Ontario Northland Transportation Commission (2004), 2004 CarswellOnt 5859, 7 C.P.C. (6th) 193, 45 C.C.P.B. 68 (S.C.J.)

In this pension class action, it was necessary to appoint representative defendants to represent the interests of a certain group of pension plan members. However the court refused to appoint the proposed representatives because the position they took was contrary to the interests of the subject group.

Conversion to or from Individual Action

Bellefeuille v. Canadian Pacific Railway, 2010 ONSC 5499, 2010 CarswellOnt 10758 (S.C.J.); additional reasons at 2011 ONSC 188, 2011 CarswellOnt 986 (S.C.J.); leave to appeal refused 2011 ONSC 2648, 2011 CarswellOnt 2832, 283 O.A.C. 119, [2011] O.J. No. 1937 (Div. Ct.)

The court has jurisdiction to convert an individual action into a class action, and did so in this case to advance the goals of the *Class Proceedings Act*.

Vennell v. Barnado's (2004), 73 O.R. (3d) 13, 2004 CarswellOnt 4196 (S.C.J.)

The court permitted an action commenced under the *Class Proceedings Act* to be converted to an individual action where notice was given to the class members and no one objected. Although the defendant consented, court approval is required.

Logan v. Ontario (Minister of Health) (2003), 2003 CarswellOnt 425, [2003] O.J. No. 418, 36 C.P.C. (5th) 176 (S.C.J.); affirmed (2004), [2004] O.J. No. 2769, 2004 CarswellOnt 2662, 71 O.R. (3d) 451, 47 C.P.C. (5th) 1, (sub nom. *Logan v. Canada (Minister of Health))* 188 O.A.C. 294 (C.A.)

A proceeding commenced under the *Class Proceedings Act* is not simply an individual action until certification is granted. Rather it is a special type of action that may be converted, at the court's discretion under s. 7, to a regular individual proceeding.

Gariepy v. Shell Oil Co. (2003), 2003 CarswellOnt 8, 63 O.R. (3d) 91, 29 C.P.C. (5th) 305 (S.C.J.)

An intended class proceeding does not lose its status as such if certification is denied. An order under s. 7 is necessary to change it to an individual action.

Notice Issues

Ducharme v. Solarium de Paris Inc., 2013 ONSC 2540, 2013 CarswellOnt 5783 (S.C.J.); additional reasons 2013 ONSC 3148, 2013 CarswellOnt 7381 (S.C.J.); leave to appeal refused 2013 ONSC 5098, 2013 CarswellOnt 11114 (S.C.J.); additional reasons 2013 ONSC 7897, 2013 CarswellOnt 17953 (S.C.J.)

Where not all class members had been identified, the court ordered notice be given by way of a combination of mailed notices and newspaper advertisements.

Silver v. Imax Corp., 2012 ONSC 1047, 2012 CarswellOnt 3621, 110 O.R. (3d) 425, [2012] O.J. No. 1352 (S.C.J.); additional reasons 2012 ONSC 4064, 2012 CarswellOnt 8512, 40 C.P.C. (7th) 60, [2012] O.J. No. 3150 (S.C.J.)

In this certified securities class action, which overlapped with an uncertified U.S. class action, the court gave directions regarding notice of certification and a press release required by s. 138.9 of the *Securities Act*.

White v. IKO Industries Ltd., 2010 ONSC 3920, 2010 CarswellOnt 4970, 98 C.P.C. (6th) 68, [2010] O.J. No. 2954 (S.C.J.)

The court provided guidance on the timing and the content of a notice to class members.

Gallagher v. Aurelian Resources Inc., 2009 CarswellOnt 4277, 81 C.P.C. (6th) 148 (S.C.J.)

The court ruled that two persons were class members and should be given notice.

Maggisano v. Skyservice Airlines Inc., 2010 ONSC 6203, 2010 CarswellOnt 8536, 6 C.P.C. (7th) 394 (S.C.J.)

In this rare case where all class members were identified by name, the court approved notice of certification by way of direct mail, a press release and a website.

Isaacs v. Nortel Networks Corp. (2001), 2001 CarswellOnt 4404, 15 C.C.E.L. (3d) 78, 16 C.P.C. (5th) 69, 31 C.C.P.B. 41 (S.C.J.)

The court ruled that the plaintiff, not the defendant, should provide the notice of certification.

Wilson v. Servier Canada Inc. (2000), 50 O.R. (3d) 219, 2000 CarswellOnt 3257, [2000] O.J. No. 3392, 49 C.P.C. (4th) 233 (S.C.J.); leave to appeal refused (2000), 52 O.R. (3d) 20, 2000 CarswellOnt 4399, 143 O.A.C. 279 (Div. Ct.); leave to appeal refused (2001), 2001 CarswellOnt 3077, 2001 CarswellOnt 3078, [2001] S.C.C.A. No. 88, 276 N.R. 197 (note), 154 O.A.C. 198 (note)

The defendants were ordered to pay the cost of notice to class members in this class action against the distributor of a weight loss pill.

Maxwell v. MLG Ventures Ltd. (1995), 7 C.C.L.S. 155 (Ont. Gen. Div.)

Where individual issues necessitated affidavits from class members and made discovery of class members a possibility, the court required the notice to state that affidavits would be required and discuss possible discovery costs.

A. (W.) v. St. Andrew's College (2008), 292 D.L.R. (4th) 427, 65 C.P.C. (6th) 18, 2008 CarswellOnt 2454 (S.C.J.)

Where the court dismissed the action for failure of the named plaintiffs to pay a costs award, the court ordered notice given to known and unknown class members.

Johnston v. State Farm Insurance Co. of Canada (2003), 38 C.P.C. (5th) 181, [2003] O.J. No. 3700, 2003 CarswellOnt 3544 (S.C.J.)

Where the court found the plaintiff's personal claim was barred by a limitation period, the court refused to order notice to the class members whose claims were within the limitation period in order to permit such a class member to be substituted as a plaintiff. Rather, the court dismissed the action in its entirety.

Lewis v. Shell Canada Ltd. (2000), 48 O.R. (3d) 612, 46 C.P.C. (4th) 378, 2000 CarswellOnt 1827 (S.C.J.)

The goal of providing effective access to justice requires that putative class members with whom a defendant wishes to negotiate individual settlements should have knowledge of the class action including an opportunity to consult class counsel. Prior to certification the court ordered the defendants to give a court approved notice to any potential class member with whom they wished to settle.

Bywater v. Toronto Transit Commission (1999), 43 O.R. (3d) 367, 28 C.P.C. (4th) 307, 1999 CarswellOnt 1139, [1999] O.J. No. 1402 (Gen. Div.)

Sections 17 to 20 are intended to ensure that at certain critical points in class actions, the class members are given specified information to make decisions that will affect their legal rights. The meaning of "notice" is to be taken in that context. A commensurate level of formality is to be expected in a document said to constitute "notice." In this case a press release concerning the court's decision granting certification and summary judgment was held not to be a "notice."

Communications with Class Members

Amyotrophic Lateral Sclerosis Society of Essex County v. Windsor (City), 2016 ONSC 676, 2016 CarswellOnt 21157, 58 M.P.L.R. (5th) 127 (S.C.J.); leave to appeal refused 2016 ONSC 1929, 2016 CarswellOnt 4634, 58 M.P.L.R. (5th) 137 (Div. Ct.)

Where the defendant went too far in conducting a multi-media opt-out campaign, the court permitted the class members to reconsider their opt-outs.

Quenneville v. Volkswagen Group Canada Inc., 2016 ONSC 959, 2016 CarswellOnt 2163 (S.C.J.)

Where the law firm that lost a carriage motion solicited individual retainers from the class members, the court ordered the law firm to send a clarifying e-mail and not accept the individual retainers.

de Muelenaere v. Great Gulf Homes Ltd., 2015 ONSC 7442, 2015 CarswellOnt 18181, 79 C.P.C. (7th) 366 (S.C.J.)

The court refused to set aside settlements made between the defendant and 24 putative class members prior to certification.

Durling v. Sunrise Propane Energy Group Inc. (2012), 2012 ONSC 6328, 2012 CarswellOnt 14079, 33 C.P.C. (7th) 42, [2013] I.L.R. I-5356 (S.C.J.)

Where an insurer sent letters to class members interfering with the opt out process, the court ordered the insurer not to communicate with class members without court approval or class counsel's consent.

1250264 Ontario Inc. v. Pet Valu Canada Inc., 2013 ONCA 279, 2013 CarswellOnt 5242, 115 O.R. (3d) 653, 34 C.P.C. (7th) 53, 362 D.L.R. (4th) 88, 305 O.A.C. 329, [2013] O.J. No. 2012

Where a group of class members urged other class members to opt out, the Court of Appeal reversed a ruling by the motions court that found the opt-out process had been subverted, set aside certain opt-outs, ordered a new notice, and provided a further opportunity to opt out. The communications did not constitute misinformation, threats, coercion, or intimidation and was not otherwise unlawful. There was no evidence to support a finding that the opt-outs by individual class members were not voluntary or fully informed.

Lundy v. VIA Rail Canada Inc., 2012 ONSC 4152, 2012 CarswellOnt 9152, 111 O.R. (3d) 628, 41 C.P.C. (7th) 347 (S.C.J.)

Prior to certification the court permitted the defendants to make offers to settle to putative class members provided (a) plaintiff's counsel was provided with advance copies, and (b) no communications be sent to putative class members who were already clients of plaintiff's counsel.

Ward-Price v. Mariners Haven Inc. (2004), 3 C.P.C. (6th) 116, [2004] O.J. No. 2308, 2004 CarswellOnt 2238, 71 O.R. (3d) 664 (S.C.J.); additional reasons at (July 8, 2004), Doc. 96-CU-103518, 2004 CarswellOnt 5764, [2004] O.J. No. 5528 (S.C.J.)

Counsel for the plaintiff becomes counsel for the class when the case is certified, not when the opt out period expires. Correspondence from class counsel to class members is privileged and cannot be waived by a single class member. *Mangan v. Inco Ltd.* (1998), 38 O.R. (3d) 703, 1998 CarswellOnt 801, 16 C.P.C. (4th) 165, 27 C.E.L.R. (N.S.) 141 (Gen. Div.) not followed.

1176560 Ontario Ltd. v. Great Atlantic & Pacific Co. of Canada Ltd. (2002), 2002 CarswellOnt 4272, 28 C.P.C. (5th) 135, [2002] O.J. No. 4781, 62 O.R. (3d) 535 (S.C.J.); leave to appeal allowed (2003), 2003 CarswellOnt 998, [2003] O.J. No. 1089, 169 O.A.C. 343, 64 O.R. (3d) 42 (Div. Ct.); affirmed (2004), [2004] O.J. No. 865, 2004 CarswellOnt 945, 50 C.P.C. (5th) 25, 70 O.R. (3d) 182, 184 O.A.C. 298 (Div. Ct.); leave to appeal refused (2004), 2004 CarswellOnt 3045, 50 C.P.C. (5th) 34 (C.A.)

The court restrained the defendant's communications with class members where the defendant had engaged in a course of conduct that was intimidating, threatening, coercive and misleading.

Pearson v. Inco Ltd. (2001), 57 O.R. (3d) 278, 2001 CarswellOnt 4340, 16 C.P.C. (5th) 357 (S.C.J.); additional reasons at (2002), 2002 CarswellOnt 52, [2002] O.J. No. 73, 45 C.E.L.R. (N.S.) 317 (S.C.J.)

Where the defendant sent out packages of material to property owners in the affected area, the purpose of which was to obtain the written consent of property owners to allow the defendant to enter into their homes and undertake an extensive indoor sampling program, the court held that the actions of the defendant did not approach the severity of conduct that would warrant court intervention under s. 12 of the *Class Proceedings Act*.

Vitelli v. Villa Giardino Homes Ltd. (2001), 54 O.R. (3d) 334, 2001 CarswellOnt 1954, 11 C.P.C. (5th) 65, [2001] O.J. No. 2119 (S.C.J.)

The court criticized defendant's counsel for improper communications with class members and ordered that, when communicating with class members, counsel must disclose that they are legal counsel and the party they represent.

Taub v. Manufacturers Life Insurance Company (April 22, 1999), Doc. 97-CU-122948, [1999] O.J. No. 2658 (S.C.J.)

The court gave directions permitting the plaintiff to communicate with class members to raise funds to pay a costs award previously made in favour of the defendant. The court did not require approval of the contents of the communications.

Mangan v. Inco. Ltd. (1998), 38 O.R. (3d) 703, 16 C.P.C. (4th) 165, 27 C.E.L.R. (N.S.) 141 (Gen. Div.)

The court held certain communications from class counsel to potential class members was a "notice" and granted injunctive relief and sanctions against class counsel for making the communications without prior court approval.

Participation of Class Members

Quenneville v. Volkswagen Group Canada Inc., 2018 ONSC 1020, 2018 CarswellOnt 2159 (S.C.J.)

Where 66 class members wished to opt-out of a court approved settlement, the court considered each of their circumstances and concluded none had a valid reason to opt-out after the deadline for doing so.

Cannon v. Funds for Canada Foundation, 2014 ONSC 2259, 2014 CarswellOnt 5159, 68 C.P.C. (7th) 180 (S.C.J.); additional reasons 2014 ONSC 4218, 2014 CarswellOnt 9703 (S.C.J.)

The court refused to permit several class members who had opted out to opt back in after a multi-million dollar settlement was reached. The opt-out procedure should be re-opened only in cases of misinformation or misconduct.

Durling v. Sunrise Propane Energy Group Inc., 2011 ONSC 266, 2011 CarswellOnt 77, 10 C.P.C. (7th) 188 (S.C.J.)

The court awarded costs against putative class members who initially opposed a motion to stay their individual actions pending determination of a certification motion, but ultimately agreed to the stay.

Soderstrom v. Hoffman-LaRoche Ltd. (2006), 2006 CarswellOnt 47, 25 C.P.C. (6th) 256 (S.C.J.)

A proceeding by a disgruntled class member attacking a court approved settlement was held to be an abuse of process, and stayed.

Webb v. 3584747 Canada Inc. (2005), 2005 CarswellOnt 499, 40 C.C.E.L. (3d) 74, [2005] O.T.C. 104, 9 C.P.C. (6th) 50 (S.C.J.); leave to appeal refused (2005), 2005 CarswellOnt 3394, 201 O.A.C. 113, 43 C.C.E.L. (3d) 147 (Div. Ct.); additional reasons at (August 30, 2005), Doc. 228/05, 2005 CarswellOnt 4029 (Div. Ct.)

Where the initial process to determine individual issues proved to be too expensive, the court amended the process, *inter alia*, by appointing less expensive referees.

Obonsawin v. Canada (2002), 26 C.P.C. (5th) 293, 2002 CarswellOnt 2066 (S.C.J.)

The court refused to permit an individual plaintiff, who was not a member of the proposed class, to join his individual action with the proposed class proceeding.

Allan v. CIBC Trust Corp. (1998), 39 O.R. (3d) 675, 18 C.P.C. (4th) 377 (Gen. Div.)

Where a class action based on only one theory of liability was dismissed, class members were permitted to sue separately to advance an alternative theory of liability. Section 27(3) limits the binding effect of a judgment to common issues described in the certification order.

Limitation Periods

LBP Holdings Ltd. v. Allied Nevada Gold Corp., 2016 ONSC 1629, 2016 CarswellOnt 6566, 130 O.R. (3d) 401 (S.C.J.); leave to appeal refused 2016 ONSC 6037, 2016 CarswellOnt 14845 (Div. Ct.); affirmed 2017 ONCA 13, 2017 CarswellOnt 38

In a securities class action, where the defendant corporation was in bankruptcy proceedings, the court permitted the plaintiff to add the defendant corporation's "underwriters" as party defendants. However it struck certain claims as legally untenable.

Canadian Imperial Bank of Commerce v. Green, 2015 CSC 60, 2015 SCC 60, 2015 CarswellOnt 18335, 2015 CarswellOnt 18336, [2015] 3 S.C.R. 801, 135 O.R. (3d) 334 (note), 44 B.L.R. (5th) 1, 77 C.P.C. (7th) 1, 391 D.L.R. (4th) 567, 478 N.R. 202, 346 O.A.C. 204, [2015] S.C.J. No. 60

Section 28 of the *Class Proceedings Act* suspends the limitation period for claims under s. 138.3 of the *Ontario Securities Act* when leave is granted under s. 138.8. If leave was sought prior to the expiry of the limitation period, the court has a discretion to grant leave *nunc pro tunc*.

Drywall Acoustic Lathing and Insulation, Local 675 Pension Fund (Trustee of) v. SNC-Lavalin Group Inc., 2015 ONCA 718, 2015 CarswellOnt 16324, 81 C.P.C. (7th) 91, 340 O.A.C. 271

The court refused to permit amendments with respect to which (a) no leave had been obtained under s. 138.8(1) of the *Securities Act* and (b) the limitation period had expired.

Green v. Canadian Imperial Bank of Commerce, 2014 ONCA 90, 2014 CarswellOnt 1143, (sub nom. *Millwright Regional Council of Ontario Pension Trust Fund (Trustess of) v. Celestica Inc.)* 118 O.R. (3d) 641, 50 C.P.C. (7th) 113, 370 D.L.R. (4th) 402, 314 O.A.C. 315, [2014] O.J. No. 419; additional reasons 2014 ONCA 344, 2014 CarswellOnt 5625, 68 C.P.C. (7th) 99; affirmed 2015 CSC 60, 2015 SCC 60, 2015 CarswellOnt 18335, 2015 CarswellOnt 18336, [2015] 3 S.C.R. 801, 135 O.R. (3d) 334 (note), 44 B.L.R. (5th) 1, 77 C.P.C. (7th) 1, 391 D.L.R. (4th) 567, 478 N.R. 202, 346 O.A.C. 204, [2015] S.C.J. No. 60

The Court of Appeal overruled its own decision in *Sharma v. Timminco Ltd.*, 2012 ONCA 107, 2012 CarswellOnt 1904, 109 O.R. (3d) 569, 19 C.P.C. (7th) 1, [2012] O.J. No. 719; additional reasons 2012 ONCA 322, 2012 CarswellOnt 6055, 19 C.P.C. (7th) 271; leave to appeal refused 2012 CarswellOnt 10678, 2012 CarswellOnt 10679, 438 N.R. 400 (note), 303 O.A.C. 389 (note) (S.C.C.) and held if an action commenced within the limitation period in s. 138.14 of the *Securities Act* pleads a s. 138.3 cause of action and an intent to seek leave to commence an action thereunder, then s. 28 of the *Class Proceedings Act* suspends the limitation period for all class members.

Coulson v. Citigroup Global Markets Canada Inc., 2012 ONCA 108, 2012 CarswellOnt 2048, 16 C.P.C. (7th) 1, 288 O.A.C. 355, [2012] O.J. No. 717

The court held that the combined effect of a previous appeal and s. 28(2) of the *Class Proceedings Act* did not prevent the expiry of a limitation period provided by s. 138 of the *Securities Act.*

Sharma v. Timminco Ltd., 2012 ONCA 107, 2012 CarswellOnt 1904, 109 O.R. (3d) 569, 19 C.P.C. (7th) 1, 345 D.L.R. (4th) 94, 289 O.A.C. 19, [2012] O.J. No. 719; additional reasons 2012 ONCA 322, 2012 CarswellOnt 6055, 19 C.P.C. (7th) 271; leave to appeal refused 2012 CarswellOnt 10678, 2012 CarswellOnt 10679, 438 N.R. 400 (note), 303 O.A.C. 389 (note) (S.C.C.)

Section 28 of the *Class Proceedings Act* does not suspend the limitation period for a claim under s. 138.3 of the *Securities Act* if leave to commence the action is not obtained under s. 138(8)(1).

Ragoonanan v. Imperial Tobacco Canada Ltd., 2011 ONSC 6187, 2011 CarswellOnt 10829, 107 O.R. (3d) 587, 38 C.P.C. (7th) 231 (S.C.J.)

The limitation period does not resume running if certification is denied. The court permitted the action to proceed as an individual action.

Smith v. Inco Ltd., 2011 ONCA 628, 2011 CarswellOnt 10141, 107 O.R. (3d) 321, 88 C.C.L.T. (3d) 1, 62 C.E.L.R. (3d) 93, 340 D.L.R. (4th) 602, 284 O.A.C. 13, [2011] O.J. No. 4386; leave to appeal refused 2012 CarswellOnt 4932, 2012 CarswellOnt 4933, [2012] 1 S.C.R. xii (note), 435 N.R. 392 (note), 300 O.A.C. 401 (note) (S.C.C.)

The court held application of the *Limitations Act* was an individual issue, not a common issue.

Coulson v. Citigroup Global Markets Canada Inc., 2010 CarswellOnt 1593, 2010 ONSC 1596, [2010] O.J. No. 1109, 92 C.P.C. (6th) 301 (S.C.J.); additional reasons 2010 CarswellOnt 2704, 2010 ONSC 2553, 92 C.P.C.

(6th) 340 (S.C.J.); affirmed 2012 ONCA 108, 2012 CarswellOnt 2048, 16 C.P.C. (7th) 1, 288 O.A.C. 355, [2012] O.J. No. 717

The limitation period for a cause of action asserted in a class proceeding is suspended even if it is later held the named plaintiff does not have a personal claim for that cause of action.

Logan v. Ontario (Minister of Health) (2004), 47 C.P.C. (5th) 1, [2004] O.J. No. 2769, 2004 CarswellOnt 2662, (sub nom. *Logan v. Canada (Minister of Health)*) 71 O.R. (3d) 451, 188 O.A.C. 294 (C.A.)

The limitation period is suspended at the date of the commencement of the proceeding, not the date of certification.

Gariepy v. Shell Oil Co. (2003), 2003 CarswellOnt 8, 63 O.R. (3d) 91, 29 C.P.C. (5th) 305 (S.C.J.)

Where certification is denied the limitation period continues to be suspended until all appeals have been finally disposed of.

Egglestone v. Barker (2001), [2001] O.J. No. 1617, 2001 CarswellOnt 1508, 9 C.P.C. (5th) 304 (S.C.J.)

Issuance of the statement of claim suspends any limitation period regarding the class members.

Pleadings

Castrillo v. Workplace Safety and Insurance Board, 2017 ONCA 121, 2017 CarswellOnt 1765, 136 O.R. (3d) 654, 37 C.C.L.T. (4th) 217

The court refused to strike a claim by injured workers against the Workplace Safety and Insurance Board for misfeasance in public office and negligence.

Turner v. York University, 2011 ONSC 6151, 2011 CarswellOnt 11051 (S.C.J.); additional reasons at 2011 ONSC 7146, 2011 CarswellOnt 14428, 38 C.P.C. (7th) 225 (S.C.J.)

The court refused to amend the statement of claim after certification had been denied. *Res judicata* prevented relitigation of the certification issue.

McLaren v. Stratford (City) (2004), 50 C.P.C. (5th) 310, 2004 CarswellOnt 2839, 50 M.P.L.R. (3d) 271 (S.C.J.); additional reasons at (2005), 2005 CarswellOnt 2353, 13 C.P.C. (6th) 113, 12 M.P.L.R. (4th) 43 (S.C.J.)

The court adjourned a certification motion where it was necessary for the plaintiff to amend the statement of claim to properly define the class and the common issues.

Blatt Holdings Ltd. v. Traders General Insurance Co. (2001), [2001] O.J. No. 949, 2001 CarswellOnt 782, 27 C.C.L.I. (3d) 308, 6 C.P.C. (5th) 174 (S.C.J.)

The court refused to order particulars of the statement of claim where it was reasonable to infer that the allegations pleaded regarding the plaintiff's claim likely applied to the class members generally. The plaintiff is not obliged to provide evidence proving the allegations at this stage.

Mangan v. Inco Ltd. (1996), 30 O.R. (3d) 90 (Gen. Div.)

The court granted leave pursuant to s. 12 of the *Class Proceedings Act* to defer service of a statement of defence until after determination of the certification motion in this action. In the preponderance of cases, a statement of defence is not required for determination of the certification motion.

Maxwell v. MLG Ventures Ltd. (1995), 40 C.P.C. (3d) 304 (Ont. Gen. Div.)

The plaintiff in a certified action was not permitted to amend the statement of claim where the proposed amendments fundamentally changed the nature of the action originally certified. Other amendments which did not change the nature of the action were allowed.

Affidavits and Cross-Examinations

K. (J.) v. Ontario, 2016 ONSC 8040, 2016 CarswellOnt 21094, 136 O.R. (3d) 67 (S.C.J.); appeal quashed 2017 ONCA 332, 2017 CarswellOnt 5949, 9 C.P.C. (8th) 22

Pre-certification, the court ordered the plaintiff to apply to the Youth Justice Court to obtain some of the plaintiff's youth records, which were subject to the *Youth Criminal Justice Act*, S.C. 2002, c. 1.

Daniells v. McLellan, 2016 ONSC 5958, 2016 CarswellOnt 16296, 2 C.P.C. (8th) 179 (S.C.J.)

On a certification motion, the court refused to require the plaintiff to produce clinical notes and other documents as they had limited relevance. Ordering production would be disproportionate.

Lambert v. Guidant Corp. (2009), [2009] O.J. No. 1910, 2009 CarswellOnt 2535, 72 C.P.C. (6th) 120 (S.C.J.); leave to appeal refused (2009), [2009] O.J. No. 4464, 2009 CarswellOnt 6512 (Div. Ct.)

It is not a legitimate approach for a defendant to file a mass of evidence relating to the merits and, when the plaintiffs do not contest the evidence on the certification motion, to argue that the evidence must be accepted as undisputed. The plaintiffs are not required to test the defendant's facts until discovery or summary judgment.

2038724 Ontario Ltd. v. Quizno's Canada Restaurant Corp. (February 8, 2008), Doc. 06-CV-311330CP, 2008 CarswellOnt 773 (S.C.J.)

Where the plaintiff raised new common issues shortly before the hearing of the certification motion, thereby depriving the defendant of the opportunity to cross-examine and introduce additional evidence, the court ordered the plaintiff not to advance such common issues at the certification motion. However, after the hearing of that motion, the plaintiff could either seek to amend the certification order to include such common issues, or reapply for certification based on such common issues, as the case may be.

Andersen v. St. Jude Medical Inc. (2003), [2003] O.J. No. 4314, 2003 CarswellOnt 5995, 2 C.P.C. (6th) 1 (S.C.J.); leave to appeal refused (January 28, 2005), Doc. Toronto 191/04, 192/04, 2005 CarswellOnt 318 (Div. Ct.)

The court adjourned a motion challenging the admissibility of evidence to be heard at the same time as the certification motion. While evidence of the merits is not directly relevant to certification, it may relate to some elements of the certification test. Costs sanctions may be appropriate where the proceedings have been protracted by an over abundance of evidence.

Price v. Panasonic Canada Inc. (December 21, 2001), Doc. Newmarket 55471/00, 2001 CarswellOnt 4639, [2001] O.J. No. 5244 (S.C.J.)

Inquiry into the merits of the action is not relevant on a motion for certification. The court dismissed a motion to compel the plaintiff to answer refused questions where there was already sufficient evidence before the court to determine the certification motion.

Hollick v. Metropolitan Toronto (Municipality), (sub nom. *Hollick v. Toronto (City))* 2001 SCC 68, [2001] S.C.J. No. 67, 2001 CarswellOnt 3577, 2001 CarswellOnt 3578, (sub nom. *Hollick v. Toronto (City))* 205 D.L.R. (4th) 19, (sub nom. *Hollick v. Toronto (City))* 56 O.R. (3d) 214 (headnote only), 24 M.P.L.R. (3d) 9, 277 N.R. 51, 13 C.P.C. (5th) 1, 42 C.E.L.R. (N.S.) 26, 153 O.A.C. 279, (sub nom. *Hollick v. Toronto (City))* [2001] 3 S.C.R. 158

The plaintiff must show some basis in fact for each of the certification requirements in s. 5, other than disclosure of a cause of action.

Caputo v. Imperial Tobacco Ltd. (1997), 34 O.R. (3d) 314, 13 C.P.C. (4th) 163, 148 D.L.R. (4th) 566 (Ont. Gen. Div.)

The defendant was permitted to examine the representative plaintiff under rule 39.03 where there would otherwise be an insufficient evidentiary record for the determination of the certification motion.

Anderson v. Wilson, [1996] O.J. 4827, 18 O.T.C. 79 (Gen. Div.)

A motion for certification is not a determination of the merits of the proceeding. In this class action arising out of an outbreak of hepatitis, the court held that questions concerning causation of the representative plaintiffs' hepatitis were not relevant to the issues on the certification motion.

Edwards v. Law Society of Upper Canada (1995), 40 C.P.C. (3d) 316 (Ont. Gen. Div.)

A motion to strike out affidavits filed in support of a motion for certification of an action as a class proceeding was allowed where the affidavits: (1) contained the reasons for judgment in a quasi-criminal proceeding; and (2) included an exhibit for which privilege was claimed and evidence as to information and belief where the source was counsel who was attempting to shield himself from cross-examination.

Discovery

Dine v. Biomet Inc., 2015 ONSC 1911, 2015 CarswellOnt 5331, [2015] O.J. No. 1857 (S.C.J.); additional reasons 2015 ONSC 3428, 2015 CarswellOnt 7771 (S.C.J.)

Prior to certification or cross-examination of the proposed representative plaintiff, production of documents, including medical records, will be ordered only if the defendant shows the documents are relevant to certification.

Brown v. Janssen Inc., 2015 ONSC 1434, 2015 CarswellOnt 3149 (S.C.J.); additional reasons 2015 ONSC 1920, 2015 CarswellOnt 3981 (S.C.J.)

The court ordered limited production of the plaintiffs' medical records prior to certification.

Fairview Donut Inc. v. TDL Group Corp., 2010 ONSC 6688, 2010 CarswellOnt 9259, 7 C.P.C. (7th) 375 (S.C.J.)

The court granted an interim confidentiality order, but refused to grant an order redacting certain documents and requiring use of pseudonyms.

Tetefsky v. General Motors Corp., 2010 CarswellOnt 1603, 2010 ONSC 1675, [2010] O.J. No. 1117 (S.C.J.); additional reasons at 96 C.P.C. (6th) 367, 2010 CarswellOnt 2717, 2010 ONSC 2539 (S.C.J.); affirmed 2011 ONCA 246, 2011 CarswellOnt 2100, [2011] O.J. No. 1390

While the court has jurisdiction to order a non-party to provide proprietary information to assist the plaintiff's certification motion, it refused to do so in this case where the plaintiff had not shown it was necessary.

Sharma v. Timminco Ltd., 2010 CarswellOnt 608, 2010 ONSC 790, [2010] O.J. No. 469 (S.C.J.); leave to appeal refused 2010 ONSC 2395, 2010 CarswellOnt 3987, [2010] O.J. No. 2161, 95 C.P.C. (6th) 1 (Div. Ct.)

The court ordered the defendant to produce insurance policy information earlier than would otherwise be required by rules 30.02(3) and 31.06(4).

Peter v. Medtronic Inc., 2009 CarswellOnt 6335, [2009] O.J. No. 4364, 83 C.P.C. (6th) 379 (S.C.J.); affirmed 2010 ONSC 3777, 2010 CarswellOnt

5221, [2010] O.J. No. 3056, 97 C.P.C. (6th) 392, 267 O.A.C. 126, 79 C.C.L.T. (3d) 26 (Div. Ct.)

The court bifurcated discovery and trial to protect the defendant's confidential information.

Pysznyj v. Orsu Metals Corp. (May 21, 2009), Doc. London 59650CP, 2009 CarswellOnt 8839 (S.C.J.)

Prior to the close of pleadings, the court ordered the defendants to produce any insurance policy which might respond to the claim.

Segnitz v. Royal & Sunalliance Insurance Co. of Canada (2003), 2003 CarswellOnt 50, 44 C.C.L.I. (3d) 248, [2003] O.J. No. 78, 29 C.P.C. (5th) 359 (S.C.J.); additional reasons at (January 20, 2003), Doc. 37188/01, 2003 CarswellOnt 139, [2003] O.J. No. 102 (S.C.J.); additional reasons at (2004), 2004 CarswellOnt 1287, [2004] O.J. No. 1376, 49 C.P.C. (5th) 167, 12 C.C.L.I. (4th) 143 (S.C.J.)

Where a summary judgment motion was served prior to certification, the court permitted the defendant to limit its affidavit of documents to documents relevant to summary judgment or certification.

Egglestone v. Barker (2003), 2003 CarswellOnt 773, [2003] O.J. No. 844, 29 C.P.C. (5th) 296 (S.C.J.)

The court refused to order production of certain class members' medical/psychiatric records which were in the possession of plaintiff's counsel or the Crown. The relevance of the records to certification was doubtful and the class members had not had an opportunity to opt out.

VitaPharm Canada Ltd. v. F. Hoffman-LaRoche Ltd. (2003), 2003 CarswellOnt 812, 223 D.L.R. (4th) 445, 23 C.P.R. (4th) 454, 30 C.P.C. (5th) 107[2003] O.J. No. 868 (C.A.); leave to appeal refused (2003), 2003 CarswellOnt 4758, 2003 CarswellOnt 4759, 28 C.P.R. (4th) vii, (sub nom. *Ford v. Hoffmann-La Roche (F.) Ltd.)* 194 O.A.C. 199 (note) (S.C.C.)

The court refused to bar the plaintiffs from seeking access from a U.S. court to information developed in a U.S. lawsuit regarding similar subject-matter. It was open to the U.S. court to make a protective order regarding the use of the information and to make the order conditional upon a similar order by a Canadian court.

Wilson v. Servier (November 22, 2001), Doc. 98-CV-158832, [2001] O.J. No. 4636, 2001 CarswellOnt 5560 (S.C.J.)

The court permitted a U.S. lawyer to attend the examination for discovery of the defendants in order to assist class counsel.

Peppiatt v. Royal Bank (1996), 27 O.R. (3d) 462, 44 C.P.C. (3d) 8 (Gen. Div.)

The court refused to permit discovery of all class members but did permit discovery of subclass representatives.

Security for Costs

Dean v. Mister Transmission (International) Ltd. (2009), 79 C.P.C. (6th) 181, [2009] O.J. No. 2550, 2009 CarswellOnt 3520 (S.C.J.)

The court refused to order security for costs where such security would not be required under rule 56, the case was not frivolous and vexatious, and requiring security would effectively end the case.

Peter v. Medtronic Inc. (2008), [2008] O.J. No. 4378, 2008 CarswellOnt 6448, 66 C.P.C. (6th) 274, 303 D.L.R. (4th) 361 (S.C.J.); additional reasons at (December 8, 2008), Doc. 05-CV-295910-CP, 2008 CarswellOnt 7523 (S.C.J.)

The court refused to order security for costs where, although the plaintiffs could not pay the defendant's full costs, they had some assets and risked losing all if the case were unsuccessful.

Sutherland v. Canadian Red Cross Society (1994), 25 C.P.C. (3d) 118 (Ont. Gen. Div.)

The court dismissed a motion for security for costs in a class action where, although the plaintiffs resided outside Ontario, they undertook to seek funding from the Class Proceedings Committee. If funding were granted, the Class Proceedings Fund would become responsible for defence costs.

Assessment and Distribution of Damages

Daniells v. McLellan, 2017 ONSC 6887, 2017 CarswellOnt 18716, 14 C.P.C. (8th) 303 (S.C.J.)

The court permitted an aggregate assessment of damages in this action for breach of confidentiality of health records.

Ramdath v. George Brown College of Applied Arts and Technology, 2015 ONCA 921, 2015 CarswellOnt 19814, 78 C.P.C. (7th) 227, 392 D.L.R. (4th) 490, 341 O.A.C. 338

The court affirmed the aggregate assessment of damages for two cohorts of the class, overturned the dismissal of the third cohort's claim, and ordered a new assessment of the third cohort's damages.

Lundy v. VIA Rail Canada Inc., 2015 ONSC 7063, 2015 CarswellOnt 17448 (S.C.J.)

The court gave directions regarding a litigation plan to resolve individual damage issues.

O'Neil v. Sunopta, 2015 ONSC 6213, 2015 CarswellOnt 16399 (S.C.J.)

The test for a *cy pres* distribution is whether a reasonable person, not a cynic, would conclude it confers a real benefit for the class members. *Sorenson v. easyhome Ltd.*, 2013 ONSC 4017, 2013 CarswellOnt 7898, 49 C.P.C. (7th) 305 (S.C.J.) not followed.

Denis v. Bertrand & Frère Construction Co. (2008), 71 C.L.R. (3d) 246, 58 C.P.C. (6th) 177, 2008 CarswellOnt 1876, [2008] O.J. No. 1284 (S.C.J.)

In this class action arising from the use of defective concrete in the foundations for 170 homes, the court conducted a trial to assess the damages for several particular homes, with the outcome to be used as a template to resolve similar claims.

Cassano v. Toronto Dominion Bank, [2007] O.J. No. 4406, 2007 CarswellOnt 7341, 47 C.P.C. (6th) 209, 87 O.R. (3d) 401, 2007 ONCA 781, 230 O.A.C. 231, 287 D.L.R. (4th) 703 (C.A.); leave to appeal refused (March 27, 2008), Doc. 32424, 2008 CarswellOnt 1729, 2008 CarswellOnt 1730, [2008] S.C.C.A. No. 15 (S.C.C.)

Where individual damages are small, the prospect of an aggregate assessment of damages is not a prerequisite for certification. If an aggregate assessment were not available, the court would have a broad discretion to determine damages individually, including determination based on the records of the defendant.

McCutcheon v. Cash Store Inc. (2006), 80 O.R. (3d) 644, [2006] O.J. No. 1860, 27 C.P.C. (6th) 293, 2006 CarswellOnt 2973 (S.C.J.)

For the purposes of the *CPA*, access to justice does not require that each claimant will receive a distribution of part of the amount for which a defendant has been found liable. Members of a class may benefit otherwise than from direct compensation.

Lewis v. Cantertrot Investments Ltd. (2006), 2006 CarswellOnt 236, 24 C.P.C. (6th) 49, 43 R.P.R. (4th) 196 (S.C.J.); additional reasons at (March 20, 2006), Doc. 04-CV-277412 CP, 2006 CarswellOnt 2737, [2006] O.J. No. 1061 (S.C.J.); additional reasons at (2006), 2006 CarswellOnt 2415, 29 C.P.C. (6th) 352, 43 R.P.R. (4th) 205 (S.C.J.); leave to appeal refused (December 6, 2006), Doc. Toronto 230/06, 2006 CarswellOnt 8009 (Div. Ct.)

Where the plaintiff proposed that damages and other individual issues be dealt with in summary trials and provided evidence that the individual damages would be between about $10,000 and $31,000 the court certified the case despite evidence from the defendant that the individual damages would average less than $500 per claimant. It was not appropriate to choose between these two estimates on the certification motion.

Pearson v. Inco Ltd. (2005), 2005 CarswellOnt 6598, 205 O.A.C. 30, 78 O.R. (3d) 641, [2005] O.J. No. 4918, 261 D.L.R. (4th) 629, 20 C.E.L.R. (3d) 258, 43 R.P.R. (4th) 43, 18 C.P.C. (6th) 77 (C.A.); additional reasons at (2006), 2006 CarswellOnt 1527, 20 C.E.L.R. (3d) 292, 208 O.A.C. 284, 25 C.P.C. (6th) 1, 79 O.R. (3d) 427, [2006] O.J. No. 991, 267 D.L.R. (4th) 111 (C.A.); leave to appeal refused (June 29, 2006), Doc. 31249, 2006 CarswellOnt 4020, 2006 CarswellOnt 4021 (S.C.C.)

The court should not take a narrow view of the goal of behaviour modification. Class actions are intended to ensure that both actual and *potential* wrongdoers do not ignore their obligations to the public. Moreover, the fact that there was a dispute regarding evidence relating to damages did not make this case an example of "certify now and worry later."

Englefield v. Wolf (2005), 2005 CarswellOnt 6609, 20 C.P.C. (6th) 157, [2005] O.J. No. 4895 (S.C.J.); additional reasons at (2006), 2006 CarswellOnt 1962, 26 C.P.C. (6th) 103 (S.C.J.); additional reasons at (2006), 2006 CarswellOnt 4983, 31 C.P.C. (6th) 174 (S.C.J.)

In this undefended class action based on a director's liability for a company's unpaid wages, the court granted judgment on motion for the aggregate unpaid wages during the period the defendant was a director.

Authorson (Litigation Guardian of) v. Canada (Attorney General) (2003), 2003 CarswellOnt 5279, 235 D.L.R. (4th) 532, 38 C.C.P.B. 193, [2003] O.J. No. 5239, 43 C.P.C. (5th) 328, 69 O.R. (3d) 129 (S.C.J.)

The court ordered an aggregate assessment of damages of this claim regarding management of disabled veterans' assets.

Tesluk v. Boots Pharmaceutical PLC (2002), 2002 CarswellOnt 1266, (sub nom. *Sutherland v. Boots Pharmaceutical PLC*) [2002] O.J. No. 1361, 21 C.P.C. (5th) 196 (S.C.J.)

Where an aggregate recovery cannot be economically distributed to individual class members the court will approve a *cy pres* distribution.

Peppiatt v. Nicol (2001), 2001 CarswellOnt 4336, [2001] O.J. No. 4711, 20 C.P.C. (5th) 290 (S.C.J.)

The court gave directions for the distribution of the proceeds of judgment by class counsel.

Discontinuance

Blair v. Toronto Community Housing Corp., 2014 ONSC 2292, 2014 CarswellOnt 4753, 68 C.P.C. (7th) 60 (S.C.J.)

After settlement of the main action, the court permitted the defendant to discontinue its third party claims with costs to the third parties fixed at $72,000.

Westland v. Ontario Hospital Association, 2013 ONSC 4631, 2013 CarswellOnt 9740, 53 C.P.C. (7th) 427 (S.C.J.)

The court approved the discontinuance of this retirement benefit claim without prior notice to the class. The class was small and no one was available to serve as the representative plaintiff.

Frank v. Farlie, Turner & Co., LLC, 2011 ONSC 7137, 2011 CarswellOnt 13816, 38 C.P.C. (7th) 266 (S.C.J.)

The court refused leave to discontinue against one of many defendants where the class might be prejudiced because there was the prospect of a future claim against him which would be statute-barred if discontinuance were granted.

Weninger Farms Ltd. v. Minister of National Revenue (2011), 2011 ONSC 6868, 2011 CarswellOnt 13162, [2012] 3 C.T.C. 35 (S.C.J.)

The court refused to permit discontinuance against the federal Crown so that the plaintiff could commence a new proceeding against it in Federal Court, where no certification costs could be awarded against the plaintiffs, while continuing this action against the provincial Crown.

Durling v. Sunrise Propane Energy Group Inc., 2009 CarswellOnt 9181, [2009] O.J. No. 5969, 98 C.P.C. (6th) 48 (S.C.J.)

Defendants in a related class action do not have standing to oppose a motion to discontinue against other defendants in a class action to which they are not a party, despite the commencement of a "composite" class action.

Duong v. Stork Craft Manufacturing Inc., 2011 ONSC 2534, 2011 CarswellOnt 2642, 18 C.P.C. (7th) 210 (S.C.J.); additional reasons at 2011 ONSC 3563, 2011 CarswellOnt 4486 (S.C.J.)

The court refused to approve discontinuance without notice to the class members, where they might be prejudiced by expiry of their limitation periods before they could assert their claims elsewhere.

Hudson v. Austin, 2010 ONSC 2789, 2010 CarswellOnt 3211, [2010] O.J. No. 2015, 96 C.P.C. (6th) 121 (S.C.J.)

The court permitted the plaintiff to discontinue this class action, and continue with her individual claim, provided certain notices be given to class members.

Campbell v. Canada (Attorney General), 2009 FC 30, 2009 CarswellNat 154, 2009 CarswellNat 858, [2009] 4 F.C.R. 211, 2009 CF 30, 342 F.T.R. 312 (Eng.), 75 C.P.C. (6th) 126

To obtain leave to discontinue it is not necessary to show lack of prejudice to the defendant. The court permitted discontinuance of this Federal Court action despite the defendant's objection, where similar actions had been commenced in various provinces.

Smith v. Crown Life Insurance Co. (2002), 2002 CarswellOnt 8437, [2002] O.J. No. 5539, 43 C.C.L.I. (4th) 123 (S.C.J.)

The court refused to approve the discontinuance of a class action without notice to the class, where some class members were being offered a settlement if the action were discontinued.

Vennell v. Barnado's (2004), 28 C.P.C. (6th) 185, 2004 CarswellOnt 4196, 73 O.R. (3d) 13 (S.C.J.)

The approval of the court is required to convert an action commenced under the *Class Proceedings Act* to an individual action. Notice of the proposed discontinuance should be given to class members.

Settlement Approval

Marchand v. Ford Motor Company, 2018 ONSC 685, 2018 CarswellOnt 2895 (S.C.J.)

The court approved a settlement of this action for defective automobile exhausts that provided partial reimbursement for the repair costs of the vehicles.

Calhoun v. Barkervill Gold Mines Ltd., 2018 ONSC 1055, 2018 CarswellOnt 2287 (S.C.J.)

The court certified this securities case on consent and approved a $250,000 settlement.

David v. Loblaw, 2018 ONSC 198, 2018 CarswellOnt 168, 14 C.P.C. (8th) 273 (S.C.J.)

The court refused to interfere with the defendant's voluntary compensation program for its price-fixing activities, and deferred determination of the issues of enforceability of the releases and credit against any ultimate damage award.

Mancinelli v. Royal Bank of Canada, 2017 ONSC 5503, 2017 CarswellOnt 14511 (S.C.J.)

The court approved the settlement of six price-fixing claims with a total value of $51.5 million.

Gerard v. Detour Gold Corporation, 2017 ONSC 3966, 2017 CarswellOnt 9956 (S.C.J.)

The court approved the $6 million settlement of this securities case, approved class counsel's $1.6 million fee, and awarded $15,000 honoraria to each of the two representative plaintiffs.

Barwin v. IKO, 2017 ONSC 3520, 2017 CarswellOnt 9580, 65 C.L.R. (4th) 137, 4 C.P.C. (8th) 305 (S.C.J.)

The court approved a $4.7 million settlement of this defective roofing shingles claim, approved class counsel's 25% fee, and awarded a $5,000 honorarium to the representative plaintiff.

Seed v. Ontario, 2017 ONSC 3534, 2017 CarswellOnt 8867, 10 C.P.C. (8th) 126 (S.C.J.)

The court approved the $8 million settlement of this institutional abuse claim, set class counsel's fees at $2.52 million, and awarded a $15,000 honorarium to the representative plaintiff.

Drew v. Walmart Canada Inc., 2017 ONSC 3308, 2017 CarswellOnt 8159, 10 C.P.C. (8th) 182 (S.C.J.)

The court approved a settlement of this data breach claim providing credit monitoring for the class members and $250,000 for class counsel's fees.

Cannon v. Funds for Canada Foundation, 2017 ONSC 2670, 2017 CarswellOnt 6889, 9 C.P.C. (8th) 431, 2017 D.T.C. 5060 (S.C.J.)

The court approved the $17.5 million settlement of this claim regarding a charitable tax donation scheme and approved class counsel's 33% contingency fee and a $50,000 honorarium for the representative plaintiff.

Ironworkers Ontario Pension Fund v. Manulife Financial Corp., 2017 ONSC 2669, 2017 CarswellOnt 6738 (S.C.J.)

The court approved a $69 million settlement of this securities action, a 22.5% fee for class counsel, and a $10,000 honorarium for each of the two representative plaintiffs.

Quenneville v. Volkswagen Group Canada Inc., 2017 ONSC 2448, 2017 CarswellOnt 6142, 9 C.P.C. (8th) 127 (S.C.J.)

The court approved a $2.1 billion settlement of this "clean diesel" case.

Keyton v. Canada Lithium Corp., 2016 ONSC 7354, 2016 CarswellOnt 18867 (S.C.J.)

Where the defendant was insolvent but had insurance coverage, the court approved a settlement applying all of the insurance proceeds to class counsel's fees.

Dow v. 407 ETR Concession Co., 2016 ONSC 7086, 2016 CarswellOnt 18617, 42 C.B.R. (6th) 315 (S.C.J.)

The court certified and approved an $8 million settlement of this claim for improper toll charges and practices, approved class counsel's 30% fee, and awarded a $10,000 honorarium to each of the representative plaintiffs.

Labourers' Pension Fund of Central and Eastern Canada (Trustees of) v. Royal Bank of Canada, 2016 ONSC 6953, 2016 CarswellOnt 18601 (S.C.J.)

The court approved $4.95 million, $4.5 million, and $6.5 million settlements with three banks regarding alleged price fixing of currency exchange rates, and approved class counsel's 25% fees.

Brigaitis v. IQT, Ltd., 2016 ONSC 6746, 2016 CarswellOnt 16914, 5 C.P.C. (8th) 406 (S.C.J.)

The court approved a $1.7 million settlement of this action for wages and termination pay, and approved class counsel's 33% fee.

McSherry v. Zimmer GmbH, 2016 ONSC 4606, 2016 CarswellOnt 11798, 3 C.P.C. (8th) 435 (S.C.J.)

The court approved the settlement of this claim for defective hip implants for up to $172,500 per class member, approved class counsel's 33% contingency fee, and approved an honorarium for the representative plaintiff.

Rosen v. BMO Nesbitt Burns Inc., 2016 ONSC 4752, 2016 CarswellOnt 12015, 133 O.R. (3d) 73, 37 C.C.E.L. (4th) 240, 100 C.P.C. (7th) 344 (S.C.J.)

The court approved this $12.5 million settlement regarding overtime pay, approved class counsel's 25% contingency fee, and a $10,000 honorarium for the representative plaintiff.

Middlemiss v. Penn West Petroleum Ltd., 2016 ONSC 3537, 2016 CarswellOnt 8785 (S.C.J.)

The court approved a $26.5 million settlement of this securities claim, and approved class counsel's 33% contingency fee.

Ramdath v. George Brown College of Applied Arts and Technology, 2016 ONSC 3536, 2016 CarswellOnt 8468 (S.C.J.)

The court approved a $2.725 million settlement of this misrepresentation case, and approved class counsel's $773,000 fees.

Bancroft-Snell v. Visa Canada Corp., 2016 ONSC 3635, 2016 CarswellOnt 8712 (S.C.J.)

The court approved a $9.9 million settlement of this price-fixing case and approved class counsel's $2.1 million fees.

McIntyre (Litigation Guardian of) v. Ontario, 2016 ONSC 2662, 2016 CarswellOnt 6668 (S.C.J.)

The court approved a $35.9 settlement regarding the operation of institutions for the developmentally challenged, and approved counsel's fees of $3.7 million representing 9.7% of the proceeds.

Waldman v. Thomson Reuters Canada Ltd., 2016 ONSC 2622, 2016 CarswellOnt 6579, 131 O.R. (3d) 367, 348 O.A.C. 210 (Div.Ct.)

In this copyright case the court approved a settlement providing for a $350,000 *cy pres* payment, $825,000 fees for class counsel, and a licence for the defendant. The court rejected "institutional fairness" as a criterion in approving a settlement.

AFA Livförsäkringsaktiebolag v. Agnico-Eagle Mines Ltd., 2016 ONSC 532, 2016 CarswellOnt 2169, 90 C.P.C. (7th) 201 (S.C.J.)

The court approved a $17 million settlement of this securities case, and approved a 29.5% contingent fee including $700,000 to be paid to a US law firm that assisted class counsel.

Silver v. Imax Corp., 2016 ONSC 403, 2016 CarswellOnt 558, 86 C.P.C. (7th) 429 (S.C.J.)

The court approved a $3.75 million settlement of this securities case, and class counsel's 33% fee, much less than their docketed time.

Bancroft-Snell v. Visa Canada Corp., 2015 ONSC 7275, 2015 CarswellOnt 17869, 80 C.P.C. (7th) 88 (S.C.J.); reversed in part 2016 ONCA 896, 2016 CarswellOnt 18625, 133 O.R. (3d) 241, 93 C.P.C. (7th) 24

The court approved settlements totaling $13.6 million in this credit card price fixing case.

Musicians' Pension Fund of Canada (Trustee of) v. Kinross Gold Corp., 2015 ONSC 3944, 2015 CarswellOnt 9329, 75 C.P.C. (7th) 158 (S.C.J.)

The court approved a $12.5 million settlement of this securities case, and approved class counsel's fee of $3.4 million representing 27.5% of the recovery, and a multiplier of 2.4.

Lundy v. VIA Rail Canada Inc., 2015 ONSC 1879, 2015 CarswellOnt 3957 (Ont. S.C.J.); additional reasons 2015 ONSC 3531, 2015 CarswellOnt 7994 (S.C.J.)

When a class proceeding reaches the individual issue stage, the court generally need not approve individual settlements. The court ordered that offers to settle to individual class members should be lump-sum offers, and that it is not the defendant's concern how the sum should be allocated between the class members and their lawyers.

Horgan v. Lakeridge Health Corp, 2014 ONSC 5209, 2014 CarswellOnt 12213, 69 C.P.C. (7th) 98 (S.C.J.)

The court approved a $1.7 million settlement of this claim regarding a tuberculosis outbreak, approved class counsel's fee of $510,000 representing 30 percent of the settlement, and awarded the representative plaintiff honoraria of $10,000 each.

Fulawka v. Bank of Nova Scotia, 2014 ONSC 4743, 2014 CarswellOnt 11626, 69 C.P.C. (7th) 134 (S.C.J.)

The court approved a $95 million settlement of this bank overtime claim, set class counsel's fees at $10.45 million, and approved a $15,000 honorarium for the representative plaintiff.

O'Neill v. General Motors of Canada, 2014 ONSC 4742, 2014 CarswellOnt 11627, 69 C.P.C. (7th) 142, 2014 C.E.B. & P.G.R. 8095 (S.C.J.)

This court approved a settlement of this retirement benefits class action with an actuarial value of $130 million, and set class counsel's fees at $1.9 million representing about 1.5 percent of the overall recovery.

Kidd v. Canada Life Assurance Co., 2014 ONSC 457, 2014 CarswellOnt 5778, 12 C.C.P.B. (2nd) 62, 56 C.P.C. (7th) 364 (S.C.J.); additional reasons 2015 ONSC 1287, 2015 CarswellOnt 2705, 21 C.C.P.B. (2nd) 69, 71 C.P.C. (7th) 412 (S.C.J.)

The court approved a revised settlement of this pension class action.

Frank v. Caldwell, 2014 ONSC 1484, 2014 CarswellOnt 2704, 60 C.P.C. (7th) 386 (S.C.J.)

The court approved a US$3.5 million settlement of this securities case, approved class counsel's fee of US$1.05 million representing 30% of the proceeds, and awarded $15,000 honourariums to the class representatives.

Waldman v. Thomson Reuters Canada Ltd., 2014 ONSC 1288, 2014 CarswellOnt 2674, 56 C.P.C. (7th) 81, 120 C.P.R. (4th) 127 (S.C.J.); appeal quashed 2015 ONCA 53, 2015 CarswellOnt 857, 71 C.P.C. (7th) 33, 127 C.P.R. (4th) 401, 330 O.A.C. 142, [2015] O.J. No. 395; reversed 2016 ONSC 2622, 2016 CarswellOnt 6579, 131 O.R. (3d) 367, 348 O.A.C. 210 (Div. Ct.)

In this copyright case the court refused to approve a settlement providing for a $350,000 *cy pres* payment, $825,000 fees for class counsel, and a licence for the defendant. The proposed settlement was unfair and unreasonable.

McKillop (Litigation Guardian of) v. Ontario, 2014 ONSC 1282, 2014 CarswellOnt 2473 (S.C.J.)

The court approved the $32.7 million settlement of this claim arising out of abuse at residences for the disabled, and approved $5,000 honouraria to the representative plaintiffs.

Hamilton v. Toyota Motor Sales, USA Inc., 2014 ONSC 785, 2014 CarswellOnt 1408, 59 C.P.C. (7th) 193 (S.C.J.)

The court approved the settlement of this defective automobile claim, certified the action on consent, and approved class counsel's fees of $4.3 million.

Glover v. Toronto (City), 2014 ONSC 305, 2014 CarswellOnt 1830, 63 C.P.C. (7th) 434 (S.C.J.)

In this case arising from a Legionnaires' disease outbreak, the court approved a $1.2 million settlement and awarded a $5,000 stipend to the representative plaintiffs.

Snelgrove v. Cathay Forest Products Corp., 2013 ONSC 7282, 2013 CarswellOnt 17592 (S.C.J.)

The court approved the $1.9 million settlement of this securities misrepresentation case, approved a 21% contingent fee for class counsel, and awarded $500 honourariums to the representative plaintiffs.

Slark (Litigation Guardian of) v. Ontario, 2013 ONSC 6686, 2013 CarswellOnt 16973, 60 C.P.C. (7th) 174 (S.C.J.)

The court approved a $35 million settlement of this residential abuse claim and approved $15,000 honourariums for the representative plaintiffs.

Roveredo v. Bard Canada Inc., 2013 ONSC 6979, 2013 CarswellOnt 15486 (S.C.J.)

The court approved a $1.375 million settlement of this medical devices class action and approved class counsel's 30% contingent fee.

Patel v. Groupon Inc., 2013 ONSC 6679, 2013 CarswellOnt 15030 (S.C.J.)

The court approved a $535,000 settlement of this coupon expiration claim, and set class counsel's fee at $235,000.

TTC v. Signorile, 2013 ONSC 6377, 2013 CarswellOnt 14890, 47 C.P.C. (7th) 173, 2013 C.E.B. & P.G.R. 8059 (S.C.J.)

The court approved a settlement dividing $5.6 million of demutualization proceeds.

Kidd v. Canada Life Assurance Co., 2013 ONSC 1868, 2013 CarswellOnt 3640, 115 O.R. (3d) 256, 3 C.C.P.B. (2nd) 169, 2013 C.E.B. & P.G.R. 8029, [2013] O.J. No. 1468 (S.C.J.)

The court should not approve an unfair settlement simply because it is the better of two unfair choices.

Glube v. Pella Corp., 2013 ONSC 6164, 2013 CarswellOnt 13746 (S.C.J.)

The court approved the settlement of this products liability case regarding defective windows and doors, and set class counsel's fee at $650,000 representing a multiplier of about 2.

French v. Investia Financial Services Inc., 2013 ONSC 6220, 2013 CarswellOnt 13538, 55 C.P.C. (7th) 206 (S.C.J.)

The court approved in principle the quantum of the settlement of this securities case, but adjourned the case so the parties could properly implement a challenge process contemplated by the settlement. The court approved class counsel's fee of $2.9 million representing about 29% of the settlement proceeds.

Mackie v. Toshiba of Canada Ltd., 2013 ONSC 5665, 2013 CarswellOnt 13129 (S.C.J.)

The court approved the settlement of this claim for defective light bulbs and set class counsel's fee at $79,500 representing a multiplier of .6.

405341 Ontario Ltd. v. Midas Canada Inc., 2013 ONSC 5714, 2013 CarswellOnt 12627, 57 C.P.C. (7th) 413 (S.C.J.)

The court approved an $8.5 million settlement of this franchise case, and set class counsel's fees at $2.1 million, representing a multiplier of 1.3.

Zaniewicz v. Zungui Haixi Corp., 2013 ONSC 5490, 2013 CarswellOnt 11949, 44 C.P.C. (7th) 178 (S.C.J.)

The court approved three settlements in this securities case, subject to varying the plan of distribution, and approved class counsel's fee of $2.8 million representing 21% of the recovery or a multiplier of 3.3.

Maksimovic v. Sony of Canada Ltd., 2013 ONSC 4604, 2013 CarswellOnt 9043, 54 C.P.C. (7th) 443 (S.C.J.); additional reasons (June 10, 2013), Doc. Toronto CV-11 425487-00CP, 2013 CarswellOnt 16103 (S.C.J.)

The court approved a largely non-monetary settlement of this claim for disruption of internet service, and approved class counsel's fee of $265,000 representing a multiplier of less than 1.

Blair v. Toronto Community Housing Corp., 2013 ONSC 4237, 2013 CarswellOnt 9409, 52 C.P.C. (7th) 399 (S.C.J.)

The court approved a $6.9 million settlement of this claim arising from a fire in an apartment building, and approved class counsel's fee of $1.15 million representing about 17% of the proceeds.

Sorenson v. Easyhome Ltd., 2013 ONSC 4017, 2013 CarswellOnt 7898, 49 C.P.C. (7th) 305 (S.C.J.)

The court approved a $2.3 million settlement of this securities case, subject to changing the *cy pres* beneficiary, and approved class counsel's fee of $562,000 representing a multiplier of about 3.

Zaniewicz v. Zungui Haixi Corp., 2013 ONSC 2959, 2013 CarswellOnt 6689, 116 O.R. (3d) 37, 51 C.P.C. (7th) 407 (S.C.J.)

The court approved a $10 million settlement of this securities claim.

Goodridge v. Pfizer Canada Inc., 2013 ONSC 2686, 2013 CarswellOnt 5615, 49 C.P.C. (7th) 342 (S.C.J.)

The court approved the $4.8 million settlement of this claim regarding the drug neurontin, and approved class counsel's fee of 25%.

Axiom Plastics v. E.I. DuPont Canada Co., 2013 ONSC 2675, 2013 CarswellOnt 5613, 51 C.P.C. (7th) 376 (S.C.J.)

The court approved the settlement of this price-fixing case.

Pryden v. Swiss Reinsurance Co., 2013 ONSC 2661, 2013 CarswellOnt 5610, 22 C.C.L.I. (5th) 121, 5 C.C.P.B. (2nd) 203, 40 C.P.C. (7th) 219 (S.C.J.)

The court approved the settlement of this pension surplus case and allowed the defendant to recover $3.8 million in legal and actuarial expenses from the pension surplus.

Markson v. MBNA Canada Bank, 2012 ONSC 5891, 2012 CarswellOnt 17304, 42 C.P.C. (7th) 202, [2012] O.J. No. 4967 (S.C.J.)

The court approved an $8 million settlement of this usury claim and approved class counsel's 30% fee, representing a multiplier of about 1.3.

Labourers' Pension Fund of Central and Eastern Canada v. Sino-Forest Corp., 2013 ONSC 1078, 2013 CarswellOnt 3361, 100 C.B.R. (5th) 30, 37 C.P.C. (7th) 135 (Commercial List); leave to appeal refused 2013 ONCA 456, 2013 CarswellOnt 8896; leave to appeal refused 2014 CarswellOnt 3023, 2014 CarswellOnt 3024, 472 N.R. 395 (note), 338 O.A.C. 400 (note), [2013] S.C.C.A. No. 395

The court approved, under the *CCAA* and *CPA*, a settlement with one defendant which included no opt outs and a full third party release.

Silver v. IMAX Corp., 2013 ONSC 1667, 2013 CarswellOnt 3202, 36 C.P.C. (7th) 254 (S.C.J.); leave to appeal refused 2013 ONSC 6751, 2013 CarswellOnt 14979, 117 O.R. (3d) 616 (S.C.J.)

The court amended the class definition to exclude persons bound by a U.S. class action settlement. The U.S. settlement was fair, and the preferable procedure was to remove such claims from the Canadian action.

Johnston v. Sheila Morrison Schools, 2013 ONSC 1528, 2013 CarswellOnt 2807, 37 C.P.C. (7th) 417, [2013] O.J. No. 1126 (S.C.J.)

The court approved the settlement of this residential school case, and approved class counsel's fee of $1 million representing 25% of the settlement, or a multiplier of 1.4.

Sa'd v. Remington Group Inc., 2013 CarswellOnt 2453, 2013 ONSC 1404, (sub nom. *Sa'd v. The Remington Group Inc.)* 115 O.R. (3d) 627, 49 C.P.C. (7th) 206 (S.C.J.)

The court approved the settlement of a claim relating to a condominium development, approved class counsel's fee of 25%, and authorized class counsel to pay part of its fee as a referral fee to U.S. counsel.

Elliot Estate v. Joseph Brant Memorial Hospital, 2013 ONSC 124, 2013 CarswellOnt 298, 44 C.P.C. (7th) 334 (S.C.J.)

The court approved the $9 million settlement of an action arising from an outbreak of the bacteria *C. difficile*, and set class counsel's fees at $1.9 million.

Woods v. Redeemer Foundation, 2012 ONSC 7254, 2012 CarswellOnt 16446, 43 C.P.C. (7th) 211 (S.C.J.)

The court approved the settlement of claims arising from a charitable donation tax avoidance scheme and approved class counsel's modest request for fees of $65,000.

Eidoo v. Infineon Technologies AG, 2012 ONSC 7299, 2012 CarswellOnt 16498 (S.C.J.)

The court approved the partial settlement of a price fixing claim regarding DRAM memory devices. No new opt out rights were provided as class members had a previous opportunity to opt out.

McSheffrey v. Ontario, 2012 ONSC 6803, 2012 CarswellOnt 15215, 1 C.C.P.B. (2nd) 167, 43 C.P.C. (7th) 199, [2012] O.J. No. 5721 (S.C.J.)

The court approved the settlement of two pension class actions and approved class counsel's fees of $575,000 and $175,000.

Toronto Community Housing Corp v. Thyssenkrupp Elevator (Canada) Ltd., 2012 ONSC 6626, 2012 CarswellOnt 14602, 44 C.P.C. (7th) 361 (S.C.J.)

The court approved a $12 million settlement of a claim for defective elevators and set class counsel's fees at $3.5 million, about 30% of the settlement.

Mignacca v. Merck Frosst Canada Ltd., 2012 ONSC 4931, 2012 CarswellOnt 13517, 33 C.P.C. (7th) 123 (S.C.J.)

The court approved a settlement in the range of $22 million to $37 million regarding the drug Vioxx and approved class counsel's interim fees, disbursements and taxes of $6 million.

Monckton v. C.B.S. Interactive Multimedia Inc., 2012 ONSC 5227, 2012 CarswellOnt 11482, 41 C.P.C. (7th) 147 (S.C.J.)

The court approved a settlement of a claim by students against their college who offered an unaccredited dental hygiene program.

Osmun v. Cadbury Adams Canada Inc., 2012 ONSC 3837, 2012 CarswellOnt 8440, 41 C.P.C. (7th) 333 (S.C.J.)

The court approved a partial settlement of a chocolate price fixing claim and approved class counsel's interim fees, subject to revision when the outcome of the case as a whole is known.

Eidoo v. Infineon Technologies A.G., 2012 ONSC 3801, 2012 CarswellOnt 8093, 41 C.P.C. (7th) 410 (S.C.J.)

The court approved the settlement of a price fixing claim regarding dynamic random access memory devices.

Robinson v. Rochester Financial Ltd., 2012 ONSC 911, 2012 CarswellOnt 1368, 27 C.P.C. (7th) 351, [2012] 5 C.T.C. 24, [2012] O.J. No. 534 (S.C.J.)

The court approved the settlement of a claim regarding a "leveraged" charitable donation program, and set class counsel's fee at $3.3 million representing 25% of the settlement or a multiplier of 1.8. The court refused compensation for the representative plaintiffs as their contribution, while commendable, was not exceptional.

Kidd v. Canada Life Assurance Co., 2012 ONSC 740, 2012 CarswellOnt 1064, 95 C.C.P.B. 73, 19 C.P.C. (7th) 378, [2012] O.J. No. 506 (S.C.J.)

The court approved the settlement of pension case and approved class counsel's fee of $4.7 million representing less than 10% of the settlement or a multiplier of 2.5.

St. John's Evangelical Lutheran Church of Toronto v. Steers, 2011 ONSC 7416, 2011 CarswellOnt 14446, 38 C.P.C. (7th) 121 (S.C.J.)

The court approved the settlement of this claim for disputed church property and approved class counsel's fee of $90,000 representing half the recovery but only about a third of their docketed time.

Voutour v. Pfizer Canada Inc., 2011 ONSC 7118, 2011 CarswellOnt 14961, 38 C.P.C. (7th) 360 (S.C.J.)

The court approved the settlement of this claim regarding the drugs Bextra and Celebrex and approved class counsel's fee of $4 million representing a third of the settlement or a multiplier of about 1.15.

Moyle v. Cash Money Cheque Cashing Inc., 2011 ONSC 7491, 2011 CarswellOnt 14405, 38 C.P.C. (7th) 327 (S.C.J.)

The court certified this usury claim for settlement purposes, approved the settlement, and set class counsel's fees at $125,000 being about 10% of the settlement and equivalent to a multiplier of 2.

St. John's Evangelical Lutheran Church of Toronto v. Steers, 2011 ONSC 7416, 2011 CarswellOnt 14446, 38 C.P.C. (7th) 121 (S.C.J.)

The court approved the settlement of this dispute over church property, and approval class counsel's fee of $90,000 representing about half of the settlement funds.

Moyle v. Cash Money Cheque Cashing Inc., 2011 ONSC 7491, 2011 CarswellOnt 14405, 38 C.P.C. (7th) 327 (S.C.J.)

The court approved the settlement of this usury claim and set class counsel's fee at $125,000 representing about 9% of the recovery.

Berry v. Pulley, 2011 ONSC 1378, 2011 CarswellOnt 1296, [2011] O.J. No. 927, 106 O.R. (3d) 123 (S.C.J.)

Settlement offers should be made to the class representative, not to individual class members. If the offer is not acceptable to the representative, it need not be disclosed to the class members.

Wein v. Rogers Cable Communications Inc., 2011 ONSC 7290, 2011 CarswellOnt 14085, 38 C.P.C. (7th) 304 (S.C.J.)

The court approved the settlement of this claim for misrepresenting long distance charges, and set class counsel fee at $100,000.

Airia Brands Inc. v. Air Canada, 2011 ONSC 6286, 2011 CarswellOnt 11396 (S.C.J.)

The court approved the settlement of a claim for price fixing cargo shipments.

General Motors of Canada Ltd. v. Abrams, 2011 ONSC 5338, 2011 CarswellOnt 9366, [2011] O.J. No. 4175, 93 C.C.P.B. 97, 2011 C.L.L.C. 220-056, 2011 C.E.B. & P.G.R. 8455, 13 C.P.C. (7th) 130 (S.C.J.)

The court approved the settlement of a claim against the plaintiff's retired employees regarding termination or alteration of their health care benefits.

Travassos v. Tattoo, 2011 ONSC 2290, 2011 CarswellOnt 3193, 19 C.P.C. (7th) 209 (S.C.J.)

The court approved the settlement of a claim regarding improper sterilization of tattoo equipment.

Wiggins v. Mattel Canada Inc., 2011 CarswellOnt 3194, 21 C.P.C. (7th) 213 (S.C.J.)

The court approved a settlement relating to a recall of toys, and set class counsel's fees equivalent to a multiplier of 1.75.

Robertson v. ProQuest Information & Learning Co., 2011 ONSC 2629, 2011 CarswellOnt 2923, 18 C.P.C. (7th) 406, [2011] O.J. No. 2013 (S.C.J.)

The court approved the settlement of a copyright claim and set class counsel's fees equivalent to a multiplier of 1.7 or 24 percent of the recovery.

Lewis v. Cantertrot Investments Ltd., 2011 ONSC 2713, 2011 CarswellOnt 2919, 18 C.P.C. (7th) 394 (S.C.J.)

The court approved the settlement of a claim by condominium purchasers and set class counsel's fees equivalent to 33 percent of the recovery, which was much less than their docketed time.

Metzler Investment GmbH v. Gildan Activewear Inc., 2011 ONSC 1146, 2011 CarswellOnt 1252, 17 C.P.C. (7th) 190, [2011] O.J. No. 885 (S.C.J.)

The court approved the settlement of a securities action, which was also subject to court approval in Quebec and the United States.

Lavier v. MyTravel Canada Holidays Inc., 2011 ONSC 1222, 2011 CarswellOnt 1105, 17 C.P.C. (7th) 161 (S.C.J.)

The court approved $2.25 million settlement of a claim against a holidaymaker for sending travelers to a resort with a norovirus outbreak.

Sayers v. Shaw Cablesystems Ltd., 2011 ONSC 962, 2011 CarswellOnt 858, 16 C.P.C. (7th) 367 (S.C.J.)

The court approved the settlement of a claim by cable installers who the defendant mischaracterized as independent contractors rather than employees, resulting in unanticipated tax liability and non-payment of statutory benefits such as vacation pay.

Mortillaro v. Unicash Franchising Inc., 2011 ONSC 923, 2011 CarswellOnt 802, 16 C.P.C. (7th) 352, [2011] O.J. No. 595 (S.C.J.)

The court approved the settlement of this payday loan usury case, and class counsel's fee.

Abdulrahim v. Air France, 2011 CarswellOnt 388, 2011 ONSC 398, 16 C.P.C. (7th) 280, [2011] O.J. No. 326 (S.C.J.)

The court approved a partial settlement of claims relating to a hard landing of an aircraft which, in addition to previous partial settlements, yielded $20.75 million.

Serhan Estate v. Johnson & Johnson, 2011 ONSC 128, 2011 CarswellOnt 40, 79 C.C.L.T. (3d) 272, 8 C.P.C. (7th) 73 (S.C.J.)

The court approved the settlement of a claim regarding defective blood glucose monitoring equipment and approved class counsel's fees and disbursements of $1.5 million.

Chrysler Canada Inc. v. Gatens, 2010 ONSC 5467, 2010 CarswellOnt 7419, [2010] O.J. No. 4185, 100 C.P.C. (6th) 295 (S.C.J.)

In a case involving a defendant class, the court approved a settlement regarding retiree health care benefits.

Waterston v. Canadian Broadcasting Corp., 2010 ONSC 4319, 2010 CarswellOnt 8028, 98 C.P.C. (6th) 364, 85 C.C.P.B. 1 (S.C.J.)

The court approved the settlement of claim regarding a pension plan surplus.

Pichette v. Toronto Hydro, 2010 ONSC 4060, 2010 CarswellOnt 5399, [2010] O.J. No. 3185, 98 C.P.C. (6th) 96 (S.C.J.)

The court approved the settlement of a usury claim against a defendant class of electric utilities.

Toronto District School Board v. Field, 2010 ONSC 3865, 2010 CarswellOnt 4797, 98 C.P.C. (6th) 36, 84 C.C.P.B. 190 (S.C.J.)

The court approved the settlement of a claim regarding the division of a pension plan surplus.

Fischer v. IG Investment Management Ltd., 2010 ONSC 7147, 2010 CarswellOnt 9886, 9 C.P.C. (7th) 444, [2010] O.J. No. 5649 (S.C.J.)

The court approved the settlement of this securities case, approved class counsel's fee of $2.8 million representing 25 percent of the settlement, and approved compensation to the representative plaintiffs of $5,000 each.

Maggisano v. Skyservice Airlines Inc., 2010 ONSC 7169, 2010 CarswellOnt 9835, 10 C.P.C. (7th) 307 (S.C.J.)

The court approved the settlement of this case arising from the hard landing of an aircraft.

Singer v. Schering-Plough Canada Inc., 2010 ONSC 6776, 2010 CarswellOnt 9273, 7 C.P.C. (7th) 344 (S.C.J.)

Where the plaintiff appealed an order refusing to certify this case, the court approved a settlement abandoning the appeal and dismissing the case without costs.

O'Neil v. SunOpta Inc., 2010 ONSC 2735, 2010 CarswellOnt 9129, 6 C.P.C. (7th) 438, [2010] O.J. No. 5251 (S.C.J.)

The court approved the settlement of this securities case based on misrepresentations in public disclosures and approved class counsel's fee of US$842,750 plus disbursements and GST.

OMERS Administration Corp. v. CP Ships Ltd., 2010 ONSC 817, 2010 CarswellOnt 9128, 86 C.C.P.B. 200, 6 C.P.C. (7th) 286 (S.C.J.)

The court approved a $12.8 million settlement of a claim based on errors in financial statements and approved a 25 percent contingent fee for class counsel.

West Coast Soft Wear Ltd. v. 1000128 Alberta Ltd., 2010 ONSC 6388, 2010 CarswellOnt 9127, 7 C.P.C. (7th) 323 (S.C.J.); additional reasons at 2010 ONSC 6687, 2010 CarswellOnt 9130, 7 C.P.C. (7th) 336 (S.C.J.)

The court approved the settlement of this securities case and approved class counsel's fee of 25 percent plus disbursements and taxes.

Speers Estate v. Reader's Digest Assn. (Canada) ULC, 2010 ONSC 6366, 2010 CarswellOnt 8749, 6 C.P.C. (7th) 416 (S.C.J.)

The court approved the settlement of a claim regarding illegal business practices in selling products to the vulnerable elderly.

Boulanger v. Johnson & Johnson Corp., 2009 CarswellOnt 6580, [2009] O.J. No. 4497, 83 C.P.C. (6th) 109 (S.C.J.)

The court approved the settlement of this class action relating to the drug Prepulsid.

Sutherland v. Hudson's Bay Co., 2009 CarswellOnt 4936, [2009] O.J. No. 3472, 77 C.C.P.B. 133, 82 C.P.C. (6th) 339, 51 E.T.R. (3d) 223 (S.C.J.)

The court approved a settlement after the plaintiffs were almost entirely unsuccessful at trial. Class counsel received a fee of approximately 17.6 percent of the settlement.

Farkas v. Sunnybrook & Women's College Health Sciences Centre, 2009 CarswellOnt 4962, [2009] O.J. No. 3533, 82 C.P.C. (6th) 222 (S.C.J.)

The court approved a settlement of claims arising from being notified by the defendant hospital about potential infection as a result of a substandard sterilization procedures.

Charmley v. Toronto Hydro-Electric System Ltd., 2010 CarswellOnt 1965, 2010 ONSC 1956, 95 C.P.C. (6th) 93 (S.C.J.)

The court approved a settlement dismissing the action without costs, where the action had no reasonable prospect of success.

Robertson v. Thomson Canada Ltd. (2009), 2009 CarswellOnt 3660, 80 C.P.C. (6th) 77, [2009] O.J. No. 2650 (S.C.J.)

The court approved the settlement of this copyright case and approved class counsel's fees of $4 million representing a multiplier of about 2.4 and 36% of the recovery.

Cassano v. Toronto Dominion Bank (2009), 2009 CarswellOnt 4052, 79 C.P.C. (6th) 110, 98 O.R. (3d) 543 (S.C.J.)

The court approved the settlement of a claim for unauthorized credit card fees and approved class counsel's fees of $11 million representing 20% of the recovery and a multiplier of 5.5.

Smith Estate v. National Money Mart Co., 2010 CarswellOnt 1238, 2010 ONSC 1334, [2010] O.J. No. 873, 94 C.P.C. (6th) 126 (S.C.J.); varied in part on other grounds 2011 ONCA 233, 2011 CarswellOnt 1920, [2011] O.J. No. 1321, 106 O.R. (3d) 37, 331 D.L.R. (4th) 208, 3 C.P.C. (7th) 223, 276 O.A.C. 237

The court approved the settlement of this usury case, set class counsel's fees and disbursements in the amount of $14.5 million and approved a $3,000 payment to the class representative.

Speevak v. Canadian Imperial Bank of Commerce, 2010 CarswellOnt 1076, 2010 ONSC 1128, [2010] O.J. No. 770, 93 C.P.C. (6th) 195 (S.C.J.)

The court approved the settlement of an action based on a bank's sending faxes containing customers' personal information to an incorrect fax number for a number of years.

Mortillaro v. Cash Money Cheque Cashing Inc. (2009), 73 C.P.C. (6th) 369, 2009 CarswellOnt 4007, [2009] O.J. No. 2904 (S.C.J.)

The court approved the settlement of a usury claim against a payday loan company.

Wamboldt v. Northstar Aerospace (Canada) Inc. (2009), 72 C.P.C. (6th) 386, 2009 CarswellOnt 3582, [2009] O.J. No. 2583 (S.C.J.)

As part of a settlement, the court ordered that class members who did not opt out were deemed to have released the defendants.

Osmun v. Cadbury Adams Canada Inc. (December 30, 2009), Doc. 08-CV-347263PD2, 2009 CarswellOnt 8132 (S.C.J.)

The court approved the partial settlement of this case alleging price-fixing of chocolate.

Abdulrahim v. Air France (December 24, 2009), Doc. Toronto 05-CV-294746CP, 2009 CarswellOnt 8104, [2009] O.J. No. 5550 (S.C.J.); affirmed 2010 CarswellOnt 3799, 2010 ONCA 403, [2010] O.J. No. 2388

The court approved a partial settlement including a bar order barring further production, discovery and crossclaims against the settling defendants.

Tourlos v. Tiffany Gate Foods Corp. (2008), [2008] O.J. No. 2891, 66 C.P.C. (6th) 14, 2008 CarswellOnt 4337 (S.C.J.)

The court approved the settlement of this class action regarding food poisoning.

Donnelly v. United Technologies Corp. (2008), 66 C.P.C. (6th) 1, 2008 CarswellOnt 3999 (S.C.J.)

The court approved the settlement of this case regarding defective furnaces.

Bilodeau v. Maple Leaf Foods Inc. (March 9, 2009), Doc. CV-08-361464CP, 2009 CarswellOnt 1301 (S.C.J.)

The court approved the settlement of this tainted food case including an interim fee for class counsel in the sum of $3 million. However, a disbursement relating to a carriage motion was disallowed.

Nutech Brands Inc. v. Air Canada (2008), 68 C.L.R. (3d) 240, 42 B.L.R. (4th) 92, 2009 CarswellOnt 888 (S.C.J.)

The court approved a settlement with some but not all defendants in this competition law action. The settling defendants paid a sum of money and agreed to co-operate in the litigation against the non-settling defendants. The settlement included a bar order prohibiting most claims for contribution and indemnity against the settling defendants.

Walker v. Union Gas Ltd. (2009), 74 C.P.C. (6th) 366, 2009 CarswellOnt 662 (S.C.J.)

The court approved a $9.2 million settlement of this criminal interest claim including legal fees and GST of $2.75 million.

Stewart v. General Motors of Canada Ltd., [2008] O.J. No. 4426, 72 C.P.C. (6th) 361, 2008 CarswellOnt 6590 (S.C.J.)

The court approved the settlement of this claim for defective intake manifold gaskets, although the court deferred final approval of class counsel's fees until the total benefit to the class was known, which depended on how many class members participated in the settlement.

Sauer v. Canada (Minister of Agriculture) (September 3, 2008), Doc. Toronto 05-CV-287428CP, [2008] O.J. No. 3419, 2008 CarswellOnt 5081 (Ont. S.C.J.); leave to appeal refused (2009), [2009] O.J. No. 402, 2009 CarswellOnt 680, 246 O.A.C. 256 (Div. Ct.)

The court approved the settlement of a claim against a cattle feed manufacturer relating to the spread of "mad cow disease." The settlement was a modified form of a "Mary Carter" agreement whereby the settling defendant would pay funds and assist the prosecution of the non-settling defendant.

Corless v. KPMG LLP (August 8, 2008), Doc. 07-CV-339348CP, [2008] O.J. No. 3092, 2008 CarswellOnt 4708 (S.C.J.)

The court approved the settlement of this overtime claim on behalf of former employees, and set class counsel's fee at $600,000.

Soderstrom v. Hoffman-La Roche Ltd. (2008), 58 C.P.C. (6th) 160, 2008 CarswellOnt 2051 (S.C.J.)

Where a settlement is approved, disposition of the common issues is binding under s. 29(3), not s. 27(3).

Markle v. Toronto (City) (May 10, 2007), Doc. 03-CV-253463CP, 2007 CarswellOnt 9464 (S.C.J.)

The court approved the settlement of this claim for retiree benefits, and approved class counsel's fee of $123,000.

Ledyit v. Bristol Myers Squib Canada Inc. (2008), 58 C.P.C. (6th) 90, 2008 CarswellOnt 116, [2008] O.J. No. 119 (S.C.J.)

The court approved the settlement of this pharmaceutical negligence case, after it was amended to delete a bar order.

National Trust Co. v. Smallhorn (2007), 2007 CarswellOnt 8217, 2008 C.E.B. & P.G.R. 8277, 66 C.C.P.B. 145, 57 C.P.C. (6th) 211 (S.C.J.)

The court approved the settlement of this pension plan surplus case.

Currie v. McDonald's Restaurants of Canada Ltd. (2007), 51 C.P.C. (6th) 99, 2007 CarswellOnt 6010, [2007] O.J. No. 3622 (S.C.J.)

The court approved the settlement of a claim regarding a fraudulent contest, set class counsel's fee, and awarded a token honourarium to the class representative.

Al-Harazi v. Quizno's Canada Restaurant Corp. (2007), 49 C.P.C. (6th) 191, 2007 CarswellOnt 4633, [2007] O.J. No. 2819 (S.C.J.)

The court approved the settlement of a franchise deposit dispute despite objections from some class members who did not appreciate the risks of continuing litigation.

Bellaire v. Daya (2007), 2007 CarswellOnt 7976, 49 C.P.C. (6th) 110, [2007] O.J. No. 4819 (S.C.J.)

The court approved the settlement, and legal fees, in this medical malpractice case.

Gould v. BMO Nesbitt Burns Inc. (2007), 2007 CarswellOnt 1720, 45 C.P.C. (6th) 360, [2007] O.J. No. 1095 (S.C.J.)

The court approved the settlement of a class proceeding, including counsel fees, in this claim involving income-participating securities.

Garland v. Enbridge Gas Distribution Inc. (December 8, 2006), Doc. 94-CQ-50711, 2006 CarswellOnt 9605 (S.C.J.)

The court approved the settlement of this criminal interest claim, set class counsel's fee and awarded compensation to the class representative for his role in the litigation.

Toronto Transit Commission v. Morganite Canada Corp. (2007), 47 C.P.C. (6th) 179, 2007 CarswellOnt 690, [2007] O.J. No. 448 (S.C.J.)

The court approved the settlement of this price-fixing class action.

Frohlinger v. Nortel Networks Corp. (2007), 2007 CarswellOnt 240, 2007 C.E.B. & P.G.R. 8233, [2007] O.J. No. 148, 40 C.P.C. (6th) 62 (S.C.J.)

The court approved the settlement of this securities class action, which was part of a global settlement of multi-jurisdictional class action litigation.

Baxter v. Canada (Attorney General) (December 15, 2006), Doc. 00-CV-192059CP, 2006 CarswellOnt 7879, [2006] O.J. No. 4968 (S.C.J.)

The court approved the settlement of this Indian Residential School case subject to minor corrections.

Joseph v. Quik Payday Inc. (2006), 2006 CarswellOnt 7681, [2006] O.J. No. 4835, 38 C.P.C. (6th) 106 (S.C.J.)

The court approved the settlement of a payday loan class action.

Garland v. Enbridge Gas Distribution Inc. (2006), 2006 CarswellOnt 6585, [2006] O.J. No. 4273, 38 C.P.C. (6th) 70 (S.C.J.)

The court adjourned a motion to approve a settlement and counsel fees to permit further evidence and amendments to the settlement.

Elliott v. Boliden Ltd. (2006), 34 C.P.C. (6th) 339, 2006 CarswellOnt 6331 (S.C.J.)

The court approved the settlement of this securities class action.

Kranjcec v. Ontario, 33 C.P.C. (6th) 290, 2006 CarswellOnt 5535, 2006 C.E.B. & P.G.R. 8221, 57 C.C.P.B. 306 (S.C.J.)

The court approved the settlement of this claim for pension benefits.

Currie v. McDonald's Restaurants of Canada Ltd. (2006), 27 C.P.C. (6th) 286, 2006 CarswellOnt 1213 (S.C.J.); additional reasons at (September 25, 2007), Doc. 02-CV-238276 CP, 2007 CarswellOnt 6010 (S.C.J.)

The court approved a settlement including a *cy pres* application of the settlement funds, notwithstanding that class members would benefit from the settlement only as members of the public.

Lau v. Bayview Landmark Inc. (2006), [2006] O.J. No. 600, 2006 CarswellOnt 835, 34 C.P.C. (6th) 138 (S.C.J.)

The court refused to approve a settlement by some but not all defendants which included a "bar order" preventing the non-settling defendants from asserting claims against the settling defendants. On the facts of this case, the bar order impermissibly affected the non-settling defendants' substantive rights.

Ford v. F. Hoffmann-La Roche Ltd. (2005), 2005 CarswellOnt 1095, [2005] O.J. No. 1118, 74 O.R. (3d) 758, 12 C.P.C. (6th) 252 (S.C.J.)

The court approved the settlement of a price fixing class action.

Kanagaratnam v. Li (2005), 2005 CarswellOnt 774, 9 C.P.C. (6th) 282 (S.C.J.)

The court approved the settlement of a claim for wages, vacation pay, *etc.* by former employees of a bankrupt corporation against the directors of the corporation.

Parsons v. McDonald's Restaurants of Canada Ltd. (2005), [2005] O.J. No. 506, 2005 CarswellOnt 544, (sub nom. *Currie v. McDonald's Restaurants of Canada Ltd.)* 74 O.R. (3d) 321, 7 C.P.C. (6th) 60, (sub nom. *Currie v. McDonald's Restaurants of Canada Ltd.)* 250 D.L.R. (4th) 224, (sub nom. *Currie v. McDonald's Restaurants of Canada Ltd.)* 195 O.A.C. 244 (C.A.)

The settlement of a foreign class action may bind Ontario class members who did not opt out if (a) there is a real and substantial connection linking the cause of action to the foreign jurisdiction, (b) the rights of the Ontario class members were adequately represented, and (c) the Ontario class members were accorded procedural fairness, including adequate notice.

Kelman v. Goodyear Tire & Rubber Co. (2005), 2005 CarswellOnt 154, 5 C.P.C. (6th) 161, [2005] O.J. No. 175 (S.C.J.)

The court approved the settlement of a Canadian class action providing for access to a joint settlement fund covering both Canadian and U.S. jurisdictions. While the settlement would be administered in the U.S., the Ontario court continued to have a statutory supervisory role in the implementation of the settlement regarding the Canadian claims.

Gilbert v. Canadian Imperial Bank of Commerce (2004), 3 C.P.C. (6th) 35, 2004 CarswellOnt 4231, [2004] O.J. No. 4260 (S.C.J.)

The court approved the settlement of a claim for unauthorized foreign currency transaction fees.

Coleman v. Bayer Inc. (2004), 47 C.P.C. (5th) 346, [2004] O.J. No. 1974, 2004 CarswellOnt 1889, [2004] O.T.C. 403 (S.C.J.); additional reasons at (2004), 47 C.P.C. (5th) 148, [2004] O.J. No. 2775, 2004 CarswellOnt 2694 (S.C.J.)

The court approved a revised settlement agreement.

Mont-Bleu Ford Inc. v. Ford Motor Co. of Canada Ltd. (2004), 2004 CarswellOnt 1207, 45 C.P.C. (5th) 292 (S.C.J.)

The court approved the settlement of this franchise dispute despite objections from several class members. The objectors could opt out and the court rejected their submission that it was an illusory right because they could not afford further litigation.

Bona Foods Ltd. v. Ajinomoto U.S.A. Inc. (2004), 2004 CarswellOnt 918, [2004] O.J. No. 908, 2 C.P.C. (6th) 15 (S.C.J.)

The court approved the settlement of a price fixing claim regarding monosodium glutamate and other food additives.

Bona Foods Ltd. v. Ajinomoto U.S.A. Inc. (November 28, 2003), Doc. 377/08, [2003] O.J. No. 4734 (S.C.J.)

The court refused to approve a settlement with some but not all defendants and adjourned the motion to permit participation of a non-settling defendant. The court was also concerned about a proposed bar order preventing claims against the settling defendants by the non-settling defendant.

McMaster University v. Robb (2001), [2001] O.J. No. 5480, 2001 CarswellOnt 5792, 37 C.C.P.B. 252, 41 C.P.C. (5th) 403 (S.C.J.)

The court approved the settlement of this pension class action.

Burleton v. Royal Trust Corp. of Canada (2003), 34 C.P.C. (5th) 182, 2003 CarswellOnt 2049, 37 C.C.P.B. 19 (S.C.J.)

The court approved the settlement of this class action regarding an actuarial surplus in the Royal Trust pension plan.

Gariepy v. Shell Oil Co. (2002), 26 C.P.C. (5th) 358, 2002 CarswellOnt 3472, [2002] O.J. No. 4022, 21 C.L.R. (3d) 98 (S.C.J.)

The court provisionally approved a settlement of this class action for use of defective materials in the manufacture of plumbing pipes and fittings.

Fraser v. Falconbridge Ltd. (2002), 24 C.P.C. (5th) 396, 2002 CarswellOnt 2357, 33 C.C.P.B. 60, [2002] O.J. No. 2383 (S.C.J.)

The court approved the settlement of this class action involving the distribution of a pension surplus.

Smith v. Brockton (Municipality) (2003), 2003 CarswellOnt 894, 3 C.P.C. (6th) 84 (S.C.J.)

The court gave directions regarding the administration of a settlement agreement.

Attis v. Canada (Minister of Health) (2003), 2003 CarswellOnt 347, 29 C.P.C. (5th) 242 (S.C.J.); affirmed (December 5, 2003), Doc. CA C39589, C39630, C40018, 2003 CarswellOnt 4868 (C.A.); leave to appeal refused (2004), Doc. 30168, 2004 CarswellOnt 2982, 2004 CarswellOnt 2983, 332 N.R. 399 (note) (S.C.C.)

The court held that a settlement with a breast implant manufacturer did not preclude an action against the government for negligence in permitting the sale of the implants.

Chopik v. Mitsubishi Paper Mills Ltd. (2003), 2003 CarswellOnt 91, 29 C.P.C. (5th) 277 (S.C.J.)

The court approved the discontinuance of this action. There was no prejudice to the class members because the limitation period was suspended until the action was discontinued. No notice of discontinuance to the class members was necessary because there had been no previous notices to class members and there was no evidence suggesting any claims were withheld in reliance on this action.

CC&L Dedicated Enterprise Fund (Trustee of) v. Fisherman, 22 C.P.C. (5th) 346, 2002 CarswellOnt 1601, [2002] O.J. No. 1855, 26 B.L.R. (3d) 281, [2002] O.T.C. 317 (S.C.J.)

The court approved the settlement of this fraudulent securities class action.

Alfresh Beverages Canada Corp. v. Hoechst AG (2002), 2002 CarswellOnt 77, [2002] O.J. No. 79, 16 C.P.C. (5th) 301 (S.C.J.)

The court approved the settlement of this price fixing case.

McMaster University v. Robb (November 1, 2001), Doc. 01-CV-216289, [2001] O.J. No. 5480 (S.C.J.)

The court approved the settlement of this pension surplus case.

Carom v. Bre-X Minerals Ltd. (2001), [2001] O.J. No. 4177, 2001 CarswellOnt 3779, 15 C.P.C. (5th) 33 (S.C.J.)

The court approved a settlement with one of several defendants.

Directright Cartage Ltd. v. London Life Insurance Co., [2001] O.J. No. 4073, 2001 CarswellOnt 3658, [2001] I.L.R. I-4013, 34 C.C.L.I. (3d) 118, 17 C.P.C. (5th) 185 (S.C.J.)

The court approved the settlement of this "premium offset" life insurance case.

Knowles v. Wyeth-Ayerst Canada Inc. (2001), 2001 CarswellOnt 2550, [2001] O.J. No. 2880, 16 C.P.C. (5th) 343 (S.C.J.)

The court approved the settlement of this diet drug class action.

McCarthy v. Canadian Red Cross Society (2001), 8 C.P.C. (5th) 350, 2001 CarswellOnt 2255, [2001] O.J. No. 2474 (S.C.J.)

A partial settlement of a class action was approved on a renewed motion based upon further and better materials.

Ho-A-Shoo v. Canada (Attorney General) (2001), [2001] O.J. No. 2330, 2001 CarswellOnt 2114, 2001 D.T.C. 5589 (S.C.J.)

The court approved the settlement of a claim for refund of tax payments.

Windsor Utilities Commission v. Ontario Hydro (May 31, 2001), Doc. 97-CV-122541, 2001 CarswellOnt 2001, [2001] O.J. No. 2173 (S.C.J.)

The court approved the settlement of a dispute between municipal electric utilities and Ontario Hydro.

Elliott v. Currie (2001), [2001] O.J. No. 1958, 2001 CarswellOnt 1783, 12 C.P.C. (5th) 233 (S.C.J.)

The court approved a settlement distributing the assets of a defunct union local.

McCarthy v. Canadian Red Cross Society (2001), 2001 CarswellOnt 509, [2001] O.J. No. 567, 8 C.P.C. (5th) 341 (S.C.J.); additional reasons at (2001), 2001 CarswellOnt 2255, [2001] O.J. No. 2474, 8 C.P.C. (5th) 350 (S.C.J.)

In considering a settlement, the court is concerned with safeguarding the interests of the absent class members, not with balancing the interests of the class members with the defendants or potential defendants. In this case, the court refused to approve a partial settlement where the evidentiary record did not satisfy certain concerns, but permitted the parties to file further and better materials.

Millard v. North George Capital Management Ltd. (2000), 47 C.P.C. (4th) 365, 2000 CarswellOnt 1450 (S.C.J. [Commercial List])

The court granted certification and approved a settlement where the action raised common issues and the settlement reached was time and cost-effective for the parties, negotiated by experienced counsel, and was fair, reasonable and in the best interests of all concerned.

Ontario New Home Warranty Program v. Chevron Chemical Co. (1999), 46 O.R. (3d) 130, 37 C.P.C. (4th) 175, [1999] O.J. No. 2245, 1999 CarswellOnt 1851 (S.C.J.)

The court approved a settlement with some but not all defendants, with various terms regarding the non-settling defendants.

Reichhold Ltd. v. Boyer (2000), 23 C.C.P.B. 182, 43 C.P.C. (4th) 263, 2000 CarswellOnt 245 (S.C.J.)

The court approved the settlement of dividing a pension plan surplus between a company and its employees.

Epstein v. First Marathon Inc. / Société First Marathon Inc. (2000), 2 B.L.R. (3d) 30, 41 C.P.C. (4th) 159, 2000 CarswellOnt 346, [2000] O.J. No. 452 (S.C.J.)

The court refused to approve the settlement of what it inferred was a "strike action" initiated by counsel simply for the benefit of counsel. The proposed settlement provided for payment of plaintiff's counsel's fees and disbursements and for dismissal of the action.

Brimner v. VIA Rail Canada Inc. (2000), 50 O.R. (3d) 114, 1 C.P.C. (5th) 185, 2000 CarswellOnt 2538, [2000] O.J. No. 2747 (S.C.J.); leave to appeal allowed (January 31, 2001), Doc. 99-GD-46301, 2001 CarswellOnt 399, [2001] O.J. No. 458 (S.C.J.); affirmed (2001), 2001 CarswellOnt 3265, 151 O.A.C. 133, 15 C.P.C. (5th) 27, [2001] O.J. No. 3684 (Div. Ct.)

An extra-judicial compensation scheme devised by the defendants did not prevent a class action from being the preferable procedure to resolve the common issues.

McKrow v. Manufacturers Life Insurance Co. (1998), [1998] O.J. No. 4692, 28 C.P.C. (4th) 104, 9 C.C.L.I. (3d) 161, 1998 CarswellOnt 4360 (Gen. Div.); additional reasons at (November 4, 1999), Doc. 24112/96, 1999 CarswellOnt 3504 (S.C.J.)

The court approved the settlement of this "vanishing premium" life insurance policy case.

Dabbs v. Sun Life Assurance Co. of Canada (1998), 41 O.R. (3d) 97, 165 D.L.R. (4th) 482, [1999] I.L.R. I-3629, 113 O.A.C. 307, 7 C.C.L.I. (3d) 38, 27 C.P.C. (4th) 243, 1998 CarswellOnt 3539, [1998] O.J. No. 3622 (C.A.); leave to appeal refused (1998), 235 N.R. 390 (note), 118 O.A.C. 399 (note) (S.C.C.)

The court held a class member did not have the right to appeal from an order approving a settlement.

Dabbs v. Sun Life Assurance Co. of Canada (1998), 40 O.R. (3d) 429, 22 C.P.C. (4th) 381, 5 C.C.L.I. (3d) 18, [1998] I.L.R. I-3575, 1998 CarswellOnt 2758, [1998] O.J. No. 2811 (Gen. Div.); additional reasons at (1998), 47 C.P.C. (4th) 105, 22 C.C.L.I. (3d) 198, 1998 CarswellOnt 5915 (Gen. Div.); set aside/quashed (1998), 41 O.R. (3d) 97, 165 D.L.R.

(4th) 482, [1999] I.L.R. I-3629, 113 O.A.C. 307, 7 C.C.L.I. (3d) 38, 27 C.P.C. (4th) 243, 1998 CarswellOnt 3539, [1998] O.J. No. 3622 (C.A.); leave to appeal refused (1998), 235 N.R. 390 (note), 118 O.A.C. 399 (note) (S.C.C.)

The court approved the settlement of a "vanishing premium" class action against a life insurer.

Dabbs v. Sun Life Assurance Co. of Canada (1997), 35 O.R. (3d) 708, 14 C.P.C. (4th) 122, [1998] I.L.R. I-3494, 48 C.C.L.I. (2d) 146, 38 O.T.C. 98 (Gen. Div.); leave to appeal refused at (1998), 36 O.R. (3d) 770, 20 C.P.C. (4th) 87, 1 C.C.L.I. (3d) 42, 48 O.T.C. 391, 1998 CarswellOnt 264 (Gen. Div.); additional reasons at (1998), 38 O.R. (3d) 781, 19 C.P.C. (4th) 18, 50 C.C.L.I. (2d) 30, 50 O.T.C. 396, 1998 CarswellOnt 521 (Gen. Div.)

Simultaneous negotiation of an agreement respecting the settlement of the action and counsel fee did not create a disqualifying conflict of interest for class counsel.

Settlement Implementation

Rowlands v. Durham Region Health, 2012 ONSC 945, 2012 CarswellOnt 1418 (S.C.J.)

The court refused to reduce the settlement Administrator's fees despite their having given a lower fee estimate. Their work was necessary and was done well.

Smith v. Brockton (Municipality) (February 27, 2004), Doc. 00-CV-192173CP, 2004 CarswellOnt 837 (S.C.J.); additional reasons at (2004), 2004 CarswellOnt 1244, 5 C.P.C. (6th) 17 (S.C.J.)

The court gave directions regarding the administration of a settlement.

Guglietti v. Toronto Area Transit Operating Authority (2000), 50 C.P.C. (4th) 355, 2000 CarswellOnt 1996 (S.C.J.)

Through the inadvertence of her counsel a class member had failed to make a claim under a court approved settlement of a class proceeding. There was no prejudice to the defendant. The court extended the time for the class member to participate.

Parsons v. Canadian Red Cross Society (2000), 51 O.R. (3d) 261, 2000 CarswellOnt 4396 (S.C.J.)

The court gave directions regarding the administration of a class action settlement.

Parsons v. Canadian Red Cross Society (2002), 26 C.P.C. (5th) 148, 2002 CarswellOnt 2353 (S.C.J.)

In order to pay down an anticipated surplus, the court ordered the payout of a portion of the settlement funds previously ordered held back.

Costs

Fehr v. Sun Life Assurance Co. of Canada, 2017 ONSC 2218, 2017 CarswellOnt 5133, 66 C.C.L.I. (5th) 201, 99 C.P.C. (7th) 67, [2017] O.J. No. 1749 (S.C.J.)

The court awarded $1 million costs of certification proceedings against the unsuccessful plaintiffs.

Green v. Canadian Imperial Bank of Commerce, 2016 ONSC 3829, 2016 CarswellOnt 9114 (S.C.J.)

The court awarded about $2.7 million costs for certification and leave motions.

Good v. Toronto Police Services Board, 2016 ONCA 250, 2016 CarswellOnt 5047, 130 O.R. (3d) 241, 82 C.P.C. (7th) 1, 396 D.L.R. (4th) 411, 347 O.A.C. 307; leave to appeal refused (November 10, 2016), Doc. 37050, 2016 CarswellOnt 17619, 2016 CarswellOnt 17620, [2016] S.C.C.A. No. 255

The court increased the plaintiff's certification cost award to $315,000 as the lower court failed to consider the impact of the costs award on access to justice.

Dine v. Biomet Inc., 2016 ONSC 857, 2016 CarswellOnt 1750 (S.C.J.)

Where the plaintiff sought $584,000 in costs of a certification motion, the court awarded $200,000 forthwith and $65,000 to the plaintiff in the cause.

Labourers' Pension Fund of Central and Eastern Canada (Trustees of) v. Sino-Forest Corp., 2015 ONSC 6354, 2015 CarswellOnt 15742 (S.C.J.); leave to appeal refused 2016 ONSC 878, 2016 CarswellOnt 1486 (Div. Ct.)

Where the plaintiffs sought $2.6 million costs of a certification and leave motion, the court awarded about $786,000 with roughly half payable forthwith and the balance in the cause.

Green v. CIBC, 2014 ONCA 344, 2014 CarswellOnt 5625, 68 C.P.C. (7th) 99

Costs of two appeals were set at $151,250 and $100,000.

Fairview Donut Inc. v. TDL Group Corp., 2014 ONSC 776, 2014 CarswellOnt 1258 (S.C.J.)

The court awarded $1.85 million summary judgment costs to the successful defendants.

Drywall Acoustic Lathing and Insulation, Local 675 Pension Fund (Trustees) v. SNC Group Inc., 2013 ONSC 7122, 2013 CarswellOnt 17348 (S.C.J.)

The court awarded costs of about $100,000 to the defendant for a post-certification motion, but with only $25,000 payable forthwith and the balance to be set off or paid later.

Smith v. Inco Ltd., 2013 ONCA 724, 2013 CarswellOnt 16202, 79 C.E.L.R. (3d) 1, 46 C.P.C. (7th) 69, 313 O.A.C. 156; leave to appeal refused 2014 CarswellOnt 7503, 2014 CarswellOnt 7504, 475 N.R. 399 (note), [2014] S.C.C.A. No. 36 (S.C.C.)

The court awarded $1.8 million in costs to the successful defendant rather than the $5.3 million it had sought.

Crisante v. DePuy Orthopaedics Inc., 2013 ONSC 6351, 2013 CarswellOnt 15417, 57 C.P.C. (7th) 399 (S.C.J.)

The court fixed the costs of a successful certification motion at $175,000 not the $700,000 requested by the plaintiff.

Lipson v. Cassels Brock & Blackwell LLP (2013), 2013 ONSC 6450, 2013 CarswellOnt 14116, 52 C.P.C. (7th) 391, [2014] 1 C.T.C. 75, 93 E.T.R. (3d) 294 (S.C.J.)

Where the plaintiff succeeded on a certification motion, the court awarded $299,000 costs, half payable forthwith and half in the cause.

Berry v. Pulley (September 3, 2013), Doc. 97-CV-135179 CP, 2013 CarswellOnt 12311 (S.C.J.)

Where the plaintiffs' claim failed at trial, and the defendants requested $1.5 million in costs, the court refused to award any costs due to the defendants' shabby and high-handed conduct.

Amyotrophic Lateral Sclerosis Society of Essex County v. Windsor (City), 2013 ONCA 254, 2013 CarswellOnt 4787, 115 O.R. (3d) 418, 41 C.P.C. (7th) 1, 306 O.A.C. 359; leave to appeal refused 2013 CarswellOnt 13700, 2013 CarswellOnt 13701, 466 N.R. 394 (note), [2013] S.C.C.A. No. 266 (S.C.C.)

Where the appellants were entirely successful on the issues appealed, the Divisional Court erred in refusing to award costs to the appellants.

Brown v. Canada (Attorney General), 2013 ONCA 18, 2013 CarswellOnt 206, 114 O.R. (3d) 355, 98 C.C.L.T. (3d) 1, 31 C.P.C. (7th) 156, [2013] 2 C.N.L.R. 15, 300 O.A.C. 290; additional reasons 2013 ONCA 256, 2013 CarswellOnt 4743

In this case regarding removing Aboriginal children from their families, the court awarded no costs of an unsuccessful certification motion where the claim involved a test case, novel points of law, and the public interest.

McCracken v. Canadian National Railway, 2012 ONSC 6838, 2012 CarswellOnt 15603, 31 C.P.C. (7th) 237, [2012] O.J. No. 5716 (S.C.J.)

The plaintiff was ordered to pay $475,000 costs of an unsuccessful certification motion. The amount claimed was reduced by issue estoppel based on the Court of Appeal's finding that the matter involved the public interest and novel points of law.

McCracken v. Canadian National Railway, 2012 ONCA 797, 2012 CarswellOnt 14475, 5 C.C.E.L. (4th) 327

Where a plaintiff's unsuccessful appeal raised novel issues and engaged access to justice concerns, the court awarded costs of only $60,000.

Smith v. Inco, 2012 ONSC 5094, 2012 CarswellOnt 11223, 70 C.E.L.R. (3d) 150, 28 C.P.C. (7th) 388 (S.C.J.)

Where an unsuccessful action involved a matter of public interest and raised a novel point of law, the court awarded costs of $1.8 million, half of what would otherwise be appropriate.

Cavanaugh v. Grenville Christian College, 2012 ONSC 4786, 2012 CarswellOnt 10174, 27 C.P.C. (7th) 326, [2012] O.J. No. 3883 (S.C.J.)

The court awarded $301,000 costs of an unsuccessful certification motion.

Williams v. Canon Canada Inc., 2012 ONSC 1856, 2012 CarswellOnt 3711, 34 C.P.C. (7th) 394 (S.C.J.)

The court awarded $200,000 costs of an unsuccessful certification motion though the defendants requested $765,000.

Plaunt v. Renfrew Power Generation Inc., 2011 ONSC 5777, 2011 CarswellOnt 10267, 13 C.P.C. (7th) 203, 63 C.E.L.R. (3d) 203 (S.C.J.)

The court awarded costs of $86,000 on a successful certification motion, after removing dockets not exclusively relating to certification.

2038724 Ontario Ltd. v. Quizno's Canada Restaurant Corp., 2010 ONSC 5390, 2010 CarswellOnt 7479, [2010] O.J. No. 4208, 100 C.P.C. (6th) 274 (S.C.J.); leave to appeal refused 2011 ONSC 859, 2011 CarswellOnt 823, [2011] O.J. No. 585 (Div. Ct.)

After the plaintiff's successful appeal of certification, the court awarded some costs payable forthwith and some costs payable in the cause.

McCraken v. Canadian National Railway, 2010 ONSC 6026, 2010 CarswellOnt 8330, 100 C.P.C. (6th) 334, [2010] O.J. No. 4650 (S.C.J.); varied 2012 ONCA 445, 2012 CarswellOnt 8010, 111 O.R. (3d) 745, 100 C.C.E.L. (3d) 27, 21 C.P.C. (7th) 57, 2012 C.L.L.C. 210-041, 293 O.A.C. 274, [2012] O.J. No. 2884; additional reasons 2012 ONCA 797, 2012 CarswellOnt 14475, 5 C.C.E.L. (4th) 327

Although there was divided success on a combined rule 21 and certification motion, the plaintiff was awarded costs.

McKenna v. Gammon Gold Inc., 2010 ONSC 3630, 2010 CarswellOnt 4352, 88 C.P.C. (6th) 83 (S.C.J.)

Where a class was certified but certain issues were decided against the plaintiff, the court granted the plaintiff modest costs of $100,000.

Singer v. Schering-Plough Canada Inc., 2010 CarswellOnt 1820, 2010 ONSC 1737, [2010] O.J. No. 1243, 87 C.P.C. (6th) 345 (S.C.J.)

The court awarded costs of $200,000 against the plaintiff on an unsuccessful certification motion.

Lambert v. Guidant Corp. (September 24, 2009), Doc. 05-CV-295630 CP, 2009 CarswellOnt 8759 (S.C.J.); leave to appeal refused (2009), 2009 CarswellOnt 7662, 256 O.A.C. 299 (Div. Ct.)

The court awarded $650,000 partial indemnity costs of a certification motion to the successful plaintiff. The defendants had taken an aggressively combative approach, filed extensive evidence solely within the knowledge of the defendants and severely hindered the plaintiff's cross-examinations of defence witnesses.

Ragoonanan Estate v. Imperial Tobacco Canada Ltd. (2009), 71 C.P.C. (6th) 394, 2009 CarswellOnt 609 (Div. Ct.)

The court denied costs to the defendant of a failed certification motion on the basis that the action involved the public interest.

Ruffolo v. Sun Life Assurance Co. of Canada, 95 O.R. (3d) 709, 2009 CarswellOnt 1743, 2009 ONCA 274, 68 C.P.C. (6th) 322, 74 C.C.P.B. 191, 247 O.A.C. 209, 73 C.C.L.I. (4th) 185, 2009 C.E.B. & P.G.R. 8336, [2009] O.J. No. 1322 (C.A.)

Costs were awarded in favour of the defendants in a proposed class proceeding that was never certified.

McNaughton Automotive Ltd. v. Co-operators General Insurance Co., (sub nom. *David Polowin Real Estate Ltd. v. Dominion of Canada General Insurance Co.)* 93 O.R. (3d) 257, 2008 CarswellOnt 6134, 300 D.L.R. (4th) 491, 62 C.P.C. (6th) 20, 69 M.V.R. (5th) 1, 2008 ONCA 703, [2009] I.L.R. I-4756, 67 C.C.L.I. (4th) 163, 244 O.A.C. 151 (C.A.)

The court awarded no costs where the Court of Appeal overruled its own previous decision and effectively ended the plaintiffs' case. The disastrous cost consequences to the class counsel who took the case on a contingency basis was not a relevant consideration.

Peter v. Medtronic Inc. (2008), 65 C.P.C. (6th) 23, 2008 CarswellOnt 2475, [2008] O.J. No. 1700 (S.C.J.)

The court awarded costs of a successful certification motion in the sum of $245,000.

Dean v. Mister Transmission (International) Ltd. (March 10, 2009), Doc. 1076/07, 2009 CarswellOnt 1308, [2009] O.J. No. 992 (S.C.J.)

The court awarded partial indemnity costs of a successful certification motion to the plaintiff in the sum of $125,000. The court inferred that the failure of the defendants to disclose their costs indicated such evidence would not assist the defendants in showing the amount claimed by the plaintiff was unreasonable.

Smith Estate v. National Money Mart Co. (2008), 92 O.R. (3d) 224, 2008 CarswellOnt 5256 (S.C.J.); additional reasons at (2008), 67 C.P.C. (6th) 260, 2008 CarswellOnt 6673 (S.C.J.)

The court ordered that costs be in the cause for the plaintiffs' failed partial summary judgment motion. However, the court ordered that costs be payable forthwith to the plaintiffs from the defendants' failed cross-motion to stay the action.

Sutherland v. Hudson's Bay Co., [2008] O.J. No. 602, 2008 CarswellOnt 801, 68 C.C.P.B. 141, 2008 C.E.B. & P.G.R. 8282, 64 C.C.E.L. (3d) 211, 51 C.P.C. (6th) 127 (S.C.J.)

The court refused to order the unsuccessful plaintiff to pay the costs of the representative defendants, who had been made parties on motion by the named defendants.

Sutherland v. Hudson's Bay Co. (2008), 68 C.C.P.B. 141, 2008 C.E.B. & P.G.R. 8282, 64 C.C.E.L. (3d) 211, 51 C.P.C. (6th) 127, [2008] O.J. No. 602, 2008 CarswellOnt 801 (S.C.J.)

Where the plaintiffs were unsuccessful at the trial of this pension case, the court ordered certain discounted defence costs paid out of one of the pension trust funds.

Poulin v. Ford Motor Co. of Canada Ltd./Ford du Canada Ltée (2007), 2007 CarswellOnt 8255, 52 C.P.C. (6th) 294, [2007] O.J. No. 4988 (S.C.J.)

The court awarded substantial indemnity costs of an unsuccessful certification motion against plaintiff's counsel, including a U.S. co-counsel.

Kerr v. Danier Leather Inc. (2007), 48 C.P.C. (6th) 205, 2007 CarswellOnt 6445, 2007 CarswellOnt 6446, [2007] S.C.J. No. 44, 2007 SCC 44, 87 O.R. (3d) 398 (note), 36 B.L.R. (4th) 95, 231 O.A.C. 348, 286 D.L.R. (4th) 601, [2007] 2 S.C.R. 331, 368 N.R. 204

The court awarded costs against an unsuccessful class representative where the dispute was predominately about private commercial interests. "Test case" means a case selected to resolve a legal issue applicable to other pending or anticipated litigation. "Matter of public interest" means a matter involving either issues of broad public importance or persons who are historically disadvantaged in society.

MacDougall v. Ontario Northland Transportation Commission (2007), 2007 CarswellOnt 5427, 61 C.C.P.B. 307, 45 C.P.C. (6th) 22 (S.C.J.)

In awarding costs against the unsuccessful plaintiff on a motion for certification, the court balanced the principle that costs follow the event against the goal of civil justice access.

Authorson (Litigation Guardian of) v. Canada (Attorney General), 2007 CarswellOnt 5501, 61 C.C.P.B. 319, 43 C.P.C. (6th) 253, 2007 ONCA 599 (C.A.)

The court refused to order that class counsel be required to indemnify the Litigation Guardian and the Litigation Administrators in this proposed class proceeding where counsel's conduct was questionable but not in bad faith.

McNaughton Automotive Ltd. v. Co-operators General Insurance Co. (2007), 2007 CarswellOnt 2233, [2007] O.J. No. 1453, 225 O.A.C. 205, 47 C.C.L.I. (4th) 56, 37 C.P.C. (6th) 120 (Div. Ct.)

The court made no order for costs where the failed certification of a class proceeding raised a novel issue of law and where, if successful, the action would have had a significant impact on insurers and insureds.

Authorson (Litigation Guardian of) v. Canada (Attorney General) (2006), 2006 CarswellOnt 8156, 57 C.C.P.B. 270, 37 C.P.C. (6th) 115 (S.C.J.)

The court refused to order a costs premium in light of the decision of the Supreme Court of Canada in *Walker v. Ritchie*, 2006 CarswellOnt 6185, 2006 CarswellOnt 6186, [2006] S.C.J. No. 45, 2006 SCC 45, 353 N.R. 265, 33 C.P.C. (6th) 1, 43 C.C.L.I. (4th) 161, 43 C.C.L.T. (3d) 1, 273 D.L.R. (4th) 240, 217 O.A.C. 374, [2006] 2 S.C.R. 428.

Arabi v. Toronto Dominion Bank (2006), 2006 CarswellOnt 7977, [2006] O.J. No. 5011, 36 C.P.C. (6th) 374 (S.C.J.)

Despite being successful, the court declined to award costs to the defendants.

Cassano v. Toronto Dominion Bank (June 22, 2005), Doc. 97-CV-128598 CP, [2005] O.J. No. 6332, 2005 CarswellOnt 10279 (S.C.J.)

Where the unsuccessful plaintiff's case involved the public interest and goals of the CPA, the court awarded no costs except $12,500 thrown away by certain abandoned claims.

Yordanes v. Bank of Nova Scotia (2006), 35 C.P.C. (6th) 86, 2006 CarswellOnt 2344, 20 B.L.R. (4th) 167 (S.C.J.)

Where the defendant was largely successful in striking out the statement of claim with leave to amend, the court awarded the defendant costs of $25,000 plus disbursements.

Vennell v. Barnado's (2004), 28 C.P.C. (6th) 185, 2004 CarswellOnt 4196, 73 O.R. (3d) 13 (S.C.J.)

The court declined to award costs to the defendant as a result of the class action being converted to an individual action.

Pearson v. Inco Ltd. (2006), 25 C.P.C. (6th) 1, 2006 CarswellOnt 1527, [2006] O.J. No. 991, 20 C.E.L.R. (3d) 292, 208 O.A.C. 284, 79 O.R. (3d) 427, 267 D.L.R. (4th) 111 (C.A.)

The court reviewed the principles applicable to an award of costs on certification motions.

McNaughton Automotive Ltd. v. Co-operators General Insurance Co., 74 O.R. (3d) 216, 2005 CarswellOnt 212, [2005] O.J. No. 179, [2005] I.L.R. I-4378, 9 C.P.C. (6th) 186 (S.C.J.); additional reasons at (2005), 2005 CarswellOnt 904, 9 C.P.C. (6th) 194 (S.C.J.)

The court awarded costs of various motions to the successful party on a partial indemnity scale. However where the claims of certain representative plaintiffs fell outside the limitation period and, the plaintiffs persisted with unsubstantiated allegations of fraud, dishonesty and deceit in order to extend the limitation period, the court awarded costs on a substantial indemnity scale.

Hague v. Liberty Mutual Insurance Co. (2005), 13 C.P.C. (6th) 37, [2005] O.J. No. 1660, 2005 CarswellOnt 1361, 21 C.C.L.I. (4th) 300 (S.C.J.); leave to appeal refused (March 29, 2005), Doc. Toronto 3-05, 2005 CarswellOnt 1830 (Div. Ct.)

It is inappropriate to defer the awarding of costs of the certification motion to the judge determining the common issues.

Pearson v. Inco Ltd. (2005), 2005 CarswellOnt 6598, 205 O.A.C. 30, 78 O.R. (3d) 641, [2005] O.J. No. 4918, 261 D.L.R. (4th) 629, 20 C.E.L.R. (3d) 258, 43 R.P.R. (4th) 43, 18 C.P.C. (6th) 77 (C.A.); additional reasons at (2006), 2006 CarswellOnt 1527, 20 C.E.L.R. (3d) 292, 208 O.A.C. 284, 25 C.P.C. (6th) 1, 79 O.R. (3d) 427, [2006] O.J. No. 991, 267 D.L.R. (4th) 111 (C.A.); leave to appeal refused (June 29, 2006), Doc. 31249, 2006 CarswellOnt 4020, 2006 CarswellOnt 4021 (S.C.C.)

A plaintiff need not show concrete and specific arrangements in place to pay defence costs awards. Such a requirement would frustrate the legislative goal of access to justice.

Andersen v. St. Jude Medical Inc. (2004), 28 C.P.C. (6th) 199, [2004] O.J. No. 3102, 2004 CarswellOnt 8144 (S.C.J.); leave to appeal allowed (2005), 75 O.R. (3d) 398, 2005 CarswellOnt 1483 (S.C.J.); affirmed (2006), 264 D.L.R. (4th) 557, [2006] O.J. No. 508, 208 O.A.C. 10, 2006 CarswellOnt 710 (Div. Ct.); leave to appeal refused (May 12, 2006), Doc. CA M333540, 2006 CarswellOnt 7749 (C.A.)

Certification motions differ from most other motions and can warrant a substantial award of costs. The court awarded $618,000 in costs to the successful plaintiffs.

Caputo v. Imperial Tobacco Ltd. (2005), 2005 CarswellOnt 856, [2005] O.J. No. 842, 74 O.R. (3d) 728, 9 C.P.C. (6th) 175, 250 D.L.R. (4th) 756 (S.C.J.)

The court declined to award any costs of an unsuccessful certification motion where the litigation raised a novel point of law and had a strong public interest component.

Cloud v. Canada (Attorney General) (2004), 2004 CarswellOnt 5026, [2004] O.J. No. 4924, 73 O.R. (3d) 401, 192 O.A.C. 239, 27 C.C.L.T. (3d) 50, [2005] 1 C.N.L.R. 8, 2 C.P.C. (6th) 199, 247 D.L.R. (4th) 667 (C.A.); additional reasons at (2005), 2005 CarswellOnt 1859, [2005] O.J. No. 733, 7 C.P.C. (6th) 137 (C.A.); leave to appeal refused (2005), 2005 CarswellOnt 1866, 2005 CarswellOnt 1867, 344 N.R. 192 (note), 207 O.A.C. 400 (note) (S.C.C.)

Where the Court of Appeal reversed lower court orders refusing to certify the case, the court referred the costs at first instance back to the motions judge but fixed the costs in the Divisional Court at $60,000 and the costs in the Court of Appeal at $42,500.

Joanisse v. Barker, 46 C.P.C. (5th) 348, [2003] O.J. No. 4081, 2003 CarswellOnt 3983, [2003] O.T.C. 733 (S.C.J.)

The court awarded no costs of an unsuccessful certification motion on behalf of former patients of a facility for the criminally insane despite the defendants' request for costs of almost $500,000.

Pearson v. Inco Ltd. (2002), 27 C.P.C. (5th) 171, 2002 CarswellOnt 3303, [2002] O.J. No. 3532, 50 C.E.L.R. (N.S.) 88 (S.C.J.); affirmed (2004), 2004 CarswellOnt 557, [2004] O.J. No. 317, 183 O.A.C. 168, 6 C.E.L.R. (3d) 117, 44 C.P.C. (5th) 276 (Div. Ct.); additional reasons at (2004), 2004 CarswellOnt 3018, 10 C.E.L.R. (3d) 307, 49 C.P.C. (5th) 267 (Div. Ct.)

The court awarded $184,000 against an unsuccessful plaintiff regarding costs of a certification motion.

Direnfeld v. National Trust (2001), 9 C.P.C. (5th) 277, 2001 CarswellOnt 1566 (S.C.J.); affirmed (2002), 2002 CarswellOnt 308, 17 C.P.C. (5th) 102 (C.A.)

Where the defendants were unaware prior to the certification motion hearing date that their motion to strike the plaintiffs' claim would be successful and were compelled to prepare for the certification motion accordingly, the court held that the defendants were entitled to party-and-party costs of both motions. The court refused to award costs against the solicitors for the plaintiffs.

Franklin v. University of Toronto (2001), 2001 CarswellOnt 4527, [2001] O.J. No. 4321, 16 C.P.C. (5th) 317 (S.C.J.); additional reasons at (April 19, 2002), Doc. 01-CV-207231CP, 2002 CarswellOnt 1236 (S.C.J.)

Where the plaintiff's motion for certification and the defendant's motion to dismiss the case were both dismissed, the court awarded no costs.

Williams v. Mutual Life Assurance Co. of Canada (2001), 2001 CarswellOnt 370, (sub nom. *Kumar v. Mutual Life Assurance Co. of Canada))* [2001] O.J. No. 445, 27 C.C.L.I. (3d) 256, 6 C.P.C. (5th) 194 (S.C.J.)

In this vanishing premium case the court refused to award costs of a certification motion against an unsuccessful plaintiff. The action raised important issues, there were potentially many class members, and the matter was novel in the sense it was the first contested vanishing premium case.

Edwards v. Law Society of Upper Canada (2000), (sub nom. *Edwards v. Law Society of Upper Canada (No. 2))* 48 O.R. (3d) 329, 188 D.L.R. (4th) 613, 1 C.C.L.T. (3d) 193, 133 O.A.C. 286, 46 C.P.C. (4th) 30, 24 Admin. L.R. (3d) 203, 2000 CarswellOnt 1964, [2000] O.J. No. 2085 (C.A.); leave to appeal allowed (2000), 266 N.R. 196 (note), 2000 CarswellOnt 4630, 2000 CarswellOnt 4631, [2000] S.C.C.A. No. 431, 142 O.A.C. 400 (note); affirmed 2001 CarswellOnt 3962, 2001 CarswellOnt 3963, [2001] S.C.J. No. 77, 2001 SCC 80, 34 Admin. L.R. (3d) 38, 206 D.L.R. (4th) 211, 277 N.R. 145, 8 C.C.L.T. (3d) 153, 13 C.P.C. (5th) 35, (sub nom. *Edwards v. Law Society of Upper Canada (No. 2))* 56 O.R. (3d) 456 (headnote only), 153 O.A.C. 388, [2001] 3 S.C.R. 562

Where a claim supported by the Law Foundation's Class Proceedings Fund was dismissed, it was required to pay party-and-party costs.

Dabbs v. Sun Life Assurance Co. of Canada (1998), 47 C.P.C. (4th) 105, 22 C.C.L.I. (3d) 198, 1998 CarswellOnt 5915 (Gen. Div.)

An award of costs against objectors to a proposed settlement of class action should be made only in rare circumstances.

Robertson v. Thomson Corp. (1999), 43 O.R. (3d) 389, 43 C.P.C. (4th) 166, 1999 CarswellOnt 2822 (Gen. Div.)

Where a defendant strenuously and unsuccessfully resisted certification the court awarded party-and-party costs payable forthwith. If the goal of enhanced access to justice is to be met, some account must be taken of plaintiffs' financial burden of carrying on litigation against wealthy and determined opponents.

Garland v. Consumers' Gas Co., 40 O.R. (3d) 479 (headnote only), [1998] 3 S.C.R. 112, 129 C.C.C. (3d) 97, 20 C.R. (5th) 44, 165 D.L.R. (4th) 385, 49 M.P.L.R. (2d) 77, 231 N.R. 1, 114 O.A.C. 1, 1998 CarswellOnt 4053, 1998 CarswellOnt 4054

A plaintiff who has obtained support from the Class Proceedings Fund should not be exposed to personal liability for any costs arising in the action, including costs of motions. The Supreme Court of Canada set aside a $500 costs award against the plaintiff personally.

Dabbs v. Sun Life Assurance Co. of Canada (1998), 38 O.R. (3d) 781, 19 C.P.C. (4th) 18, 50 C.C.L.I. (2d) 30, 50 O.T.C. 396, 1998 CarswellOnt 521 (Gen. Div.)

The court awarded solicitor-and-client costs against class members who sought to remove class counsel and cast unfounded aspersions on the integrity of class counsel.

Nantais v. Telectronics Proprietary (Canada) Limited (June 18, 1996), Windsor Doc. 95-GD-31789 (Ont. Gen. Div.)

Although certification is a procedural step, it could be determinative of the action, and should not be regarded as a simple interlocutory procedure. The court fixed the party-and-party costs of a successful certification motion in the sum of $96,113.66.

Nash v. CIBC Trust Corp. (1996), 7 C.P.C. (4th) 260 (Ont. Gen. Div.); affirmed (March 13, 1997), CA C25819 (Ont. C.A.)

The court awarded costs of the certification motion to the plaintiff to be fixed by the court and paid forthwith.

Nantais v. Telectronics Proprietary (Canada) Ltd. (1996), 28 O.R. (3d) 523, 134 D.L.R. (4th) 470 (Gen. Div.); leave to appeal to C.A. refused (1996), 28 O.R. (3d) 523n (C.A.)

A contingency fee agreement does not affect the plaintiff's entitlement to costs of motions.

Elliott v. Canadian Broadcasting Corp. (1995), 25 O.R. (3d) 302, 38 C.P.C. (3d) 332, 62 C.P.R. (3d) 19, 125 D.L.R. (4th) 534, 82 O.A.C. 115 (C.A.); leave to appeal to Supreme Court of Canada refused (March 7, 1996), Doc. 24895

Although an order striking out the statement of claim in a class action was upheld on appeal, each party was ordered to bear its own costs of the original motion and the appeal as the case involved novel and complex questions of law.

Garland v. Consumers' Gas Co. (1995), 22 O.R. (3d) 767, 17 B.L.R. (2d) 239n (Gen. Div.)

The court refused to award costs to a successful defendant where the case was a test case, raised a novel point of law, and involved a matter of public interest.

Smith v. Canadian Tire Acceptance Ltd. (1995), 22 O.R. (3d) 433, 36 C.P.C. (3d) 175 (Gen. Div.); affirmed 26 O.R. (3d) 94, 40 C.P.C. (3d) 129

The court awarded solicitor-and-client costs against an individual and organization who raised funds, purportedly to fund the class action, by holding out to the public that they could receive a share of the proceeds of the law suit, *e.g.*, up to $64,500 for a $100 investment.

Abdool v. Anaheim Management Ltd. (1995), 21 O.R. (3d) 453, 31 C.P.C. (3d) 197, 121 D.L.R. (4th) 496, 78 O.A.C. 377 (Div. Ct.)

Class members are not liable for costs except with respect to the determination of their own individual claims.

Funding Issues

Marriott v. General Motors of Canada Company, 2018 ONSC 2535, 2018 CarswellOnt 6254 (S.C.J.)

The court approved a funding agreement to pay certain disbursements and adverse costs awards in exchange for 7% of the proceeds of the case.

Houle v. St. Jude Medical Inc., 2017 ONSC 5129, 2017 CarswellOnt 13215, 9 C.P.C. (8th) 321 (S.C.J.); appeal quashed 2018 ONCA 88, 2018 CarswellOnt 1035

The court approved a Litigation Funding Agreement subject to certain amendments.

Berg v. Canadian Hockey League, 2016 ONSC 4466, 2016 CarswellOnt 10803, 89 C.P.C. (7th) 328 (S.C.J.)

The court adjourned a third party funding motion and required the plaintiff to obtain independent legal advice about the funding arrangements.

Musician's Pension Fund of Canada (Trustee of) v. Kinross Gold Corp., 2013 ONSC 4974, 2013 CarswellOnt 11197, 117 O.R. (3d) 150, 6 C.C.P.B. (2nd) 82, 55 C.P.C. (7th) 437 (S.C.J.)

The court approved an arrangement between the plaintiffs and a non-party providing financial support and an indemnity for adverse costs awards in exchange for a percentage of the proceeds of the case. The court discussed 12 principles to be applied in such cases.

Fehr v. Sun Life Assurance Co. of Canada, 2012 ONSC 2715, 2012 CarswellOnt 5632, 10 C.C.L.I. (5th) 129, 25 C.P.C. (7th) 68, [2012] O.J. No. 2029 (S.C.J.)

The court dismissed the plaintiffs' motion that sought the hearing of the approval of a third party financing and indemnity agreement be without notice to the defendant, closed to the public and documents be sealed. The court set best practices procedure for the approval of third party funding agreements.

Edwards v. Law Society of Upper Canada (1994), 36 C.P.C. (3d) 116 (Ont. Class Proceedings Committee)

Discussion of funding of class actions by the Class Proceedings Committee. The merits of the case is the most important consideration. To obtain funding the applicant should generally have a strong arguable case on the merits.

Fee Approval

McDonald v. Home Capital Group, 2017 ONSC 5195, 2017 CarswellOnt 13563, 13 C.P.C. (8th) 213 (S.C.J.)

In this securities case, the court set class counsel's fees at $2.775 million representing 15% of the recovery or a multiplier of 4.6.

Bancroft-Snell v. Visa Canada Corp., 2016 ONCA 896, 2016 CarswellOnt 18625, 133 O.R. (3d) 241, 93 C.P.C. (7th) 24

The court awarded fees of $3.45 million on a $13.6 million settlement, but disapproved part of a Fee Sharing Agreement that would have awarded fees to a law firm whose work was redundant and useless for class members.

Jeffery v. London Life Insurance Co., 2016 ONSC 5506, 2016 CarswellOnt 13691, 90 C.P.C. (7th) 313 (S.C.J.)

The court approved a $16.4 million class counsel fee, representing about 27.5% of the amount recovered, awarded $4 million costs against the defendants, and held that the Class Proceedings Fund was entitled to a $1.5 million levy regardless of whether money was paid directly to class members.

McCallum-Boxe v. Sony Corp., 2015 ONSC 6896, 2015 CarswellOnt 17439 (S.C.J.)

The court deplored and denounced an unwritten fee arrangement providing class counsel's fees would be paid by the defendant as part of a settlement agreement, and awarded $30,000 rather than the $120,000 to $225,000 requested by counsel.

Eidoo v. Infineon Technologies AG, 2015 ONSC 2675, 2015 CarswellOnt 5765 (S.C.J.)

The court refused to approve honourariums for class representatives whose contribution was valuable but not exceptional.

Slark (Litigation Guardian of) v. Ontario, 2014 ONSC 1283, 2014 CarswellOnt 2725 (S.C.J.)

The court set class counsel's fees at $14 million representing 20.68% of the proceeds of settlement of claims for abuse of residents of institutions for persons with developmental disabilities.

Cannon v. Funds for Canada Foundation, 2013 ONSC 7686, 2013 CarswellOnt 17784, [2013] O.J. No. 5825 (S.C.J.)

The court approved class counsel's one-third contingency fee on a partial settlement for $28.2 million.

Helm v. Toronto Hydro-Electric System Ltd., 2012 ONSC 2602, 2012 CarswellOnt 5761, 40 C.P.C. (7th) 310, [2012] O.J. No. 2081 (S.C.J.)

The court refused to grant an honourarium to the representative plaintiff whose contribution was not "exceptional."

Lavier v. MyTravel Canada Holidays Inc., 2013 ONCA 92, 2013 CarswellOnt 1580, 35 C.P.C. (7th) 240, 359 D.L.R. (4th) 713, 302 O.A.C. 194

The court refused to award class counsel an addition fee where the take up rate on the class action settlement was less than ten percent, and the additional fee was disproportionate to the class's actual recovery.

Baker (Estate) v. Sony BMG Music (Canada) Inc., 2011 ONSC 7105, 2011 CarswellOnt 15453, 31 C.P.C. (7th) 320, [2011] O.J. No. 5781, 98 C.P.R. (4th) 244 (S.C.J.)

In this copyright infringement case, the court approved class counsel fees of $6.3 million, representing about 13% of the settlement or a multiplier of 2.8. The court also approved an honorarium of $3,000 each for the representative plaintiffs payable out of class counsel's fees.

Ainslie v. Afexa Life Sciences Inc., 2011 ONSC 6094, 2011 CarswellOnt 12290 (S.C.J.)

The court released the balance of class counsel's fees after successful implementation of a settlement.

Smith Estate v. National Money Mart Co., 2011 ONCA 233, 2011 CarswellOnt 1920, [2011] O.J. No. 1321, 106 O.R. (3d) 37, 331 D.L.R. (4th) 208, 3 C.P.C. (7th) 223, 276 O.A.C. 237

The Court of Appeal refused to increase the fees awarded by the motions judge. The motion judge's determination was discretionary and there was no basis to interfere with it. However the court ordered that compensation awarded to the representative plaintiff be deducted from the settlement funds, not from class counsel's fees.

Fantl v. Transamerica Life Canada, 2009 CarswellOnt 6264, [2009] O.J. No. 4324, 83 C.P.C. (6th) 265, 81 C.C.L.I. (4th) 18 (S.C.J.); additional reasons 2009 CarswellOnt 7344, 83 C.P.C. (6th) 286, 81 C.C.L.I. (4th) 39 (S.C.J.); additional reasons 2010 ONSC 3113, 2010 CarswellOnt 3675, 86 C.C.L.I. (4th) 239 (S.C.J.)

A defendant who agrees in a settlement to pay class counsel fees, has standing on the motion to approve the fees. In this case the court approved a fee of $7 million.

Abdulrahim v. Air France, 2011 ONSC 512, 2011 CarswellOnt 403, 16 C.P.C. (7th) 289 (S.C.J.)

The court approved a fee of $6.225 million representing about 30 percent of the proceeds of the case.

Charles Trust (Trustee of) v. Atlas Cold Storage Holdings Inc., 2009 CarswellOnt 5789, 2009 ONCA 690, 78 C.P.C. (6th) 208, [2009] O.J. No. 4067 (C.A.)

The court affirmed the motions judge's decision to reduce the base fee and apply a multiplier of 2.6 resulting in a fee equivalent to 16% of the gross recovery. Class counsel had a right of appeal from the motions judge's decision and there was no conflict of interest between class counsel and class members in bringing the appeal. Several class members who intervened on the appeal had the same interests and were awarded only one set of costs.

Hislop v. Canada (Attorney General), 95 O.R. (3d) 81, 2009 CarswellOnt 2513, 2009 C.E.B. & P.G.R. 8339, 2009 ONCA 354, 248 O.A.C. 205 (C.A.); leave to appeal refused (October 29, 2009), Doc. 33234, 2009 CarswellOnt 6639, 2009 CarswellOnt 6640 (S.C.C.)

Section 32(3) making an approved counsel fee a first charge on any settlement funds or monetary award is subordinate to the prohibition against the assignment or charge of Canada Pension Plan benefits.

Nutech Brands v. Air Canada (2009), 71 C.P.C. (6th) 311, [2009] O.J. No. 709, 2009 CarswellOnt 888 (S.C.J.)

The court approved a fee representing about 25 percent of the recovery or a multiplier of about 1.46.

Martin v. Barrett (2008), 2008 CarswellOnt 3151, 55 C.P.C. (6th) 377, 2008 C.E.B. & P.G.R. 8296, 67 C.C.P.B. 102, [2008] O.J. No. 2105 (S.C.J.)

The court reduced the base fee by 30 percent and applied a multiplier of 2.5 resulting in a fee equal to 29 percent of the gross recovery.

Holmes v. London Life Insurance Co. (2007), 2007 CarswellOnt 268, 45 C.C.L.I. (4th) 70, 40 C.P.C. (6th) 167 (S.C.J.)

It is permissible for counsel to agree to indemnify the plaintiff for defence costs awards.

Lewis v. Cantertrot Investments Ltd. (2006), 29 C.P.C. (6th) 352, 2006 CarswellOnt 2415, 43 R.P.R. (4th) 205 (S.C.J.); leave to appeal refused (December 6, 2006), Doc. Toronto 230/06, 2006 CarswellOnt 8009 (Div. Ct.)

Subsection 20(2) of the *Solicitors Act* does not bar an award of costs to plaintiffs on a certification motion where the plaintiffs have entered a contingency agreement with their lawyers.

Ford v. F. Hoffmann-La Roche Ltd. (2005), 12 C.P.C. (6th) 226, 2005 CarswellOnt 1094, [2005] O.J. No. 1117 (S.C.J.)

The court decided that class counsel fees of 15 per cent of the actual recovered amount was fair and reasonable. When fixing class counsel fees after settlement, the court should look at the matter not only from the present perspective but should consider the challenges and risks undertaken by counsel throughout the course of the action.

Wilson v. Servier Canada Inc. (2005), 9 C.P.C. (6th) 83, 2005 CarswellOnt 1020, 252 D.L.R. (4th) 742, [2005] O.J. No. 1039 (S.C.J.); additional reasons at (April 5, 2005), Doc. 98-CV-158832, 2005 CarswellOnt 6622 (S.C.J.)

Defendants' input into the reasonableness of class counsel fee was considered because of their reversionary interest in settlement amounts.

Hislop v. Canada (Attorney General) (2004), 3 C.P.C. (6th) 42, 2004 CarswellOnt 1785, [2004] O.J. No. 1867 (S.C.J.)

In this gay pension class action, the court approved a multiplier of 4.8 for trial and appeal work and a multiplier of 1 for administrative work.

Gariepy v. Shell Oil Co. (2003), 48 C.P.C. (5th) 340, [2003] O.J. No. 2490, 2003 CarswellOnt 2466 (S.C.J.)

The court approved fees and disbursements of $4.5 million in respect of a settlement of $30 million.

Tesluk v. Boots Pharmaceutical PLC (2002), 2002 CarswellOnt 1266, (sub nom. *Sutherland v. Boots Pharmaceutical PLC*) [2002] O.J. No. 1361, 21 C.P.C. (5th) 196 (S.C.J.)

A higher percentage fee is justified where the recovery is relatively low. The court approved a fee representing about 27.4 per cent of the recovery of about $2.25 million.

Alfresh Beverages Canada Corp. v. Hoechst AG (2002), 2002 CarswellOnt 77, [2002] O.J. No. 79, 16 C.P.C. (5th) 301 (S.C.J.)

The court approved a multiplier of 3 for this price fixing claim.

Directright Cartage Ltd. v. London Life Insurance Co., [2001] O.J. No. 4073, 2001 CarswellOnt 3658, [2001] I.L.R. I-4013, 34 C.C.L.I. (3d) 118, 17 C.P.C. (5th) 185 (S.C.J.)

The court approved a fee of $7.5 million in this "premium offset" life insurance case.

McCarthy v. Canadian Red Cross Society (2001), [2001] O.J. No. 2474, 2001 CarswellOnt 2255, 8 C.P.C. (5th) 350 (S.C.J.)

In a case where class counsel have particular experience and expertise, a fee based on a base fee and multiplier may penalize class counsel's efficiency, and a lump sum fee may be more appropriate. The court awarded a lump sum fee of $2.1 million in this case.

Ho-A-Shoo v. Canada (Attorney General) (2001), [2001] O.J. No. 2330, 2001 CarswellOnt 2114, 2001 D.T.C. 5589 (S.C.J.)

In the circumstances of this case the court approved a fee representing about 60 per cent of the recovery.

Delgrosso v. Paul (2001), 10 C.P.C. (5th) 317, (sub nom. *Clients of JNP Financial Services v. Paul)* [2001] O.J. No. 1616, 2001 CarswellOnt 1532 (S.C.J.)

The court approved a fee of about 28.9 per cent of the amount recovered which was equivalent to a multiplier of about 3.5.

Parsons v. Canadian Red Cross Society (2001), 2001 CarswellOnt 182, 140 O.A.C. 348, 11 C.P.C. (5th) 16, [2001] O.J. No. 214 (C.A.); leave to appeal refused (2001), 2001 CarswellOnt 2979, 2001 CarswellOnt 2980, 275 N.R. 394 (note), 153 O.A.C. 199 (note) (S.C.C.)

The court quashed an appeal by defendants and intervenors from an order approving class counsel's fees. The appellants' rights were not affected by the order and they had no right to appeal from it.

Parsons v. Canadian Red Cross Society (2000), 49 O.R. (3d) 281, 46 C.P.C. (4th) 236, 2000 CarswellOnt 2174, [2000] O.J. No. 2374 (S.C.J.); appeal quashed (2001), 2001 CarswellOnt 182, 140 O.A.C. 348, 11 C.P.C. (5th) 16, [2001] O.J. No. 214 (C.A.); leave to appeal refused (2001), 2001 CarswellOnt 2979, 2001 CarswellOnt 2980, 275 N.R. 394 (note), 153 O.A.C. 199 (note) (S.C.C.)

The fairness and reasonableness of a fee can be assessed by a variety of corroborating tests, including the fee as a percentage against recovery, as a multiple of base fees, as against the retainer agreements, whether the fee will provide sufficient incentive in the future for counsel to take on difficult cases, a comparison to similar class proceedings, and whether the fee would impair the benefits provided for class members.

Bisignano v. Corporation Instrumentarium Inc. (1999), 47 C.P.C. (4th) 63, 1999 CarswellOnt 3667 (S.C.J.)

Where (1) the retainer agreement acknowledged the right of class counsel to seek a multiplier, (2) the retainer agreement met the requirements of s. 32, and (3) the representative plaintiff offered no objection, the court held the proposed multiplier of 2.86 was appropriate.

Smith v. Krones Machinery Co. (2000), 49 C.C.E.L. (2d) 318, 42 C.P.C. (4th) 292, 2000 CarswellOnt 68 (S.C.J.)

The court set a multiplier of 2.9 in this wrongful dismissal class action.

Gagne v. Silcorp Limited (1998), 41 O.R. (3d) 417, 39 C.C.E.L. (2d) 253, 167 D.L.R. (4th) 325, 113 O.A.C. 299, 27 C.P.C. (4th) 114, [1998] O.J. No. 4182, 1998 CarswellOnt 4045 (C.A.)

Where a multiplier fee is used, the multiplier should generally be in the range of one to four. The legislative objective of enhanced access to justice requires that solicitors conducting class proceedings have a real opportunity to obtain a multiple of the base fee.

Crown Bay Hotel Ltd. Partnership v. Zurich Indemnity Co. of Canada (1998), 40 O.R. (3d) 83, 21 C.P.C. (4th) 272, 160 D.L.R. (4th) 186 (Gen. Div.)

Percentage fee agreements are permissible. The court approved a 20 per cent fee.

Maxwell v. MLG Ventures Ltd. (1996), 3 C.P.C. (4th) 360 (Ont. Gen. Div.)

Where success in settling an action was not due to the efforts of the solicitors but rather to a settlement in a separate action, the court reduced the base fee but allowed a 1.5 multiplier since there had been some risk in accepting the retainer.

Nash v. CIBC Trust Corp. (April 24, 1996), Doc. 94-CQ-58919-CP (Ont. Gen. Div.)

The court ordered that the motion to approve the plaintiff's retainer agreement be made on notice to the defendant.

Windisman v. Toronto College Park Ltd. (1996), 28 O.R. (3d) 29, 1 R.P.R. (3d) 119, 132 D.L.R. (4th) 512 (Gen. Div.)

The court awarded the solicitors a base fee of $300,000 and a multiplier of 2.5. The court also awarded compensation to the representative plaintiff for her work on behalf of the class at the rate of $40 per hour.

Serwaczek v. Medical Engineering Corp. (September 10, 1996), [1996] O.J. 3038

The court awarded a counsel fee of approximately $2 million dollars (including disbursements and GST) to the plaintiff class counsel who had settled the litigation for some $29 million.

Maxwell v. MLG Ventures Ltd. (1996), 30 O.R. (3d) 304 (Gen. Div.)

On a motion to fix fees under s. 33 of the *Class Proceedings Act*, the court first determined the base fee and then considered whether a multiplier ought to be applied. The factors to be considered in determination of a multiplier include the degree of risk assumed by the solicitors for the plaintiff and the degree of success achieved by the solicitors. Despite the fact that the *Class Proceedings Act* does not specify a solicitor-and-client scale, a solicitor who has been successful in a class action, either at trial or by virtue of negotiating a favourable settlement for the class, would be entitled to fees on a solicitor-and-client basis so to be fully compensated for the time spent.

Nantais v. Telectronics Proprietary (Canada) Ltd. (1996), 28 O.R. (3d) 523, 134 D.L.R. (4th) 470 (Gen. Div.)

1. The fact that the plaintiff's solicitor has a contingent fee arrangement with the plaintiff is no defence to an award of party-and-party costs against the defendant. A flexible approach should be taken to problems arising from contingency fee arrangements, if only to facilitate access to the courts for more Canadians. Anything less would be to preserve the court's facilities for the wealthy and powerful.

2. All kinds of fee arrangements contingent upon success are permitted. The multiplier method referred to in s. 33(4) is simply one method authorized by use of the word "otherwise" in s. 32(1)(c).

Miscellaneous

Fanshawe College of Applied Arts and Technology v. LG Philips LCD Co., Ltd., 2016 ONSC 3958, 2016 CarswellOnt 12605, 90 C.P.C. (7th) 150, [2016] O.J. No. 4034 (S.C.J.); leave to appeal refused *Fanshawe v. LG Phillips*, 2017 ONSC 2763, 2017 CarswellOnt 8890 (S.C.J.)

In this price-fixing case, the court refused to amend the class definition to include all indirect purchasers but did expand it to include certain named entities, as had been contemplated at the time of the original certification hearing.

Irving Paper Ltd. v. Atofina Chemicals Inc., 2015 ONSC 6662, 2015 CarswellOnt 16536 (S.C.J.)

The court amended the class definition to shorten the class period.

Eidoo v. Infineon Technologies AG, 2015 ONSC 3282, 2015 CarswellOnt 7611, 74 C.P.C. (7th) 177 (S.C.J.)

The court, on its own initiative, ordered a hearing to address an issue raised by several class members that the court-approved settlement contravened the *Human Rights Code*.

Iovine v. Toronto Sun Wah Trading Inc., 2014 ONSC 6555, 2014 CarswellOnt 16167, 123 O.R. (3d) 494, 65 C.P.C. (7th) 204 (S.C.J.)

In this action arising from an outbreak of salmonella, the court refused to order public health agencies to disclose the identities of the class members. While the court has jurisdiction to order disclosure of personal health information, the plaintiffs did not establish that a disclosure order was necessary.

Trillium Motor World Ltd. v. General Motors of Canada Ltd., 2014 ONSC 4336, 2014 CarswellOnt 10782, 69 C.P.C. (7th) 161 (S.C.J.)

After certification, the court refused to add a common issue dealing with punitive damages.

Cavanaugh v. Grenville Christian College, 2013 CarswellOnt 2500, 2013 ONCA 139, 32 C.P.C. (7th) 1, 360 D.L.R. (4th) 670, (sub nom. *L.C. v. Grenville Christian College)* 304 O.A.C. 163, [2013] O.J. No. 1007; additional reasons 2013 ONCA 242, 2013 CarswellOnt 18828

The court of appeal had jurisdiction over an appeal from an order dismissing the action against one defendant as disclosing no cause of action, but refused to hear a companion appeal, which ordinarily lay to the Divisional Court, for refusal to certify the case.

Zaniewicz v. Zungui Haixi Corp., 2012 ONSC 6061, 2012 CarswellOnt 13175 (S.C.J.)

The court granted leave under s. 138.8(1) of Part XXIII.1 of the Ontario *Securities Act*, R.S.O. 1990, c. S.5.

Pardham v. Bank of Montreal, 2012 ONSC 2229, 2012 CarswellOnt 4295, 96 C.C.L.T. (3d) 173, 26 C.P.C. (7th) 99 (S.C.J.); additional reasons 2012 ONSC 4681, 2012 CarswellOnt 9946, 96 C.C.L.T. (3d) 260, 26 C.P.C. (7th) 186 (S.C.J.); leave to appeal refused 2013 ONSC 355, 2013 CarswellOnt 662, 100 C.C.L.T. (3d) 181, 303 O.A.C. 45, [2013] O.J. No. 329 (Div. Ct.)

The court extended the time to move for certification where the delay was insignificant and justified.

Nor-Dor Developments Ltd. v. Redline Communications Group Inc., 2011 ONSC 591, 2011 CarswellOnt 13452, [2011] O.J. No. 4993 (S.C.J.); additional reasons 2011 ONSC 6624, 2011 CarswellOnt 13451 (S.C.J.)

The court lacks jurisdiction to permit the plaintiffs to file a claim under Part XXIII.1 of the *Ontario Securities Act* prior to the required leave motion, though they were at liberty to request such leave be granted *nunc pro tunc*.

Dugal v. Manulife Financial Corp., 2011 ONSC 1785, 2011 CarswellOnt 1889, [2011] O.J. No. 1239, 105 O.R. (3d) 364, 18 C.P.C. (7th) 105 (S.C.J.)

The court approved a funding agreement between the plaintiff and a non-party to pay adverse costs awards and pay disbursements in exchange for 7 percent of the proceeds of the case.

Banerjee v. Shire Biochem Inc., 2010 CarswellOnt 647, 2010 ONSC 889, [2010] O.J. No. 507, 88 C.P.C. (6th) 328 (S.C.J.)

On consent, the court certified this claim regarding a drug which allegedly cause compulsive gambling and approved a pilot project to promote settlement by identifying class members with potentially compensable claims. The pilot project would suspend the ordinary progress of the action for 12 months.

McLaren v. Stratford (City) (2003), 2003 CarswellOnt 1364, 37 M.P.L.R. (3d) 231, 33 C.P.C. (5th) 253 (S.C.J.)

The court ordered that motions in this class proceeding for flooding damages take place in the community in which the flood occurred.

Boulanger v. Johnson & Johnson Corp. (2003), 2003 CarswellOnt 1405, 170 O.A.C. 333, 64 O.R. (3d) 208, 226 D.L.R. (4th) 747, 32 C.P.C. (5th) 203 (Div. Ct.)

A proceeding commenced under the *Class Proceedings Act* is a class proceeding from its commencement. It does not become a class proceeding only if and when certified.

Kanitz v. Rogers Cable Inc. (2002), 2002 CarswellOnt 628, [2002] O.J. No. 665, 21 B.L.R. (3d) 104, 16 C.P.C. (5th) 84, 58 O.R. (3d) 299 (S.C.J.)

The court stayed an action where the subject agreement provided for arbitration and none of the exceptions in the *Arbitration Act* applied.

Western Canadian Shopping Centres Inc. v. Dutton (2001), 2001 SCC 46, (sub nom. *Western Canadian Shopping Centres Inc. v. Bennett Jones Verchere)* 201 D.L.R. (4th) 385, [2000] S.C.J. No. 63, 2001 CarswellAlta 884, 2001 CarswellAlta 885, 94 Alta. L.R. (3d) 1, 272 N.R. 135, 8 C.P.C. (5th) 1, [2002] 1 W.W.R. 1, 286 A.R. 201, 253 W.A.C. 201, [2001] 2 S.C.R. 534

The court has inherent jurisdiction to fill legislative gaps regarding the mechanics of class action practice.

McNaughton Automotive Ltd. v. Co-operators General Insurance Co. (2006), 2006 CarswellOnt 8405, 43 C.C.L.I. (4th) 302, 221 O.A.C. 102, 40 C.P.C. (6th) 37 (Div. Ct.); additional reasons at (2007), 2007 CarswellOnt 2233, [2007] O.J. No. 1453, 225 O.A.C. 205, 47 C.C.L.I. (4th) 56, 37 C.P.C. (6th) 120 (Div. Ct.)

A judgment in favour of the plaintiff prior to certification does not create issue estoppel in favour of the putative class members. The class members are not privies of the plaintiff prior to certification.

Bywater v. Toronto Transit Commission (1998), 27 C.P.C. (4th) 172, 1998 CarswellOnt 4645, [1998] O.J. No. 4913 (Gen. Div.); additional reasons at (1999), 30 C.P.C. (4th) 131, 1999 CarswellOnt 201, [1999] O.J. No. 67 (Gen. Div.)

An admission of liability does not resolve or eliminate the liability issue. The issue is not *res judicata* until the case has been certified and judgment granted.

Smith v. National Money Mart Co. (2005), [2005] O.J. No. 2660, 2005 CarswellOnt 2640, 8 B.L.R. (4th) 159, 18 C.P.C. (6th) 1 (S.C.J.); affirmed (2005), 204 O.A.C. 47, 12 B.L.R. (4th) 29, 20 C.P.C. (6th) 345, 2005 CarswellOnt 4882, 258 D.L.R. (4th) 453, [2005] O.J. No. 4269 (Ont. C.A.); leave to appeal refused (2006), 2006 CarswellOnt 1202, 2006 CarswellOnt 1203, [2005] S.C.C.A. No. 528, 352 N.R. 404 (note) (S.C.C.); affirmed (2006), 18 B.L.R. (4th) 22, 28 C.P.C. (6th) 34, 2006 CarswellOnt 2774, [2006] O.J. No. 1807, 266 D.L.R. (4th) 275, 209 O.A.C. 190, 80 O.R. (3d) 81 (C.A.); leave to appeal refused (October 12, 2006), Doc. 31538, 2006 CarswellOnt 6318, 2006 CarswellOnt 6319 (S.C.C.)

The question of whether there is an enforceable arbitration clause in the contract is relevant to the preferable procedure determination. An arbitration clause in a consumer contract cannot be used to exclude class action claims.

Bunn v. Ribcor Holdings Inc. (1998), 20 C.P.C. (4th) 145, 1998 CarswellOnt 2033, [1998] O.J. No. 1790 (Gen. Div.)

The court stayed a counterclaim against the representative plaintiff based on allegedly defamatory comments made in the statement of claim.

Dabbs v. Sun Life Assurance Co. of Canada (1997), 14 C.P.C. (4th) 122, 35 O.R. (3d) 708, [1998] I.L.R. I-3494, 48 C.C.L.I. (2d) 146, 38 O.T.C. 98 (Ont. Gen. Div.); leave to appeal refused (1998), 36 O.R. (3d) 770, 20 C.P.C. (4th) 87, 1 C.C.L.I. (3d) 42, 48 O.T.C. 391, 1998 CarswellOnt 264 (Gen. Div.); additional reasons at (1998), 38 O.R. (3d) 781, 19 C.P.C. (4th) 18, 50 C.C.L.I. (2d) 30, 50 O.T.C. 396, 1998 CarswellOnt 521 (Gen. Div.)

The court denied leave to intervene on a motion for court approval of a settlement where the intervenors asserted that the settlement might be used as a precedent in a similar but unrelated action in which the intervenors were interested.

Andersen v. St. Jude Medical Inc. (2006), 33 C.P.C. (6th) 159, 2006 CarswellOnt 5612 (Master)

The case management judge may refer a motion to the master.

Hickey-Button v. Loyalist College of Applied Arts & Technology (2002), 2002 CarswellOnt 1121, [2002] O.J. No. 1198, 20 C.P.C. (5th) 377 (S.C.J.); additional reasons at (May 14, 2002), Doc. 1282/99, 1382/99, 2002 CarswellOnt 1628 (S.C.J.)

Since all motions must be heard by the same judge, once the first motion is heard all subsequent motions will be heard in the same venue, despite rule 37.03. Where this action was closely connected with a particular region, the court ordered under rule 37.03(4) that the first motion, and therefore all later motions, be heard in that region.

Chippewas of Sarnia Band v. Canada (Attorney General) (1996), 45 C.P.C. (3d) 216 (Ont. Gen. Div.)

It is for the Chief Justice or the Regional Senior Judge of the region where the case will be tried to decide whether a judge should be designated pursuant to rule 37.15(1) to hear motions in a class action. If a judge is so designated, rule 37.03 regarding venue for motions does not apply.

Potter v. Bank of Canada, 2007 CarswellOnt 1816, [2007] O.J. No. 1174, 2007 C.E.B. & P.G.R. 8238, 59 C.C.P.B. 219, 31 E.T.R. (3d) 163, 223 O.A.C. 166, 85 O.R. (3d) 9, 282 D.L.R. (4th) 553, 37 C.P.C. (6th) 104, 2007 ONCA 234 (C.A); additional reasons at 2007 CarswellOnt 3789, 2007 ONCA 442, 61 C.C.P.B. 70, 282 D.L.R. (4th) 553 at 565, 41 C.P.C. (6th) 110 (C.A.)

Section 37(a) does not preclude class actions which might otherwise be brought as a representative proceeding under the rules of court.

Crawford v. London (City) (2000), 47 O.R. (3d) 784, 1 C.P.C. (5th) 170, 2000 CarswellOnt 956, [2000] O.J. No. 989 (S.C.J.); leave to appeal refused (May 29, 2000), Doc. 30707/99, 2000 CarswellOnt 2561 (S.C.J.)

The owner of a condominium unit is not entitled to bring a representative action under the *Condominium Act* and therefore was not precluded from commencing a class proceeding under the *Class Proceedings Act.*

CLASS PROCEEDINGS ACT, 1992

S.O. 1992, c. 6

as am. S.O. 2006, c. 19, Sched. C, s. 1(1).

Summary of Contents

Section 1

Definitions

1. In this Act,

"common issues" means,

(a) common but not necessarily identical issues of fact, or

(b) common but not necessarily identical issues of law that arise from common but not necessarily identical facts;

"court" means the Superior Court of Justice but does not include the Small Claims Court;

"defendant" includes a respondent;

"plaintiff" includes an applicant.

2006, c. 19, Sched. C, s. 1(1)

Section 2

Plaintiff's class proceeding

2. (1) One or more members of a class of persons may commence a proceeding in the court on behalf of the members of the class.

Motion for certification

(2) A person who commences a proceeding under subsection (1) shall make a motion to a judge of the court for an order certifying the proceeding as a class proceeding and appointing the person representative plaintiff.

Idem

(3) A motion under subsection (2) shall be made,

(a) within ninety days after the later of,

(i) the date on which the last statement of defence, notice of intent to defend or notice of appearance is delivered, and

(ii) the date on which the time prescribed by the rules of court for delivery of the last statement of defence, notice of intent to defend or a notice of appearance expires without its being delivered; or

(b) subsequently, with leave of the court.

Section 3

Defendant's class proceeding

3. A defendant to two or more proceedings may, at any stage of one of the proceedings, make a motion to a judge of the court for an order certifying the proceedings as a class proceeding and appointing a representative plaintiff.

Section 4

Classing defendants

4. Any party to a proceeding against two or more defendants may, at any stage of the proceeding, make a motion to a judge of the court for an order certifying the proceeding as a class proceeding and appointing a representative defendant.

Section 5

Certification

5. (1) The court shall certify a class proceeding on a motion under section 2, 3 or 4 if,

(a) the pleadings or the notice of application discloses a cause of action;

(b) there is an identifiable class of two or more persons that would be represented by the representative plaintiff or defendant;

(c) the claims or defences of the class members raise common issues;

(d) a class proceeding would be the preferable procedure for the resolution of the common issues; and

(e) there is a representative plaintiff or defendant who,

(i) would fairly and adequately represent the interests of the class,

(ii) has produced a plan for the proceeding that sets out a workable method of advancing the proceeding on behalf of the class and of notifying class members of the proceeding, and

(iii) does not have, on the common issues for the class, an interest in conflict with the interests of other class members.

Idem, subclass protection

(2) Despite subsection (1), where a class includes a subclass whose members have claims or defences that raise common issues not shared by all the class members, so that, in the opinion of the court, the protection of the interests of the subclass members requires that they be separately represented, the court shall not certify the class proceeding unless there is a representative plaintiff or defendant who,

(a) would fairly and adequately represent the interests of the subclass;

(b) has produced a plan for the proceeding that sets out a workable method of advancing the proceeding on behalf of the subclass and of notifying subclass members of the proceeding; and

(c) does not have, on the common issues for the subclass, an interest in conflict with the interests of other subclass members.

Evidence as to size of class

(3) Each party to a motion for certification shall, in an affidavit filed for use on the motion, provide the party's best information on the number of members in the class.

Adjournments

(4) The court may adjourn the motion for certification to permit the parties to amend their materials or pleadings or to permit further evidence.

Certification not a ruling on merits

(5) An order certifying a class proceeding is not a determination of the merits of the proceeding.

Section 6

Certain matters not bar to certification

6. The court shall not refuse to certify a proceeding as a class proceeding solely on any of the following grounds:

1. The relief claimed includes a claim for damages that would require individual assessment after determination of the common issues.

2. The relief claimed relates to separate contracts involving different class members.

3. Different remedies are sought for different class members.

4. The number of class members or the identity of each class member is not known.

5. The class includes a subclass whose members have claims or defences that raise common issues not shared by all class members.

Section 7

Refusal to certify, proceeding may continue in altered form

7. Where the court refuses to certify a proceeding as a class proceeding, the court may permit the proceeding to continue as one or more proceedings between different parties and, for the purpose, the court may,

(a) order the addition, deletion or substitution of parties;

(b) order the amendment of the pleadings or notice of application; and

(c) make any further order that it considers appropriate.

Section 8

Contents of certification order

8. (1) An order certifying a proceeding as a class proceeding shall,

(a) describe the class;

(b) state the names of the representative parties;

(c) state the nature of the claims or defences asserted on behalf of the class;

(d) state the relief sought by or from the class;

(e) set out the common issues for the class; and

(f) specify the manner in which class members may opt out of the class proceeding and a date after which class members may not opt out.

Subclass protection

(2) Where a class includes a subclass whose members have claims or defences that raise common issues not shared by all the class members, so that, in the opinion of the court, the protection of the interests of the subclass members requires that they be separately represented, subsection (1) applies with necessary modifications in respect of the subclass.

Amendment of certification order

(3) The court, on the motion of a party or class member, may amend an order certifying a proceeding as a class proceeding.

Section 9

Opting out

9. Any member of a class involved in a class proceeding may opt out of the proceeding in the manner and within the time specified in the certification order.

Section 10

Where it appears conditions for certification not satisfied

10. (1) On the motion of a party or class member, where it appears to the court that the conditions mentioned in subsections 5(1) and (2) are not satisfied with respect to a class proceeding, the court may amend the certification order, may decertify the proceeding or may make any other order it considers appropriate.

Proceeding may continue in altered form

(2) Where the court makes a decertification order under subsection (1), the court may permit the proceeding to continue as one or more proceedings between different parties.

Powers of court

(3) For the purposes of subsections (1) and (2), the court has the powers set out in clauses 7(a) to (c).

Section 11

Stages of class proceedings

11. (1) Subject to section 12, in a class proceeding,

(a) common issues for a class shall be determined together;

(b) common issues for a subclass shall be determined together; and

(c) individual issues that require the participation of individual class members shall be determined individually in accordance with sections 24 and 25.

Separate judgments

(2) The court may give judgment in respect of the common issues and separate judgments in respect of any other issue.

Section 12

Court may determine conduct of proceeding

12. The court, on the motion of a party or class member, may make an order it considers appropriate respecting the conduct of a class proceeding to ensure its fair and expeditious determination and, for the purpose, may impose such terms on the parties as it considers appropriate.

Section 13

Court may stay any other proceeding

13. The court, on its own initiative or on the motion of a party or class member, may stay any proceeding related to the class proceeding before it, on such terms as it considers appropriate.

Section 14

Participation of class members

14. (1) In order to ensure the fair and adequate representation of the interests of the class or any subclass or for any other appropriate reason, the court may, at any time in a class proceeding, permit one or more class members to participate in the proceeding.

Idem

(2) Participation under subsection (1) shall be in whatever manner and on whatever terms, including terms as to costs, the court considers appropriate.

Section 15

Discovery of parties

15. (1) Parties to a class proceeding have the same rights of discovery under the rules of court against one another as they would have in any other proceeding.

Discovery of class members with leave

(2) After discovery of the representative party, a party may move for discovery under the rules of court against other class members.

Idem

(3) In deciding whether to grant leave to discover other class members, the court shall consider,

(a) the stage of the class proceeding and the issues to be determined at that stage;

(b) the presence of subclasses;

(c) whether the discovery is necessary in view of the claims or defences of the party seeking leave;

(d) the approximate monetary value of individual claims, if any;

(e) whether discovery would result in oppression or in undue annoyance, burden or expense for the class members sought to be discovered; and

(f) any other matter the court considers relevant.

Idem

(4) A class member is subject to the same sanctions under the rules of court as a party for failure to submit to discovery.

Section 16

Examination of class members before a motion or application

16. (1) A party shall not require a class member other than a representative party to be examined as a witness before the hearing of a motion or application, except with leave of the court.

Idem

(2) Subsection 15(3) applies with necessary modifications to a decision whether to grant leave under subsection (1).

Section 17

Notice of certification

17. (1) Notice of certification of a class proceeding shall be given by the representative party to the class members in accordance with this section.

Court may dispense with notice

(2) The court may dispense with notice if, having regard to the factors set out in subsection (3), the court considers it appropriate to do so.

Order respecting notice

(3) The court shall make an order setting out when and by what means notice shall be given under this section and in so doing shall have regard to,

(a) the cost of giving notice;

(b) the nature of the relief sought;

(c) the size of the individual claims of the class members;

(d) the number of class members;

(e) the places of residence of class members; and

(f) any other relevant matter.

Idem

(4) The Court may order that notice be given,

(a) personally or by mail;

(b) by posting, advertising, publishing or leafleting;

(c) by individual notice to a sample group within the class; or

(d) by any means or combination of means that the court considers appropriate.

Idem

(5) The court may order that notice be given to different class members by different means.

Contents of notice

(6) Notice under this section shall, unless the court orders otherwise,

(a) describe the proceeding, including the names and addresses of the representative parties and the relief sought;

(b) state the manner by which and time within which class members may opt out of the proceeding;

(c) describe the possible financial consequences of the proceeding to class members;

(d) summarize any agreements between representative parties and their solicitors respecting fees and disbursements;

(e) describe any counterclaim being asserted by or against the class, including the relief sought in the counterclaim;

(f) state that the judgment, whether favourable or not, will bind all class members who do not opt out of the proceeding;

(g) describe the right of any class member to participate in the proceeding;

(h) give an address to which class members may direct inquiries about the proceeding; and

(i) give any other information the court considers appropriate.

Solicitations of contributions

(7) With leave of the court, notice under this section may include a solicitation of contributions from class members to assist in paying solicitor's fees and disbursements.

Section 18

Notice where individual participation is required

18. (1) When the court determines common issues in favour of a class and considers that the participation of individual class members is required to determine individual issues, the representative party shall give notice to those members in accordance with this section.

Idem

(2) Subsections 17(3) to (5) apply with necessary modifications to notice given under this section.

Contents of notice

(3) Notice under this section shall,

(a) state that common issues have been determined in favour of the class;

(b) state that class members may be entitled to individual relief;

(c) describe the steps to be taken to establish an individual claim;

(d) state that failure on the part of a class member to take those steps will result in the member not being entitled to assert an individual claim except with leave of the court;

(e) give an address to which class members may direct inquiries about the proceeding; and

(f) give any other information that the court considers appropriate.

Section 19

Notice to protect interests of affected persons

19. (1) At any time in a class proceeding, the court may order any party to give such notice as it considers necessary to protect the interests of any class member or party or to ensure the fair conduct of the proceeding.

Idem

(2) Subsections 17(3) to (5) apply with necessary modifications to notice given under this section.

Section 20

Approval of notice by the court

20. A notice under section 17, 18 or 19 shall be approved by the court before it is given.

Section 21

Delivery of notice

21. The court may order a party to deliver, by whatever means are available to the party, the notice required to be given by another party under section 17, 18 or 19, where that is more practical.

Section 22

Costs of notice

22. (1) The court may make any order it considers appropriate as to the costs of any notice under section 17, 18 or 19, including an order apportioning costs among parties.

Idem

(2) In making an order under subsection (1), the court may have regard to the different interests of a subclass.

Section 23

Statistical evidence

23. (1) For the purposes of determining issues relating to the amount or distribution of a monetary award under this Act, the court may admit as evidence statistical information that would not otherwise be admissible as evidence, including information derived from sampling, if the information was compiled in accordance with principles that are generally accepted by experts in the field of statistics.

Idem

(2) A record of statistical information purporting to be prepared or published under the authority of the Parliament of Canada or the legislature of any province or territory of Canada may be admitted as evidence without proof of its authenticity.

Notice

(3) Statistical information shall not be admitted as evidence under this section unless the party seeking to introduce the information has,

(a) given reasonable notice of it to the party against whom it is to be used, together with a copy of the information;

(b) complied with subsections (4) and (5); and

(c) complied with any requirement to produce documents under subsection (7).

Contents of notice

(4) Notice under this section shall specify the source of any statistical information sought to be introduced that,

(a) was prepared or published under the authority of the Parliament of Canada or the legislature of any province or territory of Canada;

(b) was derived from market quotations, tabulations, lists, directories or other compilations generally used and relied on by members of the public; or

(c) was derived from reference material generally used and relied on by members of an occupational group.

Idem

(5) Except with respect to information referred to in subsection (4), notice under this section shall,

(a) specify the name and qualifications of each person who supervised the preparation of statistical information sought to be introduced; and

(b) describe any documents prepared or used in the course of preparing the statistical information sought to be introduced.

Cross-examination

(6) A party against whom statistical information is sought to be introduced under this section may require, for the purposes of cross-examination, the attendance of any person who supervised the preparation of the information.

Production of documents

(7) Except with respect to information referred to in subsection (4), a party against whom statistical information is sought to be introduced under this section may require the party seeking to introduce it to produce for inspection any document that was prepared or used in the course of preparing the information, unless the document discloses the identity of persons responding to a survey who have not consented in writing to the disclosure.

Section 24

Aggregate assessment of monetary relief

24. (1) The court may determine the aggregate or a part of a defendant's liability to class members and give judgment accordingly where,

(a) monetary relief is claimed on behalf of some or all class members;

(b) no questions of fact or law other than those relating to the assessment of monetary relief remain to be determined in order to establish the amount of the defendant's monetary liability; and

(c) the aggregate or a part of the defendant's liability to some or all class members can reasonably be determined without proof by individual class members.

Average or proportional application

(2) The court may order that all or a part of an award under subsection (1) be applied so that some or all individual class members share in the award on an average or proportional basis.

Idem

(3) In deciding whether to make an order under subsection (2), the court shall consider whether it would be impractical or inefficient to identify the class members entitled to share in the award or to determine the exact shares that should be allocated to individual class members.

Court to determine whether individual claims need to be made

(4) When the court orders that all or a part of an award under subsection (1) be divided among individual class members, the court shall determine whether individual claims need to be made to give effect to the order.

Procedures for determining claims

(5) Where the court determines under subsection (4) that individual claims need to be made, the court shall specify procedures for determining the claims.

Idem

(6) In specifying procedures under subsection (5), the court shall minimize the burden on class members and, for the purpose, the court may authorize,

(a) the use of standardized proof of claim forms;

(b) the receipt of affidavit or other documentary evidence; and

(c) the auditing of claims on a sampling or other basis

Time limits for making claims

(7) When specifying procedures under subsection (5), the court shall set a reasonable time within which individual class members may make claims under this section.

Idem

(8) A class member who fails to make a claim within the time set under subsection (7) may not later make a claim under this section except with leave of the court.

Extension of time

(9) The court may give leave under subsection (8) if it is satisfied that,

(a) there are apparent grounds for relief;

(b) the delay was not caused by any fault of the person seeking the relief; and

(c) the defendant would not suffer substantial prejudice if leave were given.

Court may amend subs. (1) judgment

(10) The court may amend a judgment given under subsection (1) to give effect to a claim made with leave under subsection (8) if the court considers it appropriate to do so.

Section 25

Individual issues

25. (1) When the court determines common issues in favour of a class and considers that the participation of individual class members is required to determine individual issues, other than those that may be determined under section 24, the court may,

(a) determine the issues in further hearings presided over by the judge who determined the common issues or by another judge of the court;

(b) appoint one or more persons to conduct a reference under the rules of court and report back to the court; and

(c) with the consent of the parties, direct that the issues be determined in any other manner.

Directions as to procedure

(2) The court shall give any necessary directions relating to the procedures to be followed in conducting hearings, inquiries and determinations under subsection (1), including directions for the purpose of achieving procedural conformity.

Idem

(3) In giving directions under subsection (2), the court shall choose the least expensive and most expeditious method of determining the issues that is consistent with justice to class members and the parties and, in so doing, the court may,

(a) dispense with any procedural step that it considers unnecessary; and

(b) authorize any special procedural steps, including steps relating to discovery, and any special rules, including rules relating to admission of evidence and means of proof, that it considers appropriate.

Time limits for making claims

(4) The court shall set a reasonable time within which individual class members may make claims under this section.

Idem

(5) A class member who fails to make a claim within the time set under subsection (4) may not later make a claim under this section except with leave of the court.

Extension of time

(6) Subsection 24(9) applies with necessary modifications to a decision whether to give leave under subsection (5).

Determination under cl. (1)(c) deemed court order

(7) A determination under clause (1)(c) is deemed to be an order of the court.

Section 26

Judgment distribution

26. (1) The court may direct any means of distribution of amounts awarded under section 24 or 25 that it considers appropriate.

Idem

(2) In giving directions under subsection (1), the court may order that,

(a) the defendant distribute directly to class members the amount of monetary relief to which each class member is entitled by any means authorized by the court, including abatement and credit;

(b) the defendant pay into court or some other appropriate depository the total amount of the defendant's liability to the class until further order of the court; and

(c) any person other than the defendant distribute directly to class members the amount of monetary relief to which each member is entitled by any means authorized by the court.

Idem

(3) In deciding whether to make an order under clause (2)(a), the court shall consider whether distribution by the defendant is the most practical way of distributing the award for any reason, including the fact that the amount of monetary relief to which each class member is entitled can be determined from the records of the defendant.

Idem

(4) The court may order that all or a part of an award under section 24 that has not been distributed within a time set by the court be applied in any manner that may reasonably be expected to benefit class members, even though the order does not provide for monetary relief to individual class members, if the court is satisfied that a reasonable number of class members who would not otherwise receive monetary relief would benefit from the order.

Idem

(5) The court may make an order under subsection (4) whether or not all class members can be identified or all of their shares can be exactly determined.

Idem

(6) The court may make an order under subsection (4) even if the order would benefit,

(a) persons who are not class members; or

(b) persons who may otherwise receive monetary relief as a result of the class proceeding.

Supervisory role of the court

(7) The court shall supervise the execution of judgments and the distribution of awards under section 24 or 25 and may stay the whole or any part of an execution or distribution for a reasonable period on such terms as it considers appropriate.

Payment of awards

(8) The court may order that an award made under section 24 or 25 be paid,

(a) in a lump sum, forthwith or within a time set by the court; or

(b) in instalments, on such terms as the court considers appropriate.

Costs of distribution

(9) The court may order that the costs of distribution of an award under section 24 or 25, including the costs of notice associated with the distribution and the fees payable to a person administering the distribution, be paid out of the proceeds of the judgment or may make such other order as it considers appropriate.

Return of unclaimed amounts

(10) Any part of an award for division among individual class members that remains unclaimed or otherwise undistributed after a time set by the court shall be returned to the party against whom the award was made, without further order of the court.

Section 27

Contents of judgment on common issues

27. (1) A judgment on common issues of a class or subclass shall,

(a) set out the common issues;

(b) name or describe the class or subclass members;

(c) state the nature of the claims or defences asserted on behalf of the class or subclass; and

(d) specify the relief granted.

Effect of judgment on common issues

(2) A judgment on common issues of a class or subclass does not bind,

(a) a person who has opted out of the class proceeding; or

(b) a party to the class proceeding in any subsequent proceeding between the party and a person mentioned in clause (a).

Idem

(3) A judgment on common issues of a class or subclass binds every class member who has not opted out of the class proceeding, but only to the extent that the judgment determines common issues that,

(a) are set out in the certification order;

(b) relate to claims or defences described in the certification order; and

(c) relate to relief sought by or from the class or subclass as stated in the certification order.

Section 28

Limitations

28. (1) Subject to subsection (2), any limitation period applicable to a cause of action asserted in a class proceeding is suspended in favour of a class member on the commencement of the class proceeding and resumes running against the class member when,

(a) the member opts out of the class proceeding;

(b) an amendment that has the effect of excluding the member from the class is made to the certification order;

(c) a decertification order is made under section 10;

(d) the class proceeding is dismissed without an adjudication on the merits;

(e) the class proceeding is abandoned or discontinued with the approval of the court; or

(f) the class proceeding is settled with the approval of the court, unless the settlement provides otherwise.

Idem

(2) Where there is a right of appeal in respect of an event described in clauses (1)(a) to (f), the limitation period resumes running as soon as the time for appeal has expired without an appeal being commenced or as soon as any appeal has been finally disposed of.

Section 29

Discontinuance and abandonment

29. (1) A proceeding commenced under this Act and a proceeding certified as a class proceeding under this Act may be discontinued or abandoned only with the approval of the court, on such terms as the court considers appropriate.

Settlement without court approval not binding

(2) A settlement of a class proceeding is not binding unless approved by the court.

Effect of settlement

(3) A settlement of a class proceeding that is approved by the court binds all class members.

Notice: dismissal, discontinuance, abandonment or settlement

(4) In dismissing a proceeding for delay or in approving a discontinuance, abandonment or settlement, the court shall consider whether notice should be given under section 19 and whether any notice should include,

(a) an account of the conduct of the proceeding;

(b) a statement of the result of the proceeding; and

(c) a description of any plan for distributing settlement funds.

Section 30

Appeals: refusals to certify and decertification orders

30. (1) A party may appeal to the Divisional Court from an order refusing to certify a proceeding as a class proceeding and from an order decertifying a proceeding.

Appeals: certification orders

(2) A party may appeal to the Divisional Court from an order certifying a proceeding as a class proceeding, with leave of the Superior Court of Justice as provided in the rules of court.

Appeals: judgments on common issues and aggregate awards

(3) A party may appeal to the Court of Appeal from a judgment on common issues and from an order under section 24, other than an order that determines individual claims made by class members.

Appeals by class members on behalf of the class

(4) If a representative party does not appeal or seek leave to appeal as permitted by subsection (1) or (2), or if a representative party abandons an appeal under subsection (1) or (2), any class member may make a motion to the court for leave to act as the representative party for the purposes of the relevant subsection.

Idem

(5) If a representative party does not appeal as permitted by subsection (3), or if a representative party abandons an appeal under subsection (3), any class member may make a motion to the Court of Appeal for leave to act as the representative party for the purposes of subsection (3).

Appeals: individual awards

(6) A class member may appeal to the Divisional Court from an order under section 24 or 25 determining an individual claim made by the member and awarding more than $3,000 to the member.

Idem

(7) A representative plaintiff may appeal to the Divisional Court from an order under section 24 determining an individual claim made by a class member and awarding more than $3,000 to the member.

Idem

(8) A defendant may appeal to the Divisional Court from an order under section 25 determining an individual claim made by a class member and awarding more than $3,000 to the member.

Idem

(9) With leave of the Superior Court of Justice as provided in the rules of court, a class member may appeal to the Divisional Court from an order under section 24 or 25,

(a) determining an individual claim made by the member and awarding $3,000 or less to the member; or

(b) dismissing an individual claim made by the member for monetary relief.

Idem

(10) With leave of the Superior Court of Justice as provided in the rules of court, a representative plaintiff may appeal to the Divisional Court from an order under section 24,

(a) determining an individual claim made by a class member and awarding $3,000 or less to the member; or

(b) dismissing an individual claim made by a class member for monetary relief.

Idem

(11) With leave of the Superior Court of Justice as provided in the rules of court, a defendant may appeal to the Divisional Court from an order under section 25,

(a) determining an individual claim made by a class member and awarding $3,000 or less to the member; or

(b) dismissing an individual claim made by a class member for monetary relief.

2006, c. 19, Sched. C, s. 1(1) (Table 1)

Section 31

Costs

31. (1) In exercising its discretion with respect to costs under subsection 131 (1) of the *Courts of Justice Act*, the court may consider whether the class proceeding was a test case, raised a novel point of law or involved a matter of public interest.

Liability of class members for costs

(2) Class members, other than the representative party, are not liable for costs except with respect to the determination of their own individual claims.

Small claims

(3) Where an individual claim under section 24 or 25 is within the monetary jurisdiction of the Small Claims Court where the class proceeding was commenced, costs related to the claim shall be assessed as if the claim had been determined by the Small Claims Court.

Section 32

Agreements respecting fees and disbursements

32. (1) An agreement respecting fees and disbursements between a solicitor and a representative party shall be in writing and shall,

(a) state the terms under which fees and disbursements shall be paid;

(b) give an estimate of the expected fee, whether contingent on success in the class proceeding or not; and

(c) state the method by which payment is to be made, whether by lump sum, salary or otherwise.

Court to approve agreements

(2) An agreement respecting fees and disbursements between a solicitor and a representative party is not enforceable unless approved by the court, on the motion of the solicitor.

Priority of amounts owed under approved agreement

(3) Amounts owing under an enforceable agreement are a first charge on any settlement funds or monetary award.

Determination of fees where agreement not approved

(4) If an agreement is not approved by the court, the court may,

(a) determine the amount owing to the solicitor in respect of fees and disbursements;

(b) direct a reference under the rules of court to determine the amount owing; or

(c) direct that the amount owing be determined in any other manner.

Section 33

Agreements for payment only in the event of success

33. (1) Despite the *Solicitors Act* and *An Act Respecting Champerty*, being chapter 327 of Revised Statutes of Ontario, 1897, a solicitor and a representative party may enter into a written agreement providing for payment of fees and disbursements only in the event of success in a class proceeding.

Interpretation, success in a proceeding

(2) For the purposes of subsection (1), success in a class proceeding includes,

(a) a judgment on common issues in favour of some or all class members; and

(b) a settlement that benefits one or more class members.

Definitions

(3) For the purposes of subsections (4) to (7),

"base fee" means the result of multiplying the total number of hours worked by an hourly rate;

"multiplier" means a multiple to be applied to a base fee.

Agreements to increase fees by a multiplier

(4) An agreement under subsection (1) may permit the solicitor to make a motion to the court to have his or her fees increased by a multiplier.

Motion to increase fee by a multiplier

(5) A motion under subsection (4) shall be heard by a judge who has,

(a) given judgment on common issues in favour of some or all class members; or

(b) approved a settlement that benefits any class member.

Idem

(6) Where the judge referred to in subsection (5) is unavailable for any reason, the regional senior judge shall assign another judge of the court for the purpose.

Idem

(7) On the motion of a solicitor who has entered into an agreement under subsection (4), the court,

(a) shall determine the amount of the solicitor's base fee;

(b) may apply a multiplier to the base fee that results in fair and reasonable compensation to the solicitor for the risk incurred in undertaking and continuing the proceeding under an agreement for payment only in thc event of success; and

(c) shall determine the amount of disbursements to which the solicitor is entitled, including interest calculated on the disbursements incurred, as totalled at the end of each six-month period following the date of the agreement.

Idem

(8) In making a determination under clause (7)(a), the court shall allow only a reasonable fee.

Idem

(9) In making a determination under clause (7)(b), the court may consider the manner in which the solicitor conducted the proceeding.

Section 34

Motions

34. (1) The same judge shall hear all motions before the trial of the common issues.

Idem

(2) Where a judge who has heard motions under subsection (1) becomes unavailable for any reason, the regional senior judge shall assign another judge of the court for the purpose.

Idem

(3) Unless the parties agree otherwise, a judge who hears motions under subsection (1) or (2) shall not preside at the trial of the common issues.

Section 35

Rules of court

35. The rules of court apply to class proceedings.

Section 36

Crown bound

36. This Act binds the Crown.

Section 37

Application of Act

37. This Act does not apply to,

(a) a proceeding that may be brought in a representative capacity under another Act;

(b) a proceeding required by law to be brought in a representative capacity; and

(c) a proceeding commenced before this Act comes into force.

Section 38

Commencement

38. This Act comes into force on a day to be named by proclamation of the Lieutenant Governor.

Section 39

Short title

39. The short title of this Act is the *Class Proceedings Act, 1992*.

LAW SOCIETY AMENDMENT ACT (CLASS PROCEEDINGS FUND), 1992

S.O. 1992, c. 7

Section 1

1. Section 52 of the Law Society Act is amended by striking out "53 to 59" in the first and second lines and substituting "53 to 59.5" and by adding the following definitions:

"class proceeding" means a proceeding certified as a class proceeding on a motion made under section 2 or 3 of the *Class Proceedings Act, 1992*;

"Committee" means the Class Proceedings Committee referred to in section 59.2,

"defendant" includes a respondent;

"plaintiff" includes an applicant.

Section 2

2. Subsection 55(1) of the Act is amended by adding the following paragraph:

4. The provision of costs assistance to parties to class proceedings and to proceedings commenced under the *Class Proceedings Act, 1992*.

Regulations

3. The Act is amended by adding the following sections:

Class Proceedings Fund

59.1 (1) The board shall,

(a) establish an account of the Foundation to be known as the Class Proceedings Fund;

(b) within sixty days after this Act comes into force, endow the Class Proceedings Fund with $300,000 from the funds of the Foundation;

(c) within one year after the day on which the endowment referred to in clause (b) is made, endow the Class Proceedings Fund with a further $200,000 from the funds of the Foundation; and

(d) administer the Class Proceedings Fund in accordance with this Act and the. regulations.

Purposes of the Class Proceedings Fund

(2) The Class Proceedings Fund shall be used for the following purposes:

1. Financial support for plaintiffs to class proceedings and to proceedings commenced under the *Class Proceedings Act, 1992*, in respect of disbursements related to the proceeding.

2. Payments to defendants in respect of costs awards made in their favour against plaintiffs who have received financial support from the Fund.

Application of s. 56

(3) Funds in the Class Proceedings Fund are funds of the Foundation within the meaning of section 56, but payments out of the Class Proceedings Fund shall relate to the administration or purposes of the Fund.

Class Proceedings Committee

59.2 (1) The Class Proceedings Committee is established and shall be composed of,

(a) one member appointed by the Foundation;

(b) one member appointed by the Attorney General; and

(c) three members appointed jointly by the Foundation and the Attorney General.

Term of office

(2) Each member of the Class Proceedings Committee shall hold office for a period of three years and is eligible for re-appointment.

Quorum

(3) Three members of the Committee constitute a quorum.

Vacancies

(4) Where there are not more than two vacancies in the membership of the Committee, the remaining members constitute the Committee for all purposes.

Remuneration

(5) The members of the Committee shall serve without remuneration, but each member is entitled to compensation for expenses incurred in carrying out the functions of the Committee.

Applications by plaintiff

59.3 (1) A plaintiff to a class proceeding or to a proceeding commenced under section 2 of the *Class Proceedings Act, 1992* may apply to the Committee for financial support from the Class Proceedings Fund in respect of disbursements related to the proceeding.

Idem

(2) An application under subsection (1) shall not include a claim in respect of solicitor's fees.

Committee may authorize payment

(3) The Committee may direct the board to make payments from the Class Proceedings Fund to a plaintiff who makes a application under subsection (1), in the amount that the Committee considers appropriate.

Idem

(4) In making a decision under subsection (3), the Committee may have regard to,

(a) the merits of the plaintiff's case;

(b) whether the plaintiff has made reasonable efforts to raise funds from other

(c) whether the plaintiff has a clear and reasonable proposal for the use of any funds awarded;

(d) whether the plaintiff has appropriate financial controls to ensure that any funds awarded are spent for the purposes of the award; and

(e) any other matter that the Committee considers relevant.

Supplementary funding

(5) A plaintiff who has received funding under subsection (3) may apply to the Committee at any time up to the end of the class proceeding for supplementary funding and the Committee may direct the board to make further payments from the Class Proceedings Fund to the plaintiff if the Committee is of the opinion, having regard to all the circumstances, that it is appropriate to do so.

Board shall make payments

(6) The board shall make payments in accordance with any directions given by the Committee under this section.

Applications by defendants

59.4 (1) A defendant to a proceeding may apply to the board for payment from the Class Proceedings Fund in respect of a costs award made in the proceeding in the defendant's favour against a plaintiff who has received financial support from the Class Proceedings Fund in respect of the proceeding.

Board shall make payments

(2) The board shall make payments applied for in accordance with subsection (1) from the Class Proceedings Fund, subject to any limits or tariffs applicable to such payments prescribed by the regulations.

Plaintiff not liable

(3) A defendant who has the right to apply for payment from the Class Proceedings Fund in respect of a costs award against a plaintiff may not recover any part of the award from the plaintiff.

Regulations

59.5 (1) The Lieutenant Governor in Council may make regulations,

(a) respecting the administration of the Class Proceedings Fund;

(b) establishing procedures for making applications under sections 59.3 and 59.4;

(c) establishing criteria in addition to those set out in section 59.3 for decisions of the Committee under section 59.3;

(d) establishing limits and tariffs for payments under sections 59.3 and 59.4;

(e) prescribing conditions of awards under section 59.3;

(f) providing for the assessment of costs in respect of which a claim is made under section 59.4;

(g) providing for levies in favour of the Class Proceedings Fund against awards and settlement funds in proceedings in respect of which a party receives financial support from the Class Proceedings Fund.

Idem

(2) A regulation made under clause (1)(d) may provide for different limits and tariffs for different stages and types of proceedings.

Idem

(3) A regulation made under clause (1)(g) may provide for levies that exceed the amount of financial support received by the parties to a proceeding.

Idem

(4) A regulation made under clause (1)(g) may provide for levies based on a formula that takes the amount of an award or settlement fund into account.

Idem

(5) A levy under clause (1)(g) against a settlement fund or monetary award is a charge on the fund or award.

Section 4

Commencement

4. This Act comes into force on a day to be named by proclamation of the Lieutenant Governor. [in force January 1, 1993, Ontario Gazette: Vol. 125-52, December 26, 1992, p. 3284]

Section 5

Short title

5. The short title of this Act is the *Law Society Amendment Act (Class Proceedings Funding), 1992.*

CLASS PROCEEDINGS REGULATION

Made under the *Law Society Act*

O. Reg. 771/92

as am. O. Reg. 535/95; 71/16 (Fr.).

Definitions

1. In this Regulation,

"defendant applicant" means an applicant for payment under section 59.4 of the Act;

"plaintiff applicant" means an applicant for financial support under section 59.3 of the Act;

"plaintiff recipient" means a recipient of an award of financial support under section 59.3 of the Act.

Application by plaintiffs under section 59.3 of the act

2. A plaintiff applicant shall make a separate application for financial assistance in respect of each of the following stages in a proceeding:

1. Steps taken up to the end of the hearing of a motion for an order certifying the proceeding as a class proceeding.

2. Appeals of orders relating to certification.

3. Steps other than those described in paragraphs 1 and 2 taken up to the end of discovery or cross-examination on affidavits.

4. Steps other than those described in paragraphs 1 to 3 concerning the determination of common issues.

5. Appeals from a judgment on common issues.

6. Steps other than those described in paragraphs 1 to 5.

3. (1) Every plaintiff applicant shall provide six copies of the following information and documents to the Committee:

1. If the applicant is an individual, his or her name, address, telephone number and fax number, if any.

2. If the applicant is a corporation, its name, head office address, telephone number and fax number and a copy of its articles of incorporation.

3. Each defendant's name.

4. A statement indicating which of the stages in the proceeding, as set out in paragraphs 1 to 6 of section 2, the application addresses.

5. A copy of the pleadings and any court order relating to the proceeding.

6. A description of the class and an estimate of the number of members in the class.

7. A legal opinion describing and assessing the merits of the applicant's case, and any other information and documents the applicant considers appropriate for this purpose.

8. If the applicant has not yet applied for certification of the proceeding as a class proceeding, a statement indicating when the applicant will do so.

9. If the proceeding has not yet been certified as a class proceeding, a legal opinion assessing the likelihood that it will be certified.

10. A statement of the financial support being requested, itemized according to the purposes for which it is being requested.

11. Such information and documents as the applicant considers appropriate to address each of the matters described in clauses 59.3(4)(b) to (d) of the Act.

12. An affidavit by the applicant stating that the information provided by him, her or it in connection with the application is true.

13. Authorization to the Committee and to the board to verify the information provided by the applicant in connection with the application.

14. The name and address of the applicant's lawyer.

15. A statement by the lawyer indicating that he or she will accept payments from the Class Proceedings Fund in connection with the application and will use them for the purposes for which the payments are made.

(2) Despite subsection (1), a plaintiff applicant who makes more than one application in respect of a proceeding is not required to resubmit information and documents provided on a previous application.

(3) A plaintiff applicant is entitled to make oral submissions to the Committee concerning the applicant's first application for financial support relating to a particular proceeding.

4. The Committee shall not award financial support in respect of a particular expert unless the Committee approves the use of the expert and the amount of the disbursements relating to the expert.

Criteria for decisions respecting plaintiff's applications

5. In making a decision under subsection 59.3(3) of the Act, the Committee may have regard to the following matters:

1. The extent to which the issues in the proceeding affect the public interest.

2. If the application for financial support is made before the proceeding is certified as a class proceeding, the likelihood that it will be certified.

3. The amount of money in the Fund that has been allocated to provide financial support in respect of other applications or that may be required to make payments to defendants under section 59.4 of the Act.

Conditions of financial support for plaintiffs

6. (1) A plaintiff applicant is not entitled to receive payment of an award under section 59.3 of the Act until he, she or it provides the board with,

(a) a statement of disbursements to which the award relates, certified by the lawyer who made the disbursements to be complete and accurate; or

(b) such other proof that the disbursements have been made as the board considers appropriate.

(2) The board may make a payment relating to a disbursement that the plaintiff recipient's lawyer has not yet paid if the board considers that, in the circumstances, the plaintiff recipient would otherwise suffer undue hardship.

7. (1) The plaintiff recipient shall use the money paid under section 59.3 of the Act only for the purpose for which financial support is authorized in the award.

(2) If the plaintiff recipient wishes to use any money awarded for a different purpose, he, she or it shall obtain the consent of the Committee before doing so.

(3) A plaintiff recipient who fails to comply with this section shall repay the amount of the payment.

8. (1) The conditions set out in this section apply with respect to every payment of financial support made under section 59.3 of the Act.

(2) A plaintiff recipient who fails to comply with a condition set out in this section shall, at the request of the board, repay the amount of the payment.

(3) The plaintiff recipient shall notify the defendant in the proceeding,

(a) that the recipient has received financial support from the Class Proceedings Fund in respect of the proceeding;

(b) that there is a charge in favour of the Fund on any award and settlement funds in the proceeding; and

(c) that the amount of the charge is determined under section 10.

(4) If the proceeding is certified as a class proceeding, the plaintiff recipient shall notify the other class members.

(a) that the recipient has received financial support from the Class Proceedings Fund in respect of the proceeding;

(b) that there will be a levy that reduces the amount of any award or settlement funds to which the class members may become entitled;

(c) that the amount of the levy is the sum of,

(i) the amount of any financial support paid under section 59.3 of the Act, excluding any amount repaid by a plaintiff, and

(ii) 10 per cent of the amount of the award or settlement funds, if any, to which one or more persons in the class is entitled.

(5) The plaintiff recipient shall give the notice required by subsection (4) on the first occasion that he, she or it is required to give any notice to other class members under the *Class Proceedings Act, 1992* that falls after he, she or it is first awarded financial support in the proceeding by the Committee.

(6) The plaintiff recipient shall give notice to the board of all motions in the proceeding relating to settlement.

(7) The plaintiff recipient shall provide the board with the following information and documents:

1. Details respecting any change in the information provided in the application for financial support.

2. On request, a copy of every document filed with the court in the proceeding.

3. On request, a copy of every order made by the court in the proceeding.

(8) The plaintiff recipient shall allow the board to review records relating to disbursements for which financial support is claimed or paid.

9. If the proceeding to which the award relates is discontinued or abandoned, the plaintiff recipient shall, at the request of the board, repay the amount of any payments from the Class Proceedings Fund.

Levies against awards and settlement funds

10. (1) This section applies in a proceeding in respect of which a party receives financial support from the Class Proceedings Fund.

(2) A levy is payable in favour of the Fund,

(a) when a monetary award is made in favour of one or more persons in a class that includes a plaintiff who received financial support under section 59.3 of the Act; or

(b) when the proceeding is settled and one or more persons in such a class is entitled to receive settlement funds.

(3) The amount of the levy is the sum of,

(a) the amount of any financial support paid under section 59.3 of the Act, excluding any amount repaid by a plaintiff; and

(b) 10 per cent of the amount of the award or settlement funds, if any, to which one or more persons in a class that includes a plaintiff who received financial support under section 59.3 of the Act is entitled.

(4) [Revoked O. Reg. 535/95, s. 1.]

O. Reg. 535/95, s. 1

Applications by defendants under section 59.4 of the act

11. Every defendant applicant shall provide the following information and documents to the board:

1. If the applicant is an individual, his or her name, address, telephone number and fax number, if any.

2. If the applicant is a corporation, its name, head office address, telephone number and fax number.

3. An affidavit by the applicant containing.

    i. a statement that costs have been awarded in favour of the applicant against the plaintiff, and indicating the stage of the proceeding at which the order was made,

    ii. a statement whether the court order fixed the amount of the costs to be paid by the plaintiff and, if so, setting out the amount,

    iii. a statement that the order awarding costs has not been appealed and that the certificate, if any, of the assessment officer has not been appealed, and

    iv. a statement that the time for appealing the order and the certificate, if any, has expired.

4. If the court order did not fix the amount of the costs to be paid by the plaintiff, either a certificate of assessment of costs or an agreed bill of costs.

5. The name and address of the person to whom payment from the Class Proceedings Fund is to be made.

6. The name and address of the applicant's lawyer.

Administration of the fund

12. Payments from the Class Proceedings Fund to a plaintiff recipient shall be made only to the recipient's lawyer.

13. The board shall compile the following information each year for inclusion in its annual report:

1. The number of applications under section 59.3 of the Act that were made, listed by those stages in the proceeding that are set out in paragraphs 1 to 6 of section 2.

2. The number of those applications, listed by stages in the proceeding,

    i. in which an award was made, and

    ii. in which no award was made.

3. The number of proceedings for which financial support was awarded under section 59.3 of the Act.

4. The total amount of money awarded to applicants under section 59.3 of the Act, listed by type of disbursement.

5. The total amount of money paid from the Class Proceedings Fund to applicants under section 59.3 of the Act.

6. The number of applicants who received financial support under section 59.3 of the Act before the proceeding was certified as a class proceeding and whose proceedings were certified.

7. The number of applicants who received financial support under section 59.3 of the Act,

i. who received judgment on common issues in their favour at trial, or

ii. whose proceedings settled.

8. The number of applications by defendants under section 59.4 of the Act.

9. The total amount of money paid from the Fund to defendants under section 59.4 of the Act.

10. A brief description of each proceeding for which a plaintiff was awarded financial support under section 59.3 of the Act and the amount awarded for each type of disbursement.

Commencement

14. This Regulation comes into force on the 1st day of January, 1993.

RULE 12 — CLASS PROCEEDINGS AND OTHER REPRESENTATIVE PROCEEDINGS

[am. O. Regs. 770/92; 465/93; 288/99; 504/00 (Fr.); 113/01; 575/07; 82/17, s. 2]

DEFINITIONS

12.01 In rules 12.02 to 12.06,

"Act" means the *Class Proceedings Act, 1992*;

"Foundation" means The Law Foundation of Ontario;

"Fund" means the Class Proceedings Fund of the Foundation.

O. Reg. 770/92, s. 5; 465/93, s. 2(2)

TITLE OF PROCEEDING

12.02 (1) In a proceeding commenced under subsection 2(1) of the Act, the title of the proceeding shall include, after the names of the parties, "Proceeding under the *Class Proceedings Act, 1992*".

(2) In a proceeding referred to in section 3 or 4 of the Act, the notice of motion for an order certifying the proceeding, the order certifying it and all subsequent documents shall include, after the names of the parties, "Proceeding under the *Class Proceedings Act, 1992*".

O. Reg. 770/92, s. 5

DISCOVERY OF CLASS MEMBERS

12.03 (1) For the purpose of subrule 31.11(1) (reading in examination), a class member who is examined for discovery under subsection 15(2) of the Act is examined in addition to the party.

(2) Rule 31.10 (discovery of non-parties) and clause 34.15(1)(b) (sanctions for default or misconduct) do not apply when a class member is examined for discovery under subsection 15(2) of the Act.

O. Reg. 770/92, s. 5

COSTS

Application of Rule

12.04 (1) This rule applies to class proceedings in which the plaintiff or applicant has received financial support from the Fund.

Notice to Foundation, Opportunity to Participate

(2) If the court is of the opinion that the defendant or respondent may be entitled to an award of costs, the court shall direct the plaintiff or applicant to give notice to the Foundation.

(3) When the court has made a direction under subsection (2),

(a) no order for costs or assessment of costs shall be made unless the Foundation has had an opportunity to present evidence and make submissions in respect of costs; and

(b) the Foundation is a party for the purpose of an appeal in relation to costs.

Failure to Accept Defendant's Offer

(4) Subrule 49.10(2) (costs consequences of offer) does not apply.

O. Reg. 770/92, s. 5; 113/01, s. 1

CONTENTS OF JUDGMENTS AND ORDERS

12.05 (1) A judgment in a class proceeding or an order approving a settlement, discontinuance or abandonment of a class proceeding under section 29 of the Act shall contain directions with respect to,

(a) the distribution of amounts awarded under section 24 or 25 of the Act, and the costs of distribution;

(b) the payment of amounts owing under an enforceable agreement made under section 32 of the Act between a lawyer and a representative party;

(c) the payment of the costs of the proceeding; and

(d) the payment of any levy in favour of the Fund under clause 59.5(1)(g) of the *Law Society Act*.

(2) An order certifying two or more proceedings as a class proceeding under section 3 of the Act or decertifying a class proceeding under section 10 of the Act shall contain directions with respect to pleadings and other procedural matters.

O. Reg. 770/92, s. 5; 575/07, s. 1, item 6

LEAVE TO APPEAL

Leave to be Obtained from Another Judge

12.06 (1) Leave to appeal to the Divisional Court under subsection 30(2), (9), (10) or (11) of the Act shall be obtained from a judge other than the judge who made the order.

Motion in Writing

(1.1) The motion for leave to appeal shall be heard in writing, without the attendance of parties or lawyers.

Certification Order — Grounds

(2) Leave to appeal from an order under subsection 30(2) of the Act shall be granted only on the grounds provided in subrule 62.02(4) with necessary modifications.

Order Awarding $3,000 or less or Dismissing Claim — Grounds

(3) Leave to appeal from an order under subsection 30(9), (10) or (11) of the Act shall not be granted unless,

(a) there has been a miscarriage of justice; or

(b) the order may be used as a precedent in determining the rights of other class members or the defendant in the proceeding under section 24 or 25 of the Act and there is good reason to doubt the correctness of the order.

Procedure

(4) Subrules 61.03.1(2) to (19) apply, with the following and any other necessary modifications, to the motion for leave to appeal:

1. References in those subrules to the Court of Appeal shall be read as references to the Divisional Court.

2. For the purposes of subrule 61.03.1(6), only one copy of each of the motion record, factum, any transcripts and any book of authorities is required to be filed.

3. For the purposes of subrule 61.03.1(10), only one copy of each of the factum, any motion record and any book of authorities is required to be filed.

Subsequent Procedure if Leave Granted

(5) If leave is granted, the notice of appeal required by rule 61.04, together with the appellant's certificate respecting evidence required by subrule 61.05(1), shall be delivered within seven days after the granting of leave, and from then on Rule 61 applies to the appeal.

O. Reg. 465/93, s. 2(3); 170/14, s. 1; 82/17, s. 2

PROCEEDING AGAINST REPRESENTATIVE DEFENDANT

12.07 Where numerous persons have the same interest, one or more of them may defend a proceeding on behalf or for the benefit of all, or may be authorized by the court to do so.

O. Reg. 465/93, s. 2(3)

PROCEEDING BY UNINCORPORATED ASSOCIATION OR TRADE UNION

12.08 Where numerous persons are members of an unincorporated association or trade union and a proceeding under the *Class Proceedings Act, 1992* would be an unduly expensive or inconvenient means for determining their claims, one or more of them may be authorized by the court to bring a proceeding on behalf of or for the benefit of all.

O. Reg. 288/99, s. 9

U.S. FEDERAL RULES OF CIVIL PROCEDURE RULE 23. CLASS ACTIONS

(a) Prerequisites. One or more members of a class may sue or be sued as representative parties on behalf of all members only if:

(1) the class is so numerous that joinder of all members is impracticable;

(2) there are questions of law or fact common to the class;

(3) the claims or defenses of the representative parties are typical of the claims or defenses of the class; and

(4) the representative parties will fairly and adequately protect the interests of the class.

(b) Types of Class Actions. A class action may be maintained if Rule 23(a) is satisfied and if:

prosecuting separate actions by or against individual class members would create a risk of:

(A) inconsistent or varying adjudications with respect to individual class members that would establish incompatible standards of conduct for the party opposing the class; or

(B) adjudications with respect to individual class members that, as a practical matter, would be dispositive of the interests of the other members not parties to the individual adjudications or would substantially impair or impede their ability to protect their interests;

(2) the party opposing the class has acted or refused to act on grounds that apply generally to the class, so that final injunctive relief or corresponding declaratory relief is appropriate respecting the class as a whole; or

(3) the court finds that the questions of law or fact common to class members predominate over any questions affecting only individual members, and that a class action is superior to other available methods for fairly and efficiently adjudicating the controversy. The matters pertinent to these findings include:

(A) the class members' interests in individually controlling the prosecution or defense of separate actions;

(B) the extent and nature of any litigation concerning the controversy already begun by or against class members;

(C) the desirability or undesirability of concentrating the litigation of the claims in the particular forum; and

(D) the likely difficulties in managing a class action.

(c) Certification Order; Notice to Class Members; Judgment; Issues Classes; Subclasses.

(1) *Certification Order.*

(A) *Time to Issue.* At an early practicable time after a person sues or is sued as a class representative, the court must determine by order whether to certify the action as a class action.

(B) *Defining the Class.* Appointing Class Counsel. An order that certifies a class action must define the class and the class claims, issues, or defenses, and must appoint class counsel under Rule 23(g).

(C) *Altering or Amending the Order.* An order that grants or denies class certification may be altered or amended before final judgment.

(2) *Notice.*

(A) *For (b)(1) or (b)(2) Classes.* For any class certified under Rule 23(b)(1) or (b)(2), the court may direct appropriate notice to the class.

(B) *For (b)(3) Classes.* For any class certified under Rule 23(b)(3), the court must direct to class members the best notice that is practicable under the circumstances, including individual notice to all members who can be identified through reasonable effort. The notice must clearly and concisely state in plain, easily understood language:

(i) the nature of the action;

(ii) the definition of the class certified;

(iii) the class claims, issues, or defenses;

(iv) that a class member may enter an appearance through an attorney if the member so desires;

(v) that the court will exclude from the class any member who requests exclusion;

(vi) the time and manner for requesting exclusion; and

(vii) the binding effect of a class judgment on members under Rule 23(c)(3).

(3) *Judgment.* Whether or not favorable to the class, the judgment in a class action must:

(A) for any class certified under Rule 23(b)(1) or (b)(2), include and describe those whom the court finds to be class members; and

(B) for any class certified under Rule 23(b)(3), include and specify or describe those to whom the Rule 23(c)(2) notice was directed, who have not requested exclusion, and whom the court finds to be class members.

(4) *Particular Issues.* When appropriate, an action may be brought or maintained as a class action with respect to particular issues.

(5) *Subclasses.* When appropriate, a class may be divided into subclasses that are each treated as a class under this rule.

(d) Conducting the Action.

(1) *In General.* In conducting an action under this rule, the court may issue orders that:

(A) determine the course of proceedings or prescribe measures to prevent undue repetition or complication in presenting evidence or argument;

(B) require — to protect class members and fairly conduct the action-giving appropriate notice to some or all class members of:

(i) any step in the action;

(ii) the proposed extent of the judgment; or

(iii) the members' opportunity to signify whether they consider the representation fair and adequate, to intervene and present claims or defenses, or to otherwise come into the action;

(C) impose conditions on the representative parties or on intervenors;

(D) require that the pleadings be amended to eliminate allegations about representation of absent persons and that the action proceed accordingly; or

(E) deal with similar procedural matters.

(2) *Combining and Amending Orders*. An order under Rule 23(d)(1) may be altered or amended from time to time and may be combined with an order under Rule 16.

(e) Settlement, Voluntary Dismissal, or Compromise. The claims, issues, or defenses of a certified class may be settled, voluntarily dismissed, or compromised only with the court's approval. The following procedures apply to a proposed settlement, voluntary dismissal, or compromise:

(1) The court must direct notice in a reasonable manner to all class members who would be bound by the proposal.

(2) If the proposal would bind class members, the court may approve it only after a hearing and on finding that it is fair, reasonable, and adequate.

(3) The parties seeking approval must file a statement identifying any agreement made in connection with the proposal.

(4) If the class action was previously certified under Rule 23(b)(3), the court may refuse to approve a settlement unless it affords a new opportunity to request exclusion to individual class members who had an earlier opportunity to request exclusion but did not do so.

(5) Any class member may object to the proposal if it requires court approval under this subdivision (e); the objection may be withdrawn only with the court's approval.

(f) Appeals. A court of appeals may permit an appeal from an order granting or denying class-action certification under this rule if a petition for permission to appeal is filed with the circuit clerk within 14 days after the order is entered. An appeal does not stay proceedings in the district court unless the district judge or the court of appeals so orders.

(g) Class Counsel.

(1) *Appointing Class Counsel*. Unless a statute provides otherwise, a court that certifies a class must appoint class counsel. In appointing class counsel, the court:

(A) must consider:

(i) the work counsel has done in identifying or investigating potential claims in the action;

(ii) counsel's experience in handling class actions, other complex litigation, and the types of claims asserted in the action;

(iii) counsel's knowledge of the applicable law; and

(iv) the resources that counsel will commit to representing the class;

(B) may consider any other matter pertinent to counsel's ability to fairly and adequately represent the interests of the class;

(C) may order potential class counsel to provide information on any subject pertinent to the appointment and to propose terms for attorney's fees and nontaxable costs;

(D) may include in the appointing order provisions about the award of attorney's fees or nontaxable costs under Rule 23(h); and

(E) may make further orders in connection with the appointment.

(2) *Standard for Appointing Class Counsel.* When one applicant seeks appointment as class counsel, the court may appoint that applicant only if the applicant is adequate under Rule 23(g)(1) and (4). If more than one adequate applicant seeks appointment, the court must appoint the applicant best able to represent the interests of the class.

(3) *Interim Counsel.* The court may designate interim counsel to act on behalf of a putative class before determining whether to certify the action as a class action.

(4) *Duty of Class Counsel.* Class counsel must fairly and adequately represent the interests of the class.

(h) Attorney's Fees and Nontaxable Costs. In a certified class action, the court may award reasonable attorney's fees and nontaxable costs that are authorized by law or by the parties' agreement. The following procedures apply:

(1) A claim for an award must be made by motion under Rule 54(d)(2), subject to the provisions of this subdivision (h), at a time the court sets. Notice of the motion must be served on all parties and, for motions by class counsel, directed to class members in a reasonable manner.

(2) A class member, or a party from whom payment is sought, may object to the motion.

(3) The court may hold a hearing and must find the facts and state its legal conclusions under Rule 52(a).

(4) The court may refer issues related to the amount of the award to a special master or a magistrate judge, as provided in Rule 54(d)(2)(D).

LIMITATION PERIODS

TABLE OF CONTENTS

ONTARIO LIMITATION PERIODS

Table of Contents

1. ACCESS TO INFORMATION AND PRIVACY

Action	Limitation	Accrues From	Statute
1.1 Person affected by request for access to record may make representations concerning disclosure	20 days	after receiving notice of the request	**Freedom of Information and Protection of Privacy Act, R.S.O. 1990, c. F.31, ss. 28(1), (5), 48(1), (2) [re-en. 1996, c. 1, Sch. K, s. 7]:** 28.1 (1) Before a head grants a request for access to a record, (a) that the head has reason to believe might contain information referred to in subsection 17(1) that affects the interest of a person other than the person requesting information; or (b) that is personal information that the head has reason to believe might constitute an unjustified invasion of personal privacy for the purposes of clause 21(1)(f), the head shall give written notice in accordance with subsection (2) to the person to whom the information relates. . . . (5) Where a notice is given under subsection (1), the person to whom the information relates may, within twenty days after the notice is given, make representations to the head as to why the record or the part thereof should not be disclosed. . . . 48. (1) An individual seeking access to personal information about the individual shall, (a) make a request in writing to be institution that the individual believes has custody or control of the personal information; (b) identify the personal information bank or otherwise identify the location of the personal information; and (c) at the time of making the request, pay the fee prescribed by the regulations for that purpose. (2) Subsections 10(2), 24(1.1) and (2) and sections 25, 26, 27, 27.1, 28 and 29 apply with necessary modifications to a request made under subsection (1).
1.2 Appeal decision of head of institution concerning disclosure of record	30 days	after notice of decision is given	**Freedom of Information and Protection of Privacy Act, R.S.O. 1990, c. F.31, ss. 28(7)–(9), 48(2) [re-en. 1996, c. 1, Sch. K, s. 7]:** 28. (7) The head shall, within thirty days after the notice under subsection (1) is given, but not before the earlier of, (a) the day the response to the notice from the person to whom the information relates is received: or (b) twenty-one days after the notice is given,

Action	Limitation	Accrues From	Statute
			decide whether or not to disclose the record or the part thereof and give written notice of the decision to the person to whom the information relates and the person who made the request. (8) Where a head decides to disclose a record or part thereof under subsection (7), the head shall state in the notice that, (a) the person to whom the information relates may appeal the decision to the Commissioner within thirty days after the notice is given; and (b) the person who made the request will be given access to the record or to a part thereof, unless an appeal of the decision is commenced within thirty days after the notice is given. (9) Where, under subsection (7), the head decides to disclose the record or a part thereof, the head shall give the person who made the request access to the record or part thereof within thirty days after notice is given under subsection (7), unless the person to whom the information relates asks the Commissioner to review the decision. . . . 48. (2) Subsections 10(2), 24(1.1) and (2) and sections 25, 26, 27, 27.1, 28 and 29 apply with necessary modifications to a request made under subsection (1).
1.3 Appeal decision respecting access to a record, personal information or correction of personal information	30 days	after notice of decision is given	**Freedom of Information and Protection of Privacy Act, R.S.O. 1990, c. F.31, ss. 50(1), (1.1) [re-en. 1996, c. 1, Sch. K, s. 7]:** 50. (1) A person who has made a request for, (a) access to a record under subsection 24(1); or (b) access to personal information under subsection 48(1); or (c) correction of personal information under subsection 47(2), or a person who is given notice of a request under subsection 28(1) may appeal any decision of a head under this Act to the Commissioner. (1.1) A person who appeals under subsection (1) shall pay the fee prescribed by the regulations for that purpose. (2) An appeal under subsection (1) shall be made within thirty days after the notice was given of the decision appealed from by filing with the Commissioner written notice of appeal.

2. ALTERNATIVE DISPUTE RESOLUTION

Action	Limitation	Accrues From	Statute
2.1 Appeal award or apply to set aside award of arbitrator (except in case of alleged corruption or fraud)	30 days	after receiving award, correction, explanation, change or statement of reasons on which appeal or application is based	**Arbitration Act, 1991, S.O. 1991, c. 17, s. 47(1), (2):** 47. (1) An appeal of an award or an application to set aside award shall be commenced within thirty days after the appellant or applicant receives the award, correction, explanation, change or statement or reasons on which the appeal or application is based. (2) Subsection (1) does not apply if the appellant or applicant alleges corruption or fraud.
2.2 Commence a proceeding to enforce an arbitration award under the Arbitration Act, 1991	no limitation	—	**Limitations Act, 2002, S.O. 2002, c. 24, Sch. B, s. 16(1)(d):** 16. (1) There is no limitation period in respect of, . . . (d) a proceeding to enforce an award in arbitration to which the *Arbitration Act, 1991* applies.

3. BARRISTERS AND SOLICITORS

Action	Limitation	Accrues From	Statute
3.1 Commence a proceeding in respect of a claim	2 years	day on which the claim was discovered	**Limitations Act, 2002, S.O. 2002, c. 24, Sch. B, ss. 4, 15(2):** 4.(1) Unless this Act provides otherwise, a proceeding shall not be commenced in respect of a claim after the second anniversary of the day on which the claim was discovered. . . . 15.(2) No proceeding shall be commenced in respect of any claim after the 15th anniversary of the day on which the act or omission on which the claim is based took place.
3.2 Application to reopen an agreement with solicitor where amount has already been paid pursuant to Solicitors Act (Ont.)	12 months	date of payment	**Solicitors Act, R.S.O. 1990, c. S.15, s. 25 [am. S.O. 2002, c. 24, Sch. B, s. 46(2)] [also see ss. 4 and 15(2) for the Limitations Act, 2002]:** **25. Where the amount agreed under any such agreement [agreement between solicitors and clients] has been paid by or on behalf of the client or by any person chargeable with or entitled to pay it, the Ontario Court (General Division) may, upon the application of the person who has paid it, if it appears to the court that the special circumstances of the case require the agreement to be reopened, reopen it and order the costs, fees, charges and disbursements to be assessed, and may also order the whole or any part of the amount received by the solicitor to be repaid by him or her on such terms and conditions as to the court seems just.**

Action	Limitation	Accrues From	Statute
3.3 Application by client for order for taxation of a bill already delivered under Solicitors Act (Ont.)	**1 month**	**date of delivery**	**Solicitors Act, R.S.O. 1990, c. S.15, s. 3:** 3. Where the retainer of the solicitor is not disputed and there are no special circumstances, an order may be obtained on requisition from a local registrar of the Ontario Court (General Division). (a) by the client, for the delivery and assessment of the solicitor's bill; (b) by the client, for the assessment of a bill already delivered, within one month from its delivery; (c) by the solicitor, for the assessment of bill already delivered, at any time after the expiration of one month from its delivery, if no order for its assessment has been previously made.
3.4 Application by solicitor for taxation of bill where no previous order made	one time limit	one month from delivery of bill	**Solicitors Act, R.S.O. 1990, c. S.15, s. 3:** 3. Where the retainer of the solicitor is not disputed and there are no special circumstances, an order may be obtained on requisition from a local registrar of the Ontario Court (General Division), (a) by the client, for the delivery and assessment of the solicitor's bill; (b) by the client, for the assessment of a bill already delivered, within one month from its delivery; (c) by the solicitor, for the assessment of a bill already delivered, any any time after the expiration of one month from its deliver, if no order for its assessment has been previously made.
3.4.1 Action for recovery of fees	2 years	one month from delivery of bill	**Solicitors Act, R.S.O. 1990, c. S.15, s. 2** **Solicitors to deliver their bill one month before bringing action for costs** 2. (1) No action shall be brought for the recovery of fees, charges or disbursements for business done by a solicitor as such until one month after a bill thereof, subscribed with the proper hand of the solicitor, his or her executor, administrator or assignee or, in the case of a partnership, by one of the partners, either with his or her own name, or with the name of the partnership, has been delivered to the person to be charged therewith, or sent by post to, or left for the person at the person's office or place of abode, or has been enclosed in or accompanied by a letter subscribed in like manner, referring to such bill.

Action	Limitation	Accrues From	Statute
			(2) In proving compliance with this Act it is not necessary in the first instance to prove the contents of the bill delivered, sent or left, but it is sufficient to prove that a bill of fees, charges or disbursements subscribed as required by subsection (1), or enclosed in or accompanied by such letter, was so delivered, sent or left, but the other party may show that the bill so delivered, sent or left, was not such a bill as constituted a compliance with this Act. (3) A solicitor's bill of fees, charges or disbursements is sufficient in form if it contains a reasonable statement or description of the services rendered with a lump sum charge therefor together with a detailed statement of disbursements, and in any action upon or assessment of such a bill if it is deemed proper further details of the services rendered may be ordered.
3.5 Application for taxation of a bill where there are special circumstances	no time limit	—	**Solicitors Act, R.S.O. 1990, c. S.15, s. 4(1):** 4. (1) No such reference shall be directed upon an application made by the party chargeable with such bill after a verdict or judgment has been obtained, or after twelve months from the time such bill was delivered, sent or left as aforesaid, except under special circumstances to be proved to the satisfaction of the court or judge to whom the application for the reference is made.
3.6 Assessment of bill which has been paid	12 months *[also see Limitations Act, 2002, ss. 4, 15(2)]*	payment	**Solicitors Act, R.S.O. 1990, c. S.15, s. 11 [am. S.O. 2002, c. 24, Sch. B, s. 46(1)] [also see ss. 4 and 15(2) of the Limitations Act, 2002]:** **11. The payment of a bill does not preclude the court from referring it for assessment, if the special circumstances of the case, in the opinion of the court, appear to require the assessment.**

4. CLASS PROCEEDINGS

Action	Limitation	Accrues From	Statute
4.1 Apply for order certifying proceedings	90 days	later of: delivery of statement of defence, notice of intent to defend or notice of appearance; or, if no delivery, after the date for delivery expires	**Class Proceedings Act, 1992, S.O. 1992, c. 6, s. 2:** 2. (1) One or more members of a class of persons may commence a proceeding in the court on behalf of the members of the class. (2) A person who commences a proceeding under subsection (1) shall make a motion to a judge of the court for an order certifying the proceeding as a class proceeding and appointing the person representative plaintiff. (3) A motion under subsection (2) shall be made, (a) within ninety days after the later of,

Action	Limitation	Accrues From	Statute
			(i) the date on which the last statement of defence, notice of intend to defend or notice of appearance is delivered, and (ii) the date on which the time prescribed by the rules of court for delivery of the last statement of defence, notice of intend to defend or notice of appearance expires without its being delivered; or (b) subsequently, with leave of the court.
4.2 Suspension in favour of class member of limitation period applicable to cause of action asserted in a class proceeding	indefinite	Settlement, discontinuance, decertification of proceeding or withdrawal or exclusion of class member	**Class Proceedings Act, 1992, S.O. 1992, c. 6, s. 28:** 28. (1) Subject to subsection (2), any limitation period applicable to a cause of action asserted in a class proceeding is suspended in favour of a class member on the commencement of the class proceeding and resumes running against the class member when, (a) the member opts out of the class proceeding; (b) an amendment that has the effect of excluding the member from the class is made to the certification order; (c) a decertification order is made under section 10; (d) the class proceeding is dismissed without an adjudication on the merits; (e) the class proceeding is abandoned or discontinued with the approval of the court; or (f) the class proceeding is settled with the approval of the court, unless the settlement provides otherwise. (2) Where there is a right of appeal in respect of an event described in clauses (1)(a) to (f), the limitation period resumes running as soon as the time for appeal has expired without an appeal being commenced or as soon as any appeal has been finally disposed of.

5. CONTRACTS

Action	Limitation	Accrues From	Statute
5.1 Commence a proceeding in respect of a claim	2 years	day on which the claim was discovered	**Limitations Act, 2002, S.O. 2002, c. 24, Sch. B, ss. 4, 15(2):** 4. (1) Unless this Act provides otherwise, a proceeding shall not be commenced in respect of a claim after the second anniversary of the day on which the claim was discovered. . . . 15. (2) No proceeding shall be commenced in respect of any claim after the 15th anniversary of the day on which the act or omission on which the claim is based took place.

6. CONVERSION AND DETINUE

Action	Limitation	Accrues From	Statute
6.1 Commence a proceeding in respect of a claim	2 years	day on which the claim was discovered	**Limitations Act, 2002, S.O. 2002, c. 24, Sch. B, ss. 4, 15(2):** 4. (1) Unless this Act provides otherwise, a proceeding shall not be commenced in respect of a claim after the second anniversary of the day on which the claim was discovered. . . . 15. (2) No proceeding shall be commenced in respect of any claim after the 15th anniversary of the day on which the act or omission on which the claim is based took place.
6.2 commence a conversion proceeding against a purchaser of personal property for value acting in good faith	2 years	day on which the property was converted	**Limitations Act, 2002, S.O. 2002, c. 24, Sch. B, ss. 15(3):** 15. (3) Despite subsection (2), no proceeding against a purchaser of personal property for value acting in good faith shall be commenced in respect of conversion of the property after the second anniversary of the day on which the property was converted.

7. CROWN

Action	Limitation	Accrues From	Statute
7.1 Commence a proceeding in respect of a claim	2 years	day on which the claim was discovered	**Limitations Act, 2002, S.O. 2002, c. 24, Sch. B, ss. 4, 15(2):** 4. Unless this Act provides otherwise, a proceeding shall not be commenced in respect of a claim after the second anniversary of the day on which the claim was discovered. . . . 15. (2) No proceeding shall be commenced in respect of any claim after the 15th anniversary of the day on which the act or omission on which the claim is based took place.
7.2 Notice of claim to be served on Crown before commencing action against Crown except in case of counterclaim or claim by way of set-off [*see also 7.3*]	60 days notice [*but see s. 7(2) of Proceedings Against the Crown Act (Ont.) as to extension of limitation period*]	before commencement of action	**Proceedings Against the Crown Act, R.S.O. 1990, c. P.27, s. 7(1), (2):** 7. (1) Subject to subsection (3), except in the case of a counterclaim or claim by way of set-off, no action for a claim shall be commenced against the Crown unless the claimant has, at least sixty days before the commencement of the action, served on the Crown a notice of the claim containing sufficient particulars to identify the occasion out of which the claim arose, and the Attorney General may require such additional particulars as in his or her opinion are necessary to enable the claim to be investigated.

Action	Limitation	Accrues From	Statute
			(2) Where a notice of a claim is served under subsection (1) before the expiration of the limitation period applying to the commencement of an action for the claim and the sixty-day period referred to in subsection (1) expires after the expiration of the limitation period, the limitation period is extended to the end of seven days after the expiration of the sixty-day period.
7.3 Notice of claim to be served on Crown before commencing action in respect of the Crown's breach of duties that attach to the handling of property	10 days	date claim arose	**Proceedings Against the Crown Act, R.S.O. 1990, c. P.27, s. 5(1)(c), 7(3):** 5. (1) Except as otherwise provided in this Act, and despite section 11 of the *Interpretation Act*, the Crown is subject to all liabilities in tort to which, if it were a person of full age and capacity, it would be subject, . . . (c) in respect of any breach of the duties attaching to the ownership, occupation, possession or control of property; and . . . 7. (3) No proceeding shall be brought against the Crown under clause 5(1)(c) unless the notice required by subsection (1) is served on the Crown within ten days after the claim arose.
7.4 Application for order declaring a person's interest in forfeited property	60 days	date of forfeiture	**Fines and Forfeitures Act, R.S.O. 1990, c. F.13, s. 6 [s. 6(2) found in Sch. to the Limitations Act, 2002]:** **6. Where there is a forfeiture of personal property to the Crown, any person who claims an interest in the property forfeited as owner, mortgagee, lien-holder or holder of a similar interest may, upon seven days notice to the Attorney General, apply for an order declaring the person's interest in the property immediately before forfeiture.** **(2) An application under subsection (1) shall be made within sixty days of the date of forfeiture to the Ontario Court (General Division).** **(3) On such application, where the claimant establishes to the satisfaction of the court,** **(a) that the claimant had an interest in the property forfeited to the Crown; and** **(b) that the claimant exercised reasonable care with respect to the person given possession of the property so as to be satisfied that the person was not likely to use the property contrary to any Act of the Legislature,**

Action	Limitation	Accrues From	Statute
			the court shall make an order declaring the interest of the claimant in the property immediately before forfeiture.
7.5 A proceeding brought by the Crown or delivery agent under the Ontario Disability Support Program Act, 1997 or the Ontario Works Act, 1997 relating to social, health or economic programs	**no limitation**	—	**Limitations Act, 2002, S.O. 2002, c. 24, Sch. B, ss. 16(1)(j), (2), (3), (4):** 16. (1) There is no limitation period in respect of, . . . (j) a proceeding described in subsection (2) that is brought by, (i) the Crown, or (ii) a delivery agent under the *Ontario Disability Support Program Act, 1997* or the *Ontario Works Act, 1997*; or 2. Clause (1)(j) applies to proceedings in respect of claims relating to, (a) the administration of social, health or economic programs; or (b) the provision of direct or indirect support to members of the public in connection with social, health or economic policy 2002, c. 24, Sched. B, s. 16(2). (3) Without limiting the generality of subsection (2), clause (1)(j) applies to proceedings in respect of claims for, (a) the recovery of social assistance payments, student loans, awards, grants, contributions and economic development loans; and (b) the reimbursement of money paid in connection with social, health or economic programs or policies as a result of fraud, misrepresentation, error or inadvertence. 16. (4) This section and section 17 prevail over anything in section 15.
7.6 Commence a proceeding to recover fines, taxes and penalties, or interest owing to the Crown	no limitation	—	**Limitations Act, 2002, S.O. 2002, c. 24, Sch. B, ss. 16(1)(i), (4):** (1) There is no limitation period in respect of, . . . (i) a proceeding to recover money owing to the Crown in respect of, (i) fines, taxes and penalties, or (ii) interest that may be added to a tax or penalty under an Act; 16. (4) This section and section 17 prevail over anything in section 15.

8. DEBTOR AND CREDITOR

Action	Limitation	Accrues From	Statute
8.1 Commence a proceeding in respect of a claim	2 years	day on which the claim was discovered	**Limitations Act, 2002, S.O. 2002, c. 24, Sch. B, ss. 4, 15(2):** 4. Unless this Act provides otherwise, a proceeding shall not be commenced in respect of a claim after the second anniversary of the day on which the claim was discovered. 15. (2) No proceeding shall be commenced in respect of any claim after the 15th anniversary of the day on which the act or omission on which the claim is based took place.
8.2 Action to establish claim under Assignments and Preferences Act (Ont.)	30 days	receipt of notice of contestation of claim (*or within such further time as judge allows)	**Assignments and Preferences Act, R.S.O. 1990, c. A.33, s. 26(1), (2) [s. 26(2) found in Sch. to the Limitations Act, 2002]:** 26. (1) At any time after the assignee receives from any person claiming to be entitled to rank on the estate proof of the person's claim, notice of contestation of the claim may be served by the assignee upon the claimant. (2) Within thirty days after the receipt of the notice, or within such further time as the judge allows, an action shall be brought by the claimant against the assignee to establish the claim, and a copy of the statement of claim in the action, or of the claim in case the action is brought in the Small Claims Court, shall be served on the assignee, and in default of such action being brought and statement of claim or claim served within the time limited the claim to rank on the estate is forever barred.
8.3 Proceedings in respect of offence of furnishing false information in any application, statement or return under provisions of Collection Agencies Act (Ont.)	1 year	time facts upon which proceeding based first came to knowledge of Director of Consumer Protection Division of Ministry of Consumer and Commercial Relations	**Collection Agencies Act, R.S.O. 1990, c. C.14, s. 28(1), (2) [to be amended by 2004, c. 9, ss. 6(2), (3), 24(2) (not in force)], (4), (5)]:** 28. (1)(I) Every person who, knowingly, (a) furnishes false information in any application under this Act or in any statement or return required to be furnished under this Act or the regulations; (b) fails to comply with any order, direction or other requirement made under this Act; or (c) contravenes this Act or the regulations. and every director or officer of a corporation who knowingly concurs in such furnishing failure or contravention is guilty of an offence and on conviction is liable to a fine of not more than $25,000 or to imprisonment for a term of not more than one year, or to both. [Editors Note: When amending statute 2004, c. 9, subs. 6(2) comes into force, the maximum fine will be changed to "$50,000", and the maximum term of imprisonment will be changed to "two years, less one day".]

Action	Limitation	Accrues From	Statute
			(2) Where a corporation is convicted of an offence under subsection (I), the maximum penalty that may be imposed upon the corporation is $100,000 and not as provided therein. [Editors Note: When amending statute 2004, c. 9, subs. 6(3) comes into force, the maximum penalty will be changed to "$250,000".] . . . (4) No proceeding under clause (1)(a) shall be commenced more than one year after the facts upon which the proceeding is based first came to the knowledge of the Director. (5) No proceeding under clause (1)(b) or (c) shall be commenced more than two years after the time when the subject-matter of the proceeding arose.
8.4 Proceedings in respect to offence of failing to comply with any order, direction or other requirement under Collection Agencies Act (Ont.) or contravention of any provision of the Act	2 years	time subject-matter of proceedings arose	**Collection Agencies Act, R.S.O. 1990, c. C.14, s. 28(5):** 28. (5) No proceeding under clause (1)(b) or (c) shall be commenced more than two years after the time when the subject-matter of the proceeding arose.
8.5 Apply to a judge for an order allowing creditor's claim and determining amount where claim is contested	8 days	receipt of notice of contestation of claim	**Creditors' Relief Act, 1990, c. C.45, s. 12(2) [s. 12(2) found in Sch. to the Limitations Act, 2002]:** 12. (2) The claimant whose claim is contested may apply to the judge for an order allowing the claim and determining the amount, and, if the claimant does not make such application within eight days after receiving notice of the contestation or within such further time, if any, as the judge allows, the claimant shall be taken to have abandoned the claim.
8.6 Apply to a judge for an order adjudicating contestation of proposed scheme of distribution	8 days	day notice is given to sheriff of objection to scheme	**Creditors' Relief Act, 1990, c. C.45, s. 32(1), (2) [am. S.O. 1994, c. 27, s. 44(1)], (3) [am. S.O. 1994, c. 27, s. 44(2)], (4), (5), (6) [s. 32(6) found in Sch. to the Limitations Act, 2002]:** 32. (1) Where at the time for distribution the money is insufficient to pay all claims in full, the sheriff shall first prepare for examination by the debtor and the debtor's creditors a list of the creditors entitled to share in the distribution, with the amount due to each for principal, interest and costs. (2) The list shall be so arranged as to show the amount payable to each creditor and the total amount to be distributed, and the sheriff shall deliver or send by regular lettermail a copy of the list to each creditor or creditor's solicitor.

Action	Limitation	Accrues From	Statute
			(3) If within 10 days after all the copies have been delivered or posted, or within such further time as the judge may allow, no objection is made as provided by this Act, the sheriff shall make distribution forthwith pursuant to such list. (4) If objection is made, the sheriff shall forthwith distribute rateably so much of the money made, and among such persons, as will not interfere with the effect of the objection in case it should be allowed. (5) Any person affected by the proposed scheme of distribution may contest it by giving, within the time mentioned in subsection (3), a notice in writing to the sheriff stating the person's objection to the scheme and the grounds thereof. (6) The contestant shall within eight days thereafter apply to the judge for an order adjudicating upon the matter in dispute, otherwise the contestation shall be taken to be abandoned.
8.7 A proceeding by a debtor in possession of collateral to redeem it	no limitation	—	**Limitations Act, 2002, S.O. 2002, c. 24, Sch. B, ss. 16(1)(f), (4):** 16. (1) There is no limitation period in respect of, . . . (f) a proceeding by a debtor in possession of collateral to redeem it; 16. (4) This section and section 17 prevail over anything in section 15.
8.8 A proceeding by a creditor in possession of collateral to realize it	no limitation	—	**Limitations Act, 2002, S.O. 2002, c. 24, Sch. B, ss. 16(1)(g), (4):** 16. (1) There is no limitation period in respect of, . . . a proceeding by a creditor in possession of collateral to realize on it; 16. (4) This section and section 17 prevail over anything in section 15.

9. DEFAMATION

Action	Limitation	Accrues From	Statute
9.1 Commence a proceeding in respect of a claim	2 years	day on which the claim was discovered	**Limitations Act, 2002, S.O. 2002, c. 24, Sch. B, ss. 4, 15(2):** 4. Unless this Act provides otherwise, a proceeding shall not be commenced in respect of a claim after the second anniversary of the day on which the claim was discovered. 15. (2) No proceeding shall be commenced in respect of any claim after the 15th anniversary of the day on which the act or omission on which the claim is based took place.

Action	Limitation	Accrues From	Statute
9.2 Notice of action for libel in newspaper or broadcast under Libel and Slander Act (Ont.)	6 weeks	time alleged libel has come to knowledge of plaintiff	**Libel and Slander Act, R.S.O. 1990, c. L.12, ss. 5(1), (3):** 5. (1) No action for libel in a newspaper or in a broadcast lies unless the plaintiff has, within six weeks after the alleged libel has come to the plaintiff's knowledge, given to the defendant notice in writing, specifying the matter complained of, which shall be served in the same manner as a statement of claim or by delivering it to a grown-up person at the chief office of the defendant. . . . (3) This section does not apply to the case of a libel against any candidate for public office unless the retraction of the charge is made in a conspicuous manner at least five days before the election.
9.3 Action for libel in newspaper or broadcast, under Libel and Slander Act (Ont.)	3 months	time libel has come to knowledge of person defamed	**Libel and Slander Act, R.S.O. 1990, c. L.12, s. 6 [s. 6 found in Sch. to the Limitations Act, 2002]:** 6. An action for a libel in a newspaper or in a broadcast shall be commenced within three months after the libel has come to the knowledge of the person defamed, but, where such an action is brought within that period, the action may include a claim for any other libel against the plaintiff by the defendant in the same newspaper or the same broadcasting station within a period of one year before the commencement of the action.

10. EMPLOYMENT STANDARDS

Action	Limitation	Accrues From	Statute
10.1 Commence a proceeding in respect of a claim	2 years	date on which the claim was discovered	**Limitations Act, 2002, S.O. 2002, c. 24, Sch. B, ss. 4, 15(2):** 4. (1) Unless this Act provides otherwise, a proceeding shall not be commenced in respect of a claim after the second anniversary of the day on which the claim was discovered. . . . 15. (2) No proceeding shall be commenced in respect of any claim after the 15th anniversary of the day on which the act or omission on which the claim is based took place.
10.2 Prosecution under Employment Standards Act, 2000 (Ont.)	2 years	date on which the offence was committed or alleged to have been committed	**Employment Standards Act, 2000, S.O. 2000, c. 41, s. 139:** 139. No prosecution shall be commenced under this Act more than two years after the date on which the offence was committed or alleged to have been committed.

Action	Limitation	Accrues From	Statute
10.3 Complaint under Employment Standards Act, 2000 (Ont.)	2 years	date of the contravention	**Employment Standards Act, 2000, S.O. 2000, c. 41, s. 96(3) [re-en 2001, c. 9, Sch. I, s. 1(18)]:** 96. (3) A complaint regarding a contravention that occurred more than two years before the day on which the complaint was filed shall be deemed not to have been filed.
10.4 Order to pay wages or compensation or a notice of contravention under Employment Standards Act, 2000 (Ont.)	2 years [*also see Limitations Act, 2002, ss. 4.15(2)*]	date on which complaint was filed, another employee's complaint was filed, or an inspection was commenced	**Employment Standards Act, 2000, S.O. 2000, c. 41, ss. 81(10), 114(1) [also see ss. 4 and 15(2) of the Limitations Act, 2002]:** 81. (10) A limitation period set out in section 114 prevails over a limitation period in any other Act, unless the other Act states that it is to prevail over this Act. . . . 114. (1) An employment standards officer shall not issue an order to pay wages or compensation or a notice of contravention with respect to a contravention of this Act concerning an employee. (a) if the employee filed a complaint about the contravention, more than two years after the complaint was filed; (b) if the employee did not file a complaint but another employee of the same employer did file a complaint, more than two years after the other employee filed his or her complaint if the officer discovered the contravention with respect to the employee while investigating the complaint; or (c) if the employee did not file a complaint and clause (b) does not apply, more than two years after an employment standards officer commenced an inspection with respect to the employee's employer for the purpose of determining whether a contravention occurred.
10.5 Review by Board of order to pay wages, for compensation or reinstatement, or to comply under Employment Standards Act, 2000 (Ont.)	30 days	date the order, letter advising of the order or letter advising of the refusal to issue an order is served	**Employment Standards Act, 2000, S.O. 2000, c. 41, ss. 116(1) [am. 2001, c. 9, Sch. I, s. 1(25)], (2)-(5) [re-en. 2001, c. 9, Sch. I, s. 1(26)]:** 116. (1) A person against whom an order has been issued under section 103, 104, 106, 107 or 108 is entitled to a review of the order by the Board if, within the period set out in subsection (4), the person, (a) applies to the Board in writing for a review; (b) in the case of an order under section 103, pays the amount owing under the order to the Director in trust or provides the Director with an irrevocable letter of credit acceptable to the Director in that amount; and (c) in the case of an order under section 104, pays the lesser of the amount owing under the order and $10,000 to the Director in trust or provides the Director with an irrevocable letter of credit acceptable to the Director in that amount.

Action	Limitation	Accrues From	Statute
			(2) If an order has been issued under section 103 or 104 with respect to an employee, the employee is entitled to a review of the order by the Board if, within the period set out in subsection (4), the employee applies to the Board in writing for a review. (3) If an employee has filed a complaint alleging a contravention of this Act or the regulations and an order could be issued under section 103, 104 or 108 with respect to such a contravention, the employee is entitled to a review of an employment standards officer's refusal to issue such an order if, within the period set out in subsection (4), the employee applies to the Board in writing for such a review. (4) An application for a review under subsection (1), (2) or (3) shall be made within 30 days after the day on which the order, letter advising of the order or letter advising of the refusal to issue an order, as the case may be, is served. (5) The Board may extend the time for applying for a review under this section if it considers it appropriate in the circumstances to do so and, in the case of an application under subsection (1), (a) the Board has enquired of the Director whether the Director has paid to the employee the wages or compensation that were the subject of the order and is satisfied that the Director has not done so; and (b) the Board has enquired of the Director whether a collector's fees or disbursements have been added to the amount of the order under subsection 128(2) and, if so, the Board is satisfied that fees and disbursements were paid by the person to whom the order was issued.
10.6 Withdraw complaint under the Employment Standards Act, 2000 in order to commence civil proceeding for wrongful dismissal	2 weeks	filing of complaint	**Employment Standards Act, 2000, S.O. 2000, c. 41, s. 97(2), (4):** 97. (2) An employee who files a complaint under this Act alleging entitlement to termination pay or severance pay may not commence a civil proceeding for wrongful dismissal if the complaint and the proceeding would relate to the same termination or severance of employment. . . . (4) Despite subsection (1) and (2), an employee who has filed a complaint may commence a civil proceeding with respect to a matter described in those subsections if he or she withdraws the complaint within two weeks after it is filed.

11. FAMILY LAW

Action	Limitation	Accrues From	Statute
11.1 Commence a proceeding in respect of a claim	2 years	day on which the claim was discovered	**Limitations Act, 2002, S.O. 2002, c. 24, Sch. B, ss. 4, 15(2):** 4. Unless this Act provides otherwise, a proceeding shall not be commenced in respect of a claim after the second anniversary of the day on which the claim was discovered. . . . 15. (2) No proceeding shall be commenced in respect of any claim after the 15th anniversary of the day on which the act or omission on which the claim is based took place.
11.2 Proceedings for offence under Child and Family Services Act (Ont.)	2 years	date on which the offence was committed	**Child and Family Services Act, R.S.O. 1990, c. C.11, s. 176 [s. 176 found in Sch. to the Limitations Act, 2002]:** 176. (1) A person who contravenes subsection 141(1), (2) or (3) (placement for adoption) and a director, officer or employee of a corporation who authorizes, permits or concurs in such a contravention by the corporation is guilty of an offence, whether an order is subsequently made for the child's adoption or not, and on conviction is liable to a fine of not more than $2,000 or to imprisonment for a term of not more than two years, or to both. (2) A person who contravenes subsection 141(4) (receiving child) is guilty of an offence and on conviction is liable to a fine of not more than $2,000 or to imprisonment for a term of not more than two years, or to both. (3) A person who contravenes subsection 143(2) (interference with child) is guilty of an offence and on conviction is liable to a fine of not more than $1,000 or to imprisonment for a term of not more than one year, or to both. (4) A person who contravenes subsection 175 and a director, officer or employee of a corporation who authorizes, permits or concurs in such a contravention by the corporation is guilty of an offence and on conviction is liable to a fine of not more than $25,000 or to imprisonment for a term of not more than tree years, or to both. (5) A proceeding under subsection (1), (2) or (4) shall not be commenced after the expiration of two years after the date on which the offence was, or is alleged to have been committed.

Action	Limitation	Accrues From	Statute
11.3 Application for entitlement to family property	2 years *[see s. 7(3) of Family Law Act (Ont.)]*	termination of marriage	**Family Law Act, R.S.O. 1990, c. F.3, s. 7:** 7. (1) The court may, on the application of spouse, former spouse or deceased spouse's personal representative, determine any matter respecting the spouses' entitlement under section 5. (2) Entitlement under subsections 5(1), (2) and (3) is personal as between the spouses but, (a) an application based on subsection 5(1) or (3) and commenced before a spouse's death may be continued by or against the deceased spouse's estate; and (b) an application based on subsection 5(2) may be made by or against a deceased spouse's estate. (3) An application based on subsection 5(1) or (2) shall not be brought after the earliest of, (a) two years after the day the marriage is terminated by divorce or judgment of nullity; (b) six years after the day the spouses separate and there is no reasonable prospect that they will resume cohabitation; (c) six months after the first spouse's death.
11.4 Make application re entitlement to family property	6 years	day spouses separate and there is no reasonable prospect of resuming cohabitation	**Family Law Act, R.S.O. 1990, c. F.3, s. 7(3) [s. 7(3) found in Sch. to the Limitations Act, 2002]:** 7. (3) An application based on subsection 5(1) or (2) shall not be brought after the earliest of, (a) two years after the day the marriage is terminated by divorce or judgment of nullity; (b) six years after the day the spouses separate and there is no reasonable prospect that they will resume cohabitation; (c) six months after the first spouse's death.
11.5 Application to determine entitlement to family property	6 months	death of first spouse	**Family Law Act, R.S.O. 1990, c. F.3, s. 7(3) [s. 7(3) found in Sch. to the Limitations Act, 2002]:** 7. (3) An application based on subsection 5(1) or (2) shall not be brought after the earliest of, (a) two years after the day the marriage is terminated by divorce or judgment of nullity; (b) six years after the day the spouses separate and there is no reasonable prospect that they will resume cohabitation; (c) six months after the first spouse's death.

Action	Limitation	Accrues From	Statute
11.6 Application for variation	6 months	making of order of support or disposition of another application for variation in respect of same order	**Family Law Act, R.S.O. 1990, c. F.3, s. 37(3):** 37. (3) No application for variation shall be made within six months after the making of the order for support or the disposition of another application for variation in respect of the same order, except by leave of the court.
11.7 Commence a proceeding to obtain support under the Family Law Act or enforce a provision for support or maintenance in a contract or agreement filed under s. 35	No limitation	—	**Limitations Act, 2002, S.O. 2002, c. 24, Sch. B, s. 16(1)(c), (4):** 16. (1) There is no limitation period in respect of, . . . (c) a proceeding to obtain support under the *Family Law Act* or to enforce a provision for support or maintenance contained in a contract or agreement that could be filed under section 35 of that Act; 16. (4) This section and section 17 prevail over anything in section 15.
11.8 Bring motion to suspend operation of support deduction order	30 days	service of notice of intention to enforce order	**Family Responsibility and Support Arrears Enforcement Act, 1996, S.O. 1996, c. 31, s. 21(2)–(4):** **21. (2) The Director shall give notice to the payor of the Director's intention to enforce the support order under this Part.** **(3) The support deduction order shall, 30 days after the notice is served on the payor, be deemed to have been made by the court that made the support order or,** **(a) if the support order was made under the *Divorce Act* (Canada) by a court outside Ontario, by the Ontario Court (General Division) or, where applicable, the Family Court;** **(b) if the support order (other than an order under the *Divorce Act* (Canada) was made by a court outside Ontario, by a court in Ontario that is the same level as the court that has the jurisdiction to make the order enforceable in Ontario;** **(c) if the support order is a domestic contract or patiently agreement, by the Ontario Court (Provincial Division) or the Family Court.** **(4) The payor may, within 30 days after being served with the notice under subsection (2), commence a motion under section 28 in the court that is deemed to have made the support deduction order for its suspension.**
11.9 Appeal any decision under the Interjurisdictional Support Orders Act, 2002 (Ont.) to the proper appellate court	**90 days**	**date the Ontario court's decision is entered**	**Interjurisdictional Support Orders Act, 2002, S.O. 2002, c. 13, s. 40(2):** 40. (2) An appeal shall be commenced within 90 days after the date the Ontario court's decision is entered as a judgment.

12. HIGHWAY TRAFFIC

Action	Limitation	Accrues From	Statute
12.1 Commence a proceeding in respect of a claim	2 years	day on which the claim was discovered	**Limitations Act, 2002, S.O. 2002, c. 24, Sch. B, ss. 4, 15(2):** 4. (1) Unless this Act provides otherwise, a proceeding shall not be commenced in respect of a claim after the second anniversary of the day on which the claim was discovered. . . . 15. (2) No proceeding shall be commenced in respect of any claim after the 15th anniversary of the day on which the act or omission on which the claim is based took place.

13. HIGHWAYS AND STREETS

Action	Limitation	Accrues From	Statute
13.1 Commence a proceeding in respect of a claim	2 years	day on which the claim was discovered	**Limitations Act, 2002, S.O. 2002, c. 24, Sch. B, ss. 4, 5, 15(2):** 4. Unless this Act provides otherwise, a proceeding shall not be commenced in respect of a claim after the second anniversary of the day on which the claim was discovered. 5.(1) A claim is discovered on the earlier of, (a) the day on which the person with the claim first knew (i) that the injury, loss or damage had occurred, (ii) that the injury, loss or damage was caused by or contributed to by an act or omission, (iii) that the act or omission was that of the person against whom the claim is made, and (iv) that, having regard to the nature of the injury, loss or damage, a proceeding would be an appropriate means to seek to remedy it; and (b) the day on which a reasonable person with the abilities and in the circumstances of the person with the claim first ought to have known of the matters referred to in clause (a). (2) A person with a claim shall be presumed to have known of the matters referred to in clause (1)(a) on the day the act or omission on which the claim is based took place, unless the contrary is proved. . . . 15.(2) No proceeding shall be commenced in respect of any claim after the 15th anniversary of the day on which the act or omission on which the claim is based took place.

Action	Limitation	Accrues From	Statute
13.2 Notice of claim against municipality in respect of action for damages that result from the presence of any nuisance on a highway	10 days	occurrence of the injury	**Municipal Act, 2001, S.O. 2001, c. 25, s. 46, s. 44(10):** 46. Subsections 44(6) to (15) apply to an action brought against a municipality for damages that result from the presence of any nuisance on a highway. . . . 44. (10) No action shall be brought for the recovery of damages under subsection (2) unless, within 10 days after the occurrence of the injury, written notice of the claim and of the injury complained of has been served upon or sent by registered mail to, (a) the clerk of the municipality; or (b) if the claim is against two or more municipalities jointly responsible for the repair of the highway or bridge, the clerk of each of the municipalities.

14. HOSPITALS AND HEALTH CARE

Action	Limitation	Accrues From	Statute
14.1 Commence a proceeding in respect of a claim	2 years	day on which the claim was discovered	**Limitations Act, 2002, S.O. 2002, c. 24, Sch. B, ss. 4, 15(2):** 4. Unless this Act provides otherwise, a proceeding shall not be commenced in respect of a claim after the second anniversary of the day on which the claim was discovered. . . . 15. (2) No proceeding shall be commenced in respect of any claim after the 15th anniversary of the day on which the act or omission on which the claim is based took place.
14.2 Proceeding for contravention of Health Facilities Special Orders Act (Ont.)	1 year	date facts upon which the proceeding is based first came to the knowledge of the Minister of Health	**Health Facilities Special Orders Act, R.S.O. 1990, c. H.5, s. 16 [re-en. 2002, c. 18, Sched. 1, s. 7]:** **16. Every individual who knowingly fails to comply with an order under this Act is guilty of an offence and on conviction is liable,** **(a) for a first offence, to a fine of not more than $25,000 or to a term of imprisonment of not more than 12 months, or to both;** **(b) for each subsequent offence, to a fine of not more than $50,000 or to a term of imprisonment of not more than 12 months, or to both.** **(2) Every corporation that knowingly fails to comply with an order under this Act is guilty of an offence and on conviction is liable to a fine of not more than $50,000 for a first offence and to a fine of not more than $200,000 for a subsequent offence.**

Action	Limitation	Accrues From	Statute
			(3) A director or officer of the corporation who authorizes or permits a contravention by the corporation under subsection (2) is guilty of an offence and on conviction is liable to a fine of not more than $50,000 for a first offence and to a fine of not more than $200,000 for a subsequent offence. **(4) The court that convicts a person of an offence under this section may, in addition to any other penalty, order that the person pay compensation or make restitution to any person who suffered a loss as a result of the offence.** **(5) Section 76 of the *Provincial Offences Act* does not apply to a prosecution under this section.**

15. JUDGMENTS AND ORDERS

Action	Limitation	Accrues From	Statute
15.1 Commence a proceeding in respect of a claim	2 years	day on which the claim was discovered	**Limitations Act, 2002, S.O. 2002, c. 24, Sch. B, ss. 4, 15(2):** 4. (1) Unless this Act provides otherwise, a proceeding shall not be commenced in respect of a claim after the second anniversary of the day on which the claim was discovered. . . . 15. (2) No proceeding shall be commenced in respect of any claim after the 15th anniversary of the day on which the act or omission on which the claim is based took place.
15.2 Commence a proceeding to enforce an order of a court or any other order that can be enforced in the same way	no limitation	—	**Limitations Act, 2002, S.O. 2002, c. 24, Sch. B, s. 16(1)(b):** 16. (1) There is no limitation period in respect of, . . . (b) a proceeding to enforce an order of a court, or any other order that may be enforced in the same way as an order of a court;
15.3 Commence a proceeding for a declaration if no consequential relief is sought	no limitation	—	**Limitations Act, 2002, S.O. 2002, c. 24, Sch. B, s. 16(1)(a):** 16. (1) There is no limitation period in respect of, . . . (a) a proceeding for a declaration if no consequential relief is sought;

Action	Limitation	Accrues From	Statute
15.4 Application for registration of foreign judgment in Ontario court having jurisdiction under Reciprocal Enforcement of Judgments Act (Ont.)	6 years	date of judgment	**Reciprocal Enforcement of Judgments Act, R.S.O. 1990, c. R.5, s. 2(1) [s. 2(1) found in Sch. to the Limitations Act, 2002]:** 2. (1) Where a judgment has been given in a court in a reciprocating state, the judgment creditor may apply to any court in Ontario having jurisdiction over the subject-matter of the judgment, or, despite the subject-matter, to the Ontario Court (General Division) at any time within six years after the date of the judgment to have the judgment registered in that court, and on any such application the court may, subject to this Act, order the judgment to be registered.
15.5 Application by judgment debtor to set aside registration of foreign judgment under Reciprocal Enforcement of Judgments Act (Ont.)	1 month	date judgment debtor had notice of registration	**Reciprocal Enforcement of Judgments Act, R.S.O. 1990, c. R.5, s. 6:** 6. In all cases in which registration is made upon an order made without notice, the registering court may on the application of the judgment debtor set aside the registration upon such terms as the court thinks fit, and such application shall be made within one month after the judgment debtor has notice of the registration, and the applicant is entitled to have the registration set aside upon any of the grounds mentioned in section 3.
15.6 Registration of judgment from foreign court	6 years	date of judgment	**Reciprocal Enforcement of Judgments (U.K.) Act, R.S.O. 1990, c. R.6, Sch., art. III, s. 1 [art. III, s. 1 found in Sch. to the Limitations Act, 2002]:** Article III 1. Where a judgment has been given by a court of one Contracting State, the judgment creditor may apply in accordance with Article VI to a court of the other Contracting State at any time within a period of six years after the date of the judgment (or, where there have been proceedings by way of appeal against the judgment, after the date of the last judgment given in those proceedings) to have the judgment registered, and on any such application the registering court shall, subject to such simple and rapid procedures as each Contracting State may prescribe and to the other provisions of this Convention, order the judgment to be registered.

16. LANDLORD AND TENANT

Action	Limitation	Accrues From	Statute
16.1 Commence a proceeding in respect of a claim	2 years	day on which the claim was discovered	**Limitations Act, 2002, S.O. 2002, c. 24, Sch. B, ss. 4, 15(2):** 4. Unless this Act provides otherwise, a proceeding shall not be commenced in respect of a claim after the second anniversary of the day on which the claim was discovered. . . . 15. (2) No proceeding shall be commenced in respect of any claim after the 15th anniversary of the day on which the act or omission on which the claim is based took place.
16.2 Tenant to apply to Tribunal for order	1 year	day alleged conduct giving rise to application occurred	**Tenant Protection Act, 1997, S.O. 1997, c. 24, s. 32(1) [am. 1999, c. 6, s. 62(3); 2005, c. 5, s. 67(4)] (2):** 32. (1) A tenant or former tenant of a rental unit may apply to the Tribunal for any of the following orders: 1. An order determining that the landlord has arbitrarily or unreasonably withheld consent to the assignment or sublet of a rental until to a potential assignee or subtenant. 2. An order determining that the landlord breached the obligations under subsection 24(1). 3. An order determining that the landlord, superintendent or agent of the landlord has illegally entered the rental unit. 4. An order determining that the landlord, superintendent or agent of the landlord has altered the locking system on a door giving entry to the rental unit or the residential complex or caused the locking system to be altered during the tenant's occupancy of the rental unit without giving the tenant replacement keys. 5. An order determining that the landlord, superintendent or agent of the landlord has withhold the reasonable supply of any vital service, care service or food that it is the landlord's obligation to supply under the tenancy agreement or deliberately interfered with the reasonable supply of any vital service, care service or food. 6. An order determining that the landlord, superintendent or agent of the landlord has substantially interfered with the reasonable enjoyment of the rental unit or residential complex for all usual purposes by the tenant or a member of his or her household. 7. An order determining that the landlord, superintendent or agent of the landlord has harassed, obstructed, cocreed, threatened or interfered with the tenant during the tenant's occupancy of the rental unit.

Action	Limitation	Accrues From	Statute
			8. Where a notice under section 51 has been given in bad faith and the tenant vacates the rental unit as a result of the notice, an order determining that the notice has been given in bad faith and neither the landlord, the landlord's spouse nor a child or parent of one of them has occupied the rental unit within a reasonable time after that termination. 9. Where a notice under section 52 has been given in bad faith and the tenant vacates the rental unit as a result of the notice, an order determining that the notice has been given in bad faith and neither the purchaser, the purchaser's spouse nor a child or parent of one of them has occupied the rental unit within a reasonable time after that termination. 10. Where a notice under section 53 has been given in bad faith and the tenant vacates the rental until as a result of the notice, an order determining that the notice has been given in bad faith and the landlord has not demolished, converted or repaired or renovated the rental unit within a reasonable time after that termination. (2) No application may be made under subsection (1) more than one year after the day the alleged conduct giving rise to the application occurred.
16.3 Claim in respect of tenant's goods by tenant's estate	6 months	death of tenant	**Tenant Protection Act, 1997, S.O. 1997, c. 24, s. 50(3), (4), 112:** 50. (3) If, within six months after the tenant's death, the executor or administrator of the estate of the tenant, or if there is no executor or administrator, a member of the tenant's family claims any property of the tenant that the landlord has sold, the landlord shall pay to the estate the amount by which the proceeds of sale exceed the sum of, (a) the landlord's reasonable out of pocket expenses for moving, strong, securing or selling the property; and (b) any arrears of rent. (4) If, within the six month period after the tenant's death, the executor or administrator of the estate of the tenant, or if there is no executor or administrator, a member of the tenant's family claims any property of the tenant that the landlord has retained for the landlord's own use, the landlord shall return the property to the tenant's estate . . . 112. Sections 49 and 50 do not apply if the tenant owns the mobile home.

Action	Limitation	Accrues From	Statute
16.4 Bring motion to Tribunal to set aside order voiding eviction order	10 days	issuance of order voiding eviction order	**Tenant Protection Act, 1997, S.O. 1997, c. 24, s. 72(6) [en. 2000, c. 26, Sch. K, s. 6(17)], (9) [en. 2000, c. 26, Sch. K, s. 6(17)]:** 72. (6) If before the eviction order becomes enforceable the tenant pays the amount due under subsection (4) either in whole to the landlord or in part to the landlord and in part to the Tribunal, the tenant may make a motion to the Tribunal, without notice to the landlord, for an order determining that the tenant has paid the full amount due under subsection (4) and confirming that the eviction order is void under subsection (4). . . . (9) Within 10 days after an order is issued under subsection (6), the landlord may, on notice to the tenant, make a motion to the Tribunal to have the order set aside.
16.5 Tenant to remove abandoned property	30 days	landlord's obtaining order to dispose of abandoned property	**Tenant Protection Act, 1997, S.O. 1997, c. 24, s. 79(1)–(4):** 79. (1) A landlord may dispose of property in a rental unit that a tenant has abandoned and property of persons occupying the rental unit that is in the residential complex in which the rental unit is located in accordance with subsections (2) and (3) if, (a) the landlord obtains an order terminating the tenancy under section 78; or (b) the landlord gives notice to the tenant of the rental unit and to the Tribunal of the landlord's intention to dispose of the property. (2) If the tenant has abandoned the rental unit, the landlord may dispose of any unsafe or unhygienic items immediately.
16.6 Tenant to claim proceeds of abandoned property sold by landlord	6 months	date of giving notice to tenant of intent to dispose of property	**Tenant Protection Act, 1997, S.O. 1997, c. 24, s. 79(1), (7):** 79. (1) A landlord may dispose of property in a rental unit that a tenant has abandoned and property of persons occupying the rental unit that is in the residential complex in which the rental unit is located in accordance with subsections (2) and (3) if, (a) the landlord obtains an order terminating the tenancy under section 78; or (b) the landlord gives notice to the tenant of the rental unit and to the Tribunal of the landlord's intention to dispose of the property. . . .

Action	Limitation	Accrues From	Statute
			(7) If, within six months after the date the notice referred to in clause (1)(b) is given to the tenant and the Tribunal or the order terminating the tenancy is issued, the tenant claims any of his or her property that the landlord has sold, the landlord shall pay to the tenant the amount by which the proceeds of sale exceed the sum of, (a) the landlord's reasonable out of pocket expenses for moving, storing, securing or selling the property; and (b) any arrears of rent.
16.7 Apply to Tribunal for order evicting unauthorized occupant	60 days	time landlord discovers occupancy	**Tenant Protection Act, 1997, S.O. 1997, c. 24, s. 81:** 81. (1) If a tenant transfers the occupancy of a rental unit to a person in a manner other than by an assignment authorized under section 17 or a subletting authorized under section 18, the landlord may apply to the Tribunal for an order evicting the person to whom occupancy of the rental unit was transferred. (2) An application under this section must be made no later than 60 days after the landlord discovers the unauthorized occupancy.
16.8 Apply to Tribunal for order evicting overholding subtenant	60 days	after end of subtenancy	**Tenant Protection Act, 1997, S.O. 1997, c. 24, s. 82:** 82. (1) If a subtenant continues to occupy a rental unit after the end of the subtenancy, the landlord or the tenant may apply to the Tribunal for an order evicting the subtenant. (2) An application under this section must be made within 60 days after the end of the subtenancy.
16.9 Make claim to mobile home or proceeds of mobile home	6 months	giving of notice of intent to sell or retain for own use	**Tenant Protection Act, 1997, S.O. 1997, c. 24, s. 111(2)–(5):** 111. (2) The landlord shall not dispose of a mobile home without first notifying the tenant of the landlord's intention to do so. (a) by registered mail, sent to the tenant's last known mailing address; and (b) by causing a notice to be published in a newspaper having general circulation in the locality in which the mobile home park is located. (3) The landlord may sell, retain for the landlord's own use or dispose of a mobile home in the circumstances described in subsection (1) beginning 60 days after the notices referred to in subsection (2) have been given if the tenant has not made a claim with respect to the landlord's intended disposal.

Action	Limitation	Accrues From	Statute
			(4) If, within six months after the day the notices have been given under subsection (2) the tenant makes a claim for a mobile home which the landlord has already sold, the landlord shall pay to the tenant the amount by which the proceeds of sale exceed the sum of, (a) the landlord's reasonable out of pocket expenses incurred with respect to the mobile home; and (b) any arrears of rent of the tenant. (5) If within six months after the day the notices have been given under subsection (2) the tenant makes a claim for a mobile home which the landlord has retained for the landlord's own use the landlord shall return the mobile home to the tenant.
16.10 Apply for relief in respect of agreed rent increase	2 years	time rent increase becomes effective	**Tenant Protection Act, 1997, S.O. 1997, c. 24, s. 131(1), (2):** 131. (1) A tenant or former tenant may apply to the Tribunal for relief if the landlord and the tenant or former tenant agreed to an increase in rent under section 130 and, (a) the landlord has failed in whole or in part to carry out an undertaking under the agreement; (b) the agreement was based on work that the landlord claimed to have done but did not do; or (c) the agreement was based on services that the landlord claimed to have provided but did not do so. (2) No application may be made under this section more than two years after the rent increase becomes effective.
16.11 Apply for rent reduction	1 year	after reduction or discontinuance of service or facility	**Tenant Protection Act, 1997, S.O. 1997, c. 24, s. 142:** 142. (1) A tenant of a rental unit may apply to the Tribunal for an order for a reduction of the rent charged for the rental unit due to a reduction or discontinuance in services or facilities provided in respect of the rental unit or the residential complex. (2) A former tenant of a rental unit may apply under this section as a tenant of the rental unit if the person was affected by the discontinuance or reduction of the services or facilities while the person was a tenant of the rental unit. (3) The Tribunal shall make lindings in accordance with the prescribed rules and may order, (a) that the rent charged be reduced by a specified amount; (b) that there be a rebate to the tenant of any rent found to have been unlawfully collected by the landlord;

Action	Limitation	Accrues From	Statute
			(c) that the rent charged be reduced by a specified amount for a specified period if there has been a temporary reduction in a service. (4) An order under this section reducing rent takes effect on the day that the discontinuance or reduction first occurred. (5) No application may be made under this section more than one year after a reduction or discontinuance in a service or facility.
16.12 Apply for money collected illegally	1 year	after money collected or retained in violation of Tenant Protection Act (Ont.), Rent Control Act, 1992 (Ont.) or Landlord and Tenant Act, Pt. IV (Ont.)	**Tenant Protection Act, 1997, S.O. 1997, c. 24, s. 144:** 144. (1) A tenant or former tenant of a rental unit may apply to the Tribunal for an order that the landlord, superintendent or agent of the landlord pay to the tenant any money the person collected or retained in contravention of this Act, the *Rent Control Act, 1992* or Part IV of the *Landlord and Tenant Act*. (2) A prospective tenant may apply to the Tribunal for an order under subsection (1). (3) A subtenant may apply to the Tribunal for an order under subsection (1) as if the subtenant were the tenant and the tenant were the landlord. (4) No order shall be made under this section with respect to an application filed more than one year after the person collected or retained money in contravention of this Act, the *Rent Control Act, 1992* or Part IV of the *Landlord and Tenant Act*
16.13 Appeal order of Tribunal	30 days	after being given order	**Tenant Protection Act, 1997, S.O. 1997, c. 24, s. 196(1):** 196. (1) Any person affected by an order of the Tribunal may appeal the order to the Divisional Court within 30 days after being given the order, but only on a question of law.
16.14 Commence proceeding in respect of offence	2 years	date on which facts came to attention of Minister of Municipal Affairs and Housing or date on which alleged **offence committed**	**Tenant Protection Act, 1997, S.O. 1997, c. 24, s. 206(2)(1) [am. 2000, c. 26, Sched. K, s. 6(31)], (8), (9):** **206. (2) Any person who does any of the following is guilty of an offence:** **1. Furnish false or misleading information in any material filed in any proceeding under this Act or provided to the Tribunal, an employee or official of the Tribunal, an inspector, an investigator, the Minister or a designate of the Minister.** . . . **(8) No proceeding shall be commenced respecting an offence under paragraph 1 of subsection (2) more than two years after the date on which the facts giving rise to the offence came to the attention of the Minister.**

Action	Limitation	Accrues From	Statute
			(9) No proceeding shall be commenced respecting any other offence under this section more than two years after the date on which the offence was, or is alleged to have been, committed.
16.15 Application by ex parte motion to have default judgment set aside	**7 days**	**time of service of judgment or order**	**Commercial Tenancies Act, R.S.O. 1990, c. L.7, s. 113(8) [rp 1997, c. 24, s. 213(4)]:** 113. (8) Where the local registrar signs an order or judgment under subsection (7), the respondent may, within seven days after the service thereof, by motion, without notice, apply to the judge to have the order or judgment set aside and the judge may so order upon being satisfied that reasonable grounds for dispute exist.
16.15.1 Application regarding lawfulness of rent or rent increase	1 year	date that rent was first charged or that increase was first charged	**Residential Tenancies Act, 2006, S.O. 2006, c. 17, s. 136** Rent deemed lawful 136. (1) Rent charged one or more years earlier shall be deemed to be lawful rent unless an application has been made within one year after the date that amount was first charged and the lawfulness of the rent charged is in issue in the application. 2006, c. 17, s. 136 (1). Increase deemed lawful (2) An increase in rent shall be deemed to be lawful unless an application has been made within one year after the date the increase was first charged and the lawfulness of the rent increase is in issue in the application. 2006, c. 17, s. 136 (2). s. 122 prevails (3) Nothing in this section shall be interpreted to deprive a tenant of the right to apply for and get relief in an application under section 122 within the time period set out in that section. 2006, c. 17, s. 136 (3).

17. LIMITATIONS OF ACTIONS

Action	Limitation	Accrues From	Statute
17.1 Commence a proceeding in respect of a claim	2 years	day on which the claim was discovered	**Limitations Act, 2002, S.O. 2002, c. 24, Sch. B, ss. 4, 15(2), 24:** 4. (1) Unless this Act provides otherwise, a proceeding shall not be commenced in respect of a claim after the second anniversary of the day on which the claim was discovered. . . . 15. (2) No proceeding shall be commenced in respect of any claim after the 15th anniversary of the day on which the act or omission on which the claim is based took place.

Action	Limitation	Accrues From	Statute
			. . . 24. (1) In this section, "effective date" means the day on which this Act comes into force; "former limitation period" means the limitation period that applied in respect of the claim before the coming into force of this Act. (2) This section applies to claims based on acts or omissions that took place before the effective date and in respect of which no proceeding has been commenced before the effective date. (3) If the former limitation period expired before the effective date, no proceeding shall be commenced in respect of the claim. (4) If the former limitation period did not expire before the effective date and if no limitation period under this Act would apply were the claim based on an act or omission that took place on or after the effective date, there is no limitation period. (5) If the former limitation period did not expire before the effective date and if a limitation period under this Act would apply were the claim based on an act or omission that took place on or after the effective date, the following rules apply: 1. If the claim was not discovered before the effective date, this Act applies as if the act or omission had taken place on the effective date. 2. If the claim was discovered before the effective date, the former limitation period applies. (6) If there was no former limitation period and if a limitation period under this Act would apply were the claim based on an act or omission that took place on or after the effective date, the following rules apply: 1. If the claim was not discovered before the effective date, this Act applies as if the act or omission had taken place on the effective date. 2. If the claim was discovered before the effective date, there is no limitation period.
17.2 The Limitations Act, 2002 will prevail over all other Acts unless a provision establishing a limitation period is listed in the Schedule to the Act	—	—	**Limitations Act, 2002, S.O. 2002, c. 24, Sch. B, s. 19:** 19. (1) A limitation period set out in or under another Act that applies to a claim to which this Act applies is of no effect unless, (a) the provision establishing it is listed in the Schedule to this Act; or (b) the provision establishing it, (i) is in existence on the day this Act comes into force, and (ii) incorporates by reference a provision listed in the Schedule to this Act.

Action	Limitation	Accrues From	Statute
			(2) Subsection (1) applies despite any other Act. (3) The fact that a provision is listed in the Schedule shall not be construed as a statement that the limitation period established by the provision would otherwise apply to a claim as defined in this Act. (4) If there is a conflict between a limitation period established by a provision referred to in subsection (1) and one established by any other provision of this Act, the limitation period established by the provision referred to in subsection (1) prevails. (5) Section 6, 7 and 11 apply, with necessary modifications, to a limitation period established by a provision referred to in subsection (1).
17.2.1 Claim for contribution or indemnity	2 years	date of service of claim of which contribution or indemnity is sought	**Limitations Act, 2002, S.O. 2002, c. 24, Sch. B, s. 18** Contribution and indemnity 18. (1) For the purposes of subsection 5(2) and section 15, in the case of a claim by one alleged wrongdoer against another for contribution and indemnity, the day on which the first alleged wrongdoer was served with the claim in respect of which contribution and indemnity is sought shall be deemed to be the day the act or omission on which that alleged wrongdoer's claim is based took place. Application (2) Subsection (1) applies whether the right to contribution and indemnity arises in respect of a tort or otherwise.
17.3 Limitation period not to run for minors and incapable persons not represented by litigation guardian, or	—	—	**Limitations Act, 2002, S.O. 2002, c. 24, Sch. B, ss. 6–8, 15(4), (5):** 6. The limitation period established by section 4 does not run during any time in which the person with the claim, (a) is a minor; and (b) is not represented by a litigation guardian in relation to the claim. 7. (1) The limitation period established by section 4 does not run during any time in which the person with the claim, (a) is incapable of commencing a proceeding in respect of the claim because of his or her physical, mental or psychological condition; and (b) is not represented by a litigation guardian in relation to the claim. (2) A person shall be presumed to have been capable of commencing a proceeding in respect of a claim at all times unless the contrary is proved.

Action	Limitation	Accrues From	Statute
			(3) If the running of a limitation period is postponed or suspended under this section and the period has less than six months to run when the postponement or suspension ends, the period is extended to include the day that is six months after the day on which the postponement or suspension ends. (4) This section does not apply in respect of a claim referred to in section 10. 8. If a person is represented by a litigation guardian in relation to the claim, section 5 applies as if the litigation guardian were the person with the claim. . . . 15. (4) The limitation period established by subsection (2) does not run during any time in which (a) the person with the claim. (i) is incapable of commencing a proceeding in respect of the claim because of his or her physical, mental or psychological condition, and (ii) is not represented by a litigation guardian in relation to the claim; (b) the person with the claim is a minor and is not represented by a litigation guardian in relation to the claim; or (c) the person against whom the claim is made, (i) wilfully conceals from the person with the claim the fact that injury, loss or damage has occurred, that it was caused by or contributed to by an act or omission or that the act or omission was that of the person against whom the claim is made, or (ii) wilfully misleads the person with the claim as to the appropriateness of a proceeding as a means of remedying the injury, loss or damage. (5) Subject to section 10, the burden of proving that subsection (4) applies is on the person with the claim.
17.4 Effect of acknowledgments under the Limitations Act, 2002	—	—	**Limitations Act, 2002, S.O. 2002, c. 24, Sch. B, s. 13:** 13. (1) If a person acknowledges liability in respect of a claim for payment of a liquidated sum, the recovery of personal property, the enforcement of a charge on personal property or relief from enforcement of a charge on personal property, the act or omission on which the claim is based shall be deemed to have taken place on the day on which the acknowledgment was made.

Action	Limitation	Accrues From	Statute
			(2) An acknowledgment of liability in respect of a claim for interest is an acknowledgment of liability in respect of a claim for the principal and for interest falling due after the acknowledgment is made. (3) An acknowledgment of liability in respect of a claim to realize on or redeem collateral under a security agreement or to recover money in respect of the collateral is an acknowledgment by any other person who later comes into possession of it. (4) A debtor's performance of an obligation under or in respect of a security agreement is an acknowledgment by the debtor of liability in respect of a claim by the creditor for realization on the collateral under the agreement. (5) A creditor's acceptance of a debtor's payment or performance of an obligation under or in respect of a security agreement is an acknowledgment by the creditor of liability in respect of a claim by the debtor for redemption of the collateral under the agreement. (6) An acknowledgment by a trustee is an acknowledgment by any other person who is or who later becomes a trustee of the same trust. (7) An acknowledgment of liability in respect of a claim to recover or enforce an equitable interest in personal property by a person in possession of it is an acknowledgment by any other person who later comes into possession of it. (8) Subject to subsections (9) and (10), this section applies to an acknowledgment of liability in respect of a claim for payment of a liquidated sum even though the person making the acknowledgment refuses or does not promise to pay the sum or the balance of the sum still owing. (9) This section does not apply unless the acknowledgment is made to the person with the claim, the person's agent or an official receiver or trustee acting under the *Bankruptcy and Insolvency Act* (Canada) before the expiry of the limitation period applicable to the claim. (10) Subsections (1), (2), (3), (6) and (7) do not apply unless the acknowledgment is in writing and signed by the person making it or the person's agent. (11) In the case of a claim for payment of a liquidated sum, part payment of the sum by the person against whom the claim is made or by the person's agent has the same effect as the acknowledgment referred to in subsection (10).

Action	Limitation	Accrues From	Statute
17.5 A statute temporarily suspending limitation periods in times of emergency	—	—	**Emergency Management Act, R.S.O. 1990, c. E.9, s. 7.1(1)–(8) [en. S.O. 2002, c. 14, s. 11] [am. 2003, c. 1, s. 14]** 7.1 (1) The purpose of this section is to authorize the Lieutenant Governor in Council to make appropriate orders when, in the opinion of the Lieutenant Governor in Council, victims of an emergency or other persons affected by an emergency need greater services, benefits or compensation than the law of Ontario provides or may be prejudiced by the operation of the law of Ontario. (2) If the conditions set out in subsection (2.1) are satisfied, the Lieutenant Governor in Council may, by order in council made on the recommendation of the Attorney General, but only if the Lieutenant Governor in Council is of the opinion described in subsection (1), (a) temporarily suspend the operation of a provision of a statute, regulation, rule, by-law or order of the Government of Ontario; and (b) if it is appropriate to do so, set out a replacement provision to be in effect during the temporary suspension period only. (2.1) The conditions referred to in subsection (2) are: 1. A declaration has been made under subsection 7(1). 2. The provision, i. governs services, benefits or compensation, including. A. fixing maximum amounts, B. establishing eligibility requirements, C. requiring that something be proved or supplied before services, benefits or compensation become available, D. restricting how often a service or benefit may be provided or a payment may be made in a given time period, E. restricting the duration of services, benefits or compensation or the time period during which they may be provided, ii. establishes a limitation period or a period of time within which a step must be taken in a proceeding, or iii. requires the payment of fees in respect of a proceeding or in connection with anything done in the administration of justice. 3. In the opinion of the Lieutenant Governor in Council, the order in council would facilitate providing assistance to victims of the emergency or would otherwise help victims or other persons to deal with the emergency and its aftermath. (3) The order in council may, if it so provides,

Action	Limitation	Accrues From	Statute
			(a) come into force on the day it is issued; or (b) have retroactive effect to a date no earlier than the beginning of the emergency. (4) Subsection 5(3) of the *Regulations Act* does not apply to the order in council, but the Lieutenant Governor in Council shall take steps to publish the order in council in order to bring it to the attention of affected persons pending publication under the *Regulations Act*. (5) The period of temporary suspension under an order in council shall not exceed 90 days, but the Lieutenant Governor in Council may. (a) before the end of the period of temporary suspension, review the order in council and, if the conditions set out in subsection (2.1) continue to apply, make an order in council renewing the original order in council for a further period of temporary suspension not exceeding 90 days; (b) at any time, make a new order in council under subsection (2) for a further period of temporary suspension not exceeding 90 days. (5.1) An order in council that has previously been renewed under clause (5)(a) may be renewed again, and in that case clause (5)(a) applies with necessary modifications. (6) The order in council may be general or specific in its application. (7) In the event of conflict, the order in council prevails over the statute, regulation, rule, by-law or order to which the temporary suspension relates. (8) If a provision establishing a limitation period or a period of time within which a step must be taken in a proceeding is temporarily suspended by the order in council and the order in council does not provide for a replacement limitation period or period of time, the limitation period or period of time resumes running on the date on which the temporary suspension ends and the temporary suspension period shall not be counted.

18. MOTOR VEHICLES

Action	Limitation	Accrues From	Statute
18.1 Commence a proceeding in respect of a claim	2 years	day on which the claim was discovered	**Limitations Act, 2002, S.O. 2002, c. 24, Sch. B, ss. 4, 15(2):** 4. Unless this Act provides otherwise, a proceeding shall not be commenced in respect of a claim after the second anniversary of the day on which the claim was discovered. . . .

Action	Limitation	Accrues From	Statute
			15. (2) No proceeding shall be commenced in respect of any claim after the 15th anniversary of the day on which the act or omission on which the claim is based took place.
18.2 Proceedings arising out of furnishing false information under the Motor Vehicle Dealers Act (Ont.)	1 year	date facts upon which proceeding based first came to knowledge of Director	**Motor Vehicle Dealers Act, R.S.O. 1990, c. M.42 [to be repealed by 2002, c. 50, Sched. E, ss. 12, 22 (not in force)], s. 22(1), (4), (5):** 22. (1) Every person who, knowingly, (a) furnishes false information in any application under this Act or in any statement or return required to be furnished under this Act or the regulations; (b) fails to comply with any order, direction or other requirement made under this Act; or (c) contravenes any provision of this Act or the regulations. and every director or officer of a corporation who knowingly concurs in such furnishing failure or contravention is guilty of an offence and on conviction is liable to a fine of not more than $25,000 or to imprisonment for a term of not more than one year, or to both . . . (4) No proceeding under clause (1)(a) shall be commenced more than one year after the facts upon which the proceeding is based first came to the knowledge of the Director. (5) No proceeding under clause (1)(b) or (c) shall be commenced more than two years after the time when the subject-matter of the proceeding arose.
18.3 Proceedings arising out of failure to comply with any requirement or contravention of any provision of the Motor Vehicle Dealers Act (Ont.)	2 years	time subject-matter of proceeding arose	**Motor Vehicle Dealers Act, R.S.O. 1990, c. M.42 [to be repealed by 2002, c. 50, Sched. E, ss. 12, 22 (not in force)], s. 22(1), (4), (5):** 22. (1) Every person who, knowingly, (a) furnishes false information in any application under this Act or in any statement or return required to be furnished under this Act or the regulations; (b) fails to comply with any order, direction or other requirement made under this Act; or (c) contravenes any provision of this Act or the regulations, and every director or officer of a corporation who knowingly concurs in such furnishing, failure or contravention is guilty of an offence and on conviction is liable to a fine of not more than $25,000 or to imprisonment for a term of not more than one year, or to both. . . .

Action	Limitation	Accrues From	Statute
			(4) No proceeding under clause (1)(a) shall be commenced more than one year after the facts upon which the proceeding is based first came to the knowledge of the Director. (5) No proceeding under clause (1)(b) or (c) shall be commenced more than two years after the time when the subject-matter of the proceeding arose.

19. MUNCICIPAL CORPORATIONS

Action	Limitation	Accrues From	Statute
19.1 Appeal from order or decision of chief building official	20 days	After order or decision made	**Building Code Act, 1992, S.O. 1992, c. 23, s. 25(1), (2)** Appeal to court 25. (1) A person who considers themself aggrieved by an order or decision made by the chief building official, a registered code agency or an inspector under this Act (except a decision under subsection 8 (3) not to issue a conditional permit) may appeal the order or decision to the Superior Court of Justice within 20 days after the order or decision is made. 2002, c. 9, s. 40 (2). Extension of time (2) A judge to whom an appeal is made may, upon such conditions as the judge considers appropriate, extend the time for making the appeal before or after the time set out in subsection (1), if the judge is satisfied that there is reasonable grounds for the appeal and for applying for the extension. 1992, c. 23, s. 25 (2).

20. NEGLIGENCE

Action	Limitation	Accrues From	Statute
20.1 Commence a proceeding in respect of a claim	2 years	day on which the claim was discovered	**Limitations Act, 2002, S.O. 2002, c. 24, Sch. B, ss. 4, 15(2):** 4. Unless this Act provides otherwise, a proceeding shall not be commenced in respect of a claim after the second anniversary of the day on which the claim was discovered. . . . 15. (2) No proceeding shall be commenced in respect of any claim after the 15th anniversary of the day on which the act or omission on which the claim is based took place.

21. RAILWAYS

Action	Limitation	Accrues From	Statute
21.1 Commence a proceeding in respect of a claim	2 years	day on which the claim was discovered	**Limitations Act, 2002, S.O. 2002, c. 24, Sch. B, ss. 4, 15(2):** 4. Unless this Act provides otherwise, a proceeding shall not be commenced in respect of a claim after the second anniversary of the day on which the claim was discovered. . . . 15. (2) No proceeding shall be commenced in respect of any claim after the 15th anniversary of the day on which the act or omission on which the claim is based took place.

22. REAL PROPERTY

Action	Limitation	Accrues From	Statute
22.1 Call a meeting to elect new board of directors	30 days	registration of amendments to declaration and description creating new phase	**Condominium Act, 1998, S.O. 1998, c. 19, s. 152(6)** Election of directors 152(6) If, 30 days after the registration of the amendments to the declaration and description required for creating a phase, the declarant owns a majority of the units in the corporation, the board shall, at the request of the declarant, call a meeting of owners to elect a new board which shall hold office until a board is elected as required by subsection 43 (1). 1998, c. 19, s. 152(6).

23. REPLEVIN

Action	Limitation	Accrues From	Statute
23.1 Commence a proceeding in respect of a claim	2 years	day on which the claim was discovered	**Limitations Act, 2002, S.O. 2002, c. 24, Sch. B, ss. 4, 15(2):** 4. Unless this Act provides otherwise, a proceeding shall not be commenced in respect of a claim after the second anniversary of the day on which the claim was discovered. . . . 15. (2) No proceeding shall be commenced in respect of any claim after the 15th anniversary of the day on which the act or omission on which the claim is based took place.

Action	Limitation	Accrues From	Statute
23.2 Action for replevin	6 years *[also see Limitations Act, 2002, ss. 4, 15(2)]*	time cause of action arose	**Real Property Limitations Act, R.S.O. 1990, c. L.15 [Title of Act rp. & subs. S.O. 2002, c. 24, Sched. B, s. 26(2)], s. 45(1)(g), (2) [rp. S.O. 2002, c. 24, Sch. B, s. 26(1)] [also see ss. 4 and 15(2) of the Limitations Act, 2002]:** 45. (1) The following actions shall be commenced within and not after the times respectively hereinafter mentioned. . . . (g) an action for trespass to goods or land, simple contract or debt grounded upon any lending or contract without speciality, debt for arrears of rent, detinue, replevin or upon the case other than for slander, within six years after the cause of action arose, . . . (2) Nothing in this section extends to any action where the time for bringing the action is by and statute specially limited.

24. TORTS

Action	Limitation	Accrues From	Statute
24.1 Commence a proceeding in respect of a claim	2 years	day on which the claim was discovered	**Limitations Act, 2002, S.O. 2002, c. 24, Sch. B, ss. 4, 15(2):** 4. Unless this Act provides otherwise, a proceeding shall not be commenced in respect of a claim after the second anniversary of the day on which the claim was discovered. . . . 15. (2) No proceeding shall be commenced in respect of any claim after the 15th anniversary of the day on which the act or omission on which the claim is based took place.
24.2 Commence an action for assault or sexual assault where the plaintiff is incapable of commencing the proceeding because of his or her physical, mental or psychological condition	No limitation	—	**Limitations Act, 2002, S.O. 2002, Sch. B, s. 10:** 10. (1) The limitation period established by section 4 does not run in respect of a claim based on assault or sexual assault during any time in which the person with the claim is incapable of commencing the proceeding because of his or her physical, mental or psychological condition. (2) Unless the contrary is proved, a person with a claim based on an assault shall be presumed to have been incapable of commencing the proceeding earlier than it was commenced if at the time of the assault one of the parties to the assault had an intimate relationship with the person or was someone on whom the person was dependent, whether financially or otherwise.

Action	Limitation	Accrues From	Statute
			(3) Unless the contrary is proved, a person with a claim based on a sexual assault shall be presumed to have been incapable of commencing the proceeding earlier than it was commenced.
24.3 Commence an action for assault or sexual assault where the defendant had charge of the plaintiff, was in a position of trust or authority, or was someone on whom the plaintiff was dependent	No limitation	—	**Limitations Act, 2002, S.O. 2002, Sch. B, s. 16(1)(h), (4):** 16. (1) There is no limitation period in respect of, . . . (h) a proceeding arising from a sexual assault if at the time of the assault one of the parties to it had charge of the person assaulted, was in a position of trust or authority in relation to the person or was someone on whom he or she was dependent, whether financially or otherwise; 16. (4) This section and 17 prevail over anything in section 15.

25. *TRESPASS*

Action	Limitation	Accrues From	Statute
25.1 Commence a proceeding in respect of a claim	2 years	day on which the claim was discovered	**Limitations Act, 2002, S.O. 2002, c. 24, Sch. B, ss. 4, 15(2):** 4. (1) Unless this Act provides otherwise, a proceeding shall not be commenced in respect of a claim after the second anniversary of the day on which the claim was discovered. . . . 15. (2) No proceeding shall be commenced in respect of any claim after the 15th anniversary of the day on which the act or omission on which the claim is based took place.
25.2 Action for trespass to goods or land	6 years *[also see Limitations Act, 2002, ss. 4, 15(2)]*	time cause of action arose	**Real Property Limitations Act, R.S.O. 1990, c. L.15 [Title of Act rp. & subs. S.O. 2002, c. 24, Sched. B, s. 26(2)], s. 45(1)(g), (2) [rp. S.O. 2002, c. 24, Sch. B, s. 26(1)] [also see ss. 4 and 15(2) of the Limitations Act, 2002]:** 45. (1) The following actions shall be commenced within and not after the times respectively hereinafter mentioned. . . . (g) an action for trespass to goods or land, simple contract or debt grounded upon any lending or contract without speciality, debt for arrears of rent, detinue, replevin or upon the case other than for slander, within six years after the cause of action arose, . . . (2) Nothing in this section extends to any action where the time for bringing the action is by and statute specially limited.

Action	Limitation	Accrues From	Statute
			Victims' Right to Proceeds of Crime Act, 1994, S.O. 1994, c. 39 [Act rp. S.O. 2002, c. 2, s. 17], s. 5 [am. 1997, c. 23, s. 14(1); am. S.O. 2002, c. 24, Sch. B, s. 49] [also see ss. 4 and 15(2) of the Limitations Act, 2002]: **5. Despite subsection 61(4) of the *Family Law Act* and section 45 of the *Limitations Act*, a person who considers themselves to be a victim may bring an action for the recovery of damages against an accused or convicted person if the person does so within five years after the date on which the Public Guardian and Trustee first receives money under section 2 in respect of the crime.**

LIMITATION PERIODS
CASE LAW

LIM — *CASE LAW*

Authors' Note: The following case digests relate to various limitation period issues. Cases decided before the *Limitations Act, 2002* may be affected by that statute and should be treated with care.

Limitation Period Cases — Generally

Cassidy v. Belleville Police Services, 2015 ONCA 794, 2015 CarswellOnt 17790, 128 O.R. (3d) 387, [2015] O.J. No. 6096

Discovery of sufficient material facts to trigger the commencement of the limitation period does not depend on precise knowledge of the applicable standard of care.

Lochner v. Toronto Police Services Board, 2015 ONCA 626, 2015 CarswellOnt 13965, 128 O.R. (3d) 318; additional reasons 2015 ONCA 703, 2015 CarswellOnt 15827

Not knowing whether the defendants are culpable or liable for the disclosure of the plaintiff's criminal record to his employer did not prevent the limitation period from running.

Lingard v. Milne-McIsaac, 2015 ONCA 213, 2015 CarswellOnt 4226, 125 O.R. (3d) 118, 71 C.P.C. (7th) 288, 382 D.L.R. (4th) 294, 77 M.V.R. (6th) 1, [2015] I.L.R. I-5722, 331 O.A.C. 258

Where the plaintiff in this motor vehicle case relied on a statement in the police report that the defendant was insured, the limitation period against his own insurer under the uninsured motorist coverage did not begin to run until he discovered the defendant was in fact uninsured.

Ali v. O-Two Medical Technologies Inc., 2013 ONCA 733, 2013 CarswellOnt 17092, 118 O.R. (3d) 321, 369 D.L.R. (4th) 347, 313 O.A.C. 189

Where a party to a contract commits an anticipatory breach by repudiating the contract and the innocent party does not accept the breach but rather presses for performance, the limitation period runs not from the date of the repudiation but rather from the date the repudiating party fails to perform the original contract.

Smith v. Toronto (City) (2005), 13 C.P.C. (6th) 212, 2005 CarswellOnt 1533, 197 O.A.C. 137, 8 M.P.L.R. (4th) 90 (Div. Ct.)

The court dismissed the plaintiff's personal injury action where damage was apparent within days of her fall but no action was brought within the limitation period.

Roy v. North American Leisure Group Inc. (2004), 3 C.P.C. (6th) 387, [2004] O.J. No. 4767, 2004 CarswellOnt 4821, 246 D.L.R. (4th) 306, 192 O.A.C. 209, 73 O.R. (3d) 561 (C.A.)

As a general rule in tort actions, the choice of substantive law is the law of the jurisdiction where the activity occurred even where the application of this rule means a tort claim is statute-barred.

Chenderovitch v. John Doe (2004), 44 C.P.C. (5th) 243, [2004] O.J. No. 681, 2004 CarswellOnt 784, 8 C.C.L.I. (4th) 1, 48 M.V.R. (4th) 190, 183 O.A.C. 284 (C.A.)

In this motor vehicle case, the court permitted the plaintiff to pursue her claim despite the fact that it was commenced more than two years after the plaintiff knew she had a claim for pecuniary damages.

Edwards v. Law Society of Upper Canada (2000), (sub nom. *Edwards v. Law Society of Upper Canada (No. 1))* 48 O.R. (3d) 321, 133 O.A.C. 305, 50 C.P.C. (4th) 231, 2000 CarswellOnt 1963, 36 E.T.R. (2d) 192 (C.A.); leave to appeal refused (2000), 265 N.R. 400 (note), 2000 CarswellOnt 4459, 2000 CarswellOnt 4460, 143 O.A.C. 396 (note) (S.C.C.)

Claims of fraud and fraudulent breach of trust against an estate trustee were not statute-barred despite the passage of more than two years. Where claims against an estate trustee could be found to be negligent (and not fraudulent) and, therefore covered by insurance, the action should not be dismissed on the basis of *plene administravit*.

Dreifelds v. Burton (1998), 38 O.R. (3d) 393, 20 C.P.C. (4th) 17, 108 O.A.C. 262, 156 D.L.R. (4th) 662, 1998 CarswellOnt 935 (C.A.); leave to appeal refused (1998), 232 N.R. 194 (note), 117 O.A.C. 399 (note) (S.C.C.); leave to appeal refused (1998), 232 N.R. 197 (note), 119 O.A.C. 398 (note) (S.C.C.)

This action concerning a scuba diving accident was not subject to the limitation period provided by Canadian maritime law because it was not connected with navigation or shipping.

Aguonie v. Galion Solid Waste Material Inc. (1998), 38 O.R. (3d) 161, 17 C.P.C. (4th) 219, 107 O.A.C. 114, 156 D.L.R. (4th) 222, 1998 CarswellOnt 417, [1998] O.J. No. 459 (C.A.)

The "discoverability rule" applies to all limitation periods to avoid the injustice of precluding an action before the plaintiff is able to sue.

Belanger v. Pittsburgh Penguins Inc. (1998), 17 C.P.C. (4th) 245 (Ont. Gen. Div.)

The court permitted a case to proceed notwithstanding the limitation period under the law of Pennsylvania, where the subject tort occurred, had expired. In international litigation, if the limitation period of the *lex loci delicti* would work an injustice, it does not prevail over the *lex fori*.

Ford v. Baxter International Inc. (1996), 6 C.P.C. (4th) 188 (Ont. Gen. Div.)

Where a breast implant recipient first began to experience pain in 1974 but did not sue until 1994, her claim was dismissed as statute barred.

Stefina v. Dominion of Canada General Insurance Co. (1996), 4 C.P.C. (4th) 190 (Ont. Gen. Div.)

Where the defendant insurer conducted an investigation into whether there was coverage for certain matters, the limitation period commenced when the defendant advised the plaintiff there was coverage. The plaintiff had relied on the defendant to investigate.

Alton Renaissance I v. Talamanca Management Ltd. (1996), 3 C.P.C. (4th) 229 (Ont. Div. Ct.)

Promissory notes executed under corporate seal were held to be subject to a 20-year limitation period.

Kalla v. Wolkowicz (1994), 26 C.P.C. (3d) 131 (Ont. Gen. Div.)

Discussion of the discoverability rule for limitation periods.

Karais v. Guelph (City) (1992), 11 O.R. (3d) 89, 12 C.P.C. (3d) 243 (Gen. Div.)

An action against a municipal corporation commenced beyond the applicable three-month limitation period was permitted to proceed where the words and conduct of the municipality's employee and its insurance adjuster raised triable issues based either on the principle of estoppel or waiver.

Carter v. W.H. Den Ouden NV (1991), 7 C.P.C. (3d) 107 (Ont. Gen. Div.)

The discoverability rule applies to latent damage cases only and not to personal injury cases where the damage incurred is immediately obvious and known to the plaintiff.

Sharma v. Ouellette, 2 C.P.C. (3d) 289, [1991] I.L.R. 1-2762 (Gen. Div.)

Although the plaintiffs' direct action against their insurer had been dismissed as being statute-barred, the plaintiffs were permitted to add their insurer as a party in a related action in order to assert a claim for declaratory relief. That claim was not statute-barred, and as the direct action had not been determined on its merits, the doctrine of *res judicata* did not apply.

Larche v. Middleton (1989), 69 O.R. (2d) 400, 37 C.P.C. (2d) 174 (H.C.); leave to appeal to Ont. Div. Ct. refused 1 W.D.C.P. (2d) 190

The court refused to summarily dismiss a defamation action as limitation-barred, applying the "discoverability rule" to the alleged defamation.

Walton v. Cote (1989), 69 O.R. (2d) 661, 36 C.P.C. (2d) 113, 20 M.V.R. (2d) 171 (H.C.)

Where a limitation period is expressed as a number of years, the period within which an action may be commenced includes but ends on the anniversary of the day of the event giving rise to the action.

Central & Eastern Trust Co. v. Rafuse, [1986] 2 S.C.R. 147, 34 B.L.R. 187, 37 C.C.L.T. 117, 42 R.P.R. 161, 31 D.L.R. (4th) 481, 75 N.S.R. (2d) 109, 186 A.P.R. 109, [1986] R.R.A. 527; varied [1988] 1 S.C.R. 1206, 44 C.C.L.T. xxxiv

A tort action was deemed not to "arise," nor the limitation period to commence, until the damage was discovered or ought with reasonable diligence to have been discovered by the plaintiff; this "discoverability" principle is a rule of general application, and a statutory limitation period of six years "after the cause of action arose" did not bar the plaintiff's claim.

Limitation Period Cases — Re Limitations Act, 2002

Murphy v. Hart, 2018 ONSC 1648, 2018 CarswellOnt 3819 (S.C.J.)

Discoverability applies to claims for contribution and indemnity under s. 18 of the *Limitations Act, 2002*. *Demide v. Canada (Attorney General)*, 2015 ONSC 3000, 2015 CarswellOnt 7529, [2015] O.J. No. 2611 (S.C.J.) followed. *Miaskowski (Litigation Guardian of) v. Persaud*, 2015 ONSC 1654, 2015 CarswellOnt 3313, [2015] O.J. No. 1208 (S.C.J.); additional reasons 2015 ONSC 2776, 2015 CarswellOnt 6202 (S.C.J.); reversed 2015 ONCA 758, 2015 CarswellOnt 16827, [2015] O.J. No. 5817 not followed.

Bailey v. Milo-Food & Agricultural Infrastructure & Services Inc., 2017 ONSC 1789, 2017 CarswellOnt 5109, 138 O.R. (3d) 144, 2017 C.L.L.C. 210-039 (S.C.J.); reversed in part 2017 ONCA 1004, 2017 CarswellOnt 20047, 2018 C.L.L.C. 210-022

The court struck a wrongful dismissal and severance pay claim started more than two years after notice of termination was given, but allowed claims for intentional infliction of mental distress and age discrimination to proceed.

Weinbaum v. Weidberg, 2017 ONSC 1040, 2017 CarswellOnt 3205, 136 O.R. (3d) 537, 67 B.L.R. (5th) 147, 62 C.L.R. (4th) 263, 412 D.L.R. (4th) 326 (Div. Ct.)

A contractual limitation provision can override s. 18 of the *Limitations Act, 2002* and preclude a claim for contribution and indemnity.

Winmill v. Woodstock (Police Services Board), 2017 ONCA 962, 2017 CarswellOnt 19263, 138 O.R. (3d) 641

Where the plaintiff was acquitted of assaulting a police officer and resisting arrest, the court held that the date of acquittal was the discoverability date for his battery and negligent investigation claims.

Presidential MSH Corp. v. Marr, Foster & Co LLP, 2017 ONCA 325, 2017 CarswellOnt 5780, 135 O.R. (3d) 321, [2017] 6 C.T.C. 93, 413 D.L.R. (4th) 391, 2017 D.T.C. 5049

The court applied the appropriateness criteria under s. 5(1)(a)(iv) of the Act and determined that it was not appropriate for the plaintiff to bring its claim against its accountants until the CRA responded to the plaintiff's notice of objection and that it intended to confirm its initial assessment.

Dale v. Frank, 2017 ONCA 32, 2017 CarswellOnt 332, 136 O.R. (3d) 315, [2017] O.J. No. 216; leave to appeal refused 2017 CarswellOnt 15889, 2017 CarswellOnt 15890 (S.C.C.); leave to appeal refused *Melanie Ann Dale, et al. v. Cathy Sheila Frank, et al.*, 2017 CarswellOnt 15891, 2017 CarswellOnt 15892 (S.C.C.)

The court confirmed the test for discoverability set out in *Lawless v. Andersen*, 2011 ONCA 102, 2011 CarswellOnt 626, [2011] O.J. No. 519, and rejected the assertion that a plaintiff must know that the acts or omissions are culpable ones for the claim to be discovered.

407 ETR Concession Co. Ltd. v. Day, 2016 ONCA 709, 2016 CarswellOnt 14831, 133 O.R. (3d) 762, [2016] O.J. No. 5006; leave to appeal refused 2017 CarswellOnt 6258, 2017 CarswellOnt 6259, [2016] S.C.C.A. No. 509

The court enforced a 15-year contractual limitation period. Parties may by contract extend the statutory two-year limitation period. They may shorten it if it is a "business agreement" but not if one party is a consumer.

Weinbaum v. Weidberg, 2017 ONSC 1040, 2017 CarswellOnt 3205, 136 O.R. (3d) 537, 67 B.L.R. (5th) 147, 62 C.L.R. (4th) 263, 412 D.L.R. (4th) 326 (Div. Ct.)

Section 18 (contribution and indemnity) is subject to the law in *Giffels Associates Ltd. v. Eastern Construction Co.*, 1978 CarswellOnt 381, 1978 CarswellOnt 595, [1978] 2 S.C.R. 1346, 4 C.C.L.T. 143, 5 C.P.C. 223, 84 D.L.R. (3d) 344, 19 N.R. 298. Accordingly, the right of a defendant to claim contribution and indemnity is lost where the plaintiff's rights to advance a claim have been extinguished by contract.

Independence Plaza 1 Associates, L.L.C. v. Figliolini, 2017 ONCA 44, 2017 CarswellOnt 374, 136 O.R. (3d) 202, 410 D.L.R. (4th) 747

A two-year limitation period applies to actions on foreign judgments and begins to run, at the earliest, when the time to appeal expires, or if an appeal is made, on the date of the appeal decision.

Crombie Property Holdings Ltd. v. McColl-Frontenac Inc., 2017 ONCA 16, 2017 CarswellOnt 202, 6 C.E.L.R. (4th) 1, 406 D.L.R. (4th) 252; leave to appeal refused *Avondale Stores Ltd. v. Crombie Property Holdings Ltd.*

(June 1, 2017), Doc. 37473, 2017 CarswellOnt 8290, 2017 CarswellOnt 8291, [2017] S.C.C.A. No. 85

The court permitted this hydrocarbon contamination claim to proceed where the plaintiff did not know of the contamination more than two years before commencing the litigation.

Galota v. Festival Hall Developments Ltd., 2016 ONCA 585, 2016 CarswellOnt 11684, 133 O.R. (3d) 35, 58 C.C.L.I. (5th) 78, 53 C.L.R. (4th) 175, 352 O.A.C. 140

In this occupier's liability case, the plaintiff's claim against the landlord was not discoverable until she had examined the tenant. The lack of investigation by the plaintiff prior to discoveries was not a stand-alone ground to find the claim out of time.

Grant v. Equifax Canada Co., 2016 ONCA 500, 2016 CarswellOnt 10240, 132 O.R. (3d) 318; leave to appeal refused (March 23, 2017), Doc. 37327, 2017 CarswellOnt 4218, 2017 CarswellOnt 4219 (S.C.C.)

The *Limitations Act, 2002* has no application to the *Consumer Reporting Act*, R.S.O. 1990, c. C.33. Debts over two years old would not be removed from the applicant's credit score.

1702108 Ontario Inc. v. 3283313 Canada Inc., 2016 ONCA 420, 2016 CarswellOnt 8415, 132 O.R. (3d) 237

The court found a defendant's e-mail did not acknowledge liability for a liquidated amount for purposes of s. 13 of the *Limitations Act, 2002*.

Lauesen v. Silverman, 2016 ONCA 327, 2016 CarswellOnt 6786, 130 O.R. (3d) 665, 85 C.P.C. (7th) 257

The plaintiff's claim against her former lawyer for making an improvident settlement was not discovered until she obtained an expert opinion that her injuries warranted more compensation.

Brown v. Baum, 2016 ONCA 325, 2016 CarswellOnt 6735, 84 C.P.C. (7th) 231, 397 D.L.R. (4th) 161, 348 O.A.C. 251

In a case where a physician continued to treat a patient to correct damage occurring in a surgery, the limitation period did not begin to run until after the last ameliorative surgery.

Cook v. Joyce, 2016 ONSC 2164, 2016 CarswellOnt 4885, 130 O.R. (3d) 114 (S.C.J.); reversed 2017 ONCA 49, 2017 CarswellOnt 571

The plaintiff's claim arising from an alleged sexual assault was not barred as it was not until she spoke to her lawyer that she obtained substantial awareness of the harm she suffered. Furthermore, the defendant did not show that the plaintiff had the capacity of commencing the proceeding earlier.

Arcelormittal Dofasco Inc. v. Industrial Alliance Insurance and Financial Services Inc., 2016 ONCA 224, 2016 CarswellOnt 4245, 129 O.R. (3d)

792, 2016 C.E.B. & P.G.R. 8173 (headnote only), [2016] I.L.R. I-5885, 346 O.A.C. 196, [2016] O.J. No. 1505

In a dispute between two insurers, the secondary payor insurer's claim was not barred as it could not have reasonably known it had a claim until the first payor insurer's policy was disclosed.

Bonaccorso v. Optimum Insurance Co. Inc., 2016 ONCA 34, 2016 CarswellOnt 361, 129 O.R. (3d) 544, 59 C.C.L.I. (5th) 111

The appellant's claim for income replacement benefits was barred as she commenced her claim more than two years after being advised that her benefits were being discontinued.

Hughes v. Dyck, 2016 ONSC 901, 2016 CarswellOnt 2413, 129 O.R. (3d) 495 (S.C.J.)

Claims for contribution and indemnity under s. 18(1) are not subject to the principles of discoverability.

Novello v. Glick, 2016 ONSC 975, 2016 CarswellOnt 1760, 129 O.R. (3d) 275 (Div. Ct.)

The court dismissed this dental malpractice claim. There is no blanket rule that in all medical malpractice cases, the limitation period runs from the date the relationship ends.

Daverne v. John Switzer Fuels Ltd., 2015 ONCA 919, 2015 CarswellOnt 19750, 128 O.R. (3d) 188, 52 B.L.R. (5th) 1, 57 C.C.L.I. (5th) 79, [2016] I.L.R. I-5841, 344 O.A.C. 123

The court held that a contractual one-year limitation in an insurance policy overrode the statutory two-year limitation period.

Brown v. Wahl, 2015 ONCA 778, 2015 CarswellOnt 17253, 128 O.R. (3d) 583, 128 O.R. (3d) 588

Lawless v. Anderson, 2011 ONCA 102, 2011 CarswellOnt 626, 81 C.C.L.T. (3d) 220, 276 O.A.C. 75, [2011] O.J. No. 519 did not establish a new four-part test for discoverability in respect of professional malpractice claims. The test remains when a prospective plaintiff has all of the material facts necessary to determine that she had *prima facie* grounds that a prospective defendant had been negligent.

Chelli-Greco v. Rizk, 2015 ONSC 6963, 2015 CarswellOnt 17431, 128 O.R. (3d) 136 (S.C.J.); additional reasons 2016 ONSC 520, 2016 CarswellOnt 850 (S.C.J.); affirmed 2016 ONCA 489, 2016 CarswellOnt 9670

Where a dentist repeatedly and negligently told the plaintiff that her problems were due to poor dental hygiene, the court held the plaintiff's claim was not discovered until the dentist-patient relationship ended.

Hodaie v. RBC Dominion Securities, 2011 ONSC 6881, 2011 CarswellOnt 14418, 108 O.R. (3d) 140, [2011] O.J. No. 5282 (S.C.J.); additional reasons 2011 ONSC 1721, 2012 CarswellOnt 4141 (S.C.J.); affirmed 2012 ONCA 796, 2012 CarswellOnt 14482

It is not possible to contract out of s. 11 of the *Limitations Act, 2002* which provides limitation periods are suspended if the parties agree to have an independent third party assist them in resolving their dispute.

Beuthling v. Hayes, 2011 ONSC 1203, 2011 CarswellOnt 1169, 17 C.P.C. (7th) 176, [2011] O.J. No. 858 (S.C.J.)

A claim against a criminal lawyer for incompetence resulting in a wrongful conviction is not "discovered" for purposes of s. 5 of the *Limitations Act, 2002* until it is determined that the conviction is wrongful.

Commission de la Construction du Québec v. Access Rigging Services Inc., 2010 ONSC 5897, 2010 CarswellOnt 8852, 104 O.R. (3d) 313, 7 C.P.C. (7th) 365 (S.C.J.)

The two-year limitation period in the *Limitations Act, 2002* applies to foreign judgments. The court dismissed an Ontario action to enforce a Quebec judgment where the Ontario action was commenced more than two years after the Quebec judgment.

i Trade Finance Holdings Inc. v. Ramsackal (2009), 2009 CarswellOnt 994, 74 C.P.C. (6th) 391 (S.C.J.)

Where the plaintiff obtained judgment for fraud, a proceeding to enforce the judgment by tracing the proceeds of the fraud was held to be subject to no limitation period as provided in s. 16(1)(b) of the *Limitations Act, 2002*.

Camarata v. Morgan, [2009] O.J. No. 621, 2009 CarswellOnt 770, 94 O.R. (3d) 496, 69 C.P.C. (6th) 31, 78 M.V.R. (5th) 165, 2009 ONCA 38, (sub nom. *Camarata Estate v. Morgan)* 246 O.A.C. 235 (C.A.)

Where a person dies after a motor vehicle accident, the two-year limitation period from the date of the accident under the *Limitation Act, 2002* applies, not the two-year limitation period from the date of death under the *Trustee Act*, R.S.O. 1990, c. T23.

Placzek v. Green, 2009 ONCA 83, 2009 CarswellOnt 383, [2009] O.J. No. 326, 245 O.A.C. 220, 69 C.P.C. (6th) 42, 307 D.L.R. (4th) 441 (C.A.)

Where motor vehicle collision occurred before the *Limitations Act, 2002* came into force, and an action was commenced after the Act was in force, a counterclaim for contribution and indemnity was held to be subject to the usual two-year period, and not subject to the transition provisions of the Act.

York Condominium Corp., No. 382 v. Jay-M Holdings Ltd., 2007 CarswellOnt 345, 220 O.A.C. 311, 84 O.R. (3d) 414, 30 M.P.L.R. (4th) 161, 59 C.L.R. (3d) 15, 36 C.P.C. (6th) 233, 2007 ONCA 49 (C.A.); additional reasons at (2007), 2007 CarswellOnt 1775, [2007] O.J. No. 240, 59 C.L.R. (3d) 29, 31 M.P.L.R. (4th) 218 (C.A.); leave to appeal refused (2007), 2007

CarswellOnt 5635, 2007 CarswellOnt 5636, 378 N.R. 391 (note), 245 O.A.C. 398 (note) (S.C.C.)

Under the transition provisions in the *Limitation Act, 2002*, the limitation period for a claim which was not discovered before January 1, 2004 begins to run on January 1, 2004. The plaintiff was therefore permitted to maintain an action for an alleged act of negligence that occurred over 15 years previously.

Limitation Period Cases — Various Statutes

John v. Ballingall, 2017 ONCA 579, 2017 CarswellOnt 10611, 136 O.R. (3d) 305, 415 D.L.R. (4th) 520

The notice requirements in the *Libel and Slander Act*, R.S.O. 1990, c. L.12 apply to an online newspaper article. The time that a plaintiff must give notice and bring an action begins to run when the libel has come to the knowledge of the plaintiff.

Azzeh (Litigation Guardian of) v. Legendre, 2017 ONCA 385, 2017 CarswellOnt 7165, 135 O.R. (3d) 721; leave to appeal refused *Julia A. Gagnon, et al. v. City of Greater Sudbury, et al.*, 2018 CarswellOnt 2058, 2018 CarswellOnt 2059 (S.C.C.)

In a motor vehicle case commenced by a person under a disability, the court dismissed the claim against the city for failure to keep a road in a proper state of repair, due to the failure to give notice within ten days of the occurrence.

Harvey v. Talon International Inc., 2017 ONCA 267, 2017 CarswellOnt 4549, 137 O.R. (3d) 184, 412 D.L.R. (4th) 553, 81 R.P.R. (5th) 1

The claim for the deposit on a condominium unit was within the definition of an action for recovery of land under the *Real Property Limitations Act*, R.S.O. 1990, c. L.15 and therefore the 10-year limitation period applied.

Roulston v. McKenny, 2017 ONCA 9, 2017 CarswellOnt 16, 135 O.R. (3d) 632, 407 D.L.R. (4th) 157, 23 E.T.R. (4th) 187

The doctrine of fraudulent concealment applied to the actions of the estate trustee with the result that the two-year limitation period under the *Trustee Act*, R.S.O. 1990, c. T.23 was tolled.

Bonilla v. Preszler, 2016 ONCA 759, 2016 CarswellOnt 16115, 134 O.R. (3d) 478; leave to appeal refused *Bonilla v. Personal Insurance Company of Canada*, 2017 CarswellOnt 4222, 2017 CarswellOnt 4223 (S.C.C.)

The limitation period to pay income replacement benefits ("IRBs") is triggered by the refusal of an insurer to pay the IRBs claim. It is not a rolling limitation period.

Watkins v. Western Assurance Co., 2016 ONSC 2574, 2016 CarswellOnt 13678, 133 O.R. (3d) 381, [2016] I.L.R. I-5908 (S.C.J.)

A minor dependent was barred from claiming accident benefits, as he failed to comply with the statutory timelines for the filing of an application. In addition, he brought the action outside the two-year limitation period.

Fanshawe College of Applied Arts and Technology v. AU Optronics Corp., 2016 ONCA 621, 2016 CarswellOnt 12776, 132 O.R. (3d) 81, 407 D.L.R. (4th) 128, 351 O.A.C. 308

Subsection 36(4)(a)(i) of the *Competition Act*, R.S.C 1985, c. C-34 is subject to the discoverability principle. A statutory limitation period will generally be subject to the discoverability principle when the running of the limitation period is linked either to the plaintiff's knowledge about an event or to an event related to the plaintiff's cause of action.

Elaiathamby v. State Farm Mutual Automobile Insurance Co., 2016 ONSC 2258, 2016 CarswellOnt 6389, 130 O.R. (3d) 535 (S.C.J.)

The plaintiff's added claim for punitive damages for bad faith and for negligence in the handling of his accident benefits claim was barred by the limitation period in s. 281.1(1) of the *Insurance Act*, R.S.O. 1990, c. I.8.

Intact Insurance Co. of Canada v. Lombard General Insurance Co. of Canada, 2015 ONCA 764, 2015 CarswellOnt 20062, 128 O.R. (3d) 658, 55 C.C.L.I. (5th) 94, 393 D.L.R. (4th) 329, 89 M.V.R. (6th) 1, 341 O.A.C. 240; leave to appeal refused *Zurich Insurance Co. v. TD General Insurance Co.* (May 5, 2016), Doc. 36803, 2016 CarswellOnt 7204, 2016 CarswellOnt 7205, [2016] S.C.C.A. No. 11; leave to appeal refused *Lombard General Insurance Co. of Canada v. Intact Insurance Co. of Canada* (May 5, 2016), Doc. 36804, 2016 CarswellOnt 7206, 2016 CarswellOnt 7207, [2016] S.C.C.A. No. 10

The doctrine of laches cannot defeat a "loss transfer claim" made under s. 275 of the *Insurance Act*, R.S.O. 1990, c. I.8.

Conde v. Ripley, 2015 ONSC 3342, 2015 CarswellOnt 7607, 125 O.R. (3d) 689, 57 R.P.R. (5th) 146, [2015] O.J. No. 2627 (S.C.J.); additional reasons 2015 ONSC 5250, 2015 CarswellOnt 12592 (S.C.J.)

A claim under the *Fraudulent Conveyance Act*, R.S.O. 1990, c. F.29 regarding real property is subject to the ten-year limitation period in the *Real Property Limitations Act*, R.S.O. 1990, c L.15.

Buik v. Canasia Power Corp, 2015 ONCA 352, 2015 CarswellOnt 7061, 73 C.P.C. (7th) 235, 9 E.T.R. (4th) 1

Section 38(3) of the *Trustee Act* does not apply to promissory notes that mature after the creditor dies. The cause of action is that of the estate, not the deceased.

Seif v. Toronto (City), 2015 ONCA 321, 2015 CarswellOnt 7170, 125 O.R. (3d) 481, 74 C.P.C. (7th) 74, 36 M.P.L.R. (5th) 18, 334 O.A.C. 339

The court permitted this slip-and-fall action to continue despite the plaintiff's failure to give notice to the city within ten days of her injury. The issue of prejudice was left for trial.

Sakka (Litigation Guardian of) v. Air France, 2011 ONSC 1995, 2011 CarswellOnt 2129, 18 C.P.C. (7th) 150 (S.C.J.)

The two-year limitation period under the *Warsaw Convention* is not tolled while the plaintiff is under disability.

Mosregion Investments Corp. v. Ukraine International Airlines, 2010 ONCA 715, 2010 CarswellOnt 8123, 270 O.A.C. 152, 93 C.P.C. (6th) 19

The two-year limitation period in the *Warsaw Convention* regarding carriage by air is satisfied by commencing the proceeding. It is not necessary to serve the originating process within two years.

Lewis v. Bangma Estate, 2010 ONSC 878, 2010 CarswellOnt 712, (sub nom. *B.L. (P.T.) v. B. (P.) Estate)* 100 O.R. (3d) 110, 82 R.F.L. (6th) 296 (S.C.J.); leave to appeal refused 2010 ONSC 3614, 2010 CarswellOnt 5588, 103 O.R. (3d) 59 (S.C.J.); additional reasons 2010 ONSC 4723, 2010 CarswellOnt 6407, 61 E.T.R. (3d) 322 (S.C.J.)

In an action involving sexual assault, the court found that it was not plain and obvious that the claim against the deceased's estate was statute barred by operation of s. 38(3) of the *Trustee Act*, R.S.O. 1990, c. T.23.

Yugraneft Corp. v. Rexx Management Corp., 2010 SCC 19, 2010 CarswellAlta 949, 2010 CarswellAlta 950, [2010] 1 S.C.R. 649, 482 A.R. 1, 401 N.R. 341, 490 W.A.C. 1, [2010] 6 W.W.R. 387, 318 D.L.R. (4th) 257, 22 Alta. L.R. (5th) 166, 84 C.P.C. (6th) 201, 68 B.L.R. (4th) 1

A foreign arbitral award is not a judgment or court order and, under Alberta law, is therefore subject to a two-year limitation period, not a ten-year limitation period.

Alexis v. Darnley, 2009 ONCA 847, 2009 CarswellOnt 7518, [2009] O.J. No. 5170, 100 O.R. (3d) 232, 79 C.P.C. (6th) 10, 259 O.A.C. 148; leave to appeal refused 2010 CarswellOnt 2637, 2010 CarswellOnt 2638, 407 N.R. 397 (note), 271 O.A.C. 399 (note) (S.C.C.)

General limitation periods apply to claims for personal remedies under s. 24(1) of the *Charter*.

Bikur Cholim Jewish Volunteer Services v. Langston, 2009 CarswellOnt 1105, 2009 ONCA 196 (C.A.)

The court held that a claim against one executor based on the fraud of another executor was barred by the limitation period in s. 38(3) of the *Trustee Act*, R.S.O. 1990, c. T.23.

Kramarz v. KMH Cardiology & Diagnostic Centres (2007), 51 C.P.C. (6th) 343, 2007 CarswellOnt 5430, 87 O.R. (3d) 120 (S.C.J.)

The court dismissed this action based on the two-year limitation period in s. 38(3) of the *Trustee Act*, which is not affected by the *Limitations Act, 2002*.

Castillo v. Castillo (2005), 21 C.P.C. (6th) 50, 2005 CarswellAlta 1887, 2005 CarswellAlta 1888, [2005] S.C.J. No. 68, 343 N.R. 144, 52 Alta. L.R. (4th) 199, 260 D.L.R. (4th) 439, 26 M.V.R. (5th) 1, [2005] 3 S.C.R. 870, 2005 SCC 83, 36 C.C.L.T. (3d) 167, 376 A.R. 224, 360 W.A.C. 224, [2006] 3 W.W.R. 595

Where an Alberta resident involved in an accident in California commenced an action in Alberta within Alberta's two-year limitation period but after the one-year limitation applicable in California, the Alberta action was dismissed as statute-barred.

Giroux Estate v. Trillium Health Centre (2005), 74 O.R. (3d) 341, 2005 CarswellOnt 241, 30 C.C.L.T. (3d) 88, 13 E.T.R. (3d) 1, 194 O.A.C. 231, 249 D.L.R. (4th) 662, [2005] O.J. No. 226 (C.A.); additional reasons at (2005), 2005 CarswellOnt 721, 7 C.P.C. (6th) 358 (C.A.)

The court dismissed the defendants' motion to strike out the statement of claim on the basis that the common law doctrine of fraudulent concealment can be used to toll the limitation period prescribed by s. 38(3) of the *Trustee Act* and that the facts as pleaded are capable of supporting a finding of fraudulent concealment.

Coutanche v. Napoleon Delicatessen (2004), 49 C.P.C. (5th) 34, 2004 CarswellOnt 2655, 72 O.R. (3d) 122, 8 M.V.R. (5th) 193, 188 O.A.C. 15 (C.A.); additional reasons at (2004), 2004 CarswellOnt 4731, 2 C.P.C. (6th) 224, 8 M.V.R. (5th) 206 (C.A.)

The court adjourned to trial several issues regarding the extension of the limitation period under the *Family Law Act*.

Lax v. Lax (2004), 70 O.R. (3d) 520, [2004] O.J. No. 1700, 2004 CarswellOnt 1633, 239 D.L.R. (4th) 683, 186 O.A.C. 20, 3 R.F.L. (6th) 387, 50 C.P.C. (5th) 266 (C.A.); additional reasons at (2004), [2004] O.J. No. 5146, 2004 CarswellOnt 5343, 247 D.L.R. (4th) 1, 4 C.P.C. (6th) 194, 75 O.R. (3d) 482, 12 R.F.L. (6th) 112 (C.A.)

Under the former *Limitations Act*, R.S.O. 1990, the limitation period for an action to enforce of a foreign judgment is six years after the judgment debtor returns to Ontario.

Elliott v. Canadian Forces Housing Agency (2003), 68 O.R. (3d) 661, 2003 CarswellOnt 5172 (C.A.)

Where there was a genuine issue whether the discoverability principle applied to postpone the commencement of the limitation period under section 269(1) of the *National Defence Act*, the court set aside a summary judgment which had been granted in favour of the defendant.

Berendsen v. Ontario, 13 C.P.C. (5th) 187, 2001 CarswellOnt 3338, 2001 CarswellOnt 3339, 2001 SCC 55, 204 D.L.R. (4th) 318, 275 N.R. 175, 150 O.A.C. 270, 8 C.C.L.T. (3d) 1, 42 C.E.L.R. (N.S.) 1, [2001] 2 S.C.R. 849

Since the plaintiffs' claim did not relate to the exercise by the province of a public power or duty, the six-month limitation period in the *Public Authorities Protection Act* did not apply and the dismissal of the plaintiffs' action was, therefore, overturned.

Mattick Estate v. Ontario (Minister of Health) (2001), 8 C.P.C. (5th) 39, 2001 CarswellOnt 1, [2001] O.J. No. 21, 195 D.L.R. (4th) 540, 52 O.R. (3d) 221, 139 O.A.C. 149 (C.A.)

On appeal, the plaintiff was found to have complied with the notice requirements of the *Proceedings Against the Crown Act* by providing a notice identifying the claim even though the notice did not express an intention to commence legal proceedings.

Girsberger v. Kresz (2000), 47 O.R. (3d) 145, 45 C.P.C. (4th) 77, 2000 CarswellOnt 349, [2000] O.J. No. 266 (S.C.J.); affirmed (2000), 50 O.R. (3d) 157, 1 C.P.C. (5th) 250, 2000 CarswellOnt 4506, 143 O.A.C. 228 (C.A.)

An *in personam* foreign judgment should be characterized as a "judgment" within the meaning of the *Limitations Act* and a 20-year limitation period applies.

Waschkowski v. Hopkinson Estate (2000), 47 O.R. (3d) 370, 184 D.L.R. (4th) 281, 129 O.A.C. 287, 32 E.T.R. (2d) 308, 44 C.P.C. (4th) 42, 2000 CarswellOnt 470, [2000] O.J. No. 470 (C.A.)

The discoverability principle does not apply to the two-year limitation period contained in the *Trustee Act*, R.S.O. 1990, c. T.23 regarding claims on behalf of deceased persons.

Smith Estate v. College of Physicians & Surgeons (Ontario) (1998), 28 C.P.C. (4th) 389, 115 O.A.C. 146, 167 D.L.R. (4th) 78, 41 O.R. (3d) 481, 26 E.T.R. (2d) 103, 1998 CarswellOnt 4206 (C.A.); leave to appeal refused (1999), 243 N.R. 396 (note), 127 O.A.C. 397 (note) (S.C.C.)

The wife and trustee of the estate of the deceased brought an action seeking damages for the wrongful death of the deceased, *Family Law Act* damages for herself and her children. The action was commenced outside of the two-year period provided by the *Trustee Act*. The "principal claim" on behalf of the deceased was statute barred and, as a result, the *Family Law Act* derivative claims were also statute-barred.

Grenier v. Canadian General Insurance Co. (1999), 118 O.A.C. 204, 43 O.R. (3d) 715, 9 C.C.L.I. (3d) 225, 32 C.P.C. (4th) 267, 1999 CarswellOnt 789, [1999] O.J. No. 852 (C.A.)

Although the discoverability rule is a rule of interpretation and not a general substantive rule, it is a strong rule. The court held the discoverability rule applied to the limitation period contained in s. 258(2) of the *Insurance Act*, R.S.O. 1990, c. I.8.

Appleyard v. Ontario (1999), 28 C.P.C. (4th) 329, 1999 CarswellOnt 1129, [1999] O.J. No. 3940 (Gen. Div.); affirmed (1999), 38 C.P.C. (4th) 309, 1999 CarswellOnt 2771, [1999] O.J. No. 3942 (C.A.)

The court refused to dismiss a slip-and-fall action by a prisoner against a prison for failure to provide the notice required by the *Proceedings Against the Crown Act*. The rules of the prison restricted his ability to retain counsel, although he persevered and ultimately did retain counsel after 56 days. Further, it was likely the prison conducted a timely investigation of the incident.

Des Champs v. Prescott-Russell (Conseil des écoles séparées catholiques de langue française) (January 20, 1997), Docs. CA C17424, C17720 (Ont. C.A.); leave to appeal allowed (1997), 108 O.A.C. 159 (note), 224 N.R. 317 (note) (S.C.C.); leave to appeal allowed (1997), (sub nom. *Abouchar v. Conseil scolaire de langue française d'Ottawa-Carleton)* 109 O.A.C. 200 (note), (sub nom. *Abouchar v. Conseil scolaire de langue française d'Ottawa-Carleton)* 225 N.R. 159 (note) (S.C.C.)

The court dismissed an action by separate school superintendents whose positions were declared redundant and who were assigned to be school principals where the action was not commenced within the six-month limitation period set by the *Public Authorities Protection Act*.

Smallwood v. Hill (1997), (sub nom. *Smallwood (Litigation Guardian of) v. Hill)* 31 O.R. (3d) 769, 96 O.A.C. 278 (Ont. C.A.); leave to appeal refused (1997), 104 O.A.C. 319 (note), 223 N.R. 223 (note) (S.C.C.)

The court extended the limitation period under the *Canada Shipping Act* where the plaintiff had a *prima facie* case and the defendants would suffer no real prejudice.

Corkhill Estate v. Public Trustee (1996), 30 O.R. (3d) 30 (Gen. Div.)

Where the plaintiff exercised reasonable diligence and did not discover that they had a right of action against the deceased's employer until after the death of the deceased, the court held that the discoverability rule applied and granted the plaintiff's motion to add the deceased's employer as a defendant.

Gluchowski v. McEniry & Eisenberg (1996), 48 C.P.C. (3d) 290, 2 O.T.C. 344 (Gen. Div.)

The plaintiff, treated by the defendant chiropractor in 1987, did not issue a statement of claim until 1994. In response to the defendant's motion to have the action dismissed as statute barred, the plaintiff relied on the discoverability principle arguing that it was not until he received a doctor's letter in 1991 that he discovered that he had a cause of action and arguing that he instituted proceedings three years after the date of the letter within the six-year limitation period required by the *Limitations Act*. It was held that the plaintiff had become aware of his cause of action 1991, two years before the limitation period expired. The discovery rule was not intended to apply to a situation such as this and the action was statute-barred.

Clark v. 449136 Ontario Inc. (1996), 46 C.P.C. (3d) 19, 27 O.R. (3d) 658 (Gen. Div.)

A claim by a plaintiff injured in motor vehicle accident against a tavern owner is subject to the general six-year limitation period for torts, not the two-year limitation period for motor vehicle accidents under the *Highway Traffic Act.*

Caruso v. Guarantee Co. of North America (1996), 31 O.R. (3d) 339, 141 D.L.R. (4th) 421 (C.A.)

The two-year limitation period provided in respect of actions or proceedings against an insurer in respect of bodily injury or death in the case or uninsured motorists, applies to actions for declaratory relief. The cause of action for declaratory relief accrues when an insured who is legally entitled to recover damages from the owner or operator of an uninsured or unidentified vehicle knows or ought to know that the tort feasor was uninsured.

Murphy v. Welsh, [1993] 2 S.C.R. 1069, 14 O.R. (3d) 799 (note), 18 C.P.C. (3d) 137, 18 C.C.L.T. (2d) 101, 47 M.V.R. (2d) 1, 106 D.L.R. (4th) 404, 157 N.R. 372, 65 O.A.C. 103

The effect of s. 47 of the *Limitations Act* is not specifically excluded by the two-year limitation period contained in s. 180(1) of the *Highway Traffic Act*, and accordingly an infant injured in a motor vehicle accident may bring an action within two years of attaining majority.

Peixeiro v. Haberman (1995), 25 O.R. (3d) 1, 127 D.L.R. (4th) 475, 85 O.A.C. 2 (C.A.)

The "discoverability rule" applies to the two-year limitation period in the *Highway Traffic Act*. The plaintiff was allowed to commence the lawsuit more than two years after the date of the accident where the plaintiff did not learn of the severity of the injury until later.

Bair-Muirhead v. Muirhead (1994), 20 O.R. (3d) 744 (Gen. Div.)

The two-year limitation period contained in s. 206 of the *Highway Traffic Act* is not subject to the "discoverability rule."

Superior Propane Inc. v. Tebby Energy Systems (1992), 9 O.R. (3d) 769, 9 C.P.C. (3d) 330, 2 C.L.R. (2d) 144 (Gen. Div.)

The limitation period for asserting a claim for contribution and indemnity under s. 2 of the *Negligence Act* is six years.

Mero v. Waterloo (Regional Municipality) (1992), 7 O.R. (3d) 102, 6 C.P.C. (3d) 250, 10 C.C.L.T. (2d) 197, 37 M.V.R. (2d) 56, 8 M.P.L.R. (2d) 1, 89 D.L.R. (4th) 533, 54 O.A.C. 334 (C.A.); leave to appeal to Supreme Court of Canada refused 9 O.R. (3d) xii, 141 N.R. 399 (note), 58 O.A.C. 239 (note)

The language of the three-month limitation period contained in the *Municipal Act* is broad enough to embrace claims framed in nuisance and negligence.

Rostland Corp. v. Toronto (City) (1991), 2 O.R. (3d) 421; additional reasons 2 O.R. (3d) 735 (Gen. Div.)

The plaintiff brought an action in negligence and nuisance against a utility in respect of leakage of salt water from a steam heating plant. The action in negligence was barred by the six-month limitation period in s. 32 of the *Public Utilities Act*, R.S.O. 1980, c. 423, but as the leakage was ongoing, the claim of nuisance was not barred.

Sjouwerman v. Valance (1990), 46 C.P.C. (2d) 113, 37 O.A.C. 294 (C.A.); leave to appeal to Supreme Court of Canada refused (1991), 46 C.P.C. (2d) 113n, (sub nom. *Sjouwerman v. Canada Post Corp.)* 46 O.A.C. 12 (note), 126 N.R. 336 (note)

The limitation period in the *Public Authorities Protection Act* does not apply to the federal Crown.

Keuhl v. Beachburg (Village) (1990), 1990 CarswellOnt 412, 1 O.R. (3d) 154, 75 D.L.R. (4th) 193, 45 C.P.C. (2d) 225, (sub nom. *Keuhl v. Renfrew (County))* 42 O.A.C. 387 (C.A.)

The three-month limitation period in s. 284 of the *Municipal Act* is not discriminatory and is constitutionally valid.

Mirhadizadeh v. Ontario (1989), 69 O.R. (2d) 422, 36 C.P.C. (2d) 1, 47 C.R.R. 342, 60 D.L.R. (4th) 597, 34 O.A.C. 393 (C.A.)

The six-month limitation period contained in s. 11 of the *Public Authorities Protection Act*, R.S.O. 1980, c. 406, did not offend the equality provisions contained in s. 15 of the *Charter of Rights*.

Martin v. Listowel Memorial Hospital (1989), 34 C.P.C. (2d) 303; additional reasons 34 C.P.C. (2d) 303 at 311 (Ont. H.C.); affirmed (1992), 3 W.D.C.P. (2d) 421 (Ont. C.A.)

Section 47 of the *Limitations Act* gives absolute protection to a minor, which is not lost by the appointment of a litigation guardian. Accordingly, an infant plaintiff was permitted to add certain physicians as defendants to a proceeding more than five years after the action was commenced.

Clark v. Cdn. National Railway Co., [1988] 2 S.C.R. 680, 32 C.P.C. (2d) 97, 47 C.C.L.T. 1, 54 D.L.R. (4th) 679, 89 N.R. 81, 89 N.B.R. (2d) 116, 226 A.P.R. 116

A limitation period in the *Railway Act*, R.S.C. 1970, c. R-2, was *ultra vires*, as a federally imposed limitation provision regarding a personal injury action was not an integral part of the federal jurisdiction.

Papamonolopoulos v. Bd. of Education for Toronto (City) (1986), 56 O.R. (2d) 1, 10 C.P.C. (2d) 176, 38 C.C.L.T. 82, 30 D.L.R. (4th) 269, 16 O.A.C. 249 (C.A.); leave to appeal to Supreme Court of Canada refused

(1987), 58 O.R. (2d) 528n, 35 D.L.R. (4th) 767n, 76 N.R. 240n, 21 O.A.C. 319n

Section 47 of the *Limitations Act*, providing that a limitation period in respect of minors' claims does not commence to run until the age of majority is reached, is a law of general application which supersedes a specific limitation in another statute in the absence of clear overriding wording in the other statute; since there was no clear overriding provision in the *Public Authorities Protection Act* the one-year limitation period in that Act did not start to run against the infant plaintiff until he reached the age of majority.

JUDICIAL REVIEW PROCEDURE ACT

R.S.O. 1990, c. J.1

as am. S.O. 2002, c. 17, Sched. F, s. 1; 2006, c. 19, Sched. C, s. 1(1).

Case Law

INTRODUCTION

The *Judicial Review Procedure Act* establishes a common procedural mechanism for seeking appellate review of public law decision-making: an application for judicial review. Under this single adjudicative procedure, the Act makes available the remedies of the prerogative writs of certiorari (to quash a public decision), mandamus (to compel performance of a public duty) and prohibition (to prevent or stop a public body from taking an action), as well as the remedies of declaration and injunction.

Section 1

Definitions

1. In this Act,

"application for judicial review" means an application under subsection 2(1);

"court" means the Superior Court of Justice;

"licence" includes any permit, certificate, approval, registration or similar form of permission required by law;

"municipality" has the same meaning as in the *Municipal Affairs Act*;

"party" includes a municipality, association of employers, a trade union or council of trade unions which may be a party to any of the proceedings mentioned in subsection 2(1);

"statutory power" means a power or right conferred by or under a statute,

(a) to make any regulation, rule, by-law or order, or to give any other direction having force as subordinate legislation,

(b) to exercise a statutory power of decision,

(c) to require any person or party to do or to refrain from doing any act or thing that, but for such requirement, such person or party would not be required by law to do or to refrain from doing,

(d) to do any act or thing that would, but for such power or right, be a breach of the legal rights of any person or party;

"statutory power of decision" means a power or right conferred by or under a statute to make a decision deciding or prescribing,

(a) the legal rights, powers, privileges, immunities, duties or liabilities of any person or party, or

(b) the eligibility of any person or party to receive, or to the continuation of, a benefit or licence, whether the person or party is legally entitled thereto or not,

and includes the powers of an inferior court.

2002, c. 17, Sched. F, s. 1; 2006, c. 19, Sched. C, s. 1(1)

Cross Reference: Re "statutory power of decision," see also cases under the *Statutory Powers Procedure Act*, s. 1(1), below.

Case Law

Statutory Power of Decision — s. 1 — Cases Where Power or Right Held to Be Statutory Power of Decision

Goebel v. Robertson, 2015 CarswellOnt 10513, 2015 ONSC 4454, 42 M.P.L.R. (5th) 141 (S.C.J.)

A decision of a Justice of the Peace to issue a warrant for Toronto Fire Services to enter and assess the fire safety of an alleged hoarder's home is an exercise of statutory power of decision pursuant to the *Fire Protection and Prevent Act, 1997*. The Act authorizes a Justice of the Peace to grant an inspector the legal right to enter another's property where there are "reasonable grounds" to believe that entry is necessary to assess fire safety. The court refused to quash the warrant, holding that an anonymous complaint about hoarding from a member of the public was reasonable grounds to issue the warrant.

Endicott v. Ontario (Director, Office of the Independent Police Review), 2014 CarswellOnt 5857, 2014 ONCA 363, 70 Admin. L.R. (5th) 59, 373 D.L.R. (4th) 149, 319 O.A.C. 324, [2014] O.J. No. 2189

A decision of the Independent Police Review director not to deal with a complaint about the conduct of a police officer is an exercise of a statutory power of decision and not the exercise of discretion. The *Police Services Act* grants a person the legal right to have her complaint pursued unless the director decides that the complaint should be screened out. A director's decision not to pursue a complaint decides the complainant's legal rights.

Co-Operative Housing Federation of Canada v. York (Regional Municipality), 2009 CarswellOnt 858, 89 Admin. L.R. (4th) 305, 58 M.P.L.R. (4th) 68, 81 R.P.R. (4th) 236, 247 O.A.C. 90, [2009] O.J. No. 696 (Div. Ct.)

A municipality's decision to sell a co-operative housing project was the exercise of a statutory power of decision under the *Social Housing Reform Act, 2000*.

Hasan v. 260 Wellesley Residence Ltd. (1995), 24 O.R. (3d) 335, 126 D.L.R. (4th) 363, 83 O.A.C. 280 (Div. Ct.).

In signing a judgment in relation to an application brought under the *Landlord and Tenant Act*, the local registrar was engaged in the exercise of a statutory power of decision as defined in s. 1 of the Act. However, as s. 113(8) of the *Landlord and Tenant Act* provided an adequate alternate remedy to that of judicial review, an application for judicial review of the local registrar's decision was dismissed.

MacPump Developments Ltd. v. Sarnia (City) (1994), 20 O.R. (3d) 755, 24 M.P.L.R. (2d) 1, 120 D.L.R. (4th) 662, 75 O.A.C. 378; additional reasons (January 19, 1995), Doc. CA C16439 (C.A.).

Resolutions were passed by a city council pursuant to s. 100(1) of the *Municipal Act* establishing a judicial inquiry into the sale of land. The resolutions constituted an order or direction made in the exercise of the power granted by statute and had the force of subordinate legislation. The resolutions therefore constituted the exercise of a statutory power within the meaning of that phrase as defined in s. 1 of the Act.

Middlesex (County) v. Ontario (Minister of Municipal Affairs) (1993), 10 O.R. (3d) 1, 9 Admin. L.R. (2d) 206, 12 M.P.L.R. (2d) 208, 95 D.L.R. (4th) 676, 60 O.A.C. 185 (Div. Ct.).

Actions taken by the Minister of Municipal Affairs under the *Municipal Boundary Negotiations Act* in relation to the resolution of a boundary dispute were taken in the exercise of a statutory power, and therefore were reviewable by the court.

Hamilton-Wentworth (Regional Municipality) v. Ontario (Minister of Transportation) (1991), 2 O.R. (3d) 716, 49 Admin. L.R. 169, 45 C.L.R. 257, 78 D.L.R. (4th) 289, 46 O.A.C. 246 (Div. Ct.); leave to appeal to Ont. C.A. refused (August 12, 1991), Doc. A-48/91.

A decision by the Minister of Transportation not to provide any further funding for the construction of a highway project is not subject to judicial review. To rule otherwise would be trenching on the exclusive control of the legislature in relation to fiscal matters.

Ainsworth Electric Co. v. Exhibition Place (1987), 58 O.R. (2d) 432, 35 M.P.L.R. 56, 36 D.L.R. (4th) 299, 19 O.A.C. 216 (Div. Ct.).

A decision by a board of governors to hire a single in-house electrical contractor rather than continue with a system which had resulted in business for a number of contractors was a commercial decision. The courts have no authority, in the exercise of their prerogative jurisdiction, to review a commercial business decision.

Collins v. Pension Comm. (Ont.) (1986), 56 O.R. (2d) 274, 21 Admin. L.R. 186, 33 B.L.R. 265, 31 D.L.R. (4th) 86, C.E.B. & P.G.R. 8019, 16 O.A.C. 24 (Div. Ct.).

Where the Ontario Pension Commission had consented to the removal of surplus funds from a pension plan, the consent was subject to review as a statutory power of decision, because it determined the legal rights of both the employer and the pension plan members.

Metro. Bd. of Commrs. of Police v. Ont. Mun. Employees' Retirement Bd. (1985), 53 O.R. (2d) 83, 23 D.L.R. (4th) 414, 13 O.A.C. 19 (Div. Ct.).

Where a board purported to exercise a statutory authority in determining the applicant's pension plan contributions, the decision was subject to judicial review as it affected the rights of the applicant.

Prysiazniuk v. Hamilton-Wentworth (Reg. Mun.) (1985), 51 O.R. (2d) 339, 10 O.A.C. 208 (Div. Ct.).

Where the decision of a commissioner effectively deprives the applicant of his livelihood, and seriously threatens the well-being of the residents being cared for by the applicant, the decision is subject to judicial review.

Re Temple and Ont. Liquor Licence Bd. (1982), 41 O.R. (2d) 214, 145 D.L.R. (3d) 480 (Div. Ct.).

The Liquor Licence Board of Ontario, in deciding whether an applicant is entitled to a liquor licence (pursuant to s. 6 of the *Liquor Licence Act*), exercises a statutory power of decision.

Re Grant Bus Lines Ltd. and Ont. Pension Comm. (1980), 30 O.R. (2d) 180, 116 D.L.R. (3d) 336; affirmed (1981), 33 O.R. (2d) 652, 125 D.L.R. (3d) 325 (C.A.); leave to appeal to Supreme Court of Canada refused 41 N.R. 374.

Where the Ontario Pension Commission declares that an employer's contributions vest in the employees, it exercises a statutory power of decision and the employer is entitled to a hearing before the decision is made.

Re Aamco Automatic Transmissions Inc. and Simpson (1980), 29 O.R. (2d) 565, 113 D.L.R. (3d) 650 (Div. Ct.).

The Director of the Consumer Protection Division who proposes an order to cease and desist from unfair practices pursuant to s. 6(2) of the *Business Practices Act* exercises a statutory power of decision which is subject to judicial review.

Re Keeprite Workers Independent Union and Keeprite Products Ltd. (1980), 29 O.R. (2d) 513, 114 D.L.R. (3d) 162 (C.A.); leave to appeal to Supreme Court of Canada refused 35 N.R. 85.

An arbitrator appointed by a collective agreement subject to the *Labour Relations Act* who makes findings of facts and evidence exercises a "statutory power of decision".

Re Olympia & York Devs. Ltd. and Toronto (1980), 29 O.R. (2d) 353, 113 D.L.R. (3d) 695 (Div. Ct.).

A municipality, in refusing to permit development pursuant to a by-law passed under s. 35(a) of the *Planning Act*, exercises a statutory power of decision.

Re Chadwill Coal Co. and McCrae (1976), 14 O.R. (2d) 393, (sub nom. Chadwill Coal Co. v. Ont. Treasurer & Min. of Economics) 1 M.P.L.R. 25 (Div. Ct.).

Where hearing officers appointed pursuant to the *Ontario Planning and Development Act*, 1973 made a decision to make recommendations, the decision was held to be the exercise of a statutory power of decision within the definition of the Act.

Statutory Power of Decision — s. 1 — Cases Where Power or Right Held Not to Be Statutory Power of Decision

McLeod v. City of Brantford, 2018 CarswellOnt 1896, 2018 ONSC 943, 71 M.P.L.R. (5th) 259 (Div. Ct.)

The court transferred an application for declaratory relief to the Superior Court under s. 110 of the *Courts of Justice Act* where it lacked jurisdiction under the *JPRA* to declare that the applicant's forced removal from a bus terminal for distributing Falun Gong pamphlets violated his *Charter* rights; the applicable legislation did not create a statutory power of decision-making.

PC Ontario Fund v. Ontario (Chief Electoral Officer), 2012 CarswellOnt 8041, 2012 ONCA 453, 351 D.L.R. (4th) 374, [2012] O.J. No. 2908; additional reasons 2012 ONCA 531, 2012 CarswellOnt 9700, [2012] O.J. No. 3709

The court affirmed dismissal of an application for judicial review of the Ontario Chief Electoral Officer's (CEO) alleged failure to conduct a proper investigation of the applicant's complaint regarding purported unlawful campaign financing. The CEO's decision regarding how to deal with the applicant's complaint was not a decision affecting the legal rights, interests, property, privileges or liberty of any person or party. It was therefore not amenable to review under the traditional prerogative writs, nor as an exercise of a statutory power of decision.

Batacharya v. College of Midwives (Ontario), 2012 ONSC 1072, 2012 CarswellOnt 2060, 37 Admin. L.R. (5th) 165, [2012] O.J. No. 697 (Div. Ct.)

A decision by the registrar of the College of Midwives not to investigate a complaint about one of its members is an exercise of discretion and not a statutory power of decision. The *Regulated Health Professions Act, 1991* provides that upon receipt of a complaint the registrar "may appoint" an investigator to determine whether a member has committed an act of professional misconduct.

Apotex Inc. v. Ontario (Lieutenant Governor in Council), 2007 CarswellOnt 5197, 2007 ONCA 570, (sub nom. *Apotex Inc. v. Ontario (Minister of Health))*) 229 O.A.C. 11, [2007] O.J. No. 3121

The rules governing procedural fairness and natural justice do not apply to public bodies exercising legislative functions. Whereas the power of a public body to issue a regulation is a statutory power, it is not a statutory power of decision. The validity of a regulation is reviewable only if the public body has failed to observe a condition precedent set forth in the enabling statute or if the power to issue a regulation exercised in a manner contrary to the purpose of the legislation.

Masters v. Ontario (1994), 18 O.R. (3d) 551, 27 Admin. L.R. (2d) 152, 115 D.L.R. (4th) 319, 72 O.A.C. 1 (Div. Ct.).

The government retained outside counsel to investigate and report on allegations of sexual harassment made against the Agent General for Ontario in New York. The Agent subsequently resigned, but brought an application for judicial review claiming certain declaratory relief, and an order in the nature of *certiorari* quashing the report. A motion to strike out the requests for declaratory relief was granted, and upheld on appeal. The application was not brought in relation to the exercise of a statutory power of decision as required by s. 2(1)2 of the Act, and therefore declaratory relief was not available.

Aboutown Transportation Ltd. v. London (City) (1992), 9 O.R. (3d) 143, 10 M.P.L.R. (2d) 164 (Gen. Div.).

In awarding a contract for the provision of transit services to the physically disabled, a municipality was not exercising a statutory power of decision. The court should be wary about undertaking judicial review of commercial decision-making by municipal corporations, absent very extraordinary circumstances.

Ayerst, McKenna & Harrison Inc. v. Ontario (Attorney-General) (1992), 8 O.R. (3d) 90, 88 D.L.R. (4th) 763, 54 O.A.C. 230 (Div. Ct.).

Recommendations made by a committee to the Ministry of Health regarding the designation of a generic drug were not a statutory power of decision, as no legal rights of the applicant were prescribed by the committee's actions.

Apotex Inc. v. Ontario (Minister of Health) (1989), 71 O.R. (2d) 525, 44 Admin. L.R. 130, 65 D.L.R. (4th) 622, 36 O.A.C. 355 (Div. Ct.).

A decision by the Minister of Health to recommend the designation of a generic drug under the Ontario Drug Benefit Formulary, and a decision by the Lieutenant-Governor to make such a designation, are decisions which are subject to judicial review.

Haber v. Wellesley Hospital (1986), 56 O.R. (2d) 553, 31 D.L.R. (4th) 607, 16 O.A.C. 215; additional reasons 56 O.R. (2d) 553 at 569, 31 D.L.R. (4th) 607 at 624 (Div. Ct.); affirmed (1988), 62 O.R. (2d) 756, 46 D.L.R. (4th) 575, 24 O.A.C. 239 (C.A.); leave to appeal to S.C.C. refused 63 O.R. (2d) x, 46 D.L.R. (4th) vi, 88 N.R. 317, 30 O.A.C. 77n.

The recommendations of a Medical Advisory Committee are not subject to judicial review where the recommendations are not automatically acted upon, and the applicant is entitled to receive a fair hearing after the recommendations are made.

Re Medhurst and Medhurst (1984), 45 O.R. (2d) 575, 4 Admin. L.R. 126, 7 D.L.R. (4th) 335 (H.C.).

The decision of a hospital therapeutic abortion committee to grant a certificate where life or health is endangered is not the exercise of a statutory power of decision. The onus is on the applicant to demonstrate that the committee lacked any evidence to support its opinion.

Re Head and Ont. Prov. Police Commr. (1981), 40 O.R. (2d) 84, 127 D.L.R. (3d) 366 (C.A.).

The Commissioner of the Ontario Provincial Police does not exercise a statutory power of decision when he accepts the resignation of a police officer not given under duress or coercion.

Paine v. Univ. of Toronto (1981), 34 O.R. (2d) 770, 131 D.L.R. (3d) 325 (C.A.); leave to appeal to Supreme Court of Canada refused (1982), 42 N.R. 270.

The court will be slow to exercise its discretion to review a university's process of appointing teaching staff where the university itself provides adequate internal appeal mechanisms. It is doubtful if the general reference in the *University of Toronto Act* to the power of the governing council to appoint members of faculty is a "statutory power of decision".

Re Hancock and Algonquin College of Applied Arts & Technology Bd. of Governors (1981), 33 O.R. (2d) 257, 124 D.L.R. (3d) 148 (H.C.).

A board of governors of a community college which recommends annual estimates to the Council of Regents pursuant to the *Ministry of Colleges and Universities Act* does not exercise a statutory power of decision. The duty imposed by the Act is distinct from a power of discretion.

Re Arts and London & Middlesex County R.C. Sep. Sch. Bd. (1979), 27 O.R. (2d) 468, 106 D.L.R. (3d) 683 (H.C.).

A school board which decided to close a school under the *Education Act*, 1974, was not exercising a statutory power of decision within the meaning of s. 1(f)(i).

Re S & M Laboratories Ltd. and Ont. (1979), 24 O.R. (2d) 732, 99 D.L.R. (3d) 160 (C.A.).

The decision by the General Manager of the Ontario Health Insurance Plan under the *Health Insurance Act* that an overpayment has been made to a medical laboratory and that it should be recovered by deductions from future payments is not a statutory power of decision.

Re Dodd and Chiropractic Review Ctee. (1978), 23 O.R. (2d) 423, 3 L. Med. Q.48, 95 D.L.R. (3d) 560 (Div. Ct.).

The referral to a review committee of the practice of a chiropractor because of questioned claims by the General Manager of the Ontario Health Insurance Plan is not a statutory power of decision.

Re Midnorthern Appliances Industs. Corp. and Ont. Housing Corp. (1977), 17 O.R. (2d) 290 (Div. Ct.).

A decision of the Ontario Housing Corporation that it will no longer consider tenders submitted by a former supplier because of threatened legal action is not an exercise of statutory power of decision as defined in s. 1(f), and consequently is not subject to judicial review.

Re Florence Nightingale Home and Scarborough Planning Bd., [1973] 1 O.R. 615, 32 D.L.R. (3d) 17 (Div. Ct.).

A planning board does not exercise a statutory power of decision when it meets to consider whether a proposed change in an official plan and zoning by-law should be recommended to council for enactment.

Re Robertson and Niagara South Bd. of Educ. (1973), 1 O.R. (2d) 548, 41 D.L.R. (3d) 57 (Div. Ct.).

A motion by a board of education purporting to close a school was not an exercise of a statutory power of decision, but was an administrative decision not subject to judicial review.

Re Lamoureux and Reg. of Motor Vehicles, [1973] 2 O.R. 28, 20 C.R.N.S. 254, 10 C.C.C. (2d) 475, 32 D.L.R. (3d) 678 (C.A.).

The automatic suspension of the driver's licence of a person convicted of impaired driving under the *Highway Traffic Act* is not the exercise of a statutory power.

Statutory Power — s. 1

Bezaire v. Windsor Roman Catholic Separate School Board (1992), 9 O.R. (3d) 737, 8 Admin. L.R. (2d) 29, 94 D.L.R. (4th) 310, 57 O.A.C. 39 (Div. Ct.).

Whether a school board's decision to close a school was a "statutory power of decision" as defined in either the J.R.P.A. or the S.P.P.A. did not have to be determined where there was a duty of fairness owed, and that duty had been breached.

Tomen v. O.P.S.T.F. (1986), 55 O.R. (2d) 670, 29 D.L.R. (4th) 638, 17 O.A.C. 189 (Div. Ct.).

A by-law passed under a general statute governing the internal membership of a corporation without share capital is not subordinate legislation, and therefore is not subject to judicial review.

Re McGill and Brantford (1980), 28 O.R. (2d) 721, 12 M.P.L.R. 24, 111 D.L.R. (3d) 405 (Div. Ct.).

A municipal council's decision to close a road pursuant to s. 466 of the *Municipal Act* decides the "legal rights of persons" and is a statutory power "to make ... any by-law ... having force as subordinate legislation."

Mississauga Hydro Electric Comm. v. Mississauga; Re Murray and Mississauga (1975), 13 O.R. (2d) 511, 71 D.L.R. (3d) 475 (Div. Ct.).

A municipal council resolution is a "regulation, rule, by-law or order, or ... any other direction having force as subordinate legislation" within the meaning of s. 1, bringing the power thus conferred within the definition of "statutory power," and subject to judicial review by the Divisional Court.

Section 2

Applications for judicial review

2. (1) On an application by way of originating notice, which may be styled "Notice of Application for Judicial Review", the court may, despite any right of appeal, by order grant any relief that the applicant would be entitled to in any one or more of the following:

1. Proceedings by way of application for an order in the nature of mandamus, prohibition or certiorari.

2. Proceedings by way of an action for a declaration or for an injunction, or both, in relation to the exercise, refusal to exercise or proposed or purported exercise of a statutory power.

Error of law

(2) The power of the court to set aside a decision for error of law on the face of the record on an application for an order in the nature of certiorari is extended so as to apply on an application for judicial review in relation to any decision made in the exercise of any statutory power of decision to the extent it is not limited or precluded by the Act conferring such power of decision.

Lack of evidence

(3) Where the findings of fact of a tribunal made in the exercise of a statutory power of decision are required by any statute or law to be based exclusively on evidence admissible before it and on facts of which it may take notice and there is no such evidence and there are no such facts to support findings of fact made by the tribunal in making a decision in the exercise of such power, the court may set aside the decision on an application for judicial review.

Power to set aside

(4) Where the applicant on an application for judicial review is entitled to a judgment declaring that a decision made in the exercise of a statutory power of decision is unauthorized or otherwise invalid, the court may, in the place of such declaration, set aside the decision.

Power to refuse relief

(5) Where, in any of the proceedings enumerated in subsection (1), the court had before the 17th day of April, 1972 a discretion to refuse to grant relief on any grounds, the court has a like discretion on like grounds to refuse to grant any relief on an application for judicial review.

Where subs. (5) does not apply

(6) Subsection (5) does not apply to the discretion of the court before the 17th day of April, 1972 to refuse to grant relief in any of the proceedings enumerated in subsection (1) on the ground that the relief should have been sought in other proceedings enumerated in subsection (1).

Case Law

Procedural Requirements

Aviva Canada Inc. v. Taylor, 2017 CarswellOnt 6314, 2017 ONSC 2661, 67 C.C.L.I. (5th) 71 (Div. Ct.)

Absent exceptional circumstances, parties to an administrative proceeding cannot engage the court system until the administrative process has run its course. Typically, concerns about procedural fairness and natural justice do not qualify as exceptional circumstances.

Ontario (Attorney General) v. CUPE, Local 27, 2015 CarswellOnt 12396, 2015 ONSC 5172, [2015] O.J. No. 4308 (Div. Ct.)

An applicant should name all other participants in an administrative hearing as respondents to a judicial review of that hearing.

N. (J.) v. Durham Regional Police Service, 2012 CarswellOnt 7776, 2012 ONCA 428, 284 C.C.C. (3d) 500, [2012] O.J. No. 2809

Jurisdiction is fundamental to a court's authority to deal with a matter and cannot be created by consent, attornment or assumption. The Court of Appeal set aside the quashing of a decision made on an application to the Superior Court of Justice under rule 14.05, where the application was for judicial review and ought to have been made to the Divisional Court.

Ontario College of Art v. Ontario (Human Rights Commission) (1993), 11 O.R. (3d) 798, 99 D.L.R. (4th) 738, 63 O.A.C. 393, 19 C.H.R.R. D/199 (Div. Ct.).

The court ruled that an application for judicial review was premature where the board of inquiry had not yet commenced proceedings. The court should not fragment proceedings before administrative tribunals, and it is preferable to consider the issues raised against the backdrop of a full record, including a reasoned decision by the board or tribunal.

550551 Ontario Ltd. v. Framingham (1991), 4 O.R. (3d) 571, 4 B.L.R. (2d) 75, 5 C.B.R. (3d) 204, 91 C.L.L.C. 14,031, 49 O.A.C. 376; additional reasons (October 22, 1991), Doc. 29/91 (Div. Ct.).

The court ruled that an application for judicial review was not premature where the parties bringing the application sought review of an order to pay, even though a statutory right of appeal was available. A writ of execution had already been issued against one of the parties, and in order to exercise their right of appeal, the parties were required to pay the amount due under the order.

Peel Condominium Corp. No. 199 v. Ont. New Home Warranties Plan (1989), 69 O.R. (2d) 438, 61 D.L.R. (4th) 351 (Div. Ct.).

The court ruled that an application for judicial review was premature, although the decision in issue had been made without the required notices, as the applicant had an alternative remedy available in the form of a *de novo* hearing. The court also found that the original decision had not involved a jurisdictional error, and noted that affidavit evidence on the issue of jurisdiction should only rarely be permitted.

N. v. D. (1986), 54 O.R. (2d) 550, 16 O.A.C. 75 (*sub nom. N. (R.) v. D. (M.)*) (Div. Ct.).

The decision of a lower court on a Charter point should not be subject to judicial review until the proceedings in which the point arose have been disposed of by the lower court.

Re Ont. Prov. Police Commr. and Perrier (1983), 41 O.R. (2d) 550, 147 D.L.R. (3d) 157 (Div. Ct.).

Where delay in bringing an application may cause serious prejudice to its resolution and where the relief sought is largely academic, the court may quash the application.

Re Seaway Trust Co. and Ont.; Re Crown Trust Co. and A.G. Ont. (1983), 41 O.R. (2d) 501 at 532, 37 C.P.C. 8 at 50, 6 C.R.R. 365 (C.A.); leave to appeal to Supreme Court of Canada refused 37 C.P.C. 8n, 6 C.R.R. 365n, 52 N.R. 235.

Where an action would be more appropriate than an application for judicial review in terms of the relief sought, the necessity of *viva voce* evidence, and the potential effect of the decision on non-parties, the Divisional Court properly exercises its discretion in refusing to hear the application.

Koumoudouros v. Metro. Toronto (1982), 37 O.R. (2d) 656, 29 C.P.C. 99, 67 C.C.C. (2d) 193, 136 D.L.R. (3d) 373 (H.C.).

A s. 24(1) *Charter of Rights* challenge of a municipal by-law for alleged infringement or denial of guaranteed rights and freedoms is essentially an application for judicial review. The Divisional Court is the "court of competent jurisdiction".

Re Forestell and Niagara College of Applied Arts & Technology (1981), 33 O.R. (2d) 282 (H.C.).

Where an originating notice of motion failed substantially to comply with the former Rules of Practice (Form 39), the application for judicial review was dismissed.

Re Rymal and Niagara Escarpment Comm. (1981), 129 D.L.R. (3d) 363 (Ont. C.A.).

Where notices of appeal were filed one day late due to postal disruptions and the failure of a government employee to pick up a notice of appeal within the time limit, the Divisional Court properly exercised its discretion in dismissing an application to prohibit the Minister of Housing from proceeding with the hearing of an appeal from a decision to grant a development permit.

Re Innisfil and Barrie; Oro v. Barrie (1977), 17 O.R. (2d) 277, 3 M.P.L.R. 47 (Div. Ct.).

During proceedings before an administrative tribunal, an application for judicial review may be brought at any time, and an applicant need not wait until proceedings are concluded.

Where Right of Appeal Available — s. 2(1)

1439957 Ontario Inc. v. Benkoe, 2017 CarswellOnt 13029, 2017 ONSC 4984 (Div. Ct.)

Where the legislature has expressly denied a right of appeal, the *JRPA* does not provide a surrogate right of appeal on the merits.

Volochay v. College of Massage Therapists of Ontario, 2012 CarswellOnt 10146, 2012 ONCA 541, 111 O.R. (3d) 561, 40 Admin. L.R. (5th) 307, 355 D.L.R. (4th) 518, 295 O.A.C. 164, [2012] O.J. No. 3871

The applicant's failure to make use of the appeal route mandated by statute deprived him of a right to seek judicial review. Although s. 2(1) of the *JRPA* provides that judicial review may be sought "despite any right of appeal," judicial review before exhaustion of a statutory appeal process is only available in exceptional circumstances.

John Doe v. Ontario (Information & Privacy Commissioner) (1993), 13 O.R. (3d) 767, 19 Admin. L.R. (2d) 251, 106 D.L.R. (4th) 140, 64 O.A.C. 248 (Div. Ct.).

The Information and Privacy Commissioner under the *Freedom of Information and Protection of Privacy Act* is required to develop and apply expertise in the management of many kinds of government information, and thereby acquires a unique range of expertise not shared by the courts. Accordingly, the Commissioner's decision, already protected by the lack of any right of appeal, ought to be accorded a strong measure of curial deference even where the legislature has not insulated the tribunal by means of a privative clause.

Kuntz v. W.C.B., Ont. (1985), 56 O.R. (2d) 497, 22 Admin. L.R. 226, 31 D.L.R. (4th) 630, 17 O.A.C. 170 (C.A.).

The privative clause contained in the *Workers' Compensation Act* bars judicial review unless the Board's interpretation of the statutory provision in issue is patently unreasonable.

Williams v. Kemptville Dist. Hospital (1986), 55 O.R. (2d) 633, 29 D.L.R. (4th) 629 (H.C.).

On an application for judicial review of a hospital board decision, it was found that the board's conduct had been contrary to the rules of natural justice. However there was no order for judicial review, as the applicant had a statutory right of appeal pursuant to the *Public Hospitals Act*.

O.P.S.E.U. v. Forer (1985), 52 O.R. (2d) 705, 15 Admin. L.R. 145, 23 D.L.R. (4th) 97, 12 O.A.C. 1 (C.A.).

Where an administrative tribunal is protected from judicial review by a privative clause, the tribunal should be permitted to perform its functions free of judicial interference, unless the tribunal's actions are patently unreasonable.

Re R. and Burns (1983), 41 O.R. (2d) 774, 5 C.C.C. (3d) 381, 5 C.R.R. 215, 148 D.L.R. (3d) 188 (H.C.).

Where an indictment is quashed on substantive grounds, and there is available an ordinary right of appeal, *mandamus* is not an appropriate remedy.

Re Woodglen & Co. and North York (1983), 42 O.R. (2d) 385, 23 M.P.L.R. 13, 149 D.L.R. (3d) 186 (Div. Ct.).

In the absence of exceptional circumstances, and where there exists a specific alternative remedy, the court ought not to exercise its discretion to grant the extraordinary remedy of mandamus.

Re V.S.R. Invts. Ltd. and Laczko (1983), 41 O.R. (2d) 62, 33 C.P.C. 245 (Div. Ct.).

Where particular difficulties might arise in an appeal by way of stated case of a decision by the Residential Tenancies Commission, the appeal should be stayed pending the disposition of an application for judicial review.

Re A.G. Ont. and Rae (1983), 44 O.R. (2d) 493, 40 C.P.C. 68, (sub nom. *Rae v. Rae)* 4 D.L.R. (4th) 465 (H.C.).

Notwithstanding s. 2 of the Act, where an appeal is provided, judicial review or relief in the nature of *certiorari* should be foregone.

Pronto Cabs Ltd. v. Metro. Toronto Licensing Comm. (1982), 39 O.R. (2d) 488 (Div. Ct.).

Where there exists a statutory right of appeal from a decision of the Metropolitan Licensing Commission, judicial review by way of *certiorari* and *mandamus* is not simultaneously available.

Re Reddall and Ont. College of Nurses (1981), 33 O.R. (2d) 129, 123 D.L.R. (3d) 568; reversed in part (1983), 42 O.R. (2d) 412, 1 Admin. L.R. 278, 149 D.L.R. (3d) 60 (C.A.).

Where the Divisional Court has broad review powers under a provision of the *Health Disciplines Act*, an application for judicial review is redundant.

Mississauga v. Dir., Environmental Protection Act (1978), 8 C.P.C. 292, 6 M.P.L.R. 115, 7 C.E.L.R. 139 (H.C.).

A judicial review of a decision by way of prerogative remedies, such as *certiorari*, should not be granted where there exists an express right of appeal from the decision complained of within the Act itself, except in very special circumstances.

Standard of Review — s. 2(1)

Novaquest Finishing Inc. v. Abdoulrab, 2009 CarswellOnt 3474, 2009 ONCA 491, (sub nom. *Abdoulrab v. Ontario (Labour Relations Board))* 95 O.R. (3d) 641, 95 Admin. L.R. (4th) 121, (sub nom. *Abdoulrab v. OLRB)* 2009 C.L.L.C. 210-033, 251 O.A.C. 28, [2009] O.L.R.B. Rep. 480, [2009] O.J. No. 2524; additional reasons 2009 ONCA 639, 2009 CarswellOnt 5163

Where employment standards legislation provides that its interpretation by an employment tribunal is reviewable on a standard of reasonableness, the court does not apply a "margin of error" test on judicial review by determining the correct statutory interpretation and then assessing whether the tribunal's interpretation is sufficiently close to the correct one. In such a case, the task of a judicial review court is not to determine whether the tribunal's interpretation is correct or wrong, but whether its interpretation falls within a range of acceptable interpretations.

Dunsmuir v. New Brunswick, 2008 CSC 9, 2008 SCC 9, 2008 CarswellNB 124, 2008 CarswellNB 125, [2008] 1 S.C.R. 190, 329 N.B.R. (2d) 1, 69 Admin. L.R. (4th) 1, [2008] A.C.S. No. 9, [2008] S.C.J. No. 9

Two standards of review apply on judicial review: reasonableness and correctness. As a general rule, questions of fact, discretion, policy and questions of inseparably mixed fact-and-law are subject to the deferential standard of reasonableness; whereas, issues of jurisdiction and law are generally subject to the non-deferential standard of correctness. To be reasonable, a tribunal's decision must be justifiable, transparent, and intelligible, and it must fall within a range of possible, acceptable outcomes which are defensible in respect of the facts and law.

Availability of Judicial Review — s. 2(1) para. 1

Graff v. New Democratic Party, 2017 CarswellOnt 8842, 2017 ONSC 3578, 28 Admin. L.R. (6th) 294 (Div. Ct.)

Decisions made by a federal political party about which candidates it puts forward have a serious effect on the rights of the voting public and are subject to judicial review.

West Toronto United Football Club v. Ontario Soccer Assn., 2014 CarswellOnt 14061, 2014 ONSC 5881, 327 O.A.C. 29, [2014] O.J. No. 4773 (Div. Ct.)

Basic principles of fairness are an important building block of social order. The question whether a children's sports association has acted fairly towards child players was subject to judicial review.

Setia v. Appleby College, 2013 CarswellOnt 17425, 2013 ONCA 753, 118 O.R. (3d) 481, 64 Admin. L.R. (5th) 91, 370 D.L.R. (4th) 356, 313 O.A.C. 264, [2013] O.J. No. 5736

Availability of judicial review under s. 2(1)1 of the *JRPA* turns on whether the decision for review has a sufficient public law element, not whether it was the exercise of a statutory power. Relevant factors include: the character of the matter for which review is sought; the nature of the decision-maker and its responsibilities; the extent to which the decision is informed by law as opposed to private discretion; the decision-maker's relationship to other statutory schemes or government; whether the decision-maker is an agent of government or is directed, controlled or significantly influenced by a public entity; the suitability of public law remedies; the existence of a compulsory power; and whether the result of the decision has attained a serious public dimension.

Sabados v. Can. Slovak League, 1982 CarswellOnt 846, 35 O.R. (2d) 718, 133 D.L.R. (3d) 152 (Div. Ct.).

The Divisional Court, a division of the High Court of Justice, has jurisdiction to review by certiorari, mandamus, or prohibition the decision of the board of directors of a federally incorporated fraternal benefit society to terminate the membership of one of its members. The powers of the board are analogous to private powers exercisable by an ordinary corporation created under a federal statute

Availability of Judicial Review — s. 2(1) para. 2

McLeod v. City of Brantford, 2018 CarswellOnt 1896, 2018 ONSC 943, 71 M.P.L.R. (5th) 259 (Div. Ct.)

Declaratory relief on judicial review is available only under s. 2(1)2 in relation to the exercise, refusal to exercise or proposed or purported exercise of a statutory power.

Ontario (Director, Racing Commission) v. Ontario Racing Commission, 2016 CarswellOnt 8068, 2016 ONSC 3312 (Div. Ct.)

A court has jurisdiction to judicially review a penalty imposed by a tribunal or administrative body.

Volochay v. College of Massage Therapists of Ontario, 2012 CarswellOnt 10146, 2012 ONCA 541, 111 O.R. (3d) 561, 40 Admin. L.R. (5th) 307, 355 D.L.R. (4th) 518, 295 O.A.C. 164, [2012] O.J. No. 3871

The court set aside a judicial review order quashing a professional disciplinary body's decision to investigate the applicant, despite finding that the disciplinary body deprived the applicant of procedural fairness. A breach of natural justice does not deprive an administrative body of jurisdiction so as to permit judicial review on jurisdictional grounds.

Canadian College of Business & Computers Inc. v. Superintendent, 2010 CarswellOnt 9555, 2010 ONCA 856, 17 Admin. L.R. (5th) 245, 272 O.A.C. 177, [2010] O.J. No. 5435

A reasonable apprehension of bias by an adjudicator violates the duty of fairness owed by a tribunal and is subject to judicial review. To show a real or perceived bias, mere suspicion is not enough; a real likelihood or probability of bias must be demonstrated.

Clifford v. Ontario (Attorney General), 2009 CarswellOnt 5595, 2009 ONCA 670, 312 D.L.R. (4th) 70, 98 O.R. (3d) 210, 93 Admin. L.R. (4th) 131, [2009] O.J. No. 3900; leave to appeal refused 2010 CarswellOnt 439, 2010 CarswellOnt 440, 405 N.R. 388 (note), 270 O.A.C. 395 (note), [2009] S.C.C.A. No. 461

An administrative tribunal's failure to give reasons can constitute a denial of procedural fairness. Relevant factors include: the nature of the decision and the process followed in making it; the nature of the statutory scheme being administered; the importance of the decision to the affected individual; the legitimate expectations of the person challenging the decision; and respect for the choice of procedures made by the administrative tribunal.

Peck v. Residential Property Management Inc. (July 15, 2009), Doc. Toronto 506/08, 2009 CarswellOnt 4330, [2009] O.J. No. 3064 (Div. Ct.)

As a general rule, a court will only interfere with a decision of the Small Claims Court on judicial review if the order was made without jurisdiction or in breach of the principles of natural justice.

R. v. S. (R.D.), 1997 CarswellNS 301, 1997 CarswellNS 302, [1997] 3 S.C.R. 484, 161 N.S.R. (2d) 241, 1 Admin. L.R. (3d) 74, 118 C.C.C. (3d) 353, 10 C.R. (5th) 1, 151 D.L.R. (4th) 193, 477 A.P.R. 241, 218 N.R. 1, [1997] S.C.J. No. 84

It is a well-established principle that all adjudicative tribunals and administrative bodies owe a duty of fairness to the parties who must appear before them.

St. Lawrence Cement Inc. v. Ontario (Minister of Transportation) (1991), 3 O.R. (3d) 30, 50 B.L.R. 319 (Gen. Div.).

The Minister of Transportation's decision to disqualify a tender for a provincial government contract was not subject to *certiorari*, as the decision concerned a commercial contract that did not affect the public interest.

Re Rees and P.P.F., Loc. 527 (1983), 43 O.R. (2d) 97, 4 Admin. L.R. 179, 83 C.L.L.C. 14,067, 150 D.L.R. (3d) 493 (Div. Ct.).

The decision of a trade union disciplinary committee to suspend and fire a union member is subject to judicial review on application by the member seeking relief that would be available in proceedings in the nature of *certiorari*.

Pestell v. Kitchener-Waterloo Real Estate Bd. Inc. (1981), 34 O.R. (2d) 476, 131 D.L.R. (3d) 88 (Div. Ct.).

The decision of an appeal board of a private real estate corporation to expel a voluntary member was not an exercise of statutory power and was not subject to review by way of *certiorari* by the Divisional Court.

Re Ont. Prov. Police Assn. and Ont. (1974), 3 O.R. (2d) 698, 46 D.L.R. (3d) 518 (Div. Ct.).

Individual judges of the High Court have a common law jurisdiction to grant a remedy in the nature of *certiorari* in restricted circumstances. This jurisdiction is vested, pursuant to s. 2(1), in the Divisional Court, which can determine whether a consensual board of arbitration has acted illegally in making a decision.

Re S.E.I.U., Loc. 204 and Broadway Manor Nursing Home (1984), 48 O.R. (2d) 225, 13 D.L.R. (4th) 220, (sub nom. *Durham Bd. of Educ. v. O.S.S.T.F. Dist. 17; O.P.S.E.U. v. A.G. Ont.)* 5 O.A.C. 371.

Where the Inflation Restraint Board did not exercise or propose or purport to exercise a statutory power, the Divisional Court was held to lack jurisdiction to hear an application for judicial review or to grant declaratory relief.

Re Olympia and York Devs. Ltd. and Toronto, 1980 CarswellOnt 493, 29 O.R. (2d) 353, 113 D.L.R. (3d) 695, 12 M.P.L.R. 219 (Div. Ct.).

Where a city has exercised a statutory power of decision under a statute, the court has jurisdiction to consider an application for a declaration if the interpretation of the statute could have been disposed of in an application by way of mandamus.

Re Selkirk and Schorr (1977), 15 O.R. (2d) 37, 2 C.P.C. 249 (Div. Ct.).

The Divisional Court has jurisdiction pursuant to s. 2 of the *Judicature Act* to superintend the conduct of its own officers including taxing officers, and has jurisdiction pursuant to s. 2 of the *Judicial Review Procedure Act* to control its officers by way of order of prohibition or by declaratory or injunctive order.

Re Maurice Rollins Const. Ltd. and South Fredericksburg (1975), 11 O.R. (2d) 418 (H.C.).

Although a municipal council by-law de-registering a subdivision plan under the *Planning Act* is not an exercise of a statutory power of decision, it is nevertheless an exercise of a statutory power and is subject to judicial review by way of declaratory relief pursuant to s. 2(1)1 of this Act.

Mississauga Hydro Elec. Comm. v. Mississauga; Re Murray and Mississauga (1975), 13 O.R. (2d) 511, 71 D.L.R. (3d) 475 (Div. Ct.).

Where a notice of application for judicial review has been made, the issuance of a concurrent claim by writ is not necessary to invoke the court's power to make a declaration or to grant an injunction.

Availability of Judicial Review — Motion to Quash Application

Weidenfeld v. Talaat, 2014 CarswellOnt 16132, 2014 ONSC 6520 (S.C.J.)

The court quashed as premature a tenant's application for judicial review of an order requiring the payment of rent arrears. The tenant had not exhausted the appeal process available under the *Residential Tenancies Act, 1996*.

Deeb v. Investment Industry Regulatory Organization of Canada, 2012 CarswellOnt 2115, 2012 ONSC 1014, 289 O.A.C. 81, [2012] O.J. No. 691 (Div. Ct.)

The test on a motion to quash an application for judicial review is whether it is plain and obvious that the application cannot succeed. There are two elements to this inquiry: (i) is there jurisdiction to hear the application under s. 2(1) of the *JRPA*; and (ii) even if there is, should the application be quashed because it is premature?

Smith v. Ontario (Securities Commission), 2008 CarswellOnt 7435, [2008] O.J. No. 4980 (Div. Ct.)

The court quashed as premature an application for judicial review seeking an order of prohibition against the Ontario Securities Commission. While OSC proceedings were pending against the applicants, the chair of the OSC publicly questioned their honesty and integrity. The applicants sought termination of the OSC proceedings on the grounds that they would be denied a fair process. The application was premature as the OSC proceeding had not been completed. Even where allegations of bias are raised, the proceedings below must generally be completed before judicial review can be sought.

Certified General Accountants Assn. (Canada) v. Canadian Public Accountability Board, 2008 CarswellOnt 243, 77 Admin. L.R. (4th) 262, [2008] O.J. No. 194 (Div. Ct.); additional reasons 2008 CarswellOnt 998 (Div. Ct.)

The court refused to quash an application for judicial review of the decision-making of the Canadian Public Accountancy Board. Although the board is a not-for-profit corporation and does not exercise a statutory power of decision, given its public interest mandate, it was not clear that its decision-making was immune to judicial review.

Canadian Pacific Ltd. v. Matsqui Indian Band, 1995 CarswellNat 264, 1995 CarswellNat 700, 85 F.T.R. 79 (note), [1995] 1 S.C.R. 3, [1995] S.C.J. No. 1

A court may strike out an application for judicial review where an adequate or better alternative statutory appeal mechanism exists. A variety of factors should be considered by courts in determining whether they should enter into judicial review, or alternatively should require an applicant to proceed through a statutory appeal procedure. These factors include: the convenience of the alternative remedy, the nature of the error, and the nature of the appellate body's investigatory, decision-making and remedial capacities.

Error of Law — s. 2(2)

U.S.W.A., Local 14097 v. Franks (1994), 16 O.R. (3d) 620, 19 Admin. L.R. (2d) 165, 2 C.C.E.L. (2d) 23, 94 C.L.L.C. 14,011, 110 D.L.R. (4th) 762, 69 O.A.C. 148 (C.A.); leave to appeal to Supreme Court of Canada refused 19 O.R. (3d) xvi (note), 19 Admin. L.R. (2d) 165n, 7 C.C.E.L. (2d) 41 (note), 114 D.L.R. (4th) vii (note).

Where a referee under the *Employment Standards Act* makes a decision involving the interpretation of the constituent statute, and that decision is within his jurisdiction, the applicable standard of review is one of reasonableness. The presence of a privative clause does not mean the court should mechanically defer to a tribunal. The significance of the privative clause depends on an analysis of the provision in light of the purpose, nature and expertise of the tribunal in relation to the decision in issue.

Re O.P.S.E.U. and Ont. (1984), 45 O.R. (2d) 70, 5 D.L.R. (4th) 651, (sub nom. *O.P.S.E.U. v. Min. of Correctional Services)* 2 O.A.C. 351 (Div. Ct.).

Where a tribunal commits an error of law or mixed law and fact, as where it fails to evaluate a relevant portion of the evidence, its decision is subject to judicial review as a denial of natural justice.

Connie Steel Products Ltd. v. Greater Nat. Building Corp.; Interprice Elec. Ltd. v. Bank of N.S. (1977), 3 C.P.C. 327 (Div. Ct.).

The purpose of s. 2(2) of the Act is to extend the Supreme Court's superintendence over inferior tribunals and it does not permit the review of decisions taken by other divisions or emanations of the Supreme Court.

Absence of Evidence — s. 2(3)

Wong v. Globe and Mail Inc., 2014 CarswellOnt 15512, 2014 ONSC 6372, 123 O.R. (3d) 28, 88 Admin. L.R. (5th) 294, 247 L.A.C. (4th) 323, 2015 C.L.L.C. 220-008, 327 O.A.C. 324, [2014] O.J. No. 5186 (Div. Ct.)

Where the applicant employee asserted that her representation by a union in a grievance arbitration was so deficient as to amount to a breach of natural justice, the court admitted fresh affidavit evidence describing the arbitration hearing, holding that admission was justified under the "natural justice" exception identified in *142445 Ontario Ltd.*

142445 Ontario Ltd. v. I.B.E.W., Local 636, 2009 CarswellOnt 2701, 95 Admin. L.R. (4th) 273, (sub nom. *142445 Ontario Ltd. v. International Brotherhood of Electrical Workers, Local 636)* 251 O.A.C. 62, [2009] O.J. No. 2011 (Div. Ct.)

The Ontario Court of Appeal's 1980 decision in *Keeprite* is binding. Affidavits describing the evidence that was before a tribunal are only permitted where necessary to show a complete lack of evidence on an essential point or to disclose a breach of natural justice that cannot be proven by a mere reference to the record. The court declined to follow *Denby* and *Brookfield* where such affidavits were admitted on a more liberal basis. A factual finding of a tribunal is only reviewable on the basis that there was no evidence to support it.

Brookfield Lepage Johnson Controls Facilities Management Services Ltd. v. Ontario (Labour Relations Board), 2007 CarswellOnt 709, 56 Admin. L.R. (4th) 319,

2007 C.L.L.C. 220-015, 221 O.A.C. 70, [2007] O.L.R.B. Rep. 285, [2007] O.J. No. 490 (Div. Ct.)

Where an issue for judicial review turned on a question of fact concerning what a party had or had not known, and there was no transcript of the lower tribunal hearing, the court permitted the parties to tender affidavits describing the evidence and submissions at the hearing. Citing *Denby*, the court held that fresh affidavit evidence may be admissible in support of an application for judicial review where a party would otherwise be prejudiced on a fundamental issue.

Denby v. Ontario (Agriculture, Food & Rural Affairs Appeal Tribunal), 2005 CarswellOnt 6724, 40 Admin. L.R. (4th) 128, 204 O.A.C. 146, [2005] O.J. No. 4952 (Div. Ct.)

Where the applicant for judicial review asserted that the tribunal below misconstrued and failed to consider evidence, but the tribunal hearing was not recorded, the court permitted the applicant to file affidavits describing the evidence before the tribunal. The court addressed the respondent's concern that the applicant's affidavits were partial and self-serving by permitting the respondent to file its own affidavits.

Great Lakes Power Ltd. v. Ontario (Information & Privacy Commissioner) (1996), 48 C.P.C. (3d) 364 (Ont. Div. Ct.).

In respect of the judicial review of a decision reached following an inquisitorial process where the parties were to be heard in the absence of one another, the court refused to strike from the record affidavit material supplementing the text of the decision. The affidavit material would either cause no harm or would avoid difficulties in understanding the applicant's argument based on abuse of process which might arise if based only on the text of the decision.

Re Securicor Investigations & Security Ltd. and O.L.R.B. (1985), 50 O.R. (2d) 570, 10 Admin. L.R. 189, 18 D.L.R. (4th) 151, 8 O.A.C. 372 (Div. Ct.).

On an application for judicial review, affidavit evidence as to what evidence was before the tribunal can only be used to demonstrate complete absence of evidence on an essential point.

Re Keeprite Workers Independent Union and Keeprite Products Ltd. (1980), 29 O.R. (2d) 513, 114 D.L.R. (3d) 162 (C.A.); leave to appeal to Supreme Court of Canada refused 35 N.R. 85.

On judicial review under s. 2(3) of the *JRPA*, the record of the proceeding below may only be supplemented with fresh affidavit evidence where necessary to demonstrate a complete absence of evidence on an essential point.

Unauthorized Decision — s. 2(4)

Godfrey v. Ontario Police Commission (1991), 5 O.R. (3d) 163, 7 Admin. L.R. (2d) 9, 83 D.L.R. (4th) 501, 53 O.A.C. 338 (Div. Ct.).

The court set aside an order of the Ontario Police Commission where the Commission made a jurisdictional error in construing the scope of its dispositive powers under regulations made pursuant to the *Police Services Act*.

O.S.S.T.F., District 53 v. Haldimand Board of Education (1991), 5 O.R. (3d) 21, 6 Admin. L.R. (2d) 177, 15 C.H.R.R.D./475, 83 D.L.R. (4th) 762, 52 O.A.C. 15 (Div. Ct.).

The court set aside the finding of an arbitration board where the board failed to interpret a collective agreement in accordance with the *Human Rights Code*. That constituted an error in law, as the governing legislation expressly provided that, where there was a conflict between a collective agreement and a provision in an Act, the Act governed.

Biscotti v. Ontario (Securities Commission) (1991), 1 O.R. (3d) 409, 76 D.L.R. (4th) 762, 45 O.A.C. 293 (C.A.); leave to appeal to Supreme Court of Canada refused 3 O.R. (3d) xii, 136 N.R. 407 (note), 50 O.A.C. 160 (note).

The court set aside an interlocutory ruling of the Ontario Securities Commission, where it had made a jurisdictional error by making a blanket ruling, in advance of the calling of any witnesses, that it would not consent to the production of any transcripts supplied under s. 11 of the *Securities Act*, R.S.O. 1980, c. 466 for the purpose of cross-examinations.

Ontario (Employment Standards Officer) v. Equitable Management Ltd. (1990), 75 O.R. (2d) 506, 47 Admin. L.R. 75, 33 C.C.E.L. 114, 90 C.L.L.C. 14,044, 74 D.L.R. (4th) 422, 40 O.A.C. 384 (Div. Ct.).

The court set aside the decision of a referee appointed under the *Employment Standards Act*, R.S.O. 1980, c. 137 where the referee misinterpreted the meaning of s. 13(2) of that Act.

Re Hussey and A.G.Ont. (1984), 46 O.R. (2d) 554, 4 Admin. L.R. 147, 43 C.P.C. 230, 13 C.C.C. (3d) 81, 14 C.R.R. 369, 9 D.L.R. (4th) 696, 3 O.A.C. 166 (Div. Ct.).

Where superintendents of correctional institutions exercise or purport to exercise statutory powers, the court has jurisdiction to review possible violations of prisoners' rights under the *Charter of Rights*.

Re Milstein and Ont. College of Pharmacy (1978), 20 O.R. (2d) 283, 87 D.L.R. (3d) 392, 2 L. Med. Q. 297 (C.A.).

On an application for judicial review of a decision of a disciplinary tribunal, the court may interfere with an improper penalty imposed by the tribunal, as where the penalty is beyond the jurisdiction of the tribunal or demonstrates an error of law.

Parties

Re Ronark Devs. and Hamilton (1974), 4 O.R. (2d) 195 (Div. Ct.); leave to appeal to Ont. C.A. granted without written reasons, appeal dismissed on consent 5 O.R. (2d) 136n (C.A.).

Where a municipality strenuously resists the application by a development corporation for a *mandamus* compelling the issuance of a building permit, a ratepayers' association ought not to be added as a party to the proceedings.

Noddle v. Toronto (1982), 37 O.R. (2d) 421 (H.C.).

Because an application seeking judicial review of a decision by a municipality to issue a building permit to a bus company contained allegations with respect to employee rights, the applicant, a union representative and employee of the company, was permitted to make the application.

Re Metro. Toronto and Bremner (No. 1) (1980), 29 O.R. (2d) 531, 114 D.L.R. (3d) 224 (H.C.).

In an application for judicial review of an order directing that writs of possession be executed against homes on Toronto Island, the court added the residents of the homes as "interested parties" but refused to add the City of Toronto.

Re Durham and A.G Ont. (1978), 23 O.R. (2d) 279, 95 D.L.R. (3d) 327 (H.C.).

In an application for judicial review of a regulation closing a registry office, affected individuals and municipalities have a greater interest than the general public and thus have standing. As the decision to close for reasons of fiscal restraint was a policy decision, no hearing was necessary.

Re Kingston and Mining & Lands Commr. (1977), 18 O.R. (2d) 166 (Div. Ct.).

Where a tribunal's order inaccurately embodies a settlement agreement, an affected party may bring an application for judicial review.

McDonald's Restaurants of Can. Ltd. v. Etobicoke (1977), 5 C.P.C. 55 (Ont. Div. Ct.).

The court refused to add as a party a ratepayer who sought to intervene in an application for judicial review for a building permit, on the ground that his interests were already adequately represented by the municipality.

Re Starr and Puslinch (1976), 12 O.R. (2d) 40 (Div. Ct.).

Two companies whose legal rights and financial positions would be directly affected by the determination of a ratepayer's challenge of a designation in a township's official plan were added as respondents to the application for judicial review.

Re Multi-Malls Inc. and Min. of Transportation & Communications (1975), 7 O.R. (2d) 717 (Div. Ct.).

Where an adjoining municipality has a conflicting interest in a proposed scheme for land development, it should be added as a party respondent to the application for judicial review.

Re Orangeville Highlands Ltd. and Mono; Re Orangeville Highlands Ltd. and A.G. Ont. (1974), 5 O.R. (2d) 266 (Div. Ct.).

A neighbouring municipality, whose interest is the protection of ratepayers and the business community, is not a proper party to an application for a *mandamus* order in a judicial review concerning the granting of a building permit.

Section 3

Defects in form, technical irregularities

3. On an application for judicial review in relation to a statutory power of decision, where the sole ground for relief established is a defect in form or a technical irregularity, if the court finds that no substantial wrong or miscarriage of justice has occurred, the court may refuse relief and, where the decision has already been made, may make an order validating the decision, despite such defect, to have effect from such time and on such terms as the court considers proper.

Case Law

Borton v. Ontario, 2013 CarswellOnt 14272, 2013 ONSC 6418, 53 M.V.R. (6th) 41 (S.C.J.)

The court dismissed an application for judicial review arising from defects and irregularities in a Notice of Suspension of a truck driver's driving licence. Although the notice failed to state the remedial steps required to be taken by the applicant and referenced a long-repealed statutory provision, other communications from the Deputy Registrar of Motor Vehicles to the applicant made clear that no substantial wrong or miscarriage of justice had occurred.

Martin v. Ontario (Municipal Employees Retirement Board), 2002 CarswellOnt 3717, 47 Admin. L.R. (3d) 100, 33 C.C.P.B. 224, 2002 C.E.B. & P.G.R. 8447 (headnote only), [2002] O.J. No. 2286 (Div. Ct.)

Where the decision of a tribunal was delivered by a panel that included a tribunal member who had not been present for the hearing, the presence of the member was only a defect in form and did not result in a substantial wrong or miscarriage of justice. The record made clear that the member had not participated in the decision.

Ellis-Don Ltd. v. Ontario (Labour Relations Board), 10 O.R. (3d) 729, 6 Admin. L.R. (2d) 314, [1992] O.L.R.B. Rep. 764, 57 O.A.C. 11 (Div. Ct.).

The court dismissed a motion to stay a decision of the Ontario Labour Relations Board pending adjudication of an application for judicial review, as the applicant had failed to establish a strong *prima facie* case.

Sobeys Inc. v. U.F.C.W., Local 1000A (1993), 12 O.R. (3d) 157, 93 C.L.L.C. 14,041, 62 O.A.C. 78 (Div. Ct.).

An application to stay the implementation of a decision of the Ontario Labour Relations Board should not be allowed unless a strong *prima facie* case is established that the decision in question is patently unreasonable.

University of Toronto v. C.U.E.W., Local 2 (1988), 65 O.R. (2d) 268, 30 Admin. L.R. 310, 52 D.L.R. (4th) 128, 28 O.A.C. 295 (Div. Ct.).

The court should discourage the interruption of labour relations hearings by declining to decide judicial review applications from interim awards, and by imposing appropriate costs orders, unless the proceeding arises out of exceptional circumstances.

Gardner v. Cornwall Bd. of Commrs. of Police (1986), 56 O.R. (2d) 189, 13 C.C.E.L. 143, 16 O.A.C. 238 (Div. Ct.).

An interim order was granted staying appeal to the Police Commission, pending final determination of a judicial review.

Metro. Toronto School Bd. v. Ontario (Min. of Education) (1985), 53 O.R. (2d) 70, 6 C.P.C. (2d) 281, 23 D.L.R. (4th) 303, 13 O.A.C. 113 (Div. Ct.).

Where a regulation is the subject of an application for judicial review, the regulation should be presumed valid until the application is heard, particularly where the applicants will not suffer irreparable harm if there is no interim order made.

Re United Headwear, Optical & Allied Workers Union of Can., Loc. 3 and Biltmore/Stetson (Can.) Inc. (1983), 41 O.R. (2d) 287, 83 C.L.L.C. 14,037; reversed on other grounds 43 O.R. (2d) 243, (sub nom. *Employees of Biltmore/Stetson (Can.) Inc. v. H.C.M.W., Hat Workers Union, Loc. 82)* 6 Admin. L.R. 281, (sub nom. *Hat Workers Union, H.C.M.W., Loc. 82 v. United Headwear, Optical & Allied Workers Union of Can., Loc. 3)* 83 C.L.L.C. 14,062, 150 D.L.R. (3d) 577 (C.A.).

Notice to bargain given by a trade union to a successor employer before the sale of the business is not effective as a certification. A motions court judge has jurisdiction to hear an application under this section.

Wells Fargo Armcar Inc. v. O.L.R.B. (1981), 34 O.R. (2d) 99 (H.C.).

The High Court has the power, using the criteria applicable to injunctions, to stay a decision of the Ontario Labour Relations Board. However, a strong *prima facie* case of entitlement to relief is not established where the actions of the board do not appear to involve an improper construction of s. 12 of the *Labour Relations Act*.

Re Hayles and Sproule (1980), 29 O.R. (2d) 500 (Div. Ct.).

Pending a judicial review of a disciplinary decision made under the *Police Act*, the court may order a stay of the hearing of the appeal pursuant to s. 4 of this Act.

Re Dylex Ltd. and A.C.T.W. Union Toronto Joint Bd. (1977), 17 O.R. (2d) 488, 77 C.L.L.C. 14,105 (H.C.).

Where a negative vote in a certification drive provides a *prima facie* case for an employer, and if irreparable harm would otherwise result, the court has inherent jurisdiction to stay an order for certification, despite a finding of no urgency and a lack of such express provision in the Rules of Practice or in the Act.

Re I.W.A. and Patchogue Plymouth, Hawkesbury Mills (1976), 14 O.R. (2d) 118, 2 C.P.C. 98 (H.C.).

An application for judicial review of an arbitration award does not effect an automatic stay of its operation. A stay may be obtained by interim order of the Divisional Court under s. 4 of this Act.

Section 4

Interim order

4. On an application for judicial review, the court may make such interim order as it considers proper pending the final determination of the application.

Case Law

Aviva Canada Inc. v. Taylor, 2017 CarswellOnt 6314, 2017 ONSC 2661, 67 C.C.L.I. (5th) 71 (Div. Ct.)

Where the Licence Appeal Tribunal twice refused to grant an insurer an adjournment, the court dismissed the insurer's s. 4 motion to stay the Licence Appeal Tribunal proceeding pending the insurer's application for judicial review of the refusals. There was no evidence that the insurer would suffer irreparable harm.

Ontario Provincial Police Commissioner v. MacDonald (December 11, 2008), Doc. Toronto 564/08, 2008 CarswellOnt 7511, [2008] O.J. No. 5053 (Div. Ct.)

The three-part test for interlocutory relief articulated in *RJR-MacDonald Inc. v. Canada (Attorney General)*, 1994 CarswellQue 120F, 1994 CarswellQue 120, [1994] 1 S.C.R. 311, 54 C.P.R. (3d) 114, 111 D.L.R. (4th) 385, [1994] S.C.J. No. 17, applies to a motion to stay tribunal proceedings pending an application for judicial review. The moving party must show that: (a) the application raises a serious question; (b) irreparable harm will result if the stay is not granted; and (c) the balance of convenience favours the granting of a stay.

Section 5

Extension of time for bringing application

5. Despite any limitation of time for the bringing of an application for judicial review fixed by or under any Act, the court may extend the time for making the application, either before or after expiration of the time so limited, on such terms as it considers proper, where it is satisfied that there are apparent grounds for relief and that no substantial prejudice or hardship will result to any person affected by reason of the delay.

Case Law

Leo Alarie & Sons Ltd. v. R., 2003 CarswellOnt 1698, (sub nom. *Alarie (Leo) & Sons Ltd. v. Ontario (Minister of Natural Resources))* 171 O.A.C. 381, [2003] O.J. No. 1777 (Div. Ct.)

Applying *Cessland*, the court confirmed that the limitation provisions of the *Mining Act*, which specifically states that s. 5 of the *JRPA* does not apply, prevails over s. 5 of the *JRPA* and precludes an extension of time to bring an application for judicial review.

Re Cessland Corp. and Fort Norman Explorations Inc. (1979), 25 O.R. (2d) 69, 100 D.L.R. (3d) 378 (H.C.).

Where a specific provision of the *Mining Act* precluded an extension of the time for bringing an application for judicial review, an application received after the expiry of the statutory 30-day period was dismissed.

Section 6

Application to Divisional Court

6. (1) Subject to subsection (2), an application for judicial review shall be made to the Divisional Court.

Application to judge of Superior Court of Justice

(2) An application for judicial review may be made to the Superior Court of Justice with leave of a judge thereof, which may be granted at the hearing of the application, where it is made to appear to the judge that the case is one of urgency and that the delay required for an application to the Divisional Court is likely to involve a failure of justice.

Transfer to Divisional Court

(3) Where a judge refuses leave for an application under subsection (2), he or she may order that the application be transferred to the Divisional Court.

Appeal to Court of Appeal

(4) An appeal lies to the Court of Appeal, with leave of the Court of Appeal, from a final order of the Superior Court of Justice disposing of an application for judicial review pursuant to leave granted under subsection (2).

2006, c. 19, Sched. C, s. 1(1)

Case Law

General Principles — s. 6(2)

Asa v. University Health Network, 2015 CarswellOnt 13181, 2015 ONSC 5389 (Div. Ct.)

The two-factor test for leave under s. 6(2) requires a limited review of the merits. It is sufficient if the application is not clearly devoid of merit.

Granting of Leave for Hearing by a Judge — s. 6(2)

Gymnopoulos v. Ontario Assn. of Basketball Officials, 2016 CarswellOnt 3250, 2016 ONSC 1525, [2016] O.J. No. 1097 (S.C.J.)

A case for an urgent hearing by a single judge was made out where the impugned tribunal decision would preclude the applicant basketball coach from participating in the end of the game season.

Kuki v. Ontario (Ministry of Training, Colleges, and Universities), 2013 CarswellOnt 12275, 2013 ONSC 5574 (S.C.J.)

Leave to be heard on an urgent basis was denied where the application for review was without merit.

Boehringer Ingelheim (Canada) Ltd./Ltée v. Canadian Agency for Drugs & Technologies in Health, 2008 CarswellOnt 6754, [2008] O.J. No. 4331 (Div. Ct.)

Leave to be heard by a single judge was denied where the application for judicial review could be heard by a panel of the Divisional Court later in the same week.

Korea Data Systems Co. v. Chiang, 2007 CarswellOnt 6831, 36 C.B.R. (5th) 311, (sub nom. *Chiang (Trustee of) v. Chiang))* [2007] O.J. No. 4085 (S.C.J. [Commercial List]); affirmed 2009 ONCA 3, 2009 CarswellOnt 28, (sub nom. *Chiang (Trustee of) v. Chiang)* 93 O.R. (3d) 483, 49 C.B.R. (5th) 1, 78 C.P.C. (6th) 110, 305 D.L.R. (4th) 655, (sub nom. *Mendlowitz & Associates Inc. v. Chiang)* 257 O.A.C. 64, [2009] O.J. No. 41; additional reasons 2009 ONCA 153, 2009 CarswellOnt 769, 50 C.B.R. (5th) 13, 68 C.P.C. (6th) 32; additional reasons 2010 ONCA 67, 2010 CarswellOnt 345, 63 C.B.R. (5th) 201, [2010] O.J. No. 285

The requirement of urgency was met in an application to quash the decision of the parole board granting parole to a person incarcerated for contempt of court.

Provan v. Ontario (Registrar of Gaming Control) (1994), 20 O.R. (3d) 632 (Div. Ct.).

Where the applicant would suffer substantial and irreparable pecuniary loss as a result of delay, leave was granted as the case was one of sufficient urgency that any delay would involve a failure of justice.

Jafine v. College of Veterinarians (Ontario) (1991), 5 O.R. (3d) 439, 6 Admin. L.R. (2d) 147 (Gen. Div.).

The court dismissed an application for judicial review to be heard by a single judge, where the apprehension of the consequences of a negative result from a discipline committee hearing did not form the basis of a valid argument of urgency, or establish that the delay was likely to involve a failure of justice. It was also inappropriate to refer the matter to Divisional Court until after a decision had been rendered by the committee.

Re Passmore and St. Marys (1984), 47 O.R. (2d) 262 (H.C.).

A municipality was granted leave to apply for judicial review, to be heard by a single judge, of a board's decision approving a dump site where the present site was fully used and the municipality intended to start construction on a new site in the near future.

Re T and Western Region Bd. of Review (1983), 44 O.R. (2d) 153, 3 D.L.R. (4th) 442 (H.C.).

Leave was granted as a matter of urgency for judicial review of a decision of a board authorizing electroconvulsive therapy for an involuntary, unconsenting patient.

Re Emerson and L.S.U.C. (1983), 44 O.R. (2d) 729, 41 C.P.C. 7, 5 D.L.R. (4th) 294 (H.C.).

In a case of urgency and likely failure of justice, the court will grant leave for judicial review of the decisions of the discipline committee of the Law Society before consideration by convocation.

Re United Headwear, Optical & Allied Workers Union of Can., Loc. 3 and Biltmore/Stetson (Can.) Inc. (1983), 41 O.R. (2d) 287, 83 C.L.L.C. 14,037; reversed on other grounds 43 O.R. (2d) 243, (sub nom. *Employees of Biltmore/Stetson (Can.) Inc. v. H.C.M.W., Hat Workers Union, Loc. 82)* 6 Admin. L.R. 281, (sub nom. *Hat Workers Union, H.C.M.W., Loc. 82 v. United Headwear, Optical & Allied Workers Union of Can., Loc. 3)* 83 C.L.L.C. 14,062, 150 D.L.R. (3d) 577 (C.A.).

Where a board's decision wrongly caused substantial delay to an application for certification as a bargaining agent, leave to apply for judicial review to a High Court judge was granted.

Wells Fargo Armcar Inc. v. O.L.R.B. (1981), 34 O.R. (2d) 99 (H.C.).

Where delay does not emasculate the certification of a trade union or place the parties in an irredeemably adversarial position, neither urgency nor a failure of justice has been established so as to justify leave under subs. (2) for judicial review of a decision certifying a trade union.

Re Clarke Institute of Psychiatry and C.C.A.S. of Metro. Toronto (1981), 31 O.R. (2d) 486, 20 C.P.C. 46, 119 D.L.R. (3d) 247 (H.C.).

A determination of whether a ten-month-old child was in need of protection or should be returned to his mother, where the Children's Aid Society was planning to put the child up for adoption, presented a matter of urgency and leave was granted for a hearing before a High Court judge.

Re C.P. Express Ltd. and Snow (1980), 31 O.R. (2d) 120, (sub nom. *C.P. Express Ltd. v. Min. of Transportation & Communications)* 19 C.P.C. 16, 118 D.L.R. (3d) 148; affirmed 32 O.R. (2d) 45, 121 D.L.R. (3d) 511 (C.A.).

Leave to apply for judicial review was granted where the delay in answering the question of whether a petition to the Lieutenant-Governor in Council operates as a stay of proceedings was likely to involve a failure of justice.

Re Metro. Toronto and Bremner (No. 1) (1980), 29 O.R. (2d) 531, 114 D.L.R. (3d) 224 (H.C.).

Where the delay in placing an application for judicial review before the Divisional Court calls into question the integrity, wholeness, adequacy, and validity of the judicial process, a failure of justice has occurred so as to justify a hearing of the application by a judge of the High Court.

Re Chapples Ltd. and Thunder Bay (1980), 27 O.R. (2d) 444, 106 D.L.R. (3d) 707; reversed on other grounds 29 O.R. (2d) 522 (C.A.).

Where the status of a nearly completed construction work was questioned, leave to make an application for judicial review to a judge of the High Court was granted, as the delay required for an application to the Divisional Court was likely to involve a failure of justice.

Re Bennett and Belleville (1979), 24 O.R. (2d) 121 (H.C.).

Where there is urgency and where the delay involved in an application for judicial review to the Divisional Court is likely to involve a failure of justice, an application may be heard by a single judge.

Smith v. Zeiger (1978), 2 R.F.L. (2d) 324 (Ont. H.C.).

Due to the protracted nature of an affiliation proceeding, sufficient urgency and potential failure of justice were established to justify an application for judicial review to the High Court.

Re Brendon and Univ. of Western Ont. Bd. of Governors (1977), 17 O.R. (2d) 721, 81 D.L.R. (3d) 260 (H.C.).

When an application for judicial review by a dismissed university teacher could not be heard by the Divisional Court before the start of a new academic year, it was held to be a case of such urgency and possible failure of justice as to justify judicial review by the High Court.

Bay Charles Centre v. Toronto (1977), 3 C.P.C. 343 (Ont. H.C.).

Prospective financial loss and delay are normally insufficient to constitute urgency within the meaning of subs. (2) and do not justify judicial review by a single judge when the Divisional Court is sitting.

Re Simpson and Henderson (1976), 13 O.R. (2d) 322, 71 D.L.R. (3d) 24 (H.C.).

The mere fact that an application to the Divisional Court will cause some delay is not *per se* a matter of emergency. Where, however, an application concerns an upcoming election and requires speedy disposition in the public interest, leave should be granted.

Re Taller and Assessment Commr. (1974), 7 O.R. (2d) 501 (H.C.).

Where the matter is urgent and the delay required for an application to the Divisional Court is likely to involve a failure of justice, the application may be heard in Weekly Court — but the mere consent of counsel is not sufficient for such change in jurisdiction.

Section 7

Summary disposition of mandamus, etc.

7. An application for an order in the nature of mandamus, prohibition or certiorari shall be deemed to be an application for judicial review and shall be made, treated and disposed of as if it were an application for judicial review.

Case Law

Re Beke and R. (1977), 15 O.R. (2d) 603, 34 C.C.C. (2d) 548 (Div. Ct.).

Applications for prohibition in relation to quasi-criminal matters (provincial offences) are governed by this Act and are heard by the Divisional Court; whereas applications for *certiorari, mandamus*, and prohibition in relation to criminal matters are heard by a single judge.

Re Brown and R. (1975), 11 O.R. (2d) 7, 30 C.C.C. (2d) 300, 64 D.L.R. (3d) 605 (H.C.).

An application by motion pursuant to s. 69 of the former *Judicature Act* was not an application for an order in the nature of *certiorari* within the meaning of s. 7.

Section 8

Summary disposition of actions

8. Where an action for a declaration or injunction, or both, whether with or without a claim for other relief, is brought and the exercise, refusal to exercise or proposed or purported exercise of a statutory power is an issue in the

action, a judge of the Superior Court of Justice may on the application of any party to the action, if he or she considers it appropriate, direct that the action be treated and disposed of summarily, in so far as it relates to the exercise, refusal to exercise or proposed or purported exercise of such power, as if it were an application for judicial review and may order that the hearing on such issue be transferred to the Divisional Court or may grant leave for it to be disposed of in accordance with subsection 6(2).

2006, c. 19, Sched. C, s. 1(1)

Case Law

South-West Oxford v. A.G. Ont. (1983), 44 O.R. (2d) 376, 40 C.P.C. 86, 8 Admin. L.R. 30 (H.C.).

The burden of proving grounds for transfer of an action to the Divisional Court to be dealt with as an application for judicial review rests with the party making the application. Where the applicant fails to establish sufficient grounds, the matter should proceed as an action.

Loblaws Ltd. v. Gloucester (1979), 25 O.R. (2d) 225, 10 C.P.C. 232, 100 D.L.R. (3d) 536 (Div. Ct.).

An application for summary judicial review under this section should not be made before the pleadings are completed. The onus is on the party seeking s. 8 review to establish that the case is an appropriate one for review by the Divisional Court.

Section 9

Sufficiency of application

9. (1) It is sufficient in an application for judicial review if an applicant sets out in the notice the grounds upon which he is seeking relief and the nature of the relief that he seeks without specifying the proceedings enumerated in subsection 2(1) in which the claim would have been made before the 17th day of April, 1972.

Exerciser of power may be a party

(2) For the purposes of an application for judicial review in relation to the exercise, refusal to exercise or proposed or purported exercise of a statutory power, the person who is authorized to exercise the power may be a party to the application.

Idem

(3) For the purposes of subsection (2), any two or more persons who, acting together, may exercise a statutory power, whether styled a board or commission or by any other collective title, shall be deemed to be a person under such collective title.

Notice to Attorney General

(4) Notice of an application for judicial review shall be served upon the Attorney General who is entitled as of right to be heard in person or by counsel on the application.

Case Law

Riddell v. The Law Society of Upper Canada, 2017 CarswellOnt 14733, 2017 ONCA 734

Section 9(2) of the *JRPA* confers on the impugned decision-making body a right to participate in the judicial review hearing, but does not confer an automatic right to participate in a subsequent appeal. The court denied a s. 9(2) tribunal the right to participate on appeal where the tribunal would not assist the court.

Children's Lawyer for Ontario v. Goodis, 2005 CarswellOnt 1419, 253 D.L.R. (4th) 489, (sub nom. *Ontario (Children's Lawyer) v. Ontario (Information & Privacy Commissioner))* 75 O.R. (3d) 309, 29 Admin. L.R. (4th) 86, 17 R.F.L. (6th) 32, 196 O.A.C. 350, [2005] O.J. No. 1426 (C.A.)

An administrative tribunal whose decision is attacked by way of judicial review has standing to participate in the review proceedings, but the scope of its standing is within the court's discretion.

Sutcliffe v. Ontario (Minister of Environment), 2004 CarswellOnt 1409, 242 D.L.R. (4th) 709, 69 O.R. (3d) 257, 14 Admin. L.R. (4th) 294, 7 C.E.L.R. (3d) 184, [2004] O.J. No. 277 (C.A. [In Chambers])

Pursuant to s. 9(4), the Attorney General may intervene as of right in an appeal from a judicial review decision of the Divisional Court, regardless of whether the Attorney General intervened in the original judicial review hearing appealed from.

Re Consolidated Bathurst Packaging Ltd. and I.W.A., Loc. 2-69 (1985), 51 O.R. (2d) 481, 16 Admin. L.R. 37, 14 C.L.L.C. 14,031, 20 D.L.R. (4th) 84, 10 O.A.C. 34 (Div. Ct.); reversed on other grounds (1986), 56 O.R. (2d) 513, 21 Admin. L.R. 180, 31 D.L.R. (4th) 444, 15 O.A.C. 398 (C.A.); affirmed (1990), 73 O.R. (2d) 676 (S.C.C.).

In s. 9(2), the word "may" confers on the person who is authorized to exercise the statutory power the right, but not the obligation, to be a party. Once a tribunal is properly a party to the proceedings, it becomes a rule of court, rather than a rule of law, to decide the extent to which it will be entitled to participate in the argument.

Section 10

Record to be filed in Ontario Court (General Division)

10. When notice of an application for judicial review of a decision made in the exercise or purported exercise of a statutory power of decision has been served on the person making the decision, such person shall forthwith file in the court for use on the application, the record of the proceedings in which the decision was made.

Case Law

K.D. v. Peel Children's Aid Society, 2017 CarswellOnt 19400, 2017 ONSC 7392 (Div. Ct.)

The court dismissed a respondent's motion to have additional materials included in the record of proceedings filed by the applicant where the additional materials were not relied upon by the decision-maker.

Misra v. CUPE, Local 79, 2016 CarswellOnt 14401, 2016 ONSC 5713 (Div. Ct.)

As a general rule, the record of proceedings should comprise only those materials that were before the decision-maker at the time the decision was made.

Pritchard v. Ontario (Human Rights Commission), 2003 CarswellOnt 182, 63 O.R. (3d) 97, 22 C.C.E.L. (3d) 201, 223 D.L.R. (4th) 85, 27 C.P.C. (5th) 223 (C.A.); affirmed 2004 CarswellOnt 1874, 2004 CarswellOnt 1875, 319 O.R. (3d) 322 (S.C.C.); additional reasons 2004 SCC 31, 2004 CarswellOnt 1885, 2004 CarswellOnt 1886, [2004] 1 S.C.R. 809, 72 O.R. (3d) 160 (note), 47 C.P.C. (5th) 203, 19 C.R. (6th) 203, [2004] S.C.J. No. 16

An in-house legal opinion prepared by a tribunal in aid of its decision need not be included in the record of proceedings. Nothing in the drafting of s. 10 suggests that the section was intended to abrogate solicitor-client privilege.

Payne v. Ontario (Human Rights Commission), 2000 CarswellOnt 2717, 25 Admin. L.R. (3d) 255, 2 C.C.E.L. (3d) 171, 192 D.L.R. (4th) 315, [2000] O.J. No. 2987 (C.A.)

An applicant for judicial review has the right to have a full and accurate record of what went on before the tribunal put before the court. Exercising its inherent jurisdiction, the court may insist upon the production of an adequate record of the proceedings before the tribunal being reviewed, and may order an inferior tribunal to complete the record.

Section 11

References in other Acts, etc.

11. (1) Subject to subsection (2), where reference is made in any other Act or in any regulation, rule or by-law to any of the proceedings enumerated in subsection 2(1), such reference shall be read and construed to include a reference to an application for judicial review.

Proceeding under Habeas Corpus Act

(2) Nothing in this Act affects proceedings under the *Habeas Corpus Act* or the issue of a writ of certiorari thereunder or proceedings pursuant thereto, but an application for judicial review may be brought in aid of an application for a writ of *habeas corpus*.

Case Law

Re Brown and R. (1975), 11 O.R. (2d) 7, 30 C.C.C. (2d) 300, 64 D.L.R. (3d) 605 (H.C.).

Since an application pursuant to s. 69 of the former *Judicature Act* was not an application for an order in the nature of *certiorari*, s. 12 did not apply.

STATUTORY POWERS PROCEDURE ACT

R.S.O. 1990, c. S.22

as am. S.O. 1993, c. 27, Sched.; 1994, c. 27, s. 56; 1997, c. 23, s. 13; 1999, c. 12, Sched. B, s. 16; 2002, c. 17, Sched. F, s. 1; 2006, c. 19, Sched. B, s. 21, Sched. C, s. 1(1), (2), (4); 2006, c. 21, Sched. C, s. 134, Sched. F, s. 136(1), Table 1; 2009, c. 33, Sched. 6, s. 87; 2015, c. 23, s. 5.

Section 1

Definitions

1. (1) In this Act,

"Committee" [Repealed 1994, c. 27, s. 56.]

"electronic hearing" means a hearing held by conference telephone or some other form of electronic technology allowing persons to hear one another;

"hearing" means a hearing in any proceeding;

"licence" includes any permit, certificate, approval, registration or similar form of permission required by law;

"municipality" has the same meaning as in the *Municipal Affairs Act*;

"oral hearing" means a hearing at which the parties or their representatives attend before the tribunal in person;

"proceeding" means a proceeding to which this Act applies;

"representative" means, in respect of a proceeding to which this Act applies, a person authorized under the *Law Society Act* to represent a person in that proceeding;

"statutory power of decision" means a power or right, conferred by or under a statute, to make a decision deciding or prescribing,

(a) the legal rights, powers, privileges, immunities, duties or liabilities of any person or party, or

(b) the eligibility of any person or party to receive, or to the continuation of, a benefit or licence, whether the person is legally entitled thereto or not;

"tribunal" means one or more persons, whether or not incorporated and however described, upon which a statutory power of decision is conferred by or under a statute;

"written hearing" means a hearing held by means of the exchange of documents, whether in written form or by electronic means.

Meaning of "person" extended

(2) A municipality, an unincorporated association of employers, a trade union or council of trade unions who may be a party to a proceeding in the exercise of a statutory power of decision under the statute conferring the pow-

ers, shall be deemed to be a person for the purpose of any provision of this Act or of any rule made under this Act that applies to parties.

1994, c. 27, s. 56; 2002, c. 17, Sched. F, s. 1; 2006, c. 21, Sched. C, s. 134(1), (2)

Case Law

Statutory Power of Decision — Not Being Exercised — s. 1(1)

B. v. W. (1985), 52 O.R. (2d) 738, (sub nom. *B. (Y.) v. W. (R.))* 16 Admin. L.R. 99, 23 D.L.R. (4th) 248 (H.C.).

When a university decides to suspend a student, the *Statutory Powers Procedure Act* does not apply as such a decision is not made in the exercise of a specific power conferred by statute.

Re Hancock and Algonquin College of Applied Arts and Technology Bd. of Governors (1981), 33 O.R. (2d) 257, 124 D.L.R. (3d) 148 (H.C.).

A college board of governors in carrying out its duty under the *Ministry of Colleges and Universities Act* to recommend annual budget estimates to the Council of Regents exercises an administrative duty and hence does not exercise a statutory power of decision.

Re Weston and Chiropody (Podiatry) Review Ctee. (1980), 29 O.R. (2d) 129, 112 D.L.R. (3d) 343 (C.A.).

Where a review committee considers claims referred to it by the General Manager of the Ontario Health Insurance Plan, its function is purely administrative and thus it does not exercise a statutory power of decision.

Re McGill and Brantford (1980), 28 O.R. (2d) 721, 12 M.P.L.R. 24, 111 D.L.R. (3d) 405 (Div. Ct.).

The function of closing a road is not a statutory power of decision. The power to do so by by-law is a "statutory power" reviewable under the *Judicial Review Procedure Act*, s. 1(g)(i), but that does not attract the application of the *Statutory Powers Procedure Act*.

Re All Ont. Tpt. Ltd. and Ont. Highway Tpt. Bd. (1979), 26 O.R. (2d) 202 (Div. Ct.).

The Board does not exercise a statutory power of decision with regard to an intervenor. A decision would not affect an intervenor's eligibility to receive any benefit nor would a decision from the Board be deciding an intervenor's legal rights.

Re O.S.S.T.F. and Shelton (1979), 28 O.R. (2d) 218, 109 D.L.R. (3d) 59 (Div. Ct.).

The Relations and Discipline Committee of the O.S.S.T.F. does not exercise a statutory power of decision as it only recommends courses of action to the Federation.

Re Webb and Ont. Housing Corp. (1977), 18 O.R. (2d) 427; affirmed 22 O.R. (2d) 257, 93 D.L.R. (3d) 187 (C.A.).

A decision by the Ontario Housing Corporation to terminate a tenancy is not a statutory power of decision.

Re Polten and Univ. of Toronto Governing Council (1975), 8 O.R. (2d) 749, 59 D.L.R. (3d) 197 (Div. Ct.).

The determination of academic appeals by a university faculty committee, where permitted by statute, is not the exercise of statutory power of decision unless the committee was specifically required by law to permit the applicant to be heard before reaching a decision.

Re Raney and Ont. (1974), 4 O.R. (2d) 249, 47 D.L.R. (3d) 533 (C.A.).

The Ministry of Transportation and Communications Qualification Committee is an internal administrative body without statutory existence, thus it cannot be said to be exercising a statutory power of decision.

Re Lamoureux and Reg. of Motor Vehicles, [1973] 2 O.R. 28, 20 C.R.N.S. 254, 10 C.C.C. (2d) 475, 32 D.L.R. (3d) 678 (C.A.).

The automatic suspension of a driver's licence of an individual convicted of impaired driving does not involve any decision-making. Thus, the suspension is not a result of a statutory power of decision.

Re Robertson and Niagara South Bd. of Educ. (1973), 1 O.R. (2d) 548, 41 D.L.R. (3d) 57 (Div. Ct.).

The power exercised by the Board of Education to order the closing of a particular school is not a statutory power of decision. Furthermore, the decision to close a particular school does not affect the rights or privileges of children attending the school as there is no legal right or privilege to have one's children attend a particular school.

Re Florence Nightingale Home and Scarborough Planning Bd., [1973] 1 O.R. 615, 32 D.L.R. (3d) 17 (Div. Ct.).

The conducting of a meeting by a planning board to determine whether or not to recommend changes in zoning by-laws to a council is not an exercise of a statutory power of decision.

Re Thomas and Ctee. of College Presidents, [1973] 3 O.R. 404, 37 D.L.R. (3d) 69 (Div. Ct.).

Where a university committee has decision-making functions transferred to it by a university, this is not a statutory power of decision as the enabling legislation does not impose any duty upon the committee to make decisions.

Statutory Power of Decision — Being Exercised — s. 1(1)

Re Temple and Liquor Licence Bd. of Ont. (1982), 41 O.R. (2d) 214, 145 D.L.R. (3d) 480 (Div. Ct.).

In deciding whether or not to issue a liquor licence to an applicant, the Liquor Licence Board exercises a statutory power of decision.

Re Grant Bus Lines Ltd. and Pension Comm. of Ont. (1980), 30 O.R. (2d) 180, 116 D.L.R. (3d) 336; affirmed (1981), 33 O.R. (2d) 652, 125 D.L.R. (3d) 325 (C.A.); leave to appeal to Supreme Court of Canada refused (1981), 41 N.R. 374.

The Pension Commission of Ontario in making its decisions under the *Pension Benefits Act* affects the legal rights and the eligibility of a person to receive a benefit. Hence, the commission exercises a statutory power of decision.

Re Forde and O.S.S.T.F. (1980), 30 O.R. (2d) 169, 115 D.L.R. (3d) 673 (Div. Ct.).

A statutory obligation to belong to the Federation means that decisions regarding a member's conduct will affect his rights and privileges. Thus the Federation when deciding these matters is exercising a statutory power of decision.

Re Paine and Univ. of Toronto (1980), 30 O.R. (2d) 69, 115 D.L.R. (3d) 461; reversed on other grounds (1981), 34 O.R. (2d) 770, 131 D.L.R. (3d) 325 (C.A.); leave to appeal to Supreme Court of Canada refused (1982), 42 N.R. 270.

The awarding of tenured appointments by a university president, where such power is conferred on that individual by the governing council, is an exercise of a statutory power of decision.

Re Stone and L.S.U.C. (1979), 26 O.R. (2d) 166, 102 D.L.R. (3d) 176 (Div. Ct.).

The Discipline Committee of the Law Society of Upper Canada exercises a quasi-judicial function and its proceedings involve a "statutory power of decision" within s. 1 of the Act.

Re Grant and Metro. Toronto (1978), 21 O.R. (2d) 282 (Div. Ct.).

The discretionary power of a municipal council to pay the legal costs incurred by police officers in defending themselves against charges is a statutory power of decision.

Re Windsor and I.A.F.F. Loc. 455 (1974), 5 O.R. (2d) 690, 51 D.L.R. (3d) 346 (Div. Ct.).

In carrying out its functions, an arbitration board acting under s. 6 of the *Fire Departments Act* exercises a statutory power of decision.

Re Thompson and Lambton Bd. of Educ., [1972] 3 O.R. 889, 30 D.L.R. (3d) 32 (H.C.).

A board of reference convened and acting under the *Schools Administration Act* exercises a statutory power of decision. Despite the fact that the board reports to the Minister of Education, the function of the Minister is purely mandatory — to "direct the implementation of the direction of the board of reference".

Tribunal — s. 1(1)

Re Windsor and I.A.F.F. Loc. 455 (1974), 5 O.R. (2d) 690, 51 D.L.R. (3d) 346 (Div. Ct.).

A board of arbitration acting under s. 6 of the *Fire Departments Act* is a tribunal as defined in the *Statutory Powers Procedure Act*. [*cf. s. 1(1)(d), s. 15.*]

Re Raney and Ont. (1974), 4 O.R. (2d) 249, 47 D.L.R. (3d) 533 (C.A.).

The Ministry of Transportation and Communications Qualification Committee is an internal administrative body without statutory existence, thus it cannot be said to be exercising a statutory power of decision.

Section 2

Interpretation

2. This Act, and any rule made by a tribunal under subsection 17.1(4) or section 25.1, shall be liberally construed to secure the just, most expeditious and cost-effective determination of every proceeding on its merits.

1999, c. 12, Sched. B, s. 16(1); 2006, c. 19, Sched. B, s. 21(1)

Section 3

Application of Act

3. (1) Subject to subsection (2), this Act applies to a proceeding by a tribunal in the exercise of a statutory power of decision conferred by or under an Act of the Legislature, where the tribunal is required by or under such Act or otherwise by law to hold or to afford to the parties to the proceeding an opportunity for a hearing before making a decision.

Where Act does not apply

(2) This Act does not apply to a proceeding,

(a) before the Assembly or any committee of the Assembly;

(b) in or before,

(i) the Court of Appeal,

(ii) the Superior Court of Justice,

(iii) the Ontario Court of Justice,

(iv) the Family Court of the Superior Court of Justice,

(v) the Small Claims Court, or

(vi) a justice of the peace;

(c) to which the Rules of Civil Procedure apply;

(d) before an arbitrator to which the *Arbitrations Act* or the *Labour Relations Act* applies;

(e) at a coroner's inquest;

(f) of a commission appointed under the *Public Inquiries Act, 2009*;

(g) of one or more persons required to make an investigation and to make a report, with or without recommendations, where the report is for the information or advice of the person to whom it is made and does not in any way legally bind or limit that person in any decision he or she may have power to make; or

(h) of a tribunal empowered to make regulations, rules or by-laws in so far as its power to make regulations, rules or by-laws is concerned.

1994, c. 27, s. 56; 2006, c. 19, Sched. C, s. 1(1), (2), (4); 2009, c. 33, Sched. 6, s. 87

Case Law

Application of Act — s. 3(1)

Masters v. Ontario (1994), 18 O.R. (3d) 551, 27 Admin. L.R. (2d) 152, 115 D.L.R. (4th) 319, 72 O.A.C. 1 (Div. Ct.).

The government retained outside counsel to investigate and report on allegations of sexual harassment made against the Agent General for Ontario in New York. The Agent subsequently resigned, but brought an application for judicial review, and an order in the nature of *certiorari* quashing the report. It was held that the Act had no application to the original investigation nor to the preparation of the report in the circumstances of the case. No statutory power of decision had been exercised within the meaning of the Act; no hearing was required either by statute or "otherwise by law".

Re Grant and Metro. Toronto (1978), 21 O.R. (2d) 282 (Div. Ct.).

As the *Police Act* imposes no requirement that a trial-type hearing be held, the only other requirement would be "otherwise by law". As the Metropolitan Council makes administrative type decisions, it is not bound in law to provide the trial-type hearing and is not subject to the *Statutory Powers Procedure Act.*

Re Krofchick and Prov. Ins. Co. (1978), 21 O.R. (2d) 805, 91 D.L.R. (3d) 744 (Div. Ct.).

Insurance appraisers are not required by the *Insurance Act* or "otherwise by law" to provide the parties with an opportunity to be heard. Therefore the *Statutory Powers Procedure Act* does not apply to the appraisers.

Re Doctors Hosp. and Min. of Health (1976), 12 O.R. (2d) 164, 1 C.P.C. 232, 68 D.L.R. (3d) 220 (Div. Ct.).

The *Statutory Powers Procedure Act* is not binding on the Crown. However, where the Lieutenant Governor in Council decides to revoke the approval of certain hospitals as public hospitals no right of the Crown is affected by the proceedings.

Exceptions — s. 3(2)(d) — Before an Arbitrator

Re H.F.I.A. and Master Insulators Assn. of Ont. (1979), 25 O.R. (2d) 8, 99 D.L.R. (3d) 757 (Div. Ct.).

The Ontario Labour Relations Board in hearing a grievance regarding a collective agreement comes to a final binding result. The board sits as an arbitrator and decides as an arbitrator. Thus, the *Statutory Powers Procedure Act* does not apply to the board.

Where There is an Investigation and Report — s. 3(2)(g)

Hryciuk v. Ontario (Lieutenant Governor) (1994), 18 O.R. (3d) 695, 115 D.L.R. (4th) 227, 71 O.A.C. 289 (Div. Ct.).

A Commissioner appointed under s. 50 of the *Courts of Justice Act* to determine whether a Provincial Court Judge should be removed from office exercised a statutory power of decision, but s. 3(2)(g) removed the proceeding from the application of Part I.

Re Emerson and L.S.U.C. (1984), 44 O.R. (2d) 729, 41 C.P.C. 7, 5 D.L.R. (4th) 294 (H.C.).

Since the Discipline Committee of the Law Society is the first stage of a single disciplinary proceeding, it does not come within the hearing exemption of s. 3(2)(g).

Re Abel and Dir., Penetanguishene Mental Health Centre; Re Abel and Advisory Review Bd. (1979), 24 O.R. (2d) 279, 46 C.C.C. (2d) 342, 97 D.L.R. (3d) 304; affirmed (1980), 31 O.R. (2d) 520, 56 C.C.C. (2d) 153, 119 D.L.R. (3d) 101 (C.A.).

The Advisory Review Board created under the *Mental Health Act* annually reviews applicants' cases and makes recommendations to the Lieutenant Governor. As the board's report is not binding on the Lieutenant Governor, the board comes within the exception in s. 3(2)(g)(i) therefore the *Statutory Powers Procedure Act* does not apply to the board.

Re Peterson and Atkinson (1978), 23 O.R. (2d) 266, 95 D.L.R. (3d) 349 (Div. Ct.).

A hospital selection committee does not come within the s. 3(2)(g) exception. The committee does much more than recommend, and its recommendations "amount to executive action".

Section 4

Waiver of procedural requirement

4. (1) Any procedural requirement of this Act, or of another Act or a regulation that applies to a proceeding, may be waived with the consent of the parties and the tribunal.

Same, rules

(2) Any provision of a tribunal's rules made under section 25.1 may be waived in accordance with the rules.

1994, c. 27, s. 56; 1997, c. 23, s. 13

Case Law

MacCosham Van Lines (Can.) Co. v. Ontario (Minister of Transportation & Communications) (1988), 66 O.R. (2d) 198, 30 O.A.C. 124 (Div. Ct.).

Where the Ontario Highway Transport Board and a party applying for a rewritten certificate under the *Public Commercial Vehicles Act* both waived a hearing of the board, a third party could not require the board to hold a hearing before rewriting the certificate.

Section 4.1

Disposition without hearing

4.1 If the parties consent, a proceeding may be disposed of by a decision of the tribunal given without a hearing, unless another Act or a regulation that applies to the proceeding provides otherwise.

1994, c. 27, s. 56; 1997, c. 23, s. 13

Section 4.2

Panels, certain matters

4.2 (1) A procedural or interlocutory matter in a proceeding may be heard and determined by a panel consisting of one or more members of the tribunal, as assigned by the chair of the tribunal.

Assignments

(2) In assigning members of the tribunal to a panel, the chair shall take into consideration any requirement imposed by another Act or a regulatoin that applies to the proceeding that the tribunal be representative of specific interests.

Decision of panel

(3) The decision of a majority of the members of a panel, or their unanimous decision in the case of a two-member panel, is the tribunal's decision.

1994, c. 27, s. 56; 1997, c. 23, s. 13

Section 4.2.1

Panel of one

4.2.1 (1) The chair of a tribunal may decide that a proceeding be heard by a panel of one person and assign the person to hear the proceeding unless there is a statutory requirement in another Act that the proceeding be heard by a panel of more than one person.

Reduction in number of panel members

(2) Where there is a statutory requirement in another Act that a proceeding be heard by a panel of a specified number of persons, the chair of the tribunal may assign to the panel one person or any lesser number of persons than the number specified in the other Act if all parties to the proceeding consent.

1999, c. 12, Sched. B, s. 16(2)

Section 4.3

Expiry of term

4.3 If the term of office of a member of a tribunal who has participated in a hearing expires before a decision is given, the term shall be deemed to continue, but only for the purpose of participating in the decision and for no other purpose.

1994, c. 27, s. 56; 1997, c. 23, s. 13

Section 4.4

Incapacity of member

4.4 (1) If a member of a tribunal who has participated in a hearing becomes unable, for any reason, to complete the hearing or to participate in the decision, the remaining member or members may complete the hearing and give a decision.

Other Acts and regulations

(2) Subsection (1) does not apply if another Act or a regulation specifically deals with the issue of what takes place in the circumstances described in subsection (1).

1994, c. 27, s. 56; 1997, c. 23, s. 13

Section 4.5

Decision not to process commencement of proceeding

4.5 (1) Subject to subsection (3), upon receiving documents relating to the commencement of a proceeding, a tribunal or its administrative staff may decide not to process the documents relating to the commencement of the proceeding if,

(a) the documents are incomplete;

(b) the documents are received after the time required for commencing the proceeding has elapsed;

(c) the fee required for commencing the proceeding is not paid; or

(d) there is some other technical defect in the commencement of the proceeding.

Notice

(2) A tribunal or its administrative staff shall give the party who commences a proceeding notice of its decision under subsection (1) and shall set out in the notice the reasons for the decision and the requirements for resuming the processing of the documents.

Rules under s. 25.1

(3) A tribunal or its administrative staff shall not make a decision under subsection (1) unless the tribunal has made rules under section 25.1 respecting the making of such decisions and those rules shall set out,

(a) any of the grounds referred to in subsection (1) upon which the tribunal or its administrative staff may decide not to process the documents relating to the commencement of a proceeding; and

(b) the requirements for the processing of the documents to be resumed.

Continuance of provisions in other statutes

(4) Despite section 32, nothing in this section shall prevent a tribunal or its administrative staff from deciding not to process documents relating to the commencement of a proceeding on grounds that differ from those referred to in subsection (1) or without complying with subsection (2) or (3) if the tribunal or its staff does so in accordance with the provisions of an Act that are in force on the day this section comes into force.

1999, c. 12, Sched. B, s. 16(3)

Section 4.6

Dismissal of proceeding without hearing

4.6 (1) Subject to subsections (5) and (6), a tribunal may dismiss a proceeding without a hearing if,

(a) the proceeding is frivolous, vexatious or is commenced in bad faith;

(b) the proceeding relates to matters that are outside the jurisdiction of the tribunal; or

(c) some aspect of the statutory requirements for bringing the proceeding has not been met.

Notice

(2) Before dismissing a proceeding under this section, a tribunal shall give notice of its intention to dismiss the proceeding to,

(a) all parties to the proceeding if the proceeding is being dismissed for reasons referred to in clause (1)(b); or

(b) the party who commences the proceeding if the proceeding is being dismissed for any other reason.

Same

(3) The notice of intention to dismiss a proceeding shall set out the reasons for the dismissal and inform the parties of their right to make written submissions to the tribunal with respect to the dismissal within the time specified in the notice.

Right to make submissions

(4) A party who receives a notice under subsection (2) may make written submissions to the tribunal with respect to the dismissal within the time specified in the notice.

Dismissal

(5) A tribunal shall not dismiss a proceeding under this section until it has given notice under subsection (2) and considered any submissions made under subsection (4).

Rules

(6) A tribunal shall not dismiss a proceeding under this section 25.1 respecting the early dismissal of proceedings and those rules shall include,

(a) any of the grounds referred to in subsection (1) upon which a proceeding may be dismissed;

(b) the right of the parties who are entitled to receive notice under subsection (2) to make submissions with respect to the dismissal; and

(c) the time within which the submissions must be made.

Continuance of provisions in other statutes

(7) Despite section 32, nothing in this section shall prevent a tribunal from dismissing a proceeding on grounds other than those referred to in subsection (1) or without complying with subsections (2) to (6) if the tribunal dismisses the proceeding in accordance with the provisions of an Act that are in force on the day this section comes into force.

1999, c. 12, Sched. B, s. 16(3)

Section 4.7

Classifying proceedings

4.7 A tribunal may make rules under section 25.1 classifying the types of proceedings that come before it and setting guidelines as to the procedural steps or processes (such as preliminary motions, pre-hearing conferences, alternative dispute resolution mechanisms, expedited hearings) that apply to each type of proceeding and the circumstances in which other procedures may apply.

1999, c. 12, Sched. B, s. 16(3)

Section 4.8

Alternative dispute resolution

4.8 (1) A tribunal may direct the parties to a proceeding to participate in an alternative dispute resolution mechanism for the purposes of resolving the proceeding or an issue arising in the proceeding if,

(a) it has made rules under section 25.1 respecting the use of alternative dispute resolution mechanisms; and

(b) all parties consent to participating in the alternative dispute resolution mechanism.

Definition

(2) In this section,

"alternative dispute resolution mechanism" includes mediation, conciliation, negotiation or any other means of facilitating the resolution of issues in dispute.

Rules

(3) A rule under section 25.1 respecting the use of alternative dispute resolution mechanisms shall include procedural guidelines to deal with the following:

1. The circumstances in which a settlement achieved by means of an alternative dispute resolution mechanism must be reviewed and approved by the tribunal.

2. Any requirement, statutory or otherwise, that there be an order by the tribunal.

Mandatory alternative dispute resolution

(4) A rule under subsection (3) may provide that participation in an alternative dispute resolution mechanism is mandatory or that it is mandatory in certain specified circumstances.

Person appointed to mediate, etc.

(5) A rule under subsection (3) may provide that a person appointed to mediate, conciliate, negotiate or help resolve a matter by means of an alternative dispute resolution mechanism be a member of the tribunal or a person independent of the tribunal. However, a member of the tribunal who is so appointed with respect to a matter in a proceeding shall not subsequently hear the matter if it comes before the tribunal unless the parties consent.

Continuance of provisions in other statutes

(6) Despite section 32, nothing in this section shall prevent a tribunal from directing parties to a proceeding to participate in an alternative dispute resolution mechanism even though the requirements of subsections (1) to (5) have not been met if the tribunal does so in accordance with the provisions of an Act that are in force on the day this section comes into force.

1999, c. 12, Sched. B, s. 16(3)

Section 4.9

Mediators, etc., not compellable

4.9 (1) No person employed as a mediator, conciliator or negotiator or otherwise appointed to facilitate the resolution of a matter before a tribunal by

means of an alternative dispute resolution mechanism shall be compelled to give testimony or produce documents in a proceeding before the tribunal or in a civil proceeding with respect to matters that come to his or her knowledge in the course of exercising his or her duties under this or any other Act.

Evidence in civil proceedings

(2) No notes or records kept by a mediator, conciliator or negotiator or by any other person appointed to facilitate the resolution of a matter before a tribunal by means of an alternative dispute resolution mechanism under this or any other Act are admissible in a civil proceeding.

1999, c. 12, Sched. B, s. 16(3)

Section 5

Parties

5. The parties to a proceeding shall be the persons specified as parties by or under the statute under which the proceeding arises or, if not so specified, persons entitled by law to be parties to the proceeding.

Case Law

Re Temple and Ont. Liquor Licence Bd. (1982), 41 O.R. (2d) 214, 145 D.L.R. (3d) 480 (Div. Ct.).

Where an individual is permitted to make representations before the Liquor Licence Board with regard to an application for a liquor licence, that individual is a party within the meaning of s. 5 of the *Statutory Powers Procedure Act.*

Section 5.1

Written hearings

5.1 (1) A tribunal whose rules made under section 25.1 deal with written hearing may hold a written hearing in a proceeding.

Exception

(2) The tribunal shall not hold a written hearing if a party satisfies the tribunal that there is good reason for not doing so.

Same

(2.1) Subsection (2) does not apply if the only purpose of the hearing is to deal with procedural matters.

Documents

(3) In a written hearing, all the parties are entitled to receive every document that the tribunal receives in the proceeding.

1994, c. 27, s. 56; 1997, c. 23, s. 13; 1999, c. 12, Sched. B, s. 16(4)

Section 5.2

Electronic hearings

5.2 (1) A tribunal whose rules made under section 25.1 deal with electronic hearings may hold an electronic hearing in a proceeding.

Exception

(2) The tribunal shall not hold an electronic hearing if a party satisfies the tribunal that holding an electronic rather than an oral hearing is likely to cause the party significant prejudice.

Same

(3) Subsection (2) does not apply if the only purpose of the hearing is to deal with procedural matters.

Participants to be able to hear one another

(4) In an electronic hearing, all the parties and the members of the tribunal participating in the hearing must be able to hear one another and any witnesses throughout the hearing.

1994, c. 27, s. 56; 1997, c. 23, s. 13

Section 5.2.1

Different kinds of hearings in one proceeding

5.2.1 A tribunal may, in a proceeding, hold any combination of written, electronic and oral hearings.

1997, c. 23, s. 13

Section 5.3

Pre-hearing conferences

5.3 (1) If the tribunal's rules made under section 25.1 deal with pre-hearing conferences, the tribunal may direct the parties to participate in a pre-hearing conference to consider,

(a) the settlement of any or all of the issues;

(b) the simplification of the issues;

(c) facts or evidence that may be agreed upon;

(d) the dates by which any steps in the proceeding are to be taken or begun;

(e) the estimated duration of the hearing; and

(f) any other matter that may assist in the just and most expeditious disposition of the proceeding.

Other Acts and regulations

(1.1) The tribunal's power to direct the parties to participate in a pre-hearing conference is subject to any other Act or regulation that applies to the proceeding.

Who presides

(2) The chair of the tribunal may designate a member of the tribunal or any other person to preside at the pre-hearing conference.

Orders

(3) A member who presides at a pre-hearing conference may make such orders as he or she considers necessary or advisable with respect to the conduct of the proceeding, including adding parties.

Disqualification

(4) A member who presides at a pre-hearing conference at which the parties attempt to settle issues shall not preside at the hearing of the proceeding unless the parties consent.

Application of s. 5.2

(5) Section 5.2 applies to a pre-hearing conference, with necessary modifications.

1994, c. 27, s. 56; 1997, c. 23, s. 13

Section 5.4

Disclosure

5.4 (1) If the tribunal's rules made under section 25.1 deal with disclosure, the tribunal may, at any stage of the proceeding before all hearings are complete, make orders for,

(a) the exchange of documents;

(b) the oral or written examination of a party;

(c) the exchange of witness statements and reports of expert witnesses;

(d) the provision of particulars;

(e) any other form of disclosure.

Other Acts and regulations

(1.1) The tribunal's power to make orders for disclosure is subject to any other Act or regulation that applies to the proceeding.

Exception, privileged information

(2) Subsection (1) does not authorize the making of an order requiring disclosure of privileged information.

1994, c. 27, s. 56(12); 1997, c. 23, s. 13(11)

Section 6

Notice of hearing

6. (1) The parties to a proceeding shall be given reasonable notice of the hearing by the tribunal.

Statutory authority

(2) A notice of a hearing shall include a reference to the statutory authority under which the hearing will be held.

Oral hearing

(3) A notice of an oral hearing shall include,

(a) a statement of the time, place and purpose of the hearing; and

(b) a statement that if the party notified does not attend at the hearing, the tribunal may proceed in the party's absence and the party will not be entitled to any further notice in the proceeding.

Written hearing

(4) A notice of a written hearing shall include,

(a) a statement of the time and purpose of the hearing, and details about the manner in which the hearing will be held;

(b) a statement that the hearing shall not be held as a written hearing if the party satisfies the tribunal that there is good reason for not holding a written hearing (in which case the tribunal is required to hold it as an electronic or oral hearing) and an indication of the procedure to be followed for that purpose.

(c) a statement that if the party notified neither acts under clause (b) nor participates in the hearing in accordance with the notice, the tribunal may proceed without the party's participation and the party will not be entitled to any further notice in the proceeding.

Electronic hearing

(5) A notice of an electronic hearing shall include,

(a) a statement of the time and purpose of the hearing, and details about the manner in which the hearing will be held;

(b) a statement that the only purpose of the hearing is to deal with procedural matters, if that is the case;

(c) if clause (b) does not apply, a statement that the party notified may, by satisfying the tribunal that holding the hearing as an electronic hearing is likely to cause the party significant prejudice, require the tribunal to hold the hearing as an oral hearing, and an indication of the procedure to be followed for that purpose; and

(d) a statement that if the party notified neither acts under clause (c), if applicable, nor participates in the hearing in accordance with the notice, the tribunal may proceed without the party's participation and the party will not be entitled to any further notice in the proceeding.

1994, c. 27, s. 56; 1997, c. 23, s. 13; 1999, c. 12, Sched. B, s. 16(5)

Case Law

Re Central Ont. Coalition Concerning Hydro Transmission Systems and Ont. Hydro (1984), 46 O.R. (2d) 715, 8 Admin. L.R. 81, 27 M.P.L.R. 165, 10 D.L.R (4th) 341, 4 O.A.C. 249, 16 O.M.B.R. 172 (Div. Ct.).

Where a new Ontario Hydro "system plan" is proposed, individuals affected by the proposals are entitled to notice of any hearing. The notice must be reasonable, such that the individual may know the case to be met.

Re Seven-Eleven Taxi Co. and Brampton (1975), 10 O.R. (2d) 677, 64 D.L.R. (3d) 401 (Div. Ct.).

Reasonable notice entails notice sufficient to give an individual whose rights are "in jeopardy" an opportunity to meet the case against him.

Section 7

Effect of non-attendance at hearing after due notice

7. (1) Where notice of an oral hearing has been given to a party to a proceeding in accordance with this Act and the party does not attend at the hearing, the tribunal may proceed in the absence of the party and the party will not be entitled to any further notice in the proceeding.

Same, written hearings

(2) Where notice of a written hearing has been given to a party to a proceeding in accordance with this Act and the party neither acts under clause 6(4)(b) nor participates in the hearing in accordance with the notice, the tribu-

nal may proceed without the party's participation and the party is not entitled to any further notice in the proceeding.

Same, electronic hearings

(3) Where notice of an electronic hearing has been given to a party to a proceeding in accordance with this Act and the party neither acts under clause 6(5)(c), if applicable, nor participates in the hearing in accordance with the notice, the tribunal may proceed without the party's participation and the party is not entitled to any further notice in the proceeding.

1994, c. 27, s. 56

Section 8

Where character, etc. of a party is in issue

8. Where the good character, propriety of conduct or competence of a party is an issue in a proceeding, the party is entitled to be furnished prior to the hearing with reasonable information of any allegations with respect thereto.

Case Law

Re Commodore Bus. Machines Ltd. and Ont. Min. of Labour (1984), 49 O.R. (2d) 17, 10 Admin. L.R. 130, 84 C.L.L.C. 17,028, 14 D.L.R. (4th) 118, (sub nom. *Olarte v. Commodore Bus. Machines Ltd.)* 6 O.A.C. 176 (Div. Ct.).

Section 8 is not intended to preclude the introduction of evidence arising from issues raised by an opposing party at a hearing.

Re Cwinn and L.S.U.C. (1980), 28 O.R. (2d) 61, 108 D.L.R. (3d) 381, 33 N.R. 358n (Div. Ct.).

It is not a denial of natural justice for the Law Society to present evidence at a hearing before the Discipline Committee, though not specified in the complaint, if full particulars of this evidence are provided to the affected member prior to the hearing.

Re All Ont. Tpt. Ltd. and Ont. Highway Tpt. Bd. (1979), 26 O.R. (2d) 202 (Div. Ct.).

The section does not apply to intervenors because, though there may be allegations made challenging their competence, their legal rights are not affected by the immediate proceedings.

Re Don Howson Chevrolet Oldsmobile Ltd. and Reg. of Motor Vehicle Dealers & Salesmen (1974), 6 O.R. (2d) 39, 51 D.L.R. (3d) 683 (Div. Ct.).

The section is not intended to limit cross-examination. Rather it is to permit the person against whom the allegations are made the opportunity of preparing an answer.

Re DiNardo and Ont. Liquor Licence Bd. (1974), 5 O.R. (2d) 124, 49 D.L.R. (3d) 537 (H.C.).

Where the Liquor Licence Board decides to suspend an individual's licence, the combination of the board's "show cause" letter and police and fire department reports is sufficient to satisfy the requirements of s. 8.

Section 9

Hearings to be public, exceptions

9. (1) An oral hearing shall be open to the public except where the tribunal is of the opinion that,

(a) matters involving public security may be disclosed; or

(b) intimate financial or personal matters or other matters may be disclosed at the hearing of such a nature, having regard to the circumstances, that the desirability of avoiding disclosure thereof in the interests of any person affected or in the public interest outweighs the desirability of adhering to the principle that hearings be open to the public,

in which case the tribunal may hold the hearing in the absence of the public.

Written hearings

(1.1) In a written hearing, members of the public are entitled to reasonable access to the documents submitted, unless the tribunal is of the opinion that clause (1)(a) or (b) applies.

Electronic hearings

(1.2) An electronic hearing shall be open to the public unless the tribunal is of the opinion that,

(a) it is not practical to hold the hearing in a manner that is open to the public; or

(b) clause (1)(a) or (b) applies.

Maintenance of order at hearings

(2) A tribunal may make such orders or give such directions at an oral or electronic hearing as it considers necessary for the maintenance of order at the hearing, and, if any person disobeys or fails to comply with any such order or direction, the tribunal or a member thereof may call for the assistance of any peace officer to enforce the order or direction, and every peace officer so called upon shall take such action as is necessary to enforce the order or direction and may use such force as is reasonably required for that purpose.

1994, c. 27, s. 56; 1997, c. 23, s. 13

Case Law

Pilzmaker v. Law Society of Upper Can. (1989), 70 O.R. (2d) 126 (Div. Ct.).

A discipline committee's decision to conduct a hearing in public was made within its jurisdiction. The committee had heard argument on the point, and concluded that the matter was not within the exceptions enumerated in s. 9(1)(b). There was not a strong *prima facie* case that the committee's decision in this regard was wrong.

Ottawa Police Force v. Lalande (1986), 57 O.R. (2d) 509 (Dist. Ct.).

A hearing that affects the public should not be heard *in camera*, unless there are compelling reasons which outweigh the desirability of an open hearing.

Section 9.1

Proceedings involving similar questions

9.1 (1) If two or more proceedings before a tribunal involve the same or similar questions of fact, law or policy, the tribunal may,

(a) combine the proceedings or any part of them, with the consent of the parties;

(b) hear the proceedings at the same time, with the consent of the parties;

(c) hear the proceedings one immediately after the other; or

(d) stay one or more of the proceedings until after the determination of another one of them.

Exception

(2) Subsection (1) does not apply to proceedings to which the *Consolidated Hearings Act* applies.

Same

(3) Clauses (1)(a) and (b) do not apply to a proceeding if,

(a) any other Act or regulation that applies to the proceeding requires that it be heard in private;

(b) the tribunal is of the opinion that clause 9(1)(a) or (b) applies to the proceeding.

Conflict, consent requirements

(4) The consent requirements of clauses (1)(a) and (b) do not apply if another Act or a regulation that applies to the proceedings allows the tribunal to combine them or hear them at the same time without the consent of the parties.

Use of same evidence

(5) If the parties to the second-named proceeding consent, the tribunal may treat evidence that is admitted in a proceeding as if it were also admitted in another proceeding that is heard at the same time under clause (1)(b).

1994, c. 27, s. 56; 1997, c. 23, s. 13

Section 10

Right to representation

10. A party to a proceeding may be represented by a representative.

1994, c. 27, s. 56; 2006, c. 21, Sched. C, s. 134(3)

Case Law

B. v. W. (1985), 52 O.R. (2d) 738, (sub nom. *B. (Y.) v. W. (R.)*) 16 Admin. L.R. 99, 23 D.L.R. (4th) 248 (H.C.).

Where there is no issue of credibility in a proceeding, there is a discretion to prohibit cross-examination.

Re Merrick and Dir. of Vocational Rehabilitation Services Branch of Ont. Ministry of Community and Social Services (1985), 49 O.R. (2d) 675, 7 O.A.C. 255 (Div. Ct.).

Where a statute permits a document to be filed, there are no grounds to complain of lack of procedural fairness because the author could not be cross-examined.

Re Ladney and Moore (1984), 46 O.R. (2d) 586, 26 M.P.L.R. 140, 10 D.L.R. (4th) 612, 5 O.A.C. 390, 16 O.M.B.R. 70 (Div. Ct.).

Generally, a party should be permitted to make submissions and adduce evidence before the tribunal reaches its decision.

Re Ellis and Min. of Community & Social Services (1980), 28 O.R. (2d) 385, 110 D.L.R. (3d) 414 (Div. Ct.).

The right to conduct cross-examinations of witnesses, provided for in s. 10(c), does not include the right to require the calling of these witnesses. Specifically, where a statute permits an individual to make his submissions in writing, there is no obligation for that individual to appear as a witness.

Re Henderson and Ont. Securities Comm. (1976), 14 O.R. (2d) 498, 74 D.L.R. (3d) 165 (H.C.).

Any person who has been made a party to the proceedings is entitled to all the rights specified in the section.

Section 10.1

Examination of witnesses

10.1 A party to a proceeding may, at an oral or electronic hearing,

(a) call and examine witnesses and present evidence and submissions; and

(b) conduct cross-examinations of witnesses at the hearing reasonably required for a full and fair disclosure of all matters relevant to the issues in the proceeding.

1994, c. 27, s. 56

Section 11

Rights of witnesses to representation

11. (1) A witness at an oral or electronic hearing is entitled to be advised by a representative as to his or her rights, but such representative may take no other part in the hearing without leave of the tribunal.

Idem

(2) Where an oral hearing is closed to the public, the witness's representative is not entitled to be present except when that witness is giving evidence.

1994, c. 27, s. 56; 2006, c. 21, Sched. C, s. 134(4), (5)

Section 12

Summonses

12. (1) A tribunal may require any person, including a party, by summons,

(a) to give evidence on oath or affirmation at an oral or electronic hearing; and

(b) to produce in evidence at an oral or electronic hearing documents and things specified by the tribunal,

relevant to the subject-matter of the proceeding and admissible at a hearing.

Form and service of summons

(2) A summons issued under subsection (1) shall be in the prescribed form (in English or French) and,

(a) where the tribunal consists of one person, shall be signed by him or her;

(b) where the tribunal consists of more than one person, shall be signed by the chair of the tribunal or in such other manner as documents on behalf of the tribunal may be signed under the statute constituting the tribunal.

Same

(3) The summons shall be served personally on the person summoned.

Fees and allowances

(3.1) The person summoned is entitled to receive the same fees or allowances for attending at or otherwise participating in the hearing as are paid to a person summoned to attend before the Superior Court of Justice.

Bench warrant

(4) A judge of the Superior Court of Justice may issue a warrant against a person if the judge is satisfied that,

(a) a summons was served on the person under this section;

(b) the person has failed to attend or to remain in attendance at the hearing (in the case of an oral hearing) or has failed otherwise to participate in the hearing (in the case of an electronic hearing) in accordance with the summons; and

(c) the person's attendance or participation is material to the ends of justice.

Same

(4.1) The warrant shall be in the prescribed form (in English or French), directed to any police officer, and shall require the person to be apprehended anywhere within Ontario, brought before the tribunal forthwith and,

(a) detained in custody as the judge may order until the person's presence as a witness is no longer required; or

(b) in the judge's discretion, released on a recognizance, with or without sureties, conditioned for attendance or participation to give evidence.

Proof of service

(5) Service of a summons may be proved by affidavit in an application to have a warrant issued under subsection (4).

Certificate of facts

(6) Where an application to have a warrant issued is made on behalf of a tribunal, the person constituting the tribunal or, if the tribunal consists of more than one person, the chair of the tribunal may certify to the judge the facts relied on to establish that the attendance or other participation of the person summoned is material to the ends of justice, and the judge may accept the certificate as proof of the facts.

Same

(7) Where the application is made by a party to the proceeding, the facts relied on to establish that the attendance or other participation of the person is material to the ends of justice may be proved by the party's affidavit.

1994, c. 27, s. 56; 2006, c. 19, Sched. C, s. 1(1)

Case Law

Carter v. Phillips (1988), 66 O.R. (2d) 293 (C.A.).

A commissioner proceeding pursuant to s. 105(1) of the *Residential Tenancies Act* has jurisdiction to order production of records pursuant to s. 12 of the *Statutory Powers Procedure Act.*

Section 13

Contempt proceedings

13. (1) Where any person without lawful excuse,

(a) on being duly summoned under section 12 as a witness at a hearing makes default in attending at the hearing; or

(b) being in attendance as a witness at an oral hearing or otherwise participating as a witness at an electronic hearing, refuses to take an oath or to make an affirmation legally required by the tribunal to be taken or made, or to produce any document or thing in his or her power or control legally required by the tribunal to be produced by him or her or to answer any question to which the tribunal may legally require an answer; or

(c) does any other thing that would, if the tribunal had been a court of law having power to commit for contempt, have been contempt of that court,

the tribunal may, of its own motion or on the motion of a party to the proceeding, state a case to the Divisional Court setting out the facts and that court may inquire into the matter and, after hearing any witnesses who may be produced against or on behalf of that person and after hearing any statement that may be offered in defence, punish or take steps for the punishment of that person in like manner as if he or she had been guilty of contempt of the court.

Same

(2) Subsection (1) also applies to a person who,

(a) having objected under clause 6(4)(b) to a hearing being held as a written hearing, fails without lawful excuse to participate in the oral or electronic hearing of the matter; or

(b) being a party, fails without lawful excuse to attend a pre-hearing conference when so directed by the tribunal.

1994, c. 27, s. 56; 1997, c. 23, s. 13

Case Law

Re Ajax & Pickering Gen. Hosp. and C.U.P.E. (1981), 32 O.R. (2d) 492, 81 C.L.L.C. 14,102, 122 D.L.R. (3d) 109; reversed on other grounds (1982), 35 O.R. (2d) 293, 82 C.L.L.C. 14,164, 132 D.L.R. (3d) 270 (C.A.); leave to appeal to Supreme Court of Canada refused 35 O.R. (2d) 293n, 132 D.L.R. (3d) 270n, 42 N.R. 353.

The section is one of general application and exists as a remedy for contempt in spite of compliance.

Section 14

Protection for witnesses

14. (1) A witness at an oral or electronic hearing shall be deemed to have objected to answer any question asked him or her upon the ground that the answer may tend to criminate him or her or may tend to establish his or her liability to civil proceedings at the instance of the Crown, or of any person, and no answer given by a witness at a hearing shall be used or be receivable in evidence against the witness in any trial or other proceeding against him or her thereafter taking place, other than a prosecution for perjury in giving such evidence.

(2) [Repealed 1994, c. 27, s. 56(29).]

1994, c. 27, s. 56

Case Law

Re O.S.S.T.F. and Shelton (1979), 28 O.R. (2d) 218, 109 D.L.R. (3d) 59 (Div. Ct.).

In deciding that Part I of the *Statutory Powers Procedure Act* does not apply to the Relations and Discipline Committee of the Ontario Teachers' Federation, a committee that merely recommends, the court also decided that s. 14 of the Act does not apply to the above committee.

Section 15

What is admissible in evidence at a hearing

15. (1) Subject to subsections (2) and (3), a tribunal may admit as evidence at a hearing, whether or not given or proven under oath or affirmation or admissible as evidence in a court,

(a) any oral testimony; and

(b) any document or other thing,

relevant to the subject-matter of the proceeding and may act on such evidence, but the tribunal may exclude anything unduly repetitious.

What is inadmissible in evidence at a hearing

(2) Nothing is admissible in evidence at a hearing,

(a) that would be inadmissible in a court by reason of any privilege under the law of evidence; or

(b) that is inadmissible by the statute under which the proceeding arises or any other statute.

Conflicts

(3) Nothing in subsection (1) overrides the provisions of any Act expressly limiting the extent to or purposes for which any oral testimony, documents or things may be admitted or used in evidence in any proceeding.

Copies

(4) Where a tribunal is satisfied as to its authenticity, a copy of a document or other thing may be admitted as evidence at a hearing.

Photocopies

(5) Where a document has been filed in evidence at a hearing, the tribunal may, or the person producing it or entitled to it may with the leave of the tribunal, cause the document to be photocopied and the tribunal may authorize the photocopy to be filed in evidence in the place of the document filed and release the document filed, or may furnish to the person producing it or the person entitled to it a photocopy of the document filed certified by a member of the tribunal.

Certified copy admissible in evidence

(6) A document purporting to be a copy of a document filed in evidence at a hearing, certified to be a copy thereof by a member of the tribunal, is admissible in evidence in proceedings in which the document is admissible as evidence of the document.

Case Law

B. v. Catholic Children's Aid Society (Metropolitan Toronto) (1987), 59 O.R. (2d) 417, (sub nom. *B. (J.) v. Catholic Children's Aid Society (Metropolitan Toronto))* 27 Admin. L.R. 295, 7 R.F.L. (3d) 441, 38 D.L.R. (4th) 106 (Div. Ct.).

A party applying to have his name expunged from the Child Abuse Register was denied natural justice when hearsay evidence of the alleged abuse was admitted on the hearing. The admission of the evidence had precluded the appellant from cross-examining the alleged victim.

Re Commodore Bus. Machines Ltd. and Ont. Min. of Labour (1984), 49 O.R. (2d) 17, 10 Admin. L.R. 130, 84 C.L.L.C. 17,028, 14 D.L.R. (4th) 118, (sub nom. *Olarte v. Commodore Bus. Machines Ltd.)* 6 O.A.C. 176 (Div. Ct.).

A board of inquiry of the Human Rights Commission is within the jurisdiction of the *Statutory Powers Procedure Act*, and therefore the board is entitled to admit and base its decision on similar fact evidence and hearsay evidence.

Lischka v. Criminal Injuries Comp. Bd. (1982), 37 O.R. (2d) 134 (Div. Ct.).

Section 15(1) permits the admission of hearsay and opinion evidence, though in some cases the admission of such evidence could amount to a denial of natural justice.

Lynch v. Ottawa (1974), 7 L.C.R. 7 (Land Compensation Bd.).

In proceedings before the board, hearsay evidence in appraisal reports of sales and offers to purchase is admissible as relevant.

Re Windsor and I.A.F.F. Loc. 455 (1974), 5 O.R. (2d) 690, 51 D.L.R. (3d) 346 (Div. Ct.).

A brief prepared by a union is not evidence. The contents of the brief are representations by the union and, thus, should not be relied upon by the Labour Relations Board in reaching its decision.

Section 15.1

Use of previously admitted evidence

15.1 (1) The tribunal may treat previously admitted evidence as if it had been admitted in a proceeding before the tribunal, if the parties to the proceeding consent.

Definition

(2) In subsection (1),

"previously admitted evidence" means evidence that was admitted, before the hearing of the proceeding referred to in that subsection, in any other proceeding before a court or tribunal, whether in or outside Ontario.

Additional power

(3) This power conferred by this section is in addition to the tribunal's power to admit evidence under section 15.

1994, c. 27, s. 56; 1997, c. 23, s. 13

Section 15.2

Witness panels

15.2 A tribunal may receive evidence from panels of witnesses composed of two or more persons, if the parties have first had an opportunity to make submissions in that regard.

1994, c. 27, s. 56

Section 16

Notice of facts and opinions

16. A tribunal may, in making its decision in any proceeding,

(a) take notice of facts that may be judicially noticed; and

(b) take notice of any generally recognized scientific or technical facts, information or opinions within its scientific or specialized knowledge.

Section 16.1

Interim decisions and orders

16.1 (1) A tribunal may make interim decisions and orders.

Conditions

(2) A tribunal may impose conditions on an interim decision or order.

Reasons

(3) An interim decision or order need not be accompanied by reasons.

1994, c. 27, s. 56

Section 16.2

Time frames

16.2 A tribunal shall establish guidelines setting out the usual time frame for completing proceedings that come before the tribunal and for completing the procedural steps within those proceedings.

1999, c. 12, Sched. B, s. 16(6)

Section 17

Decision

17. (1) A tribunal shall give its final decision and order, if any, in any proceeding in writing and shall give reasons in writing therefor if requested by a party.

Interest

(2) A tribunal that makes an order for the payment of money shall set out in the order the principal sum, and if interest is payable, the rate of interest and the date from which it is to be calculated.

1993, c. 27, Sched.; 1994, c. 27, s. 56

Case Law

Leung v. Ontario (Criminal Injuries Compensation Board) (1995), 24 O.R. (3d) 530, (sub nom. *So v. Criminal Injuries Compensation Board (Ont.)*) 82 O.A.C. 43 (Div. Ct.).

On an appeal from a decision of the Criminal Injuries Compensation Board, the appellant argued that the Board had erred in applying Board policy guidelines with respect to, *inter alia*, wage laws. The Board had given no reasons for its decision but on appeal it was found that it could not be said that the Board exercised its discretion unreasonably. While it would have been desirable for the Board to have given reasons, there was no evidence to suggest that the appellant had requested that the Board give reasons, and accordingly s. 17 of the Act did not apply.

Re Temple and Ont. Liquor Licence Bd. (1982), 41 O.R. (2d) 214, 145 D.L.R. (3d) 480 (Div. Ct.).

Because a member of the public making representations before the Liquor Licence Board is a party to the proceedings, that person is entitled to reasons from the board concerning the decision reached.

Re DiNardo and Ont. Liquor Licence Bd. (1974), 5 O.R. (2d) 124, 49 D.L.R. (3d) 537 (H.C.).

Where in response to a request for reasons for their decision the Liquor Licence Board furnished the party with a summary of the proceedings, it was held that this was not sufficient to satisfy the written reasons requirement of the section.

Section 17.1

Costs

17.1 (1) Subject to subsection (2), a tribunal may, in the circumstances set out in rules made under subsection (4), order a party to pay all or part of another party's costs in a proceeding.

Exception

(2) A tribunal shall not make an order to pay costs under this section unless,

(a) the conduct or course of conduct of a party has been unreasonable, frivolous or vexatious or a party has acted in bad faith; and

(b) the tribunal has made rules under subsection (4).

Amount of costs

(3) The amount of the costs ordered under this section shall be determined in accordance with the rules made under subsection (4).

Rules

(4) A tribunal may make rules with respect to,

(a) the ordering of costs;

(b) the circumstances in which costs may be ordered; and

(c) the amount of costs or the manner in which the amount of costs is to be determined.

Same

(5) Subsections 25.1(3), (4), (5) and (6) apply with respect to rules made under subsection (4).

Continuance of provisions in other statutes

(6) Despite section 32, nothing in this section shall prevent a tribunal from ordering a party to pay all or part of another party's costs in a proceeding in circumstances other than those set out in, and without complying with, subsections (1) to (3) if the tribunal makes the order in accordance with the provisions of an Act that are in force on February 14, 2000.

Submissions must be in writing

(7) Despite sections 5.1, 5.2 and 5.2.1, submissions for a costs order, whether under subsection (1) or under an authority referred to in subsection (6), shall be made by way of written or electronic documents, unless a party satisfies the tribunal that to do so is likely to cause the party significant prejudice.

(8) [Repealed 2015, c. 23, s. 5.]

(9) [Repealed 2015, c. 23, s. 5.]

1999, c. 12, Sched. B, s. 16(7); 2006, c. 19, Sched. B, s. 21(2); 2015, c. 23, s. 5

Section 18

Notice of decision

18. (1) The tribunal shall send each party who participated in the proceeding, or the party's representative, a copy of its final decision or order, including the reasons if any have been given,

(a) by regular lettermail;

(b) by electronic transmission;

(c) by telephone transmission of a facsimile; or

(d) by some other method that allows proof of receipt, if the tribunal's rules made under section 25.1 deal with the matter.

Use of mail

(2) If the copy is sent by regular lettermail, it shall be sent to the most recent addresses known to the tribunal and shall be deemed to be received by the party on the fifth day after the day it is mailed.

Use of electronic or telephone transmission

(3) If the copy is sent by electronic transmission or by telephone transmission of a facsimile, it shall be deemed to be received on the day after it was sent, unless that day is a holiday, in which case the copy shall be deemed to be received on the next day that is not a holiday.

Use of other method

(4) If the copy is sent by a method referred to in clause (1)(d), the tribunal's rules made under section 25.1 govern its deemed day of receipt.

Failure to receive copy

(5) If a party that acts in good faith does not, through absence, illness or other cause beyond the party's control, receive the copy until a later date than the deemed day of receipt, subsection (2), (3) or (4), as the case may be, does not apply.

1994, c. 27, s. 56; 1997, c. 23, s. 13; 2006, c. 21, Sched. C, s. 134(6)

Case Law

Re Powell and Min. of Justice (1980), 31 O.R. (2d) 111, 118 D.L.R. (3d) 158, (sub nom. *Re Powell and A.G. Ont.)* 11 O.M.B.R. 193 (Div. Ct.).

A decision of the Ontario Municipal Board was quashed when an interested party did not receive notice of the decision until after the time for petitioning the Lieutenant Governor in Council had expired.

Section 19

Enforcement of orders

19. (1) A certified copy of a tribunal's decision or order in a proceeding may be filed in the Superior Court of Justice by the tribunal or by a party and on filing shall be deemed to be an order of that court and is enforceable as such.

Notice of filing

(2) A party who files an order under subsection (1) shall notify the tribunal within 10 days after the filing.

Order for payment of money

(3) On receiving a certified copy of a tribunal's order for the payment of money, the sheriff shall enforce the order as if it were an execution issued by the Superior Court of Justice.

1994, c. 27, s. 56; 2006, c. 19, Sched. C, s. 1(1)

Case Law

WMI Waste Mgmt. of Can. Inc. v. Metro. Toronto (1981), 34 O.R. (2d) 708, 23 R.P.R. 257, 24 L.C.R. 204 (H.C.).

Filing under the section does not incorporate a substantive right to interest on taxed costs. The right to interest in respect of an expropriation claim is a substantive right that must be found in the legislation governing the claim.

Section 20

Record of proceeding

20. A tribunal shall compile a record of any proceeding in which a hearing has been held which shall include,

(a) any application, complaint, reference or other document, if any, by which the proceeding was commenced;

(b) the notice of any hearing;

(c) any interlocutory orders made by the tribunal;

(d) all documentary evidence filed with the tribunal, subject to any limitation expressly imposed by any other Act on the extent to or the purposes for which any such documents may be used in evidence in any proceeding;

(e) the transcript, if any, of the oral evidence given at the hearing; and

(f) the decision of the tribunal and the reasons therefor, where reasons have been given.

Section 21

Adjournments

21. A hearing may be adjourned from time to time by a tribunal of its own motion or where it is shown to the satisfaction of the tribunal that the adjournment is required to permit an adequate hearing to be held.

Section 21.1

Corrections of errors

21.1 A tribunal may at any time correct a typographical error, error of calculation or similar error made in its decision or order.

1994, c. 27, s. 56

Section 21.2

Power to review

21.2 (1) A tribunal may, if it considers it advisable and if its rules made under section 25.1 deal with the matter, review all or part of its own decision or order, and may confirm, vary, suspend or cancel the decision or order.

Time for review

(2) The review shall take place within a reasonable time after the decision or order is made.

Conflict

(3) In the event of a conflict between this section and any other Act, the other Act prevails.

1994, c. 27, s. 56; 1997, c. 23, s. 13

Section 22

Administration of oaths

22. A member of a tribunal has power to administer oaths and affirmations for the purpose of any of its proceedings and the tribunal may require evidence before it to be given under oath or affirmation.

Section 23

Abuse of processes

23. (1) A tribunal may make such orders or give such directions in proceedings before it as it considers proper to prevent abuse of its processes.

Limitation on examination

(2) A tribunal may reasonably limit further examination or cross-examination of a witness where it is satisfied that the examination or cross-examination has been sufficient to disclose fully and fairly all matters relevant to the issues in the proceeding.

Exclusion of representatives

(3) A tribunal may exclude from a hearing anyone, other than a person licensed under the *Law Society Act*, appearing on behalf of a party or as an adviser to a witness if it finds that such person is not competent properly to represent or to advise the party or witness, or does not understand and comply at the hearing with the duties and responsibilities of an advocate or adviser.

1994, c. 27, s. 56; 2006, c. 21, Sched. C, s. 134(7)

Case Law

L.I.U.N.A., Local 183 v. L.I.U.N.A., Locals 506, 527, 837, (sub nom. *Universal Workers' Union, Labourers' International Union of North America, Local 183 v. Laborers' International Union of North America)* 70 O.R. (3d) 435, [2004] O.L.R.B. Rep. 471 (S.C.J.)

The Ontario Labour Relations Board has jurisdiction under ss. 23(1) and 25.0.1 of the *Statutory Powers Procedure Act* as to whether there is a conflict of interest which justifies the disqualification of solicitors representing a party involved in proceedings before the Board.

Re Stone and L.S.U.C. (1979), 26 O.R. (2d) 166, 102 D.L.R. (3d) 176 (Div. Ct.).

The procedure to be followed on a motion for severance of charges before the Discipline Committee of the Law Society of Upper Canada is the same as the procedure to be followed on an application to sever counts on a multiple count indictment against an individual accused of committing a crime.

Re Henderson and Ont. Securities Comm. (1976), 14 O.R. (2d) 498, 74 D.L.R. (3d) 165 (H.C.).

Where an individual has been made a party to the proceedings, a board may not refuse the individual's counsel the right to cross-examine.

Section 24

Notice, etc.

24. (1) Where a tribunal is of opinion that because the parties to any proceeding before it are so numerous or for any other reason, it is impracticable,

(a) to give notice of the hearing; or

(b) to send its decision and the material mentioned in section 18,

to all or any of the parties individually, the tribunal may, instead of doing so, cause reasonable notice of the hearing or of its decision to be given to such parties by public advertisement or otherwise as the tribunal may direct.

Contents of notice

(2) A notice of a decision given by a tribunal under clause (1)(b) shall inform the parties of the place where copies of the decision and the reasons therefor, if reasons were given, may be obtained.

Case Law

Re Rose (1982), 38 O.R. (2d) 162, 29 C.P.C. 235, (sub nom. *Re Rose and Reg. of Collection Agencies)* 137 D.L.R. (3d) 365 (Div. Ct.).

In seeking a stay of execution of a tribunal's decision, absent special circumstances, an applicant ought to apply to the tribunal before making application to the Divisional Court.

Re C.P. Express Ltd. and Snow (1980), 31 O.R. (2d) 120, (sub nom. *C.P. Express Ltd. v. Min. of Transportation & Communications)* 19 C.P.C. 16, 118 D.L.R. (3d) 148; affirmed 32 O.R. (2d) 45, 121 D.L.R. (3d) 511 (C.A.).

A petition to the Lieutenant Governor in Council does not operate as an automatic stay of a decision of the Ontario Highway Transport Board because (1) it does not qualify as "an appeal ... to a court or other appellate tribunal" within the meaning of s. 25 of the *Statutory Powers Procedure Act*, and (2) pursuant to s. 18(a) of the *Ontario Highway Transport Board Act*, only ss. 2–24 of the *Statutory Powers Procedure Act* apply.

Re Schiller and Scarborough Gen. Hosp. (1973), 2 O.R. (2d) 324 (Div. Ct.).

Where an applicant seeks an order removing a stay arising from an appeal, the onus is on the applicant to convince the court that in light of all relevant circumstances the stay should be removed.

Section 25

Appeal operates as stay, exception

25. (1) An appeal from a decision of a tribunal to a court or other appellate body operates as a stay in the matter unless,

(a) another Act or regulation that applies to the proceeding expressly provides to the contrary; or

(b) the tribunal or the court or other appellate body orders otherwise.

Idem

(2) An application for judicial review under the *Judicial Review Procedure Act*, or the bringing of proceedings specified in subsection 2(1) of that Act is not an appeal within the meaning of subsection (1).

1997, c. 23, s. 13

Section 25.0.1

Control of process

25.0.1 A tribunal has the power to determine its own procedures and practices and may for that purpose,

(a) make orders with respect to the procedures and practices that apply in any particular proceeding; and

(b) establish rules under section 25.1.

1999, c. 12, Sched. B, s. 16(8)

Section 25.1

Rules

25.1 (1) A tribunal may make rules governing the practice and procedure before it.

Application

(2) The rules may be of general or particular application.

Consistency with Acts

(3) The rules shall be consistent with this Act and with the other Acts to which they relate.

Public access

(4) The tribunal shall make the rules available to the public in English and in French.

Part III (Regulations) of the **Legislation Act, 2006**

(5) Rules adopted under this section are not regulations as defined in Part III (Regulations) of the *Legislation Act, 2006*.

Additional power

(6) The power conferred by this section is in addition to any power to adopt rules that the tribunal may have under another Act.

1994, c. 27, s. 56; 2006, c. 21, Sched. F, s. 136(1), Table 1

Section 26

Regulations

26. The Lieutenant Governor in Council may make regulations prescribing forms for the purpose of section 12.

1994, c. 27, s. 56

Section 27

Rules, etc., available to public

27. A tribunal shall make any rules or guidelines established under this or any other Act available for examination by the public.

1999, c. 12, Sched. B, s. 16(9)

Section 28

Substantial compliance

28. Substantial compliance with requirements respecting the content of forms, notices or documents under this Act or any rule made under this or any other Act is sufficient.

1999, c. 12, Sched. B, s. 16(9)

Section 29

29. [Repealed 1994, c. 27, s. 56.]

Section 30

30. [Repealed 1994, c. 27, s. 56.]

Section 31

31. [Repealed 1994, c. 27, s. 56.]

Section 32

Conflict

32. Unless it is expressly provided in any other Act that its provisions and regulations, rules or by-laws made under it apply despite anything in this Act, the provisions of this Act prevail over the provisions of such other Act and over regulations, rules or by-laws made under such other Act which conflict therewith.

1994, c. 27, s. 56

Case Law

Re Thompson and Lambton Bd. of Educ., [1972] 3 O.R. 889, 30 D.L.R. (3d) 32 (H.C.).

As Part I of the *Statutory Powers Procedure Act* applies to a board of reference under the *Schools Administration Act*, where a section of the *Schools Administration Act* is found to be in conflict with the *Statutory Powers Procedure Act*, the latter prevails.

Section 33

33. [Repealed 1994, c. 27, s. 56.]

Section 34

34. [Repealed 1994, c. 27, s. 56.]

Forms 1 and 2 [Repealed 1994, c. 27, s. 56.]. ***See now O. Reg. 116/95.***

FORMS

Made under the *Statutory Powers Procedure Act*

O. Reg. 116/95

as am. O. Reg. 271/15, ss. 1 (Fr.), 2–4.

1. A summons issued under subsection 12(1) of the Act shall be in the form entitled "Summons", labelled as Form 1 and dated November 2014, that is available on the website of the Government of Ontario Central Forms Repository.

O. Reg. 271/15, s. 2

2. A warrant issued under subsection 12(4) of the Act shall be in the form entitled "Warrant for Arrest (Defaulting Witness)", labelled as Form 2 and dated November 2014, that is available on the website of the Government of Ontario Central Forms Repository.

O. Reg. 271/15, s. 3

3. This Regulation comes into force on April 1, 1995.

FORM 1 — SUMMONS

***Statutory Powers Procedure Act*, O. Reg. 116/95**

[Repealed O. Reg. 271/15, s. 4.]

[Editor's Note: Pursuant to O. Reg. 116/95, s. 1, the form entitled "Summons", labelled as Form 1 and dated November 2014 is available on the website of the Government of Ontario Central Forms Repository. For your convenience, the government form is reproduced below.]

Name of the Act under which the proceeding arises

Summons to a witness before
Name of tribunal

Name of witness

Last name	**First name**	**Middle initial**

Address of witness

Unit/Apt. number	**Street number**	**Street name**

City/Town	**Province**	**Postal Code**

Oral Hearing
***You are required to attend to give evidence* at the hearing of this proceeding on**

Date (yyyy/mm/dd)	**Time (hh:mm)**

Address

Unit number	**Street number**	**Street name**

City/Town	**Province**	**Postal Code**

and to remain until your attendance is no longer required.
***You are required to bring with you* and produce at the hearing the following documents and things: (Set out the nature and date of each document and give sufficient particulars to identify each document and thing.)**

Document/Item name	**Nature of document or item**	**Date (yyyy/mm/dd)**

If you fail to attend or to remain in attendance as this summons requires, the Superior Court of Justice may order that a warrant for your arrest be issued, or that you be punished in the same way as for contempt of that court.

Electronic Hearing
You are required to participate in an electronic hearing on

Date (yyyy/mm/dd)	**Time (hh:mm)**

in the following manner: (Give sufficient particulars to enable witness to participate.)

If you fail to participate in the hearing in accordance with the summons, the Superior Court of Justice may order that a warrant for your arrest be issued, or that you be punished in the same way as for contempt of that court.

Name of tribunal	**Signature by or on behalf of tribunal**	**Date (yyyy/mm/dd)**

***Note*: You are entitled to be paid the same fees or allowances for attending at or otherwise participating in the hearing as are paid to a person summoned to attend before the Superior Court of Justice.**

November 2014

FORM 2 — WARRANT FOR ARREST (DEFAULTING WITNESS)

***Statutory Powers Procedure Act*, O. Reg. 116/95**

[Repealed O. Reg. 271/15, s. 4.]

[Editor's Note: Pursuant to O. Reg. 116/95, s. 2, the form entitled "Warrant for Arrest (Defaulting Witness)", labelled as Form 2 and dated November 2014 is available on the website of the Government of Ontario Central Forms Repository. For your convenience, the government form is reproduced below.]

Superior Court of Justice

....
Date (yyyy/mm/dd)

Name of Judge ....
(Last name, first name)

....
Title of proceeding

(Court Seal)

Warrant for Arrest

***To all* police officers in Ontario**

***And to* the officers of all correctional institutions in Ontario**

***Whereas* the witness**

Last name	**First name**	**Middle initial**

Address

Unit/Apt. number	**Street number**	**Street name**

City/Town	**Province**	**Postal Code**

was served under section 12 of the *Statutory Powers Procedure Act* with a summons to witness to give evidence at the hearing of .... Title of proceeding before .... Name of tribunal on .... Date (yyyy/mm/dd) at .... Time (hh:mm),

***And whereas* the witness failed to attend or to remain in attendance at the hearing (or, in the case of an electronic hearing to participate in the hearing in accordance with the summons),**

***And whereas* I am satisfied that the witness' attendance or participation is material to the ends of justice,**

***You are ordered to arrest* and bring the witness .... (Last name, first name) before .... Name of tribunal to give evidence in the proceeding, and if the tribunal is not then sitting or if the witness cannot be brought forthwith before the tribunal, to deliver the witness to a provincial correctional institution or other secure facility, to be admitted and detained there until his or her presence as a witness is no longer required, or until otherwise ordered.**

Name of Judge (Last name, first name)	**Signature of Judge**	**Date (yyyy/mm/dd)**